W9-BIO-653
900 ELI

Praise for Yaffa Eliach's

There Once Was a World

"A massive compendium. . . . In encyclopedic detail, Eliach covers nearly a millennium of religious practice, commerce, agriculture, transportation, medical care, and education. . . . The important point is that the Jews of Eishyshok, their lives and community vaporized, now live on."

— Jonathan Dorfman, *Boston Globe*

"An endlessly fascinating work. . . . Yaffa Eliach's monumental *There Once Was a World* is so vital. It enables us to tap into the actuality of what occurred in Europe in the 1930s and 1940s. . . . Eliach has been a faithful and painstaking chronicler." — Michael J. Bandler, *Houston Chronicle*

"Although Eliach's tale speaks specifically about Eishyshok, it represents the life and demise of all Jewish shtetls, and therein lies the book's great value. . . . The writer's strength is her intimate familiarity with the daily life of Jews in the shtetl and her ability to give context to traditions and rituals of so many of our ancestors." — Pnina Levermore, *Jewish Bulletin*

"Exhaustively researched and well-written. . . . In *There Once Was a World*, the Jewish bones under Poland's earth are alive. They have bodies and faces, and they tell their stories." — Howard Lovy, *Detroit News*

"*There Once Was a World* is so complete in detail and in spirit. . . . It attempts to capture every aspect of life during those many years — the early settlements; migrations; disease; massacres; wars; religious practice; family dynasties; education; folk tales; and commerce. . . . More than just a document, though, Yaffa Eliach has given us a legacy by which we can remember an entire way of life — indeed, a world — that was obliterated by hate."

— Edward R. Silverman, *Newark Star-Ledger*

"A massive, lavishly illustrated volume. . . . Yaffa Eliach's portrayal of these events is heartbreaking and gripping." — David G. Roskies, *The Forward*

"Eliach has written a compendious work, the equivalent of a one-volume encyclopedia that makes massive use of archives and historical documents no less than oral sources and deals with every aspect of a shtetl's life."

— Hillel Halkin, *Commentary*

"Heartbreaking and gripping. . . . An exhaustive and kaleidoscopic history of a town whose 3,500 Jews were nearly all slaughtered."

— Stephen J. Dubner, *New York Times Book Review*

"I am deeply grateful to this Jewish woman for this work, exquisitely simple, brilliantly profound."

— John Cardinal O'Connor

"A massive and entirely enthralling history. . . . *There Once Was a World* serves as a moving monument not only to her lost town but to the entire Eastern European Jewish experience."

— *Publishers Weekly*

"A mesh of memoir, a fascinating and tragic history, a handbook on Eastern European Jewry, and a window on a way of life now vanished. . . . By revealing so much about one small place, Eliach offers a sense of the unfathomable scope of what was lost in the century's most terrible war."

— Michael Pecker, *Dallas Morning News*

"*There Once Was a World* is impressive in its layers of research and details, and the deep underlying passions of the author, a pioneering scholar in Holocaust studies and daughter of one of the founding families of Eishyshok."

— Sandee Brawarsky, *Jewish Week*

"What Eliach has accomplished is a scholarly masterpiece . . . endlessly fascinating. . . . Highly recommended."

— Paul M. Kaplan, *Library Journal*

"The shtetl that was Eishyshok is gone, but, in its surviving sons and daughters, and in their sons and daughters — and in Yaffa Eliach's *There Once Was a World* and tower of photographs — it lives on. . . . A monumental history. . . . The story Eliach tells would have merited telling even if there had been no Holocaust."

— Patrick T. Reardon, *Chicago Tribune*

"A textured, many-hued portrait of shtetl life and history. . . . Eliach uncovers a fascinating picture of the role of women in the shtetl. Though official documents show men as community leaders, it was the women who were often the ones with the economic power. . . . Reading Eliach's book makes you care about her hometown almost as much as if it were your own."

— *Jewish Woman*

"Yaffa Eliach understands the greatness that was Jewish Europe before the war — and hence the magnitude of what was lost. . . . This book is without a doubt a great testimonial to the continuity of the Jews of the shtetl Eishyshok."

— Micah D. Halpern, *Jerusalem Report*

"A comprehensive, exhaustive recording of life in an archetypal Lithuanian shtetl and its vital community over time. Through discriminating scholarship, painful reflection, and searing vision, Eliach masterfully interweaves *halakhot*, history, mores, legends, and personal experience. . . . The text is at once universal and intimate, momentous and everyday, profound and ordinary. Through its topical, rather than chronological, arrangement, Eliach describes in minute detail the town's religious and academic institutions, effective leaders, and brisk commerce, and endeavors to commemorate each of its 3,500 prewar residents." — Lisa Thaler, *Shemot*

"The details are gripping. . . . Eliach is not afraid to chronicle foibles and weaknesses alongside triumphs and achievements. I found the section on family life especially fascinating, as Eliach admits that the shtetl's multigenerational, multifamily households were not always the loving, cohesive units we know from myth and idealized memory."

— Anne Sebba, *Jewish Chronicle*

"Thoroughly involving. . . . An exhaustive chronicle of memory, history, and ethnography, interwoven with rare ingenuity and acumen."

— Dr. Luba K. Gurdus, *Martyrdom and Resistance*

ALSO BY
YAFFA ELIACH

HASIDIC TALES
OF THE
HOLOCAUST

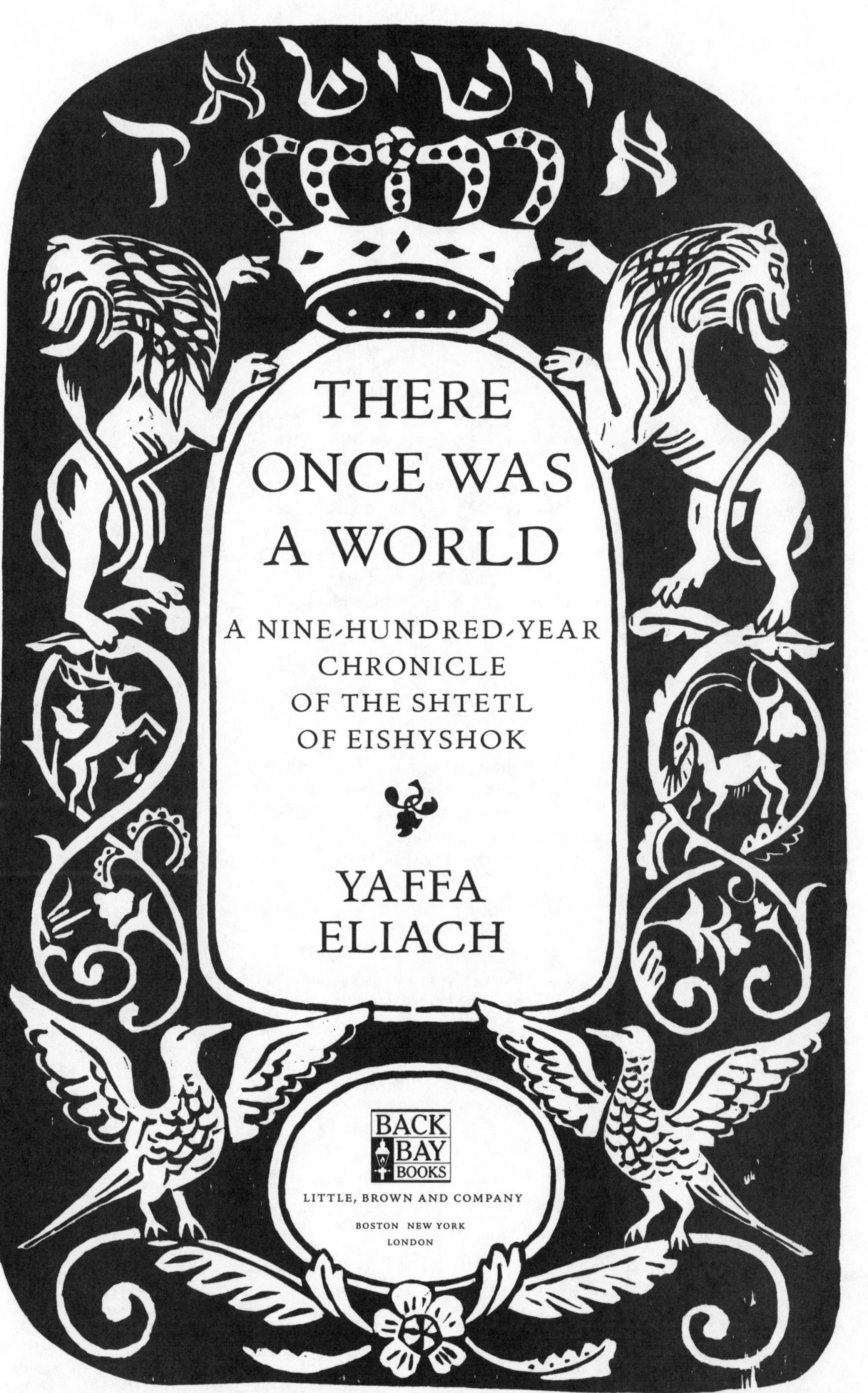

THERE ONCE WAS A WORLD

A NINE-HUNDRED-YEAR CHRONICLE OF THE SHTETL OF EISHYSHOK

YAFFA ELIACH

BACK BAY BOOKS

LITTLE, BROWN AND COMPANY

BOSTON NEW YORK
LONDON

Copyright © 1998 by Yaffa Eliach
All rights reserved. No part of this book may be reproduced in any form or by any electronic or mechanical means, including information storage and retrieval systems, without permission in writing from the publisher, except by a reviewer who may quote brief passages in a review.
Originally published in hardcover by Little, Brown and Company, 1998
First Back Bay paperback edition, 1999
Library of Congress Cataloging-in-Publication Data
Eliach, Yaffa.
There once was a world : a nine-hundred-year chronicle of the shtetl of Eishyshok / Yaffa Eliach.
p. cm.
Includes index.
ISBN 0-316-23252-1 (hc)/0-316-23239-4 (pb)
1. Jews—Lithuania—Eišiškės—History. 2. Eišiškės (Lithuania)—Ethnic relations. I. Title.
DS135.L52E36 1998
947.93—dc21 97-43504
10 9 8 7 6 5 4 3 2 1
RRD-IN
Designed by Misha Beletsky
Maps drawn by Mikhail Magaril
Printed in the United States of America

IN MEMORY OF MY DEAR
PARENTS, ZIPPORAH
KATZ SONENSON, THE
GREAT LOVER OF
HUMANITY, AND MOSHE
SONENSON, THE GREAT
STORYTELLER, WHOSE
DEDICATION TO THEIR
CHILDREN, FAMILY, AND
COMMUNITY HAVE
INSPIRED ME ALL MY
LIFE. IN MEMORY ALSO
OF ALL THE OTHER
MEMBERS OF THE KATZ
AND SONENSON FAMILIES,
AND ALL OF THE
MARTYRS OF EISHYSHOK MURDERED
DURING THE HOLOCAUST
AND POST-LIBERATION PERIOD.

MAY THEIR MEMORY
LIVE FOREVER AND EVER.

CONTENTS

PART ONE: BEGINNINGS AND ENDINGS

Introduction: The Quest for Eishyshok: Restoring a Vanished Past *3*

1 · Origins and History of Eishyshok: 1065–1941 *15*

PART TWO: THE SHULHOYF

2 · The Synagogue and Beth Midrash *63*

3 · Rabbis and Rebbetzins *90*

4 · Other Members of the Clergy *119*

5 · Heder Education *147*

6 · The Yeshivah: Town and Gown *175*

7 · The Bathhouse: The Perfect Rest *203*

8 · Mutual Aid Societies *210*

9 · The Old and New Houses of Eternity *228*

PART THREE: THE SHTETL ECONOMY

10 · Agriculture *255*

11 · Commerce *270*

12 · Handicrafts *289*

13 · Transportation *300*

14 · Market Day *313*

PART FOUR: FAMILY AND COMMUNITY

15 · The Shtetl Household *331*

16 · Rites of Passage *348*

17 · Life on the Fringe *376*

18 · Holidays *405*

19 · Medical Care *435*

PART FIVE: MODERN TIMES

20 · Entering Modernity: The Haskalah 451
21 · Zionism 482
22 · Cultural Life 513
23 · Emigration to America 544

PART SIX: THE BITTER END: 1933–41

24 · On the Eve of the Storm 559
25 · Di Shehita (The Slaughter) 575
26 · In Ghetto Radun 595
27 · In Hiding 610
28 · In the Forests 629
29 · Liberation and Its Aftermath 655

Notes 699
Sources 749
Glossary 773
Index 785

ACKNOWLEDGMENTS

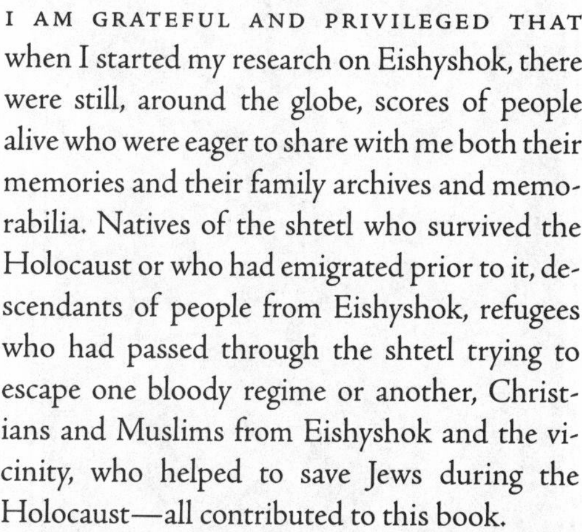

I AM GRATEFUL AND PRIVILEGED THAT when I started my research on Eishyshok, there were still, around the globe, scores of people alive who were eager to share with me both their memories and their family archives and memorabilia. Natives of the shtetl who survived the Holocaust or who had emigrated prior to it, descendants of people from Eishyshok, refugees who had passed through the shtetl trying to escape one bloody regime or another, Christians and Muslims from Eishyshok and the vicinity, who helped to save Jews during the Holocaust—all contributed to this book.

Over the years, I interviewed an entire generation whose members are no longer among the living. Their love for Eishyshok, their involvement in every aspect of shtetl life, their personal links with people from the nineteenth century, greatly enhanced this book. Among the many individuals who were particularly generous with their time were my father, Moshe Sonenson, my uncle, Shalom Sonenson Ben-Shemesh, Zosza Aliashkewicz, Sarah Plotnik Avrahami, Naftali and Dora Berkowitch, Luba Ginunski Deutch, Shlomo Farber, Rina Lewinson Fenigstein, the Glombecki family, Faivl, Hillel, and Ettl, Rebbetzin Zivia Hutner Hadash, Elka Szulkin Jankelewicz, Moshe Kaganowicz, Peretz Kaleko Alufi, Kazimierz Korkuc, Shaul Schneider, Zipporah Lubetski Tokatli, Szeina Blacharowicz Wiszik, Malka Matikanski Zahavi, Atara Kudlanski (Goodman) Zimmerman, and Philip Zlotnik. May their memory be blessed.

I would like to thank the Holocaust survivors who are still among the living. Their testimonies, documents, and photos were of great importance. My brother, Yitzhak Sonenson, opened important doors to the past, giving on to vistas of both a historical and a personal nature. I thank him for his outstanding photo collection, his detailed testimonies about the children and young people of the shtetl, and the very moving information he gave me about our family. Many thanks as well to Reuven Paikowski. His memory of events during the interwar years, the Holocaust, Liberation, and its aftermath are accurate and astonishing. At whatever hour of night or day, whenever I needed to verify a name or an event or to resolve a contradiction in testimonies, Reuven was on the other end of the line with accurate facts. I am very grateful for his private archive, located in his head and his heart.

Among the others who survived as partisans and in hiding, I am especially grateful to my father's cousin, Miriam Kabacznik Shulman, for her excellent testimony about various Zionist youth organizations in the interwar years, and to Avraham (Avremke) and Liebke Asner, Avraham Lipkunski Aviel, Dora and Israel Dimitro (Dimitrowski), Leon Kahn (Liebke Kaganowicz), Sol Lubek (Zalman Lubetski), Zvi Michalowski, and Zahava (Zlatke) Garber Paikowski.

A number of Eishyshkian descendants were eager to assist in restoring the shtetl's past and uncovering their own families' roots in that past. I am especially grateful to Judy Baston for the hundreds of Bastunski family letters she shared with me, as well as for other documents she provided and for introducing me to Yakov Shadevich, who made my access to state archives in Lithuania and Belarus immeasurably easier. Thanks also to Rosalind Rosenblatt for the many photos from her summer 1932 tourist days in Eishyshok, and for scores of additional photos and documents covering a period of more than a hundred years; Pnina Berkowitch Ivzan for assistance in gathering photos and documents of the Zlotnik and Berkowitch families; Ann Greenspan Greenstein for her material regarding the Broida family throughout America and Israel; Shirley Grynbal for collecting the Shlanski photos and documents; Neora Barkali Yahav for helping me to find her father's and grandfather's diaries, documents, and photos; Temira Wilkanski Orshan for the outstanding material on her father, Meir, and the entire Wilkanski family, gathered from private and public archives covering a period of two hundred years; Rachel and Shmuel Rabinowitch for additional material on the Wilkanski-Rabinowitch families.

Thanks to the many individuals associated with the creation of the United States Holocaust Memorial Museum in Washington, D.C., both those who were responsible for choosing to include my exhibit, the "Tower of Life," in the museum, and those who graciously allowed me to participate in decisions about the design and content of that exhibit: Jeshajahu Weinberg, Dr. Michael Berenbaum, Ralph Appelbaum, Cindy Miller, Martin Smith, Raye Farr, and Arnold Kramer.

I appreciate the photographers in Israel and America who assisted me with copying original photos and documents, at times under severe pressure: Yohanan Schwartz, Otto Katz, Stephen J. Weitz, and Bob Barker. Thanks also to Jeff Bieber from WETA-TV for producing the documentary *The Tower of Life* based on my photos and this book, and to the cameraman, Kevin Cloutier. Many thanks to Professor Mark Liwszyc, my college professor of Slavic languages, for his assistance in ensuring my accurate translation of Russian and Polish material; the poet Julius Keleras for his translation of Lithuanian material and research in various archives in Lithuania; Yakov Shadevich for finding the official Pinkasim of Eishyshok in various archives in Lithuania and the former USSR;

Yaffa Eliach with Ralph Applebaum in the "Tower of Life" at the United States Holocaust Memorial Museum in Washington, D.C., February 24, 1993. Ralph Applebaum was the designer of the interior of the museum including the "Tower of Life." PHOTO: VON CHRISTINE BRINCK, YAFFA ELIACH SHTETL COLLECTION (YESC), Y. ELIACH

Jeshajahu Pery for the research assistance he provided at the early stages of this book; Rochel Licht for the meticulousness of her research assistance during the past ten years; Mollie Fried for typing parts of the manuscript; Shani Rosenblum for her outstanding assistance in completing the typing of this manuscript and bringing it into the new era of computers; Jill Sanders, whose linguistic skills brought clarity and accuracy to a number of the illustration captions in my book; Uri Assaf for invaluable assistance with interviews, and with research in public and private archives in Israel, and also for the important advice he offered regarding the founding of my private archive, "The Yaffa Eliach Shtetl Collection"; the librarians at the

Yeshivah of Flatbush Joel Braverman High School, Rabbi Abraham Kurtz and Yael Penkower; Richard Z. Chesnoff for the stimulation of his unflagging intellectual curiosity about Jewish cultural life in both the small shtetls and the large urban centers of Eastern Europe; the Guggenheim Fellowship of 1987, which enabled me to do research in Eishyshok (Eisiskes), Vilnius, Riga, Moscow, Helsinki, Oxford, and London; Brooklyn College for its Broeklundian Professorship.

It is a special blessing to have a literary agent like Miriam Altshuler. Her constant support, sound advice, and wise counsel have helped to safeguard the integrity of my work.

To Sarah Crichton, publisher, and everybody else at Little, Brown and Company, I am grateful for their patience in understanding the many delays in the completion of this book, due in part to the time devoted to creating my exhibit, the "Tower of Life," and also to the political changes in the former Soviet Union, which greatly increased the amount of research material available to me and therefore the time I had to spend on it. Thanks to Anne Montague, copyeditor, for restructuring some of the chapters; to Peggy Freudenthal, copyediting manager, for her thorough work in reviewing every detail of the book; to Martin Barabas, for the energy and intelligence of his work on the publicity for my book; to Misha Beletsky for his beautiful interior design, which so accurately recreates the look of an East European book; to Jennifer Josephy, editor, for her patience and dedication over what turned out to be an unexpectedly long period of time, for her excellent assistance in the final choice of photos and illustrations, which so unerringly reflects her sensitivity to the text, and for her commitment to bringing this book to as wide an audience as possible; and to Abigail Wilentz and Emily Fromm, Jennifer's able assistants.

Very special thanks to Beth Rashbaum, who brought this book to Little, Brown in the first place and has continued to play a key role in the editing and writing ever since. Our editor-author relationship dates back to my earlier book, *Hasidic Tales of the Holocaust*, and has developed into an enduring friendship. It is a special privilege to work with such an editor, whose formidable skills are reflected in her understanding of every element of shtetl life, from its local roots to its universal influence, and in her ability to remain true to the unique flavor of the book's many different kinds of materials, translated from many different languages, while molding them into a harmonious whole. She greatly enriched and enhanced the final result.

Most of all, I am very grateful to my family. They inspired me and gave me strength during years of intense research.

My son, Yotav Eliach, is an expert in Zionism. His interest in the Zionist activities in Eishyshok and its practical implications was very important to me, as was the love for the shtetl of my daughter-in-law, Hildy. My daughter, Smadar Rosensweig, a professor of history, was very interested in my research. We frequently discussed and analyzed many historical issues, particularly those pertinent to the Jewish family and to the role of women in Eastern Europe. My son-in-law, Rav Dr. Michael Rosensweig, is a brilliant Talmud scholar who helped me with the verification of important halakhic elements in shtetl life.

Yotav's children, Ayalon, Adiva, Aitan, Ariel, Liam, and Noa, and Smadar's children, Ariel, Moriah, Itamar, Avigdor, Ayalah, and Avigail, were all born during the research and writing of this book, between the years 1983 and 1998. From the minute of their birth, all twelve of my grandchildren have been an inspiration and a joy. For many of them the first word they spoke was Ei-shy-shok! They are enchanted with Eishyshok, and have heard its stories at every stage of their lives so that it occupies a special place in their hearts and minds. To hold them in my arms and look at their smiling faces is a statement of life, the most positive response I can make to the

Yaffa Eliach holding in her arms her granddaughter Adiva Eliach, next to a photo of Ayalon, Adiva's brother and Yaffa Eliach's oldest grandson, May 1987. PHOTO: DAVID ELIACH, YESC, Y. ELIACH

Yaffa Eliach with eleven of her twelve grandchildren at Liam Eliach's birthday party. Top row (right to left): Ayalon Eliach, Yaffa Eliach holding Avigail Rosensweig in her arms, Adiva Eliach, and Ariel Rosensweig. Middle row (right to left): Moriah and Itamar Rosensweig, Aitan and Ariel Eliach, and Avigdor Rosensweig. Front row: Ayalah Rosensweig with two-year-old Liam Eliach, the birthday boy. (His sister, Noa, was born a few days later.) May 1998. PHOTO: SMADAR ROSENSWEIG, YESC, Y. ELIACH

tragic murder of my mother and the two dead babies she held in her arms; to stand with them in the midst of my "Tower of Life" in the museum, or on the mass grave in Eishyshok, is a victory statement, a confirmation that the life of my family and my shtetl will transcend the tragedies of history.

My husband, Rabbi Dr. David Eliach, a world-renowned Jewish educator, my high school principal, and my friend, has been constantly at my side supporting my research on Eishyshok. For the past nineteen years all of the trips we took together were related to my research, and a large segment of our income was spent on that research, on creating the "Tower of Life" and on writing this book.

David has "lived" in Eishyshok for close to two decades. The rooms of our house are filled with photos, documents, books, and memorabilia from Eishyshok, and even the food on our table has sometimes come from Eishyshok or, to be precise, from old Eishyshkian recipes that were given to me during my interviews. Many of our conversations, at home and abroad, begin—or end up—on themes relevant to Eishyshok.

Recently, I stood on the spot in my grandmother Sonenson's house where my mother and baby brother were murdered. David stood next to me with our daughter, Smadar, and two of our grandchildren, Ariel and Moriah. Without their presence, I would not have had the emotional strength to go back to that place, where I was able to complete a crucial section of the book.

But without the help and support of all those mentioned above, and many others whose names I am unable to mention for reasons of space, this book could never have come into being at all. You made it possible. Needless to say, its shortcomings are all mine.

New York City
July 14, 1998
20th of Tamuz, 5758

· ONE ·

BEGINNINGS AND ENDINGS

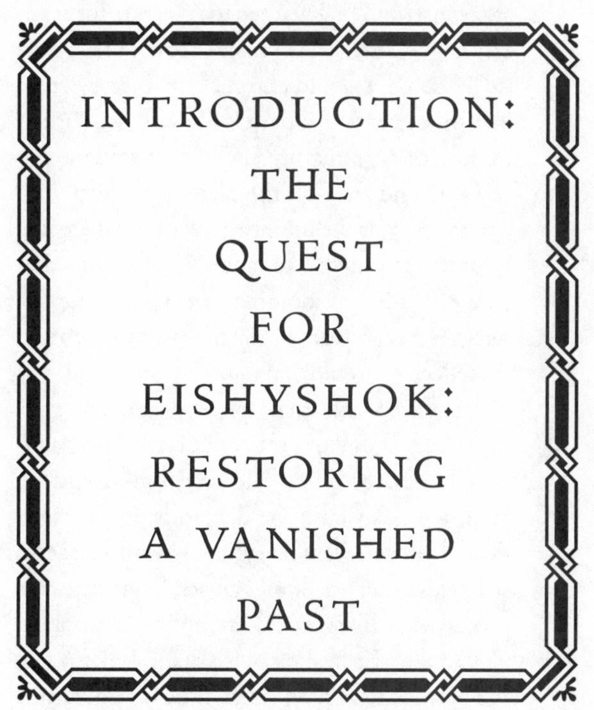

INTRODUCTION: THE QUEST FOR EISHYSHOK: RESTORING A VANISHED PAST

PERHAPS THE EASIEST WAY OF MAKING A TOWN'S ACQUAINTANCE IS TO ASCERTAIN HOW THE PEOPLE IN IT WORK, HOW THEY LOVE AND HOW THEY DIE.

Albert Camus
THE PLAGUE

IN AUGUST 1979 I WAS ON MY WAY TO RUSSIA, IN THE MIDST OF A FACT-FINDING MISSION to Eastern Europe. As a member of President Carter's Holocaust Commission, which was charged with making a recommendation for an appropriate United States memorial to the victims of the Holocaust, I had spent several days traveling to the various capitals of the Holocaust Kingdom — Warsaw, Treblinka, Auschwitz-Birkenau, and Plaszow among them. Now, flying south of Vilna (Vilnius), on a plane from Warsaw to Kiev, I became aware that somewhere beneath the clouds lay the town of Eishyshok, home to the early years of my brief, interrupted childhood.

Eishyshok (the Yiddish name for Ejszyszki, as it is known in Polish, and Eisiskes in Lithuanian) had been home not just to my family and to several thousand other Jews just before the Holocaust, but home to generation upon generation of Jews, going back to the eleventh century. In fact, Eishyshok is the site of one of the oldest Jewish settlements in that part of the world. My paternal ancestors had been among the first five Jewish families to settle there in that long-ago time, and their descendants had lived on its soil for all the centuries since then, under all the various governments that had fought for control of it: Lithuanian, Polish, German, Russian, and Soviet. But now, in the post-Holocaust era, it was for the first time in all those hundreds of years a town without Jews.

Nine hundred years of Jewish history in Eishyshok had been wiped out. In Eishyshok, as elsewhere in Poland and Lithuania, nearly a millennium of vibrant Jewish life had been reduced to stark images of victimization and death. During my travels I had been struck by the fact that, insofar as the world knew anything about the Jews of Eastern Europe, it knew them as skeletal concentration camp survivors and huge piles of corpses, ashes in crematorium ovens, pitiful targets of history's most astonishing epidemic of mass genocide. What kind of memorial could possibly transcend those images of death and do justice to the full, rich lives those people had lived, I wondered. At the time, the question seemed merely rhetorical to me, a question that could never find a satisfactory answer.

Thinking these grim thoughts as I flew over my former home, while remembering what I could of the colorful, intricately detailed tapestry of my own family life before that tapestry was so brutally shredded, I suddenly saw that there was a possible answer, and that I might be able to play a role in providing it. With great clarity my mission began to unfold before me: Regardless what kind of memorial my distinguished colleagues recommended to the president, I decided, I would set out on a path of my own, to create a memorial to life, not to death. Rather than focusing on the forces of destruction as most memorials do, mine would be an attempt at reconstruction. I wanted to re-create for readers the vanished Jewish market town I had once called home. I would chronicle its history, from its earliest years as a place of Jewish settlement to the tragic, premature end of that settlement.

There and then on the plane, with little understanding of the implications of my decision, I committed myself to a course of action that would completely dominate and consume the next seventeen years of my life (not to mention the effect it would have on my husband, my two children and their spouses, and my ever-expanding brood of grandchildren). The financial burden of doing the research would be enormous, as would the demands on my time. For all those seventeen years I would have to struggle to balance family, an academic career as professor of history and literature at Brooklyn College, and Eishyshok (with Eishyshok tipping the balance heavily in its own favor, my family often felt, particularly during the final stages of the research). There were to be no vacations during these years, but my travels in search of source material would require me to circle the globe many times, taking me to six continents and hundreds of cities, towns, and villages. The speaking engagements that helped finance this research took me to even more. In sum, every minute and every mile of these travels were devoted to either my research or its financing.

Eventually the Eishyshok project assumed a whole new dimension. During another trip to Europe, in August 1987, when a Guggenheim fellowship enabled me to do further field research, I returned to Eishyshok itself for the first time. I had not been there since 1945, when my brother and I visited our father, Moshe Sonenson, in the jail cell where he was being held by the Soviet authorities.

Members of President Carter's Holocaust Commission were sworn in on February 1, 1979, in the White House Roosevelt Room. Yaffa Eliach is sworn in by Thomas P. (Tip) O'Neill, Speaker of the House. Elie Wiesel, chairman of the president's Holocaust Commission, holds the Bible. That Bible was one of thousands of books looted by the Germans from the Vilna ghetto. After liberation, it was recovered by American forces. YAFFA ELIACH SHTETL COLLECTION [YESC]

As part of my tour of the town, I went to one of the mass graves, which had been both killing field and burial ground to thousands of Jewish women and children from Eishyshok, Olkenik, and the surrounding villages, who had all been murdered on September 26, 1941. The place was marked only by a drab concrete plaque bearing the misleading dedication: to "The Victims of Fascism, 1941–1944."

Standing on the grass-covered grave, with yellow buttercups dotting the ground everywhere I looked, I found myself riveted to the spot. I could feel my beloved grandmothers Hayya Sonenson and Alte Katz holding on to me, my aunts, cousins, friends, and neighbors pulling at me. And I could hear the voices of those buried beneath my feet. By this stage of my research I had read many of their diaries and letters,

President Jimmy Carter greets Yaffa Eliach in the White House Rose Garden, September 29, 1979. That day Elie Wiesel (at Carter's side) gave President Carter the Holocaust Commission's report, written by historian Michael Berenbaum, recommending the establishment of the Holocaust Museum in Washington, D.C. YESC

collected their birth and marriage certificates, pored over their photographs. They surrounded me now, my family, my parents' friends, and my own little friends, asking with new urgency to be remembered, not as heaps of skulls and bones but as the vibrant, dynamic people I'd known. They wanted the world to see them as they had looked at their weddings, on their picnics, in their social clubs, and during the course of their daily lives.

My husband, David Eliach, who was standing a short distance away, later told me he seemed to see me sinking into the mass grave, aging before his eyes. But I was brought back to life by the mental image of one of my little grandchildren, whose face appeared out of nowhere, smiling up at me, giving me strength to leave the grave.

During my long vigil at the killing field, Ezekiel's vision of the valley of dry bones had assumed new meaning for me. "Behold," he heard the Lord say to the bones, "I will cause breath to enter into you, and ye shall live. And I will lay sinews upon you, and will bring up flesh upon you, and cover you with skin, and put breath in you, and ye shall live . . ."

When I left Eishyshok that time, I had a new mission — or at least a new component to my original mission. In addition to the book I was writing, I wanted to create a photographic exhibit depicting every man, woman, and child of twentieth-century Eishyshok, bringing them all back to life, and all together in one place: "Beloved and cherished, never parted in life or in death" (II Samuel, 1:23). The 1,500 photographs that line the walls of the Tower of Life in the United States Holocaust Memorial Museum in Washington, D.C., were the ultimate result of that decision. Like this book, they are part of my commemoration of my lost home. Thus my own vision of a memorial found a place in the official memorial that President Carter and the U.S. Congress had commissioned to be built on the banks of the Potomac.

For both personal and historical reasons, Eishyshok seemed to me to be an ideal candidate for the kind of memorial — or memorials — I had in mind. Given my family's ancient roots in Eishyshok and my own early years there, the personal reasons are obvious. But my instincts as a historian were also at work in the decision to document the long life of this particular community.

First of all, from the practical point of view of a researcher (and this may have been the only "practical" aspect of my decision), the size of Eishyshok's Jewish population, which ranged in its last five hundred years between 1,000 and 3,500, made it seem like a manageable subject. This factor was particularly important to me since I was determined to find some kind of authentic documentation, visual or written, archival or anecdotal, on every Jewish person who had lived in the shtetl in the twentieth century, including those who had emigrated from it, those who had been privileged to die a natural death in it, those who had perished there or nearby during the Holocaust, and the handful of Holocaust survivors who had somehow lived to tell the tale.

Eishyshok, insignificant and obscure as it may at first appear, seemed to me to be not just a manageable subject but a very important one, particularly in the context of Jewish history. The fact that it had been in existence since about 1061; its geographical position at the crossroads of Poland, Lithuania, and Russia, the three countries that for hundreds of years were home to the largest concentration of Jews in the world; its proximity (forty miles) to Vilna, a major intellectual and cultural center of Jewish life; the world-renowned yeshivah it supported during the nineteenth century, which made it a wellspring of Jewish intellectual life itself — all these factors and more allowed me to see in Eishyshok the very paradigm of the small Jewish market town — the shtetl, as such towns were called, using the Yiddish diminutive of *shtot* or *stadt*, the Yiddish and German words for "town."

The shtetl, typically a town ranging in size from about one thousand to twenty thousand people, was a uniquely Eastern European phenomenon, the product of a very specific time and place. We can trace its origins to the eleventh and twelfth centuries, when Jews from Babylonia, Germany, and Bohemia began trickling into Eastern Europe. Many of them settled in large urban centers, and a few lived in isolated rural areas, but most would eventually make their homes in one of the thousands of shtetlekh that came to serve as trading centers for both country and city folk in the vicinity.

Given that shtetl life was for hundreds of years the predominant mode of existence for the majority of East European Jewry, and that during that period Eastern Europe was the principal domain of the Jews, the shtetl had clearly played a central role in Jewish cultural history. Indeed, no history of Jews in the Diaspora would be complete without an understanding of the shtetl. And yet, as I discovered to my surprise when I began my preliminary researches, no serious, comprehensive, in-depth account of shtetl life had ever been done. For a historian whose areas of specialization are Eastern European intellectual history in general and the Eastern European Jewish community in particular, such a gap in the literature presented a unique opportunity. By studying Eishyshok, I felt, I could create a portrait that would reflect the various historical, social, cultural, economic, educational, and religious phases of shtetl life from the time of its origins until its destruction during the Holocaust.

It is true, of course, that each shtetl had its own distinctive character, its own folklore, which varied according to geographic location, political and economic conditions, level of scholarship, patterns of leadership, relations between Jews and Gentiles, and so forth. But the towns had enough in common with one another, and enough to set them apart from any other kind of settlement in history, to make the study of one relevant to the study of all. Eishyshok, I decided, would be that one.

And I came to realize as I did my research that Eishyshok was not just a paradigm of Eastern European shtetl life, but a veritable microcosm of Western civilization, and beyond that of the entire family of humankind. There is hardly any major trend in the last nine hundred years of history that did not manifest itself in Eishyshok. From the Crusades to World War I to the Holocaust, from the pagan worship of the early Lithuanians to the European Age of Enlightenment to the secularization that occurred throughout much of the Western world in the twentieth century, Eishyshok has seen and experienced it all.

And yet, even as it reflected events and trends from the world at large, Jewish Eishyshok remained true to itself. In this shtetl as in so many others, the Jews lived and thrived in the midst of pagan, Muslim, and Christian neighbors, managing to be both of that world and apart from it, for many centuries. By maintaining a strict adherence to their own customs, they created a Jewish homeland thousands of miles from the original homeland, a kind of Jerusalem of the spirit. Napoleon himself is said to have called nearby Vilna the Jerusalem of Lithuania on account of the strong ethnic identity of its Jewish population. Perhaps at no time since the destruction of the Second Temple in Jerusalem in 70 C.E., and at no other place in the Diaspora, had there been a more successfully autonomous and intact set of Jewish institutions than those preserved in the shtetlekh of Eastern Europe.

Every stage of life in the shtetl — birth, circumcision, bar mitzvah, marriage, divorce, death and burial — was observed according to ancient law and tradition. So complete was the immersion in pre-Diaspora Jewish culture that the children of Eishyshok perceived the very topography of their surroundings as being a replica of the ancient Land of Israel. In their lively imaginations, the local Kantil stream was the Jordan river, the plaza that was home to the synagogue and the two houses of study was Mount Moriah, the sacred grounds of the Temple in Jerusalem.

But even though Eishyshok was a place whose very heart and soul were dedicated to religion — with a bit of superstition thrown into the mix — its people, like Lithuanian shtetl-dwellers in general, were so intellectually rigorous and questioning that other Jews expressed doubts about their piety. Hence the popular Yiddish expression "Litvak zelem-kop," an almost untranslatable phrase meaning, literally, "Lithuanian cross-head." It conveys the notion that every Lithuanian Jew has a little Christian cross inside his head. (It also conveys, in even more untranslatable fashion, the extreme stubbornness of Lithuanian Jews, who are known for never yielding to another opinion.)

If they were sometimes stubborn and unyielding, they were also open-hearted. Eishyshok's Jews supported the yeshivah in their midst with a generosity so extraordinary that they were frequently invoked as models of devotion to Torah-learning.

But these generous people were also such aggressive traders that they were known as *albe levones* — half moons — because they would even try to buy the dark side of the moon.[1] In short, Eishyshkians were complicated, contradictory, multifaceted, and fascinating, true representatives of the family of man in all its complexity and beauty.

When I embarked on my work, upon returning from the Holocaust Commission trip in the summer of 1979, I had no idea what kind of documentation I would be able to find for it, or where it would be. But I was soon to learn the truth of Goethe's warning that the most valuable materials are not to be found in official archives — not those of Europe and the Soviet Union, nor those of Israel and the United States. While I never ceased in my efforts to get access to those archives — a particularly difficult challenge during the Cold War years, when it involved dealing with the wary officialdom of Poland, the Soviet Union, and, after the breakup of the Soviet bloc, Lithuania — I found that what I could learn about Eishyshok from these sources was very limited. In fact, the official documents give no clue as to who lived in the town of Eishyshok, or what happened to them. The text of a history of Eishyshok, part of a multivolume work on the towns of Lithuania that was commissioned during the last years of the Soviet regime, published in 1983, reads as follows:

During World War II Eisiskes suffered great losses. The majority of the people were shot, the economic life was paralyzed, and the town center was destroyed. Despite this devastation, during the years 1941 to 1944 the borough remained a district center, its administrative offices continuing to function.[2]

A footnote to the text mentions the fact that 3,446 people were shot near the town, "Jews and Soviet activists *among* them" (my emphasis). During the massacre of the men on September 25, 1941, and of the women and children

September 26, *only* Jews were murdered — not a single Russian or Lithuanian or Pole — and there were about 5,000 victims, not 3,446. In the years that followed, the town did indeed continue to function, but it did so without the people who had constituted the majority of its population, for there were no Jews left. Those who had survived were in hiding, as they would remain until liberation, in July 1944.

By contrast, the material I eventually found in private family archives and collections was astonishing in both quality and quantity, exceeding by far my most hopeful expectations.

When I began my systematic research, there were still a significant number of living Eishyshkians scattered around the globe to whom I could turn for memories and material. One of my first priorities was to interview as many of them as I could before age, illness, and death silenced them. During my years as founder and director of Brooklyn's Center for Holocaust Studies, the first in the United States, I had learned important lessons about the possible uses and abuses of oral history, lessons that enabled me to establish basic criteria for conducting interviews and for verifying their accuracy. These proved crucial in the hundreds of interviews I now began to conduct.

Because of their diversity of age and experience, all the people I interviewed brought something different to the process of reconstruction. Some of the older people, for example, still had strong personal links to the shtetl of the nineteenth century; their memories encompassed not just their own experiences but stories passed down by parents, grandparents, and great-grandparents.

To listen to these old men and women, to look over their written documents and photos with them, was to reexperience the dynamic life of the shtetl, to be privy to its folklore, to enter its past. Indeed, I felt as though I was touching history itself when I heard Shlomo Farber repeating his grandfather's account of Emperor Napoleon's visit to nearby Olkenik during the Russian campaign.

I was in touch with another kind of history — literary history — courtesy of Szyrke Groshman (whose Hebrew name is Shira Gorshman). Szyrke was not herself from Eishyshok, but her life had touched, and been touched by, several people who were: Sarah, Mordekhai, and Rivka Rubinstein. The gifted Sarah had been her Hebrew teacher in Krok, the shtetl of her birth, and Sarah's brother and sister were, like Szyrke, members of a socialist group called the Labor Battalion in Jerusalem. To earn money for the impoverished Labor Battalion, Szyrke accepted a 40-piaster-a-day job as a maid in the household of Sh. Y. Agnon (1888–1970), future Nobel laureate in literature. Though Agnon was immensely taken with her beauty and her free-spirited ideology, complimenting her frequently on her expressive eyes (as well as her gefilte fish), she saw in him merely the epitome of the starched-collar, coat-and-tie bourgeoisie. And then one day in 1927 the beautiful Szyrke disappeared — to Russia. She, Mordekhai, and Rivka, along with about a hundred other disillusioned leftists who felt they could not achieve the socialist utopia they had dreamed of creating in Palestine, had taken the absolutely unheard-of step of emigrating from there to Communist Russia. But it was during her time in Jerusalem that Szyrke's life entered literature, for Agnon almost certainly modeled the protagonist of his posthumously published novel *Shira* after the lively young woman he had known so many years before.[3]

Szyrke's brilliant Hebrew teacher, Sarah, came by her talents naturally, being the daughter of one of Eishyshok's most beloved teachers and scholars, Reb Tuvia der Yeremitcher (from the shtetl of Yeremitch). My uncle Shalom Sonenson, who had been privileged to study with him, re-created for me the image of his heder (the religious elementary school attended by all shtetl boys). There was Reb Tuvia Rubinstein, seated at the head of a long wooden table, sipping his steaming glass of tea and sucking a chunk of white sugar during the occasional pauses in his eloquent declamations of whole chapters from the Prophets, to which he appended his own brilliant commentaries and interpretations. And there were the pale-faced little heder boys, lined up on the backless benches to either side of the table, listening spellbound and silent to their teacher's display of intellect. My uncle was but one of many former students I met during my research who could still quote passages they had learned over half a century before from the Yeremitcher rebbe.

Rivka Remz, close to a hundred years old when interviewed, could still conjure up the awe she felt during Yom Kippur services in the closing decades of the nineteenth century. Through her eyes I saw the worshippers dressed all in white from head to toe, standing in their white socks on heaps of fresh-cut straw, beseeching the Almighty God to inscribe them in the Book of Life for the coming year. And so vivid was Morris Shlanski's account of the Big Fire of 1895, which he had experienced as a seven-year-old child, that I could almost feel the hot cobblestones scorching his feet as he ran from the encroaching flames.

Several decades later, there was Faivl Glombocki astride a white horse in a torch-lit parade that drew the entire shtetl in its wake. Everybody had turned out to say goodbye to the Schneider family, who were leaving for the Bastun train station, on their way to Eretz Israel (the Land of Israel, as the Jews called Palestine before it became a state). Recalling what had been a momentous event for the shtetl some sixty-five years before, the aging Faivl was suddenly transformed into the enthusiastic young Zionist he had been in 1924.

Most of those who were still alive when I began my research were not Holocaust survivors, of whom there were very few, but people who had emigrated before the war in search of a better life, generally to either the United States or Eretz Israel. Having left the shtetl during the 1910s, '20s, and '30s, they had no firsthand knowledge of it during its final years. But there was also a group of survivors who had remained in the shtetl up to and beyond the fateful June day in 1941 when the German troops marched across a centuries-old bridge into Eishyshok, and who had managed one way or another to escape the subsequent massacres. They had been eyewitnesses to the shtetl's final days, its ultimate destruction, and the grim aftermath of its liberation. Additionally, there was a small contingent of people who had chosen to go to Russia or had been exiled there in 1940–41.

The prewar emigrants, unlike the survivors of the German occupation, had not just memories to share but ample memorabilia. When they'd left Eishyshok they had taken with them family records and heirlooms, photos, diaries, letters, and official documents that would prove invaluable to my effort to reconstruct life in the shtetl. Many of them were able to show me souvenirs and keepsakes that shed considerable light on the modernizing, secularizing trends that transformed the shtetl during the twentieth century: for example, the script of a play they had had a role in prior to their departure, or the program for a cultural event in Eishyshok or nearby Vilna, or the lyrics to one of the topical songs performed in the local cabaret revue.

Many of these emigrants still had in their possession a wealth of traditional materials their parents had sent with them when they left: candlesticks to light and kiddush cups to drink wine from on the Sabbath and other festival days, portraits that were to be hung over the beds of their new homes so that the ever-watchful eyes of Papa and Mama would always be there to remind them not to abandon their traditions or their faith. The ongoing bond between the emigrants and those they left behind was amply documented by the bundles of photos, letters, and postcards exchanged after their departure, as well as the souvenirs they had kept of their occasional returns to the shtetl, as tourists taking sentimental journeys home.

The Holocaust survivors' items were, of course, fewer in number, and often much more damaged, due to the perils of the journeys they had made. Many of the photos, written documents, and artifacts that managed to survive the war had been buried in the ground or stashed away in other hiding places, or deposited with friendly Christian and Muslim neighbors, then retrieved by their owners after liberation. Also included among the survivors' keepsakes were various items that helped tell the story of the Holocaust period itself: yellow stars and other grim mementos of the Nazi invasion; diaries and letters describing the lives of their authors in nearby ghettos, and in the surrounding forests, where many went either to hide or to join up with the partisans; death certificates from the post-liberation era of murder and mayhem.

That I had so much material to draw upon was little short of miraculous. To track the history of any given artifact in its post-shtetl days is to follow the twentieth-century trials and tribulations of its owner, and often of the owner's new homeland as well. For example, I was very eager to see anything that the Wilkanski family had taken from Eishyshok, because Reb Layzer Wilkanski (1824–1915), his wife Batia, and their six children had all played such prominent roles in the ethical, cultural, intellectual, and political life of Eishyshok. When they emigrated to Eretz Israel in 1914, following in the footsteps of their children, Reb Layzer and Batia brought with them not just the usual family memorabilia but official records relating to his fifty years of service as the shtetl dayyan (judge). In 1915, however, fearful of being deported from Palestine by the Turks as a foreigner, Reb Layzer buried all his shtetl documents and photos. With the assistance of the Wilkanski family, I was able to retrieve some of those materials; but termites and other underground creatures had gotten to many of them before me. Fortunately, several books about Eishyshok written by Reb Layzer's son Meir Wilkanski still survive to bear witness to the Wilkanski legacy.

Internal Zionist politics could pose just as much of a threat to family archive materials as termites did. In the 1940s, Peretz Kaleko-Alufi, who had emigrated from Eishyshok in 1933, was appointed principal of a Labor Party school in Zikhron-Yaakov. Fearing that a former affiliation with the rightist Beitar youth organization could jeopardize his relations with Labor and hence his job, he buried all his shtetl documents, including, of course, photographs of himself wearing a Beitar uniform. As a key member of one of the families that had inherited the mantle of intellectual leadership from the Wilkanskis, Peretz was a very important source for me. I wanted those documents badly. So in 1987, armed with a digging permit and accompanied by the aging Peretz and my brother Yitzhak, I went on an archaeological expedition. Alas, the main beam of a small building stood just above the spot where Peretz had performed the burial.

My brother Yitzhak and I experienced firsthand how challenging it was to preserve family papers. In 1945, with my mother dead and my father in exile in Siberia, I began the journey toward my new homeland with my uncle, whose papers listed me as his child. Though I was only a little girl, I knew enough to treasure my few remaining family photos — and to hide them in my shoes in order to conceal my true identity. I kept them there during all the months of our travels, from Poland to Czechoslovakia to Germany and eventually to Marseilles, where we boarded a boat that sailed the Mediterranean to the Suez Canal. Only after we arrived in Palestine on a train from Egypt on April 4, 1946, did I remove them.

The following year my brother attempted to reach the shores of Eretz Israel on one of the many ships that were transporting "illegal" Jewish immigrants (*maapilim*), almost all of whom were Holocaust survivors from Eastern Europe. The *Lanegev* left France on January 18, 1947, but was intercepted by three British gunboats off the shores of Haifa. During the fierce battle that ensued, Yitzhak jumped into the water with his share of our family photos strapped around his waist. Along with many of the other maapilim from the *Lanegev*, he was captured and exiled to Cyprus. In August 1947 he finally made it back to Haifa, his photos still strapped to his body. During the entire War of Independence, in which he fought and was wounded, he carried those precious photos with him, unwilling to part with his last paper link to the past.

Another man who managed to save his family photos was Yossele Hamarski, who had fought as a partisan in the forests around Eishyshok during World War II. In his case the danger came from the army troops of the newly formed Israeli government, who were cracking down on freelance defense militias such as the Irgun, which was supposed to have disbanded after the declaration of the State of Israel. In June 1948, Yossele was on the ill-fated Irgun ship the *Altalena*, which was carrying men and arms to Israel from Europe. At one of its clash-ridden stops along the coast, Yossele was forced to disembark, with the result that when the ship was fired on by the military and up in flames in Tel Aviv, he and his photos were at a safe distance.

Even as recently as 1991 the precious documents so crucial to my research were endangered in Israel. During the Gulf War that year, a Scud missile hit a home in Ramat-Gan. Though it caused no loss of human life, it did destroy many photos and papers. These would have helped shed additional light on the war years, because they documented the experience of one of the 15,000 refugees who passed through Eishyshok from 1939 to 1941, availing themselves of the community's assistance in illegal border crossings as they tried to make their way to safety.

Much of the memorabilia brought to the United States by the 1,500 Eishyshkians who emigrated there between 1873 and 1940 fell victim not to war, terrorism, or politics, as happened in Israel, but to lack of interest, particularly among the immediate descendants of the immigrants. The "old country" seemed too remote to these products of the melting pot. Ethnicity and family roots were quickly forgotten in the rush to Americanization.

Since most of the second-generation Americans had assimilated so thoroughly that they could not read Yiddish, Hebrew, or any of the other foreign languages in which their family correspondence had been conducted, and likewise could not read the inscriptions on the back of the family photos, or any of the diaries or official documents that had been brought over, they were likely to consign a lot of that material to the trash.

Ironically, even as memories have faded and memorabilia disappeared, recent decades have seen a revival of interest in the story they tell. The new fascination with family roots has resulted in an active effort by American Jews to search for and preserve those materials that still remain to bear witness to the past. But for many family archives, including a number of those from Eishyshok, the change came too late. They are lost to the world forever.

The bulk of emigrant material that survived in the United States (and in other places around the globe) was in the possession of individuals who had a direct physical or emotional link to the shtetl, many of whom had assumed the role of family historians. They included the emigrants themselves, as well as children who had been born in the new land but felt strong ties to the old one, either because they had visited it with their parents or had grown to love it through listening to their nostalgic stories.

Some of the material that survived in the United States was deposited in official archives maintained by synagogues and fraternal societies set up by Eishyshkian emigrants. However, since so many of the synagogues in cities like Chicago, Boston, and Detroit either disappeared without leaving a trace or were converted to churches as their congregants left the inner cities and moved out to the suburbs, I was able to rescue only a few shreds of the records they had once contained. But the Eishyshok Society of America (Hevrah Bnei Avraham Shmuel Anshei Eishyshker) proved to be a storehouse of information — about both the people who had been left behind in Eishyshok and those who had come to the new land. Despite the fact that some of the records were "cleaned out" and discarded when the leadership of the Society was taken over by the Holocaust survivors' generation during the 1970s, there was still a significant body of intact documentary material that covered a period of over a hundred years, beginning when the first emigrants arrived on American shores. This material is now in my possession.

The breakup of the Soviet Union, which began in 1989, had a considerable impact on my research, because it meant that many official government archives, most notably those of the newly independent Lithuania, were now at least theoretically open to researchers from the West — for a price. By going through various public and private channels, and paying a very high price indeed, I was able to obtain from the Lithuanian archives comprehensive records pertaining to the Jews of Eishyshok and the villages under its jurisdiction between the years 1792 and 1940. Births, marriages, divorces, illnesses, deaths, and taxes are the subjects of these records, which I used to fill in many gaps not just in the research I did for this book, but the biographical data I assembled on many of the people who appear in the photos displayed on the walls of the Tower of Life at the United States Holocaust Memorial Museum.

Valuable as such public records are, they are not nearly as useful as the material from private family archives. The differences between the two kinds of documentation — differences in accuracy as well as personal detail, richness, and color — are enormous. One crucial area in which the public records fall short has to do with the male population. Many of these inaccuracies stem from the attempt to spare young men and boys from the military draft, and the distortions took a number of different forms.

When Reb Layzer and Batia Wilkanski's first child Yitzhak was born in 1879, he was entered into the records as a four-year-old boy. This was done on the advice of the shtetl expert on draft laws, who said that this way when Yitzhak was called up for military service, he would be eligible for exemption as a son supporting an aging father, because there would be no other sons close in age, even if other male children had been born in the meantime. A distortion of a different kind had to do with "only sons." Since only sons were exempt from conscription into the tzarist army, during the nineteenth century and the early years of the twentieth it was a common practice to give each brother a different last name. Thus ten brothers would appear in the records as "only sons" of ten different sets of parents. Other males were falsely recorded as having died in infancy. As for females, since the government had no particular interest in them, they were often simply omitted from the official records.

Another problem with trying to interpret the information contained in the public records is that it has often been distorted by the political uses to which it is put. In order to disguise the fact that the majority of the people in Eishyshok were Jewish, for example, the Polish records cited statistics that referred to the total number of people in the entire district of Eishyshok, only 10 percent of whom were Jewish, rather than the number of people in the town itself.

Sometimes I was able to get to the truth behind the distortions in the government records by looking at private archives, where I found such items as postcards announcing the birth of a child, photographs with identifying inscriptions on the back, diary entries, wedding invitations, and so forth. Yet, the inaccuracies in the public records notwithstanding, I was able to use them to glean considerable amounts of valuable demographic information about the Jewish population of the shtetl. And the discrepancies between public and private records were themselves of interest, revealing much about the relations between the Jews and the governments they lived under.

The difficulties I faced in gaining access to government archives in what were formerly Iron Curtain countries were different in kind from, but no more severe than, many of the obstacles I came up against in my search for private materials. First there was the problem of finding them. This often required a detective's skills in tracking people down, especially since there was enormous confusion about people's names. People in the shtetl were rarely called by their family names. Even if they weren't going under a false name to avoid army service, their real surnames were often lost to history, submerged under names that indicated the family's place of origin (Matikanski from the village of Matikan, Paikowski from Pajkoi, Bastunski from Bastun, Radunski from Radun, and so forth) or the family occupation (Shuster meaning shoemaker, Portnoy the tailor, Kabacznik the innkeeper, Hutner the glassmaker). Or else they were known mainly by their nicknames, for there were as many nicknames as there were people. The nicknames could refer to a person's occupation (Pessie di Zigele = Pessie the Goat Shepherdess, Nahum der Kvoresman = Nahum the Gravesman); character or personality (Moshe der Shtiller = Moshe the Quiet One, Hayyaike di Berie = Hayyaike the Diligent); disability or deformity (Soreh di Kalike = Soreh the Lame, Israel Leib der Eiker = Israel Leib the Hunchback); or physical appearance (Benyomin der Boof = Benyomin the Fat, Isik Berishe Lape = Isik the Bear Paw, who had huge hands). Some of these nicknames were applied to family members for generations to come.

On one occasion, for example, a single clue, consisting of a family nickname (die meizalekh = the mice), took me from the old age home in Worcester, Massachusetts, where I first heard the nickname, to Melbourne, Australia. There I did at last find the material I sought. The man who gave it to me was a descendant of a turn-of-the-century heder teacher who had been nicknamed "the mouse" after a hilarious mishap involving that animal (see chapter 5).

Once I located the people with the family archives, I then had to persuade them to share the material with me. Generally speaking, those who had emigrated at a young age or were the children of emigrants were more cooperative than the survivor/exiles. People like Atara Zimmerman (née Kudlanski; in America Kudlanski was changed to Goodman), who emigrated to the United States as a teenager in 1930; Rosalind Rosenblatt (née Foster, of the Michalowski family), who was born in the United States but visited her grandmother in Eishyshok in 1932, when she was a young college student; and Judy Baston, a descendant of the Bastunski family who was born in Oakland — these women were all eager to participate in my project, in hopes of learning more about their roots, and/or reliving happy memories of the shtetl.

Some people, understandably, were reluctant to share their memories and memorabilia. Those who had lost their families in the Holocaust sometimes found it too painful to part with whatever mementos they'd managed to preserve. Their photos, letters, and other artifacts were their only physical link with families now vanished, a past forever destroyed. Occasionally I was able to overcome this reluctance by bringing a photographic crew to the house of the interviewee, so that we could reproduce the material on the spot. But in other cases I was not even given that option, for some of the Holocaust survivors, especially the older ones, were suspicious about my motives. In at least two cases this meant the permanent closing of a door, because with the death of these individuals, all their materials vanished.

Money helped smooth my way more than once. These business transactions could be very expensive. For one photograph of the market square on market day I paid with a color TV, a VCR, a radio, four jogging suits, and four pairs of Reebok sneakers. On another occasion I paid four thousand dollars for a batch of photographs.

The fact that my family was from Eishyshok often proved helpful, as I had expected it would. All of the emigrants and survivors knew my family very well, and some had had close associations with them. A few even remembered me as an infant or a small child. Thus I was accepted as an insider and entrusted with material and information they would never have shared with strangers.

Such cordiality was not universal, however. Old class conflicts occasionally surfaced. Some members of the working class (the bale-melokhe) still nursed grievances against my family as prime representatives of the householder or upper class (the balebatim). Their treatment of me was a way of evening up the score. As I should have anticipated, given the nature of small-town life, there were also those who had personal grudges against my family, some of them dating back to the nineteenth or even eighteenth century. They used me to settle old family accounts. One woman I approached, for example, refused even to respond to my initial greetings and good wishes until I apologized. What was her complaint? It seemed that some seventy years before, my grandfather, Shael Sonenson, in his capacity as neeman ha-kahal (head of the community), had voted against her widowed mother's request to lease a store in the prime commercial district, thereby consigning the family to a life of poverty. In more recent times, my mother, she claimed, had made a negative remark about the looks of her newborn baby. After apologizing on behalf of my entire family, I was granted an interview, and access to her photos and documents from Eishyshok.

On the whole, my relationships with former Eishyshkians and their descendants were very warm. I came to feel close to many of them, and in some cases, especially where the elderly were concerned, felt it incumbent upon me to assume responsibility for them. I arranged for leaky roofs to be repaired and hot water tanks installed in their apartments; I bought them electrical appliances, medicines, clothes, and blankets.

The kindnesses were mutual. Peretz Kaleko-Alufi summoned me to his deathbed in the Hadassah Hospital in Jerusalem, in order to deliver to me his last will and testament. For him this was a matter not of material goods, but of his expectations for the research I was doing about Eishyshok. These were his last words: "I trust you, that you will present Eishyshok the way it was: small, beautiful, and full of life." A few hours later he was gone. I felt that I had received a great blessing.

I asked a friend and fellow Eishyshkian, Moshe Szulkin, what he hoped I could accomplish with my book. His answer: "To understand Russia, one must be a Russian. To appreciate America, one must be American. If you want your readers to comprehend what Eishyshok was, you will have to transform every reader into an Eishyshkian. Since your Eishyshkian ancestors are nine centuries old and so is your Eishyshkian soul, your pen will be able to do its job."

I hope that Szulkin's confidence proves justified — that the portrait I have drawn will bring back to life many of the shtetl's admirable traditions; that it will offer knowledge of the past and hope for the future; that it will build bridges between the world that once was and the world still to be; and that the world of the future will be a better one because of those bridges.

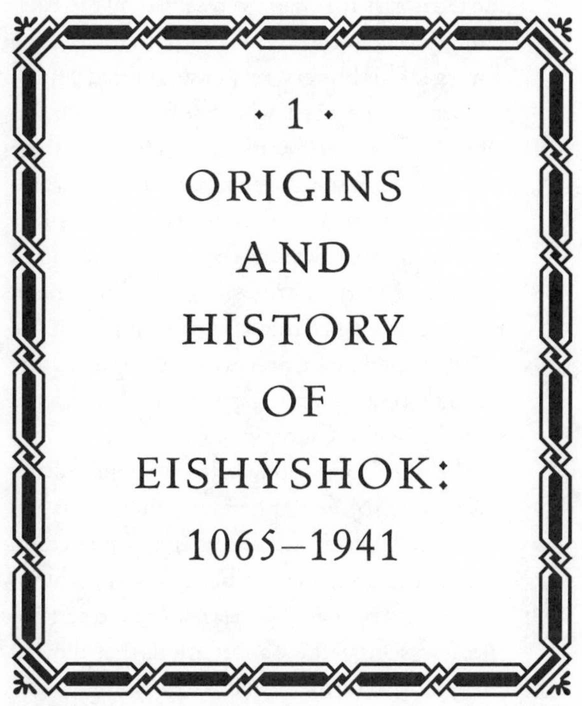

1 ORIGINS AND HISTORY OF EISHYSHOK: 1065–1941

IF I SHOULD TRY TO DESCRIBE EISHYSHOK, THE SHTETL OF MY BIRTH, ALL THE TIME OF MY LIFE ON THIS EARTH WILL NOT SUFFICE. FOR WHO COULD KNOW BETTER THE TOWN AND ITS PEOPLE, THEIR GREATNESS, AND WHAT THEY HAVE GIVEN TO THE WORLD?

Rabbi Meir Stalevich (1887–1951), shortly before his death, in EISHYSHOK KOROTEAH VE-HURBANAH

HISTORY HAS ITS OWN FASCINATING METHOD OF CHOOSING MATERIAL FOR THE PERmanent record. Who would have predicted that the obscure little town of Eishyshok would have a substantial entry in that record? But almost from the beginning, Eishyshok was a small town with big-city aspirations. During a span of nearly a thousand years, every one of the major events that shaped the destiny of Europe sooner or later meandered its way through little Eishyshok as well. Not only was Eishyshok a paradigm for a very specific kind of Eastern European Jewish town — the shtetl — but it was also a mirror to the wider world around it, its fate reflective of events hundreds and even thousands of miles away.

Neither the Eishyshkians themselves nor the world at large could ever quite seem to decide whether it was indeed just a small town or something much more significant. And if the latter, what did it signify? Whatever else it was, numerous sayings about it indicate that it was famous for being obscure. Until well into the twentieth century it was the town you named to make a point about something being remote, or primitive, or old-fashioned — the Eastern European Jewish equivalent of Podunk.

For example, a common Yiddish proverb to describe those who lost their way said that they were "farkrokhn in Eishyshok" — lost in Eishyshok. And the town was always ending up in the headlines in unexpected ways — as when the legendary Zionist hero Vladimir Jabotinsky singled it out in one of his famously flamboyant speeches during the 1920s. Urging a crowd in Warsaw to establish a Jewish self-defense system, he admonished that "even Eishyshok has a fire department to save the shtetl from fires." Isaac Bashevis Singer also cited Eishyshok when he wanted to contrast the urban addiction to timeliness and topicality with a small shtetl's sleepy, backward ways, writing, "New York is not Blendev or Ejszyszki, where people hold on to their newspapers forever!"[1]

On the other hand, when Judah Leib Gordon, the poet of the Haskalah (Jewish Enlightenment), wanted to point to the greatest concentration of scholarly minds in Lithuania, he advised people to go stand "at the crossroads of Mir, Volozhin, and Eishyshok." For a small shtetl, Eishyshok loomed large in many minds, and not just as a symbol of obscurity!

THE FOUNDING OF EISHYSHOK

Eishyshok might also stand as a symbol of antiquity. The history of Eishyshok begins in 1065, when the legendary Lithuanian military commander Eisys, serving under the Samogitian tribal duke Erdvilas, helped recapture some of the territories that had been seized by the Russian prince Yaroslav the Wise (980–1054). As a reward for his bravery, Eisys was granted land in a clearing in the forest, where he built a town and named it Eisiskes after himself.[2] Or so the story is recounted in the ancient Lithuanian Chronicles, a sixteenth-century compilation of historical writings that recount the transformation of a group of warring tribes into the Lithuanian Duchy, and thence into a partnership with the Polish Kingdom, a process that began in the eleventh century and was formally completed with the Lublin Union in 1569.

Meir Wilkanski, Eishyshok's nineteenth-century chronicler, in 1905, the year he emigrated to Eretz Israel, where he became one of the prominent authors of the Second Aliyah. PHOTO: M. L. SHERA. YESC, WILKANSKI

After the Tatar–Mongolian invasions of Russia (1223–1240), areas previously under Russian rule were left empty as the Russians fled, and some of the Lithuanian tribal dukes were able to annex parts of these war-torn, deserted territories. It was one of these annexations that allowed Eishyshok to further expand its holdings.[3]

The town founded by Eisys was among the earliest settlements in the region of Lida and Vilna, its name frequently preceded by the phrase "the ancient city of." Although there are other versions of when it came into being, including one that suggests Eishyshok was not established until the middle of the thirteenth century,[4] the existence of Jewish tombstones in the Old Cemetery that bore dates as early as 1097, for which there is evidence in a number of different sources, Lithuanian, Russian, and Polish, as well as Jewish, refutes that theory.[5]

Besides the several versions of the founding of Eishyshok, there are also other versions of the name of its founder — Eiksys and Aiksys among them — and numerous other versions of the name of the town: Ejszyszki in Polish; Eisisken and Eisiskes in Lithuanian; Aishishek, Aishishok, and Aishishuk in the late-nineteenth-century record books and correspondence of the shtetl's own landsman society in New York. In 1384 an agreement between the Crusaders and Grand Duke Witold of Lithuania bore the seal of a functionary who signed himself "Sigillum Sudemond de Wesisken" — "Wesisken" being a clear reference to Eisisken.[6] Around the same time, the Crusaders themselves left descriptions of the town, which they referred to variously as Eyksischeken, Eykshissken, and Eyksiskindorf (a "dorf" being a village, though Eishyshok appears in other documents as "eine stadt" — a town).[7] In late-fourteenth- and early-fifteenth-century Russian chronicles, the town appears as Eishishki, Jeshishki, Eikshishki, and Ekshishki,[8] and in later centuries it appears in an even greater variety of spellings.[9] Indeed, if posted vertically, the names would probably occupy a column as long as the huge market square at the town's center.

Just as there is no agreement on what the name of the town is, there is no consensus on how it got its name. Many of the Poles in the region, who didn't accept the idea that the Lithuanians had been there first, believed that the name came from the word *sheshkes*, meaning conifers or pine cones, a reference to the abundance of pine trees in the region. Their version, too, entered the local mythology, and then, after World War I, when Eishyshok came under the rule of the Second Polish Republic, it found its way into the visual shorthand of heraldry as well: In 1935 the Poles created a new coat of arms for Eishyshok consisting of three pine cones beneath which the year of its founding, 1065, was inscribed. Whether there were any antecedents for this in earlier coats of arms is not yet known.[10]

Another possible explanation, at least for the last part of the name, has to do with a Lithuanian coin called the *shok*, which was a currency common among many taxpayers in the Middle Ages. The Yiddish translation of *shok* was the number 60. Some scholars have suggested that the many Lithuanian shtetlekh whose names end in *shok* (Eishyshok, Vasilishok, Deveneshok, and so on) were called so to indicate that they were about sixty kilometers from the town or government facility where they paid their taxes — in shoks.

Local Jewish folklore had its own account of how the name of the town came into being: Once upon a time in the early days of the shtetl, a man came home and was greeted by his wife with a special treat of freshly cooked varenie (preserves), made from the berries that grow in such abundance in the region. Not realizing they were still sizzling hot, he took a big bite and scorched his tongue, which caused him to yell "Heishe-shok!" (Hot sauce!) at the top of his lungs. The scorched-tongue story is also used to account for the peculiar way in which Lithuanian Jews, especially those from small towns, often reverse their pronunciations of *s* and *sh*.

JEWISH EISHYSHOK

As one of the oldest Jewish communities in Lithuania, Eishyshok has a history that encompasses much of the drama and vitality, the triumph and tragedy, of nine centuries' worth of Jewish settlements throughout Eastern Europe. Indeed, its history can be seen as a paradigm for that of hundreds and even thousands of small Jewish towns in Lithuania and beyond.

Located on a wide plateau between the Neimen and the Wilja rivers and their many tributaries, Eishyshok is part of a landscape of gentle rolling hills and thick, deep, quiet forests. Its rivers flow peacefully, its lakes and marshes are still. But its mild, tranquil scenery is in sharp contrast to the natural disasters and devastating plagues that have afflicted it, and the violent wars that have been fought there during the long course of its lifetime — wars waged in the name of land, of faith, of riches, of ideology, of nationality, and of sheer ethnic hatred. For this is a region teeming with different peoples — Lithuanians, Tatars, Byelorussians, Russians, Germans, Poles, and Gypsies — and different religions — pagan, Catholic, Provoslavic (Russian Orthodox), Muslim, and Jewish — with all of them battling one another for control, or for mere survival. Alliances among the different groups would be formed, only to be renounced at a later date in favor of others deemed more advantageous when circumstances changed. Each group had its moments of ascendancy when it claimed Eishyshok as its own and attempted to reshape it (and rewrite its history) in its own image.

But in the midst of this multihued, many-threaded, and ever-changing tapestry, composed of peoples who were constantly assuming new identities as they transformed themselves into the image of whatever new power had assumed sovereignty for the moment, were the Jews. The Jews of Eishyshok, like those of the Jewish settlements throughout this part of the world, belonged to a strong community with remarkable cohesiveness and continuity. Their social, religious, cultural, and familial institutions, rooted in a tradition thousands of years old whose legacy was always being passed on and renewed, would remain in place until the towns themselves came to an end in the Holocaust. (And even then many of them would set seed in new places, better times.)

The Lithuanian Jews in particular held fast to the qualities that made them unique. No matter where the latest national boundaries lay or what flag flew above them, they remained within the fixed, permanent borders of their cultural identity. To be a Lithuanian Jew — a Litvak — was to have traits, values, and cultural ideals that set you apart not just from your non-Jewish neighbors, but from the Polish Jews, the Hasidim, and the Jews who lived in the Pale of Settlement. The Jews of Eishyshok were the very embodiment of these Lithuanian Jewish characteristics — sharpness of intellect, pungency of wit, a deep dedication to scholarship, intense religiosity, stubborn self-sufficiency, and unceasing industriousness — especially during the shtetl's last four centuries. They were to remain so even under the influence of Polish Jewry, which had an ever greater impact from the sixteenth century on.

EARLY SETTLERS

From the evidence of the tombstones in the Old Jewish Cemetery, Jewish Eishyshok is almost as old as the military settlement founded by Eisys. A chain of memories, stretching across the generations, supports that claim. Such memories were passed on during the traditional visits paid to the graves in the Old Cemetery, which were occasions for the elders to tell the family history to the young people.

One man interviewed in 1984 could remember being taken by his grandfather to pray at the site of the tombstone of one of his ancestors, dating back to the eleventh century. Though the stone itself was no longer there, having either sunk into the ground or been destroyed by Christian farmers from nearby Juryzdyki, the grandfather said that *his* grandfather had seen the stone and had been able to read the inscription. Until the destruction of the Jewish community in 1941, it remained the custom for young people to visit the Old Cemetery with their families on the Ninth of Av, a Jewish fast day (and on other dates on both the religious and the personal calendar), there to listen to their parents, grandparents, and great-grandparents tell stories about the ancestors at rest beneath their feet.

According to the evidence of the Old Cemetery tombstones, as recounted during such visits, the founding families of Jewish Eishyshok bore the names Ben-Yossef, Ben-Asher, and Azrieli. (Actually, there are thought to have been five founding families, but the original Hebrew names of the other two — whose descendants included the Senitski and Shimshelewitch fam-

Karaite Jews in Troki. YESC, KARAITE MUSEUM TRAKAI

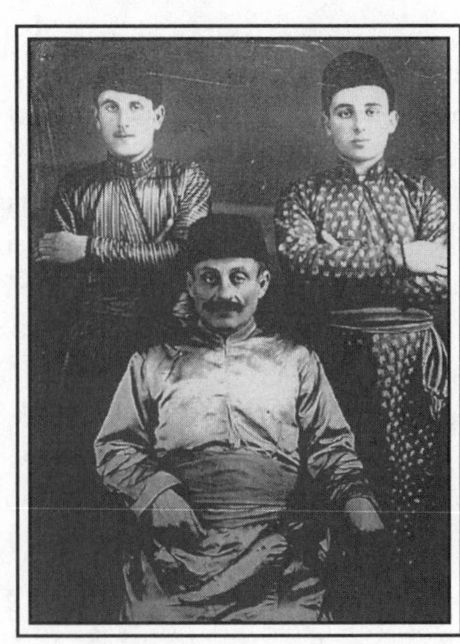

ilies — have been lost.) The Ben-Yossefs were later known by the Russified Hebrew version of their name, Josephowitch, and the Slavic version, Kabacznik; similarly, the Ben-Ashers became Asherowitch and Yurkanski; the Azrielis became Azrielowitch and, through marriage, Edelstein.

These families are believed by some to have been Karaite Jews — a sect dating from eighth-century Babylonia, which by the eleventh century had shifted one of its centers from the Middle East to Europe.[11] Unlike the main body of Jewry, known as Rabbinites, who recognize the authority of both Scripture and the Talmudic, rabbinical tradition, the Karaites looked to the Holy Scriptures as the sole and direct source of religious law. (The word *Karaites* is from the Hebrew *Kraraim* or *Benei Mikra* or *Baale Mikra*, meaning "People of the Scripture.")

Whether the original Jewish settlers in Eishyshok were Karaites or Rabbinites, no one really knows. Some remnants of distinctly Karaite practices survived into the twentieth century in several families, but they hardly constitute proof of any kind.[12] Also unknown is the geographic origin of those first settlers; but local tradition, official records, the ancient tombstones in the Old Cemetery, and family histories all seem to confirm the hypothesis of the Orientalist scholar of Jewish history and literature Abraham Elijah Harkavy (1835–1919), who maintained that the first Jews who settled in Lithuania came from Babylonia, other places in the Middle East, Crimea, and the Khazar Kingdom, which existed from the seventh to the tenth century between the Black and Caspian seas.

What is known is that the Jewish settlers who came to Eishyshok in the eleventh century, whoever they were and wherever they came from, were later joined by a continual influx of Jews from Germany, France, Spain, and other parts of Western Europe where Jews were made unwelcome. In the late fourteenth century there may also have been an influx of Karaite Jews from Crimea, because Crimean Karaites were among the prisoners Grand Duke Witold brought back

A Karaite woman of Crimea and her children, in an 1837 lithograph. YESC, LITHOGRAPH BY RAFFET

Five-year-old Layzer Szczuczynski (right) and his two-year-old brother Israel, who is wearing a Karaite hat during a family wedding in 1909. The custom was common till World War I among several families descended from the original settlers of Eishyshok. Both brothers were killed during the Holocaust, Israel and his family by the Armia Krajowa (AK). PHOTO: YITZHAK URI KATZ. YESC, SZCZUCZYNSKI

to Lithuania after defeating the Tatars in 1392. They settled in Troki, Lutsk, and other locations, which may have included Eishyshok.

By some time in the sixteenth century, a turning point had been reached, with Jews gradually changing from a minority to the majority of the town's population. From then until the end of the Jewish community in 1941, all the Jews of Eishyshok, including the descendants of the original settlers, were Rabbinites.

No matter how distinct a niche an ethnic group carves out for itself, however, nor how much it may try to remain apart from the conflicts consuming its neighbors, there is no escaping history. The story of Jewish Eishyshok, of Lithuanian Jewry, and beyond that of all of Eastern European Jewry, cannot be told apart from the history of the region. Just as it was said, in tribute to the excellence and impact of the legal scholars of Eishyshok, that the learning that took place at its distinguished yeshivah had ramifications as far away as the British Parliament in London, so, too, the people of Eishyshok found their fate bound up with that of their neighbors, and beyond them with events on the national and even global scale.

If the Duke of Lithuania married the Princess of Poland and converted to Catholicism in 1386, there were far-ranging consequences — both good and bad — for the Jews of Eishyshok. If the Crusaders were on the march in the vicinity during the fourteenth and fifteenth centuries, the Jews lost lives, land, and property as readily as the pagans and Muslims did. If the Cossacks and the Tatars joined together in a revolt against the Polish nobility in the mid-seventeenth century, the Jews suffered massive devastation too. And so it went, until the worldwide conflagration that began with the German invasion of Poland and resulted in the murder of 6 million Jews, including nearly all of the Jews of Eishyshok.

EISHYSHOK IN EARLY LITHUANIAN HISTORY

Given its location at a strategic intersection of the roads leading to the fortified cities of Lida and Navaredok, it is natural that Eishyshok should have begun its life as a military settlement. It was responsible for protecting the southern borders of what would later become Lithuania against the many different invaders who would try to stake claims to the land: the Russians and Tatars from the south and east, the Crusaders from the north and west.

In 1323 the Grand Duke of Lithuania, Prince Gediminas (c. 1275–1341), moved the capital of the country from Troki to the new city of Vilna, which meant that the safety of the three major roads that ran from Eishyshok to Vilna, including one that went on to Cracow, became of primary importance. Probably it was around this

Shaul Dubrowicz (right) and friend at the ruins of the Navaredok castle in 1931. PHOTO: BEN ZION SZREJDER

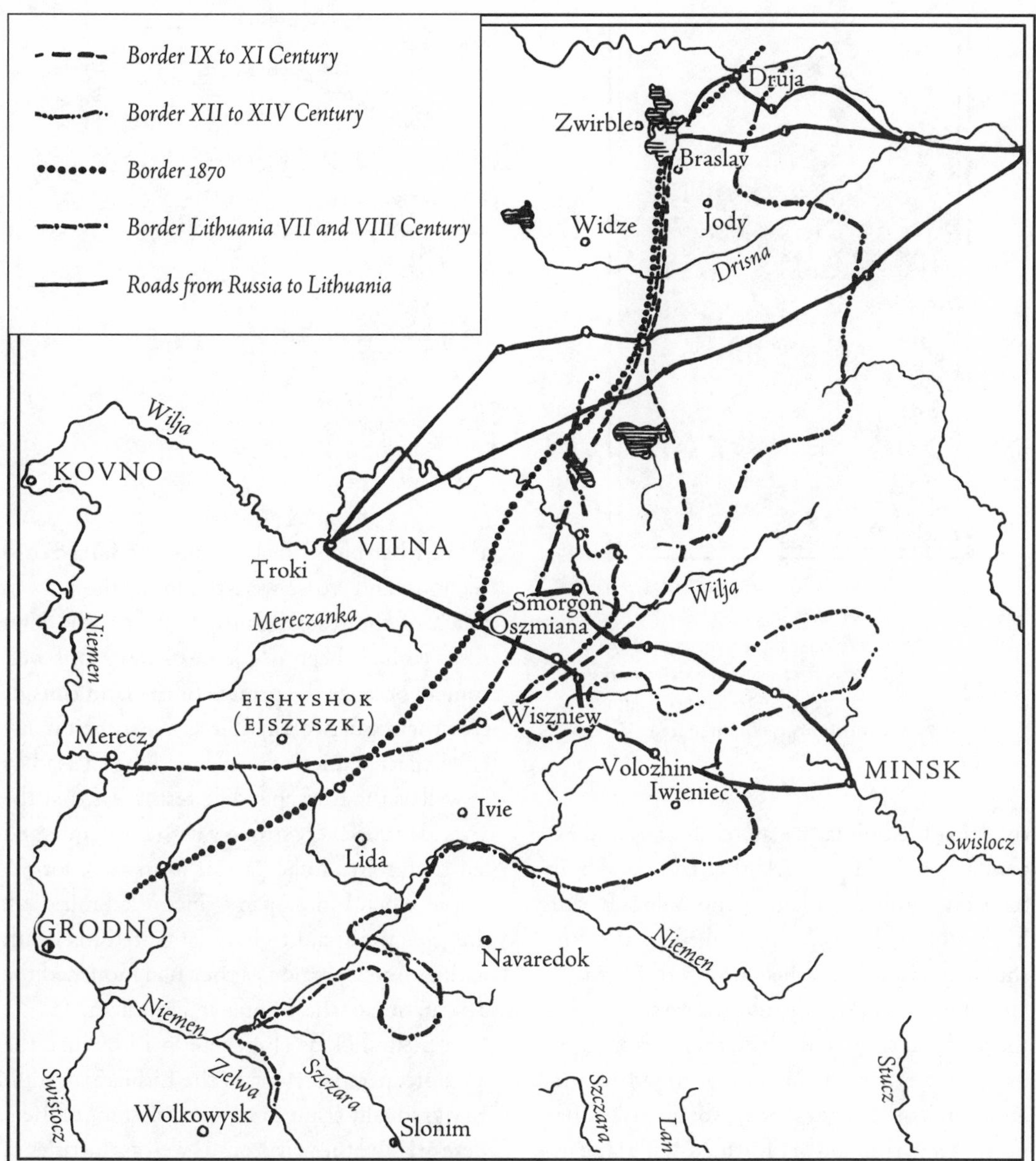

Borders of Lithuania from the seventh to the nineteenth century.

The entrance to Troki (now Trakai), capital of Lithuania until 1323. (Yaffa Eliach is on the extreme right with the Krisilov family.) The beautiful ancient town has been reconstructed; its castles are a museum and tourist attraction. PHOTO: DAVID ELIACH, AUGUST 10, 1987. YESC

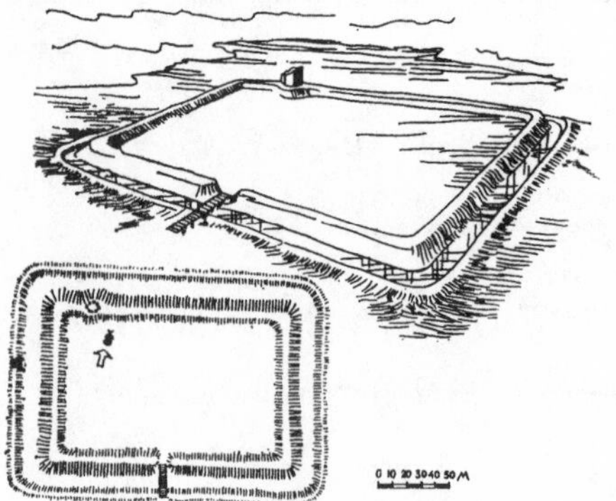

The position of the Eishyshok castle in the thirteenth century. YESC, LIETUVOS TSR URBANISTIKOS *PAMINKLAI* NO. 6, P. 26

time that Gediminas began reinforcing and expanding the ancient castle that had been built high on a hill overlooking the Vilna–Radun highway near Eishyshok. Flanked by the Virshuki, the Kantil, and the Dumbla rivers, which are tributaries of the Vistula, the castle guarded the road and the town nearby, thus becoming an important factor in the steady growth of the area, for, as the historian S. Abramauskas has noted, "Construction of a fortified castle is an inseparable aspect of settlements."[13]

LOYAL LITHUANIANS

Part of Eishyshok's original vitality can perhaps be attributed to the tolerance with which the Lithuanians treated the Jews. The Lithuanians prided themselves on being the last pagan people in Europe, which was one of the factors in their tradition of religious tolerance — a tradition that made the Jews feel relatively secure at a time when blood libels, expulsions, forced conversions, and worse were the lot of the Jews in much of the rest of Europe. In fact, the Jews seem to have been not just tolerated but welcomed, because the princes of the land considered them trustworthy allies against their many Christian enemies, who included the Crusaders as well as the Russians. The result was that the Jews identified very strongly with Lithuania, and felt themselves to be part of it. In 1288, for example, when Lithuanian Prince Vladimir died, the Jews were said to have lamented his death with as much passion as they had mourned the destruction of the Temple in Jerusalem.[14]

In Eishyshok as elsewhere in Lithuania, the Jews prospered, serving in the Lithuanian military, gradually rising in status until some of them were granted the privileges as well as the titles of nobility, being rewarded with land in recognition of their services to the rulers of the duchy. On the evidence of the size of the tracts of land that were owned by descendants of the original Jewish settlers in Eishyshok, it seems that their services were very highly valued indeed. Their emotional connection to that land, a tie forged over the many centuries the land remained in their families, proved enduring. (Their ownership rights, alas, did not, for the land was taken

The ancient castle of Grodno was typical of the region. YESC, MINSK 1986

from them in the nineteenth century, by a series of decrees issued by the Russian tzars.)

As long as Lithuania remained pagan — and for some time thereafter — the tradition of tolerance for the Jews continued. This was fortunate for the Jews, because Lithuania persisted in its pagan beliefs long after the rest of Europe had abandoned them. Well into the fourteenth century the Grand Duke of Lithuania, Prince Gediminas, still put his faith in Perkunas, the god of thunder and forests, who ruled over the many other gods and goddesses in the Lithuanian pantheon. When emissaries of the pope attempted to convert the prince to Christianity in 1324, the prince told them he would like to be treated by them as he treated those within his domains: He did not interfere with the Christians who worshipped their God according to their laws, and he hoped that he and his subjects would be left to worship God in their own way. He concluded his remarks by saying, "We all share one God, our Creator." The papal emissaries left without accomplishing their mission. Some see in Prince Gediminas' response, with its monotheistic theme, a sign of the influence of his Jewish subjects, who were then concentrated mainly in southern Lithuania.[15]

Whether this is true or not, there was no doubt that the Jews of Eishyshok prospered during the reign of Gediminas, as did the Jews throughout his realm, and the country as a whole. An empire builder who issued an open invitation to people of various nationalities, religions, and occupations to come and settle in Lithuania, Gediminas presided over an expanding economy, which was receptive to the contributions of the many peoples he had welcomed within his borders.

The religious tolerance and goodwill of Gediminas' reign continued to prevail during the reign of two of his sons. For example, when the Black Death of 1348–1350 took its toll on Lithuania, as it did throughout Europe, no one thought to blame the Jews for the devastating tragedy, although they were a common scapegoat in much of Christian Europe. And Gediminas' legacy of tolerance was furthered by Grand Duke Witold, known as Vytautas the Great, who on June 24, 1388, granted a charter to the Jews of Troki, Brisk (the Jewish name for Brest-Litovsk), and, a year later, Grodno, spelling out their legal and economic rights, guaranteeing them personal and religious security, and allowing them certain tax exemptions (on synagogues and cemeteries, for example). According to the Russian historian Sergei Bershadsky, this charter laid the foundation for a system of Jewish autonomy under which the Jews would flourish for several centuries.[16]

Their economic and political well-being was also enhanced by the eventual routing of the Crusaders. Indeed, it was the frequent attacks by the Livonian and Teutonic Knights against that population which forced the many tribal clans of the area, most prominent among them the Samogitians, to try to protect themselves by uniting into the state of Lithuania some time in the middle of the thirteenth century.[17] After the Battle of Grunwald in Prussia in 1410, a major international battle in which the Teutonic Knights were defeated, the final decline of the

Crusaders was set in motion.[18] As a result, the roads and the countryside, as well as the towns and villages themselves, became much safer. The Jews of Lithuania were now joined by Jews who migrated from Bohemia, Crimea, France, Germany, Italy, and Spain in the hope that they, too, would be able to benefit from the peace, prosperity, and religious freedom that had begun to spread throughout the land. The followers of the Czech Christian reformer Jan Hus (1369–1415) also found a haven under the tolerant regime of Grand Duke Witold, after years of persecution in Germany.

With its large tracts of land that had been cleared from the surrounding forest, its abundance of water and timber, its central location, and its proximity to major roadways, Eishyshok was in an excellent position to benefit from the commercial prospects that came with this new security. Inns and other businesses now began to spring up along the now safe roads, to service the many noblemen, and other civilians and soldiers, who passed through Eishyshok or came there for business.

Over the following centuries Eishyshok continued to grow in importance, gradually being transformed from a military settlement to a market town, a place where tradespeople, artisans, and farmers as well as soldiers could flourish, and where many of the new emigrants found a home. Sometime in the fifteenth century the town became a district seat, one of the administrative centers of Lithuania, along with nearby Grodno and Lida.[19]

What would have been one of its greatest moments of glory occurred — or rather, didn't occur — in 1429, when Grand Duke Witold, who was to be crowned the ruler of Lithuania, arranged to have his coronation take place in Eishyshok, which some historians believe was the birthplace of his wife Anne. Upon arrival in Eishyshok, he was met by the bishop of Vilna and a group of nobles, but the coronation they had all gathered for never took place, because Witold's cousin and rival, Jagiello, now the king of Poland, withdrew his consent.[20] Witold died the following year.

In 1433 the Livonian Order of Knights burned the town down, but it was quick to rise from its ashes, once again showing the vitality that was to characterize it for many centuries to come.[21] In 1453, at a time of tension between Poland and Lithuania, Eishyshok was chosen to host the Council of Lithuanian Lords. By the beginning of the sixteenth century it was being referred to as one of the most important towns in the Grand Principality of Lithuania. In 1513 records show that it was paying a "war tax" equal to that of Troki and other prominent settlements, which was an indication of the size of the town. Its military status was evident from the number of noblemen who resided there: 238 in 1528–1529, a significant number of whom were cavalrymen.[22]

THE UNION OF LITHUANIA AND POLAND: 1386–1569

The long dominion of the pagan gods over Lithuania had come to an end in 1386, with the politically impelled marriage of the Lithuanian ruler Jogaila (1351–1434) — Jagiello in Polish — and the Polish princess Jadwiga. She was eleven years old, her pagan husband three times her age. Their union, and the resulting political union of Poland and Lithuania, created a state that was much more powerful than either state alone.

Both the union and the subsequent conversion of Lithuania to Christianity would have a monumental impact on Lithuanian Jewry, with consequences spanning the entire spectrum of their lives: religious, economic, social, and legal.

THE CHRISTIANIZATION OF LITHUANIA

After the wedding and coronation in Cracow, Jagiello, now king of Poland and Lithuania, returned to his castle in Vilna. There he decreed the abolition of the pagan gods. Perkunas's grove of sacred oaks was felled, the statue of Perkunas overturned, the eternal fire at its base extinguished. The people were baptized, sometimes forcibly, in droves, and many pagan practices were Christianized. Shortly after the conversion, Grand Duke Witold built the Church of the Ascension in Eishyshok (though certain relics of the pagan era would remain in existence until some time in the nineteenth century, tucked away in a hidden corner of the church, and later transferred to the church built in nearby Juryzdyki).[23]

As part of the Catholic church's ascendancy, it, like the Polish nobility, began amassing large tracts of land in Lithuania. The dean of the Catholic church in Eishyshok fought for control and ownership of the land around his church, just as churches throughout the region were doing, and eventually it was granted, probably some time in the late fourteenth century or early fifteenth century. Hence the name of the town that grew up around it: Juryzdyki, meaning "under Church jurisdiction." Enclaves that were exempt from the authority of the central government, being owned by the nobility or the church or both, were often called Juryzdyki, in acknowledgment of their autonomous jurisdiction, which explains why from the fourteenth century on there were towns named Juryzdyki throughout the Polish–Lithuanian commonwealth.[24] Unfortunately for the Old Jewish Cemetery in Eishyshok, the grant of additional land to the church meant that the cemetery's grounds were now immediately contiguous to the boundaries of Juryzdyki, and were constantly being encroached upon by the Christian villagers.

Between 1386, when the personal union began, and 1569, when the Act of Union was signed at Lublin and Lithuania came more completely under the domination of Poland, Lithuania was gradually Polonized, particularly the region around Vilna. Not only did its non-Jewish people adopt the Catholic faith of the Poles, they also adopted Polish laws and customs. Eventually the church itself would lose the battle to retain Lithuanian as the language of its sermons.[25]

Though the Lithuanian Jews retained their right to own land under these new laws — unlike the Polish Jews, who had never had landowning rights — they lost many of their other rights, including their access to the privileges and titles of the nobility, for which Christianity was now a prerequisite. The exclusion of the Jews from the ranks of the nobility was part and parcel of their being segregated as a separate estate under the new Polish–Lithuanian regime. Where previously the Jews had been integrated into Lithuanian society, from top to bottom, they now constituted one of the five estates that emerged during the Jagiellonian period (which ended with the death of the last Jagiellonian king in 1572).

Membership in each estate — the clergy, the nobility, the burghers, the Jews, and the peasants — was determined largely by birth and religion, and each estate had its own rights, rules, and responsibilities. Since birth largely determined one's place in the social order, it was very difficult to move from one estate to another, the way being strewn with obstacles. This was a dramatic change for Lithuania, which had been a mainly military-oriented society, in which all classes, including the nobility, earned their land and privileges in service to the duchy, and there was a great deal of social mobility. For the Lithuanian nobility, the change would prove to be empowering. Previously dependent on the grand duke, under Polish influence the Lithuanian nobles began to aspire to the same rights and privileges accruing to the Polish nobility, who enjoyed considerable independence from their own crown.

For the Jews the various changes would result in mixed consequences. One of the effects of Lithuania becoming Christian was that it began to turn anti-Semitic, like the rest of Christian Europe, and even staged its own expulsion, in 1495, three years after the expulsion from Spain (which had resulted in an influx of Jews into Lithuania). Grand Duke Alexander Jagiello (1461–1506) hoped that by expelling the Jews he could cancel all the loans they had given him and seize all their properties, which would allow him to install Christian settlers from Germany and Sweden in their homes, and fill his empty state treasury. None of his plans worked out, however; the Christian settlers did not come, and the treasury remained empty. By 1503 the grand duke had permitted the Jews to return from their lands of exile, which in the case of the Jews from southern Lithuania were in Crimea and Turkey. Jews from Troki, Grodno, Brisk, and probably Eishyshok had gone to Poland—where the grand duke's own brother, King Jan Olbracht (1459–1501) had given them a warm welcome. Returning to Lithuania, especially to the Troki–Grodno–Brisk–Eishyshok area, the Jews had both their public and private properties restored to them.[26]

In 1538, the Diet of Piotrkow issued anti-Jewish provisions regulating the relations between Christians and Jews. Jews were not allowed to own Christian serfs, hire Christian servants, or wear Christian-style clothing—provisions that signaled a greater determination than ever to set the Jews apart, even if many of the restrictions were ignored in practice. In 1550 and again in 1569–71, during the reign of Sigismund II Augustus, the last Jagiellonian monarch, Lithuania was struck by a series of epidemics. Under the influence of the Polish church and parliament, which did not share the king's spirit of religious tolerance, the local population put the blame for the epidemics on the Jews and other nonbelievers. Now Lithuania was following the example of the rest of Europe in using the Jews as scapegoats, a distinct departure from its behavior two centuries before during the Black Death.

Lithuanian farmers in their typical dress. YESC

Despite these outbreaks of religious hatred, which were new in the case of Lithuania and which followed long precedent in Poland, the union of the two states ushered in a true age of opportunity for the Jews of Eastern Europe. The Polish nobles, whose power in the state was steadily increasing, may sometimes have been anti-Semitic in their personal sentiments, but they found the Jews to be of considerable use in their ever-expanding commercial ventures, and therefore often protected them against the church and the burghers.

THE LUBLIN UNION

On July 1, 1569, a more far-reaching agreement, binding Poland and Lithuania into one indivisible body and bringing Lithuania much more firmly under Polish influence, was signed in Lublin. Afterward, King Sigismund II Augustus ushered the entire assembly of notables who had gathered to witness the sealing of the union into the Church of St. Stanislaw, where he knelt before the altar and led them in prayer — a symbol of the ever-greater role the church would be playing in what was now the kingdom or commonwealth of Poland and Lithuania.

POLONIZATION OF LITHUANIA AND THE JEWS

For the Jews of Lithuania, the Lublin Union meant coming ever more under the influence of Polish Jewry, adopting their educational system and many of their communal institutions and organizations as well. Lithuanian Jews also found that their status within the state was changing, so that it conformed more fully to that of the Polish Jews. The latter had until the mid-sixteenth century been under the protection of the Polish crown (Servi Camerae). But at the Diet of Piotrkow in 1539, it had been decided that those Jews who had settled in the estates, towns, and villages owned by the great Polish magnates would now come under the magnates' jurisdiction.

After the signing of the Lublin Union, the Lithuanian nobility received full legal equality with the Polish nobility, which meant that many of the Jews in Lithuania were also now under the jurisdiction of the local nobility — or else under the jurisdiction of the Polish nobility, who had been steadily migrating into Lithuanian territory during the centuries when the union was being cemented. No longer were the Jews under the direct protection of the Lithuanian grand duke.

The Polonization of Vilna and its vicinity, and with it the arrival of a large number of Polish nobles in the countryside, resulted in the proliferation of small, mainly Jewish market towns nearby, many of them under the direct jurisdiction of the nobility. Such towns were known in Yiddish as *shtetlekh* (literally, "small towns"). The spread of these Jewish towns was part of a process taking place throughout Lithuania and Poland, and eventually to the south and east as Poland moved into Byelorussia and the Ukrainian steppes — an area that was later to become part of the Pale of Settlement. For wherever the nobility went — and they were on the move to all these places — they made the Jews welcome, because they had need of their services. They used the Jews as tax collectors and administrators, shopkeepers and traders, land managers and farmers. Eager for employment, Jews began coming from Austria, Germany, France, Bohemia, and Turkey, and from other areas within Poland itself. They settled both in already established areas and, in larger numbers, in the frontier areas along the eastern borders, because these were considered lands of opportunity. Some of the towns grew as large as 20,000 people, but most were in the 1,000–5,000 range.

As is well known, the Jews in these areas emerged as the principal middlemen — traders — between the peasants and nobles, and between them and the European community at large. They traveled east to the borders of Russia, west as far as Germany and even France. At the local level they went out to the villages in the countryside to buy and sell, and held once-a-week markets in the shtetl, where the peasants could sell their wares and produce, and buy whatever merchandise they needed from the Jewish shopkeepers and artisans. Many people preferred to buy from them rather than their Christian competitors because their prices — and their profit margins — were often lower. This was so because, having been barred from membership in the Christian guilds because they were Jewish, the shtetl craftsmen were free to set their own prices.

In addition to the weekly market days, some shtetlekh also held large annual or semiannual fairs. Eishyshok, for example, had a horse fair that drew traders from hundreds of miles away.

Jews earned a living not just through trade, but through the leasing, managing, and even farming of the magnates' country estates, and all the many commercial transactions associated with those estates. For the Jews, the development of private towns and estates under the jurisdiction of the magnates proved a great economic opportunity. For the nobility, who made good use of the managerial skills of the Jews, these towns and landed estates were among their most profitable ventures.

Eishyshok was different from many of the shtetlekh that grew up around this time in that it was an old town with an already long history of Jewish settlement. But as the Polish magnates built new private towns to which the Jews flocked, while also taking under their jurisdiction existing towns, Eishyshok's Jews would benefit from the same social, economic, and even legal forces at work in all of them. Thus in the middle of the sixteenth century we find the first official mention of a market and shops in Eishyshok.[27] By 1603 Eishyshok is no longer referred to as a military town, but rather a market town, with regular, organized market days. The transition from military settlement to Jewish trade shtetl was ultimately the result of the successive acts of union which created the Polish–Lithuanian kingdom. The gradual Polonization of the area was another long-lasting result of the Lublin Union. In fact, Eishyshok and the area around it would remain a mostly Polish enclave until World War II.

JEWISH AUTONOMY UNDER THE LUBLIN UNION

For the Jews, one of the most significant developments to occur in the wake of the Lublin Union was the formation of the Jewish Councils: the Council of the Four Lands of Poland and the Council of the Land of Lithuania. These were ruling bodies made up of elected officials and legal scholars (rabbis and judges), whose original mandate was to be the official collector of taxes from the Jewish community for the Polish–Lithuanian crown. It was this responsibility that caused the Councils to come into being, and that constituted the legal basis of their power, for the rulers had found it difficult to collect the taxes they levied. Needing a central administrative organ to assess and collect what was owed them, they found it in their interest to grant the Jews a measure of self-government and autonomy. But from that one very specific function of tax collection, the Councils would expand their powers into every aspect of Jewish communal life, much to the benefit of most of the Jews under their domain (expressions of dissatisfaction and tension between many of the smaller communities and the Councils notwithstanding).

The Councils represented the highest form of autonomy ever achieved by European Jews. The years of their existence, from the mid-sixteenth century to 1764, coincided with a tremendous growth in the size (as well as the economic and political power) of the Jewish population of Eastern Europe. Polish Jewry, for example, grew from somewhere between 20,000 and 30,000 at the end of the fifteenth century to 300,000 by the mid-seventeenth century.[28]

In both Poland and Lithuania the Councils were established on the foundations of Jewish communal organizations that had been in existence for thousands of years. The concept of the Jewish community as an administrative body — the kehilah — had first come into existence during the Babylonian exile, and it eventually took root wherever Jews lived in the Diaspora. With the destruction of the Second Temple in Jerusalem in 70 C.E., and the loss of the Jewish homeland, the kehilah became the organization responsible for the official conduct of Jewish affairs. It offered to its members religious, educational, judicial, financial, and charitable services, which helped the Jews of the Diaspora achieve a degree of self-sufficiency that would otherwise have been impossible. This independence would reach unprecedented levels under the rule of the Polish–Lithuanian kingdom.

The elected officers of the Jewish community served on a board known as the *kahal* (though sometimes the terms *kahal* and *kehilah* were used interchangeably, as was the case during the last hundred years or so of Eishyshok's existence). The number of elected officials varied with the size of the community. Their titles and functions, which were designated in Hebrew (the language of scholarship and of officialdom in the Jewish community, even in the Diaspora), included the rosh ha-kahal (head of the community); parnasim (aldermen); neemanim (trustees); gabbaim (supervisors and tax collectors); shamaim (tax assessors); kotev (literally "writer"— the council's clerk); shtadlan (diplomatic spokesman or court lobbyist, who interceded between the Jewish community and the state authorities). These board members achieved a sort of de facto recognition on the part of the governments under whom the Jews lived, because it was a convenience for the rulers to be able to deal with a central Jewish authority. With the formation of the Councils, the recognition became more formal and official.

By 1580 the Council of the Four Lands of Poland was fully functioning. It included representatives from the four major districts: Great Poland, Little Poland, Ruthenia, and Volhynia. These larger Jewish communities generally controlled and took responsibility for the smaller ones in the area. The Lithuanian Council, for which we have records going back only to 1623 but which may have come into being even earlier than the Council of the Four Lands, included representatives from the super-kehilot of Brest-Litovsk, Grodno, and Pinsk, which were later joined by Vilna and Slutsk. Although the two Councils functioned independently of each other with respect to their constituent communities, the Lithuanian Council was dependent on the Council of the Four Lands for representation before the central government of the Polish–Lithuanian kingdom.

Both Councils consisted of two distinct houses, a parliamentary-style body made up of elected delegates from the major communities, and a Supreme Court–type body, made up of legal scholars, all of whom were rabbi-judges (dayyanim). The judicial branch formulated the legislation; the parliamentary branch was responsible for executing and enforcing it. Though the means of electing delegates varied from one community to another within each Council, what they all had in common was the principle of very limited voting rights. Only a small percentage of male householders — as low as 1 percent in Lithuania and probably never more than 5 percent in Poland — participated in the elections.[29] This meant that the Councils were elected by and made up of an oligarchy of well-to-do householders and powerful rabbis.[30]

Mirroring the traditional community board, the kahal, the Councils were made up of officials bearing similar titles and functions. At the head of the Council was a "parnas of the House of Israel for the Four Lands" (in Poland), who presided over the Council in both external and internal matters and was always chosen from the delegates to the parliamentary branch; in the Lithuanian Council the comparable leadership position was held by a rabbi well versed in Jewish law, and for a long period of time this was always the head of the rabbinic court (av beth din) of Brest-Litovsk. Second in the hierarchy was the neeman (trustee), who acted as treasurer and chief secretary. This position could be held by candidates from either the legislative or the judicial house. There was a shtadlan, who was obliged to be on hand at the royal court or the state assemblies (sejms) to represent Jewish interests before the government. He had to be fluent in local languages, and conversant with court customs and fashions. And of course there were the shamaim (tax assessors), whose function was so integral to the existence of the Councils.

The Council of the Four Lands met twice yearly, at the fairs of Lublin and Jaroslav, though less frequently during the eighteenth century. The Lithuanian Council did not meet as regularly or as often, the time and venue of its meetings being decided as circumstances required. From 1623 to its last year, 1764, it held thirty-seven meetings in a number of different places, with fifteen of those meetings taking place in the first thirty years. In 1695 they met in Olkenik, next door to Eishyshok.[31]

All the transactions conducted during the meetings were written down in the official record book — the pinkas — maintained by each Council. The records that survive give a very good idea of how far-reaching and comprehensive the legislation was. Though only a few remnants of the Council of the Four Lands pinkas still exist, we have the complete proceedings of the Lithuanian Council from 1623 to 1764 (which made it clear that the Lithuanian Council had been in existence for a considerable time prior to 1623).[32] The Lithuanian Council's pinkas contains detailed descriptions of its tax collections, the financial status of each community, and the sum of money it paid. It also records ordinances and regulations issuing from the Council that governed every aspect of Jewish life: social, ethical, religious, and legal. An astonishing range of subjects was addressed by the Council: food; dress; family life; education; commerce; clergy; religious festivals; the use of the herem (excommunication) as a form of punishment; the status of women, minors, and the homeless; economic competition between Jews; ethical and legal questions regarding credit and interest rates; relations among Jews; Jewish–Christian relations and the crises that issued from them (including blood libels, which prior to Christianity had never occurred in Lithuania). Even matters beyond the borders of Eastern Europe came up for consideration, as indicated by the minutes on the subject of charity for Jews in Palestine.

The two Councils sometimes adopted divergent approaches to problems, based on differences in their respective national histories. The Lithuanian Jews, for example, had had a relationship with their sovereign that gave them much more of a sense of security about their place in the state than the Polish Jews had enjoyed. Coming out of a period in which religious persecution of the Jews had been unknown, and with a long tradition of land ownership and cultivation behind them, they felt themselves to be an integral part of the country and its economy. The Polish Jews, with a different experience of history, felt their position to be more precarious.

Thus the Polish Council of the Four Lands prohibited the Jews from engaging in the sort of economic activities — the leasing of salt mines, or collecting local tax and customs revenues — that might put them in competition with the nobility. These leases were an extension of the arenda, the system by which a Jew leased a magnate's land and estates for a fee, in exchange for which he managed the properties and received the income from them. The custom, which began in the sixteenth century, pertained not just to commodities but to a variety of revenue transactions, like the collecting of local tolls and levies (which was subcontracted out in an arrangement known as tax farming). Though in many places the nobility were happy to assign these leases to the Jews, in others they held on to them for themselves or assigned them to family and friends. The Polish Council felt that for Jews to press their claims and compete with the nobility for such revenues would mean harming the whole community.

By contrast, the Lithuanian Council felt that the Jewish community would benefit if customs revenues were kept in Jewish hands. In reality, neither Council was ever able to ensure that their decisions were followed to the letter. The communities over which they presided often proved too recalcitrant for them to exercise effective control.

The tensions between the Councils and their constituent communities (which had their own regional councils, intermediate between them and the national Councils) were usually related to money, particularly to the Councils' tax-collecting practices. Part of the tax revenue, of course, went into the coffers of the national government, for it was as tax collector for the state that the Council had its official standing. Another part went back to the communities in the form of support for internal social welfare needs. These revenue distributions were perceived as being weighted in favor of the larger, wealthier communities; the smaller communities felt their own interests were not well represented. And it was true that the super-kehilot — the five principal communities, in the case of Lithuania — often slighted the smaller constituent communities, since the latter had no direct representation and no voice in the decision-making. Over time, the smaller communities began to fund their own social services organizations, paying for them with a kind of sales or service tax — the korobka, or "shopping basket" tax — levied on certain consumer items, particularly kosher meat. Naturally, this made them even more resistant to paying the taxes levied by the Council.

There were also tensions between the two national Councils, also over money issues. A third part of the tax revenues collected by the Councils was for the purpose of maintaining the effectiveness of the Councils vis-à-vis the central government. This involved gifts, outright bribery, the costs of legal and diplomatic intercession, and so on. The Council of the Four Lands expected the Lithuanian Council to share in the expenses it incurred in trying to buy favor from the state, which it deemed a crucial part of its mandate. Often the Lithuanian Council deemed these payments excessive.

Despite all the conflicts and resentment, in general the Council system proved a success. It allowed the Jews a degree of self-government — reasonably effective, fair, enlightened self-government — which helped the Jewish communities of Poland and Lithuania to survive and even, during much of the war-torn seventeenth and eighteenth centuries, to thrive.

TIMES OF TROUBLE: MASSACRES, WARS, PLAGUES, AND FAMINES

As the nobles flourished, and with them many of "their" Jews, the peasants felt ever more burdened and oppressed. In 1648 Bogdan Chmielnicki led the Cossacks and their allies the Tatars in a revolt against the Polish nobility, whom they regarded as exploiters of the Ukrainian peasantry. Despite the fact that most shtetl Jews were completely at the mercy of the Polish magnates, who often abused and exploited them, too, they were perceived as the noblemen's allies, and were targeted accordingly.[33] Chmielnicki and his Cossacks inflicted terrible devastation on the Jews. Nathan of Hanover, the eyewitness chronicler of the Chmielnicki massacres, describes these atrocities in language that calls to mind the Nazi cruelties that would be committed some three centuries later:

Children were slaughtered in their mothers' bosoms and many children were torn apart like fish. They ripped up the bellies of pregnant women, took out the unborn children, and flung them in their faces. They tore open the bellies of some of them and placed a living cat within the belly and left them alive thus, first cutting off their hands so that they would not be able to take the living cat out of the belly . . . and there was never an unnatural death in the world that they did not inflict upon them.[34]

Many Jews were taken into captivity by the Tatars and sold into slavery in the markets of Turkey. Some managed to escape; a large number were redeemed through ransom payments made by Jews in other locations. The Lithuanian Council, for example, passed a resolution imposing taxes and tariffs specifically for the redemption of these captives (pidyon shvuyim). Regarding the "many souls of Israel which were taken into captivity," the Council wrote: "We have written an authorization to all communities and to every place where there is a minyan [quorum of ten Jewish males] . . . to redeem every soul." The refugee problem that resulted as tens of thousands of Jews fled in the wake of the massacres was another of the issues the Lithuanian Council confronted: "Because so many of our people have been expelled from their places and properties and as yet have not returned to home and safety . . ." was the beginning of one Council recommendation concerning the heavy obligations it expected the community to shoulder in support of the refugees.[35]

The massacres had a devastating impact on the family. Surviving children too young to remember their families did not know their identity, which was a matter of grave concern to the Council.[36] In Italy some years later, two surviving children were about to marry each other when it was discovered, only moments before the ceremony, that they were brother and sister.[37] Children born to women who had been raped by Chmielnicki's soldiers and the Tatars were yet another problem the communities had to come to terms with, both socially and halakhically (legally).

Prior to the Holocaust, the Chmielnicki massacres of 1648–49 constituted the largest tragedy ever to befall Eastern European Jewry. Though it is impossible to make an accurate determination of the number killed, it was in the tens of thousands. Jewish chroniclers of the time mention 100,000 murdered, 300 communities destroyed.[38] In 1650 the Lithuanian Council decreed three years of mourning and prohibited the wearing of elaborate clothes and ornamentation during that period; it also dictated that "no musical instruments be heard in the House of Israel, not even the musical entertainment at weddings, for one full year."[39] The twentieth day of the Jewish month of Sivan (which falls in May–June) was established as the official day commemorating the massacre. In many communities it was observed until the Holocaust.

In 1654 Chmielnicki and his followers took the oath of allegiance to Tzar Alexis of Russia (1645–76). This alliance and the resulting hostilities between Russia and the Polish–Lithuanian state from 1654 to 1667 brought about a new round of horrors for the Jews. Large sections of Lithuania were devastated, including Vilna and the surrounding region. The Jews lost property and lives at the hands of the invading Cossacks, who killed every Jew they met. After Alexis banished the Jews, most of the Jews of Vilna escaped, leaving with only what they could carry.[40] The Lithuanian Talmudist Rabbi Moshe Rivkes described the catastrophe: "And on the fourth day of the week on the 23 of Tammuz in 5415 [1655], the whole congregation fled for its life from the city of Vilna as one man. . . . Some escaped in carriages, others carried on their shoulders their small children and belongings."[41] Many of those who managed to escape Tzar Alexis and the Cossacks fell prey to Swedish forces in the area, who were fighting the Poles in what would be a devastating forty-year war known as the Deluge (1650s–1690s).

Jewish individuals and communities throughout the Diaspora, especially in Turkey, Italy, Amsterdam, and Hamburg, offered food, clothing, money, and shelter to the refugees. Gluckel of Hameln (1646–1724) described how her family opened their doors and their hearts to them:

About this time, the Vilna Jews were forced to leave Poland. Many of them, stricken with contagious diseases, found their way to Hamburg. Having as yet neither hospital nor other accommodations, we needs must bring the sick among them into our homes. At least ten of them, whom my father took under his charge, lay in the upper floor of our house. Some recovered; others died. And my sister Elkele and I both took sick as well.

My beloved grandmother tended our sick and saw that they lacked for nothing. Though my father and mother disapproved, nothing could stop her from climbing to the garret three or four times a day, in order to nurse them. At length she too fell ill. After ten days in bed she died, at a beautiful old age, and left behind her a good name. For all her seventy-four years she was still as brisk and fresh as a woman of forty.[42]

Eishyshok was one of the many shtetlekh to suffer under this latest onslaught. The town became nearly deserted and only fifty or sixty houses remained.[43] Ancestors of the Wilkanskis, one of the most important families in nineteenth- and twentieth-century Eishyshok, were in such a state of despair that they saw no future for Jewish life in Poland–Lithuania. One of the surviving members of the decimated family, an elderly man who was sure the massacres signaled the end of their line, ordered that the scroll depicting the family tree be buried with him in his coffin. Fortunately, his dire predictions proved false; unfortunately, the scroll was indeed buried with him, and lost forever to his family, who not only survived but eventually thrived. Among the other Eishyshkians who escaped were the ancestors of Yaffa Eliach's maternal grandfather, Yitzhak Uri Katz, who fled Vilna and managed to board a ship for Amsterdam. Eventually they were able to return to start their lives anew in the place of their birth.

In order to help the destroyed shtetl rebuild, the Polish Sejm (parliament) passed a resolution in 1662 freeing Eishyshok from the payment of taxes for a period of four years. But during this same period, 1661–67, the shtetl was burned down by the Russians.[44] In 1672 or 1673, following the requests of the town elder, J. Kaleckis, new efforts were made to revive the economy of the town by stimulating trade in the region. Tolls for crossing the bridges over the Dumbla and the Virshuki rivers were lowered to one Lithuanian coin per cart, in the hope that more peasants would make the trip to the market in Eishyshok. Local artisans were allowed to bypass legislation that had previously served to exclude them from competing with monopolies held by other groups. And then in 1678, Eishyshok received its greatest boon to trade, when John III Sobieski, the king of Poland and a man who often acted as a friend to his Jewish subjects, granted it Magdeburg Rights, which were commercial privileges usually awarded only to much larger towns.[45]

The economic revival that was set in motion by these changes was brutally disrupted by the Great Northern War, 1700–1721, a massive conflict that involved Sweden, Russia, and Poland–Lithuania (among other disputants). In 1702 King Charles XII of Sweden marched straight through the Polish–Lithuanian commonwealth, occupying Vilna, Warsaw, and Cracow. In 1704 the Swedish-sponsored Confederation of Warsaw produced its own claimant to the Polish–Lithuanian throne, Stanislaw Leszczynski, whom they crowned in 1706, forcing King Augustus II to flee Poland.

In 1706 Eishyshok was devastated by the Swedish army. The town was burned down and many of its people were murdered, while many others fled. Known for the brutality of their behavior, the Swedish conquerors were particularly cruel to the Jews. A long tradition of anti-Semitism — Jews having been prohibited from settling on the Scandinavian peninsula since early times — ensured that the Jews would be especially singled out for vicious treatment.[46]

The loss of life during the Great Northern War was all the greater because of the famine and plagues that accompanied the war. Again, many Jews were of course among the victims. In fact, it was during the cholera epidemic that the Jews of Eishyshok dedicated their New Cemetery, engraving the cemetery gate with words expressing their hope that the plague would now end. The tombstones of the victims of 1706–08 and 1710 remained in existence through World War II, as did the cemetery gates. They would survive the Holocaust, only to be demolished during the postwar years by the Lithuanian municipality of Eisiskes, which destroyed the entire New Cemetery sometime in the late 1960s.

In January 1708 Sweden's King Charles was forced to leave his command post in Grodno and fight the Russians. The next year, 1709, Tzar Peter the Great defeated Charles and his army at Poltava. This proved to be a turning point in Russian history, for Russia now became an important force in European politics, supplanting Sweden as the major power in the Baltics. Its dominance was consolidated by the two new ports Peter won as prizes of war: the city he named St. Petersburg on the Baltic Sea, and Sebastopol on the Black Sea. The tzar's victory was also an important turning point in the relationship between Russia and Poland–Lithuania, for Russia was clearly the superior power, which the Poles looked to, at least for the moment, as their liberator.

Among the other consequences of the defeat at Poltava was the removal of the Swedish-appointed king and the restoration of Augustus II as king of Poland in 1710.[47] On his royal tour of places that had been devastated by the Swedes, Augustus included a stop in Eishyshok — testimony both to the importance of the town and the severity of its losses at the hands of King Charles and his army. To commemorate his visit, the Jews of Eishyshok commissioned an elaborate new covering for the Holy Ark in the synagogue, which was displayed every year on Simhat Torah until the shtetl's last celebration of that holiday, in 1940.

During King Augustus's visit, he ordered that a new church be built in Juryzdyki, and increased the royal grant of money and land to the church. There is no record of his having done anything for the Jews.

THE PARTITIONING OF POLAND: 1772–95

Poland's Saxon monarchy had been restored, and would endure until the death of Augustus's son, Augustus III, in 1763, but Russia's new dominance in the region would soon lead the Polish Lithuanian commonwealth into the Russian camp. There it would remain until the end of the Cold War in the 1990s — with brief interruptions during World War I and the period that followed, 1918 to 1939, when the Polish state reemerged as the Second Polish Republic, and again during World War II.

In the years after Poltava, the Polish kings would lose their powers, the Polish Sejm would collapse, and the government of the country would for all intents and purposes be in the hands of an oligarchy of Polish magnates, whose interests were mainly personal and provincial. Unlike Russia, which had a powerful central government with lines of authority stretching into the smallest village, Poland–Lithuania during the years 1709–72 had a weak central government presided over by an elected (rather than hereditary) monarchy, which consisted mainly of foreigners, such as the Saxons, who had taken the Polish throne in 1697. Conditions in Poland were described as "anarchy tempered by civil war." Thus Poland would prove helpless before the three mighty absolutist states — Russia, Austria, and Prussia — which would set about carving it up as political spoils beginning in 1772.

All three partitions took place during the reign of Poland's last king, Stanislaw Poniatowski, the partly Italian monarch who had been elected king under pressure from his one-time lover, Russia's Catherine the Great.[48] He would reign from 1764 to 1795, she from 1762 to 1796. With a lust for land at least as great as her lust for men, Catherine took 12.7 percent of Poland–Lithuania's territory and some 1.8 million in-

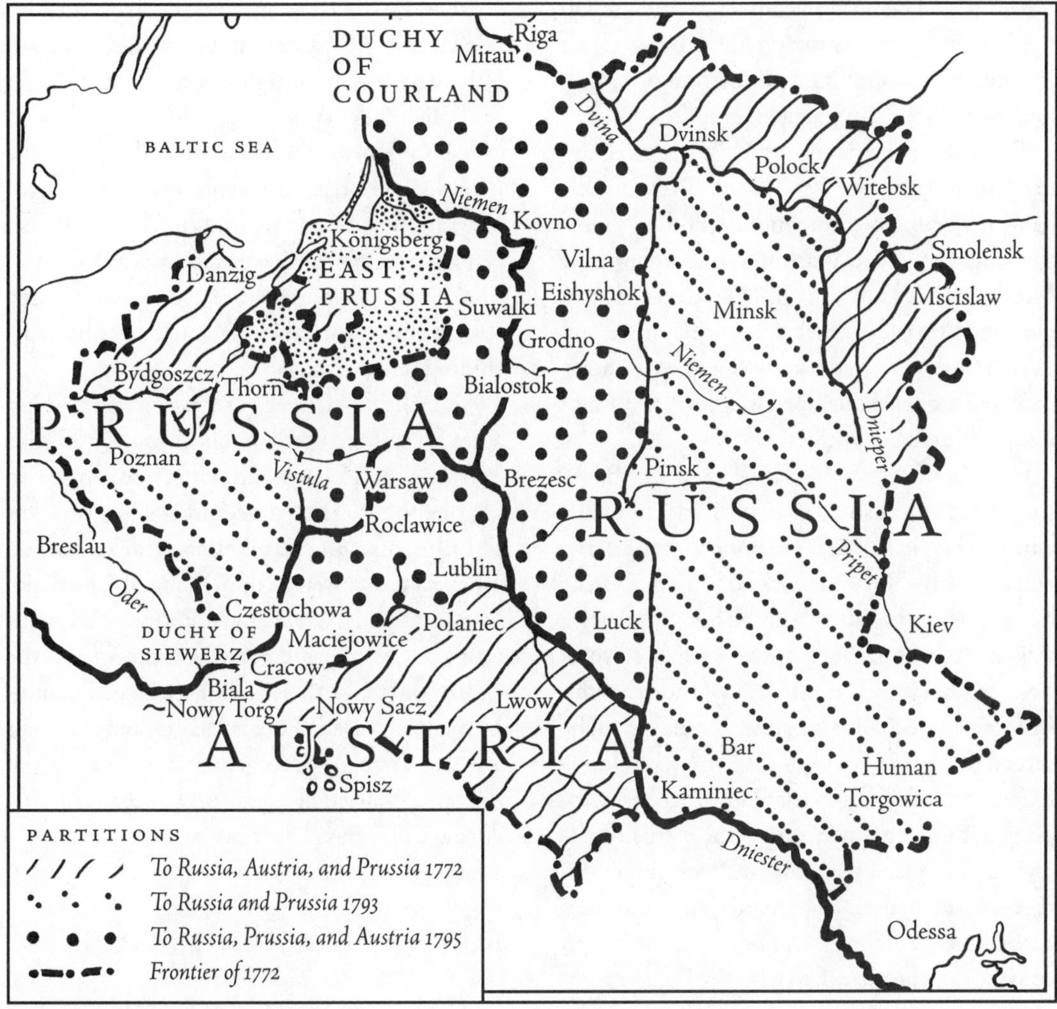

The Partitions of Poland, 1772.

habitants in the First Partition, while Austria took 11.8 percent and 1.7 million, Prussia 5 percent and 416,000. The partition treaty was signed in St. Petersburg in the summer of 1772.[49]

After the disaster of the First Partition, the Poles tried to enact some basic reforms in the hope of creating a strong central government that could hold the aggressors at bay and stem the escalating anarchy within their state. Beginning in 1773 and culminating in the activities of the Four-Year Sejm of 1788–92, their work was embodied in the constitution of May 3, 1791, which called for a hereditary monarchy with effective executive power; legislative authority vested in a two-chamber Sejm, which for the first time would include representatives of the middle class; and a cabinet of ministers organized along modern lines. All reforms would prove short-lived, however, because the May 3 constitution brought matters to a head with the Russians, who were not happy at the thought of a more powerful central government in Poland.

Joined by the Prussians, the Russians invaded Poland and began the Second Partition in January 1793. This time Russia took most of Lithuania and the western Ukraine, with a total population of 3 million. In addition, Russia obtained the right to move its troops into what remained of Poland, and control its foreign policy. Prussia seized Danzig, Thorn, and Great Poland, with a combined population of 1.1 million. Austria did not participate.

The Poles responded in 1794 with a massive national uprising led by Tadeusz Kosciuszko, the same brilliant commander who had joined the army of George Washington to fight in the North American War of Independence, distinguishing himself in the battles of Saratoga and West Point.[50] Kosciuszko was a great military man and a great Polish patriot, born to a Polonized Lithuanian family.

Fighting alongside him in Poland was Berek Joselewicz, a Jewish colonel born in Lithuania, who had begun his career in public service in the employ of Bishop Massalski of Vilna. During his travels on behalf of the bishop, Joselewicz visited Paris on the eve of the French Revolution, drinking in its heady brew of ideas about freedom and equality for all. After his return he settled in a suburb of Warsaw, where he closely followed the debates in the Four-Year Sejm, especially those that concerned the status of the Jews in Poland–Lithuania and the hopes for their emancipation. Like many Jews who were excited by the reforms embodied in the May 3 constitution, he identified with the Polish struggle against partition and was eager to join in. So when the Poles went to war against Russia, Joselewicz, along with another Jewish officer named Jozef Aronowicz, formed a separate Jewish light cavalry regiment numbering about five hundred men who went to the support of Kosciuszko, fighting "like lions and leopards."

A number of the Jews of Vilna also took part in the uprising, and their kahal made donations to the participants. In Eishyshok, too, many of the Jews in the shtetl and the surrounding villages supported the Polish uprising, especially those whose families had close ties with the Polish nobility.

Despite the great courage displayed by the Polish patriots and their supporters, they were crushed by the Russians and the Prussians. Joselewicz fled to Austria, but he would return to Poland a number of times to continue the fight for Polish independence.[51] In May 1809, he was killed in Kock, while fighting alongside the Napoleonic forces in defense of the Duchy of Warsaw. During the years of the Second Polish Republic, Joselewicz's reputation as a Polish national hero got a new lease on life, with many streets and squares being named after him, including one in Eishyshok.

After the failed uprising, Austria rejoined her allies for a share in the spoils of war. The Third Partition of Poland–Lithuania took place in October 1795. Russia acquired what was left of Lithuania and the Ukraine, with 1.2 million inhabitants, as well as the Duchy of Courland; Prussia took Mazovia, including Warsaw, with 1 million people; and Austria appropriated the Cracow area, with 1 million people. Poland–Lithuania ceased to exist as an independent state, disappearing altogether from the map of Europe. Eishyshok came under Russian rule during this Third Partition.

RUSSIA IN ASCENDANCE

Catherine the Great's greed for land now had to come to terms with tzarist Russia's longstanding anti-Jewish policy, which had prohibited Jews from living there since the end of the fifteenth century. With the land seized during the partitions, Russia found itself home to the largest Jewish population in the world. To cope with this new development, Russia created the Pale of Settlement, a territory within the borders of tzarist Russia, consisting mainly of the annexations of the preceding twenty years, where Jews were authorized to live. Though the Pale of Settlement remained in effect from 1791 until the Russian Revolution of 1917, its borders were always in flux, expanding and contracting according to Russia's latest acts of aggression and

SWEDEN
BALTIC SEA
BALTIC PROVINCES
St. Petersburg
Novgorod
Lake Ilmen
Lake Pskov
KOVNO
VITEBSK
Moscow
GERMANY
VILNA
SUWALKI
Eishyshok
Smolensk
Tula
PLOCK
LOMZA
MOGILEV
KALISZ
GRODNO
MINSK
WARSAW
SEDLITS
RUSSIA
PIOTRKOW
RADOM
Voronezh
KIELCE
LUBLIN
CHERNIGOV
Kursk
VOLHYNIA
Kiev
Kharkov
POLTAVA
AUSTRIA-HUNGARY
PODOLIA
KIEV
EKATERINOSLAV
KHERSON
Nikolayev
RUMANIA
BESSARABIA
TAURIDA
SEA OF AZOV
KUBAN
Sevastopol
Yalta
BLACK SEA
TURKEY
The Pale of Settlement. Russian Jews were confined to this area by laws of 1795.
Towns within the Pale which were themselves barred to Jews without special residence permits.
Towns outside the Pale with Jewish inhabitants (figures for 1897).

The Pale of Settlement, 1795–1917.

colonization, and the whim of its rulers. Sometimes exceptions would be made, permitting Jews to reside in heretofore "forbidden" territories if they were perceived as vital to the interests of a newly colonized region in need of development. Sometimes there were new expulsions, as when the Jews were ordered to begin leaving the villages by an 1804 order of Tzar Alexander I.

In 1897, the Pale covered an area of about 386,100 square miles from the Baltic to the Black Sea. According to the census of that year, 4,899,300 Jews lived there, forming 94 percent of the total Jewish population of Russia, and about 11.6 percent of the general population of the area.[52]

Under Catherine, Russia's system of government was reorganized, so that the country was divided into fifty administrative units, or provinces, called *gubernia*, which were further subdivided into districts, ten per gubernia. Each gubernia had about 300,000 inhabitants, each district about 30,000. It was an abstract, numbers-driven system, with boundaries being drawn for administrative convenience but in complete ignorance of historical factors, and of the religious and ethnic origins of the people within those boundaries.

Eishyshok belonged to the gubernia of Vilna, and the district of Lida. What sounded clear-cut on paper was less so in real life, however, for the division of power between the district and the gubernia officials was always shifting. On many occasions during the next 120 years or so, the kahal of Eishyshok found that it had to report to, pay, and bribe officials in both Vilna and Lida, as well as in other towns where official business was conducted, for example Aran (Varena), where induction to the army took place.

Nonetheless, like so many of the other Lithuanian shtetlekh and towns that were now part of the Russian empire, Eishyshok thrived. Though Russia imposed many anti-Jewish laws, put restrictions on where Jews could live, and created a variety of new economic obstacles for the Jews, by comparison with the preceding war-torn century and a half — years that had encompassed the Chmielnicki massacres, the Thirty Years' War, the Deluge, the Great Northern War, and the wars for Polish independence — the rule of the tzars constituted an era of relative peace, which would endure until World War I.

There would be periods of turbulence, such as the Napoleonic wars of 1808–12, and the Polish uprisings of 1831 and 1863. And there would be periods of persecution and suffering, particularly after the assassination of Tzar Alexander II in 1881, which was followed by violent, murderous outbreaks of anti-Semitism — the "Southern Tempest" pogroms — on the part of the masses, and by a new and harsher round of anti-Semitic legislation — the May Laws — on the part of the government. But whether benevolent or harsh, committed to integrating the Jews or determined to uproot and expel them, tzarist rule was never as destructive as the blood and strife that characterized many of the decades leading up to it.

For the Jewish shtetlekh of the former Poland–Lithuania, the period from the second half of the eighteenth century up to the 1880s (and in some cases beyond that to World War I) was a time of unprecedented growth. There was a population explosion, and a flowering of political, cultural, intellectual, and religious creativity surpassing anything that had yet occurred in East European Jewish history.

INSTITUTIONS OF JEWISH AUTONOMY AFTER THE PARTITIONS

THE KAHAL One sign of the vitality of the Jews in Eastern Europe during this period was the resurgence of the kahal, their traditional, local form of self-government, which was sparked by the demise of the Councils, the centralized organs of autonomy called into existence by the Polish–Lithuanian state.

A Lithuanian Jewish woman of the eighteenth century. YAHADUT LITA, VOL. I, 1959, P. 137

The Councils had come to an end even before the partitions began, the way having been prepared by events both internal and external to the Jewish community. As far as internal events were concerned, tensions between the Councils and the individual communities they presided over had increased in the wake of the Chmielnicki massacres, when so many communities were brought to the brink of ruin. At the same time that many communities found it particularly difficult to pay the high taxes levied by the Councils, the Councils were spending large amounts to maintain Jewish representation in government circles, to bribe officials when necessary, to provide physical protection, and to defend against the increasingly frequent blood libels and charges of desecration of the host. Over the years the tensions continued to increase, and it became harder and harder for the Councils to collect the taxes. Finally in 1721, feeling that they were bearing a disproportionately large amount of the tax burden and getting disproportionately few benefits, the smaller communities in Lithuania united in protest. Just as the central government of the Polish Lithuanian state was weakening and giving way to anarchy, so, too, were the central organs of Jewish autonomy, which reported to that state.

As the individual communities became more self-sustaining, thanks to increasing reliance on the korobka tax, and the Councils became less effective at doing the job they had been established to do — collect taxes for the crown — the central government withdrew its support. In 1764 the Polish Sejm passed a resolution introducing a different system of collecting the Jewish poll tax. This spelled the end of the Councils, after nearly two hundred years of being recognized by the state as the central institutions of Jewish self-rule. The last Council meeting convened that same year, 1764.

For many Jews in Poland and Lithuania, the Councils had been the prime symbol of Jewish social power. Nathan of Hanover, the chronicler of the Chmielnicki massacres, had compared the Councils to the Sanhedrin, the seventy-one-man judicial body which constituted the Supreme Court of the Land of Israel prior to the destruction of the Temple in Jerusalem. When the Councils were dismantled, the "heads of the lands" stripped of their authority, many Jews of the time felt that they had lost their major source of status within the state.

But the disintegration of this centralized form of autonomy helped pave the way for a revival of local forms of leadership and authority — and for a new religious movement known as Hasidism as well. The new forms of leadership that Hasidism gave rise to were quite influential. But since Hasidism never successfully took root in the vicinity of Eishyshok, thanks in part to the strong stand taken against it by Eishyshok's neighbor Rabbi Eliyahu ben Shlomo Zalman, known as the Gaon (Sage) of Vilna, who was the leader of Lithuanian Jewry, it is a subject outside the scope of this book.

In towns like Eishyshok, strongholds of the Mitnaggedim (opponents of Hasidism), it was usually the local kahal that filled the leadership vacuum left by the Councils. Throughout the

Rabbi Eliyahu ben Shlomo Zalman, the Gaon (Sage) of Vilna (1720–1797), the leading scholar of Ashkenazic Jewry in the eighteenth century. YESC

A Lithuanian Jew with his wife and daughter, 1802. A HISTORICAL ATLAS OF THE JEWISH PEOPLE, 1992, P. 163

period of the Councils, the local kahals had remained active in serving their communities. But since the Councils were the tax collectors and makers of economic policy, the kahals, deprived of the power of the purse, had been under the thumb of the super-kehilot, which made up the Councils. After the Councils were abolished, the kahals continued to fulfill their old obligations, and, in the process of freeing themselves from the yoke of the super-kehilot, assumed additional responsibilities as sole representatives of their local Jewish communities. They offered religious, educational, judicial, financial, and social services to the Jews, and sometimes, particularly in times of crisis, to the non-Jews living in their communities as well. Their range extended to all the Jews living in the immediate vicinity — those in the shtetl as well as in nearby villages and on isolated farms, and those acting as managers or lessors of estates belonging to the local magnates. Thus the kahal of Eishyshok had jurisdiction over Jews in Kalesnik, Dumbla, Arodnoy, Nacha, Rubishok, Dociszki, Okla, and other villages.

The members of the kahal were balebatim (householders), most of whom were well-to-do merchants. They were the shtetl's oligarchy, its patrician class. In shtetlekh that had a strong contingent of Hasidim, this oligarchy was often severely undermined, but in Eishyshok, as in many non-Hasidic Lithuanian shtetlekh, the balebatim retained their exclusive grip over the community until the twentieth century. And indeed the kahal would remain the central, if not always the only or dominant, authority until the final days of the shtetl.

That authority was challenged in several ways, however. Externally, the principal challenge at this time came from the Russian government. In 1844 it prohibited the kahal from using its most potent form of social control, the herem (excommunication). For a Jew to be excommunicated from the Jewish community, when the community was the sole bulwark standing between him and the hostile world outside, was a virtual death sentence, and a fate few would risk. Thus the attempt to ban the herem was a direct strike against the power of the kahal. Moreover, by making the kahal responsible for providing military recruits for the dreaded tzarist army, as happened during the

Reb Shael Sonenson served as Eishyshok's rosh ha-kahal (head of the community) or as a member of the kahal from the late 1880s until his death in 1935. He was one of the shtetl's most powerful individuals and a strong supporter of Modern Orthodoxy. PHOTO: YITZHAK URI KATZ. YESC, M. SHEFSKI

Meir Kiuchefski was one of the shtetl's leaders in the early twentieth century. He served as rosh ha-kahal and as a member of the kahal. He and Shael Sonenson were allies. YESC, R. ROSENBLATT

cantonist period (1827–56), the Russian government turned many people in the community against their own leaders. Later the Russians banned the kahal altogether. The effect in Eishyshok, as in many other communities, was minimal, for the residents resisted all attempts to undermine the kahal, and it remained one of the most vigorous institutions of Jewish life. The shtetl continued to elect members to the kahal, and to employ the power of the herem against those it deemed harmful to the community, until the bitter end.

Within the Jewish community itself, the challenges to the kahal, in Eishyshok as elsewhere, would prove to be of several different kinds: Hasidism, which, as mentioned above, never made any inroads in Eishyshok; the Haskalah (the Jewish offshoot of the Enlightenment), an intellectual and cultural rebellion that was causing turmoil in many shtetlekh by the mid-nineteenth century, and eventually began to have an impact on Eishyshok in the 1880s; Zionism, which swept the shtetl at the beginning of the twentieth century, and was gradually taken up by many of the foremost balebatim themselves; and the growing power of the artisan class, which allied itself with various socialist and Communist movements in the years between the two world wars. In that same period, money sent as charity from America posed another threat to the establishment, because the individuals who received the funds and decided how to distribute them operated outside the shtetl's traditional network of mutual aid societies. But Eishyshok's kahal had a tendency to meet all challenges by absorbing and thereby co-opting the challengers, changing with the times as necessary. This is one reason the conflicts in Eishyshok never reached the fever pitch they did in other shtetlekh, where the kahal was attacked by followers of the Haskalah as a "force of darkness."

Moreover, the authority of Eishyshok's kahal, its central position as the framework within which all community decisions were made, had a basis in factors transcending the social and economic class of its members. A typical instance of the behavior that earned it the loyalty of its constituents occurred in the twentieth century, the period of its greatest internal challenges. In 1921 the Poles were back in Eishyshok, following the signing of the Treaty of Riga on March 18. When they demanded a large quantity of meat to supply the Polish army stationed nearby, the shtetl was unable to meet the demand, whereupon the Poles arrested a number of men and threatened them with twenty-five lashes if the meat was not delivered by the next day. Faced with such an ultimatum, the head of the kahal, Reb Shael Sonenson, and several fellow members of the kahal, including Reb Itche (Yitzhak) Streletski and Reb Isser Velvl Abelowitch, gave up their own cows and used money from their own pockets to buy additional cattle from Polish peasants in the countryside. The deadline was met. Each kahal during its years of tenure was likely to face similar trials, and over the centuries each had held itself to similarly high standards of behavior. The feeling of safety and security that the kahal thereby gave the community was its greatest guarantee of its own continued existence.

The Assistance Committee who worked with the kahal in distributing money from America. The photo was taken in honor of Aharon Don Becker (front row, third from left), who in 1920 brought a large donation to the shtetl from the Eishyshker society in New York. Seated to the right of Aharon Don is his relative Sarah Kaganowicz; to his left are Hayya Sonenson, head of the Froyen Farain (Union of Women); Libe-Gittel Rudzin; her daughter Miriam Kaganowicz; and Miriam's husband Shael, relatives of Aharon Don. Among others in the photo are members of the Pachianko family (Aharon's last name before he changed it in America), members of the kahal, and clergy. Standing in the back, between Aharon Don and Hayya Sonenson, is Reb Hertz Mendl Hutner, the shtetl dayyan. Most people in the photo who did not emigrate to America or die a natural death were murdered during the Holocaust in Eishyshok, Radun, or Majdanek. Shael Kaganowicz was killed by the AK. PHOTO: YITZHAK URI KATZ. YESC, HINSKI

Every shtetl had its own rules pertaining to the election, makeup, and duties of the kahal. In Eishyshok the kahal had seven members, who were all elected to a three-year term, except for the head of the kahal (neeman ha-kahal, or rosh ha-kahal), who served four years. The titles and responsibilities they held were similar to those of ancient times.[53] They made decisions pertaining to every aspect of shtetl life, from the yeshivah to the synagogue, the cemetery to the slaughterhouse, and they appointed all key religious personnel. They also maintained official relations with whatever national government was in place.

There was no limit on the number of terms the officials of the kahal could serve, and no financial compensation for serving. Until the twentieth century, when money sent from America had a democratizing influence on the makeup of the kahal, no one from the artisan class was

A banquet at the Shlanski home in 1936, in honor of Dr. Morris Shlanski and his brother Louis, visiting from America. They gave a large donation to the kahal. Seated (left to right): Yossl Rochowski, leader of the shoemakers' shtibl and Tehilim Society; Avraham Dubitski; Eliyahu Bastunski; Dovid "der Kichier" Moszczenik; Dr. Morris Shlanski; Leib "der Pochter" Berkowicz; Szymen Rozowski, the shtetl rabbi; Avraham-Mordekhai Shlanski, father of the visitors; Louis Shlanski; Markl Koppelman; two unidentified people; and Reuven-Beinush Berkowitch. Standing (left to right): Baruch Matikanski, assistant shammash of the Old Beth Midrash; Faivl Epstein; Benyomin Tshorny; Rephael "der Meller"; two unidentified people; Zelig Shlanski, brother of the visitors; Isaac Shlanski; Dodke Schwartz; Yudl Dwilanski; and Mote Yosl Kremin. The identity of the people in the third row is unknown. With the exception of the Shlanski brothers, all these people were killed in the September 1941 massacre. Markl Koppelman and his family were murdered by the AK.
YESC, SHLANSKI

eligible for election. Women never became eligible, despite the fact that some of them earned enough money to become large-scale contributors to the various benevolent societies within the shtetl.

Elections took place once a year on a Saturday night, in the home of the shtetl dayyan, and under his supervision. Meir Wilkanski, the son of the man who was the dayyan of Eishyshok for over fifty years, describes one such election that took place in the late 1880s:

All the town notables assembled in our house on Saturday night. They sat around the table and spoke with great excitement. Father cut with a pair of scissors a number of pieces of paper and distributed them among the people seated at the table. Each of them wrote something on the paper, rolled it up and placed it in a kippah — a headcovering we were using that night as a ballot box — which was in the center of the table.

Another kippah was in Father's hand. There he placed many rolled-up pieces of paper on which nothing was written. Then he dipped his hand into both of the kippoth and scrambled together the blank and the written ballots.

My brother Yitzhak and I were called in and told to remove the ballots from the boxes. Alternating turns, he took out a piece of paper from one box, I from the other, and we continued to alternate until all the papers had been removed. Then each ballot was examined. The blank ones were torn up, as were the others, once the names written on them had been entered on a special sheet of paper. And this is how, one by one, the wondrous pieces of paper became fewer and fewer until all were gone.[54]

After the announcement of the results, cake, cookies, and bottles of brandy were brought out, and all the assembled ate and drank in honor of the newly elected officials. One of these officials would host a large festive meal in his home the following day, after which all left for the Old Beth Midrash for the ceremonial inscribing of the new members' names in the record book — the pinkas — maintained by the kahal. Then one of them — usually the one who was considered the best orator in the group — gave a short speech.

In Eishyshok, as in Jewish communities for thousands of years, the pinkas was the document of record for everything the community considered to be important about itself. Because it went into such detail, the pinkas made it possible for the shtetl to hand down a complete diary of its past. All dates referred to the Jewish lunisolar calendar, and most entries were in Hebrew, though there were occasional entries in Yiddish, and a smattering of words from other languages as well. The person chosen to write the entries was a member of the kahal, an individual known for his penmanship, his artistic talent, his command of Hebrew, his scholarship, his accuracy, and his pleasant disposition.

In some shtetlekh the pinkas went back many hundreds of years. In Eishyshok, alas, the ancient book was destroyed in the Big Fire of 1895 — this despite the fact that the kahal had taken the precaution of storing it in a large box on wheels so that it could be quickly rolled out into the street in the event of fire.[55] The new pinkas ha-kahal, along with the pinkasim of other key shtetl organizations, such as that belonging to the burial society and the one in which the rabbi recorded all the births, deaths, marriages, divorces, illegitimate children, and so on, were all lost in the Holocaust.

THE CLERGY It would not be farfetched to suggest that many shtetlekh were governed by a two-chamber assembly consisting of an executive branch, the kahal, and a judicial branch, the clergy. The executive branch was elected and unpaid. Because it was made up of and elected by members of the balebatim, its attitudes toward the community it served were shaped sometimes by self-interest, sometimes by concern for the greater good, and at all times by class, character, and tradition.

The judicial clergy branch was appointed — by the kahal — and salaried. Its members included the rabbi, the dayyanim (judges), the hazzan (cantor), the shammash (beadle), the shohet (ritual butcher), the sofer (scribe), and the melamed (teacher) for the school for the poor (the Talmud Torah). The shtetl rabbi was the spiritual leader of the community, and often took on many temporal responsibilities as well.

The rabbi was appointed by the kahal and technically accountable to it, but as the spiritual leader of the community, in a society whose very essence had to do with its religious beliefs and institutions, his stature was greater than anybody's. As a symbolic acknowledgment of the rabbi's superiority, Eishyshok's kahal members used to come to the rabbi's house every Friday afternoon to sweep his floor, thereby obeying the admonition to "Be like servants who minister to their master not for the sake of a reward."[56] This practice continued through Zundl Hutner's tenure as rabbi (which ended only with his death in 1919).

Eishyshok was remarkably well served by both its kahal and its clergy. With few known exceptions, both groups of men were public-spirited and of very high moral caliber. Which is not to say they always worked together in perfect harmony. There were times of bitter strife between the kahal and the rabbi. Though Jewish Eishyshok has disappeared from under the skies, remnants of those conflicts linger on to this day, in Israel and America, where descendants of the two groups are still settling scores with one another.

THE JEWS UNDER RUSSIAN RULE

The fortunes of the Jews under the tzars waxed and waned depending on the individual tzars, for their attitudes toward the Jews, and their ideas for how to handle the "Jewish problem," varied enormously. As a non-Christian group, numbering in the millions, with its own distinct cultural identity, traditions, beliefs, loyalties, and institutions of self-government, the Jews constituted a challenge to an absolutist regime determined to exercise control over every aspect of its citizens' lives.

Generally speaking, the two approaches to dealing with this "problem" were to try to integrate the Jews into the legal, economic, social — and, it was hoped, religious — framework of Russian society, or to make life so unbearable for them that large numbers of them would either die out, emigrate, or convert. Sometimes the two approaches seemed equally oppressive, especially when the "integrationist" policies of the more enlightened tzars made it their goal to eradicate over two millennia of Jewish tradition and belief. To be forced to give up their language, their educational institutions, their Talmud-centered curriculum, their form of self-government, in many cases their customary means of making a living (estate-leasing, innkeeping, manufacture and sale of alcohol), their places of residence (the villages), and ultimately their religion, was a spiritual and cultural death as alarming to many Jews as the pogroms that were the sequelae of the regimes of the crueler, more explicitly anti-Semitic tzars.

MILITARY SERVICE One of the darkest chapters in the history of tzarist rule over the Jews was the cantonist period, ushered in by Tzar Nicholas I, who reigned from 1825 to 1855. Though a policy of general conscription had been in effect in Russia ever since the days of Peter the Great, the founder of the modern Russian army, when the Jews first came under Russian rule during the reign of Catherine the Great they were allowed to buy themselves out of military service. Since the period of service was twenty-five years, and could begin as early as age twelve, the Jews had proved willing to pay whatever price was necessary to avoid it. But this policy changed in 1827 when Nicholas, as part of his program to "reform" the Jews and integrate them into Russian life, abolished the payment option.

Though many of the wealthier Jews were still able to bribe their sons out of service, there were quotas to be filled, and the community was responsible for filling them. Often they were filled in the most brutal way: by kidnapping. Every community in the Pale of Settlement had individuals of questionable character who were given the official task of kidnapping children (generally the children of the poorest, most vulnerable families) for army conscription. The dreaded officials were known in Yiddish as *khapers* (kidnappers). In Hebrew this period of history is known not as the cantonist period, but the era of the Hatufim — the Kidnapped.

The 1827 statute set twelve to twenty-five as the minimum and maximum age for Jewish draftees, and provided that boys "under eighteen years of age shall be placed in preparatory establishments to train them for the military."[57] Many of those seized were indeed as young as twelve, for their youth, inexperience, and physical weakness made them easy prey for the kidnappers. In fact, many of them were younger. One writer tells of a child in Grodno who was five when recruited.[58]

Jewish families lived in constant dread of the kidnappers, who could strike at any time, any place. The same writer who cited the case of the five-year-old child in Grodno described the kidnappers at work in Minsk. A coach stopped near a Jewish home, and six thugs jumped out and burst through the door. Soon they emerged dragging a small child, whom they had gagged to silence his screams. The child's mother wrestled frantically with them to free him from their grasp, but to no avail; they threw her to the ground and galloped off with her little boy. The desperate mother, bloody and bruised, beat her head against the pavement and set up an endless lament of "my son, my little chick, my nestling."[59] Her anguish was for very good cause, for these separations were final in most cases, and often tantamount to a death sentence for the child.

The Jewish community's despair over the drafting of their young children made itself felt even in the cold language of officialdom. Russian government documents describe Jewish mothers rushing to the graves of their parents to plead for divine intervention, sometimes dying themselves of their grief and heartbreak.[60]

The children were usually sent to military training schools as far away as possible, beyond the boundaries of the Pale of Settlement, deep in the interior of Russia, in cantonments in Kazan, Orenburg, Perm, and Siberia. The journeys took months, often under the most deplorable conditions, which included long forced marches. The Russian author Alexander Herzen gave a graphic description of one such cantonist march, which he witnessed during a trip he made in 1835, in the vicinity of Perm:

The officer who escorted them said, "They have collected a crowd of cursed little Jew boys of eight or nine years old. Whether they are taking them for the navy or what, I can't say. At first the orders were to drive them to Perm; then there was a change and we are driving them to Kazan. I took them over a hundred versts farther back. The officer who handed them over said, 'It's dreadful, and that's about it; a third were left on the way' (and [he] pointed to the earth). 'Not half will reach their destination,' he said."

"Have there been epidemics, or what?" I asked, deeply moved.

"No, not epidemics, but they just die off like flies. A Jew boy, you know, is such a frail, weakly creature, like a skinned cat; he is not used to tramping in the mud for ten hours a day and eating biscuit — then again, being among strangers, no father, nor mother, nor petting; well, they cough and cough until they cough themselves into their graves. And I ask you, what use is it to them? What can they do with little boys?". . .

They brought the children and formed them into regular ranks; it was one of the most awful sights I have ever seen, those poor, poor children! Boys of twelve or thirteen might somehow have survived it, but little fellows of eight and ten . . . not even a brush full of black paint could put such a horror on canvas. Pale, exhausted, with frightened faces, they stood in thick, clumsy, soldiers' overcoats, with stand-up collars, fixing helpless, pitiful eyes on the garrison soldiers who were roughly getting them into ranks. The white lips, the blue rings under their eyes, bore witness to fever or chill. And these sick children, without care or kindness, exposed to the icy wind that blows unobstructed from the Arctic Ocean, were going to their graves.[61]

Once in their training camps, the boys who somehow survived these cruel journeys were then faced with the most brutal treatment until they accepted forced baptism. This, too, was part of Tzar Nicholas' attempt to "integrate" the Jews into Russian life, in essence to obliterate their identity as a separate cultural and religious group. They were forbidden to practice any Jewish religious observances, speak Yiddish, visit Jewish homes, or fraternize with one another. Those who refused to accept Christianity were starved, flogged, and deprived of sleep. The culminating ceremony of their "education" was baptism, after which their names were changed to those of their Christian sponsors. They continued their training in the cantonments until the age of eighteen, and they then served in the army for twenty-five more years.

Those who resisted baptism, becoming martyrs to their faith, were celebrated in myth and legend, song and poetry.[62] Inspirational stories about their spiritual strength were told and retold through the ages. One of the best known of these stories concerns a visit Tzar Nicholas himself made to one of the cantonments, in Kazan. As he was reviewing the troops, he got to that part of the ceremony where the Jewish cantonists were to undergo public baptism in the Volga River. At the command of the tzar they submerged themselves in the water — never to rise again. The young cantonists had made a pact among themselves to weight themselves with stones, committing suicide rather than submit to baptism.[63] There were a number of these mass suicides.

Like every other shtetl, Eishyshok lost children to the tzar's army. But a few of those who managed to survive came back after their twenty-five years of service, drawn to their native town by the longing to live in proximity to Eishyshok's famed yeshivah, to hear the chants of the Torah learners. One of these returnees was Berl the Cantonist, or Nikolaievitz (as conscriptees into Nicholas' army were called), a well-known character in nineteenth-century Eishyshok, who was colorfully sketched by the shtetl chronicler Meir Wilkanski. Such returns were rare, however. After twenty-five and more years, the men were so cut off from their roots that it was too hard to make the journey — physical and emotional — to reclaim them. Their connections to their families had been permanently severed. Indeed, some were so young when they were seized, and had undergone such drastic changes in their identities, including their names, that they didn't even know who their families were. Since the cantonists' service to the tzar made them eligible for land grants outside the Pale of Settlement, most of them retired to places far from the homes of their youth.

It is difficult to determine the number of Jewish cantonists during the twenty-nine years the statute of 1827 remained in effect, but estimates are between 30,000 and 40,000.[64] Other sources say about 25,000.

Long after the cantonist law was abolished in 1856, the memories of its brutality lingered on, poisoning the attitude of the Jewish villagers toward both the community leaders who had enforced it and the government that had issued it. One result would be a permanent distrust of the tzarist monarchy. For the promoters of the Jewish Enlightenment, the Haskalah, this would prove a major stumbling block. Their cooperation with the Russian authorities, who shared their enthusiasm for "reforming" and

Aaron Paley, an Eishyshkian by marriage, in the tzarist army during the Russo–Japanese War. He later emigrated to America. YESC, E. LANDSMAN

Hirsh-Faivl Kremin, who in civilian life was one of Eishyshok's master tailors, in the tzarist army, 1907. He was murdered in Ghetto Grodno in 1942. PHOTO: YITZHAK URI KATZ. YESC, D. & I. DIMITRO

"integrating" the Jews (albeit from a different perspective, with different ultimate aims), made them suspect to their own community.

Tzar Alexander II's ascension to the throne in 1855 resulted in many reform-minded changes in government policy toward the Jews, including the rescinding of the cantonist law. Jews now did the same kind of military service everyone else did, their years of service were reduced (to five years, by 1874), and until 1887, when the offer was rescinded, they were made eligible to join the ranks of the petty officers.

Even with all the obstacles they faced, some Jewish soldiers managed to distinguish themselves in the tzars' armies. Prominent among them was Leo Pinsker, decorated for his services as an army doctor during the Crimean War (1854–55), at the height of the cantonist persecutions. Yossef Trumpeldor, a second-generation army man, also had a distinguished record in the tzarist army, and sustained severe wounds resulting in the amputation of his left arm in 1904, during the Russo–Japanese War. He, too, of course, became a leading Zionist, whose military exploits in World War I and later in Palestine made him a legend in his own time, a soldier hero still revered and celebrated in ours.

There were others, too, like Zvi Hertz Zarum, who was kidnapped in 1852 at the age of nine and went on to become a Jewish career officer with a thirty-five-year record of service (not including six years as a cantonist). He was the only high-ranking Jewish career officer in the tzarist army who did not convert to Christianity. In contrast to the prevailing notion that Jews evaded their military obligations, the percentage of Jews in the army exceeded their percentage in the general population. In the census of 1897 there were 55,000 Jews in service.[65]

Despite their achievements, the Jews were treated very badly in the army. Whereas for most of the non-Jewish soldiers in Russia, life in the army was an improvement over life in their native villages — it offered better food, clothing, and shelter, a workload lighter than on the farm, and a spirit of camaraderie among them and their coreligionists — for the Jews it was a nightmare. For most East European Jews, military service meant maltreatment, constant harassment, and heavy pressure to convert, on top of the normal hardships and dangers of the military. But at least there was a five-year limit on compulsory service after 1874, thanks to Tzar Alexander.

The first part of Alexander II's reign (1855–81) saw a return to a more benevolent policy toward the Jews in areas besides military service, it being the opinion of this tzar and a number of his counselors that carrots might work better than sticks to encourage the Jews to assimilate. Certain residency restrictions were removed, as were bans on some forms of employment and government service. But soon government policy and public opinion would go the other way — part of the constant pattern of liberalization alternating with backlash that prevailed throughout the rule of the tzars.

THE NINETEENTH CENTURY: EISHYSHOK'S GOLDEN AGE

Though Eishyshok, like the rest of Jewish Russia, found itself in flux during much of the nineteenth century, it is nonetheless probably safe to say that this was its golden age. One indicator of a flourishing community in those days was population growth, but those statistics are hard to interpret until the middle of the century, when the growth of the Jewish population in Eishyshok became rapid, large, and indisputable. Earlier the statistics are erratic, many pertaining only to tax-paying, male members of the community — in other words, the balebatim (and affluent members of the non-Jewish community as well). Some figures record only the number of houses paying the chimney tax (again, this refers mainly to the affluent), others the physical size of the shtetl, or the number of "Jewish farmsteads," or "Jewish households."[66] Such figures can be manipulated to prove virtually anything you want them to prove.

The figures are also distorted by the inaccuracy of the information the Jews themselves provided to the authorities. As noted in the Introduction, many families didn't register the birth of their male children, or registered them as dead at birth, or as only sons, in order to avoid having them drafted into the tzarist army. One town near Eishyshok, Aran, was known as Araner Meisim (Aran of the dead) because its residents registered most of their male children as victims of infant mortality in order to save them from military service. Official government records also underreported the numbers of Jews, in order to show that the Jews were a minority rather than a majority in the shtetl, again so that fewer Jewish men would have to serve in the army.

Nevertheless, the general impression one gets of Eishyshok in the first several decades of Russian rule is of a town that was flourishing. Twice a year it was host to a big international horse fair that attracted people from all over Europe; from the beginning to the end of the nineteenth century it supported with its own resources a yeshivah of global renown; and its population was comfortable enough to maintain a tradition of tolerance for other minorities, including the Tatars and the Gypsies. This tolerance meant that it attracted ethnic groups who were not welcome elsewhere. Indeed, from 1780 to 1802 Eishyshok was considered the Gypsy capital of Lithuania, since it was home to the man known as the King of the Gypsies, J. Znamierovskis. Not finding life in one location interesting enough, the Gypsies eventually left the shtetl, but they continued to come to Thursday market day until the very end.[67]

Fortunately for them, the Gypsies left Eishyshok in time to escape one of the most serious catastrophes to afflict the town in the first

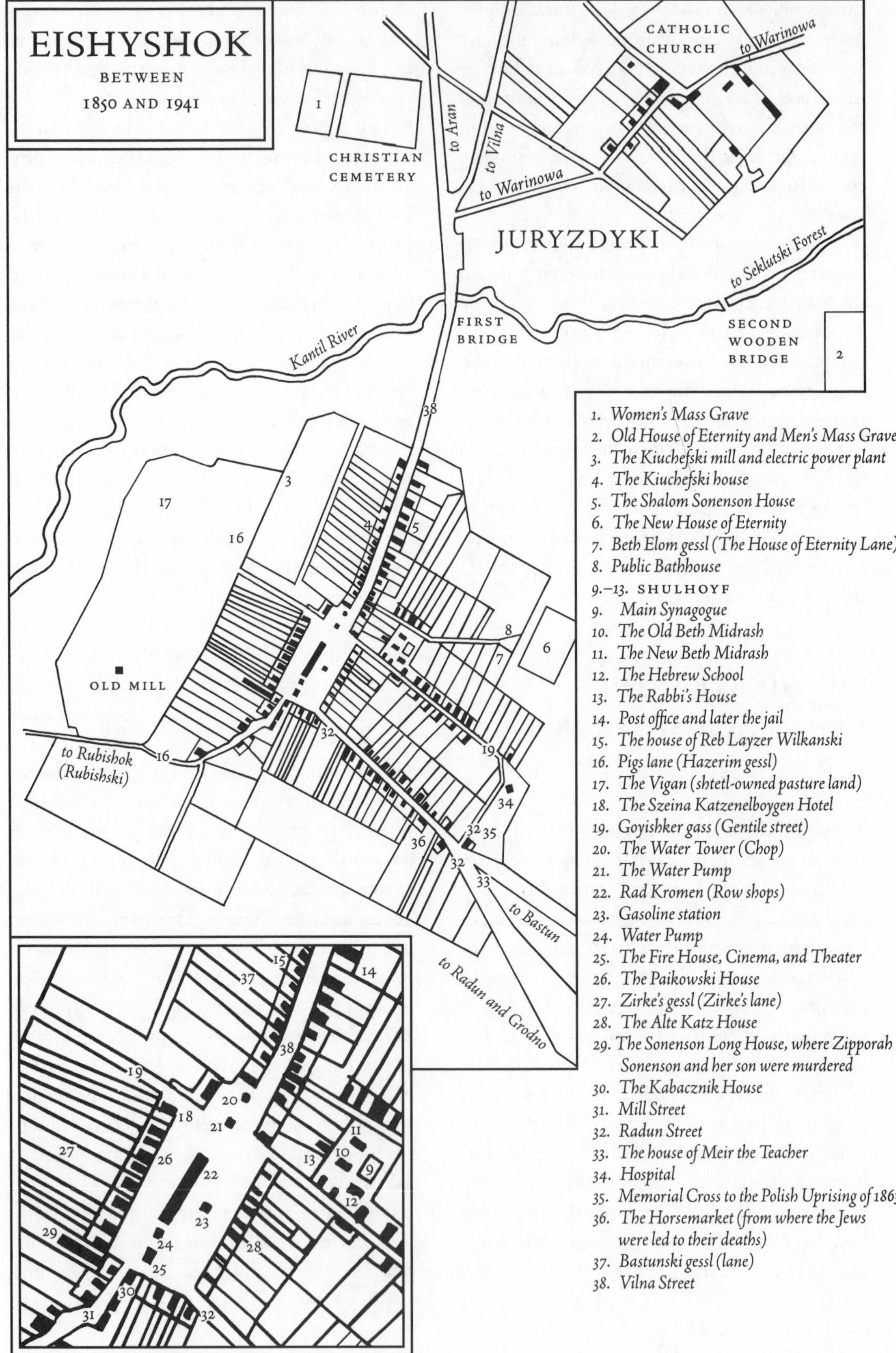
EISHYSHOK
BETWEEN
1850 AND 1941
CHRISTIAN
CEMETERY
to Aran
to Vilna
to Warinowa
CATHOLIC
CHURCH
to Warinowa
JURYZDYKI
to Seklutski Forest
Kantil River
FIRST
BRIDGE
SECOND
WOODEN
BRIDGE
OLD MILL
to Rubishok
(Rubishski)
to Bastun
to Radun and Grodno
1. Women's Mass Grave
2. Old House of Eternity and Men's Mass Grave
3. The Kiuchefski mill and electric power plant
4. The Kiuchefski house
5. The Shalom Sonenson House
6. The New House of Eternity
7. Beth Elom gessl (The House of Eternity Lane)
8. Public Bathhouse
9.–13. SHULHOYF
9. Main Synagogue
10. The Old Beth Midrash
11. The New Beth Midrash
12. The Hebrew School
13. The Rabbi's House
14. Post office and later the jail
15. The house of Reb Layzer Wilkanski
16. Pigs lane (Hazerim gessl)
17. The Vigan (shtetl-owned pasture land)
18. The Szeina Katzenelboygen Hotel
19. Goyishker gass (Gentile street)
20. The Water Tower (Chop)
21. The Water Pump
22. Rad Kromen (Row shops)
23. Gasoline station
24. Water Pump
25. The Fire House, Cinema, and Theater
26. The Paikowski House
27. Zirke's gessl (Zirke's lane)
28. The Alte Katz House
29. The Sonenson Long House, where Zipporah Sonenson and her son were murdered
30. The Kabacznik House
31. Mill Street
32. Radun Street
33. The house of Meir the Teacher
34. Hospital
35. Memorial Cross to the Polish Uprising of 1863
36. The Horsemarket (from where the Jews were led to their deaths)
37. Bastunski gessl (lane)
38. Vilna Street

decades of the nineteenth century: the retreat of Napoleon's army in 1812. On the way to Moscow the soldiers had been in a good mood; Napoleon himself had visited nearby Olkenik, where he had greatly admired the beauty of its synagogue. But defeat turned the army into a ragtag mob of sick and wounded men who went on a furious rampage. Twenty Eishyshkians were killed, and others died as a result of fevers that the soldiers brought with them into the shtetl. For some years after, Eishyshok remained so devastated by the losses suffered during the ransacking that it was unable to pay taxes.[68]

Slowly, however, it began to recover and grow. Physical conditions improved: swamps were drained, the shulhoyf expanded onto some of the newly drained land, and the town grew in size. Other kinds of progress were being made, too. In 1830 a remarkable technological innovation was built on the site of the ancient castle: the St. Petersburg–Warsaw telegraph tower. New brick buildings were put up around the tower, possibly to house the guards who had been posted there to protect it.[69]

Any celebrations for the telegraph tower must have been short-lived, however. In March 1831, the Polish Rebellion reached Lithuania. The Jews were caught in the middle, their loyalty demanded by both sides. Near Eishyshok a fierce battle took place between a Russian regiment and the Polish rebels, which ended in defeat for the Poles. Blaming their defeat on the Jews, the Poles murdered all the members of a wedding party traveling between two shtetlekh, and Jews in several other locations as well. In fact, loyalties were divided, some Jews having maintained

German aerial photo of Eishyshok taken on May 27, 1944. The photos were later used by the Allied military intelligence. NATIONAL ARCHIVES, WASHINGTON, D.C., RECORD GROUP 373

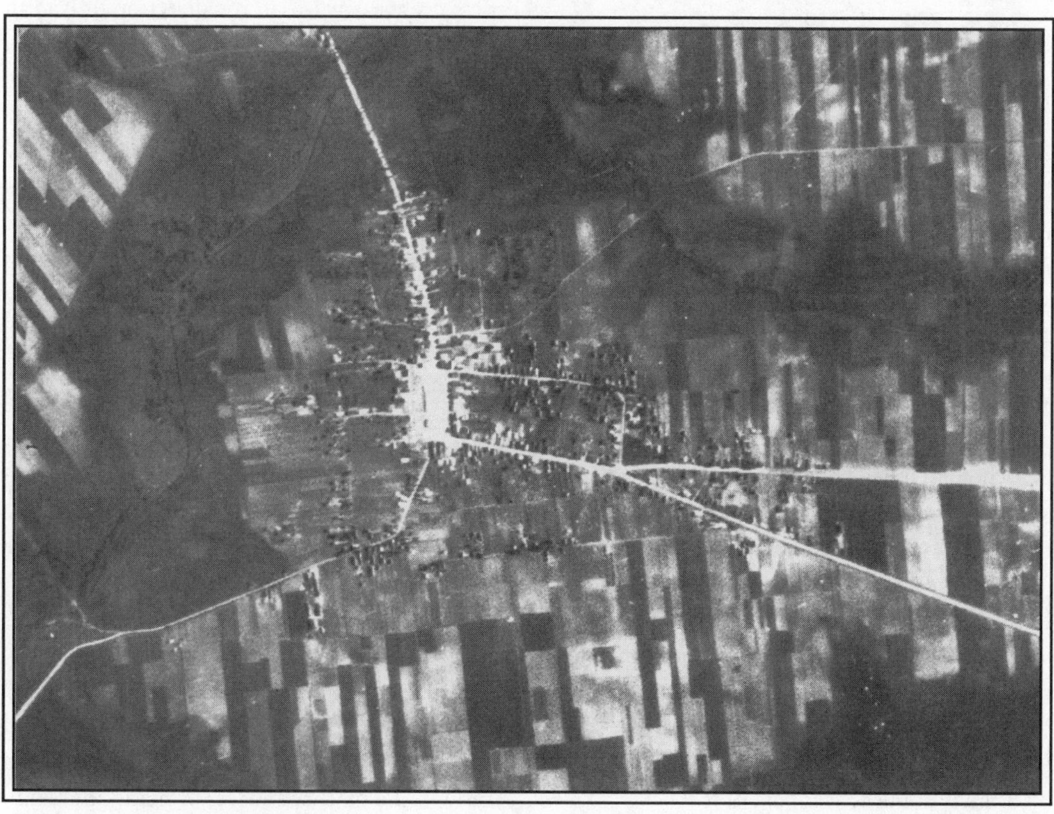

The Kiuchefski family in their house on Vilna Street, August 12, 1937. The Kiuchefskis enjoyed special privileges during the Second Polish Republic, because Frade-Leah Kiuchefski had saved Ludwik Narbutt (1832–1863), the local commander of the 1863 Polish uprising, by hiding him in bed under her blanket. Standing (left to right): Shlomo Kiuchefski and his wife Masha; Shlomo's sister Masha and husband Velvke Kaganowicz, Mordekhai (Motke) and Yossef Kiuchefski. Seated (left to right): Rochel Kiuchefski; Yefim; a Kiuchefski relative; Esther Kiuchefski, wife of Yefim; Berl and Sonia Kiuchefski. Motke and Yossef Kiuchefski survived the war in Russia. All the others were murdered in the September 1941 massacre in Eishyshok and in the Ponar section of Vilna. Shlomo Kiuchefski and his family were murdered by the AK. YESC, M. KAGANOWICZ

Wounded victims of the Polish uprising of 1863, during which the Kiuchefski family and other Jews from Eishyshok and the vicinity assisted the Poles against the Russians. PAINTING BY S. WITKIEWICZ

close ties with Poles, others having forged new ones with Russians.

Nonetheless, when the rebellion was at last put down, Russian officials from a number of cities, including Vilna, Grodno, and Bialystok, thanked the Jews for their support.[70] Even the anti-Semitic Prince Dolgoruky expressed gratitude to the Jews. In Eishyshok, one of the families who had indeed been loyal to the Russians, the Paikowskis, were given land and other benefits as a reward for their help.[71] These privileges, political as well as financial, exempted the Paikowskis from a number of the tzars' punitive measures, including the 1835 restrictions on Jews' voting in municipal elections. Over all, however, the price paid by Eishyshkians during the Polish Rebellion was a heavy one. Cholera, brought by Russian soldiers, was part of it.[72]

Another cholera epidemic raged through the town in 1848. But still Eishyshok kept growing — from 72 households, 53 of which were Jewish, in 1847, to 124 households, 80 of them Jewish, in 1850. To accommodate increases in the shtetl's population as well as in its trading activities, the market square was expanded, and the town grew eastward, in the direction of Radun and Dumbla, in an area that would be known from the 1860s on as "The New Plan." New streets and new homes were built, in a different kind of configuration from before. The lots grew narrower, the houses closer together. At this time most of the buildings still stood with their back to the market square and the front facing the shtetl gardens and the fields beyond, a legacy of Eishyshok's strong agricultural ties. But this would gradually change as the Jews lost their lands due to one or another of the tzarist decrees. Then most of the stables attached to the houses disappeared (though a few kept their stables to the very end), and the houses began to be built with their main entrances facing the square and the streets.

In 1863 the shtetlekh were again thrown into turmoil by another Polish uprising. Once more, Jewish loyalties were called into question by both sides, and as usual both sides attacked the Jews. Drunken Russian Cossacks rampaged through the market squares of many shtetlekh, seizing and beating people; Polish rebels went so far as to conduct hangings on the outskirts of shtetlekh where Jews were accused of disloyalty.[73] Eishyshok, too, was drawn into the uprising, as host to an elite tzarist fighting unit that had been sent in as reinforcements to the permanent army encampment (part of which was based in the brick fortifications around the telegraph tower). The tzarist soldiers fought a fierce battle with the Poles not far from Eishyshok. During the subsequent rout of the Polish forces, one of the local Polish commanders, a man named Ludwik Narbutt, took refuge in the home of the Kiuchefski family. Just as the Paikowski family were granted certain favors by the Russians for the helpful role they played in the 1831 uprising, so the Kiuchefskis obtained valuable privileges from the Poles for their aid to a man who turned out to be a Polish national hero — though the awarding of those privileges would have to await the founding of the Second Polish Republic, after World War I.

Three years after the uprising, in 1866, the district of Lida was divided into court zones, and Eishyshok became the seat of the justice of peace.[74] Though this conferred considerable prestige upon the town, many of the residents, Jews and non-Jews alike, continued to prefer the judgments of Reb Layzer the Wise, the shtetl dayyan.

One of the most profound changes within the shtetlekh during the nineteenth century was the appropriation of Jewish-owned land by a series of tzarist decrees. This was a huge blow, for throughout all its centuries of change the shtetlekh had maintained a deep connection to their agricultural past, an image of themselves as towns of landowners. But during the reigns of Alexander I and Nicholas I, ancestral lands that had been in the hands of old Jewish families for centuries were taken away. More still was taken away under Alexander II, who confiscated various properties to give to the serfs after he freed them in 1861.

In Eishyshok the land was taken from twenty-one Jewish families, among them the descendants of the original Jewish settlers, particularly the Kabacznik, Yurkanski, and Senitski families. Thirty-five landless peasants who had been sent in by the government, as well as fourteen local peasants, were the beneficiaries. The official rationale for this land grab was that this was "state-owned land" which was not in use.[75] In reality, it was family-owned land under constant cultivation. Another tzarist decree in 1869, this one aimed at giving grants of land to veterans of the army, deprived Eishyshkians of even larger tracts, and left the shtetl surrounded by a belt of Christian settlers.

Refusing to accept the legality of these thefts, the Jewish families fought to reclaim their land, pursuing their cases in the courts even after the country came under Polish rule following World War I. Indeed, they never stopped fighting, until the last days of the shtetl. But the Poles proved no more sympathetic than the Russians had.

Toward the end of the nineteenth century an attempt was made to bring industry to Eishyshok, with the building of a match factory. But apparently even then it was difficult for the shtetl to accept that it was no longer a primarily agricultural town, for the official permission for the building of the factory contains a clause stating that if the land should be needed for a farm, the factory would be removed.[76]

With the addition of the Christian farmers and their families, as well as increases in the native population, Eishyshok kept growing apace — from 1,250 residents in 1868, for example, to 2,616 in 1880. Over half the population was Jewish, and the total number of Jews did not include the several hundred students who were studying at the Kibbutz ha-Prushim yeshivah in Eishyshok at the time.[77]

The Big Fire of 1895 proved to be a landmark in Eishyshkian life — emotional, spiritual, practical, and historical. The fire began on a market day in May, when the town was buzzing with activity, and before it ended it had destroyed almost everything in its path. It was one of a series of fires known as the "Red Rooster" or "Red Cockscomb" that were sweeping the shtetlekh of Eastern Europe that spring.

People tried desperately to save their homes and their possessions, especially their books and their family heirlooms and records, but that proved impossible. The flames were faster than the people, and eventually all the townspeople had to make their way to the banks of the river, with clouds of smoke filling the skies behind them. By sunset all that remained of Eishyshok were the three burned-out shells of the synagogue and the Old and New Houses of Study (batei midrash), part of Radun Street, and a few homes near the bridge.[78] Jews from nearby villages drove in with their horses and wagons to offer shelter to the newly homeless Eishyshkians.

Twelve people lost their lives during the Big Fire. They included the one-year-old granddaughter of Reb Layzer Wilkanski, who died in her crib. Her father had tried to save her, but in the confusion grabbed a pillow and left the baby behind. Another casualty, Hayyim Berkowitch, drowned in the swamps while trying to save his horses.

Even after such total devastation, Eishyshok recovered — although the yeshivah never did (see chapter 6). Donations from the Eishyshok Society in America, from people as far away as Siberia who had read about the fire in the Jewish press, from former students of the yeshivah, and from local well-to-do balebatim paid for the rebuilding of the synagogue and the houses of study.[79] Generous gifts from friends and relatives in America helped with the construction of new homes.

For many Eishyshkians, the fire of 1895 was a turning point, a moment when they began to consider whether they wanted to put their lives in Eishyshok back together again or move. They were touched, surprised, and impressed by the generosity of Eishyshkian émigrés in America, whose gifts of money were helping the townspeople to rebuild with such speed that the houses seemed to rise from the ashes like mushrooms after a rain. Before that, America had had a reputation in the shtetl as a godless, materialistic place, a place where people lost their identities and their very souls. Many decided to emigrate.

Two years after the fire, in 1897, a census was taken throughout the Russian empire. Eishyshok had 3,196 people, 2,376 of them Jews, 820 non-Jews. In the province of Vilna, to which Eishyshok belonged, there were 204,686 Jews, constituting 12.9 percent of the general population. The greatest concentration of Jews in the empire was to be found in the nearby province of Grodno, which had 280,489 Jews, who made up 17.5 percent of the general population.[80]

Eight years later, in 1905, there were 2,448 people in Eishyshok — a decrease of 748. How to account for the decline? The official Soviet-commissioned history of the shtetl, part of the same multivolume history of Lithuanian towns that so completely misrepresented the facts about the massacres that were committed against the Jews in September 1941, states: "The decrease in population was thought by some authors to be related to emigration to America, but this was hardly important in Eisiskes, because the majority was made up of Jewish people, and they did not emigrate."[81] In fact, emigration — mainly to North America but also to Palestine, England, France, South Africa, and countries in South America and elsewhere — took considerably more than 1,500 Jews from Eishyshok and the vicinity between 1880 and the outbreak of World War I. After the war, changes in the immigration laws of America stemmed the tide from Eastern Europe and diverted much of it elsewhere — mainly to Palestine. From the very beginning of the emigrations to the end, in 1939–40, the number of those who left probably totals something like 4,000, if people from the villages under Eishyshok's jurisdiction and from the surrounding countryside are included along with those from Eishyshok proper.

One of the primary incentives for the 1880–1914 wave of emigration that carried millions of East European Jews to American and other foreign shores was to escape conscription into the Russian army, which never ceased to be a humiliating, nightmarish experience, thanks to the ingrained anti-Semitism of the military. As a regular stopping-off place on the route of newly drafted soldiers, Eishyshok witnessed firsthand the deplorable treatment of Jewish recruits. Escorted by military policemen who were supposed to maintain order, the young soldiers would arrive in town, and the Christian ones would proceed to wreak havoc: drinking heavily, looting stores, and beating every Jew they encountered, especially the recently drafted Jews in their own company. All the new draftees were readily recognizable by the red scarves they wore around their necks, but somehow the policemen generally contrived not to be in their vicinity during these rampages. Meanwhile, the Jewish recruits could always be distinguished from the others; though they too wore the red scarves, they were the ones who remained apart from the rowdy crowd, sad gazes fixed on the ground as they walked along, accompanied by weeping parents who followed behind as though in a funeral procession.[82]

A German postcard of Eishyshok's Vilna Street during World War I. YESC, ELLIS

Many changes had occurred in the Russian military during that portion of the nineteenth century that Jews had been required to serve — but some things seemed never to change. Anti-Semitism remained as strong as ever. (The same observation could be made about the experience of Jews in the Polish army in the next century.)

Another of the incentives for the massive departures that began in the last quarter of the nineteenth century, after so many hundreds of years of persecution and economic oppression, was a new round of violence against the Jews in southwestern Russia. The assassination of Tsar Alexander II in 1881 was followed by an outbreak of anti-Jewish pogroms known as the Southern Tempests, an eruption of hatred that was tolerated by the authorities and indeed fueled by the virulent anti-Semitism of Tzar Alexander III's new minister of the interior, Nikolai Ignatiev.

During the years to come, years that encompassed the rise of Zionism as a major world movement, World War I, the Russian Revolution, the civil war in Russia, the establishment of the Second Polish Republic, and the Polish–Russian War, the Jews would find more and more reasons — and opportunities — to leave. And leave many of them did. The general turbulence of the area and the persistence of anti-Semitism long after the ideals of the Enlightenment had raised hopes for universal brotherhood and equality would have been sufficient cause; but there was also yet another new wave of blood libels and of ever more violent and murderous pogroms. Hundreds of thousands of Jews would be savagely beaten, raped, and murdered in the pogroms of the first two decades of the twentieth century.

Eishyshok's experience of emigration could be

seen as a paradigm for the average Eastern European shtetl. Though the majority of its emigrants to the United States got started on their journeys somewhat later than those from other shtetlekh, and the emphasis on Zionism and emigration to Palestine in the years after World War I was more intense than in many other Jewish centers — thanks to the Wilkanski family, whose commitment to Zionism had inspired the entire community — it was a town, like so many other Jewish towns in that part of the world, that would lose many of its best and brightest to the lure of a new life in a new land.

TWENTIETH-CENTURY EISHYSHOK

The Eishyshok that rose from the ashes of the Big Fire was physically very different from the one that had gone up in flames, and for the most part — with the exception of the synagogue, which had been extraordinary — much more attractive. The houses were bigger, some two stories high. There was more space between them, thanks to a new fire law that required that they be over two feet apart in order to prevent the kind of instant spreading of flames that had consumed the shtetl in 1895. The streets were longer and wider, with a network of small lanes connecting the biggest streets: Vilna Street, Radun Street, Goyishker (Gentile) Street, Mill Street, and Pigs Lane (so named for the pigs who were given the run of the street, for this was where a large concentration of the Christian settlers lived, and they were pork eaters, unlike their Jewish neighbors). The shops in the center of the market square were more spacious. The new

After a few fires in the years between the two world wars, Vilna Street was rebuilt. A parade of Jews and Poles on Vilna Street marks Polish Independence Day, May 3. On the right is the studio of the photographer Rephael Lejbowicz. YESC, B. KALEKO

iron water pump on the northern end of the market square was much larger than the old one.

All in all, Eishyshok was a far more modern place than it had been, and this process of modernization would only accelerate in the years to come — years of great change. These years are covered in depth in Part Five.

World War I was perhaps the principal catalyst in Eishyshok's transition to modern life. Though Eishyshok endured its share of suffering in that war as the Russians, Germans, Poles, and Lithuanians fought for control of it, and the Jews were made scapegoats with each of the seven shifts in sovereignty that occurred during these years, it in fact fared much better than many other towns — thanks to the Germans. Most of the war (1915 to 1918) was spent under German rule, and the Germans proved a relatively benevolent occupying force. Not only did they assist the kahal in caring for the victims of hunger and typhus, they improved many of the physical conditions in the shtetl. Houses and shutters were painted, wooden sidewalks were constructed, additional trees were planted, new crops such as tomatoes and cultivated strawberries were introduced, and some of the side streets were paved with cobblestones like those lining the main streets and the market square.

Even more striking, the Germans were able to maintain such a level of civil order and well-being that a cultural renaissance was able to blossom, even in the midst of war. German support for the arts, in the form of money, patronage, and even participation, helped contribute to the new explosion of interest in musical events, theater performances, secular libraries, co-ed education, and so forth. Moreover, the constant and revolving presence of successive groups of outsiders in the shtetl, invaders as well as refugees, meant that Eishyshkians were exposed to a wide variety of cultural experiences, for some of these outsiders were highly educated and sophisticated urbanites. Suddenly Eishyshok was becoming cosmopolitan, in a way it had never been before.

After the Germans fled came a period of chaos, while Russia, Poland, and Lithuania fought for control over the region. By 1921 Eishyshok was officially under the rule of the Polish Second Republic, where it would remain until the confusion of the power shifts that followed the outbreak of World War II, when Lithuanian and Soviet rule would alternate until the Nazi troops arrived in June 1941.

The years of Polish rule were marked by anti-Semitism in both government policy and public

Moshe Kaplan of Warinowa, a shtetl near Eishyshok, served in the Polish army in 1938. He recounted incidents from his military service that could just as easily have occurred in the Russian army during the cantonist period. At bedtime he and the three other Jewish soldiers in his regiment would cover their heads with blankets to try to dull the bite of their comrades' belt buckles into their flesh, as the Poles administered their nightly beating. On an educational trip devoted to the history of Vilna, where they were stationed, they had to listen to an officer once again invoking the perennial blood libel, as he explained how the Jews in the area used the blood of Christian children to bake their Passover matzot. YESC, MOSHE KAPLAN

sentiment, with the Jews being expelled from one area after another of economic and professional endeavor.

Even young Jewish men who excelled in the army found their hopes trampled. The four Asner brothers, for example, who were from a village near Eishyshok, served with distinction, becoming among the best riders and sharpshooters in their unit of the Polish cavalry. Their reward was not promotion but rather a piling up of demeaning duties, with a special emphasis on assignments that had to be completed on the Jewish holidays. Their meager pay was often so delayed that they had to turn to the Jewish community, and the Bnei Hail Society, for help. During the Holocaust, three of the four Asner brothers, all of whom were fighting as partisans in the forest, were killed by Polish bullets — bullets from their former comrades-in-arms, bullets from men fighting the same enemy they were fighting. There would be many such stories, in Eishyshok and elsewhere.

Pogroms were also part of the Jewish experience of these years, particularly during the 1930s, after the death of chief of state Jozef Pilsudski (native of a village near Eishyshok), who many felt had acted as a brake against the anti-Semitic violence.

Not surprisingly, then, these were also years when more and more people tried to leave the shtetl. Unfortunately, the doors to the United States began to close to the Jews of Eastern Europe during the 1920s, thanks to new immigration laws. Thus emigration to America slowed to a trickle, and people had to look to new lands where the welcome mat was out. Of the approximately 1,500 Jews from Eishyshok who made aliyah ("ascended") to Palestine, the largest number emigrated during the 1920s and part of the 1930s, until the increasingly severe British re-

A map of Lithuania prior to World War I.

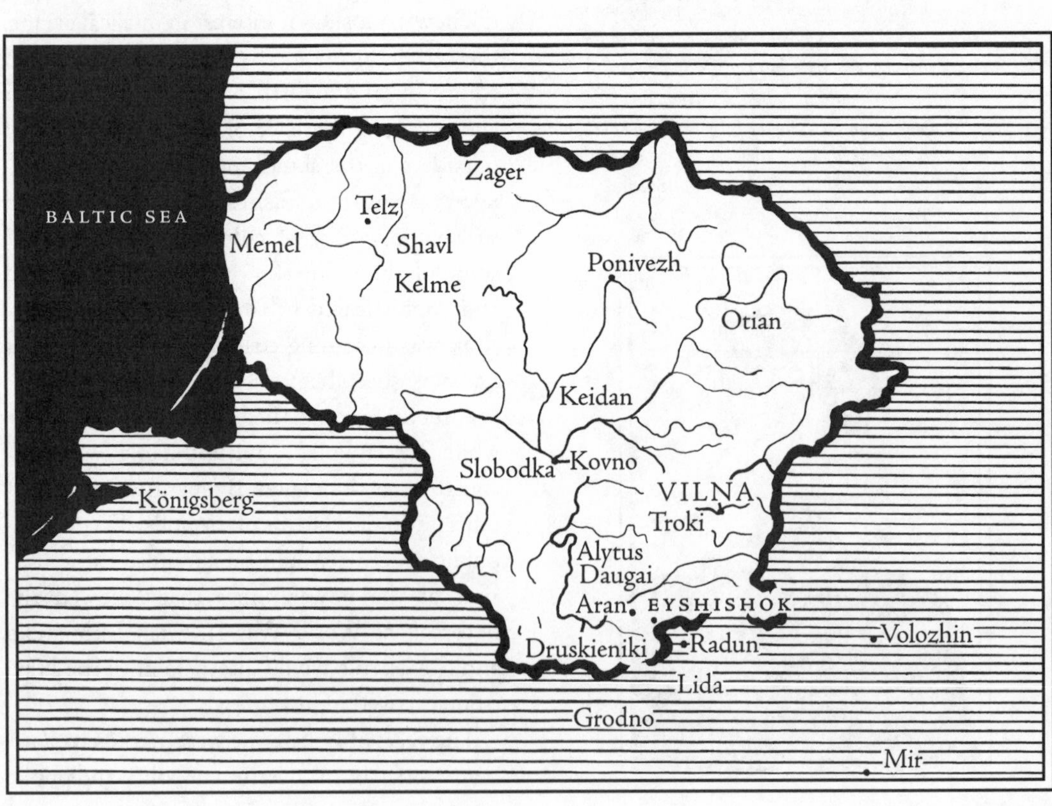

strictions on emigration reduced that flow to a trickle, too.

But not everyone left. In 1919 there were 2,344 people in Eishyshok. In 1931 there were 2,839. By 1939 there were about 5,000, of whom 3,500 were Jewish.[83]

News of Nazi atrocities began filtering into Eishyshok in 1939, carried by the 15,000 refugees who passed through the shtetl in flight from the German occupation. Many people dismissed the stories, unable to believe that the sons of the "good Germans" of World War I could be so different from their fathers. With the fall of Poland at the outbreak of World War II, Eishyshok went to the Soviets, then was ceded to Lithuania, and returned again to the Soviets before meeting its final fate at the hands of the Germans, who invaded in June 1941.

The following September, 3,500 Jews from Eishyshok along with about 1,000 from Olkenik and 500 from the surrounding countryside were murdered, in the course of a two-day massacre conducted by the Germans and their Lithuanian collaborators. Many of the Polish townspeople assisted in transporting their neighbors to the killing fields, and either looked on as their fellow Eishyshkians were slaughtered or used the time to begin looting their homes.

Unlike other massacres of this period, this was no anonymous act of brutality, where victim and executioner were strangers. Christians were witnessing and participating in the murder of their Jewish neighbors, alongside of whom they had lived in peace, and sometimes even in friendship, for 876 years. The twentieth-century Catholics of Eishyshok had much to learn from the eleventh-century pagans of Lithuania.

LOSS AND LEGACY

The rest of this book is an account of life before death, of what was lost in the massacre of 1941. Who were these people, what were their beliefs, how did they maintain their ability to rise, phoenixlike, from the ashes of the numerous wars and disasters that afflicted them through the ages, and what is their legacy to us?

In the 1930s, Anshel Virshubski of Eishyshok wrote a letter to his old friend and townsman Meir Wilkanski, who was by then living in Palestine:

Time has probably erased from our memories many of the details of our early lives in the shtetl. But as I write this letter I recall the childhood days we spent together in the heder, the teenage years inside the walls of the beth midrash learning Talmud. . . . And I remember how we used to walk together, you and your brother Yitzhak and I, roaming the woods and fields beyond the shtetl, filled with youthful optimism, inspired with the ideals of Zionism. Those magical days of youth, spent in the shtetl of our birth, were the most beautiful days of our lives.

Anshel would die in World War II, a victim of the Holocaust, one of the many who had hoped to make aliyah but were unable to do so. But he and Meir Wilkanski were such typical Eishyshkians in so many ways — in their love of learning, their kindness to their fellow man, their bravery, their industriousness, their closeness to the land around them, and their idealism about the Land of Israel — that they offer the beginnings of an answer to the question of what kind of legacy Eishyshok has left.

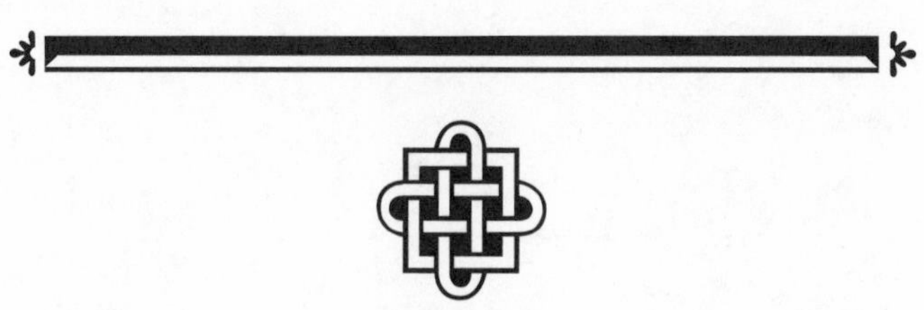

· TWO ·

THE SHULHOYF

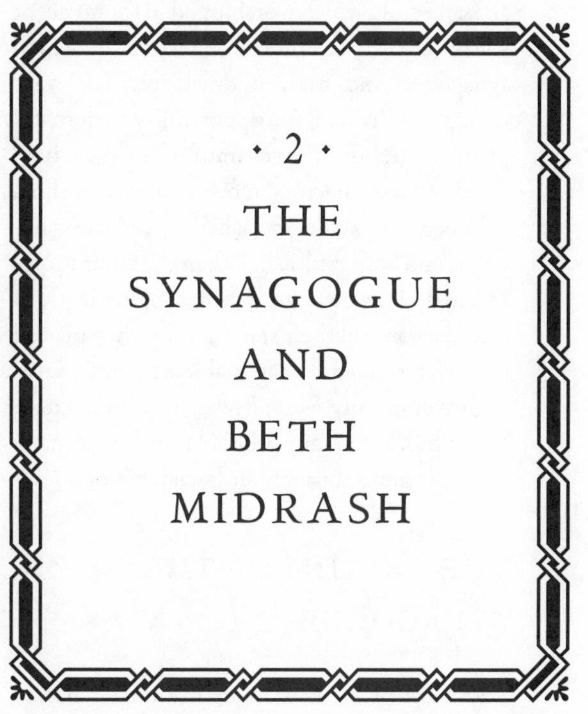

· 2 · THE SYNAGOGUE AND BETH MIDRASH

WITH THE SYNAGOGUE BEGAN A NEW TYPE OF WORSHIP IN THE HISTORY OF HUMANITY . . . IN ALL THEIR LONG HISTORY, THE JEWISH PEOPLE HAVE DONE SCARCELY ANYTHING MORE WONDERFUL THAN TO CREATE THE SYNAGOGUE.

Robert Travers Herford, THE PHARISEES (1924)

THE SYNAGOGUE (SHUL) AND ITS IMMEDIATE NEIGHBOR, THE HOUSE OF STUDY (BETH midrash), were the soul of shtetl life, the very essence of its existence. As the physical structure of the synagogue was the dominant architectural feature of the Jewish skyline, so the melodious chants of prayer and study that emanated from it were the sovereign voice of the Jewish community. Not that the everyday cadences of shtetl life were foreign to the synagogue. There one heard not just the sounds of devotion and exaltation, but from beyond its walls the voice of Jacob in ceaseless struggle against Esau; the cacophony of the marketplace.

The synagogue was the house of God and the dwelling place of every Jew. It and the beth midrash were the places where the Jewish male spent most of his life, from birth to death, making him a virtual guest in his own home. All the formal turning points in his life, as well as the mundane days in between, came to pass within the walls of the house of God and the house of study. All significant religious and personal events were observed there, all grievances stated, all community affairs conducted. It is where every stranger in need made his way, and each member of the community could look for solace in time of trouble. These houses were the ultimate expression of the Jew's pride in his heritage. Few other places throughout the centuries have witnessed more scholarship, friendship, devotion, humility, charity, love, longing, joy, hope, tears, and sorrow than the rooms enclosed by the walls of the shtetl synagogue and beth midrash.

The synagogue and beth midrash expressed the noblest yearnings of the human soul, while also embodying many of the obstacles the soul encounters in its search for spiritual perfection and community harmony. Together the two institutions formed a ladder with the top reaching toward heaven, the base firmly grounded in the shtetl's muddy soil. Upon its rungs a simultaneous two-way traffic of ascent and descent took place, as the people of the shtetl shuttled back and forth between the angels and the marketplace.

The synagogue had a social significance within the community that counted just as much as its spiritual, scholarly, and psychological roles. One's ranking in the synagogue determined one's position in the shtetl, and one's status in the shtetl expressed one's standing in the synagogue. Yet, despite this apparently rigid and inescapable class stratification, the synagogue and beth midrash also provided an intricate system of checks and balances, of parliamentary-style procedures, that allowed the disadvantaged to challenge the entrenched power brokers of the community oligarchy. This was a world in which the conclusion of the services in the main sanctuary of the synagogue or beth midrash waited on the participation of a quorum from the poor artisans' guild which worshipped in the adjacent shtibl (small prayerhouse), a world in which synagogue and beth midrash offered every wronged individual the opportunity to demand justice by holding the community a virtual hostage until a satisfactory agreement was reached.

When the people flourished, so did the synagogue and beth midrash. When the community was in decline, these most central of institutions also lost some of their standing. Yet they proved to have a resilience that enabled them to serve their community when it was most in need, in Eishyshok as in many other places, and at many different times throughout Jewish history.

The main synagogue in the center of the shulhoyf. Standing in front of the synagogue are siblings from the Schneider, Sonenson, Wilenski, Kabacznik, and Resnik families and Shlomo Farber from Olkenik. PHOTO: YITZHAK URI KATZ. YESC, ROZOWSKI

THE ORIGINS OF THE SYNAGOGUE

Like most of the shtetl's institutions, major or minor, the synagogue and beth midrash were part of its inheritance from a long distinguished history, to which it added its own significant contributions. The institution of the synagogue was governed by halakhic codes, customs and traditions that shaped every aspect of the life lived within its walls, down to the very location and architecture of those walls.

It is generally accepted that the synagogue originated during the Babylonian captivity in the aftermath of the destruction of the First Temple in Jerusalem in the year 586 B.C.E.[1] The exiles who returned to Jerusalem from Babylonia with Ezra and Nehemia brought with them the rudiments of the synagogue. And those who left during the course of the Diaspora carried the nascent institution with them, establishing synagogues wherever they set down roots, not only in Babylonia but in Syria as well as in Alexandria, Ptolemais, Rome, and other cities of the Jewish Diaspora.[2] By the first century C.E., the synagogue had emerged as an established institution, unrivaled as the very center of the social and religious life of the Jews in the Diaspora, and co-existing harmoniously with the newly built Second Temple in Jerusalem.

Throughout the Land of Israel, where both synagogue and Temple flourished, there were an impressive number of synagogues — in Tiberias, Dor, Caesarea, Capernaum, and Lod, to mention a few.[3] By the time of the destruction of the

Second Temple in 70 C.E., there were 480 synagogues in Jerusalem alone, according to one source, 390 by another count, and as many batei midrash.[4] Ruins of about a thousand synagogues have been discovered throughout the country. In Rome, which was the destination of many exiles, inscriptions from about thirteen synagogues from the same period have been found.[5]

With the destruction of the Second Temple, the synagogue became the exclusive focus and center of Jewish religious life. Many customs and rituals previously practiced only in the Temple were transferred to the synagogue, but some were forbidden or altered significantly, even though the terms referring to them may have continued to be used. The ceremony of animal sacrifice, for example, was replaced by the prayer service. Hence the word *avodah,* which previously referred to the sacrificial ritual in the Temple, was now applied to prayer, which came to be known as "avodah of the heart."[6] Other practices were transferred intact. The order of the daily and Sabbath services as set down in the first chapter of the Brakhot tractate, and the order of the services celebrated on festival days as written in the Megillah, remained fundamentally unchanged, though additions did get made over the ages.[7] Additions notwithstanding, the institution of the synagogue, its services, its functions, and the duties of its officials, have remained remarkably stable and consistent throughout 2,500 years of history in numerous countries of the Diaspora, among both Sephardic and Ashkenazic communities.

THE SYNAGOGUE OF EISHYSHOK

The first synagogue in Eishyshok was probably built immediately upon the arrival of the Jewish settlers which, according to the ancient Lithuanian Chronicles, took place in 1171, or, according to other, probably better, sources, almost a century earlier, in 1065. And indeed, in the Old Jewish Cemetery, located atop one of the two highest elevations in the shtetl, tombstones dating back as far as 1097 have been documented, as noted in chapter 1. One can safely assume that a Jewish community large enough to have a cemetery in one of the most prominent locations in the vicinity would also have had a synagogue, since a halakhic requirement stipulates that any settlement with more than ten Jews (a quorum, or minyan) must establish a synagogue.[8]

Another halakhic law states that the property on which the synagogue is built must be community-owned and, preferably, near a body of water. The first-century Jewish historian Flavius Josephus alludes to this custom when he writes about Hellenistic Jewish communities "who make their places of worship near the sea." And Paul refers to gatherings by the side of a river "where prayer was casually held."[9] Many explanations are offered for the proximity of the synagogue to a body of water. Perhaps the practical element should not be overlooked: The mikvah, the ritual purification bath, was part of the larger synagogue complex.

The builders of the Eishyshok synagogue meticulously followed all halakhic and traditional requirements. The synagogue was indeed built near one of the shtetl's two rivers, the Virshuki, on community-owned land, which was, as stipulated, one of the two highest elevations in the shtetl. Also as stipulated, the synagogue was the tallest building in the shtetl.[10]

In many towns, in both Christian and Muslim countries, Jews were unable to fulfill these requirements. Among the many discriminatory laws against the Jews in such places were restrictions on the size and style of the synagogue. For example, in 1661 King Jan Kazimierz (John Casimir) of Poland and Lithuania issued a letter of privileges to the Jewish community of Kameneta-Litovsk, permitting the Jews to build a synagogue provided it would not be taller than the local cloisters and churches and not surpass them in splendor or beauty.[11]

Eishyshok, however, escaped such restrictions, at least in the beginning, because when its Jewish community was established Lithuania was still pagan. The temple dedicated to Perkunas, the god of forests and thunder who ruled over a pantheon of other assorted gods and goddesses, existed in Vilna as late as 1387.[12] Enemies of Perkunas (and of the Lithuanian princes he protected) who were captured on the battlefield were sacrificed live, horse and rider alike, on Perkunas's altar. But the Jews were not counted among those enemies. In that respect, pagan Lithuania was among the most tolerant countries in medieval, largely Christian Europe. And so it was that the height of the Jewish synagogue in Eishyshok was not a problem, having apparently been deemed acceptable to Perkunas and his entourage of lesser deities.

Whether the church that was built in Eishyshok shortly after Lithuania's conversion to Christianity in the late fourteenth century posed a challenge to the height of the synagogue is not known. Nor is it known how long that church stood. We know only that a quite substantial church was erected in nearby Juryzdyki in the late eighteenth century, and that there had been a Tatar Muslim mosque in nearby Nekraszunca, which had been built, like the synagogue, in pagan times. Within Eishyshok itself beginning in pagan times and then from the eighteenth century on, if not continuously since pagan times, the synagogue was the dominant feature of the skyline, a fact attested to by Polish documents dating from the eighteenth century in which considerable displeasure is expressed over this state of affairs.[13]

Were it not for a terrible accident, the penultimate synagogue in Eishyshok's history would have been even taller than it was. But during construction of the magnificent building in the seventeenth century the builder fell to his death from the upper scaffold, and it was decided to call a halt to further construction immediately and pitch the roof on what was there.[14] Even so, this synagogue towered over everything else in the shtetl, including the two batei midrash on either side, which were the next-tallest buildings but were only half its size and height.

The plot on which the synagogue and the other community buildings were located was an open, elevated space of about four acres. To comply with ancient tradition, no trees or shrubs were planted on it. This custom dated to the synagogue's earliest days, in pagan times, when trees were worshipped as deities;[15] it continued to be observed in shtetl practice throughout Eastern Europe for hundreds of years, until the synagogues themselves were destroyed during the Holocaust.

The stark, bare, treeless courtyards often made for a sharp contrast with the elaborate architecture of the buildings surrounding them. But in Eishyshok the courtyard underwent a dramatic change during the late spring and summer months, when nature, uninhibited by tradition, covered the shulhoyf ground with lush green grass and wild flowers. Much to the delight of the students at the Eishyshok yeshivah and the young boys at Eishyshok's many hadarim, the courtyard was then transformed into a beautiful public plaza — a perfect place for the older students to take a leisurely stroll between afternoon (minhah) and evening (maariv) prayers, and for the younger ones to play.[16]

In the center of the shulhoyf was the main synagogue, flanked by the Old and the New batei midrash, the three buildings forming a triangle with the synagogue at the apex. The rest of the shulhoyf complex included the rabbi's house, the public bath (bod) and the ritual bath (mikvah), the shack where fowl were killed by the shohet, a shelter for the homeless, a water well, and two huge stones to support the canopies used during wedding ceremonies. At the rear of the shulhoyf were the public outhouses. In 1932 the Hebrew-school building was added to the complex, to the right of the synagogue. But even with the addition of the new building and its adjoining playground, the huge shulhoyf remained uncluttered, its spacious plaza unenclosed by walls or gates. This was in sharp contrast to the situation in urban areas, where due to lack of space and to anti-Jewish restrictions by the government, the shulhoyf was usually confined to a small, walled-in plot of land on which a maze of buildings huddled closely together.

THE FOUR-PILLARED STYLE

Eishyshok's synagogue was built in the style of the Grodno–Bialystok region, which meant a four-pillared configuration with a three-tiered pagodalike wooden roof atop an elaborate wooden interior framed by massive stone walls. (Until the closing years of the nineteenth century, the synagogue and the two houses of study that flanked it were the only stone buildings in the shtetl.) The synagogue's stained-glass windows glittered from on high in an assortment of vivid colors. Both the synagogue and the Old Beth Midrash (and probably the new one as well, but that is no longer known for certain) had intricately carved wooden interiors with the four columns surrounding the elevated central platform (bimah), as well as a magnificent, almost lacelike hand-carved Holy Ark.

The magnificent Olkenik synagogue was built between 1798 and 1802. PHOTO: HENDEKE. YESC, SH. FARBER

Similarly styled synagogues in the Grodno–Bialystok region, including those of Wolpa and Olkenik, only a few miles from Eishyshok, were considered among the jewels of Eastern European synagogue architecture. Ultimately the area owed these architectural splendors to the economic hardships imposed upon Jews in Prussia and Austria by anti-Semitic ordinances that first banned them from owning stores, then forbade them to peddle their goods, and ultimately forced them to settle elsewhere. The traders and merchants who moved to Grodno–Bialystok during the seventeenth and eighteenth centuries as a result of these restrictions were responsible for the great economic revival the region enjoyed at this time, and for the construction of its beautiful synagogues as well.[17]

The central bimah of the Olkenik synagogue. PHOTO: SHLOMO FARBER, 1933. YESC, SH. FARBER

Eishyshok shared in the general prosperity of the region, its fertile lands and rich forests a fine source of livelihood, as was the biannual Horse Fair for which it was known. So it was natural for the community to spend part of its wealth to adorn its holy buildings. Elsewhere, however, the magnificence of a small shtetl's synagogues sometimes owed as much to the local gentile gentry as to the economic prosperity of the Jewish community itself. Such was the case in Olkenik, a community of fewer than a thousand people, whose internationally renowned wooden synagogue was a joint venture between well-to-do local Jewish merchants and the benevolent Polish magnate who owned the land on which the shtetl was built. Count Granowsky was eager for "his" Jews to have an impressive prayer-house as a sign of his own success.[18] The beauty of the Olkenik synagogue was to inspire many, including one of its most famous visitors, Napoleon Bonaparte.

An outstanding example of the four-pillared style was the Great Synagogue in Vilna, which was built in 1573 and burned during anti-Jewish riots in 1592, then rebuilt in brick and stone.[19] It was the most famous big-city shulhoyf in the Pale of Settlement, known far and wide for the glories of both its religious and its secular life. Behind the small iron gate that had marked the entrance since 1640, when the Tailors' Guild presented it as a gift, was an extensive collection of buildings: the Old Kloiz, one of the most beautiful synagogues in Europe, built originally in 1573; the Gaon's Kloiz; over twenty additional synagogues and batei midrash; the renowned Strashun Library, built in 1885; community office buildings; ritual baths; a fountain; a slaughterhouse; shelters for the homeless; and bookseller stands.[20]

Although inspired by the Italian Renaissance, the four-pillared style as it was developed in Eastern Europe constituted an original Jewish architectural contribution, a direct outgrowth of the way the affairs of the community were conducted.

The canopy above the central bimah in the Olkenik synagogue, with an eagle on the pedestal and the four pillars surrounding the bimah. PHOTO: SHLOMO FARBER, 1933. YESC, SH. FARBER

THE SIGNIFICANCE OF THE BIMAH

In such buildings the ceiling or dome rested on the four massive columns in the center of the sanctuary, framing the bimah and creating a dramatic subspace that called attention to it. Thus was the building's shell linked structurally to the centrality of the bimah, expressing in the language of architecture the increasing concentration on the bimah that had been occurring since the sixteenth century, when the Council of the Four Lands was established in Poland and Lithuania. All of the Council's decisions and regulations were announced from the bimah.

The central position of the bimah was emphasized by Rabbi Moses ben Israel Isserles of Cracow, the great sixteenth-century legal codifier of Ashkenazic Jewry, and it would long remain a major issue for East European scholars. Rabbi Isserles wrote: "A bimah is constructed in the center of the synagogue so that the Torah reader stands where all may hear him, and he himself faces the Holy Ark."[21] This idea was restated by the Gaon of Vilna and the Hatam Sofer of Bratislava in the eighteenth century,[22] and it became one of the hallmarks of Orthodox synagogues, setting them apart from Reform and Conservative sanctuaries, architecturally and in many other ways as well.

The bimah was used as a pulpit by the Torah reader and by speakers at various nonreligious assemblies, and as the platform from which most of the community's secular affairs were conducted. Clearly, it had achieved a social and practical significance transcending even that of the Holy Ark. It also had political significance, for it was here that the legally binding decrees and decisions of the Council of the Four Lands were communicated to the community. Thus the four-columned, bimah-centered synagogue was, in its earliest days, an architectural manifestation of Jewish sovereignty, an expression of the autonomous status of the Jewish community under the jurisdiction of the Council.

With the decline of the Council of the Four Lands and its final collapse in 1764, the function of the bimah changed. Though it continued to serve as the platform from which local decisions about community affairs were announced, it was no longer the link between the shtetl's religious and legal authority (as represented by the men who sat on the kahal) and the federal authority (as represented, formerly, by the Council). Once it lost its political centrality, it also lost its physical prominence. The bimah as an independent structure dominating the sanctuary began to disappear. Though it continued to be located in the center, it became a more integrated part of the synagogue interior, and the Holy Ark became the more imposing structure.

Liberal Judaism went even further and challenged the physical position of the bimah as well, moving it away from the center of the synagogue and closer to the Holy Ark, which was located on the eastern (mizrah) wall. This was in part to bring synagogue architecture more closely in line with church interiors, in part to emphasize the division between church and state, in the spirit of the Enlightenment. For just as the central position of the bimah had affirmed the unity of civil and religious authority, so its removal from that place of honor was a declaration that civil authority now resided elsewhere, outside the synagogue. But Liberal Judaism did not prevail everywhere. In traditional synagogues in Eastern Europe, large and small, and in many Orthodox prayerhouses throughout the world, the bimah has retained its position in the center of the sanctuary down to the present day,[23] even though it is used mainly as the place where the Torah is read, and its role as platform for the conducting of community affairs is minuscule.

REBUILDING AFTER THE BIG FIRE

Beautiful as the Eishyshok synagogue was, such magnificence could prove ephemeral. In the Big Fire of 1895, the entire town of Eishyshok burned down. The exquisite hand-carved interiors of the synagogue and the Old Beth Midrash, the work of a fabled artist, were now forever lost, as was the shtetl record book, its pinkas. The flames also consumed religious articles that had graced the shulhoyf for generations: treasured ancient holy scrolls and an impressive library of sacred books, including many rare editions. These books were the pride of many a student at Eishyshok's famed Kibbutz ha-Prushim yeshivah. Some of them were inscribed by students who had gone on to achieve fame, and by distinguished visitors who had sat and learned amid the books in the Old Beth Midrash. One such inscription was by the famed eighteenth-century poet Y. L. Gordon, who, while visiting relatives in the shtetl, had written one of his poems on the blank page at the back of a Gemara.

When the Big Fire started, Meir Wilkanski was among the many students studying in the two batei midrash.

In the middle of the day Mother burst into the beth midrash and carelessly bypassed the other prushim [students]. She reached a bench near the eastern wall, grabbed me by the hand and pulled me outside, exclaiming over and over "Fire! A fire has started in one of the houses on the marketplace and who knows how it will end!"[24]

Batia Wilkanski's fears were justified. By the end of the afternoon, Eishyshok was in ruins. Her son, the shtetl's faithful chronicler, records: "The city of Torah has disappeared from under the skies. All that remains are the three naked scorched ruins of the batei midrash and the synagogue."[25]

The Big Fire occurred in the first week of May 1895. The rebuilding of the shtetl was done at a frantic pace in order to beat the cold weather of winter, and to have the batei midrash and the synagogue ready for the High Holiday season. The challenge was to recapture some of the glory of what had been destroyed, while creating structures that would be fireproof. The shtetl dayyan, Reb Layzer Wilkanski, born in Eishyshok in 1827 to one of its oldest families and father of town chronicler Meir, was among the individuals entrusted with supervising the replacement of the shulhoyf buildings.

Support for the rebuilding was extensive, locally and even internationally. Assistance came from many former Kibbutz ha-Prushim students, some of them now eminent writers and editors, others prosperous businessmen. Emigrants to the new world, both as individuals and as members of the Eishyshok Society, Hevrah Bnei Avraham Shmuel Anshei Eishyshker, responded so generously to the tragedy that, Meir Wilkanski wrote, "The hands of Elisha the postman [were] tired from carrying the load of letters and money arriving from America."[26] Some of the funds were sent for the general needs of the shtetl, others were earmarked specifically for the rebuilding of the synagogue and batei midrash, where so many of the donors had sat and learned during their student years. Though the contributions did not cover all the town's building expenses, they were sufficient for the houses of prayer and study.[27]

Young Meir Wilkanski, as the son of the shtetl dayyan, had a close-up view of the reconstruction. Fascinated by the activities of the contractor, architects, builders, and artists under his father's supervision, he followed the restoration intently and later recorded it for posterity:

But if in Noah there is the spirit of Torah, the spirit of God is in Bezalel and Oholiab, who came from afar and labored in their holy work on the batei midrash. The ancient pillars that supported the ceiling pillars were taken out, the sanctuary became wider. No longer will people bump into them when passing by or rushing to the bimah for an aliyah to the Torah. The new ceiling is pitched on a void, suspended on a miracle! The roof is constructed of massive interlocking beams, horizontal and vertical, and somehow this heavy load does not collapse under its own weight and tumble down! We walk safely high up on the beams and look down, and we stand safely below on the ground and inspect the ceiling above.*[28]

THE INTERIOR AND ITS FURNISHINGS

The newly spacious sanctuary that resulted from the removal of the four columns surrounding the bimah was an innovation. But other aspects of the rebuilt synagogue were in keeping with tradition, some of which was dictated by religious law, some by regional style. The new wooden three-tiered ceiling that so intrigued Meir Wilkanski ("pitched on a void, suspended on a miracle!") was, like the one it replaced, in the time-honored style of the Grodno–Bialystok region. Its intricate architecture created an illusion of height far greater than the actual four stories of its interior, and allowed for a freer, more complex interplay of forms than would have been possible with a roof of brick or stone. Each of the roof's three tiers ended in a richly carved pendant and was crowned with a decorative balustrade. (In other synagogues, like that in nearby Olkenik, the balustrades were real.) The overall effect for those within the sanctuary was of being inside a wondrous wooden tent.[29]

The Eishyshok synagogue was rectangular in shape. As in many synagogues since the seventeenth century, this basic rectangular layout included both the polesh (vestibule) and, on the second floor, the women's gallery.[30] (In other synagogues in the Grodno–Bialystok region, however, they were located in separate annexes surrounding the main hall.)[31] The women's gallery was a rectangular space above the polesh, running north to south along the western wall, and jutting into the sanctuary below. Because religious rules dating to the time of the Temple required the segregation of the sexes, not only was separate seating established for men and women, but separate entrances as well. The women's gallery was reached through a doorway on the northern wall, leading to an internal staircase. The men's entrance, on the western wall, was the main one, consisting of a heavy wooden door inlaid with carved rectangular slabs.

Overlooking the main sanctuary through a row of arched windows cut into a three-foot-thick stone wall, each window covered with lacy white curtains, the women's gallery faced the Holy Ark and offered an excellent view of everything below. Stained-glass windows lined its other three sides, the western, southern, and northern walls, filling the gallery with beautifully colored light and allowing the women views outside into the shulhoyf.

Though the women were separated from the main sanctuary, and had no official role to play in the synagogue, administrative or ritual, in

*Noah was an accomplished Eishyshkian builder of the time; Bezalel and Oholiab were the two skilled artists who constructed the Tabernacle and its vessels (Exodus 31:1–11).

Lithuania there was at least one breach in the barrier: The rabbinic authorities granted women permission to recite the mourner's Kaddish in memory of their parents if there was no male member of the family available.[32] Several known instances of this permission being granted occurred in Eishyshok and the vicinity, which suggests that a number of other occasions have probably been lost to memory. After the devastating typhus epidemic of World War I, for example, the teenage daughters of a number of the victims recited Kaddish, and not from the women's gallery, but in the main sanctuary, standing in front of the entire community, to the right of the hazzan's lectern, wearing berets on their heads. In the 1920s, a four-year-old girl recited Kaddish for her father in the main sanctuary of the synagogue of Radun, in the presence of its illustrious rabbi, the Haffetz Hayyim. And in 1934, Zipporah Hutner, daughter of the shtetl dayyan Hertz Mendl Hutner, recited Kaddish for her father in the main sanctuary and at graveside. Though she had two brothers, they were not in the shtetl at the time.

As prescribed by tradition, the main sanctuary had twelve windows, located high above the floor. On bright days the light passing through their stained glass filled the sanctuary with a vivid interplay of colors. On overcast days and at dusk, however, the interior was immersed in dim shadows that gave rise to many stories and legends about strange encounters with spirits and demons. The other source of light besides the stained-glass windows was the skylight in the dome just above the bimah, through which rays of light fell directly onto the table where the Torah was read. The effect was striking and dramatic.

Those who walked through the main entrance found themselves in the polesh, directly beneath the women's gallery. To the right was the shtibl of the Hevrat Mishnayot, the Mishnah society, where its daily classes convened. It was the only heated place in the synagogue, and the only part of it that was in regular use throughout the winter. The rest of the sanctuary was closed for winter, and it was therefore known as the summer shul to optimists, the cold shul to pessimists.[33]

Also located in the polesh was a table with a sandboxlike top (orla tish). In the sand of the orla tish were kept the foreskins of circumcised baby boys prior to burial. Next to the orla tish stood an elaborate old chair known as the Elijah chair in honor of the prophet Elijah, who is the invisible participant at every circumcision.[34] There the godfather (sandak) of the baby sat, holding him during the circumcision. Above, hanging on the wall, were a handbasin and a towel.

On the eastern wall of the polesh stood the lectern for the shliah zibbur ("the messenger of the congregation"), who led the afternoon and evening prayers there on weekdays. The main sanctuary was used for prayers only on the Sabbath and on holidays.

One passed from the polesh through a set of carved wooden swinging doors into a gazebolike structure with stained-glass windows and intricately carved, lacy woodwork complementing that of the ceiling. To either side of it were two small staircases leading down to the sanctuary. The tradition of placing the sanctuary at a level lower than the vestibule is attributed by some historians to a ritual requirement, as expressed by the psalmist: "Out of the depths I call you, O Lord."[35] Others see it as an architectural response to the prohibition against Jewish houses of worship rising higher than those of the Christians. In some synagogues the floor itself was not made lower, only the lectern where the hazzan prayed. Hence the expression in Hebrew is "to go down to the lectern," rather than "to go up."

The interior walls of the sanctuary were smooth, white-washed surfaces. Above the entrance to the sanctuary, on either side of the gazebo, hung two massive clocks, one with Roman numerals and huge long chains, the other with Arabic numerals. Beneath this second clock was a framed Hebrew inscription reading: "May God console you among the other mourners of Zion and Jerusalem," which was addressed to the congregation's mourners, who sat on a bench nearby.

Along the eastern wall, the mizrah, on both sides of the Holy Ark, ran an elaborate hand-carved wooden bench, seating for the community's most prominent members — the so-called Mizrah Jews — each of whom had a free-standing lectern (shtander) in front of him. The other members of the community sat on benches flanking the central bimah. The long benches were in pairs that shared a common back, so that those who sat on one side faced east, and those who sat on the other faced west. This seating arrangement permitted the congregation to follow what went on at the two most vital centers of the synagogue, the Holy Ark and the bimah. One simply turned around in his seat if the action was in the direction opposite from the way he was facing. The benches had hinged seats that opened into cubbyholes where one's personal books and other items were kept, and where children loved to hide their bags of goodies and other precious items.

The seating arrangement in the women's gallery followed in general principle that of the men's, with the most prominent and well-to-do women near the windows overlooking the main sanctuary. The price of the seat decreased as the distance from the windows increased.

To the right of the Holy Ark was the cantor's lectern which, in the years after World War I, was of bronze, presented as a gift from Eishyshok's Jewish veterans in gratitude for their safe return from the war, and in memory of those who were not so fortunate. On the black center panel of the lectern were engraved the names of the dead and missing-in-action; on the right and left panels were the names of the donors. The old pulpit, the one replaced by the veterans' gift, was moved to the vestibule of the synagogue.

THE HOLY ARK

The Holy Ark, where the scrolls of the Torah are kept, is a synagogue's most sacred place. Eishyshok's was located in a specially built niche in the wall, above the platform (also called a bimah, but different from the central bimah) from which the rabbi and the maggid delivered their sermons, and the kohanim their priestly benedictions.

Though the Eishyshok Ark was lost in the Big Fire, it lives on in the description left by Meir Wilkanski, who spent many hours of his youth in the synagogue and remembered it vividly.

Gone forever is the ancient splendor of the Holy Ark that was consumed by flames. It was carved entirely of wood like the Ark in the Tabernacle. Gone forever those miraculous sea creatures, half man and half fish. So true to life were they it was as though their very scales were endowed with a living spirit. A wondrous artist who came from a miraculous place created those creatures. The world will not see his like, nor that of his creations, again.*[36]

The magnificent wooden Ark in the synagogue of neighboring Olkenik may have been the work of the same "wondrous artist." Or it may be that Reb Yaakov, the Olkenik artist, inspired the man who did the work at Eishyshok, for the two Arks were strikingly similar in style, according to individuals who knew both very well. Though the Ark at Olkenik is also now lost to us, destroyed in 1941 during the Holocaust, its appearance and that of the synagogue's central bimah live on in the original artists' drafts from

*The Ark in the Tabernacle was made of acacia wood and overlaid with pure gold both inside and out (Exodus 25:10–22 and 37:1–9). No such sea creatures were mentioned in the Bible; their origins can be found, rather, in the mystical tradition and in folktales.

the eighteenth century and in the detailed photographs Shlomo Farber, a teacher from Olkenik, took in 1933, just prior to his emigration to Eretz Israel in 1934.

The Olkenik Ark, an elaborate four-level structure, was about thirty feet high and twelve feet wide. Steps led up from the sanctuary to the first level, a small wooden platform surrounded by a carved railing.

On the second level was the Ark itself, where the Torah scrolls were kept. It was flanked by two wooden columns, Yakhin and Boaz, in commemoration of the two main pillars of the Temple in Jerusalem. On top of Yakhin was a plaque bearing the name of the benefactor who paid for the construction of the Ark; on top of Boaz was a plaque honoring the donor's wife. And between the two columns was a carving of the legendary leviathan with its tail in its mouth. According to the legend, if the leviathan lets go of its tail, a flood will once more engulf the world. Attached to Yakhin and Boaz were two movable planks, each one inscribed with part of an intricate, 448-year calendar beginning in 1798 when the synagogue was completed, and ending in 2246. Little did anyone suspect when the calendar was created that in 1941 all the Jews of Olkenik would be taken to Eishyshok and murdered along with their neighbors — some 305 years before the calendar on their Holy Ark ran out. Extending from each side of the calendar were the wings of the Ark, elaborately carved with plants, birds, and animals, among them a mythic half-lion, half-fish creature whose tail was covered with shimmering silver scales. These carvings were very close in spirit to the "miraculous sea creatures" Meir Wilkanski described in the Eishyshok synagogue, which, some 140 years after they were made, appeared to him "as if they were created and completed just yesterday."

The third level of the Ark, above eye level, consisted of a hand-carved tableau of the giving of the Law at Sinai. The Ten Commandments at the center were surrounded by numerous figures and symbols, topped by the Crown of Torah, and flanked by two lions.

The fourth level depicted the crown of majesty, its chief adornment a double-headed eagle, the emblem of Imperial Russia, which had been adapted to its surroundings, for it clutched a three-foot-long shofar in one claw, a lulav of the same length in the other. Eagles identical to this one appeared in several other synagogues that we know of, including one in Cracow. There

According to legend, if this carved wooden leviathan, part of the Holy Ark of the Olkenik synagogue, let go of his tail, a flood would once more engulf the world. ORIGINAL SKETCH BY THE ARCHITECT-BUILDERS, 1790S. YESC, SH. FARBER

On the top of the Olkenik Holy Ark was a double-headed eagle, the emblem of Imperial Russia, clutching a three-foot-long shofar in one claw, a lulav in the other. ORIGINAL SKETCH BY THE ARCHITECT-BUILDERS, 1790S. YESC, SH. FARBER

The right wing of the Olkenik Holy Ark, elaborately carved with plants, birds, animals, and a half-lion, half-fish creature whose tail was covered with shimmering silver scales. PHOTO: SHLOMO FARBER, 1933. YESC, SH. FARBER

was also a huge carved eagle on the canopy of the central bimah, this one being the emblem of the Polish kingdom. It might have been included in honor of the Polish nobleman Count Granowsky, who was instrumental in the construction of the synagogue, donating the wood, among other generous acts.

Reb Yaakov, son of Shlomo of Rasein, did not get to complete the magnificent Ark of Olkenik. As he was moving into the final phase of his work on its fourth level, Reb Yaakov informed the shtetl notables that he was close to death, and that they should search for another artist to finish his work. His dying wish was that this artist be someone who could execute what remained of the work in a style as close as possible to his own, and that that same artist be hired to build the bimah, thus completing the Ark. But this proved impossible, and the new artist's creations, while also highly accomplished, clearly were the work of a different hand.[37]

The Ark in Olkenik was one of the last of its kind, for by the turn of the century those that were lost to fire or other kinds of devastation — and they were many — were usually replaced with something quite different, in materials and consequently in style, as happened in Eishyshok. As Meir Wilkanski said about the Eishyshok Ark that went up in flames in 1895, the world would not see the likes of such work again. And indeed, because of its vulnerability to fire, it would not be attempted again.

To safeguard Eishyshok's new Ark from the fate of its predecessor, a niche for it was carved out of the stone walls of the synagogue, and its ornaments were made of plaster. The new bimah was of polished brass. Though the new Ark lacked the ancient majesty of the old handcarved wooden one, Meir Wilkanski consoled himself that because it was fireproof, it would last a long time. Having followed the artists through each step of the molding and shaping of this new creation, he described their work in his usual vivid language:

Like clay in the hands of the creator, so is the plaster in their hands. Above the Holy Ark they made the Tablets of the Law, on which the Ten Commandments are written in big, bold shining letters. Lions stand to either side, their tables forming an arc like a rainbow beneath the Tablets. Above the Tablets an eagle hovers in mid-flight, his wings spread just as they were when he carried the chosen people to the Promised Land during the exodus from Egypt.[38]

RELIGIOUS ARTICLES

The losses in the Big Fire were great, but some of the synagogue's most precious religious artifacts escaped the flames because they were stored elsewhere, in the home of the neeman (trustee) or gabbai (elected official) of each prayerhouse, and brought to the synagogue only on specific holidays or other special occasions. Among the articles that thereby survived were covers (caporot) for the table where the Torah was read, mantles for the Torah's holy scrolls, and curtains (parokhot) for the Ark where they were stored. Some of these parokhot were made of ancient national flags commemorating various historic events, such as the visit of King Augustus II of Poland to Eishyshok in 1710; others were elaborately embroidered and appliquéd. Once a year, from a few days before Sukkot until after Simhat Torah, for a period of about two weeks, they were brought out of storage and hung on the wall of the Old Beth Midrash.

Although Eishyshok's sacred treasures could not compare to those of a city like Vilna, for a small town they were quite impressive and had managed, quite remarkably, to survive centuries of war and plunder, thanks in part to the devotion of the townspeople. Each of the many silver and brass religious objects, each parokhet and caporet had a story attached to it, bearing testimony to the history of Eishyshok, or perhaps to the life of the individual who had donated the article, or helped to protect it. The last of the treasures to be given to the synagogue was an elaborate parokhet for the Holy Ark, donated by

The treasured Ark curtain of Olkenik, a gift from Napoleon to the community on his stop in Olkenik during the Russian campaign. PHOTO: SHLOMO FARBER, 1933. YESC, SH. FARBER

the Shlanski brothers, who had emigrated to America, on the occasion of their return visit to the shtetl in 1936. In large embroidered golden letters, they thank the Almighty for their success in the golden land of America.

Most of the stories that the religious objects of Eishyshok told are now lost. By the period between the two world wars, only a handful of people remained who still knew them. Reb Itche the melamed, over a hundred years old and virtually blind at the time of his death, was the most knowledgeable. In his younger years he had shared these stories with the heder boys who were his students during his many decades of teaching; and later, when he was no longer teaching, he would tell the stories to visiting classes of schoolchildren. But when he was murdered by the Germans and their Lithuanian collaborators on September 25, 1941, he took with him to the mass grave his knowledge of the ancient parokhot of Eishyshok. Almost no one survived who could tell the stories. Nor can anyone today find any trace of those ancient Ark coverings. As their last guardian, Reb Itche had stored them in a huge yellow trunk on wheels, so that it could be pushed out into the street in case of fire. No precaution, however, could have protected against the kind of conflagration that eventually consumed both those historical treasures and their dedicated keeper.

When the local Polish population seized Reb Itche's beloved Ark curtains (along with many of the other precious objects from the synagogue) during the years of the Holocaust, they made them into bedspreads, wall hangings, carpets, tablecloths, throw pillows, wedding gowns, and even lunch bags. And yet some traces did remain for a while: Itzle Kanichowski, the last Jewish child in Eishyshok, who lived there until the late 1950s, remembers becoming acquainted with the aleph beth, the Hebrew alphabet, while doing her Russian and Lithuanian homework lessons in the homes of her Christian girlfriends. There she saw the Hebrew letters on velvet tablecloths and other objects that had been made from the desecrated Holy Ark coverings.

The only existing pictorial record of a parokhet from the vicinity of Eishyshok is Shlomo Farber's 1933 photograph of the famous Napoleon Ark curtain of Olkenik. According to tradition, during the Russian campaign Napoleon visited many of the beautiful synagogues and churches in the area. To show his admiration for the Olkenik synagogue, Napoleon ordered that part of his magnificent Gobelin saddle blanket, embroidered with gold and silver crowns, the name of Napoleon Bonaparte, and the words *Gloria et Patria,* be cut off and given as a gift to the community. It was made into an Ark curtain that was the synagogue's most cherished possession.

Nothing could persuade Olkenik to part with its beloved parokhet. Museums in St. Petersburg offered substantial amounts of money for it, but it was not for sale. And neither would the community allow it to be stolen from them. During World War I, high-ranking Russian officers marched off with the Napoleon Ark curtain and carried it away to Vilna. Reb Yossef Dvorcen, the synagogue's trustee, took a delegation of Olkenik Jews to Vilna in hot pursuit. After long negotiations and the payment of a substantial bribe, they were able to redeem the parokhet and bring it back to its rightful place in the synagogue. There it remained, covering the Holy Ark throughout the year (except on the Ninth of Av, when it was removed as an expression of mourning for the destruction of the Temple), until a certain homeless stranger came along.

Like so many others who had passed through Olkenik before him, this man took shelter in the synagogue one night. To get some protection from the cold, he covered himself with the famed Ark curtain, and walked away with it in the morning. Upon entering the synagogue for morning prayers shortly thereafter, the shamash (beadle) realized that the Ark curtain was missing and gave chase. A few miles beyond the shtetl he caught up with the drifter and reclaimed the synagogue property. Again the Napoleon Ark curtain had been saved, but this time it was minus Napoleon's name, for the drifter had unstitched its golden threads and the shamash did not notice until it was too late.

After this episode, which occurred during the years between the wars, the Napoleon curtain was not returned to its place in the synagogue but was stored in the home of one of the trustees. In 1934, Shlomo Farber tried to persuade the shtetl elders to let him take it with him when he emigrated to Eretz Israel, to preserve it from the destruction he saw coming, but to no avail. The elders felt that Olkenik was the only proper place for the Napoleon Ark curtain and they would not be parted from it. Some Holocaust survivors from Olkenik say that after the German occupation, the shtetl elders held a secret meeting and decided to burn the Ark curtain rather than allow it to fall into Nazi hands. These reports seem dubious, though, since they stand in sharp contrast to numerous attempts in towns large and small to save religious objects in the hope that normalcy would one day return and the objects could once more be used. At any rate, all that remains of it today are the stories about it, and Shlomo Farber's photographs.[39]

THE OLD AND THE NEW BATEI MIDRASH

The synagogue and the Old Beth Midrash that were destroyed in the Big Fire of 1895 were only the latest editions of buildings that had stood in the shulhoyf for some seven centuries. The New Beth Midrash of Eishyshok, however, was less than seven decades old at the time of the fire. Its origins dated to one of the fierce disputes so common in shtetl history, a dispute involving a bar mitzvah boy in the 1830s and his claim to the coveted title of *morenu* —"our teacher."

One of the most prestigious designations among Eastern European Jewry, *morenu* signified a high level of scholarship and therefore entitled its bearer to special privileges. It was so important an honor that the Lithuanian Council discussed it repeatedly over the course of many years, continually redefining the requirements for eligibility. In its meeting of 1667, the Council stated that rabbis were not allowed to confer the title *morenu* on any individual until he had reached the age of thirty and been married eleven years, and unless the study of Torah was central to his life and all other work peripheral.[40] In 1695 these requirements were modified, and the Council decreed that the *morenu* candidate had to have been married eight years and to be teaching a Gemara class to other scholars. In 1761, in the last recorded session prior to the dissolution of the Council, the *morenu* issue was still being discussed.[41]

Eishyshok, while adhering to the general guidelines of the Council with regard to the awarding of the title, did practice its own variations on them as well. When an Eishyshkian boy was called up to the Torah on his bar mitzvah, local custom dictated that he be given the title if he had prepared a scholarly sermon for the occasion, for this was regarded as an incentive to scholarship among the young. If the boy had not prepared a sermon, he was given the title *haver,* which was less prestigious than *morenu*, but still an honor.

For generations no one seems to have challenged this local practice. But in the 1830s, when one of the Yurkanski family's boys reached bar mitzvah age, it became an issue. The Yurkanskis were one of the five founding families of Eishyshok, and Asher Leib, its head at that time, was himself a scholar and a prominent baalbait (householder). His ten sons and their children, however, were ignorant and boorish individuals with no respect for scholarship. They could barely even read the prayer book. Nonetheless, when one of these boys was about to have his bar mitzvah, the Yurkanski family demanded that he be given the title *morenu* when he was called up to the Torah, despite the fact that he had not prepared a scholarly sermon. They claimed that since the title was granted even to some of the sons of poor shoemakers and tailors on *their* bar mitzvah days, the honor should not under any circumstances be denied to a member of the great Yurkanski family. To no avail, however; the kahal was firm in its decision not to grant the title to the boy.

The Yurkanskis did not accept this decision and solved the impasse in their own way: they established a new prayer group (minyan) in one of the family homes, where not only the bar mitzvah boy but all other individuals called up to the Torah were granted the title *morenu*. The Yurkanski minyan introduced other changes in the service as well, omitting some religious piyyutim (poems) and various prayers that had been added to the basic prayers, thus shortening the duration of the services.

The new minyan soon attracted a growing number of worshippers and needed more spacious quarters. On a plot of land owned by the Yurkanskis, they constructed an impressive wooden building and then, under cover of night, moved the building to the shulhoyf and placed it directly across from the existing beth midrash. They named their building "the shul," thus designating it the equal of Eishyshok's official synagogue. Such a serious challenge to the authority of the kahal could not be tolerated, especially once it was learned that the Yurkanski clan had bypassed the kahal and, bribe in hand, gone directly to the local Russian authorities for the necessary building permit.

The kahal demanded the removal of the building from community property. The Yurkanskis refused. It was open war. The kahal mobilized its supporters and marched on the shulhoyf to dismantle the building. This was deemed so important a mission that the melamdim gave an almost unprecedented early dismissal to their heder students so that they might join their elders in the fight against the upstart camp. The Yurkanskis retaliated by having a number of prominent members of the opposition arrested by tzarist officials and taken in chains, like common criminals, to the district prison, from which they later had to be redeemed by payment of a substantial sum at community expense.

The battle was still not over. The Yurkanskis completed work on the new building and, for the High Holidays, hired a renowned hazzan, a shofar blower, and all the other religious functionaries required for running a full-fledged synagogue. All went well until the holiest of all days, Yom Kippur. No one could later recall what triggered the fight, but soon after the solemn prayer of Kol Nidre the two opposing camps were once again at war, hurling benches, lecterns, and even lighted candles at each other. The Day of Judgment had been violated!

For years the dispute rekindled on Yom Kippur continued to smolder. Only when Avraham Shmuel Rabinowitch was appointed shtetl rabbi in 1848 were its flames finally quenched. First he abolished the custom of granting the title *morenu* — to anyone. Instead, all those who were called up to the Torah for any reason, and regardless of their status, were called *Reb*, an honorary title that was less descriptive of its possessor's level of scholarship than *morenu* and *haver*. The building constructed by the Yurkanskis was henceforth to be known as the New Beth Midrash, and the other one as the Old Beth Midrash. Thus did Rabbi Rabinowitch settle a dispute that had divided the shtetl for close to twenty years.[42]

Despite the peaceful resolution, the New Beth Midrash never effaced the blemish of its past, not even when the original building was supplanted by any of the three that succeeded it at the same location. For the nearly one hundred years of its existence, it would lack the prestige of the Old, its ceremonies and rituals never quite meeting the standards of the strict traditionalists. In the Old Beth Midrash, for example, clean-shaven hazzanim were not permitted to lead the congregation in prayer.[43] Mordekhai Lawzowski, whose family was a prominent one in Eishyshok, recalls that as a young boy in the pre–World War I era he once ventured into the New Beth Midrash to listen to a world-renowned — but clean-shaven! — hazzan who was making a guest appearance in Eishyshok. So serious a violation of his family's customs was this that a synagogue trustee who spotted young Mordekhai advised him to leave and go back to the Old Beth Midrash where he belonged, or else he would have to throw him out.

The Old Beth Midrash would remain home to some of the most ancient and most cherished traditions of the shtetl, such as the once-a-year hanging of the Ark curtains on the wall and the telling of the story behind each one. During the winter, it was the Old Beth Midrash that would serve as the official synagogue, where all the shtetl's public functions took place. There members of the congregation would gather every night during Hanukkah to watch the shammash mount the ladder to light the three-foot-long candles that burned through the night and into the early-morning prayers. There local elections, emergency meetings, and the leasing of various community enterprises took place, as well as sermons by visiting preachers and receptions for visiting dignitaries. And there during the heyday of the Kibbutz ha-Prushim yeshivah the advanced students gathered to hear the lectures and discussions that were at the core of their education. By contrast, the New Beth Midrash was where the yeshivah's most junior students were sent to study; only when they had established their scholarly ability and achieved proper seniority could they progress to studies in the Old Beth Midrash.

The last rabbi of Eishyshok, Rabbi Szymen Rozowski, tried to be more evenhanded in his use of the two batei midrash. He worked out an elaborate schedule that stipulated his presence in each of the community's three houses of prayer on specific days of the religious calendar. For example, he would appear in the Old Beth Midrash on the first day of Rosh Hashanah, the new one on the second day, and the synagogue for Yom Kippur. Naturally, wherever the rabbi prayed, the hazzan and the choir followed. But even before Rabbi Rozowski made it a matter of policy to do so, the community had in an informal way incorporated the New Beth Midrash into its daily life (albeit without ever elevating the new to the status of the old). It was common practice among Eishyshkians to make the rounds of all three prayerhouses during services and other community functions that occurred in summertime. Men bedecked in prayer shawls strolled through the shulhoyf as they made their leisurely way between the two batei midrash and the synagogue, occasionally stopping for a chat with one another or simply enjoying the works of nature. During the winter months they rushed back and forth between the two batei midrash, wrapped in fur-lined coats which they would remove as soon as they entered the polesh, placing them against the oven to store up extra warmth for the dash they would soon make to the next house of prayer.

Physically the Old and New Batei Midrash

were mirror images of each other, and different in many respects from the synagogue.[44] Each was two stories high, with windows halfway up the wall, and square windows notched into the walls of the second-story gallery where the women sat overlooking the sanctuary; each bore a mezuzah on its doorpost, and each, being heated, was available for use twenty-four hours a day, year round. Their ceilings were white-washed, with handsome corolla-style moldings surrounding the hanging fixtures. On the right side of the western wall of the Old Beth Midrash was a huge brass Hanukkah menorah, much larger and more elaborate than the one in the New Beth Midrash. Also on the western wall were bookcases filled with sacred books and rabbinic texts.

Lining the polesh of each building were several small rooms, including storage closets for firewood. In the Old Beth Midrash the polesh also included a candle room, a genizah (the room where old, worn sacred books were kept prior to burial), and the shoemakers' and psalms reciters' shtiblekh, both of which insisted on using candlelight until the very end, despite the introduction of electricity.[45] The tailors' and mixed minyan shtiblekh were located in the polesh of the New Beth Midrash.

The cleaning of all three of Eishyshok's houses of prayer and of the other buildings in the shulhoyf was done by a Christian family named Aliova, who had been employed by the shtetl for generations. Before them, during the time of the Kibbutz ha-Prushim yeshivah, however, the New Beth Midrash was cleaned by new arrivals among the students, and the more senior students had the honor of cleaning the Old Beth Midrash.

The seating arrangement in both the Old and New batei midrash followed the same general principles as that in the synagogue, with the best seats being those near the eastern wall, and the affluence and prominence of the seat owners decreasing the nearer one got to the entrance. The physical configuration of the seats, however, was different, consisting of benches at long rectangular tables. Some shtot (seat) owners held seats in both the summer synagogue and the batei midrash.[46] This was true for women, too, who might own a seat in the women's gallery of one, two, or all three. Near the oven were the benches of those who could not afford to purchase seats of their own. Even among the poor a hierarchy existed, however, with one bench in particular, known as the brooding bench, reserved for the most wretched of all because of its proximity to the large woodburning oven. There the unfortunates could be found, between the afternoon and evening prayers, warming themselves at the oven and sharing with each other their tales of misery and woe.[47]

BUSINESS TRANSACTIONS IN THE OLD BETH MIDRASH

The many and diverse secular activities carried on at the bimah of the Old Beth Midrash in the post-Sabbath hours included the election of members of the kahal to their four-year terms. This bimah also served as the community's official platform for business transactions. On regularly scheduled Saturday nights, following the close of Sabbath, the lease rights to certain profit-making community enterprises were auctioned off. The transactions were presided over by the judges of the kahal, who sat on the bimah while the auction took place. Only residents of Eishyshok and of villages under its jurisdiction were eligible to offer bids, thus ensuring that in case of any negligence or breach of contract the offenders would be legally bound by the decisions of the local kahal.

Some of these leasing auctions made for high drama and were widely attended by members of the community; others were of less interest. The leasing of the public bathhouse was among the latter, since the outcome was usually known in advance. The leasing of the two community-owned grazing fields traditionally went to the same family over a period of many generations, and was therefore similarly predictable. But because the constant conflict between the family who leased the fields and members of the community who used them virtually guaranteed an evening of interesting verbal exchanges when it was time to renew the lease, this particular event was popular among Eishyshkians, who always enjoyed a good fight.

Though other leasing auctions may have been more popular among the community as a whole, none was more important than the leasing of the korobka (the kosher meat tax). Since the korobka affected the price of meat in every shtetl household, it might have been expected that such a major event would have been attended by everybody. But this was an event mainly for the shtetl power brokers — the well-to-do balebatim — and for the tanners, cattle merchants, salt dealers, shoemakers, stitchers, ritual slaughterers, and other individuals whose income was directly affected by the meat tax.

For those who did attend, it was extremely exciting. Women lined up at the windows of the women's gallery, and among the other onlookers were gentiles who were associated with the meat business either as independent merchants or as employees of Jewish merchants. The bidding among the affluent families of the shtetl was fierce and protracted, sometimes lasting until well into the night as a tense audience watched the proceedings and voiced their feelings about issues that would affect the pocketbooks of each and every one of them. Meir Wilkanski, who seems not to have missed a single event in the life of the shtetl, describes the leasing of the korobka on a typical night in the closing decade of the nineteenth century:

Again it was Saturday night, and in the Old Beth Midrash the Gemarot were put away and learning was brought to a halt. As a crowd gathered, the most diligent of the prushim went off to the New Beth Midrash for the rest of the night. This was the night when the newly elected members of the kahal would be leasing the korobka.

While the masses crowded 'round the bimah, the most distinguished and respected members of the community, wrapped in their magnificent fox tail coats, stood somewhat at a distance, near the eastern wall. The members of the kahal sat on the bimah, and next to them stood the shammash, who served as auctioneer at these events.

"Who will increase the sum," he asks; "who will make a higher offer?" More and more people crowd ever more closely around the bimah as the excitement intensifies. The loud voices of the bidders increasing their offers reverberate throughout the sanctuary. The shammash begins his spiel anew, and as he gets to the part where he announces "going twice," the storm subsides and for a moment there is silence in God's sanctuary. After the silence is a whispering, as friends deliberate with friends in hushed voices. The shammash resumes the count, seeming on the verge of closing the bidding. "Going thrice!" All eyes are on the shammash and on the last, highest bidder.

The shammash laughs quietly, as though pleased with what he has wrought. Is his laughter for real, or does he fear he has trapped himself in his own deception, having meant to force the bidding higher still? His bluff is not called, so we will never know. No sooner does he announce the "going thrice" than another bid is hurled at the bimah. He starts anew. "Going once, going twice," and on and on, into the night. He's come a long way since those early, small bids — bids that previously looked so large! A number of bidders have dropped out. And the bidding is much less enthusiastic now, proceeding in ever smaller increments offered in quiet voices which, it is hoped, will not incite one's wealthy opponents to still higher bids. Hearts are heavy with anticipation.

And now a mighty voice rises from the bench facing the eastern wall, surging over the heads of the crowd and into the bimah with a bid decisively larger than any yet heard.

Whose was that powerful roar, which made all hearts tremble? Yehudah, the Son of Reuben! Yehudah the horse dealer, the bandit! The korobka now belongs to him.[48]

EXORCISMS IN THE OLD BETH MIDRASH

Another of the community activities that took place in the Old Beth Midrash was the exorcism of a dybbuk (a transmigrated soul that possesses a living being and transforms that person) or a gilgul (a transmigrated soul that enters but does not take over a living being). Eishyshok, being a bastion of Talmudic scholarship, was less prone to such superstitious occurrences. In the wake of the establishment of Hasidism in the mid-eighteenth century, it was also less willing to allow those that did take place to be discussed in public, since they seemed more appropriate to the folklore-loving Hasidim than to the rational, scholarly Lithuanian community Eishyshok prided itself on being. But even Eishyshok was subject to the occasional visitation from beyond.

The last exorcism in the Old Beth Midrash of Eishyshok occurred just prior to World War I when the renowned scholar Zundl Hutner was the shtetl's rabbi. That case, however, turned out to be one of mistaken identity: the transmigrated soul was revealed to be a small but very squeaky mouse that had taken up residence in the shoulder padding of an absentminded melamed.

When it came to exorcisms, Eishyshok was upstaged by the town next door, Radun. In the nineteenth century a young girl there was possessed by a dybbuk while bringing drinking water to the horses in her father's stable. After much suffering, the girl was brought by her parents to the shtetl's world-renowned scholar, the Haffetz Hayyim. In the presence of ten men in Radun's old wooden beth midrash, the Haffetz Hayyim ordered the dybbuk to leave the girl's body. The dybbuk obeyed the great sage, departing through her finger.[49] Then the sound of breaking glass was heard and the dybbuk exited the beth midrash through a clearly visible hole in one of its windows.[50]

Radun was a bit embarrassed that one of its most distinguished scholars had exorcised a dybbuk for all the world as though he were a Hasidic master, and it permitted the story to be told only during Purim festivities.

CHANGE COMES TO THE HOUSES OF PRAYER

During the turmoil of war, old traditions and practices were wont to fall by the wayside, as the young seized the moment and sought new alternatives to the customary way of doing things. The rigid social stratification of the shtetl, which was so clearly manifested in the customs of the houses of prayer, was among the many aspects of traditional shtetl life challenged by those advocating social and political change in the aftermath of World War I. Led by a number of young married men, there was a movement afoot for a more egalitarian ethos, and for other changes as well, such as the introduction of new melodies and more communal singing during services. As part of this democratizing initiative, these young men demanded more frequent opportunities for community-wide socializing under the auspices of the synagogue, and suggested that there be a kiddush for the entire synagogue congregation after Saturday-morning prayers. (This would replace the centuries-old practice whereby each Saturday one of the various charitable societies in the shtetl hosted the post-services kiddush in the polesh or the women's gallery, but invited only their own members and friends.) Though the community did not yield to the young men's demands, they were given permission to establish their own prayer minyan, with the stipulation that women not be allowed to attend either the services or the kiddush afterward — thus effectively preventing the functions from becoming full-fledged social events.

Unlike the founders of the New Beth Midrash, who had built their own building in the 1830s and inflicted it on the community, these young men of the 1920s met in a private house belonging to Berl Slepak which, since it was on the shulhoyf, was under community jurisdiction. The hazzan was Shmuel Gross, a young cantor with a voice so golden that years later former Eishyshok cantor Ruben Boyarski would recommend him to the great Caruso, who asked Gross to join his concert tour. (Gross, like Boyarski before him, declined Caruso's invitation, in favor of becoming a pioneer farmer in Eretz Israel.) The Torah was read by Yehuda Lawzowski, a member of the Mizrahi, a Zionist movement founded in 1902, and a former student at the yeshivah in Lida run by Rabbi Yitzhak-Yaakov Reines, who cofounded the Mizrahi. Each time one of the new minyan's members was called up to the Torah, he made a monetary donation, which the group used for the purchase of food and drink for the kiddush following services. There they discussed the week's events and mulled over their relevance to the prevailing political issues, and sang Hebrew and Yiddish songs. Saturday nights they gathered in the home of one of the other men in the minyan and held the melaveh malkah, the traditional meal in honor of the departure of the Sabbath Queen, accompanied by the singing of cantorial music and various Hebrew and Yiddish songs, the reading of poetry and short stories, and more discussion of current events.

The men in the independent prayer group continued to meet for a number of years, until receiving a challenge from a very unexpected source: their wives. The women complained that their husbands' schedule on Saturday conflicted with the prayer time observed in the synagogue, and hence disrupted their lives and those of their children on the Sabbath. In part because of these complaints, and in part because so many of their members (among them Shmuel Gross and Yehudah Lawzowski) were emigrating to Eretz Israel at this time, the minyan dissolved.

But these were only the superficial reasons for its demise. More profoundly, the synagogue and its sister institutions were no longer as central to the life of the shtetl as before. There were now alternative outlets for socializing, sponsored by the youth clubs of the various political and cultural movements that were proliferating in the 1920s. Membership in Zionist organizations had taken its toll on synagogue attendance, which had been declining substantially except on the major holidays. Many young men and women were no longer interested in making changes in the practices of the synagogue; they now spent their Saturday mornings in a youth club or in informal gatherings in the Seklutski forest, enjoying the lectures or the singing and dancing that were offered there. Saturday nights they might attend coed parties (held in the clubhouses, or private homes, or at the fire house in the center of town), rather than attending one of the traditional melaveh malkah celebrations at the synagogue. Increasingly it was only the older people and those too young to go their own way who were still to be found bidding farewell to the Sabbath Queen in the traditional manner.

Though the two batei midrash and the synagogue would experience a brief revival in Eishyshok's final years, their undisputed centrality in the life of the shtetl was effectively at an end after World War I, and soon the community that had given life to them would come to its own end.

SOCIAL PROTEST IN THE SYNAGOGUE: THE DELAYING OF THE TORAH READING

Even in a time of change, a number of synagogue-based activities survived. Indeed, at least one not only survived but actually flourished in the midst of the social upheaval, since it offered a kind of recourse and relief to members of the community that was not otherwise available. The ikuv kriah — the Delaying of the Torah reading — was a shtetl practice rich in local color and tradition, with its roots in the Middle

Ages.[51] It was one of the last vestiges of a time when the community had a great deal of power and autonomy, and the bimah was the platform where its deliberations were conducted, its decisions delivered. Though the historian H. H. Ben-Sasson refers to the "delaying" process as "an authorized scandal," it was more like a people's court which gave every member of the community access to justice, and a role in meting it out.[52] During the harsh interwar years when Jews were subject to severe economic restrictions imposed upon them by the government, the ikuv kriah took on new significance, its proceedings having become the last — and only — court of appeal for those suffering the injustices of the Polish legal system, and looking to their own community in hope of some kind of relief.

Public readings of the Torah from the bimah were held on Monday, Thursday, the Sabbath, and holidays. The holiday and Sabbath readings, which attracted the entire congregation, were the forum for those wanting to make a public statement of their grievances. Days in advance of these events, excitement would start building in the shtetl, for word of the plaintiff's intent usually spread rapidly via the grapevine as the Sabbath approached. On the day of the event itself, many people would forgo their regular seat for one in whichever house of prayer had been chosen as the venue for the proceedings (which, in Eishyshok, meant wherever the rabbi would be praying that Sabbath); while other people, particularly the elderly and sick, might be moved out of the designated prayer-house into another one so that they would be spared the inconvenience of the prolonged proceedings and the excitement of the showdown.

As the moment for the Torah reading approached, the congregation's excitement kept escalating, until at last the plaintiff mounted the bimah, banged three times on the table, and announced: "I am delaying the Torah reading." He would then describe the nature of his complaint (or that of the group he was representing) and explain why he had chosen to present his case directly to the community, instead of to the judges in either the shtetl or gentile courts. In conclusion he would tell the members of the community that he was depending on them for advice, truth, and Torah justice, thus placing full moral and ethical responsibility in their hands. In Eishyshok this was the moment at which the neeman of the synagogue would step up to the bimah and, on behalf of the congregation, accept the responsibility for mediating the issue before them.

A consultation period followed, during which the neeman, the rabbi, and other notables would gather at the eastern wall to discuss the issue. The community, for its part, was eager to show itself worthy of the trust placed in it, and there was much heated debate among its members, much movement back and forth between small clusters of people taking sides and offering suggestions, and a constant flow of traffic as men made their way to the eastern wall with their recommendations. Though women were officially excluded from the process, unofficially they often had input by way of their menfolk. Watching the drama from the women's gallery, they could express opinions or make requests for further information, using their children as messengers to communicate with the men in the sanctuary. Or perhaps a husband would look up to the gallery for a sign from his wife, the nod of her head serving as a crucial element in the outcome of a case.

Once a decision was reached, the gabbai rishon (the first-ranking elected official of the synagogue) would mount the bimah and make a public offer on behalf of the community. He would announce the name of the three borerim (arbitrators) who had been selected and the deadline for settling the grievance. If the offer was acceptable to the plaintiff, the reading of the Torah would resume; if it was rejected, the whole process would begin anew, with the community remaining hostage to the plaintiff's dissatisfaction until some kind of agreement was reached and services could be resumed.

The delay of the Torah reading proved a potent social weapon, quite often providing the community with a satisfactory and speedy resolution to extremely knotty problems. And during the interwar years, as one of the few means of alleviating the economic hardships inflicted on the Jewish community by the Polish state, it was resorted to with increasing frequency. Typical of the problems it addressed was that of Jewish soldiers who were drafted into the Polish army. Many young men from Eishyshok and the villages under its jurisdiction served in the Polish army, among them the four Asner brothers from nearby Nacha, whose widowed mother and sister suffered greatly due to their absence. But it wasn't just the families of the soldiers who suffered; it was the soldiers themselves, for they were discriminated against in a variety of ways because of anti-Semitism. Harassed, kept from advancement, assigned the most demeaning jobs by their Polish officers, often denied furloughs on the most sacred Jewish holidays and sometimes not even paid the wages due them, they were quite a destitute group, especially those who came from poor homes that could not afford to supplement their army pay.

Since it was clear that the Polish government would not respond to their grievances, the soldiers turned to the kehilah (community). Dressed in their army uniforms, a number of the Jewish soldiers from Eishyshok and vicinity surrounded the bimah, while others stood near the door to assure that no one would leave the synagogue. Their spokesman took up his position near the Torah, banged the customary three times on the table, and announced the delay of the Torah reading. Stating their grievances, he demanded that the community pay monthly allowances to the soldiers to alleviate the hunger, hardship, and humiliation that were their lot. The soldiers won their case. The kehilah of Eishyshok stepped in where the Polish government had abdicated, agreeing to pay a regular allowance to needy Jewish soldiers from the area.

Another of the problems brought before the community was also a result of the anti-Jewish policies of independent Poland in the grim interwar years. This time the issue had to do with the korobka, the tax levied on consumers of kosher meat, the proceeds from which paid not only for the salaries of the clergy but for many community services, such as hospitals, old age homes, soup kitchens, and so on. In 1936, on the pretext of preventing cruelty to animals, the practice of shehita (kosher animal slaughter) was curtailed by the Polish government, which decreed that Jews had to reduce the number of animals ritually slaughtered to half the previous year's total. Since the tax revenues would thereby also be cut in half, depriving the Jewish communities of money they desperately needed to minister to their sick, their poor, and their elderly, this was a severe blow to an already impoverished population. In order to be able to meet their financial responsibilities to the needy, some communities, Eishyshok among them, increased the korobka, which was itself a hardship for individual consumers. The vicious cycle of lower tax revenues and higher meat prices led more and more consumers to look for a way to outmaneuver both the Polish government and the community.

So it happened that a group of butchers in Eishyshok began slaughtering the animals outside the community in a nearby village, thus avoiding the legal taxes and making it possible for them to give their customers better prices on meat that had been prepared under strict rabbinic supervision. Many of the shtetl Jews flocked to these underground butchers in order to purchase meat that was free of the onerous korobka. As a result, the butchers who were not part of the underground group were left with virtually no income. The complaint they brought before the community was that it had abdicated its responsibility to see to it that all meat consumed within its boundaries be prepared under its jurisdiction. Again the community found in favor of the plaintiffs, and ritual slaughter was brought back to Eishyshok. Even then further conflict ensued, with some butchers getting more than their fair share of the now severely limited quota of animals that could be used for kosher slaughter, and Rabbi Rozowski had to intervene. He decided that all the butchers would have to join a cooperative and distribute the animals more equitably among themselves. This would at least mean that everyone suffered equally under the new legislation, which had been initiated by Janina Prystor, a female member of the Polish parliament, who was from nearby Bastun. Hence the response of the shtetl wits to this painful situation: "Long live the Rabbi and the goya."

HEREM (EXCOMMUNICATION)

In addition to all its other functions, the synagogue complex served as a place of judgment for the sentencing of those who had disobeyed the law or run afoul of the community in other ways. During the hegemony of the Council of the Four Lands in the sixteenth and seventeenth centuries, for example, and in some communities for many years thereafter, the vestibule of the synagogue was fitted out with a kuna, a makeshift form of restraint for prisoners awaiting punishment. And at certain times in the long history of the shtetl, the shulhoyf was also where the punishment of whipping was meted out.

The most powerful and most dreaded of the community's punishments was the herem — excommunication — and it too took place in the synagogue. In practice since biblical times (see Joshua 7:10–26), the herem had many different manifestations and degrees of severity, depending on the locale, but in Europe was similar to a church excommunication.[53] As the community's most powerful weapon against disobedience and intellectual dissent, it was a constant threat hanging over the heads of great and small alike, as evidenced by the haramot against Uriel Acosta and Baruch Spinoza in the seventeenth century. Indeed, its power within the community never waned, even after it was officially banned by the civil authorities in the mid-nineteenth century, and in Eastern Europe it continued to be used until the end.

Eishyshok's last excommunication occurred in 1940, at a time when waves of panic-stricken refugees were passing through the shtetl. Warmly welcomed by the townspeople, they were clothed, fed, furnished with new identification papers, ransomed from border guards when necessary, put on the bus to Vilna, or smuggled over the border into next-door Byelorussia. But it happened that the shtetl tradition of hospitality to strangers in need was violated by a handful of local border smugglers who took advantage of a few hapless refugees, mainly single women, extorting from them their most valuable possessions. To punish the smugglers, Rabbi Szymen Rozowski resorted to the most effective weapon he had: the herem.

It had been a long time since the shtetl had witnessed this terrifying ceremony. Standing before the open doors of the Holy Ark in the main synagogue, accompanied by the sounding of the shofar, Rabbi Rozowski pronounced the herem, while ten members of the kahal and the beth din stood holding the Torah scrolls, and others held aloft flaming black candles. After the excommunication was declared, the candles were extinguished, to symbolize the punishment of the thieves. Smuggling was declared anathema, warnings to any future offenders were issued, and a call for law-abiding behavior was made. Then there came a plea on behalf of the shtetl population that they be forgiven for the crime that had taken place in their midst, and the ceremony concluded with a prayer for the welfare of both the community and the thousands of refugees in search of a safe haven.

A few days after the herem, most of the stolen goods were returned to their rightful owners. By a strange twist of fate, all but one of the men who participated in the enactment of the herem were murdered by the Nazis, while almost all the thieves survived.

THE REFUGEE PERIOD

By another ironic twist, during the final two years of the shtetl's existence the synagogue and the Old and New batei midrash were once again restored to their preeminent position in the community. The prayerhouses that had had so many empty seats due to both emigration and secularization were once again filled to capacity, thanks to the thousands of refugees passing through the shtetl on their flight eastward. Regardless of their level of religious commitment, most refugees attended services — perhaps feeling that a prayer would be worthwhile baggage to take with them on their perilous journey into the unknown.

The shulhoyf buildings were put to practical as well as spiritual uses: The women's galleries were converted to sleeping quarters for the overflow of refugees who could not be housed in shtetl homes, a soup kitchen was set up in the polesh, and the various shtiblekh were used as clandestine offices by the Vaad ha-Pletim (the Refugee Committee), which had to keep its location secret because of the nature of its activities. These included providing illegal papers, paying ransom to border guards for the release of refugees who had been arrested, and making arrangements for border crossings and journeys to Vilna. Once more the shulhoyf and its three

Sitting on the fence of the Jewish grazing field in the early 1930s is Geneshe Kaganowicz, with her best friend Matle Sonenson. (The two eventually became sisters-in-law when Geneshe married Matle's brother Leibke.) In the background is the Catholic church at Juryzdyki.
PHOTO: BEN ZION SZREJDER. YESC, Y. SONENSON

distinguished buildings were filled to overflowing with the life of a vital, activist community.

For the religious life of the community, the crowning glory of this two-year period was the arrival in Eishyshok of a section of the Radun yeshivah, which had eclipsed the importance of the Kibbutz ha-Prushim of Eishyshok by the beginning of the twentieth century. Now, in 1939, the yeshivah was on the run from Bolshevik persecution and had come to Eishyshok, which was then under Lithuanian rule, in search of a temporary haven. Overjoyed that the Crown of Torah had once more returned to them, the people of Eishyshok turned out to greet the newest refugees. First to arrive from Radun were horse-drawn cartloads of Torah scrolls, hundreds of them, stacked like firewood. Of beautiful workmanship, they came from around the globe and had been given as gifts to the yeshivah and its world-renowned master and founder, the late Haffetz Hayyim, a graduate of the Eishyshok yeshivah. Great excitement gripped the shtetl when these scrolls were carried into the batei midrash.

Following the scrolls of law came 198 yeshivah students. The Old Beth Midrash, once the home of the Haffetz Hayyim, was now their house of study, too, much to Eishyshok's delight.

The joy reached its climax during Simhat Torah, the celebration of the annual completion of the reading of the Torah and the beginning of a new cycle. This year the native Eishyshkians would be joined in their celebrations by many hundreds of refugees, including those from the Radun yeshivah, as they all took hold of the hundreds of Torah scrolls and danced in honor of the great occasion. Children holding flags and lighted candles stuck in red-cheeked apples sat happily on their fathers' shoulders, their voices joining with those of the adults as their fathers danced and sang with the yeshivah students.

Little did they know that this joyous Simhat Torah would be for most their last. Soon the same wagons that brought the holy scrolls into Eishyshok would take the women, children, and old people out to the killing fields.

That Simhat Torah was a strange finale, a curtain call to a thousand years of loving dedication to Torah study, to community service, to dreams and aspirations, to coexistence with their gentile neighbors, all carried on in the face of suffering, persecution, and poverty. Yet no one was willing to admit on that Simhat Torah night that the circle was about to close; that the spirit and culture nurtured within the holy walls of the shtetl's prayerhouses for a millennium were nearly at an end; that a mere handful of people would survive to tell us of that heritage.

The walls of the shulhoyf prayerhouses, built with love, filled and transformed by the sounds of life — the cries of infants brought into the covenant, the melodious voices of Torah learners, the chants of the maggidim, the sobbing of women, the sermons of rabbis, the joyful buzz of children untangling the mysteries of the aleph beth, the rhythms of a community in prayer — would soon revert to the silence of wood, brick, and stone.

The shul, for years a sports complex, is now an empty, crumbling building; the New Beth Midrash is a theater; the Old Beth Midrash is gone, demolished. The church of Juryzdyki towers over the Eishyshok skyline.

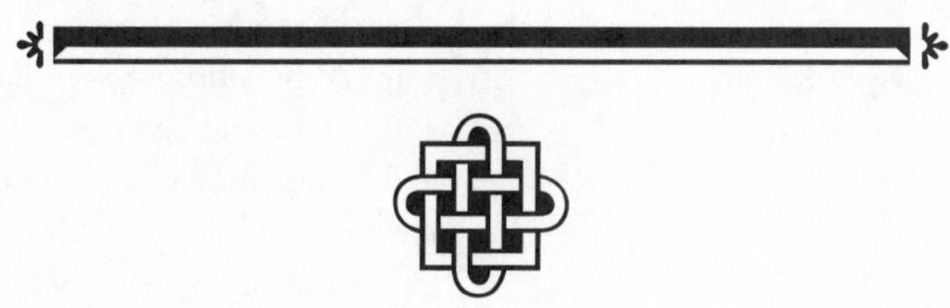

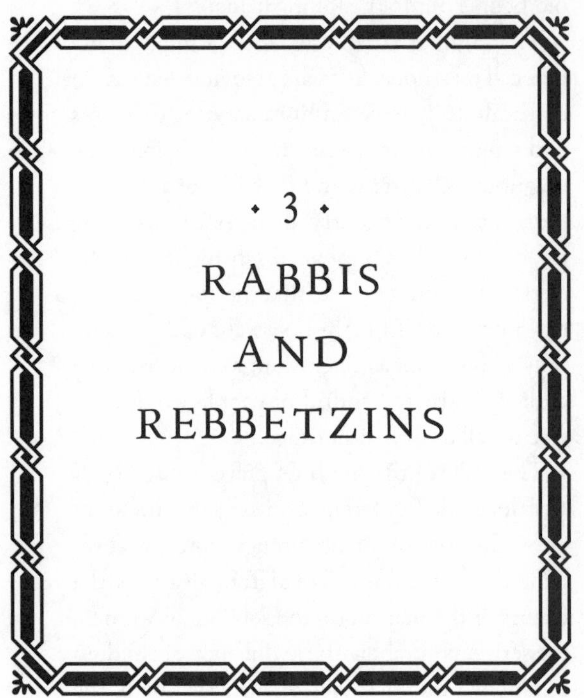

• 3 • RABBIS AND REBBETZINS

LATE IN THE NIGHT
WHEN I SAW THE
BURNING CANDLE IN
THE RABBI'S WINDOW,
MY HEART WAS FILLED
WITH JOY, AND MY HEAD
WITH HOPE FOR A
BRIGHT FUTURE.

Hayya Streletski Kosowski

THE EAST EUROPEAN RABBINATE WAS A CONSTANTLY EVOLVING INSTITUTION, ITS roots going back to the time of the Second Temple. Until the destruction of the Second Temple in 70 C.E., the rabbi was a teacher and a scholar but had no official power, for all ultimate authority resided within the Temple itself. Though the rabbinate was profoundly altered in the centuries that followed the loss of the Second Temple, it did retain many of its ancient characteristics, including the very title *rabbi* (which dates from the first century, and comes from the Hebrew for "great one, master"), the tradition of scholarship and teaching, and some aspects of the ordination ceremony.

To be a rabbi one had to be ordained, in what was a formal acknowledgment that a very high level of scholarship had been achieved. Ordination had its origins with Moses, who placed his hands on Joshua, his successor, thereby investing him with some of his own stature.[1] Later, ordination was granted only after the candidate had passed examinations on various religious texts, particularly those pertaining to Jewish law. Traditionally, only an ordained rabbi can confer the title of *rabbi* on another — on the principle that "only the ordained may ordain." The ordination consists of the Hebrew words "Yoreh yoreh, yadin yadin," meaning "The candidate may surely give a decision, may surely pronounce judgment."

It wasn't until the end of the tenth century that the title *rabbi* or *rav* came to mean not simply a scholar who had passed certain examinations, but a person who was the spiritual leader of his community, having been elected to serve in that capacity by the townspeople. No one who was not married could be elected. Men who were ordained rabbis often took other kinds of clerical posts, if they couldn't (or didn't choose to) become the rabbi of a community. Dayyanim (judges), for example, were always ordained rabbis, since the job required a thorough knowledge of Jewish law; many hazzanim (cantors and prayer readers) were rabbis too.

The title *rabbi* was not, however, restricted to practicing members of the clergy. Even as the institution of the clergy began to be formalized after the tenth century, the title continued to be adopted by all those who had passed their examinations and been ordained, many of whom had no intention of seeking election or appointment to a rabbinic post. Gradually the title began to lose some of its luster because it was perceived as being too freely granted.[2] In the seventeenth

Szymen Rozowski (1874–1941) was an ardent religious Zionist leader, a member of the Mizrahi movement, and the beloved last rabbi of Eishyshok. During the September 1941 massacre, Rabbi Rozowski was kept alive on the edge of the mass graves so that he would witness the murder of each member of his community. After the murder of the last person, the rabbi was buried alive. PHOTO: BEN ZION SZREJDER. YESC, ROZOWSKI

century, with Eastern Europe's emergence as the center for Jewish scholarship, came a profusion of yeshivah graduates who had studied Torah for the sake of Torah and been ordained. With the establishment of the renowned Lithuanian yeshivot of the nineteenth century, which attracted even more young men who studied sheerly for the sake of studying, the title was ever more commonly used, to the point where it eventually became simply a respectful and very widespread form of address. Conversely, some of the most distinguished of the ordained rabbis of Eastern Europe (and elsewhere) didn't use the title at all, but were known by various other titles that expressed reverence and affection, such as the Gaon (sage) of Vilna, the Godol (great scholar) of Minsk, and Yossef Zundl Hutner of Eishyshok, who was simply called by his middle name. Other rabbis, like the Haffetz Hayyim, were known by the titles of one of their publications.[3]

As it developed over time, the East European rabbinate, as a clerical body, was very much a kehilah (community) rabbinate — a product of the strengthening of Jewish communal organizations, and of a number of other factors as well, within both the Jewish community and the community at large. Developing in response to these various historical circumstances, many of which were similar to those that produced the parish priest and the mullah, the rabbinate gradually came to fill the void left by the Temple, and its evolution was encouraged by the secular authorities.

In 1334, for example, among the privileges the king of Poland granted the Jews was permission for the Jewish "judge," meaning the rabbi, to "teach" the Jews, though only with the permission of the Jews — which simultaneously empowered both the people, for they elected their own rabbi, and the people's rabbi, for once elected he had considerable authority and decision-making powers within his community, and as his community's representative to the outside world. Though these privileges were intended as a gift to the Jewish people, a way of inducing tax-paying subjects to be loyal to the king by simultaneously giving them a leader who had real power and making that leader accountable to them, sometimes the granting of such powers led to conflict. This was particularly likely to happen in the larger towns and cities, where the powers granted the rabbi by the secular authority had the potential to confer considerable financial benefits on him and his family, and some rabbis did not hesitate to petition the crown to protect those rights if they felt they were being infringed upon by the community.

Thus in 1531, Menachem Mendl Frank, the rabbi of Brisk (as Brest-Litovsk was known to the Jews), complained to the grand duke of Lithuania that the Jews of Brisk were bypassing his rabbinic court in favor of the Tribunal of the

Starosta ("the elder"— a local government official), and moreover had even summoned him before that court. The grand duke's father, Sigismund I, king of Poland, got involved in this issue, and ordered the Jews of Brisk to use the rabbi's court.[4] In case they didn't comply, he said, the rabbi could impose a herem (excommunication) and punish them according to Jewish law. Still not satisfied, since he felt the ruling did not go far enough toward giving him full legal authority and autonomy within his own community, Mendl Frank appealed to the crown once more — this time to the queen, Bona Sforza. Her verdict said explicitly that the rabbi himself was not answerable to any court but that of the grand duke — a judicial privilege that gave Mendl Frank virtual parity with the upper strata of the Polish and Lithuanian nobility. In the privileges granted by King Sigismund II Augustus two decades later, in 1551, there is a stern warning that all those who oppose a rabbi elected by the community will have their property confiscated and be liable to physical punishment.[5] Clearly, the community-based Lithuanian rabbinate was growing steadily in power, which again was both an indirect tribute to the Jewish people — since they had a leader equal in status to the nobility — and an affirmation of the rabbinate, a way of securing its loyalty to the crown.

THE COMMERCIALIZATION OF THE RABBINATE

The rabbinate as a commercial enterprise is a relatively recent phenomenon in the history of Judaism, dating to the era of the Council of the Four Lands and the Lithuanian Council (1569–1764), when the privileges granted the Jews by the various Polish and Lithuanian kings resulted in substantial economic opportunities and benefits for the rabbis. For most of its history, the office of the rabbi was an honorary one, based on the principle, upheld by Maimonides, that the Torah had to be taught free of charge.[6] Thus many of the most noted rabbi-scholars, since the time of the first century, had to do other kinds of work to earn a living. Old Hillel was a woodcutter, Rabbi Yohanan was a shoemaker, Korna was a wine taster, Huna was a water drawer. But even as early as the time of the Second Temple, a legal concept that would later be used as a basis for paying rabbis for their services was beginning to be worked out. This occurred when Rabbi Huna, who was asked to serve as a dayyan, requested compensation for those hours he could not do his job as waterbearer because of his service to the community. The legal concept was that of the *sekhar battalah*, a sort of unemployment compensation.[7]

The principle was reinvoked in 1391, when a community in Algiers asked Rabbi Shimon ben Zemah to become their rabbi. He told them he couldn't accept the post because he was penniless and had to earn a livelihood. So he, like Rabbi Huna, was paid not a salary for his services, but a compensation for the income his rabbinic duties kept him from earning. The use of the sekhar battalah concept in ben Zemah's case has remained the legal basis in Jewish law for paying rabbis who hold rabbinic posts.

Only since the seventeenth century, however, has it been common practice for a rabbi to receive emolument. And even then the phenomenon of the merchant rabbi, the rabbi who sought his office specifically because of its financial advantages, was only a problem in the superkehilot (cities and towns that had jurisdiction over all the other Jewish communities in the vicinity) and other large communities, for those were the only places where there was real money to be made, both from the privileges granted by the crown and from the salary and various service fees the rabbi was paid by his community.[8]

In places where the rabbinate was a lucrative profession, the office was sometimes abused. Indeed, rabbinic posts could be so profitable that some rabbis and their families purchased them outright for stipulated periods of time.[9] This was so even though the fact that the rabbi was elected by the community should have made him accountable to them. But since only the balebatim members of the kahal were eligible to elect the rabbi, and they themselves stood to profit from the purchasing of these posts, they sometimes went along with it. Thus the community often had great difficulty ridding itself of these bribe-giving rabbis.

THE RABBINATE AS VOCATION

The purchasing of the rabbinate was more the exception than the rule, and rarely occurred outside the large communities. Not that being a city rabbi necessarily meant that a man had sought the post for its financial benefits. Professor Rabbi Hayyim Heller (1878–1960), a rabbinical and biblical scholar, became rabbi of Lomza, Poland, a most prestigious post, in 1911. However, to the great disappointment of the people of Lomza, he resigned a few months later. He had learned that, prior to his appointment, his rich father-in-law had donated substantial sums of money to local charities, and he saw in that act a touch of bribery he could not condone.[10]

Notwithstanding the occasional big-city rabbi who bought his way into the job, most rabbis were chosen for their posts on the basis of their spiritual and their scholarly credentials, their saintly personalities, their commitment to justice. And many East European rabbis actively preferred the less prestigious, less powerful, and less lucrative rabbinical posts in small shtetlekh to those in the large towns, because they wished to study and write without the demands that the latter would make on their time. Generally their salaries were quite modest, being drawn from a community fund created by the korobka, the tax on all kosher meat. The rabbi's small salary could be supplemented by whatever his wife earned, by various gratuities received for rendering services, and by a tax called the RaHaSh — short for "rabbi, hazzan, and shammash"— which was divided among the clergy who officiated at bar mitzvahs, circumcisions, weddings, and other ceremonies.[11] In certain eras he was given a percentage of all wedding expenses. All of these earnings were tax-exempt. Still, in the average shtetl, the total from all these sources didn't add up to much.

Rabbis who wished to study and write usually preferred a community known for its reverence for scholarship, particularly one with a yeshivah that had a sound nucleus of prushim (a group of committed learners). After the establishment of the Hasidic movement in the mid-eighteenth century, many Lithuanian rabbis also sought out shtetlekh with no Hasidic enclaves, because the Hasidim and their many dynasties presented a constant challenge to the rabbis' authority. The more homogeneous the town, the fewer the problems.

In some communities, however, the local yeshivah itself was a challenge to the rabbi's authority, sometimes subtle, sometimes quite direct. In Radun, for example, the yeshivah that had been founded by the Haffetz Hayyim in 1869 was so powerful by comparison with the timid community organizations of the shtetl that it was known as the Tzarski Dvor, the Tzar's Court. And in Mir, the struggle between the rabbi who headed the yeshivah and the town rabbi culminated in a court battle whose outcome gave legal approval to the independence and autonomy of the family-owned yeshivah as a completely separate entity from the town and the town's rabbi.[12]

For all the difficulties he sometimes faced, all the challenges to his authority that were posed in various places, all the resentment directed against him for fees he may have exacted from the community for his services, the East European rabbi in general and the shtetl rabbi in particular was a guiding and unifying force. The light that shone from his window as he studied into the late hours of the night was for centuries a ray of hope and solace to his people. He was perceived as the highest moral authority in the community, the embodiment of Judaism itself, and honored accordingly. The respect paid to the rabbi exceeded even that due one's parents.

As the Av Beth Din, the head of the shtetl rabbinic court, the rabbi was expected by the Jews of the community, and in many instances the non-Jews, to settle all disputes justly, and to resolve all conflicts wisely. In time of trouble, natural or man-made, he was expected to guide the community to safety, to rescue it from misfortune at the hands of its adversaries. He opened all public and private events with a speech or a benediction, he maintained the shtetl register (pinkas) where all births, deaths, marriages, and divorces were recorded, he was invited to every family affair, and he was expected to attend every important ceremony in the lives of the members of his community, for his presence was perceived as the presence of the Torah, indeed of God. Services in the synagogue began only after the rabbi's arrival, and, with the guidance of the hazzan (who led the congregation in prayer and took his cues from the rabbi), proceeded at the rabbi's pace. When the hazzan heard the rabbi pronounce the word emeth (truth), he could proceed with the rest of the Shema Israel, and when he concluded the Amidah, that was the hazzan's sign that he could move to the next part of the service. The shtetl expressed its reverence for the rabbi, as a community and as individuals, by rising in his honor whenever he entered a public or private place.

RABBIS' WIVES

If the rabbi's wife commanded respect among scholars and laymen, she too was accorded this honor. Indeed, many clergymen's wives, or rebbetzins, played a prominent role in shtetl life, due not just because of their husbands' positions as rabbis, dayyanim, hazzanim, or other clergy (Klei Kodesh, meaning Holy Vessels), but because of their own personality, conduct, erudition, and wisdom.

It was not at all unusual for the rebbetzin to be impressively knowledgeable about Jewish scholarly subjects, or at the very least to have a profound respect for such scholarship, for most of these women came from backgrounds that valued learning highly. Some of them were daughters of successful businessmen whose money was able to purchase that most coveted of acquisitions, a Talmudic scholar for a son-in-law. Frequently, part of the purchase price was the *kest* arrangement, whereby the bride's parents agreed to support the young couple for a number of years so that the husband could continue his studies. Parents of more modest means who aspired to a scholar for a son-in-law were willing to deprive themselves of many of life's most basic amenities in order to provide the kest that would make their extravagant dream a reality.

Some rebbetzins were daughters of men who were themselves prominent scholars and clergymen and had devoted all their lives to the study of Torah. Simply by living in such homes, these women would have absorbed an impressive amount of learning, regardless of whether they received any formal education, because most rabbinic affairs were conducted at home. It was there that the rabbi responded to various inquiries from his congregation, wrote his responsa, conducted rabbinic courts, or simply studied for hours on end. The erudition that pervaded the domestic atmosphere is well expressed in the Yiddish proverb, "At the rabbi's home, even the Christian maid is knowledgeable enough to issue a rabbinic (halakhic) verdict."

Since Jewish scholarship is heavily text oriented, knowledge acquired by women through mere listening was looked down upon. But in some instances a woman did have firsthand acquaintance with the texts, for in a tradition dating back to the Talmudic scholar Rashi in eleventh-century France, who educated his three daughters, many rabbis who had been blessed only with daughters would lavish upon them the scholarly knowledge that was customarily passed on to sons. These women did not have to resort to disguising themselves as men to pursue their studies, as Yentl did in the Isaac Bashevis Singer story (and Barbra Streisand movie). Hence the saying "The wife of a scholar is like a scholar," and hence the status they enjoyed both at home and in the community, or even beyond it.[13] Their range of knowledge was impressive. They could cite parts of Talmudic lore with fluency and ease, and were versed in many of the halakhot that governed dietary laws, family purity (conjugal relations),[14] and the Sabbath and holiday observances. Some offered their own interpretations of rabbinic literature and were even quoted by their husbands in their published works. Included among the rebbetzins of Lithuania were some of Judaism's most lively female scholars.

Many of these women had been tutored in their father's home by private teachers, not only in the basic reading, writing, and arithmetic skills, but also in languages, such as German, Russian, Polish,[15] even French — and, on rare occasion, in the playing of a musical instrument. They were among the most loyal subscribers to foreign-language newspapers, and if in later years their husband's meager earnings could not pay for subscriptions, they often looked to their parents to continue to send them their favorite publications. With the advent of the Haskalah movement, the Hebrew language and its newly emerging literature and newspapers also became part of the tutorials.

Most of these women had a deep love and reverence for scholarship, and had always dreamed of marrying a scholar. In the song Zaidl sings to the matchmaker in *Fiddler on the Roof*, the lyrics might just as well be "For *me* make him a scholar" as "For Papa make him a scholar." But there was nothing easy about the position they aspired to, and they were well aware that in marrying a scholar they would face a life of struggle. Since rabbinical contracts were generally for limited periods (typically three years), they would almost certainly move around a great deal, forfeiting any chance of a permanent residence, much less a permanent residence in their hometown. A rabbi's wife was expected to be in a state of constant readiness to move from community to community in search of more favorable opportunities for her husband's scholarship. In Eishyshok, for example, during the hundred years prior to the destruction of the Jewish community none of the rebbetzins who lived there had been born there. Batia Wilkanski, wife of dayyan Reb Layzer, suffered such culture shock when she moved in the 1860s to the humble Lithuanian shtetl from her elegant family home in Prussia that she cried her heart out into her pillow every single night for months — which must have been an experience shared by many of these women.

A rebbetzin would also be expected to work very hard to support her husband while he studied, for, as noted earlier, the remuneration he received would in all but the larger communities be very modest — which helps to explain why so many rabbis praised their spouses in the forewords to their books, thanking them for not just the moral but the financial support that made it possible to write them. The wife's status as chief wage-earner was acknowledged in the contract between the community and the rabbi, which often stipulated that the rabbi's wife would be given a store, and exclusive rights to sell certain items, such as candles, yeast, wine for kiddush and havdalah, salt, sugar, and kerosene.

THE RABBI'S ELECTION AND CONTRACT

The election of a new rabbi was a major event in the community, regulated by an elaborate structure of laws, amendments to laws, customs, and local traditions. In Vilna, which was a super-kehilah, only the highest levels of society — the parnasei ha-eidah (official leaders of the community), the tovei ha-yir (the town notables), and all those with the title *morenu* (literally, "our teacher," an indication of scholarly achievement) — were eligible to vote. But in Eishyshok, as in many smaller communities, a wider cross-section of the town, consisting of all dues-paying male balebatim, could vote on the new rabbi (after the admittedly smaller, more select group who made up the search committee had chosen a candidate).

Once the rabbi had been elected, his contract was drawn up, defining in great detail his privileges and obligations. It would stipulate the term of office (usually three years); the salary and any additional emoluments and gratuities to which he would be entitled; the commercial rights, if any, that the kahal would grant to the rebbetzin so that she might supplement his income; their place of residence; the title by which he would be addressed, such as Moreh Zedek (Teacher of Justice) or Av Beth Din (head of the court); the days he would pray in the various batei midrash; his position in the sequence of men called up to the Torah; the number of major sermons he was expected to deliver (usually two, one on Shabbat Teshuvah, the Sabbath of Repentance, between Rosh Hashanah and Yom Kippur, and one on Shabbat ha-Gadol, the Sabbath before Passover); his duties as head of the rabbinic court; the local yeshivot, if any, under his stewardship; his obligations to yeshivah students who were candidates for ordination, and to students at the community-run Talmud Torah schools; the charities and community organizations he was expected to oversee; his role as supervisor of the slaughter, production, and sale of kosher meat; and so on, down to such details as whether he was to wear a shtreimel (fur hat) or a bowler, and other particulars pertaining to the local dress code.[16] It was also the rabbi's duty to represent the community to the non-Jewish authorities outside the shtetl (since the shtetlekh, unlike the larger communities, did not have a shtadlan, an official who was the intercessor with the secular world).

No item was viewed as too trivial to be included in the contract. By being spelled out in sufficient detail, the contract could help the rabbi and the town leadership to divide up their duties fairly, and thus avoid bitter disputes later.

Once the contract had been accepted and signed by the rabbi, a date was set for the inauguration ceremony, and festivities were arranged to welcome him to his new home. In Eishyshok, the town notables, accompanied by the shtetl klezmers (musicians), went out to greet the rabbi at the bridge that symbolized the shtetl's boundaries, and then the entire population greeted him with lighted torches and lanterns when he entered the shtetl proper. With the rabbi and other dignitaries in the lead, the procession then made its way from the marketplace to the main synagogue or the Old Beth Midrash, depending on the season. There the rabbi delivered his first sermon, followed by a lavish meal for him and the town notables, and some simpler refreshments for the rest of the community.

That night, after the festivities, the shtetl would watch in suspense to see how long the candle burned in the rabbi's window. If it burned late into the night, the townspeople knew they had made a good choice and had been blessed with a diligent scholar.

THE RABBIS OF EISHYSHOK

From the late eighteenth century, the era of our first detailed records documenting the lives and works of the rabbis of Eishyshok, until the death of the last Eishyshker rabbi in the massacre of 1941, the town was well served by a remarkable group of rabbis and their wives. This was the golden age of the rabbinate, in Eishyshok as in Eastern Europe in general. In their scholarship, their publications, their personal lives, the intricate partnership they worked out with the community leadership, their relationship to both the Jewish and the non-Jewish population of their community, their ability to manage crises from within and without, their attempts in later years to respond to the ever-accelerating process of secularization, the rabbis of Eishyshok tell us much about the ethos of the shtetl rabbi. Some of them rose to extraordinary moral, spiritual, and scholarly heights; others were more modest in their accomplishments. But during this golden age, the men who occupied the rabbinic chair of Eishyshok, and the women who shared their lives, offer as fine an example as can be found of the Lithuanian rabbinate.

RABBI MOSHE BEN AARON HALEVI HOROWITZ SEGAL

Reb Moshe, the first Eishyshok rabbi about whom we have a substantial body of information, was born in Kruzh in the eighteenth century, and eventually became so accomplished a scholar that the Gaon of Vilna hired him to teach his own sons. According to tradition, he became an intimate of the Gaon's, one of the few he allowed to interrupt his studies.

Reb Moshe is thought to have been the founder of the Kibbutz ha-Prushim in the 1790s, thus making Eishyshok the virtual mother of Lithuanian yeshivot.[17] However, his community-owned yeshivah was different from the other great Lithuanian academies of the nineteenth century, which, in a departure from centuries of tradition, were under the jurisdiction of family dynasties, rather than the community and its rabbi.

Reb Moshe's devotion to the Kibbutz ha-Prushim knew no bounds. One Friday night, when the flimsy doors of the beth midrash would not close, Reb Moshe did not take his customary place among the prushim studying Torah there. At dawn the following day the shammash found him outside, nearly frozen to death, for he had stood all night long in subzero temperatures, ensuring that his students would be warm by propping the doors closed with his own body.[18]

After a number of years as rabbi of Eishyshok, Reb Moshe returned to Vilna, where he served as a Maggid Meisharim (Preacher of Righteousness). In 1811 he lost his voice and was given a post as dayyan so that he might earn a living. He died in 1821, a renowned scholar and a well-known preacher, whose parables were quoted for many years to come.[19]

RABBI AVRAHAM SHMUEL RABINOWITCH

Reb Avraham Shmuel (1809–1868) is a representative of the best of the Lithuanian shtetl rabbis of the nineteenth century: a brilliant scholar, author of an important halakhic work, student of prominent Lithuanian yeshivot, and protégé of some of the most famous Talmudic scholars. The Amud Esh (Pillar of Fire), as he is known, for the collection of responsa his son gathered and published posthumously, would become one of Eishyshok's most beloved rabbis.

Born in Turetz, Lithuania, Avraham Shmuel was among the first students at the Mir yeshivah. From there he went on to study at the Navaredok yeshivah, and then to Minsk, where he studied with the renowned rabbi of Minsk, David Tebeli, a relative of his who recognized his promise early on.[20] Eventually Avraham Shmuel too became well known in Lithuanian scholarly circles, and was offered high-paying posts in prominent communities. But he declined such offers for fear that they would interfere with his scholarship, preferring a smaller, less demanding place. In 1848 he went to Eishyshok as rabbi and head of the yeshivah.

Three factors attracted Reb Avraham Shmuel to Eishyshok: It was a genuine Lithuanian shtetl without a single follower of the Hasidic movement; it had no church in its midst; and it was the home of a great yeshivah.[21] The Kibbutz ha-Prushim would enjoy its golden age during his tenure, attaining a stature fully equal to that of the distinguished academies in Volozhin and Mir.[22] Thanks in part to the strength of his personality and the vast scope of his knowledge, which enabled him to do brilliant in-depth textual analysis, the yeshivah attracted students of very high caliber. Prominent among them was the Haffetz Hayyim, who probably modeled certain aspects of his own public person after that of Reb Avraham Shmuel.

After seven fruitful years in Eishyshok, during which he made great contributions to the community and to the scholarly world, poor health and poverty forced Reb Avraham Shmuel to accept a higher-paying post in Roseini, near Kovno. But he longed for the prushim at his beloved yeshivah so much that he returned two years later, in 1857, even though his salary in Roseini had been many times that which he would receive in Eishyshok. There he remained until his death in 1868.

Though he lived a life totally devoted to scholarship, Reb Avraham Shmuel had a major impact on his time. In fact, the study group he formed among the balebatim of Roseini would determine the future of that town, since it served as the base for a formidable opposition to the Haskalah followers who later attempted to dominate the shtetl.

Throughout his life he was in constant touch with other scholars, who asked his opinion on halakhic matters, sought his endorsements for their books, and admired him for both the extreme modesty of his demeanor and the profundity of his thought. Reb Yaakov Lifshitz, an author from Kovno, wrote the following after his initial encounter with Reb Avraham Shmuel, at a din Torah they were both mediating:

The great gaon, renowned zaddik, who in addition to his greatness in Torah is endowed with the virtue of truth, this magnificent man spiritually towers over others. Though there is nothing in his appearance to indicate either his righteousness or his kindness, yet the imprint of ultimate truth is apparent. He conducted himself in a just manner, always striking at the heart of truth and never missing its target.

As head of the rabbinic court, Reb Avraham Shmuel inspired awe in the plaintiffs who stood before him, for they knew that his penetrating gaze and his great knowledge would enable him to find the truth. Even gentiles came to his court, knowing that his verdict was always just, his insight profound. Once when Reb Avraham Shmuel traveled with a gentile coachman, the man failed to cross himself when they passed a crucifix. The rabbi told the coachman to halt the carriage, and then dismounted, reasoning that "A person who has no reverence and fear for his own God may eventually prove a murderer."[23] Reb Layzer Wilkanski, dayyan of Eishyshok for over fifty years, considered Reb Avraham Shmuel the finest of the many rabbis under whom he served during his long tenure.

Because of his reputation for both wisdom and probity, Reb Avraham Shmuel was called upon to mediate many notorious disputes, among them the conflict between town and gown in the shtetl of Mir, where he himself had once been a student. The city of Lomza also sought his advice on halakhic and other questions, and eventually invited him to accept the rabbinic post there. Claiming that he was not accomplished enough to hold such a prestigious post, which previously had been occupied by scholars of great distinction, Reb Avraham turned it down.[24]

Indeed, his modesty was legendary. He once received a book in which he had been referred to as *gaon* — a title frequently accorded him — and he became greatly upset. First he tore out his hair, then the page on which the offending word occurred, saying "How will I face in the world to come the great sage, the only true bearer of this title, the Gaon of Vilna?"[25] Modesty was so much part of his identity that he never even signed his name with any rabbinic title, but closed his communiqués with: "Stationed here in the holy community of Eishyshok, Avraham Shmuel."

His devotion to scholarship, which had caused him to choose service in a small shtetl rather than a well-paid rabbinic post in a larger community, meant that he lived a life of stark poverty, apparently unrelieved by his wife's income. He was so poor that he could not even afford a warm coat to protect him against the harsh winters, and his shoes were so shabby that his toes were visible through the holes in them. Not surprisingly, his health was affected by the grim conditions in which he lived, as he acknowledged in a letter he wrote to a colleague, which he signed "From the overburdened and fatigued." Yet he continued to study, write, and teach, day and night, as well as to guide his community and to travel to various places as a mediator. Moreover, his door was always open to anyone in need of a meal or a place to sleep, and it was said he never sat down to his table without sharing food with a guest.[26] He did not regret the choices he made, for he saw wealth as a burden and distraction, poverty as a virtue. Indeed, he said that a person should always pray for his sons not to be rich.

In 1868, on the verge of departing for Eretz Israel, where he was planning to settle, Reb Avraham Shmuel went to the seaside town of Palangian to attend the funeral of one of his colleagues, and to take his leave of several others whom he expected to see at the ceremony. There he died, apparently while swimming in the Baltic, and there he was buried. "Lithuania was in an uproar when the news of his death became known," according to Reb Shalom David Meirowitch, who wrote that "one who had not seen the magnitude of his charity, purity, temperance, and modesty, had never witnessed holiness . . . His judgment was the embodiment of the ultimate truth of the Torah [delivered] with restraint and moderation. There were eulogies in all the countries, and I too was among the eulogizers."[27]

Reb Avraham Shmuel left behind many unpublished manuscripts, including the responsa that his son gathered and later published as *Amud Esh*, with a glowing endorsement from the great Rabbi Yitzhak Elhanan Spektor of Kovno. Though the book contained only a fragment of the vast body of halakhic verdicts Reb Avraham Shmuel rendered, it reflects both the magnitude of his knowledge of the law and his sensitivity to the social and economic realities faced by the individuals who would be affected by his decisions. Because he did extensive research in the field before reaching some of his verdicts, his responsa still stand as a rich source of information about the life and times of those in the communities he served as mediator and judge.

By the time of his death, Reb Avraham Shmuel had amassed a comprehensive knowledge of the Talmud and of the accompanying rabbinic and halakhic literature, and had achieved the spiritual wealth that comes of leading a life according to the highest ethical and humanitarian standards. He made such an impression on the town he served for nearly twenty years that, twenty-one years after his death, the association founded by the Eishyshker immigrants to America was named in his honor.

RABBI YOSSEF ZUNDL HUTNER AND REBBETZIN HENDL HUTNER

When the position of rabbi of Eishyshok became open in 1896, a notice appeared in the popular Hebrew-language newspaper *Ha-Melitz* on September 14, signed by several members of the Eishyshok kahal:

We find it necessary publicly to announce that our Rabbi, after much honor, was taken by the town of Vilkovisk. Therefore, we announce and caution the honorable rabbis in every location, please do not extend yourselves; remain at home and do not travel to Eishyshok in connection with the rabbinical post. For only the rabbi we choose shall we contact and place upon the Rabbi's chair.

Apparently this was written with Rabbi Yossef Zundl Hutner in mind, for shortly thereafter, emissaries from the Eishyshok kahal showed up late one night, rabbinic contract in hand, in Derechin, where Hutner was serving as rabbi, and offered him the post. Hutner accepted the offer — a move that seems to have come as quite a shock to the people of Derechin, for their kahal was to complain that "they came at night and stole our Rabbi." And indeed, Rabbi Hutner would prove to be quite a prize for Eishyshok, a brave and saintly man, one in the line of distinguished rabbis who preferred a post in a small shtetl to one in a large town because it would leave more time for their scholarly pursuits.

Reb Yossef Zundl Hutner (1844? 46?–1919) was born in Dvinsk (Dunaburg), Latvia, the "son of Rabbi Hayyim from Bialystok," as he later referred to himself.[28] The family was originally from Ilya, where they were involved in glass manufacturing.

In his youth Reb Zundl, as he came to be called, did not attend a yeshivah, but studied alone, most likely under the supervision of his father. He felt that both his personality and his scholarship bore the marks of this early education. As he wrote: "I did not study with hair-splitting students, nor did I have study partners. All my reasoning and theoretical debate were carried on in solitude, and with much labor and toil, which gave me strength . . . for His holy studies."[29]

As was the custom of the time, he married early, to the daughter of a well-to-do Dvinsk scholar. But she soon died, as he lamented in the eloquent foreword to his first book, *Bikkurei Yossef*: "God has stricken me and my young wife, Hayyia Dvorah of sainted memory, who died in the spring of her life. . . . In purity she ascended to heaven at the age of twenty-two, on Thursday, the 22nd. of Tamaz, 1870 . . . Her pure innocent soul will bring our memory before the Master of all Souls . . ."[30]

Zundl Hutner, an eminent scholar who served as rabbi in Eishyshok from 1896 until his death in 1919. He and his family (most of whom eventually emigrated to Eretz Israel) had a great impact on shtetl life. The photo was taken during World War I. On his lapel is an ID badge issued by the German occupation force; it included the wearer's last name and a number. PHOTO: YITZHAK URI KATZ. YESC, HUTNER-HADASH

In 1872 he moved from Dvinsk to Bialystok, where he married Hendl, one of the three daughters of Reb Yehudah Leib Krechmer. His love of scholarship made a lifelong impression on them: All three girls married prominent scholars, and supported them throughout their lives, despite having been impoverished by their father's early death. The spunky, erudite Hendl gave birth to two sons while she and Reb Zundl

Hendl Hutner (1850–1928), one of the most powerful rebbetzins in the history of Eishyshok. She was an outstanding businesswoman, a fine scholar, and an expert manager of her husband's personal life and his relationship with the community. She emigrated to Eretz Israel in 1925.
PHOTO: YITZHAK URI KATZ. YESC, HUTNER-HADASH

lived in Bialystok: Yehudah Leib and, five years later, Naftali Menahem (later known as Hertz Mendl), both of whom would become rabbinic judges. Rebbetzin Hendl used to say that for her two sons, one bed was sufficient, since one loved to study through the night and sleep a few hours during the day, while the other rose to study at the crack of dawn and retired to bed early in the evening.

Hendl Krechmer Hutner soon became the most important factor in her husband's life, for her respect for scholarship and diligence made her a ferocious defender of the many hours he devoted to his studies, and her own learning and good sense enabled her to answer for him when people came to the house with routine halakhic questions, and to be the helpmate he himself would consult on the life-and-death issues they faced during World War I. Her reverence for scholarship was matched only by her respect for an honest day's work. "God save me from idle time and scot-free money" was the prayer she later taught her granddaughters to recite, after the traditional one for the kindling of the Sabbath candles. Apparently God granted her her prayer, for she worked very hard. The income she earned from the store she owned in Bialystok, and the exclusive sales concession she had from a Russian paint and dye company, enabled her to provide her family with a comfortable home and complete economic security, so that her husband could study and write without interruption.

For a short while Reb Zundl was the head of an academy in Bialystok, but he soon gave that up to devote full time to his studies. The pinkas of the old beth midrash of Bialystok lists him among the prominent scholars who studied there between 1879 and 1881.[31] During the Bialystok period he was offered a prestigious, well-paid position as rabbi in his hometown of Dvinsk, but declined the offer, for both he and most especially his wife felt that it would occupy too much of his time. Later he accepted the position of rabbi of Derechin, a small shtetl near Slonim with a history of prominent rabbis. There he moved into the rabbi's comfortable house in the shulhoyf, and continued to immerse himself in his studies and halakhic writings, while Hendl continued to supplement his meager salary with her paint and dye sales commissions. And it was while they were there that Hendl helped find wives for both their sons. The townspeople of Derechin had great admiration for the tireless Rebbetzin Hendl, who took upon herself so many of her husband's community obligations, and they had great reverence for her husband, whose saintly personality and brilliant scholarship were already much in evidence.

Shlomo Yudson, a friend of the rabbi's younger son Naftali during this period, later wrote a brief memoir, in which he offered glimpses into Rabbi Yossef Zundl Hutner as both man and scholar. Shlomo was a young boy at the time he first met Reb Zundl, who had asked him to pay a visit. When Naftali told

Shlomo that his father wished to see him, Shlomo was very anxious about meeting this man, whom his own father had described as "the embodiment of the Torah."

When we arrived at the Rabbi's house, my friend led me to his father, who sat in a deep armchair with his extraordinary, huge head bent over an immense Gemara in which he kept searching with his near-sighted eyes. He sensed that someone was standing near him, lifted his head, and upon seeing me said, "Good, Shleimke, that you came." Then he got up and started to walk to a special room, motioning me to follow. The small room to which he led me was lined with book cabinets. It contained a large table on which there were many rolls of paper and numerous writing utensils, and next to it stood a very comfortable chair.[32]

This was the table and chair at which Shlomo was to work. For what the rabbi wanted from Shlomo was for him to use his beautiful penmanship to transcribe the rabbi's latest manuscript on the *Shulhan Arukh* (Rabbi Yossef Caro's sixteenth-century, four-volume codification of all writings on Jewish law, topic by topic, which became a standard text for Sephardic Jews that scholars continue to write about, revise, and update) into a document that the rebbetzin could deliver to the printers. As payment for copying the rabbi's illegible handwriting, Shlomo would receive the same 3 kopecks per double sheet that the rabbi had paid the student from the Derechin beth midrash who had previously done the work.

That first day, Shlomo earned 11.5 kopecks, but as he mastered the rabbi's difficult handwriting, he was able to increase his earnings to 20 kopecks a day. However, one sunny summer day, instead of going to the rabbi's house, Shlomo went to play in the beautiful gardens that had belonged to Duke Serfia when he ruled Lithuania from Derechin. Thinking that young Shlomo had not come because the pay was too low, Reb Zundl suggested an increase to 5 kopecks per sheet, and for the next seven months Shlomo worked at copying the entire manuscript, sometimes taking home as much as 3 rubles a week, which was more than some of Lithuania's most prominent rabbis earned.[33]

When Eishyshok invited Reb Zundl to become its rabbi, his wife urged him to take the job, for she reasoned that in Eishyshok, a town known for its devotion to Torah and for the excellence of its yeshivah, her husband's scholarship would be even better appreciated than it was in Derechin, and he would be allowed even more time to devote to his studies. When he accepted, the people were overwhelmed with joy at being blessed with another renowned scholar like their beloved late Rabbi Avraham Shmuel. To express their great reverence for him, members of the kahal and several other of Eishyshok's most prominent citizens swept the floors of the rabbi's residence in the shulhoyf complex, in fulfillment of the words "Be like servants who serve their rabbi without expecting a reward; and let the fear of God be upon you."[34]

When they moved to Eishyshok, Rebbetzin Hendl continued her work as an agent for the Russian dye company. But her husband's studies were always her main objective in life, and in Eishyshok as elsewhere she saw to it that he pursued them with as few distractions as possible. She told the people that her husband's presence in their midst was a great honor, for which they could express their appreciation by making very few demands on his time — an attitude much resented by Reb Layzer Wilkanski's wife, Batia, who no doubt hoped that the Hutners would share some of the burdens she and her husband had taken on when Reb Zundl's predecessor proved unequal to the job. Batia considered the rabbi as well as the dayyan to be a public servant, whose duty it was to serve the people and the community at all times. Accordingly, the Wilkanski home was always open and Reb Layzer was always available, while Hendl Hutner, maintaining that the rabbi's house was the holy of holies, a place for learning, not for socializing, kept the rabbi's study (and the rabbi himself) strictly off limits to most of the community.

However, Rebbetzin Hendl's own knowledge of Scripture, Hebrew grammar, the Talmud, and halakhic principles was considerable enough that she was able to speak for her husband in many mundane matters, and so in part to make up for his unavailability. When congregants came with one of the usual dilemmas, such as "Is the chicken kosher if it has a broken wing?" or "Can we eat the chicken soup if a drop of milk was accidentally splashed into it?", she would listen intently, at times consult the appropriate books, then dismiss it as a "minor question" that even she could issue the halakhic verdict for. "For such issues that even the rebbetzin can handle," she would say, "there is no need to disrupt the rabbi from his holy work, the study of the Torah."

Once, it is told, a stubborn man insisted on consulting with the rabbi himself. Reminding the rebbetzin that Eishyshok had hired her husband, not her, he moved toward the door to the rabbi's study and found himself physically blocked by the rebbetzin. When he attempted to force his way past her, he received a resounding slap in the face — a stern warning to the shtetl that it was not to question the rebbetzin's authority.

Not only did congregants call upon the rebbetzin, her husband's colleagues did so as well, among them some of the most renowned Talmudic scholars of Lithuania, who paid her the same honors as were customarily paid to rabbis. When she entered a room, students and scholars alike all stood. Many of these men she knew from the travels she undertook on business related to her husband's publications, and others she knew from their visits to her husband and to the yeshivah in Eishyshok.[35] Indeed, she was so at ease in the company of scholars that she felt free to engage them in academic and ideological debates.

In an exchange that caused quite a commotion in the scholarly community, she used her considerable skill in textual analysis to challenge Reb Yeruham Yehudah Leib Perlman, the Godol (great scholar) of Minsk, in his reading of a biblical verse, going so far as to ask the brilliant Talmudist whether his interpretation meant that he was a supporter of the Haskalah, and using the text as an opportunity to discourse at length on one of her favorite themes: the spiritual as well as intellectual dividends resulting from the long, slow, diligent search for knowledge.

In addition to textual exegesis, she filled her conversations with midrashic and homiletic imagery, quotations from the Scripture, and parables worthy of a maggid. During her time in Derechin, she was called to the deathbed of a man who greeted her with: "Nu, Rebbetzin, what do you have to say about my wretched condition, you who are always filled with so much faith?" The rebbetzin was quick to respond: "I am surprised that you of all people should talk that way. When a baby is in his mother's womb and floating there in all that filth, the baby is content and pleased, because as yet he has no other experience. So it is with you. Soon you will be ushered from this world of filth to a world of truth. You should be pleased that you are embarking on such a great new experience — the journey to the eternal land of truth." The man thanked the rebbetzin for her comforting words, and lived for another few months, serene and at peace.

The stories of her intellectual accomplishments should not be allowed to obscure the down-to-earth good sense and the day-to-day kindnesses of this remarkable rebbetzin, who is remembered as much for these latter qualities as for her scholarship. One woman whose family's home in Bialystok was a stopping-off place for Rebbetzin Hendl during her traveling days still recalls the homemade gifts the rebbetzin brought her and her sister each time she came to visit — not to mention the fact that the rebbetzin was tolerant enough to stay in a non-kosher home! "She would bring a bagful of bread that had been toasted in the oven, and we kept a separate glass and spoon for her tea. . . . When I was ten or eleven she took me for a visit to Eishyshok by horse and wagon. I can still remember the gracious atmosphere in the house."

Eishyshok had many fine rebbetzins, but in the shtetl's last hundred years, only one became known as "the Eishyshker Rebbetzin," and her name was Hendl Hutner. The people's love for her was matched only by their affection and admiration for her husband.

From his long hours of study, Reb Zundl produced a number of halakhic works that brought him ever more fame, and increased the shtetl's pride in having him as their rabbi.[36] Eishyshkians loved to tell stories about his fortitude and perseverance, and the respect paid him by other famous scholars of his time. One of their favorites concerned the Haffetz Hayyim from neighboring Radun, who was among the many scholars who so admired Reb Zundl's halakhic books that they asked him to write endorsements to their own.[37] Since his student days at the Kibbutz ha-Prushim yeshivah, the Haffetz Hayyim had been a frequent visitor in Eishyshok, but he did not want to intrude on Reb Zundl during his visits, nor on the other hand did he want to offend him by failing to call upon him. The Haffetz Hayyim resolved the dilemma in his own unique style.

On his way back to Radun one day he sent an emissary to Reb Zundl to ask him for a blessing. When the emissary returned, the Haffetz Hayyim stood up to receive the blessing, but the man seemed reluctant to pass on the words Reb Zundl had spoken, and explained: "Rabbi, forgive me, but to me they did not sound like much of a blessing." After some coaxing from the Haffetz Hayyim, he reluctantly blurted out, "Reb Zundl blessed you, that you should walk barefoot and carry stones on your chest." Tears of joy began to stream from the Haffetz Hayyim's eyes, and his small, frail body began to turn in a dance, as if to the tune of a melody that only he could hear. The messenger looked on in bewilderment, until the Haffetz Hayyim explained: "As you know, I am a kohen, and as such it is my duty to work in the temple. In the Holy Temple in Jerusalem the priests walked barefoot and the high priest wore a breastplate of precious stones. Reb Zundl blessed me that I might be worthy to witness the coming of the Messiah and the rebuilding of the Holy Temple, and to serve our benevolent God there."

Another story told of two young students from the Haffetz Hayyim's yeshivah in Radun, Eliezer Yehudah Finkel and Yossef Kahaneman, both of whom were later to become significant figures in the scholarly community, who paid a visit to Finkel's uncle in Eishyshok. He took them to meet Reb Zundl, who was bent over his Gemara and responded to their greetings without ever lifting his eyes, but invited them to sit down. After a long silence, Finkel's uncle announced with great pride that his nephew knew the entire Talmud. At that, Reb Zundl looked up and asked Eliezer how old he was. "Seventeen," he replied. "So what is so extraordinary? It is about time you should know the entire Shas [Talmud]!" For Eliezer's friend, Yossef Kahaneman, Reb Zundl had the following advice: "People think that one has to study for very long hours, but it is not necessary to do so, and in fact may be detrimental to one's health. To study only fourteen hours a day may be quite sufficient."[38]

Yet in times of great trouble, Reb Zundl abandoned his holy books and instantly became a man of the people, putting their welfare above all else. World War I was such a time, and both rabbi and rebbetzin rose to the occasion brilliantly, proving themselves true leaders of the community, and inspiring all with their courage and dedication. As the battlefront neared Eishyshok, many residents ran away, either to Vilna and other large cities that they hoped would be safe havens from the havoc of war, or to small villages that they hoped would simply be overlooked by the approaching troops. Indeed, the rabbi and rebbetzin urged their son Reb Hertz Mendl (by that time the dayyan) and his wife Kreindl, for the sake of their children, to join those refugees headed for Vilna, which they did.

Reb Zundl and his wife stayed in Eishyshok, however, for "it is the duty of a shepherd to be with his flock," Rebbetzin Hendl kept saying. As the shtetl changed hands repeatedly, going back and forth among the Russians, Germans, Lithuanians, Soviets, and Poles, chaos reigned (except for a period of relative stability during the peaceful German occupation of World War I, when the Hutners were joined by their grandchildren from Warsaw). No matter who was in power, the Jews were always the prime targets for torture, plunder, rape, and murder. But Reb Zundl and Rebbetzin Hendl remained in the shtetl with the sick, the very old, the poor who could not afford to buy transportation, and the many young women whose husbands had been drafted into the tzarist army at the outbreak of the war. Those left behind always remembered the dedication of their rabbi and his wife during this period, how they helped all those in need and fulfilled their roles as God's guardians of the shtetl.

One of Reb Zundl's finest moments came on the eve of a Yom Kippur during a period of Russian occupation. Families dressed all in white in honor of the holiday walked cautiously toward the synagogue, hoping to escape the bullets and the sabers of the Russian troops. But as services were about to begin, a young girl was shot. During the Kol Nidre prayer, the congregation wept uncontrollably. Loud sobs arose from the upstairs gallery, as the women tried to drown out with their tears the sounds of drunken Russian cavalrymen rampaging in the streets below.

On the bimah stood Reb Zundl, surrounded by members of the kahal and other notables. Rebbetzin Hendl came down from the women's gallery and made her way toward the bimah. Reb Zundl stepped down to meet her, and they held a hurried consultation.

Next the shammash banged on the bimah table to get the attention of the congregation, and a hush fell over the room. Reb Zundl then announced that on this holy day he would go to the Russian headquarters in Juryzdyki to plead for the safety of the shtetl. With God's help, the people's prayers, and the merit of their holy forefathers, he hoped he would succeed in his mission. A red-bearded coachman responded to the rabbi's request for a volunteer driver. Beaming with excitement as the rabbi beckoned him forward from a bench at the back of the room, he mounted the bimah, there to stand next to the rabbi on the holiest of holy days, just like one of the balebatim — an honor he had never dreamed of.

Rabbi and coachman then set out on their dangerous mission, accompanied by a member of the kahal who was fluent in Russian. When they arrived in Juryzdyki they met with the Soviet commander, who was impressed with Reb Zundl's frail, saintly appearance, and with his excellent "political" record as a man who was a protector of the poor and needy in wartime — a man known to all by his first name had to be a man of courage, dedicated to the people, a true revolutionary, the commander proclaimed. Then he signed an order stating that any soldier who harmed a Jew in the shtetl of Eishyshok would be punished severely, after which he sent the rabbi and his party home in their carriage, under the protection of two of his cavalrymen.

It was long past midnight when the entire congregation, which had taken shelter in the cemetery for the night, returned to the shulhoyf to welcome the three men who had risked their lives on behalf of the shtetl. Once more the rabbi stood on the bimah, flanked by his brave companions, and told the congregation about the righteous, God-fearing Russian commander and his order. There was not a dry eye in the house as the community resumed its Yom Kippur prayers, with only the twenty-four-hour candles that burned in memory of the dead and in honor of the living to light the dark interior of the synagogue. Each detail of that remarkable Yom Kippur was recorded in the shtetl's pinkas.

Rebbetzin Hendl went on a comparable mission herself, during another of the shtetl's many occupations. The events that led to her journey began one day when shots were fired on the Soviet troops, and the Russians were told the shots had come from the direction of a house occupied by some monks who had fled to Eishyshok during the war. In retaliation, the Russians arrested all the monks and took them to Vilna as prisoners of war. A few days later, Eishyshok changed hands again and Polish troops marched in, only to be told by a Polish informer that the Jews were responsible for the arrest of the monks. The Polish commander issued a decree that "if all the monks are not returned unharmed within ten days, the entire Jewish population of Eishyshok will be put to death."

Panic-stricken, the people of the shtetl gathered at the Old Beth Midrash to discuss the situation. The Poles refused to believe that the Jews were innocent of any wrongdoing with respect to the monks, and reiterated their threat, placing a loaded pistol to the rabbi's head, warning that he would be the first to be shot if the monks were not returned. After some discussion, it was decided that a community representative would have to go to Vilna. Since battle lines would have to be crossed, and anyone who crossed them would risk being suspected as an enemy spy, this was a dangerous journey. A long silence now filled the beth midrash.

Suddenly the rebbetzin walked up to the center of the bimah and announced, in her decisive manner, "I am going to Vilna." Knowing that when Rebbetzin Hendl had made up her mind there was no point in further discussion, the townspeople accepted her offer. A coachman volunteered to take her to Vilna, and the rebbetzin said her farewells, taking with her only a red kerchief in which she wrapped several hard-boiled eggs and matzah. Upon arriving in Vilna, she went directly to the Russian headquarters, where, in her eloquent Russian, she stated her shtetl's case.

Ten days later Eishyshok witnessed a sight it was never to forget. A coachman drove into the shtetl with Rebbetzin Hendl, wearing her usual composed expression, by his side. Inside the carriage, seated in two rows facing each other, were eleven monks.

The entire population gathered in the marketplace to weep tears of joy over their deliverance. When the rebbetzin was asked how she had accomplished this bold, heroic feat, she had a one-word answer: "Faith." Pressed to elaborate, she said: "Angels must have walked before me because I was on a holy mission to save our beloved shtetl."

With the death of Reb Zundl on January 28, 1919, an era in Eishyshok's history came to an end. No longer would the rabbi's home be the undisputed royal household of the shtetl, no longer would the rabbi's authority rest solely in his scholarship and saintly personality, no longer would the crown of Torah scholarship reign supreme, and never again would there be a rabbi's wife like Hendl, the last regal rebbetzin of Eishyshok. For the shtetl that mourned Reb Zundl's death was a totally different place from the one that had welcomed him with such joy two decades before.

Reb Zundl's tenure as Eishyshok's rabbi, 1896–1919, coincided with what were until then the most dramatic and crucial years in the history of East European Jewry in general, and Eishyshok in particular.[39] This was a period when centuries-old traditions were overshadowed by secular movements: Zionism, socialism, and Communism.

In Basel, during the summer of 1897, the First Zionist World Congress was convened. Its reverberations were felt throughout Eastern Europe, as people reacted to the call of Zionism itself, and to the appeal of the magnetic personality of its founder, Theodor Herzl. That same year saw the founding of the Bund, the socialist workers' organization, in Vilna, and its rapid spread to much of the rest of Eastern Europe. After these dramatic events came the Kishinev pogrom of 1903, the revolution of 1905, the infamous Beilis blood-libel case,[40] the outbreak of World War I, the Russian Revolution of 1917, the Balfour Declaration, the San Remo Conference, the abolition of the Pale of Settlement, the massacre of hundreds of thousands of Jews during the Russian civil war, and the reshaping of the entire Eastern European map, which resulted in an independent Poland and Lithuania, and the emergence of Soviet Russia — all of which events helped spell the beginning of the end for the shtetl.

It seemed as if the only thing that remained stable in Eishyshok during that stormy period was the light that shone from Reb Zundl's window, illuminating his tranquil face bent over the holy books. But his failure to participate in the ideological debates that fired the heart, mind, and hopes of East European Jewry in general, and of his fellow Eishyshkians in particular, was very much the exception, not the norm for his time. Vilna being the very eye of the storm, most of his fellow rabbis and scholars in the vicinity, men like the Haffetz Hayyim of Radun, who was a founder of the anti-Zionist group Agudat Israel (Union of Association of Israel), and Rabbi Reines of Lida, a cofounder of the religious Zionist organization Mizrahi, were passionately committed to one ideological trend or another. As Eishyshok's youth, among them Reb Zundl's own granddaughters, took up the Zionist cause, and Reb Layzer Wilkanski and his family made aliyah to Eretz Israel, leaving the shtetl without any firm day-to-day guidance from its traditional leadership, Reb Zundl remained aloof in his study. His lack of involvement was much appreciated, however, by young Shaul Kaleko, who was among those who took on the mantle of Zionist leadership from the Wilkanski children after they departed for Israel. To him it meant that he would have a free hand in organizing the youth of the shtetl, as he later wrote:

The Rabbi Gaon, Reb Zundl, sat days and nights immersed in his Torah studies and did not persecute us. He was a gentle person who disliked conflict. When Meir Shalom Dubitski came and asked him if, as a God-fearing Jew, he may purchase the shekel *[a fee for membership in the Zionist movement], the Rabbi responded that, as far as the Torah is concerned, it is not a transgression.*[41]

Eishyshok was delighted with his response, and chose to interpret it as his endorsement of Zionism. The fact that his grandchildren were ardent Zionists seemed further confirmation of the rabbi's stand on this vital issue.

Shortly after Reb Zundl's death, however, many of the conflicts that his studied neutrality had kept beneath the surface erupted, as a struggle over his successor split the shtetl into two camps. On one side were Rebbetzin Hendl and followers from the Old Beth Midrash, all of them fervent opponents of the new secular tendencies, who wanted to see the post given to the very conservative Hertz Mendl, the rabbi's son and the dayyan of the shtetl.

The opposition came from men of the New Beth Midrash, led by Meir Kiuchefski and Shael Sonenson, who were also the leaders of the kahal.[42] Their choice was Rabbi Szymen Rozowski from Kapolia (Kopyl), who was both a scholar from one of the great Lithuanian yeshivot (where Sonenson had first made his acquaintance), and an active religious Zionist.

Because Rozowski was willing to embrace certain aspects of modernity, he was someone they hoped would be able to carry on a dialogue with the shtetl's youth, and thereby curb their secular zeal.

Rozowski was the winner in this contest. An ardent Zionist and member of Mizrahi, he was never accepted as the legitimate rabbi by any member of the Hutner family, but was always referred to by them as "the Kappuler rabbi."

For a while after Reb Zundl's death, the rabbi's official residence continued to be occupied by his widow Hendl, his son Hertz Mendl the dayyan, who served as acting rabbi during this interim period, and Hertz Mendl's family. But when the new rabbi was appointed, the Hutners were asked to move, and were offered a number of different accommodations, all of which were rooms in other people's homes. Understandably, they felt they deserved a home to themselves, but none was available, and finally the kahal converted several rooms in the hekdesh (the shelter for the homeless) into a residence, and asked the Hutners to move there — despite the complaints from both Rebbetzin Hendl and her granddaughter Zivia about the terrible injustice of their having to live in such degrading lodgings. One evening as Zivia was milking the cow behind their new home, the candle that had been left in the window to illuminate her path to the cowshed set fire to a curtain, and soon the whole house was in flames. Reb Hertz Mendl risked his life to save his father's precious library, but in vain. The wooden structure burned to the ground, and with it the holy books.

From there the Hutner family moved to a succession of houses in different localities, most of them small and uncomfortable, and so damp and chill as to affect the health of the younger children. Shoshana Hutner Hinski, who caught rheumatic fever during this period, still speaks bitterly about the humiliation and physical distress they suffered in the shtetl that her illustrious grandparents had risked their lives to save.

In 1923 Rebbetzin Hendl decided it was time to leave Eishyshok, where she had spent some of the richest years of her life, to join her other beloved son, Rabbi Yehudah Leib Hutner, an eminent dayyan in Warsaw. There she became a prominent voice in the three courts over which he presided from his home at 24 Franciskanka Street, and a very visible presence in his household, which was filled with the activities of his six children. But she longed to go to Eretz Israel, and during the two years she lived in Warsaw she fought constantly for the necessary emigration certificate. British restrictions on emigration to Palestine, however, excluded the old and those without property, which meant, as one official explained to her, that her chances were nil. Never one to take no for an answer, she bypassed the official and went over his head directly to the British consul in Warsaw.

The meeting between the consul and the rebbetzin was a memorable one. "My dear lady," he

Rabbi Hertz Mendl Hutner (seated), son of Rabbi Zundl and Rebbetzin Hendl, was the shtetl dayyan (judge) from 1921 until his death in October 1934. With him are (top row, right to left) daughters Zipporah Hutner Kravitz, Zivia Hutner Hadash, Shoshana Hutner Hinski, and son Shimon Hutner; (seated) Rebbetzin Kreindl Epstein Hutner, holding granddaughter Shulamit Hadash; Rabbi Hertz Mendl is holding grandson Aaron Hadash. The photo was taken in honor of Zivia's visit with her two children from Eretz Israel in 1933. Zivia's siblings and their widowed mother emigrated to Eretz Israel two years later. PHOTO: REPHAEL LEJBOWICZ. YESC, SH. & Z. HINSKI

addressed her, "I need not ask your age, for it is apparent; but what is the extent of your property?" In her typically terse, pointed style, she replied: "Unlimited faith." She was granted a visa on the spot.

Eventually all the family she left behind would follow her to Eretz Israel, except for her two sons, both of whom died (of natural causes) before they could get there, Yehudah Leib in 1927 and Hertz Mendl in 1935. The first to make the journey, even before Hendl, was Zivia, the oldest daughter of Hertz Mendl. As a member of the halutz (pioneer) movement that trained Eastern European youth for agricultural work in Eretz Israel and an active member of Mizrahi, she was able to get papers for passage. Though her family was reluctant to let a beautiful young girl travel by herself, she convinced them, telling them in words as vivid as Hendl herself might have used that she would be the golden thread to pull all of them to Eretz Israel. And indeed she was soon followed by her brother Zvi Hayyim and her grandmother Hendl.

Luba Hutner Lewin and husband Abraham Lewin. Luba was the daughter of the Zundl Hutners' son Yehuda Leib. She came from Warsaw to live with her grandparents in Eishyshok during World War I. Luba and Abraham were outstanding educators who worked in Eretz Israel and Poland. In the Warsaw Ghetto, Abraham kept a diary, which survives. Luba, Abraham, and daughter Ora apparently perished at Treblinka. PHOTO: ZACHETA, WARSAW. YESC, RUBINSTEIN

Zivia did not escape the turbulence of that troubled time. On August 30, 1929, Arab rioters attacked the Slobodka yeshivah (which had moved from Kovno, Lithuania, to Hebron in Palestine), killing sixty-seven men, women, and children.[43] Zivia was among the sixty wounded. When one of the Arabs checked the bodies for signs of life, slashing each one with a long sabre, Zivia was lucky enough to have only her foot slashed, and she was somehow able to maintain her pretense of being dead. Several years later, in 1933, Zivia returned to Eishyshok for a visit, and soon thereafter arranged for her parents to follow her to Palestine. Though Hertz Mendl's heart gave out in October 1934, on the eve of the family's departure, and he never reached the promised land, Zivia's widowed mother Kreindl and the rest of her siblings were able to emigrate. Thus all the Hutners of Eishyshok were spared the wrath of the Holocaust, as were all the Hutners in Warsaw, except granddaughter Luba.

Luba, too, had gone to Palestine in the 1920s, where she helped to found a school in Kibbutz Ein Harod, but she returned to Warsaw after a bout with malaria. There she married Abraham Lewin, a prominent educator who ran the Yehudia School for girls. Luba joined the staff, and, with what a friend called her "special love of learning and research . . . warm heart, and compassion for her fellow man," became a great asset to the school.[44]

On August 13, 1942, her husband, living in Ghetto Warsaw, made the following entry in his diary:

I will never be consoled as long as I live. If [Luba] had died a natural death, I would not have been so stricken, so broken. But to fall into the hands of such butchers!

She went out in a light dress, without stockings, with my leather briefcase. How tragic it is! A life together of over 21 years (I have been close to her since 1920) has met with such a tragic end.

That day was also their daughter Ora's fifteenth birthday. Luba's husband and daughter also perished. Only the diary survived, their tombstone and epitaph.[45]

All six of Rebbetzin Hendl's other grandchildren made it to Palestine. And there she lived out her last years, her home in Jerusalem a center for the Lithuanian religious elite, just as her previous homes had been. Young and old made the pilgrimage to see the aging Eishyshker Rebbetzin, among them the chief rabbi of Palestine, Rabbi Yitzhak ha-Cohen Kook, father-in-law of Hava, one of her granddaughters from Warsaw, and a great admirer of the rebbetzin's pearls of wisdom. Batia Wilkanski, however, did not visit, though she had preceded Rebbetzin Hendl to Eretz Israel by a number of years. In Eretz Israel, as in Eishyshok, the two women remained worlds apart.

When Hendl Hutner died in 1928, hundreds came to bid her a last farewell. She was buried on the Mount of Olives in Jerusalem, where eventually she would be joined by a number of her grandchildren and their children. Down below in the bustling city of Jerusalem is a large, thriving network of her descendants, many named in memory of her, her husband, her sons, and her daughters-in-law. Among them are prominent rabbis, scholars, teachers, heads of academies, community works volunteers, and the director of the Encyclopedia of the Talmud, her grandson Rabbi Yehoshuah Hutner.

Grandmother Hendl is remembered on many family occasions, and stories are told about her remarkable life. But Hendl Hutner is more than a family legend. She is representative of a group — at least two centuries' worth of Lithuanian rebbetzins — whose lives confound stereotypes.

They used their husbands' status to gain entrée to the intellectual elite, but they secured their place there on their own merits.

Many rebbetzins initiated community projects and could be counted on to be present wherever and whenever they were needed. Some, like Rebbetzin Hendl, went further and played a very public role in their communities, though she was exceptional, indeed extraordinary, in her leadership abilities. Most, however, shared Rebbetzin Hendl's reverence for scholarship, and her commitment to the survival of the Jewish community. Indeed, her belief in the value of perseverance, the faith that long, grinding hours of Torah study would bestow both intellectual and spiritual wealth on even those students who were poor in talent, was integral to the Lithuanian ethos.

A common Yiddish proverb that became popular in Lithuania after the death of the Gaon of Vilna (in 1797) sums it up: "Will nor vestu zain a goen" (With a strong will, a commitment, you too can be a gaon, a genius).

THE LAST RABBI OF EISHYSHOK: RABBI SZYMEN ROZOWSKI

Though he would later become a voice for change, Rabbi Rozowski had a very traditional beginning. Born in 1874 in the impoverished shtetl of Kapolia (Kopyl), Byelorussia, a town with a great love for the Torah and the study of it, Szymen nurtured the typical bright young shtetl boy's ambition to become a Talmudic scholar.[46] He studied at the yeshivah of Volozhin and then, probably after the Russian government forced it to close its doors, continued his studies at the newly founded yeshivah of Slobodka. Both institutions were to leave a profound imprint on his life, on everything from the brilliance of his scholarship to the elegance of his appearance (the latter being a hallmark of both institutions).

His promise was obvious early on, for he had

a keen analytic mind, a quickness of comprehension, and a profound interest in the social and political changes taking place within and beyond the Jewish community. A well-to-do family in Volozhin was quite impressed with young Szymen, and chose him to marry one of their three daughters. (Their wealth enabled them to acquire brilliant scholars for each of their daughters.) As was customary in such circumstances, under the arrangement known as *kest*, the young couple was supported by the bride's parents for the first several years of their marriage, so that the groom could delay getting a job while he pursued his studies.

Miriam Rozowski was a striking contrast to her extraordinary-looking husband: plain, timid, and reserved, utterly lacking in the flamboyance, vivacity, and erudition of rebbetzins like Hendl Hutner and Batia Wilkanski. But she would prove to be an exceptionally loving mother to their three children, Avraham, Uri, and Bat-Sheva, and a hardworking, generous, uncomplaining helpmate to her husband, her door always open to all the people of the communities he served.

The first rabbinic post Rabbi Rozowski was appointed to was in Simonis (Shimantzi) in 1904. From there he was invited to serve as rabbi of his native Kapolia, where his tenure coincided with World War I, the Russian Revolution, the Balfour Declaration, and the Russian civil war. As an ardent Zionist, an active participant in Zionist congresses and Mizrahi conventions, and a frequent contributor to various religious Zionist publications in Poland and Israel, writing about Zionist issues and their relation to Jewish halakha and thought, Rabbi Rozowski became a political target.[47] He was singled out for persecution by the Soviets, and especially by the Yevsektsia (the Jewish section of the propaganda department of the Communist Party, whose generally youthful members tended to be extremely harsh on their fellow Jews). Eventually the Yevsektsia forced him to give up his post in Kapolia, to the great distress of his wife, who never forgot their suffering at the hands of the Revolution, and till her last days feared the vengefulness of the Jewish Communists.

When Eishyshok notables arrived in Kapolia to deliver the contract that would bring Rabbi Rozowski and his wife to their town, the move to a shtetl that was then part of Poland, not the Soviet Union, was a welcome one. And to the kahal members and other community leaders who had favored him over their late rabbi's son, Hertz Mendl Hutner, and who had finally prevailed in the two-year power struggle that had torn the shtetl in two, the dynamic Rabbi Szymen Rozowski seemed like just what they were looking for. They liked his Mizrahi Zionist orientation, his activism, his involvement in community affairs, as well as his scholarship; and they hoped that someone with his qualifications would be able to turn the overwhelming tide of secularism that was sweeping the shtetl youth toward the shores of secular Zionism, socialism, and Communism. Even in his dress he seemed the perfect bridge between old and new, for while embracing many other aspects of modernity, he wore traditional rabbinic garb, consisting of top hat and silk tails.

The challenges faced by Rabbi Rozowski in Eishyshok were typical of those confronting the East European rabbinate in the chaotic post–World War I years. Spreading from the larger cities to the shtetlekh over the course of several decades, the newly emerging political, cultural, and social movements that began to undermine traditional religion at the turn of the century all had their power bases outside the shtetl. This meant that they posed a direct threat to the authority of the rabbi, whose power, both symbolic and real, was completely centered in the community he served.

Communities that lacked a prominent yeshivah or a strong, viable Hasidic movement, both of which served as bulwarks against the forces of secularization, were particularly vulnerable.

Thus Eishyshok, whose yeshivah never really recovered from the Big Fire of 1895, was rapidly turning away from religion and tradition, while Telz and next door Radun, home to the renowned yeshivah founded by the Haffetz Hayyim, remained much more religious shtetlekh.[48] But Rabbi Rozowski had a genuine faith that halakhic Judaism and modernity could coexist, indeed even enhance each other. He saw in religious Zionism and its ideologies the main vehicle for achieving that goal.

Thus he would write in 1936, on the subject of contributing to the Jewish National Fund (a fund for buying land and planting trees in Eretz Israel):

We do not have any other option but to redeem our land with our money, our dedication, and our blood. Every individual who contributes to the Jewish National Fund is redeeming the Land of Israel and fulfilling the commandment.

Therefore my heart rejoices when I see that most honorable people of my town are lovers of Zion and are fulfilling the great mitzvah (precept) by contributing to the Jewish National Fund. My joy is particularly great in these days when the National Fund has introduced a major amendment, that all people who reside on Jewish National Fund lands are obligated to keep the Sabbath. . . .[49]

Despite the opposition his appointment had faced from many of the shtetl's most prominent balebatim, Rabbi Rozowski eventually endeared himself to a wide spectrum of people in the community, for he was someone whom young and old alike could turn to for guidance, and he made a point of maintaining cordial relations with people of many diverse views. Peretz Kaleko-Alufi would remember some sixty years later the advice the rabbi gave him on a long stroll through the Seklutski forest when Peretz discussed his feelings about switching his allegiance from a religious to a secular Zionist group: "As much as tradition depends on people for its survival, people's need for tradition is vital."

And as strong a believer in tradition as Rabbi Rozowski was, he knew when a tradition had run its course. He loved the shtetl, for example, but was particularly eager to encourage emigration to Palestine, even going so far as to pay the fees for the necessary birth certificates out of his own purse. "Hayyiale," he told Hayya Streletski when she went to him for the papers she would need to emigrate, "make aliyah, for there is no future for Jews in Poland." Yet he would prove equally warm, hospitable, and concerned to shoemaker Moshe Szulkin, a non-Zionist affiliated with the political left, when Szulkin went to him for the papers he needed for emigrating to Russia.

Rabbi Rozowski was also careful to live in harmony with his peers in the immediate vicinity, despite religious and political differences that could have divided them. In his youth and during the first years of his rabbinic career, as a member of Hovevei Zion and later of Mizrahi, he had been in the majority of Lithuanian rabbis. But in later years, in the period between the two world wars, as more and more of the rabbis of Poland and Lithuania became disillusioned with Zionism because of its secular tendencies and joined the much more conservative Agudat Israel, he found himself increasingly in the minority. The most prominent local member of Aguda in the area was Radun's Haffetz Hayyim, who had been one of its founders and had opened its first world convention. Out of respect for the Haffetz Hayyim, Rabbi Rozowski often asked his advice, and even showed him articles he had written to get his approval. On one such occasion, when the Haffetz Hayyim voiced no objections to an article expressing Zionist views, Rabbi Rozowski dashed off to Vilna to get it printed in the next day's paper — and was followed shortly thereafter by an emissary with a message for the editor from the Haffetz Hayyim: "I know that in R'Szymen's zealous commitment to his ideals, he may sometimes perceive a non-objection as an endorsement."

Rabbi Rozowski's courtesy toward his peers was not always reciprocated. When his daughter Bat-Sheva married Rabbi David Zalmanovitz in 1932, the wedding was a major event in the shtetl, attended by many prominent rabbis, including a veritable "Who's Who" of the Mizrahi movement in Vilna and the vicinity. Conspicuously absent, however, were the Haffetz Hayyim and all the other Aguda rabbis and academy heads, who had declined the invitation. Yet Rabbi Rozowski, with his cheerful disposition, overlooked the slight, and would go on to attend many functions and weddings where he was ever more frequently in the minority. Chaim Grade immortalized one of these events, the wedding of the daughter of the rabbi of Olkenik, in a poem containing a stanza dedicated to Rabbi Rozowski.[50]

Dancing in the circle is the Eishyshker of the Mizrahim,
Agudaniks besiege him in a wreath,
"And all shall unite," the young men tease him
"In the party of Aguda"
But the elder rabbi revels in the dance with all his breath.[51]

Rabbi Rozowski's tolerance of difference extended to his children, too, as did his wife's, even though Uri and Avraham had moved to the leftist, secular end of the Zionist spectrum, and both did on occasion cause their parents embarrassment with their embrace of modern ways. In many other families, however, political and religious differences divided the generations.

The rabbi's son Avraham Rozowski lived with his wife and children in Eishyshok, where his business as an insurance agent took him to many non-Jewish homes. Since it was common for a variety of Jewish craftsmen, peddlers, and merchants to spend some time in Christian and Muslim (Tatar) homes in the course of doing business, non-Jews had become familiar with the essentials of Jewish dietary laws, and some kept a "Jewish pot" exclusively for the boiling of potatoes that would be served to their guests. They even knew that by Jewish law the Jew must kindle the fire under his own potato pot. Imagine, then, the scandal when the rabbi's son went to the home of some gentile peasants and, instead of eating from the Jewish potato pot, insisted on eating food cooked in the regular household pots. The woman of the house was stunned when she related this scandalous story about the rabbi's son to a Jewish friend. The friend tried to calm her, describing to her the process of secularization that was occurring in the shtetl and the decline of religious observance among the young. But the peasant woman would not hear of such a thing, not about the rabbi's son. Finally another Jew from the shtetl was able to placate the anxious woman. He told her that when the rabbi's son ate food from regular pots, he acted upon doctor's orders, for there was a kind of curative that could be found only in food cooked in non-Jewish pots. She was pleased with this explanation and reassured that, in giving Avraham nonkosher food, she had not sinned before either her own Lord or that of the rabbi's son.

This story, like most others about events that occurred in the shtetl, circulated for some time, being told and retold in endless variations with numerous embellishments. The rebbetzin was not spared the telling. Far from it. She heard it many times, especially from those belonging to the camp that had opposed her husband's appointment. But as always, when it came to her children, she preferred to dwell on their virtues, not their shortcomings, and in the "Jewish pot scandal" she saw only signs of her son's honesty, and his popularity among Jews and gentiles alike.

The rabbi's other son, Uri Rozowski, an ardent Zionist and Hebraist who was one of Eishyshok's political activists, inherited his father's good looks, his love of people, and his strong social and political concerns — but not his political views. He too caused his parents problems, despite his being extremely sensitive to the fact that he was "the rabbi's son" and therefore needed to be constantly on guard to spare his parents any embarrassment. With him as with Avraham, his mother deflected all criticism. Thus when Uri and his wife Fania and their two children made a family visit to Eishyshok in the summer of 1939, Uri's first trip back since emigrating to Palestine several years before, the rebbetzin overlooked many a snide remark from members of the Old Beth Midrash about Fania's immodest style of dress. Defending her daughter-in-law, she told people that her son and his family had brought with them to Eishyshok the sunshine of the Holy Land, and therefore dressed accordingly — in shorts. Although the youth of the shtetl were enchanted by the young Rozowski family, and inspired by their Zionist idealism, the elders clucked disapprovingly at everything from their clothes to the informality of their speech and their behavior.

Bat-Sheva, the youngest of Szymen and Miriam Rozowski's children, was a well-educated young woman who in matters of religion and politics followed in her parents' footsteps. But even she and her husband were not immune to the gossipy criticism directed at the rabbi's household. David Zalmanovitz, the bridegroom her parents had chosen for her, was a young rabbi who had had a secular education as well as the traditional one — cause enough for comment. At their wedding the amiable young husband was told by one of Rabbi Rozowski's opponents that love must indeed be blind, for he had failed to notice the hair on his bride's face, or perhaps he didn't mind since it would simply fit in with his theories about evolution and the origin of the species. There was a long silence, and then Reb Dovid'l, as he was known in the shtetl, replied: "Hair is always associated with beauty in a woman. The more beautiful the woman, the more hair she has. As to evolution," he continued, the snide allusion to his secular education not having been lost on him, "some people's level of intelligence may indeed be an additional proof for those who believe in Darwin's theory."

Until R'Dovid'l accepted a rabbinic post in a shtetl near Bialystok, he served as his father-in-law's assistant, helping him in what was the main objective of Rabbi Rozowski's service in Eishyshok: educating the young. For it was through a return to the best aspects of a more traditional religious education that Rabbi Rozowski intended to halt the process of secularization, just as changes in education had been partly responsible for setting that process in motion in the first place.

By the time of Rabbi Rozowski's arrival in Eishyshok, the main educational institution was a coed Hebrew day school. Naturally the Hebrew-school curriculum reflected the educational philosophy of its founders, who were secular Zionists. After a long struggle, however, Rabbi Rozowski reached a compromise with the principal of the school, Moshe Yaakov Botwinik, and the Parents' Board of Education, under which a certain amount of religious subject matter would be included and would be taught according to the curriculum developed by the educational network of the religious Zionists. Rabbi Rozowski also saw to it that the boys wore hats during classes, and each schoolday began with morning prayers. Eventually a student synagogue with a Holy Ark was constructed.

Rabbi Rozowski made his presence felt in the school in many other, much more immediate ways. Each Thursday, the traditional testing day in the heder, the rabbi came and quizzed the children in the weekly portion, always emphasizing the biblical passages associated with the

Land of Israel. He attended Rosh Hodesh celebrations at the beginning of each month, and school performances. He even came to the kindergarten plays, where he sat in the front row, beaming with satisfaction, as he listened to the young tots speaking and singing in Hebrew.

The 1920s and '30s were extremely eventful years for the Rozowskis. The rabbi threw himself into the task of becoming a leader who could guide the shtetl through a time of rapid transitions. He and his wife made all the people of the shtetl welcome in their home, the official rabbi's residence, which had been remodeled after their arrival in Eishyshok. A constant stream of visitors, not just townspeople but visiting Mizrahi party members and teachers, as well as guests from Palestine and America, flowed through their comfortable, spacious rooms. Miriam Rozowski was always there, serving tea from her shining samovar, dishing out cakes, fruits, varenie, and even special delicacies for the children. Though she was a plain woman, in both her appearance and her taste, which elicited a lot of criticism in the fashion-conscious shtetl of those years, her unassuming manner made everyone comfortable.

The accomplishments of previous years notwithstanding, both the rabbi and the rebbetzin would display their finest qualities in the two years following the outbreak of World War II in September 1939. The preceding summer, when their son Uri had been visiting from Palestine, and it was clear that war was imminent, he had pleaded with them to emigrate, but to no avail. Rabbi Rozowski would not abandon his community.

In October 1939, after a brief takeover by the Soviet Union, Lithuania, including the area around Vilna, became an independent nation, which meant that Eishyshok was now under Lithuanian rule. Because of Eishyshok's location — it was a mere forty-mile bus ride away from Vilna and all the consulates and the many Zionist, socialist, and Communist political groups headquartered there, and it was practically on the border with the USSR, the Republic of Byelorussia being only a few miles away — it became a magnet for Jewish refugees seeking to escape Hitler, a strategic point on the route to freedom.

To accommodate the 15,000 refugees who would eventually make their way through Eishyshok, Rabbi Rozowski and the shtetl leadership organized a Refugee Committee, of which he was the head.[52] The committee saw to it that the 3,500 residents of Eishyshok were able to give efficient, effective aid to the thousands of people in need of food and shelter.

Rabbi Rozowski also saw to it that when nearly two hundred students from the Radun yeshivah arrived seeking safe haven in Eishyshok, they and the cartloads of holy Torah scrolls they brought with them were made welcome. Indeed, he was overjoyed to have them, for their presence made Eishyshok a center of Torah learning once again.

Although the rebbetzin did not herself assume any position of leadership, she worked alongside the other shtetl women in the soup kitchen, polished the muddy boots of refugees who had been smuggled over the marshy border, delivered food, and assisted wherever she was needed. The photographer Ben Zion Szrejder, who worked in Alte Katz's photo studio, snapped a picture of Miriam Rozowski in those days, which he displayed in a showcase in front of Alte Katz's house on the marketplace. There she was, plainly dressed as always, seated next to a coachman in a horse-drawn wagon filled with coal that she was delivering to the soup kitchen. Some praised the picture; others wanted a more regal-looking rebbetzin.

In 1940, during another of Eishyshok's short-lived Soviet occupations, the local Revolutionary Committee, which in Eishyshok consisted of Jewish Communists, including Ruvke Boyarski, known as "di bulbichke" (the potato), Luba Ginunski, and Hayyim Shuster, ousted the rabbi and his family from their comfortable home and installed a poor family with eight children in their place. Since they deemed the rabbi a prime member of the exploiting class, they persecuted him while sparing the local Catholic priest a similar indignity, even though he occupied a much more spacious home.[53]

From their new home, a very humble residence, the rabbi and rebbetzin continued to work for the well-being of the people of Eishyshok. Bearing her hardships in silence, Miriam served tea to the many who came to their home for comfort and advice. And Rabbi Rozowski did what he could to sustain the shtetl's religious institutions and activities, although they had to go underground to avoid the wrath of the Jewish Communists. He even organized clandestine classes after they forced the closing of the Hebrew day school. As a large segment of European Jewry faced the German executioner, Rabbi Rozowski was frantically trying to salvage some fragments of a traditional Jewish life from the zealous Russification process the Communists were forcing on Eishyshok.

When the Germans entered Eishyshok on June 23, 1941, the sixty-seven-year-old rabbi saw in the invasion yet another challenge, but was hopeful that the shtetl could weather this one too. His hopes were short-lived. Indeed, Rabbi Rozowski was among the first to understand that total destruction was near.

To aid them in their plans, the Germans turned to the shtetl's traditional leadership. Once more the rabbi was to bear the brunt of the responsibility. A Nazi official named Webber charged Rabbi Rozowski with the task of establishing a Judenrat, a council of Jewish residents forced to assist the Germans. (The term *Judenrat* was not used by the Eishyshkians themselves, since to them it implied "collaborator." Their own term was *Juden Kommittet.*) When the rabbi assembled all the community leaders from the pre-Soviet days, they all refused to serve, until lots were cast and twelve men were appointed. The main function of the Kommittet was to provide the Germans with supplies and carry out their orders. At the Germans' behest, they not only requisitioned food and other necessities, they confiscated all gold, silver, precious stones, furs, linen, radios, light bulbs, and medical supplies possessed by the Jews in the shtetl.

The rabbi and his fellow Kommittet members were singled out for especially cruel abuse, torture, and humiliation by the Nazis. A variety of grotesque episodes ensued, including one in which German dogs chased them into the river, fully clothed, after which they were forced to roll down the main highway of the shtetl.

The synagogue and the two batei midrash were also targets. Stripped of all their silver, gold, and brass candelabras, the ancient candlesticks, the exquisite Ark curtains, and all the furniture, they were turned into stables for the German horses.

Twice during those days, Rabbi Rozowski convened clandestine meetings of the traditional shtetl leadership. The first meeting took place sometime in August, after the rabbi learned that many Eishyshkians were hiding their valuables with local Christians. "You are turning the goyim [gentiles] into your enemies. They will hasten your death so that they may inherit your property," he warned. But his warning was not heeded and the practice continued, for people relied on the hope that their hidden goods would help them rebuild their lives in the postwar years.

The second meeting took place on September 11, 1941, after the rabbi dispatched a gentile messenger to Aran (Varena) to check the validity of rumors saying that the Jewish community there had been slaughtered.[54] Upon his return, the messenger reported that the streets of Aran were strewn with the bodies of murdered Jews. It was clear to the rabbi that Eishyshok would be next on the Einsatzgruppen hit list, as his words to the assembled leaders reveal: "Jews, you can see that our end is hastily nearing. God did not want our rescue. Our fate is sealed and we have to accept it! But if we must die, let us die with honor. Let us not offer our throats to the slaughter like sheep. With the money still left in our hands, which is otherwise useless, let us buy ammunition. Let us defend ourselves until our last breath. Let us not go like sheep to the slaughter. 'Let me die with the Philistines.'"[55]

Opinion was divided about the rabbi's call to arms. Ephraim Karnowski, a member of the Juden Kommittet and the prewar head of the kehilah, supported it. But one of the most affluent members of the kehilah, R. Yossl Weidenberg, vehemently opposed it, warning that it would only result in the total destruction of the shtetl. He took Karnowski to task for his militant stand, and accused him, as a non-native who was a relative newcomer to Eishyshok, of having no understanding of the shtetl's traditional relations with the gentile world. The Germans and their Polish and Lithuanian collaborators were only after Jewish money, he insisted. The meeting was dispersed with no consensus having been reached.

Rabbi Rozowski's stand on Jewish armed resistance was a most unusual one for the time. Having sensed that the Germans intended the total annihilation of all Jews under their occupation, he did not share the fear that arming the community would provide the Germans with a pretext for something they would otherwise not have done, nor did he feel there were any other options that could be explored.[56] Though it was only the summer of 1941, and the true extent of the Germans' genocidal plans had not been revealed, he felt certain that all the Jews of Eishyshok would die, and he saw armed resistance as the only honorable death.

On the eve of Rosh Hashanah 5702 (1941), Rabbi Rozowski and the rest of the shtetl Jews were herded into the synagogue and the batei midrash, where they were joined in their last hours by Jews from Olkenik and its vicinity. After three days of torture, they were herded to the Horse Market, and from there marched in groups to their final destination.

At the Horse Market, the rabbi led his congregation and their neighbors from Olkenik in the last prayer, the Vidduy Gadol (confession of the dying). He was joined in his prayer by Rabbi Waldshan of Olkenik, at whose daughter's wedding he had once danced with such joy, by Waldshan's younger son-in-law, Reb Hayyim Berger, and by the Eishyshker hazzan, Moshe Tobolski. Then they set out on their death march.

Dressed in his black silk coat and his top hat, Rabbi Rozowski led the procession, in company with the handsome Tobolski, who was holding the holy Torah scrolls. By order of Ostrauskas, the Lithuanian chief of police who carried out the German orders for the massacre of the Jews, the rabbi was kept alive until the last member of his beloved shtetl was murdered, including his son Avraham, his son's wife and children, and his own wife. He was then buried alive.[57]

On the 26th of September, 1941, all was quiet in Eishyshok, but for one drunken peasant who staggered about the center of the marketplace, dressed in Rabbi Szymen Rozowski's top hat and his long black coat, holding the rabbi's cane in one hand, a bottle of vodka in the other, and screaming in Yiddish, with uncontrolled glee, "Yidden, in shul arain!" (Jews, go to shul!)

For the drunken Pole, the rabbi and the synagogue were the very symbols of Judaism, and now both were destroyed.

THE RABBINATE IN TRANSITION

What sort of institution the East European rabbinate would have evolved into during the latter part of the twentieth century and beyond we shall never know. The rabbinate was blamed, in

Eishyshok as elsewhere, for all the imperfections and shortcomings within the Jewish community, but in the years after World War I certain changes were beginning to be made, as exemplified by Rabbi Szymen Rozowski's work in Eishyshok. The Holocaust put a permanent end to the process of change he and his supporters had initiated.

Still, we can see in him, and in many of the rabbis who managed to emigrate before the Holocaust, and in their descendants, intimations of where the rabbinate was headed. Indeed, we need only look at the modern American Orthodox rabbi. With his active involvement in the social, political, and intellectual life of his community, and his position not just as scholar but as veritable social worker and psychotherapist to his congregation, he is heir to the tradition that the East European shtetl rabbis were in the process of reshaping before the Holocaust.

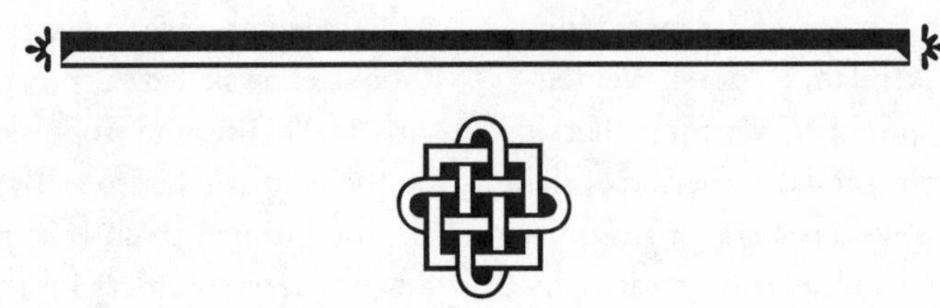

SOCIAL AND POLITICAL ACTIVISTS IN CLOSE TOUCH WITH THE NEEDS AND YEARNINGS of the people among whom they live — perhaps no group better exemplified that conception of the role of the rabbi than the maggid, whose name means, literally, "to preach," "to say." And indeed the maggidim very often did serve as the voice of the people.

The institution of the maggid, the scholar/preacher/rabbi, has existed since antiquity, and by the seventeenth century had become so well established in Germany and Eastern Europe that there were then two kinds of maggidim: stationary and itinerant. The stationary maggid was often appointed by the community, in which case he bore the title *Maggid Meisharim,* the Preacher of the Righteous, in reference to the biblical verse "Speaking the truth and declaring what is right."[1] He was also known as the "shtetl maggid," or town preacher, and his salary was paid out of the korobka, like that of the other community-employed clergy. His major function was to preach, and thereby to enlighten, encourage, instruct, admonish, and lift up his audience. Unlike other rabbis, he did not offer advice on halakhic issues; nor did he usually perform weddings, bar mitzvahs, or other life ceremonies. But he did give eulogies in honor of distinguished rabbis and scholars, whose lives were the occasion for many of his most penetrating observations about morality and spirituality. Moral rather than legal issues were his main subject.

Generally it was only the larger communities such as Vilna, which was known for its outstanding maggidim, that could afford to have their own town preachers. This was so particularly after the tzarist government's May Laws of 1882, which had such a devastating economic effect on Eastern European Jewry. Communities newly impoverished by that round of anti-Semitic legislation often had to cut back on the number of clergy they employed, and the maggidim were often let go during these years. But during better times, even some of the smaller communities could afford to engage them. Thus, during the heyday of its Kibbutz ha-Prushim yeshivah, even little Eishyshok had its own maggidim, who were among the finest in Lithuania.

The other kind of maggid, the itinerant preacher, was referred to by the people as a *Pechotni,* or infantry, maggid, a reference to one of the infantry divisions of the tzarist army. He was not affiliated with a particular town but

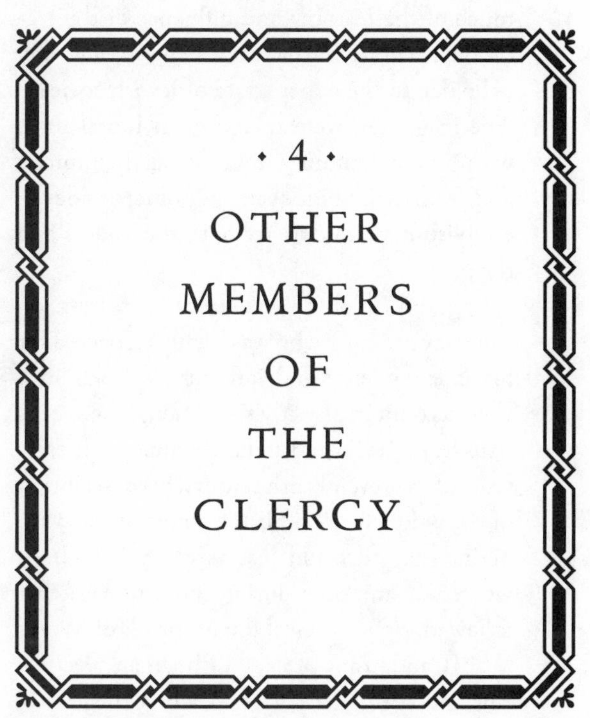

THE MAGGID: VOICE OF THE PEOPLE

BEING THE DAUGHTER OF A GREAT MAGGID WAS LIKE BEING PART OF THE DIRECT LINE OF COMMUNICATION BETWEEN THE ALMIGHTY GOD AND ORDINARY PEOPLE.

Rachel Shekowitski Hadash

simply made rounds, from one shtetl to another and even to remote rural communities, delivering his sermons wherever he went, and earning a living from the donations of those who came to hear him.

Some historians view the maggidim, particularly the itinerant ones, who drew no salary and had no community position to protect, as a kind of non-establishment intelligentsia, having much of the learning and influence of the traditional scholar but without being in any way beholden to the upper strata of Jewish society.[2] The maggidim were thus a great moral force within the community, free to speak their minds and, from their unique vantage point outside the establishment, to criticize both the leaders and the people.

Ephraim Shlomo ben Aaron Luntschitz, an itinerant preacher who was highly respected for his independence and integrity, left behind a vivid account of his activities. Though he speaks to us from the Poland and Lithuania of the early years of the seventeenth century, his description of the uniquely nonaffiliated status of the wandering maggid could just as easily have been written at any time during the centuries that followed, right up until the outbreak of World War II, and in any place — Lithuania, Palestine, England, the United States — where the Jews of Lithuania settled, bringing their traditions with them.[3]

In my later years, yielding to the importunities of prominent men, I preached in Lublin, especially during the great fairs, where Jewish leaders as well as large masses of the people gathered. There I used to express myself quite freely on the shortcomings of the rabbis as well as of the laity, undeterred by any consideration or fear. This boldness, naturally enough, created for me numerous enemies who heaped slander upon my name and otherwise persecuted me. Of course I could well have avoided all this wrath and uproar had I been willing to be more restrained in my utterances, or were I more chary of my personal honor. But I had long ago resolved to put the honor of God above my own.[4]

Such boldness of speech and independence of spirit were sometimes so radical that they could find expression only in various reformist and revolutionary movements, such as Hasidism and Zionism or even Communism. Maggidim such as Dov Baer (1707–1772), the great maggid of Mezrich, were among the leaders of the Hasidic movement. Hayyim Zundel Maccoby (1858–1916), known as "the Zionist Preacher," was responsible for the establishment of about three hundred Zionist societies throughout the Pale of Settlement — his brand of Zionism being religious, as opposed to Theodor Herzl's more secular version.[5] And then there was Rabbi Hayyim Pesachowitz (1877–1956), an alumnus of the Eishyshok yeshivah, who was known as the "Red Maggid of Minsk" because of his Communist sympathies. The Red Maggid eventually emigrated to Palestine in 1931, but he remained a lifelong Communist, true to his ideals to the end.[6]

Even the most outspoken maggid had a respected place within the traditional confines of the community, where he was allowed unrestricted freedom of speech and movement. Acting as a sort of gadfly, he carried on dialogues with all factions of society, from the Gaon of Vilna (who was a great admirer of the maggid of Dubno, Yaakov ben Wolf Kranz [1741–1804]), to Reb Shaye Ginunski, a twentieth-century Eishyshkian from the artisan class who never missed an opportunity to engage in conversation with any maggid he encountered.

Because of their wanderings, the maggidim were intimately acquainted with every aspect of Jewish life throughout a far-flung network of shtetlekh, and were involved with the people of these communities not just as observers, but as human beings who cared deeply about the fate of their fellow Jews. Their sermons included parables, fables, stories, and folkloristic material taken directly from the people they encountered, which makes them an excellent source of information about Jewish life in Eastern Europe over a period of several centuries.[7] And just as the maggidim got to know the people on their rounds, so the people became familiar with the details of the maggidim's lives and ideologies. The interactions between the maggid and the people he encountered on his journeys were of such interest to both parties that they were the subject of a special genre of storytelling. The following is a popular tale from that genre:

There once was a maggid who always traveled from shtetl to shtetl with the same coachman. Since the maggid used to practice his sermons aloud, the coachman eventually became familiar with his entire repertory. One day the maggid suggested that he and the coachman exchange roles. When they arrived at a nearby shtetl, it was the coachman who mounted the bimah, dressed in the maggid's clothes, to deliver the sermon, while the maggid stood near the door of the beth midrash, the coachman's whip in his hand and the coachman's clothes on his back. The coachman delivered a very fine sermon which pleased the audience greatly. At the conclusion of the sermon, a young man approached the bimah and addressed a scholarly question to the maggid, who was quick to respond: "Such an easy question even my coachman can answer," he said, motioning to the "coachman" to approach the bimah.

The story is a tribute both to the maggid for his display of trust in a mere coachman, member of one of the lowest echelons of shtetl society, and to the coachman himself, who, though a simple man, rose to the occasion when given the chance and displayed considerable wit, ability, and presence of mind. Stories in praise of the simple man were one of the maggid's staples, and a healthy antidote to the class consciousness of the society he lived in.

A typical well-structured sermon would be a complex fabric of anecdote, parable, epigram, and folklore, all woven together in a triumph of homiletic artistry. In constructing these sermons, the maggid drew upon the vast treasury of Jewish halakhic and kabbalistic material, combining it with stories that could be understood by any layperson or child. Alternating between words of comfort and stern reproof, hope and admonition, his sermons both encouraged and terrified the listeners, whipping them into an emotional frenzy. Generally the first response heard would be the faint, hushed weeping of the women in their gallery, gradually rising to a loud sobbing. Once it filtered down to the main sanctuary, it would swell with the uncontrolled sobbing of many of the men and children, and continue to rise and fall as the subject of the sermon warranted, until the end was reached and the maggid concluded with the traditional prayer of the maggidim, "And a redeemer shall come to Zion, speedily, in our days, Amen."

In the twentieth century, maggidim frequently delivered eulogies in honor of various Zionist activists and sympathizers: settlers in Palestine who had been murdered by Arabs, victims of pogroms who had longed to make aliyah but had never gotten the chance, and of course the leaders of the movement. Rivka Remz recalled that her first exposure to Zionism was a maggid's eulogy in the crowded Old Beth Midrash of Eishyshok. It was 1904; the eulogy was in memory of Theodor Herzl. Eighty-five years later, the mere sight of a photograph of Herzl could still bring back to her the magic chant of the maggid's voice, and with it the tears she had shed so freely that day.

In general the goal of the maggid as he preached his sermons was to reach as many people as possible, quickening their religious and spiritual receptivity and awakening in them an active commitment to improve the imperfect present. But the maggid was also sometimes more specific, in both his choice of subject matter and his intended audience.

Women's issues were a frequent topic, since women made up a significant portion of the audience for these sermons and the maggidim were careful to pay them special attention. Women were rarely addressed or included as equal participants in the life of the community, so they looked forward to the coming of a maggid with particular excitement. Women also responded enthusiastically to the sheer melodrama of the sermons which, like the Greek tragedies of old, seemed to offer a cathartic release for pent-up emotions. At times the uncontrolled sobbing associated with these events may have had less to do with the actual subject matter of the sermon than with the fact that it was one of the few occasions in shtetl life when such uninhibited emotionalism was sanctioned, indeed welcomed, as an enhancement of the general atmosphere.

The dedication of the Jewish mother to her children's education and their physical well-being was one subject much favored by the maggidim; the suffering of poor widows and of orphan brides was another. During the 1890s the rising tide of emigration from the Pale of Settlement spawned a new thematic development in the sermons of the maggid: the plight of the agunot, women deserted by husbands who had gone in search of a new life and had presumably settled abroad, whereabouts unknown, usually somewhere in America. And with the spread of various political movements at the turn of the twentieth century, the maggidim took as one of their main subjects the problem of young Jewish women who were leaving their sheltered, pious domestic routines for the excitement of dedicating themselves to furthering socialism or Zionism or some other revolutionary belief. Though these sermons spoke very directly to real issues confronted by the women of the shtetl, they were usually cloaked in parable, metaphor, allegory, and a broad spectrum of literary and scholarly allusions.

THE MAGGID AND EISHYSHOK

When a maggid was due to arrive in Eishyshok, a few days prior to the event an announcement was made from the bimah in each of the shtetl's prayer quorums, and handwritten notices were posted in the polesh of the shul and the two batei midrash. Like all community-sponsored events in Eishyshok, the maggid's sermon would be preached in the Old Beth Midrash — unless the maggid was known for socialist, Zionist, or other unorthodox views, or had some other kind of blemish on his reputation, in which case he was assigned to the New Beth Midrash.

Though these restrictions were relaxed at the start of the twentieth century, as late as the 1890s they were to be the cause of a major uproar in the shtetl, based, as it happened, on a complete misunderstanding. A very prominent maggid arrived in Eishyshok one day and, to his astonishment, was directed to the New Beth Midrash. Highly insulted, not to mention mystified as to the reason for such an insult, he refused to deliver his sermon. Only later was the mystery unraveled. It turned out that a very conservative member of the kahal had misread the announcement, in which the maggid was touted as "excellent." In Hebrew the words *excellent* and *from Zion* are spelled similarly, the only difference being in pronunciation. As a staunch opponent of the Enlightenment and of Zionism, but not much of a Hebraist, the kahal member had concluded that the maggid was a Zionist and therefore not suitable for an Old Beth Midrash audience.

Like all shtetl mishaps, this one lived on for years in the many stories told about it. Particularly pleased to recount and relive those stories were certain yeshivah students who were known for their Zionist activities and had as a result been blacklisted by the same kahal member responsible for the terrible misunderstanding.

Upon the arrival of a favorite maggid, the entire community would flock to the Old (or

New) Beth Midrash. The sanctuary, the women's gallery,* and even the polesh would be filled to capacity, and many of the children could be squeezed in only by perching them on window-sills or, if necessary, on top of the oven.

If his visit fell during the summer, the maggid delivered his sermon in the synagogue, from the bimah near the Holy Ark. Bedecked in his prayer shawl, he would begin by mounting the bimah, opening the Holy Ark, and burying his head among the sacred scrolls, at which time a fearful silence would descend upon and grip each person in the audience. From out of this silence the sobs of the maggid at the Holy Ark would ascend heavenward, as he pleaded with God to have mercy on His children and redeem them from their sufferings. He would then turn to the audience, his face awash in tears, and, in that special heart-rending East European maggid chant that moved and touched the very foundations of the soul, would set about preaching his sermon.

Though the sermons were almost always highly emotional, for sheer intensity nothing matched the performance of a maggid delivering a eulogy. The fire and brimstone he conjured up rained down on his listeners' heads as he stirred them to new frenzies of soul-searching and repentance. Meir Wilkanski describes one such eulogy, delivered on the occasion of the death of a prominent rabbi in the closing decades of the nineteenth century, by a maggid making his first appearance in Eishyshok:

The beth midrash filled up to capacity. On the bimah near the Holy Ark, in his prayer shawl, stood the unknown maggid. The candles in the House of God dimmed. The maggid turned to the right and to the left, addressing his audience, and from time to time raised his eyes to heaven. Then he turned to the Ark and opened it.

"Torah, Torah, gird yourself in sackcloth, mourn like a virgin for the husband of her youth! Alas! the zaddik [pious one] has passed away. Because of man's iniquity, and the horrors that will henceforth be the lot of the world and of Israel, the righteous man has died, that he might be spared such horrors. God did not want the zaddik to witness the disaster and feel compelled to intercede on behalf of the wicked, as Abraham did for Sodom and Gomorrah, so he has taken the zaddik away.

"Who will pray for us?

"Who will ask mercy for us?

"Let us search our souls.

"Let us sink to the ground in silence.

"Like mourners we will tear our clothing! Beat our breasts! and weep like jackals.

"A person must shed tears on the death of a scholar taken by God.

"Woe unto those whose eyes remain dry and cannot shed tears!"

. . . . Dogs were barking outside. Was the angel of death coming to town? God, are you about to bring the end upon the chosen people of Israel? Tears rolled down cheeks and onto the floor. A broken heart lamented in pain and the entire House of God cried vociferously.[8]

These itinerant preachers proved adept at updating their material as the eras passed, and thus could count on attracting a large crowd, even in the twentieth century, when many of the younger people were turning away from the shulhoyf, being more interested in political movements and current events than in religion. The last maggid to appear in Eishyshok delivered his sermon on the eve of the High Holidays of 1940, when the shtetl was under Communist occupation. Using the biblical story of Jonah and the whale, always a great favorite, he cleverly adapted its universal message to the concerns of a particular time and place, complete with references to local characters. In the words of a woman who

*In some communities in the twentieth century, women dared to stand at the entrance to the sanctuary when space was tight.

heard it firsthand, the sermon went something like this:

A little-known fact about this famous episode is that Jonah was not alone in the belly of the big fish. With him was a young, talkative woman wearing red boots and a red scarf to match. Just like Jonah, she too was spewed out onto dry land by the fish, but for different reasons. In her case it was not prayer that resulted in her ejection, for unlike Jonah she did not spend her time in the belly of the fish praying; rather, it was that the fish could no longer tolerate the painful stab of her boots in his ribs or the sound of her marathon lecturing sessions.

Once arrived in Nineveh, the woman in the red boots delivered long speeches about the differences between various classes of people, while by contrast Jonah told the King and the people that they were all the children of one man and one God and should therefore repent and stop oppressing their own brothers and sisters.

The King of Nineveh, though a gentile, listened to Jonah and he and his people repented and were saved. Disappointed, the woman in the red boots made her way back to her comrades, whom she found in great danger from a nearby tribe of cannibals. One day, when the cannibals nearly took over the town, all of the woman's comrades hastily boarded their vehicles and fled. The woman in the red boots tried to find a place on one of the eastward-bound vehicles, but was pushed aside and told, "There is no place for you among us. You are a Jewess and must pray to your own God to save you." Then they sped away, leaving behind the woman in the red boots.

To all those assembled in the Old Beth Midrash that evening, the meaning of this allegory was completely clear, for the woman in red boots was their own Luba Ginunski, who was one of the highest-ranking Communists in the vicinity.

While the names differed from locale to locale— it was Luba Ginunski in Eishyshok, Esther Frumkin in Minsk, and so forth — the phenomenon of the young, bright, idealistic Jewish woman playing an active role in the Communist Party was widespread, and the maggid might well have delivered a similar sermon in many places. But in the outcome of this particular case, history proved more creative than even the fertile imagination of the maggid, ringing its own strange variations on the theme of the Jewess who rejects her heritage.

Luba, the woman who was the protagonist of the last maggid's sermon to be given in Eishyshok, did indeed escape the advancing German troops, on her own, and made her way to Russia. After much suffering there, she had a chance encounter on a train with a young Austrian Jewish refugee from a Hasidic family and fell in love. When the war ended they settled in Israel, where Luba became an ardent Zionist and dedicated her life to helping impoverished immigrants from Asia. So her story in its final version is that of a young Jewish woman swept away by the fierce storms of the twentieth century who somehow reaches safe shores and finds her way back to the people she'd renounced. But there is no longer a beth midrash in Eishyshok where a wandering maggid might update Luba's story and build a new parable around its unforeseeable, ironic ending. Her pious Uncle Shaye, who never missed a chance to hear a maggid in the Old Beth Midrash, was murdered by the Nazis in his beloved Eishyshok, as was her younger brother Moshe. Her older brother Gedalia, once a hazzan in the New Beth Midrash, was murdered in Auschwitz. Thus all that is left is an orphaned allegory by an East European maggid who was never to learn the true ending of his tale.

THE LAST MAGGID OF MINSK: A MAN OF EISHYSHOK

"Rabbi Benyamin Ha-Cohen Shekowitski, The Maggid of Minsk, A Man of Eishyshok"— so read the letterhead of the last town preacher of Minsk, who exemplified in his life and his work the best of the East European preacher, with all the fire and compassion and commitment to public welfare that we associate with that class of men. Born in 1871 or 1872, he may also serve as an exemplary twentieth-century maggid, his life spanning the turbulence of the tzarist regime in Russia, the Kishinev pogrom of 1903, the Beilis blood-libel case of 1911, World War I, the Russian Revolution, the Russian civil war, the terrors of the Yevsektsia, and finally the travails of emigration to Palestine and life in Tel Aviv under the British Mandate.

Reb Benyamin Shekowitski was the son of Mordekhai Yossef Shekowitski of Eishyshok and a woman from the Dolinski family of next-door Radun. From his brief stays on the farm leased by his father's family, Reb Benyamin acquired a great love of gardening and the outdoors, while from his mother, a magnificent storyteller, he received his great gift of oratory.

His vocation was evident early on. Even as a small child in heder he showed his love of preaching. Each night as the other boys were leaving for home, in the dim light of the beth midrash he would mount the bimah to preach to an audience of empty lecterns and benches. By the age of nine he had left home to study at the famous Ramailes yeshivah in Vilna.[9] There his early practice sessions seem to have paid off, for by the time he was seventeen he had made a reputation for himself as an excellent preacher and teacher, even in a town filled with brilliant, gifted young men.

Rabbi Benyamin Ha-Cohen Shekowitski (1871–1938), one of the leading maggidim of Eastern Europe, with his wife and four of his five children: (right to left) his wife; daughter Rina Shekowitski Leibowitz; son Aaron; and daughters Rachel Shekowitski Hadash and Sarah Shekowitski Hazzan. The photo was taken in Minsk in honor of Aaron's departure for Eretz Israel in 1927. Some of the family emigrated to Eretz Israel, others to England and the United States.

By his early twenties Shekowitski's fame had spread beyond Vilna, and he was being invited to preach and deliver eulogies in prominent communities all over Lithuania and White Russia. His masterly command of language, his melodious maggid delivery, and his sincere commitment to social justice made him a memorable speaker. And his stirring delivery was only enhanced by his striking appearance, for he was a tall, handsome man with burning eyes above a jet-black beard. Zalman Shazar, third president of the State of Israel, could still recall, decades after the event, the effect of one of Reb Benyamin Shekowitski's eulogies, delivered on the occasion of the passing of one of the Grand Rabbis of Israel, when Shazar himself was but a child.

Each time I think back on it, the melody in which he spoke swells up in my heart, quivers, and brings back to life an entire bygone world . . .

The synagogue was filled with an overflow crowd. On the bimah stood a bearded man, wrapped in a prayer shawl, his voice that of a lion, his eyes two streams of water. In what followed, story was linked to story, parable gave rise to parable, sayings of renowned personalities alternated with folkish wisdom that would bear repetition for many years to come, and all was delivered in language that was picturesque and well seasoned with smatterings of Russian.

In his commanding, fatherly tone the Maggid begged the congregation, in the name of the deceased, to abandon their sinful ways, to change their behavior, and to purify their thoughts so that the soul of the dead man could approach the Heavenly seat in their behalf. Like a baby who had been hurt, the Maggid sobbed.... He enumerated in detail all the misfortunes faced by the present generation, all the perils of the times and the evil instincts of the spirit. He alternately beseeched and ordered the soul of the deceased to approach the gates of mercy, to fall at the feet of the heavenly Father, and to remain there until He agrees to have mercy on Israel and send them His just redeemer....

Burying his head in the Holy Ark, among the Torah scrolls, he let out a heart-rending scream, imploring: "Master of the Universe, how long will you hide your face from us? ... Have pity on Zion, for it is time to redeem it."

All the people in the synagogue, young and old, men and women alike, began to sob, trembling in fear and awe....

Much time has passed since then ... but that cry remains in my ear forever, and the kinship born of that weeping still lives in my heart ...[10]

At the age of twenty-three, Reb Benyamin heard that Minsk was searching for a Maggid Meisharim. He applied for and was appointed to the position — despite the fact that at that time he was still single, and such jobs usually went only to married men. As one of the oldest communities in the region, a commercial center with a large population of Jewish working-class people as well as many Torah scholars, Minsk was a most prestigious post.

Like most Maggidei Meisharim, Shekowitski was paid as a community employee, his salary being drawn from the korobka. His contract stipulated that he preach in the synagogues of Minsk and its suburbs for ten months out of the year. The rest of the year he was free to preach elsewhere — a common source of additional income for the Maggidei Meisharim.[11]

During the several decades Reb Benyamin spent in Minsk, he became one of the best-known, most accessible, and most beloved figures in the Jewish community, active in many benevolent societies, respected as much for his endless generosity as for his eloquence and his scholarship. The spacious home he shared with the woman he married shortly after being appointed town preacher had an open-door policy, which applied to Jew and gentile alike. People from all walks of life came to him for help and hospitality, which he and his wife offered freely, she being as dedicated to the public welfare as he. A poor traveling coachman whose horse had collapsed and died was as welcome as the many distinguished rabbis and preachers who used the Shekowitski home almost as a hotel when they had occasion to be in Minsk. And Reb Benyamin's reach within the local community was also wide-ranging. He was on friendly terms with the Episcopus of the Provoslavic Church, whose home was nearby and with whom he was in the habit of exchanging neighborly gifts: gefilte fish from his own kitchen, to reciprocate for fruits from the bishop's garden. Reb Benyamin also knew the poor of his community, and even a number of its crooks.

Thus when a refugee woman who had been swindled of her diamonds — her portable wealth — asked him for help, he knew who to go to. Summoning the thieves, men who prayed at the rag shul, which was the synagogue of the junk dealers as well as a number of denizens of the underworld, he urged them to change their crooked ways. Whereupon one of the thieves replied: "Everything is the work of the Creator. God could have created you a thief and me a preacher. But you were fortunate, for you are the preacher and I am the thief. This is my preordained way of life. How can I be blamed for it?" But after he had delivered himself of this theological discourse, he was nonetheless susceptible to the maggid's entreaties, and soon agreed to return the stolen goods.[12]

During the difficult years of World War I, the maggid of Minsk displayed his finest qualities as a community leader. Not only was he one of the most active members of the central relief committee, he turned his home into a virtual refugee center for many of the thousands of people streaming through Minsk on their way out of the war zone. The refugees included Jews who had been evicted from the war zone on suspicion of "espionage," families trying to escape the perils of life amid warring armies, and entire yeshivot (including those of the Slobodka yeshivah of Kovno and the Radun yeshivah) which were on the run from the German occupying forces. At night the doors of the household would be removed from their hinges to serve as beds for the refugees, and in the morning the maggid and his wife rose early to feed them. He kneaded the bread dough, she formed it into loaves and baked them.[13] She also nursed a number of critically ill people back to life, including refugees from Eishyshok, her husband's hometown, and Radun, her own.

The end of World War I marked the end of an epoch of Jewish history within Russian borders, and the end of an era for the maggidim as well. For after the Russian Revolution, the maggid, like other Jewish religious leaders, became a target for the Yevsektsia, the Jewish section of the propaganda department of the Russian Communist Party, staffed by secular Jews. For the duration of its existence, from 1918 to 1930, the Yevsektsia took as its mandate the destruction — via assimilation — of a distinctly Jewish identity. Not to be outdone by the Poles or the Germans, the Yevsektsia zealously pursued its own method of persecuting the Jewish religion. And although it would be reductivist to assign this a merely psychological meaning, it is nonetheless true that many of the Yevsektsia's key members were the sons and daughters of rabbis.*

In line with the policies of the Yevsektsia, and in the name of "the people," the Shekowitskis' home was confiscated — the very home that had offered so much comfort to so many people in need. His magnificent six-thousand-volume library was dispersed. Only one room was made available for the use of the maggid's family (which by then included five children), and that they qualified for only on the grounds that one daughter, Rachel, was a kindergarten teacher, and as such a "productive" member of society, unlike the clergy, who were "parasites."

On the eve of Yom Kippur 1919, Shekowitski was arrested and thrown into jail. Through a mutual friend, Esther Frumkin was asked to intercede for him. As one of the leading members of the Yevsektsia and a Central Bureau member in charge of political education, Frumkin had the power to do so, but no one could be sure whether she would, for she had what was obviously a very complex and ambivalent attitude toward religion. She was the granddaughter of a rabbi and had formerly been married to one herself. But her politics, her ideology, and her restless, boiling temperament had seemingly sundered all her ties to that past. As she put it: "Whoever has breathed the stifling air [in the synagogue on Yom Kippur], has heard the wailing and sighing of hundreds of people, the trembling voice of the cantor — for the rest of his life he cannot free himself of the memory of this oppressive spirit."[14]

On that Yom Kippur of 1919, Esther Frumkin seems to have allowed herself to succumb to "the trembling voice of the cantor," or perhaps she simply acknowledged that the maggid, like herself, was a person of the people and for the people. In any case, she allowed the imprisoned maggid to have his prayer shawl, his prayer book, and his kittl (white robe) brought to him, and that night in his cell he held Kol Nidre services, which were attended by about sixty other political prisoners.[15] The next day, with 150 workers having signed a petition asking for Shekowitski's release, Frumkin ordered him to be set

*The members of the Yevsektsia were persecuted in their turn. Once their mandate as destroyers of a separate Jewish identity and culture in the USSR had been deemed fulfilled, they lost their lives in Stalin's purges during the 1930s.

free. When his wife answered his knock on the door, she passed out immediately at the sight: her husband, who had left the house with black hair, had returned a mere twenty-four hours later having gone totally gray.

For many years to come, Shekowitski would endure numerous humiliations and hardships, these being the standard lot of the religious leaders of the Jewish community in the new Soviet state. In 1925 he was arrested and tortured along with about twenty of his fellow rabbis from Minsk, who were then forced to sign a document attesting to the fact that there was no religious persecution in Russia. This was only one in a whole series of arrests, one of which resulted in his losing the right to reside in Minsk. By now all five of the maggid's children had emigrated, and they began the struggle to get their parents out of Russia. Though they were able to obtain the necessary certificates of emigration to Palestine, the Russian government refused to honor them. Finally their daughter Rachel, back in Russia for a six-month stay, appealed for help to Yekatrina Pavlovna, Maxim Gorky's first wife, who was an admirer of Zionism, and to Mikhail Ivanovich Kalinin, a leading Russian revolutionary who was then the ceremonial head of the Russian state. With their assistance, Shekowitski and his wife were finally able to leave. In 1934 they arrived in Tel Aviv, where they were met by their youngest son and their two daughters, all of whom had emigrated there in 1931.

In 1938, Zalman Shazar, who had never forgotten the magnificent eulogy Reb Benyamin Shekowitski had given almost four decades before, was walking down the streets of Tel Aviv when he saw an obituary notice announcing the maggid's death. Canceling his plans to attend a political meeting that afternoon, he soon found himself in a synagogue listening to another eulogy — this time in honor of Reb Benyamin. There on the bimah stood a maggid who was delivering the eulogy in the same heart-wrenching melody Shazar remembered from all those years before. And there beside Shazar stood a young boy of about the same age he had been, his large, burning eyes feverishly following every word of the eulogy.[16]

THE DAYYAN: VOICE OF JUSTICE AND COMPASSION

JUSTICE SHALL BE THE
GIRDLE OF HIS LOINS,
AND FAITHFULNESS THE
GIRDLE OF HIS WAIST.

Isaiah 11:5

The dayyan (judge) was part of a judicial system dating back to biblical days, when the Children of Israel were commanded to appoint judges in each town.[17] Eventually, under the leadership of ordained rabbis, the beth din (rabbinical court) continued to operate in communities throughout the Jewish Diaspora, even at times when the Jewish courts had minimal authority because of restrictions imposed by the host country. Whenever possible, however, Jews did go to Jewish rather than secular courts — by preference, and out of respect. Going to a non-Jewish court was severely criticized as *hillul ha-shem* (profanation of the divine name) — a term applied to an unworthy action that reflected discredit upon Judaism.

THE EASTERN EUROPEAN JUDICIAL SYSTEM

At some periods and in some places of the Diaspora, various host countries allowed their Jews almost total self-government. From 1569 to 1764, when the Council of the Four Lands represented the Jewish communities of Poland and Lithuania to the crown, the Jews enjoyed perhaps their greatest measure of autonomy, which was reflected in their judicial system. In fact, during parts of the sixteenth, seventeenth, and eighteenth centuries, the Jews in many areas of Poland and Lithuania had full authority to render judgment in most criminal, financial, and civil cases, including those that involved non-Jewish litigators. Jews and non-Jews alike used the Jewish courts. After the dissolution of the Council in 1764, however, all major criminal offenses were judged in the non-Jewish courts.

Even before then, however, the reality was that most cases involving a severe punishment, or serious accusations between Jews and non-Jews, or any prominent non-Jewish personality usually went to a gentile court. Highly placed, wealthy Jews, and those with connections to the gentile authorities, could also choose the gentile court system when it suited them, as happened in the sixteenth century with Rabbi Menachem Mendl Frank, of Brest-Litovsk, who wanted it to be clear that only the grand duke himself, not anyone in the Jewish community, had authority over him. Similarly, in the latter part of the eighteenth century, Rabbi Shmuel ben Avigdor of Vilna used the crown courts when he did not obtain the rulings he wanted from Jewish courts.

Besides the beth din, which consisted only of ordained rabbis but nonetheless incorporated aspects of both Jewish and civil law in its rulings, there was also a "Jewish Court" that combined Jewish and secular authority. The Jewish Court operated only in the larger cities and towns, though people from the shtetlekh and villages under the jurisdiction of the local "mother town" sometimes went to it for judgments in cases that required a court of higher standing than the local beth din. Its membership consisted of the pod-wojewoda, the sub-governor of the province, who was always a gentile; a general prosecutor (instigator) who was sometimes a gentile, especially if there was a large sum of money being contested; a Jewish judge, who was a rabbi; a shammash (the synagogue beadle, who also summoned the litigants to court); a Jewish clerk; and, when necessary, one or more consulting dayyanim (also rabbis). In reality the pod-wojewoda generally sat only when large sums of money were at stake.[18] Unless the proceedings required the presence of the pod-wojewoda, or the wojewoda (governor) himself, in which case they were held at the official residence, the Jewish Court convened in the community room of the shulhoyf complex, and, like the beth din, operated quite autonomously. From the seventeenth century on, however, many of the Polish provincial governors took advantage of their role in the Jewish Courts to impose their own restrictions not just on the running of the court, but on the powers of the kahal members as well. Sometimes they even meddled in community elections.

Whether their power was official or not, and regardless of prevailing political circumstances, many Eastern European rabbis had a moral authority that could not be denied. Indeed, it wasn't just Jews but gentiles too who had great faith in the wisdom and compassion of these rabbis. One of the most notable of these beloved figures was Avraham Dov Popl (1870–1923), rabbi of Mariampole, delegate to the Lithuanian parliament, and former student at the Kibbutz ha-Prushim of Eishyshok. His humanitarian qualities were so remarkable, and so ecumenical, that a story about him made it into a Lithuanian high school textbook on government. When a young Lithuanian university student was arrested and sentenced to death for his involvement with the outlawed Communist Party, Rabbi Popl went before the parliament and delivered an eloquent speech against capital punishment, and a plea for the life of the young man. The story in the textbook is illustrated by a picture of the young man's mother kissing the rabbi's feet, as he tells her that her son has been set free.[19]

Besides the formal proceedings that transpired in the Jewish Court or the beth din, there was yet another form of arbitration known as a *din Torah*, a quasilegal and usually rather informal procedure in which the litigators agreed to be bound strictly by Jewish law, custom, and even folk wisdom. Anyone in the Jewish community could be called to a din Torah to account for a wrongdoing, including God. Gentiles, too, resorted to the din Torah, particularly if they had a lot of trust in the dayyan.

In turn-of-the-century Eishyshok, an argument over the location of the slaughterhouse would become the stuff of high drama — yet another occasion for the factions within the shtetl to do battle with one another — and a case for a five-man din Torah. It all began with a proposal by Shael Sonenson, who had married into the powerful Kabacznik family and thereby acquired both that family's prestigious position in the community and its traditional enemies. When the old slaughterhouse in the shulhoyf collapsed, Reb Shael proposed relocating it to the outskirts of the shtetl, which would spare the population the foul odors as well as the cries of the animals. Conveniently enough, there was a spacious brick building at the very end of Mill Street that would serve the purpose nicely — and that also happened to be owned by Reb Shael, who had bought it when the match factory it housed went out of business.

Meir Kiuchefski, then the shtetl neeman (trustee) and a supporter of the New Beth Midrash, favored the Sonenson proposal, while Reuven Dubitski, a longtime Kabacznik foe and supporter of the Old Beth Midrash, opposed it. Soon balebatim from both houses of study had entered into the fray, which became so heated that Rabbi Zundl Hutner, the shtetl rabbi at the time, decided that the issue would have to be resolved by rabbis from nearby towns, since only they would be able to assess the pros and cons in an unbiased manner.

Five distinguished rabbis, including the renowned Rabbi Reines of Lida, met to consider this case. The opposition was claiming that the proposed location was unsuitable because it would require herding the animals through Goyishker Gas (Gentile Street) and Hazerim Gessl (Pigs Lane), where, they said, the gentiles would set their dogs after the cattle, the cattle would stampede and thereby injure themselves and render the meat nonkosher, and everybody, including the consumers who would have to pay higher prices for scarcer meat supplies, would lose money. To determine whether this was an accurate description of the hazards of the new location, the rabbis who were to adjudicate in the din Torah proceeding ordered a trial cattle drive through Gentile Street and Pigs Lane. All the gentiles stood in front of their gardens to witness the strange procession, cattle in front, distinguished-looking rabbis and shtetl notables following closely behind. Suddenly, at a narrow bend in the road, a pack of dogs attacked the cattle and pandemonium broke out. Fortunately the wild chase ended without injury to man or beast, though the rabbis' silk coats and top hats were somewhat the worse for the experience.

Things didn't look good for Reb Shael's proposed slaughterhouse, until it came out in court that the dogs had been set not by gentiles, but by a Jew the opposition had hired. Rabbi Reines was furious at the deception: "If two-legged dogs had not unleashed four-legged dogs," he thundered, "all would have been well." A verdict in favor of the modern brick building on the outskirts of town was issued shortly thereafter, and it served as the slaughterhouse until the final days of the Jewish community in 1941.

From moral indignation to incarceration, physical punishment, and even execution, the range of sentences available to the Jewish Court and to the beth din, especially before the dissolution of the Council of the Four Lands, was considerable. Minor transgressors might simply be punished with thirty-nine lashings, or less,[20] administered within or in front of the synagogue. Until well into the nineteenth century in some communities, the kuna — a set of metal rings attached to the wall of the vestibule of the synagogue — was also used: a prisoner would be locked up in the kuna, his neck and hands secured by the metal rings, and passersby would be expected to spit on him, the degradation and humiliation constituting the punishment. Or he would be held there while awaiting his beating or some other form of punishment.

Imprisonment was also possible, for many Jewish communities maintained their own jails, sometimes two of them: one a simple room or holding cell which was usually near the beth din's meeting place, the other a more secure lockup. After the Big Fire of 1895, Eishyshok's jail was located in a building on Vilna Street, which it shared with the post office. There is no longer any record or memory of where the jail was before then.

Though it is not clear whether he ever exercised it, and most of the prominent rabbis of the time opposed it, the Chief Rabbi of Little Poland, Rabbi Shalom Shakhna ben Yossef of Lublin (the founder of Talmudic scholarship in Poland), possessed the right of capital punishment, as spelled out in his 1541 letter of appointment from the crown.[21]

But since capital punishment was rarely if ever used in Eastern European Jewish life, the herem (excommunication), an expression of moral indignation with dire practical consequences, was, realistically speaking, the most dreaded of all the sentences that could be passed. Indeed, it sometimes came close to being a death sentence, so totally was the excommunicated individual cut off from the Jewish community, at a time when it was extremely difficult for a Jew to survive in the world outside. A herem was pronounced by the shtetl rabbi, in the synagogue itself. While there were categories of excommunication, and the specifics varied in different eras and in different communities, the purpose was always to remove the person from society.[22] No one in the community was allowed to associate with the banished person; if he was single at the time of the herem, he could not marry; his children could not be circumcised, attend school, or be married; his wife was expelled from the synagogue; and, when he died, he was to be denied a Jewish burial.

THE SHTETL DAYYAN

Eishyshok, like many other shtetlekh, had a rabbinic court that consisted of three dayyanim. The head of the court was the shtetl rabbi, and the other two judges were the shtetl dayyanim, both of whom were also ordained rabbis, qualified to judge in family and money matters, in issues pertaining to hazaka (property), and in problems of civil law. While the larger towns and cities had separate and sometimes very grand judicial chambers, the shtetl beth din met in the home of either the rabbi or one of the dayyanim.

Besides the rabbinic court, there was also a lay court, which was basically a court of arbitration. It consisted of one scholar, generally the shtetl rabbi or a dayyan, and two laymen, chosen by the two warring parties subject to the approval of the presiding judge, who acted as the borerim (arbitrators).

While the shtetl rabbi was always the head of the court and the final legal authority within the community, the dayyan played an unusually prominent role at certain times — not just in legal proceedings, but as a leader of the community. The circumstances that led to this state of affairs were always particular to the individual shtetl: the personalities of the people involved, the needs of the community, custom, and tradition.

REB LAYZER DAYYAN Ever since the establishment of the Kibbutz ha-Prushim yeshivah in Eishyshok in the 1790s, the town had been fortunate enough to attract a number of men of very high caliber to serve as dayyanim. But none would be a greater asset to the community than its native-son dayyan who guided the shtetl through some of its most turbulent years, Reb Eliezer Yehoshuah Wilkanski, known affectionately as Reb Layzer Dayyan, or Reb Layzer der Hokhem (the wise). Reb Layzer studied in

Vilna, with a man who had been a student of the Gaon. He was appointed an Eishyshok dayyan in 1860, and held that post for over fifty years, until his departure for Eretz Israel in 1914. Five different rabbis would serve Eishyshok during Reb Layzer's tenure. It wasn't just his longevity in office but his remarkable personal qualities that made Reb Layzer the shtetl's most stable, enduring source of leadership in this period. When Maimonides summed up the seven qualifications of a true judge — wisdom, humility, reverence for God, disdain of gain, love of truth, love for his fellow men, and a good reputation — he could have been talking about Reb Layzer.[23]

He so impressed some students at the Eishyshok yeshivah that after his first wife died, they made a match between him and a young relative of theirs: the beautiful, spirited, and very well educated Batia Altshul. Though the students forgot to mention to her that Reb Layzer was thirty-one years her senior and a widower with four children, she eventually overcame her initial shock, which was considerable, and became enchanted with him. Their home, filled with the comings and goings of the children from his first marriage and the six children they had together, became a hub for the entire shtetl. Not only did the Wilkanski home serve as a court of law for the shtetl and the surrounding villages, people came to consult with both Reb Layzer and Batia about all manner of personal problems, the shtetl intellectuals congregated around the Wilkanski dining table to discuss current events over homemade pastries and a steaming glass of tea from Batia's gilded Russian samovar, and many community events took place in their home too, including the periodic Saturday-night elections to the kahal.

Jews, Christians, and Muslims, Russians, Poles, Lithuanians, and Tatars, all went to Reb Layzer for legal arbitration, for they knew that his justice was swift and fair, unlike that available to them in the Russian judicial system. Confident that before Reb Layzer all men were equal, all were created in the image of God, all deserving of justice and compassion, they spoke to him through their interpreters, and waited for his verdict while he consulted his many books. His name was as highly praised in the church of Juryzdyki and the mosque in Nekraszunca as it was in the three prayerhouses of Eishyshok. He also commanded the respect of the secular authorities, because in his capacity as judge during a time of harsh anti-Jewish decrees he always acted from one of the basic principles of rabbinic law: "Dina de-mallkhuta dina" (In civic matters, the law of the land where Jews reside is binding).[24] To him this meant that the impact of the

Eliezer Yehoshua Wilkanski (1824–1918), known as Reb Layzer Dayyan, was the shtetl dayyan (judge) for fifty years. His personal qualities and scholarship made him the most influential and trusted leader in the shtetl, even among the non-Jewish residents. He and his second wife Batia made their house Eishyshok's intellectual center. Their six children introduced Zionism into the town. The entire family, including the children from Reb Layzer's first marriage, emigrated to Eretz Israel, where they had a great impact as well. PHOTO: M. GROSSMAN, VILNA, 1913. YESC, WILKANSKI

tzar's legislation had to be confronted legally, not evaded or undermined. So strict was his adherence to this principle that once when the tzarist authorities were searching for a yeshivah student who lodged with the Wilkanskis, Batia hid the young man — not just from the police, but from Reb Layzer. That way she made it possible for her husband to say in all honesty that he had no knowledge of the young man's whereabouts.

No problem was too large or small to bring to Reb Layzer. "Today, in moments of crisis, we call the police or an ambulance. When I was a little girl we ran to Reb Layzer," former Eishyshkian Elka Szulkin Jankelewicz recalled. When Eishyshok burned down in the Big Fire of 1895, and the shtetl rabbi, Zvi Hirsh Ma-Yafit, departed soon thereafter, it was Reb Layzer who was entrusted with supervising the rebuilding of the synagogue and the Old and New batei midrash. It was also Reb Layzer who was asked to render judgment on many of the ongoing battles and lawsuits over the korobka (the kosher meat tax). His son Meir's description of one of them conveys the courage and charisma that characterized Reb Layzer's judicial style, and the universal respect he commanded:

Once again the leaders of the kahal gathered in our house, as well as many ordinary people. They stood crowded together inside the house, and mobbed the windows on the outside, to witness the din Torah between the kahal and Reb Yehudah, the leaser of the korobka. Reb Yehudah did not want to fill his part of the bargain with respect to the korobka, for he claimed that so much of the slaughtered meat had been declared treifah *[unkosher] that he could not pay what he had agreed to. The heads of the kahal argued, Reb Yehudah argued. Suddenly Reb Yehudah became excited and roared at the top of his powerful lungs while banging his hand on the table. The table squeaked, the lamp tottered and nearly fell to the floor extinguished, and the elders of the kahal remained seated, looking distressed, pale and sorrowful. Father, who had been sitting on the bench listening intently to the argument, now rose to his feet: "Yehudah!" Father said. "Me you cannot force, me you will not be able to intimidate! . . . I do not fear you and I shall deliver my verdict!" The faces of the kahal leaders grew paler still. As Father returned to his place, a heavy silence hung inside the house and outdoors as well. But soon afterward, Reb Yehudah nodded to my father and in a hushed voice said: "To you I will always listen."*[25]

It was also Reb Layzer whom Eishyshkians went to in moments of personal trouble of all kinds: property disputes, monetary conflicts, even marital problems. So it came as no surprise to the Wilkanski family when Soreh-Reizl, shaking and hysterical, burst into their house one Friday afternoon, followed by her husband, Hayyim-Barukh, a heavy-set coachman whose beard and shirt were covered in noodles. Tall, skinny Soreh-Reizl was obsessed with cleanliness. Each week she welcomed the Sabbath by polishing every item in the house, scrubbing the furniture, putting pure white starched linens on the beds, and spreading sparkling yellow sand on the clay floor. Alas, her husband had little respect for her efforts. Between sobs, Soreh-Reizl told Reb Layzer that when her husband had returned from his latest journey, just after she had finished cleaning the house from top to bottom for the Sabbath, he had walked across her spotless floor in his mud- and pitch-covered boots and thrown himself onto the fresh white linen of their bed — whereupon she had hurled a pot of just-cooked noodles at him. Now both were demanding a get (bill of divorcement).

After taking Hayyim-Barukh into the kitchen to wash up, and telling Soreh-Reizl to run back and fetch a clean shirt for her husband, Reb Layzer was able to calm them down and send them home to welcome the Sabbath together. But the peace was short-lived. Their fights continued in the days that followed, escalating to the point where Reb Layzer had to take further action. His solution was to use community money to rent a room for Soreh-Reizl and Hayyim-Barukh in the home of the shammash. There the shammash and his family kept the warring couple under observation for a period of time, at the end of which it was concluded that the initiator of the fights was the wife, who seemed to have a particular fondness for throwing kitchen utensils at her husband. Soreh-Reizl, who was again demanding a get, was again sent home with her husband and told to reconcile. Later the couple would be blessed with a son.[26]

During his final years in Eishyshok, as a brand-new shtetl arose from the ashes of the 1895 fire, Reb Layzer witnessed many profound changes in the town of his birth, including those promulgated by his and Batia's six brilliant children. One by one their three daughters and three sons left the world of the Torah for that of the Haskalah and secular Zionism. They studied at German and Swiss universities, attended Zionist congresses, then brought their new ideas home to the shtetl, where they were involved in establishing a library, a theater, and a club for Hebrew-speaking girls. But the bitter rift that divided the generations of so many Haskalah-influenced families never divided theirs.

With Batia's constant encouragement, Reb Layzer always tried to bridge the differences with their children, and to support them in their interests, even giving in to his daughter Sarah's demands that she and her sisters receive a formal education, though he knew his decision would be a controversial one, sure to elicit harsh criticism in many quarters. The voluminous correspondence between the parents and the children, Batia's letters in Yiddish, Reb Layzer's in his magnificent Hebrew, provide a fascinating and moving look at the generations meeting at the crossroads between tradition and secularism.

Not everybody in Eishyshok was so accepting. The behavior of the Wilkanski children was fiercely opposed by some of the shtetl leaders, and seems to have been one of the sources of friction between the households of Reb Layzer and Zundl Hutner, the rabbi. This may explain why Reb Layzer's son Meir Wilkanski, the shtetl's gifted and ubiquitous chronicler, never mentions the Hutner family, who were major figures in the shtetl and its mainstay during World War I—an otherwise unaccountable omission, given that a number of the years covered by his memoirs coincide with Hutner's tenure as rabbi.

Batia and Reb Layzer followed their children to Eretz Israel in 1914, where both lived into their nineties. His tombstone reads:

Here is the resting place of Eliezer Yohoshuah Wilkanski (Reb Layzer) b. Yekutiel.

He served a number of the greatest scholars of his generation and for fifty years sat on the dayyan chair in his native town of Eishyshok, a town of Torah since the distant past.

In Tamuz, 1914, he made aliyah to Yaffo and settled in Ben-Shemen. On the 7th. of Heshvah, 1918, he closed his eyes forever. His eyes were undimmed and his vigor unabated.

To the question of his granddaughter, "What was Eishyshok to my grandfather?" there could be only one answer: Reb Layzer *was* Eishyshok.

THE SHAMMASH: FAITHFUL SERVANT OF GOD AND COMMUNITY

THE SHAMMASH OFTEN ACTED AS A DIPLOMAT OR WAS OFTEN SENT AS AN ENVOY TO ANOTHER COMMUNITY.

Encyclopedia Judaica

The shammash (beadle, or sexton) was one of the shtetl's triumvirate of essential public servants, the other two being the rabbi and the hazzan. They were collectively known by the acronym RaHaSh (the same as the acronym for the tax from which they received part of their income). More, perhaps, than any of the other Klei Kodesh, the shammash was expected to serve a multitude of functions, and to be able to fill in for other members of the clergy when they were unable to do their jobs. His domain was the synagogue, the batei midrash, the shtetl at large, and, during the years between the two world wars, the Hebrew day school. All of which suggests that, until the secularization of the shtetl during the twentieth century, when many of the activities previously based in the synagogue moved to different locations, the duties of the shammash had changed little since the third century, when the Jews of Simonia in Palestine went to their leader, Judah the Prince, and asked him for one person who could be a preacher, a dayyan, a hazzan, and a scribe — as well as someone who could take care of all their other needs![27] Since the obligations of the shammash were so many, synagogues often employed two official shammashim, the upper, who performed the more prestigious tasks, and the lower, who did the more menial ones.

The shammash was the faithful servant of God, his duties alternating between the mundane and the exalted. He summoned the people to the Lord's service, made sure that the service was conducted properly, provided the congregation with all amenities while they were at prayer, and saw to the upkeep of the synagogue when prayers were not in session.

During the hours between services, he performed his maintenance chores, ensuring that the synagogue was clean, warm, and well lit, arranging the lecterns and benches, posting notices pertinent to the services of the day, week, and season, winding the synagogue clocks, and so forth. During the holidays it was his responsibility to decorate the synagogue according to the dictates of tradition and local custom, which might mean decking the Holy Ark, the reading table, and the scrolls of the Torah all in white for the High Holidays, or adorning the sanctuary with greenery during Shavuoth.

Before services in the morning, it was the shammash who opened the synagogue doors and asked the spirits of the dead to return to their resting places. And after services at night, it was he who closed the doors, making sure that all earthly worshippers had left the shul for the safety of their homes, so that there would be no unexpected encounters between them and the inhabitants of the Houses of Eternity. Meir Wilkanski, whose best friend in childhood was the grandson of Zechariah the shammash, gave a vivid description of what Mikha ben Abba had told him about his grandfather's awesome responsibilities:

In the hands of his grandfather are the lives of the old and the young. If, God forbid, he would lock the synagogue while a person remained inside, that person would be found dead in the morning. Therefore, at the conclusion of the evening prayers, with candle in hand, R'Zechariah canvasses the length and breadth of the synagogue. The sanctuary is big, and sunk in half darkness, so the eye may deceive. He searches above and beneath the benches: perhaps a man or a child has fallen asleep, or someone is so immersed in thought that he did not hear the synagogue being cleared. Then he ascends the bimah, bangs forcefully on the lectern, and announces: "Leave the synagogue!" He comes down, searches the sanctuary once more, extinguishes the last candles, then mounts the steps leading to the shulhoyf. Now, holding his lantern, he closes the door, locks it with a noisy click and with a huge key knocks on the door. Then he waits for a moment and listens, to see if perhaps a child he overlooked will wake up and cry. If all is quiet he takes his leave. The synagogue remains in darkness, the habitation for the dead.

Having emptied the synagogue of the living the night before, Reb Zechariah returned the next day, just before dawn, to empty it of the dead:

At ashmoret (the third watch), he rises to serve the Creator. He takes the huge keys, which are too heavy for a child to lift, lights the lantern and walks alone through the shtetl's empty streets. In his hand he carries a book of Psalms, for one should not approach the dead with hostility, with a whip or sword. He puts his ear to the door and listens attentively, then knocks three times and announces: "Return to your eternal rest!" He waits a while, then noisily turns the weighty key, opens the heavy door, and enters the sanctuary. Everything fades away and disappears. He mounts the bimah, places the lantern on the table, and begins to recite Psalms. He recites the Psalms continuously until the crack of dawn, when the first vatikin arrive for the morning prayers.[28]

These picturesque rituals continued until electricity arrived in Eishyshok in the winter of 1930–31, when the lighting of the synagogue made it, in the perception of Eishyshkians, a less foreboding place for the living, and less hospitable to the nocturnal visits of the dead.

The shammash was expected to be present at all religious services, on weekdays, Saturdays, holidays, and other special days of the calendar, for it was his responsibility to see to it that all services were conducted according to tradition as well as local custom. In the absence of any individual who had a role in the services, such as a hazzan, a Torah reader, or a shofar blower, he was expected to substitute.

The shammash also saw to it that every Jew had a private invitation to prayer. No public tolling of bells nor loud muezzin call from a minaret summoned the shtetl Jew to services. Instead, no matter what the weather, the shammash made his way through the dim, silent dawn (or, during penitential periods, through the darkness of predawn), tapped on the wooden shutters of each sleeping house, and sang his wake-up call, in a special melody reserved for this occasion: "Yidden, shteit uf le-avodat ha-Boyreh!" ("Jews, get up to serve the Creator!")

It was the shammash who maintained decorum in the shul. With the resounding bang of his hand on the bimah table, he called the congregation to order on all religious, community, and social occasions. At times it seemed as if the shtetl lived by the cadence of this echoing hand bang. And woe to those children who didn't heed its warning, or who acted up during services. Older children feared his admonishing finger, while younger ones were subject to having their ears pulled if they were boys, their braids yanked if they were girls.

Friday at sundown it was once more the shammash who alerted the shtetl, ushering in the Sabbath Queen by standing in the marketplace and announcing "Vaiber, tzind di likht" ("Women, light the candles), and "Yidden, in shul arain" (Jews, go to shul). At the conclusion of the Friday-evening services, he stood at the synagogue door and distributed platten to all who needed them. These were special pieces of wood on which were engraved the names of people who had agreed to serve as Sabbath hosts for those who were visiting the shtetl. In the absence of a host from the synagogue, the shammash usually invited the visitor to his own Sabbath table. Alexander Zisl Hinski, son of Eishyshok's last upper shammash, remembers many a Friday evening when their family played host to outsiders Reb Israel Yossef Hinski brought home with him. Though they were at times very crude people, who spat on the floor and made strange conversation, the family treated them with respect, for they were honored Sabbath guests.

The shammash was the rabbi's right hand, an indispensable assistant who helped him in matters of ritual and in his many administrative duties, serving, when necessary, as notary, tax collector, bailiff, and on occasion even policeman.[29] At public functions the rabbi was rarely seen without the shammash at his side. From a twentieth-century anecdote one may learn how Eishyshkians viewed the rabbi–shammash relationship. On the shulhoyf lived a family of roofers. Though they were known by the nickname "di ketz" (the cats) due to their agility at climbing roofs, the pet they owned was a dog. The dog was a constant source of irritation to some of the shul-goers. On several occasions Rabbi Szymen Rozowski admonished "the cats," but to no avail. Finally, after an incident involving an elderly person, the rabbi asked "the cats": "Tell me, why does a Jew need a dog?" In the best shtetl tradition, the question was met with a question: "And why does the rabbi need a shammash?"

Despite the multitude of duties performed by the shammash, and the long, irregular hours he worked, the pay was very low and many a shammash had to look for an additional source of income. The most common second occupation was to be a melamed. Nineteenth-century Eishyshok had a number of these hardworking, overburdened men, including Reb Yitche der Butchan (the stork) and Reb Itche der Shammash, both of whom were beadles in the Old Beth Midrash and both of whom thereby suffered a double dose of pranks from their young charges — first in the heder, then in the house of study. For a while during his youth, Reb Itche der Shammash also had a third job as mohel, but failing eyesight put an end to that.

Reb Itche took great pride in his job as the shammash of the Old Beth Midrash. Indeed, the painstaking care he took in arranging the lecterns in the sanctuary was so well known throughout the shtetl that some worshippers came early to afternoon prayers, just to catch a glimpse of the beautifully arranged stands before services began and they were once more cast into disarray.

The heder boys also liked Reb Itche's lecterns, but for a different reason: They were among their favorite playthings. Whenever they had some free time, which happened especially often when they were between semesters, they would go to the beth midrash and rearrange Reb Itche's configurations into circles, zigzags, or whatever other formation appealed to the whim of the moment, so long as it met the primary objective: that the lecterns were close enough together that when one was pushed, all the others would crash to the floor one after another, domino-style. The resulting ear-splitting bangs were accompanied by the cheers of the delighted heder boys.

Upon hearing the echoing reverberations from the beth midrash, Reb Itche would rush to the sanctuary, only to find all his meticulously arranged lecterns now lying flat on the floor. And with his old, aching back and his weak, shaky hands, he would once more have to put the stands in good order for the afternoon prayer. Reb Itche knew well who was responsible for the prank. He would walk briskly to the space behind the oven and there, around the table, would be seated a dozen boys deeply engrossed in their studies, as evidenced by the sweet, melodious Talmud chant issuing from their lips. Undeceived, he would thunder at his young charges: "Even if your faces were like that of our patriarch Abraham and your voices like Jacob's, Reb Itche would know that your hearts are the hearts of bandits!" And then he would take the long towel from the ritual washstand and snap it at them as he chased them out of the sanctuary. A few days later the entire scenario was likely to be repeated again, the boys performing their usual mischief, Reb Itche delivering his usual tirades.

Among the shammashim who had to endure such pranks, on top of performing their already backbreaking tasks and catering to the whims of the balebatim, were accomplished scholars worthy of being rabbis, judges, and heads of academies; indeed, some were finer scholars than the rabbis they served. For this was a society that produced an enormous number of scholars but offered few positions appropriate to their abilities. In order to provide for their families, these scholarly young men were pleased to accept any position that kept them in the social stratum of the Klei Kodesh.

Israel Yossef Hinski, Eishyshok's last upper shammash, was typical. A fine scholar, he had first studied at the Radun yeshivah and then at the Kibbutz ha-Prushim in Eishyshok. Reb Zalman Kabacznik, one of Eishyshok's most prominent balebatim and a member of one of the five founding families, was impressed enough with both Hinski's scholarship and his personality that he chose him as a husband for his gentle beautiful blond daughter, Taibe-Edl.

Despite his many duties, Reb Israel der Shamesh, as he became known, continued to study all his life, while also giving a daily Torah class to the local members of Tiferet Bahurim, an organization of Polish and Lithuanian working-class youth, mainly artisans' apprentices, who went to study in the beth midrash between afternoon and evening prayers each day.[30] Reb Israel's students so appreciated his dedication to them that they presented him with a beautiful kerosene lamp, on which was inscribed the name of the society, and their thanks for bringing the light of Torah into their lives.

On the eve of Rosh Hashanah 1941, Reb Israel der Shamesh made his rounds from house to house on the market square. But he was not awakening the shtetl Jews to summon them to God's service. That custom had been discontinued in Eishyshok sometime during World War I. And in any case the Jews of Eishyshok had already been awakened that morning by the German Einsatzgruppen and their Lithuanian collaborators, who would soon enough chase them to the synagogue and the Old and New batei midrash for their last prayers.

Reb Israel, instead of searching for possible routes of escape for his family and himself, was rushing from house to house to ask for forgiveness. He sensed that time was running out, and that he might never again have the chance to ask the people of the shtetl for their forgiveness, as it had been his custom to do each year on the eve of Yom Kippur. Perhaps in his capacity as upper beadle he had wronged some people. Perhaps he had not called this one up to the Torah as often as he would have wished, or had spoken harshly to that one, or had been too stern with the children while trying to maintain decorum in the synagogue. As the Lithuanians and the Germans went from house to house to collect all the Jews, Reb Israel ran ahead of them, trying desperately to complete his rounds.

Reb Israel Yossef Hinski (middle row, third from right), a scholar who was devoted to the community, was Eishyshok's last upper shammash. In this family portrait he is joined by (top row, right to left) daughter Golda-Brahah, his brother Yekutiel, niece Masha Hinski; (middle row) son Alexander Zisl, Reb Israel's wife Taibe-Edl (née Kabacznik), and his sister-in-law Esther Hinski; (bottom) daughter Hayya-Sheine, niece Golda Koppelman, and son Avraham-Yaakov. Alexander Zisl emigrated to Eretz Israel in 1939. Hayya-Sheine died a natural death during the German occupation in the summer of 1941. All the others were murdered in the September 1941 massacre and elsewhere. YESC, HINSKI

On September 26–27, 1941, Reb Israel Yossef Hinski, his wife Taibe-Edl, and three of their children were murdered, together with some five thousand other shtetl Jews. The only member of their family to survive was the oldest son, Alexander Zisl, who had emigrated to Eretz Israel in 1939.

THE HAZZAN, BAAL-TEFILLAH, AND ZOGERKE: LEADING THE CONGREGATION IN PRAYER

PRAYER IS THE SERVICE OF THE HEART.

Taanit, 2/a

THE HAZZAN

Nineteenth- and twentieth-century Eishyshkians, like other East European Jews, had a great weakness for hazzanim (cantors), the singers who lead the congregation in its prayers on the Sabbath and on holidays. A hazzan with an excellent voice, perfect diction, and a God-fearing personality was a highly desirable ornament to the synagogue, and Eishyshok had many gifted men who filled these requirements over the years.

The duties of the job, and the qualifications for it, have changed little since the Middle Ages. The hazzan is required to have a pleasant voice and appearance, wear a beard, have complete familiarity with the liturgy, and be married, possessed of a blameless character, and acceptable in all other respects to the community he serves.[31] The Council of the Four Lands made additional provisions, some of them pertaining to the remuneration of the hazzan, including his being exempt, like the other Klei Kodesh, from taxation, and his drawing a salary from the RaHaSh tax. Because many hazzanim were given to showmanship and self-display, the Council also made a point of restricting the number of prayers the hazzan could chant during Sabbath services, lest prayers go on too long and overtax the congregation's patience.[32] Occasionally a prominent rabbi would castigate the hazzanim for needless repetition of the prayers, when done for the sole purpose of displaying the beauty of their own voices.

The popularity of the East European cantor rose to new heights during the period known as the Golden Era of the Hazzanim, which began sometime in the nineteenth century, and continued until World War II put an end to the communities in which their talents had been nurtured. This was a time when renowned hazzanim had equal standing with the great operatic tenors, and were invited to perform on European and eventually American stages. Gershon Sirota (1874–1943) of Vilna, for example, gave an annual concert for Tzar Nicholas II.

Fame had its drawbacks, however, for the shtetlekh were often ambivalent about these men and their dual roles as clergy and artistic performer. As a result, the hazzanim found that their movements were all closely scrutinized, their piety always suspect. And indeed, some of them did succumb to the worldly temptations of stardom. The most famous of these fallen hazzanim was Joel David Loewenstein-Strashunski (1816–1850), who at the age of fifteen succeeded his father, Zvi Hirsch Loewenstein, as the hazzan of Vilna. Because a hazzan had to be a married man, Joel had been married off in his fourteenth year, and so became known as "der Vilner Balebessl" (the little householder of Vilna).

In Warsaw, however, he fell in love with a Polish opera singer, went on stage as an opera singer himself, and left his wife and child behind in Vilna. Overcome by guilt after a while, he gave up both his lover and his career and went into "voluntary exile," a form of self-punishment in which one becomes a vagabond. He spent the rest of his days wandering from one hekdesh (homeless shelter) to another, eventually returning to Vilna, where he froze to death as a street beggar. The tragic life and death of the Vilner Balebessl were to become the stuff of legend and literature, known even to the youngest of shtetl children, and casting their shadow over the reputations of hazzanim for many decades to come.[33]

Eishyshok was very cautious about hazzanim,

Ruben Boyarski (1885–1975) was a hazzan in Eishyshok. He and his wife Alte were active in the shtetl Zionist organization. Boyarski's outstanding voice so impressed Enrico Caruso that the opera star invited him to perform with him. After leaving Eishyshok, Boyarski was a renowned cantor in England, the United States, and Israel. PHOTO: SUWALKI, POLAND. YESC, BOYARSKI

The famous Vilna Hazzanim Quartet, which continued to be known as such even after it expanded. Gedalia Ginunski (standing, far left), a native Eishyshkian, was an accomplished hazzan who for a period of time led the prayers in the New Beth Midrash. At Auschwitz, the Germans forced him to perform for them. Gedalia perished there with his wife and children. YESC, L. GINUNSKI

not just those who took jobs in the shtetl, but world-famous visiting artists as well. These visitors were subjected to the most intense scrutiny. Was their behavior exemplary, their piety beyond reproach? And if they met those standards, were their beards trimmed appropriately? Might there be any other blemishes on their personal character or style? If a visiting hazzan did not pass the test, he could not appear in the Old Beth Midrash, but might still be permitted to sing in either the New Beth Midrash or the summer shul. Gershon Sirota, the Vilna hazzan who was regarded as one of the finest tenors of his generation, capable of moving his listeners to tears by the emotional intensity he brought to the liturgy, was among those denied permission to perform in Eishyshok's Old Beth Midrash. The fact that he had sung for Tzar Nicholas disqualified him. Yossele Rosenblatt (1882–1933), who stopped in Eishyshok on his East European tour, was approved by the trustees of the Old Beth Midrash — begrudgingly, since he was single at the time. Indeed, he was a child prodigy, who conducted synagogue services with his father.

Eishyshok's own hazzanim included some remarkable singers, among them Ruben Boyarski, who served the shtetl during the opening years of the twentieth century. Hazzan Boyarski, his sister Ida, and his beautiful wife Alte were popular among the youth, for they belonged to Zionist organizations and were members of the newly formed drama club. But the shtetl's cantor was careful to abide by the restrictions placed on him by Reb Zundl Hutner, which meant singing his role off stage when he appeared in a play. The golden-voiced Ruben Boyarski would go on to have a very distinguished career, however, and would eventually appear on many stages. Indeed, he was so good that the great Enrico Caruso invited him to perform with him — an offer he turned down, as he later came to regret. He served for a while as the cantor of

Moshe Tobolski, Eishyshok's last cantor, with children at the Dumbla summer camp, where he was cultural director. Tobolski's magnificent voice, dedication to young people, and close relationship with many shtetl inhabitants won him and his family an honored place in the community. Together with Rabbi Szymen Rozowski, Tobolski walked at the head of the procession to the killing fields of September 1941 and led the community in prayer. Tobolski and his entire family were murdered there. PHOTO: BEN ZION SZREJDER. YESC, D. & I. DIMITRO

the Central Synagogue in Manchester, England, going on to Glasgow from there, and eventually moving to America, where he became the cantor of the Beth Tefila Emanuel Synagogue in Detroit.

In Eishyshok, Ruben Boyarski was succeeded by Asher Markus, who was given the post even though, at age forty, he was long past the prime age for a cantor, and didn't indulge in the kind of showmanship for which many cantors were known. But Reb Asher had such a melodious voice and prayed with such great devotion that his chanting of the prayers during the High Holidays, accompanied by his grandson Lolke Markus and Lolke's friend Fishke Cofnas, was remembered by many as the most moving prayer experience they ever had. Reb Asher was also a shohet (kosher slaughterer) and a mohel (one who performs circumcisions), jobs that were often given to the hazzan if the cantor's job alone could not provide him with a living wage. The job of shohet was in fact considered a way of ensuring the hazzan's always suspect piety, for a shohet had to know Jewish law well enough to pass an annual examination in it.

Gedalia Ginunski nearly became the official hazzan of Eishyshok in the 1920s, but even though he was a native son with a magnificent voice, his yihus (pedigree) was against him. His mother was a seamstress, his father a shoemaker, and his sister Luba an ardent Communist. A brilliant voice and unimpeachable piety were not enough to overcome the opposition that the balebatim of the Old Beth Midrash mounted against his candidacy. For a while he led prayers in the New Beth Midrash, to the delight of many, but eventually left Eishyshok to launch a successful singing career. During one phase of that career he was a member of a noted singing group known as the Vilna Hazzanim Quartet.

The last of Eishyshok's cantors was a man named Moshe Tobolski, who, like Reb Asher Markus, was also one of the shtetl shohatim. Young, handsome, and popular, he had a pretty wife, Rivka, and two little daughters, Sheindele and Zina. Like many other young, fashion-conscious women in the shtetl during the 1930s, Rivka wore short-sleeved dresses and did not cover her hair, for she was determined that neither she nor her daughters be "stigmatized" by their role as female members of a clergyman's family. Tobolski was such a presence in the shtetl, for reasons owing as much to his good looks as to his magnificent voice, that he drew the attention of everyone in it. The women followed his every move, and were particularly delighted to discover that he loved to help out in the kitchen. Soon his fine-cut noodles were a legend among housewives.

Eager to safeguard Reb Tobolski's piety, the older members of the Old Beth Midrash and the young yeshivah students were equally watchful — sometimes perhaps a bit overzealously so, as appears to have been the case during the episode of the berries. It seems that one Saturday the Tobolski family went walking in the Seklutski forest with another young family, and, according to two yeshivah students who were nearby, violated the Sabbath by picking berries. When summoned for questioning by Rabbi Szymen Rozowski, the hazzan and his wife acknowledged that they had been in the forest that day, but insisted that when he bent down and moved his hands toward the berries it was only to point out to the children the differences among various species. Their testimony was corroborated by the other young couple who had been with them that day, Moshe and Zipporah Sonenson.

On the eve of World War II, Tobolski had a number of prestigious offers from central synagogues in Europe and abroad, but he remained in Eishyshok until the end. He and his wife loved the shtetl, had close friends there, and were actively involved in various Zionist community organizations and in the shtetl's summer camp in Dumbla, where Tobolski was the cultural director. Although they expected to leave eventually, they weren't yet ready to say goodbye to a place that had become such a happy home. Thus it happened that Moshe Tobolski was on hand to join Rabbi Rozowski at the head of the procession as it marched to the killing fields.

THE BAAL-TEFILLAH

With six houses of prayer in Eishyshok, three major and three minor ones, quite a number of people were kept busy leading the different congregations. The generic name for all such people was *shliah zibbur,* meaning "messenger of the congregation," and there were several species within that genus. Besides the cantor, who led services only on the Sabbath and on the holidays, there was a baal-tefillah, who did the cantor's job at daily services and, on holidays, performed that portion of the service not specifically related to the holiday. Though the baal-tefillah was expected to have a good but not necessarily great voice, some people preferred his more modest style of praying, for they felt it did not distract them from the content of the prayers, as the showmanship of the typical cantor sometimes did.

The baal-tefillah was an honorary, generally unpaid position, but not just anyone was allowed to fill it. During the 1920s Yude-Yankl the shoemaker was barred from leading the congregation in prayer at the Old Beth Midrash, despite a voice so magnificent that people stood outside his humble dwelling just to hear him sing, because it was not thought suitable for a lowly shoemaker to have such an honor. He was allowed to sing in the New Beth Midrash and the smaller prayerhouses, however. During the 1930s, Yitzhak Broide, a teacher at the yeshivah, sang in the Old Beth Midrash, as did lumber merchant Eliyahu Bastunski — reluctantly, to hear him tell it, in a letter on September 11, 1935, to his son Shlomo in California:

We are awaiting the Day of Atonement — I prayed, thank God, before the Cantor's stand, at the morning prayers in our beth midrash. . . . I can tell you, my son, that this year I did not want to lead the services, but what should I do, all the people pleaded with me. I could not refuse them. . . . Thank God I prayed well. It should not be worse on Yom Kippur.

In reality, people loved to lead the congregation in prayer, and very little persuasion was needed. There were many eagerly awaiting their chance, hoping that the aging Eliyahu Bastunski would soon step aside so that they might take his place near the cantor's stand in the Old Beth Midrash.

THE ZOGERKE

The female version of the baal-tefillah was the zogerke, who sat among those women who did

Golde Moszczenik with husband Honeh. Golde was one of the last zogerkes in Eishyshok. She chanted the prayers in the women's gallery for those who could not follow the hazzan or did not know how to pray. Golde and Honeh were murdered in the September 1941 massacre. A number of their children emigrated to the United States, South America, and Israel.
PHOTO: YITZHAK URI KATZ. YESC, MOSZCZENIK

not know how to read and explained the chants of the hazzan and the baal-tefillah. In a special section of the women's gallery the women gathered around the zogerke to hear her chant the prayers, and repeat them after her. She was paid by the women individually, usually in food, clothing, or firewood. Among the shtetl's last zogerkes were Golde Moszczenik; Mere Ratz, who was fluent in Hebrew and knew the Bible by heart, and was the mother of Frume-Rochl Ratz, the leading lady of Eishyshok's theater; and a woman remembered only as Yache.

THE FINAL PRAYER

Many of Eishyshok's cantors and prayer readers were killed during the Holocaust, including several who were murdered right in the town. Yitzhak Broide the baal-tefillah was shot by a Lithuanian guard near the Kantil River as he attempted to escape. Yache the zogerke was being herded to the synagogue along with all the other Jews when she realized she had forgotten her prayer book. As she raced back home to get it, she was struck by a bullet from the gun of a Lithuanian collaborator and fell into a pool of her own blood in the middle of the market square. Moshe Tobolski the hazzan, dressed in the tall black satin hat, flowing robes, and prayer shawl he wore in shul, and holding a Sefer Torah, recited the Vidduy Gadol as he led the congregation in prayer for the last time on the way to the Old Cemetery. His wife Rivka, holding on to Sheindele and Zina, was struck by the murderers' bullets and fell into the large pit that had been dug for the bodies.

Hazzan Gedalia Ginunski, who had had to leave his beloved shtetl to launch his career, died far away. His wife and children were murdered at Auschwitz, but he was at first spared, for the Germans liked to hear him sing. But when he developed a leg infection he too was sent to the gas chambers.

THE SHOHET: A STEADY HAND AND A RIGHTEOUS HEART

FOR THE SHTETL HOLOCAUST SURVIVORS, THE CONCEPT OF SHEHITA CHANGED FROM THE SLAUGHTER OF ANIMALS TO THE MURDER OF JEWS.

East European Holocaust survivors

Every Jewish community was responsible for hiring a shohet, the person who performed the ritual slaughter of animals and thereby rendered them kosher. Eishyshok usually had two or three people doing this job. Until the codification of the law by Moses ben Israel Isserles, both men and women could serve as ritual slaughterers. But after his 1525 decision, women were barred from the profession in the Ashkenazic communities. Down to the present, however, there has been the occasional shohetet (female shohet) in Sephardic communities.[34]

A member of the Klei Kodesh, the shohet was expected to be well versed in all the laws governing shehita (kosher slaughter), and, according to the Lithuanian Council in 1623, had to be certified annually after being tested for his proficiency in those laws by the community rabbi.[35] Given his clerical standing, the shohet was required to be God-fearing and of fine character; given the nature of his task, he had to be a nondrinker, steady of hand, friendly, and not prone to fainting. So long as he passed his annual test, and did not violate any of the laws governing his profession, the shohet was usually granted hazaka (perpetual tenure).

There were two types of shohatim — those of fowl and those of cows, sheep, and goats. The shehita of the large animals was done in the community slaughterhouse, while that of fowl was usually done in a small shack near the shohet's house. It was the custom in Eishyshok, as in other communities, to have the younger members of the family take the birds to the shack of the shohet. In their later years, many former Eishyshkians recalled those visits to the shohet as among their most vivid memories of childhood. Decades afterward, people remembered (some with horror) every detail of the process: how the birds' legs were tied together so that the youngster could carry it to the shohet bound to a stick or bundled into a wicker basket; how the shohet would wipe his knife until it was spotlessly clean, then gently run the edge of its blade back and forth against his fingernail to make sure that it was completely smooth, without a single notch or dent; and how he recited a benediction immediately before the slaughter: "Blessed art thou, Lord our God, King of the Universe, who hast sanctified us with thy commandments and commanded us to perform the shehita." The shehita consisted of one swift cut to a prescribed spot in the neck, the goal being to make the killing as instantaneous and painless as possible, in order to prevent *zaar baalei hayyim* (cruelty to animals). Whatever blood spilled to the ground, the shohet covered with sand or soil, after which he pronounced another benediction: "Blessed art thou, Lord our God, King of the Universe, who hast sanctified us and commanded us to cover the blood." This benediction applied to all undomesticated animals, who, unlike domesticated animals, owed man nothing and whose slaughter was therefore somewhat shameful.

Animals killed in the slaughterhouse had to be inspected by the shohet in his other role as bodek (examiner), so that he could confirm that the lungs of the animal had not been punctured or in any other way rendered defective, hence nonkosher. (In some communities the shohet was known as *shub*, an acronym for *shohet* and *bodek*.) A verdict of *treifah* (nonkosher) could cause quite an uproar, and the shohet and his customers might then seek a second opinion from the shtetl rabbi or dayyan. Meir Wilkanski recounts one such case, when his father the dayyan received the shohet and several angry butchers.

They did not come unencumbered, but brought along a number of lungs. On a bench the butchers placed one huge lung, stuck a straw in it, and began to inflate it, in which they were assisted by Shalom the shohet and by my father too. The lung did inflate. What a beautiful sight. But on the faces of the blowers there was no sign of joy. Apparently something was wrong. My father began leafing through various books, as did Reb Shalom, while the butchers stood silently next to the oven awaiting the verdict. "Treifah, treifah, there is no legal loophole to make it kosher. Hurry, remove the treifah from the house!"[36]

A verdict of *treifah* meant trouble for a number of people: for the butchers, who would have to sell the meat to gentiles at a loss, for the leaser of the korobka, who was usually allowed to collect the meat tax only on kosher meat, and ultimately for all consumers, since the butchers passed their losses on to the customer in the form of higher prices. The community at large was also affected, for proceeds from the korobka were one of its main sources of revenue, out of which came the salaries of the Klei Kodesh, and money for many vital community services.

The poor were the most deeply affected of all, as it was they who were most dependent on various forms of community support, and they who could least afford to pay a higher price for meat.

Yitzhak Burstein, Reb Itche der Shohet, was among the last shohatim (ritual slaughterers) of Eishyshok. During the September 1941 massacre one of his Polish neighbors told the Germans of Reb Itche's occupation. The Germans ordered him to bring his halaf (knife). They slashed his throat with it. PHOTO: YITZHAK URI KATZ, 1924. YESC, ELLEN MURAD

But centralized control over the slaughter and sale of kosher meat was a millennia-old tradition, which can be traced to the tenth century in Israel and in Egypt; its yoke would continue to weigh heavily on the poor until the mid-eighteenth century, when the founder of Hasidism, Rabbi Israel ben Eliezer, the Baal Shem Tov (1700–1760), took a stand against the monopoly of the kahal over the slaughter and the tax by providing his own shohatim to some communities, sometimes even free of charge. Many historians attribute much of the popularity of the Hasidic movement to this act.[37] In Eishyshok, however, the Hasidim never gained a foothold, and until well into the twentieth century the korobka remained a frequent source of conflict within the community, and the shohatim were often in the midst of it.

Indeed, the problems of the shohatim did not end with their own communities. In the mid-1930s the Polish government took it upon itself to try to ban the shehita, on the grounds that it constituted cruelty to animals. As it happened, this national movement coincided with a local event in Eishyshok that had aroused the alarm of the entire shtetl population. One day two young children, a brother and a sister, had gone to the shohet's shack, as generations of youngsters before them had done. While watching the shohet slaughter their chicken, the girl apparently suffered a freak heart attack and died instantly. The town was in a state of shock at the news. No one could recall such a tragedy, and people could talk of little else. Mothers and grandmothers debated the wisdom of sending young children to the shohet, while teachers in the Hebrew school devoted entire lessons to discussions of the humane aspects of the Jewish shehita.

Eventually the furor died down and custom prevailed. Youngsters continued to perform their centuries-old chore in Eishyshok until the very end. The Polish government managed to curtail the number of animals that went under the knives of the shohatim, but the resulting meat shortage was just another of the many indignities and hardships inflicted on the Jewish community at this time.

In the not very distant future, the question of cruelty to animals would be quite forgotten, overshadowed by far greater cruelties to humankind — as revealed by the following story of the Polish veterinarian of Eishyshok and a young Jewish girl in his household.

Dr. Shemitkowsky employed the girl as a babysitter for his small children. There was great mutual respect and admiration between the young babysitter and the Shemitkowsky family. Thus it was to them that she ran when she escaped from the Horse Market where the Jews had been locked up on the eve of the human shehita in September 1941. Mrs. Shemitkowsky greeted her at the door with a glass of water and said, "My child, drink the water. When animals drink water prior to their slaughter, it makes their death easier."

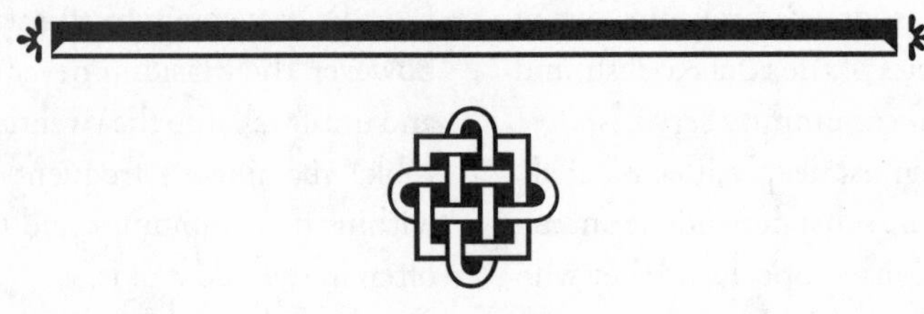

THE HEDER — LITERALLY "ROOM"— WAS NOT STRICTLY A PRODUCT OF THE SHTETL. Different aspects of its identity can be traced to Jerusalem during the Second Commonwealth, to Babylonia, and to the medieval Ashkenazic community. Once the shtetlekh of Eastern Europe embraced the heder, however, they shaped it according to their own needs and endowed it with their own unique, unmistakable character. So successful was the adaptation that for centuries the heder was viewed as the backbone of East European Jewish education, all but synonymous with Jewish boyhood. As such it came to be a prime target for criticism from those who disapproved of the insularity and provincialism of East European Jewry, and a magnet for praise among those who supported that community in its effort to preserve its identity.

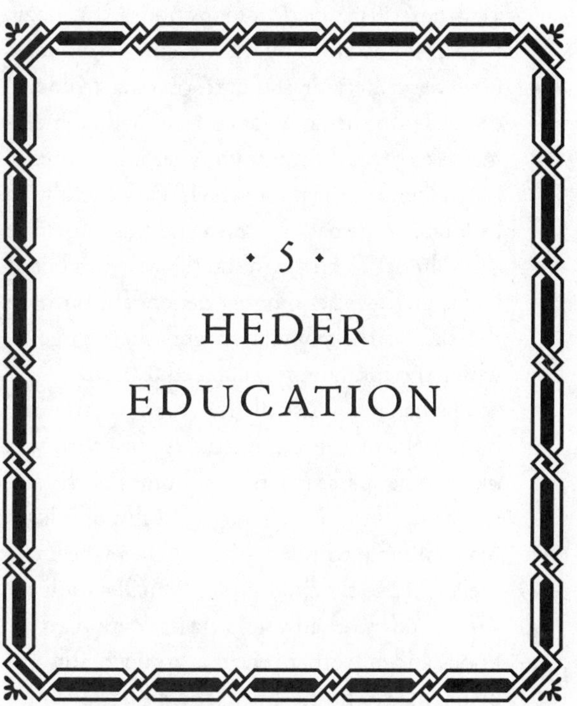

5 HEDER EDUCATION

THE HEDER EMERGED FROM THE CORE OF JEWISH LIFE. IT WAS CREATED IN THE IMAGE OF THE COMMUNITY AND BECAME THE PEOPLE'S SACRED PILLAR OF STRENGTH.

A. M. Lifshitz,
HA-HEDER *(1920)*

An integral part of shtetl life, the heder was both an extension of and preparation for the intellectual and spiritual life of the synagogue and beth midrash. Like all the male adults he knew, the heder boy studied Torah, and he, like them, was brought up to believe that "Teireh is die beste Sheyreh" (Torah is the best merchandise).

The heder was the first and most important of the institutions responsible for molding the boy in the image of the community and preparing him to take his place in it. Once the little charges were given over to the melamed (teacher), it was accepted by all that the basic aim was to produce a God-fearing, mitzvot-observing, knowledgeable, charitable Jew, well versed in halakhic sources, well trained for a traditional way of life, ready to take his place in his community. Thanks to the large amount of individual attention most of the boys received, and the rigorous twice-weekly testing to which they were subjected (once at heder, once at home), this goal was generally fulfilled.

The crowning achievement of heder life, however, was to produce a Talmid haham, a Talmudic scholar, the elite of East European Jewish society. Requiring a certain combination of money, talent, application, and interest, this was a goal reached only by a relatively small number. Not until the Haskalah (the Jewish Enlightenment), however, would any other goal be accorded the same high value.

For a detailed description of the heder, we can look to the Cracow Ordinance (c. 1594 or 1595), one of the first written documents concerning Eastern European Jewish education. A summary of the Cracow Jews' educational practices, which were largely based on those the German Jewish settlers had brought into the community, it can be seen as the basic blueprint for heder education throughout Eastern Europe, well into the twentieth century.[1]

Originally the heder was located in a room at the synagogue or beth midrash that was set aside specifically for the schooling of young children, a custom still in practice among non-Ashkenazic Jews. As prescribed by the Cracow Ordinance, however, it became standard practice to locate the heder in the home of each individual melamed, except for the community-supported heder for the sons of the poor, which was generally to be found at the beth midrash and was known as the Talmud Torah. Each shtetl had a number of hadarim, the exact number dependent both on the size of the population and the degree to which the community valued education.

The heder was usually the main room in the household of the melamed. Its furniture was likely to be sparse (as in most homes of the sixteenth century), consisting, typically, of a large wooden table with wooden benches where the melamed and the children sat, a smaller table for the second, more advanced class, a cupboard for books and any other precious family heirlooms belonging to the melamed, and a huge oven for cooking and for heat. The oven had other purposes, too: its flat top could be used as a sleeping place, and a compartment at the bottom, known as the *katukh*, often served as a hen roost. At times, an education-conscious yishuvnik (rural Jew) from a village too small to have a heder of its own would send his bright son to a heder in a neighboring town, in which case the melamed's already crowded room became the boy's dormitory, its clay floor, covered with a batch of straw, his bed. The melamed's livestock, generally consisting of a goat or two and a few chickens, also boarded in these cramped quarters during the cold winter months.

A modern heder in Eishyshok, March 28, 1927. Seated in the center is the melamed, Eliezer David Mordekhai Krapovnitski, who was known as Reb Adam. The heder boys are (standing, right to left) Shlomo Pilushki, Moshe Dovid Katz, Shmuel Shlanski, Avraham Kabacznik, and Shlomo Dugaczanski; (seated) Sander Nochomowicz, Alexander Zisl Hinski, Yehiel Blacharowicz, and a boy known as Hishveh from the village of Golmecziszki. Shmuel and Hishveh eventually emigrated to America, Sander to Argentina, Alexander Zisl to Eretz Israel. Of the others, Avraham died a natural death; the rest were murdered during the September 1941 massacre. PHOTO: YITZHAK URI KATZ. YESC, SH. & Z. HINSKI

In an adjacent room, usually the bedroom, the melamed's wife, daughters, and infant sons went about their daily life. (Older boys were of course in the heder or yeshivah.) It was not uncommon for the wife to run a business from her home, in order to supplement her husband's meager income, such as growing vegetables, pickling herring, sauerkraut, or cucumbers, raising goats or chickens, or running a small wig factory — perhaps in the very room where the boys sat. A spinning wheel threaded with women's hair was a not unusual sight in many a heder. With or without a business to attend to, however, the melamed's wife was likely to be a constant presence in the lives of her husband's small charges, and her personality did much to establish the tone of the school.

Meir Wilkanski retained fond memories of the woman who presided over his melamed's household, especially of the pleasant greetings she gave the children when they arrived, before her husband had returned from morning services. But in other homes such harmony was not always the rule, and Wilkanski recalled hearing about one melamed whose yishuvnik boarders witnessed the corporal punishment of his children — including his young daughters, though he would first bind their legs for the sake of modesty — and on occasion his wife as well.[2]

The melamed's other family affairs were similarly visible to the heder pupils. They witnessed the hectic preparations for a wedding, the pain and suffering of a sick child. Mordekhai Zanin, the founder and editor of the Yiddish newspaper *Die Letzte Naeis*, recalls that in his heder in Sokolov, at the turn of the century, the melamed did not have sufficient food for a bedridden son, and the students would share their lunches with him. This sharing may not have been completely voluntary, for one episode that remains vivid in his mind is the time the melamed cautioned one of his students not to eat his hard-boiled egg, lest it have a drop of blood in the yolk, thus rendering it nonkosher. The offending egg was tossed into the sick child's bed, ostensibly for him to play with, as the melamed put it, but more likely as food for the starving child to eat once the students returned to their studies and left him alone with it.

THE MELAMDIM

There were three basic levels of melamdim, one for each of the three stages of heder education. Melamdei dardakei (Aramaic for "small children") or melamdei tinokot (Hebrew for "tots") were teachers in the early-childhood heder, where the main goal was to learn to read the aleph beth (Hebrew alphabet) and acquire basic reading skills in Hebrew; melamdei Humash were teachers in the middle heder, where the subject was the Pentateuch; and melamdei gapat (an acronym for Gemara, Peirush [Rashi commentary], and tosafot) were teachers in the advanced heder, where the subject was Gemara with commentaries. Melamdim of early-childhood and middle hadarim were paid less than those who taught at advanced hadarim.

Melamdim were not subject to any formal community supervision, nor did they have to receive any pedagogical training, pass any exam, or be granted any kind of certification.[3] Insofar as the community did concern itself with the schools, it was to monitor the students' level of accomplishment, rather than the knowledge of their teachers. Occasionally it happened that a man who sought employment as a teacher would be given an oral test by the town rabbi, but this was mainly for the purpose of protecting local melamdim from outside competition.

Though their competence varied considerably, many melamdim were yeshivah graduates, accomplished scholars who had hoped to use their gifts in some more prestigious and rewarding position. But since this was a society that trained most of its bright male population for a life of scholarship without offering them jobs commensurate with this training, many men never got the chance to realize their intellectual ambitions. Employment as a melamed was often undertaken as a last resort, the only means available for supporting a growing family. Teaching in a heder was considered a degrading occupation, the word *melamed* a derogatory term. When the nineteenth-century Russian intellectual Daniel Khwolson said he would rather be a professor in St. Petersburg than a melamed in Eishyshok, he was not only explaining his reasons for converting to Christianity, but giving voice to sentiments shared by many of his brilliant but frustrated peers.

Many a heder student must have shared the wish that his teacher could be elsewhere, for accomplished as some of these yeshivah graduates may have been as scholars, they had no training as teachers and thus lacked the most rudimentary pedagogical skills. Some teachers — usually melamdei dardakei in small, remote shtetlekh without access to institutions of higher learning — lacked both knowledge and teaching skills. Still, a number of melamdim had a natural gift for teaching that would be the envy of many a well-trained teacher today. Eishyshok seems to have been generously endowed with such teachers, thanks to the prestigious yeshivah in its midst.

A melamed's hours were long and the salary was not only low (a very basic fee was recorded in the pinkas of Eishyshok, for example), it was often not even in cash; rather, it might be paid in the form of food, wood for the oven, grazing rights for the melamed's livestock, or housing for the melamed and his family. Moreover, it was unstable, since it depended on the number of students the melamed could attract, and parents frequently moved their sons from one melamed to another, always in search of the one who would take the boys to new heights of academic achievement.

The bottom line was that the melamed had to satisfy the fathers, who were the tuition payers. This system had both its positive and its negative aspects. Since the melamed knew he was being judged primarily by the boys' accomplishments, this meant he had an investment in achieving good teaching results. However, it also meant that the eldest son of a well-to-do father of five or six promising young boys, all potential heder students, was likely to attract a teacher's best efforts. Conversely, the sons of the poor, or of families where the father was not very interested in academic achievement or not able to judge it effectively, or lacking in additional sons, were often ignored.

CHOOSING A MELAMED

A father took many factors into account when choosing a melamed. In a society that put such a high value on a Torah education — for one half of its population, anyway — selecting the right melamed was a weighty matter that required serious thought. Over and above the question of the level of scholarship the various candidates had achieved, which was particularly important in a Gemara teacher, they were closely scrutinized for their command of diction and pronunciation, their knowledge of Hebrew vocabulary and grammar, their fluency in the many prayer chants to be recited on different days of the religious calendar, their ability to maintain order, and the saintliness of their behavior.

Like many another shtetl with an elite yeshivah in its midst, Eishyshok was blessed with an overwhelming number of melamdim during its last 150 years, some of very high quality indeed. One of the finest among them was "the Yeremitcher rebbe," Reb Tuviah Rubinstein, an awe-inspiring figure. Though he was subject

Reb Tuvia Rubinstein, "the Yeremitcher rebbe," was one of the shtetl's most beloved and inspiring melamdim. His perfect Hebrew and his love for the Bible and the Holy Land were engraved on his students' minds. Eight decades later, they could still quote the Yeremitcher word for word. Reb Tuvia emigrated with his family to Eretz Israel in the early 1920s. YESC, S. RUBINSTEIN

to breathing difficulties in moments of excitement and even to occasional fainting spells, the eloquence and power of his classes in the Prophets held his students spellbound. He was a master teacher whose excellent command of Hebrew was gracefully transmitted to his students, as was his love of the Prophets and the Holy Land. Eighty years later, his former students — some of them sprightly paragons of health, others attached to life support systems in hospitals, or confined to nursing homes — still lit up at the mention of his name. Without hesitation they could quote, out of the depths of their cluttered memories, whole chapters from the Prophets, complete with the appropriate commentaries, and this would be done in perfect diction, with all proper grammatical emphases, as if these old men had just stepped out from the Yeremitcher's heder to the cobblestone-paved market square of Eishyshok.

COMPULSORY EDUCATION: EARLY-CHILDHOOD HEDER

A boy's education was considered to commence when he began to speak, at which time it was the duty of the father to teach him to recite selected verses from the Bible. Great value was placed on the education a boy received in these early years, which was a matter not just of academic but of moral training, with the child being inculcated in the habit of observing the mitzvot.* About this much, there was general agreement. But agreement broke down on the question of when to begin a boy's compulsory education outside the home. An ancient ordinance said: "At five years the age is reached for studying the Bible."[4] Alternately, Rav (Abba ben Aivu, also known as Abba Arikha), the famed third-century Babylonian scholar, advised: "Do not accept a pupil under the age of six; but at the age of six, stuff him with knowledge like an ox."[5]

The various kehilot (communities) that made up the Council of the Four Lands did not follow either of those pieces of advice, determining in their wisdom that three was an acceptable age for a heder yingl (heder boy). For sons of the poor and for orphans, whose education was the responsibility of the community, the ancient ordinance was followed, and their formal education did not commence until age five — thus saving the community two years of tuition, which was probably the justification for the practice.

While the age at which it began was not fixed, the education of boys was mandatory and it was the father's legal obligation to provide for it. Any father who failed to send his sons to heder or to hire a private tutor was punished by the community, the punishments ranging in severity from various monetary sanctions to the extreme measure of revoking residency rights. As a result, the Jewish male population was highly literate, with illiteracy to be found mainly among the yishuvniks — Jews who resided in remote rural areas outside the shtetl.[6]

Virtually all Jewish boys received at least an elementary education and attended school until sometime between the ages of seven and nine. The first statistics available, dating from the end of the nineteenth century, when they were prepared by the Jewish Colonization Association (I.C.A.), showed that in the Pale of Settlement there were 375,000 children in hadarim registered with Russian government agencies. Since many hadarim were not registered with the government, the actual number of children in school was actually much higher.[7]

On the day a boy was brought to school to become a heder yingl, he left his childhood behind,

*The observance of the mitzvot included wearing a four-fringed garment known as a zizit, saying a short prayer such as "Moses commanded us a law, an inheritance of the Congregation of Jacob" (Deuteronomy 33:4), and reciting the blessing over bread and other foods.

embarking on the journey toward manhood. This dramatic event was marked by a ceremony that evolved through many centuries, but always retained certain common aspects. During the Middle Ages, at the beginning of every new zeman (semester), each boy who had come of age was wrapped in a prayer shawl in the early hours of the morning, carried to the heder, and turned over to the melamed. The melamed took the boy in his arms, gave him an aleph-beth tablet smeared with honey, a small cake called a kilorit, and a hard-boiled egg with passages from the Bible written on the shell. Legend has it that Rabbi Eleazar Kallir, the famed liturgical poet of long ago, took his name as well as his talent from the kilorit he ate at the ceremony commencing his education.[8]

The next step in the ceremony was for the melamed to whisper a few magical words above the boy's head, as a charm against Pura, the angel of forgetfulness. After the boy listened to the melamed read from the aleph beth and recite the biblical passages inscribed on his egg, he was allowed to lick the honey and eat the cake. By way of concluding the ceremony, the melamed took the boy to the shore of a flowing river or other source of fresh water, both because the Torah was often likened to a stream of water and because running water was thought to be conducive to memory and study.[9]

Elements of this ceremony continued to be practiced well into the twentieth century. Wrapped in a prayer shawl, the boy was carried to the heder by one or both of his parents, handed over to the melamed, and given a tablet imprinted with the aleph beth or else with the words *emeth* (truth) or *Torah*.* Then he was showered with fruits, coins, and candies, as described by Rabbi Moshe ben Henich Brantshpigl, writing at the beginning of the seventeenth century: "When a boy begins his education he is greeted with soothing, flattering words. His rebbe showers upon him fruits from above, and says, 'An angel is throwing these treats to you, so that you should study with eagerness.'"[10]

In his autobiography, Eishyshok chronicler Meir Wilkanski recounts his own first day at heder in 1886, when he was four years old:

One sunny day after the holiday of Sukkot, I burst into the house and announced to my mother, "I want to go to the heder. Take me to the heder." At that moment my mother was engrossed in a conversation with my father, holding in her hand the huge two-pronged key to their store. Both looked at me with great satisfaction. But Mother asked me to wait a while, and Father explained that the Inspector was in town, making his rounds. It was important for Mother to be at the store when he arrived, so that she could open it up for him . . .

Though I continued to plead, "to the heder, to the heder," and even tried tears, it was to no avail. Mother slipped out of the house and left. I then started to chase after her, running through the marketplace toward her store on nearby Shop Row, where all the shopkeepers were standing at their store entrances awaiting inspection. When I finally caught up with her, I got hold of her apron and would not let go. "To the heder, to the heder," I kept on pleading.

A neighboring shopkeeper, hearing my pleas and seeing my tears, offered to open our shop for examination when the Inspector arrived, so that he would indeed see it in all its stark emptiness. Mother considered and accepted her offer, handing her the large two-pronged key.

We then departed for the heder, steering our way through the crowds on Shop Row, squeezing between barrels filled with fragrant apples, then at last turning into a long alley where my mother exclaimed: "Here is

*According to the Gaon of Vilna, the three letters of the word *emeth* are the essence of the entire Torah: The letter *aleph* is at the beginning of the Torah, *mem* in the middle, and *taf* at the end.

In this eighteenth-century drawing, an angel welcomes the young heder boy by showering him with fruits, coins, and candy. On the left is a melamed with kanchik in hand. EDUCATIONAL ENCYCLOPEDIA, 1964, VOL. IV, P. 390

the heder!" As we neared a small house from which two windows stared down at us, I saw a man leaning out one of them. His beard was red, his eyes were bleary, and he wore blue spectacles. He looked at us and smiled, whereupon Mother announced, "Here is the rebbe. How he will rejoice to welcome you!"

But a sudden sadness came over me just then, and I let go of my mother's apron and ran away. I ran with all my strength, never looking back, retracing my steps through the long alley, across the marketplace, and finally into our home. Sensing my presence, Father looked up from his Gemara, over at me, and asked, "Have you seen Mother? Did she take you to the heder? Where is she? Why have you come back?" I stood in the corner, thumb in mouth, eyes downcast, silent. Father paced the room, back and forth, back and forth, until he went over to the window and stood there motionless, staring outside. Only the squeak of the door, signaling Mother's return, interrupted the heavy silence.

Mother told Father the entire episode, and both demanded an explanation. But I continued to look at the floor in silence. Then they asked if I was now willing to go back to the heder. I shook my head in the negative.

I was carried to the next room and placed on a windowsill, surrounded by my mother, my father, and my brother-in-law, all of them speaking soothing and comforting words. Mother promised me the best goodies the market could offer. Father told me about the generosity of the Angel toward those who studied Torah. My brother-in-law tried reason: "You are already four years old and still don't know how to pray. A young man who behaves like a coachman! All your friends already learn Torah, and you're still playing with horses . . ." When I continued to shake my head in defiance, my brother-in-law became angry. His red pointed beard moved from side to side and his mouth uttered stern words. "This worm needs a strong hand. Otherwise you will be like Yashka and Petrushka, a goy! And like them you will be sitting on the ground and digging up potatoes. . . ."

Hand in hand Mother and I crossed the marketplace, stopping before one of the barrels in order to buy red-cheeked apples and raisins. From there we turned into the small long alley, and neared the small house. Once again I saw the rebbe, framed in the window, his beard red, his eyes bleary behind his blue spectacles. I let go of my mother's hand but this time she realized what was happening and gripped me tightly. The rebbe came out, swinging a leather strap. After him came a troop of children who caught me and began dragging me toward the house. Though I pushed, kicked, scratched with my nails, and lay stretched out on the ground, holding on to anything and everything I could grasp to delay my progress, my strength was no match for theirs, and I at last found myself inside the heder.

There I was placed at a long table, the aleph-beth tablet before me. As tears streamed from my eyes, two apples fell onto the table from above, followed by a shiny copper penny, a gift from the good Angel. The rebbe smiled.

Mother distributed raisins, giving a double portion to my friend Israel. He ate with a great appetite while staring at me. Through the fog of my tears I inspected the room. When I tried to get up from the bench, I found I was riveted to it. Four hands were holding me down, and a voice was telling me "Do not cry, do not cry."[11]

Though their versions were much less dramatic than Meir Wilkanski's, Eishyshkians Moshe Kaganowicz and Peretz Kaleko vividly remembered their own first days in heder, in 1904 and 1912 respectively. Wrapped in prayer shawls, they were carried to the heder by their mothers through the same huge market square where Meir Wilkanski and thousands of other tots had begun their journey toward Torah education. Once arrived, they too were met by a melamed who gave them the aleph-beth slate while coins were rained down upon them from above. But they belonged to the last generation of Eishyshkians for whom this ancient ceremony was the norm rather than the exception. (And Peretz would spend only a short time in the traditional heder, soon switching to a more modern school.)

The Eastern European Jew's world, which was centered on the synagogue and on scholarship, was text-oriented, requiring a reading knowledge of the central texts of the faith. A boy's education therefore commenced with learning to read from the Siddur (prayer book), the same book that would accompany him throughout his adult years, the book that was the earliest and most visible sign of the lifelong bond between the synagogue and every male of the community. As the boy's primary reader, the Siddur opened with a page on which the aleph beth and the vowels were printed — a standard teaching tool used in hadarim throughout Eastern Europe. Standing before his charges, the melamed displayed a chart that was an enlarged version of the one in the Siddur, and as he pointed to each letter on the chart he spoke its name. The children repeated what he said in unison, making a loud chant.

To assist him in the difficult task of teaching his charges the secrets of the aleph beth, the melamed employed a bahelfer (assistant), who was usually a young man in his early teens. Bahelfers were mandatory in early-childhood hadarim, but since they were paid by the melamed, who was himself very poorly paid, their services were dispensed with whenever possible. Nonetheless, they played an official and well-recognized role in the educational system of the shtetl, and they even had their own professional "conventions." Twice a year, during the intermediary days of Passover and Sukkot, the bahelfers held regional fairs, where they exchanged information about job opportunities and other pertinent topics. So important did the young men consider these job fairs that many traveled considerable distances, at no small cost to themselves, to attend them.[12]

How well the youngsters mastered their studies often depended on the personality and ability of the bahelfer, for he was an integral part of every aspect of their early educational experi-

Mina Kaleko with five of her children (right to left): Shmuel, little Peretz, Shaul, Simha, and Rachel standing in the front. The photo was taken in 1912 to commemorate little Peretz's entering the heder at the age of three. All his life Peretz remembered his mother wrapping him in a prayer shawl and carrying him to the school. The photo was mailed to his father, Mordekhai Munesh Kaleko, who was living in Boston at the time. The entire Kaleko family, with the exception of Shmuel, emigrated to Eretz Israel in the 1930s. Shmuel and his family were killed in Ghetto Grodno. PHOTO: YITZHAK URI KATZ. YESC, KALEKO-ALUFI

ence. Depending on local custom, his working day might begin in the homes of the smallest boys, where he would help them to wash and get dressed. At dawn and dusk, with lantern in hand, he guided his little charges to and from the heder, sometimes even carrying them in his arms. Once arrived at the heder, he prayed with them, fed them, and brought them their lunches when necessary. For the youngest pupils, the bahelfers did a lot to help soften the rigors of heder life.

Appeals to the youngsters' imagination in the early stages of their training in literacy were another of the concessions made to their youth. Avraham Hayyim Schorr (d. 1632) advised melamdim how to bring life to the monotonous process of learning the aleph beth: for example, tell the little ones that the letter *gimel* has what looks like a pouch hanging from its side; the *aleph* can be likened to a person drawing water while carrying one pitcher in his hand and another on his back; the letter *beth* has a wide-open mouth, a reminder that one should widen his mouth with knowledge.[13]

With or without the aid of their teachers, the little children who sat in the heder from dawn to dusk looked to their imaginations for help in memorizing their lessons, seeking to associate the letters of the aleph beth with all the sights and sounds of the world that was just outside their windows, yet ever far away. One particularly imaginative child, Hayyim Nahman Bialik (1873–1934), who would grow up to be the Hebrew poet of the National Awakening, described in his autobiography his own first encounter with the challenges of the aleph beth:

From the first day on which the assistant showed me the letters of the aleph beth set out in rows, I saw leaping forth the measured ranks of soldiers like those who at times passed in front of our house, with their drummer rattling "tum tararum tum" at their head. Those that most resembled this were the alephs, *all arms swinging and legs striding, and the* gimels *with their boots moving off to the left, particularly when they had the* kubbutz *vowel beneath them, its three dots like a ladder. These were real soldiers, armed head to foot. The* alephs *had their knapsacks on their backs and strode along somewhat bowed under their burden, proceeding to manoeuvres, while the* gimels *began to search the sides and flanks of the hornbook.*

"Whom are you looking for?" asked the assistant.

"For the drummer," said I, my eyes searching.

The assistant dropped the pointer, took me by my chin, raised my head slightly and stared at me with animal-like eyes. Suddenly he roused and said, "Get down!" Two syllables, no more. And at once another child took my place and I went down vexed and went off into a corner so as not to know what the assistant wanted. All day long I daydreamed about armies and soldiers. Next day, when I went up again, the assistant showed me the form of an aleph *and asked me: "Can you see the yoke and a pair of pails?"*

"That's true, upon my soul; a yoke and a pair of pails!"

"Well, that's an aleph,*" testified the assistant.*

"Well, that's an aleph,*" I repeated after him.*

"What's this?" the assistant asked again.

"A yoke and a pair of pails," I replied, highly delighted that the Holy and Blessed one had sent me such fine utensils.

"No, say aleph!*" repeated the assistant, and went on, "Remember:* aleph, aleph.*"*

. . . And the minute I went down the aleph *flew away and was replaced by Maryusa, the gentile girl who drew water. She never budged all day long. I saw her just as she was, with her bare shanks, her thick plaits, and the yoke and pails on her shoulders. . . .*

"What's this?" the assistant asked me the next day, showing me the aleph.

"Oh, Maryusa," quoth I, happy to find her again.[14]

It is interesting to note that the assistant, the bahelfer, is using the same imagery — the two pails or pitchers — suggested three hundred years earlier by Avraham Hayyim Schorr. Even the appeal to the imagination, and the precise form it took, had become part of the tradition.

Learning to read Hebrew (Yivre) was the main objective of the early-childhood heder. The process was divided into three major phases lasting from one to two years each, depending on the child's ability. Phase one consisted of mastering the aleph beth, learning the names of the letters and their proper order. This was a task both practical and spiritual since, according to some, the letters are endowed with a special holiness, a mystical quality.[15] In phase two, the youngster embarked on an intensive program of reading exercises in which he mastered syllables, then words, phrases, and entire sentences, leading up to phase three, in which he learned to read and pronounce the prayers and gained familiarity with the customs surrounding them. To achieve the desired fluency in reading Hebrew, students performed countless repetitions and drills. When a student made mistakes, the ever-present rod was not spared.

Knowing the right prayers, the right chants, and the correct pronunciation of the Hebrew words offered the youngster his first initiation into the adult male fellowship of the synagogue. Such mastery was considered the most elementary level of education to be attained by every Jewish male. It stopped short of translation, however, which was taught in the middle heder. Since many youngsters from poor families were not able to continue their studies past early-childhood heder, and thus never learned much about the meaning of the prayers they pronounced, they were cut off forever from the intellectual and spiritual wealth of Humash (see below) and Talmud. Moreover, as lifelong members of the shtetl's uneducated class, they would find any hope of social mobility within the rigid class structure of the shtetl permanently foreclosed.

HUMASH (MIDDLE) HEDER

Toward the end of the third phase of the education received in early-childhood heder, the students were given a preview of the subject matter that would occupy them in middle heder: the Humash, consisting of the Five Books of Moses, also referred to as the Torah or the Five Books of the Law (Genesis, Exodus, Leviticus, Numbers, and Deuteronomy). This, along with the commentary of Rashi, the eleventh-century biblical and Talmudic scholar, would be their central study for a number of years to come, constituting the Book of Books that was to accompany the young men throughout their lives, another manifestation and reinforcement of the bond between them and the synagogue. And the material would be studied in the original. As in the early-childhood heder, no books specifically designed for children were used in the Humash heder. Like all the adult men they knew, the heder boys learned directly from the sacred texts.

Physically the middle heder was much like the early-childhood heder — same tables, same backless benches, same familiar household setting — but the differences were perhaps more striking than the similarities. Not only was the melamed himself different, for the Humash melamdim belonged to a more prestigious caste than those who taught the youngest children, the course of study was very different and so was the psychological atmosphere. The children no longer had the assistance of bahelfers, and the children were in fact no longer considered children: They were addressed as "bohrim" (young men), not as "heder yingls."

Admission to the Humash heder was marked by a special ceremony that took place on a Saturday sometime after the beginning of the new semester. The festivities were to mark the boy's acceptance of the Yoke of Torah and the responsibilities of Judaism — not in the legal, halakhic sense, but as a "Jew in training." Family, friends, and classmates were invited to the honoree's home, where tables set with special sweets and fruits marked the occasion. Dressed in his Sabbath best, which was likely to include a pocket watch with a golden chain, the family heirloom, the young man received his guests. Then the ceremony began.

Placed atop a table surrounded by other heder boys, the "Jew in training" faced the man who had been asked to pose the series of questions that was part of the standard initiation ceremony. Though the details varied slightly from region to region to allow for local idiosyncrasies, the basic shape of the ceremony was the same throughout Europe. It went like this:

QUERIST: *What's your name, graceful child?*

BOY: *I am no longer a child but a proper young man who has begun to study Humash with mazl and blessing.*

QUERIST: *What is Humash?*

BOY: *Humash is five.*

QUERIST: *What is five, maybe five rolls for a penny?*

BOY: *No. Five are five Books of the Torah that God gave to Moses.*

QUERIST: *What are their names?*

BOY: *Genesis, Exodus, Leviticus, Numbers, Deuteronomy.*

QUERIST: *And, if indeed you are a proper young man, tell me which one of the five books will you be studying?*

BOY: *I will be studying Vaikra (Leviticus).*

QUERIST: *What is the meaning of Vaikra? Who called upon whom? Maybe Bezalel, the shtetl's sexton, called upon another Jew to come to the synagogue?*

BOY: *No, God called upon Moses to command him about the sacrifices in the Holy Temple.*

QUERIST: *And what do you have to do with laws regarding sacrifices?*

BOY: *Because the sacrifices were pure, and I am a pure Jewish child. Let an innocent child study about the holy sacrifices.*

QUERIST: *And why is the letter* aleph *in the word* Vaikra *a tiny one?*

BOY: *Because I am a small child and I will be studying Torah.* Aleph *means studying, and the Torah exists only among those who humble themselves on her behalf and are not arrogant.*

QUERIST: *Why are you arrogant?*

BOY: *God forbid! I am not arrogant.*

QUERIST: *So why are you standing on the table?*

BOY: *I am listening to you and I am stepping down.*

As the boy did so, family and friends showered him with blessings and small gifts. The day was an especially proud one for his mother.

The following morning in the Humash heder he joined the other students in the study of the weekly portion, one of the fifty-four portions into which the Five Books of Moses are divided for the synagogue's annual cycle of public readings.

Every Saturday that week's entire portion is read in the synagogue, and the first three sections of the portion are also read during the preceding week at Monday and Thursday morning services. In preparation for assuming his proper role in the synagogue, the boy now began to learn how to chant each week's portion aloud to the accompaniment of a rhythmic swaying of the body — a practice that was followed by everyone in the synagogue, but may in fact have originated in the heder. Though swaying during prayer is a tradition not just in Judaism but in other faiths as well, this particular swaying motion, which came to typify the Eastern European Jew at prayer in the synagogue, probably got its start on the backless benches of the early-childhood heder, when the boys tried to compensate for the discomfort of sitting there for hours at a stretch. As for the chant, it was a special one prescribed for heder boys learning Humash, and it differed from the cantillations used in the synagogue (though in the Sephardic and the Yemenite hadarim, the heder boys' chant is the same as the synagogue chant).

Proficiency in reading the weekly portion was the most essential goal of a Humash heder education. Since the days of the Cracow Ordinance, proficiency had been deemed to mean not just the literal act of reading, but comprehension; therefore the readings were translated word for word into Yiddish, albeit using a translation that dated back to medieval Germany — a translation still used today by heder students around the world, from Brooklyn to Jerusalem. Some of its strange German words are so ancient and rare that they are now known only to those Jewish school boys, and to a handful of scholars of pre-Reformation German. (The old German words known to the heder boys predated Luther's sixteenth-century translation of the Bible, which was one of the milestones in modernizing the German language.)

As the melamed read and translated the weekly portion, which the students repeated in unison after him, he also incorporated various homiletic and midrashic commentaries into his recitation. This he typically did so seamlessly that for the rest of their lives the students made no distinction between the text proper and its numerous exegeses; in their minds all these elements were part of one long, carefully wrought, continuous work.

At the beginning of this new stage in their education, the students learned only the first of the three sections of each week's portion of the Law, but gradually they were expected to increase their reading to include the second and third sections, until they had reached the goal of being able to complete the entire weekly portion. As noted by the heder's critics, this goal was rarely achieved, which meant the Humash heder did not in fact give the youngsters the comprehensive knowledge of the Five Books that was its central mandate.

In the second and most crucial phase of the Humash heder education, the study of Humash was done in conjunction with the study of the Rashi commentary. Mastery of the commentary was accepted as the very yardstick of the level of learning deemed appropriate for an ordinary Jew, placing him above the ignoramus and below the Talmudic scholar.

The method of teaching was monotonous and boring. The melamed translated from his huge Humash, followed by numerous repetitions by melamed and students, which went on from dawn to dusk, with a few short breaks, until the students had memorized the material.

At this stage of his education the young man was also expected to learn Hebrew, some sections from the Prophets, penmanship, composition, and the various customs governing the Jewish calendar in the synagogue and at home — all of this in preparation for the next stage, the pinnacle of Jewish scholarship, the study of the Talmud.

Thursday, examination day, was the most dreaded day of the week in the heder. The humiliation and the corporal punishment that were the lot of those who failed left scars that often lingered.

Those teachers who were natural pedagogues as well as being talented in arts and crafts sometimes created teaching aids to enliven the material and make it more comprehensible. Favorite props included a model of the Tabernacle and its furnishings, maps of the Holy Land, and dolls dressed in the uniforms worn by priests serving in the Temple. But with or without these teaching aids, the students were expected to know the material, and were called upon regularly to demonstrate that they did. First the teacher would call upon the bright children, then the others. Many hadarim had a buddy system, in which the more gifted youngsters were seated next to the slower ones and were held responsible for them.

Although there were no grades or report cards as such, the system encouraged fierce competition, and each boy was acutely aware of his place in the pecking order. At times brother competed against brother, their rivalry extending from heder to home. Some seventy years after the fact, Shaul Schneider could still recall his own rivalry with his brother, which came to a head one day during the Thursday testing, and had a number of lasting ramifications. Little Shaul was blessed with an excellent memory. While still in the early-childhood heder, he knew by heart all the prayers and the first and second sections of the weekly portion. He was a favorite of his grandmother Malke Roche's Schneider, who pressured her son Velvel, Shaul's father, to transfer him to the Humash heder at a tender age. Though the melamed agreed to accept Shaul, he did so on the condition that the underage pupil was only to listen in the heder, not to talk. Thus Shaul found himself in the heder of Reb Itche der Shamesh, and in a class with his older brother Yaakov.

Then came Thursday, not just any dreaded Thursday, but the most dreaded one of all, the Thursday when the youngsters were tested on their understanding of the weekly portion of Mishpatim in Exodus, one of the most difficult of all the portions of the Five Books. The whole heder was awestruck, the students trembling on their benches in anticipation of the wrath of their melamed. Reb Itche began firing his questions rapidly at one boy after another. Paralyzed with fear, no one responded — until at last little Shaul volunteered. Reb Itche reminded him of the terms of his acceptance to the Humash heder, and Shaul obediently remained silent. Again Reb Itche began asking his questions; again no one responded. And now, unable to control himself any longer, little Shaul took advantage of the silence and explained the entire issue according to Rashi, repeating verbatim the melamed's words on the subject. Furious that he had been upstaged by his younger brother, Yaakov smashed the glass of the kerosene lamp which was lighting the heder that dark day, and received a deep cut in the palm of his hand.

At home that night, Grandmother Malke was delighted with the story of her favorite grandson's bravura performance and happily rewarded him not only with candies, a common enough treat, but, since she had had a profitable day at the market, with what was for a child the rather large sum of 10 kopecks. Her great enthusiasm for her grandson's academic excellence was typical of that of many shtetl women, who, unable to go to school themselves, had to live out their dreams of achievement through their male kin.

To have given any thought to how the events of that day might have affected the other child in this story was simply beyond the worldview of anyone in the shtetl. But Yaakov was indeed much affected. He refused to return to Reb Itche's heder and was eventually sent to study in nearby Olkenik. Until the day of his death in Jerusalem, he bore the mark of that incident on his palm. However, Yaakov's own story about what had happened to his hand differed from the account just given, which is based on Shaul's recollection. Throughout his life, Yaakov attributed the scar not to that humiliating childhood drama, but to an event that occurred many years later, in a confrontation he had with an Arab builder in Palestine. Wanting to prove that a Jewish halutz could drive a nail into a wall with his bare hands, he did — to which victory his scar bore witness, he said.

In addition to learning Humash and Rashi, students were also expected to spend several hours each week on the study of writing, which consisted of both composition and penmanship. Composition consisted of learning to write cordial letters and contracts; the goal of penmanship was to achieve a beautiful hand. If the melamed was not accomplished in this area — and since no shortcomings ever went unremarked upon in the shtetl, this would be a matter of public knowledge — a scribe was hired. Depending on the age and reputation of both scribe and melamed, the scribe either came to the heder or the heder boys went to the scribe.

To achieve the desired facility and beauty of handwriting, it was common practice to assign the students to copy a given text within a designated space. Sometimes a very fanciful exercise, this could involve copying the Song of Songs within the outline of a dove, for example, or the Scroll of Esther within the shape of a scroll. Both of these texts were used frequently, since they are the only two texts in the Bible that do not contain the name of God, and any paper on which the name of God appears cannot be discarded, nor can the name of God itself ever be erased. Thus those two texts were particularly useful for purposes of practice and training.

GEMARA HEDER

As the youngsters neared the last stage of their education in the Humash heder, they were introduced to the crowning glory of all their studies, which would be the focus of the next step of their education, if they were fortunate enough to progress that far: the Talmud. They began with the Gemara, which consisted of the traditions, rulings, and discussions of the amoraim, the Jewish scholars of the third to the sixth centuries, in Eretz Israel and Babylonia, who had composed the Talmud. However, a significant number of students did not proceed to the next stage; most of those who left school after Humash heder were artisans' sons, who now began work as apprentices in the family trade.

For those who did continue, there was no official ceremony to mark the entry into the Gemara heder. The young man's only reward was the bliss he felt at having finally arrived at the enchanted shore of the sea of the Talmud, and the gratification and pride he saw in the eyes of his family and his community. The one very modest rite of passage consisted of his receiving a used copy of the Bava Kama tractate from the Talmud (the first tractate to be studied in the Gemara heder), one that had belonged to an older brother or other family member, and carefully taking his newly acquired treasure to the bookbinder in order to claim it as his own.

The new melamed he would be studying with at this stage of his education usually enjoyed an even more prominent place in the shtetl's social hierarchy than the man who had taught him in Humash heder. The classes were smaller, not to exceed ten or twelve students, and they were usually conducted in the beth midrash rather than in the melamed's home. The curriculum of the Gemara heder still included penmanship, selected passages from the Prophets, the weekly portion of the Law, and other basic sources in Judaism. But the main preoccupation of the Gemara heder, from dawn to dusk, was the study of the Talmud.

As in the early and middle hadarim, the education in this school was divided into three major phases. The main object of the first two was bekiut (proficiency). To achieve the desired proficiency, the melamed first presented a sugia (Talmudic topic), complete with text commentaries and his analysis of the commentaries. The class then repeated what the melamed had said, in unison, after which each student was called upon to explain the topic under discussion. Teacher and classmates made whatever corrections were necessary when a presenter was in error. Numerous repetitions, of both the basic text and the teacher's explanations of it, were the key to this style of pedagogy, which dated back to the Mishnah: "He who has repeated his chapter a hundred times is not to be compared to the man who has repeated it a hundred and one times."[16] As to repeating the teacher's commentary verbatim: "One is obligated to use the language of one's teacher."

During the third stage of Talmud studies, however, the emphasis on repetition gave way to methods designed to develop the student's analytical abilities and his creativity, so that he would be able to understand a Gemara text on his own. Thus each student was assigned a topic in the Talmud, which he was expected to prepare and present to the class as proof of his having mastered the necessary techniques of analysis. In the days leading up to his presentation, the young man might spend many a long, cold winter night at the beth midrash, studying his Talmud lesson by the dim light of a burning candle, with only the encouragement of his melamed, his family, and his peers to warm and inspire him.[17] Much was riding on the quality of his performance, for a student who excelled could establish himself early on as an illui (prodigy), the highest status a boy could attain.

Naturally, the ultimate aim of the Gemara heder was to send the young man on to a renowned yeshivah, where he would at last become a master of the Talmud, a true Talmid haham. This he would do not for the sake of being ordained as a rabbi, but for the pure love of Torah and scholarship.

THE RHYTHMS OF HEDER LIFE

To achieve its highly ambitious academic goals, the heder became a virtual home to its students from early childhood on. In his family's home, the boy was treated as a very precious, welcome little guest who slept there and spent the Sabbath and holidays there; most of the rest of his life was spent in the heder, where, even for the youngest boys at the very beginning of their education, there was virtually no attempt to make the long hours of study more pleasurable or agreeable. By ancient tradition and shtetl practice, education was considered a serious business that demanded sacrifice. Still, a pattern of short breaks was built into the rigorous schedule of academic life.

On Friday the hadarim in Eishyshok were open only until noon. In the afternoon the boys were expected to be busy preparing to welcome the Sabbath. This took the form of going to the public bath with the other menfolk in their families, doing any necessary chores, and becoming active participants in the shtetl's charitable organizations. Meir Wilkanski fondly recalled one such Friday afternoon in the 1880s, when he and his friend Israel, both of whom had beautiful penmanship, were therefore given the honor of going door to door to seek contributions toward the purchase of a new set of Talmud books for Eishyshok's famed yeshivah:

On that Friday at noontime, we got dressed in our Saturday best and made our way to those houses that were listed in the notebook that had been given to us. One of us held on to the notebook, the other a tied kerchief. The money was tossed into the kerchief, while next to each name we entered the amount of the contribution. We canvassed the marketplace and all the streets that gave on to it. Our knees were deep in snow, and the heavy copper change was stinging our frozen hands. But the kerchief grew heavier and heavier as sundown approached, and we were ecstatic. All this money was earmarked for a sacred purpose — to purchase an additional Talmud for the beth midrash![18]

Saturday was the day when the unity of heder, home, and synagogue was reinforced, the day when their shared emphasis on the values of scholarship came into particular focus. At the synagogue the boy's performance and behavior during the services and the reading of the weekly portion were closely watched. Back home, he was tested by his father or other knowledgeable men of the family, sometimes in the presence of the melamed. If there was an erudite person in the household, he added to the child's knowledge. If not, it was the child himself who brought Torah into the house. At the conclusion of the test, assuming the child did well, the proud, delighted mother would set the table with special delicacies, as a reward for her son and, if he were present, her son's melamed. The quality and quantity of the treats depended on the quality of the child's performance.*

Saturday afternoon was also the day for the youngster to see the heder in a different light. After the second Sabbath meal at home, he went to the heder, where he would find the huge study table covered in a white tablecloth, and the melamed, his family, and the other students dressed in their Sabbath finery. In this atmosphere the boys would study for an hour or two, focusing on books that were specific to the season, such as the Passover Haggadah. While they studied, most of the rest of the male population of the shtetl, as well as many of the older women, were also reading and learning, for the afternoon of the Sabbath was the time traditionally set aside for such activities.[19]

The heder year was long and vacations were few. Semesters ran from the holiday of Sukkot to the holiday of Passover, approximately October to April; and from Passover to Rosh Hashanah, April to October. Students were given a few days off in honor of these and other holidays. All the fasts were half-day vacations. But even on the Sabbath, the holidays, and the between-semester breaks, there were set hours for studying in the heder.

HOLIDAYS

Each holiday had its unique symbols and ceremonies to mark it — and many of the items particular to a given holiday were prepared in the heder. For Simhat Torah, the boys made flags on whose flagpoles their mothers would later place an apple and a candle. For Hanukkah they made the dreidels (toplike toys of wood and lead) that were great favorites of the younger boys. For Tu Be-Shevat, the New Year for Trees, they made necklaces of carob pits for their sisters. For Purim the youngsters constructed noisemakers, often with the help of the shtetl blacksmiths.

Bows and arrows were brought out for Lag ba-Omer, the late-spring holiday that celebrated the bravery of the great second-century scholar Rabbi Akiva and his students. Armed with their fierce weapons, and provisioned with lunches prepared by their mothers, the Eishyshok students and their melamdim went out into the verdant Seklutski forest to hear again the magnificent story of the martyred Rabbi Akiva and his valiant students, who fought under the military leader known as Bar Kokhba. With the aid of the melamed's stories and their own active imaginations, it was easy for them to see themselves fighting alongside Bar Kokhba on his fierce lion, overpowering Hadrian and his Roman legions (and thereby rewriting history).

They carried wooden swords (and were additionally protected by cloves of garlic worn in their clothing) on Tishah be-Av, which was the ninth day of the month of Av (late July or early August), the day of mourning for the destruction of the Temples and the capture of Jerusalem. It was the custom for the entire shtetl to go to the cemetery that day, where they would watch the heder boys reenact the war between the Jews and the Romans, partly in pantomime. Barefoot or wearing only socks (since on this day, as on Yom Kippur, the wearing of leather was not permitted), the boys refought the old battle — with a difference. Like the Lag ba-Omer reenactment, this one ended in Jewish victory and Roman defeat, thus departing from the description of the battlefield events as recorded by the historian Flavius Josephus. At the end of the mock battle the boys left their swords

*Orphans who attended the community-owned Talmud Torah were tested by their melamed, or else by an official of the community, by a childless man who had chosen to act as their spiritual godparent, or by a relative. This testing might be done in their homes on Saturday, or at the Talmud Torah on a certain set day of the week, not necessarily Saturday.

in a mound of earth, to symbolize their belief that the Messiah would soon come and there would be no more need for swords.

The fast that was observed on the Ninth of Av concluded the three-week period of mourning for the Temple, and put an end to various restrictions that pertained during that time — including, alas, the prohibition against corporal punishment.[20]

One event that was always looked forward to with great anticipation by the heder boys as well as the melamed's family was the Sium (completion) celebration, a festive meal held in honor of the boys' completing their study of one of the Talmud tractates. The boys brought money to pay for the meal, which was prepared by the melamed's wife. The borscht, herring, and potatoes that she cooked would be supplemented by fruits and baked goods brought by boys from the wealthier families.

SWIMMING

Swimming was the only athletic activity sanctioned by the heder (and thus one of the boys' few physical outlets), since it is written in the Talmud that it is a father's responsibility to teach his son to swim. Shortly after Lag ba-Omer, youngsters in tow, the melamed would march through the market square and on to where the river passed the old watermill and became wide like a lake. This was the place where the men of the shtetl swam.[21] But for the boys, the river was not the Kantil, Eishyshok's small tributary of the Vistula; no, this was the River Jordan in the Land of Israel. And they were not ordinary heder boys from Eishyshok on an outing with their melamed, but promising young scholars swimming alongside the Amorah Rabbi Yohanan and his brother-in-law Rabbi Reish Lakish, the brigand-turned-rabbi in order to marry the beautiful sister of his handsome companion, she who was as beautiful as the barefoot shikses they could see in the distance, carefully stepping over the slippery beaver dam.

The river they swam in, like all rivers, flowed into the sea, as they had learned in Ecclesiastes. At the coming of the Messiah, a paper bridge would be built across this sea to the Holy Land, and the righteous would march over it, as every heder boy hoped to do. Little Meir Wilkanski cried bitterly on Tishah be-Av because he knew that the tears of babes who study Torah can reach the heavenly throne and hasten the arrival of that momentous day. Until then, however, all empty joy and laughter were prohibited, a difficult restriction for a young heder boy who could find so many things to laugh at, including the melamed himself.

COLORFUL CHARACTERS

While some melamdim were known for their scholarship or their pedagogical gifts, and others for the strictness of their discipline, yet another group made their reputation on the basis of their eccentricities. Since the heder boys were practically members of the melamed's household, any peculiarities he had were sure to become common knowledge, from his relations with his wife and children down to his manner of eating, drinking, napping, and dressing. And anything his students missed seeing in the heder, they were able to pick up at the public bath on Friday, where many of the shtetl's most intimate secrets were revealed to the eyes of the curious. For the high-spirited but hardworking boys of the heder, these quirks were sources of amusement and fun in an otherwise rather spartan, severe environment. Their former students love telling tales of these colorful characters, many of whose idiosyncrasies have also been chronicled in various written memoirs.

The kuperne kantel (copper mug) rebbe, for example, was a melamed who drank his tea in noisy gulps from a huge copper mug that he held with both hands. To the despair of their mothers, many of his students adopted his teatime manners. Reb Yitche der Butchan (the stork), a tall man who was a shammash in the Old Beth

Midrash as well as a melamed, liked to stand while doing his teaching, most of the time in the one-legged stance that resulted in his nickname. Di wilde katchke (the wild goose) was a melamed who in moments of anger would throw up his hands in the air and make strange noises with his tongue, which reminded one class of heder boys of a wild goose surprised on the riverbank. The name they gave him stuck through several generations of students. Der fledermaus (the bat), like his colleague di wilde katchke, was quick to lose his temper, at which moments he would remove his belt and swoop down on his prey, his loose black kapote billowing in his wake, making him look like a bat on the wing. The tzen por ploidern (ten pairs of pants) rebbe got his name from the multiple layers of trousers he wore to keep warm during the cold winter months (there for all his students to see in the public bath!).

But no Eishyshok melamed was a more vivid character in the folklore of the shtetl than the man known as the maizele (tiny mouse). Until the bitter end of the shtetl, his descendants continued to be known as Maizalekh, and his story is still told. At the turn of the century, a God-fearing melamed who at that time went by the name of Reb Meyshe-Yude was already preparing for bed one early winter's night as the heder boys, lanterns in hand, were still struggling through the deep snow on their way home. He put on his long kapote in order to keep warm in bed, and waited for the angel of sleep, who was usually so quick to visit him. But on that particular night he was kept awake by a peculiar wheezing sound he kept hearing in his left ear. When he complained to his wife, she applied a warm compress and tied it around his head with a piece of flannel, but this merely diminished the sound of the squeak, rather than eliminating it, and Reb Meyshe-Yude became concerned. So the next day he visited the feldsher. But the feldsher's medicine also failed to stop the nocturnal noises in his ear.

After many sleepless nights in bed followed by irritable days in the heder, Reb Meyshe-Yude realized that matters were very serious. He reached the conclusion that his affliction must be a case of transmigration of souls. Clearly a stray soul — a gilgul — had entered his body and settled in his ear. He went to the shtetl rabbi, Yossef Zundl Hutner, to tell him the grave news. Reb Zundl called upon the shammash from the Old Beth Midrash, instructing him to make all the necessary arrangement for an exorcism. Before an assembly of ten men in prayer shawls, in a room lit only by the flickering black candles of the exorcism ceremony, the shammash called upon the gilgul to take leave of Reb Meyshe-Yude's body.

But this, too, was to no avail. The very same night, the squeak in his ear resumed. Reb Meyshe-Yude grew desperate. He became convinced that it was the restless wandering soul of a student he had wronged, come back to haunt him. Since it is through the ears of his students that the melamed tries to reach their hearts and minds, he reasoned, it was natural that the soul of a vengeful student should settle in his ear! And it was natural, too, that he should come only at night, since during the day the voices of the innocent students studying Talmud kept him away.

Reb Meyshe-Yude decided he should go tell Reb Zundl what he had figured out. But just as he was about to leave and his wife began to help him on with his kapote, she noticed that the seam above his left shoulder was split. Thimble, needle, and thread in hand, she set about mending the kapote when, from the shoulder padding of the coat, a tiny, frightened mouse jumped out!

Within moments, the story of Reb Meyshe-Yude's gilgul had spread through the shtetl like wildfire. That very night he was given the name "maizele."

As to the mystery of why the melamed had heard the sounds only at night, this too was now clear: During the day Reb Meyshe-Yude did not wear his kapote; he wore it only when he went to bed or went out at night, for only then did he need it to ward off the biting chill.

OTHER AMUSEMENTS

The occasions on which it was thought permissible for the melamed to dismiss his young charges from their studies were few indeed. Planting a tree in the Holy Land or welcoming the Messiah were two of them, but needless to say, the long history of the shtetl was short on such occasions. Consequently, unscheduled holidays were extremely rare events in the lives of the heder yingls.

The heder day was a long one, beginning in the early hours of the morning and lasting into the evening, as decreed by ordinance: "He sits and studies the entire day and part of the night as well . . ."[22] There were no bells to break up the day into different periods, and only two official recesses, one at lunchtime, the other after the evening prayer.

There was also no going home during heder hours, except for serious matters, and then only by request of the family or because of the child's bad behavior or an illness. However, the boys ardently made the most of every possible chance, inside and outside the heder walls, to interrupt their routine. The primary window of opportunity was that presented by the melamed himself. Studying in his home, immersed in the habits of his daily life, the boys knew all his idiosyncrasies and how to take advantage of them. They knew, for example, precisely when he would tire and his attention would wane.

Meir Wilkanski recalled that he and the other boys knew to the minute the two times a day when their Gemara melamed would place his red kerchief as a bookmark in his tractate of Bava Metzia and allow both the book and his eyelids to fall shut. During such catnaps, the "Tower of Clothing" in the corner, the repository for the heavy outer garments the students wore on their way to school, became their playground. Sliding, hiding, and burrowing amid the clothes, throwing mufflers and coats at one another, or standing atop the pile and shaking their milk bottles under the guidance of a yishuvnik student who was instructing them in the mystery of turning milk to butter, the students exulted in their brief reprieve. Moments later, their faces still flushed with excitement, they were all back in their assigned places on the long benches, their little hands stretched out on the table awaiting the lashes of the melamed. The fun was deemed worth the punishment, and the following day the Tower of Clothing would once more teem with activity as the rebbe dozed off.[23]

Sometimes official breaks could be extended by various devious means if the boys were sufficiently determined. In the early years of the twentieth century, Shalom Sonenson and several of his classmates one day took a great risk to prolong their melamed's absence from the heder during afternoon prayer. Climbing the steep walls of the synagogue at a time when no one else was in it, they moved the hand of the official town clock backward. For weeks the whole of Eishyshok did not pray on time, thanks to the students of Reb Yitche der Butchan. When the prank was discovered, the rod was not spared and the humiliation was public.

Another moment ripe for exploitation by fun-starved heder boys was "repetition time," when the melamed was occupied with one group of students at the main table, and the other group was left to its own devices at the repetition table, which was often simply a board placed on a barrel of herring, sauerkraut, or pickles. At such interludes it was often the case that very little repetition took place. Instead, a variety of trinkets, especially buttons, changed hands, and games were played.

Even when the boys could find no recess time, scheduled or otherwise, their minds were apt to wander while their bodies remained still. The heder's little windows were windows to the world, allowing the curious eyes of the students to observe a cross-section of the shtetl population going about its business — doing their daily chores; visiting the public outhouse nearby, or opting for the open spaces of gardens in back of their homes. Nature in all its splendor and drama was also an endless source of diversion. The little plot of land outside the heder could, with summer's magic, turn into a garden so lush that the bean stalks all but invaded the classroom.[24] The rumble of a thunderstorm sounded to the frightened youngsters like the war of Gog and Magog, though to the nearly deaf melamed it was merely the faint echo of a faraway carriage passing over the shtetl's cobblestones. And winter too had its way with the boys' imaginations; the frosty designs it etched on the heder windows drew a lacy curtain on the outside world and encouraged the boys to daydream away the hours in the kingdom of Uncle Schneur (Snow).[25]

PUNISHMENT

For many of these unscheduled recesses, as indeed for any slacking off in their studies, the boys paid a price. The rod and the kanchik (leather strap) were ever present. Corporal punishment was an accepted reality in the heder, as it was in all other educational systems of the time, and had been for centuries. Indeed, Jewish education had been addressing itself to the issue as early as the Gemara days, when the sages gave specific advice about acceptable limits on such punishment and warned against injuring the child. Rav's directive to teacher Samuel ben Shilat in Babylonian times included the following: "When you punish a pupil, hit him only with a shoe latchet. The attentive student will learn of himself; the inattentive one should be placed next to one who is diligent."[26] Much later ordinances prescribed similar guidelines: "A melamed should not hit a child with a cruel enemy blow, but only with a small strap."[27]

Despite these admonitions, teachers had in their arsenals a wide assortment of punishments, both corporal and psychological. Some placed the errant child in the corner, with or without a dunce cap adorned with soot-covered feathers atop his head; some ordered the youngster to ride a broom with his pants down; others resorted to more violent measures.

Meir Wilkanski recalls a cold winter day when the upper class was studying Gemara and the lower class, his own, was sitting at the repetition table. But instead of repeating the difficult verses they had been assigned in the Book of Job, they found the lacy handiwork of Uncle Schneur more interesting, and were trying to improve upon his intricate designs with the imprints of various coins. All this was accompanied by much giggling, to the great displeasure of the melamed, who had not yet fallen into his morning catnap. Though he warned the youngsters that anyone who continued to laugh would be tied with a sturdy rope to the table, the warning came too late for Meir Wilkanski, who was unable to stop his giggles. The next thing he knew, Reb Yitche, rope in hand, was dragging him to the table, whereupon little Meir, screaming and scratching, fought back. Then blood began to run from the scratches Meir had inflicted, and someone was sent off in search of Meir's parents. The results were almost immediate. While teacher and student were still wrestling, the door opened and Meir's mother rushed in, screaming: "Woe to the eyes that are beholding such a sight." Meir refused to go home with his mother and instead ran away to seek refuge in a dark corner of the Old Beth Midrash, as far as he could get from his father's seat. Later that day when he worked up the courage to return to the heder, he found his father and the melamed waiting for him. Before four benches of attentive classmates, Meir received his dressing down, which was so severe that his ears were unable to absorb a single word.[28]

When a father was searching for the ideal melamed for his sons, a reputation for relying on corporal punishment was not necessarily a deterrent; on the contrary, it was sometimes viewed as a plus. Such was the case with Shael Sonenson, one of the leaders of the kahal and the neeman (trustee) of the New Beth Midrash, who, in his search for the appropriate melamed for his boys, had decided he wanted a stern disciplinarian. The mild-natured melamed who had taught Avraham and Israel, his two oldest sons, would not do, he felt, for his next two, the mischievous Shalom and Moshe — especially since he was hoping they would follow in his own footsteps and spend a few semesters at a renowned yeshivah (his own had been the Slobodka academy in Kovno) before entering the business world.

To set his boys on the course he thought most likely to lead in that direction, Reb Sonenson chose "the pickeler rebbe." This man was a fine scholar who, like so many others, had had to resort to the degrading work of teaching in order to support his family. His reputation for scholarship was rivaled only by his renown for a particular form of corporal punishment: He liked to discipline his wayward charges by ordering them to stretch out on a mat, face down, bare buttocks up, then scattering seeds on their exposed skin and inviting his flock of chickens to pick. When the chickens rushed out from the katukh for their feast, their pickings included not just the seeds, but bits of flesh. Hence his nickname, the pickeler rebbe, and hence his dreaded reputation, which so appealed to Shael Sonenson.

When the two Sonenson boys learned about their intended fate, however, they decided that their bare buttocks were not going to serve as a feeding ground for the pickeler rebbe's chickens, and they worked out a stunt to foil their father's plan. When the fateful day arrived, Reb Shael entered the melamed's house, Moshe in one hand, Shalom in the other. As the two men began to negotiate the terms of payment for the first semester, Shalom suggested that he and his brother bring chairs so that their father and the teacher might sit comfortably during their negotiations. Delighted by his sons' politeness, Reb Shael loosened his firm grip on them, and they ran off to get the chairs. As the melamed smoothed his kapote and made ready to sit down, the youngsters pulled the chair out from under him, causing him to tumble to the floor. Red with rage, the pickeler rebbe pointed to the door and screamed, "Out! Rascals like these I do not teach even if they are sons of the shtetl rich man and even if he has a houseful of heder boys!"

The boys' dubious reward for their cleverness was to escape the heder of the pickeler rebbe for that of Yankl der Cymbler, a melamed known for his erudition and his thorough knowledge of the Bible. Though he was the lesser of two evils, Yankl Rachowsky had come by his nickname honestly, as a generation of Eishyshkian males, who some sixty- and seventy-odd years later were still dodging at the sight of a raised hand, can attest. Yankl was known as "der Cymbler" because the blows he aimed at his students' heads used to echo in their ears like the sound of cymbals.

THE POWERS OF THE HEDER BOY

Despite their naughtiness and many other personal shortcomings, of which they were ceaselessly reminded, the boys knew that in their identity as babes who study Torah they possessed special powers. Not only could they hasten the coming of the Messiah with their tears, they could protect against evil spirits. So it was that when a baby boy was born, the heder yingls were called into action on the night prior to his circumcision, the fateful night on which, it was thought, Lilith, the Queen of the Demons, set out to snatch male infants. The boys would march directly from the heder to the home of the new baby. There they would gather around the mother's bed and recite the Shema Israel and various prayers from Psalms, which would create a pure, unseen screen around mother and child, shielding them from evil. For this the boys were handsomely rewarded, with gifts of fruit, candy, and baked goods, provided in particular abundance to the siblings of the new baby and their close friends.[29]

Rituals and rewards like these, reinforced by other treats conferred on them for their Torah studies by their anxious, adoring mothers, grandmothers, sisters, and aunts, did much to enhance the self-esteem of each young heder boy. They also helped forge the bonds linking the outer and inner worlds of Jewish life, the material and the spiritual. For the heder boy, the unseen evil forces lurking in the bedroom of the newborn baby were as real as the mother and child, the opportunity to hasten the coming of the Messiah vivid enough that more than one little boy was known to squeeze out tears in the effort to do so.

So, too, were the biblical personalities and places they heard about each day as real to them as people and places in the shtetl. They read of them in the weekly portion, learned about them in the heder, encountered them again in the synagogue, and were tested on them at home. After such an immersion, was it any wonder that the big oven in the melamed's home was not just a stove but the furnace where their forefather Abraham was cast into billowing flames and rescued by the Angel Gabriel? That a market-day brawl between a Jew and a gentile was seen as but another manifestation of the eternal struggle between Jacob and Esau, Jerusalem and Rome, destined to end, after no matter what momentary setbacks, in Israel's triumph? And that the tall man the shtetl called Abba Arikha (Long Daddy), who appeared to the untrained eye as a mere cobbler but knew by heart the entire Six Orders of the Mishnah, was in fact, as any heder boy could have told you, none other than Elijah the Prophet, who had chosen to grace Eishyshok with his presence?

THE MIXED HEDER (HEDER IRBUVIA)

Until the end of the nineteenth century, the entire enterprise of formal, compulsory education was restricted to the male population since, according to Jewish law, only men are obligated to study. There were of course the usual exceptions to the rule: Some extraordinary women attained the highest levels of education and became accomplished scholars, such as the daughters of Rashi, who assisted him in the writing of his commentary. These women generally received their education with the help of a concerned male family member, most often a father blessed with daughters only. But by and large women did not study. Or if they did, their education was considered to be merely a status symbol, as had been true since at least the time of the first-century sage Abbahu, who "allowed his daughters to be taught Greek as a social accomplishment."[30]

Before the 1890s, those Eishyshkians who believed in education for girls and were affluent enough to be able to pay for it (and to dispense with their daughters' labor) had to provide them with private tutors, for there were no hadarim that admitted girls until that date; even then there were very few.[31] The statements of second-century sage Rabbi Eliezer ben Horcanus had clearly not fallen on deaf ears: "A woman's place is at the spinning wheel," he wrote, and "Better the Torah be burned than to be studied by women," and "He who teaches his daughter the Law teaches her frivolity."[32] In a society in which the learning and teaching of the Torah were core values, such pronouncements had a great impact on the role and status of women. And yet they seem not to have pertained in the rabbi's own family, for he was married to Ima Shalom, a scholar and one of the few women mentioned in the Talmud.[33]

Prior to the twentieth century, girls did of

course learn a great deal about their religion at home, and were taught the particular precepts that were pertinent to their roles as daughters, mothers, wives, housekeepers, and businesswomen. That is, they learned the practical aspects of halakhah, and they learned to recite those prayers and benedictions they would use in daily family life. Girls who were tutored might also receive some instruction in reading the prayers, in basic arithmetic, in a foreign language or two, and perhaps in the playing of a musical instrument. But this was only at the discretion of the parents, and not mandated by law or by community practice. Some shtetlekh also offered organized classes for girls, but again this depended entirely on private initiative.

The majority of girls were not tutored or, after the advent of the mixed heder, sent to class, but did manage on their own to acquire basic reading skills — at times by standing outside the heder window after delivering a younger brother to school in the morning, or bringing him his lunch at midday. There they would stay, peering in through the window, trying to learn the secrets of the aleph beth from the melamed's huge chart.

In 1620, *Zeenah U-Reenah* (Go Forth and Gaze) was published by Jacob Ashkenazi of Janow. This Yiddish work, which became immensely popular among women, caused a revolution in their education. In it women read biblical stories and aggadic and midrashic homilies, as well as comments on Jewish life, customs, and morals, all in the voice of a remarkable raconteur. The book became a virtual handbook of Judaism for women, which would accompany them throughout their lives.[34]

To have such a book was some small mitigation of a woman's lot in life, but it would be almost three centuries before any change more substantial than that would be made. Until then, women were for the most part removed from the intellectual as well as the spiritual life of the shtetl. This meant that, for all intents and purposes, they were also cut off from virtually all means of bettering themselves socially and economically. Not that the shtetl was an open society for men, either. Wealth and property were in large part the practical measures of one's standing in it, and, generally speaking, one was born to them, with little opportunity to achieve them from scratch. But the only true aristocracy in Judaism consisted of the intellectual elite — the scholars. For a man this meant that upward social mobility was always at least theoretically possible via the road of scholarship. For a woman, denied the opportunity of an education, there was no such avenue; she was doomed to remain in the class of her birth. Her exclusion from the world of scholarship was tantamount to a life sentence. Virtually her only real hope of improving a lowly social position was to give birth to a son who would himself become a scholar.

Most women rejoiced vicariously in the Torah-learning experience, through fathers, husbands, brothers, sons, sons-in-law, and other male relations. As a young virgin, a girl would bake hallah for her brother's heder entrance ceremony. As the new mother of a son, she was grateful for the visit of the heder boys whose prayers helped protect her and her infant from evil. As the mother of a young boy, she took pleasure in rewarding her son and his melamed with an assortment of goodies after the Sabbath testing hour. It was she who hosted the Humash heder admission ceremony for her son, and in many cases she who paid his tuition from her own meager earnings. And, as in Meir Wilkanski's story, it was usually she who brought him to the heder at the very beginning of his studies. In the synagogue, the shtetl woman sat in the women's gallery, basking in the reflected glory of the male members of her family whenever one of them was called up to the Torah or delivered a learned discourse.

In the late nineteenth century, the ideas of the Haskalah and National Awakening movements posed the first major challenge to the lack of organized, compulsory education for Jewish women, for the leaders of these movements saw the absence of an educational system for women as a serious obstacle to achieving their goals. The "new Jew" envisioned by the Haskalah was a member of a universal and egalitarian "brotherhood," which was also to include women; the National Awakening's "new Jew" was a pioneer working the land of Eretz Israel, and both men and women were to be trained for this sacred task. Thus the 1889 constitution of Bnei Moshe (Sons of Moses, one of the earliest of the Zionist groups), talks about the necessity for the Jewish community "to educate its young boys and girls . . . so that they will know the Hebrew language, and the history and teachings of the Nation of Israel"; and the founding statement of the Mizrahi Zionist organization in 1902 similarly speaks of the need to educate girls in the spirit of faithful Judaism.[35]

The mixed heder (heder irbuvia) was one of the first and in some ways most dramatic responses to the new movements. First in the larger cities, which were centers of the Haskalah, and then gradually in the smaller towns and shtetlekh, families inspired by the hope for change began sending their daughters to heder. Though it was the most familiar of educational institutions, the very fact that it was now admitting girls was revolutionary.

Not that the change was overnight or universal. Very few melamdim were willing to accept girls into their schools, and only a handful of parents wanted to send their daughters to study in the first place. And even families who had begun to believe in education for girls might not be able to afford it, or might see it as a desirable but unattainable luxury. Perhaps they would send only the brightest of their daughters, or the one who could most readily be released from household chores. Or, as one woman recalled, they might rotate: In her family the opportunity to go to school was limited by the fact that there was only one pair of shoes among three girls, so the girls took turns going to school, one eager pair of feet making its way to the heder one day, another the next, and so forth. Those girls who did attend were generally sent to the early-childhood heder at a much older age than their brothers, and remained there for a longer period of time.[36]

Besides the economic obstacles and the difficulty of changing a community's millennia-old attitude toward women, there were also external factors limiting the enrollment of girls in the mixed heder. The Russian authorities did not permit girls to attend heder past the age of eleven, and in the mid-1880s they prohibited the opening of new hadarim for girls. Ironically, they justified their action by citing that old Talmudic dictum of Rabbi Eliezer ben Horcanus: "He who teaches his daughter the Law teaches her frivolity."[37]

Despite the limited enrollment and the fact that the girls could attend only until age eleven, the heder irbuvia produced an elite group of women with a fine knowledge of Humash, the Prophets, and midrashic sources. Until the end of his days the great scholar Rabbi Isser Zalman Meltzer would turn to his wife, Rebbetzin Beile Hinde, the product of a heder irbuvia, whenever he was searching for a particular biblical quotation. It was she who copied out his first great work, *Even ha-Azel* (1938), prepared it for publication, and paid for its printing with the earnings from her leather business.[38]

The struggle for a heder irbuvia in Eishyshok was led by the high-spirited Sarah Wilkanski, assisted by her two brothers, Yitzhak and Meir, and two younger sisters, Esther and Leah. Though Reb Layzer the dayyan and his wife Batia were proud of the courage exhibited by their children in this battle, they knew well the scandal it would create, and dreaded it. Finally Reb Layzer yielded to his daughter's demands

Sarah Wilkanski, who demanded equal education for girls, and was the first girl in Eishyshok to study at the boys' heder. She was also the shtetl's first female to receive a diploma from a university. YESC, WILKANSKI

and approached Reb Kalman, a melamed known for his secret sympathy for the Haskalah. Kalman agreed to accept the girls into his heder, but only on certain conditions: When a stranger was about to enter the heder, the girls were to hide under the table or, if there was time, in the katukh.[39] Years later Sarah loved to recall how she, Esther, and Leah spent many painful moments under that table at the mercy of ten pairs of kicking feet — or, alternately, in the katukh, where the torment was supplied by the beaks of hungry chickens instead.

To supplement his sisters' heder education, Meir ordered Hebrew grammar books from the "big city" (presumably Vilna). This put the entire shtetl in an uproar. The holy language, profaned by girls! Once again the Wilkanski household was leading the shtetl astray. But when one sister claimed that she wanted to learn Hebrew in order to dig potatoes in Eretz Israel, and another that she aspired to the wisdom of Beruria, the second-century female scholar, the Wilkanskis won.[40] The winds of change were blowing with them, and women's education in Eishyshok, as elsewhere, was about to enter a new phase. What had begun "under the table" would soon lead to a formal system of education for women — and, for Sarah Wilkanski, to the teachers' seminary in Königsberg.

THE RECONSTRUCTED HEDER (HEDER METUKAN)

The late nineteenth century's heder metukan, the reconstructed or reformed heder, was another manifestation of the changes introduced by the National Awakening movement in its effort to create the "new Jew." Education was to be a major factor in achieving this goal, but the Russian schools previously advocated by the Haskalah were considered inadequate for this purpose, as were the traditional hadarim, whose customs were seen as antiquated and harmful. Leveling harsh criticism against the heder system, the National Awakening movement demanded drastic changes in every aspect of it, from its use of corporal punishment to its methodology, from its long, grueling hours down to the very dress and hygiene of its population.

The new reconstructed heder was to be moved out of the home of the melamed into much more pleasant quarters, and the students were to undergo a similar improvement. As envisioned by the National Awakening movement, under this new order there were to be "large houses with spacious rooms, clean fresh clothing without patches and other signs of wear for both the melamdim and his students, and cleanliness in body as well. The boys will sit up straight as is proper according to the Torah, and will not sway back and forth, for it is logical that in a serene body will dwell a serene soul."[41] Following the recommendations of the Haskalah paper *Ha-Meassef*, many communities located the new heder in a special house set aside for educational purposes only, and furnished like a regular school. What had formerly been a dawn-to-dusk day was shortened to eight hours, there were regularly scheduled recesses throughout the day, and the students were divided into classes according to age.

The first heder metukan was founded in Yeketrinislav in the closing decades of the nineteenth century, under the leadership and guidance of Menahem Ussishkin (the first such school in Eishyshok was not established until 1903). To encourage the founding of additional hadarim metukanim, a society by the name of Hinukh (Education) was established in 1899 in Odessa at the behest of the Russian Zionist leader and writer Ahad Ha'am (the pen name, meaning "One of the People," of Asher Ginzberg), who would later coin the slogan "Conquer the Schools!" At the Zionist conference held in Minsk in 1902, education reform was one of the central issues, and it would attract many supporters, including National Awakening poet Hayyim Nahman Bialik, a product of a traditional heder. A fervent advocate of reform, Bialik wrote that "the greatest gain that Zionism can bring is to establish a reconstructed heder."[42]

Meir "der Lerer" Shewitski, one of Eishyshok's most accomplished and modern heder teachers in the shtetl's final days. He also tutored and taught many shtetl girls. His penmanship style was adopted by a significant number of Eishyshok's young women.
PHOTO: YITZHAK URI KATZ. YESC, RUTH KAAN

The guiding principle of the reconstructed heder was the combination of traditional and secular knowledge, despite the resistance of both the Russian authorities (who wanted to jettison the religious part of the curriculum) and the Jewish community (which did not want to admit secular studies into the classroom). The entire heder curriculum was revised, including the very language in which it was taught. Yiddish as the language of instruction and translation gave way to Hebrew, which was to be restored as the native language of the Jewish people. "Yivrit be-Yivrit" (Hebrew in Hebrew) was the methodology for teaching Hebrew as the mother tongue. In addition to Hebrew as a spoken language, other new subjects in the curriculum included Jewish history, Russian language, and arithmetic; this left virtually no time for Gemara, in accordance with the Haskalah's negative attitude toward the Talmud. Instead of using original sources, special primers for children were introduced, and the centuries-old practice of teaching the weekly portion gave way to a systematic study of the twenty-four books of the Bible, with only a few hours a week devoted to the weekly portion.

Although the concepts underlying the reconstructed heder represented an almost complete break with tradition, the name *heder* was retained. There were several reasons for this, some related to the legal status of Jewish education in Imperial Russia, others to internal matters within the Jewish community. In Russia at the time, it was illegal to establish a new school whose official language was anything other than Russian. Also, the government had stipulated that any new Jewish schools that opened had to employ teachers who had taken a special exam or had obtained teaching certificates from the teachers' seminary in Zhitomir or Vilna. Since the number of such teachers was limited, the number of new schools that could be opened was also limited.[43] By calling them hadarim metukanim, the Jews were able to bypass these regulations. This meant that they could continue to open new schools surreptitiously, and to employ as melamdim anyone who paid 3 rubles a year for a heder teacher's license (as called for by a law passed in 1893). Staffing the hadarim metukanim was thus no problem.

Keeping the traditional name was also a way of minimizing the wrath of the ultra-Orthodox groups within the Jewish community, though the success of that strategy proved short-lived. Critics of the new heder were quick to see it as an institution that alienated the child from his synagogue, his community, and his home, and they punningly dubbed it "heder mesukan" (the dangerous heder). Most of the critics were opponents of Zionism, but even some within the Zionist movement shared the concern of more conservative members of the community, and in 1902 the Mizrahi Zionists issued a statement that called on its members "to vigorously protect the old heder, which produced the great scholars of our people." Despite all the opposition, however, the heder metukan made great inroads on the traditional educational system, its success climaxing in 1889–93, by the end of which 774 new schools had been established.[44]

After the establishment in 1897 of the anti-Zionist Bund, which had its own very successful educational program, and the sudden death of Theodor Herzl in 1904, the reconstructed heder began to decline. By 1910, only 500 hadarim metukanim were reported in Russia and Poland, representing 2 percent of the total number of hadarim and about 10 percent of the total Jewish student population (which in 1913 was estimated at about 400,000).[45]

The heder metukan was slow to reach Eishyshok, though its merits and shortcomings had been feverishly debated there for some years. The shtetl rabbi of the time, Rabbi Zundl Hutner, opposed it, as did the Haffetz Hayyim and a number of the balebatim who prayed in the Old Beth Midrash.[46] The immediate cause for these heated debates was the son of Shmuel Senitski the lawyer, who attended a heder metukan in Vilna in the 1890s. On school vacations the boy used to come home to Eishyshok speaking Russian and wearing a short jacket with brass buttons and a cap with a visor and insignia. To the local heder boys he was an enigma, and since they were never quite sure whether he was a Jew or the son of Polish nobility, they never associated with him. For the adults he was the personification of all the shortcomings of the reconstructed heder, and as such both source and target of their disdain.[47]

During and after World War I, a variety of educational options began to be offered in the shtetl: a Polish school, a coed Hebrew day school, and a number of independent study groups. The traditional hadarim coexisted with these other ventures, but steadily lost ground to them until eventually, sometime in the 1930s, only one remained open, which was attended mainly by the sons of the clergy.

THE TWENTIETH-CENTURY HEDER

And even the traditional hadarim had begun to show the effects of change, especially in the postwar years. Melamdim were addressed not only as "Rebbe" but as "Lerer" (teacher). The day was shorter, the rooms more spacious, and some, such as the heder of Eliezer David Mordechai Krapovnitski, even had a dress code. Hebrew was now the language of instruction, and students like Alexander Zisl Hinski can to this day recall phrases they learned in the hadarim of Eliezer David Mordechai Krapovnitski and Maneh Michalowski, just as students of a generation earlier could with equal vividness recall biblical passages they were taught by the Yeremitcher rebbe. Corporal punishment was used with much greater discrimination, in conformity with the new attitudes. Thus Moshe Edelstein, a scion of one of the five founding families of Eishyshok, whose parents were among the few who continued to send their sons to a traditional heder in the 1930s, recalled that his teacher, Meir "der Lerer" Shewitski, kept the kanchik on top of the stove some distance away, rather than on the table, within arm's reach. A small change, perhaps, but symbolically large.

Though the traditional heder of Eishyshok attracted only a small number of students in the 1930s, by which time it had changed substantially in form as well as content, it continued as a viable educational alternative. Closed down by local Jewish Communists in 1940, when Eishyshok was briefly under Soviet rule, the town's last remaining heder reopened during the Lithuanian occupation, only to be closed down again when the Russians reoccupied the shtetl.

On June 23, 1941, the Germans entered Eishyshok. On that day the heder, like all the other millennia-old Jewish institutions in the shtetl, came to an abrupt and tragic end.

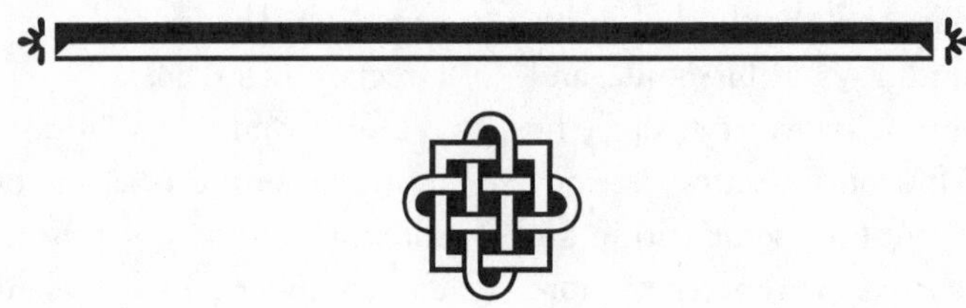

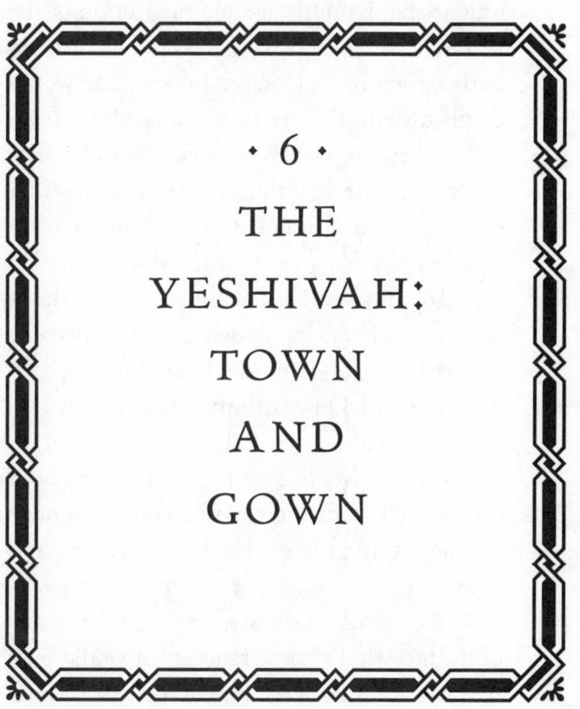

• 6 •
THE YESHIVAH: TOWN AND GOWN

WHEN STUDENTS IN THE KIBBUTZ HA-PRUSHIM YESHIVA OF EISHYSHOK WERE LEARNING WITH GREAT DILIGENCE AND DEVOTION, THE IMPACT ON LEGISLATION IN THE BRITISH PARLIAMENT IN LONDON WAS FELT IMMEDIATELY.

Rabbi Simhah Zisl Broida, the Grand Old Man of Kelme[1]

SINCE THE TIME OF THE DIASPORA, THE INSTITUTION OF THE YESHIVAH HAS BEEN the portable homeland of the Jew. An academy devoted to the highest realms of Jewish scholarship, it has always been at the core of Jewish life. From Palestine to Babylonia, Spain, Provence, Germany, Poland, and finally to Lithuania, which saw the last pre-Holocaust flowering of this ancient institution, the yeshivah has gone everywhere the Jews have gone, and has flourished wherever the Jewish communities of the Diaspora have flourished.

As one of the fundamental institutions of the Jewish people, the yeshivah has shared its fate. Where the Jews enjoyed a favorable political, religious, and economic climate, the yeshivah has prospered. But when the Jews' status in a host country became precarious and they were forced to uproot to avoid persecution, the yeshivah suffered as well. As the number of students and prominent rabbis decreased, the yeshivah either moved elsewhere or closed its doors permanently, and Torah studies declined until a new center of Jewish life emerged, creating the circumstances for yet another intellectual and cultural revival.

Somehow the seeds for these continuous rebirths have always been planted, no matter how complete the devastation may have seemed. In the wake of the Holocaust, which destroyed what were at the time the world's preeminent Jewish scholarly academies, Israel's yeshivot have arisen as the new leaders in Torah scholarship, and yeshivot have also taken root in the United States, which is now the leading Jewish intellectual center of the Diaspora.

It is the yeshivah's endless capacity for regeneration that has been one of the keys to the continuity and stability of Jewish spiritual life. And the yeshivah's capacity to reinvent itself, to adapt time and again to the needs, demands, and cultural styles of the communities in which it is based, to respond to criticism and innovation, may be one of the keys to its own continuity — as can be seen from a look at nearly four hundred years of Eastern European Torah studies.

Prior to the sixteenth century, the Polish and Lithuanian yeshivot followed the Ashkenazic model that had been imported from the declining Jewish centers of Western and Central Europe. Loosely affiliated with the local community, the typical academy of this era was often a semi-private institution belonging to a prominent scholar who headed it and was responsible for its finances.[2] The students, who paid their own upkeep if they could afford to and were supported by the community if they couldn't, were from both local and distant towns.

With the consolidation of the East European Jewish settlement by the end of the fifteenth century, and the strengthening of its communal institutions in the years to come, the stage was set for this vital community to put its own unique stamp on the age-old institution of the yeshivah. Gradually, changes would be made in both structure and methodology that would distinguish the Eastern European yeshivot from the Ashkenazic models on which they had originally been based. Within two centuries, further evolutionary developments would culminate in what would be a new, distinctly Lithuanian model of the yeshivah. The Lithuanian model — or, more accurately, models — would become the very acme of Talmud scholarship throughout the world. Only with the Holocaust would Lithuania's supremacy end. The Lithuanian yeshivot themselves live on, however, having been transported from their native land to centers of scholarship in Israel, the United States, and elsewhere.

By the middle of the sixteenth century, many of the historical circumstances that would pave the way for the development of the Lithuanian model had crystallized. With the Jews of Poland flourishing under the enlightened rule of the Jagiellonian dynasty, the center of Torah scholarship moved eastward, from Germany to Poland, and the Polish Jews created their own style of yeshivah, which was different in structure and organization from the German model. The Polish-style academy, a community-supported yeshivah under the directorship of the community rabbi, existed alongside the semi-private yeshivah of earlier times, and the two kinds of yeshivah mirrored the education system for younger students, which also was divided into community-owned (Talmud Torah) and private (heder) schools. This duality of community and private educational institutions would continue for centuries, with sometimes one kind, sometimes the other, predominating; but the ascendancy of the communal would persist until the late eighteenth century.

Four Radun yeshivah students from Eishyshok in 1934: (standing, right to left) Shaul Rogachewski and Alexander Zisl Hinski; (seated, right to left) Shlomo Dubczanski and Sander Nochomowicz. Hinski emigrated to Eretz Israel and Nochomowicz to Argentina. Rogachewski and Dubczanski were murdered in the September 1941 massacre.
PHOTO: BEN ZION SZREJDER. YESC, HINSKI

Intellectually, the Polish yeshivot were heavily influenced by those of Germany, whose traditions went back to the Middle Ages. Their methodology emphasized the making of hillukim (fine distinctions) arrived at via pilpul (a highly refined, extremely complex dialectical method of disputation). The founders of native Polish scholarship were direct descendants of that intellectual lineage, and brought with them the old German ways when they started their own yeshivot.

Rabbi Jacob Pollak (b. 1460? 1470?, d. sometime after 1532), who became head of a distinguished yeshivah in Cracow and Poland's first halakhic authority, was not from Poland originally, but from Bohemia. It was there that he came under the influence of the German-style yeshivah that was then the dominant model. Later he married into the wealthy, prominent Fischel family of Cracow, and, since they were on intimate terms with the Polish court, was eventually appointed Rabbi of Little Poland by Grand Duke Alexander Jagiello. Thus Pollak was a transitional figure in the world of Polish scholarship: A foreigner by birth, whose roots were in the intellectual traditions of Germany, he was also, because of his yeshivah in Cracow and the great prestige of his crown appointment, a man in a position to promulgate those traditions throughout Poland, and from there to much of the rest of Eastern Europe.

Pollak's most distinguished student, who like his master would become Rabbi of Little Poland, was Shalom Shakhna ben Yossef (d. 1558), the true progenitor of the native Polish line of Talmud and Torah scholarship. The yeshivah he headed in Lublin, whose methodology was a direct offshoot of the pilpulistic model he had learned from Rabbi Pollak, was a great intellectual center, and a highly influential one. Having come from all over Europe to study there as disciples of Rabbi Shakhna, the students disseminated the pilpul methodology to many far-flung geographic outposts. But pilpul would find its purest expression in the communities of Eastern Europe, and the scholars they produced — men like Rabbi Shakhna's brilliant student (and son-in-law) Rabbi Moses ben Israel Isserles, known as the Rema (c. 1525–1572), who would become the great Ashkenazic codifier of Jewish law.

Rabbis Pollak and Shakhna and their successors relied heavily on the pilpul style of logic out of the belief that it would enable their students to think independently, to make intelligent comparisons of different legal works, and most of all to penetrate through to the very spirit of the text. During the sixteenth and seventeenth centuries the ability to excel in pilpulistic disputations was the yeshivah student's supreme mark of distinction, and a virtual prerequisite for achieving any kind of status in the world of scholarship. Nonetheless, even then there were scholars who objected to it, who saw that, when deployed by some mentally agile scholar who cared less for comprehension than for the opportunity to indulge in some showy intellectual acrobatics, it had the potential to distort the plain truth, to seduce its practitioners into mere displays of hairsplitting. They argued that pilpul should always be used in service to the text, not as an end in itself.[3] Many modern historians of Jewish culture in Eastern Europe are also critical of pilpul, yet the method has persisted to the present day. Until well into the eighteenth century, it was part of the mainstream curriculum in most of the yeshivot in Poland and Lithuania.

Sixteenth- and seventeenth-century Poland–Lithuania saw a tremendous proliferation of yeshivot, because the Jewish community under the Council of Four Lands had so much judicial power that large numbers of legal scholars were needed. Every mother and father hoped that at least one of their sons would be able to attend yeshivah, and everyone in the community was involved in supporting these institutions, on both the individual and the communal level. Indeed, scholarship became the hallmark of the Eastern European community at this time. An entire people lived for it. Nathan of Hanover (d. 1683) describes its central place in the culture:

The study of Torah was nowhere so widespread as in Poland. Every community had its Talmudic academies. The head of the yeshivah was paid generously so that he might be able to devote himself to it entirely, heart and soul, without extraneous worries. The whole year through he would not cross the threshold of the academy except to go to the synagogue, but would sit and study Torah day and night. The students of the yeshivah were also maintained by the community, and each would receive a fixed stipend every week. Every student would be given at least two boys to teach so that he might accustom himself to transmit to others what he himself had learned and become proficient in pilpul. Meals were provided for the students from the community charity fund or from the communal soup kitchen. A community of fifty householders would support no fewer than thirty Talmudic students. Each student, with the two boys he was teaching, would live with a householder . . . [who] would feed him as though he were his own son. . . . In the whole land of Poland there was hardly a single home where Torah was not studied. Either the master of the house himself, or his son, or his son-in-law, or a student who took his meals in his home, was a scholar. Often all of them together were students and scholars . . . For this reason, every community was rich in students.[4]

Much of what Nathan of Hanover described in detail illustrates the implementation of the Council's numerous takkanot (regulations) pertaining to the yeshivot. From the 1620s on, the Council addressed itself repeatedly to the community's obligations to the yeshivah and its students, to admission policies, academic standards, recompense for the head of the academy, and so forth.[5] The frequency with which the Council issued such regulations was in part an expression of the community's intense concern with education, and in part an indication that the community did not always live up to its ideals and had to be legislated into doing so.

Occasional failings notwithstanding, nothing was more prestigious in Eastern European Jewish culture than a life devoted to scholarship, and everyone wanted a scholar in the family. A revealing anecdote that circulated in the seventeenth century concerned a wealthy merchant who had availed himself of the matchmaking opportunities at one of the great trade fairs. Thousands of yeshivah students gathered at these annual and semiannual fairs, trading information about the various yeshivot, looking for new positions, and, not incidentally, searching out advantageous marriages. This rich man announced to a neighbor whom he encountered at the Lublin fair that he had just acquired a brilliant young scholar for a son-in-law. Since the neighbor knew that his friend did not have any daughters, he was rather puzzled by this announcement. When he expressed his surprise, the wealthy merchant responded: "So what? Among all my other precious possessions back home, why should I not also have a son-in-law who is a scholar?"

The period of peace, prosperity, and stability that allowed the yeshivot of sixteenth- and seventeenth-century Eastern Europe to flourish came to a devastating end with the Bogdan Chmielnicki massacres of 1648–49, which were followed by the forty-year period known as the Deluge, when Russia, Sweden, and Poland–Lithuania were at war, and all of Eastern Europe was in chaos. The subsequent period of decline in the Jewish community followed the classic pattern, with the yeshivot suffering the same fate as the people who sustained them. Leading scholars from Eastern Europe began migrating west to become rabbis and heads of yeshivot in German and other European communities. Academies like Ez Hayyim, a Sephardic yeshivah in mid-seventeenth-century Amsterdam, attracted large numbers of these fine East European students and rabbis, who brought with them their high standards of achievement — and the renown accruing to those standards.

Though much of Poland was slow to recover from the devastation, the Lithuanian community's resilience enabled it to make a remarkable comeback by the mid-eighteenth century. Now a new type of yeshivah was established, which would make Lithuania the world center for Torah and Talmud scholarship. These new Lithuanian academies, which were usually under the ownership and administration of dynasties of scholars, rather than of the community, as had been the case in earlier times, became very powerful in their independence, eventually attracting funding from all over the globe. And it was because of this new-found strength that they were able to act as a bulwark against yet another challenge to the community, this one deriving from within.

The Hasidic movement was founded in Podolia (a province in the southwestern Ukraine) by Rabbi Israel ben Eliezer (1700–1760), the Baal Shem Tov (Master of the Good Name). With its emphasis on prayer, pious behavior, and storytelling as the means to creating direct channels of communication between man and his fellow man and between man and God, Hasidism posed a challenge to many of the accepted hierarchies of the Jewish community. Moreover, its distinctly populist tone gave new dignity to the common man and woman, new hope and optimism to the downtrodden. And such changes inevitably meant an undermining of some of the traditional routes to leadership. Even scholarship was in danger of losing its position of primacy. No longer was there universal acceptance of the idea that scholarship was the only or the highest form of communion with God.

The new-model, dynastically organized Lithuanian academies proved quite able to meet the challenge of Hasidism, and to serve as a stronghold for those who opposed it, thus preventing it from ever becoming as powerful in Lithuania as it did elsewhere in Eastern Europe and the Austro-Hungarian Empire. What these academies stood for, at their best, was represented by one man.

Just as Hasidism had the figure of the Baal Shem Tov to stand for the values of the heart and the emotions at this time, so there was an equivalent figure among the mitnaggedim (opponents of Hasidism) who would stand as the symbol of the intellect. A contemporary of the Baal Shem Tov, and a man whose influence on subsequent generations of yeshivah students and yeshivot would be profound, Reb Eliyahu ben Shlomo Zalman, the Gaon (sage) of Vilna (1720–1797), was a brilliant scholar, but interestingly enough had never himself been a student at a yeshivah. When still very young he achieved a reputation as a prodigy, and therefore from boyhood on studied independently, never coming under the influence of pilpul.

At the age of twenty the Gaon left his home to wander about the world and, in the phrasing of the time, "to suffer exile." In the course of five years he made his way through Lithuania to Poland, Germany, and perhaps even England. (According to some, his signature is to be found in a visitors' book in London's British Museum.) There are numerous legends about this period, among them one treasured by Eishyshkians, who believed that during his years of wandering incognito the Gaon came to their shtetl and spent time in the beth midrash.[6] Whether true or false, this story was commemorated by a plaque in the Old Beth Midrash, which every heder boy and every yeshivah student came to gaze at, in hopes that they too would be able to become a Gaon.

The Gaon's early experience of independence taught him to stand by his own views and to seek his own way along the paths of scholarship. A similar independence of mind would be the hallmark of his students, and of the yeshivot they founded, which included some of the finest and most influential institutions of this second flowering of the Eastern European Jewish academic community.

THE VOLOZHIN-STYLE YESHIVAH

The leading disciple of the Gaon of Vilna was Reb Hayyim of Volozhin, who in 1801 founded the Volozhin yeshivah (later called Ez Hayyim — Tree of Life — in a play on words that incorporated his name while referring to the Torah as well).[7] Due to the dissolution of the Council of the Four Lands several decades earlier, and the fact that for many years even before then the Jewish community had been losing more and more of its judicial autonomy, this was a time when there was much less practical need for scholars steeped in the intricacies of Jewish law. But Reb Hayyim made it part of the philosophy of his yeshivah that every male Jew should aspire to be a Torah scholar. Even though a man might earn his living as a merchant or a clerk, a trader or a landowner, ideally he would spend some years in a yeshivah, pursuing knowledge for its own sake, scholarship for the sake of scholarship.

Volozhin became the prototype and inspiration for the great Talmudic academies of Eastern Europe, which were among the most influential institutions of nineteenth- and twentieth-century Jewish life. Along with the heder, the yeshivah was, in the words of former Volozhin student and National Awakening poet Hayyim Nahman Bialik, the place where "the soul of the people was forged."

Volozhin's yeshivah attracted students from all over Lithuania and Poland, as well as from Germany, England, and even the United States, which meant that it could pick the best and brightest from among all the applicants. In the interest of fairness as well as diversity, the leaders established a quota system in Lithuania, so that only a certain number of students from each shtetl could be accepted; but some aspiring students were so eager to attend that they would even move in with relatives in another shtetl to ensure their eligibility.

The methods of instruction at Reb Hayyim's yeshivah were as demanding as the standards for admission, and they departed from the traditional Polish methodology in several ways — particularly with regard to pilpul. Like his master the Gaon of Vilna, Reb Hayyim was fearlessly independent in his scholarly endeavors, having little regard for the complicated dialectics of pilpul, which until then had ruled the academy. He insisted on *iyyun yashar* (straight thinking) as the most direct route to that which was paramount at Volozhin: a genuine understanding of the meaning of the text.[8] Dazzling displays of intellectual gymnastics he considered to be beside the point. Another departure in methodology instituted by Reb Hayyim was the system of *hevruta* (collegial study) which he preferred to individual study, in part because he felt it would help students to refrain from going off on solitary intellectual flights into the empyrean. He wanted them to stay focused on the text, not on their own intellectual dexterity.

A daily program was established for the students. Prayers were held at 8:00 A.M., followed by breakfast, and a reading and explanation of the weekly portion by the rosh yeshivah (head of the academy). Supervised study time was between 10:00 A.M. and 1:00 P.M., during which the supervisor checked to make sure none of the students was absent. A shiur (lecture) followed the midday meal. Students returned to the yeshivah at 4:00 for minhah (afternoon prayer), and studied until 10:00, when they broke for maariv (evening prayer) and supper. After supper many returned to the yeshivah to study until midnight. Others would sleep until 3:00 A.M. and then return to the yeshivah to study until morning. The rosh yeshivah would test the students once each term.

ROSH YESHIVAH VS. COMMUNITY RABBI

As a privately owned institution, the academy at Volozhin was housed in its own building, unlike the community-owned yeshivot, whose students sat and learned in the beth midrash. As symbolized by its separate building, Reb Hayyim's yeshivah was totally independent of the community, its methodology and philosophy accountable to no one but its founder and his descendants. Although this placed a considerable financial burden on the rosh yeshivah, who was fully responsible for its upkeep, successful letter-writing campaigns and fund-raising tours by the rosh yeshivah and other emissaries kept money flowing in from throughout the entire Jewish Diaspora.[9]

At Volozhin and wherever else the new dynastic model of yeshivah had come into being, the academy's independence from the community in which it was located created a constant potential for dissension — a variation on the age-old town and gown conflict. But not until 1867, when a bitter power struggle divided the shtetl of Mir, would there be a beth din verdict that spelled out the legal rights of these privately owned institutions.

Mir, a town in the province of Minsk, had become world-renowned for its yeshivah. Founded by Shmuel Tiktinski, a well-to-do merchant and rabbi, the Mir yeshivah was first headed by his son, Avraham Tiktinski, who was a fine scholar as well as an excellent administrator. Like many other Lithuanian yeshivot of the time, it was virtually family property, with the majority of its funding coming from outside the community. Nonetheless, sometime after the founding of the school the rabbi of the community, Rabbi Avraham Moshe, had been given a role in the administration.

When Rabbi Avraham Moshe died, the town of Mir elected his son-in-law, Rabbi Hayyim Zalman Bressler, to be their new rabbi, at which time he demanded a role in the governing of the yeshivah.[10] Citing the precedent of his father-in-law, and invoking the principle of hazaka, he engaged in battle with Reb Hayyim Yehudah Leib Tiktinski, who was then the head of his family's yeshivah.

In the best shtetl tradition, Mir split into two feuding camps, one supporting the town rabbi, the other the head of the yeshivah. When contributions to the yeshivah suffered a severe decline because of the ongoing dispute, both parties agreed to submit to the judgment of a rabbinic court which would be composed of five great scholars they would jointly choose. Whereupon five of the finest rabbis of that era, all of them known for their qualities of leadership, erudition, and commitment to the yeshivah world, were chosen. Among them were Rabbi Yitzhak Elhanan Spektor of Kovno and Rabbi Avraham Shmuel Rabinowitch of Eishyshok.[11] Rabbi Rabinowitch was himself an alumnus of the Mir yeshivah, having been among its first students, and he knew the son of the current head of the academy, who was a student at the yeshivah in Eishyshok.

After a thorough examination of the case, the rabbis delivered a verdict that was unequivocally in favor of the yeshivah. They stated that the shtetl rabbi had no claims to any post or partnership in the yeshivah, and that the fact that the previous town rabbi had been given such a role was not a precedent, but rather an extraordinary event, which could be explained by the fact that the founder of the yeshivah and his son had both died, leaving an heir, Reb Hayyim Yehudah Leib Tiktinski, who was a mere twelve years old at the time, but who was now fully competent. Only because of those unfortunate circumstances had Rabbi Avraham Moshe been brought in to assist with the management of the yeshivah. As an institution funded almost exclusively by contributions from outside the community, the Mir yeshivah was not subject to community authority, management, or partnership, and was not accountable to the community rabbi. In the words of one of the five rabbis on the rabbinic court:

The rabbinate is a separate entity and has no part in the yeshivah. The yeshivah will be governed by the head of the academy and God-fearing supervisors who will control all its income and expenditures. The rabbi elected by the shtetl majority will govern and judge all shtetl affairs, but in the yeshivah he has no share whatsoever . . . And if the grand balebatim of Mir will not accept my advice, then it is my opinion that the head of the yeshivah, may his light shine, should leave Mir and choose another town and another yeshivah where his wish will be honored by the local leaders.[12]

To ensure that their verdict would be implemented, Rabbi Spektor used financial pressure, in the form of a letter he wrote to the rabbi of St. Petersburg, who presided over a very well-to-do Jewish community which had made significant contributions to the Mir Yeshivah:*

I ask that you not give money to the holy community of Mir unless its emissary has in hand a letter signed by R'Hayyim Leib Tiktinski, may his light shine, who is the head of the academy, not Rabbi Hayyim Zalman Bressler. Please adhere to these guidelines for the sake and honor of Torah study. . . .[13]

Rabbi Bressler accepted the painful verdict of the beth din, as did all the future rabbis of Mir, among them some of Lithuania's finest scholars, such as Rabbi Yom Tov Lippman. The verdict was important, for it provided legal guidelines for yeshivot that were privately owned, albeit publicly funded. Though such academies had been in operation for many decades by this time, this was the first legal acknowledgment they had received, and it would have a significant impact on their well-being.

By conceding private ownership, with all the rights and benefits that attach to it, the verdict sanctioned the family dynasties who now ran so many of the leading academies. The new legal backing gave them the incentive they needed to establish and maintain their yeshivot — sometimes against great odds.

A group of students at the Volozhin yeshivah in 1925; seated second from right is Yossef Goldstein from Eishyshok. YESC, GOLDSTEIN

DYNASTIC POWER

In 1886 the Volozhin yeshivah would meet one of its most serious challenges. On a Friday afternoon that summer, the town of Volozhin burned down, including the yeshivah complex. By Sunday morning the students were discussing whether to return home, or, since the semester was not yet over, to try to enroll at another yeshivah to finish out the term. Before they even had an opportunity to reach a decision, a directive was issued by Rabbi Naftali Zvi Yehudah Berlin, known by the acronym "the Neziv," who had married into Reb Hayyim's family and was at that time the head of the academy: "No one should travel or budge from this place. Tomorrow morning studies will resume. The yeshivah of Volozhin is in existence!"[14] The following day, classes were held in a makeshift shelter. The firm stand taken by the Neziv, thanks in part to his vested interest in preserving the family dynasty's "royal court" (as the Volozhin academy was known), had saved the day, as would happen in many family-owned yeshivot.

*Though St. Petersburg was outside the Pale of Settlement, Jewish businessmen crucial to Russian commerce were granted special permission to reside there.

Torah scholarship flourished under the dynastic model. The families who owned and managed each yeshivah had a financial stake in the institution that ensured their commitment to its well-being and its excellence; the generational succession guaranteed continuity and stability; and the fact that the line did not strictly follow primogeniture but was constantly infused with new talent, via sons-in-law — the brilliant young men chosen as husbands for the daughters of the dynasty — meant that the yeshivot were in a state of perpetual renewal. The Volozhin dynasty is a perfect example of these strengths. Down to the present day, its members have remained among the most prominent of the Jewish intellectual elite.[15]

Ultimately, despite the conflicts these dynastic institutions often caused, they proved beneficial to their communities — indirectly, because they were a source of prestige, and directly, because their students were a source of income to the townspeople. Not that the communities necessarily acknowledged these benefits. In Volozhin, for example, the yeshivah students had to organize a strike against the shtetl butchers and bakers in order to get their fair share of the korobka and yeast taxes, which they needed to help pay their medical expenses. As consumers of meat and bread who through their purchases paid taxes to the shtetl, the students were fully entitled to these funds, but even the strike, and a subsequent physical confrontation between the students and eight ax-wielding butchers in which some of the students proved that their intellect was matched by their physical strength, did not succeed in settling the dispute. The Neziv had to ask for a din Torah.[16]

Students at Volozhin became activists in other ways as well, for they were sharply attuned to the political and ideological movements of their time. In 1885 they organized a group called the Nes Ziona (Banner of Israel), and in 1890 Nezah Israel (The Eternity of Israel), which future National Awakening poet Hayyim Nahman Bialik joined. The students also published their own papers, *Ha-Boker* (The Morning) and *Ha-Hayyim* (The Life), in which many of the new views were expressed.

Yeshivot similar to the Volozhin model were established throughout Lithuania, in Mir (1815), Radun (1869), Telz (1875), and Navaredok (1896). Though organized along similar dynastic lines, each yeshivah had its own style and character, based on the personality and philosophy of its founder and of the dynasty of scholars who continued the line.

Current educational trends were another influence. In mid-nineteenth-century Lithuania, for example, the Musar movement had a tremendous impact on many yeshivot. A philosophy founded by Rabbi Israel Lipkin Salanter in Vilna, Musar stressed strict ethical behavior in the spirit of halakhah.[17] Rabbi Salanter's emphasis was on living a moral life, and he saw education as a means to that end. This emphasis on morality, on the real-life implications of lessons studied in the classroom, would become one of the distinctive characteristics of many Lithuanian yeshivot. Some incorporated Musar into the curriculum; others, such as those of Slobodka, Kelme, and Navaredok, made it their main focus.[18]

The Lithuanian yeshivot of the nineteenth and early twentieth centuries produced an extraordinary group of scholars and leaders, who would play significant roles in both the religious and the secular worlds. At a time of great intellectual and social ferment, when the yeshivot were enjoying a golden age, their students, unlike previous generations of scholars, were often at the very eye of the storms that were sweeping through Eastern Europe. Having been educated to believe that they were responsible for shaping the destiny of their own people, and for improving the lot of all mankind, yeshivah students were active participants in the Haskalah,

Zionism, the Bund, and various Russian socialist movements. With many of them having manned the barricades (sometimes quite literally) in their ongoing feuds with the people of the towns in which they resided, they were familiar with the tools of political protest, and even, as was true of the students who fought the butchers of Volozhin, with violence. These experiences toughened them and served them well in their future lives. Some went on to become chief rabbis and heads of yeshivot, others became political party leaders, Bund members, and strike organizers in Moscow, St. Petersburg, and Vilna. But wherever their paths took them, the students of Volozhin, Mir, Telz, Navaredok, and other similar academies had something in their demeanor that marked them forevermore.

KIBBUTZ HA-PRUSHIM OF EISHYSHOK

There was another kind of yeshivah at this time, which had also been founded by students of the Gaon of Vilna. These yeshivot were originally intended for young married men who wished to become members of the clergy: rabbis, judges, teachers, and preachers. As such they were designed to provide the students with an in-depth, systematic knowledge of the Talmud and of the other sources most frequently consulted by rabbis and judges. The students were known as prushim, meaning "abstainers," because they had left their families to go study Torah — usually for the purpose of seeking ordination and a clerical post, but in some cases because the yeshivah served as a refuge from an unhappy marriage, a legitimate opportunity for escaping a quarrelsome household. These academies were known as *kibbutzim* after the Hebrew word *kibbutz* meaning "together," because the students were supposed to share everything, to live collectively. (Though the word was used to refer to these yeshivot long before it was applied to the kibbutz movement in Israel, the earlier use has been all but forgotten. Actually, the usage goes back further still — to the Karaite Jews, who as early as the Middle Ages referred to their community as a *kibbutz*. The fact that many of the Lithuanian yeshivot went by this name is one of several indications that the original Jewish settlers of Lithuania, from the eleventh century on, may have included a number of Karaites.)

COMMUNITY SUPPORT

Unlike Volozhin and the other nineteenth-century Lithuanian yeshivot organized along dynastic lines, the kibbutzim of prushim retained many of the characteristics of the sixteenth- and seventeenth-century yeshivot, including their close relationship with the local community. These academies, of which there were a number in White Russia, in Zamut, and in Lithuania, were heavily dependent on local support, at both the individual and the kehilah level.

Though several sources place the Eishyshok yeshivah in the same category with those at Volozhin and Mir,[19] it was in fact one of the kibbutzim of prushim, and moreover would become the largest and most renowned of its kind. It was Eishyshok's great love for Torah, and the extraordinarily generous support the townspeople extended to those who were studying in their midst, as well as the high caliber of its brilliant rabbis, maggidim, and dayyanim, that would make its yeshivah such a success, and the town itself the very symbol of "love of learning."[20] Graduates of the Eishyshok yeshivah were among the most outstanding scholars of their generation, and went on to become renowned leaders of Lithuanian and world Jewry, distinguished academics, journalists, political activists, and even the occasional flaming revolutionary.

According to shtetl tradition, Eishyshok's Kibbutz ha-Prushim was founded in the 1790s by a man named Reb Moshe, who most probably was Rabbi Moshe ben Aaron Halevi Horowitz Segal. He was the rabbi of the community, a friend of the Gaon of Vilna, and one of the rabbis who had been called upon to mediate during a bitter dispute between the rabbi and the kehilah of Vilna — which may have been why he founded a yeshivah that was intimately bound up with the community in which it was based. By uniting the authority of town rabbi and rosh yeshivah in one man, according to the old model, he perhaps thought he could minimize the potential for conflict between town and gown.

Perhaps Reb Moshe also knew, on the basis of his experience as the rabbi of Eishyshok, that the people of that town could be counted on to express their love and admiration for scholarship in practical ways — as indeed they would do for generations to come, even in times of severe hardship. Fortunately, however, Reb Moshe's era was one of prosperity, an auspicious moment for the founding of a yeshivah dependent on community support. Eishyshok was at that time known for its huge biannual Horse Fair, which attracted buyers from hundreds of miles away, and for the bounty of the surrounding countryside, where Jewish farmers and land managers cultivated rich, fertile fields. As expected by Reb Moshe, the man who stood outside the beth midrash one freezing night to make sure the doors didn't blow open and chill those who were studying inside, Eishyshkians were nearly as fervent in their devotion to the young prushim as he himself was.

Everything from firewood to candles, medical expenses to food, books to bathhouse fees and laundry expenses, was supplied to the prushim by the generosity of the community. Eishyshok's beth midrash, where the students did their studying, was so well heated, at community expense, that it was said the Gaon of Vilna, who ordinarily allowed himself to sleep only eight hours out of every forty, fell asleep there — giving rise to the expression "farshlofen in Eishyshok" (to fall asleep in Eishyshok). Some considered the expression an insult, a suggestion that Eishyshok was so dull and backward, even a man who rarely slept could not stay awake there. Most Eishyshkians, however, considered the story and the saying a tribute to their love and generosity toward those who studied Torah.

In Eishyshok, as in many towns with kibbutzim of prushim throughout Lithuania, during weekdays the food for the students was brought to the batei midrash, where they ate in the vestibule or the women's gallery. This spared them time as well as the humiliation sometimes associated with "eating days," when students went to the homes of balebatim for their meals. The food was prepared by housewives who made extra portions as they cooked for their own families, and it was picked up and delivered by individuals who volunteered for the task. Several of these people are still remembered, having joined the shtetl's crowded pantheon of colorful characters.

Berl the Cantonist, or Nikolaievitz (as conscriptees into Tzar Nicholas' army were known), had been kidnapped from Eishyshok as a child, was forced to serve the standard twenty-five-year term in the military, and, like all cantonists, was baptized a Christian. Nonetheless, with the sturdy stubbornness that characterized so many of these conscriptees, he had secretly held on to his faith and, when his compulsory service was up, had come back to his native shtetl, even though as a cantonist he was entitled to a plot of land and a farm outside the Pale of Settlement. Now at last he could return to the Torah, he thought. But he found that his head was as rusty as his old sword, as he put it, so he found another way of immersing himself in the Torah. By bringing food to the prushim, he could hear all around him the sounds and voices of Torah learners; and by his service to these servants of God, he hoped not only to absorb some of their learning, but to atone for the many transgressions he had been forced to commit during his years in the military. A tall, lean man who was very adept at his food delivery duties, Berl was described by Meir Wilkanski thus:

Berl was a military man from the days of Tzar Nicholas. He wore army belts from his service days all strung with iron and clay cooking pots. In addition, each of his hands balanced its own tower of pots. As he walked he was engulfed in a steamy cloud of hot soup and the aroma of meatballs.[21]

Berl's assistant pot carrier was Hayyim der Tregger (porter), also a cantonist, who did a nice balancing act himself, according to one who remembered him; but Hayyim was no match for the other old soldier, and had to make several trips to accomplish what Berl did in one.

Berl Nikolaievitz and Hayyim der Tregger had a female counterpart in Hiene di Frume (the pious one), who took it upon herself to make sure that the prushim were provided with warm nourishment every morning, after their long night of study. Neither hail, snow, rain, nor ice stopped Hiene. Each morning at sunrise, just as the shliah zibbur (reader) reached the Kedushah in the Eighteen Benedictions, Hiene would arrive at the shulhoyf and, hearing the words, put down her pails and rise three times onto her toes, like the most graceful of dancers, reciting "Kadosh, Kadosh, Kadosh" (holy, holy, holy). It was quite a performance, and the prushim used to follow it intently from behind the beth midrash windows. On days when the gentiles' pigs, who were also familiar with Hiene's punctual appearances, wandered on to the shulhoyf in search of her food pails, the students got an even better show than usual. Trying to recite the Kedushah between attempts to fend off the pigs called for some heroic efforts from Hiene the Pious, who could be heard uttering some distinctly unholy sounds between her repetitions of "Kadosh." But once the prayers and her ordeal were concluded, she promptly distributed her pails of food along with freshly baked rolls, which were a gift from Rivke Nohum's bakery. As the prushim ate their breakfasts and eavesdropped, Hiene headed directly for the Holy Ark of the Old Beth Midrash, where she opened the door and addressed God:

Good morning, Gotenu [a term of endearment for God]. It is me, Hiene, thy servant. In your great wisdom, which I accept, you have created me a woman, and thus prevented me from studying Torah. So Gotenu, thank you for granting me the privilege and pleasure to serve those whom you have created in order to study thy Holy Torah.

Hiene's love and reverence for the Torah were shared by most Eishyshkians, and expressed via their generosity to those who studied it. Whatever they had, they gave some to the prushim, and when they had nothing to give they were crestfallen. Shlomo the Vegetable Man, for example, was sad during the long, bleak months of winter when his garden was covered in snow, but during the summer, when it was at its peak, his joy knew no bounds. Daily he would gather his crop, place it in the folds of his coat, and bring it to the beth midrash. There he would place the vegetables on a bench, as though making an offering at an altar, then stand out of sight, watching the prushim as they divided his gift equally among themselves.[22]

On Saturdays and holidays the prushim ate in shtetl homes, they and their hosts having been matched according to scholarship, yihus (status), age, and even personality. Some of the students, especially the more mature ones, and those who had relatives in the shtetl, boarded in private homes, while others slept on the hard benches of the beth midrash.

By the late nineteenth century, towns that supported their own yeshivah in this manner were a declining phenomenon. Indeed, Eishyshok was considered an anachronism in its devotion to its yeshivah, a backward shtetl clinging to outdated ways. For some, however, it seemed a beacon, a reminder of the values of a better time. In what would prove a futile rallying call in which the shtetlekh of Eastern Europe were urged to establish and maintain their own academies, Rabbi Israel Salanter cited Eishyshok as the very model of devotion to the Torah:

Why do you not emulate the piety of the small town of Eishyshok where they have taken it upon themselves — rich and poor alike — not to eat their bread themselves unless they have first given some to the students of the Law who sit there before the Lord. In joy they bring their food, like the first crops, each one at a specified time, to His house of study.[23]

Many of the prushim later looked back on their student days in Eishyshok with great affection, going so far as to pay tribute to the town and its people in the books they wrote. Rabbi Yehezkiel Hafetz, an important Lithuanian scholar, wrote in the foreword to one of his in 1875:

They are holding on to Ez Ha-Hayyim (The Tree of Life), the Torah. With all their efforts, they support the Torah learners, and with great dignity they look after their needs . . . And toward me, too, the insignificant one, they showed their goodness, during the three and a half years I lived among them and learned at the academy, sitting at the feet of our master and teacher, the great Sage and Saint, Rabbi Avraham Shmuel of blessed memory. May God remember them with favor and bless them, shine His countenance upon them, glorify them and enhance their prestige.[24]

A contemporary of Hafetz's, Uri David Apirion, rabbi of Old Zager, used similar language:

I would like to acknowledge with a blessing and gratitude all the householders, kindhearted individuals and great respecters of scholars in the holy community of Eishyshok where, for a number of years, I studied in their beth midrash . . . They treated me with great dignity, shared with me their bread, and gave me the best portions of their food. God, remember all the good they did for us, and for all the great rabbis and scholars who found shelter in their homes. May God lengthen their days and bless them in all their endeavors.[25]

AN UNSTRUCTURED ENVIRONMENT

The townspeople of Eishyshok had nothing but admiration for the students in their midst, and rightly so, for they were of the very highest caliber. Indeed, they had to be, because the course of study was quite rigorous. Moreover, because the curriculum was an unstructured one, it required a level of self-discipline and willpower that would deter all but the truly committed, and would be virtually impossible to find in the younger, single men who attended the other kind of yeshivah.

At Eishyshok and similar kibbutzim of prushim, the students worked mainly on their own — either alone, or in the hevruta, or buddy, system that had been instituted by Reb Hayyim of Volozhin. The only structured events were the weekly classes given by the rosh yeshiva (who was also the shtetl rabbi), and by the other instructors. While the shtetl dayyanim, the maggid, and those balebatim who were known for their scholarship were always available to students who needed help resolving difficult issues, and the most advanced and knowledgeable of the students were also consulted, for the most part the students were on their own.

An atmosphere that valued independent study encouraged a corresponding independence of mind, which was one of the hallmarks of the Eishyshok yeshivah. Students were permitted to pursue their Talmudic learning according to methodologies and trends of their own choosing. When Rabbi Salanter's Musar movement became popular in the Lithuanian yeshivot, for example, many students at Eishyshok chose to study Musar even though it was not an official part of the curriculum, nor was it compatible with the ideology of the school.

As difficult as it was, the unstructured curriculum of the yeshivah in Eishyshok was preferred by many. In combination with the excellence of the faculty and the remarkable hospitality of the townspeople, it was a curriculum that made Eishyshok the preeminent academy of its kind, and induced great loyalty in its students.

Nonetheless, a considerable number of students moved frequently from one yeshivah to another. Though some students stayed at Eishyshok for extended periods, sometimes as long as seven or eight years, others left after only a semester or two, for it was common practice for students to attend several schools in the course of their studies. The poet Judah Leib Gordon, a frequent visitor to Eishyshok, described the back-and-forthing in quite literal terms. "Stand at the crossroads of Mir, Eishyshok, and Volozhin," he said, "and you will see young, poor students walking in great haste . . ."

The usual pattern was to start at the Eishyshok yeshivah, in order to master the ability to think and study independently before being exposed to the more structured curricula at the other schools. But some students, once having experienced the Eishyshok approach, did not want a more structured school, and if they left it was for an even more solitary and independent atmosphere. Either they went home, where they continued their studies on their own or with a father or grandfather or some other learned individual, or they chose the kloiz, a shul in one of the larger towns or cities, where they studied in almost complete solitude, becoming known as *kloizniks*.

Even after the mid-nineteenth century, when the makeup of the student body of the Eishyshok yeshivah gradually began to change until it became predominantly young, single boys and men studying for the sake of study, not married men whose goal was a clerical post, the unstructured curriculum continued to attract brilliant students. They came from far and wide, as was evident from their names, which, in keeping with the custom of the times, reflected their geographic origins: "der Bastuner" (from Bastun), "der Vilner" (from Vilna), "der Olkeniker" (from Olkenik), "der Ashkenazer" (from Germany).

Until unforeseen events toward the end of the century inflicted a near mortal blow on the Eishyshok yeshivah, it remained one of the premiere academic institutions in Lithuania, its alumni between 1835 and 1895 a veritable "Who's Who" of Torah scholarship. Large numbers of Lithuania's most prominent rabbis were among its graduates. Indeed, to study there became an obligatory rite of passage for many of the era's most gifted minds.

OUTSTANDING YESHIVA STUDENTS

THE HAFFETZ HAYYIM Most Kibbutz ha-Prushim students retained a special relationship with their alma mater. But none would be closer than that between the yeshivah and its most illustrious student, Israel Meir Ha-Kohen (1838–1933), better known as the Haffetz Hayyim. The people of Eishyshok knew him for over eighty years — first as a student, later as friend, mentor, founder of a yeshiva in next-door Radun, and distinguished author of twenty-one books. The people of the world came to know him as the most saintly figure in modern Judaism.

If his reputation were based solely on his scholarly achievements, it would be an enduring one. His first book, *Haffetz Hayyim* (by whose title he is called), published anonymously in Vilna when he was thirty-five, is devoted to an exposition of the laws pertaining to slander, gossip, and tale-bearing.[26] It is typical of all the writings that poured from his pen in its emphasis on the practical, its concern not with hairsplitting academic issues but with the moral fabric of everyday Jewish life. His best-known and most widely studied book, an indispensable reference work on halakhic matters that can be found in every Orthodox home, is the six-volume *Mishnah Berurah* (1894–1907). It is a comprehensive commentary and updating of the *Orah Hayyim* section of *Shulhan Arukh*, the Sephardic scholar Rabbi Yossef Caro's early-sixteenth-century codification of all writings on Jewish law, and of the changes Rabbi Moses ben Israel Isserles, the Rema, had made a few decades later when he revised it to take into account the interpretations of the Ashkenazim.

Since the Haffetz Hayyim hoped for and believed in the imminent coming of the Messiah, he emphasized the study of laws related to the restoration of the Temple, and he lived his own life accordingly. Because he was a kohen, and was therefore destined to work in the restored Temple, he made sure that he observed the laws of purification so that he was in a state of perpetual readiness to assume his duties. Among other things, this meant immersing himself in the river each day, even in the dead of winter. Believing that the return of the Messiah was at hand also meant rejecting the political activism of his Zionist contemporaries in favor of messianic redemption. Hence the Sage of Radun opposed secular and political Zionism, and in 1912 became one of the founders of the anti-Zionist Agudat Israel movement.

The Haffetz Hayyim's goodness was as rooted in immediate, practical realities as it was in messianic expectations. He lived very modestly, refusing to make the rabbinate his calling card, or to benefit from his yeshivah.[27] To this day, stories illustrating his ethical behavior, piety, humility, integrity, and caring for others are still being told. A favorite of his contemporaries — among them the tzarist postal officials

The Haffetz Hayyim (1838–1933), one of the most illustrious students of the Eishyshok yeshivah, became a world Jewish leader who in 1869 founded the yeshivah in Radun. YESC, FARBER

The Haffetz Hayyim (with white beard), sitting in front of his house in Radun in the 1930s, facing his son-in-law, Rabbi Lewinson. Among the others are (second from left) Rabbi David Zalmanovitz, son-in-law of Rabbi Szymen Rozowski of Eishyshok; Velvke Natzir, Shlomo Vishniver; Rabbi Scholem Wilenski of Eishyshok; Reb Chafetz; his son Berl; the maid of the household; the wife of the Haffetz Hayyim; Yehudah Breskin (behind the pole); and Shmuel Walkin. YESC, CHAFETZ

who made it one of his most talked-about "miracles"— described the Haffetz Hayyim setting what must have been unprecedented ethical standards with regard to the post office. Because he supported himself by selling his books, the Haffetz Hayyim made considerable use of the mail. And when, for reasons of expediency, he occasionally sent books via tourists or travelers, he felt that he was depriving the post office of its legitimate revenues. Therefore, before handing the books over to his couriers he would weigh them, complete with wrapping paper and string, and then go down to his local post office to pay the money he felt he owed!

The relationship between the Haffetz Hayyim and the people of Eishyshok was close enough that they felt they could turn to their distinguished neighbor if for some reason the wisdom of their own sages was deemed insufficient. For example, a bitter property dispute arose that even Reb Layzer the dayyan was unable to resolve, when a fence that had marked the division between Nahum Koppelman's land and that of his brother Markl was consumed in a fire. Accompanied by Reb Layzer, the two brothers, and everyone else in the shtetl, the Haffetz Hayyim paid a visit to the two empty, burned-out lots. He went to the center of one Koppelman property, bent down and put his ear to the ground, listening intently. Then he did the same to the other. When at last he stood, his face shining under his simple workman's cap, he said: "First I listened to each of you tell your tale. Next I listened to the earth itself. What you have told me you are quite familiar with and there is no need to repeat. But let me tell you what the good earth has said: 'Tell the Koppelman brothers that in the end, all that a person needs are four cubits of land.'" With the dispute resolved, new houses were built and new fences went up. But alas, neither of the Koppelmans was to have his four cubits of earth. During the Holocaust, both brothers and their families were savagely murdered by local Poles, and thereby denied even the "privilege" of being buried in the mass grave that received the thousands of Eishyshkians killed by the Nazis.

REB HAYYIM OZER GRODZINSKI Another student of the Eishyshok yeshivah (as well as of the one in Volozhin) who would go on to have a lasting impact on the political and cultural fiber of twentieth-century Jewish life was Reb Hayyim Ozer Grodzinski (1863–1940), who came to the Eishyshok yeshivah at the age of eleven. Even at a school known for its outstanding students, his brilliance set him apart; he was known as "the prodigy from Ivie." When he celebrated his bar mitzvah in the Old Beth Midrash, his fellow prushim asked him to deliver a sermon, but since he had not prepared a discourse he volunteered to recite by heart any section that they cared to pick, at random, from two recondite, highly complex rabbinic works, *Ketzot ha-Hoshen* and *Netivot ha-Mishpat*. This was only the beginning of what would be a long and dazzling scholarly career.[28]

Reb Hayyim Ozer eventually inherited his father-in-law's position on the beth din of Vilna, thus becoming one of the most prominent rabbis in Eastern Europe at the age of twenty-three. When he heard that people were concerned about his youth, he remarked, "There is nothing to worry about. Youth is an imperfection that passes with time."

Like his friend and close associate the Haffetz Hayyim, Reb Hayyim Ozer opposed Zionism, and joined with him in helping found the anti-Zionist Agudat Israel. As the spiritual leader of Orthodox Lithuanian Jewry, and a member of every important ultra-Orthodox organization of his time, he was also firmly opposed to secular education, indeed to all manifestations of secularism in shtetl life. In 1924 he founded the Vaad ha-Yeshivot (Council of Yeshivot) for the spiritual and material support of the Lithuanian academies, which he saw as a stronghold against the creeping secularism of the shtetlekh, among

Rabbi Yitzhak Yaakov Reines (1839–1915), a product of Eishyshok's Kibbutz ha-Prushim. He attended the First Zionist Congress in 1897, was one of the cofounders of Mizrahi, and founded the Reines yeshivah in Lida. YESC

them the towns of his youth, Ivie, Eishyshok, and Volozhin. Despite his overwhelming preoccupation with these and other public affairs, he was a brilliant writer whose responsa, titled *Ahiezer,* is one of the most essential texts in Torah scholarship.

When Reb Hayyim Ozer died in Vilna, in August 1940, the Communist regime that was then in place permitted no public announcement of his death or his funeral. Nonetheless, the news spread like lightning and tens of thousands of mourners followed his coffin to the grave. Among them were Moshe and Zipporah Sonenson, and their two young children, Yitzhak and Yaffa. Though the Sonensons were staunch Zionists themselves, their admiration for this great leader transcended all political boundaries.

RABBI YITZHAK YAAKOV REINES Not all Eishyshok alumni shared the conservative politics of the Haffetz Hayyim and Reb Hayyim Ozer. Rabbi Yitzhak Yaakov Reines (1839–1915), who was one of the first rabbis to answer Theodor Herzl's call, would put quite a different stamp on his era. After attending the First Zionist Congress in 1897, he became one of the cofounders of Mizrahi, the religious Zionist movement, and its first head.

As evidenced by his Zionist activities, he was committed to effecting a reconciliation between tradition and modernity within a halakhic framework, and he believed that education was a means to that end. Hence his deep concern with education, for both men and women, and his willingness to incorporate secular studies into the curriculum of the yeshivah he founded in Sventsyan (Swieciany); it later moved to Lida. Another innovation in the curriculum was his rigorously logical approach to rabbinic scholarship, which was influenced by his readings of Maimonides. His own distinctive contribution to Talmudic scholarship was a methodology known as *higgayon* (logic).

The Reines yeshivah attracted a significant number of Eishyshkians. There was much disappointment when it closed after the death of its founder, for it had been the perfect solution for those who wanted their sons to attend a Zionist yeshivah that had an integrated curriculum, but paid meticulous attention to tradition.[29]

What the Haffetz Hayyim, Reb Hayyim Ozer, and Rabbi Reines all had in common, their political differences notwithstanding, was more than a shared academic background in Eishyshok, more than their fame, more than the reverence they still compel. They were the epitome of what was special about the scholars who came of age in the Lithuanian yeshivot of the nineteenth century: brilliant in their scholarship, profoundly committed to public life, highly ethical and moral in their personal lives. They all lived modestly, declining to benefit from their renown. And while all three were fully deserving of their illustrious reputations, there were many other distinguished individuals to come out of the Eishyshok yeshivah, some well known, others not, who were imbued with the same high ideals, and who made their own marks on Torah scholarship, and on the destiny of world Jewry.[30]

CHANGE COMES TO EISHYSHOK'S KIBBUTZ HA-PRUSHIM

Even tiny Eishyshok, with its love of Torah learning and its extraordinary yeshivah, did not remain untouched by time. Changes did occur, albeit for many decades at a somewhat slower pace than in other places.

REACTION TO THE HASKALAH

The Haskalah (the Jewish Enlightenment) finally reached the shtetl in the 1860s. It was not carried on the bayonets of Napoleon's soldiers, as happened in other towns, but rather was hidden between the Talmud pages of yeshivah students from the larger cities, where the Haskalah had made great inroads among scholars and intellectuals. The shtetl rabbi, Avraham Shmuel Rabinowitch, was a staunch opponent of Haskalah ideas, and did not hesitate to use the prestige of his pulpit to discredit them. But that didn't stop the yeshivah students from trying to foster them.

Open conflict eventually broke out between the rabbi and the student supporters of the Haskalah, but Reb Layzer the dayyan, whose own family would later prove to be a hotbed of Haskalah activism, was able at that earlier time to foil the students. His intervention occurred as he accompanied the rabbi to shul, where Avraham Shmuel was to deliver one of his fiery anti-Haskalah discourses. Without the rabbi noticing what he was doing, Reb Layzer quickly picked up and read a note that had been dropped in their path. The note was an announcement of the death of Avraham Shmuel's ailing mother, but Reb Layzer recognized it for the false alarm that it in fact was, realizing it had been penned in an attempt to prevent the rabbi from making his much-publicized speech. Unaware of the behind-the-scenes drama, the rabbi gave the speech as planned. It was a fierce attack on the Haskalah, which made a great impact on all the people present in the Old Beth Midrash.[31]

All of Eishyshok's traditional leadership joined forces to fight the spread of the Haskalah among the yeshivah students. The rooms of the prushim were searched for Haskalah books and newspapers, which were then turned to ashes in a public burning held in front of the rabbi's official dwelling on the shulhoyf. Afterward the prushim tried to evade the ever-searching eyes of the censors by tearing out the title pages of forbidden books, but this tactic was soon discovered, and the vigilance merely increased.[32] In the summer of 1877, a bookseller who passed through Eishyshok with Haskalah books was confronted by Reb Layzer, who presented him with a written edict stating that such publications were to be deposited with the shtetl neeman for the period of his stay in Eishyshok, to ensure that they never reached the eyes of the prushim.[33]

Eventually, students who were known for their activism in promoting the Haskalah and supplying the forbidden literature were expelled from the yeshivah. Some of those who were expelled would go on to have careers as distinguished as those of the alumni the yeshivah boasted about, and indeed many of the former students in later years would go out of their way to read the newspapers and books published by those who had been driven away.

Among the banished students were Elhanan Leib Levinski (1858–1910), Yehuda Leib (Leon) Rabinowitz (1862–1938), and Israel Isser Goldbloom (1863–1925). All three became prominent in the Jewish literary establishment. Levinski was the author of a number of books, as well as editor and contributor to many Enlightenment newspapers, including *Ha-Melitz* (The Mediator), a leading organ of the Haskalah movement. Rabinowitz, who studied at Mir and Volozhin as well as Eishyshok, also went on to study medicine in Königsberg, and physics and chemistry at the Sorbonne. In 1890 he was awarded a gold medal in Paris for one of his inventions. His major contributions were in journalism and literature, however, and in 1893 he became the editor-in-chief of *Ha-Melitz*. Goldbloom, who was ousted from Eishyshok in 1879, went on to study at Volozhin, where his room became the unofficial headquarters for students interested in the new ideas. It was there that many Volozhin students first succumbed to the charms of the Haskalah.[34] Goldbloom later became a publicist for various Haskalah organizations and publications, as well as a noted bibliographer, who studied ancient Hebrew manuscripts in Berlin, Paris, the Vatican, London, and Oxford.[35]

Despite their expulsion from its yeshivah, Rabinowitz and Levinski remained lifelong friends of Eishyshok, assisting it in both a personal and a public capacity. When it burned down in the Big Fire of 1895, for example, they put out calls in the pages of *Ha-Melitz* for help in rebuilding. There had been a wave of fires in various Lithuanian shtetlekh that spring — the "Red Rooster" must have been hungry. But Eishyshok's received the most extensive press coverage, thanks to its two former yeshivah students. Goldbloom, however, remained bitter about his treatment in Eishyshok, and used his journalistic skills to discredit the town at every opportunity.

Eishyshok's initially vehement opposition to the Haskalah slowly mellowed with time. By the 1880s and '90s, some of the balebatim from the New Beth Midrash were among its sympathizers.

The restrictions against Haskalah publications in the yeshivah began to loosen. No longer were newspapers forbidden. Though only a handful of students could in fact afford them, those who did buy them shared them generously. It was common to see a group of prushim in the beth midrash huddled around a single copy of *Ha-Zefirah* (The Dawn) or *Ha-Melitz* — the latter a special favorite among the students, "for its editor came from this very beth midrash, and was expelled from this very study hall; now he is a renowned person, a glory to our academy," as Meir Wilkanski described Levinski. Yeshivah students didn't just read the newspapers of the Haskalah, but contributed to them as well, and even, as was the case with the young man known as "der Bastuner," engaged in correspondence with distinguished socialist authors.[36]

As a reflection of the changing times, a new type of prushim began arriving in Eishyshok. Their bundles of books, which they displayed openly, no longer consisted exclusively of sacred texts. Gimpel der Maskil (follower of the Enlightenment), a student from a town near the German border, brought a trunk filled with German books, including a selection of the best contemporary German poetry. A student from Keidan, north of Kovno, brought with him the works of Kalman Shulman, a leading Haskalah author who wrote books on health and geography, and about the self — how to improve it, adorn it, and develop its intellectual, spiritual, and emotional potential (concepts that were completely novel in Eishyshok).[37]

In both the Old and the New batei midrash it was possible to hear heated debates about current events and issues, particularly among those students who, like der Bastuner, had been active socialists and had come to the sleepy town of Eishyshok to escape the attention of the tzarist authorities. As well known for his socialist ideology as for the excellence of his Hebrew grammar and his poetry (praised by no less an authority than Y. L. Peretz), der Bastuner had had to flee the Russian secret police, after the factory workers he had befriended in the large industrial town where he formerly attended yeshivah involved him in some of their revolutionary activities against the regime.

Around the same time der Bastuner was active, a less radical form of socialism was being promulgated in Eishyshok by another student, "der Zargodian," whose ideas about a just society were based not on the tenets of the gentiles, but on the words of the prophets Isaiah and Micah. An accomplished scholar as well as a stirring speaker, der Zargodian preached in the tailors' shtibl, where his ideas about a new world in which class distinctions would disappear were received with great delight.[38]

COURTSHIP

During the late 1880s the yeshivah students in Eishyshok took another step into the future, this one involving their relations with young women. Though many a match had been made between the red-cheeked maidens of the shtetl and the pale, studious prushim in the years since the founding of the yeshivah, all such marriages had been arranged ones. During the 1880s and 1890s, however, the prushim began openly courting the girls of their choice. In a courtship that became the talk of the shtetl, since the girl's father was a poor itinerant tailor, a student named Zusmann lavished gifts on his beloved Beila.[39] Meanwhile, Rachel Rosenheim had captured the imagination of a number of prushim, who courted her in secret missives written in Hebrew. But it was der Bastuner who actually got to spend time with her, having been hired to tutor this lovely bluestocking in Hebrew grammar. Reb Layzer and Batia Wilkanski's beautiful and intellectually active daughter Sarah was also drawing attention — from a handsome, brilliant young man, formerly a student at Volozhin, who courted her under her parents' close supervisory gaze, while trying to convince her to leave the narrow confines of the shtetl to pursue her studies in a large city.

A serene birch grove that cynics labeled "the sin grove" was the meeting place for many of the prushim and the young women they courted. But as they strolled its quiet paths, it was intellectual, not carnal, passions to which they gave rein. "The sin grove" was a rendezvous for young minds ablaze with new ideas, a place where books, ideologies, and the intricacies of Hebrew grammar were hotly debated, and the "sins," if any, were those of heresy.

PERSONAL GROOMING

Around this same time, the students' appearance began to change dramatically. No longer unkempt and disheveled, as the typical yeshivah student of the past had been, the prushim began to pride themselves on their clean, well-groomed look, which was part of the self-improvement program that the Haskalah was urging on the "new Jew." An elegant appearance became the hallmark of a number of Lithuanian yeshivot. In fact, the leadership of many of the yeshivot encouraged this attractive new image, in the hope that it would help their students

Meir Wilkanski, the shtetl chronicler and prominent author of the Second Aliyah. While a student at Kibbutz ha-Prushim of Eishyshok in the 1890s he changed his style of dress from traditional to modern. PHOTO: M. KOPPLON, MEMEL. YESC, WILKANSKI

to resist the lure of the snappy, well-tailored uniforms of the gymnasiums and universities. When an observer remarked disapprovingly that the students at Slobodka were sharp dressers, "the Grandfather of Slobodka" (as the rosh yeshivah Neta Zvi Hirsh Finkl was affectionately known) replied: "So what is their crime, since they are also sharp Talmudic scholars?"

Meir Wilkanski was among the many students in Eishyshok eager to keep in step with their peers elsewhere. Encouraged by his friend Gimpel der Maskil, who wore a short, tailored jacket, a small, neatly trimmed, almost invisible beard, and gold-rimmed glasses, Meir too began to look into the mirror and to devote time to his personal grooming. After all, as Gimpel told him, the sages of antiquity had done the same.[40]

OUTSIDE INFLUENCES

This new breed of Eishyshok student received reinforcement from a contingent of Volozhin prushim who arrived in Eishyshok in the winter of 1892, shortly after the tzarist government closed their school.[41] Many of them were as handsome and elegantly dressed as they were brilliant, and the combination — "they not only studied Torah but were also preoccupied with worldly matters," as Meir Wilkanski put it — made a big impression in Eishyshok.[42] Still, the town of Eishyshok was comparatively slow to embrace change, and some of its most intellectually precocious students were eager to taste the world beyond. Again it would be the Wilkanskis who would be in the forefront of this group.

Yitzhak, the oldest of Batia and Reb Layzer's sons, wanted to leave Eishyshok to study at the yeshivah in Telz, near the Prussian border.[43] Since its rosh yeshivah, Rabbi Eliezer Gordon, had been appointed by Rabbi Israel Salanter of Vilna, in whom Reb Layzer had unlimited trust, Reb Layzer overcame his misgivings and gave Yitzhak his grudging consent. While pursuing

Elegantly dressed Avraham Peretz was a student at the Eishyshok yeshivah and a close friend of Tuviah Rubinstein, the Yeremitcher rebbe. YESC, RUBINSTEIN

Yitzhak Wilkanski, a leading scientist in Eretz Israel, was one of the candidates for the Israeli presidency in the 1950s. During his years at the Telz yeshivah, he dressed in the European university fashion, as was the style among Lithuanian yeshivah students. YESC, WILKANSKI

his yeshivah studies, Yitzhak also became an "external student," following a secular curriculum outside the yeshivah as part of his plan to prepare himself to enroll at a university — all of which he reported on in the letters he wrote back home, which his adoring brother Meir shared with his fellow yeshivah students in Eishyshok. The letters were so eagerly awaited, for both what he had to say about the new ideas he had encountered in Telz and the fine style in which he said it, that the arrival of each one became an event among the prushim. Meir's friend Gimpel, who was well read in Schiller and Heine, was especially appreciative of their literary merits.

The students' enthusiasm for Yitzhak's letters was not, however, shared by Zalman Leib, one of the more pious but not particularly scholarly balebatim of the shtetl. He stormed into the Wilkanski household one day, complaining that the letters were a harmful diversion from Torah learning, and accusing Reb Layzer of maintaining a home that was a snakepit where all the dangerous modern heresies were being incubated. Reb Layzer and Batia were stunned into silence, but not Meir. Having overheard the attack on his beloved brother and his parents, he rushed in with a stick and chased the unwelcome visitor away — to the great pleasure of Reb Layzer and Batia, who saw in his act the ultimate expression of brotherly love.[44]

Yitzhak Wilkanski was a student at Telz during the stormy 1890s, when it, like many other Lithuanian yeshivot, bore more than a passing resemblance to the Russian university campuses of the time, with their political unrest, their conflicting ideologies, their clandestine societies, their fiery publications, and their strikes. Indeed, the student strike against the authorities at the Telz yeshivah was so serious that it caused the school to close down for a while, and the resulting negative publicity had such a chilling effect on contributions that it forced the discontinuation of financial aid to the students. Yitzhak was an eager participant in this world, where he reinforced not only his analytic powers, but his desire for a university education, his commitment to social justice and Zionism, and his leadership abilities. In this way he was representative of a significant number of "sharp Telzians," as they were known.

His hometown, however, despite the many changes it had experienced, remained relatively tranquil, its yeshivah still well integrated into and supported by the community. While the students there were attempting to reshape the shtetl, especially its youth, they were doing it at a slower pace, and in a relatively peaceful fashion. Meanwhile, those who wished merely to sit and study in the beth midrash, as their predecessors had been doing ever since the founding of the yeshivah, were free to do so, their quiet hours undisturbed by strikes or strife.

THE DECLINE OF EISHYSHOK'S KIBBUTZ HA-PRUSHIM

After close to a hundred years of existence, and the passage of thousands of students through the doors of the batei midrash, the yeshivah of Eishyshok experienced a sudden, dramatic setback. No tzarist decree was responsible, nor were the dazzling attractions of the Haskalah. Instead, it was the Big Fire of 1895, which leveled the entire shtetl, including the shulhoyf complex where the yeshivah was located.

After a similar fire in Volozhin, the quick action of the rosh yeshivah, Rabbi Naftali Zvi Yehudah Berlin, had saved the day. By contrast, Rabbi Zvi Hirsh Ma-Yafit, the rosh yeshivah of Eishyshok, was among those who fled when his school and town burned down. As soon as he was offered a good post in Vilkovisk, he left. The difference may perhaps be explained by the fact that Berlin had a vested interest, monetary and legal, in his yeshivah; Ma-Yafit did not. Thus the yeshivot owned and run by dynasties of scholars proved more enduring than the community-owned model, even in a town like Eishyshok, where the people of the community had offered such consistently generous and devoted support.

Eishyshok was rebuilt with help from many sources, including a number of former yeshivah students, even some who had been expelled, as noted earlier. The Haffetz Hayyim, the most illustrious of all the alumni of the Eishyshok yeshivah, who now the head of his own yeshivah and enjoyed world renown, enlisted the help of the Rothschilds and their wealthy friends, the Strausses and the Rosenheims of Germany. Not only did they contribute money to the rebuilding of the batei midrash and the synagogue, they also allocated 5,000 marks annually, for a number of years, to be used to bring former Eishyshker prushim back to their old yeshivah to teach.[45]

Alas, nothing could return the yeshivah to its former glory. The town itself rose from the ashes better planned and more sturdily built than ever before, with two spacious batei midrash, still known as the "Old" and the "New," and a beautiful synagogue. And Reb Zundl Hutner, who came to Eishyshok as the new community rabbi and rosh yeshivah after the departure of Rabbi Ma-Yafit, was a renowned scholar who had published a number of highly respected halakhic works. Yet only about fifty boys and young men came to study when the yeshivah reopened in 1897, and of those, only a few had been among the two hundred who had been there at the time of the fire. In the less than two years during which the Eishyshok yeshivah had been closed, time seemed to have passed it by.

One new arrival who surely thought so was Issic Meir Devenishki (1878–1919), later known as A. Weiter, who came in the fall of 1896. Though his family had roots in Eishyshok — both his maternal great-grandfather and his paternal grandfather were sons of the Eishyshker hazzan Reb Yehoshua Heshl Devenishki, and other family members still resided there[46] — his distressed parents chose to send him to study in Eishyshok for reasons having nothing to do with family ties. Rather, they were hoping to rescue their son from what they saw as a dissolute life.

Like many other parents, Weiter's mother and father had decided that their son was to become a rabbi. Instead, at the yeshivah in Smargon, where he had studied before coming to Eishyshok, he had become a revolutionary, one year there having forever altered his outlook on the world. He had joined the socialist movement that was active among the unhappy factory workers of that town, used his journalistic skills to contribute to the underground press, and begun to write poetry and plays with a social message. And like der Bastuner before him, he too was in correspondence with Y. L. Peretz, and with several well-known socialist authors as well. When news of these dangerous activities reached his parents, they were shocked. They thought they could save him from himself by sending him to Eishyshok, a shtetl without an industrial base and hence without an active workers' movement, a place known for the piety of its people and the excellence of its yeshivah. So it was that A. Weiter, the would-be revolutionary, found himself living in Eishyshok, in the home of "Reb Israel, Reb Hayyim, Reb Moshe" (as the host styled himself, in honor of his lineage). The grandson of the founder of the Eishyshok yeshivah, this man had such a reputation for piety that Weiter's parents had bypassed their own relatives' homes in favor of his, no doubt in the hope that some of that piety would rub off on their son.[47]

Eishyshok proved a great disappointment to Weiter. Its involvement in Haskalah issues was on a completely different level from what he was used to in Smargon. In Eishyshok the students were interested in religious reform; in Smargon, in fundamental social change and the remaking of society. In Eishyshok they were discussing cultural matters that had been the hot topics two decades before; in Smargon they had engaged in heated debates about assimilation, political Zionism, and socialism. In Eishyshok they were reading Dr. Isaac Erter's 1858 publication *Ha-Zofeh Le-Veit Israel* (The Watchman of the House of Israel), an attack on Hasidism, which had been a favorite Haskalah target more than thirty years before, as well as Moshe Leib Lilienblum's *Hatteot Neurim* (Sins of Youth), the several-decades-old autobiography of an East European yeshivah prodigy gone astray, having succumbed to the attractions of the Haskalah; in Smargon the favorite authors included Y. L. Peretz as well as Aaron Lieberman, one of the pioneers of Jewish socialism.[48]

A. Weiter left Eishyshok on the eve of Passover, 1897, depressed and dismayed by what he considered the waste of his time in such a backward place. But he soon made up for this lost time, filling the remaining years of what would be a very short life with action and excitement. He became a Yiddish writer, political agitator, active member of the Bund, and participant in the revolution of 1905. In 1912 he was exiled to Siberia, where he remained until 1917. He settled in Vilna in 1918, where he was shot by Polish Legionnaires in 1919.

THE END OF AN ERA

Tranquil Eishyshok was not a suitable place for a firebrand like A. Weiter. But other students also found it unsatisfactory, for quite different reasons. Those students who still wanted a yeshivah education were increasingly drawn to the structured yeshivot, many of them under the leadership of charismatic personalities such as the Haffetz Hayyim. They preferred a yeshivah with a well-defined ideology, philosophy, and methodology, and they also looked for schools that could offer substantial financial assistance to their students, as only the dynastic, family-owned academies, which charged fees and were supported by donations from around the world, could afford to do. Though a handful of prushim continued to come to study in the shtetl's community-owned academy, it would never again be what it had been at its height.

OTHER YESHIVOT

Many young Eishyshkians who had once aspired to go no further than the superb yeshivah in their own town square now traveled elsewhere to attend school. With the decline of Eishyshok's Kibbutz ha-Prushim, next-door Radun became the undisputed center of Torah studies in the vicinity.[49] Its yeshivah was a thriving institution under the leadership of the Haffetz Hayyim. In some Eishyshok families the Radun yeshivah became a two- and even three-generation tradition. So close was the relationship between the two shtetlekh that when the Radun yeshivah's new building was dedicated in 1913, the press reported that "almost all of the young people from nearby Eishyshok [were among those who] filled the beautiful hall."[50] And the traffic back and forth between the two towns was considerable. Eishyshkians who missed their prushim would frequently walk to Radun, which was just an hour or so away; while yeshivah students from Radun who loved the more economically prosperous and "cosmopolitan" atmosphere of the neighboring town often took advantage of the time between minhah (afternoon prayer) and maariv (evening prayer) to take a leisurely stroll to Eishyshok.

While the more conservative Eishyshkians, mainly Old Beth Midrash people, such as the Lawzowski, Lewinson, Zlotnik, and Hutner families, sent their sons and grandsons to traditional schools like the Radun yeshivah, others looked for schools where Talmud scholarship was combined with secular studies. The Lida yeshivah of Rabbi Yitzhak Yaakov Reines, himself an Eishyshok alumnus, was very popular with that group, which included Shael Sonenson, Yaakov Resnik, and Mekhil Wilenski.

But even yeshivot that had not incorporated

The new building of the yeshivah in Radun was dedicated in 1913. YESC

A group of students at the Radun yeshivah in 1938, among them eight Eishyshkians: (top row, from right) Hersh (last name unknown), his friend Yitzhak Matikanski, and (sixth from right) Hayyim Zvi Solcianski; (middle row, second, sixth, and eighth from right): Yaakov Zubizki, Alexander Zisl Hinski, and Alter Eishyshki; (bottom row, fourth and seventh from right): Shalom Shimonowitch and another Eishyshkian. Seated on the ground on the right is Avraham-Yaakov Hinski, Alexander Zisl's brother. Of the Eishyshkian students, only Alexander Zisl Hinski made aliyah to Israel. All the others perished in the Holocaust. YESC, HINSKI

secular studies into their curriculum attracted their share of forward-thinking students, simply on the basis of their distance from home and family, and their proximity to intellectual centers where the ideas of the Haskalah and other social movements were brewing. It was on that basis that Meir Wilkanski, one of the fifty students who had for a while attended Eishyshok's yeshivah when it reopened after the 1895 fire, chose his school. Following in the footsteps of his brother Yitzhak, he turned his back on the yeshivah whose final years of greatness he had so faithfully recorded, and set off for Telz, and the beginning of a different kind of life. Like many students of his era, including his own brother, he saw this more urban yeshivah as an intermediary step, a chance to break with home, family, and tradition in a more gradual way, as opposed to going directly to the university:

My friend Israel and I are on our way to the big city. It has much to offer — for my father it is Torah, for me and my friend it is secular wisdom.

Avraham-Hayyim the coachman came to take me to the train station, the first stop on my way to the big world outside. In the total darkness before dawn, the sound of his carriage wheels was clearly heard.

All the lamps in my house had been placed on the window sills, to light up the dark alley and my good fortune. All the family members came out of the house to stand outdoors and see me off.

In the midst of the glowing light, my father's face darkened, as if covered by a cloud. His hands were shaking as he hugged me, his voice was choked as he blessed me. My two little sisters tried to cheer him up, and to me, too, they spoke encouraging words, all in Hebrew.

The carriage pulled out. My father's house was left behind. And soon our little alley and all it contained retreated into the distance. Then Reb Avraham-Hayyim turned his head toward us and, with great joy, announced that the morning star had risen![51]

Reb Layzer dayyan, wise man that he was, well understood the ramifications of his son's departure. He knew that Meir was leaving behind not only his home, but the light of Torah, a light that had for generations illuminated the dark alleys of the shtetl. For young Meir, the morning star was shining above a new city, and a new way of life.

By the closing years of the nineteenth century, universities were attracting more young Jewish men in Eastern Europe than yeshivot were. Those whose parents would not send them to a university were likely to choose a yeshivah like the famed Ramailes yeshivah of Vilna, founded in 1831. It satisfied their parents' requirements but did not supervise the students closely enough to interfere with their goal of broadening their experience. For them such a yeshivah was not so much a way station as a pretext. Shaul Kaleko, one of the last Eishyshkians to study at Ramailes, is the perfect example of this phenomenon.

Shaul was the son of Mina and Mordekhai Munesh Kaleko, grandson of the legendary shopkeeper Malke Roche's Schneider. While his father was away in America, working on the docks of Boston but as yet unable to send money back home, Shaul convinced his mother, who was trying to support six small children on her own, that the Ramailes yeshivah was an important step on the road to becoming a great Talmudic scholar. Since it was Mina Kaleko's greatest wish that her bright son Shaul become a rabbi, she consented. But in fact Shaul, who had been studying at the yeshivah in Eishyshok and living at home under the watchful eye of his mother, saw the Ramailes yeshivah as his chance at freedom, and it was this that he had in mind when he set out for Vilna in the spring of 1914. Upon his arrival on June 2, he began keeping a diary in Hebrew, part of it devoted to an accounting of the world he longed to escape. The diary offers an insight into the life young yeshivah students led in the early years of the twentieth century:

My years are few, numbering only fifteen, but as the poet has said, already I am filled with misery, like an old man . . . Like my peers I have learned in yeshivot, suffered "eating days" and starved, endured sleepless nights on hard benches and on equally hard brick ovens, with a bundle of straw as my mattress. I have experienced the rage of balebatim and their wives, ladies with thin, withered lips, as I went from door to door begging for my "days." I have tasted all that is troublesome in our lives, all that evokes in us the will to run away to save ourselves from our precarious lives. Indeed, I truly drank from the bitter cup until the last draught. . . .

Already by the time I was seven I was in Vasilishok; there I experienced the same things that most other poor yeshivah students did. . . . In Vasilishok I learned only one year. From there I returned home and learned in my own shtetl. In those days I excelled in my studies and my parents saw in me a future Talmud scholar.[52]

Once in Vilna, Shaul rarely attended the yeshivah. His goal was to pursue secular studies so that he could qualify for a gymnasium diploma from the Russian school system, which would make him eligible for the university. Soon after he arrived, he began tutoring students in Hebrew in order to pay for his Russian lessons. But life in Vilna was as difficult as it had been in his Vasilishok days, and once again he suffered hunger and sickness. Though he gave up his tutoring for better-paying jobs, first as a clerk, then as a bookkeeper, he still had to work long hours, which kept him from his studies. Packages from his mother sent via the Vilna coachmen, help from his older brother Simha, also a student in Vilna, and the friendship of a poor young girl who was a seamstress alleviated his despair. And after not very many months, the outbreak of World War I put an end to Shaul Kaleko's eight years of yeshivah education. He returned to Eishyshok, and was very pleased to taste his mother's cooking once again.[53]

YESHIVAH KETANAH

Shaul Kaleko's difficult life as a yeshivah student was typical for many of his generation. The hardships faced by these students, from a very young age, in combination with other changes that were occurring at the time, resulted in the establishment of a new institution. This was known as the yeshivah ketanah — the middle or small yeshivah — which could not grant rabbinic ordination. After World War I, Eishyshok was among the relatively few places where this new kind of school, for boys who were past heder age but still quite young, had begun to emerge.

The middle yeshivah, also known as the *mekhina* (preparatory school), was a structured school with a well-defined curriculum, the main goal of which was to prepare students for the yeshivah for older students (now known, technically, as the yeshivah gedolah).[54] At the conclusion of the course of study a diploma was granted. Classes were organized by age and achievement level, and went by the names of the first four letters of the Hebrew alphabet: *Aleph, Beth, Gimel,* and *Daleth.* In addition to the Talmud, the main subjects were the Bible, Hebrew grammar, and some arithmetic. Allowance was made for the youthful energies of the students, with occasional outings to the forest and swimming in the river.

Though community-owned, the yeshivah ketanah of Eishyshok was supplemented by tuition and outside contributions. Perhaps as a sign of the less intimate relation between the town and its new yeshivah, some of the more picturesque customs of the Eishyshkians were abandoned. Thus, the food distribution of the Kibbutz ha-Prushim gave way to the "eating days" system prevalent in most yeshivot, and students ate in the homes of designated balebatim on their assigned days. Avraham Lipkunski from Dugalishok, later to become the youngest witness at the Eichmann trial, ate at the home of Moshe and Zipporah Sonenson. Avraham Asner, from Nacha, ate at the home of Hayya Sonenson. Students also ate at the home of Yehiel Lewinson, but never on Wednesday, because his itinerary as a Lida coachman required that he be absent from home on that day and it would have been improper for young male students (probably in their early teens) to be alone in the house with his wife and daughters.

One thing that hadn't changed was the quality of the education offered in Eishyshok, for the faculty was outstanding. Some of its more charismatic teachers included Rabbi Tuvia Rothberg, a rosh yeshivah who was married to the daughter of Reb Hersh, the Haffetz Hayyim's maggid; the brilliant Tuviah Rubinstein, the Yeremitcher rebbe; Scholem Wilenski, a former revolutionary turned mystic; and Rabbi Zusha Lichtig.

During World War I the yeshivah ketanah of Eishyshok grew by leaps and bounds, due to the influx of refugees. But after the war, despite the devoted efforts of Rabbi Szymen Rozowski, who spent much of his time collecting funds for the yeshivah, it was eclipsed by the coed Hebrew day school, where the majority of young shtetl boys were educated.[55]

Like all other Jewish religious institutions, the yeshivah Ketanah would eventually fall victim to the local Jewish Communists. During their brief period of power in September-October 1939, and when they were in power again from June 1940 to June 1941, they closed what was left of this already dying academy.

FINAL DAYS

In October 1939, Radun became part of the Russian Republic of Byelorussia, Eishyshok part of Lithuania. To escape Russian persecution, a section of the Radun yeshivah, consisting of 198 students, moved to Eishyshok, while another group moved to Otian.[56] Under the dynamic leadership of Rabbi Rozowski, Eishyshok lavished attention on the students from Radun. Many rejoiced at hearing the Old and New batei midrash echoing day and night with the voices of Torah scholars; some even saw those sounds as a favorable omen, a sign from heaven that Eishyshok would be spared the havoc of war.

On Simhat Torah of 1939, the Radun yeshivah

students led the entire town of Eishyshok in fervent dancing and singing. Their festivities overflowed both batei midrash and the summer synagogue, and spilled out into the grounds of the shulhoyf. Older Eishyshkians, who still remembered the glory days of the Kibbutz ha-Prushim, wept with joy during this spectacular celebration of the Torah. Why else would God send Eishyshok nearly two hundred yeshivah students, along with hundreds of holy Torah scrolls and sacred books, if not to send a message — that their beloved shtetl was to be rewarded for years of devotion to the Torah and its scholars?

They were convinced that Eishyshok would escape the destruction others were warning against. Looking at the writing on the wall, the ancient, beautiful Ark coverings that were brought out only for this one holiday period each year, they reassured each other. For there, hanging in the Old Beth Midrash, they could see gold and silver letters, glistening in the light, spelling out the words that promised life.

Moshe Sonenson, with his little daughter Yaffa-Sheinele on his shoulders, stopped to greet his elders, and listened silently to their tearful expressions of hope. "Be careful with the candle," Reb Itche the melamed warned, for the child was holding a Simhat Torah flag topped with an apple and a burning candle. Moshe Sonenson responded: "Reb Itche, it is already too late. Our shtetl is burning, but we fail to see the flames."*

*"Our shtetl is burning" is a line from a popular song of the same name, written by the Yiddish poet Mordekhai Gebirtig (1877–1942).

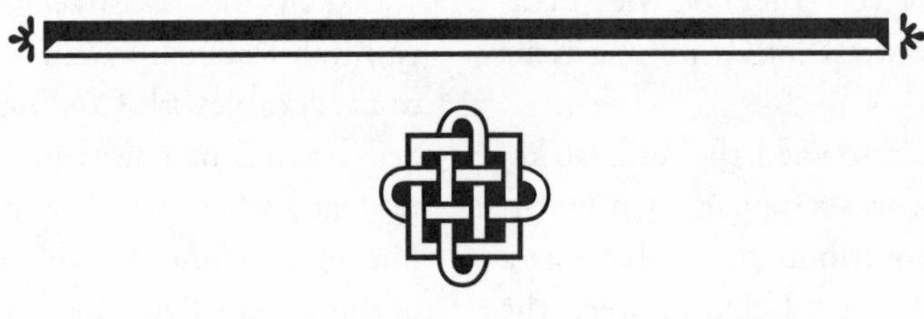

THE PUBLIC BATH HAS BEEN ONE OF THE MOST ESSENTIAL INSTITUTIONS OF JEWISH community life, from the time of the Second Temple, when a mandate required each settlement to have a public bathhouse, throughout the Diaspora. Although most Jewish homes are of course equipped with baths today, the mikvah, or ritual bath, which was always part of the public bath complex, is still maintained in a community-supported building in many cities; and, because of its strictly observed ritual role in a woman's monthly cycle, it still occupies a central position in Orthodox Jewish family life.

Hillel the Elder considered bathing a religious obligation: "For just as the custodians scour and wash the statues of the kings," he told his disciples, "likewise must man, created in God's image and likeness, do to his own body."[1] Bathing was equated with being civilized. Indeed, primitive people were defined as those who "sit in the darkness without a candle and do not bathe in the bathhouse."[2] Among the Talmud's voluminous discourse on the subject is a passage stating that a scholar — who of course set the standard for all that was good and civilized — may not reside in a city that does not have a communal bathhouse.[3]

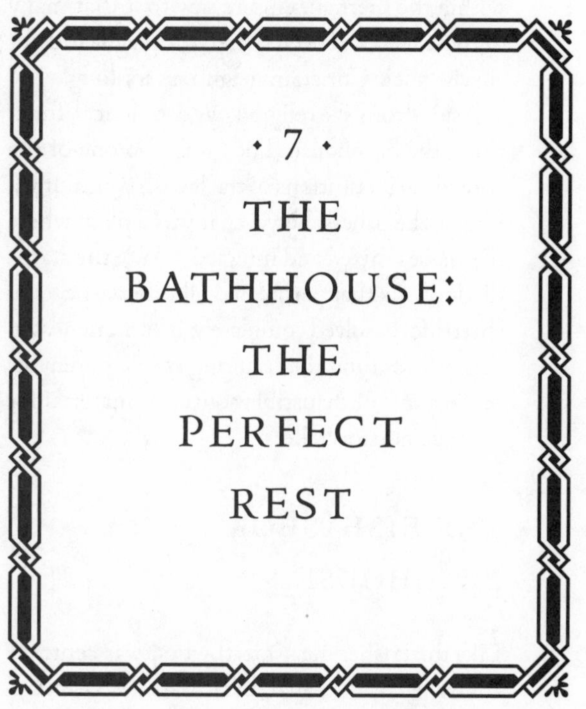

· 7 ·
THE BATHHOUSE: THE PERFECT REST

THE BATHHOUSE FOR THE JEW IS HIS HOMELAND, HIS DEMOCRACY. PROMINENT AND MEEK ALIKE, EACH CAN ASCEND, STEP BY STEP, TO THE TOP OF THE BLEACHERS IN THE BATHHOUSE. THERE EACH CAN CHEER HIS GLOOMY SOUL, CAST OFF HIS BURDENS OF WOE AND SORROW, AND FIND AN HOUR OF CONTENTMENT IN THIS WORLD, A PERFECT REST.

Mendele Mokher Sefarim
THE TRAVELS OF BENJAMIN THE THIRD

Like the Jews, the Romans were known for their devotion to bathing, and even at a time of general animosity toward their rule were praised by a number of rabbis for the magnificent bathhouses they built during their reign over Judea.[4] But in Roman culture the luxurious public bathhouses were a form of pleasure and entertainment, in a civilization that prized those aspects of life, while in Judaism the public bath and the mikvah were expressions of the culture's commitment to physical cleanliness and spiritual purity.[5] And this commitment remained constant, regardless of the wealth or stature of the community. Affluent communities had Jewish bathhouses noted for their size and splendor, like the landmark Badenhaus in Augsburg and the ones in Barcelona, but even the most modest communities also built the mandated bathhouses, in a style commensurate with their means.[6] Moreover, they continued to build, maintain, and frequent them even at times in history when bathing was generally considered a rare luxury, and kings boasted that they seldom or never bathed.

The centrality of the bathhouse in Jewish culture is probably one reason that during times of epidemic and plague, the mortality rate among Jews tended to be lower than among the neighboring non-Jewish population. In fact, during the Black Death of 1348–49, the disparity between the numbers of Jews and non-Jews who were killed by the plague was so great that the Jews were accused of poisoning the wells as part of a plan to destroy the whole of Christendom.[7] The resulting massacres of Jews in many places within the German empire saw to it that many of those who had been spared the plague did not survive their Christian neighbors for long.

Aside from its religious and practical functions, the bathhouse (bod) was also one of the core social institutions of the Jewish community. Unlike the others, however, it was a place where the classes mixed and mingled, where the status distinctions that permeated all other aspects of shtetl life dissolved completely. Its uniqueness in this respect (and the resulting comic potential) made it an inexhaustible source of material for writers and storytellers.

THE EISHYSHOK BATHHOUSE

Like the kosher meat tax, the bod was centrally controlled by the kahal, and leased at a Saturday-night public auction in the Old Beth Midrash to a member of the community, who assumed responsibility for all management and maintenance. While the bathhouse itself may have been a democratic society, the usual rigid class distinctions pertained to the position of bedder (bathhouse manager), which was not one of the more prestigious jobs in the shtetl; thus the person who leased the bathhouse was never, unlike the korobka-leaser, a member of the balebatim (householder) class. His job was, however, an essential one, taken seriously by most of the men who performed it, and the communal bath was generally very well maintained.

Still, by its very nature the bathhouse was filled with potential hazards, which the rabbis of the Roman period had devised prayers to protect against. "May it be Thy Will, O Lord, my God, to deliver me from the flames of the fire and the heat of the water and protect me from cave-in," one was to say upon entering. "I thank Thee, O Lord, my God, for having delivered me from the fire," one said as one left.[8] Tongues of flame, scalding water, and building collapse were only the natural hazards; according to the Talmud, there were also supernatural dangers to worry about, in the form of non-Jewish sorcerers who sometimes found their way into the Jewish bathhouse.[9] Though there is no shtetl record of bathhouse sorcery, the physical hazards the rabbis' prayers were intended to ward off proved as real in late-nineteenth-century Eishyshok as they had been in first-century Judea, for there were two accidents in the 1880s, during the tenure of Yossef der Bedder.

The public bath building in Eishyshok in 1996. On the outside the building, dating from the interwar period, is unchanged. PHOTO: GLORIA BLUMENTHAL. YESC, KABACZNIK

The first occurred when the bathhouse became overheated. One woman passed out, and many others were on the verge of doing so, but all were revived when a doctor was rushed to the bathhouse to administer first aid. The day ended without serious mishap but with an abundance of dramatic stories, which Dr. Ezra was happy to share with a group of eager yeshivah students who gathered that night at the beth midrash.[10]

The second accident had a much more tragic outcome. A number of men were in the bathhouse when suddenly there was a huge fiery blast — the boiler had exploded! The prushim from the beth midrash were the first to arrive at the scene, which was a terrible one indeed. More than a dozen men died, and many others were critically wounded.[11]

One hazard that went unmentioned by the Roman-period rabbis was the pack of dogs that lived behind the Eishyshok bathhouse with a gentile family named Alvokove. Before electricity shed its bright light on the dark streets, it was the Alvokoves' practice to sic their dogs on women who were leaving the bathhouse at night, whereupon it became the bedder's responsibility to chase away the dogs and ensure that the women got home safely.

The bath in Eishyshok was part of the shulhoyf complex, as was customary, and was located near a tributary of the river Kantil on Bod Gessl (Bathhouse Lane). It was a two-part brick structure consisting of a small section called the bedl (small bath) containing a mikvah and several bathing tubs as well, and, connected to the bedl but with its own entrance, a larger section with three rooms, which was the public bath. Like the synagogue itself, a mikvah had to be built to certain specifications. For example, it could not be constructed elsewhere and transported to the site, but had to be carved out of or built on the site. It had to be watertight and had to hold at least 120 gallons of water, which were to come from a natural source, and to be running, not drawn (one reason the bath was usually part of the shulhoyf complex, since the shul also had to be near a natural body of water).

Although the bedl was open to Jewish men at certain times, it was mainly for the use of Jewish women, and was strictly off-limits to all non-Jews, for it was in that sanctum that the laws regarding "family purity" were observed. Dating back to biblical times, these laws were observed by all women in Eishyshok until the shtetl's final days.[12] By Jewish law, a menstruating woman can resume marital relations only after an immersion in the mikvah, which takes place at the conclusion of the "seven clean days" following the cessation of her monthly flow. Failure to observe the laws relating to menstruation was one of the three transgressions for which women might be punished by dying in childbirth.[13] Immersion in the mikvah at the close of a prescribed period of time is also necessary for resumption of marital relations after childbirth. Immersions were required at other special times as well, such as on the eve of the Sabbath and on various holidays. Men used the mikvahs too, both the one in the bedl and the two that were in the main bath area, but the immersions safeguarding family purity were the most important ones.

A female attendant known as the tokerin or tokerke (from the Yiddish for "to immerse") supervised each woman's immersion in the mikvah, pronouncing it kosher once she had ascertained that all had been done according to law and custom. She also assisted in grooming tasks that were part of the mikvah ritual, such as nail cutting and hair combing, for which she received small fees as well as tips, on top of a salary. To supplement what was still a very modest income from her bathhouse duties, Rochel-Leye, one of Eishyshok's last tokerkes, stood in the marketplace in wintertime, selling frozen apples.

Mothers who needed to go to the mikvah at the end of their "seven clean days" were occasionally accompanied by their older daughters. There the daughters had the opportunity to bathe, and to learn from their mothers both the basic laws of family purity and the traditions particular to their own family, such as immersing oneself in the mikvah six or nine times instead of the three required by law. There too the girls might learn something about the facts of life, either from their own mothers or from some of the other women.

Facts were mixed in with folklore. Looking back with affection on the hours she and her two sisters spent with their mother at the mikvah,

Dobke Kremin Dimitrowski (now Dora Dimitro) remembers her mother turning to catch a glimpse of the bedder as she departed from the bathhouse, out of the ancient belief that a child conceived the night of a woman's immersion in the mikvah would resemble the first living thing she saw as she left it. Women had been observing this custom at least since the Talmudic era, when, it was said, the handsome Rabbi Yohanan (180–279 C.E.) made a habit of sitting opposite the bathhouse door so that the women could see him on their way out.[14] And they were still observing it in Eishyshok in the 1930s, which prompted Yude-Yankl, shoemaker and shtetl wit, to tell the good-looking Moshe Tobolski that he should consider supplementing his hazzan's salary by sitting near the bathhouse window and charging the departing women for a look. Reb Ele, Eishyshok's last bedder, was not as physically attractive as Rabbi Yohanan or Hazzan Tobolski, but he was a God-fearing, hardworking, honest Jew who had fathered a brilliant Talmud scholar, and for some, like Dobke Kremin Dimitrowski's mother, the model sufficed.

The bathhouse had a regular weekly schedule, but because there were so many exceptions to it due to holidays and other special events, the bedder gave both oral and written notice of its calendar of operations in the polesh of all three houses of prayer. The text was always the same: "Today the bathhouse is being heated." While the bedl was open every night of the year (except Yom Kippur) for women whose time of the month dictated that they immerse themselves in the mikvah, the main section had a much more abbreviated schedule: Wednesday was for the women of the shtetl; Thursday was specifically for gentile men, mainly from the countryside; and Friday was for the men of the shtetl. The logistics involved in any emergency adjustments to this schedule could be daunting. Reb Alter "the Long," for example, was once in urgent need of a bath after falling into the public outhouse. Nonetheless, since it was Wednesday, he was made to wait until the last woman had left the bathhouse before being allowed in.[15]

Thursdays, when the bathhouse was open to the peasants who had come to town for market day, were particularly busy during the winter, because the farmers could no longer bathe outdoors in the ponds and rivers. On those frigid winter days they would take off their lice-infested sheepskin coats, hang them high above the highest bleachers in the steam room, and wait until the clouds of vapor rising from below had killed off all the lice before reclaiming their garments. Whereupon many a peasant emerged flushed and grinning from the baths, joking about how his coat had walked in of its own volition, but had had to be carried out. This may explain why many of the local Eishyshkian gentiles preferred to go to the bathhouse with their Jewish neighbors on Friday!

Friday, between ten in the morning and sundown, was the day when the bathhouse was at its peak of activity, and the bedder at the height of his command. "Balebatim un shkhenim, in bod arain" (Householders and tenants, time to go to the bathhouse), he would call out from the market square, and would then proceed to several other main streets, where he would make the same announcement. Within minutes, entire families of men, two, three, and sometimes four generations at a time, began streaming out of their houses, converging from all the streets, lanes, and courtyards of the shtetl upon one destination: the bathhouse. Some carried wicker baskets heaped with towels, soap, clean underwear, Sabbath shirts, and socks. Others simply rolled a few clean articles of clothing in a towel and tucked it under their arm.

Once arrived at the bathhouse, the men filed past a small table in the entrance hall where the bedder and his son or other male family members collected the bathing fees. There one could also purchase soap and other bathing accessories, such as the small bundles of dried birch twigs used in the steam room. And there the bedder took pleasure in extending his personal greetings to members of the clergy and other prominent men in the community, as Meir Wilkanski recalls a bedder named Yossef doing with his father, Reb Layzer the dayyan:

With respect he welcomes my father. "Let his honor look and see the huge stack of firewood in the backyard," he says, as he conducts my father on a tour of his domain. "The flames in the oven are well stoked, no firewood is spared, everything is given with an open hand to keep up the heat and the steam. This year the bathhouse did not bring in much profit. But Yossef ben Hayyim is a man of his word, and he remains faithful to the bargain he struck."[16]

Then he sent Reb Layzer on his way, after selecting for him the finest bundle of birch twigs.

The first stop was the "cold room," where one undressed and left one's clothes, and to which one returned after bathing. Because the dressing room was unheated, there was less of a shock to the system when passing between it and the outdoors after bathing in wintertime, and therefore less chance of getting sick. Next was the "lukewarm room," where some people liked to immerse themselves (at least in warmer weather) in the cold mikvah, and where all the shtetl boys and men got their hair cut and their peot (sidelocks) and beards trimmed. Here, during Meir Wilkanski's time, Shraga Feibush the barber reigned supreme, master not just of the shears but of the cupping glass and the leech bottle. With candle in hand he would ignite the spirit-smeared glass cups and place them, in row upon flaming row, on his customers' aching backs and ribs. Or, for those with other ailments, he would reach into his bottle of leeches, extract several hefty black specimens, and deposit them around the neck, whence they would make their leisurely way down the man's naked body, leaving long trails of blood in their wake.[17]

Some fifty years later, little had changed. The lukewarm room was now the domain of Alter der Sherer (the barber), and he had so many customers that he employed a number of assistants: Muslim Tatars who were experts in local folk medicine, and Christians who were fine masseurs.[18] But this room and the other two, as well as the bathing procedures that were observed in them, would have been familiar to Meir Wilkanski in the 1880s, as indeed they would have been to the scholar Rashi in the eleventh century. Rashi's Talmudic commentaries on bathhouse and bathing procedures reveal the continuity through the ages.[19]

The third of the three bathhouse chambers, the steam room, was where most people did their actual bathing, and where they immersed themselves in the mikvah after bathing. In both it and the lukewarm room there were buckets of water to be poured over the body, and a shallow gutter that drained the water away. The bathhouse attendant was kept busy bringing bucket after bucket of hot water, both for bathing and for pouring over the burning coals that were under a grate in one corner of the room.

Ringing the room were five steplike wooden bleachers, which one ascended according to one's tolerance of the heat level. Young boys stayed at the first level, most adults at the second, third, or occasionally fourth, and the bravest of all, the elite of the classless bathhouse society, climbed to the fifth. Stretched out on the top bleacher, wreathed in steam, glistening with sweat, the men abandoned their bodies to the intensity of the heat, and revived each other with the thrashings of the twigs. Not only did these little birch bundles improve the circulation, but when the moist steam penetrated the wood, it released wonderful fresh smells, recalling the meadows and forests from which it had been gathered by local shepherds. Meir Wilkanski describes the ritualized pleasures of the fifth bleacher:

Up there in the fog and the mist, the faces can barely be seen. People scream and thrash each other with heated birch twigs, attacking the back, shoulders and posterior.... Yossef the bath attendant perpetually augments the clouds of vapor and mist with fresh supplies of boiling water, while from out of the steamy clouds invisible beings utter strange cries and harsh, guttural breathing sounds.[20]

During the years between the two world wars, a local official from the Polish Department of Health claimed that the wooden bleachers constituted a fire hazard and demanded that the shtetl replace them with concrete, which was done. But there were those connoisseurs who claimed that the quality of steam in the third room was never again the same, even though the new concrete benches were covered with wooden planks. In fact, some were convinced that the fire code was just a screen for yet another of the Polish government's anti-Semitic acts, this one designed to rob the Jew of one of his greatest pleasures: the perfect rest that could only be achieved on a wooden bleacher in the shtetl bathhouse.

Though the shtetl was a society governed by strict laws of modesty, these customs were as little observed in the bathhouse as those that kept the classes apart. Young and old, fathers and sons, rich and poor, all saw one another in the nude, stripped of the last vestiges of privacy, and disregarding certain biblical injunctions against such behavior. Indeed, little Meir Wilkanski had to exercise some mental ingenuity to explain to himself why the curse that afflicted Noah's son Ham for looking at his naked father would not apply to those in the Eishyshok bathhouse. Pondering the passage from Genesis in which Ham encounters the drunken Noah in his tent, Meir resolved his dilemma thus: "But Noah was outdoors, not in the bathhouse. Here everything is permitted."[21]

As the sun descended to the treetops and the Sabbath approached, the attendant often had a difficult time persuading the last bathers to leave. While other shtetlekh employed people specifically for this purpose,[22] in Eishyshok the responsibility for shooing people out before the Sabbath was the bedder's — as were so many other tasks. Meir Wilkanski recounts that once when his shoes got lost or stolen in the late-Friday-afternoon bathhouse tumult, Yossef der Bedder, embarrassed that such a mishap could have occurred in "his" bathhouse, carried Meir home on his shoulders.[23]

With the weekly closing of the bathhouse, those who emerged in their gleaming white starched shirts and other Sabbath finery resumed their usual places behind the rigid class lines that separated them from their fellow man. And soon those who just hours before might have been among the bathhouse elite of the fifth bleacher now sat at the synagogue entrance, far from the prestigious mizrah wall.

Not long after the arrival of the Germans in Eishyshok in 1941, the commanding officer known as "der Wiesser Rekele" (White Jacket, in reference to the spotless garment he always wore) marched down to the bathhouse and ordered his men to close it, and to destroy the mikvaot. For a while, however, he lingered at the mikvaot and examined them closely. Perhaps he saw in their clear waters the millennia-old procession of beautiful, bashful young Jewish brides whose immersions preceded their wedding days; or the hopes and dreams of all the women who had bathed in the waters after giving birth; or the awe and trepidation of Jewish men emerging from the waters on the eve of Yom Kippur; or the face of an old, sainted scribe immersing himself prior to writing the name of God in the Holy Scrolls. Or perhaps he saw reflected in the quiet ripples of the water the terror-stricken eyes of the beautiful young girl, daughter of Reb Scholem Wilenski the shtetl mystic, whom he had raped immediately before his visit to the bathhouse. Or perhaps he simply contemplated the slaughter still to come.

On September 25, 1941, the men of the shtetl were marched from the Horse Market, in groups of 250, to Besoylem Gessl (Eternity Lane), which took them to the Old Cemetery. There they were ordered to undress, which they did, neatly folding their clothes as they had done so many times before in the bathhouse. Naked, facing the trench which had long ago been dug around the cemetery to protect it, they were gunned down. And, in a return to the democracy of the bathhouse, grandparents, fathers, sons, and grandsons, rich and poor, saintly scholars, ardent Zionists, devoted Communists — all fell into the trench, their common grave. From there their blood flowed into a tributary of the Kantil River, meandering through green meadows till it reached the shtetl bathhouse.

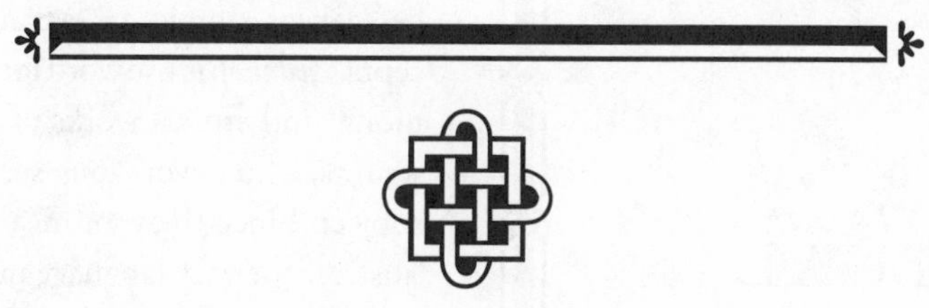

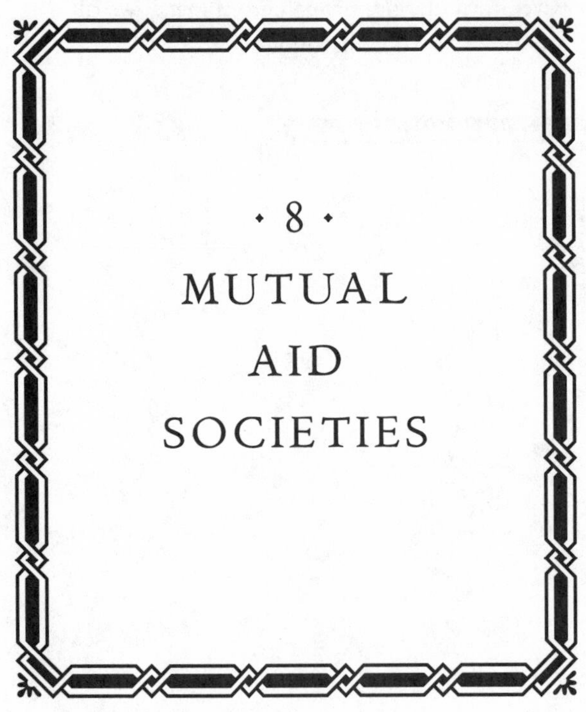

· 8 · MUTUAL AID SOCIETIES

WHEN ONE IS LOOKING FOR ASSISTANCE FOR THE NEEDY AND CARE FOR THE SICK, ONE SHOULD ALWAYS CHOOSE A PERSON FROM EISHYSHOK. IN THEIR NATIVE SHTETL THEY TOOK CARE OF THE PEOPLE IN NEED WITH LOVE, DEVOTION, AND COMPASSION.

Rabbi Avraham Yitzhak ha-Cohen Kook, Chief Rabbi of Eretz Israel, 1921–35

SINCE BIBLICAL TIMES, THE JEWS HAVE VIEWED POVERTY AS A PERMANENT SOCIAL ILL, which the community has not just a moral but a legal obligation to address: "For the poor shall never cease out of the land; therefore, I command thee saying thou shalt open thy hand unto the poor and needy in thy land." (Deuteronomy 15:11). Because the Jews of the Bible were an agricultural society, many of the laws relating to the poor refer quite specifically to the harvest: the Torah speaks of the practice of leaving the post-harvest gleanings for the poor, of leaving one corner of the field for them to reap, and of giving them one-tenth (tithe) of the harvest. The basic concepts established in the Bible — that these gifts are the legal property of the poor, and that the owner of the fields has no choice about whether to give, or to whom — have remained viable throughout Jewish history, in agricultural, shtetl, and urban communities alike.

Indeed, all subsequent discussions in Jewish literature of society's obligation to the poor can be seen as simply an expansion of these concepts. *Zedakah* is the word for charity in the legal, moral, and ethical works of postbiblical Jewish writers, who devote long sections of text to the subject. Since the root meaning of the word is "justice," the very language in which the concept is discussed conveys the notion that charity is not just a matter of voluntary philanthropic impulses on the part of individuals, but a legal, ethical obligation, central to the Jewish home and community, which must be fulfilled by all the more fortunate members of society.

Eastern European Jewish communities developed an elaborate network of relief organizations to deal with the ever-present needs of the poor. In the days of centralized government, under the Council of Four Lands of the sixteenth and seventeenth centuries, it was the Council that oversaw the efforts to feed, clothe, shelter, marry, educate, nurse, and bury. When the Council ceased to operate, the relief system, like all the other functions under its purview, decentralized, reverting to local community jurisdiction. Before, during, and after the Council it was an extremely effective system, in both normal and emergency situations, perhaps all the more effective because the society that sustained it consisted of a minority people in an often hostile environment, constantly living on the brink of destitution and disaster. The system had to cope with everything from routine crop failures, fires, and floods to the Chmielnicki massacres of

Both Shael (Shaul) and Hayya Sonenson served as chairpersons and members of many shtetl mutual aid societies. Hayya was the chairwoman of the Froyen Farain, the association of women's societies in the shtetl. Reb Shael died a natural death in 1935. Hayya was murdered in the September 1941 massacre. PHOTO: YITZHAK URI KATZ. YESC, Y. ELIACH

1648–49, the cholera epidemic of 1708, and the anti-Semitic May Laws of 1882 (which led to a massive influx of yishuvniks into the shtetl)—and it did.

So successful was it, in fact, that a myth has persisted, wherever Jews have lived, that they have no poor among them. But the occasional observant outsider has been able to see beyond that myth to the reality. Thus Lancelot Addison, an English travel writer of the late seventeenth century who became fascinated by the Jews of Barbary, goes to some length to dispel the belief that "the Jews have no beggars." This is an error, he says, which must be attributed to the "regular and commendable" methods by which the Jews met the needs of their poor and thereby "much concealed their poverty."[1]

Never were the challenges to the Eastern European Jewish relief system greater than in the twentieth century, and nowhere was the need greater than in the shtetlekh. During the calamitous years of World War I, the majority of the shtetl population was starving. Even in Eishyshok, where the German occupation had brought relative peace and order to the shtetl, and allowed, indeed encouraged, its cultural activities, food was often in extremely short supply and many people went hungry. During the interwar years, under the harsh anti-Jewish economic policies of the Polish government, perhaps as much as 30 percent of Eastern Europe's shtetl population required assistance in one or more vital areas, such as food, clothing, shelter, medicine, or tuition. The situation was made even more dire by the fact that the shtetl population was an aging one during these years, since so many of the young had made aliyah or had moved to one of the larger European cities in search of better opportunities, leaving behind them elderly parents who often required some form of public assistance. Through all these years, the shtetlekh continued to struggle valiantly to meet the needs of their poor.

RELIEF SOCIETIES IN EISHYSHOK

While charity was considered a universal duty, and even the poor were taxed for the relief of their own class, in Eishyshok as elsewhere it was the balebatim who were responsible for supplying the lion's share of charity, and the balebatim who made up the membership of most of the charitable societies. Belonging to these societies was thus not only an obligation on the part of the well-to-do, but, despite the demands it made on both time and money, a privilege, even a status symbol. The many activities associated with these societies also provided their members with a social outlet.

Each society had a designated Sabbath in the synagogue, during which its members were honored by being allowed to conduct parts of the service, and its treasury was replenished by donations from the congregation. Afterward a kiddush would be held in the women's gallery, where members of the society and their friends would meet and socialize. Usually the society's annual date was chosen because an event chronicled in that Sabbath's weekly portion had some relevance to its charitable mission. Thus the passage from Genesis about Matriarch Rachel dying in labor was the epigraph of the society that was devoted to aiding women at childbirth, and their Sabbath always coincided with the reading of the weekly portion in which that story was told. On the Saturday night following each society's annual Sabbath, elections were held to choose its new officers, and on the next day, Sunday, the society celebrated with its annual feast.

Like everything else in the shtetl, the relief societies were organized not only along class lines, but gender lines. Only one society in Eishyshok was coed, the soup kitchen (Billige Kikh), established during World War I in a time of great need — and changing mores. A number of the men's organizations did have a female auxiliary, but the men and the women always convened separately.

Eishyshok's traditional mutual aid organizations generally bore names that had their roots in sacred texts. Societies of more recent vintage, many of which were under the umbrella of a Zionist, socialist, Communist, or Bundist organization, had names that reflected the new secular ideologies overtaking the shtetl. But whatever their names or ideologies, and whenever they were founded, they were all reflections of the Jewish mandate to provide for the poor. The same was true in shtetlekh throughout Eastern Europe, where the mutual aid societies of the twentieth century, under names similar if not identical to those in Eishyshok, continued to fulfill the age-old obligations set forth in the Torah and Talmud.

BIKKUR HOLIM (VISITING THE SICK)

Ben Sira, writing at the time of the Second Temple, counsels, "Do not hesitate to visit a man who is sick."[2] According to one statement in the Talmud, whoever visits a sick person takes away one-sixtieth of the illness; another tells us that visiting the sick is among the religious duties to which no limit has been set.[3] Post-Talmudic writers continued to view the obligation to the sick as an issue of major moral importance, and gave detailed advice to the visitor about proper bedside etiquette and demeanor.[4]

The shtetl's response to the millennia-old ethical code pertaining to the welfare of the sick was Bikkur Holim, whose annual Sabbath was marked by the reading of the Va-Erah in Genesis, which describes God's visit to Abraham when he was convalescing from his circumcision.[5] Members of the society took as their mandate the responsibility to visit the ailing poor; indeed, *bikkur holim* means "visiting the sick." Some of its members were professionally trained, among them Rivka Lewinson Shanzer, who was a nurse, and all were imbued with a strong sense of community obligation and Jewish tradition. Thus it was natural that when Rabbi Avraham Yitzhak ha-Cohen Kook, then the chief rabbi

Rivka Lewinson Shanzer, a member of Eishyshok's Bikkur Holim (Visiting the Sick society), in 1925. After emigrating to Eretz Israel, she became a nurse in the Bikkur Holim hospital in Jerusalem. YESC, FAM LEWINSON

of Palestine, was looking for a compassionate, reliable nurse to take care of his sick daughter, Rivka was the one who was recommended and ultimately chosen. She had brought with her to Palestine the valuable ethos and traditions of the shtetl.

In addition to visiting the sick, Bikkur Holim saw to it that they got the doctors and medications they could not afford. For generations these bills were paid by the kehilah from the korobka, candle, and yeast taxes, supplemented by donations from individual balebatim. During the closing decades of the nineteenth century, however, Reb Benyomin Kaganowicz der Kapeliushnik (the derby man, after the derby hat he always wore) established a new source of income, the Kuppat Holim (sick fund) charity boxes, which were placed in each home in Eishyshok. Prior to lighting the Sabbath and holiday candles, the women of the house dropped their donations into the boxes, and twice a year Reb Benyomin came around to empty them.[6] Thus women constituted the main contributors to the fund, but, as was typical at the time, it was the male gabbaim (trustees) who managed it.

Yaffa Sonenson Eliach with her granddaughter Moriah Rosensweig on a visit in 1997 to the house that had been Hayya Sonenson's (Yaffa's grandmother's). They are standing in front of the closet where Hayya kept supplies for needy mothers and their newborn infants. PHOTO: SMADAR ELIACH ROSENSWEIG. YESC, Y. ELIACH

LINAT ZEDDEK (THE RIGHTEOUS BEDSIDE)

As the name (which comes from Isaiah 1:21) indicates, this was another of the shtetl organizations dedicated to offering personal care to the sick. Its members, men and women alike, provided round-the-clock nursing care for the needy, and it was common for even the most respected balebatim to spend the night at a poor sick person's bedside. A very prestigious society into which boys and girls were initiated at an early age, it trained its members thoroughly. They might begin, as Rivka's sister Rina Lewinson Fenigstein remembers doing, as messengers, progress to being orderlies, and eventually assume full-fledged nursing responsibilities.

EZRAT YOLEDET (AIDING A WOMAN AT CHILDBIRTH)

One of the busiest societies in the shtetl, Ezrat Yoledet, was made up exclusively of women, who provided midwife and postnatal services for mother and child. The midwife was paid out of the society's treasury, and was assisted by society members, who made themselves available at any hour of the day or night. When they arrived at the home of the needy mother, they brought all necessary supplies: fresh linens, nightgown, towels, blankets, a pot to boil water and firewood to heat the pot, diapers and swaddling for the newborn. They also stayed on to nurse the mother and child after a difficult delivery, and, in the event of complications or maternal death, assisted the family with infant care until other arrangements could be made.

Hayya Sonenson, who was for a while the

head of the society, even took one such child into her own home for several years. When Velvke Saltz's mother died giving birth to him in 1909, Hayya, who had recently borne a son of her own, said, "What if I had given birth to twins? God and Kashka [the Sonenson maid] will help." And she proceeded to raise Velvke and her son Leibke together, until it was time for Velvke to go to heder, when she returned him to his maternal grandfather. Velvke and Leibke remained good friends until Velvke's departure for America to join his father.

Hayya Sonenson was a very active member of this society; she had a special closet in her bedroom set aside for the supplies she took with her when she went out on call. Every time one of her two daughters and five daughters-in-law gave birth, they had to make a contribution to the Ezrat Yoledet closet, adding new articles that could be used by less fortunate mothers and their infants. Thanks to the constant expansion of Hayya's family, the closet was very well stocked. Next to its many neatly folded items Hayya kept her special Ezrat Yoledet lantern, which lit her way on many a dark and snowy evening to the bedside of a mother in labor. Though it was her wish that this lantern be lit once a year at her grave, on the anniversary of her death, this was not to be. Hayya Sonenson was

Four young friends (right to left): Velvke Saltz, Motke Kiuchefski, Leibke Sonenson, and Israel Szczuczynski. Velvke Saltz's mother died giving birth to him in 1909. Hayya Sonenson, the chairwoman of Ezrat Yoledat (Aiding a Woman at Childbirth society), raised Velvke with her son Leibke, who was born in the same year. Velvke eventually emigrated to America, Motke to the Soviet Union, Leibke was murdered in the September 1941 massacre, and Israel was killed by the AK.

PHOTO: YITZHAK URI KATZ. YESC, Y. ELIACH

murdered with the other women and children of Eishyshok on September 26, 1941; her lantern, like all of her family heirlooms, was looted; and what had once been her charity closet bore a crucifix, hung there by the new Polish occupants of her home.

HAKHNASAT KALLA (PROVIDING A DOWRY)

While the marrying off of a daughter is a father's responsibility, there has always been a tradition within the Jewish benevolence system of providing dowries for daughters from poor families — orphaned or not — and for girls with disabilities. Depending on the circumstances, the community might pay not just for the dowry, but for all wedding expenses and even for a matchmaker to find a proper bridegroom. According to Maimonides, to do so is to fulfill one aspect of the "Love thy neighbor as thyself" commandment.[7] Moreover, for the sake of peaceful relations with their non-Jewish neighbors, Jewish communities were also advised to assist poor gentile brides.

During the days of the Lithuanian Council, there was very detailed legislation, dating from the 1620s, that covered everything from the size of the dowry the community was required to provide, to the father's eligibility for assistance, limitations on the possible extravagance of the father, and the number of brides eligible for assistance within each district under the Council's jurisdiction. Poor brides were not allowed to marry until the age of fifteen, and for the preceding three years they were required to work toward their dowries by acting as domestic servants in the homes of prosperous Jewish families at a set wage per year. The money was payable to a community trustee, who set it aside for the girl and allowed neither her nor her father any access to it, except for the purpose of buying materials for a Sabbath dress she could make for herself — with the prior permission of the trustee. At the end of her service she was given her wages as a dowry, minus about 15 percent of the total, which went into the community treasury. Girls who did not work were not eligible for community assistance.

With the collapse of the Council, the burden of marrying off poor brides reverted to the individual communities, which met their responsibility via Hakhnasat Kalla (which means, literally, the ushering of the bride under the bridal canopy). The society funded its work from various sources, including a tax on weddings (the size of the tax depending on the expense of the wedding), individual contributions, and a Purim collection in honor of Queen Esther, the heroine of the holiday, who was an orphan.[8] In Eishyshok the male members of the society kept its written records and did much of the fund-raising, while the women performed most of the actual services, such as preparing the bride's trousseau, arranging the wedding feast, and so forth.

Occasionally, in times of trouble, such as war or plague, the community undertook at its own expense to marry off a poor or disabled bride to an equally unfortunate bridegroom, perhaps two residents of the local shelter for the homeless, because it was thought that the charitable deed would ward off evil. Such weddings took place in the cemetery, and were attended by everyone in the shtetl.

MALBISH ARUMIM (CLOTHING THE NAKED)

The main function of the Malbish Arumim society was to clothe the poor. New clothing was distributed on the eve of Passover, used clothing the rest of the year, with the donations coming from store owners, shoemakers, tailors, and whoever else chose to give. The society distributed the merchandise from the vestibule of the Old Beth Midrash, or took it to the homes of people who did not want to be seen receiving community assistance.

MAOT HITTIM (WHEAT MONEY)

Since the days of the Talmud, community members paid a compulsory "wheat money" tax to provide the poor with matzot and wine at Passover.[9] In later years the term was interpreted more broadly and the tax paid for all Passover essentials.

In Eishyshok as in other communities, a man who had the hazaka on collecting the tax (for a set period of time, or in perpetuity) made annual door-to-door rounds with an assistant (for all charity funds had to be collected by two people). The last Maot Hittim collector in Eishyshok was Reb Itche Velvel, who, as a true mavin of good conversation, tea, baked goods, and varenie (preserves), enjoyed these annual visits and looked forward to them as a chance to catch up on the news of people he may not have seen for a while. After Purim, he began calling on the homes of everyone who had lived in the shtetl for at least twelve months, as all those who met the residency requirement were eligible to be either contributors to or beneficiaries of the tax. Each of the donations he put into his big black bag usually elicited Reb Itche's farewell blessing: "We should live and be well and next year be able to see each other again and give with an open, warm hand."

One Passover eve during the years between the two world wars, Reb Itche Velvel called on Zirl di Garberke (tannery owner) Yurkanski, who had been widowed during the year but continued to run the family business successfully on her own. After the usual formalities, Reb Itche asked for the amount of Maot Hittim money Zirl's late husband Layzer had traditionally given, but to his surprise she refused to pay. After ordering his assistant to close the bag and making a notation in his impressive-looking pinkas, Reb Itche turned to Zirl and explained: "In my book are listed only two categories of people: those who give and those who receive." Accordingly, the next day his assistant showed up at Zirl's house with a Maot Hittim donation — which was both an insult and a suggestion that she would find herself impoverished the following year.

HAKHNASAT ORHIM (HOSPITALITY SOCIETY) AND HEKDESH (HOMELESS SHELTER)

Hospitality, in the form of welcoming a guest to one's home, offering food and shelter, is among the hallmarks of Jewish life and is discussed repeatedly throughout Jewish sacred writings. The first discussion of hospitality concerns Abraham, whose tent near a crossroads had four openings, so that he could receive people coming from any direction. Abraham gave food, drink, and lodging to all, thus becoming the standard against which all other hosts would be measured.[10] Hospitality continued to occupy a prominent place in the ethical and halakhic writings of the Talmudic sages, who had a higher regard for the welcoming of guests than for the greeting of the Shekhinah (Divine Presence). And they concerned themselves specifically with the hospitality to be extended to the needy: "Let your house be wide open; treat the poor as members of your own family."[11]

On both the individual and the institutional level, hospitality in the shtetl was a continuation of millennia-old Jewish practices. In Eishyshok, people were so eager to welcome travelers and other guests into their homes that they vied for the privilege of doing so, especially on the Sabbath, when it was the practice of the synagogue shammash to match up would-be guests and hosts at the close of Friday-night services. As he ushered the congregation out of the synagogue, the shammash would hand the shtetl guests platten, little pieces of wood on which were engraved the names of their hosts for the night.

Since the poor could ill afford the extra food for a guest, they were usually not given the honor of playing host, an omission that some of them regretted keenly. On one occasion Yude-Yankl the poor shoemaker begged so insistently to be assigned a guest that finally the shammash gave in early Friday morning and wrote out by hand on a piece of cardboard a platten bearing Yude-Yankl's name. That Friday night, in full view of the congregation, Yude-Yankl left the synagogue with a guest.

When the two men arrived at the house for dinner, Yude-Yankl's wife and a roomful of hungry children were astonished to see that he had brought with him yet another mouth to feed. But Yude-Yankl made kiddush over the wine, washed his hands, and said the blessing over the hallah, just as he did every Friday night, after which he and his family ate one piece of bread after another, while the guest eagerly awaited the Sabbath meal to follow — until it finally became obvious that there was none. In answer to his guest's puzzled look, the beaming host explained: "We share with you everything that we have, even our hunger. You see, for many years no guest has crossed our threshold. Never before have I been able to show the members of the congregation that I too can have a guest, just like the balebatim. But today I did. I walked from the shul through the marketplace with you by my side, and your presence has filled the hearts of a poor Jewish shoemaker and his family with pride and joy. Don't you think that is worth the price of an empty stomach?"

This story notwithstanding, very few guests went hungry in Eishyshok. And Eishyshkians were hosts to many: to travelers from the countryside, people without families, yeshivah students who were regulars on the Sabbath and holidays, visitors from the Holy Land collecting money for yeshivot there, emissaries from various Zionist and other political organizations.

Generally speaking, when it was the shammash who was responsible for making a match between guest and host, he did try to take social status and scholarship into consideration. Not just any drifter passing through town would be welcomed into the home of one of its prominent citizens. Nonetheless, accommodations were available for all. In shtetlekh throughout Eastern Europe, drifters could always count on the doors to the synagogue or the batei midrash being open for a stay of a night or two, where they could sleep on a bench in the women's gallery.

Indeed, the theft of the famous Napoleon Ark curtain from the synagogue in Olkenik involved just such a drifter. When the shammash noticed that their overnight guest had made off with the Ark curtain and chased him down, the man returned it, but it was subsequently found to be missing the gold threads spelling out Napoleon's signature. Haikl Lunski, the librarian and folklore expert who later wrote the detailed history of this historic artifact, left the incident of the drifter out of his story. Asked why, he responded as though the future of the whole tradition of hospitality might rest with him: "How can I write that a transient beggar stole the Holy Ark curtain? To do so might cause the locking up of the synagogue doors in the face of the destitute homeless."[12]

Beggars in Eishyshok could be sure of not just a bench to sleep on, but a handout on Friday, the official begging day in Eishyshok. Jute bags slung over their shoulders, the beggars (both local and transient) went from door to door on that day — the day after the shtetl's market day, when people's pockets were still full and their homes newly redolent with the odors of the Sabbath meal being prepared.

Poor people in need of shelter for more than a few nights had two options, both of them under the aegis of the official hospitality society, the Hakhnasat Orhim. The society oversaw a hospitality house, which was a very simple inn that was leased out at public auction. The leaseholder was responsible for putting up travelers of modest means who passed through town. Eishyshok's last Hakhnasat Orhim was in the attic of Alter Korelanski, the barber, where one could rent a bed, or, for 10 cents more, a bed and a pillow. Until the bitter end, the shtetl's prayer-houses and its hospitality inn remained open for short-term stays.

For those visitors in need of longer-term accommodations, there was the hekdesh (homeless shelter). The hekdesh took its name from Leviticus 27:14–25, where it was Hebrew for "consecrated property, dedicated to the needs of the Temple." In the Middle Ages the word *hekdesh* came to connote property that had been set aside for charitable purposes, and generally referred to an institution that provided shelter for the sick and the homeless. Beginning sometime in the seventeenth century, the hekdesh became a permanent feature in most Eastern European communities. In larger towns it often served as a makeshift hospital as well as a communal shelter.

The size of the hekdesh depended on local needs, and ranged from one room to a house or even a group of small buildings. Most often located near the cemetery, as it was in Eishyshok, the hekdesh was usually a dirty, malodorous place, viewed with no small degree of horror by the locals. In Yiddish, the word *hekdesh* became synonymous with disorder and disarray, and could be applied as readily to a person as to a room or a home.

In Eishyshok the hekdesh was a community-owned house with several rooms, administered by the Hakhnasat Ohrim. In one of its rooms the shtetl undertaker stored his tools, and the Hevrah Kaddishah society prepared the bodies of yishuvniks and strangers for burial. The other rooms were fitted out, very modestly, for those who needed a place to stay for a while. The furnishings included tables, benches, a central oven, and rows of bunk beds with straw mattresses.

The stay in the hekdesh was limited to two distinct periods: from the beginning of the High Holiday season (sometime in September) through the end of Passover (sometime in April or early May), and from the end of Passover to the beginning of the High Holidays. The designated periods took into consideration weather and holidays, as well as the school year, for many of the transients had children, who were allowed to attend the community-funded Talmud Torah school. Restrictions on the period of hekdesh residency were also meant to prevent transient beggars from staying in the shtetl for longer than twelve months at a stretch, because after that one acquired permanent residency and the right to share in the privileges of the local poor, thereby straining the resources of the community even further.

Not all beggars took advantage of the full period of time allotted to them, for some of them were always on the lookout for a hekdesh in a location that might be more beneficial to them — such as a rich shtetl, or one with a big fair or an impending wedding in a wealthy family.

Some beggars arrived alone, some in pairs, some in groups or families. Some came on foot, others in covered wagons like those used by local Gypsies. Some were momentarily down on their luck, others were professional mendicants who enjoyed a nomadic lifestyle, wandering from one hekdesh to another.[13] Still others had organized themselves into small gangs of thieves who used the hekdesh as a temporary base of operations. All were viewed with suspicion.[14]

The beggars came to be both very persistent and very troubling figures in modern Jewish society. Particularly since it didn't have separate quarters for men and women, the hekdesh developed a reputation for promiscuity and scandal. Thus it was at the Eishyshok hekdesh that Meir Wilkanski and several other heder boys learned the facts of life, after viewing a graphic encounter between a man and woman sharing a bed there.[15] Though the trustee of the Hakhnasat Orhim visited the hekdesh daily, in an attempt to impose some form of order and morality on the residents, he was rarely successful.

Attempts were also made, by both the Hospitality Society and the kehilah, to find some employment for the hekdesh beggars, especially those who stayed for a few months. They might be paid to clear the snow in the shulhoyf, to carry water, or to work as domestics in a shtetl home.

Occasionally a man or woman from the hekdesh would marry a local resident—usually someone with a dubious yihus who would otherwise have had trouble finding a mate, such as a person born out of wedlock. In the mid-nineteenth century one such marriage occurred between Berl the Cantonist, who had served in the army of Tzar Nicholas I for twenty-five years (and therefore had been baptized), and a young, healthy woman from the hekdesh (who was his fifth wife).[16] The newlyweds were given a room in the hekdesh, which remained in the possession of their descendants (by right of hazaka) until the very end. Berl's great-grandson, who still resided there at the outbreak of World War II, was the last caretaker of the hekdesh.

Generally speaking, the hekdesh served its intended purpose well. It was a considerable burden on the community, but the community was realistic about poverty, and practical about dealing with it. East European Jewry acknowledged the existence of the homeless, knew that there had always been and perhaps always would be homeless people, and accepted its obligation to provide shelter for them in the present, while trying on a long-term basis, through employment and education, to strike at the root of their problems and pave the way toward a better future.

GEMILUT HESSED (PRACTICE OF KINDNESS)

For centuries, Gemilut Hessed societies throughout Eastern Europe provided interest-free loans to needy people in the Jewish community. Generally the loans were guaranteed by an object of value that was left with the society, and stored in the home of the town trustee. If the loan was repaid within a year, the object was returned; if not, it was sold along with all the other unredeemed articles at the annual public auction held in the Old Beth Midrash, under the gavel of the upper shammash.

Auction day was a time of commotion and excitement. People gathered in the shulhoyf after morning prayers to inspect the merchandise, which was laid out on a long table and which typically included fur coats and hats, candlesticks, strings of pearls, sacred books, down blankets, pillows, and wedding gowns. Often family and friends of a person who had been unable to redeem a precious heirloom would purchase it for him, thus preventing it from falling into the hands of a stranger. All proceeds from the auction went into the Gemilut Hessed treasury.[17]

Sometimes matters were complicated by the theft of the pawned articles. Bandits would break into the house of the town trustee and make off with the valuables. During the reign of Yehudah the Brigand, the late-nineteenth-century Robin Hood of Eishyshok (and one-time lessee of the korobka), the stolen goods were always retrieved, but before and after his time, these episodes rarely had such happy endings.

During the interwar years most of the Gemilut Hessed's activities were taken over by individual moneylenders, especially Eishyshkians who had made money in America and returned to the shtetl with some capital; by the Merchants and Artisans Alliance; by the Volksbank (the Jewish Cooperative People's Bank); and by the Gemilut Hessed Kassa, a new Polish Jewish loan organization with many ties to various socialist workers' groups.

PIDYON SHVUYIM (RANSOMING OF CAPTIVES)

The ransoming of captives is considered to be one of the most sacred obligations of a Jewish community—a higher duty, by law, than the feeding and clothing of the poor. And within the hierarchies of Jewish law, the ransoming of a mother takes precedence over a father or a teacher, the ransoming of a scholar over that of a king (for the scholar is irreplaceable, while the position of king can, theoretically, be filled by anyone).[18]

According to the community pinkas, a charitable group dedicated to freeing prisoners existed in Eishyshok until the late nineteenth century, when it was abolished. Like many other organizations, however, this one found a new lease on life during the shtetl's final years. In 1939 it was revived for the purpose of ransoming refugees who were fleeing Nazi-occupied territories and fell into the hands of Lithuanian or Byelorussian border patrols. Most of its members belonged to various Zionist organizations.

BILLIGE KIKH (SOUP KITCHEN)

At certain times of crisis the traditional social welfare organizations were unable to meet the demands, and then people organized new societies, some of which survived beyond the immediate emergency. Such was the case with Eishyshok's Billige Kikh (literally, inexpensive kitchen), which was formed during World War I to prevent wholesale starvation in the shtetl. Here both gender and social barriers broke down, as men and women, young and old, balebatim and artisans joined together to distribute hot meals on a daily basis. Women were its mainstay, as they were not subject to military or forced-labor drafts, but men too played a role — in the case of one of the Abelowitch brothers, a role that proved fatal. On one of their many food-foraging expeditions to the countryside,

Members of Eishyshok's Billige Kikh (soup kitchen). It was established during World War I and was the shtetl's first coed society. Among the people in the photo are Meir Kiuchefski, Maneh Michalowski, the Lewinson sisters, Zivia Hutner, Sonenson siblings, the Abelowitch brothers, and members of the Schneider family. YESC, Z. HUTNER-HADASH

the three brothers took off in different directions, despite the dangers of traveling solo. Though they managed to outmaneuver nearby German troops, one brother, Leizerke, fell victim to anti-Semitic Poles, who ambushed him and then killed him with repeated blows from an ax. Bearing his mutilated body, his horse and buggy returned to town and stopped in front of the house of his fiancée, Rivka Lewinson.

The irony of this brutal murder was that the soup kitchen the Abelowitch brothers were working to supply catered not just to Jews, but also to gentiles. Indeed, the gentiles, among them many hungry Poles, sometimes outnumbered the Jews at the soup kitchen.

Shtetl inhabitants, Jews and non-Jews, await food distribution in front of the soup kitchen. German soldiers helped to distribute the food. The building that housed the soup kitchen belonged to Leib der Grober ("the fat one"), who emigrated to the United States, the middle house to Avraham-Asher, the third house to Hayyim Leibke Paikowski. PHOTO: YITZHAK URI KATZ. YESC, KALEKO-BARKALI

BNEI HAIL (SONS OF VALOR)

Another of the organizations formed to cope with the disasters of World War I was Bnei Hail, named after a passage from Deuteronomy (3:18): "Ye shall pass over armed before your brethren the children of Israel all the men of Valor." With scores of wounded, shell-shocked Jewish soldiers left behind in Eishyshok each time the shtetl was taken over by another army, not to mention deserters fleeing their anti-Semitic commanders and comrades-in-arms, the community needed to mobilize to care for their needs. The members of Bnei Hail were assisted by women from the shtetl, since so many men had been drafted into the army or into the local German labor battalions; it was quite a departure from tradition to have women providing

Eliyahu Plotnik, the shtetl's last POW to return from captivity in Germany after World War I. He was an active member of Bnei Hail (Sons of Valor), the Jewish veterans' society. Reb Eliyahu was killed in the September 1941 massacre.
PHOTO: YITZHAK URI KATZ. YESC, S. AVRAHAMI

Eliyahu Plotnik's wife and their daughter Sarah. Despite many objections, little Sarah played a major role in the welcoming ceremonies in the Old Beth Midrash in honor of her father and other POWs who had returned home. Sarah emigrated to Eretz Israel in 1940. Her mother was murdered in the September 1941 massacre. PHOTO: YITZHAK URI KATZ. YESC, S. AVRAHAMI

nursing care for men. In addition to medical assistance, the society's members also gave food and shelter to needy soldiers.

Several years after the founding of Bnei Hail, in the summer of 1920, when the last of the shtetl's enlisted men had returned from POW camps, the society gave itself an official inauguration. During the festivities, which took place in the main synagogue, war veterans donated a cantor's podium inscribed with the names of the twenty-one POWs and the two Eishyshkians killed in action, special passages were read from the Torah, the hazzan and his choirboys offered several liturgical renditions, and each of the children of the men who had fought in World War I held aloft a small scroll. Although one of the more conservative members of the Old Beth Midrash objected to allowing girls to play a role in the ceremonies, he was told that their participation was warranted by the fact that they had suffered as much from the absence of their fathers during the war as the boys had.

The father of one of those little girls, Eliyahu Plotnik (the shtetl's last returning POW), told a story during the ceremony, which, in combination with many other stories that were similar in tone, would help to influence an entire generation's view of the Germans. While in captivity in Germany, he said, he had worked as a farmhand for a German family whose patriarch took a liking to him. Reb Eliyahu asked the old German for a Bible, but when he got it he was not happy to see that it included the New Testament, whereupon the old man went to a nearby town and exchanged it for a Hebrew Bible with a Yid-

Yekutiel Ginunski served in the tzarist army during the Russo-Japanese War. During World War I, when this photo was taken, he ended up a Russian POW *in German captivity. He was one of the shtetl's most active war veterans. A great admirer of the good Germans he met during World War I, Yekutiel was murdered during the September 1941 massacre.* PHOTO: MAKOVSKI, BRIANSK. YESC, L. GINUNSKI

dish translation — and no New Testament. This Bible became one of Eliyahu Plotnik's most cherished possessions, which during the summer of 1939 he would give to his daughter Sarah as a wedding present — a memento of both his suffering and the kindness of a man who had tried to alleviate it.

The Bnei Hail society continued to function during the interwar years, becoming basically a Jewish veterans' society that cared for the veterans and their families, as well as for Jewish enlisted men in the Polish army. Their annual Sabbath, which preceded the Ninth of Av and was timed to the weekly portion from Deuteronomy that had given the society its name, also coincided with the anniversary of the outbreak of World War I (early August) and the drafting of many soldiers from the shtetl.

On the basis of their experiences in German captivity, most of the World War I veterans had great faith in the German respect for law and order, as did their fellow Eishyshkians, who had spent the better part of two years under a very peaceful German occupation. Thus when the "new Germans" invaded Eishyshok on June 23, 1941, all efforts at resistance or escape were rejected by the older people. The former POWS kept reassuring the younger generation that the "new Germans" of World War II would prove worthy heirs to the "good Germans" (gutte Deitschen) of World War I.

But the Plotnik Bible would be a casualty of the "new Germans" of the next world war. Sarah had had her father's wedding present shipped to her after she emigrated to Palestine, but its journey was interrupted by the outbreak of war, and it was returned to Eishyshok.

When these "new Germans" and their Lithuanian collaborators murdered 4,000 people in Eishyshok, their victims included most of the World War I veterans who had so highly praised the civility of their fathers. Eliyahu Plotnik was among them.

HEVRAH BNEI AVRAHAM SHMUEL ANSHEI EISHYSHKER

The landsmanshaft was a form of mutual aid society transplanted to America by emigrants. Half benevolent society, half lodge or clubhouse, the landsmanshaften brought together men from the same area of the old country, for purposes both practical and nostalgic. On October 16, 1891, men from Eishyshok founded the Hevrah Bnei Avraham Shmuel Anshei Eishyshker in New York, one of the earliest of what would eventually be thousands of similar Eastern European emigrant organizations.[19]

By naming the society in honor of Rabbi Avraham Shmuel Rabinowitch, whose tenure as rabbi in Eishyshok coincided with the childhood and adolescent years of most of the emigrants of the 1880s, the men were paying tribute to a man known as the very embodiment of spirituality — which many back in Eishyshok found to be highly ironic, since those who left at that time were generally motivated by material, not spiritual, aspirations. Nonetheless, the group would eventually prove itself a worthy vessel of at least some of the shtetl's more exalted aims, most specifically (as far as the Eishyshkians at home were concerned) those having to do with charity.

As was so often the case with newly formed, shtetl-inspired institutions, this one reflected both its origins and the strange world in which it found itself. Thus the twenty-one articles of the constitution of the Eishyshker society read like a cross between the bylaws of the kehilah and the rulebook for a Masonic lodge.[20]

Since most of the emigrants at this time were young men from the artisan class and from small villages and farms, men who were not educated and did not know Hebrew, the constitution is in Yiddish and it provides that all of its records be kept in Yiddish — a departure from two thousand years of Jewish record-keeping tradition. There were other departures, too, but perhaps more interesting are the many ways in which these new Americans strove to maintain the old ways. All members who were married had to be married according to Jewish Law; anyone who was not would be expelled. Care for the sick was one of the group's central concerns, and the provisions concerning visiting the sick and the payment of sick benefits were modeled in some respects after those of the Bikkur Holim society in Eishyshok. The subjects of old age, death, burial, and mourning were also given ample attention, taking up a large section of the constitution. Most of the customs relating to the society's burial plots, its burial society (Hevrah Kaddishah), and even the burial society's annual meal closely resemble those followed in Eishyshok. Similarly, all the customs at the society's synagogue, the Eishyshker shul on Clinton Street on the Lower East Side, followed shtetl tradition.

Though the constitution makes no mention of any obligation the men owed the community they had left behind, in fact the New York Ei-

One of the original record books of the New York Eishyshker society. PHOTO: MELVIN LEVINE, 1997. YESC, Y. ELIACH

Front page of the constitution of Hevrah Bnei Avraham Shmuel Anshei Eishyshker, a society composed of Eishyshok émigrés founded in New York on October 16, 1891. PHOTO: MELVIN LEVINE, 1997. YESC, Y. ELIACH

קאנסטיטושאן

— דער —

חברה

בני אברהם שמואל

אנשי איישישקער

געגרינדעט י״ד תשרי תרנ״ב

דען 16טען אקטאבער 1891

אין ניו יארק.

נדפס בשנת תרפ״ו

— ביי —

אברהם יצחק פיינמאן, 192½ דילענסי סט., נ. י.

shyshker society proved a generous friend to the shtetl from the time of the Big Fire in 1895 until 1940 (after which it was impossible to send letters and money from America into Eastern Europe). As the society grew in numbers and its members grew in wealth, the size of its donations kept increasing.

In addition to the elaborate network of community-sponsored mutual aid societies, a number of individuals, some of them virtual shtetl institutions themselves, dedicated themselves to taking care of the needy. Hiene di Krume (the lopsided one) was such a person.

At dawn when the men of the shtetl were on their way to the synagogue, they would see the crooked little figure rushing off on one of her charitable missions. There she'd go, wrapped in her checked woolen shawl, delivering a pair of shoes to a little girl born out of wedlock so that she could go to school with the rest of the children, or taking a warm breakfast to a sick old widower. Hiene knew everybody's needs and made it her personal business to see to it that they were met.

There were also people in America who chose to give as individuals rather than as members of one of the landsmanshaften. Dr. Morris Shlanski proved a generous donor to the shtetl of his birth. During his visit to Eishyshok in 1936, several decades after his departure, he saw firsthand its problems, and made a large contribution to the kahal, as well as to the yeshivah of Radun, which he had been so eager to escape when he was a student there. An ardent Zionist, he also committed himself to sponsoring the shtetl's Zionist organizations — a promise he kept after returning to America.

Dovid der Kichier (R'Dovid Moszczenik from Kitchie) was another of these one-person charities. All but one of his children had emigrated to America, where they prospered and eventually formed a Detroit branch of the Eishyshker society, which sent substantial sums

The celebration of the fifty-second anniversary of the Eishyshker society in New York, March 9, 1940. More than 1,500 Eishyshkians emigrated to the United States between 1873 and 1940. PHOTO: ARROWHEAD PHOTOGRAPHERS, NEW YORK. YESC, SHLANSKI

of money to Reb Dovid in Eishyshok for distribution to the poor. Reb Dovid carried the money in a leather pouch he wore around his neck and he distributed it — most generously — as he saw fit. Indeed, during the interwar years it was rumored in the shtetl that he had personally distributed more money than all of the mutual aid societies combined. Thanks to that leather pouch, he eventually became one of the most prominent individuals in Eishyshok, elected to a number of important posts in community organizations. But since he made his contributions without consulting either the rabbi or the kahal, he found himself at odds with them, and the money became a source of acrimony in the shtetl. Moreover, though his motives were noble, the results were not always ideal, for by establishing an independent financial power base in the shtetl, he essentially took money that would otherwise have gone into the coffers of the established aid organizations and left many of their needy clients on the brink of starvation. When other families who received money from America followed suit, and when various socialist and Zionist organizations made their own claims on the pocketbooks of the shtetl's philanthropists, it was a virtual death knell to many of the traditional charitable groups.

Reb Dovid "der Kichier" Moszczenik sitting on the porch in front of his house on Mill Street. Reb Dovid controlled and distributed all of the funds sent by the Detroit branch of the Eishyshker society from the late 1920s until his death in the '30s. YESC, A. ZIMMERMAN

THE LAST HURRAH

In 1939–41, however, they would come back to life to launch one more massive aid campaign. This period constituted a severe test for the network of community relief institutions in Eishyshok — one that all the experience of the preceding years enabled them to pass with honors. Because of its geographical location, so close to the border of Russia and also to the consulates, political organizations, and relief agencies of Vilna, Eishyshok ended up playing host to 15,000 refugees who passed through the shtetl in search of freedom and safety. Young and old, rich and poor, all the townspeople helped. They not only fed, clothed, and housed the refugees, but gave them financial assistance when necessary, made available to them Eishyshok's two telephones and its telegraph and postal services, directed them to Vilna, where the headquarters of most Zionist organizations were located, as were other immigration agencies and the foreign consulates of a number of countries whose doors were still open, and even risked their own lives to help with illegal border crossings into Byelorussia. All this was done within the framework of centuries-old traditions and practices, to which a superstructure of new social and political relief efforts had been added.

Working in concert with the newly established Refugee Committee headed by Rabbi

Szymen Rozowski, and the Zionist organizations, the mutual aid societies had their finest hour. Their long-established traditions helped to mobilize the entire community into one big unified relief organization that drew on the resources of every home in the shtetl. This last glorious flowering ended when the Communists took over the shtetl in June 1940 and abolished all Jewish organizations and societies (though many of their activities were continued clandestinely, on a smaller scale).

Many Eishyshkians were certain that the Soviet rule would be short-lived, as indeed it was. The Germans invaded in June 1941. Three months later, when they murdered most of the Jewish population, they also destroyed a millennia-old tradition of human kindness, love, and justice. Never again would the walls of the synagogue and the Old and New batei midrash echo the words of the prayer that had been recited there every morning for generations:

These are the things the fruits of which a man enjoys in this world, and the stock of which remains for him in the world to come: honoring one's father and mother, and charity, and making peace between man and his fellow. . . .[21]

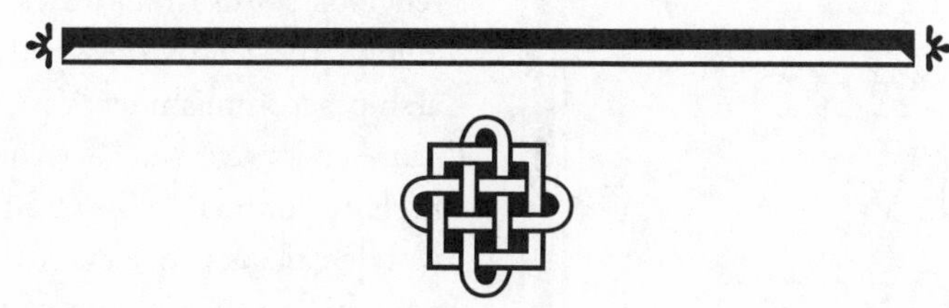

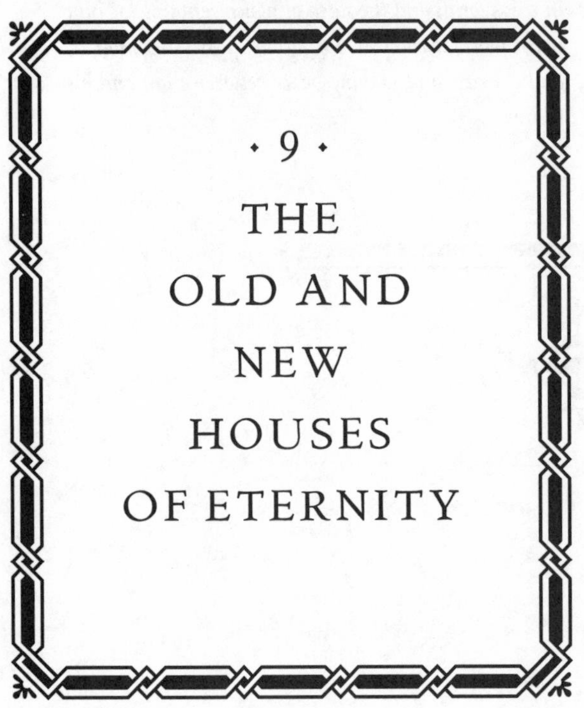

• 9 • THE OLD AND NEW HOUSES OF ETERNITY

THE WHOLE WORLD IS A VERY NARROW BRIDGE AND THE MAIN THING TO RECALL IS TO HAVE NO FEAR AT ALL.

Rabbi Nahman of Braslav

THE CEMETERY OCCUPIED A PROMINENT PLACE IN THE LIFE OF THE SHTETL, AND WAS in many ways a mirror image of that life. In its rituals, its physical configuration, and its location, we can see a reflection of the essence of a world now vanished — just as the cemetery itself is now vanished. The cemetery spoke eloquently of the shtetl's social and economic life, its religious beliefs, and its family relationships, in all their diversity and divisiveness as well as their cohesiveness. Its stones survived centuries of natural and man-made catastrophes — until the years following the Holocaust, that is — to tell of events in the lives of individuals and the community as a whole. Its written records, in the large black leather pinkas maintained by the local burial society, told the story not only of each burial, but of all that the community believed about this life and the afterlife.

By their location, size, inscription, and illustration, the tombstones were stone pages in the chronicle recounting each individual's life history within the community. In one section of the cemetery were the elaborate stones of the town notables, engraved with symbols depicting their religious status and virtues, and with lengthy epitaphs bearing witness to the departed's scholarship, accomplishments, piety, suffering — and sometimes even their shortcomings. These stood in sharp contrast to the small, sparsely engraved wooden planks that marked the graves of the poor, before slipping out of sight forever in the mud of the lower part of the cemetery. It was as though the cemetery were the afterworld's version of the shtetl itself, maintaining in death the same divisions and stratifications that had prevailed in life. As the houses of the balebatim were grand in scale and occupied the choicest locations around the market square, and the houses of the poor were modest dwellings lining the back lanes on the outskirts of the shtetl, so it was with the graves as well.

The cemetery spoke also of shtetl history — its length, and the events that had marked it, many of them part of the larger history of the region, and of the world. One could read in the engravings on the stones the story of the fires, accidents, epidemics, wars, and martyrdoms that had afflicted Eishyshkians through the centuries.

Among the most ancient tombstones in the Old Cemetery — for the shtetl actually had two cemeteries — were ones bearing dates as early as 1097 (not many years after the founding of Ei-

Hanneh-Beile Kudlanski (née Moszczenik) (left) with daughter Atara (right) and other family members, bidding farewell to ancestors in 1933 before emigrating to America (where Hanneh-Beile's husband had changed the family name to Goodman). On right is the tombstone of Hanneh-Beile's uncle Reb Zvi Hersh Moszczenik, the "Garden Preacher"; on the left the tombstone of his wife Gelle. PHOTO: BEN ZION SZREJDER. YESC, A. ZIMMERMAN

Reb Zvi Hersh Moszczenik and wife Gelle. PHOTO: YITZHAK URI KATZ. YESC, A. ZIMMERMAN

shyshok). Elka Szulkin Jankelewicz, the daughter of the shtetl's last kvoresman (undertaker), Nahum Szulkin, used to hear her father talk about twelfth-century tombstones bearing the names of Ben-Yossef, Ben-Asher, and Azrieli — the original Hebrew names of three of the founding families of Jewish Eishyshok.

The oldest tombstone in the New Cemetery to survive into the 1940s was from 1706. The last markers were those placed on the graves of Zipporah Sonenson and her infant son Hayyim, who were murdered by the Polish Armia Krajowa and townspeople after liberation from the Germans in 1944. They were buried on October 22, 1944 — the last burials to take place in the New Cemetery.

Between them, the stones and markers in the two cemeteries recounted nearly nine centuries of life and death in one Lithuanian Jewish shtetl. The fate of the cemeteries in the late 1950s and early 1960s under what became the Lithuanian Socialist Republic of the USSR — total obliteration — is as revealing in its fashion as their former eloquence had been. For the obliteration of the cemeteries echoed the obliteration of an entire way of life and an entire community. Just as there is virtually nothing left in Eishyshok to suggest that Jews once lived there, there is nothing to show that Jews died there, either. No sooner was the last terrible chapter of Eishyshok's history as a Jewish settlement written than it was erased. All that now remains of nine hundred years of Jewish tombstones is a handful of photographs.

BELIEFS ABOUT DEATH

The laws, customs, and folkways governing the treatment of the shtetl dead were the culmination of thousands of years of Jewish culture, and as such an expression of the beliefs central to that culture. One could read in all the rituals performed — in the home of the deceased, during the funeral, and in the cemetery afterward — the philosophy of a people, the East European shtetl Jew's fundamental belief that the transitory is a reflection of the lasting, just as the lasting is a reflection of the transitory.[1]

So intricate was the relationship between the ephemeral and the enduring that it was sometimes hard for the shtetl-dwellers to draw a line between them. The folklore of the cemetery was part of an elaborate network of beliefs which held that death was not a final ending, but merely a transition whereby one traded one's earthly attire for more enduring shrouds.[2] The cemetery was the permanent home, to which one moved after completing one's brief stay in the shtetl. As the place where the dead were buried and the living came to visit, the cemetery provided a bridge between them, where the creatures of the fleeting present could commune with the eternity of past and future.

Shtetl Jews believed in an ongoing interaction between the living and the dead, with the deceased playing an active role in the shtetl's daily routine, as well as in its special events, both joyful and sorrowful. As part of the traffic between the two realms, visits were paid to the graves on special days of the calendar consecrated to them, and on many other occasions when the dead were beseeched to intervene on behalf of the living.

It was also believed that the dead often returned to the shtetl, especially after the clock struck midnight, when they assembled to pray at the main synagogue. Thus it was understood that Besoylem Gessl (Eternity Lane), the street that led from the shtetl to the cemetery, was by no means a one-way street. In order to avoid unwelcome encounters with the dead, Eishyshkians were careful not to walk alone on that street. However, it sometimes happened that people in great haste forgot to take the necessary precautions, and shtetl tradition held that there was no telling what could happen under such circumstances.

One oft-told story recounted the strange adventure of an Eishyshkian who took a solitary walk to a village beyond the cemetery. As he neared the stretch near the cemetery, he accelerated his pace. Just then he noticed someone walking toward him. Delighted to see a fellow human being, he greeted the stranger with a sigh of relief and told him how glad he was to meet another living soul in that particular place. The stranger smiled and said, "I understand your feelings perfectly. When I was alive, I too feared to venture here alone."

The shtetl did not originate the tradition of spirits and demons, but inherited it. In the Talmud the cemetery is mentioned as the dwelling place of defiled spirits, who have so much power that they can transform an individual into a sorcerer. The Talmud also warns that sleeping in the cemetery can endanger one's life. But even in the Talmud the dead were not always viewed negatively. The story is told of a pious man who, after being taunted by his wife, left the house and spent the night in the cemetery. There he heard two spirits conversing with each other. When he went back a second time he had the same experience, and eventually was able to benefit greatly from the information that had been passed on from the next world.[3]

THE OLD HOUSE OF ETERNITY

Eishyshok had two cemeteries, the old house of eternity (der alter besoylem) and the new house of eternity (der nayer besoylem).[4] As noted in chapter 1, the Old Cemetery was dedicated as a burial place shortly after the Jews arrived in Eishyshok, which was probably in the last quarter of the eleventh century, though the Lithuanian Chronicles puts the date at 1171. It was built in accordance with Jewish law, which stipulates that the burial ground be located at a considerable distance from town — at least 50 cubits from the nearest house.[5] It was not just a considerable trek from the town, but an uphill one at that, for the cemetery was situated on the highest hilltop in the vicinity. Since this was the spot that would usually be reserved for a military outpost overseeing the defense of a city — thus a prestigious and much-coveted site — it is reasonable to see it as one of a number of the indicators suggesting that the early Jews of Eishyshok were accorded substantial privileges by the ruling powers of Lithuania. Such privileges would have been consistent with an era when the Lithuanian princes looked to the Jews as valuable allies in the fight against Christianity.

The eventual decline of the privileged position the Jews enjoyed in those early years proved unkind to the ancient graveyard, as did the ravages of time. The result was that by the closing days of the nineteenth century, the old tombstones were rapidly sinking into the ground. In 1798, there had still existed in the Old Cemetery tombstones with Hebrew inscriptions dating back to the original settlers. But a century later, Polish peasants in the vicinity were constantly claiming parts of the cemetery for their farms, destroying the old tombstones, plowing the land, and planting their crops. The battle over the graveyard became a source of constant friction between the Jewish community and the Christian farmers whose fields bordered the cemetery. Though the Jews appealed to the authorities, their pleas fell on deaf ears.

Among the best known of the many stories and legends about the Old Cemetery was one that explained how it had come to survive at all, given the constant raids upon its grounds. It is the tale of a land-greedy, Jew-baiting farmer from the village of Juryzdyki. The farmer claimed the Jewish cemetery as his land and decided to stake his claim publicly. In the presence of a number of other local Christian farmers who came to watch the groundbreaking, he set out to plow the cemetery. No sooner did his horse set foot in the cemetery than it collapsed and broke its two front legs. The determined farmer returned to the cemetery with a fresh horse. The poor beast suffered the same fate as its predecessor. And so it happened with several horses until the farmer understood that these were no mere coincidences, and gave up his claim. Thus was the cemetery saved from total obliteration.[6]

What was saved was a small strip of land about 100 by 330 feet long, elevated 6 to 10 feet above the surrounding fields. To ensure that no further depredations would be made against this last surviving strip, and to prevent farmers and their horses and grazing cattle from desecrating it, a deep trench was dug around its perimeter. Little did anyone then know the terrible use to which this trench would be put in the final days of the shtetl.

The Old Cemetery continued to be a holy place, revered by young and old alike, long after it had ceased being used for burials. The very fact that it continued to attract so many visitors says volumes about its meaning to the community, for it was very difficult to reach. Until 1827 the walk there had been a pleasant one — along a path through tranquil meadows, then over a small bridge spanning the Kantil River. But in 1827 a tzarist edict took the surrounding fields away from the Jews for redistribution among gentile landowners, so that while the cemetery itself was left to the Jews, the path that led to it no longer belonged to them. Over the years the new owners' neglect saw to it that this path was covered over by the muddy green waters and thick undergrowth of an encroaching swamp, and even the bravest townspeople were afraid to walk that way, for fear of drowning in the swamp's murky depths.

The alternate route to the Old Cemetery, the extremely roundabout one Eishyshkians had to take after the edict of 1827, followed the main highway to Vilna, across the bridge over the Virshuki River, then continued on the road leading to Warinowa past the village of Juryzdyki and the Seklutski forest. There they had to leave the main road for a narrow path through fields owned by gentiles. It was this last leg of the long journey that made the visit to the cemetery so harrowing, for the gentile peasants of Juryzdyki liked to sic their dogs on the Jews as they passed by. Not once but many times did such visits end with torn clothes and bloody wounds.

Despite the hardships involved in reaching the Old Cemetery, Eishyshkians never ceased to visit it, never loosened their emotional ties to it. In times of religious and ethnic trouble, the elderly and the pious made the difficult pilgrimage to the cemetery to ask that the merit of the dead protect the shtetl Jews against their adversaries. The young went because they were fascinated by the challenge of deciphering the Hebrew inscriptions on the old tombstones, eager for any insight this would give them into the ancient past.

The hilltop location of the Old Cemetery also contributed to its popularity as a destination for warm-weather outings, for it offered one of the few beautiful views in this region of southern Lithuania. Indeed, only the church steeple in Juryzdyki offered a comparable vista. From the cemetery one could see the shtetl as clearly as if one were holding it in the palm of one's hand: the small houses with their back gardens, the complicated web of alleys and streets converging on the market square, the two beautiful batei midrash flanking the grand synagogue, the synagogue itself with its three-tiered roof giving it the appearance of a structure wearing three hats, the whole scene quite picturesque from afar.

For children, the Old Cemetery was a place filled with mystery, its legends and lore luring them to adventure, promising to unlock the secrets of the past, the riddle of the future. As recounted in the following story by Eishyshkian Shaul Kaleko, many a child was unable to resist the temptation.

We were the shtetl's triplet rascals, Hayyim-Nahman, Mendel Menahem, and I. One day Hayyim-Nahman said to me, "Shaul, let's go to the Holy Martyr's Grave."

Who was that Holy Martyr? There was an old story in our shtetl about him, and this is how it went. In bygone days the shtetl was the property of a wicked cruel magnate who loved to malign the Jews. But worse than the magnate himself were his many dogs, who were even more vicious than their master, particularly his most beloved dog, called Caesar, who was the most atrocious and treacherous creature in the pack. When the magnate came to the shtetl, accompanied by his dogs, all the people stayed home behind locked doors.

One night Caesar died suddenly, and the magnate blamed his death on the Jews. He issued a proclamation warning that if within two days no one came forward to take responsibility for the death of his dog, then all the Jews of the shtetl would be put to death. The entire community of Eishyshok prayed, cried, and fasted, calling upon God's mercy to nullify the evil decree.

In the shtetl there was a Jew by the name of Moishe Mordekhai, a simple man who made his living as a woodcutter. When he heard about the terrible fate awaiting his fellow Jews, he left his house, telling his family that he was going to the forest to cut wood, as was his daily custom. But instead of going to the woods, Moishe Mordekhai headed for the estate of the wealthy landowner, where he "confessed" to the crime of killing Caesar. The magnate punished the innocent man with the most excruciatingly deadly instruments of torture, until finally his body gave way and his pure soul returned to his Maker.

By sacrificing himself, Moishe Mordekhai had saved the entire shtetl. He was buried in the Old Cemetery with great honor, whereupon he became known as the "Holy Martyr," his resting place as the "Holy Martyr's Grave."

Many years after those terrible events we three rascals decided to visit the Holy Martyr's Grave, because Hayyim-Nahman said that the Holy Martyr himself had appeared to him in a dream and told him that if he would come to the Old Cemetery, he would reveal to him the secret truth about when the Messiah would come.

We went to the cemetery the long way. All was well until we reached the path through the fields of the goyim, when a giant goy gave chase and caught us, then thrashed us with a stick until we were a bloody mess. He claimed that we had been vandalizing his fields.

Beaten, bloody, and covered with cuts and scratches, we returned home. There we received no hero's welcome, but the anger and anguish of our worried parents, who didn't know where we had disappeared to. That is how our visit to the Holy Martyr's Grave ended. We never succeeded in learning the secret of when the Messiah will come.[7]

THE NEW HOUSE OF ETERNITY

Around the beginning of the eighteenth century, the Jews of Eishyshok began burying their dead in the New Cemetery, probably because they ran out of space in the old one after outbreaks of the deadly cholera epidemic in 1706, 1708, and 1710. The earliest surviving tombstones from the New Cemetery dated to those years, and they were still in existence until the final days of the shtetl.

If the usual custom had been followed, the New Cemetery would have been dedicated with a marriage ceremony between two poor orphans, paid for and organized by the community. Paying for the marriage of an orphan couple and providing for their living expenses for a number of years to come was an act of charity that was thought to have the power to nullify evil decrees.[8]

The New Cemetery was located in much friendlier territory than the old one. It was about a half a mile from the synagogue, behind the public bath, down a small, well-trodden path, named Besoylem Gessl (Eternity Lane), and it backed on a large farm owned by a Jew named Meishke Abelowitch, who had bought back the land from Christian farmers. For the children of the shtetl, a visit to the cemetery was often combined with a side trip to the Abelowitch farm.

As required by tradition, the cemetery was fenced off, surrounded on three sides by a stone wall, on the fourth and ever-expanding side by a wooden fence cut from weeping willows. During the summer months this fence was covered with dazzling wildflowers. Inside the cemetery, amid the graves and grass, grew fine old apple trees which the children loved to raid, and tall aspens that fluttered in the lightest breeze, whispering a steady stream of secrets.[9]

One entered the cemetery through a black iron gate, which was engraved with words expressing the hope that the cholera plague would soon stop. To the right was the house of the kvoresman and his family, to the left a well, where one washed one's hands upon leaving. Not far from there was the taharah shtibl, the purifying house, where the bodies of the dead from nearby villages were prepared for burial.

Within the cemetery were three types of soil, the finest being the yellow sand located in the highest part of the cemetery, which made for excellent drainage. There the shtetl buried its most esteemed citizens: the rabbis, scholars, and other notables, including the balebatim. In the center of the cemetery, where the soil was a mixture of yellow sand and red clay, the shtetl buried its artisans and those among the poor who were known for their good character, their piety, or their learning. Where the cemetery sloped gently down toward the public bath, the soil was all of red clay, which turned to mud after the thaw and during the rainy season. This was the final resting place for the poor, simple, uneducated Jews, whose humble wooden grave markers sank rapidly into the ground. Within each of these general divisions, of course, were even more finely demarcated burial zones.

There were also special sections allocated to specific groups — for example, the rows reserved for women who had died in childbirth, rows set aside for infants, and yet other rows for those who had met a violent death.[10] Baptized Jews, persons of ill repute, and suicides were all buried together in their own dark corner. And along one wall of the cemetery — one of the walls that would never be moved to make way for expansion — was a special section for the kohanim (priests). Because all members of the priestly families had to observe special purity regulations about keeping a certain physical distance from the dead, the kohanim had to be buried in a part of the cemetery that would permit their family members to see their graves without actually entering the cemetery and walking among the dead.[11]

Any family who wished to challenge the shtetl's rigid caste system would find the battle a difficult one, as Yitzhak Uri Katz discovered. Reb Yitzhak Uri himself was descended from a prominent rabbinic family related to the Gaon of Vilna. He married Alte Rochel Yehudit Dwilanski from Eishyshok, and when her father, a pious man and a scholar, died, Reb Yitzhak Uri requested permission to bury him in the cemetery's most prestigious section, and offered to pay whatever the burial society assessed them for the plot. But permission was not granted, for despite his intellectual interests, Avigdor Dwilanski had been a lowly baker. A mild man by nature, Reb Yitzhak Uri fought this decision with unaccustomed vigor, horrifying the establishment with the threat that when his time came, his family would be instructed to bury him alongside his father-in-law in the more humble sand/clay section of the cemetery. Such a dire threat stunned the shtetl and had the desired effect: After the proper payment was made, Avigdor Dwilanski was buried in the cemetery's yellow sand section.

After these events, three more deaths occurred in the Katz family within a very short span of years, all on the fifth day of Hanukkah.

Avigdor Dwilanski (center) with his brothers Rabbi Moshe-Leib Krisilov (left) and Rabbi Kosolewicz (first name unknown). Each brother had taken a different name in order to avoid service in the tzarist army. Reb Avigdor studied at the Volozhin yeshivah and was an accomplished scholar, but became a bakery owner rather than a rabbi. PHOTO: YITZHAK URI KATZ. YESC, RESNIK

Yitzhak Uri Katz, a scholar, photographer, and pharmacist, triumphed over the cemetery's caste system and got his father-in-law buried in the most prestigious section. YESC, Y. ELIACH

Avraham Yaakov Katz, rabbi of Delyatichi, father of Yitzhak Uri and husband of Rebbetzin Hannah-Batia, a descendant of the Gaon of Vilna. PHOTO: YITZHAK URI KATZ. YESC

The first to die was Yossele Katz, the talented young son of Yitzhak Uri and Alte, who succumbed to an infection that was the after-effect of a skiing accident; the next was Rabbi Avraham Yaakov Katz, the father of Yitzhak Uri; and the third was Yitzhak Uri himself. To some of the older people in the shtetl, the three Hanukkah-season deaths in the Katz family seemed an omen, a warning to those who would dare challenge the established burial practices in the cemetery.

When Avraham Yaakov and his son Yitzhak Uri were buried, an elaborate white ohel (mausoleum) was built over the two graves, just diagonally from Avigdor Dwilanski's tombstone. Its impressive inscription spoke eloquently of their lives, while omitting one important piece of information: the fact that Yitzhak Uri had received a college education in New York City. His wife, Alte, was urged not to include it, in order not to "blemish" her husband's yihus, for even as late as 1930, some people considered America a godless country, not suitable for a man of quality.

TOMBSTONE MOTIFS AND EPITAPHS

The New Cemetery's tombstones, and the motifs and epitaphs inscribed on them, reflected ancient Jewish traditions of commemoration, and were therefore typical of what was to be found in cemeteries throughout the shtetlekh of Eastern Europe. Some of the tombstones were cast and cut in Vilna, then brought to Eishyshok aboard the wagons of the Vilner coachmen. Others were carved from local stone, including black basalt, or constructed of red brick, which was then whitewashed. Carving and engraving was officially a man's domain, and Eishyshok's local masons did most of the work, but Malka Dina Szulkin, the wife of Nahum Szulkin, the shtetl's last kvoresman, was a gifted artist who sometimes clandestinely assisted in the designing and engraving of tombstones.

The shtetl's last kvoresman (undertaker), Nahum Szulkin, pictured here in 1932, was murdered in the September 1941 massacre.
PHOTO: ROSALIND ROSENBLATT. YESC, R. ROSENBLATT

The tombstone of Arieh-Leib Asner. Since Arieh-Leib means lion, a lion was engraved on the headstone. He was the grandfather of the American actor Ed Asner. Standing next to the tombstone is Beile, Reb Arieh-Leib's widow.
PHOTO: YITZHAK URI KATZ. YESC, ASNER

Tombstones were often marked with such universal Jewish symbols as a menorah (a candelabra) or a shofar (a ram's horn), a practice that dates to the Jews of the Roman period. Over the years, the universal symbology became intertwined and overlaid with motifs specific to the region, but much of the iconography would have been clear to Jews from anywhere in the world.[12] Without even reading the epitaphs, they would have been able to glean a fund of essential information about the deceased. The tombstones of rabbis and scholars often bore the image of a book, or of the Ten Commandments — the latter symbolic of the fact that the deceased had been a preacher and a teacher of the Law. The tombstones of kohanim always depicted two hands raised in the gesture the kohanim use to bless the congregation during the priestly benediction. The image of a ewer and bowl signified that the tombstone belonged to a Levite, descendant of the tribe of Levi, since one of the duties of the Levites is to wash the priest's hands prior to the benediction.

It was common practice to use images illustrative of the name of the deceased: a lion, for example, symbolizing Aryeh (Hebrew for lion) Leib (Yiddish for lion). The lion was also a general symbol for membership in the tribe of Judah. A man whose name was Zvi (Hebrew for hart) Hirsh (Yiddish for deer) might have a galloping hart on his tombstone, and a verse with an allusion to it, such as "Be strong as a leopard, light as an eagle, fleet as a hart, and bold as a lion, to do the will of thy Father who is in heaven."[13] Sometimes the symbols were a combination of the personal and specific, like those just described, and something more general, like the cut trunk of a tree, which symbolized untimely death. After World War I, some tombstones also included a photograph of the deceased.

Women's tombstones drew on a more limited range of symbols than men's, the most com-

Yude-Mendl Kremin (center), with son-in-law Hirshl Tatarski (right), daughter Rivka Tatarski, son Hayyim-Itchke, and granddaughter Hayya-Rochke Shmidt. Yude-Mendl had a clubfoot. That leg was broken during a severe beating by Lida coachmen in 1936, because he was one of the shareholders of the newly formed Lida truck company, and therefore posed a threat to the coachmen's livelihood. Yude-Mendl died a natural death; all the others perished in the September 1941 massacre. YESC, ELLIS

The family of Yude-Mendl Kremin at his tombstone in 1932: (right to left) son Hirsh Faivl, daughters Rivka Tatarski and Nehamah Shmidt, son-in-law Notl Krashunski, Notl's wife Hayya, and son Hayyim-Itchke Kremin. All perished during the Holocaust in Eishyshok, Lida, and Grodno. PHOTO: REPHAEL LEJBOWICZ. YESC, ELLIS

mon one being a candelabra, which alluded to a woman's duty to light the candles on the eve of the Sabbath and other holidays. The accompanying inscription might also be an allusion to this most central of duties, like the description of a woman of valor, whose "lamp never goes out at night," or the praise of matriarch Sarah, whose light "burned Friday evening to Friday evening."[14] A dove in flight from a nest filled with chicks was often engraved on the tombstones of mothers who left behind a houseful of small children when they died.

As with men's tombstones, illustrations alluding to the deceased's namesake in the Bible were a common motif. For a Rachel, there might be a carving of the well where Rachel met Jacob; for a Rebecca, the weeping willow where Rebecca's wetnurse was buried; for a Miriam, a stream of water and the inscription "Miriam died there and was buried there. The community was without water . . ."[15]

With or without complementary symbols, the epitaphs constituted a form of poetry that could reach great heights of compression and complexity. Some were written in acrostics or anagrams of the person's name. Some combined standardized laudatory descriptions with specific personal data. Quotations from the Psalms, from other books of the Bible, and from a variety of other sacred texts were common, often chosen because they included or alluded to the name and character of the deceased.

VISITING THE GRAVES

The Old and New Cemeteries were the place where Eishyshkians went in moments of despair, when they were in need of comfort. They did not go there to pay tribute to world-renowned personalities, for there were none buried in the Eishyshok cemeteries. If they wanted to make such a pilgrimage, to worship at the site of a great man's grave, they went, like other Lithuanian Jews, to the Zaretche cemetery in Vilna, where the Gaon of Vilna and Count Valentine Potocki, a noted convert to Judaism, were buried, or to nearby Radun, final resting place of the Haffetz Hayyim.

Eishyshkians were particularly drawn to the

grave of the Haffetz Hayyim, whose funeral in 1933 was attended by the entire shtetl. His mausoleum would become a pilgrimage destination for people from around the world, including even some non-Jews, and among the constant stream of worshippers there was always an impressive number of Eishyshkians. Thanks to the years he had spent at the yeshivah in Eishyshok, and the close ties he retained with the town throughout his long life, they viewed the Haffetz Hayyim as their own. During the Holocaust and its aftermath, his grave would take on a special significance in the lives of the survivors, who believed that it had protective properties.

Within Eishyshok itself, visits to the cemetery were not in the nature of pilgrimages. Rather, they were mainly family affairs that took place on prescribed dates, on both the religious and the personal calendar. It was an ancient custom for everyone to visit the graves twice a year, on Tishah be-Av (the ninth day of the month of Av, which was July–August), and sometime during the month of Elul (August–September).[16] One also visited on the yahrzeit (the anniversary of the death of the deceased) and in time of trouble, as well as on many other personal dates of one's own choosing.

On Tisha be-Av, the day the First and Second Temples were destroyed, and on the final day of the three weeks of mourning commemorating the destruction, the entire shtetl went to the cemetery. There they visited the family graves, and watched the heder boys reenact the war between the Jews and the Romans. The visit to the cemetery was concluded with a solemn hakafot, a ceremonial procession around the perimeter of

The body of the Haffetz Hayyim being taken from the Radun yeshivah before his funeral, September 1933. In the left corner are Reb Hertz Mendl Hutner and his son Shimon. PHOTO: REPHAEL LEJBOWICZ. YESC, Y. HUTNER

At the grave of Meir Yaakov Polaczek, his wife (left) and daughter Mariyasl. Mrs. Polaczek was murdered in the September 1941 massacre, Mariyasl Yurkanski by the AK. YESC, FANNY YORK

Alexander Zisl Hinski (right) and David Hirsh in 1938 at the tombstone of the Haffetz Hayyim in Radun. PHOTO: REPHAEL LEJBOWICZ. YESC, SH. & Z. CHINSKI

the cemetery walls. Meir Wilkanski describes some of the events of one such day during the closing decade of the nineteenth century:

At noon on Tishah be-Av, after the reciting of the lamentations, all flocked to the cemetery. Everyone rushed to the family graves. From various tombstones could be heard the piercing wails of widows, bereaved mothers, and orphan girls.

The men and the lads went from tombstone to tombstone seeking the graves of the great zaddikim [pious ones] who were buried in Eishyshok. Their tombstones are already sunken into the ground, so everyone took extra care not to step on the graves. When they reached the row of the ohalim [mausoleums] where the great rabbis are interred, they entered the ohalim and prostrated themselves in prayer, just as they do in times of trouble . . .[17]

For the visit that took place during Elul, the month of repentance, it was common in some communities to hire klogerins (professional mourners) to fall upon the graves, weeping and wailing. This practice was not followed in Eishyshok. Instead, the cemetery visit was a private one, an occasion for family members from the shtetl and from elsewhere to come together to pay their respects to the ancestral graves. There, on what was the eve of the coming new year, they beseeched the dead to intervene on behalf of the living. Prayers were recited, contributions made to the Hevrah Kaddishah (burial society) and the kvoresman for the maintenance of the family graves, and alms distributed among the shtetl poor.

For the kvoresman it was quite a busy time, particularly so in the first decades of the twentieth century. With emigration from Eishyshok ever on the increase, especially among the youth, the return visit to the ancestral graves during the month of Elul became an important link between the emigrants and those they had left behind, and even people who ignored many other traditions were eager to observe this one. Those emigrants who could not be there during Elul timed their visits as closely as possible to it.

The graves of family members, and of the scholars and martyrs, were frequently visited prior to important events in one's personal life, such as weddings, bar mitzvahs, or, in the twentieth century, emigration.

People also visited the cemetery in times of personal trouble, to call upon the deceased to act as virtuous advocates on behalf of the living.[18] If a mother was having a difficult labor, a member of her family would take a piece of yarn to measure the perimeter of the cemetery, or the tombstone of an illustrious ancestor or some other prominent personage, and the figure denoting the length in meters, or a multiple of that length, would then be used to calculate a charitable donation — how many wax candles, how many lengths of wood, how many pud of kerosene. Women who had difficulty conceiving, and single people desiring a mate, might also go to the cemetery in search of otherworldly help. In fact, visits to the Eishyshok cemetery may have resulted in as many tales of matrimony as were recorded in the little notebooks of the shtetl's matchmakers.

One of the most appealing of these stories concerned Elka Szulkin, the last kvoresman's own daughter. As a child she had smallpox, which left her with a scarred face. Covered with a veil to conceal the pockmarks, she roamed the cemetery, preferring the silent company of the dead to the cruel comments of the shtetl's youth. She would make her rounds among the tombstones, read the inscriptions, and pray for a better future. One day, while wandering through the area of the ohalim, where candles were often lit by

Hayya Kabacznik Sonenson with her six sons at the grave of her husband Shael Sonenson, who died in 1935 and was buried in the most prominent section of the cemetery. Standing according to age to the right of the tombstone are Hayya, Israel, Moshe, and Leibke (Aryeh). To the left of the tombstone, Avraham, Shalom, and Shepske (Shabtai). A tradition in the Kabacznik family decreed that young women were not to go to the cemetery. PHOTO: BEN ZION SZREJDER. YESC, Y. ELIACH

Members of the Levittan family who resided in Kovno, Lithuania, were granted permission by the Lithuanian and Polish governments to come to Eishyshok to visit their husband and father's grave in the 1930s (right to left): wife Breine Levittan, daughter Mina, son Hayyim, and granddaughter Henia-Hayya. PHOTO: REPHAEL LEJBOWICZ. YESC, H. LEVITTAN

visiting supplicants, she encountered a young man, a soldier of about her own age. He was an army deserter who had sought refuge among Eishyshok's illustrious dead. Before long, the two young people fell in love. For Nahum der Kvoresman the wedding of his daughter was quite an event. Instead of bringing people to the cemetery for their final rest, for once he had the chance to reverse that journey, to lead his daughter out of the cemetery toward the wedding canopy and a new life.

The Yitzhak Sonenson cemetery story was another Eishyshkian favorite. Young Yitzhak was a brilliant scholar, known as "der Minsker illui" (the prodigy from Minsk), and became a rabbi at an early age. Whenever he visited his brother Shael in Eishyshok, he never missed a chance to visit the cemetery. One day he heard from among the ohalim the sound of a woman's voice, pleading and sobbing, begging the martyrs to send her a bridegroom. Upon concluding her prayers, she placed a folded piece of paper in one of the tombstone crevices. A gentle wind from the aspen trees blew the paper straight to the feet of Rabbi Yitzhak Sonenson. At first he ignored the slip of paper, but when the wind blew again, carrying it practically into his hands, he unfolded it and discovered that it was a heartbreaking note written by the woman whose cries he had heard. In it the young woman listed all her deficiencies: her homely looks and undersize stature, her family's poverty, her humble origins. Yet despite all these obstacles, the woman wrote, she still hoped that she could somehow fulfill her only wish in life, which was to marry a scholar and to serve him day and night with her full devotion, thus enabling him to spend all his time studying and learning. Since she knew she stood no chance among the shadkhanim (matchmakers) of this world, she was taking her appeal directly to the dwellers of "the world of truth." As required by custom when writing such a note, she signed her first name and those of her father and mother.

Rabbi Yitzhak Sonenson went immediately to the shtetl matchmaker to seek the hand of the notewriter. The shadkhan was stunned, for Rabbi Sonenson was not only a brilliant scholar but a very handsome young man, blond with burning blue eyes. In short, he was one of the most eligible, sought-after young men in the vicinity, whom many prominent scholars and wealthy merchants wanted as a son-in-law. Fearing that he would be ridiculed for such a mismatch, the shadkhan tried to dissuade the young scholar from pursuing the matter, but to no avail. Yitzhak's brother Shael flew into a rage when he heard about his brother's decision. But Yitzhak paid no heed to his brother's outrage either. He stated that the matter was closed; there was no changing his mind. The only explanation he would offer was that "one can't put to shame a daughter of Israel who beseeched the graves of the martyrs with so much faith and self-abnegation."

The marriage between the brilliant, handsome Yitzhak Sonenson and Hannah, his short, homely bride, did take place. Eishyshok remembered her as one of the happiest brides ever. They married and settled in Mir, and for ten years it was a childless marriage. (In Jewish law, having no children after ten years of marriage is grounds for divorce.) Though Rabbi Yitzhak was advised to seek a divorce, once again he followed his conscience with regard to his wife. For her part, she prayed at the tombstones of various saints and rabbis, turning to the dead for help, just as she had done in Eishyshok, until finally her prayers were answered. The couple was blessed with two children, a daughter, Ruhama, and a son, Alter. Later they emigrated to Eretz Israel and settled in Jerusalem. There Rabbi Yitzhak studied day and night, occasionally publishing a scholarly pamphlet, while his wife catered to him devotedly, as she had promised. Until the last days of their lives they were supported financially by Yitzhak's brother Shael back in Eishyshok. Yitzhak and his wife Hannah are buried on the Mount of Olives in Jerusalem, their graves overlooking the Temple Mound.[19]

During times of war or epidemic or other community catastrophe, the entire population of the shtetl might take refuge in the cemetery. In the midst of World War I, as a fierce battle was waged on the outskirts of town between the retreating Russians and the advancing Germans, Eishyshok's Jews shuttled back and forth between the house of prayer and the house of eternity. As recounted in the memoirs of Pessia Moszczenik, who was thirteen years old at the time:

At night we used to leave for the cemetery, which was not too far from the shulhoyf. As the battle continued to rage, we lay next to the graves, trembling with fear that a bullet might hit us. . . . Friday morning, September 9, 1915, on the eve of Yom Kippur, we returned to the shulhoyf . . . Russian soldiers entered the Old Beth Midrash and fired a few shots, one of which hit a young girl who was a refugee from Aran, a shtetl not far from Eishyshok . . . Friday evening we again assembled at the cemetery, as the bullets of the "haters of Zion" flew over our heads and bright flashes of gunpowder lit the skies above us. But nobody, thank God, was hit. We survived. At sundown, there among the graves, we recited the Kol Nidre.[20]

HEVRAH KADDISHAH

It was the sacred duty of the Hevrah Kaddishah (Sacred Brotherhood) society to assure a dignified burial for the dead. The origins of this charitable group date to antiquity. Its first members were individuals who joined a brotherhood dedicated to serving the public welfare without any monetary reward. Burial of the dead was included among their functions, but it was only one of many.[21] Members of the brotherhood were greatly appreciated, as they continue to be today; prayers for their well-being that were composed many centuries ago are still being recited in the synagogue.

Over time, however, their various functions were gradually assumed by other benevolent societies, until the Hevrah Kaddishah became a group dedicated exclusively to purifying and burying the dead. They took it upon themselves to provide a burial for all the members of the community, and those under its jurisdiction. Every burial was to be performed with the greatest dignity and expediency, as prescribed by Jewish law and local custom, even if the dead person was a complete stranger.

Each year in Eishyshok the spring thaw brought its share of such strangers into the hands of the Hevrah Kaddishah. Unidentified corpses that had been covered by ice and snow would be revealed when the warm weather came, and if they were found anywhere in the area under shtetl jurisdiction, they became the responsibility of the shtetl's burial society. Though technically the burial of the body of a met mitzvah (an unknown) is everyone's responsibility, in fact it was the Hevrah Kaddishah, assisted by the shtetl leadership, who carried out and paid for the preparations. The community performed its part when the Hevrah Kaddishah shammash announced, "Jews, go to the funeral of a met mitzvah," whereupon everyone turned out to follow the casket of the anonymous stranger to the final resting place.

During periods of strife, war, and epidemic, when the number of victims overwhelmed the members of the Hevrah Kaddishah, they sometimes had to enlist the assistance of particularly pious members of other fraternal societies to ensure proper burials for the deceased. But their dedication to their duty never flagged, sometimes even prompting them to endanger their own lives. This happened during World War I, for example, when the large number of bodies placed an extraordinary burden on the Hevrah Kaddishah of Eishyshok. Their fellow Jews were dying in battle, in the crossfire between the various armies, and in the raging typhus epidemic of 1918; others succumbed to starvation, or the vicious attacks of local peasants. While people were streaming out of the shtetl in a mass evacuation, many members of the brotherhood remained behind, refusing to compromise their commitment to the dead.

Sometimes the Hevrah Kaddishah was required to mediate with the secular authorities. When the boiler in the shtetl's public bathhouse exploded sometime during the 1880s, more than a dozen men were killed, and their bodies were promptly buried. An informer (rumored to be a maskil who had been expelled from the yeshivah) reported the terrible mishap to the tzarist county officials, insinuating that it was homicide rather than an accident. A committee led by a high-ranking government bureaucrat arrived with orders to exhume the bodies so that autopsies could be performed. The shtetl went into a state of shock, since in Jewish tradition autopsies are considered the ultimate desecration of the dead, and the entire population followed the official party to the New Cemetery. Meir Wilkanski, then a young heder boy, described the event from the perspective of a child:

Boys pushed through the crowd. How does the body look after being interred for several weeks? How does the face of a dead person look? Does it look like the faces of the dead who appear in the synagogue at night, after the second watch? Do the holy faces of our ancestors who were not embalmed resemble these dead?[22]

While the heder boys were pondering these mysteries, the leaders of the community, including the Hevrah Kaddishah, were negotiating with the government officials. Reb Leib, the neeman of the kahal, made a hurried trip to Vilna, carrying with him a handsome sum taken from the coffers of the Hevrah Kaddishah and the kahal, and augmented by private donations from leading citizens of the community. The bribe was apparently satisfactory to the officials, for the bathhouse victims were allowed to rest in peace. As Kaddish was recited, and the crowd in the cemetery sobbed, the dead were returned to their graves, untouched by the medical examiner's knife. Snow started to fall, soon covering the raw gashes in the ground.[23]

THE BROTHERHOOD

Membership in the Hevrah Kaddishah was a much coveted honor. Only the most prominent, scholarly, and pious of the balebatim were supposed to be eligible for membership. It also helped to be related to someone who was already a member, for membership was often hereditary. To ensure a family's continuing presence in the brotherhood, young men, children, and even infants were sometimes initiated when an opening became available.[24] Thus Shalom Sonenson, a grandson of one of the Kabaczniks, began his participation as a bar mitzvah boy. The Kabaczniks, who were one of the five founding families of Eishyshok, had been in the Hevrah Kaddishah for generations, often serving as trustees, but all the mature male members of the Kabacznik family had by this time either died or emigrated. Shalom Sonenson received his final initiation when he was in his twenties. As the group's youngest member, however, he was not eligible to be elected to the post of trustee.

THE SISTERHOOD

The Hevrah Kaddishah's women's auxiliary was an equally prestigious group, equally limited in membership. But women didn't covet membership in the burial society as highly as men did, and membership was usually along marriage lines, not hereditary lines. Thus the women's group, unlike the men's, excluded the unmarried, and the society was made up chiefly of the wives and widows of Hevrah Kaddishah members. (There was also an associated group of women who sewed shrouds, but they were not actual members of the society, and thus did not participate in its main social activities.) The women didn't have their own leader; they were under the jurisdiction of the neeman of the men's group. However, one or two prominent women usually assumed unofficial leadership roles.

THE HEVRAH KADDISHAH PINKAS

The Hevrah Kaddishah was strictly governed by a set of rules (takkanot), which were written down in its pinkas. Originally compiled by the Maharal of Prague in 1564, and eventually augmented by local custom and tradition, these rules became the guidelines for burial for most Ashkenazic Jews. The Hevrah Kaddishah pinkas also recorded all the decisions, elections, and events pertinent to the local society, as well as the date of death for every member of the community whom they buried. In Eishyshok the last pinkas kept by the brotherhood dated only from 1895, the year the previous one, which was one of the oldest pinkasim in Lithuania, was lost in the Big Fire. It was a black book about three by two feet in size, its pages divided into two sections. In the first section were written the names of the deceased and the death and burial dates; in the second section was a record of all the other business of the society. Another pinkas, which recorded not only the name, date, and place of burial for all the dead but also the inscriptions on the headstones, was kept in the house of the kvoresman. All entries were in Hebrew.

There was also an official death record, kept for the government, where deaths, as well as in some instances the causes of death, were recorded. This record was kept in Hebrew and Russian when Eishyshok was part of the Pale of Settlement, and in Hebrew and Polish when Eishyshok was part of the Polish Republic (during the interwar years).[25]

THE ANNUAL HEVRAH KADDISHAH FEAST

The fraternal aspects of the Hevrah Kaddishah were observed in various ways, the most notable being a once-a-year feast. Though the date of the meal differed from one community to another, a popular choice was the seventh day of the month of Adar (March–April), which, according to oral tradition, is the anniversary of the birth and death of Moses. In Eishyshok and its vicinity, however, the burial society usually held its feast on the Sunday in October or November when the weekly portion reading was the Hayei Sarah.[26] It recounts the death of Matriarch Sarah at the age of 127, and her burial in the cave of Makhpela, a site that had been purchased by her husband Abraham for use as a family grave.[27] According to tradition, Adam and Eve are buried there also. Perhaps this date was chosen because this particular reading seemed a better expression of the shtetl's attitude toward death and the keeping of ancestral graves than the reading about Moses did, for Moses' burial place is unknown, while Sarah's, which was to become the final resting place for all three Patriarchs and two of the Matriarchs, is a deeply venerated site. Needless to say, the Hayei Sarah reading has an additional significance for women. There may also have been a history-based reason for the choice of dates: the shtetl's possible Karaite origins would have dictated a scriptural rather than an oral tradition.

The Sunday of the big banquet began with a fast, and, for the men in the burial society, with a ritual immersion in the mikvah, which had been specially heated the night before. The men then proceeded to the synagogue for the selihot (penitential prayers) that were recited in addition to the usual morning prayers, and from there to the cemetery. As they made their way from grave to grave, checking to be sure that each burial site had been properly maintained during the preceding year, they asked forgiveness of the dead in case any inadvertent disrespect had been shown them during their purification and burial rites. The members then performed a ceremony culminating in their donating money to a special fund for the benefit of the shtetl rabbi. For the rest of the day they sat with the rabbi in the beth midrash, reviewing all the laws and customs that pertained to their duties.

Meanwhile the women, who were also fasting, spent the entire day in their respective kitchens, cooking and baking their contributions to the banquet. A typical menu included sweet hallah, stuffed whole pike, roasted turkey or goose, a variety of kugels, an assortment of side dishes, special round cookies made particularly for this feast because they symbolized the continuity of life, and vodkas and wines. Since children were not invited to the feast that their mothers and grandmothers were preparing under their very noses, they were permitted to indulge in a ritual food-snatching prank, with each community's children favoring a different treat. In Eishyshok the most coveted targets were the potato kugels.

Each year the feast rotated to the home of one or another of the members (though in other towns the festivities took place in the women's section of the synagogue). The women ate in one room, the men in another, their enjoyment enhanced by the opportunity to hear their rabbi or some other learned person deliver a special scholarly discourse for the occasion. The women who sewed the shrouds were not invited to the banquet, but food was sent to them at their homes.

The events of the day were of interest not just to the celebrants, but to the shtetl as a whole, which avidly followed all the activity, some people even going so far as to eavesdrop at the windows and doors. Every syllable that slipped from the lips of these important personages, every gesture they made, was scrutinized in the belief that it might be some kind of omen for the future. Unfortunately, the consumption of so much good food and drink sometimes loosened tongues, leading those usually restrained pillars of the community to air their grievances and attempt to settle accounts with one another in ways they would later regret. Needless to say, the shtetl gossips awaited those lapses with great interest.

One such event, which occurred in nearby Olkenik, would have ramifications that lasted for years, engulfing much of the Jewish population of Lithuania in a fiercely contested dispute. Abba Yossef ben Ozer ha-Kohen Trivash, the rabbi of Olkenik, was one of the most prominent Lithuanian scholars of his time, and scion of an illustrious family which traced its lineage to Rashi. It was the Lithuanian branch of the Dreyfus family of Alsace. At the Hevrah Kaddishah feast of 1873, he was accused of allowing nonkosher fat to be used for the baking of the kugels. The accusation, which was reported in the pages of *Ha-Shahar*, the leading Hebrew newspaper, tore Olkenik asunder. Though Rabbi Trivash was defended by Rabbi Yitzhak Elhanan Spektor of Kovno, the most prominent sage of Lithuania, it was to no avail. Olkenik's notables were determined to be rid of him, and after a few years of bitter fighting they succeeded. Rabbi Trivash spent the rest of his life in

Vilna, studying in the kloiz (synagogue) of the harness-makers. One Saturday, he accidentally tipped a burning paraffin lamp onto his Gemara, engulfing it in flames. After the accident he became sick, never to recover.[28]

DEATH AND BURIAL

Until Eishyshok's final days, most people died in their own homes, surrounded by their family. Immediately upon death, the family notified the Hevrah Kaddishah and the kvoresman. Philip Zlotnik remembered that when his grandfather died, he and his cousin Naftali, both ten years old at the time, were dispatched to deliver the news. Breathless and in unison, they recited their important message to the kvoresman and waited for it to have its effect. However, instead of saying the customary phrase upon hearing of a death—"Blessed be He, the Judge of all Truth"[29]—the kvoresman clapped his hands in joy, his gloomy face alight with excitement, and murmured happily to himself "a fetter hecht, a fetter hecht" (a fat cat, a fat cat). The deceased grandfather was Reb David Kabacznik, the powerful neeman of the Hevrah Kaddishah. For the funeral of such a notable, the kvoresman's fixed fee was sure to be handsomely supplemented, by both the dead man's well-to-do family and the organizations to which he had belonged.

When someone died, the kvoresman would arrive at the house of the deceased carrying the taharah bret, the board on which bodies are laid for cleansing before burial; he then returned to the cemetery to dig the grave, leaving the actual purification of the body to the burial society, whose members arrived at the house soon afterward. The corpse was placed on the taharah bret, feet facing the door of the house, with candles to either side of head and feet. The Hevrah Kaddishah members cleansed the body according to ancient tradition and local custom. Men performed the rites for males, women for females.

At the conclusion of the Hevrah Kaddishah's ritual, the body was wrapped in white linen shrouds. A man's shrouds would then be covered with his prayer shawl, which was shorn of one of its fringes to symbolize that he was no longer obligated to observe the 613 precepts of the Torah. For both men and women, two pieces of broken pottery, known as sharves, were placed over the eyes, and if the deceased had procured a small bag of earth from the Holy Land (a practice adopted throughout the Diaspora), it would be placed under the head like a little pillow. A forked twig was put in each hand, so that at the coming of the Messiah the body would be supported as it rose from the dead.[30] From the beginning of the cleansing ritual to the conclusion of the burial, members of the Tehilim (Psalms) society, an organization made up of the shtetl's less-educated citizens, remained in the home of the deceased, reciting psalms.

If the deceased had been murdered, however, there were no cleansing rites; instead, the corpse was wrapped in shrouds while still wearing its bloodstained clothes, for since "the blood is the soul" (Deuteronomy 12:23), it must all be buried along with the body. For infants less than a month old, there was no shroud. The baby was wrapped in a sheet of white linen and the kvoresman came to the house and carried the child away, tucking the tiny body into the flap of his jacket or coat—a sight that did not endear him to the shtetl children, who saw him as the living angel of death, ready to snatch them away.[31]

Prior to the funeral, the Hevrah Kaddishah shammashim appeared at the marketplace, the synagogue courtyard, and on all major streets, to make the announcement: "Yidden, geit zu di levaieh" (Jews, go to the funeral). For the duration of the funeral, all the shops in the shtetl were shut down, all business was suspended, the yeshivah, hadarim, and all other schools were closed.[32] Everyone joined the funeral procession as it passed their home, shop, or school, with the exception of the kohanim, who had to stay at a distance from the coffin. If the deceased had belonged to the Hevrah Kaddishah, or was a prominent scholar, a member of the balebatim class, or a person of some other kind of distinction within the community, the casket was carried by pallbearers. Otherwise, it was placed in a black carriage.[33] At the head of the funeral procession were the members of the Hevrah Kaddishah, who carried huge charity boxes which they rattled ceaselessly, all the while reciting the Hebrew phrase "Zdakah tazil mi-mavet" (Alms save from death).[34]

Upon reaching the synagogue, the funeral procession came to a halt. If the deceased was a man, his body was carried inside and placed at his regular seat. All the other people, with the exception of the kohanim, also took their regular seats, and the rabbi delivered the eulogy. If the rabbi and the deceased had quarreled, however, and the dispute had not been settled at the time of death, the rabbi did not deliver the eulogy — not out of enmity, but out of respect for his dead rival, who could no longer defend himself against anything the rabbi might say. Thus when Reb Dovid Moszczenik der Kichier died in the late 1930s, his eulogy was delivered by Reb Hayyim Paltiel, one of the shtetl's dayyanim, because the rabbi, Szymen Rozowski, and Reb Dovid had been feuding for years over who had the authority to distribute charitable funds from America.

The eulogy for a woman was given not in the shul but in front of whichever prayerhouse she regularly attended. At the conclusion of the eulogy, for either a man or a woman, the funeral cortege proceeded to the cemetery. Over the fresh grave the sons recited Kaddish. In Eishyshok, as in other Lithuanian shtetlekh, if the deceased had no sons or they could not be present at the funeral, the daughters were allowed to recite Kaddish. The body was then lowered into the earth. If the deceased was a man, pages taken from books of sacred writings too timeworn to remain in use might be buried with him. Known as *shemot* (divine names) because they contained God's name and as such were to be treated with great respect, the pages (or sometimes whole books) might have belonged to the deceased, or might have come from the genizah, the special room in the synagogue where worn-out sacred books were stored.

After Kaddish, the congregation formed two lines and comforted the bereaved as they passed down the middle, on their way out of the cemetery. Upon exiting the cemetery gates, all who had attended the funeral washed their hands at the well nearby, thus symbolically cleansing themselves of the impurity associated with the dwelling place of the dead. The men of the Hevrah Kaddishah then went to the mikvah and immersed themselves prior to taking a small meal at the home of one of the members, while the bereaved family returned to their own home for the seudah havraah, the customary meal of condolence prepared by friends and neighbors. It usually included round foods like eggs and lentils, to signify the circle of life, and bread, because of its symbolism as the staff of life. During both the shivah (seven-day) and sloshim (thirty-day) phases of mourning that followed, prayers and Mishnah studies took place in the home of the deceased, with the Hevrah Kaddishah responsible for seeing to it that a minyan was always present. While it is customary to have the ten-man quorum in the home of the mourners for the shivah, in Eishyshok the minyan convened for the entire shloshim.

Fundamental principles of Judaism were expressed in all the laws and practices relating to death, with every detail of the rituals informed by an acknowledgment of the honor, dignity, and respect owed to the dead, and concern for the mental, emotional, and spiritual needs of those left behind. But even within this highly ritualized and regulated process, there was room for families to create their own traditions, to honor the dead and tend to the living in their own way. Some families, for example, did not allow the young children of the deceased to attend the funeral and burial, a custom still observed by many families in Jerusalem; others did not allow young female members of the family to visit the grave on the yearly anniversary of death.

There was also room for the community to express its feelings toward the deceased — for better and sometimes for worse — and room even for distinctly alien practices to be imported into the shtetl, as happened with the yishuvniks.

FUNERALS EXALTING AND DEGRADING

If the deceased had been particularly well liked by the community, respected for some combination of scholarship, leadership, and piety, the entire shtetl mourned the death as though it were that of a family member. Though not mandated by law, a ban on music at shtetl weddings would be observed for a month after the death, and public celebrations postponed. Boys born in the year following the death of a revered scholar might be named in his honor, baby girls in honor of a pious woman.

If, however, the deceased was persona non grata in the community, the burial and mourning were considered ideal occasions for the settling of grievances. Despite the strict commandment that burial must take place as soon as possible after death, if the deceased had not paid his community dues or made charitable donations in proportion to his wealth, or had in some other way offended his neighbors, interment might be delayed as a punitive measure, pending the settling of accounts with the bereaved family. As early as 1761 the Lithuanian Council had warned against such delays;[35] nonetheless, they continued to be used, and indeed were still being practiced in Eishyshok in the 1920s and 1930s. For three days in the 1930s, for example, the Hevrah Kaddishah refused to bury the body of the shtetl Scrooge. Only after his widow had paid all his debts to the community was the body of Reb Alter Plock interred, even though Nahum Szulkin, the kvoresman, had taken pity on her and tried to mediate on her behalf.

If the deceased was a criminal or an informer, he was given a disrespectful funeral. In the Middle Ages he would have been buried outside the cemetery fence without shrouds or the recitation of the Kaddish. In some communities the casket of an informer was placed in the garbage wagon rather than in the community hearse. Such a funeral was known as a "donkey interment," and was justified as part of the process of atonement that the dead person had to go through, in order to alleviate the harsh punishment that would otherwise be levied in "the world of truth."[36]

YISHUVNIK FUNERALS

Yishuvniks (rural Jews) from the surrounding villages under Eishyshok's jurisdiction were well known in the shtetl, and made use of its cemetery as they did all of its vital institutions. Many were connected to the shtetl by ties of blood or by business and social bonds; in death they were treated with the same ceremony and respect as shtetl natives. But their practices sometimes deviated from those observed by Eishyshkians.

The deceased yishuvnik was brought to the special taharah shtibl at the hekdesh, the shelter for the homeless. There the Hevrah Kaddishah prepared the body for burial with the usual rites and rituals. But since most of these country Jews had resided among gentiles for generations and possessed only a minimal Jewish education, they had adopted some of the customs of the Christian population among whom they lived — to the occasional exasperation of those responsible for seeing to it that standard practices were observed. For example, the family members of former soldiers in the Russian army (Nikolaievtzky) often insisted on displaying the body dressed in uniform, rather than in the customary shrouds. Others, including the survivors of Arieh-Leib Asner, a pious Jew from the village

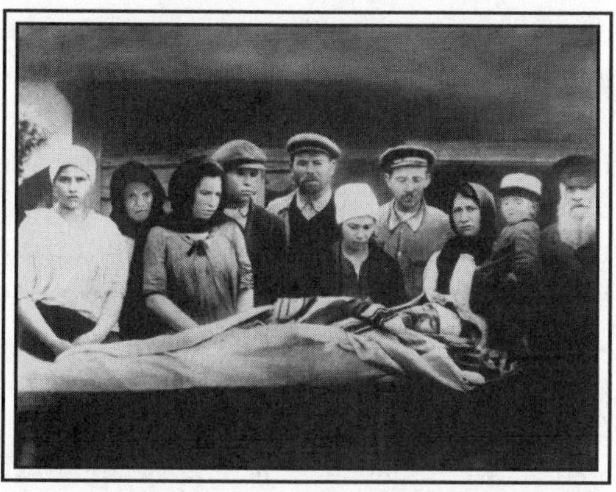

Posing with the body of Reb Arieh-Leib are members of the Asner family in the village of Nacha. The face of the deceased had been left uncovered, in accordance with a local non-Jewish village custom. YESC, A. ASNER

of Nacha (and grandfather of the American actor Ed Asner), demanded to pose with the deceased for photographs. The resulting photo, which was sent to family members who had emigrated to Kansas City, Missouri, depicted the Asners gathered around a corpse whose face had been left uncovered. Although the shtetl Jews considered this "open casket" practice disrespectful to the deceased, it was tolerated if not officially approved by the shtetl rabbi and the Hevrah Kaddishah. In general the community tried to honor the wishes of their country cousins so as not to alienate them — but they did love to tell stories about their peasant ways, which were a source of much amusement to the Eishyshkians.[37]

One particularly popular story concerned the funeral of a yishuvnik from nearby Kalesnik. The son followed his father's coffin in a very composed, restrained fashion, until a member of the Hevrah Kaddishah advised him that it was proper for a son to demonstrate some signs of grief. In instant compliance, the son began a lament, delivered with the rolling *r*'s of the yishuvnik-accented Yiddish spoken in the countryside: "Woe unto me, if only I had had two fathers, one would be dead in his coffin, while the other would still be alive and walking beside me at this very funeral."

PREPARING FOR THE ANGEL OF DEATH

While shtetl customs provided an elaborate system by which the living could avoid unnecessary confrontations with death, all death-related needs being taken care of by members of the Hevrah Kaddishah, the angel of death himself was a different matter. Ultimately there was no avoiding him, and every Jew knew that sooner or later the angel would make his unscheduled call. On that day one made one's passage into eternity, life having been but a brief stop along the way. Many shtetl Jews prepared for that inevitable departure time with great care, much as they did for other sacred occasions in life. They prepared their shrouds in advance, obtained if they could a bag of soil from the Holy Land so they would have a pillow on which to rest their heads, selected their own gravesite and even their coffin. Some requested that the coffin be made from the dining room table upon which they had shared their meals with the poor and the needy, so that the table would serve as their melitz yosher (champion of right) before the heavenly court.

Mordekhai-Leib the tailor was one such planner. He had his bag of soil, a much-cherished gift from a son who had emigrated to England and become a dentist; he'd purchased his plot in a suitable section of the cemetery; and he visited his gravesite often, lying down on the ground and taking measurements to confirm that the space was still adequate for his proportions. He also prepared his shrouds; in fact, the Hevrah Kaddishah knew that whenever they needed shrouds in great haste, they could always count on Reb Mordekhai-Leib. He would eagerly give his up on request, since to do so was considered a good omen for longevity. And it was for him. Mordekhai-Leib lived to a ripe old age. Alas, he never made use of his soil from the Holy Land, nor his shroud, nor his gravesite, for he was murdered by the Nazis with their Lithuanian collaborators, and buried in the mass grave with the rest of his neighbors.

MODERNITY AND SECULARISM

Even during Eishyshok's evolution toward modernity and secularization, the cemetery continued to retain its central position.

Taking photos at the cemetery became a farewell ritual: Prior to their departure, the émigrés posed for farewell shots near the tombstones of relatives, especially their own namesake. The photographs became cherished mementos, reminders of all the deceased loved ones who had been left behind. And now, in the wake of the post-Holocaust destruction of the cemeteries, they are the only such reminders their descendants will ever have. Family members in Eishyshok frequently included among the photos sent abroad to their relatives a picture of the family clustered around an ancestor's tombstone. Individuals who left the shtetl for larger cities and even some of those who emigrated overseas still made occasional trips back home, during which they made a point of visiting the ancestral graves. In the summer of 1932, for example, when Annie Foster, daughter of Nehemia der Feldsher (medicine man), came back to Eishyshok from America on a visit, bringing her daughter Rosalind with her, their cemetery stop was one of the highlights of their trip. Accompanied by Annie's widowed mother and by other relatives who had come back to Eishyshok from points far and near for the occasion, they were shown around the cemetery by Nahum der Kvoresman and Reb Hertz Mendl Hutner, the shtetl dayyan. To commemorate the special day, pictures were taken of the family at Nehemia's grave.

The most visible change in attitude toward the cemetery was demonstrated by Eishyshkians who were members of the Bund or were Communist sympathizers in the 1920s. These revolutionaries did not challenge the shtetl's rigid class structure in the market square, which was the center of the shtetl's economic life, or at the synagogue, the center of its religious life, but rather in the cemetery, among its tombstones. And even there the rebellion was limited. The funeral and burial customs remained unchallenged, Bundists and Communists going to

Annie Foster on a visit from America in 1932, with brother Anshel Virshubski at the grave of their father, Nehemia der Feldsher (medicine man). Anshel was murdered during the Holocaust. PHOTO: ROSALIND ROSENBLATT. YESC, R. ROSENBLATT

Hanneh-Beile Kudlanski with daughter Atara, prior to emigration to America in 1933, parting from Atara's grandmother Kreine, for whom Atara was named. YESC, A. ZIMMERMAN

their family graves as their fathers and forefathers had before them, observing the same rituals. But the sanctity of the cemetery land itself was challenged, the fertile soil presenting an irresistible temptation to those who wished to redistribute Eishyshok's worldly goods.

The New Cemetery was known for its luscious tall grasses, but no one could graze animals there because that was forbidden by Jewish law.[38] With the secularization of the shtetl, a number of individuals challenged that prohibition. Among them was a poor coachman, a sympathizer with the Russian Revolution. He led his horse to the cemetery and left the beast to graze to its heart's content. Though he was admonished several times for this practice, he continued to loose his horse among the graves. The townspeople solved the problem in their typical shtetl way. One late afternoon, when the coachman returned to the cemetery to take his horse back to the stable, he froze in his tracks. On the horse was seated a rider wrapped in shrouds, with pottery fragments around his eyes, and the horse itself was covered with sweat as though just returning from a long journey. After this incident, the poor coachman's horse was never again seen grazing in the cemetery. As to the identity of the mysterious rider, it remained one of Eishyshok's best-kept secrets.

The younger revolutionaries and reformers were much more radical in their rebellion than the older coachman. To him, the revolution meant that a poor man's horse was entitled to green pastures just like the rich man's horse; for them, the issue was more basic. In their zeal to change the world, they saw the cemetery as what Mount Carmel had been to Elijah the Prophet: a battleground of confrontation between two Gods, the place where the true God would decisively triumph over the false one. They believed in revolution, not in a supreme being.

Isaac Deutscher (1907–1967), on his road from tradition to revolution, ate his first ham sandwich in the Jewish cemetery, on his grandfather's grave, on Yom Kippur! During his act of defiance he called upon God "if indeed he exists," to smite him for violating his commandments. Apparently neither God nor Isaac's grandfather responded to the young revolutionary's call for punishment.[39]

In at least one case, the attempt to cast aside tradition foundered unexpectedly, with the confrontation between the revolutionary and the deceased ending in a surprise victory for the latter.

During the Soviet rule of Eishyshok in 1940–41, the local Jewish Communists were especially active. The local Communist cell, the comitet, included among its many objectives the reeducation of the shtetl youth. The goal was to create a new Jew, a loyal Communist, godless and fearless. During the day the young people were kept busy marching and singing Russian revolutionary songs, while their nights were taken up with talks dedicated to the denial of God. The central theme was that "everything is from nature, nothing is from God."

The cemetery, however, was proving a real stumbling block on the road to reeducation, its inhabitants an eternal reminder of the realm of the spirit. Even the most politically correct youth feared the cemetery, especially at night when the dead were thought to roam. To overcome this fear, Ruvke Boyarski, one of the comitet leaders, decided to take a group of youngsters on a nocturnal visit to the cemetery. Zvi Michalowski, a member of the youth group, described the visit:

It was a very dark night, terrifying. But they are members of the comitet, and you cannot refuse them. Everyone was shaking. And while the leader was preaching against God, explaining that there are no ghosts in the cemetery, the dead are dead and they cannot come back, all of a sudden a white shadow appeared, perhaps fifteen meters [fifty feet] from us. I thought I would die of fright. Meanwhile this fellow is preaching against everything we believed, and this white figure is coming closer and closer. The boy who was sitting closest to the speaker grabbed him by the hands, shook him and said,

"Ruvke! Look! Vos is dos?*" Everyone turned around to see, trying not to show that we were terrified, as the white shadow passed by.*[40]

The white figure who made such a timely appearance turned out to be a mentally ill young gentile from a nearby village, who used to roam the Jewish cemetery at night. However, Ruvke the Red never succeeded at convincing his young disciples of this. Unlike Isaac Deutscher, whose challenge went unmet, Ruvke was defeated. That was his last attempt to deny God on the cemetery grounds.

To the very end, the cemetery maintained its position as one of the shtetl's most venerated institutions, in no way undermined by the threat mounted by the Communists. Among the 15,000 Jewish refugees who passed through Eishyshok in flight from the Nazis, many stopped to pray at the graves of the Old and the New Cemeteries, begging the dead martyrs and sages to guide them to a safe haven, and thanking them for the warm hospitality and generous assistance of their descendants. Many of those 15,000 survived the war and its perilous aftermath; the Old and the New Cemeteries did not.

During the expulsion from Spain in 1492, the exiles were able to take along the tombstones of their ancestors. The Jews of Eishyshok were not so fortunate. The handful who somehow lived through the Holocaust and returned to their hometown found themselves facing a pogrom staged in 1944 by some of the local Poles. Those who survived the pogrom escaped with only their lives, leaving behind them the graves of their ancestors, the two mass graves that contained the thousands who had been massacred by the Germans and their Lithuanian collaborators in September 1941, and two fresh graves, belonging to Zipporah Sonenson and her infant son, the most recent victims. Those stones that still survived in the Old and New Cemeteries were soon to disappear, crushed into gravel by the new residents — Poles, Lithuanians, and Russians — who moved in. Now those pulverized tombstones pave the town's roads.

Perhaps at night, the shattered letters embedded in the pavements emerge and hasten to the synagogue, which became a social hall and disco. There in the dark, desecrated shul they assemble and take flight, hanging suspended above the hollow sanctuary, burning like prushim's candles. And perhaps then the letters arrange themselves to spell out the mourner's Kaddish, their silent weeping scream sounding the ancient words: "Itgadal, ve-yitkadash, Sh'me Rabba" (Magnified and sanctified be His great Name in the world which He created according to His will).

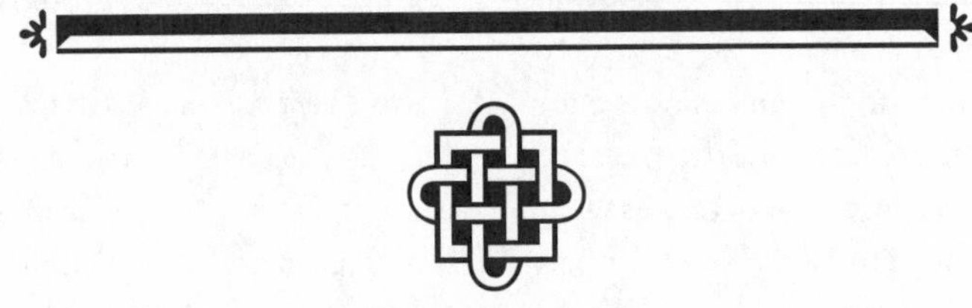

· THREE ·

THE SHTETL ECONOMY

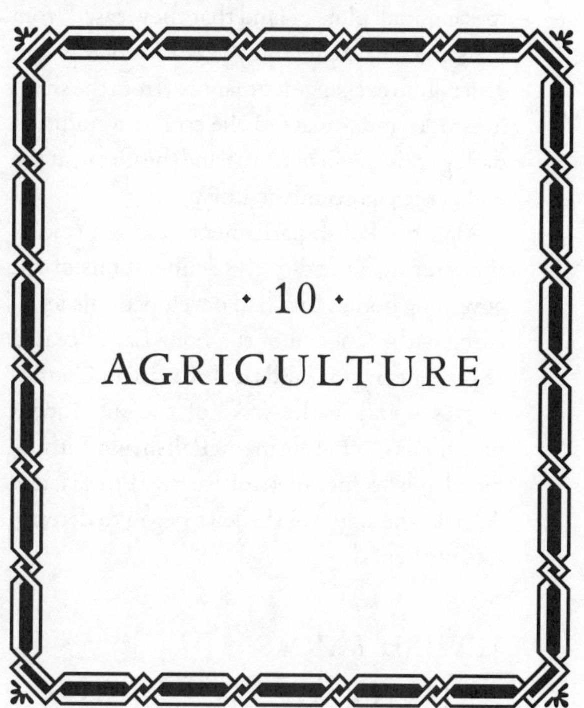

· 10 · AGRICULTURE

HE WHO TILLS HIS LAND SHALL HAVE FOOD IN PLENTY.

Proverbs 12:11

THE EISHYSHOK OF LIVING MEMORY WAS, LIKE ALL SHTETLEKH, A MARKET TOWN WITH trade as its main economic base. But it had begun its existence as a military and agricultural settlement, its location having been chosen in part because, as a natural "island in the forest," it was deemed highly suitable for cultivation.

Eishyshok was deeply marked by its centuries-long agrarian history, as were many of the families whose ties to the land went back for generations. This past lived on even within the shtetl proper: Men who had been students at Eishyshok's famed Kibbutz ha-Prushim during the mid-nineteenth century remembered that each morning, as they made their way to the yeshivah in the early hours of dawn, they would hear the shtetl's farmers in their barns, threshing the wheat as they recited Psalms.[1]

According to the records, Jewish ownership of land to the south and west of Eishyshok proper dated at least to 1145, and probably went back another half a century or so.[2] The founders of the shtetl, the Yurkanski, Kabacznik, Shimshelewitch, Edelstein, and Senitski families, were eventually to own vast tracts of land in the area. Many other Jewish families had holdings of various sizes, in some cases managing to maintain their ownership long after it was illegal to do so; and the shtetl itself owned der vigan, community pastureland on which anyone could graze cattle and goats. Jews, Poles, Lithuanians, and Russians, rich and poor, peasant and nobility, farmed the area for centuries, cultivating wheat and rye, raising cattle, goats, pigs, chickens, and other livestock, harvesting the timber from its forests, and growing fruits and vegetables in small plots they owned in town, or leased in the countryside nearby.

Grain was the major crop in the region, and because the grain trade did not require any manufacturing process other than milling, it did not foster the development of any of the skills, techniques, or forms of organization that are conducive to industry, which meant that Eishyshok and its vicinity remained a primarily agrarian culture until well into the twentieth century.[3] The grain was grown mainly on land owned by the Polish nobility (szlachta), and by Jews who lived either on estates or in villages in the countryside, or within the shtetl proper.[4]

While relations between Jews and gentiles may not always have been ideal, they coexisted, their lives bound up with each other in many and complex ways. Jews in the vicinity managed or leased Christian estates and forests for or from absentee landowners, lived amid Christian and Muslim farmers in Polish and Lithuanian villages like Kalesnik, Okla, Paradin, and Dumbla,[5] owned mills to which all the farmers brought their grain for processing, and ran small businesses patronized by Jews and gentiles alike. Many of those who lived in the shtetl grew potatoes on small plots of land that they leased from the same Christian family year in and year out, generally in exchange for manure (from the shtetl livestock) and a share of the crop — a tradition dating to the reign of Catherine the Great, at the end of the eighteenth century.

After the Polish parliament passed a resolution putting an end to the deliberations of the governing bodies that had developed this legislation — the Council of the Four Lands ceased to convene in 1764, and the Lithuanian Council in 1765 — and in the wake of the subsequent partitioning-off of formerly Polish and Lithuanian lands to the rulers of Russia, Prussia, and Austria, the status of the Jews began to deteriorate further.

Fortifications in the midst of agricultural land.
M. M. IVANOV

The Vistula grain trade: "God and Corn will repay."
ANON

JEWISH FARMS AND VILLAGES

For centuries the countryside around Eishyshok was dotted with a considerable number of Jewish farms. Some of these farmers lived in Christian villages, but many of them lived in predominantly Jewish villages under the jurisdiction of various nearby shtetlekh: Selo (Dekeshene), Panashishok, and Leipun, which belonged to Olkenik; Dugalishok, which belonged to Radun; and Nacha and Kalesnik, which belonged to Eishyshok.[6]

Having been founded by Jewish families, Dugalishok and Nacha remained almost exclusively Jewish. Dugalishok eventually became something of a Jewish resort, attracting numerous summer vacationers from the neighboring shtetlekh during the 1920s and '30s. The most illustrious of its visitors was the Haffetz Hayyim himself, who brought with him many of the yeshivah students from Radun. Drawn to the countryside by the beautiful pine forest, the excellent agricultural produce, and the warm hospitality of the farmers, the young tourists kept the village abuzz all during the summer months.

The villages of Dugalishok and Nacha stood on land that had been granted to the Asner, Paikowski, and Lipkunski families by a Russian general named Stalewitch. Members of these families were known as excellent farmers and as brave, courageous people. In fact, it was their courage that had won them their special land-

The old water mill in Eishyshok, where peasants and shtetl people milled their grain for centuries. PHOTO: YITZHAK URI KATZ. YESC, RESNIK

Brothers Morris (right) and Yitzhak Asner. Both emigrated from Nacha to America. Morris remained in America; he is the father of actor Ed Asner. Yitzhak returned to Nacha. His entire family perished during the Holocaust, with the exception of one son, Avraham, who survived. Many were killed by the AK. PHOTO: KANSAS CITY, 1910(?). YESC, A. ASNER

owning privileges: Stalewitch had given them a charter to the land in thanks for their having helped save his life during the Polish uprising of 1831.[7] The charter, which was to serve them very well by allowing them to continue to own land long after the time when most of the Jews in the Eishyshok area had had their land taken away, also granted them voting rights in the landowners' assembly under the name Paikowski-Stalewitch, and later exempted them from other anti-Jewish legislation such as the 1882 May Laws (see below).

In addition to the Jewish farmers in the countryside, there were many Jewish villagers and country people working in typically Jewish professions: millers, tavern owners, liquor manufacturers, blacksmiths, locksmiths, tailors. There were also Jewish fishermen, mainly from Doig (Daugai). Until World War I, they came to Eishyshok each week for market day to sell their fish. They were particularly popular with children, because they would give them blown-up fish bladders — the shtetl version of balloons.

ANTI-SEMITIC LEGISLATION IN THE NINETEENTH CENTURY

Russia, whose acquisitions by the end of the eighteenth century included Lithuania and, specifically, all the land around Vilna, including Eishyshok, would prove to be a harsh ruler. Responding to allegations from the gentile peasantry that the Jews were a major source of competition and therefore of poverty in rural areas, the Russian authorities commenced a commercial war against the Jews. Jews who had owned land for centuries found themselves dispossessed, their property distributed to non-Jews as a reward for army service; Jews who for generations had leased Christian farms or worked as estate managers on them were prevented by law from doing so; and various occupations that had been traditional to Jews in the surrounding villages and towns were now off-limits to them.

Not long after the beginning of his reign, Tzar Alexander I passed the 1804 Statute, the first comprehensive law pertaining to the Jews to be enacted in Russia.[8] Though its edict that Jews were to leave the countryside proved impossible to enforce, it established a legislative framework for subsequent expulsions and restrictions against the Jews that were more successful. In the 1820s, for example, Jews were expelled from villages in the Mogilev, Vitebsk, and Grodno provinces, and in 1825 the government took steps to remove all Jews to a 50-verst distance (about 35 miles) from the western frontier in order to prevent smuggling. In 1845 the war against the village Jews escalated as the authorities tried to prevent them from manufacturing or selling liquor in rural areas. The war escalated further with Tzar Alexander III's May Laws of 1882, which stipulated that no new Jewish settlers could move into the villages and hamlets of the Pale (formerly Polish and Lithuanian territory, where the Russian government had allowed Jews to live); no Jews could own or manage real estate or farms outside the cities of the Pale; and all Jews had to refrain from doing business on Sunday and on other Christian holidays.[9]

Most of the ancestral lands belonging to the individual Jews of Eishyshok and to the community in common had already been taken away during the reigns of Alexander I (1801–25) and Nicholas I (1825–55), or in the wake of the 1861 Emancipation of the Serfs, under Alexander II (1855–81). A tzarist decree issued in 1869 had proved particularly devastating to Eishyshkian landowners, depriving them of a substantial part of their holdings. These vast tracts of land now owned by non-Jewish army veterans surrounded the shtetl. The street where some of the settlers built their houses was known to the Jews of Eishyshok as Hazerim Gessl (Pigs Lane) because of the pigs which the new arrivals — unlike their kosher Jewish neighbors — raised for food.

The May Laws of 1882 had their main effect not so much on the Jews within Eishyshok, who had already lost most of their lands, but on those in the surrounding rural areas and small villages under the jurisdiction of Eishyshok. Those who had been farming were now landless; those who had been shopkeepers and artisans now found it almost impossible to make a living. Of course, there were always means of avoiding the laws. Even the man who drafted them, Count Nikolai Pavlovich Ignatiev, was not immune to bribery. While the May Laws awaited the tzar's signature, Ignatiev arranged through his mother to grant twelve-year contract renewals to all his own Jewish land managers in the province of Kiev. Apparently he did not regard the Jews as a menace to his own estates.[10]

What happened among the high and mighty in the upper echelons of the Russian government also took place in little Eishyshok. People with connections to local nobility and money with which to bribe them were often able to remain on the land. A large number, however, had neither connections nor money and thus became uprooted. Some emigrated to America at this time; others moved into Eishyshok, where they overloaded the community's resources and competed with townspeople who were already economically threatened. On market day these new inhabitants did business with Christian and Tatar villagers who preferred buying from their former neighbors. In a place with a hand-to-mouth economy, the loss of even a few customers on market day could have a devastating impact.

Many of the Eishyshkian Jews who lost their land to government decrees never gave up hope of reclaiming it. And while they pursued one futile lawsuit after another through the maze of the tzarist judicial system, exhausting family and community funds along the way, they made sure that their kin did not forget the days when all the land, as far as the eye could see, was theirs. It was important to them that their families should always feel a link to the land. In the 1890s three men from the Yurkanski clan, Arie-Leib the tailor and his two butcher brothers, would gather their sons on Saturday afternoons and walk the fields that once belonged to them, thus affirming the bond between their family and its lost heritage.[11] Shlomo Farber's grandfather Shlomo Sczervak vividly remembered Napoleon staying in the vicinity as he made his way toward Moscow, and Farber's mother, Hanneh-Feige, retained her father's love of the countryside and in her turn tried to pass it on to her

Zirl Yurkanski, the head of the Yurkanski clan in the twentieth century. She was a descendant of the Ben-Asher (Asherowitch) family, one of the founding Jewish families of Eishyshok. Zirl was murdered by the Poles in 1944. PHOTO: YITZHAK URI KATZ. YESC, B. YORK

Members of the Yurkanski family in 1928 (standing right to left): Gutke Kanichowski (née Yurkanski) and husband Haikl; Liebke Kabacznik (née Moszczenik); Yitche-Mendke Yurkanski and wife Miriam (née Kanichowski); (seated) Ida Kaganov (née Kanichowski) and husband Leibke. Leibke Kaganov was murdered in the September 1941 massacre, Gutke Kanichowski was murdered in Ghetto Radun, Ida Kaganov and Liebke Kabacznik were murdered by the AK. The others survived the war, in the forest. PHOTO: YITZHAK URI KATZ. YESC, B. YORK

son. Farber remembers being taken to walk amid the fields around Olkenik at harvesttime, and watching his mother borrow a sickle from one of the young reapers in order to display the skills she had learned as a Jewish farm girl in Meretch (Merkine) many years before.

Later, even such symbolic expeditions would be too dangerous. When Eishyshok was under the rule of the Second Polish Republic, during the years between the two world wars, and Hayya Kabacznik Sonenson could no longer walk on her ancestors' land, she would gather her grandchildren around her at dusk on Saturday afternoon, point to where the setting sun met the forests, and talk of how they were the rightful owners of all the gardens and fields that stretched between them and that blazing red horizon. The tzars had taken the land away from her family, she said, but one day it would be returned to them.

The Poles, of course, proved no more sympathetic to such claims than the Russians had been. When the individual Jewish land claimants and the community of Eishyshok continued to press their still unsettled claims in the Polish courts, renewing their old lawsuits in 1923, they lost almost everything. A mere 37 hectares of community pastureland was awarded to Eishyshok.[12] And even this was only the most hollow of victories. Some of the land was unusable as grazing land, for it was part of the infamous Dumbla blotes, the marshes where cows and horses would often sink when grazing. Moreover, while it was true that the tall grasses that grew there could, at great risk, be cut and used for hay for the shtetl livestock, Alter der Dumbler and his three brothers claimed that these fields actually belonged to them. So the resolution of one set of claims merely led to others, the new arrangement being a source of constant litigation within the community.

Despite the constant legal harassment they faced, some Jews managed to hold on to their land until the bitter end, even at the cost of great

The Sonenson family in 1934 in their orchard, a parcel of land that was not taken away by the tzarist government. Sitting in the center surrounded by their children are Hayya Kabacznik Sonenson and Reb Shael. Hayya was a direct descendant of the Ben-Yossef (Josephowitch) family, who came to Eishyshok from Babylonia in the tenth century. Top row (right to left): Avraham and Ida (née Goide) Sonenson; Israel and Matle (née Sonenson) Shereshefski; Israel Sonenson; Hinda Sonenson Tawlitski. Second row from top (right to left): Moshe and Zipporah (née Katz) Sonenson; Hayya and Reb Shael; Miriam and Shalom Sonenson; on Shalom's lap is nephew Shmuel (Mulke). Third row from top (right to left): Leibke and Geneshe (née Kaganowicz) Sonenson; Shepske Sonenson. Children's row (right to left): Benyamin (Niomke), Gittele, and Yitzhak Sonenson, Leah and Hannkeh Tawlitski. Two spouses and twelve grandchildren are missing from the photo; nine were born between 1935 and 1941. Reb Shael died a natural death in May 1935. During the war, Gittele died from TB while in hiding; the others were murdered in the Baranowicz, Radun, and Eishyshok massacres and by the AK. Matle, Israel, Moshe, Shalom, and Yitzhak survived. PHOTO: ALTE KATZ. YESC, Y. ELIACH

A joint birthday party for cousins Shula and Yaffa Sonenson in May 1941. Most of Hayya Sonenson's grandchildren who resided in Eishyshok were there. To these children, every Saturday at sunset, Hayya would point out that all the land to the horizon was rightfully theirs and had been confiscated by the tzar. Back row (right to left): Hannkeh Tawlitski; Elisha Koppelman; Shalom and Miriam Sonenson, the hosts of the party; Shmuel (Mulke) Sonenson; Hayyim Tawlitski; and Meir Sonenson. Front row (right to left): Shaul Replianski; Yaffa and Yitzhak Sonenson; Sheinke Dwilanski; Benyamin (Niomke), Gittele, and Shula Sonenson; and Leahke Tawlitski. Hanging on the wall are a photo of Miriam's parents and a painting of Jerusalem flanked by marble reliefs of Theodor Herzl and Hayyim Nahman Bialik. Shalom, Yitzhak, and Yaffa survived the war; Elisha Koppelman was murdered by the AK, Gittele died from TB in hiding; Miriam and Shula in the Radun massacre, all the others in the Eishyshok massacre, September 1941. PHOTO: BEN ZION SZREJDER. YESC, Y. ELIACH

hardship. During the interwar years, for example, many families from Eishyshok continued to tend land they owned in what had now become Lithuania, whose border was about nine miles away. They were given special permission, during the planting and harvest seasons, to cross the border and work their land, providing that by 5 P.M. each day they reported back to the Polish municipal officer in Eishyshok.

The links between the Jews of Eishyshok and the land around them could not be broken, so long as there were Jews alive to recall those links. The history was too venerable, the hold of the land upon them too strong. Through all the many centuries of Jewish habitation, regardless of the varying difficulties posed by the successive regimes to which they were subject, the Jews in this area continued to own farmland. Some, like the Yurkanski family, purchased it illegally — in many cases it was land that had once been their own, before one or another confiscation — from the local peasantry. Others owned land within the shtetl proper, even if it was just a patch of earth behind the house where vegetables could be grown for the family larder. The Jews of Eishyshok may have looked to commerce and ar-

Seated on a wagon loaded with hay in the late 1930s are (right to left) Miriam Koppelman Rushkin, an unidentified visitor, Shepske Sonenson, Malka Nochomowicz, and baby Elisha Rushkin. Miriam died a natural death; all the others but Elisha were murdered in the September 1941 massacre. PHOTO: BEN ZION SZREJDER. YESC, RESNIK

Moshe Sonenson in the summer of 1939, after a day laboring in the fields of Jaszka Aliszkewicz, once Sonenson family property; with Moshe are wife Zipporah and children Yitzhak and Yaffa. Zipporah was murdered by the AK; Moshe and the children survived. PHOTO: BEN ZION SZREJDER. YESC, Y. SONENSON

Yehiel Blacharowicz with Dobke (Dvorah) Deutch (right) and a friend on the Radunski family's farm, August 11, 1937. All three were murdered in the Eishyshok massacre, September 1941. YESC, RADUNSKI

tisanship for their daily sustenance, and to the world-renowned yeshivah in their midst for a sense of community pride and identity, but the feeling of being connected to the land was also and always a major part of who they were.

LAND MANAGERS

There was a longstanding Eastern European tradition of Jews managing the estates belonging to local magnates, predominantly members of the Polish and Lithuanian nobility, but also some Russian aristocrats. While the nobleman and his family spent their time in various fashionable European capitals, returning home only for the occasional holiday or hunting spree, the Jewish manager supervised every aspect of the estate. He managed the farmlands, forest, livestock, and household and was also responsible for the marketing of all that the estate produced. In fact, the Jews played such an important role in the economy of the countryside that even anti-Semitism had to give way.

In the fifteenth century, for example, King Casimir IV (1427–1492) of Poland and Lithuania came under church pressure to deny the Jews their economic privileges. In 1454 John of Capistrano, a church official known for his intense dislike of the Jews, coerced King Casimir into signing the Statute of Nieszawa, which nullified the rights of the Jews since "they are contrary to Divine Law and the Law of the Land." The king quickly disregarded his own statute, however, because of the detrimental effect it had on the country's economy. Once more he allowed the Jews to lease and manage land, and also to trade freely and to collect tolls at the frontiers and city gates (another traditional source of income for the Jews).[13]

The terms and conditions of the land-management agreements, which were specified in private arrangements made between the Jewish manager and the Christian landholder, were partially under the supervision of the kahal. But the kahal was often superseded by the nobility's own body of custom and law, leaving the estate manager very much at the mercy of his powerful employer. The life and death of Avigdor, a Jew from Eishyshok who managed the estate of Count (Graf) Potocki in the early years of the nineteenth century, well illustrates the precarious state of those in his position.

AVIGDOR THE MARTYR

Under the supervision of Avigdor, the estate of Count Potocki flourished. Its wheat and rye were known for their high quality and were in great demand by grain dealers. One day two Jewish dealers from Vilna, eager to purchase the Potocki grain, made a substantial offer to Avigdor. He declined to sell to them, however, as he had a long history of good trade relations with other grain dealers, also Jews from Vilna.

Undeterred, the two returned to the Potocki estate and renewed their offer several times, even offering Avigdor a handsome bribe for the grain contract. But Avigdor continued to turn them down, for he felt that the longstanding arrangement he had with the other dealers was in the best interest of Count Potocki. To avenge their disappointment, the two grain dealers returned to the estate once again, this time under cover of night, and poisoned Potocki's favorite watchdogs. Count Potocki arrested the night watchman and several farmhands (parobkis) who had been on duty when the poisoning occurred, and had them interrogated in the estate prison. There they recounted overhearing several heated debates between Avigdor and the two visiting grain dealers, whom they suspected of the crime.

Avigdor was then arrested and interrogated, and told that if he would not confess to the crime himself or reveal the identity of the other suspects, ten shtetl notables, including the rabbi himself, would be arrested, and each day one of them would be hanged in public, between two pigs, except for the rabbi, who would be tortured to death.

For a number of days Avigdor was held in solitary confinement, where he continued to proclaim his innocence and his loyalty to Potocki, to refuse to reveal the names of his fellow Jews, despite their crimes, and to make fervent pleas on behalf of the rabbi and the other members of the kahal whom Potocki had arrested. The count's own wife (the Grafina) and his son Adam also proclaimed Avigdor's innocence and begged Potocki to free him as well as all the unjustly arrested Jews from the shtetl. The estate priest, however, convinced the count to continue the "investigation." When all other means proved unsuccessful at eliciting a confession from Avigdor, or the names of the two suspected Vilna Jews, Count Potocki ordered the public torture of his former estate manager to begin.

Avigdor was conveyed to the main courtyard of the estate, stripped naked, and burned over every inch of his body with hot iron frying pans.[14] Through all the days of his ordeal, Avigdor chanted psalms and continued to proclaim his innocence. Finally, on the eighth day, when he thought his end was near, he recited the Vidduy Gadol (the confession of the dying), pronounced the words of the Shema Israel, and collapsed.

Avigdor's scorched body was wrapped in white linen, placed in his two-horse carriage, and returned to Eishyshok by Count Potocki's servants.

For six months his soul clung to his burned body. The people of the shtetl did all they could to save his life. Prayers were recited in his behalf day and night at the Old Beth Midrash. Doctors were brought in from Vilna, and medicine men, both Jewish and Tatar, from the entire region, but to no avail. After months of suffering, his body gave up the struggle. His funeral procession was led by the rabbi and the other kahal members (who had since been freed), and thousands of people from all over the area came to pay their last respects to the martyred Avigdor.

After his death, Avigdor's widow was sure that her husband came back every Friday, Saturday, and holiday to sit at his desk and study the holy books, as was his custom when he was among the living. She could even see the pages turn and hear the sad, melodious sound of his chanting.

Eventually Count Potocki learned the truth and Avigdor's innocence was completely vindicated. To atone, the count brought money and gifts to the grieving widow, but she refused to accept them. For many years after, the count and his wife donated firewood to heat the Old Beth Midrash, in honor of Avigdor who had prayed there so faithfully. Potocki also issued a permanent exemption from military service to all of Avigdor's relatives and descendants, who now went by the name of Pachianko, "the burned one," to commemorate Avigdor.[15]

LEASEHOLDERS (ARENDATORS)

While some Jews like Avigdor Pachianko were employed as estate managers by absentee Christian landowners, others leased such estates for a fee (arenda). In return, they managed the activities of the estate and received an income from it. This practice, which began sometime in the sixteenth century, became so prevalent in this area of Eastern Europe that the census for 1765–91 used the term *arendator* interchangeably with *Jew*, describing a village as having "no leaseholders," when in fact it meant "no Jews."[16] Unlike the arrangements between landowners and their estate managers, all dealings between the land magnate and the arendator were subject to the governance of the local kahal, under legal guidelines established by the Lithuanian Council. During the years of the Polish–Lithuanian state, an entire body of law devolved to govern relations between the Jews who leased land in the countryside and the Polish and Russian magnates who owned it. Its rulings were honored by both the Jews and the landowners. The term of lease and the fee were set in advance and remained the same, regardless of the success or failure of the crops, the health of the livestock, or any of the numerous natural or man-made disasters that might ensue.

The arenda was a major source of income not just for many Jewish families in the area who earned their living on the estates, but for their communities as well, thanks to the tax revenues it yielded. Because it was so lucrative, the lease was the subject of fierce competition among the arendators themselves, and a frequent occasion for brutal treatment of the arendators by the Christian magnates.[17]

Both the importance of the arenda and the trouble it caused can be inferred from the complexity of the Council's legislation, which attempted to deal with every conceivable legal, economic, and social implication of the arrangement, and from the frequency with which such legislation was revised. The Council specified that each community was to record all transactions relating to the arenda in two separate pinkasim (record books), one original and one copy, and to keep both in a secret place known only to the head of the local kahal. Each community was given the authority to interpret the arenda decisions of the Council according to local circumstances, which meant that on occasion the kahal could overrule the Council.[18]

Moreover, the only Jews eligible for the arenda were Lithuanian Jews; no outsiders could lease property in Lithuania. Once an arendator had held a lease for three years, he had the right to keep renewing it (the right of possession, or hazaka) for the rest of his life; this right was not, however, inherited by his children. After his death they could keep the arenda only until it expired, when it would again be placed on the open market — unless they lived in an area where no community had jurisdiction over the arenda, in which case they could inherit the hazaka.[19]

Other regulations specified that a Jewish arendator could employ only as many non-Jewish female domestics as were needed; and if a Jewish arendator failed to fulfill his contractual obligations and the lease was then given to a non-Jew, no other Jew could subsequently lease that property unless given permission by the kahal.[20] And so forth and so on.

LEASEHOLDING NEAR EISHYSHOK

Under the community jurisdiction of the Eishyshok kahal were a significant number of arendators who leased estates, forests, mills, ponds, and rivers, and continued to do so, relatively unimpeded by the legal restrictions against Jewish arendators that prevailed in other areas of Eastern Europe, until well into the twentieth century. The Gruznik family, for example, leased a mill. Five miles from Eishyshok, in Paradin, a Jewish family who became known as di kezalakh (the cheese people) leased a dairy farm. And Hayyim Dovid Shapira, a tall, handsome man, leased a huge estate on which he raised his thirteen daughters. Its stables were filled with horses, its barns with cattle, the land was fertile, and Hayyim Dovid himself was very much the gentleman, riding in a carriage driven by three horses in the style of the Polish nobility (a special dispensation, since Jews were ordinarily forbidden to harness more than one horse to a carriage). But eventually he met his downfall, in a manner typical of many leaseholders. Natural disasters ruined his crops, and then the old magnate died, to be succeeded by a son who gambled away the estate. Afterward the two eldest Shapira daughters opened a store in the shtetl.[21]

One of the most prominent arendators in the vicinity was a Pole who had worked for a Jewish arendator in his youth and converted to Judaism — hence his name, Moshe Polak. An affluent businessman who owned much land in Lida, Moshe Polak also leased a large estate in Arodnoy, about nine miles from Eishyshok. On the estate were huge fields of grain, stables of racehorses, herds of cattle, many hectares of forest land, and a magnificent wooden palace to which the Polish nobleman who owned the estate returned only during the summer months.

Moshe Polak's beautiful, spacious home served as a gathering place for the other Jewish arendators in the vicinity, a place of worship, a makeshift heder, and even, after the Big Fire of 1895, a temporary residence for many Eishyshkians who had been made homeless.[22] After Moshe Polak died, his son Meir Yankel and Meir's wife Golde Roche continued to lease the estate, and to maintain the traditions of hospitality and charity for which Meir's father had been known. It was quite common, for example, for them to feed as many as twenty beggars each day. During the summers of 1910–13, Moshe Kaganowicz, their grandson and Moshe Polak's namesake, lived on the estate at Arodnoy with them. He remembers learning much about the grain trade and forestry there that he would later put to work in his businesses in Eishyshok and Vilna, and eventually in Jerusalem.

Reb Arieh-Leib "der Rubishker" (from Rubishok) Kudlanski supplied milk to a number of Eishyshok residents. Every Saturday morning, in his prayer shawl, he used to walk to the shtetl's Old Beth Midrash. When he passed by, Christian and Muslim farmers removed their hats in his honor. All of his children emigrated to America; he visited them but returned to his beloved shtetl. He did not like a country "where people love more the people who walk on the walls [actors in the movies] than real people who walk on the fields and streets." He was in his eighties when the Germans cut his beard and then murdered him in the September 1941 massacre. YESC, A. ZIMMERMAN

THE YISHUVNIKS

Though there were some learned individuals among the various Jews who lived in the countryside, and many of the estate managers and arendators were very prosperous and therefore likely to have acquired some refinement, in general the country Jews were considered to be coarser and less educated than the shtetl Jews and were known as *yishuvniks* — a word that might best be translated as "hicks." Their speech, with its rolling *r*'s, their peasantlike dress and mannerisms, and their sturdy, healthy physiques made them instantly identifiable, and a source of amusement to the shtetl-dwellers, who considered themselves more sophisticated than their country cousins.

They did, however, intermingle frequently, on certain holidays and on other occasions as well. For example, the yishuvniks were required by the kahal of Eishyshok to spend Passover in the shtetl, so that the community could supervise their preparations and thereby ensure that all the dietary and other Passover restrictions were properly observed. An area of the synagogue was set aside for the yishuvniks' communal Seders, which were held on both the first and second nights of the holiday.

The yishuvniks also intermarried with people from the shtetl, and, after the passage of the May Laws and various other crackdowns on the rights of Jews in the Pale, they came to live there too, bringing with them in the form of their family names the names of the villages where they were born: the Matikanski family from Matikan, Kiuchefski from Kitchie, Bastunski from Bastun, Dumblianski from Dumbla, and so forth. Sometimes the names were in the form of nicknames, which actually superseded family names in daily usage. Thus nobody thought of Reb Dovid der Kichier (from Kitchie) as Dovid Moszczenik.

The country people were a breath of fresh air in Eishyshok — men and women who had grown up among wheatfields, rivers, and pine forests. Their healthy constitutions and physical strength were an asset to the community in good times; their intimate knowledge of the surrounding countryside a veritable lifesaver during the Holocaust, when it helped those who had been able to escape the massacres in Eishyshok and Radun to survive in the forest.

Reb Dovid "der Kichier" Moszczenik and his wife Leah, working in their garden in back of their home, July 25, 1932. Reb Dovid died a natural death, Leah was murdered in the September 1941 massacre. PHOTO: BEN ZION SZREJDER. YESC, A. ZIMMERMAN

Yudaleh Kabacznik in the flower garden of Hayya Sonenson, July 16, 1939. Yudaleh was murdered by the AK in February 1944. PHOTO: BEN ZION SZREJDER. YESC, A. ZIMMERMAN

AGRICULTURE WITHIN THE SHTETL

The Jews of Eishyshok were avid gardeners, cultivating small orchards and growing whatever vegetables they could on the land behind their own homes or on small plots of land they leased nearby. In the orchards they grew apples, pears, cherries, and a variety of berries; in their vegetable gardens they grew cucumbers, radishes, squash, pumpkins, red beets, cabbage, peas, beans, kohlrabi, tomatoes, onions, garlic, carrots, dill, and even tobacco. Potatoes were also grown, mainly on leased land outside the shtetl proper. Families lavished great care on their gardens and orchards, since they were a major source of food — fresh during the summer, pickled and preserved during the winter. Often Eishyshkians even slept in small huts in their gardens during the summer months, to protect them from the thieves who came at night.

In the two or three days before Rosh Hashanah, it was common for young men to accompany their mothers and sisters to the village farm where the potatoes were grown so that they could assist in digging them up, then transporting them back to the family cellar for storage, but during the rest of the year most gardening was considered women's work. Young Rina Lewinson was typical of the hardworking women and girls of the shtetl. Not only did she work in her mother's store and become an accomplished seamstress by the age of ten, she was responsible for the family vegetable garden as well as the family potato patch. She even sold the surplus produce in the village of Rubishok.

No one, however, was a more dedicated gardener than Reb Zvi Hersh Moszczenik, one of the few men who performed this kind of work in Eishyshok. Known popularly as "Reb Hersh the Garden Preacher" — a nickname that delighted him as much as his fabulous vegetables did — he used to talk to his vegetables every day, believing that it enhanced their growth.[23]

Though vegetable gardens were common, flower gardens were very rare. People might grow sunflowers and poppies for their seeds, but except for Hayya Sonenson and the Tzimbalist family, Jews in Eishyshok did not grow flowers.

Cows returning at dusk from pasture to the streets of Warinowa, a shtetl near Eishyshok. YESC, MOSHE KAPLAN

Leah Moszczenik on her way to the barn to milk the family cow in the mid-1930s. PHOTO: BEN ZION SZREJDER. YESC, A. ZIMMERMAN

In fact, until after World War I, growing flowers was considered "un-Jewish," in the same way that owning a dog was.

One family who briefly deviated from the general pattern soon reverted to tradition — to the distress of their children, as Meir Wilkanski recounted in his memoir. Sometime in the 1880s the Wilkanski children planted the seeds of sweetpeas and other flowers that had been sent to them by a relative in the countryside. The flower garden in their front yard was very successful. All the seeds blossomed, and sweetpea vines climbed the house, covering it with a dazzling array of flowers which delighted the children. Their parents, too, were proud, until the day Reb Layzer overheard a Jewish beggar standing before his house debating in a loud monologue whether to enter it and ask for alms. Deciding on the basis of its flowers that it must be the house of a gentile, he passed it by. Reb Layzer promptly went out to the garden and uprooted all his children's beautiful flowers, whereupon the children, fighting back their tears, vowed to have a beautiful flower garden as soon as the family emigrated to the Land of Israel, where, they felt sure, it would be proper for a Jew to grow flowers.[24]

Flowers may not have been welcome in the shtetl, but cows and other livestock were. Cows in fact were a status symbol, marking their owners as affluent. Owning only a goat placed one a few notches below cattle owners on the social scale, and owning chickens counted for nothing, since everyone owned them.

Those fortunate enough to own cattle grazed them on the vigan, the common pastureland, paying the kahal a per-head fee that covered not only the use of the land but the wages of a shepherd. Every morning from May to November the shepherd's horn could be heard at dawn, calling the cows and goats. All around the shtetl, barn doors would open and the animals would emerge to walk themselves down to the market square, there to meet their shepherd, who would lead them to the vigan. At dusk the shepherd blew a pipe (the horn was only for morning), and soon a cloud of dust and the smell of cow manure would herald the return of the herd. The women and girls would then lead them home for the evening milking. The goats were sometimes a problem, however. Before the Big Fire, when

Ted (right) and brother Leo Simons (Tuviah and Layzer Shimonowitch) with their beloved cow in front of their home in Nacha. Ted was so attached to the cow that when the family emigrated to America in 1914, he attempted to have it board the boat. YESC, TED SIMONS

Professor Yitzhak Wilkanski, the pioneer scholar of scientific agriculture in Israel, in 1912 at Ben-Shemen, where he started his agricultural projects. With him on his horse is daughter Zafrira; standing next to them is his wife Sarah. YESC, WILKANSKI

the houses were small and had thatched roofs, the goats were likely to leap onto the roofs to continue their grazing, and would have to be chased down and led home by horns and beards.[25]

To the best of people's recollections, all the shepherds, almost until the end of the shtetl, were Jewish and had been approved by the kahal. The last Jewish shepherd was Naftolke, the son of Hashe Golde. His beautiful melodies were succeeded in the final years by those of Shavelis, a Lithuanian lad, who called the cows to pasture with a bark pipe, and new, unknown melodies.

EMIGRANT FARMERS

Even after they emigrated, many Eishyshkians maintained their ties with the soil. Shaul Kaleko (known as Shaul Barkali in Israel) wrote his dissertation at the University of Berlin on the agrarian state of Lithuania. Among the hundreds who emigrated to Palestine between 1902 and 1939, a significant number turned to agriculture, including some who would make a lasting contribution to the productivity of their new land. The brothers Wilkanski, who had longed for their own flower garden, were among them, particularly Yitzhak Wilkanski (1880–1955), known in Israel as Yitzhak Elazari-Volcani. An agronomist by profession, he was the father of scientific agriculture in Israel, operating out of an experimental station that he founded and managed until 1951. The Institute of Agricultural Studies of the Hebrew University in Rehovot, which he helped to found, was later renamed the Volcani Institute in his honor. His contribution was so great that he was among the candidates considered for the presidency of Israel in the 1950s. The youngest of the Wilkanski brothers, Dr. Mordekhai Elazari-Volcani Wilkanski, was also a pioneer in scientific agriculture, and introduced many new plants to Palestine. In fact, he died, in 1935 at age forty-four, of blood poisoning incurred from a boil he developed on his neck while working in the field that was his laboratory for experiments with cultivating a nicotine-free tobacco.

Meir Wilkanski, the Eishyshok chronicler, began his years in Palestine as an agricultural worker, enduring the hardships of manual labor for four years, before becoming secretary of the Palestine Office (responsible for surveying and acquiring new land) under Dr. Arthur Rupin. Eventually Meir became head of the Palestine Land Development Company, where he worked from 1918 until his retirement in 1942. He spent his retirement years on a farm in Kfar Vitkin growing flowers and vegetables — a passion of his ever since his childhood in Eishyshok.

Shaul Schneider, another native Eishyshkian, who had a degree in agriculture from the University of Grenoble in France, became an expert on growing citrus fruit in Israel, a project on which he and his townsman Mordekhai Wilkanski collaborated.[26]

Many emigrants to the United States, Canada, and South America became farmers as well. In the 1880s a few Eishyshkians along with a small group of villagers who were still yearning for their land after being displaced by the 1882 May Laws settled in Argentina with the assistance of the Jewish Colonization Association.[27] In the 1940s, the Kabacznik brothers, Meir and Shepske, who were among the shtetl's few survivors of the Holocaust, bought huge ranches in Brazil. Their cousin Moshe Sonenson eventually became a farmer in Israel. Over a century after their land in Eishyshok was taken away by the tzarist government, the Kabacznik family once again owned land.

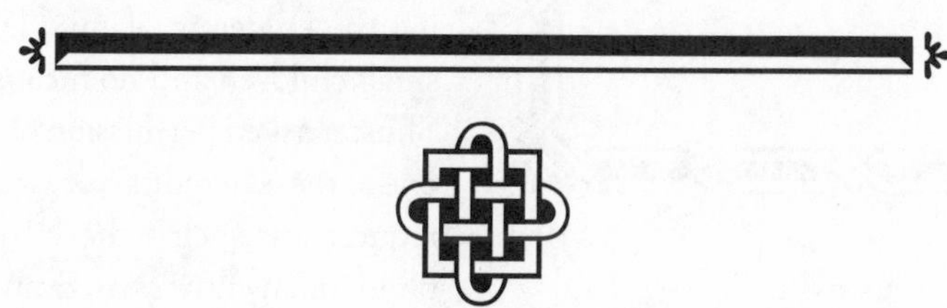

FOR HUNDREDS OF YEARS IT WAS THE MERCHANT CLASS THAT CONTROLLED THE shtetl. Their preeminence was not just a matter of custom and tradition, but of law as well — as dictated by the Lithuanian Council and the kahal. The worldwide depression of the 1920s and '30s brought economic changes that impoverished many of the balebatim and threatened their status, but even these changes did not put an end to it, for it was too deeply rooted. Since those who sat on the kahal were among the most powerful balebatim in the shtetl, they saw to it that the rights of their class were well protected — insofar as local governance could offer any protection against the rapacious policies of the Polish Republic.

· 11 · COMMERCE

A WOMAN OF VALOR WHO CAN FIND? . . . HER HUSBAND DEPENDS ON HER, AND HE HAS NO LACK OF GAIN. SHE BRINGS HIM GOOD AND NOT EVIL ALL THE DAYS OF HER LIFE. SHE SEEKS OUT WOOL AND FLAX, HER HANDS MOVE GLADLY AT THEIR LABOR. . . . SHE RISES WHILE IT IS STILL NIGHT, APPORTIONING FOOD TO HER HOUSEHOLD, AND DUTIES TO HER MAIDENS.

Proverbs 31:10–15

SHOPKEEPERS

One means of exercising control over commerce was by putting a limit on the number of shops that could occupy the choicest locations, and deciding who their proprietors would be. Thus the same families owned or maintained the right to lease the best stores in the best locations for generations, and the number of such stores was kept constant for centuries, making the leasing of a store by a member of the artisan class, or a gentile or a newcomer, a virtual impossibility.[1]

One woman who tried to rent in the prime district discovered just how rigid the rules were. When her husband Yossef died of typhus during the epidemic of 1918, leaving her with six small children and no means of support, Hodl Shuster asked permission of the kahal to obtain one of these hereditary leases. The denial of that request was such a shock to her that she went blind for an entire year. Eventually she opened a store on a side street and, with the assistance of her oldest daughter, Basha, who was forced to quit school at age nine, was able to eke out a meager living. The Shuster children never forgave the community for the family's hardships. The two surviving sons became ardent Communists — David a Trotskyite and Hayyim a Stalinist. And during the Soviet occupation of Eishyshok in 1940–41, Hayyim and two other comrades, Ruvke Boyarski and Luba Ginunski, would rule the town with an iron hand, making the merchants and the clergy their primary targets of abuse.

Hayya-Sarah Shuster (right), her sister Basha, and a friend, Ruth Matikanski Rubin. Hayya-Sarah perished in Treblinka, Basha survived the war by hiding in the forest, and Ruth emigrated to the U.S.
YESC, LANDSMAN

The old Rad Kromen, or row shops, one long building in the center of the market square, which housed back-to-back stores, the major shtetl shops. It was the ideal location for business. The old row shops burned down in the mid-1930s and were replaced with new ones.
PHOTO: YITZHAK URI KATZ. YESC, RESNIK

In Eishyshok the best locations were in the houses around the market square, each of which had one or more stores within, or in the double row of back-to-back shops — the Rad Kromen, or row shops — that occupied one long building in the center of the market. (This was where Hodl Shuster had hoped to do business.) Though the number of stores and their locations remained fixed by law, their appearance changed often: the many fires that swept through the shtetl meant that they were constantly being rebuilt. One description of them, which appeared in the Hebrew-language newspaper *Ha-Shahar* in 1878, was penned by Israel Isser Goldbloom, who had been expelled from the Eishyshok yeshivah for his Haskalah views — which perhaps explains the vivid dyspepsia that colored his writings about the shtetl for many years:

In the center of the market, green with age, are the 30 stores. The town wisemen believe that at night satyrs dance there in riotous merriment. The stores are small in size, like chicken coops. The entrance is on the side and a person can enter only with great difficulty. The revenue is meager and most of it is earned on the Thursday, market day. There is constant fighting among the old women, the noise and cursing as bad as on Yatkeve Street in Vilna. Their bread and cakes are black as raven's wings, and are purchased only when sickness prevents people from baking for their own needs.

One thing the writer got right was the dominance of women in the stores and on market day. Until World War I, when the rising tide of secularism emptied the beth midrash of many of the younger men in the community, freeing them to work beside (or on occasion replace) their wives and daughters, it was women who ran most of the stores. They were not just old crones like the ones described above, but women of all ages — and all temperaments too. Take the lovely widow Malke Roche's Schneider, descendant of one of Eishyshok's oldest families. Her generous nature, incredible industriousness, and apparently considerable personal charms (as well as her amply provisioned store, which was in the row shops), were described in loving detail in the memoirs of her daughter Mina's husband, Mordekhai Munesh Kaleko:

My mother-in-law, may she rest in peace, was a young, beautiful woman, real gorgeous, a divorcee. Though she wore a filthy apron, stained with kerosene, pitch tar, and lubricant grease that smelled from a distance, it did not detract from her beauty. She owned a store that appeared small from the outside, but was well stocked. There were sacks of flour, a few pud sugar, raisins, barrels of herring, kerosene, pitch tar, lubricant grease. There was plenty of everything, and she bought all for cash, for she did not suffer from lack of business, but was popular with Jews and Christians alike.

Her stock also included tailoring and shoemaking supplies like spools of thread, cobbler's lacing from pig bristles, awls, wooden nails, horse shoes, wax, and black polish. She sold clothing and drugstore items too — babushkas, ribbons, socks which she herself knitted, zizit, castor oil, epsom salts, a homemade ointment she concocted as a remedy against mange in cattle, snuff tobacco, bark snuff boxes, nine kinds of spices, coffee, cinnamon, salt, pepper . . .

In addition to being an attractive lady, my mother-in-law was religious. She always kept her hair covered with a tzipeck, trimmed with lace and tied with two white ties — a true kosher Jewish woman! Everyone loved her. Some of her Christian customers called her by the endearing name of Michalowitchka. She used to give them cigarettes which she herself rolled, and candies for their children.

She got up every weekday at three to open her store for her early-bird customers, the Jews who prayed at the vatikin [the dawn quorum]. They would stop at her store on the way to the beth midrash to purchase a candle, a pinch of snuff, cigarettes. She also closed later than all the other shopkeepers.

All week she looked filthy, but came the Sabbath and the holidays, and she dressed up in her shaitl [wig] and the beautiful black dress she made for her wedding, on top of which she wore a short velvet coat. Then the weekday shopkeeper looked like a princess.[2]

Malke Roche's Schneider, one of the shtetl's most respected store owners, with her grandson Simha Kaleko. YESC, SCHNEIDER

A Saturday night party at the home of Dina Weidenberg, one of the shtetl's most prosperous shopkeepers: (right to left) David Leib Levin; Miriam Kabacznik; her brother Shepske (in the back); Dina Weidenberg; Yehiel Blacharowicz; Kreinele Kanichowski; Dov Wolotzki; Frumele Abelov, also a successful shopkeeper; an unidentified visitor; and Sarah Lejbowicz, sister of photographer Rephael. David Leib survived the war in the forest, Miriam and Shepske in hiding, and Dov at Dachau. Kreinele was killed by members of the AK, including Pietka Barteszewicz, the caretaker of the Polish school where Kreinele once studied. All the others were killed in the September 1941 massacre. PHOTO: REPHAEL LEJBOWICZ. YESC, M. KABACZNIK

Like Hodl Shuster, those who could not rent around market square or in one of the thirty row shops opened stores on the side streets and alleys leading away from the market, where virtually every house ran some kind of commercial enterprise, no matter how small. Many of them were very small indeed, their proprietors possessed of no more than 10 or 20 zlotys of capital — enough for perhaps half a dozen herring or so — and even that borrowed.[3] During the hard times caused by the Polish government's anti-Jewish economic policies, these smaller stores would prove particularly vulnerable.

The Compulsory Sunday Rest Law was enforced in Eishyshok beginning in January 1921, when Vilna and the surrounding vicinity first came under Polish rule. This set the stage for the government's attempt to solve its economic problems by forcing Jews out of traditionally Jewish occupations so that Poles could take their places. Sunday had always been the second most profitable day in the shtetl, since many Christians shopped at the Jewish stores after church services. Closing on Sundays, as well as on the Jewish Sabbath, which began at sundown on Friday, and on all the Jewish holidays, as many shopkeepers continued to do, meant that Jewish stores were closed 134 days of the year, while Christians closed down on only 62 days.[4] Occasionally merchants attempted to outmaneuver the Sunday Rest Law — for example, Yossl Weidenberg built a discreet side entrance to his textile shop which came to be known in the shtetl as the "Sunday Door" — but, as in Yossl's case, the bribes they had to pay the Polish officials to overlook the violation ate up most of the additional income.

Margolia Saposnikow, granddaughter of Nehemia der Feldsher, at the entrance of a store at a summer dacha near Vilna that sold sweets, soda, and ice cream, August 6, 1932. Margolia's fate during the Holocaust is unknown. PHOTO: ROSALIND FOSTER ROSENBLATT. YESC, R. ROSENBLATT

The taxes paid by the small shopkeepers were particularly high, the licensing requirements complex and burdensome, the fines and bribes extorted from them by minor Polish officialdom outrageous. On top of all their other troubles, their extremely limited capital meant they were unable to buy in quantity and therefore unable to price their goods competitively enough to hold on to their customers, even the Jewish ones.

In Eishyshok the small shopkeepers who suffered the most from the anti-Jewish economic policies of the 1920s and '30s were the grocers. Since the grocery business was the most important branch of trade within the shtetl, providing an income for a large segment of the population, the radical decline in the number of Jewish food stores — from fifty-one in 1925 to thirty-one in 1935 — led to the impoverishment of many struggling families.[5]

Though some of the Jewish representatives to the Polish parliament fought hard to safeguard the ever-diminishing economic rights of their people, Yitzhak Gruenbaum and Heshl Farbshtein being among the most ardent fighters,[6] it was a losing battle. Many shopkeepers, even those whose families had leased stores in the Rad Kromen for centuries, gave up the struggle and emigrated, yielding the hazaka that had been passed from one generation to another to newcomers. Such was the fate of the store owned by Malke Roche's Schneider. When she died in 1925, her son, Velvel Schneider, emigrated to Palestine, taking with him his entire family.

In 1936, after yet another of the shtetl's numerous fires, the stores in the Rad Kromen were rebuilt again, this time in a modern structure that the young people of the shtetl liked to refer to as the Halles, after the fashionable new market in Vilna, which was named for the market in Paris. The customary thirty stores had now been increased to thirty-five, the additional stores being reserved for Christians only — just one more step in the inexorable process of Polonization.

The anti-Jewish policies were working. More and more stores were taken over by non-Jews. The number of Jewish merchants, which had been in constant decline since the middle of the nineteenth century, reached its lowest point during the years of the Second Polish Republic and the Soviet occupation of 1941.

MERCHANTS AND MIDDLEMEN

Shopkeepers were not the only people in the shtetl who earned their living in business (handl). There were merchants and middlemen of all kinds — livestock traders, fur traders, foresters, owners of restaurants, inns, and taverns who sold alcoholic beverages, tobacconists, flax seed processors and sellers, middlemen who traded in goods produced on land that might once have belonged to them, roving merchants who made their rounds from village to village, buying whatever was in season or for sale at a good price at the local market.

The bulk of business reflected the regional resources: agriculture, livestock, and the yield of the rivers, lakes, and forests. The grain trade provided a livelihood for a number of families, both those who exported the local grain (mainly wheat), and those who imported wheat and flour from the Ukraine. Locally produced sugar, made from white beets, was also sold, while the finer-grained sugar, made from cane, was imported, as was salt, both of them considered luxuries.

Trading in horses, pigs, and cattle was one of the largest branches of commerce in Eishyshok, as it had been since the days when the shtetl was host to the gigantic biannual Horse Fair. Though the end of the Horse Fair in 1860 when trains took over meant that horse trading in the shtetl was done on a much smaller scale thereafter, it did continue until well into the twentieth century. One of the last of the big traders was Mendl Kabacznik. When the railroad bypassed Eishyshok (the nearest station being about thirteen miles away, at Bastun), he moved his business to Vilna, which was on the railway line, and also became a food supplier, catering to a select clientele. His horses populated the personal stables of the tzar, it was his fodder transported in railway cars bearing his name on which they feasted, and geese from his sources that were served at the tzar's table. So close was his relationship to the tzar's household that he was arrested as a Russian supporter and spy after the establishment of the Second Polish Republic. He was freed only because of the personal intervention of Lucjan Zelikowski, a general in the Polish army who had liberated Vilna from the Germans in 1920, and of Marshal Jozef Pilsudski himself, who was born in the Eishyshok region and had known Kabacznik since his earliest days.

The forest was one of the richest natural resources in the region, providing pleasures and treasures through all four seasons. Its beauty attracted many vacationers from nearby shtetlekh

Avraham Sonenson (right) and his brother-in-law Israel Shereshefski, returning to Eishyshok from a business trip. Israel survived the war in Siberia; Avraham was murdered by the AK in February 1944. YESC, Y. SONENSON

Young Moshe Sonenson during one of his business trips, visiting his girlfriend and future wife Zipporah Katz (right) in Lida, where she was studying photography with Glauberman. On the left is Zipporah's sister Esther (Etele). Esther emigrated to Colombia; Moshe survived in hiding. Zipporah was murdered by the AK October 20, 1944. YESC, RESNIK

who stayed in their dachas (summer villas) or in bungalow colonies, and sent their children to one of the neighboring summer camps. Its earth yielded an abundance of mushrooms, nuts, and wild strawberries and blueberries that could be sold in local shtetl markets as well as in larger city markets. And the animals to which the forest was home, among them fox, raccoon, mink, and beaver, were the source of a flourishing fur trade.

Moshe Sonenson was one of the shtetl's youngest, most energetic fur traders. To the great disappointment of his parents, he had quit the prestigious Epstein Hebrew gymnasium in Vilna in order to join his older brother Israel in the business. During a brief stint on the road (1926–28), he made regular stops in Navaredok, Lachowice, Anozewicz, Kleck, Neshwis, Garadie, Slonim, Pinsk, Wishnowitz, and various regions of the Ukraine in order to buy furs, then shipped them to his American buyers. Since life on the fur route was not conducive to domestic happiness, however, Moshe returned to Eishyshok prior to his marriage. There he diversified his trade, expanding into honey, flax, and flaxseed, and later reopening one of the old family tanneries.

Logging was another well-developed source of income from the forest. Because restrictions against Jewish ownership of forest land were not nearly so strictly enforced as those that pertained to agriculture, many families continued to make a good living from the forest for years

Forest merchants and their workers shipping their rafts of logs, with their personal insignia, downriver to various locations. CENTRAL ARCHIVES FOR THE HISTORY OF THE JEWISH PEOPLE, JERUSALEM, FILE LI\3

Eliyahu Bastunski, daughter Batia, and wife Ettl. Eliyahu was a successful forest merchant and an active member of the kahal. Financial support from his sons in America and a grocery store sustained him during the economic crisis in the 1930s. Batia joined two of her brothers in America; Eliyahu and Ettl were murdered in the September 1941 massacre. YESC, BASTUNSKI-BASTON

after most of the Jews had been dispossessed of their farms. Each forest merchant shipped raftloads of lumber marked with his personal insignia downriver to various sawmills (some of them quite a distance away), where it would be cut either for construction materials or for firewood, the only heating fuel.

During the 1890s, however, the tzarist government began to regulate logging in the Eishyshok district, stipulating that only one-fourth to one-third of a forest could be logged. Though this did immediate damage to the shtetl's economy,[7] the misfortunes of the forest merchants did not peak until the 1920s and '30s, when the Poles issued additional restrictions on logging, especially by Jews. Then even once-prosperous families like the Bastunskis found themselves impoverished, as their many letters to family members in America attest. In 1935, forest merchant Eliyahu Bastunski wrote to his son Shlomo in Oakland, California: "It is a very bad time by us. The livelihood is meager. Once there was the trade from the forest. Today it is down completely. . . . The trade of wheat is not good either; it is cheap and there is no one to sell it to." And the Bastunskis were among the lucky ones, because they belonged to the minority kept afloat by gifts and loans from relatives in America. Those who had no relatives there (or whose relatives had no money to spare) struggled to get by on loans from various Jewish banks and benevolent associations.

Another traditionally Jewish branch of business that suffered badly during the interwar years was the liquor trade. Ignoring precedent shaped by legislation going back to 1639 (when the Lithuanian Council began laying down its rules and regulations concerning the manufacture and sale of alcohol by Jews), the Polish government decided that Jews should make up only 9 percent of the business, that being their proportion of the general population.[8] To accomplish this, the government awarded the alcohol monopolka (the exclusive concession to sell liquor and alcoholic drinks) only to wounded Polish veterans or to the widows of fallen soldiers. By definition this excluded all the soldiers from Eishyshok, for they had been part of the Russian empire during World War I and had therefore served in the tzarist army.

In a place like Eishyshok, where virtually all the inns, taverns, and restaurants that sold alcoholic beverages were leased or owned by Jews, such a policy spelled economic disaster. Once-thriving businesses, which had often engaged in ferocious competition with one another for customers,

Yankl Bastunski and his brothers Shmuel and Mordekhai, like their father, were forest merchants. Shmuel was also successful in the liquor business. Yankl and Mordekhai moved to Vilna and ran their business from the big city. Yankl, Shmuel, Mordekhai, and their families were murdered in Eishyshok and at Ponar near Vilna. YESC, BASTUNSKI-BASTON

now found themselves fighting for their very survival rather than for a larger share of the trade.

There were, of course, many ways around the law. Some of the eighteen Jewish establishments that continued to sell hard liquor in Eishyshok leased the concession from Polish veterans; others simply operated outside of the law, using tactics similar to those of the bootleggers during America's Prohibition.

But two Eishyshok families actually possessed the monopolka. Herman Weitz, a Polish Jew who had served in the German army during World War I before deserting and joining up with the Polish army, was granted an alcohol concession as a reward for his wartime service. And the Kiuchefski family was given the coveted concession for an act performed in the 1863 Polish uprising against the tzar. When a man named Ludwik Narbutt, a local commander of the rebellion, took shelter from the pursuing Russians in the humble house of Dovid Kiuchefski, Dovid's wife Frade-Leah, who was sick in bed at the time, hid the officer under her huge down coverlet. The Russians searched every nook and cranny of the house — except Frade-Leah's bed. During the Second Polish Republic the story of this Polish commander was revived and he became a local hero, in whose reflected glory the Kiuchefski family were able to bask, to their great good fortune, which came in various forms, including not just the liquor monopolka but a tobacco monopolka as well.

For those who did not enjoy such special favors, the liquor trade was a difficult one during these years. The bribes the Jewish merchants had to pay were steep, and the fear of being informed on quite real, since there was a local Polish informer by the name of Koszczuk who had a concession to run a liquor store in Eishyshok and didn't relish competition. Still, these obstacles didn't stop the Jewish liquor trade, much of which was in the hands of a very plucky group of women. Besides Rochel Kiuchefski, whose business was legal (thanks to her in-laws Dovid and Frade-Leah), and Fruml Blacharowicz, who leased her business from a wounded Polish veteran, there were Zlate Blacharowicz, Basha Kaganowicz, Gitta Gross, and the beautiful young divorcee Shoshke Wine.[9] The strain of doing business illegally was too much for some, however. Gitta Gross, for example, used to get help from Rochel Kiuchefski, who always set aside part of her shipments of liquor for her pregnant friend. Gitta would then show up to haul baskets filled with bottled whiskey back to the customers waiting eagerly in her small tavern. Rochel used to joke that Gitta's baby would be born a drunk. Gitta gave birth to a healthy baby boy, but she and her husband Shmuel couldn't take the constant fear of arrest and eventually emigrated to Eretz Israel, where they became farmers.

Yehoshuah Gross, born healthy and beautiful despite the fact that during her pregnancy his mother Gitta used to haul large baskets filled with whiskey, vodka, and other liquor to the tavern she ran. YESC, SH. & G. GROSS

Gitta Gross, her husband Shmuel, and son Yehoshua in 1927. Gitta was one of the most diligent liquor traders. The photo was taken in Jerusalem after their aliyah to Eretz Israel. YESC, SH. & G. GROSS

Rochel Kiuchefski, the shtetl's most successful woman in the legal liquor trade. She was murdered in the September 1941 massacre. YESC, M. KAGANOWICZ

Shoshke Yurkanski Wine and ex-husband Zeev Wine in Eretz Israel. Shoshke was a Jewish tavern owner beloved among the Christian population of Eishyshok. Zeev emigrated to Argentina; Shoshke returned from Eretz Israel to Eishyshok. She was murdered by Russian partisans in the forest in 1944 during a rape attack on young Jewish girls whom Shoshke tried to protect. PHOTO: BY BEN-NOAM, PETAH-TIKVAH. YESC, Z. & R. PAIKOWSKI

Tobacco and saccharin were among the other products for which a monopolka was required, and in those trades, too, economic hardship forced many who did not have the licenses to continue to operate illegally. One such businessman, Szymen Kaganov, was to pay dearly for his crime — though ultimately it would also be his salvation. When his coachman was caught with an illegal shipment of saccharin, Kaganov received a stiff jail sentence. Managing to escape from prison, he emigrated to Palestine and returned clandestinely to retrieve his wife Judith and small son Yankele, whom he had not seen for six years. Because of that saccharin, and the necessity of leaving Poland for Palestine, they were saved from the Holocaust.

For most of the merchants who remained in Eishyshok, the years between the two world wars were one long decline. The elderly saw their businesses die, the young saw no future for themselves. Eliyahu Bastunski's letters have already been quoted on the subject. His daughter Batia's letter in response to her brother Zusl's invitation to join him in America in 1937 tells the story from her point of view: "As you know, the Jewish situation is a strained one. Here, more and more, the pessimistic mood prevails. The long exile is etched on everyone's face. It is especially difficult for a young person who wants to settle down." Batia Bastunski emigrated to California in 1938.

Benyamin Kabacznik (left), a grain merchant, with friend Shlomo Dubczanski. For many years, Benyamin's parents managed a huge Polish estate near Eishyshok, in Paradin. Benyamin was murdered by the AK in February 1944. YESC, SHEFSKI

The merchant class of the shtetl, the balebatim, were losing the economic base that gave them their power in the community. Even when they became impoverished, they still clung to their status, of course, but they were mocked by people from the artisan class. Long accustomed to being the underclass of the shtetl, the artisans and small shopkeepers were much more likely to have gone off to seek new lives in America than their more affluent neighbors. Now they were sending money to their relatives back home, thereby altering the class structure of the shtetl. Those who were newly affluent thanks to relatives in America called those who were newly impoverished *zaidene torbes* — "the silk beggars" — an allusion to the longtime beggars in the shtetl, who made their rounds from house to house with sacks of jute, not silk, slung over their shoulders.

MANUFACTURING

Because of the predominantly agricultural nature of the region, Eishyshok, like other shtetlekh in the area, never developed any significant industry. The grain trade, however, did require a flour mill, and for centuries there had been a tradition in Poland and Lithuania of predominantly Jewish millers who owned or leased the local mills, and resided there with their families. So it was that during outbreaks of anti-Semitism, which often coincided with hard times (and the tendency to blame the Jews for them), the miller and his family were likely to be among the first casualties. Such incidents increased during the interwar years, and so did the number of Jewish millers forced out of their centuries-old profession.

In 1920, the Zlotnik family of Eishyshok barely escaped with their lives when their mill was set upon by Ulans, the Polish army gangs (also known as the Lancers) who terrorized the Jews of the countryside with their violent attacks. Hearing the sound of horses' hooves galloping across the wooden bridge that led to their mill, the Zlotniks jumped out the windows and hid. A Jewish miller and his family in the next village were less fortunate that day. They were murdered by the same gang of thugs. In nearby Rudna, Zvi Hayyim Gruznik and his wife leased a mill, which they had to give up after a fight with a local peasant. They then moved to Eishyshok and leased a mill on New Plan land (the addition that had been incorporated into Eishyshok as part of a turn-of-the-century redesign of the shtetl), but times were hard and they were not able to hold on to it. The children of both the Zlotnik and the Gruznik families emigrated to Palestine since they saw no future in milling, which left the shtetl with only one mill, that owned by the Kiuchefski family.

Modern industrialization first came to Eishyshok in 1878–79, with the building of a match factory. The abundant raw material provided by the nearby alder groves must have made Eishyshok a natural choice for such an enterprise. But in 1893 the factory was destroyed by fire, the "Red Rooster" that was always feeding on the shtetl. All attempts to douse the flames, which made a spectacular fireworks display as they engulfed the factory's sulfur and wood supplies, proved futile.[10]

Some years later, Jossef Stalewitch, a bespectacled scholar/entrepreneur who was an admirer of the Haskalah movement and a staunch believer in its productivization ideology, settled in Eishyshok (to be near his relatives, the Wilkanskis) and decided to rebuild the match factory. He formed a partnership with a native Eishyshkian named Arkeh Puzeritsky. This time the factory was located in a large, fireproof, red brick building, behind a tall fence, on a spacious lot near the Kabacznik tannery. An expert from Vilna supervised production, and 150 workers, mainly young women, performed the tasks of packing the matches in boxes and pasting labels on the boxes. The workers' modest income was a welcome addition to the family coffers, in many cases providing the girls with their dowries. Burdened with the high taxes imposed by the Russian government (up to 50 percent of the retail price), and the bribes that had to be paid to the inspectors who showed up periodically, Eishyshok's largest industrial venture nonetheless managed to keep turning a profit until the early years of the twentieth century, when a lawsuit brought by Russia's largest match factory (over brand-name infringement)

Mary (Margolia Dragutski) Kaplan-Gottlieb, one of 150 young shtetl women who worked in the match factory. She was so short, she had to stand on a box in order to reach the table. She emigrated to America. YESC, R. ROSENBLATT

Itte Lewinson with daughter Pesie and husband Yehiel. Itte, who made linseed oil, was considered one of the shtetl's smartest businesswomen; Reb Yehiel, a Lida coachman, was an accomplished Talmud scholar. Itte, Yehiel, Pesie, and a son, Ephraim, were murdered in the September 1941 massacre. Three daughters had already made aliyah to Eretz Israel. YESC, LEWINSON FAMILY

Reb Ephraim Kirschner, one of Eishyshok's wool and linen manufacturers in the nineteenth century, supplied nearby tzarist army bases with fabric for uniforms and underwear. He, his second wife, and his children from both marriages emigrated to America. His son Walter was a supporter and close friend of President Franklin Roosevelt. PHOTO: BIALYSTOK, I.I. SOLOWEITZIK. YESC, SHANBERG-KAPLAN

caused it to shut down.[11] The building that housed it would later be bought by Reb Shael Sonenson, who converted it into the shtetl slaughterhouse.

In the years prior to World War I, Eishyshok also was home to three wool and seven linen manufacturers that supplied nearby tzarist army bases with fabric for uniforms and underwear. The flax plant from which linen was made had other uses, too, and its various processing stages provided revenues for a number of shtetl families. Moshe Sonenson developed an export trade in flaxseed, shipping it in large quantities to a factory in the Ponar section of Vilna, and several enterprising women in the shtetl, such as Moshe's mother Hayya Sonenson and Itte Lewinson, ground locally grown seeds for linseed oil. Itte's husband Yehiel, a Lida coachman and a pious Talmud scholar, used to make unannounced inspections of the scales on which his wife weighed the seeds she purchased from the peasants, to make sure that her scales did not shortchange them. "Love me, not the peasants," she used to chide him on such occasions.

A rather unusual little industry that had a brief life in Eishyshok was made possible by a machine sent to the daughters of textile manufacturer Ephraim Kirschner by their sisters in America. Hoping to save the shtetl innocents from the decadent life they themselves had encountered in the new world, the young women sent their siblings a wool-sock knitting machine. If the girls could make a respectable income in Eishyshok, the émigré sisters reasoned, perhaps they would stay there. After mastering the secrets of the machine with the help of an instructor from Vilna, they did indeed achieve success — so much so that they were able to use their earnings to purchase steamboat tickets and sail for America! The wondrous machine that had caused so much commotion in the shtetl upon its arrival was left behind.[12]

World War I, and the grim economic realities it left in its wake, halted any further development of small industry in Eishyshok, while making the rebuilding of old ones unprofitable. In addition, by 1929 the newly paved highway linking Eishyshok to Vilna, Grodno, and Lida made it so much easier for manufacturing plants in those cities to ship goods that it was even less likely that any sort of industrial initiative would be fostered in the shtetl. Thus the modest number of enterprises, which stood at only twenty-one before the war, had shrunk to thirteen by 1937.[13] The wool and linen manufacturers were gone, as were the knitting machine enterprise and the match factory, the number of wax factories remained the same, tanneries had dropped from five to three, mills from two to one, and the only new enterprises were several kvass and ice factories, two trunk factories, an electric power plant, and a volickes (felt boots) manufacturer.

This last industry is a perfect example of how the Second Polish Republic's anti-Jewish policies frustrated any nascent entrepreneurial instincts. Dovid Paretski, the one felt-boot manufacturer in Eishyshok, used such slow, primitive methods that he could not fill the local demand during the cold winter months, and his customers had to turn to suppliers whose boots were imported from Lida, Vilna, and Swen-

Ella Kirschner Levin and husband Solomon. Ella, born in Eishyshok in 1861, was one of the daughters of Reb Ephraim Kirschner who mastered the use of a wool-sock knitting machine. With her earnings she bought steamboat tickets for emigration to America. PHOTO: MITCHELL, KANSAS CITY, MISSOURI. YESC, SHANBERG-KAPLAN

An owner of an ice cream factory selling products to his young customers at the entrance to Eishyshok's Vilna Street near a special welcoming gate built in honor of a visiting Polish Catholic church official. The inscription in Hebrew reads: "May you be blessed at your arrival and departure." There is a Jewish Star of David on the right and the Polish eagle on the left. PHOTO: YITZHAK URI KATZ. YESC, RESNIK

czian. Even so, there were not enough to go around, which left the shtetl tradesmen with empty shelves and the customers with cold feet.

But then there occurred an event with the potential to transform the felt-boot manufacturing process. In 1931 an electric power plant jointly owned by Moshe Kaganowicz and his brother-in-law Berl Kiuchefski ushered the shtetl into the modern era. Batia Bastunski reported the upcoming grand event in a letter to her brother in San Francisco: "I am writing you that here in Eishyshok there will be electricity for the winter. Just imagine; by us it is a great happening. In little Eishyshok that there should run buses and there should be electricity!" And when the big day arrived, February 1, 1931, Reuven-Beinush Berkowitch described it in a letter to his sons in Palestine:

The inauguration in 1931 of the electrical power plant building, which also housed the new electric flour and saw mills. It was built and owned by the Kiuchefski family and Moshe Kaganowicz. Standing in front of the building are (left to right) Shlomo Kiuchefski, Dora Zlotnik Berkowitch, Zeev Kaganowicz, and wife Masha (née Kiuchefski). Two Kaganowicz brothers, Moshe and Zeev, married two Kiuchefski sisters, Hannah and Masha. Moshe and Hannah later moved to Vilna. In addition to his partnership in the electric power plant, Moshe was also an agent for a cosmetic company. Dora made aliyah to Eretz Israel; Zeev and Masha were murdered by Germans during the war, Shlomo by the AK. PHOTO: REPHAEL LEJBOWICZ. YESC, M. KAGANOWICZ

Today is a jubilant time. There is light! Electricity came to Eishyshok. We all assembled in the Old Beth Midrash and there electricity was turned on. The electric light shows people more animated. They look just like in the movies. The little boys ran around, the old ones followed them. It is a delight. There is joy and gladness here in Eishyshok.

This was indeed a great improvement in shtetl living conditions. Electricity was available in private homes from 4 P.M., and the dark streets were now illuminated with streetlights.

Dovid Paretski saw electrification as an opportunity to put the techniques of mass production to work in the manufacture of felt boots. If he could come up with the thousands of zlotys necessary for the purchase of new machines and of raw material in bulk, he could dramatically increase his output and hire a number of additional people for the production line.[14] Encouraged by the prospects of this new business, the Jewish Distribution Committee tried to find a source to lend Paretski the money he needed, and various people in the shtetl, among them Moshe Sonenson, agreed to guarantee the loans. The ambitious project was never to materialize, however, because the Polish authorities were not willing to issue a manufacturing permit to a Jew.

Tanneries were another of the industries affected by the anti-Jewish policies of the Polish government in the 1920s and '30s. Long before such policies ate into the profits of this business, it had been marked by ferocious competition. In Eishyshok (as elsewhere), the tanneries belonged to the oldest families, in this case the Yurkanskis and the Kabaczniks, who had a history of acrimonious relations going back centuries. One thing they did agree on, however, was the necessity of outwitting the government, which they attempted to do by registering their tanneries as workshops rather than manufacturing plants, as that would allow them to avoid the high taxes and prohibitive licensing arrangements required of all Jewish industries. To create the impression of many small workshops owned by many different individuals, they shipped their bundles of leather to the local trade center under an assortment of names — all of which they had copied from tombstones in the New Jewish Cemetery of Eishyshok. But an informer tipped off the Polish inspector about the "dead souls" scheme, and Zirl Yurkanski and Sorl Kabacznik (both women) spent a number of months in the Lida jail.

Since Moshe Sonenson had recently purchased and reopened an old family tannery, thus putting himself in competition with them, the Yurkanskis suspected that he had been the informer. Years later he and his family were to pay dearly for that groundless suspicion.

Feuds like those between the Yurkanskis and the Kabacznik-Sonensons were common in the shtetl, and were kept well fueled by the difficulties the Jews faced during successive tzarist, Polish, and Soviet regimes. The anti-Semitic policies of these various governments, which levied ever higher taxes and made the business of staying in business ever more impossible, pitted the Jews against each other in deadly rivalries. But by the time of the Second Polish Republic, their struggles had less to do with greed and success than sheer survival. At last they were being destroyed by the Polish merchants and artisans who had for centuries attempted, through their guilds and with the support of their church, to put them out of business. No longer could the Polish crown and aristocracy protect them as they once had done, if only in the spirit of enlightened self-interest. No longer could the Jews in the shtetl even be counted on to protect each other.

HELP FROM EMIGRANT KIN

Eishyshok had a post office since the 1870s, and almost from its inception it brought not just news and gossip and packages from those who had emigrated abroad, but money, too. The first post office, a small room on Goyishker Street, was leased to the postman by the kehilah, which in turn had leased it from the Russian authorities.

During the closing decades of the nineteenth century, the shtetl postman was Elisha, a round-faced, round-bellied man whose eagerly awaited appearances were often greeted with a steaming glass of tea and homemade delicacies. His tenure as postman encompassed the beginnings of the mass emigration to America, which started in the 1880s and reached its peak in the years before World War I, and the golden days of the Eishyshok yeshivah, whose students came from all over Europe. Thus there were many people relying on his services, and they could always count on them to be performed in a highly personal way, for discretion was not one of Elisha's strong points (notwithstanding the prohibitions of the eleventh-century sage Rabbenu Gershom ben Judah regarding mail and the right to privacy).[15] Who received which newspapers, for example, was information Elisha seemed to think it his duty to disseminate — much to the discomfiture of those yeshivah students whose secret subscriptions to Haskalah publications thus became general knowledge. But Elisha's personal touch proved invaluable in the months that followed the disastrous Big Fire of 1895, for he made it his duty to search out all the people living in temporary, makeshift lodgings and get their mail to them. Money from relatives in America who wanted to help rebuild the shtetl thus found its way into the pockets of those in need, and enabled the community to rise from the ashes.[16]

Elisha also performed indispensable services for the wives of men who had gone abroad in

Arie-Leib "der Grober" (the fat one) Dragutski, the former shtetl postmaster, in a photo taken after his emigration to America. YESC, ROSENBLATT

search of a better life for their families. Eager to perform his job in the most efficient way possible, and, again, not much concerned about his customers' privacy, Elisha was wont to skip several steps. As Meir Wilkanski wrote:

In the post office he opens the letters. In the post office he writes the responses. Why should he lose two or three days until the next mailcoach? So he brings to the women both the letters they received from their husbands and the responses he already wrote on their behalf.

Since Elisha was not just a postman but a teacher, who had taught many of the women of Eishyshok the art of writing letters (in Yiddish), he had their complete trust. Indeed, the women of the shtetl were very pleased with Elisha's system. Not only did it save them both time and money, but since everyone in the shtetl knew everyone else's business (as Elisha pointed out, by way of justifying his methods), there was usually nothing to add to his comprehensive, beautifully written accounts of their lives.[17]

Letters from America were anxiously awaited in the shtetl. The letters brought not only astounding news of the new land and spicy, gossipy tales about Eishyshkian emigrants, but material gifts in the form of green American dollars. A significant number of Eishyshkian emigrants sent money to their families, money that was used to enlarge businesses, build homes, help with medical needs and children's education, or, more basically, buy food and clothing. Thus most of the letters from the shtetl acknowledging the American ones begin with some version of the phrase, "We have received your beloved letter with the dollars for which we thank you greatly."

Elisha's successors included Arie-Leib der Grober (the fat one) Dragutski and Reuven the Postman, who were the last Jews to fill the position. During the interwar years, the post office moved to a Vilna Street building that the Polish government leased from the Kiuchefski family, and the entire staff was Polish. The economic hardships of those years, combined with the restrictions on immigration to both America and Palestine that kept many families divided for long periods of time, made the mail more eagerly welcomed than ever. Batia Bastunski wrote to her brother in 1934 about the excitement caused by the arrival of his letter from Oakland, California: "It is hard for me to put in writing the effect it had on us when the letter-carrier delivered the letter. Overwhelmed and pale, I went to the synagogue to tell Father the good news."

THE JEWISH VOLKSBANK AND THE GEMILUT HESSED KASSA

The hard years between the two world wars inflicted nearly lethal blows on the shtetl economy, and in Eishyshok, as elsewhere, much more substantial kinds of help were now needed. Not only were Jews being barred from their traditional occupations, denied access to the state loans granted their Polish Christian counterparts, and prevented from holding any civil or government job but, because of immigration restrictions after World War I, they had few hopes of escaping their economic woes by going abroad.

In addition to getting help from abroad and from the traditional mutual aid societies that had been their recourse in times of trouble for hundreds of years, the Jews in Poland also created new financial aid institutions, among them the Jewish Cooperative People's Bank (Volksbank) and a benevolent fund, the Gemilut Hessed Kassa. By 1922 the Volksbank had forty-six branches in the shtetlekh, including one in Eishyshok, which had a membership of 264. By 1936 the Eishyshok branch membership had risen to 283. In 1931, the average loan in Eishyshok was 519 zlotys, the maximum 2,000 zlotys. In 1936 the range was from 50 to 1,500 zlotys, at an annual interest rate of 10 percent, on top of which there were various transaction and business fees.[18]

The Eishyshok branch of the Gemilut Hessed Kassa was founded in December 1926. Its main purpose was to help those who were facing the severest economic hardship and thus were frequently ineligible for bank loans. When it was established, its funds consisted of 5,310 zlotys ($600) contributed by Eishyshkians in America, 2,000 zlotys contributed by local Eishyshkians, and 4,000 zlotys on loan from EKOPO (the letters standing for Hebrew and Yiddish words that mean the Jewish Loan Association of Eastern Europe). The Eishyshok Kassa had its ups and downs, but under the leadership of Moshe Shalit, the EKOPO representative from Vilna, it was eventually to become the shtetl's most vital loan fund — and one of the most efficiently run funds in Poland.[19]

By 1936 the Eishyshok branch of the Gemilut Hessed Kassa had increased its funds by almost a third, was making loans ranging from 20 to 200 zlotys, benefiting some 80 percent of the shtetl's working population, and had a dues-paying membership (at 6 zlotys a year) of 330. From 1932 to 1936 it granted 2,415 loans totaling 156,185 zlotys to 1,168 people (many of them repeat borrowers, obviously, and many of them nonmembers).[20] Without the assistance of the Kassa, much of the Jewish population of the shtetl would have faced total ruin.

One case, only too typical of the hundreds they handled, will illustrate the work done by the Kassa, which was modest in scale, and emphasized self-help, not handouts, wherever possible. A middle-aged man came to the Kassa with tears in his eyes, asking for a loan of 20 zlotys, for his family had nothing to eat. Since he was unemployed, the management of the Kassa proposed to buy him a horse and wagon with which he could transport merchandise between Vilna and Eishyshok, and they then persuaded various merchants and shopkeepers to use his services. The arrangement worked out well, and each week the man turned over a certain percentage of his earnings to repay the Kassa for the horse and wagon. Though he was eventually able to support his family, he asked for and received five additional loans.[21]

Because the ever-worsening state of the economy put a severe strain on the resources of the Kassa, in 1936 the management came up with a creative fund-raising promotion: the publication of a Golden Pinkas in which, for a fee, individuals and organizations could inscribe their names and those of their loved ones. In what seems in hindsight like an eerie premonition of the approaching doom of the shtetlekh, the first organization to buy a page in the pinkas was the Hevrah Kaddishah — the burial society.

Unzer Hilf (Our Help), a booklet published in Eishyshok in conjunction with the issuing of the Golden Pinkas, made an emotional appeal on

Members of the younger generation who in the 1930s secured money for the shtetl from outside political and educational Zionist organizations: (standing right to left) Moshe Kaganowicz, Yankele Jankelewicz, Zeev Kaganowicz, Motke Burstein, Yankl Levin, and Israel Krisilov (Israel worked in the shtetl bank); (seated right to left) Hanche Berkowitch, Shlomo Kiuchefski, Rachel Kaleko, and Avraham Ele Politacki. Rachel emigrated to Eretz Israel. Shlomo was murdered by the AK; others were murdered during the September 1941 massacre and elsewhere. PHOTO: ALTE KATZ. YESC, RESNIK

behalf of the fund, complete with practical instructions on how to enter one's name in the pinkas:

To all Eishyshker Jews and Eishyshker landsleit (émigrés) overseas:

At this time of economic destruction, a community numbering 3 million souls is being devastated. Hundreds of thousands of Jewish families are standing on the edge of economic disaster and are fighting a bitter struggle for their very survival. At a time when the process of eliminating the Jew from the economy proceeds with lightning speed, no one is safe. The one who was spared today may be ruined tomorrow.

We turn to you with a passionate plea that we join together to strengthen our Gemilut Hessed Kassa, which has helped over 100 families in our shtetl.

Edited by Mordekhai Replianski, *Unzer Hilf* was modeled after a similar publication by the same name, reporting similarly grim news, that had been appearing twice a month in Vilna since 1921.[22] In a poignantly revealing mixture of old and new, traditional and secular, religious and political, the Eishyshok version opened with a brief article in Hebrew on the importance of charity, written by the shtetl rabbi, Szymen Rozowski, which was followed by reports in Yiddish detailing the activities of the shtetl's financial-aid societies; it ended with a plea signed by members of the rabbinate as well as by officials of the merchants' and artisans' alliances. The publication date was December 12, 1936, the Hanukkah Sabbath, traditionally one of the most festive dates on the shtetl calendar.

The very name *Gemilut Hessed Kassa* reflected the alliance between the centuries-old traditions of the shtetl and the modern political, secularizing forces that were taking it by storm: *Gemilut Hessed* ("practice of kindness") was an ancient term for the benevolent societies that had been supplying interest-free loans to the needy for centuries; *Kassa*, "safe," was the word used by various socialist workers' organizations to denote the loan funds they established for their members.

This last-ditch effort to save their beloved community was jointly undertaken by members of the older generation, who still had control of many of the shtetl's financial resources, and the younger, more secular-minded generation, who had access to money from political movements and umbrella organizations from outside the shtetl. But all such efforts could only be temporary, stopgap measures. Besides being marked by official Polish government policy for economic destruction, Eishyshok, like so many other shtetlekh, was also at risk because of modernization. With paved roads and new methods of transportation reshaping the system for the distribution of goods, it was inevitably losing its importance as a market town.

Even if history could be rewritten to undo the devastation created by nearly two decades of Polonization, which pushed the Jews out of their traditional professions and simultaneously closed all the doors to new ones; even if many of the best and brightest of the young people had not concluded there was no future for them in the shtetl and left for more promising lands; and even if the Holocaust had never occurred, the shtetlekh of Eastern Europe would still have faced serious challenges in the twentieth century. Their very reason for being — the vital economic role they had played since the Middle Ages as centers for the exchange of goods — was slipping away from them. Their survival would have depended on their ability to change with the times.

For that very reason Eishyshok might have numbered itself among the survivors. As a look at the second of the two major social groups in the shtetl, the artisan class, reveals, many people in Eishyshok were proving surprisingly capable of moving forward, embracing the modern world.

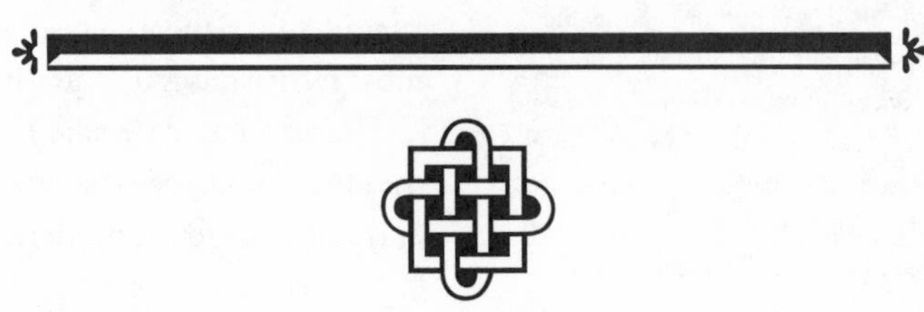

• 12 • HANDICRAFTS

FOR A TAILOR TO WORK
THE ENTIRE WEEK WAS
HIS GOAL
YET HE EARNED ONLY A
BAGEL WITH A HOLE.

A shtetl song

THE ARTISANS AND CRAFTSMEN WERE PERHAPS THE MOST PICTURESQUE MEMBERS OF the shtetl population, thus the most enduring of the quaint images handed down to us in the art and literature celebrating the shtetl. Yet in Eishyshok, as elsewhere, they were also among the most progressive, actively adapting their skills to the trends of the day, becoming champions of social change, and joining political movements — the Bund, the Communist Party, the Zionists — they hoped would improve the lot of the Jewish workingman and woman. Their commitment to change was both personal and political, for as the low end of the social totem pole, the bale-melokhe, they had the least investment in the status quo.

The shtetl hierarchy was quite intricate in structure and quite difficult to alter, however. Besides the basic division between the balebatim and the bale-melokhe, there were distinctions between crafts, and many fine gradations of rank within each craft. Tailors, for example, were generally looked down upon by many of their fellow craftsmen, the consensus being that their business ethics were rather shady; they were thought to have a tendency to cheat their customers. In fact, this stigma did not pertain in Eishyshok, but the usual social distinctions within the tailoring profession did apply, based, as they were in each profession, on the individual's skill, his clientele, his product, and other criteria less easily defined. A tailor of suits for the shtetl notables and the gentry ranked higher than a tailor of riding pants, for example, although many of the latter's clients were also members of the gentry. Shoe stitchers were higher on the social scale than shoemakers, and even began slowly to make their way into the balebatim as their prosperity increased and they became property owners.

In larger towns, each craft had its own synagogue. In Minsk, for example, there was a tailors' shul, a haberdashery shul, a masons' shul, a rag dealers' shul, and even a thieves' shul. But in Eishyshok only the shoemakers and the tailors, the two largest groups of artisans, had their own shtiblekh (which convened in separate rooms within the Old and New batei midrash, respectively). All other craftsmen prayed together in what became known as the mixed minyan.

Occasionally, as with the stitchers in and around Eishyshok, a group as a whole might gradually rise in social rank because of an overall increase in its income. And occasionally individuals within a given craft would so far transcend the boundaries of their class, by some combination of character, charisma, and scholarship, that they too would be honored, not just by the esteem of their peers, but by the grudging acceptance of the balebatim. These, of course, were the very few, their learning so deep or their saintliness so pronounced that even the boots, apron, cap, and roughened hands of the craftsman could not detract from or disguise their worth. For most people in the shtetl, however, at least until the twentieth century when the barriers began to fall, the class one was born into was the class one expected to live, marry, die, and be buried in.

TAILORS AND SEAMSTRESSES

The makers of clothing were one of the two largest artisan groups in Eishyshok, and the only one to include a significant number of women in its ranks.

Among the older tailors in the 1920s and '30s, the traditions of the kehilah (community), and most particularly its religious institutions, were a strong influence on everything they did. Tradition shaped their ethics, dictated how they spent their time, and was sewn into the very seams of the clothes they made. Dovid Matikanski, for example, was very active in the Hevrah Kaddishah, his tailor shtibl, and daily Talmud class. Another old tailor, whose clients were all Christians, prided himself on the positively biblical propriety of his dealings with them. He saved every thread and every tiny scrap of fabric left over from the clothes he made for a customer and pinned them to a piece of paper with the customer's name on it, and offered it to that client. Of course nobody wanted the scraps, so the old man requested that when his time came he would be buried with them, as proof that he had fulfilled the injunction in Genesis 14:23: "Not even one thread have I taken from them." But he and his family, having escaped the massacre in Eishyshok in 1941, were murdered in Radun, and this request could not be fulfilled.

The older tailors were known not just for their ethics, their excellent tailoring skills, and their economical use of fabric, but for their ability to make clothes that could last many years. A suit commissioned for a young groom, or a Sabbath dress for a bride, would be made a few sizes larger, with extra fabric at the seams, so that it could accommodate the additional pounds expected to come with age and respectability.

Many of the shtetl's tailors, however, especially the younger ones, knew that they had to move with the times, and their products showed it. These younger tailors understood that many people were no longer interested in garments that could last forever, but in up-to-the-minute clothes like the ones they saw in nearby Vilna, in

Reb Dovid Matikanski, his wife Nehama (née Pecker), and two of their younger sons, Haikl (standing left) and Yitzhak, posing with three young relatives in front of their house. The Matikanskis were among the shtetl's elite tailors and most popular individuals. Reb Dovid, the three young children, and the people in the window were all murdered in the September 1941 massacre. Nehama, Haikl, and Yitzhak perished at Majdanek.
YESC, PORTNOY-LEVIN

the fashion supplements of daily papers like Warsaw's *Haint* (Today), the most popular Yiddish newspaper of its time, or in the movies and newsreels playing at the local makeshift movie house, the Swjat. The world was coming to Eishyshok, and more and more Eishyshkians, especially those who boarded the frequent buses to Vilna, were quick to aspire to more worldly dress. Being well dressed mattered, even in the midst of an economic depression, and it mattered not just to the balebatim, but to the sons and daughters of the artisans, too, because it offered them a means of minimizing class distinctions.

Rochel Szulkin (right), the shtetl's finest seamstress, with some of the talented young seamstresses employed in her workshop: (right to left) Rochel Slonimski, who rented the workshop to Szulkin; Gittke Demitrowski; Beileh-Rivkeh Radunski (seated); Sarah Jankelewicz, Rochel Szulkin's niece; Gitta Politacki Ginsberg at the sewing machine. Gitta and Sarah survived the war, in Russia; all the others were murdered in the September 1941 massacre. YESC, Z. & G. GINSBERG

To keep up with the new demands, many young tailors and seamstresses took courses from their fashion-conscious counterparts in Vilna. Rochel Szulkin, for example, became an elite seamstress (at the same time that she was an ardent supporter of the Communist Party), and employed a number of talented young women in her workshop. Her beautiful clothes were known throughout the region.

The rapidity with which the sewing machine was adopted in Eishyshok was another sign of people's eagerness to change with the times. The Singer sewing machine concession had originally belonged to Szeina Blacharowicz's grandfather, around the turn of the century, and she eventually took it over from her father. Young and energetic, she traveled the countryside to sell new machines and collect payments on those already sold (at 2 zlotys a month, payable in twenty-eight installments). By the 1920s not only had most tailor and seamstress workshops bought the machines, so had virtually every shtetl household with a young wife or teenage

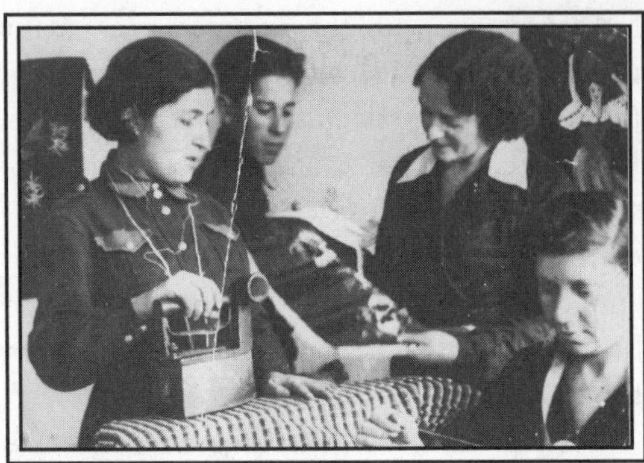

Rochel Szulkin (second from right) in her workshop with a young apprentice, Hayyim-Yoshke Bielicki, and Gitta Politacki Ginsberg (left), who is wearing a Beitar uniform. Seated on the right is one of Rochel's seamstresses. Hayyim-Yoshke and Gitta survived the war, in Russia; the two others were killed in the September 1941 massacre. YESC, M. SZULKIN

Tailors Dovid Matikanski (second from right) and son Albert (first on right), with relatives, apprentices, and other tailors celebrating the purchase of a new Singer sewing machine. Albert emigrated to Paris and from there to America. Dovid and most of the other people in the photo were murdered during the Holocaust in Eishyshok, Radun, Lida, and Majdanek. YESC, PORTNOY-LEVIN

daughters. On a summer day when all the windows were open, one could hear the constant hum of the sewing machine issuing forth from homes and workshops throughout the shtetl, its sound blending with the songs of the young apprentices and their teachers.

In the homes of the balebatim the machines were mainly for personal use, but among the bale-melokhe a new cottage industry was forming. The machine increased the number of working youth, enabling many young women to assist their families during hard times, and even to become the major breadwinners when necessary. Fruml Slepak, for example, had supported her brother and herself with the Singer sewing machine Szeina Blacharowicz had sold her before she married Hirshke Slepak, and she continued to sew as a source of income after her marriage. She was briefly separated from her machine when she and her husband, who were Communists, had to flee Eishyshok during the eight months of Lithuanian rule in 1939–40. But a Communist friend, truck driver Yankele Krisilov, delivered it to her in Byelorussia, where they had taken refuge, and it would later follow her into exile in Siberia, where it once again enabled her to support her family. Eventually it accompanied the Slepak family to Israel.

Ready-made clothes (tandet) seemed to present another great opportunity for the shtetl's entrepreneurial set, since they were clearly the wave of the future, but this opportunity faded in the face of certain financial realities. To compete with the Polish ready-to-wear garments that were taking over the local market in the 1930s, nine forward-looking Eishyshok families, totaling twenty-six tailors and seamstresses, went into the business. They didn't have as much capital as some of the richer tailors in town, however, and were therefore unable to buy material in large enough quantities to price their clothes competitively. They raised 3,000 of the 8,000 zlotys necessary to form a cooperative, so that they could buy fabric at low cost, but the balance, which was to have come from the American JDC, never materialized.[1]

Like other artisans, the tailors and seamstresses responded to the winds of change by joining political parties. The Bund, a socialist movement dedicated to improving the Jewish workers' lot by organizing them against their exploiters, was founded in Vilna in 1897. Soon it made its way from the larger industrial towns, where factory workers were the prime recruitment target, to shtetlekh such as Eishyshok, where young people apprenticing in the various craftsmen's workshops were the focus of all the organizing activities. And indeed their lot, depending on the whims of their master, could be a bitter one. Master tailor Shlomo the Amalekite was known (as his nickname indicates)* as a particularly cruel employer, who hit his apprentices frequently and took particular pleasure in aiming his ever-present stick at cuts and bruises that had not yet healed. Other employers had a reputation for using a hot iron.

Still, the Bund could do little to help, and may even have hurt by making employers more cautious about hiring potential troublemakers. The end result was that many young people found themselves unable to get jobs. The more active Bund members then retreated to Vilna, leaving behind them little more than a longing for change and the beautiful Yiddish songs with which the workers lamented their fate. Often, however, the line between worker and master in those days was so fine, with each of them just barely managing to scrape by, that the two might even join together in a musical plaint. Moshe-Reuven Michalowski remembers the solace that came from singing those old Bundist songs, first as a tailor's apprentice in Eishyshok, where he and his fellow apprentices were often accompanied by their master, Hirsh-Faivl Kremin, then later when he himself was a master tailor in Kalesnik, and later still as a farmer in Israel.

Unlike the early years of the twentieth century, the years between the two world wars were relatively prosperous ones for the tailors and seamstresses of Eishyshok, because the fashion explosion that occurred in that era meant a greater demand for their services. But they too were quick to cast their lot with various workers' parties, including the outlawed Communist Party and various groups within the Zionist movement. In fact, shtetl workshops were such hotbeds of political activism that the Polish police made regular raids on them, looking for Communists, and often finding them with the help of informers. The raids ended in harsh jail sentences for those who were caught. Fortunately for the tailor Avraham-Meishke Kaplan, he had a sixth sense that warned him he was about to be apprehended in one such raid, and he was able to escape by fleeing his workshop for a yeshivah in a nearby shtetl. There he posed as a pious student, staying for so many years that when he emerged he was a fine Talmudic scholar, also fluent in Hebrew. After the Holocaust, he emigrated to the United States, where he became a Hebrew teacher and lecturer.

The tailors and seamstresses of Eishyshok were much less affected by the Polonization of the area in the 1920s and '30s than members of many other professions in the shtetl. Up-to-date in their fashion sense, highly skilled, known for their honesty, they continued to enjoy the patronage not just of their Jewish customers but of the gentile peasants and gentry in the vicinity as well. In fact, little competition seemed to exist between Jews and gentiles in this business; just as the Christians went to Jewish tailors, many shtetl Jews willingly patronized the Christian tailors who were constantly opening new workshops.[2] There was enough work for all, and it was work that went on year-round. Though tailoring did have its peak seasons, such as the eve of Passover and the High Holidays, a never-ending whirl of activities seemed to keep everyone employed. The elite tailors, who catered to

*The Amalekites were an enemy of Israel from wilderness times to the early monarchy. Israelites were commanded to wage a war against them through the ages, to remember always the Amalekites' vicious attack against old, sick, and tired Israelites in the desert (Deuteronomy 25:17–19).

the balebatim, the Polish and Russian gentry, and Polish army officers, made clothes for weddings, christenings, patron saints' days, parades and other military events; the less skilled tailors, whose customers were their fellow artisans and the village peasants, were busy outfitting them in workaday clothes.

Despite the anti-Semitic mood of the interwar years, Jewish tailors of both kinds continued to spend days, weeks, and even months with their Christian clients in the countryside. His sewing machine on his shoulders, Shlomo Politacki regularly set off for far-flung homesteads in the countryside, where he would sew the outer garments (burkes) and short coats (kurtkes) that were such favorites with the gentile peasants. Meanwhile, Burnik Avraham Yitzhok and his son were spending most of their winters in affluent homes in the villages, making the shearling coats so popular among the gentry. Typically, a tailor might live in a client's home long enough to outfit the entire family. While staying with Polish families, the tailors would eat boiled potatoes from the "Jewish pot" their hosts maintained for kosher guests, and go to the homes of Jews who lived nearby to spend the Sabbath and Jewish holidays.

After the German occupation in 1941, the Nazis, too, were eager to avail themselves of the superior skills of Eishyshok's tailors, though only the elite ones, the Matikanskis, would do for them. After part of the family escaped the massacre of the Jews in Eishyshok, they made their way to Ghetto Radun. There Haikl Matikanski again sewed uniforms for German officers, and his craftsmanship was so well regarded that he was spared the mass killings in Radun and taken to Lida, where once more his skill dazzled the Germans. From Lida, however, he and his wife were deported to Majdanek, which proved to be their final destination.

SHOEMAKERS AND STITCHERS

Originally the largest artisan class in Eishyshok, the shoemakers began to shrink in both numbers and prosperity after the 1861 Emancipation of the Serfs, when many of the freed Russian serfs went into competition with them. But they remained an important factor in the shtetl economy, and, like the older tailors, a colorful, tradition-bound group whose image was part of the vivid picture we have of shtetl life. For example, Yankel-Layzer, a nineteenth-century shoemaker, knew all six volumes of the Mishnah by heart. On his low shoemaker's table, next to the hammer, nails, glue, and leather that were the tools of his trade, the Mishnah could always be found, for Yankel-Layzer had devised a special system that allowed him to alternate work and study: Whenever he wasn't clenching nails between his teeth, he was chanting the Mishnah.

But the chant of the Mishnah slowly gave way to the Yiddish songs the Bundists and Communists sang about the plight of the workingman, and the Hebrew songs the Zionists sang about their yearning for Israel. Marx proved more appealing than the Mishnah to the scores of young shoemakers' apprentices in the shtetl, among whom were many of its hard-core Communists.

Indeed, the shoemakers had much to complain of, for the initial competition they faced from the serfs was exacerbated, during the interwar years, by competition from Polish cobblers and, eventually, from ready-made shoes. Even worse, however, was the competition within the ranks of the shoemakers themselves — or, more accurately, between the shoemakers and the stitchers, who were responsible for different stages of the shoemaking process.

The stitchers, who did the fittings and patterns and then cut and sewed the upper parts of custom-made boots and shoes, were the more highly skilled artisans, and therefore more afflu-

Shoemaker Moshe Szulkin with his children Matle and Avraham (Robert) and wife Feigl. Moshe was an ardent reader who had a much better command of Karl Marx than of the Mishnah. The family survived the war, in Russia. YESC, M. SZULKIN

ent. Many of them had made their way into the balebatim class, including some who had come from a long line of shoemakers but had managed to upgrade their skills and hence their status during the interwar years. Usually it was the stitchers who both sold the shoemakers the raw materials for the shoes (since they had enough money to allow them to buy leather in quantity) and sold the finished shoes and boots to the customers. The shoemakers made the soles of the shoes, but were frequently dependent on the stitchers to sew the uppers to the soles. As relatively unskilled labor, much harder hit by the economic depression of the 1920s and '30s than the stitchers were, they were more likely to join up with the Bundists and the Communists, and to view the stitchers as part of the "exploiter" class, while the stitchers were more likely to remain traditional Jews or to join up with the Zionists, and to look down on the shoemakers.

In Eishyshok, the tension between the two groups riveted the entire population. Angered by the shoemakers' constant political agitation against them, the stitchers began to give work to non-Jewish cobblers, who they said did superior work at lower prices. The Jewish cobblers fought back, uniting with the non-Jewish cobblers into a Shoemakers' Alliance, which was supposed to enable them to buy their own leather and attract their own clientele, thereby superseding many of the stitchers' functions and making them less central to the whole process. But in the long run the Alliance did not succeed. Its standard of workmanship wasn't high enough, the leather it provided was of inferior quality, and many of the finest shoemakers in the shtetl did not join, either because they were in jail for Communist activities and couldn't, or because they were dubious about the Alliance and wouldn't.

The stitchers continued in their dispute with the shoemakers. Not only did they refuse to give them work, they hindered them in the work they did have. When a cobbler brought a stitcher a pair of soles to be sewn to the uppers, the latter would go about his own business, selling leather or shoes, perhaps working on another set of uppers. Not having any other option, the shoemaker sat idly and waited, often losing an entire day's work in the process. When factory-made shoes further worsened the shoemakers' plight, many faced very dark times. Yude-Yankl, a shoemaker known both for his poverty and the gallows humor with which he endured it, told his wife on the eve of Passover one year: "For the first four days of Passover I will eat matzah and you will watch. During the last four days you will watch and I will eat."

The days of the Jewish cobbler were clearly drawing to a close. In only two years, from 1934 to 1936, the total number dropped from 62 to 32, while the number of non-Jewish cobblers rose from 9 to 37.[3] Yet there were still 19 Jewish shoemaker's apprentices in 1936 — not because there was much hope for the future of the profession, but because there was no place else for many of the young people to turn.

THE MIXED MINYAN CRAFTSMEN

In 1936, according to a chart that appeared in *Unzer Hilf* (the booklet published in conjunction with the Golden Pinkas, in order to detail the financial plight of the Eishyshok community), a total of 332 families in the shtetl were among the artisan class, about two-thirds of whom were Jewish.[4] There were Jewish locksmiths, bakers, potters, barbers, watchmakers, blacksmiths, photographers.

The builders, roofers, tinsmiths, and carpenters, who together made up the third-largest group of artisans in Eishyshok (after the tailors and seamstresses, and the shoemakers and stitch-

Gedalia Cofnas and son Pessah, accomplished carpenters, in their carpentry shop in 1935. Reb Gedalia was murdered during the September 1941 massacre. Pessah survived the war, in Russia. YESC, R. & P. COFNAS

Seated in front of their house on Eishyshok's Radun Street are Honeh the builder (Dovid Elhanan Moszczenik), his wife Golde, and family members. Honeh built the family's house with funds sent by his children who had emigrated to America. The entire European branch of the Moszczenik family was killed during the Holocaust in Eishyshok and the vicinity. PHOTO: REPHAEL LEJBOWICZ. YESC, MOSZCZENIK

A group of Jewish and Polish carpenters in 1934, rebuilding a house that was burned down. Pessah Cofnas is installing a window frame. YESC, R. & P. COFNAS

Yehudah Kaleko in the family workshop in 1923, constructing wooden wheels for carriages. Yehudah later made aliyah to Eretz Israel. YESC, KALEKO-BARKALI

ers), enjoyed a downright boom in the interwar years because there was so much building going on. Though only non-Jews were employed on the building of the Vilna–Grodno highway, as on all Polish government projects (except those involving unskilled labor), there was plenty of work to be done on private projects, and it was all done by Jewish craftsmen: the Kiuchefski electric station was built between 1928 and 1931, the Kiuchefski electric sawmill (Tartak) not long after, the Rad Kromen (row shops) were rebuilt in 1933 and again in 1935, a new shtetl school was constructed in 1932, and the frequent fires in the shtetl meant that homes were always having to be rebuilt, year in and year out.

Still, even in the midst of a building boom, the number of unemployed among the artisan class was increasing, in part because the master carpenters had decided to keep their wages high by freezing the number of carpenters at existing levels, taking on no new apprentices. Four young carpenters did manage to circumvent the limitation by opening their own workshop with raw materials and tools financed by a loan from the

Young employees in front of the Kiuchefski electric station in the 1930s. Two of them, Dov Wilenski (front right) and Munia Zahavi, (back left), made aliyah to Eretz Israel and became directors of electrical plants there. All the others were killed during the Holocaust in Eishyshok and other locations. YESC, D. WILENSKI

Young Jewish laborers working on a public government project, draining the swamps on the outskirts of Eishyshok. Only Pessah Cofnas (far left) survived the war, in Russia; all the others were killed during the Holocaust. YESC, R. & P. COFNAS

Gemilut Hessed Kassa, but many young people found themselves shut out of entry-level apprentice positions.[5] Those who were unable to get other jobs had to accept any kind of work they could find, including jobs paying as little as 1 or 2 zlotys a day. Some did occasional work as unskilled laborers on Polish government projects, planting trees along the highways, paving the highway shoulders, doing drainage along the shtetl's main streets and market square, and so forth, while many others simply left. When the United States closed its doors by changing its immigration laws in 1921, 1924, and 1929, some went to Cuba and South America, while others continued to stream into Palestine, despite the British restrictions against immigration.

Another response to the hard times was to learn new skills, which would allow them to take their place in the technologically advanced twentieth century. Parents from both the balebatim and the bale-melokhe sent their children to Vilna and other big cities for training in such fields as medicine, dentistry, pharmacology, and engineering, often at great personal sacrifice, for it was difficult to come up with the money to finance such educations; but it was obvious that if they didn't help their children to find new ways of making a living, the children could not hope to have much of a future. Many of the students viewed their training as preparation for a future in Palestine, however, not in the shtetl. Eishyshok, like shtetlekh throughout Eastern Europe, was losing the best of its younger generation.

THE SHTETL WORK ETHIC

There persist to this day certain unfounded notions about the shtetl work ethic, to the effect that most of the people in the shtetl were luftmenschen — unproductive individuals. The coarse, bumbling buffoon, by turns lazy and crafty, incompetent and slightly dishonest, is the folksy stereotype of the shtetl Jew that has been handed down to us in art and literature. Such notions were also perpetuated by the Haskalah and later by modern Zionism as well, for both movements saw it as their task to "rehabilitate" the Jew in general and the Eastern European Jew in particular, transforming him via the "productivization" philosophy through which they hoped to redefine the entire socioeconomic basis of Jewish society. The result would be the "new Jew."

In reality, however, the shtetlekh of Eastern Europe were dynamic, vibrant market towns filled with energetic, hardworking people. The majority of the shtetl tradesmen, shopkeepers, and craftsmen were Jews, and there was not a single category of labor regarded as inappropriate for Jews (with the exception, of course, of certain kinds of maintenance work that had to be done on the Sabbath, which were performed by a Shabbes goy, a non-Jew who did work that Jews were prohibited from doing on the day of rest). Perhaps the only other society in modern Jewish life that can claim to be the equal of the shtetl in its overall self-reliance and positive attitudes toward labor is the Israeli kibbutz.

Until the closing decades of the nineteenth century, the shtetl was like a living ethnographic museum of a bygone era, untouched by the Industrial Revolution. To the outsider it was both quaint and primitive, but to the Jewish outsider, whether from the West or from the larger cities of Eastern Europe, it was an embarrassment. Ashamed of this reminder of their roots, reluctant to identify with anything so foreign and remote, many urban Jews tried hard to distance themselves from their brothers and sisters in the shtetl. Even as the shtetl slowly began to change, they were unable to see beyond their prejudices, to acknowledge the vitality and resourcefulness of a way of life they hoped they had put behind them forever.

So while both the admirers and the detractors of the shtetl continued to see it as mired in tradition, frozen in time, this was not the case. In art, the Jewish cobbler was still chanting the Mishnah while mending shoes; in reality, he was unionizing. In art, the old Jewish tailor was still sewing the Sabbath dress meant to last its owner a lifetime; in reality, the young Jewish seamstress was a Communist making a dress in the very latest fashion, something its owner could flaunt on a trip into Vilna, or wear on a date with someone she hoped to impress. In art, the coachman still urged his team down winding dirt roads; in reality, his stable had been converted into a garage.

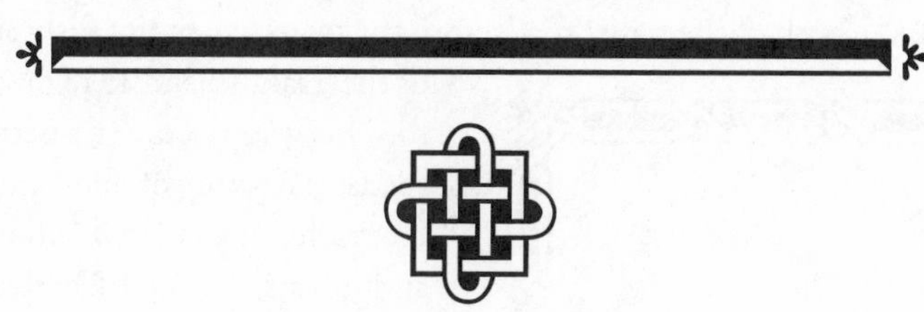

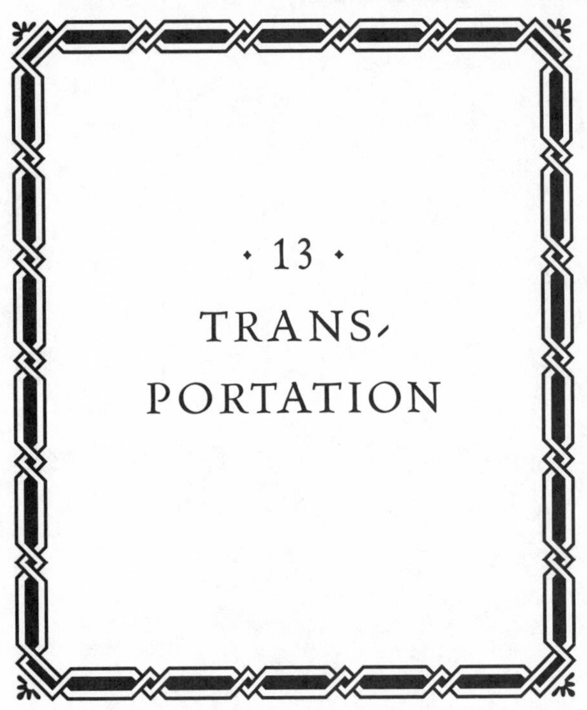

WHEN THE BUSES REPLACED THE HORSES, THE SHTETL BECAME A SHTOT (BIG TOWN) AND NEWSPAPERS REPLACED THE GEMARA.

Moshe Sonenson

UNTIL THE ADVENT OF MODERN, MECHANIZED MEANS OF TRAVEL, HORSE-DRAWN coaches were the backbone of European transportation, and in Eastern Europe, especially within the Pale of Settlement, the Jewish coachman had a virtual monopoly on the moving of goods, passengers, and mail. This monopoly would endure for many centuries; the picturesque image of the big, burly coachman, whip in hand, wearing high boots, a tall fur hat, and a rope belt, seemed a permanent feature of shtetl life.

Eishyshok's location at the junction of roads to Warsaw, Bialystok, Grodno, Vilna, and Lida was particularly auspicious for a market town. The two main highways ran from Eishyshok to Vilna and from Eishyshok to Lida, both of them dirt roads until the 1920s, when the Eishyshok–Vilna portion of the Trakt Pilsudski highway linking Warsaw to Vilna was paved; and a network of smaller dirt roads, consisting of one-lane carriage roads and footpaths, meandered among fields, swamps, and forests, linking Eishyshok with various villages, estates, hamlets, and farms in the vicinity. Two great, dense forests (puszcza), the Rudnicki and the Nacha, surrounded the plain on which Eishyshok was built, and many of the roads leading to Eishyshok had to navigate this forbidding territory.

Two powerful coachmen (baaleagoleh) groups served Eishyshok, the Vilner Forer and the Lida Forer. The occupation was hereditary, being passed from one generation to another in the same family. Each group consisted of about five families, most of the members of the two groups being related to one another through some combination of blood and marriage, and each group had its own territory. When the railroad from Warsaw to St. Petersburg bypassed Eishyshok in favor of Bastun, twelve miles away, a new coachmen's group was formed to serve Bastun, as well as a group that served Aran (Varena), a train station about nine miles away.

The Vilner coachmen left Sunday morning, between 8:00 and 9:00, traveling in a caravan of about ten wagons (sleds in winter). When the Vilner coachmen left Eishyshok, the seats would be filled with students who were returning to their schools (and parcels of food sent by mothers whose children were studying there), people in need of the medical attention that could only be found in the big city, brides and their mothers who were off to shop for the trousseau, and emigrants laden down with bundles that they somehow had to squeeze into the limited space available between the other passengers and all the commercial cargo.

Their forty-mile-long route began with a stop at an inn in Polukne, where they teamed up with the Olkenik coachmen and then made two more stops, in Popiski and Krizova, before arriving in Vilna and proceeding to the station for the Eishyshok–Olkenik coachmen, which was in the courtyard of an inn at 8 Stefanska Wielka. Once merchandise had been delivered to and picked up from various merchants in Vilna, the coaches set out on the return journey, once more crossing the perilous Rudnicki forest, and arrived back in Eishyshok on Wednesday, bearing goods for market day on Thursday.

The Lida coachmen, like the Vilner coachmen, traveled in wagons built to accommodate both merchandise and passengers. Accompanied part of the way by peddler-coachmen called *karabelniks*, they too left on Sunday morning, in a caravan of about eight wagons, and headed toward Lida, a twenty-five-mile trip that took about seven hours, including a rest stop at a tavern in Jeszance.

Holding the reins is an Eishyshkian coachman, A. Levin, with two friends or relatives, September 21, 1919. The photo is inscribed in Hebrew "For a lasting memory, I am giving my photo to the beautiful maiden, Rashi Deguchinski, from the town of Eishyshok: Better one old lover than two new ones; better a close neighbor than a distant brother." YESC, SHLANSKI

Though the price was fixed for the various destinations, someone was always trying to negotiate a cheaper rate by volunteering to walk part of the way, a proposition the coachmen usually rejected; others, unable to pay the fee, did walk, keeping close enough to the caravan that they felt secure (especially during the journey through the forests), but far enough so that they weren't considered part of it. Even some of the coachmen walked, either because it meant being able to fill another seat with a paying passenger, or because they wished to ease the load on their beloved horse. In the late nineteenth century Israel Berkowicz, one of the Vilner coachmen, walked the forty miles between Vilna and Eishyshok every week.

Shtetl businessmen had their own regular coachmen whom they trusted with valuable merchandise, such as wagonloads of silver fox furs, dried tobacco leaves, or large sums of money for the purchase of new merchandise. It could prove a costly, or even deadly, mistake to use the services of a coachman who was not one of the regulars. In 1920 Meir Kiuchefski traveled to Lida to pick up a large sum of money that had been sent from the Hebrew Immigrant Aid and Sheltering Society (H.I.A.S.) in America to assist the community in its efforts to recover from the devastation of World War I. On the way back, his coachman, who was an outsider and not well known within the shtetl, slipped poison into his tea, killed him, and made off with the money.

Those businessmen who did maintain close relationships with individual coachmen sometimes commanded such loyalty that they saw their own rivalries with their fellow businessmen reproduced in rivalries among the coachmen. Some coachmen would stop at nothing to undermine a competitor's transport of goods. But that was hardly the only threat to the safety of the coachman and his load. City thieves and roving gangs of bandits stole merchandise and money, rain caused the coaches to sink into the mud in springtime, blizzards often left the coachmen stranded in the snow, fighting off frostbite — and the notoriously vicious wolves — in wintertime.[1]

Depending on the political climate of the age, the coachmen were also sometimes targeted for attacks by anti-Semitic political groups, like those by the Ulans between 1919 and 1921, and the Endekes in the 1930s, which resulted in the looting, beating, and even murdering of coachmen and their passengers. The peddler-coachmen who traveled from village to village to trade with the peasants were similarly vulnerable to anti-Semitic attacks, like the one that befell a karabelnik named Kanichowski at the height of the Ulan riots in the early 1920s. Last seen trading in the village of Kiczie, he was not seen again until his horse and carriage parked in front of his house in Eishyshok, bearing his beheaded body. (He left behind three daughters and two sons, one named Haikl, who was such a believer in peaceful coexistence that he would later return to Eishyshok after the Holocaust and the pogrom that followed, and remain there, as the last Jew, until emigrating to Israel in the mid-1960s.)

Nonpolitical anti-Semitism inspired individuals who had no other motivation than a personal hatred for Jews to attack the coachmen. This happened to Israel Berkowicz one day when he was on his way to Vilna without any passengers and decided to take a rest from his long walk. While asleep in his wagon he felt a sharp pain at his throat, and awoke to discover his body covered in warm blood, as a man standing above him slashed away with a sharp knife. Recognizing the man as a friend of his, he managed to cry out, "Iluk, what's the matter with you? Why are you trying to kill me?" Surprised to be recognized, Iluk suddenly realized who his victim was and responded, "Oh, it is you, Srolke. I thought you were just a Jew!" Iluk was sentenced to twenty years in prison, and Israel, the Vilner coachman, remained hoarse for the rest of his life, but was otherwise strong and healthy until the day he was murdered by the Nazis in Ghetto Radun at the age of eighty-six.[2]

Benyamin Kabacznik riding one of the family horses. One of the shtetl's best riders, he led most of the shtetl parades on his horse. The photo was dedicated to Naftali Berkowitch on the eve of his departure to Eretz Israel, April 1923. PHOTO: YITZHAK URI KATZ. YESC, BERKOWITCH

WOMEN ON THE ROAD

Women who traveled in the Eishyshok coaches faced other kinds of threats. Sexual attacks, by strangers they encountered on the road or by peasant coachmen, worried them much more than anti-Semitic attacks. This had long been a problem in the region. Indeed, the issue of tendlerin (women peddlers) was such a big one that the Lithuanian Council that met in Mir in 1752 devoted an entire session to it, during which they declared numerous prohibitions, including one ordaining that "Every year on Rosh Hashanah, prior to the blowing of the shofar, it must be announced in the synagogue three times that no woman peddler should go to Christian homes."[3]

Despite efforts to ban women from the trade altogether, economic exigency saw to it that they continued to make their rounds of the countryside — and continued to face attack. Newspaper accounts of one incident delighted students at the Kibbutz ha-Prushim yeshivah around the turn of the century. A Jewish village maiden on the way to Eishyshok was set upon by a knife-wielding Christian coachman who tried to rape her. Promising to comply if he would relinquish his knife to her, she protected herself by cutting off the relevant body part just as he was about to carry out the act. The young woman was decorated for her bravery by the tsarist government.[4]

Throughout the nineteenth and well into the twentieth century, many women from Eishyshok found themselves on the road quite frequently. Yekutiel Ginunski's wife, who had three young children, had to provide for her family during the six years her husband was a World War I POW in Germany and, with her sewing machine on her shoulders, she made the rounds from village to village to sew clothes for peasant women. Batia Wilkanski, mother of six and wife of the shtetl dayyan, Reb Layzer, traveled annually to Prussia to visit her family, and went to Vilna on her husband's business, so that he might sit and study without interruption. Rebbetzin Hendl Hutner also traveled for her husband, in order to see his books into print, and did business of her own as well, covering a large area as the exclusive representative of a Russian dye company. Her equally spunky granddaughter, Zivia, began traveling in her adolescence, bringing salt and kerosene back from Vilna to be sold on market day. Sewing machine saleswoman Szeina Blacharowicz had also been traveling from village to village since her youth.

Some of the women in the shtetl whose businesses required them to travel long distances on a regular basis tried to minimize their risk by disguising themselves as men. The religious prohibition against women dressing in men's clothing was frequently suspended by rabbis who were consulted on this matter, especially when the woman's income was essential for the family's livelihood (as was true in families where the husband was occupied with studying the Torah instead of providing for his family's needs).[5]

Firsthand knowledge of the roads and countryside around Eishyshok would later prove crucial for a number of women (including Szeina Blacharowicz) who were able to escape the initial Nazi massacre in the shtetl by fleeing to the forests. Their familiarity with the landscape and their contacts with Christian friends and acquaintances in surrounding villages enhanced their chance of survival.

COACHMEN AS A SOCIAL CLASS

The coachmen were members of the artisan class; in many shtetlekh and cities they had their own synagogue. Though as a class coachmen were considered part of the simple folk, the shtetl amha, they were an extremely diverse group of individuals. Rich and poor, scholarly and ignorant, pious, profane, elegant, crude, they numbered among themselves both gentle, wise souls and cruel, hard-drinking shtarke (thugs).

Coachman Yehiel Lewinson was an ordained rabbi and scholar whose knowledge of the Talmud and reputation for rectitude earned him a prominent seat in the synagogue, but he could not overcome the class stigma that would consign his three beautiful, talented daughters to unsuitable marriages. (A coachman/scholar is still a coachman.) Only by emigrating to Palestine, as they eventually did, could the coachman's daughters marry men who were worthy of them. There were other lovers of learning among the coachmen too. It was not uncommon to see a snow-covered coachman returning from a long journey, whip still in hand, going directly to the shulhoyf to see if he could catch the afternoon or evening prayers or whatever class was in progress. And there he would sit, the snow slowly melting from his clothing and forming a puddle around him, his tired eyes shining with delight because he was in the house of study, studying or listening to the holy words. If there had been among his passengers a noted rabbi or scholar, the coachman might share his joy at such good fortune with his fellow learners. Indeed, the coachman who was privileged to drive Rabbi Yitzhak Elhanan Spektor (1817–1896), chief rabbi of Kovno, saw it as the crowning achievement of his career.[6]

On the other hand, there were coachmen with links to organized crime, and others whose horse and wagon would be stolen while they were having a bout with the bottle. The patrons of Yoshke Shneur Mordekhai's more than once had to buy him a new horse and wagon to replace those that were stolen while he slept off his latest drunk. Arke der Shtarker was a coachman who liked the bottle and who, drunk or sober, had a steel fist that was feared by Jew and gentile alike. But alas, when the Germans started to torture Jews and those who had always dreaded his violence hoped to see it put to good use, he lapsed into passivity, his powerful physique seeming to shrink before their very eyes.

Coachmen as a group were known as hard drinkers. In fact, the coachmen in the town of Bobruisk raised money to build their own shtibl by donating what they would ordinarily have spent on liquor. In less than two years, they had the sum they needed. The people of Bobruisk used to jest that their Coachmen's Synagogue was not built of brick but of vodka.[7] Had the coachmen of Eishyshok diverted their drinking money to the building of a synagogue, it would most likely have exceeded the large summer shul in height and beauty.

Like other members of the artisan class, the coachmen captured the imagination of those who wrote about the shtetl. Adam Mickiewicz, Poland's national poet, who was born in 1798 in the shtetl of Navaredok, wrote a popular ballad, "The Return of Daddy," about a coachman at-

Vilner coachman Yoshke Shneur Mordekhai's (Bleicharowicz) and his son Honke in the mid-1930s. Yoshke's clients often had to buy him a new horse and wagon. At times, they were stolen as he slept off a binge; occasionally a carriage simply collapsed or horses died, since feeding them was not always part of Yoshke's agenda. He survived the war hiding on the farm of a Polish peasant named Adamowicz and living among partisans in the forest. His son Honke, with four other siblings and their mother, were murdered during the September 1941 massacre. PHOTO: BEN ZION SZREJDER. YESC, Y. SONENSON

tacked by a band of forest robbers. A hundred years later Shimshon Melzer, writing about the world that had been destroyed by the Holocaust, would compose a ballad about a coachman who, unable to deliver his merchandise on time because he got stuck in the mud during a thaw, argued his case before God Almighty, the Supreme Judge Himself.[8]

But years before the Holocaust, even as the coachmen continued to inspire those artists and storytellers who loved the more picturesque aspects of the shtetl, they were on the verge of extinction. Dirt roads were giving way to paved highways, the horse and carriage to trucks, buses, and cars. The clatter of horses' hooves on cobblestones, so long a part of the music and cadence of shtetl life, was being drowned out by the honking of horns and the roar of motors.

Pessah Cofnas riding his bicycle from the Seklutski forest toward Vilna Street, summer 1938. Cofnas survived the war, in Russia. YESC, R. & P. COFNAS

MECHANIZED TRANSPORT

When the bicycle was introduced to the shtetl in the 1890s by a Christian doctor, it instantly captivated the youth of the town, becoming the very symbol of modernity. Meir Wilkanski described this eighth wonder of the world: "Sort of a steel vehicle, with a wheel in front and back, it races through the entire shtetl in one second. The rider is safe, unlike the men and beasts in the road before him, who can meet with harm if they are not quick to get out of his way."[9]

During the years between the two world wars, the dream of ownership became a reality for most of the shtetl youth. Those unable to afford to buy a bicycle could rent one from shoemaker Eli Dovid Michalowski, who supplemented his income with a bike-repair and -rental shop. With almost every household owning at least one, the bicycle became a significant means of transportation, and bicycle races an integral part of the shtetl's youth activities.

New feats of speed would become possible when the highway between Eishyshok and

On the Vilna Street First Bridge, Bluma Lubetski is showing off the new bike of her fiancé, Isaac Juris (Etchke Jurdyczanski) (right). Behind Bluma are (left to right) Mickhe Gruznik, Bluma's sister Etele Lubetski, and Hayyim-Yoshke Szczuczynski. Etele was raped and murdered in Eishyshok during the September 1941 massacre. The other four survived the war, in Russia. YESC, I. & B. JURIS

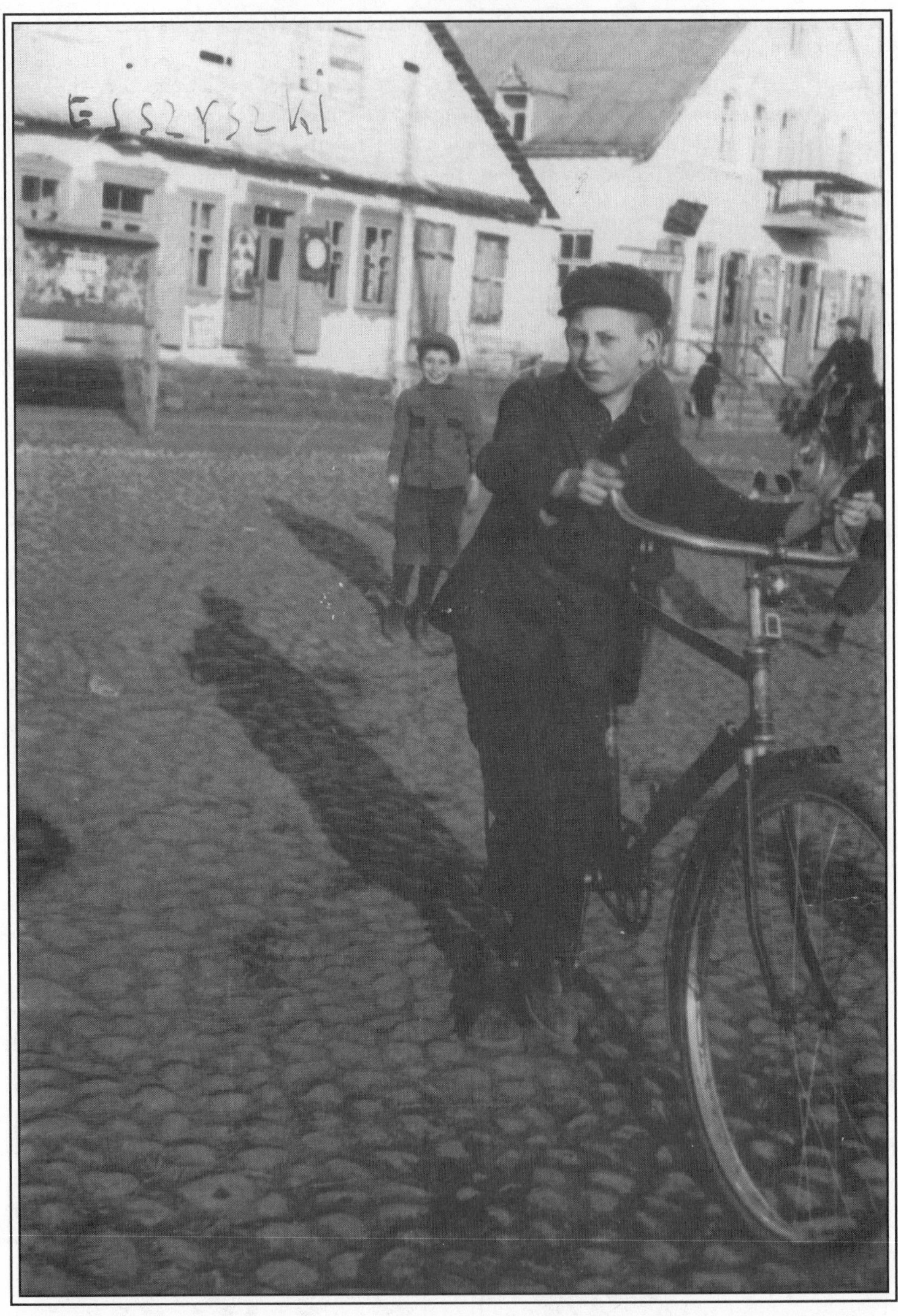

Avigdor Katz on the market square posing with his new bicycle, a birthday present. Avigdor was killed in the September 1941 massacre. PHOTO: BEN ZION SZREJDER. YESC, Y. SONENSON

Atara Kudlanski, one of the shtetl's most popular girls, riding a bicycle on the outskirts of Vilna Street, August 31, 1930. Her dress was a gift from her Aunt Sarah in America. The bicycle was rented. Atara joined her father in America in 1933. PHOTO: REPHAEL LEJBOWICZ. YESC, A. ZIMMERMAN

Newlyweds Esther (Etele) Katz Resnik (in center with white scarf) and husband Yossef (wearing a bowler hat) parting from relatives and friends as they embark on the first leg of their emigration to Colombia. Esther's family is standing next to Yossef: her brother David, mother Alte, sisters Shoshana and Zipporah, holding her baby daughter Yaffa. Esther is standing next to her best friend Szeina Blacharowicz and brother-in-law Moshe Sonenson, with his little son Yitzhak. Yankele Krisilov, the bus driver, is placing their luggage on top of the roof. Most of the people in the photo were murdered by Germans in the September 1941 massacre and in Ghetto Radun, others by the AK. Only Yankele Krisilov, Szeina Blacharowicz, Moshe Sonenson, and his two children survived the Holocaust. PHOTO: BEN ZION SZREJDER. YESC, BLACHAROWICZ WISZIK

The paving of the Pilsudski highway in 1929 at the outskirts of Eishyshok. One of these paving rollers inadvertently ran over a young Polish worker taking a lunchtime nap in its shade. His father was operating it. PHOTO: YITZHAK URI KATZ. YESC, M. KAGANOWICZ

Vilna was paved, a process that began in 1920 and was completed in 1929. Like all innovations, it was greeted with mixed reactions, and a terrible accident that occurred early on seemed to many of the naysayers to confirm their misgivings. A young Polish worker who was taking a lunchtime snooze in the shade of one of the paving rollers was run over by his father, the operator of the roller, who had not seen his son. And indeed, soon after Marshal Jozef Pilsudski rode through the shtetl in an open car to celebrate the completion of the highway named for him and the beginning of a new chapter in the shtetl's life, a new wave of accidents began. This was inevitable, since the Pilsudski highway was a busy artery that ran straight through the center of the shtetl. Eishyshok's first victim was Benyamin Slepak, struck by a speeding bus while in the act of purchasing firewood from a peasant's wagon. The second and third fatalities were a bride and groom who had embarked on a shopping trip to Vilna and were killed when the taxi they were riding in collided with a train. Soon a new phrase began to appear on tombstones in the cemetery of Eishyshok: "Life cut short by an automobile."

Almost as soon as the paving of the highway

was completed, buses began operating between Eishyshok and Vilna, which reduced the day-long journey to a mere two-hour ride. A second bus line put four or five buses a day on the road between Eishyshok and Lida, for what was now a one-hour trip; a third line ran between Eishyshok and the Bastun train station. There was also a regular cab to Bastun, driven by Yankele Hazkl Luski, who had formerly been a bus driver in Palestine, and, in case of emergency (for few people had money to take taxis for everyday purposes), a taxi owned by a Pole named Maricewicz. A Shell Oil gas station owned by Avraham Krisilov and Moshe Slonimski serviced the vehicles from its location at the very center of the market square.

The passenger bus companies were followed by trucking companies, operated by the Lida Corporation formed by some of the Vilna and Lida coachmen. The corporation bought the trucks and then converted Meir Ragachefski's stable into a garage for the Vilna line, Yehiel Lewinson's for the Lida line. Besides the Jewish trucking companies there were also Polish ones.

Though some coachmen were able to move with the times and profit from the change, and others continued to serve locations whose roads were still unpaved, the transition from the

The shtetl bus stop and transportation office in the center of the market square. On the left is the gasoline pump and a tin barrel in which gasoline was delivered to Eishyshok before being transferred to an underground tank. The people in the photo are members of the Nochomowicz–Cofnas families who posed for a photo in honor of a cousin, a former Eishyshkian, visiting from England in July 1937. All the members of the Nochomowicz family who remained in the shtetl were killed in the September 1941 massacre. PHOTO: BEN ZION SZREJDER. YESC, I. FRIEDMAN

A visitor to Eishyshok takes friends on a ride in the early 1930s. Seated next to the driver are Leibke Sonenson and his nephew Benyamin. In the back seat (left to right) are Matle Sonenson Shereshefski, Shaul Dubrowicz, and the driver's friend. The little boy without the hat on the extreme left is Leibke Kaganowicz (Leon Kahn). The houses in the background are those of the Kaganowicz family (right) and Szeina Blacharowicz. Of the passengers in the car, only Matle survived the war, in Siberia; all the others were murdered during the Holocaust. Of those next to the car, only Leon survived. PHOTO: BEN ZION SZREJDER. YESC, Y. SONENSON

After the paving of the Pilsudski highway, to own a car — or even just to ride in one — became the aspiration of the shtetl's younger generation. In the 1930s the most popular backdrop in the photography studio of Alte Katz was that of a sports car with its various accoutrements. Zipporah Katz Sonenson, "taking a ride" in her mother's studio with her two children, baby Yaffa and son Yitzhak in 1937. At the steering wheel is Zipporah's brother Avigdor Katz. Avigdor was killed during the September 1941 massacre. Zipporah was murdered by the AK. Yitzhak and Yaffa survived. PHOTO: BEN ZION SZREJDER. YESC, RESNIK

coachman era to that of buses and trucks was not a smooth ride for everyone. When the Lida Corporation bought its first truck in 1936–37, a number of the Lida coachmen, whose livelihood was at stake, staged an ikuv kriah (Torah reading stoppage) in the synagogue to bring their plight to the attention of the community. Others resorted to violence, beating up several corporation members and breaking the leg of Yude-Yankl Kremin, one of the main shareholders in the venture. The event found its way into a satirical song done by the shtetl's theater group.

But as the number of buses and trucks continued to increase, it became clear that the era of the coachman was over. And just as the coachman had to cede the roads he had dominated for so long, so too did the Jews have to cede their dominance in Eastern European transportation, for most of the bus, truck, and cab companies required government support, and Jews were not eligible for such support. Soon transportation, like so many other formerly Jewish businesses, was largely under Polish ownership.

The shtetl was transformed by these changes. When a 3-zloty fare and a two-hour bus ride was

Drivers, friends, and partners in the gasoline station at the shtetl bus stop in the 1930s: (left to right) Moshe Slonimski; Israel Erlich; Avraham Krisilov; a local Polish policeman; and two bus drivers. Slonimski and Krisilov were co-owners of the Shell Oil station. Both were murdered in the Eishyshok massacre. Erlich was killed by the AK. PHOTO: BEN ZION SZREJDER. YESC, RESNIK

On Vilna Street, Yankl Bastunski is showing off his new car to his friends (left to right) Motke and Shlomo Kiuchefski and Shimon Jurdyczanski. Motke survived the war in Russia; Shlomo was murdered by the AK. Yankl and Shimon were killed by the Germans in Ponar and Eishyshok. YESC, I. & B. JURIS

Members of various Zionist organizations dance on the riverbank near the First Bridge, in honor of halutzim who were about to make aliyah: (left to right) Fania Botwinik, Golde Kabacznik, Shepske Sonenson, Malka Matikanski, Miriam (Mirke) Koppelman, two unidentified friends, Szeina Blacharowicz, Motke Burstein (Szeina's first husband), and three more members of Zionist organizations. Malka made aliyah; Miriam died a natural death in 1940; Szeina survived the Holocaust; all the others perished. A few of the women in the photo marched to their death across this very bridge. PHOTO: BEN ZION SZREJDER. YESC, MATIKANSKI

all that separated Eishyshok from Vilna, the shtetl became a suburb of the big city virtually overnight, thus accelerating the secularization and modernization processes already under way. Young people who were eager to escape the vigilant gaze of their parents and the shtetl elders found new freedom via bus, car, motorcycle, and even bicycle. Thrilled to be able to shed their shtetl ways, they began to imitate the dress, speech, and mannerisms of the big city, and to enjoy its rich cultural fare as well. But it wasn't just the shtetl going to Vilna; Vilna came to the shtetl, in the form of artists, lecturers, and political leaders who found an avid audience there, and paid it many visits.

On the morning of June 23, 1941, German motorcycles crossed the two Vilna Street bridges that led into Eishyshok. The bridge that was closer in, known as the First Bridge, had long been the psychological boundary of the shtetl. All those who yearned for the big world beyond dreamed of crossing that bridge, and it had been the scene of many tearful partings over the centuries — newlyweds saying goodbye to their families as they left for new homes, students bidding farewell to their mothers as they departed for schools in other cities, emigrants taking a last look at their loved ones as they went off in search of a better world. The halutzim used to dance on the riverbank by the bridge whenever any of their members left for Eretz Israel. And former Eishyshkians who had returned for a visit, some from as far away as America or South Africa, others from as close as Vilna, used to pose there for photographs with their relatives — a symbolic gesture meant as a promise to the relatives that they too would one day cross that bridge to a new life.

Travel over the bridge was not just one way, of course. The bridge was the shtetl's official welcoming station. State dignitaries were greeted on the bridge with bread and salt; brides who came to Eishyshok to marry were met on the bridge by their future mothers-in-law bearing honey; the carriage of a new rabbi would be met on the bridge by the town's notables and serenaded by the shtetl klezmers.

The Rushkin family and their new motorcycle: Avraham, son Elisha, wife Miriam (née Koppelman), and daughter Sarale. Miriam (Mirke) died in 1940. Sarale was murdered in Ghetto Zhetl (Dyatlovo) in August 1942. Avraham, a dentist, went from his hiding place in the forest to a former patient, a Polish farmer, to ask for food for him and his son. After a warm reception and a gracious supper, the farmer shot Avraham at close range. Elisha was caught by the Germans. In order not to waste bullets, they split open the head of the six-year-old boy with the butt of a machine gun and left him bleeding in the snow. But Elisha survived the war. YESC, N. FRISCHER

Standing on the Second Bridge are Miriam Kabacznik (right) and Batia Bastunski, welcoming two Hebrew teachers who were returning to Eishyshok in the 1930s. Batia emigrated to America; Miriam survived the war hiding on Polish farms. The two teachers were murdered during the Holocaust. PHOTO: BEN ZION SZREJDER. YESC, RESNIK

When the Germans roared over that bridge on their motorcycles, the natives of Eishyshok, veterans of so many wars, thought it was just another troop crossing. They did not know that this one would prove fatal, that three months later, on September 26, all the women and children of the shtetl, except for the very few who were able to flee into the countryside, would walk over that bridge one last time and meet their death near the Christian cemetery, blasted by volleys of machine-gun fire.

Truck driver Yankele Krisilov had tried to save his family. As the Russians beat a hasty retreat from Eishyshok, he piled his young children in his truck and pleaded with his wife and other family members to escape with him. But to the other Krisilovs, who were not Communist sympathizers like Yankele, the retreating Bolsheviks seemed a greater evil than the advancing Germans, so they wrestled Yankele to the ground and forcibly removed his children from the truck, leaving him to drive away without his family. The man who had saved Fruml Slepak's Singer sewing machine was unable to do the same for his loved ones.

Krisilov survived the war as a supply driver in the Red Army. After the war he remarried and with his new wife settled in Vilnius (as Vilna became known in 1940), the capital of Lithuania, where he was acclaimed as one of the city's model bus drivers.[10] But the new road from Vilnius to Eisiskes (as it was renamed), which had cut the driving time to less than an hour, was not part of his route. Yankele Krisilov would die in 1976 without ever returning to Eishyshok. That forward-thinking, idealistic man of the new era, whose truck had once rumbled over the bridge to bring Vilna to Eishyshok and Eishyshok to Vilna, and who like the other young people of his time had been so eager to link the two worlds, now wished desperately to keep them apart. He wanted to remember Eishyshok as a small, bustling Jewish town with big-city aspirations, so in his mind he locked the shtetl away behind its bridges, and declined to travel the new paved highway that ran over those bridges. He preferred the meandering roads of his memory.

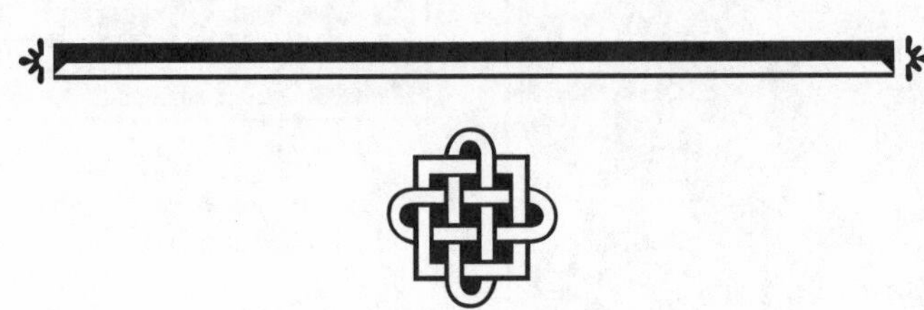

"HOW CAN ONE HAVE A MARKET WITHOUT JEWS?" THIS WAS THE QUESTION POSED BY two Eishyshkian women in 1941, by way of explaining why they were sure no harm would come to the Jews of Eishyshok in World War II. And indeed the Jews had been a key factor in European trade for centuries.

Despite the constant religious, social, and economic tensions between them and their Christian neighbors, Jews were made welcome at European fairs and markets for over a thousand years, from the Middle Ages on. They were such highly valued participants, because of their wide-ranging contacts and family connections, that the fairs were usually scheduled so as not to conflict with the Jewish calendar. This convention goes back at least to the year 825, as we know from a document in which Archbishop Agobard complained that the weekly market in Lyons had been changed from Saturday to another day to suit the needs of the Jewish traders.[1]

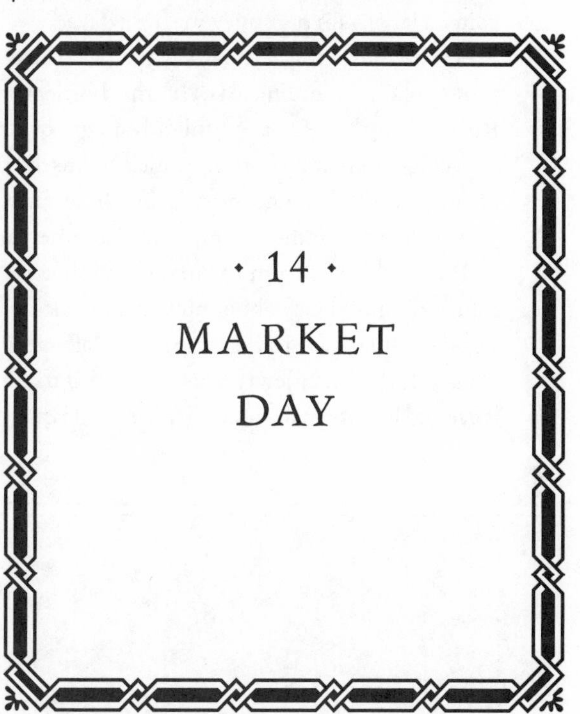

· 14 ·
MARKET DAY

THE SHUL WAS THE SOUL OF THE PEOPLE THE MARKET WAS ITS POCKET.

Shtetl proverb

FAIRS

Even during times when Christian merchants were challenging the commercial rights of Jews in every other context, when Jews were forbidden to live in many areas, when Jews faced outright persecution, they were made welcome at the fairs. The Jews may have been expelled from Breslau in 1455, for example, but they were never absent from the Breslau fair. Attempts to discourage their attendance were resisted, as when the Breslau municipal council opposed the special tax Ferdinand I intended to levy on Jewish fairgoers in 1537; at other times their participation was actively courted, as happened a century later when, at the request of the textile guilds and the imperial authorities (and despite the opposition of the local merchants), Jews were permitted to be in Breslau not just during the fairs but for several days before and after.

In Poland–Lithuania it was expressly forbidden to fix dates of fairs and markets on the Jewish Sabbath or other Jewish holidays, and when the Lithuanian crown persecuted Jews in 1539–40 with the result that they stayed away from the fairs, the nobility appealed to the king to cease the persecutions at once, for the Jews' role in the exchange and distribution of wares throughout the various regions of the country was considered vital. The commercial transactions of a merchant named Shimon, who traveled from Grodno to the Lublin fair in 1580, tell us something of that role: Furs, skins, hides, wax, peasant linen, and other local products were among the items he took to the fair and declared at the customs office; spices, sugar, rice, raisins, prunes, silk, fine linen, and ironware were some of the luxury items he brought back, at a cost of 253 golden coins, a large sum of money in those days.[2]

Permission to travel to fairs was a pan-European policy, extending east to the border of Russia, and the Jews took full advantage of it. Traveling often and far, they availed themselves of all possible benefits offered by these fairs, which were by no means limited to commerce. In Poland, leaders from the major Jewish communities and their rabbis met at the fairs of Lublin and Jaroslav to discuss matters affecting Polish–Lithuanian Jewry as a whole, and to resolve and litigate many local disputes and issues. The fairs facilitated the delivery of mail across long distances, served as meeting places for the exchange of views about Jewish affairs, functioned as convention sites for the various professions, provided a forum for intellectual discourse among yeshivah students, and more. Nathan of Hanover's account of mid-seventeenth-century fairs in Poland makes it clear that those students weren't there just for intellectual or professional reasons: "The head of the yeshivah journeyed with all his pupils to the fair on market day. And at each fair there were hundreds and thousands of Jewish youths and merchants. And whoever had an eligible son or daughter went to the fair and arranged a match, for everyone

On market day horse-drawn carriages, peasants, shtetl residents, out-of-town merchants and artisans occupied every cobblestone of the market square and the streets leading to it. The photo, taken in the 1930s from near the entrance to Radun Street, shows the right side of the market. Vilna Street is in the upper left corner. PHOTO: BEN ZION SZREJDER. YESC, Y. ELIACH

could find one to his liking."[3] Between 1675 and 1764 the majority of Jewish participants in the large European fairs came from Central Europe, but the number of East European Jews was increasing steadily, amounting to one-third of the total Jewish attendance by the early nineteenth century.

THE EISHYSHOK HORSE FAIR

Beginning sometime in the Middle Ages, Eishyshok was host to a grand biannual fair of its own, which put it on the map as a major commercial center.[4] This particular fair had none of the religious or social purposes of some of the other fairs, and it was unusual for a Jewish town because it did not specialize in any of the typically Jewish trades, such as textiles or furs. The Eishyshok fair was a horse fair — the biggest in the region, attracting an international trade. Thousands of horses were brought to the shtetl's market square and there sold to members of the local nobility, to merchants from as far away as Prussia and central Russia, and eventually to the tzarist and Prussian cavalry.

The completion of the railroad in 1860, however, meant the end of the horse fairs: the international trade was able to bypass Eishyshok and transport the horses directly from source to destination via rail. All that remained in Eishyshok from its Horse Fair days were huge stables, a few nicknames that lingered for generations (such as *di praislikhe* to denote those who had traded with the Prussians), and an abundance of legends, particularly about supplying horses to Napoleon's cavalry as it made its ill-fated march on Moscow. Horse trading did continue, but only on a local level, at the weekly market, when livestock was sold from the Horse Market on the edge of Radun Street, as well as from the marketplace itself.

The Horse Fair was replaced by an annual local yerid (fair), which continued until the onset of World War I. Meir Wilkanski attended that fair during his childhood, and described it with excitement: "Today is not just an ordinary market day. It is the yerid, the only such day in the year. Since dawn the wagons, cattle, and peasants have been streaming to town."[5]

THE WEEKLY MARKET DAY

After the disappearance of the annual fair that had so delighted young Meir Wilkanski, there was only the ordinary weekly market day to divert the children of the shtetl. "Ordinary" the Eishyshok market may have been by comparison with the once-a-year extravaganza, but it was still quite an event: a day of merrymaking and moneymaking, holiday and hard work, attracting Jews and gentiles, Tatars, Russians, Poles, Lithuanians, and Gypsies, many of whom came from miles around, as they had been doing for centuries.

With the Industrial Revolution rapidly changing the face of the world, the shtetl market was one of the last vestiges of the old economic system. It was as it had always been: the place where town and country met to provide for each other's needs. By the twentieth century, many of those needs were no doubt being met in other ways, thanks to modern methods of transportation and exchange. But market day would continue to be the lifeline of the shtetl, the very reason for its existence, the nerve center of its economy, right up until the day of the German invasion in the summer of 1941.

Market day was the only day of the week when the profane voices of the marketplace overpowered the melodious chants of the beth midrash learners. It was market day that gave the shtetl its new lease on life each week, and as such it was planned for with care and consumed an ample portion of the inhabitants' (particularly the female inhabitants') energies. The towns in a given area would have their own, nonoverlapping market day — Radun's was Tuesday, for example, Olkenik's Wednesday — so as not to compete with each other. In Eishyshok, preparations for the Thursday market began with the exit of the Sabbath Queen on Saturday night. For the next four days the shtetl Jews plunged into a feverish round of activities, each person part of an army gearing up for a major operation.

Businesspeople, shopkeepers, artisans, and everyone else in the shtetl worked frantically to get ready, because their success on that single day affected their survival during the entire week that followed. In a town where most of the inhabitants lived a hand-to-mouth existence, and all but a few particularly affluent merchants operated on minimal capital, modest stocks of supplies, and a small margin of profit, what happened or, God forbid, didn't happen on Thursday was a matter of considerable gravity. Failure on market day put everything in jeopardy. And therein lies the story of why Malke Roche's Schneider found it necessary to shed her husband.

A widow with several children, Malke married a fine young scholar from the yeshivah whom the saintly Rabbi Yossef Zundl Hutner and his flamboyant wife had found for her. Malke had been supporting her family on the income from her store, which, like the other stores in Eishyshok, had its biggest earnings on market day. On the first market day after their wedding, Malke's husband left the beth midrash to assist his wife for a few hours at the store. It was the first time in his life he had ever faced a real scale, and though he knew all the halakhic and ethical regulations pertaining to scales, he did not in fact know how to use one, as his wife discovered when she gave him a kilogram of salt and he

Market day prior to World War I, when Eishyshok was part of tzarist Russia. The photo was mailed by an Eishyshker to a relative who had emigrated to America. The Yiddish inscription reads: "I am sending you the market. Examine closely the photo and you will recognize all of our Eishyshkian Jews as they talk with the gentiles. This is the entrance to our Vilna Street."
PHOTO: YITZHAK URI KATZ. YESC, L. GINUNSKI

carefully placed both the salt and the weights on one side of the scale.

Malke was outraged. In an unprecedented move, she closed the store at the height of market day, grabbed her husband by the sleeve, and marched him through the market square to the home of Reb Zundl. When she arrived at the rabbi's house, she said, "Rebbe, you gave him to me, you take him back. I am a hardworking widow who is trying to provide for her orphans so that they will grow up to be proper human beings. I do not have the time to raise yet another child." She left her husband with the rabbi and was eventually granted a divorce.

The closer market day grew, the greater the tension and energy in the shtetl. Late Wednesday afternoon the shops in and around the market square were made ready: the floors were swept, signs printed, merchandise rearranged, scales checked for accuracy by the rabbi and his committee, barrels in front topped up with water in case of fire. The cobbler's hammer hit the nails faster, the hum of the tailor's sewing machine accelerated, and letters got shorter because there was no time to spare, and the writers needed their rest. Batia Bastunski wrote to her two brothers in Oakland in 1933: "It is already late, and tomorrow is market day for us, so I am going to sleep." On the evening before market day a few women, alone and in small family groups, could still be seen rushing to and from the public bath, since Wednesday was women's day at the baths. And then all got quiet. One light after another faded, even many of those that usually burned far into the night at the beth midrash. It was the eve of market day, the lull before the storm.

Market square near the entrance to Vilna Street, on a Thursday in 1905 (?) at the break of dawn. Peasants, merchants, and shoppers hoped that an early start would enhance their business transactions for the day. PHOTO: YITZHAK URI KATZ. YESC, KALEKO-ALUFI

Market day began Thursday at dawn. From a distance the earth could be heard rumbling as if an army were on the march — an army of merchants from the countryside. The peasants who had camped Wednesday evening on the outskirts of town were now converging on the center, joining those who were just arriving. From each of the shtetl streets, wagons overflowing with fowl, fruit, grain, and other produce were streaming toward market square, their iron-rimmed wooden wheels making a huge racket as they rolled over the granite cobblestones. There was also the click-clack of horseshoes and the chatter of the peasants. The animals contributed their sounds to the market symphony. Squawking chickens ran about everywhere, constantly attempting to escape their fate. Hogs grunted and growled as they were carried to the scales to be weighed. Horses neighed and stamped their hooves as their teeth were checked and counted by potential buyers. Cows, calves, goats, and sheep chimed in, too. Add to that the bustle of Jews on their way to the shulhoyf for morning prayers, and the frantic scramble of enterprising young people from the shtetl running to intercept the arriving peasants and get first crack at the fattest geese, the freshest vegetables, and the biggest berries, and the scene seemed a chaotic tumult of man and beast. In reality, each wagon, vendor, and pedestrian was headed toward a very specific destination.

By eight o'clock the market was in full swing. Weary horses had been unharnessed and were hungrily eating the oats in their jute feedbags,

Merchants in horse-drawn carriages arrive at the Thursday market, July 21, 1932. Dr. Zytoner, the shtetl veterinarian, checks the horses; that summer there was an outbreak of a contagious disease among horses. YESC, A. ZIMMERMAN

On a cold fall market day, peasant women wrapped in typical shawls, wearing wooden shoes, are standing in front of a Jewish store. The photo was taken by a German photographer during Warld War I. YESC, S. H. FARBER

the wagons were parked, the stands set up to display their colorful merchandise, and wares from the stores lining the market square had been moved outdoors, the better to be seen by passersby.

Each commodity had its own spot on the square: grain, fruits, vegetables, pickles, berries, mushrooms, flour, honey, eggs, butter, nuts, fish, wax, clothing, kerchiefs, shoes, boots, hats, earthenware, ironware, household goods, spoons, spools, sieves, crude oak and pine furniture, kerosene lamps, flycatchers, folk medicines, bridles, harnesses, whips, straps, wagon wheels. There were areas to get your hair cut, enjoy entertainments of various kinds, or consult with the medicine man or woman of your choice; an area where the many non-Jewish beggars and cripples congregated to place their hats before them and beg in the name of God for alms (Jews were allowed to beg only on Friday); an area consecrated to the sale of Christian religious articles — crosses, icons, rosaries, statues of saints; and even, in the nonkosher part of the market, one particular section that sold shiny roasted piglets. Contemplating that symbol of everything that was forbidden, little Meir Wilkanski laments: "Oh how difficult it is to pass that section of the market. The breath is halted, the heart beats faster and the knees are about to give way."[6]

Not just each commodity, but each vendor had a specific location on the market square, which, in Eishyshok as in other shtetlekh, had been fixed since time immemorial. So it was that an American tourist who returned to his native shtetl in the 1920s or '30s, after an absence of many years, immediately recognized the herring vendor from his childhood. There was Soreh Gittl, standing next to her herring barrel, exactly where she had stood twenty-five years before — but the tourist was soon to realize that it was not Soreh, it was Soreh's daughter Hayyeh Beileh, for these locations were passed down from one generation to the next.[7]

Market day was a huge and long-rehearsed pageant enacted each week by buyers and sellers who gradually grew into the roles previously played by their parents, and their grandparents before them, and who therefore knew exactly what to expect of each other. All of the participants were bent on the same happy but modest ends: attracting more customers, selling more goods than the competition, making a small profit, buying all the essentials at the best price, and having a good time.

The talents deployed were many and various, each vendor broadcasting the virtues of his or her merchandise in an accent, melody, and style unlike any other. The Jewish fishermen from Doig (Daugai) sang the virtues of their fish as if they were the most beautiful mermaids. The Muslim Tatars, though more reserved in their advertising than others, spoke in Polish and halting Yiddish of their sweet onions, their fresh vegetables, their excellent tobacco leaves, their huge braids of garlic. Shtetl women selling apples, pears, and cherries from huge barrels aimed an assortment of jingles at their potential customers: one jingle for heder boys, another for grandmothers, yet another for red-cheeked, barefoot shikses. Even the earthenware artisans of the Lebowicz family, quiet people who did not utter a word during the rest of the week, proclaimed the beauty of their creations. Pots, mugs, and bowls of all sizes stood row upon row, some of them painted with beautiful meadow flowers on earth-toned clay, others finished with a shiny single-hued glaze, each of which rang with a lovely hollow sound when the Lebowiczes tapped their fingers against it, like musicians playing a precious instrument. Nearby, the iron merchants' children tried to drown them out with the high-pitched tunes they played on their pots and pans.

Also part of the market's melody were the fights that broke out between vendors as they insulted each other's merchandise and performed tugs-of-war on their customers' sleeves. The Yiddish curses that were exchanged would have put even the virtuoso performances of a Sholem Aleichem character to shame.

THE MARKET IN WINTER

The market was at its peak during the summer months when a veritable cornucopia of products spilled from its stalls, but each season brought its special delights, its particular sounds and colors and smells. Undeterred by the difficulties of overland travel through the snow-covered winter countryside, many of the peasants brought their goods to market on sleds rather than wagons; the clacking of wagon wheels on cobblestones was replaced by the whir of sled runners on hard-packed, well-traveled snow, accompanied by the ringing of the Sunday bells that many of the horses wore around their necks, as protection against getting lost in a blinding blizzard, and the ceaseless stamping of boot-clad feet, for warmth.

For man, woman, and beast, keeping warm during winter market days, when the temperature often reached 40 below zero, was their biggest priority. The horses wore blankets of coarse jute sacks, while the people wore attire appropriate to their social class. Peasants dressed in a multitude of layers topped with sheepskin jackets tied with ropes, sheepskin hats on their heads, and volickes (felt boots) to cover their rug-wrapped feet. Shtetl residents swathed themselves in an array of animal skins, which included mink, rabbit, sheepskin, raccoon, dyed lamb, and fox, and wore heavy hats, gloves, and boots for additional warmth. But whether they were dressed in the coarsest of sheepskins or the silkiest of minks, everyone contributed to the overall appearance of the winter market as a congregation of large bundles moving around constantly for warmth, some gracefully, others quite clumsily.

The frigid weather took its biggest toll on the outdoor vendors, many of whom were women. To keep warm they used the "fire pot" (der Fire Top), a pot filled with burning coals concealed beneath their many-layered skirts. Some women lent their fire pots briefly to other women at the market, or warmed their children by having them take shelter under their skirts, next to the fire pot.[8] The market women and their fire pots were a staple of East European folklore, and an endless source of humor, much of it rather risqué.

Though the winter market was smaller, with fewer outdoor vendors coming from the countryside, it had its own specialties that lent their distinctive aroma to the goings-on. Fresh produce gave way to barrels filled with pickled vegetables and apples and an array of delicious preserves. And since all the buildings in Eishyshok were heated by woodstoves, the winter months brought a weekly invasion of sleds piled high with logs giving off their wonderful woodsy fragrance, promising a few more days of warmth.

Buying the wood involved a special set of skills. First it had to be selected, and only the connoisseurs knew how to pick just that special blend of pine, oak, and birch logs that would create the perfect heat level in the house, the most wonderful aroma for each room, and the tastiest results on the spit and the broiler. Then came the bargaining, between the peasant in his short sheepskin coat and tall hat on one side of the firewood sled, the shtetl buyer in a long fur coat on the other. Buyer and seller would circle the sled, clapping their hands and stamping their feet to keep warm, so that from a distance, on a cold snowy day with many such negotiations taking place, the market appeared to be staging a strange, almost dancelike ritual on a mass scale, from which each pair of partners withdrew only at the conclusion of the deal, when the sled followed the buyer home to unload the precious cargo.[9] One of the most legendary of the shtetl bargainers was Goldke di Hilzerne ("wooden Goldke"), a wood merchant whose stern manner of conducting business earned her a reputation among her peasant suppliers and her Jewish customers alike. Each Thursday she took up her place in the holtz mark, the special section of the market where the wood buyers and sellers congregated.

A WOMAN'S PLACE

Women ran much of the market. Until the changes that began toward the end of the nineteenth century, when the forces of secularization saw to it that fewer and fewer boys went to yeshivah, and many of the younger men no longer studied at the beth midrash all day, much of the male population of the shtetl was otherwise occupied on market days. Young heder boys were available to help out in the market for a few hours, as the melamed himself was busy shopping for potatoes, onions, flour, and other essential items; but aside from them, the only other Jewish males who regularly came to market were the occasional rich merchant, and men from the artisan class whose wives managed the business end of things while they produced the product. So until World War I the market was largely in the hands of the grandmothers, mothers, and daughters of the shtetl.

Perhaps that was why so many of the usual social barriers, between classes and between Jew and gentile, broke down on market day. The women of Eishyshok were more proficient than their men in the languages spoken by the gentile peasants. Many could manage conversations in Polish, Russian, and Byelorussian, and some knew the essential trade words in Lithuanian and Tataric as well. They were familiar with the religion and customs of their clients, took an interest in their families, assisted them with their practical needs, and even knew their tastes well enough to take them into account when ordering stock. Malke Roche's Schneider, for example, was considered not just a merchant but an adviser and friend to many gentiles. She knew all their woes and sorrows, and would sympathize with them when a pregnant swine was accidentally slaughtered or the crops failed. Though she was tight with her money, she sold to all the peasants on credit, and remembered all her accounts accurately without ever having to write down a name or an amount.

Most shtetl men, however, spoke only Yiddish and were totally alienated from the gentile countryside, for which reason many gentiles preferred to do business with women. When asked their destination on market day, they were apt to answer "going to Malke" or "going to Gitka," or even, with reference to shops where a man was present too, "going to Pani Yossefa" (Yossef's wife) or "going to Pani Katzowa" (Katz's wife), mentioning only the female proprietor. Thus a man in the store on market day was generally considered a liability. Batia Wilkanski, for one, was always quite relieved when her husband, Reb Layzer the dayyan, left her small ironware store. She felt that his brief appearances there chased the customers away.[10]

Every goy had his Jew, and every Jew her (or his) goy, especially in the case of the well-to-do peasants, who were considered petit nobility. They would often go to the homes of their preferred Jewish customers prior to taking their goods to market, offering them first pick, perhaps bartering for things they needed. Occasionally such transactions would conclude with a glass of vodka or tea or some special Jewish dish favored by the gentile peasants. Some of these cordial business relationships ripened into real friendships, with the gentile being asked to spend the night before market day in his Jewish friends' home, and parking his wagon in the backyard of his host.[11] Kazimierz Korkuc of Korkuciany, for example, who parked his wagon at the home of Moshe and Zipporah Sonenson in the 1930s, had an extremely close relationship with the Sonensons and their cousins, the Kabaczniks. He did business with them, selling them skins for their leather and fur trade, and he celebrated his birthday with them each year. Indeed, he owed his very life to Zipporah's parents, Yitzhak Uri and Alte Katz, for in World War I he had been left for dead by the Russians, and they had rescued him from a pile of corpses and nursed him back to health, using drugs from their own pharmacy and that of the Koppelman family.

The shtetl women were at least as busy shopping as they were selling. Every shtetl woman, regardless of her social status, shopped at the weekly market. Not to do so was to be labeled meshuggeneh (insane), as Yitzhak Dubitski's wife discovered when, as a bride new to Eishyshok, she chose to shun the market. Even women who had merchandise brought to them in their homes still had to go to market to see for themselves, for there might be someone who had a fatter goose for the Sabbath dinner or better berries for that special varenie (jam). With basket in hand, and children trailing behind ready to assist in carrying the purchases back home, mothers made their rounds from wagon to wagon, store to store. Everything was closely examined. Buying a chicken or goose, for example, was quite an exacting process: First you had to get a good grip on the bird's legs, then you had to assess the quality of the feathers, then blow the feathers apart to see the color of the skin, yellow being a sign of ample amounts of the fat you needed to make gribenes (chicken fat fried with onion). Once the fowl was selected, the bargaining could begin. To shop and not to bargain was considered a mortal sin, insulting to both seller and buyer alike. A person who failed to bargain was sure to become the laughingstock of the shtetl for weeks to come. In his 1978 memoir, *No Time to Mourn*, Leon Kahn (Leibke Kaganowicz in the shtetl) recounts his childhood shopping expeditions with his mother:

It was very exciting to follow my mother as the weekly ritual began; the thoughtful trip from wagon to wagon, looking, touching, pinching, smelling the produce. And bargaining! (Between housewives and farmers this had been refined to an art!). . . . At last my mother would choose a wriggling chicken, its feet tied together with string, and take it straight away to the shochet, the ritual slaughterer, across the square.[12]

The children of the shtetl, especially the boys, whose lives were so confined by the boundaries of the heder, found market day offered a bounty of practical education. There in the marketplace the heder boys witnessed the dynamics of the world outside the melamed's home and the synagogue. They learned about agricultural produce — where it grew and what made it flourish and how to recognize the best. They learned about measuring — liquids and solids, berries, grains, fabrics, and livestock — for there before these young scholars was a peasant woman who did not know how to read, write, or count and yet could measure out her berries exactly, being careful not to spill or crush even one berry's worth of her precious commodity, and then knew to the last grosz (Polish penny) the value of what she was selling and the change she owed out of what she was paid. And most of all they learned about people, growing familiar with various groups of peasants, their regional attire, religious and ethnic affiliations, and even their familial status. In the 1880s, while still tots, Meir Wilkanski and his heder friends could tell which young peasant woman was married, single, or about to get married, and who was Catholic, Provoslavic, or Muslim.[13]

ENTERTAINMENT

The range of entertainments offered on market day was vast. In addition to the general spectacle of the human comedy, which was free for the looking, a variety of performers did their acts for a paying audience. Among the former could be counted the team of Lemel the tailor and his partner Moishe der Guss ("the last"). Tailors to the peasants, and not terribly refined in either the materials or the techniques they used, they made their patterns by having the client lie down on a piece of paper, which they then cut to conform to his body shape. This process was much enjoyed by the children who watched (and others besides). Among the professional entertainers was the organ grinder with a monkey on his shoulder who, for a fee, would give you a piece of paper with your fortune on it. Another did a variation on the same act but was assisted by a bird rather than a monkey. Both performers were particular favorites of the children and the young, unmarried farmers and their girlfriends. Also on the bill were a dancing bear; a puppet theater (whose puppets spoke in all the regional dialects), which ranked as one of the wonders of the world to the children of the nineteenth century; and a wheel of fortune, manned in the early 1900s by Shraga Feibush, the shtetl barber.[14]

Perhaps the most colorful of all the entertainers were the Gypsies, entire families of them, who came to market in the bude (covered wagons) in which they lived. Dressed in vivid clothing that set off their olive skin, dark eyes, and gold-capped teeth, they were an exotic presence in the market, thrilling but also slightly menacing. They would tell fortunes, read cards and palms, dance with tambourines, sing sad, haunting songs, eat fire, walk ropes strung between the row shops in the center of the market and the firehouse, and send their children out into the crowd, tambourines extended, to collect their reward. Though everyone was delighted by the acts, they also remained on guard as they watched, parents holding on tight to their children, peasant women guarding the bodices in which they'd hidden their leather pouches, for the Gypsies were never able to shake their reputation as kidnappers and thieves.

A PEASANT HOLIDAY

For the peasants, market day was a mini-vacation from the farm and its laborious chores. Eager to put business matters behind them so that they could turn their attention to entertainment and certain personal concerns, they tried to empty their wagons of the goods they had brought to market, and to buy whatever items they needed, as quickly as possible.

Once the selling and buying were concluded, they could avail themselves of the many amusements and amenities of the shtetl. Since the public baths were open to non-Jewish men on market day, some of the farmers took advantage of the opportunity to bathe and to delouse their clothing there. Getting a haircut and being bled by leeches, both of which were done by the barber at his stand in the marketplace, were other popular activities. The farmers also visited various medical practitioners, who always did a brisk business on market day. There was Berl

Standing on the steps of the Alte Katz (A. Kac) drugstore and enjoying the view of the market in the mid-1930s are (right to left) Esther (Etele) Katz, her sister Shoshana, and their friend Fania Botwinik. Seated on the steps (right to left): Avigdor Katz, his nephew Yitzhak Sonenson, Yitzhak's cousin Gittele Sonenson, and two friends. To the right of the steps is the entrance to the bakery below street level. On the left is a display of photos from the Katz photography studio. Only Esther and Yitzhak survived the war. PHOTO: BEN ZION SZREJDER. YESC, RESNIK

Vasilishki, a shtetl medicine man and horse expert, who was in great demand during the 1920s and 1930s for his potions, his good advice, and the curative jingles — different ones for toothaches, stomachaches, headaches and so forth — that he taught his ailing patients; there were the Tatars, who were as famous for their medicinal skills as they were for their excellent vegetables; there were two doctors who attended to them, one in an infirmary and one in the shtetl hospital; and there were several drugstores where the farmers often went to purchase medication as a backup to the folk remedies they preferred.

From 1905 on, one of these drugstores was located on the ground floor of Alte Katz's house on the market square. Standing on its steps, which were in a straight line with the gasoline pump and the bus stop at the center of the market, one had a view of the market's entire western flank, and could even catch a glimpse of the Gypsies' covered wagons from a safe distance. Within the store, all was neatly ordered and arranged, and the activity was constant. Above the sounds of the mortar, grinding the various potions, rang the hubbub and laughter of peasants reporting on the health of their loved ones, and deciding what to buy. From huge, slender-necked blue and amber bottles wrapped in wicker baskets, medicine was poured into small individual bottles; from a clear, glass-corked bottle was dispensed a white headache powder the peasants called Kogutek, after the rooster insignia that appeared on the small yellow envelopes in which the powder was sold; and other ointments and toiletries were transferred to tiny wooden boxes bearing labels that illustrated their functions. Drawn by Alte Katz's daughter Shoshana, for the benefit of the illiterate peasants, the labels depicted a face with boils, a hand scratching a foot with a boil, an ear into which drops were being poured, a soap bar, a cologne bottle. For special customers, there were labels adorned with the image of the Dionne sisters, the Canadian quintuplets born in 1934.

On the second floor of Alte Katz's house was another establishment popular with the peasants on market day: one of the shtetl's two photography studios. Engaged couples, newlyweds, the parents and grandparents of a just-christened baby, all were eager to immortalize the turning points in their lives. Those coming in from the countryside would sling their shoes over their shoulders (for the peasants expected their shoes to last a lifetime), tie their festive attire into a kerchief or a jacket, then change into their good clothes once they had arrived. After choosing an appropriate backdrop and props, they would get into position for the picture, freeze — and, as often as not, find the enterprise interrupted by the ringing of the bell that meant Alte Katz was needed down below in the drugstore. There they would remain, frozen in place, staring into the black-draped camera manned by Alte's associate, Ben Zion Szrejder, as though watching an amazing revelation. Soon Alte would come running back upstairs, make some adjustment in the pose, and take the picture — a process that never failed to entrance her grandchildren Yitzhak and Yaffa Sonenson. The two children loved spending time in that magic kingdom, which included not just the photography atelier and the drugstore but, on yet another floor, a few steps below street level, a bakery, where peasants gathered to eat pirogen and gulp down glass after glass of tea on market day.

From Alte Katz's the children could look into Aaron the Saltman's shop next door, which was filled with farmers on shopping expeditions, and into a building across the alley where their uncle Shalom Sonenson had a fabric store. With wooden yardstick in one hand and a large pair of scissors in the other, he was the very picture of concentration as he measured and cut cloth at top speed, never noticing the watchful eyes of his little nephew and niece.

THE DARK SIDE OF MARKET DAY

The shtetl's eighteen Jewish-owned drinking places did a brisk business on market day, selling vodka, beer, and kvass, which could be downed with kielbasa, herring, pickles, black bread, and the white Jewish bread called hallah. Some peasants arrived at the saloons the moment the doors opened, leaving their wives behind to sell their goods; others went only at the conclusion of the business day, sometimes accompanied by their wives and girlfriends, who either joined them in a glass or two or, more frequently, stood vigilant guard to make sure the menfolk didn't drink all their hard-earned money away. Some of the women, however, went off on their own errands, perhaps to one of the shtetl's letter writers, women like Mariyasl Yurkanski who, for a fee, would take down the words they wished to send to distant loved ones. Meanwhile, they knew they could count on the saloonkeepers to see to it that their husbands didn't get too drunk, for most of them knew their customers well and would refuse to serve them after a certain level of inebriation had been reached, and might even send them to a back room to sleep off the effects of overindulgence. The beautiful tavern owner Shoshke Wine, for example, was very popular with the peasants for the vigilance with which she protected them from their own tendencies toward excess. But just in case, the most cautious of the women would give their husbands only a small portion of the day's earnings, sometimes hiding the rest with the saloon owner.

Despite all the precautions, however, market day was known for its drunken brawls. Young peasants would arrive at the market armed with heavy sticks, knives, and even pistols so as to be ready for the bloody encounters, some of which ended in arrest, severe injury, and even death. During the years between the two world wars these incidents bore increasingly anti-Semitic overtones.

Market day was also the day when crime in the shtetl was at its height. Shoplifting and pickpocketing were common, no matter how hard people tried to guard against them, and even though most of the thieves were well known to their victims. Yitzhak the Chicken, a notorious poultry thief, was especially active on market day, when birds were so abundant. Arie Yankel the horse thief slaughtered some of the horses he stole, in order to sell their hides and hair on the market, and traded the rest — sometimes to the very farmers he had stolen them from. When he was caught, as happened occasionally, he got his sons to assist him in the resulting brawls. In all other respects Arie Yankel considered himself an upright citizen and could be heard reciting the Eighteen Benedictions in the synagogue, long after even the rabbi had finished.

Yehudah the Brigand was the shtetl's nineteenth-century Robin Hood, who used his professional skills as well as his imposing physical prowess to go to the rescue of his fellow Eishyshkians on market day. Prior to alerting the police, robbery victims would turn to him, and they were very rarely disappointed. Once when a prayer shawl and phylacteries were taken from a Jew from one of the nearby villages, Yehudah sprang into action and very soon located the missing articles, which were hidden in the straw of a wagon belonging to a perfectly innocent-looking peasant who was parked on the market square. When asked by the amazed onlookers how he had performed this feat of detection, Yehudah pulled on his beard and replied, in his characteristic Talmudic chant, that the peasant's well-bred horse did not seem a match for his plain wagon, which meant that the horse was stolen, and if he'd stolen the horse, then he'd probably stolen other items as well.[15]

With the building of the Pilsudski highway in the 1920s, market day crime increased dramatically, as thieves from Vilna, Grodno, Lida, and other smaller towns found it simple to board buses that would take them directly to their targets. Eventually these thieves also became familiar figures to the Eishyshok merchants and their customers, so that vigilance would increase as soon as they were seen disembarking from the bus.

The local police, who came out with reinforcements from neighboring towns on market day, did offer some protection. During the tzarist regime, Eishyshok's police were Jewish, two of them legitimate and the third a tzarist informer. During World War I the Jewish police patrolled alongside the German military police, who would later be remembered fondly — especially in comparison with the Polish police who succeeded them.

These twelve Polish Catholic policemen were headquartered on the second floor of lumber merchant Eliyahu Bastunski's home, from which they had a clear view of the market square. Besides crime intervention, their duties included collecting fees from the market vendors, keeping the highway clear for traffic (a time-consuming task, since the road ran straight through the middle of the market), breaking up the increasingly frequent anti-Semitic clashes, which they were slow to do, and preventing illegal political activities, which they were much more serious about, especially when the politicking involved members of the outlawed Communist Party.

The Communists used market day as an occasion to distribute party literature, and to hang political posters on the telegraph poles in and around the market square, where everyone would see them. Pessah Cofnas, David Ejszyszki, and other comrades used to steal pigeons, tie red flags to their feet, then release them over the square. As the pigeons took flight, the strings attaching them to the red flags often became tangled in the electrical wires, and sometimes the fire department had to spend hours freeing the birds and removing the offensive flags. Such stunts often led to searches and arrests that tied up the police for the duration of the day, though the culprits were generally well known.

For a few years the Polish police were assisted by members of Beitar, a right-wing, militaristic Zionist youth group founded in 1923, who turned out in force on market day to help maintain order and direct traffic. In their uniforms and caps, with police whistles strung around their necks, they made quite an impression, and eventually became very popular and well respected. After some of the most active Beitar leaders emigrated to Palestine and South America, however, the group's police operations ceased, which left the shtetl Jews more vulnerable than ever to anti-Semitic attacks.

Such attacks were led by Poles, among them the son of the merchant Dakinewiczowa, whose pork store on the market square displayed icons of Mary and Jesus alongside signs saying "This is a Christian store" and "Patronize your own." One of Eishyshok's handful of allies of the extremist Endecja Party, an anti-Semitic, "Poland-for-the-Poles" organization, the Dakinewiczowa boy and his fellow green-armband-wearing Endekes would attempt to block the entrances to various Jewish stores on market day. Most of the peasants ignored them and continued to deal with their favorite Jewish proprietors and customers, but there were always a few younger peasants to whom the anti-Semitic jingles and slurs appealed. The resulting fistfights, broken bones, and smashed windows sometimes failed to elicit a prompt response from the police, and when the response did come it was sometimes more sympathetic to the Polish rioters than to the Jewish victims. (Later some of those same police would serve under the Nazis.) Elsewhere, for example in Grodno, the Jewish community organized very effective self-defense groups in response to the rising tide of anti-Semitism in the 1920s,[16] but that never happened in Eishyshok, perhaps because few of the Jews there recognized the gravity of their situation — and those who did, primarily the young people, were likely to have already left.

The end of a market day in July 1937. Villagers from nearby who leased the rights to clean the market square gathered the rich bounty of manure to be carted away to their farms. The last buses leave for Vilna (on the right) and Lida (on the left). To the right of the gasoline pump is the old water reservoir (der alter chop). On the left is the market's lightning rod. PHOTO: BEN ZION SZREJDER. YESC, RABBI I. FRIEDMAN

Indeed, the very regularity of market day may have lulled those who remained, for the market of Eishyshok on the eve of World War II seemed as teeming with life and color as it had for centuries. Jews and gentiles did business with each other with the same gusto and vigor as their ancestors had before them. And the cleanup that took place at the end of each market day was done with the same eye to the future as always: By arrangement with the Eishyshok kahal, villagers from nearby leased the privilege of cleaning the market square in exchange for the rich bounty of manure it yielded, which would ultimately be returned to Eishyshok in the form of the next season's tomatoes, onions, beets, and other crops.

POLONIZATION

Those who had not emigrated in the 1920s and '30s faced increasing economic hardships because of the Polish government's attempts to "Polonize" the nation's commerce by passing laws that would force Jews out of their traditional businesses and replace them with Poles. On the eve of World War II, the Jews of Eishyshok were also fearful that the local government would follow through on its threats to change market day from Thursday to Saturday, and/or require them to relocate the market from the center of the shtetl, where all the Jewish businesses were based, to the outskirts, which was the Polish sector. Either of those moves would have been the death of the shtetl economy, and never more so than at that time, when merchants were already in such dire straits.

1939–41

After the outbreak of World War II, when Eishyshok was returned to Russia, this time as part of the USSR, with a brief eight-month interlude during which it was part of an independent Lithuania, the market continued to be held on its usual day. However, because many of the villagers who had been regular traders were from Byelorussia, and could no longer legally cross the border to come to Eishyshok, the market shrank considerably. Moreover, those merchants who remained were unable to do business in the usual way for fear of being labeled bourgeoisie and deported to Siberia, so they hid much of their better merchandise and sold it on the flourishing black market. Portraits of Marx, Lenin, and Stalin appeared in many shop windows, including those of the merchant Dakinewiczowa, who was quick to substitute them for the Holy Family icons that had previously enjoyed pride of place.

It was, however, the best of times for the artisan class, who were now held in high esteem as the true sons and daughters of Mother Russia. Young people who had been jailed for their Communist activities during the Polish years were now at liberty, and were put in command of the shtetl. These new Communist commissars numbered among their many duties the supervision of Eishyshok's commerce, especially on market day.

Another new feature of market day was the presence of thousands of Jewish refugees streaming eastward to escape the German occupied territories. In the less than two years between the initial German invasion of Poland and the Germans' arrival in Eishyshok, in June 1941, 15,000 refugees passed through this town of about 3,500, often under cover of the general commotion of market day. Dressed as peasants, they mingled with the market crowd and surreptitiously made contact with the local Jews, who helped them in a variety of ways.

But despite the horrible stories the refugees told of German atrocities they'd witnessed in the occupied territories, despite Hitler's inflammatory speeches which could be heard blasting from the shtetl's few radios, most people in Eishyshok continued to enjoy a false sense of security. "This too will pass" was the consensus; the huge market square and all its inhabitants would weather this storm as they had so many others over the centuries. And indeed, market day continued, as regular as ever, during 1939, 1940, and much of 1941.

One market day in 1941 a farm wagon carrying honey overturned in the center of the market and dumped all its cargo onto the cobblestones. This caused one of the horses pulling the wagon behind it to slip, and thus to upset that wagon, which was carrying apples. The apples that spilled out of the second wagon became coated with honey and rolled all over the market square. Many people in the shtetl were delighted, for this seemed an omen that the approaching New Year, Rosh Hashanah of 5702, would be a good, sweet year for the Jews of Eishyshok.

Three days later, on Monday, June 23, 1941, German tanks and motorcycles rolled through the same market square. The daughters of Dakinewiczowa welcomed them with flowers and with the latest portrait in the rotating display that adorned their mother's shop window — that of Hitler.

Moshe Sonenson pleaded with his mother, Hayya Kabacznik Sonenson, and his mother-in-law, Alte Katz, to run away into hiding with him, his pregnant wife, and their two young children, before the German grip on the shtetl became inescapable. But both the older women had very favorable recollections of the Germans who had patrolled the Eishyshok market during World War I, bringing such good order, and they could not imagine the sons of those men being that radically different from their fathers. After a long debate, the decision was made to remain in the shtetl, for, as the women reassured themselves: "It would be unthinkable for them to destroy us. How can one have a market without Jews?"

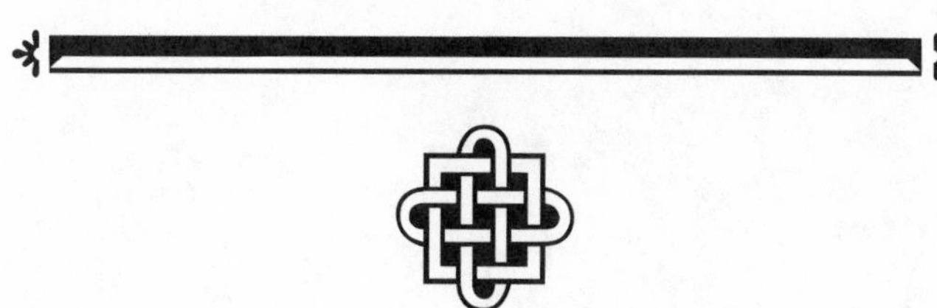

· FOUR ·

FAMILY AND COMMUNITY

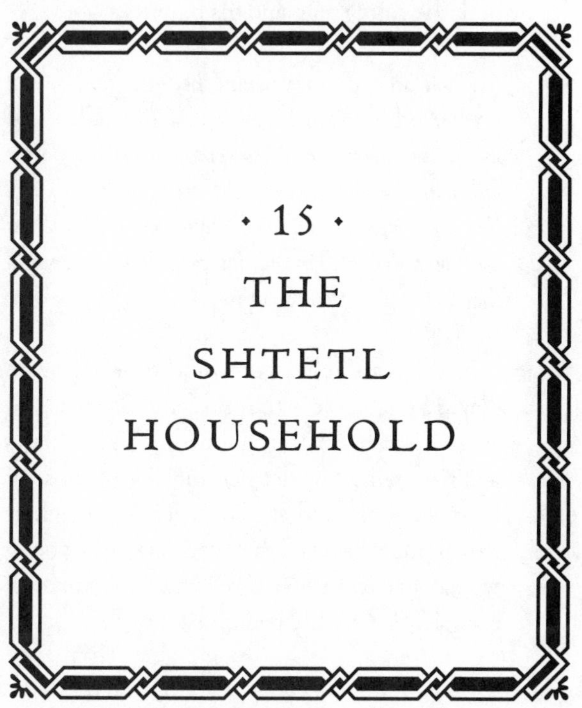

15 THE SHTETL HOUSEHOLD

THREE THINGS INCREASE A MAN'S SELF-ESTEEM: A BEAUTIFUL DWELLING, A BEAUTIFUL WIFE, AND BEAUTIFUL FURNISHINGS.

Brakhot 57/B

THE FAMILY UNITS OF THE SHTETL WERE USUALLY MATRILOCAL IN NATURE: THE pattern in Eastern Europe, dating from at least the seventeenth century, was for young couples to establish their first household in the home of the wife's family.

From the sixteenth century on, the ideal husband for an Eastern European Jewish girl was the scholar, the diligent, promising yeshivah student. Hence the criteria for the bride were that she be the daughter of well-to-do parents who were eager and able to support the scholar and his young family during the early years of their marriage, in an arrangement known as *kest.* Offering kest allowed the husband to continue his studies, while the bride, ideally an industrious, strong, healthy young woman, established a business of her own that would eventually enable her to take upon herself the financial responsibility for her husband and their children. During this period the wife (and sometimes her husband) might receive training in the family business, as preparation for becoming a worker or a partner in it, or might learn a craft or a trade, or might do agricultural work. The duration of the kest period was according to the husband's level of scholarship. The greater the scholar and the higher the hopes for his intellectual growth and achievements, the longer the kest.

If the newlyweds did not actually reside there, they usually lived close by and ate their major weekday meals as well as all their Sabbath and holiday meals there. Instantly the bridegroom became a member of a new extended family, with its own customs, quirks, and complexities.[1] Often it included three generations under one roof, for kinship responsibilities were extensive, and often the mix was further complicated by stepchildren from earlier marriages that had ended either in death or — rarely — divorce.

SONS-IN-LAW

For the new husband, this period could prove a very difficult adjustment. Though a proverb held that "a son-in-law can do no wrong," this was one of those sayings more honored in the breach than the observance, describing an ideal but seldom realized situation in which the bride's parents endlessly admired and pampered their beloved son-in-law, the highly esteemed scholar. In reality, sons-in-law were perceived as doing wrong much of the time, and treated accordingly. And the treatment must have seemed all the worse by contrast with the adoration they had received in their own homes growing up.

Thus many a young son-in-law found it difficult to fit in to his wife's family. The letters that one Shmuel of Kelme, Lithuania, wrote to his newly married son Arieh-Leib in the nineteenth century offer a glimpse into the resulting pain of both the young man and his parents:

My son, beloved of my soul! I heard a rumor, and my stomach was upset, that your father-in-law and mother-in-law (perhaps your spouse as well), and your father-in-law's entire household, are at odds with you. You never mentioned it to us — and you did not tell us that you are belittled in your father-in-law's house, and they do not pay attention to you.

In this case it was the mother-in-law who played a major role in the problems. She insulted Arieh-Leib by casting doubt on his scholarly abilities, which she deemed inferior to those of her own sons. And she so upset her daughter that Shmuel believed the miscarriage the young woman had recently suffered was the result of all the grief her mother had caused.[2]

Hayya Sonenson, mother of Reb Shael Sonenson, in the 1870s. She was a typically powerful Lithuanian matriarch: in command at home, successful in her business, and even known for her scholarship. After her son Shael married Hayya Kabacznik, he called his wife Haike to distinguish her from his mother. She was Yaffa Eliach's paternal great-grandmother.

YESC, M. SACHAROFF

CHILD BRIDES AND GROOMS

The Talmud dictated that the father of a daughter should seek to marry her off at a young age, anytime from twelve on; if she did not marry young she might break the commandments and become unchaste.[3] This practice of encouraging marriage at an early age has remained a constant feature in traditional Jewish society, owing not just to moral concerns about chastity, but to a variety of economic, cultural, and political circumstances. For example, during the cantonist period, 1827–56, when the tzarist army was drafting Jewish males as part of a pattern of anti-Semitic persecution, boys as young as their early teens, and sometimes even younger, were married off so that they could avoid army service. Fear of government decrees attempting to delay Jewish marriages — some of them real, some only rumors — merely resulted in a flood of such rushed early unions. The legal literature of the time reflects both the public and private aspects of this phenomenon, and the considerable suffering it caused.[4]

The younger the son-in-law, the harder the adjustment was likely to be; a groom who was virtually a child had few defenses or resources to fall back on. A teenage husband who was regarded as a budding scholar of promise at the yeshivah might be treated as a spoiled brat who needed to be disciplined in the home of his in-laws, with mothers-in-law often doing the disciplining.

The philosopher Salomon Maimon (1753–1800) was a child prodigy who was born in Lithuania and married off — being quite a prize — at the age of eleven. In his autobiography, he described himself as "under the lash of my mother-in-law" and recounted the indignities she visited upon him, which included not just her refusal to honor her financial obligations to him and the way she begrudged him his very meals, but physical attacks as well. "Confident by reason of my youth and want of spirit, she even ventured now and again to lay hands on me."[5] Another story, dating from around the same time, concerned a twelve-year-old boy (referred to in the responsa literature describing these events as a "babe") who married an equally young girl. Since the bride would not permit her husband to touch her, the marriage remained unconsummated. When their failure to have sexual relations was attributed to her husband's refusing her on the grounds that she wasn't a virgin, however, she yielded to pressure and agreed to fulfill her marital obligations. Unfortunately, the couple were interrupted by a knock at their door as they were trying to perform the act, and from that day on the humiliated youngsters avoided each other. Shortly after his fourteenth birthday the husband disappeared, leaving his wife an agunah (a deserted woman who cannot remarry since she was never granted a divorce).[6]

Even the brilliant scholar Naftali Zvi Yehudah Berlin (1817–1893) was not immune to the miseries and mortifications of early marriage. When the Neziv, as he was later known, was a thirteen-year-old student at the Volozhin yeshivah, he married the daughter of the head of the school. The young man's intellectual development was very closely supervised by his in-laws and, alas, found wanting, perhaps because the pressure was simply too much for him, with the result that he was not allowed to sit at the table with the family for Sabbath and holiday meals. His humiliation seems not to have robbed him of hope, however, for he worked all the harder at his studies and finally succeeded, at age sixteen, in being reinvited to the family dinner table. In later life, as a world-renowned scholar and religious leader, now head of the Volozhin yeshivah he had once attended, he used his authority to speak out against early marriages, which he opposed on medical grounds.[7] His father-in-law, Reb Itzele, continued to favor them. Attending a conference of rabbis in St. Petersburg in 1843, Reb Itzele was questioned about the practice by a priest who was well known for his hostility toward Jews. Reb Itzele responded with a smile: "Ever since the events of some 1,800 years ago when a Jewish girl reached maturity and did not marry, with results that have been calamitous to us from that day forth, we have been seeing to it that our daughters are married off young."[8]

In the closing decades of the nineteenth century, the phenomenon of early marriages sharply declined. The average age of unmarried students at the Lithuanian yeshivot rose to twenty, and eventually twenty-five. Older grooms found it much easier to be more assertive with their in-laws and with other members of the extended family. And if life at home was still unbearable, there was always the option of spending most of one's time at the yeshivah. This conception of the academy as a refuge from an unhappy marriage is reflected in the old Lithuanian proverb "A man does not become a parush if he is married to a pretty wife."[9]

In many households, of course, sons-in-law were warmly and lovingly welcomed, even in some cases held in so much esteem that their in-laws tried to keep them in the family after their wives had died. When Reb Hayyim Paltiel, the shtetl dayyan, lost his wife, her parents acted swiftly, matching him up with a cousin of their deceased daughter. His marriage to Alte meant that they would continue to have a renowned and saintly scholar in their family, for which they were most grateful.

For David Kabacznik, holding on to a son-in-law was a matter of good business rather than scholarship. When Reuven-Beinush Berkowitch, son of Reb Itche der Shammesh, married Golde Kabacznik, the beautiful blond daughter of Reb David, he proved a great asset to the family business, which consisted of supplying the tzar with horses and fodder for his stables, and geese for his table. With his fluency in Russian and Polish as well as several local dialects, Reuven-Beinush made an excellent buyer, and when his wife died in childbirth her father immediately married him off to his other pretty daughter, Rachel. Not that Reb David's appreciation for his son-in-law found any material expression. The Kabacznik family exploited their great find, paying Reuven-Beinush meager wages, sending him out on lengthy buying trips, and keeping him and his family, which came to number five sons and a daughter, in a state of abject poverty. When it came time to find his own daughter a husband, Reuven-Beinush had to sell his home to provide a dowry for her, after which he lived in a small rental apartment on one of the side streets. Since he was not flesh and blood of the Kabacznik clan, they never made him a partner. But the unhappy son-in-law in a matrilocal family structure had few options — for all that the larger structure of the society was patriarchal.

Indeed, the Jewish family has been described as basically patriarchal from biblical times on, though there has always been some degree of acknowledgment of the wife's role.[10] After all, God did tell the patriarch Abraham, with regard to the first Jewish matriarch: "In all that Sarah hath said unto thee, harken unto her voice."[11] Through the millennia, God's conversation with Abraham has received many interpretations, depending on both time and place, and both the position of the Jewish matriarch and the pitch of her voice have varied accordingly.

THE JEWISH MATRIARCH

In the Eastern Europe of the seventeenth, eighteenth, and nineteenth centuries, as many generations of sons-in-law were quick to discover, the shulhoyf and the larger worlds of business and public affairs were, as ever, the man's kingdom, but the home and its more modest commercial enterprises were definitely the woman's domain. Indeed, the matrilocal organization of the shtetl household was at the core of the kest system, and thus a woman in the household of a family oriented toward scholarship was in a particularly strong position.[12] As the main breadwinner, she had considerable power, power which had its roots in the early days of her marriage, when she was just beginning to develop some kind of business with which to support her family and thereby enable her husband to study without interruption. Even if she turned out not to be the sole breadwinner in the family, it was expected that she supplement the income of her husband. This expectation was so much the norm that the appointment letter for a shtetl

Reuven-Beinush Berkowitch and his wife Rachel Kabacznik, whom he married after the death of his first wife, Golde, Rachel's sister. David Kabacznik was eager to keep Reuven-Beinush as a son-in-law because of his outstanding business talents. Reuven-Beinush and Rachel were killed in the September 1941 massacre. YESC, BERKOWITCH

rabbi, for example, usually stipulated the economic enterprise that would be allotted to his wife. Typically the rebbetzin was given exclusive rights to sell yeast, or candles, or kiddush and havdalah wine.

While it was particularly common among the klei kodesh (holy vessels) and the lomdim (learners) for the wife to play a pivotal role in economic matters, women were important economic partners in all social classes of the shtetl from at least the seventeenth century. The strong-willed, outspoken Jewish woman has been a staple of Jewish humor and literature ever since, an inexhaustible source for East European authors and their literary descendants. The nineteenth-century Yiddish playwright Jacob Gordin, who was as popular in Eishyshok as he was on the stages of Warsaw, Vilna, and even New York, made a notable contribution to this genre, the much-beloved *Mirele Efros* (1898). Based on the true story of a woman from Grodno, his play recounted the decline and fall of the fortunes of a very wealthy woman who ran the family business with a strong hand, and managed to remain the practical as well as the emotional and spiritual center of her family even as her financial base dwindled. Though few women had Mirele's kind of money, many displayed the same kind of strength. And always there were mixed feelings about such women.

Haskalah writers advocated taking women out of the marketplace and letting men assume the financial responsibility for their families. (This didn't stop the acclaimed Hebrew writer Avraham Mapu from commending a young woman's business skills as one of the qualities that would make her a suitable match for his brother in 1862. Presumably he was a practical man, who was able to overlook certain principles of the Haskalah when the well-being of his brother was at stake.)[13] Some later writers, like Chaim Grade (1910–1982) and the Zionist leader Vladimir Jabotinsky (1880–1940), overflowed with praise for their hardworking mothers, recalling them as vigorous, vital women who had been willing to take on difficult and even demeaning work in order to provide for their families and, specifically, to earn money for their children's education.[14]

Shtetl humorists had a field day with the phenomenon of the powerful woman, their jokes reflecting the discomfort men felt in the presence of such women — though the women they disparaged were always wives, not mothers (power in a wife being a much more unnerving, apparently). Lines like the following are representative of their "wit":

Even a wife as big as a flea can sting.
One could live in peace, if not for the wife and the flies.
Eve had long hair but she made Adam's life short.
Twice in a lifetime a wife is dear to her husband: on her wedding day, and during her funeral.
When a wife wears the pants, the husband launders the dress.[15]

Perhaps an old Romanian proverb best sums up the traditional man's view of the ideal woman, who was not at all like the women of the shtetl: "A woman should be like the moon: shine at night and disappear during the day." The shtetl woman had too much to do to disappear during the day, as those who benefited from her efforts knew very well.

Nonetheless, her position was ambiguous, for her prominent role in the household and the marketplace was not reflected beyond those confines, nor was it officially acknowledged within them. Shtetl women were identified as housewives, and rarely appeared in any official documents as the proprietors of their businesses, even when they owned those businesses and ran them singlehandedly. The clarity with which all the shtetl's social and religious roles and responsibilities were defined for men and women, husbands and wives, boys and girls gave way to gray zones when it came to the home. Family life, with the exception of those religious rituals that were part of it, was left to the discretion of those who lived it, which did not necessarily benefit women. Even as late as the seventeenth century there still lingered a perception that a woman was simply property, that a man owned his wife (and children) outright — an error that seems to have been common enough that the Lithuanian Council made a point of condemning it, and in very harsh terms: "A man who will commit evil to enslave his wife, son, or daughter in a debt to a non-Jew or who, even worse, actually hands over his wife and daughters to a non-Jew because of debt — his blood is on his head."[16]

By the nineteenth century, woman's legal status may have been clearer, but her image was still problematic, current realities not matching up with the ancient customs and beliefs. Hence the complaint of Reina Batia, first wife of the Neziv, who objected to the blessing recited every morning by the men in the synagogue: "Blessed are you, Our God, King of the Universe, for not having made me a woman." Speaking not just as a woman but as an accomplished scholar and an important participant in the administration of her husband's yeshivah, she was indignant:

Every man, including the simplest, most uneducated man who does not even understand the meaning of the blessing, who would not dare to cross the threshold of my home without my permission, proudly recites that prayer daily. To add insult to injury, I must respond "Amen!" Who can sustain such an eternal insult to women?[17]

It's not surprising that the result of all these mixed messages about the role of women was often frustration and resentment on the part of the wife, anger and insecurity for the husband. Many a marriage was marred by years of silent brooding, or harsh verbal exchanges — or worse.

The strains only grew more severe in the twentieth century, especially after World War I, when the majority of shtetl men emerged from the cloistered depths of the beth midrash and the yeshivah to go out into the marketplace. With women proving reluctant to yield their prominent place in the shtetl economy and the world beyond, and men eager to consign their wives to the homemaker role as they took on the breadwinner role, the competition between the sexes was heightened. Women who refused to cede power were looked upon with contempt, and labeled shrill, aggressive, even ruthless. Hence the increasingly common portrait of the Jewish woman as a shrew, a conception that lives on to this day, passed along by writers who might seem far removed from the shtetl, but are nonetheless carriers of its legacy. In a work like Philip Roth's novel *Portnoy's Complaint*, the resentment against women has generalized beyond wives to mothers — perhaps because at the time Roth was writing about, the 1950s, the once-powerful Jewish woman had been effectively eliminated from the marketplace and therefore had no outlet for her considerable energies and talents.

No doubt the American immigration process contributed to the problem. For reasons that are not entirely clear, women who emigrated from the shtetl to America were glaringly absent from the public worlds of business and philanthropy in their new land. Perhaps because their husbands usually preceded them there by some years, it may have seemed natural for women to allow their more acclimated, experienced spouses to assume the major responsibility for earning a living, while they themselves were relegated to supporting roles. Having made up the majority of the shopkeepers and been the very backbone of the market-day economy — in Eishyshok as in many other places — they disappeared from sight in America.[18]

One of the very few émigré women from Eishyshok who retained that special shtetl flair for business was Lena Kaganowicz, who moved at the age of fifteen in 1909. She began as a seamstress living on the Lower East Side and doing

Lena Kaganowicz with her future husband, Morris Rosenberg, in New York City. Even after emigrating to America in 1909, at the age of fifteen, she retained her special shtetl female flair for business. YESC, JEAN ROTHSTEIN

piecework at home for $3 a day. Later she became a contributor to "A Bintel Brief" (A Bundle of Letters), the letters column that ran in the *Jewish Daily Forward*, her special subject being the plight of the working woman on the Lower East Side.[19] Ostensibly a forum for recent immigrants to ask an editor for advice about their various problems, the column sometimes ran short of real letters, in which case it commissioned them. Lena, a woman with an excellent command of Yiddish and a fine epistolary style, was one of their writers. She and her husband later moved to Spedden, a small town near Edmonton, Alberta, where they opened a general store that was highly popular with the local Ukrainian settlers as well as with the Cree Indians who lived on two nearby reservations. Although she was a very successful businesswoman and the mother of four daughters, Lena was one of those shtetl-style women who always had time for everything and everybody.

Of course, this could only have been because she worked incredibly hard. For the women in the shtetl there was no pause in the demand for their labor, no escape from the relentless grind of daily life. Regardless of class or even of individual temperament, the shtetl woman worked virtually nonstop, from early dawn until late at night. When shopkeeper Malka Roche's Schneider opened her store in time to serve the members of the minyan vatikin, those pious men who prayed each day at sunrise, she knew she was not the only one hard at work. Amid the clatter of boots against cobblestones, as the men made their way to the beth midrash, she could hear the sound of streams of milk flowing into tin and wooden pails, for this was the hour when the shtetl women milked the family cow. Against the dark skies, she could see smoke already issuing from most of the shtetl chimneys, could catch a whiff of Rivka Dwilanski's famous bagels being baked at No. 13 Marketplace, perhaps even pick up the smell of whatever Feige Demitrowski had put into the oven of her bakery at the corner of Vilna Street. And these women were the rule, not the exception.

No shtetl son or daughter could ever recall seeing their mother asleep. When the children went to bed their mother was still working; when they woke up in the morning she was already at it again. Moshe Kaplan, born in 1915 in a town near Eishyshok, describes his mother's daily routine:

My mother was a housewife (for lack of a more accurate word) and she worked hard all her life. She got up at three o'clock in the morning to milk the cow and to take her to pasture with the shtetl's communal herd. Then she stoked the fire in the oven, cooked, and baked bread, pastry, and donuts. When she finished her household chores she worked in the family vegetable garden, consisting of about 2.5 acres in back of our home.

In 1922 Mrs. Kaplan, the mother of six young children, was widowed. To support her children and provide for their education, she leased an additional patch of land from a Christian villager so that she could grow more vegetables to sell. During the winter months she sold clay pots, pitchers, pans, and bowls to the villagers, transporting them from the factory to her customers' homes with the help of her son Moshe. In the late 1920s another son, Asher, was arrested for Communist activities and was sent to the Vronki prison for political offenders. Out of her modest income she managed to find enough to send him a weekly food parcel, but the strain of it all was too much for her. She died in 1932, with Moshe at her bedside.[20]

The hardships of Mrs. Kaplan's life may have been more extreme than many, but they were not atypical. Most women ran a business while simultaneously managing a large household. The average shtetl woman raised between ten and twelve children, cared for aging parents and other relatives, and looked after the kest couples and their children. The businesses of many of them were located in the home, which may have been convenient in some ways, but also contributed to the overcrowding that was so common in shtetl households. The melamed's wife would have her little wig workshop in one corner of the house's main room, which was also her husband's classroom. Another woman might have a dressmaking business in her home. Alte Katz's household, with a bakery below street level, a drugstore adjacent to the living quarters on the first floor, and a photography studio on the second floor, was unusual, this being far more space than most people had, even if it did have to accommodate a home and three businesses.

In the artisan class, the husband's workshop would be in the house or attached to it, so that it was normal for three generations of family members to be living and working in the same room along with the workshop apprentices. The husband's constant presence often added greatly to the tensions of the household. Women looked forward to prayer time as a welcome respite, for all the men in the household would leave for the beth midrash as the hour approached. Similarly, women whose husbands were seasonal workers — builders, roofers, carpenters — were known to breathe a sigh of relief when winter came, for then they could count on their husbands spending long hours away from home sitting and learning in the beth midrash.

Some women had problems of a different sort. Their husbands, sole or joint proprietors of the family business, were often away on long business trips. Due to a combination of bad weather and primitive roads and transportation, these absences could last weeks or even months, during which time the women in the family had to take over, shouldering yet another burden.

DOMESTIC HELP

To ease the woman's workload, the more affluent households employed maids and other domestics, both Jews and non-Jews. The terms and conditions of Jewish maids' employment were first regulated by the Lithuanian Council, and later by the community.[21] Those who took such employment included widows, orphans, children of broken homes, women from the hekdesh, and other poor, stranded individuals. Since some of them had no home, they resided with their employer, but not everyone wanted live-in help. It was feared — and such fears were sometimes justified — that the presence of a young unmarried woman in the home would attract undesirable types, or prove too tempting for the family's young boys.

Problems of another kind attended the hiring of Christians as domestics. Throughout the centuries, the Catholic church forbade its members to work as servants in Jewish homes. Periodically these prohibitions were eased, only to be enforced with new vigor by the church and other authorities whenever it suited them. Such restrictions notwithstanding, Christians were always being employed by Jews, which often re-

Zlate Koppelman with two of her daughters, Nehama (left) and Leah. They assisted her at home and at work, especially after the death of their father, Elisha. Nehama and Leah made aliyah to Eretz Israel. Zlate was killed in the September 1941 massacre. PHOTO: YITZHAK URI KATZ. YESC, N. FRISCHER

sulted in conflict with anti-Semitic local authorities. To minimize the tension, the Jews themselves tried to curtail the practice of employing Christians, as a look at some of the seventeenth-century legislation of the Lithuanian Council makes apparent. Duration of employment was limited to one year, and the number of people who could be employed by any one household was restricted. Employment of Christian servants had to be approved and regulated by the community.[22]

Things apparently improved — marginally, to be sure — in the course of the next couple of hundred years. In Eishyshok, sometime during the first half of the nineteenth century, a local Christian woman was hired as a wet nurse for an infant Jewish boy named Todrus. But when the tzarist authorities got wind of it, they took the family to court, where their case made its slow and tortuous way through the legal labyrinth for several decades. The family was victorious in the end, though Todrus was by then a grandfather. "Todrus may nurse" was the verdict — a phrase that came to stand as shorthand for any kind of bureaucratic inefficiency in general, and that of the tzarist judicial system in particular.

The practice of hiring Christian servants had a long history in Eishyshok, with some families maintaining bonds with generations of Christian employees, bonds that endured even into the Holocaust. Kashka, the Polish Catholic maid who helped raise eight of the boisterous children born to Hayya and Shael Sonenson, was so devoted to her charges that she even made regular visits to the grave of one little Sonenson boy who died in infancy. Kashka was fluent in Yiddish, could sing Yiddish songs, and knew all the Jewish rituals concerning the dietary laws as well as those governing all the other aspects of weekday and holiday life in a Jewish household. Having come to the Sonensons by way of her mother, who had been Hayya's maid at an earlier period in her life, she passed on the legacy of ties to this one family when her granddaughter Jasza became a maid in Shalom Sonenson's house.

Jasza helped Shalom's wife Miriam raise their two daughters, Gittele and Shula. She even learned some Hebrew, since Shalom often spoke it to his little girls. During the massacre of September 1941, Jasza risked her own life by helping the family hide, then put herself in mortal danger again when she smuggled food into Ghetto Radun, where Shalom and his family were incarcerated for nine months.

DAUGHTERS

A woman's greatest helpers and most trusted allies, both at home and in her business, were her daughters. An old shtetl proverb sums up the feeling about the mother–daughter relationship: "If a woman gives birth only to sons, she probably does not deserve to bear daughters."

Until World War I, when compulsory education for Jewish girls in the Russian empire was introduced (in Eishyshok and other Lithuanian communities it was first instituted during the German occupation), girls were always at home, while their brothers were at school or apprenticing in a trade. From early childhood on, girls assisted their mother with all the chores: at home, in the garden, with the livestock, and in the family business enterprise. As they grew older they were made responsible for their younger siblings. And always they were expected to be mature and reliable.

Alte Katz with her oldest daughter, Zipporah (Feigele). Zipporah helped her mother in raising her siblings and educating them. She also assisted professionally in the photo studio after the death of her father, Yitzhak Uri Katz. Alte was killed during the September 1941 massacre; Zipporah was murdered by the AK post-liberation. PHOTO: YITZHAK URI KATZ. YESC, Y. ELIACH

While daughters were their mother's greatest helpers, they were also her greatest concern. Protecting the chastity, the morals, and the reputation of a young girl was a constant preoccupation, for anything less than ceaseless vigilance might endanger the girl's chances of making a good match. Thus a daughter was expected to be at her mother's side at all times — a virtual impossibility, given the nature of her many duties. Girls and young women were often alone in the store or the market, or even on the road. Zivia Hutner, the granddaughter of Eishyshok rabbi Zundl Hutner, traveled back and forth to Vilna on business beginning in early adolescence, and sewing machine saleswoman Szeina Blacharowicz traveled the countryside at about the same age. Though it was out of concern for the morals of these spunky entrepreneurs that Haskalah writers were so vehement about keeping girls and women out of commerce, their recommendations were not followed — if only because the girls played too important a role to be banished.[23]

The shtetl had its own ways of guarding the reputations of its young women. For example, if a girl's hymen broke due to an accident, the details of the event were entered in the shtetl record book, and the family was given a special certificate, signed by the rabbi or the dayyan, attesting to the girl's purity. Surviving fragments from the record book of one of the Lithuanian shtetlekh include descriptions of three such incidents. Seven-year-old Miriam, daughter of Hannah and Zvi the tailor, was pushed into a ditch by her girlfriends; two other girls, both teenagers, fell on thus-and-such a day, we are informed, and in thus-and-such a manner.[24] During the Big Fire of 1895, when the entire shtetl of Eishyshok burned down, one girl's virginity-loss certificate went up in the flames. Though her family had lost everything, it was this piece of paper that most concerned them, and they rushed to Reb Layzer Wilkanski, the shtetl dayyan, to ask him to issue a new certificate.[25]

The close surveillance and stringent expectations paid off. Most shtetl girls were indeed obedient, chaste, hardworking, religious. Nonetheless, there was a tradition in literature and folklore depicting the renegade daughter: She married out of the faith; or she married a non-

Three of the daughters of Nehemia der Feldsher, who sought a new life in America in the 1890s: Margolia (Cohen) (left), Lilly (Sirk), and Annie (Foster). PHOTO: GREEN, BOSTON. YESC, R. ROSENBLATT

Feigele (Fanichke) and Velvke Saltz. Shortly after their mother's death, their father emigrated to America. Feigele was devoted to her brother and helped to raise him. Years later both joined their father in America. PHOTO: KALINOWITCH, IVIE. YESC, SHULTZ–SALTZ

religious man; or she escaped her mother's watchful eye by fleeing to the big city; or she in any one of a wide variety of other ways brought shame upon her family. By the twentieth century these girls were not just characters in literature, but, increasingly, figures drawn from life. Even Eishyshok had a few, though they remained very much the minority, as they did in most places.

Still, parents lived in constant fear that their daughters would be labeled damaged goods and live out their lives as old maids (or "gray braids," as they were known). Obsessed with marrying them off as early as possible, they began preparing their daughters' trousseaux practically at birth, and agonized greatly over the cost of dowry and kest arrangements when it came time to settle the terms of the betrothal agreement. The fear of spinsterhood, considered the ultimate shame, prompted many parents to rush into marriage arrangements that were not always in the best interests of their daughters. Of course, it was not just shame that motivated them; a daughter was felt to be an economic burden. Even though the cost of her upkeep must surely have been more than compensated for by her household labor, the word on daughters was that they "eat by day and grow by night"— ceaselessly consuming food and clothes.

The mixed messages a girl received about herself from her family and her community were in stark contrast to the very clearly positive status her brother enjoyed. From birth, the male was honored and cherished: his many life-passage celebrations brought joy to his parents' home; his heder and later yeshivah accomplishments were sources of pride for them; he would recite the Kaddish for them when they were dead.

SISTERS AND BROTHERS

A girl knew that she had to take care of her brother — give him the best pair of shoes to go to heder, deliver a warm meal to him at lunchtime, offer him his choice of foods when he came home. If for some reason he needed any kind of special care or assistance, she might also be expected to stay by his side throughout the school day. For example, Rabbi Isser Zalman Meltzer of Mir (1870–1953), the only surviving male child in his family, went to heder each day in the company of his sister Fruma-Rivka. All his brothers having died in infancy, he had an entire household focused on maintaining his health and well-being, and his sister's ministrations were part of that campaign. He became a great Talmudic scholar and lived a long life.[26]

A sister was her brother's lifelong nurturer. He knew that in time of need, he could always turn to her. This Eastern European conception of sibling relationships was in sharp contrast to the practice in Mediterranean countries, where it was the role of the brother to protect his sister. But shtetl boys did value their sisters, and were expected to demonstrate their affection. Hence the many little gifts the heder boys made for their sisters at holiday time: the Hanukkah dreidels, the fruit pit jewelry for Tu Bishvat, the flag for Simhat Torah, the scroll of Esther for Purim.

With mothers so overworked, having little time to lavish affection on their children, the sister–brother relationship was a particularly important one, a source of emotional sustenance for each. Though the educational and social patterns of shtetl life afforded them little time to be in each other's company, what time they did have was precious to them; they played together on the Sabbath and holidays, and whenever else they could.

At the dawn of the twentieth century, the sister–brother relationship began to change, along with everything else. Now that girls could go to school, could embark on their own journeys of self-improvement and exploration, their brothers increasingly saw it as their duty to help them along the way. They felt responsible for molding their sisters' character, for guiding them intellectually. In this as in so many other social changes, the Wilkanskis were in the vanguard. Yitzhak and Meir devoted much time to their sisters Sarah, Esther, and Leah, encouraging them in their eager pursuit of education, advising them, and even helping them out financially from their own very limited resources. The girls' moral development was also on their minds, as one of Yitzhak's letters to ten-year-old Leah in 1904 reveals. Writing from Berlin, where he was a student, he admonishes her for her complaint about the brevity of his letters, then goes on to advise: "If you want to be rewarded, you must also learn to give to others." A couple of decades later, Shaul Kaleko would help his sister, Rachel, to make an illegal border crossing from Poland into Lithuania. He wanted her to join him in Kovno, where she would be able to continue her studies at the excellent Hebrew gymnasium of Reali, while remaining under his watchful eye.

Zusl Bastunski (left) holding the hand of sister Altke. In the center are two friends. Zusl emigrated to America in 1921. Until World War II he sent money to his siblings and parents who remained in Europe. Altke and her family were murdered in the September 1941 massacre.
PHOTO: YITZHAK URI KATZ. YESC, BASTUNSKI

STEP-SIBLINGS AND ORPHAN RELATIVES

During the eighteenth and nineteenth centuries and the first two decades of the twentieth, perhaps as many as two-thirds of the marriages in the shtetl were second, third, and even fourth marriages. Death rather than divorce was responsible for this high remarriage rate, and death also created a large number of orphans. Since many spouses brought with them the children from previous unions, the result was that many if not most shtetl households were filled with stepchildren, and often with distantly related orphans too. This was particularly true in Eishyshok, which had no orphanage because the kahal had stipulated that orphans be sent to their relatives instead.

Sometimes this worked out well. Miriam Kaplan, for example, was taken in by Alte Paltiel and her husband Hayyim, the shtetl dayyan, during World War I. Miriam's father had gone off to America, where he opened a soda shop with the hope of making enough money to send for his wife and infant child. When his business failed and World War I broke out, the few dollars he had been able to send stopped coming, and Miriam and her mother moved in with her mother's father, a miller in a small village near Eishyshok. One day a hunting party of German soldiers mistook the miller for an animal and shot him. When his daughter saw the accident through her window, she ran out into the snow to try to save him, wearing only her dress and slippers. She caught a cold that developed into pneumonia; she died only a few days after her father, leaving her little daughter Miriam for all intents and purposes an orphan, for nothing was ever again heard from Miriam's father. Though Alte Paltiel was only a distant relative, she took Miriam in, and raised her with great love.

The typhus epidemic of 1917–19 claimed hundreds of lives in Eishyshok, leaving many orphans behind. Many of them were not so fortunate as Miriam, for Alte Paltiel was unusual — if not in her willingness to shoulder a family obligation, then certainly in the loving way she did it. An orphan or a stepchild was often considered an onerous burden, and resented accordingly. The mother of Shneur Glombocki, knowing that her days were numbered, summoned the shtetl rabbi to her deathbed. With Rabbi Zundl Hutner in attendance, she spoke to her father and her husband and made them promise that the baby boy would not be raised by a stepmother, for the thought of her beloved child in the care of her husband's second wife was unbearable to her. Her father had to agree to take the baby in after her death, which he did. And just as the mother had predicted, the boy's father took no interest in him after he remarried, nor did his new wife or the children from that second marriage, even though they all lived in Eishyshok. As the saying went, "Der foter is getrai vi lang di mame is derbai" (The father is faithful as long as the mother is around).

ASSIGNED ROLES: FROM CRADLE TO GRAVE

As stories like that one reveal, these multigenerational, multifamily households were not always the warm, loving, cohesive units we know from myth and idealized memory. One way of dealing with the potentially overwhelming complexities of life in the shtetl's crowded, often impoverished homes was to assign roles to everyone, thus imposing a kind of crude order on the messiness of reality. With typical shtetl bluntness, each person was labeled, his or her future predicted, his status as winner or loser virtually preordained, with no options for escape. The clever child was identified as the scholar in the family, the "future cabinet member," while the slow one was said to have been "last in line when God granted brains"; the clumsy child had "hands of clay"; the one with calf eyes was "the beast."

A bright, attractive child was considered a good reflection on the family, and put on display, while the others were kept out of sight. If a marriage was being arranged, for example, and the prospective in-laws were coming to conduct the negotiations, the family's "winners" were brought out to greet the guests, while less impressive family members, certainly including anyone with handicaps, stayed behind closed doors. In Hayya and Shael Sonenson's family, for example, Shalom was chosen over his seven siblings to represent the family, although he was not the brightest. None of the children were unattractive, but with his blue eyes, blond curls, and captivating, dimpled smile, Shalom was picture-perfect, and his parents always used to take only him to family celebrations in other shtetlekh, without any thought to how the other children would feel.

Reinforcing the tendency to assign everybody a label were the economic difficulties faced by so many families. The hand-to-mouth existence they lived dictated that choices be made and life paths mapped out with maximum efficiency. Thus bright boys were seen as a good investment, and as such were sent to the best heder and yeshivah their families could afford; less talented boys were sent to study in second-rate institutions, and steered into the family business or apprenticed to a trade at a very early age.

Sometimes, however, death intervened and negated family choices. The favored child of a dying mother would more than likely not be favored by the stepmother who eventually replaced her. Mrs. Glombocki's fear of the stepmother syndrome was well warranted.

INHERITANCE

The same kind of blunt, often arbitrary favoritism that prevailed in other areas of family life dictated inheritance divisions as well. Favoritism rather than fairness, necessity, or even seniority decided who got what. The only shtetl guideline concerning the distribution of one's estate was the saying "It is better to give with a warm hand than a cold one"— in other words, divide it up while you're still in the land of the living. Typically one gave to the child with whom one had the closest relationship, the child in whose home one hoped to spend one's old age, loved, respected, cared for.

In the Dwilanski family, it was Alte Dwilanski Katz, youngest child of Avigdor and Rivka, who received the family inheritance, which consisted of a large orchard, a spacious three-story house on the market square, and the bakery that was the family business. Her aging parents lived with her in great harmony until their deaths, Rivka's in 1935 when she was almost one hundred. Alte's brother Hayyim Dwilanski never forgave her and her descendants for taking what he considered rightfully his. Penniless and bitter, he emigrated to Palestine. Favorite child Alte Katz and most of her family perished in the Holocaust. Hayyim Dwilanski and his family lived out the war in Palestine.

Each shtetl had its own famous inheritance feud. In Radun such a feud racked the household of its most admired and beloved resident, the saintly Haffetz Hayyim, when he died in 1933. The conflict over his house was solved by building a wall through the middle of it, dividing it into parts, one for the descendants of his first marriage, the other for the descendants of his second marriage. But disagreements over other issues, such as positions in the yeshivah and royalties from his books, continued to rage. The royalty issue was especially complicated.[27]

GRANDPARENTS

Grandparents were the bearers of wisdom and tradition, the greatly esteemed heads of the family, the living patriarchs and matriarchs. They were also much adored allies and protectors for their grandchildren, who confided in them, asked their advice, and went to them for comfort and affection. Because of the kest system, maternal grandparents, in whose home the extended family lived, sometimes for many years, played a particularly dominant role in the lives of their grandchildren.

What many people from Eishyshok remember best about their grandparents was their tales of the past. Shlomo Farber's maternal grandfather was a history buff, and filled his grandson's head not just with family lore, but with accounts of local events that had significance on the stage of world history. Farber was so enthralled by what his grandfather told him during their long walks in the fields and forests around Olkenik that he became the chronicler of that shtetl, and later built an intricately detailed model of it from memory, using the woodcarver's skill he had also learned from his grandfather.[28] In 1924–25 *Di Welt*, a Lithuanian Jewish newspaper, published a series titled "From My Grandfather's Memory," which consisted of Shaul

Shlomo Zlotnik, though a widower, helped to raise and educate his grandchildren. One of his sons abandoned his wife and daughter and ran away to America; a daughter of Shlomo's died in childbirth. The photo was taken in honor of Dora Zlotnik's aliyah to Eretz Israel. Standing, right to left: Yitzhak Broide and wife Hayya Fradl (née Zlotnik), Honeh Michalowski and wife Bluma (née Zlotnik). Center row, right to left: Yankele Sheshko, Reb Shlomo Zlotnik, Dora Zlotnik, and Sarah (Sorke) Michalowski. Front row, right to left: (first name unknown) Sheshko, Moshe Sheshko, and Zelda-Bluma Michalowski. When Hayya Fradl and Bluma attempted to escape the September 1941 massacre, they were murdered by Lithuanian guards. Yankele Sheshko was killed by Arabs in Israel. The majority of the family were killed in the September 1941 massacre. PHOTO: YITZHAK URI KATZ. YESC, BERKOWITCH

Alte Katz (center) in 1941 with her two grandchildren and other family members who lived in Eishyshok: daughter Shoshana Katz (upper right), granddaughter Yaffa-Sheinele, and son-in-law Moshe Sonenson; (seated, right to left) son Avigdor Katz, grandson Yitzhak Sonenson, and his mother Zipporah Katz Sonenson. Memories of their grandmother's love helped Yitzhak and Yaffa through terrible and lonely years. When they became grandparents themselves, Alte was their role model. Moshe Sonenson and his two children survived the Holocaust; Alte Katz and three of her children were murdered in the September massacre; Zipporah was murdered post-liberation by the AK. PHOTO: BEN ZION SZREJDER. YESC, Y. ELIACH

Yossef Ginzberg and granddaughter Tamar, May 1935. Yossef was murdered in Ponar, Vilna. Tamar survived the war, in Siberia. YESC, GLOMBOCKI

Yaffa-Sheinele was named after her paternal grandfather Shael Sonenson, her brother Yitzhak Uri after his maternal grandfather Yitzhak Uri Katz. Their mother Zipporah was convinced that both of her children had inherited the personalities of their namesakes and that her daughter was too much of a tomboy. Both children survived the Holocaust. PHOTO: BEN ZION SZREJDER, WINTER 1940. YESC, Y. SONENSON

Kaleko's retelling of his grandfather's stories about nineteenth-century Eishyshok.

The older generation made sure the young people knew about their ancestors, so that they might carry on the good name of their family and continue its traditions. During the summers Moshe Kaganowicz spent with his maternal grandparents on their farm in the 1910s, they told him about his great-grandfather's conversion to Judaism, and about his reputation for hospitality to those in need, which they in their turn were continuing, and which eventually became his own model. Grandparents also hoped that the recounting of family history would instill pride in their descendants, perhaps even inspire them to hope for the day when they could reclaim what once had been theirs. It was in that spirit that Hayya Kabacznik Sonenson made a ritual of telling her grandchildren, every Saturday at dusk, that all the land as far as they could see had once belonged to her family.

For their part, children were expected to be at their grandparents' side whenever needed. If Grandfather was too frail to walk alone to the beth midrash, a grandson would accompany him there, offering him his arm in support. If the old man's eyes were failing, his grandson was there to read to him from the Talmud; if his hands trembled, the grandson rolled his cigarettes for him, or cut tobacco for his snuff box. Similarly, a girl would assist her grandmother with the bookkeeping for the family business, would thread her needle for her, would sit next to her in the women's gallery at shul and repeat the words of the maggid's sermon.

The grandchildren were responsible for their grandparents' physical comfort and well-being too. If it was cold at night, a boy might sleep in the same bed with his grandfather, a girl with her grandmother, so that the old people were kept warm. When the grandparents were sick, their devoted grandchildren nursed them through their illnesses. And on their deathbeds, too, they were attended by their grandchildren. The young people of the household were expected to be there along with everybody else when their grandparents closed their eyes forever. It was "for the honor of the dead and the memory of the living." With watchful, curious eyes, in awe and fear, many a young child observed the ceremony that provided the final confirmation of death: the feather placed next to the mouth, proof that breathing had stopped.

Grandparents who died before their grandchildren could know them were often memorialized in their grandchildren's names. A child who carried a grandparent's name was expected to bring honor to the ancestor, to learn about him or her and pass that knowledge on, and to visit the grave, even if it was in another town. Some believed that a child would embody the character of the grandparent for whom he or she had been named. Thus it was common for parents who had named their children after their own parents to show them special preference. Yaffa-Sheinele Sonenson, named for her paternal grandfather, Reb Shael Sonenson, was the apple of her father's eye, just as her brother Yitzhak Uri, named for his maternal grandfather, was the pride of his mother. Yaffa seemed to her mother Zipporah to have inherited Reb Shael's outspoken, dynamic ways, and thereby to have been turned into a tomboy. Zipporah always felt that if her daughter had been named after her own maternal grandmother, Rivka Dwilanski, she would have been a more ladylike little girl.

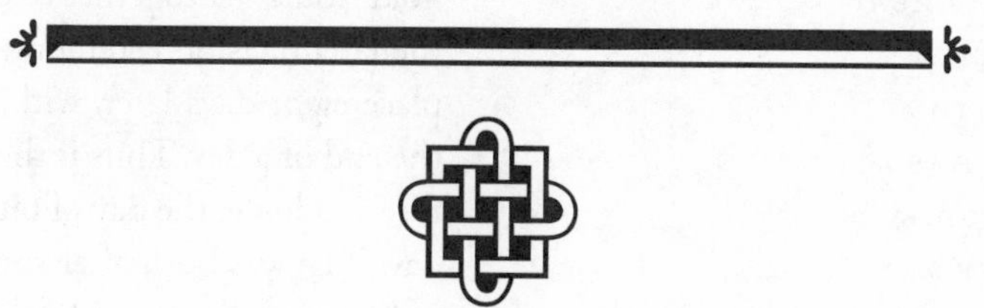

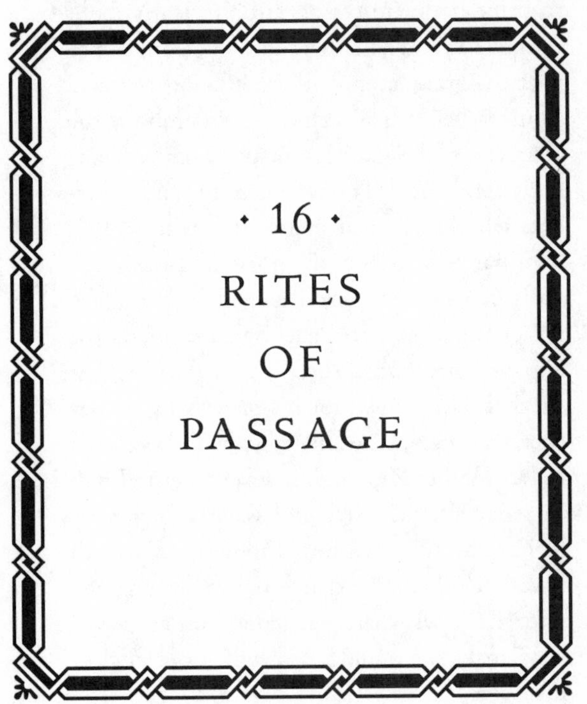

· 16 · RITES OF PASSAGE

MAZEL TOV. WITH GREAT JOY MASHA [KIUCHEFSKI] GAVE BIRTH TO A BOY. THE FAMILY HAS A PRECIOUS NEW ADDITION. THOUGH WE ARE ON THE EVE OF DIFFICULT TIMES, WE MUST HOPE FOR BETTER ONES. CIRCUMCISION WILL BE ON WEDNESDAY.

Geneshe Kaganowicz Sonenson, to brother Moshe in Jerusalem, July 31, 1939, re his sister-in-law

CEREMONIES FOR NEWBORN BOYS AND GIRLS

THE BIRTH OF A COUPLE'S FIRST CHILD WAS AWAITED WITH GREAT ANTICIPATION, not just by the parents, grandparents, and other relatives, but to some extent by the entire shtetl. There was, however, a marked difference in the ceremonies welcoming a newborn baby girl and a newborn baby boy, as one might expect from certain passages in the Talmud. For example: "The world cannot do without either males or females. Yet happy is he whose children are males, and alas for him whose children are females."[1]

Only a simple naming ceremony in the synagogue, held the first Sabbath following the birth, marked the occasion of a girl's coming into the world. During the reading of the Torah the father would be called up to name the baby girl (though in Eishyshok, if the child, either girl or boy, was a firstborn, the actual choosing of the name was the mother's privilege). Girls, like boys, were usually given the name of a deceased relative or a prominent scholar, but unlike boys, girls could have a Yiddish name as well as Hebrew — names like Yentl, Alte, Itzle, Dobrushe, Mariyasl, Geneshe, Zisl, Edl, and so forth — as part of their official name. Once the very modest naming ceremony was concluded, girls had to wait until their wedding day before they could again be cause for any kind of celebration. In between these two events they were acknowledged in supporting roles only.

For boys, the first eight days of life, from the very minute they were born, were crowded with ceremony and pageantry. After the birth, the boy's father and other male members of the household would get together to calculate the day for the circumcision ceremony, which was to take place eight days later, with sunset counting as the end of a day. Thus if the baby was born before sundown, the day of birth counted as a full day. If he was born after sundown, the first day of life was reckoned to be the following day.

On the first Friday night following the male child's birth, the shammash announced in the synagogue that a baby boy had been born to so-and-so and that all were invited to a party in his honor that evening; or, alternatively, the shammash would invite only those individuals whose names appeared on a list given to him by the family. The Friday-night celebration was known as Shalom Zakhar — Peace Unto the Male — which derived its name from the Talmudic statement, "A male comes into the world, peace comes into the world." This makes for a sharp contrast with a comparable Talmudic statement regarding girls: "Daughters come into the world, quarrels come into the world."[2] During the party, which was mainly for men, with the women of the household celebrating in a separate room, scholarly discourses were delivered, and traditional foods were served, including chickpeas, known in Yiddish as *arbes*, similar to the Hebrew word *arbe*, meaning numerous, as in the blessing God gave to Abraham: "I will bestow my blessing upon you and make your descendants as numerous as the stars of heaven and the sands of the seashore."[3]

The day and night prior to the circumcision had their own rituals, observed by most Lithuanian Jews, which were devoted to keeping Lilith and her entourage of demons away from the baby. Lilith was Adam's first wife, who after her banishment became Queen of the Demons and was always on the lookout to kidnap baby boys, especially before their circumcision. A variety of protective amulets and prayers were therefore attached to the baby's crib and to his mother's bed, and boys from the early-childhood heder — usually boys with some family connection to the mother — came to say their own prayers on behalf of the child, for the purity of such prayers was believed to have a special power. On the night before the circumcision, known as *wachnacht* (watchnight), all the males in the family, as well as the men in any study group to which the father or grandfather belonged, stayed awake, learning and reciting psalms together throughout the night. It was hoped that the merit of their learning would keep Lilith and her evil forces away. (In Eishyshok, however, very few families observed wachnacht.)[4]

Early on the morning of the eighth day, the covenant of circumcision took place, in the polesh (vestibule) of the Old Beth Midrash. There stood the chair of Elijah, in which the child's sandak (godfather) would sit, and also the orla tish (foreskin table). The day's ceremonies began with the usual morning service, led by the mohel who was going to perform the circumcision. A community employee and in many cases an ordained rabbi, the mohel was supposed to be a pious Jew, who was trained in the necessary medical procedures and well versed in halakhic provisions. At the conclusion of the service, candles were lit in the vestibule, and the married couple who had been chosen to perform this part of the ritual carried the baby in on a snow-white embroidered pillow, then placed him on the lap of his godfather. The godfather, a close friend of the family, was ideally a person known for his piety and scholarship. Among Lithuanian Jews it was often the custom for him to be godfather to more than one son in the same family, or to all of them, though this practice was frowned upon elsewhere.[5] Godfather and child were meant to form a lifelong bond.

During the circumcision covenant, the godfather held the baby, while the father of the baby recited the proper benedictions and formally named him. Afterward a mitzvah meal was held at home, supposedly limited in size to ten, the number set by the Lithuanian Council, but in most cases larger. And a very festive meal it was, as Meir Wilkanski recounted in his description of one such party, which followed the circumcision of his half-sister's infant son. While the adults feasted and drank, little Meir and his friend Israel became curious about the contents of a nearly empty liquor bottle and sampled the leftovers. Back in heder that afternoon, Meir could make no sense of his teacher's words, nor could he keep the letters of the Gemara from dancing before his eyes. His head was heavy, his face aflame, and he was sure he could hear the rattle of the wings of the Angel of Death. The teacher took pity on Meir and sent him out to the green, grassy shulhoyf for a breath of fresh air. From there he was led home by two friends, and a deep, sound sleep restored him to well-being.[6]

If the baby boy was a couple's first child (and provided the mother was not the daughter of a Kohen or a Levi), yet another ceremony awaited him at the age of one month, a Pidyon ha-Ben, Redemption of the First Born. This was deemed necessary because in biblical times all firstborn males were to have been consecrated to lifelong service to the Lord, and therefore needed to be "bought" back.[7] A simple home ceremony, the Pidyon ha-Ben began with the father bringing the infant to the kohen on a silver tray and informing him that the child is his mother's firstborn. The kohen then asked: "Which do you prefer — to give me your son or to redeem him?" The father replied, "To redeem him," and recited the appropriate benedictions, after which he turned over to the kohen the five silver coins he had been holding in his hand. With the words "This in place of this," the kohen took the money and passed it over the child's head, bringing the ceremony to a conclusion with the priestly benediction and the blessing over a cup of wine. This ceremony was also followed by a festive meal. The kohen who performed the ceremony was usually a scholar known for his saintly behavior. He was expected to donate the redemption money to charity.

In each little boy's life, the years to come were filled with ritual, pageantry, ceremony, and celebration, all of it designed to make him aware of his special place in the world. As described in chapter 5, a ceremony was held at the early-childhood heder to mark the child's first day there, another was held at home two years later to honor his progression to the next stage, and others would follow at each stage of his educational journey. On such occasions the boy was the star of the show, in whose honor home and heder were brought together in celebration. And all manner of other special occasions dotted his educational calendar, signaling the completion of a religious book, celebrating such holidays as Hanukkah, Purim, Lag ba-Omer, and so forth. Though all these celebrations were generally modest in scope, they were highly memorable to the boy. Often they included special outings, games, and food, and often, as in the pre-circumcision ceremony where little boys came to chant psalms against Lilith, they gave him the feeling that he was destined to play an important role in life.

For girls no such celebrations existed, if for no other reason than that girls didn't go to school, where most of these events took place. At best, girls could participate vicariously. As sisters of the boy who was being honored they might help in the preparation of food for his party, or, as in Germany, they might have a role in the heder initiation ceremony. And they were the occasional recipients of articles their brothers made for them at heder: the spinning tops that were part of Hanukkah festivities, the necklaces and bracelets fashioned from fruit pits to mark the fifteenth day of Shevat (Tu Bishvat), the noisemakers for Purim.

BAR MITZVAH

The many celebrations during boyhood culminated in the bar mitzvah, which marked its ending, for at age thirteen a Jewish boy is considered to have reached his religious maturity. From that point forward he is a Man of Duty, an adult who is held personally responsible for all his religious acts, who has both privileges and responsibilities accordingly. Among his privileges are reading the Torah during services, counting as a member of the minyan, and putting on tefillin (phylacteries): little leather boxes containing parchments inscribed with quotations from Scripture.

In many Lithuanian communities, including Eishyshok, the boy was called up to the Torah to

Avremele Botwinik (Epstein), sitting in the center, celebrating his bar mitzvah with his best friends in 1939. To Avremele's right is Moshe Bastunski, to his left, Avigdor Katz. Standing between Avigdor and Avremele is Moshe Kaplan; standing second from left is Elisha Koppelman. All of the boys in the photo also celebrated their bar mitzvah in 1939. Only Avremele survived the war, as a partisan. Elisha was murdered by the AK, the others in the September 1941 massacre. PHOTO: BEN ZION SZREJDER. YESC, Y. SONENSON

recite the haftarah on the Sabbath before his bar mitzvah, and was called up again, though without the privilege of reading, after his bar mitzvah. By ancient Eishyshkian custom a bar mitzvah boy who had delivered a scholarly discourse for the occasion was called up to the Torah with the title *morenu* (our teacher); if he did not deliver a sermon he was given the much less prestigious title *haver*. But this practice had to be abandoned when it led to a bitter fight with one of the most powerful families in the shtetl, as recounted in chapter 2.

The actual delivery of the Talmudic discourse took place at the boy's home on Saturday, during the festive meal that followed the Sabbath service (though families that had suffered a recent death or other tragedy were allowed to postpone the meal).[8] Some rabbinic authorities ruled that the parents should put on a banquet in honor of the occasion,[9] but in Eishyshok it was celebrated more modestly, at a meal attended mainly by family members, close friends of the bar mitzvah boy, and, depending on the family's social standing, by an assortment of shtetl rabbis, community notables, and balebatim from the various societies to which the boy's parents and grandparents belonged. For children whose parents could not afford even a modest festive meal, the community arranged one, as it did for bar mitzvah boys from the hekdesh. As the boy gave his sermon he would be interrupted frequently by questions from the rabbi and the other learned individuals who were present, and he was expected to be able to respond to all their inquiries.

For boys who reached bar mitzvah age while studying at the yeshivah in Eishyshok, the testing was done by their peers, as was the case with Reb Hayyim Ozer Grodzinski, the future leader of Lithuanian Orthodox Jewry, who celebrated his bar mitzvah at the Eishyshok yeshivah in 1876, dazzling the older prushim with his erudition and proficiency, as is described in chapter 6.

Bar mitzvah presents were limited mainly to books and small sums of money, as dictated by the Lithuanian Council. And, in line with the true meaning of the occasion, whereby the boy became a contributing member of his community, he was initiated into one of the community's mutual aid societies — this being one of the most prestigious gifts he could receive. Thus for the bar mitzvah of Shalom Sonenson, his mother's favorite son, her gift was a beginner's membership in the Hevrah Kaddishah, the burial society, which was dominated by her family. Also by way of recognizing the boy's commitment to his community, family members would make donations in his honor to the synagogue, the beth midrash, the yeshivah, and other institutions and charities. For example, David Kabacznik commemorated his grandson Avraham Fishl's bar mitzvah with a gift of 40 pud (40 Russian pounds) of kerosene to the Old Beth Midrash.

Like virtually every other aspect of shtetl life, the traditions governing bar mitzvah celebrations in Eishyshok began to change during the opening decade of the twentieth century. Though the ritual in the synagogue remained the same, the festivities surrounding it altered, becoming much more child-oriented. Less attention was paid to the boy's responsibility to the community, more to his own social, educational, and emotional needs.

Some families divided the celebrations into two parts, one for adults, the other for children, with the scholarly discourse being delivered during the festivities for the adults. No longer, however, would the boy be interrupted in order to be tested on his comprehension of the material he was covering. That was considered too rigorous a test for a child that age. (In some communities, though not in Eishyshok, there would be interruptions of another kind: the singing of songs, which was intended to prevent the boy from delivering the sermon in its entirety, and thus to take some of the pressure off him.) Another change that occurred with increasing frequency was the incorporation of personal material into the sermon, allowing the boy to devote a paragraph or two to thanking his parents and other family members for their love and care, his teachers, mentors, and friends for their guidance. The second celebration, also held on the Sabbath, was mainly for the bar mitzvah boy and friends and relatives of the same age. By the end of World War I a variety of coed youth organizations and educational opportunities had taken hold, and the tradition of separating the sexes died out among the young. Most of the parties in honor of the bar mitzvah boys were coed.

Boys had a lot of say about who was invited to their parties, and were allowed to express opinions even about very close relatives. Shneur Glombocki banned his own father. As noted in chapter 15, Shneur was raised by his maternal grandparents after his mother died while he was still in infancy, and had been entirely ignored by his father and his father's new wife. But the father did show up at the synagogue service on the occasion of Shneur's bar mitzvah, and at the party for adults at the home of his former in-laws. Young Shneur asked his father to leave the party, since he did not want his moment of triumph marred by the presence of someone who had essentially abandoned him.

Centuries-old Lithuanian Council prohibitions against certain kinds of bar mitzvah gifts — such as food products, or sums of money that went over very modest limits — were swept away by the winds of change, along with so many other traditions and customs. Now such changes may seem modest, but they made an impression that lingered for many decades thereafter. Alexander Zisl Hinski, as a man in his sixties, could still remember the taste of the bar of chocolate he had been given more than fifty years before. Shimon Hutner, son of the shtetl dayyan Hertz Mendel Hutner, received a small crate of oranges from his sister Zivia in Palestine in the 1920s. Though he eventually followed his sister there and consumed countless oranges

In honor of their bar mitzvah, two best friends, Avigdor Katz (left) and Avremele Botwinik (Epstein), pose for a photo in 1939 on the steps leading to Avigdor's house, the pharmacy and photo studio of his mother Alte Katz. PHOTO: BEN ZION SZREJDER. YESC, Y. SONENSON

during his life, none of them ever matched the fragrance or taste of those bar mitzvah oranges. Among the most popular bar mitzvah gifts in Eishyshok during the 1930s were secular as well as religious books, watches, bicycles, and subscriptions to magazines and newspapers.

One of the very last of the bar mitzvahs to be celebrated in Eishyshok was that of Benyamin Sonenson, oldest grandson of Hayya Sonenson, in September 1941. Despite the German curfew, a group of family and close friends gathered in Hayya's large dining room to celebrate the occasion. Included in the group were Rabbi Szymen Rozowski; Reb Aaron Katz, brother of Yitzhak Uri Katz, from Lida (who had come to Eishyshok for the circumcision of his brother's youngest grandson, Shaul, and stayed on for the bar mitzvah); five of Hayya's six sons (including Avraham, the father of the bar mitzvah boy); one daughter; four daughters-in-law; and thirteen other grandchildren. The heavy curtains were drawn, family members were posted as sentries near the windows so that they could warn of the approach of any German soldiers, and the service was held in hushed voices. The meal that followed was eaten at a long table which over the years had witnessed many joyous events, warmly and noisily celebrated; but that day the only sound to be heard was the clinking of silverware against china plates. When the rabbi made a brief speech, his theme was the biblical hero Samson, who chose to fight the Philistines, though he knew it would be his last fight and that he would pay for it with his life. Concluding his emotional remarks, Rabbi Rozowski quoted Judges 16:30, "Let me die with the Philistines," then kissed and hugged Benyamin and all the other children in the room, saying goodbye to each as tears ran into his long white beard.

Benyamin Sonenson's bar mitzvah in September 1941, a few days before the massacre, was the last one to be celebrated in Eishyshok. Near the house of Alte Katz, Benyamin (right) poses with a few of his cousins: (right to left) Yitzhak Sonenson, Altke Tawlitski, and Hayyim Tawlitski. Standing in the front are Meir Sonenson (right) and Oscar (Asher) Shereshefski. Yitzhak survived the war in hiding, Oscar in Siberia; all the others were murdered in the massacre.
PHOTO: BEN ZION SZREJDER. YESC, Y. SONENSON

Benyamin's bar mitzvah sermon, delivered in Hebrew, was about redemption and rebuilding in the Land of Israel. Upset that her children and grandchildren in Baranowicz could not be present, Hayya Sonenson listened with a stoic expression on her face, but the tears that glistened in her eyes betrayed her. What she didn't know was that months before, the Communists had deported her daughter Matle and Matle's husband and children from Baranowicz to Siberia. And there they remained throughout the war, unharmed, and unaware either of the bar mitzvah or of the fact that a few days after it, Benyamin, his mother Ida, brother Shmuel, grandmother Hayya, Rabbi Szymen Rozowski, and most of the other guests at that clandestine celebration were all murdered.

No bat mitzvah celebrations ever took place in Eishyshok. Though the custom of acknowledging a girl's religious maturity (which by Jewish law occurs at age twelve, a year earlier than the boy's) had been officially introduced in France and Italy in the 1840s, it never found its way to Eishyshok before the final destruction. The hearty smack a girl received from her mother when she began her first menstrual cycle was the extent of her maturity celebrations.

Among the small children who had stood guard at the window of Benyamin Sonenson's bar mitzvah, however, was a young girl who would go on to celebrate her bat mitzvah some years later, in her new home in what had just become the new nation of Israel. One of the first Eishyshkians to have a bat mitzvah, Yaffa Sonenson stood at the partition between the men's and women's sections so that she could hear the principal of her school give a speech in her honor, then delivered her scholarly discourse to her peers that afternoon. But not a single relative attended the ceremony, for most had been murdered in Eishyshok and on the killing fields of Europe. The few who had made it to Israel were off fighting the War of Independence. Still she experienced the bat mitzvah as a time of joy, sure that her dynamic, vivacious grandmother Alte Katz and her mother Zipporah, both of them among the murdered, were watching lovingly from the heavens above, as once they had done from the women's gallery of the synagogue in Eishyshok, and taking pleasure in the fact that girls too were now able to mark their religious maturity with a party.

MARRIAGE

TO MAKE A SUCCESSFUL MATCH IS AS DIFFICULT AS THE PARTING OF THE RED SEA.

Sota 2/A

In Judaism, marriage is considered the only way of life for men and women; celibacy is deemed unnatural. Marriage is not just for companionship and procreation, but for self-fulfillment. In the words of the Talmud, "He who has no wife is not a proper man," and "he lives without joy, blessing, goodness, Torah protection, or peace."[10] According to other passages in the Talmud, a man who is in financial distress may go so far as to sell a Torah scroll in order to get married, and a woman should stay in an unhappy marriage rather than live alone.[11]

Tradition held that one's partner in marriage was predestined: forty days prior to the creation of the fetus a heavenly decree announces "the daughter of so and so will marry the son of so and so."[12] On the other hand, each man is responsible for finding a wife, and for choosing her wisely, toward which end the sages of the Talmud offered many guidelines. Marriage should not be for money. A man should seek a wife who is mild-tempered, tactful, modest, and industrious. He should look carefully into her family background and status, and find someone from circumstances similar to his own, who ideally is the daughter of a scholarly father. Large differences in age are to be avoided.[13]

Early marriages are preferred; for men "eighteen is for marriage." If a man is not married by the age of twenty, God curses him. But if a man is intensively occupied with Torah study, the Talmudic sage ben Azzai suggests that he may postpone marriage, though in Babylonia it was suggested that he should marry first and study later.[14]

The positive attitude of the rabbinate toward marriage, dating from the days of the Mishnah and the Talmud, has been maintained in post-Talmudic literature, and in Jewish practice throughout the ages, thus firmly establishing the family as the foundation of Jewish life.

But over the years, particularly during the last century and a half, in the years following the Enlightenment in Western Europe and the Haskalah in Eastern Europe, some aspects of Jewish courtship and marriage practices did change.

Traditions and moral codes that were thousands of years in the making were questioned and challenged, even in that most traditional of worlds, the shtetl. During the closing decades of the nineteenth century and the first decades of the twentieth, the shtetl took a large leap into modernity and secularism. The ideologies of socialism, Communism, and Zionism, along with the rapid industrialization of the large cities, and radical changes in modes of transportation and patterns of emigration had a profound impact on marriage and courtship customs.

ARRANGED MARRIAGES

In the era of arranged marriages, choosing a mate was, of course, usually the responsibility of the parents, although during the Middle Ages, matchmaking was also conducted by prominent rabbis and community leaders. For those parents who wished to look beyond their immediate geographical range, the big commercial fairs in Lublin in the sixteenth and seventeenth centuries, which drew thousands of yeshivah students from throughout Eastern Europe, served not just as an opportunity for job-hunting, intellectual discourse, and assessing other educational options, but as a matchmaking marketplace. There prospective fathers-in-law could size up the husband material, speak to young men who looked like suitable candidates, and make inquiries about them to their fellow students and the heads of their academies.

With the eventual decline of the fairs, parents once again sought help from local matchmakers, who eagerly resumed the duties of their time-honored profession. In fact, the profession was so old that it was even discussed in the Talmud, and so honorable (in its aims, if not always in practice) that even God himself is said to be involved in matchmaking. It is he, after all, who joins "the daughter of so and so to the son of so and so."[15]

Overpriced or dishonest matchmaking was always a risk, however, as a reading of the Lithuanian Council's regulatory literature on the subject makes clear. The matchmakers' fees were to be kept in proportion to the size of the dowry and the elaborateness of the parties that would celebrate the wedding. If as a result of a failed match or other problems a matchmaker resorted to using slander against an individual or a family, the matchmaker was liable for damages.[16] Matchmakers were also warned against overstating or embellishing the virtues of the individuals they proposed as mates, but to no avail. In shtetl folklore, they were well known as unreliable; indeed, it was said that the word *shadkhan* (matchmaker) was an acronym for the Hebrew words *sheker dover kessef notel* ("speaking lies and taking money").

Besides the parents, the professionals, the sages, and the community leaders, the yeshivah played an important role in the shtetl marriage patterns. Students at the Kibbutz ha-Prushim who were from other towns and cities were recommended as mates for Eishyshok women, and young men from Eishyshok attending yeshivot in other locales were matched up there.

The yeshivah students in Eishyshok were a constant source of concern to the parents of young girls, who worried about the possibility of illicit romantic relationships. As Mordekhai Munesh Kaleko recorded in his diary:

> *In the shtetl there was a kibbutz with about 300 prushim. Mothers tied their daughters to their apron strings, careful not to let them out of their sight for even a minute. They were always on the alert, keeping their daughters under their ever-watchful eyes.*

Yeshivah students sometimes looked beyond their school for potential husbands for their sisters. In the 1830s–1840s the Altshul brothers from Prussia, who attended the Kibbutz ha-Prushim in Eishyshok, recommended a husband for their beautiful, erudite, spunky twenty-year-old sister Batia. They praised the prospective bridegroom as a great scholar, wise, gentle, of impeccable character. Their father, a merchant and scholar, was much impressed with his qualifications, and in due course the marriage was arranged and the date set — all by correspondence. When the family arrived from Prussia for the wedding, Batia and her parents were greeted by a middle-aged man with a long graying beard. Batia waited patiently to be introduced to his son, her bridegroom. But she was soon to realize that the middle-aged man with the graying beard was the bridegroom himself. He was, as promised, a scholar, the shtetl dayyan, as wise and gentle as her brothers had said, but they had failed to mention that Reb Layzer Wilkanski was more than twice her age, that he was a widower with four daughters, that he was already a grandfather. She dutifully married him, and for the first few months of her marriage wept into her pillow every night. What eventually followed were six brilliant, handsome children and fifty years of a fascinating relationship.

"Jewish geography," which refers to the propensity of Jews to have a far-flung global network of relatives whom they can call upon for help, was in part made possible by this tendency to marry mates from other towns. In Eishyshok, for example, for all that it might seem a sleepy, provincial, and inbred little shtetl, three-quarters of the marriages during the eighteenth, nineteenth, and first four decades of the twentieth centuries were to people from outside Eishyshok. This meant a constant infusion of new blood, and, in practical terms, a good likelihood of being able to find a relative no matter where one traveled.[17]

THE MEETING When possible, of course, an advance meeting between the parents of the prospective bride and groom was arranged, the logistics and circumstances of the meeting being governed by a variety of local customs. In the Vilna–Grodno region, the parties usually had their first meeting on neutral ground, perhaps at an inn midway between their respective homes. At a typical meeting, the young man would be engaged in a scholarly conversation by the father of the bride-to-be and by other members of his party to determine the level of his Talmudic scholarship. Similarly, the young woman's parents would bring samples of her needlework and knitting to the meeting, so that her future mother-in-law might examine it for clues to her personality: her patience, skill, and neatness, for example.[18] If the meeting took place at the prospective bride's house, she was expected to serve the guests a variety of her own homemade delicacies, in order to display her talents as a housekeeper, hostess, and baker.

It was not uncommon to arrange for the young couple to see each other, prior to formalizing the agreement between the two parties. But such meetings always took place in the presence of other family members, and were often so brief that the principals never exchanged a single word, indeed barely got a glimpse of each other, and thus knew little more about their future mates than they did before.

Ironically, Avraham-Heshl, the sofer gittin (divorce scribe) of Eishyshok, who might have been expected to be particularly vigilant in avoiding the possibility of an unsuitable match, was the victim of one of these cursory meetings sometime during the 1880s. He and his intended were introduced at an inn, where the bride-to-be's father explained that as she was a modest girl, not accustomed to going out much, she had found her journey tiring and would have to remain seated. There followed a second meeting, this one at her parents' home, where she served the company as expected, but managed to do so only when Avraham-Heshl was not looking in her direction. It wasn't until after the wedding that he realized his wife had a limp. He was furious with the matchmaker and with his father-in-law for their deception. But he liked his wife very well, for she was a charming woman. Avraham-Heshl proved an excellent husband, a happily married man who continued to write

Celebrating the signing of the betrothal agreement (tenaim) of Leah Dubrowicz and her groom. (Leah was a relative of the Moszczenik and Katz families.) Most of the people in the photo were murdered during the Holocaust. PHOTO: SHAUL DUBROWICZ. YESC, A. ZIMMERMAN

The celebration of Leah Dubrowicz's wedding. The groom is carried on a chair by his friends and relatives. PHOTO: SHAUL DUBROWICZ. YESC, A. ZIMMERMAN

bills of divorcement for couples who did not share his good fortune.[19]

Searching for a proper mate for a son or daughter was a cold, calculating process. In addition to investigating the character of the potential spouse, parents wanted to know the financial status of the family, their mental and physical health, their moral stature, and their standing in the community. Yet despite all the precautions, Reb Avraham-Heshl's case was far from unique, and many a marriage agreement was signed on the basis of inadequate, inaccurate, or even falsified information.

THE TENAIM The formal agreement was a document known as *tenaim* (Hebrew for "betrothal terms"), which dated from Talmudic times.[20] It was a written contract stipulating the amount of the dowry, the types of jewelry and other gifts to be given, the date and place of the wedding, the number of years of kest the bride's parents were to provide, and the place where the couple would live. As a rule, the couple themselves had no voice whatsoever in formulating the terms of the agreement.

The signing of the document was done by non-family-member witnesses, who also acted as its guarantors. At the conclusion of the signing ceremony, plates were broken, both to symbolize good luck and to commemorate the destruction of the Temple in Jerusalem. Though they didn't establish marital ties, the tenaim did make both parties subject to serious legal obligations. Once signed, they could be broken only by payment of a considerable portion of the dowry, generally half.

Despite the penalties, however, there were occasional violations of the agreement. Sometimes a young woman refused to marry the young man chosen for her, perhaps because he was so unattractive to her that his scholarly achievements were not enough. Such concerns were reflected in many folk songs of the time, such as:

Black cherries we bring home
Red cherries we leave alone

Handsome grooms we bring home
Ugly ones we leave alone.[21]

When an engagement was broken, not only did the parents of the rejecting party have to pay a penalty to the other set of parents, it was thought that bad luck would follow. The shame of it was so great that it was sometimes thought worse than divorce. Hence the popular saying, "It is better to cut up a parchment (as in a divorce) than to tear paper (the paper on which the betrothal terms were set)."

An occurrence in one Eishyshok family in the 1880s illustrates these sentiments very well. In an inn on a road near town, Reb Layzer Wilkanski was about to sign the betrothal terms on behalf of a daughter who was to marry a young man with a fine scholarly reputation. Just as the document was about to be finalized, the young man's sister intervened and aborted the signing ceremony. Reb Layzer's daughter later married someone else, gave birth to twins, and managed a store to help her father and stepmother with the kest. One day a handsome young man with a thick black beard and sad eyes appeared at the Wilkanskis' door. He had come to ask forgiveness from the woman who had been his intended until the interruption of the tenaim-signing ceremony, he explained, for ever since that day at the inn, he and his family had been struck by disasters. The sister who had opposed the marriage had gone blind; he and the wife he had eventually chosen were childless. He was certain that if Reb Layzer's daughter would forgive him, their bad fortune would be reversed. For the meeting between the two, Reb Layzer's son-in-law urged his wife to wear her Sabbath dress and look her best. Beaming with his knowledge that the other man's loss had obviously been his gain, he then had the pleasure of witnessing the requested meeting.[22]

Betrothal terms that had been arrived at by the couple, without the knowledge of their parents or other adult relatives, were not binding if the bridegroom was younger than twenty, and there was no penalty for backing out of them. This particular provision was introduced by the Council of the Four Lands in 1634, for purposes of preventing young people from marrying without the consent of the elders of their family and later becoming a financial burden upon them. It was still being observed in Eishyshok during the nineteenth century.

MARRYING FOR LOVE

Members of the artisan class and the yishuvniks enjoyed more freedom than the balebatim to marry for love. Since the financial stakes were much lower, more young people from these lower classes married for love, and married at a later age, than the children of the balebatim did. But when the ideas of the Haskalah began filtering into the shtetl during the final years of the nineteenth century, love matches ceased to be confined so exclusively to the artisan class. An ever-growing segment of the local youth became enamored of the Haskalah view of marriage, which held that traditional arrangements were a commercial transaction of a kind that was totally outdated in modern society. Scorn for such loveless unions, and a passionate advocacy of romantic courtship and marriage for love, became veritable hallmarks of Haskalah thinking at this time.[23]

The story of a young maskil (a follower of the Haskalah) from Olkenik who courted a woman from Eishyshok is a classic case of a Haskalah-influenced romance. Mordekhai Munesh Kaleko was a handsome young man who worked as a forest overseer. Often he paid visits to nearby Eishyshok, because he had relatives there. At the home of a tavern owner named Yankelewitch, he met the man's three beautiful daughters, the youngest of whom he fell in love with at first sight. His feelings were reciprocated. Frieda seemed "picture perfect" to him; to her, he appeared "tall, handsome and slim . . . a dashing figure in his boots (similar to those worn by aristocrats), his immaculately ironed shirt, and his gleaming ruby tie clasp which cost 50 kopecks — all in the latest fashion." As an accomplished seamstress, Frieda was in a position to appreciate the high quality of his elegant wardrobe.

Blessed with a beautiful voice and a good memory for all the local songs as well as the holiday and Sabbath tunes, Mordekhai Munesh loved to join the Yankelewitch family in song as they sat around the Sabbath table. Mr. Yankelewitch was delighted with the young man, and told his wife, "You know, Beile, Munesh will become my Frieda's groom. They will make a beautiful couple." The elder Kalekos, however, were unaware of the budding romance, and indeed were being besieged by matchmakers, who knew a good catch when they saw one. But as a young maskil, Mordekhai Munesh was pleased with himself for following the Haskalah philosophy and seeking to marry for love.

From his lonely cabin in the forest during the winter of the year of their courtship, Mordekhai Munesh wrote regular letters to his beloved Frieda, composed in the flowery Haskalah style and filled with charming love poems. During the spring and summer months, Frieda visited her beloved in the forest, accompanied by her older sister. Together they hiked among the beautiful pines, and admired the old wooden mansions that dotted the countryside. Mordekhai Munesh spent most of the holidays with the Yankelewitches, though he had to be careful not to interfere with Frieda's work, since the eve of the holidays was the busiest time for a seamstress.

When the marriage agreement was signed, the young man did not ask for much; he was too overjoyed by his good fortune in winning the woman he loved. "When I became a groom," he wrote in his journal, "I did not ask for a dowry or kest. I took twelve pieces of gold, for what good is paper?" The wedding took place on Hanukkah, and the celebrations lasted an entire week.

Still, Mordekhai Munesh Kaleko was the exception at the time. Though the Haskalah would have a profound impact on marriage and family life throughout Europe, it took a while to have its effect in Eishyshok, which was slow to respond to its many innovative ideas. They were gradually introduced by the students at the yeshivah, many of whom came from bigger towns in Germany and Prussia where the Haskalah had been under way for decades. They were eager to share Haskalah books and journals with their fellow students, and with other young people in the shtetl, among them Meir Wilkanski, the son of Reb Layzer and Batia.

The Wilkanski house became the meeting place for the shtetl's young intellectuals, a forum for all the new ideas, including those that concerned love and marriage. Gimpel, a yeshivah student from Germany, pronounced himself strongly in favor of marriages based on love. Arranged marriages, he said, demeaned women, by treating them like merchandise, whereas freely chosen matches had been blessed by the angel of love. To support his ideas he quoted freely from the poet Heine. Reb Layzer's son-in-law, the man who owed his own marriage to the breakdown in the betrothal agreement between his wife and a previous suitor, took issue with Gimpel. He claimed that the true angel of marriage was not the angel of love but the father-in-law, since it was he who paid the dowry and provided the kest.[24] In the years to come, indeed until the very end of the shtetl of Eishyshok, parental support continued to play a big role in making marriages possible, as did parental approval, but love entered into these choices with ever greater frequency, and so did concerns about the groom's financial status, which gradually became more important than his scholarly status. Thus Eishyshok came to be witness to a strange and unforeseen partnership, between Gimpel's angel of love and Reb Layzer's son-in-law's angel of dowry and kest. Working hand-in-hand, they ushered in a new age of marriage.

The change was visible in all strata of shtetl society, and it took root within a generation. In the Wilkanski family, for example, Reb Layzer arranged all the marriages for the four daughters from his first marriage, while the five children from his marriage to Batia who lived to adulthood (a daughter, Leah, died young) chose their own mates. Their courtships and the family's evaluation of their chosen spouses are documented in their letters to one another, letters written with the characteristic Wilkanski combination of romanticism and brutal frankness. After meeting Sarah Rubin, who came to Eishyshok in 1904 to spend some time with the family of Meir, her intended, while he pursued his studies, his sister Esther wrote to him:

Father envies you since your bride is not especially pretty and you are not paying any attention to money. He says that beauty and money blind one and get in the way of one's ability to see things objectively. And since neither beauty nor money is at issue here, that is an indication that the value lies within the bride herself.

The Wilkanskis' experiences reflected and in some respects anticipated the new trends in courtship and marriage, including the ever-increasing tendency to delay marriage. Marriage records from 1891–1903 show that in many first-time marriages, one or both of the partners were beyond their teens, unlike the typical couples of earlier times. During the 1920s and '30s, delayed marriages became the norm, for those who remained in the shtetl, those who emigrated, and the urban population, including non-Jews.[25]

MARRIAGE, MONEY, AND CLASS IN CHANGING TIMES

Another change that was taking place was the trend toward a more egalitarian society, and with it the freedom to marry outside one's class. This freedom is often overstated, however, for while it may have appeared that the ideals of the Haskalah and Zionism were sweeping through the shtetl and vanquishing the age-old barriers of class, a closer examination of shtetl marriages reveals a more complex picture. Even in this new era of love and romance, parents were much more than mere rubber stamps in the process of their children's courtship and marriage. In Meir

The engagement photo of Yitzhak Wilkanski and Sarah Krieger. They made aliyah to Eretz Israel. PHOTO: M. KOPPLON, MEMEL. YESC, WILKANSKI

The engagement photo of Meir Wilkanski and Sarah Rubin, 1904. They made aliyah to Eretz Israel prior to their wedding. PHOTO: GEBR. BARASCH, KÖNIGSBERG. YESC, WILKANSKI

Wilkanski's case, for example, his parents were well acquainted with the family of his bride-to-be since she was Batia's niece, hence Meir's first cousin. And while Reb Layzer apparently commended Meir on his indifference to dowry, most families continued to express great concern about it, and about yihus. Parents of girls also had a new yardstick to measure a prospective groom: his ability to support his family, which now counted for more than his Talmudic scholarship. Thus class distinctions by no means disappeared. Even within the Zionist movement, one could be talented, bright, good-looking, and charming, and still have trouble finding a suitable mate if one were also poor.

Many young people chose to emigrate at this time, not only to escape the difficult economic conditions of interwar Poland but also to transcend their class, and the marriage prospects it dictated. Rina Lewinson and her two sisters, all accomplished, beautiful, popular young women, knew that they would not be free to marry for love. They were the daughters of a coachman, hence their yihus was inferior by shtetl reckoning. Despite the fact that their father was also a scholar and a good businessman, their options would be extremely limited. And so in the 1920s and '30s they emigrated, "so we could choose the men of our hearts."

The engagement photo of Yitzhak Uri Katz and Alte (Rahel-Yehudit) Dwilanski (Yaffa Eliach's maternal grandparents), the pharmacists and photographers, 1905. Yitzhak Uri died a natural death in 1929. Alte was murdered in the September 1941 massacre. PHOTO: STUDIO OF YITZHAK URI KATZ. YESC, RESNIK

Sometimes even emigration did not take these young romantics far enough from the shtetl. When Hayya Sonenson got wind of her beloved son Shalom, who had moved to Jerusalem in the 1920s, dating Zipporah Lubetski, the émigré daughter of an Eishyshok blacksmith, she was furious. She threatened to disown him if he did not break off the relationship. The fact that Zipporah was beautiful, talented, educated, and a nurse by profession was of no interest to Hayya. Yihus prevailed. Shalom returned to Eishyshok from Jerusalem and married a young woman with a substantial dowry, as his mother and father wished him to do. Zipporah herself did eventually escape the chains of yihus, marrying a man from an aristocratic Sephardic family in Eretz Israel, much to the delight of her parents.

Another Sonenson son, Shalom's younger brother Moshe, was in love with another Zipporah — Zipporah Katz. After a year of courtship he proposed marriage, on the anniversary of Theodor Herzl's death, and was accepted by his beloved. The couple notified both sets of parents about their decision. Reb Yitzhak Uri Katz then met with Moshe Sonenson and told him that he accepted the fact of their engagement, though in his opinion Moshe's impulsive character was not compatible with his daughter's serene nature. Nonetheless, he offered his blessing as well as $500 and two years of kest. "Though the word in the shtetl is that I am a wealthy man, I cannot afford more than what I am offering you," he told his future son-in-law. Yitzhak Uri Katz died on the fifth night of Hanukkah, 1929, five weeks

The engagement photo of Hayya Streletski and Daniel Kosowski, Jerusalem, 1923(?). Both were halutzim in Eretz Israel. YESC, H. STRELETSKI

Zivia Hutner met Meir Hadash and became engaged to him in the 1920s after her aliyah to Eretz Israel. The photo was taken in Jerusalem. YESC, R. HADASH

prior to his daughter's wedding. Moshe Sonenson never received the dowry or the kest. Instead, he helped his widowed mother-in-law, Alte Katz, to expand her three businesses.

Peretz Kaleko, the son of the romantic maskil Mordekhai Munesh 'Kaleko and his second wife, Mina (his beloved Frieda had died in childbirth), married Leah Koppelman, Zipporah Katz's best friend. Peretz and Leah had fallen in love in the course of their activities in the Zionist organization Ha-Shomer ha-Zair and the local Hebrew literary club. Though the Koppelman family was well-to-do, the dowry they offered was only $500, out of which he was to buy a fur coat for Leah, and their only gift to Peretz was a gold watch. The meager dowry and the fur coat stipulation were expressions of their disappointment in the marriage their daughter was making. Though Peretz was handsome, well educated, popular, and one of the cultural leaders of the shtetl, he did not come from a rich family with a distinguished yihus. The Koppelmans felt that Leah could have done better.

During the years between the two world wars, dowries in Eishyshok were paid in dollars, and averaged between $500 and $1,500. When a dowry was not paid, the parents were generally obliged to help the young couple establish themselves. Eliyahu Bastunski's letters to his son Zusl in California offer an interesting commentary on the subject of marriage, and the economics thereof. In September 1934 Bastunski writes about the marriage of another son, Yankl:

I thought he would get a bride's dowry and make life easier for me. Instead he married for love, without a bride's dowry. So I am not filled with pleasure, even though it was a decent match with fitting in-laws. But what can I do? This was done without my knowledge.

Until his death in the massacre of 1941, Eliyahu Bastunski helped this son who "married for love" without a dowry.

Two months after his letter about his son's marriage, Bastunski wrote about the marriage of the shtetl's most eligible bachelor, the extremely handsome son of the wealthy Kiuchefski family:

David Levin (né Portnoy) and Zipporah Levin became engaged in Eishyshok and got married in America on August 10, 1923. PHOTO: BRUDNER, VILNA. YESC, PORTNOY-LEVIN

Altke Bastunski and Avraham Kaplan were engaged on June 16, 1925. The Kaplans and their children were murdered in the September 1941 massacre. YESC, BASTUNSKI

"Shlomo Kiuchefski got married last week. He received $1,500 as a dowry." Seven months after that, in June 1935, Bastunski wrote to ask for financial help from his émigré son, this time not for his own family, but for a community obligation: "Perhaps you, my child, can help me to perform this act of charity, that the merit of my good deed will prolong my life. A small thing — an orphan has to get married; that money which you sent me I already used to pay off my debts."

Not long after that, having successfully married off his oldest daughter, Altke, to Avraham Kaplan, a fine young merchant who was a member of the kehilah, Bastunski was already worrying about marrying off the youngest one, and seemed to be laying the groundwork for yet another request for money from his son:

Thank God you helped us to marry off Altinke. I found a husband for her, not rich but handsome; we should not receive a worse one for Bashinke! A very beautiful child she is, but with beauty nothing can be done. The world may say that "a beautiful girl is half the dowry," but still the other half is needed. And on the merit of your generosity in this matter, the beloved God will reward you and grant you success in all your endeavors.

In the spring of 1937 he decided it was time for Batia (Bashinke) to marry, and time to ask for money again:

In the meanwhile you can help us with $500, for the dowry. I thank you for it, my child. The other half of the dowry I will provide, with God's help, for a good dowry helps a pretty girl.

Batia, however, had her own plans. She harbored a secret wish to join her brothers in America, and did not want to get married at this time, which she explained by saying that she did not feel well enough to make such plans. Unbeknownst to her father, she wrote her own letter to Zusl and mailed it with her father's:

Beloved brother, I thank you very much for your willingness to help me. Meanwhile, let the $500 remain with you, for it seems to me that you are the safest place for it. If God will grant that I should feel better, then I will need it.

Batia did not need a dowry in Eishyshok, for in 1938 she did indeed emigrate to America, where she joined her brothers, and subsequently married.

The Bastunskis were fortunate to have two sons who were doing well abroad. Few Eishyshkians could count on receiving dowry dollars from America. During the hard times in interwar Poland, the inability to come up with a suitable dowry was a problem for many lovestruck couples. Some solved it by going to larger towns where, free from parental pressure and supervision, they married without parental consent. Then, struggling on their own, hoping eventually to find a way to emigrate, they remained in Vilna or Lida or Bialystok or wherever their hopes had taken them. Some couples simply kept their marriage a secret, as was the case with Hayya Sorele Lubetski, a cousin of Zipporah Lubetski (whose romance had been broken off because her father was a lowly blacksmith). In the late 1930s Hayya-Sorele, also the daughter of a blacksmith, defied yihus and economics by marrying a Hebrew teacher from outside Eishyshok, over the objections of both sets of parents — for she had neither yihus nor money, and he had no money.

Other young people tried to overcome the lack of a dowry or a suitable income by a kind of sleight of hand. Setting their tables with borrowed fine china, silverware, and crystal, and wearing elegant suits or dresses that were also on loan, they welcomed the parents of their beloved into their homes. Perhaps money issues would be forgotten if they could create the impression of a balebatish home and life. The story of one such bridegroom, eager to impress his future in-laws, became a shtetl classic. For his trip to his bride's home in Lida, he donned a borrowed suit and tie — the first time in his life he had ever worn such clothing. When he arrived only to discover that the meeting with his bride's parents had to be postponed by a day, he was frantic, for he had no idea how to tie a tie. His solution to the problem was to keep the tie on. Thus he spent the night sleeping upright in a chair, fully clothed.

Financial problems plagued parents and young couples until the very end of the shtetl's life, eventually becoming more of an issue than the yihus factor. Even as World War II broke out, and thousands of refugees began streaming through Eishyshok on their way east, parents with unmarried daughters continued to worry about coming up with the necessary dowry. When dollars gave way to gold, the more stable currency in times of trouble, parents began collecting gold coins in the hope of providing their daughters with a better life, once the war had ended. But soon they would be facing much greater problems, for which gold coins would be no solution.

SHTETL WEDDINGS

FROM THAT BYGONE WORLD, MOST OF ALL I MISS THE BEAUTY OF THE FRIDAY AFTERNOON WEDDINGS.

Rivka Remz Rewzin

Though the betrothal agreement was meant to pave the way for a trouble-free wedding, unforeseen last-minute difficulties often arose, mainly relating to travel problems and dowry renegotiations. Since a majority of weddings involved spouses from other towns and cities, travel was a major concern, with each season presenting its own challenges. Late fall and winter were the worst: snow and ice made unpaved roads impassable, blizzards trapped travelers in out-of-the-way places from which there was no escape, and bandits and wolves both went on the attack. Wedding travel disaster tales became a genre unto themselves, occupying a special place in East European lore.

Eishyshok contributed its own share of such tales, some of them tragic. Naftali Eliezer Sonenson traveled from Karelitz to Mir in the dead of winter, in order to attend the wedding of his handsome son Yitzhak, der Minsker Illui (the prodigy from Minsk). As they traveled through the forest, the wedding guests were set upon by a pack of wolves. The horses went into a wild, panicked gallop, and the sled carrying the family skidded and overturned. Reb Naftali Eliezer was killed, his wife Hayya and other members of their family were injured. Meanwhile, after a long wait for the missing guests, and with no means of learning about the tragedy that had befallen them, the wedding took place in Mir as planned. Since Reb Naftali had objected to his son's marriage to the poor, short, homely bride whom Yitzhak had met amid the mausoleums of the Eishyshok cemetery, some later claimed to see in his death the hand of providence.

Another winter wedding tale, this one with a narrowly averted tragic ending, was that of Motl, whose mother wrapped him up, mummy-style, in bundles of sheepskin and layer upon layer of heavy clothing, in order to protect him from the bitter cold on the journey from Eishyshok to the nearby shtetl of his bride. His friends parted from him with the traditional farewell ceremony at the bridge on the outskirts of town, and at the other end of his journey his future in-laws waited to welcome him. When Motl's sled arrived, they went to greet him with bread and salt, as was the custom, only to discover that his seat in the sled was empty and Motl was nowhere to be found. The horse-drawn sled was driven back in search of the missing bridegroom, who was eventually found lying in the middle of the snowy road. Having fallen off the sled during the journey, he had been unable to free himself from his swaddling, and had been lying there trapped ever since. After Motl's mishap, a special message was incorporated into the parting ceremony at the bridge, warning bridegrooms to be sure to take good care of themselves on the journey to their weddings.[26]

Even after the railroad was built, the journey to and from Eishyshok remained hazardous, since the nearest train station, in Bastun, was still thirteen miles away. A variety of tragicomical adventures occurred along every inch of those thirteen miles, many of them related to wedding journeys. After 1929, with the opening of a paved highway from Vilna through Eishyshok, automobiles gradually replaced horses, and car accidents began claiming their share of lives, including those of the bride and groom who were buried side by side under a black wedding canopy.

When man, beast, weather, and fate cooperated, wedding guests coming to Eishyshok were met at the bridge by the family, and there followed a joyous welcoming ceremony, which often included musical contributions by the shtetl klezmers. Afterward, the guests were settled in the homes of their designated hosts, and the final preparations began. But this was often a time of great tension as well as joy, filled with last-minute demands to renegotiate the terms of the dowry settlement, backed up by threats to delay or even cancel the wedding — a spectacle to which the entire shtetl was usually privy.

One winter day in the 1880s the shtetl was eagerly awaiting the marriage between the daughter of Mendl the peddler and the fine, accomplished yeshivah student who was her intended. To win such a bridegroom for their daughter, Mendl and his wife had given him all they possessed, in addition to presenting him with a gold pocket watch, the customary gift from the bride. But the day of the wedding dawned bitter cold, and it occurred to the bridegroom that a coat of fox fur would be much warmer than the one he had originally agreed to. Instead of going to his wedding, the bridegroom went to sleep, leaving the negotiations for the fur coat to his father and other members of his wedding party. Only when an agreement was finally reached did he allow himself to be rushed to his place beneath the wedding canopy. But there, too, the phlegmatic groom took his time, placing the ring on his bride's index finger with such weighty deliberation that he was urged to get on with it. "What do you think," he replied, "to marry a woman is like eating a cookie?"[27]

Meir "the wicked butcher" had a similar experience. He, too, chose for his daughter a bridegroom from the yeshivah of Eishyshok, a handsome, red-bearded parush with an excellent reputation for scholarship. Months of wooing the young scholar with choice meats from Meir's butcher shop had culminated in the signing of a very generous betrothal agreement, which stipulated a large dowry and a long-term kest. But despite all the goods and monies that were to be lavished upon him, the young man balked on his wedding day, demanding an increase in the dowry before he would proceed with the ceremony. Meir the butcher refused to be bullied. He instructed his daughter to abandon her prewedding fast, and ordered his coachman to harness his horses and drive the members of the bridegroom's party back to their respective shtetlekh. At the last moment, the bridegroom backed down and the wedding took place.[28]

Once all the final difficulties had been resolved and the bride and groom began to make their way to the wedding canopy, the entire shtetl could be heard breathing a sigh of relief — and anticipation. Weddings, after all, were entertaining as well as joyous celebrations, blending millennia-old traditions and laws with local customs and lore. The result was a picturesque pageant involving virtually everyone in the shtetl as an active participant — thanks in part to the fact that weddings were generally held on Friday afternoons, when most people were free to come.

Friday weddings were one of those instances of local custom superseding Talmudic tradition, for it is stated in the Mishnah that a virgin gets married on Wednesday, a widow on Thursday. One possible explanation for the first of these stipulations was that the rabbinical court sat on Thursdays, and would therefore conveniently be in session on the day after the wedding, should the groom wish to lodge a complaint questioning his wife's virginity. The widow married on Thursday to ensure that her husband would devote at least three days to her — Thursday, Friday, and the Sabbath — before going back to his work.

Never a market day, Friday was always a slow day in the shops of Eishyshok, since most people had already bought everything they needed in advance of the Sabbath. Stores closed early on Fridays, heder boys had a short day, and all the coachmen, merchants, and peddlers were back home from their travels, awaiting the arrival of the Sabbath Queen. Friday weddings therefore offered the least disruption to the local economy and the greatest opportunity for universal participation in the wedding festivities.

THE CEREMONY As the hour of the wedding approached, the shtetl went about its last-minute preparations for the big event. The *clink-clunk* of large metal keys turning over in heavy iron locks signaled an even earlier than usual Friday-afternoon closing for the local shops, and men could be seen hurrying out of the public bathhouse, having cut short their leisurely immersions in order to return home and get ready. Candles appeared in the windows facing the market square, in the windows overlooking the alleys, lanes, and streets that led to the shulhoyf where the wedding canopy stood, and in the windows on the streets where the bride and groom lived. The shtetl water carriers and the shtetl poor took their designated places along the route to be followed by the wedding procession, dressed in their Sabbath best and toting their heavy buckets. And when at last all was made ready, the shtetl klezmers began making their way to the groom's residence.

Meanwhile, both the bride and the groom were taking part in prewedding ceremonies. At the bride's house a badkhan (a sort of jester) was entertaining the bride and her female entourage in a ceremony known as *baveinen di kalleh* (lamenting the bride). This involved celebrating the carefree days of the childhood and youth she was leaving behind, and bemoaning the burdens of the married life she was about to assume. Custom required that the badkhan, also known in some places as the marshelik, be a married man who was a permanent resident of the shtetl. If a badkhan from a neighboring shtetl was invited, the Lithuanian Council dictated that he had to be approved by the local shtetl rabbi or the kahal.

At the residence of the bridegroom, an all-male entourage of family, friends, and dignitaries gathered for the signing of the marriage certificate, the ketubah. In the ketubah, which was written in Aramaic, the groom pledged himself to assign a certain sum of money to the bride in the event of his divorcing her or dying. Once the signing ceremony was completed, the groom was expected to deliver a scholarly discourse (though in some Eishyshok families the discourse was delivered during the festive Friday-night meal). In order to avoid embarrassing bridegrooms whose scholarship was inadequate to the occasion, it was customary to repeatedly interrupt the discourse with songs and merriment so that no one could really tell what was being said. At the conclusion of his speech, ashes were placed high on his forehead as a symbol of mourning for the destruction of the Temple in Jerusalem, and the groom and his party, following in the footsteps of the klezmers, began the walk to the home of the bride. Families dressed in their Sabbath best came pouring out of all the houses on the way, joining in the groom's procession.

Next came the badeken di kalleh ceremony: "covering the bride." The bride in her white wedding gown sat on a large, elaborately decorated chair that stood on top of an upside-down dough trough covered with a rug — the dough trough being a symbol of abundance. Placing his hands on his daughter's head, the bride's father blessed her with these words: "May God make thee as Sarah, Rachel, and Leah who built the House of Israel." If the father was a kohen, he also blessed his daughter with the priestly benediction. Then it was the groom's turn to participate in the ceremony, by lowering the veil over the face of his bride, after which everybody in the room joined in saying the next blessing: "Our sister, be thou the mother of thousands of ten thousands, and let thy seed possess the gate of those that hate them."[29]

With the conclusion of this ceremony, havdalah candles were lit, the musicians split into two groups, and the groom and his party began the walk to the shulhoyf. Leading the way were young men with burning torches and one of the two klezmer groups, behind whom were the groom and his parents, who carried the long, twisted havdalah candles, their flames flickering in the breeze. As the bride and her parents, who also carried candles, made their entrance into the wedding procession, their approach was loudly proclaimed by the second group of klezmers. At the sound of the instruments, the entire population of the shtetl joined in the candlelit procession, which made its way across the huge market square. As people marched past the water carriers, many would drop coins for good luck into their water-filled buckets. Other people, who were too old or too sick to walk in the procession, would stand on their stoops as the wedding party passed by, some holding candles, others pairs of doves to symbolize a peaceful life, and still others handfuls of wheat kernels for fertility. Some had unique blessings and comments of their own to offer, like the old woman who lived to be over a hundred. "Fools, they still believe in this kind of nonsense," she would loudly announce from her stoop as she saw the bride approaching, adding quietly, under her breath, "May God bless them for many years."

Once the groom reached the shulhoyf, he stood under the huppah (wedding canopy) awaiting the bride. There he was joined by the rabbi, who emerged from his house on the shulhoyf, and shortly thereafter by the bride. Surrounded by their townspeople, who filled the spacious grounds of the shulhoyf, the groom and bride became husband and wife.

When the ceremony was over and the procession began the journey back to the bride's home, the klezmers led the way, followed by the water carriers, into whose buckets coins were constantly dropped. As they passed through the streets of town, the married couple were showered with wheat kernels and often, if it was wintertime, with an arsenal of snowballs, courtesy of the shtetl children, while flights of doves were released into the air around them.

Upon reaching the bride's house, the couple was greeted by the bride's mother, who welcomed them with a huge braided hallah and salt. This was one of several special hallahs that were prepared for consumption at the various wedding meals and ceremonies still to come, and like all of them it had to be absolutely picture perfect. To ensure perfection, there were professionally baked backups for the homemade hallot (or *koillegim*, as these special breads were known), prepared by shtetl bakeries known for the art of koilleg baking.

The amply provisioned bride and groom were then shown to a quiet room where they could be alone together and break their fast (in a legally prescribed practice known as *yihud*), whereupon everyone else was offered slices of honey cake brought forth from two immense wicker trunks. After wishing the couple mazel tov, the men and boys of the shtetl rushed off to shul, and the women and girls rushed back home to light the Sabbath candles. Soon the bridal couple emerged, so that the groom could also go to shul.

THE CELEBRATION The Friday-evening Sabbath meal that followed was the first of the "seven-benediction" wedding meals. So called because at each such meal the seven benedictions that were recited at the wedding were repeated, these occasions were part of the weeklong festivities celebrating the marriage of a virgin. By doing honor to both the Sabbath bride and the earthly bride, thus serving a double purpose, the first of these festive meals maintained another shtetl tradition: that of thrift, for many a family was hard pressed to pay for all of this feasting. During the Sabbath, the food served was the traditional Sabbath menu. During the weekdays, a typical "seven-benediction" meal might include any or all of the following: gefilte fish, small sweet and sour meatballs, sliced veal in sauce, jellied calves feet, carrots with prunes, potatoes with prunes, sauerkraut with red berries, and pickles. Desserts included cakes, tea, preserves, and cooked apples with prunes. Preparing the food for these wedding meals was of course a major undertaking — how major depending on the affluence as well as the generosity of the bride's family. Friends, neighbors, and family did the baking, but in the cooking they were often assisted by professionals, women who had made a business out of catering special events.

On Saturday morning the groom was taken to the synagogue, escorted by male friends and relatives who sang a special "groom's melody" on the way. Seated in a place of honor on the eastern wall, next to the rabbi and other shtetl notables, the groom took precedence over all others at this service. Even if there was a bar mitzvah that morning, it was the groom who was called up to the Torah to read the haftarah — much to the chagrin of any bar mitzvah boy unlucky enough to be sharing his special day. Sixty years after his own bar mitzvah, Hayyim Sonenson could still remember the disappointment and anger he felt when his reading of the Torah was preempted by a groom.

The bride, too, went to shul that morning, escorted by an all-female entourage of friends and relatives, all of them dressed in their best for the occasion. And she, too, had a place of honor, seated in the women's section near the center window, facing the Holy Ark. At the conclusion of the services she and her entourage returned home for a special kiddush in her honor. This "sweet table" consisted of a variety of delicacies — baked goods, preserves, dried fruits — that had been prepared by her friends and brought to her home prior to noontime on Friday.

Saturday night was the height of the wedding celebrations. Though the Lithuanian Council recommended a modest gathering on that first Saturday night following the wedding, in

Eishyshok, as in many other shtetlekh, the festivities involved many more people than the ten men plus relatives envisioned by the Council. In fact, it was customary to invite the entire shtetl, including the poor people from the hekdesh.

Since there were no wedding halls in Eishyshok, the rumpl, as the celebration was known in Yiddish, took place in a spacious stable attached to a big house. The stable was cleaned for the occasion, yellow sand was spread on the floor, and strings of paper lanterns were hung from the rafters. Long tables covered in coarse white homespun linen were set up, and a stage was created by placing wooden planks atop large barrels. From the stage the wedding couple and the entertainment for the evening — the klezmers and the badkhan (usually the same man who had performed the "lamenting the bride" ceremony) — could be seen by all. Even in times of austerity, when the Lithuanian Council's mandate regarding small weddings was honored, the badkhan and the klezmers were a must. Indeed, they were explicitly excluded from the Council's numerical restrictions, in recognition of the important role they played in even the most modest of celebrations.

Part of the entertainment was the gift-giving ritual, the droshe-geshank, over which the badkhan presided as master of ceremonies. In improvised rhymes he announced the nature of each gift, and the name of the giver and his or her relationship to the bride and groom, then showed it to the crowd and placed it on the stage. The gift-givers were mainly relatives, and the gifts were generally of two kinds: religious articles and household utensils. The former category encompassed such items as silver kiddush cups, fine linen hallah covers, Hanukkah candelabra, prayer books and other religious books; the latter included pots and pans, dishes, cutlery, a samovar, down quilts and pillows. As he presented each of the gifts, the badkhan often made comments about the character of the giver, rarely mincing his words even when the subject was one of the shtetl notables. His comments also included philosophical remarks about the nature of love, marriage, and family life. On love, one such comment, which like many was repeated with slight variations at subsequent weddings, was this haunting rhyme:

What is love?
It is a small candle
Flickering on a mantel.
Briefly it leaves its mark
Then once again fades into the dark.[30]

On a respectable family known throughout the shtetl for their years of internal feuds:

The givers are like a samovar
Burning inside and shining from afar.[31]

Besides the antics of the badkhan, there was music and dancing to enliven the festivities. The music was provided by the klezmers, as well as by yeshivah students who added their own special touch by singing sad songs, typical of the Lithuanian yeshivot, about exile, God, and the Jewish people.[32] Eishyshkians also gave themselves special dispensation to sing the lively, cheerful songs of the Hasidim at weddings, despite their intense dislike for what they regarded as an upstart, anti-intellectual religious movement. Dancing was segregated, the men in one area, the women in another, as dictated both by custom and by the Lithuanian Council. On one occasion when this propriety was not observed, a furious Batia Wilkanski made her way to the center of a circle of dancers, who instantly scattered in shame.[33]

The other main attraction of the evening was the food, which was a cold pareve meal — that is, one that did not include meat or dairy. It had to be a cold meal because any cooking or warming up of food would be a desecration of the Sabbath. Among the most common offerings at such a celebration were gefilte fish, various

A winter wedding portrait of members of the Moszczenik and Rothberg families and various other relatives: (seated left to right) Yitzhak Yidl, Reb Dovid der Kichier Moszczenik, Reb Tuvia Rothberg, the bride and groom. Standing behind Reb Tuvia is Hanneh-Beile Kudlanski (née Moszczenik); between Reb Tuvia and the groom is Hanneh-Beile's daughter Atara. Hanneh-Beile, Atara, and a few others emigrated to America. Reb Dovid died a natural death; most of the others were murdered during the Holocaust. YESC, A. ZIMMERMAN

Moshe Sonenson and Zipporah Katz (Yaffa Eliach's parents) posing for their engagement picture on the shtetl's wooden bridge, July 28, 1928. Zipporah was murdered by the AK after liberation. PHOTO: YITZHAK URI KATZ. YESC, RESNIK

herring dishes (which might include pickled herring, chopped herring, or schmaltz herring with onion rings), sauerkraut, bagels, and an assortment of cakes, cookies, and dried fruits, all washed down by kvass and beer.

The last of the celebratory meals was the one held the following Saturday night, as a send-off for all the departing out-of-town guests, and for the newlyweds as well, if they were not going to reside in Eishyshok. After that, the bride's family could breathe a sigh of relief — and start saving up for the next daughter's wedding!

For centuries most weddings in Eishyshok took place during the winter months, for reasons that are no longer known. Perhaps the custom had its roots in the farming life of the founding families of Eishyshok, which meant that winter was their idle season, when they could afford to take time off for such diversions. Perhaps, too, the very nature of winter celebrations made it easier to supervise the unmarried young people, for the cold winter nights discouraged romantic outdoor rendezvous, and all the dancing took place within an enclosed space where nothing could be hidden (as the hapless dancers discovered by Batia Wilkanski learned to their chagrin). Or perhaps this tradition shared the same roots as the custom observed by the Yemenite Jews, who considered winter to be the luckiest time of the year for weddings.* One thing for

*Among the Yemenite Jews, the Hebrew months that were approximately equivalent to November, December, January, and February were considered lucky months — and they were also much more conducive to a celebration than the scorching hot months of the desert summer.

Altke Burstein sitting with her groom (name unknown) and all of the Burstein and Zlotnik relatives from Eishyshok (to avoid army service Reb Itche der Shohet, father of the bride, changed the family name from Zlotnik to Burstein) at her wedding in 1924. The bride and groom emigrated to America via Paris; Kunie Zlotnik and her husband Yehuda-Leib (top row, third and fourth from right) made aliyah. Most of the people in the photo were murdered during the September 1941 massacre; Reb Itche was slaughtered with his own knife. PHOTO: YITZHAK URI KATZ. YESC, ELLEN MURAD

Miriam Koppelman and Avraham Rushkin on their wedding day, Sunday, November 25, 1934, posing with their best friends from Eishyshok and Szetl. Standing second from left is Malka Matikanski; seated far left is Haikl Matikanski (Malka's brother); next to Haikl is Esther Katz. Malka emigrated to Eretz Israel, Esther to Colombia, before the war. Avraham was murdered by one of his dental patients while in hiding in the forest, Haikl perished at Majdanek. Most of the others were killed as well. YESC, MALIKANSKI

sure was that a winter wedding had the advantage of making it possible to maintain the freshness of large quantities of food, much of it prepared in advance of the weeklong celebrations. In the pre-refrigeration era, this must have been a major concern.

WEDDINGS IN THE 1920S AND '30S In the years between the two world wars, the tradition of winter weddings, like so many other wedding traditions that had been observed for centuries, underwent a change. While those rituals that were governed by law (halakhah) remained intact, others that were the product of local custom came close to disappearing. Thus weddings now took place throughout the year — though not, of course, on any of those days on the Jewish calendar that are expressly forbidden:† Friday weddings, with all their public pageantry and communal participation, became much less common. Couples increasingly preferred to have private weddings, and would go to some lengths to avoid having to share this special, intimate occasion with the entire shtetl. When Moshe Kaganowicz and Hannah Kiuchefski went to Vilna to get married in 1924, they became trendsetters. After all, if the children of some of the most prominent balebatim in the shtetl could get married in Vilna, surely others could do the same.

Printed invitations to the wedding replaced the old custom of extending a shtetl-wide invitation from the bimah in the beth midrash, or going door to door. Segregated dancing gave way to mixed dancing; the tango and the waltz replaced the traditional folk dances; the Israeli hora took the place of the East European sherele. And this younger generation, for all that they espoused

†The Sabbath, holidays, fasts, the first thirty-three days of the omer, which are observed as partial mourning, and the three weeks of semi-mourning that begin with the minor fast on the seventeenth of Tammuz and end with the fast on the ninth day of Av.

equality and social justice, had abandoned the shtetl tradition of inviting the poor to their weddings and setting up special tables for them.

As late as 1930, however, when Moshe Sonenson and Zipporah Katz got married, there were still occasional weddings that preserved much of the pageantry and symbolism of an earlier time, a few deviations notwithstanding. Moshe Sonenson and Zipporah Katz were married on the ninth day of the month of Shevat (February 7 on the Roman calendar), a few days prior to the full moon, a time considered the luckiest part of the month. A traditional wedding procession wound through the snow-covered, candle-lit market square, but upon leaving the bride's home, after the "lamenting the bride" ceremony, the groom, the water carriers, and the klezmers did not turn toward the shulhoyf; rather, they directed their steps to the apple orchard of Hayya and Shael Sonenson, the parents of the groom, for Reb Shael was too ill to walk to the shulhoyf. The ornate old wedding canopy had been transported from the shulhoyf to the orchard and set up on poles in the family gazebo, so that Moshe Sonenson could be married under the same huppah where generation upon generation of his family had also been married. Szymen Rozowski, who was the shtetl rabbi and a close

The wedding of Rivka Lewinson and David Shanzer in Jerusalem, June 19, 1925. The young couple is sitting among fellow halutzim from Eishyshok who also made aliyah to Eretz Israel: (top row, third and fourth from right) Yitzhak Frischer and wife Nehama Koppelman; (middle row, right to left) Motke Levittan, with wife and baby daughter; next to the groom is Rachel Dwilanski; (far left) Rachel Dwilanski's brother; seated next to him is Zipporah Lubetski (Tokatli); (seated on the ground, far right) Naftali Berkowitch and, next to him, Shalom Sonenson. YESC, N. FRISCHER

friend of Shael Sonenson, officiated. At the conclusion of the ceremony one could hear the splashing sounds of coins being dropped into water-filled buckets, and watch kernels of wheat being thrown at the young couple as they stepped forth from the gazebo. Hayya Sonenson had made sure that this ancient symbol of fertility would be a part of her son's wedding, for she abhorred the more modern custom of throwing showers of confetti. She considered even the pelting with snowballs to be preferable to *that* abomination!

The wedding of Bat-Sheva Rozowski and Rabbi David Zalmanovitz from Ilya, June 17, 1932. Bat-Sheva was the daughter of Rabbi Szymen Rozowski. This was the last wedding celebration in which the entire shtetl participated, as in pre–World War I days. Sitting next to Bat-Sheva in the shulhoyf is her mother, Rebbetzin Miriam; next to the groom is his mother, Dvorah. Standing behind them are Bat-Sheva's brother's wife and David's sisters. In the front row are their little nephews and nieces. They were all murdered during the Holocaust, the Rozowski family in the September 1941 massacre, Bat-Sheva, David, and their three children in the Treblinka gas chambers.
PHOTO: BEN ZION SZREJDER. YESC, ROZOWSKI

Though many a home in the shtetl was filled with wedding guests, among them noted rabbis and scholars from Lida, Baranowicz, Radun, Mir, and Luna, the celebrations that followed were comparatively modest ones, since the bride's father, Yitzhak Uri Katz, had died only five weeks before. Alte Katz, the mother of the bride, was a professional photographer, but was too distracted by her recent loss to photograph her own daughter's wedding celebrations.

The traditions of the shtetl were so strong, even in changing times, that at least some émigré families carried them beyond the shtetl to new lands. When beautiful Dora Zlotnik was about to leave Eishyshok to marry Naftali Berkowitch in Eretz Israel in 1931, his father, Reuven-Beinush, wrote to cousins there, hoping they would ensure that the old customs were indeed perpetuated:

My dear ones, please see to it that immediately upon Dora's arrival they should be led to the wedding canopy and marry according to law and tradition. It is painful that we cannot be present at the wedding of our most beloved son Naftali. However, we are comforted that you, dear Feigele [Zipporah] and Yaakov, will take our place and assure that all will be done the right way.

The wedding was indeed a traditional ceremony, held at the beautiful synagogue Baron Edmond de Rothschild had built in Rishon Le-Zion. There the witnesses included a number of other halutzim from Eishyshok, friends as well as family. Mordekhai Lawzowski, a friend of the groom's from back home, had taken care of the invitations and travel arrangements. The groom's cousin Yaakov Schneider, and Yaakov's wife, Zipporah, led the couple to the wedding canopy, as had been requested. And family friend Velvel Schneider, who had emigrated with his family in 1924, was host at the celebration that followed, near his own citrus grove — a dream

Rabbi Szymen Rozowski (third from left), sitting with his new son-in-law, Rabbi David Zalmanovitz, amid family, friends of the groom, and prominent members of the Mizrahi movement. (The Agudat Israel boycotted the wedding.) Most of the people in the photo, including the rabbi's son Avraham, second from right in the top row, were murdered during the Holocaust. The rabbi was buried alive, the last victim of the September 1941 massacre. YESC, ROZOWSKI

come true for him, a symbol of the melding of ancient tradition and Zionist ideals. Back in Eishyshok, Reuven-Beinush was very pleased. From the bimah of the Old Beth Midrash he read aloud the letters describing the wedding.

Not all parents were so fortunate, for among many of the young emigrants, both to Palestine and to America, the desire to reject tradition was strong, as was the peer pressure to do so. Meir Yaari, the leader of Ha-Shomer ha-Zair in Israel (both before and after it had achieved statehood), married his wife according to Jewish law — but kept that fact a secret, for fear that the religious ceremony would be considered incompatible with his commitment to Socialist ideology.

The last wedding in Eishyshok to fully recapture the old pageantry took place on Friday, June 17, 1932, when Bat-Sheva Rozowski, only daughter of Rabbi Szymen Rozowski, married Rabbi David Zalmanovitz from Ilya. For weeks in advance the shtetl was gripped in anticipation of the big event. Letters to America, like this one from Eliyahu Bastunski, were filled with news of it:

By now it is already the eve of Shavuoth. On the second Friday there will be the wedding of our Rabbi's daughter, Sheva, whom I believe you may remember. There will be great pageantry, there will be much dancing, and there will be many important guests. It will be, in one word, joyous.

Eliyahu's daughter Batia Bastunski, a contemporary of the bride's, also wrote to her brother about the wedding, which she looked forward to as a rare interruption in the dreariness of shtetl life.

My dear, you ask how I spend my time. Not too happily, as you will understand if you still remember how time passes in a shtetl. However, soon we will celebrate the wedding of the Rabbi's daughter. Many guests will be there and I hope that it will be very merry and that we will have a grand time.

The wedding seems to have lived up to all expectations, and to have remained a highly treasured, lifelong memory for many. It was removed from twentieth-century shtetl-style politics, as a look at who was missing from among the guests showed. As noted in chapter 3, many of the rabbis in the vicinity boycotted the event, since they belonged to the ultra-orthodox Agudat Israel movement, while Rabbi Rozowski was an ardent member of the religious Zionist movement, Mizrahi. Still, the dancing was joyous, the singing loud and lusty. Not even the old-timers could find a dark cloud to mar this flawless celebration under sunny spring skies.

No one could have predicted that nine years later, Bat-Sheva, David, and their three children would walk in a different procession, into the gas chambers of Treblinka.

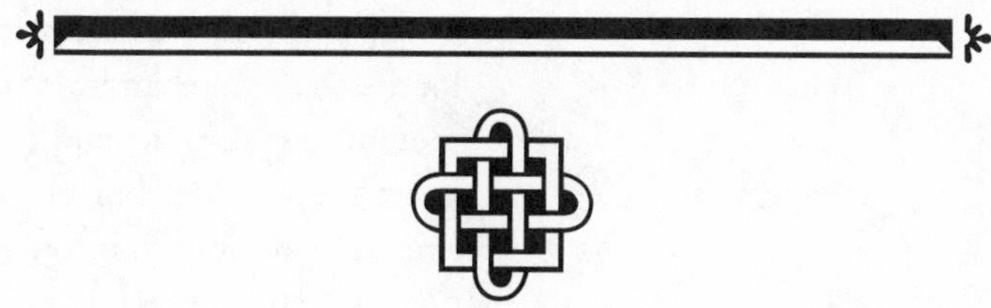

LIKE EVERY SOCIETY, THE SHTETL HAD TO DEAL WITH DEVIATIONS FROM ITS NORMS. Divorce, illegitimate children, mental illness, suicide, and conversion to other faiths were some of the departures from convention faced by certain families. There was, of course, a large body of Jewish law that had evolved over many centuries for the purpose of offering guidelines in these circumstances. But the shtetl supplemented halakhic wisdom with its own network of moral codes and social attitudes — comprehensive in nature, and typically blunt in style. Alternately punitive and supportive, the community tried to provide a safety net for the unfortunates in its midst, and deterrence for those whose misfortune it saw as self-willed.

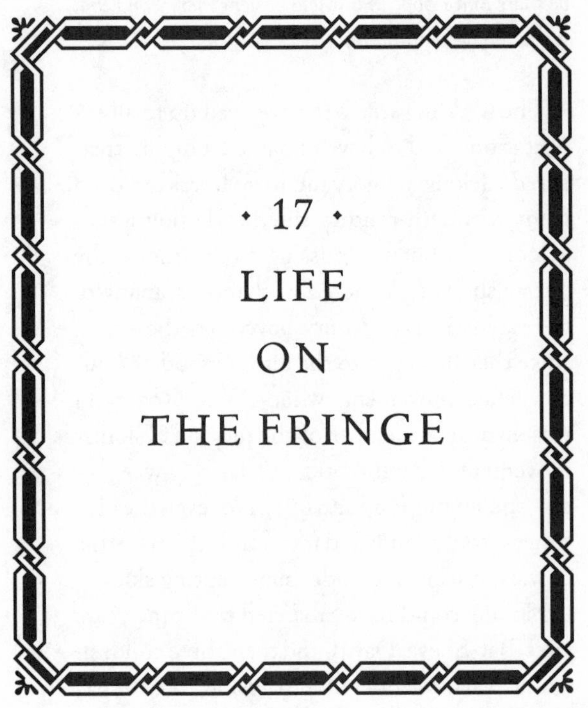

· 17 · LIFE ON THE FRINGE

JEWS IN THE DIASPORA
WHO SURVIVED FOR
TWO THOUSAND YEARS
WALKED IN THE CENTER
ON THE GOLDEN PATH.
AFTER THE HOLOCAUST
THE FRINGE BECAME
THE CENTER.

Moshe Sonenson

DIVORCE

WHOSOEVER DIVORCES HIS FIRST
WIFE, HE CAUSES EVEN THE ALTAR
TO SHED TEARS.

Gittin, 90/B

Although marriage has been viewed since biblical times as the ideal state for Jewish men and women, Jewish tradition has always acknowledged that marriage may cause so much unhappiness as to require some form of redress, of relief. Thus the Bible contains a number of references to divorce, as a legal procedure for dissolving an unhappy marriage. But divorce is only to be considered as a last resort, after all avenues of reconciliation have been explored and exhausted. To bring a feuding husband and wife back together is considered a noble accomplishment, placing one in the company of Aaron, brother of Moses and classic peacemaker.[1]

Under Jewish law, men have much more power with respect to divorce than women do, for they have much more latitude in establishing grounds for divorce, and it is they who must grant the get (the bill of divorce).[2] However, since the prohibition issued in the eleventh century by Rabbenu Gershom ben Judah (c. 960–1028), the Light of the Diaspora, it has been unlawful for a Jew to divorce his wife without her consent. Among the reasons a man can give for initiating divorce procedures are: a wife's physical disabilities (such as contagious diseases) that prevent cohabitation; her failure to bear children in the first ten years of marriage; unacceptable wifely conduct, such as transgressing the Laws of Moses, demonstrating habitual immodesty, or committing adultery; or simply his dislike for her. In the case of rape, if the husband of a woman who has been raped is a kohen, he *must* divorce her.

A woman may ask for a divorce on the grounds of a husband's physical disability that precludes cohabitation; or physical characteristics (like bad breath, or disagreeable odors related to the man's profession, such as working in a tannery) that arouse feelings of revulsion. According to Maimonides's code, *Mishneh Torah*, a woman may also be granted a divorce if her husband prevents her from participating in certain joyous functions, or if he prevents her from wearing expensive clothes and jewelry that he can afford to buy.[3]

Having received a divorce, however, the woman would find her lot a hard one. Again, the law deals more harshly with women than with men. In general, the husband was granted custody of the children, though arrangements were often made for young girls to remain with their mothers. If young boys were left with their mothers, they were to be returned to their fathers by the time they were six years old.[4] A man could remarry immediately after the divorce; a woman had to wait three months — for purposes of establishing the paternity of any child she might bear after her remarriage. A man was forbidden to remarry his divorced wife if, in the meantime, she was married to another man (though there was no similar limitation on the husband's acceptability after another marriage). And no divorced woman could marry a kohen — an indication of the stigma attached to divorced women.

The bill of divorce had to be sanctioned by a beth din (court) consisting of three men well versed in the religious laws concerning marriage and divorce. In the shtetl the court consisted of the town rabbi and the dayyanim (judges). Reb Layzer Wilkanski, like the shtetl dayyanim who preceded him and those who followed him, spent a significant amount of time with couples who were contemplating a divorce — to very good effect, it would seem: According to the official records, between the years 1891 and 1914, years that coincided with Reb Layzer's tenure, there were only six divorces in Eishyshok.[5]

In many of his attempts at reconciliation, Reb Layzer was assisted by his wife Batia, since most of the counseling and negotiating, and even the decision to grant a divorce, took place in their home. Thus their son Meir, the shtetl chronicler, was privy to these intimate transactions, which he later recorded in his autobiographical books. As he recounts, the reasons that motivated couples to seek a divorce were as diverse as the range of human emotion, as colorful as the spectrum of human life itself: miserliness, sexual abuse, incest, interfering in-laws, money, illness, children from previous marriages, violence. In this respect, the shtetl was as modern as today, as ancient as biblical times, though the particulars of the disputes often bore the unique stamp of Eastern European small-town Jewish life.

At the more humorous end of the unhappy-marriage continuum were the disputes having to do with housekeeping — for example, the noodle-throwing episode between the obsessively clean Soreh-Reizl and her grubby coachman husband, Hayyim-Barukh, which culminated in an intervention by Reb Layzer, as is recounted in chapter 4. Of course, not all of these conflicts required the mediation of a dayyan. Der Dzhik (the wild one) was a renowned shtetl humorist who was able to vent his marital frustrations with an arsenal of jokes about his wife and her compulsive housekeeping. To anyone within earshot he would complain, for example, that his house was so immaculate that there was no place for him to spit except at his wife — she being so ugly and so ceaselessly disheveled from her non-stop cleaning that a little bit of spit wouldn't matter.

Some disputes did not lend themselves to

humor of any kind, however, and often led one or both members of the couple to request a divorce. Reb Layzer could be very stern in such instances, for many years of observing marital woes had made him a shrewd judge of character, with a keen sense of how to get to the root of a couple's problems, and where to allot blame. A young wife came to Reb Layzer crying her heart out one day, for her husband and her father-in-law had made her life unbearable, she said. Having decided that she had been unfaithful, like the archetypal "defiled" wife described in Numbers 5:11–31, they were tormenting her. At night they pulled on her fingers, for according to a folk belief, this would cause a sleeping person to confess the truth. When that exercise proved futile, they had dragged her from her bed into the street in the middle of the night to force her to reveal her guilt — but to no avail, for she was not guilty and would not confess.

A postcard depicting the granting of a get (divorce) by three rabbis in a rabbinic court (beth din). The postcard was mailed to Sarah Wilkanski by someone who had received a divorce. YESC, WILKANSKI

Reb Layzer sent for the father and son, two simple shtetl hatmakers. When they arrived he angrily admonished them, telling them that they were uneducated, crude, cruel men whose behavior was inexcusable. The two men claimed that the young woman must be a witch engaged in sorcery, for they had seen her playing with cards. She in turn conceded that she did indeed use cards, but not to play — only to consult them about how long her suffering was to go on, and whether to ask for a divorce. Though she said her cards had answered in the affirmative, Reb Layzer did not grant a get. Instead, he told the woman to stop consulting her cards, since this was not a Jewish custom, and told the husband to cease his relentless harassment of his wife.[6]

Sometimes even Reb Layzer could not save a marriage, especially if the problems were compounded by in-law conflicts, as happened with Uri Zakheim and his wife. Uri was the only son and the pride and joy of two of the most respected people in the shtetl, Reb Benyomin Zakheim, the keeper of the shtetl pinkas, and his wife Miriam, who ran a large textile store and was known for her piety and charity. So eager were they to have their beloved son remain in Eishyshok after his marriage that, contrary to custom, they had agreed during the dowry negotiations that they would take care of the kest. Nonetheless, this did not endear them or their son to the young wife's father, the rabbi of Yashinowa, who was a great scholar and an equally great Scrooge.

Bearing grudges having to do with dowry and kest issues, the rabbi of Yashinowa came frequently to Eishyshok, where he never stopped trying to foment trouble between his daughter and her husband. Uri, a handsome, red-bearded young man whose fine scholarship had won him the respect of his fellow prushim, soon began spending all his time in the Old Beth Midrash, rather than at home with his young wife. And this was only the beginning of the trouble the rabbi of Yashinowa caused. He also tried to turn the Wilkanskis against the Zakheims. But Reb Layzer had known the rabbi of Yashinowa during his student days at the Eishyshok yeshivah, and remembered his miserly ways and his unpleasant demeanor even from then. When Reb Layzer would refuse to listen to him, repelled by his foul language, so unbecoming in a rabbi and a scholar, the rabbi would follow Batia into the kitchen and besiege her with nasty remarks about the Zakheim family. Finally at least some of his troublemaking paid off. His daughter demanded, and was granted, a get. This caused so much distress to Uri's mother that she tried to commit suicide, jumping into the shulhoyf well with a bag of stones tied around her neck, only to be saved by several prushim who had seen her running toward the well.

Eventually the young divorcée and her small children grew so miserable living with her father back in Yashinowa that, to the delight of the Eishyshker community, she returned and remarried Uri Zakheim. Her father, who must have had some sense that he was at fault since he was also instrumental in bringing the young couple back together, had to promise Reb Layzer and Batia that he would not interfere in his daughter's life ever again, and would abandon his use of foul language.[7]

No problem was too intimate to be brought to Reb Layzer. Too much sex was the complaint of one newlywed, the younger daughter of Reb Leib, the flour merchant. After initially rejecting her older sister's widower when he begged her to marry him, she had eventually yielded to his persistent pressure. But soon after their marriage she realized she had made a mistake; she simply could not cope with his frequent sexual demands, and now she wanted a divorce. Instead of instantly complying, Reb Layzer summoned her husband and warned him that if he repeated his offense, which is contrary to Jewish law, then his wife's request for a get would be honored.[8]

Certain Jewish marriage customs were particularly punitive to women, and these Reb Layzer and Batia tried their best to protect women from, while always remaining within a halakhic framework. The tradition of the levirate marriage, for example, which calls for a childless widow to marry her dead husband's brother unless he releases her from this obligation, could cause all manner of problems. Even if the brother had no desire to marry the widow, if he was a minor he could not formally release her to remarry anyone else until his bar mitzvah. If he wished to cause her trouble, or genuinely loved her and wanted her for himself, she could not marry anyone else, regardless of her own feelings in the matter. As prescribed in Deuteronomy 25:5–10, she was free only if he agreed to participate in a ceremony called the Halizah (Hebrew for "untying"), in which the woman removed her brother-in-law's shoe. In Eishyshok, as in many other places, the ceremony was performed with a sandal-like shoe that was maintained as community property.

If a woman's husband deserted her, or died without her being able to confirm his death, she became an agunah and could not remarry. Though this was a problem that had occurred occasionally throughout the ages, it became a painful and increasingly common side effect of the great migrations to America (and other countries) beginning in the late nineteenth century, when many men severed all ties with the wives they left behind, and completely disappeared into the new world. In fact, the great Rabbi Yitzhak Elhanan Spektor of Kovno directed much of his scholarship and his empathy to this problem, seeking halakhically acceptable ways for releasing agunahs from their wretched state. Thousands of women were thereby helped; indeed, his final deathbed act was to release yet another agunah.[9]

Reb Layzer also did whatever he could in such circumstances. Thus when a letter arrived in the shtetl bearing the shocking news that Shlomo the engraver, a heretofore God-fearing artisan from the shtetl, was about to get married in America — despite the fact that he had left a wife and four daughters in Eishyshok — all forces were mobilized to prevent the wedding from taking place. Reb Layzer, the rabbi, and the kahal immediately began collecting money throughout the shtetl, in order to outfit Shlomo's wife Rochel and her daughters in new clothing and buy them steamship tickets to America. Wife and daughters arrived in New York just in time.[10]

When it was possible to anticipate difficulties that could result in a woman's becoming an agunah, Reb Layzer might recommend a conditional get — a divorce that would take effect only if certain stipulations were met. Thus if he knew that a man was going to war, or taking part in some dangerous mission, Reb Layzer would suggest to him beforehand that he give his wife such a get, to be finalized after the passage of a specified period of time during which the wife had not received word from her husband or about him. The conditional get could be used in cases of serious illness, too, if Reb Layzer thought the imminent possibility of an undesirable levirate marriage warranted it.

When a young Eishyshkian named Munesh became ill and was taken to a hospital in Vilna, Reb Layzer and Batia became concerned about his wife. She was a childless young woman who would need a Halizah in the event of her husband's death, and what they knew of her brother-in-law promised only trouble for her. Therefore Reb Layzer traveled to Vilna to see Munesh, bringing with him the other members of the beth din and the divorce scribe. After much persuasion, Munesh agreed to the conditional get, only to die as the scribe was writing the eleventh line of the document. Munesh's wife was declared a divorcée by the beth din, which thus spared her the necessity of requesting a Halizah — and the possibility of its being denied.[11]

The divorce that came as a real shock to the shtetl was that of Menuha, a hardworking, well-respected shopkeeper, and her second husband Naphtali, an expert in Hebrew grammar who was popular with the Haskalah sympathizers among the prushim. Menuha was a tall, heavy woman who was always in competition with Malke Roche's, each shopkeeper trying to outdo the other by opening earlier or closing later. Many years after Menuha's first husband, a kohen, died, leaving her with an infant girl named Hassia, she married the red-bearded Naphtali, of whom she was very fond. She was also pleased to discover that he appeared to be a good father to the teenaged Hassia, unlike the third husband of Malke Roche's, who had been so cruel to her children from an earlier marriage that she had finally divorced him. All seemed well in the Menuha–Naphtali household.

But one day Reb Zalman, the man who kept Reb Layzer informed about shtetl events, came rushing into the Wilkanski home with startling news: Hassia, daughter of Menuha the shopkeeper and her late husband the kohen, was pregnant — by her stepfather. For the daughter of a kohen it was a very serious matter.[12] All those present in the Wilkanski household were stunned. Books were closed, conversation ceased, and people looked at Reb Zalman in disbelief.

When the heartbroken Menuha was brought before Reb Layzer to explain, through a veil of tears she tried to defend her daughter. It was not Hassia's fault, Menuha said, for she had been asleep and did not fully comprehend what was happening when her stepfather raped her. Menuha herself had been at the summer synagogue at the time, reciting the penitential prayers that begin prior to Rosh Hashanah. Despite her defense of her daughter, Menuha was devastated when informed that she could no longer cohabit with Naphtali, for she cared for him very much and did not wish to divorce him, as she was told she must do. Eventually it came to pass, however, that Reb Avraham-Heshl, the divorce scribe, wrote the get and Naphtali placed it in the cupped, trembling hands of the woman he had wronged so terribly. Afterward Naphtali was given a steamship ticket for America, bought at community expense, and was sent off to that godless country. He wrote many letters from there to Dr. Ezra, who shared them with Naphtali's friends at the yeshivah, where they were deemed quite witty.

After Hassia gave birth, the kahal married her off to a tall, handsome artisan who made steel rims for wooden barrels. Cursed with six fingers on each hand and, it was rumored, six toes on each foot, he could not find a bride without a blemish. When news about this marriage reached Naphtali in America, his comment was: "What a pity that a furnishing once used by a scholar is now being used by a boor"— a playful allusion to a passage in the Talmud which was not lost on the crowd at the yeshivah. Indeed, they were greatly amused by its cleverness (however inappropriate such cleverness might have been, given the circumstances that had occasioned it).[13]

Menuha never remarried, but helped her daughter raise her children and continued to work diligently in her shop. Avraham-Heshl the divorce scribe never wrote another get, for he was dismissed from his post shortly afterward, as was reported in the Hebrew-language publication *Ha-Melitz*. His crime? According to the satirical article, written by Israel Isser Goldbloom, a former student at the Eishyshok yeshivah who had himself been expelled because he'd been caught reading Haskalah books, Avraham-Heshl had entered the Catholic church in Juryzdyki to watch a reception being given in honor of a visiting dignitary from the Holy See.[14]

During the years between the two world wars, the shtetl no longer had control over the marriages and divorces of its population. As part of the momentous change that had overtaken the shtetl, the community and its traditions were not powerful enough to prevent people from obtaining the marriage or divorce that they wanted, for people were now free to travel outside the shtetl for such ceremonies, and there was always someone, somewhere, who would perform the service, no matter what the obstacles. This is what happened with Rochke, the pretty daughter of the tannery owner Zirl Yurkanski, who as a divorcée fell in love with Yoshke Kaplan and wished to marry him. The problem was that Yoshke Kaplan was a kohen, and as such could not marry a divorced woman. But eventually the couple found a rabbi in a large town who was of the liberal persuasion and agreed to marry them, despite the halakhic prohibition. When Yoshke and Rochke Kaplan returned to Eishyshok as a married couple, no one wanted to rent an apartment to them, for tradition still influenced people, even if it did not rule them. Finally they found one in the home of a Christian man on Vilna Street. Rochke's uncle so disapproved of her marriage that he told Rabbi Szymen Rozowski: "The union of a divorcée and a kohen is like gasoline. It will burn the shtetl down and consume us all in its flames." As it happened, Rochke and Yoshke Kaplan were the only Jewish couple in Eishyshok to survive the Holocaust and its aftermath without being so much as singed by the conflagration.

Although the interwar years saw the waning of the once-formidable powers of other shtetl rabbis, many people still chose to consult Rabbi Rozowski, the last rabbi of Eishyshok, for advice about family matters, for he had won their confidence with his wise, kindly ways. He believed that good counseling could lead to reconciliation, and he did what he could within halakhic guidelines to save troubled marriages. Even extraordinarily difficult cases like that of Meir "der Lerer" (schoolteacher) Shewitski and his wife were not without hope. After the couple opened a small tavern in their home in order to supplement Meir's small income as a teacher, his wife had run away with one of their Christian customers. Despite Meir's great humiliation, Rabbi Rozowski was able to persuade him, in the end, to take his wife back and resume the marriage.

The efforts of shtetl rabbis and dayyanim like Rabbi Rozowski and Reb Layzer to counsel couples, trying to get them to reconcile before granting them divorces, probably reduced the number of divorces. This would help to explain why the general consensus seems to be that the shtetlekh had lower divorce rates than the cities. (Though the overall divorce rate in the Jewish population was still higher than among non-Jews, the non-Jewish group includes a large number of Roman Catholics, among whom divorce is forbidden.)[15]

OUT-OF-WEDLOCK BIRTHS

While the divorce rate among Jews was higher than among non-Jews, the rate of illegitimate children among Jews was the lowest. An illegitimate child was considered a great blemish on the reputation of the family and the individual, causing severe damage to their yihus. Between 1840 and 1940 there are accounts of only eight children being born out of wedlock in Eishyshok, not including births among the hekdesh population. Four of the children were born to Jewish women who were employed as maids in Jewish households, where one of the men in the family was believed to be the father.

In all cases of illegitimate births, the community became involved. In the case of Hassia, made pregnant by her stepfather Naphtali, the kahal both paid for a ticket to America for Naphtali and saw to it that Hassia got married, so that her child would have a father. Reb Layzer intervened in the case of Minke and the klezmer. Minke's widowed mother rented a room in her house to a young fiddler who had come to Eishyshok to join the klezmer band. During the winter, Minke began spending many hours on top of the warm oven with her mother's tenant, a well-dressed, curly-haired man with a glass eye. Eventually she became pregnant and gave birth to a daughter, at which point Reb Layzer persuaded the father to do the right thing. The wedding between Minke and her fiddler lover took place on the eve of Shabbat Nahamu, and the young man's fellow klezmers provided the music.[16]

In the modern era ushered in by World War I, the community wielded less power than it once did in matters of illegitimacy, just as it had less say about marriage and divorce. Thus when the son of a prominent Jewish family fathered an illegitimate child by the Jewish maid, the boy's father made hasty arrangements to ship him to America, rather than marrying him off to the mother of his child. The family did later make some contribution to clothing and educating the little girl, having been embarrassed into doing so by the mother's ceaseless — and public — demands, but the payments were never as large as the mother would have liked, and the community itself had little to do with the arrangements.

While the community no longer had the power to enforce its moral code and see to it that men married the women they got pregnant, when necessary it did take responsibility for the offspring of such unions, supporting them financially and taking care of their education. And in the person of Rabbi Szymen Rozowski, it continued to exercise considerable moral suasion, if not absolute control. This happened in what was surely the most infamous of Eishyshok's out-of-wedlock births, which came to be known in the press as "the case of the black suitcase." When the unmarried daughter of the tailor Shlomo the Amalekite became pregnant, she concealed her condition until the last moment. Going into labor, she told her father she was having severe stomach cramps and needed to be rushed to a hospital in Vilna. There she gave birth to a boy. When her father learned the truth about her stomach ailment, in a moment of rage he took a shoelace and strangled the newborn baby.

The dead infant was placed in a black suitcase and given to the baby's father, a young Eishyshkian shoemaker, so that he could take him back to Eishyshok and bury him. On his way to the train station, however, the young man's hurried walk and nervous demeanor attracted the attention of the Polish police, who suspected that the shoemaker, a clandestine Communist, might be carrying Communist leaflets in his suitcase. When they opened the suitcase and found the dead baby, they immediately proclaimed the infant a Polish victim of a Jewish ritual murder, whose blood had been used for religious purposes.

Both Shlomo and the father of the baby made a full confession, explaining that Shlomo had killed him to try to protect the honor of his family. But the confession was to no avail. With the financial assistance of a number of people in the shtetl, and of relatives in America as well, the family of Shlomo the Amalekite hired one of the top Jewish lawyers in the country, who had defended Mendel Beilis, a poor laborer in Kiev, in an earlier blood-libel case in 1911. But the trial became complicated when the shoemaker's Communist connections were revealed, and he had to serve a longer jail term than the short sentence given to the actual murderer, Shlomo. The young shoemaker was not abandoned by the shtetl, however. Rabbi Rozowski and Shael Sonenson, and later Reb Shael's son Moshe Sonenson, all offered assistance to him and his family. And Rabbi Rozowski eventually influenced him to marry the mother of his dead child, in a wedding ceremony that took place in the jail. When he had served his term and was released, he and his wife were able to live a normal life in the shtetl, and to raise a family, much to the joy of Rabbi Rozowski as well as their families and friends.

THE MENTALLY ILL

Virtually every aspect of the shtetl's community and family life was governed by guidelines made up of some combination of Jewish law, local mores, Lithuanian Council provisions, and tradition. The Jewish community had since biblical times had an all-encompassing system for governing itself, one that showed a special sensitivity to society's most wretched members. But the safety net sometimes failed when it came to the mentally ill. Ethical and moral rules to shield these vulnerable creatures from the cruelty of the society around them were surprisingly sparse. The mentally ill lived in a gray zone where many of the regulations had to be invented by each individual shtetl, and sometimes reinvented from generation to generation.

Included among the few halakhic treatments of the subject is a definition of insanity: A person who walks alone at night, sleeps in the cemetery, tears his clothes, and loses everything that is given to him is classified a lunatic — though he did not have to display all those symptoms concurrently in order to warrant the label. Most of the rest of the halakhic guidelines were meant to protect society from the insane. Thus the insane were exempt from the responsibility of observing divine precepts, but they were also excluded from many of society's rights and protections.[17]

According to a combination of halakhah and custom, the mentally ill could not engage in the giving of gifts or any other form of property transaction, nor could they bear witness. An insane person was exempt from standing trial, and could not be held liable for injuries he caused others. However, normal members of society were liable for injuries to the insane.[18]

The insane did not have the same contractual rights as other people.[19] Since contractual aspects were central to marriage and divorce, the insane, and their spouses or would-be spouses, were affected in these areas in a number of ways. The marriage of two insane people was not valid (though this was questioned by some authorities).[20] If a married man became insane, his wife could never remarry, since he was unfit to grant a get and the husband's grant was a crucial part of the divorce process. If a married woman became insane after marriage, however, her husband could divorce her and remarry, even though she was unfit to grant her consent (as was required under normal circumstances) — but only if he obtained permission from a hundred rabbis. The rationale behind allowing the husband but not the wife of an insane person to remarry had to do with certain legal technicalities concerning bigamy. Although men had been barred from bigamy since the time of Rabbenu Gershom ben Judah — and women of course had never been allowed it — his ban was merely a rabbinic provision, not a law from the Torah, and thus it could under special circumstances be bypassed. If one hundred rabbis agreed, the husband of an insane woman could remarry, thereby becoming, technically speaking, a bigamist.

The insane, or meshuggoim, as they were known in the shtetl, represented a cross-section of the population: rich and poor, male and female, young and old, scholars and illiterates, native Eishyshkians and strangers. In a society that maintained rigid class divisions, the meshuggoim were an anomaly: a democracy of suffering, whose citizens had few pretensions to yihus. But in other ways they were strictly representative of the social strata from which they came, their appearance, dress, gestures, language, and overall frame of reference reflecting back on their origins like a distorted mirror. They were not segregated but rather were very much a part of shtetl life, and it was understood that in their craziness was a skewed lucidity; thus many of their sayings were held up as pearls of wisdom, included in the shtetl storehouse of favorite expressions, and hauled out to be quoted on suitable occasions. Their integration into the community — not total, but surprisingly extensive — was a characteristic of Jewish life, not just in the shtetl but in the cities, too. When a prominent meshuggener in Vilna died in 1929, the daily paper, the *Vilner Tog*, carried the announcement of the death of "the messiah," as he had called himself.

Not all of those who were classified as meshuggoim were deserving of the label. Some had physical deformities or other disabilities, some were slow learners, some anorexics, and some were simply eccentrics who did not fit into any of the shtetl's rigid molds. Once labeled, however, they fell under the protection of the shtetl, which was in many ways more benevolent than was required by Jewish law. Considered God's less fortunate children, in Eishyshok they were entitled to food, shelter, clothing, and compassion — and free transportation; the shtetl's bus drivers were instructed to permit them to ride without paying the fare. The shtetl's mutual aid societies helped them avail themselves of all of the above, even when the benefactors had to force community assistance on people who were not competent to understand that they needed it. And should any of the shtetl's male lunatics have a grievance, he, like any other male member of the community, was entitled to state his complaint from the bimah in the synagogue or the beth midrash during daily prayers.

Until the twentieth century, no Jewish insane asylums existed in the vicinity of Eishyshok. But around the turn of the century, in the village of Dekeshene (known among the Jews as Selo), just a mile or so west of Olkenik, Jewish farmers opened an insane asylum without walls. Selo was originally a Jewish farm community made up of land grants given to cantonists during the regime of Tzar Nicholas I in the 1840s. Since the soil was poor and the farmers had barely been able to survive, even with the assistance of Baron Maurice Hirsch, a prominent Jewish nobleman, many of the young people had emigrated to America and Palestine. When the village had dwindled in population to about forty families numbering two hundred people, one enterprising farmer decided that while the village was not suitable for agriculture, it had other possibilities. With no rivers or railroad tracks in the immediate vicinity, it was a quiet and tranquil place, and would make an ideal retreat for the mentally ill. The farmer built a pension to house the insane, and families from Vilna and Warsaw began bringing their afflicted relatives.[21]

The demand grew. More and more city people made the trip to Selo, and were eventually followed by people from the various shtetlekh in the area. Shlomo Berz, a relative of the Israeli novelist Amos Oz (born Amos Klausner) and of the renowned historian Dr. Yossef Klausner, enlarged his house to accommodate the mentally ill, as did many other farmers, until the day came when the meshuggoim outnumbered the native village population. The inmates looked upon Selo, with its unpaved streets and its small synagogue, as their private domain. In fact, the town came to be so identified with them that its name was used in a local expression: To call a person one of the "Seloyer meshuggoim" was to insult him as one of the "Selo crazies."

In Selo the mentally ill were given food and lodging and allowed the run of the town, except when they became violent and had to be locked in their rooms until they calmed down. Other than the occasional lock-up, they were given no special treatment, medical or otherwise. But many of them did have frequent visitors, friends as well as family, and they were also the beneficiaries of visits by various youth groups in the area. Olkenik, Eishyshok, Meretch, and other nearby shtetlekh sent groups to entertain the mentally ill with plays, concerts, and football games.

Though most Eishyshkians cared for their disturbed relatives at home, a few did take advantage of the facilities at Selo. After Luba Ratner's mysterious nervous breakdown, her family sent her to Selo, where she became a permanent resident and enjoyed great popularity among the other colorful inhabitants. Luba's troubles seem to have begun quite suddenly, sometime in the early 1930s, and no one ever knew the details of the events that had led to her breakdown. A very attractive, capable, well-liked young woman who managed a textile store in Eishyshok's row shops, she one day dressed up in the transparent white gauze of a bridal gown, tucked a small pillow under it, and claimed that she was pregnant by Shlomo Kiuchefski, the shtetl's most eligible bachelor.

In Selo, Luba was visited by friends from her former life. Thus when Zipporah Lubetski Tokatli returned from Palestine to visit friends and family in Eishyshok in 1938, she also went to see Luba in Selo. Asked whether she was expecting a girl or a boy, Luba told Zipporah: "Such secrets belong to the Almighty Himself. But with the little wisdom He has shared with me, I know that I will in all likelihood give birth to feathers. And after all, even feathers are better than nothing . . ." During another visit, Shepske Sonenson and Batia Bastunski showed up with a camera and asked her to pose for them. Instead, she took the camera and proposed, "How about you posing for me? On celluloid we are all equals; there one can't tell who is sane and who has lost his marbles."

TRANSIENTS

Among the meshuggoim to be seen in Eishyshok were not only native sons and daughters but also transients, who for one reason or another chose to avail themselves of the shtetl's hospitality for varying periods of time.

One of the most prominent of these transients was Reb Isserson, whose permanent residence was the famous Vilna shulhoyf, which was home to quite a number of these colorful characters. Isserson used to arrive in Eishyshok with the Vilner coachmen, and in later years on the bus, carrying with him his handwritten "calling cards"— pieces of paper on which he had inscribed his latest teachings. Upon arrival, he immediately made his way to the home of the rabbi, for in earlier years, before his mental collapse, he and Rabbi Szymen Rozowski had studied together at the renowned Volozhin yeshivah. Indeed, Isserson remained quite fond of books, and was a frequent bookstore browser. Since it was his practice to "put a wrinkle" (a kneich) in bookstore windows — his euphemism for shattering the glass — he was not a favorite among bookstore owners, though his well-to-do family could be counted on to cover the damage. Isserson frequented other stores as well. The famous Zalkind department store of

Vilna once ran a newspaper ad stating that any customer who could stump them with a request for an item that could not be found in the store would be given that item at a later date, free of charge. Among the first to enter the elegant doors after the appearance of that ad was Reb Isserson, who demanded a zizit — the fringed garment worn by observant Jewish men. The store honored its promise and eventually presented him with the garment.

Another of the Vilna lunatics who used to visit Eishyshok was Sander der Rechisnik, whose nickname, "buckwheat pudding," resulted from his craving for that dish — a craving that had brought him to Eishyshok, where rechisnik was a local specialty. Sander was a well-educated man from a good family, whose members included B. A. Kletskin, the head of the most important modern Yiddish publishing house in Vilna. Well read in Yiddish, Polish, Russian, Hebrew, and German literature, Sander spoke only in rhymes, which were usually a hodgepodge of all his languages, and which he never repeated. Much of his "conversation" consisted of begging for food; when he ran out of rhymes, he stopped begging until he could replenish his font of poetry. A typical rhyme went something like this:

Girl, give me a halleh
Or you will never be a kalleh [bride]

Shneyer and Meyer [common local names]
Give me eyer [eggs]

In the skies soars a feigl [bird]
Into my hand flies a bagel.

Please call me Kugel Tzimmes [carrot pudding]
for Rechisnik is nimes [boring].

Hirshele Rohe Sheftle's was a meshuggener from Olkenik who came to Eishyshok to seek refuge from his older brothers.[22] They had stolen one of the Olkenik synagogue's oldest Torah scrolls and had hidden the scroll itself in a katukh (hen roost under an oven), the two wooden handles (known as the atzei hayyim, or "trees of life") in a bed. Hirshele, the shtetl simpleton, had told on them to the shtetl rabbi: "The Torah is in the katukh and the twigs are in bed." The message was understood, and the rabbi was able to retrieve the valuable scrolls and return them to the Holy Ark of Olkenik's famed wooden synagogue, thus foiling the brothers' plan to smuggle them out of town and sell them for a high price. For his trouble, Hirshele was severely beaten by his brothers, after which he ran away to Eishyshok, where he had relatives, Shoshke and Dodke Dimitrowski, who opened their home to him. While in Eishyshok Hirshele did his best to be useful. When he wasn't in the Old Beth Midrash reciting the Kaddish for the dead from an upside-down prayer book, he was drawing water at the public well and getting paid by the pail. Whenever he was given a new suit, he would try to keep it from wrinkling by leaning against walls, rather than sitting

Hirshele Rohe Sheftle's, a mentally ill man from Olkenik, who came to Eishyshok to seek refuge from his older brothers. YESC, SH. FARBER

Liebke Kaminetski, a mentally ill person who came to Eishyshok during World War I. Here she is standing in the shulhoyf, her favorite haunt; to her left is the New Beth Midrash. Liebke was murdered in the September 1941 massacre. YESC, BLACHAROWICZ-WISZIK

down, even during the hours he spent in the beth midrash.

Not all the transients remained transient. Itchke and Liebke Kaminetski, the children of a mentally ill mother, appeared in Eishyshok during the turmoil of World War I, built themselves an intricate underground dwelling known in local dialect as a *lipianka,* and eventually made their permanent home in the shtetl, remaining there until the end. Their lipianka, on the outskirts of town near the slaughterhouse, became something of a local attraction. As winter gave way to spring, Eishyshkians made it one of the stops on their weekly Sabbath-afternoon strolls, marveling at the Kaminetskis' handiwork, the rope bridges that connected the interior spaces, the trapdoors and furniture that had been carved out of tree trunks and branches.

After a while Itchke Kaminetski, who, unlike his sister, had not inherited their mother's mental illness, left the lipianka, got married, and moved to a small shack near the public bath. Eventually his wife, their eight children, and his sister all lived there together. To support them, Itchke cleaned the public outhouses, assisted local builders, sold soap and other toiletries on market day, and did other odd jobs, including that of chimney sweep. Liebke also worked, fetching water from the public pump for certain homes that the kahal assigned to her, and being paid by the kahal for each pail.

Liebke's favorite place was the shulhoyf, where, much to the delight of passersby, she used to do dances on request, with each dance having its own name and price. Tourists, especially those from America, used to request special performances, consisting of her usual dances accompanied by certain suggestive gestures and sounds. At a dollar per performance, both the price and the currency were right, and Liebke was happy to oblige.

Like many other shtetl girls, sane and insane, Liebke had a crush on Shlomo Kiuchefski, and was constantly accosting him. He must have had a soft spot in his heart for her, because when the Kiuchefskis built an electric power plant in Eishyshok, Itchke Kaminetski's humble dwelling was the first to be hooked up to the electrical network, free of charge. As a gift from the Kiuchefski family, the Kaminetskis never had to pay an electric bill, a policy that continued until the Communist takeover of Eishyshok in 1940.

Under Soviet rule the local Jewish Communists made an effort to one-up the generosity of the "exploiting class." Thus the Kaminetskis became the beneficiaries of the action taken by Ruvke Boyarski, Hayyim Shuster, and Luba Ginunski to evict Rabbi Szymen Rozowski from his spacious home so that a poor family could be installed there.[23] But although Itchke's wife, children, and sister moved into the house, Itchke himself remained in his humble hut, out of respect for Rabbi Rozowski.

The transient meshuggoim passed through

with ever increasing frequency after the building of the Pilsudski highway, which made trips from Vilna into the very heart of the shtetl easier. However, there weren't enough of his fellow lunatics in the shtetl to suit at least one man who took the bus in from Vilna: When he asked whether the meshuggoim had their own prayer minyan, or whether there were nine insane men in town for whom he could be the tenth and thus form a minyan, the answer to both questions was no. Whereupon he reboarded the bus to go back to Vilna, announcing, "A shtetl without a minyan of meshuggoim is not for me!"

THE NATIVE MENTALLY ILL

Most of the mentally ill in the shtetl of Eishyshok were native born, and most lived with their own families, who did the best they could to control their sometimes troublesome relatives. Bashke Yurkanski, a daughter of one of the five founding families of Eishyshok, was only intermittently afflicted, but when she had one of her sudden fits of violence they were so extreme that her mother and brothers had to lock her up. Hidden away in the storage room of the family tannery, she would go into a strange frenzy during which she cut leather soles with such uncanny perfection that hardly a scrap of leather was wasted. Her leather-cutting feat had a certain appropriateness for a woman who during her sane periods was a fine businesswoman and a valued partner in the tannery. Shtetl wits used to joke about her leather cutting, saying, "The rich have mazel (luck), and even from insanity they profit."

Benchke der Meshuggener was the victim of a head injury suffered while working with his father, Shmuel, a builder of ovens. During his occasional attacks of violent behavior, Benchke would have to be restrained. At such times his family chained him down with heavy leg irons and locked him in the house, until he calmed down. On one occasion Benchke became involved in a fight with a band of youngsters and suffered a finger injury. Feeling wronged and mistreated, Benchke made his way to the Old Beth Midrash to exercise his rights. There he mounted the bimah, the platform for all grievances, banged on the table to command the attention of the congregation, and announced, "Either you treat me well, or you can find yourselves a new lunatic!" Benchke never carried out his threat to leave; like most of the other mentally ill in the twentieth century who were native to Eishyshok, he remained in the shtetl until the bitter end.

During the heyday of Eishyshok's yeshivah, one meshuggener was especially fond of the prushim. One day he appeared at the Old Beth Midrash with his hands folded over his stomach, claiming that he was into his fifth month of pregnancy, bearing a child that had been fathered by one of the prushim. After a thorough investigation by the prushim themselves, it was determined that a member of their community had indeed sexually abused the man. The perpetrator was the son of the pickeler rebbe, the notorious melamed who used to scatter grain on the bare bottoms of his students and then watch as his chickens picked at them. Not surprisingly, the melamed also abused his own children, and seemed to have passed the behavior down to his son. The son's punishment was a severe beating administered by his fellow prushim on a table in the beth midrash.[24]

Arke Rabinowitch was the shtetl's most brilliant and talented twentieth-century meshuggener. A man with an acute sensitivity to changes in the political climate, he had a running stock of political commentaries and witticisms that his fellow Eishyshkians loved to quote. As the son of one of Reb Layzer's daughters, he had been born into a prominent, accomplished family, which included scientists, writers, Talmudists, and a brother who was an engineer in Paris. Arke himself had once been a fine artist, his paintings winning praise from critics as far away as Palestine and Paris. But when he emigrated to

Palestine to join relatives (who included two brothers and various other members of the Wilkanski family), something happened to him — a failed love affair, some said; a bout with malaria, according to others — that resulted in a mental breakdown. Afterward he was sent back to Eishyshok.

Arke was one of the mentally ill whose condition was highly unpredictable. After periods of seemingly normal behavior, he could quite suddenly become violent and dangerous. But his outbursts always eventually subsided, and were followed by long stretches of apparently curative sleep, from which he would emerge with the long, unkempt beard of a wild man. Reuven Paikowski used to be able to look out a window of his own house into Arke's house on Vilna Street, where he could see Arke stretched out on a wooden bench, sleeping off one of his attacks, Rip Van Winkle–style. (Actually, the Jews had their own version of Rip Van Winkle, Honi-ha-Me'aggel, a renowned miracle worker in the period of the Second Temple, first century C.E., who went to sleep for seventy years. Thus the local expression for Arke's protracted sleep was a reference to Honi-ha-Me'aggel.)[25]

After a fire in which Vilna Street nearly burned down, Arke became so dangerously violent that his family took him to Selo for a few months. There he had numerous visitors, most frequent among them Pessah Cofnas and other youths known for their socialist and Communist sympathies, for Arke's satiric political commentaries had endeared him to them. Arke always greeted his visitors by asking, "Do you come to our Utopia as an inmate or a guest?"

Back in Eishyshok, Arke had a close call when the Polish minister for agriculture came to visit one day, bringing with him his wife, who attracted Arke's attention. Arke had been following the official entourage with his usual fascination for anything political, and for a brief moment found himself in the company of the minister's wife, when she was left alone in the market square. Taking advantage of the moment, he complimented the woman on her looks and her good taste, only to have her complain to her husband as soon as he came back about the "dirty Jew" who had accosted her. Without batting an eyelash, the minister took out his revolver and aimed it at Arke. Equally composed, Arke turned to Moshe Sonenson, one of the shtetl officials who was accompanying the minister, and said, "Meishke, tell him I am a lunatic." This soon became one of the most quoted lines in the shtetl, and the most memorable episode from the minister's visit.

During the Lithuanian occupation of 1940, Arke became violent again, then lapsed into his Honi-ha-Me'aggel sleep, only to jump into a well upon awakening. Fire department volunteers saved him that time. When the Russians took over the shtetl later that year, Arke was at his best, his wit sharper than ever. The appointment of Yoshke Aronowitch to a policeman's post particularly amused him, for Yoshke had recently been operated on to have part of his intestines removed. "If Yoshke, having no stomach, can be a policeman," Arke proclaimed upon hearing of the appointment, "then I, Arke Rabinowitch, having no head, can be a government minister."

A similar comment made during the German occupation would have dire consequences. Shortly after the Germans occupied the shtetl in June 1941, Arke approached the Wehrmacht commander and announced, "If Hitler, a former painter, is now the world's leader, then I, Arke Rabinowitch of Eishyshok, a deranged painter, am qualified to be a Fuehrer." Unamused by Arke's keen political observation, the commander ordered his execution. Two Lithuanian policemen, taking Reuven Paikowski with them, escorted Arke to the back of the Kiuchefski mill, shovels in hand. When Arke's sister saw the small processional with their shovels, she immediately grasped the fate awaiting Arke and ran to plead for her brother's life, but to no avail. The policeman ordered Arke to dig his own grave, which he did. Serene and silent, as though somehow aware through his political intuition that these representatives of the state were different from any he had faced before, Arke stood in his grave and faced the guns of the Lithuanian policemen head on. Thus Arke Rabinowitch became the first victim of the Nazis in Eishyshok. Reuven Paikowski buried him.[26]

Sorke Leah's was as obsessed with love and death as Arke Rabinowitch was with politics. A member of an old Eishyshok family, Sorke had once been married to a prominent rabbi, but after she became mentally ill, he obtained a divorce signed by the requisite one hundred rabbis. Unlike so many of the other women in the shtetl, both sane and otherwise, Sorke was in love not with one of the irresistible Kiuchefskis, but with a handsome Polish county official named Bukeika. Sorke di Meshuggeneh constructed her own romantic drama starring herself and Bukeika, celebrating the imaginary relationship in a series of narrative poems. Standing under the window of her beloved at the Polish municipality building in the shtetl, she serenaded him in Polish, Yiddish, Russian, and Hebrew. Many of the love songs she had inherited from her predecessor, a lovesick lunatic by the same name who lived in the nineteenth century. That earlier Sorke used to run practically naked through the streets, her long black hair flying in the wind, as she alternated between songs to her beloved and curses upon her father for not allowing her to marry him. After these episodes her brothers would pull her back home with ropes.[27]

Sorke Leah's stopped singing about love when the Germans occupied the shtetl. From then on, she sang only about death. One morning she knocked on the window of Sorl Kabacznik and pointed to the people whom the Germans had put to work, scrubbing the cobblestones of the market square. "You see all the people out there?" she said. "They are all corpses." A few days later her words proved prophetic.

THE MISIDENTIFIED

A number of individuals in the shtetl who had been categorized as insane, and therefore had been denied normal participation in shtetl life, were in fact not deserving of the label. Cut off from the community and forced into quiet, marginal existences, this unfortunate group numbered among its members the occasional eccentric, some (though by no means all) of the physically disabled, and certain people with minor disorders who were quite capable of functioning at their own pace if given proper care and assistance and not provoked.

Temke "shtekele fekele" Politacki was among the physically disabled: she was nearly mute. A very pretty woman who worked as a domestic, she was rumored to have been intimate with various German soldiers during their World War I occupation of Eishyshok. Legal and ethical guidelines for the treatment of the deaf and the mute notwithstanding,[28] the shtetl children used to love to tease Temke. One of their favorite torments was to arrange their hands in the shape of a pointed German helmet, by way of alluding to her supposed sexual escapades. This would send her into a screaming rage, during which she uttered strange sounds and made-up words, including the nonsense syllables that had given her her nickname, *shtekele fekele*. Another who was similarly afflicted, Zisl Maculski, was known as "der Shtumak" (the mute one). A good-looking man, an excellent baker, and clever enough with his hands that he had made a hobby of constructing plane models, Zisl was nonetheless classified among the meshuggoim, and was treated accordingly.

Some of the Eishyshkians who had been the victims of damaging accidents or other mishaps did not fare any better. Malka, the only child of Avraham Asher Koppelman, had been a cute baby, but her grandmother had felt that her head was too big and tried to reshape it, apparently by squeezing it with great vigor. The result was that Malka was slow in movement and speech, which made her a target of other children's cruelty. To protect her from their mockery, her family always kept her at home.

As a young child, Katke Remz was kicked in the head by a horse, which resulted in his being retarded — or, as any mental condition was known in the shtetl, "not fully baked" (nit kin dabakener). Unlike lonely Malka, Katke roamed the streets, where he was free to indulge his fascination with animals, especially horses and chickens. Unfortunately, for the creatures who attracted his attention, it was a love–hate relationship. Katke would ride and beat a horse to the point of collapse, then try to revive it with a long, gentle "conversation." He would caress a chicken, then pluck its feathers. His father, Eliezer Remz, one of the most respectable balebatim in the shtetl, was constantly having to pay animal owners for the damage inflicted by his son.

Nohem the Pope, the most colorful among the Eishyshkian meshuggoim (lunatics), standing on Vilna Street in front of the Kaleko house, August 15, 1932. The left side was a barn, the right side the living quarters. The inscription on the back of the picture reads, "The City Nut." Nohem was murdered by the Germans a few days prior to the September 1941 massacre. PHOTO: ROSALIND FOSTER ROSENBLATT. YESC, R. ROSENBLATT

Henia di Meshuggeneh was a sane but highly eccentric old spinster who lived alone. For many decades, going back to the 1870s, she had been the shtetl's goat shepherdess, with only the goats to keep her company, for no one associated with her and no one spoke to her. Early each morning she collected everybody's goats on the market square, and at sundown each day she brought them back from pasture, without ever exchanging a single word with another human being. Her own goats were snow white, and went everywhere with her, even on occasional strolls through the shtetl streets. And in what must have been one of the last scenes from another era, they could occasionally be found grazing on the straw-thatched roof of her small house, an image straight out of a Marc Chagall painting.

Another of the women who had been wrongly classified as a meshuggeneh was the well-educated wife of Shmuel Senitski, the shtetl lawyer. She was painfully thin, having refused to eat and nearly starved herself to death. Her problem was probably anorexia, a condition for which the shtetl had no name — and no sympathy. Indeed, she was the subject of much gossip and criticism on account of her appearance, and became a virtual prisoner in her own home in order to avoid the sharp tongues and pointed stares of the other women. She went out only to pray in the shul or the New Beth Midrash.

The most colorful among the Eishyshok meshuggoim during the 1920s and '30s was Nohem the Pope, whose hair, which he wore long in the style of the Russian Orthodox priests, had earned him his nickname.[29] Nohem appeared in Eishyshok during World War I, his background and origins a mystery from then until the day he was murdered by the Nazis. The mystery gave rise to many speculations. According to one version, he came from Kovlo and suffered from melancholy. Another theory was that he had been a saintly man, an accomplished scholar, who had gravely sinned. To atone for his wrongdoing he had exiled himself, choosing Eishyshok as his new home because of its once-renowned yeshivah. In support of this version was the fact that Nohem the Pope knew the Talmud, the Bible, and Hebrew, and had a great appreciation for scholars and scholarship. So profound was this respect that it spilled over even to the daughter of one of the shtetl scholars: If he ran into Rivka Remz, he would interrupt his usual lunatic shtick in order to say to her, in a quiet mumble, "I know who you are; you are Reb Yehuda Leib Remz's daughter, and your father sits in the beth midrash and learns day and night."

It was suggested that Nohem the Pope was once an ardent revolutionary but had become so disillusioned that his mental balance was affected; that he had been a high-ranking officer in the tzarist army who lost his mind on the battlefield and deserted, ending up in Eishyshok by chance; or that he had deserted and become mentally ill due to a long period of starvation, after which he traveled to Eishyshok to find his brother, who agreed with Nohem the Pope that they would keep his identity, and their relationship, a secret.

Nohem the Pope's physical strength was as much the stuff of legend as were the theories about his origins. When it came time to give him a haircut, wash him up under the public pump, and dress him in clean clothes and shoes, an annual ritual in honor of Rosh Hashanah, it took a number of di starke (the shtetl strongmen) to subdue him. Once when he became ill and was desperately in need of medical attention, di starke had to be called upon again, for only then could he be brought to the hospital and treated. The doctor at the hospital marveled at his stamina, and the toughness of his skin, which was like an animal hide.

During warm weather, Nohem the Pope slept under the bridge or in various gardens in the shtetl, some belonging to Jews, others to Christians. During the winter, the door to the heated Old Beth Midrash was always kept unlocked for him, as well as for any of the homeless people who preferred the beth midrash to the hekdesh (the poorhouse). There Nohem the Pope regularly slept in the women's gallery. No Jewish lunatic in Eishyshok shared the fate of the Christian unfortunate Olesh, who was found one morning frozen to death on a shtetl street.

Like the beth midrash, many shtetl homes were open to Nohem the Pope and to his fellow meshuggoim. Nohem paid regular visits to a number of homes, announcing his arrival with the phrase that always served as his calling card: "Tfu. Ich faif af di reiche" (literally "I whistle on the rich," meaning "To hell with the rich"). His unmistakable odor also preceded him, as Leon Kahn recalled in his account of the Pope's visits to his parents' home:

Nochem was in the habit of appearing at our home every afternoon for tea, which my mother's mother would serve from our huge samovar. She reserved a glass especially for him, and gave him his own spoon to stir it with; no one else ever had the courage to use these dishes. Then because of the stench from his unwashed body, he would be required to sit apart from the rest near the door. There he drank his tea and departed without a word.

Sometime before the invasion, we acquired a German shepherd dog which took an instant dislike to poor Nochem, and he was obliged to drink his tea outside after that to avoid the dog. One afternoon, I looked down my bedroom window to see Nochem drinking directly below. Impulsively, I put my head out and shouted at him, "Ich feife auf de orime!" (to hell with the poor).

With one swift movement, Nochem threw the scalding tea up into my shocked face, and disappeared into the crowd in the square. I raced downstairs to tell my mother and grandmother. Instead of sympathy, I got a scolding for teasing a poor, crazy man.[30]

At night, especially during the winter, Nohem the Pope visited the warm bakery of Alte Katz. There he ate freshly baked rolls, pastry, and — his special passion — raw eggs. He would puncture a tiny hole in the shell, suck the contents of the egg directly into his mouth, then return the empty shells, which sometimes numbered as many as a few dozen, into the egg baskets. To wash down his meal, he drank scalding tea sweetened with heaps of sugar chunks. Upon completion of his meal, wherever he was, he walked backward toward the door, in the same manner that one takes leave of the Holy Ark in the synagogue. Nohem the Pope also got "room service" of a type: Hiene di Frume (the pious) would prepare his favorite dishes and bring them to him in the women's gallery in the beth midrash. When not eating, Nohem the Pope loved to materialize, as if from nowhere, and startle people — particularly pretty girls, his favorite targets — with his trademark statement: "Tfu. Ich faif af di reiche."

Nohem the Pope himself was a favorite with photographers, who found him highly picturesque. During World War I his picture appeared in German newspapers, as a bit of local color, and between the wars he posed often and eagerly for American visitors as well as local photographers.

When the Germans occupied Eishyshok in the summer of 1941, they photographed Nohem the Pope as a representative of East European shtetl Jews, the archetype of degraded Jewry. After the photography session, they ordered him to shave, wash, and change his clothes, or else be executed as a menace to public health. The old ritual at the barber and the public pump was repeated, as it had been so many times before; but after a few days, the same old Nohem emerged, as he always had, in tattered, filthy clothes. Defiantly he flung his favorite words into the faces of the Germans: "Tfu. Ich faif af di reiche." Nohem the Pope was taken to the Seklutski forest and shot, becoming the shtetl's second victim of the Nazi occupation.[31]

THE MAD IN A WORLD GONE MAD

A few days later, the rest of the shtetl suffered the same fate as the two murdered meshuggoim, Arke Rabinowitch and Nohem the Pope. About sixty severely mentally ill people from Selo were also rounded up to be included in the Eishyshok massacre (the less severely afflicted ones having apparently been reclaimed by their families after the war broke out in 1939).

On Monday, September 22, 1941, the Germans and the Lithuanians armed the Selo lunatics with large sticks and appointed them "overseers." Huddled together with the rest of the people from their shtetl, the Eishyshok lunatics engaged in their characteristic activities, so far as was possible: Hirshele recited the Kaddish nonstop; Sorke sang her love songs for Bukeika, who was standing among the German and Lithuanian executioners. Luba Ratner could only curl up like a snake. Hours later they were all murdered, joining the rest of their community in death, as they had lived among them in life.[32]

After the liberation of Eishyshok on July 13, 1944, thirty-six Jews who had somehow managed to survive drifted back in small groups. Among the many unfriendly faces who "welcomed" them were the shtetl's Christian mentally ill, men and women who had been fed and clothed by the Jews in pre-Holocaust times, just as the Jewish mentally ill had been. There was Vladuk, who used to carry water to Jewish homes; Patrushka's son, the sleepwalker, who always wore a white nightgown; and Rishula, who had a passion for cigarette butts and for Jewish food. They lined the streets with the other Christians, telling the handful of Jews who had returned that they should go back to the grave where they belonged. To illustrate their point, they moved their hands across their throats, in unison, like members of an orchestra.

Watching the whole lot of them, in a world as crazy as any insane asylum, Moshe Sonenson remarked: "I wonder what pearls of wisdom Arke Rabinowitch would have had to offer about this bizarre 'welcoming committee.' "

APOSTATES (MESHUMODIM)

I ACCEPTED BAPTISM ENTIRELY
OUT OF CONVICTION — THE
CONVICTION THAT IT IS BETTER TO
BE A PROFESSOR IN THE IMPERIAL
ACADEMY IN ST. PETERSBURG
THAN A MELAMED IN EISHYSHOK.

Daniel Khwolson

In the Jewish shtetl, where religion bound everyone together, apostates — converts from Judaism — brought shame and pain upon their families, tainting the family yihus, causing individual family members both personal grief and public humiliation. Such wounds were so deep that in some cases even time could not heal them.

Despite the high costs it exacted, apostasy was a constant presence in the Jewish community. Though it was rare — as were conversions from Christianity to Judaism — it was still more frequent than anyone cared to admit. For many Jews throughout the ages, voluntary apostasy was the price they decided to pay for upward mobility, social and economic. For a smaller number of others, it was a matter of belief, motivated purely by theological considerations, or an act of love, which enabled them to marry someone of another faith.

Some apostates founded influential families whose Jewish origins were well known among Christians, such as the Pierleone family in Rome, who produced a number of popes,[33] the patrician Jud family in Cologne, and the Josefowicz-Hlebickis family in the Polish–Lithuanian commonwealth. Indeed, a significant number of converts were to become prominent members of the gentry and the nobility, especially in Eastern Europe, where their socioeconomic progress was encouraged by legislation like the Third Lithuanian Statute of 1588, which conferred noble status on many of the converts and their descendants.[34] Having achieved their social and economic goals, some converts used their newly acquired power to help their Jewish brethren; others never looked back, or if they did it was only to denounce their origins, to undermine their community. They used theological disputation and even outright falsehood to attack Judaism, to remove themselves from any taint of it.

By the eighteenth century, the Enlightenment, with its belief in the brotherhood — hence the equality — of all mankind, had stirred large numbers of Jews to strive for cultural, political, and social emancipation. Once they realized this was not going to occur, many looked to assimilation as the answer, which often translated into religious conversion. Conversion was a particularly strong trend in the upper circles of Jewish society, for it was considered the Jew's passport into elite European society. Most Jews who became Christians in the years between the French Revolution and World War II chose conversion on their own initiative, and for primarily pragmatic reasons.[35] Isaac D'Israeli, a British Jewish man of letters who had great aspirations for his son Benjamin, had him baptized at age eleven in 1817. Six-year-old Karl Marx and his seven siblings were baptized in 1824. Their father, Heinrich, was a successful lawyer who had converted from Judaism in 1817, when a Prussian edict banned Jews from the practice of law. The nineteenth-century German poet Heinrich Heine converted in order to be accepted by European society.

In the nineteenth century there were about 204,500 Jewish apostates throughout the world, approximately 84,500 of them in Eastern Europe. Of these about 69,000 were Russian Jews who were baptized into the Russian Orthodox church; the rest were in the Polish provinces, where about 75 percent of them converted to Catholicism, the rest to various Protestant denominations. Unlike the situation in Western Europe, many of the Russian conversions were not voluntary, for during the reign of the tzars the Jews were under relentless pressure to be baptized.[36]

During the reign of Nicholas I (1825–55), for example, it is estimated that some 30,000 to 40,000 Jewish child cantonists (draftees into the Russian army) were forcibly baptized into the Russian Orthodox church.[37] During the reign of Alexander III (1881–94), the government's attempts to "Russify" the Jews went hand in hand with a policy of religious orthodoxy. Indeed, Konstantin Pobedonostsev, director general of the Most Holy Synod of the Russian Orthodox church, saw baptism as one of the keys to "solving the Jewish question" in Imperial Russia. By imposing quotas on the Jews, as the government did in 1887, limiting their numbers in some institutions of higher learning, totally excluding them from others, and later restricting them from practicing medicine and law, the Russians hoped to force the Jews to convert.

Sometimes such coercion worked. The restriction on Jewish enrollment in the universities was particularly effective, for it cut off educational opportunities for anyone too poor to go abroad to study. In a culture that valued education so highly, and that depended on it as one of its few routes to upward mobility, this was disastrous. Hundreds of university-bound students from poor Jewish homes went on frantic searches for a Provoslavic "godfather"— a conversion sponsor.[38] Some Jewish students were able to obtain quick baptismal certificates by traveling to Viborg, Finland, then under Russian rule, where Pastor Arthur Peer would issue the coveted piece of paper for a few rubles. (Later these Peer certificates were revoked by Provoslavic clergymen, and the Jewish students had to be rebaptized by Russian Orthodox clerics.)

The renowned Orientalist Daniel Khwolson was probably the best known among this type of apostate; his witticism about his motivation for conversion is still being quoted as an apt summary of the frustrations of an entire generation of Russian Jews. As a poor kloiznik (yeshivah student who sits and learns in a kloiz — a prayer and study house), Khwolson saw no future for himself, and converted to Russian Orthodoxy in 1855. After his conversion, he not only became a professor at the Imperial Academy of St. Petersburg, as he had hoped, but also a professor in the Provoslavic and Catholic seminaries, which put him in a position to shape the intellectual lives of Russia's future clergymen. He used his position well, for he maintained close ties with the Jewish community — at first to the maskilim, later to traditional Jewish Orthodox circles — and came to its defense when necessary. His writings at the time of the Saratov blood libel made him a legendary figure among shtetl Jews.[39]

The Russian community of Jewish apostates included a gallery of famous intellectuals, professionals, artists, and merchants, as well as former cantonists, and it also included a fair number of individuals who had had skirmishes with the law — for until 1862, any Jew convicted of a crime in Russia could have his sentence reduced, commuted, or totally lifted upon baptism.

Though some converts maintained their relationship with the Jewish community, this did not always redound to the benefit of the community. Converts like Jacob Brafman, one of the most infamous of the censors the Russians inflicted upon the Jews in the nineteenth century, were employed by the government in Jewish-related matters, and did not hesitate to use their first-hand knowledge of the community to intimidate it. Brafman was not only a stern censor, but an anti-Semite who published a book of error-filled propaganda that only intensified the already strong distrust of the Jews among Russians.[40]

Women — ordinary, poverty-stricken young women, who saw baptism as their only option for escaping a wretched fate — were also targets for conversion by the Russians. In 1737 in Vilna, the Catholic priest Torczinowicz was given a church from which to operate his missionary society, Maria's Covenant. When he failed to win many converts among the male population of Jews, he turned to the female sector, focusing on Jewish girls from Vilna and the vicinity. There he was much more successful, perhaps because of the 80-gilden wedding gift he was able to offer those Jewish girls who embraced Catholicism.[41]

Vilna was also the home of the Lithuanian consistory of the Russian Orthodox church, whose files for the years 1819–1911 include 244 detailed descriptions of Jewish conversion. As analyzed by Michael Stanislawski, these files yield very interesting data about the socioeconomic factors involved in conversion. Most of the converts were drawn from among the destitute and desperate, and most were young, the median age for men being 21, for women 18. Of the 244, 58 percent were men, 42 percent women, with the proportion of women rising steadily through the decades, from zero percent in 1830 to 65 percent between 1900 and 1911, perhaps because over the course of the nineteenth century, men, even Jewish men, came to have more options for radically altering their lives than women did, with conversion being one of the very few available to women.[42] Conversion allowed one to alter the social and psychological boundaries of life, without moving beyond the familiar geographical boundaries.

APOSTATES IN EISHYSHOK

In Eishyshok there were no native-born residents who converted for the purpose of achieving educational or professional advancement. But there were some distinguished converts to be found among former students of the Eishyshok yeshivah, and their descendants — for example, the children and grandchildren of Hayyim Zelig Slonimski (1810–1904), the Hebrew popular science writer and editor. Apostates from the Slonimski family, including the prominent Polish poet and novelist Antoni Slonimski (1895–1976), swelled the ranks of the twentieth-century Russian and Polish intellectual elite.[43]

Another non-native apostate who spent time in Eishyshok was a Polish commandant by the name of Gottlieb, a Jew from Warsaw who had converted to Catholicism in order to further his advancement in the army and was stationed in Eishyshok around 1924–25. He was kind to the Jewish population, granting permission for Zionist parades and even participating in some of them, a crisp military figure astride his white horse. Such behavior, however, did not go over well with the local anti-Semitic Polish intelligentsia — the priest, the doctor, and the pharmacist — and they campaigned successfully for his removal to another post.

Most of the converts in Eishyshok and the vicinity were either cantonists, who had been forcibly baptized into the Russian Orthodox church, or converts for love, who joined the Catholic church.

Though most cantonists did not return to their native towns after concluding their service in the army, choosing instead to live outside the Pale, in Russia proper or in Finland, a handful did come back, a number of them to Eishyshok and Olkenik.[44] Berl Nikolaievitz, whose services to the yeshivah students were detailed by Meir Wilkanski (see chapter 6), was representative of this group: a man who had never ceased longing for his faith, or his native land, through the twenty-five years of his military service.

Five of the six Ejszyszki siblings posing for a photo upon their move to Eishyshok from their village of Golmecziszki: brothers (right to left) David, Benyamin, Israel, and Gedaliah, and sister Zipporah. The family had left their hometown in disgrace because their pretty sister Peshke married a Catholic. David and Israel survived the war, in Russia. Israel died post-liberation. The parents and the other three siblings in this photo were murdered in the September 1941 massacre. Peshke and her two daughters survived. Her Catholic husband was killed by the AK because he was married to a Jewish woman. YESC, EJSZYSZKI

Other former cantonists who came to Eishyshok had no family ties there, but were drawn by its famed yeshivah. Even if the long, hard years of service in the army of the tzar had left them unable to study, or to remember anything of their religious past, they were eager simply to be in the presence of Torah scholars. Included in this group was a man known only as "Abraham the son of Abraham," for he had been torn from his family and baptized at such a young age that he could not remember his Jewish name, nor that of his father. After his father appeared to him in a dream, he had left his Christian wife and their many children and returned to Judaism, though he was always haunted by the fear that he would be tracked down, rebaptized, and exiled to Siberia. Sometime in the 1880s he moved to Eishyshok, where he spent long hours sitting and praying in the Old Beth Midrash.

As for those who married out of the faith and converted for love, the story of Peshke Ejszyszki is only too typical, especially in the effect it had on her family. The Ejszyszki family lived in the village of Golmecziszki, where the father was one of the last of the region's arendators (a Jewish holder of a lease from a Christian landowner). Working the Polish magnate's Bastun estate, which covered 300 hectares of land, 250 of them given over to farmland, the rest to pine forests, Ejszyszki became a prosperous farmer, who provided comfortably for his wife Hannah and their six children, all of whom also worked on the land. Ejszyszki was known as a God-fearing Jew, respected by both his Christian neighbors in the village and the Jews of the shtetl. But all his good fortune came to an end when his pretty sixteen-year-old daughter Peshke fell in love with a local Catholic boy and ran away with him on Yom Kippur, while the rest of the family was praying at the synagogue in Eishyshok.[45]

Disappearing with the family jewelry and a substantial sum of money, Peshke left no trace. Her father, who hoped to find her before she took the drastic step of converting, offered a handsome reward for information on her whereabouts, which only resulted in his spending large sums of money on false leads.[46] So obsessed with finding his daughter that he neglected the farm, Ejszyszki soon found himself in near ruin. After having to sell off his livestock and equipment at half price, he moved to Eishyshok. There the family encountered social humiliation that was utterly devastating.

Peshke's father was forced to give up his regular seat in the more prominent section of the shul, and to move to a bench located near the synagogue entrance, among the poor and lowly; he was never to be called up to the Torah. Peshke's four brothers were beaten up by the melamed and their fellow heder boys. Peshke's younger sister Zipporah became a loner. The experience was so embittering that the boys grew up to be angry young men whose reliance on their powerful fists earned them the nickname *di Golmeczikskier shleger* (the hitters from Golmeczyszki). David Ejszyszki, who was just eight years old when his sister ran away, carried the emotional scars for the rest of his life. "I see my father almost as Sholem Aleichem describes Tevya the milkman in 'Fiddler on the Roof.' Though my father was well-to-do, the conversion of his daughter ruined him," he wrote many years later.[47]

While Peshke's apostasy had a huge impact on her family, it left little trace in the collective memory of the shtetl. But Goldke di Meshumeideste was quite a different story, her apostasy having caught the imagination of all the people of Eishyshok. She was the hot-tempered daughter of an even more hot-tempered father, the blacksmith Yekutiel Slonimski, of the nearby village of Zaidres. A widower, he did not spare the rod when there was any question of wrongdoing by his pretty, red-headed Goldke. To escape her father's temper she began spending time in the home of a Polish family who belonged to the petty nobility and lived in a small village near Dugalishok. There she found warmth and comfort and, eventually, romance. To the horror of her father, she converted to Catholicism and married the oldest son of the family, a widower with two grown sons of his own. Like other major local events, Goldke's conversion was material for the shtetl's satiric cabaret revue, a theatrical enterprise that was launched in 1920. One of the songs from that revue that remained on the local "hit parade" for a number of years went something like this:

Beautiful she was,
Like the flower rose.
Now all the people hum,
"You should be deaf and dumb."
Goodbye, Goldke, you are no longer brave,
Goodbye, Goldke, you did misbehave.
For your sins you should ever after have to pay,
While slaving in the fields among stacks of hay.

After her marriage Goldke di Meshumeideste became an enthusiastic churchgoer, never missing an opportunity to attend services. Dressed in her Sunday best, riding in a fancy carriage drawn by horses with rows of bells hanging around their necks, she would pass through the shtetl, which was on the way to the church in Juryzdyki. On such occasions all Jewish doors and shutters would be slammed shut, and mothers and grandmothers would whisper to the children, "Do not look; Goldke di Meshumeideste is on her way to church." On her way back from services Goldke often stopped for a drink at a Jewish-owned tavern, where shtetl pranksters would remove the pins from her carriage wheels if one of her husband's sons wasn't standing guard.

Goldke was one of those apostates who tried, despite their conversion, to maintain ties with the Jewish community. In the context of a discussion of Benjamin Disraeli, Hannah Arendt described such behavior as "flaunting one's Jewishness."[48] Others have called it "the Jewish Syndrome." Daniel Khwolson's way of explaining similar behavior in his own case was summed up in his declaration, "Now that I am Christian it is as if I am not Christian" (in Hebrew: Akhshav shenozarti keilu lo nozarti) — his acknowledgment that in his basic identity he remained Jewish even after conversion, indeed felt so then more than ever.

Whatever its causes, the desire to stay connected to one's Jewish roots was a characteristic of many apostates, and was expressed in a variety of ways. Goldke's participation in the Jewish Syndrome was on both the family and the community level. Though her family had sat shivah for her after her conversion, mourning her as if she were dead, she paid secret visits to her sister. And though the Jewish community lost no opportunity to express its revulsion toward her, she continued to patronize Jewish stores, and to perform acts of charity such as distributing potatoes to the shtetl poor.[49] But her most pointedly symbolic acknowledgment of her Jewishness was her habit of donating firewood to the Old Beth Midrash. Every so often Goldke's shkotzim (as her two sons by marriage were known in the shtetl) would drive up to the shulhoyf in their sled, unload a large supply of neatly stacked firewood, and leave it in the woodpile that was located in a shack behind the Old Beth Midrash. Goldke never accompanied them on these missions, and they never lingered in the shtetl after completing their task.

Eishyshok's most notorious male convert in the 1920s was Meir Hilke, the son of Mendl the builder. A lazy man who rarely worked, Meir used to spend his days sitting on the stoop, daydreaming. When his wife complained that she and their two children were hungry, he advised her to "eat stones." Their next-door neighbor was a tall, energetic woman, the wife of a Polish policeman, and a fanatical Catholic. Eventually Meir Hilke fell in love with his neighbor, left his family, converted to Catholicism, and married his neighbor. The day of his conversion, June 29, 1921, was also a Catholic holiday, Corpus Christi, and his conversion was celebrated as a major event in the Juryzdyki church, just as it was mourned as a disaster in his hometown. Church bells tolled throughout the day, their first peals signaling the beginning of a procession that traversed the entire length of the shtetl, as it headed out toward Juryzdyki. Leading the procession was Meir Hilke, who carried a huge cross; behind him were the members of the church, who carried red pillows on which all the church icons and relics were displayed. Not a single Jew was to be found on the streets of Eishyshok, and all the doors and windows were shut tight against the terrible sight. The shtetl resembled a ghost town.

From that time on, whenever any of the shtetl Jews encountered Meir der Meshumad, they insulted him with a phrase meant specially for apostates: the demand that he return all the Sabbath and holiday kugels he had eaten while he was a Jew. In Jewish folklore the kugel is a noodle or potato dish that is associated (for reasons long since lost to memory) with apostates. Thus even their insults were rooted in tradition, ritualistic rather than spontaneous.[50]

One particularly noteworthy example of intermarriage, and highly unusual for the time because it did not involve the conversion of either party, was that of Ossip Gabrilowitsch (1878–1936), who was related to Shael Sonenson, and Clara Clemens, the daughter of Mark Twain. They met at a concert in Vienna. By 1909, the year of their marriage, Ossip was an accomplished musician, and in 1916 he became the conductor of the Detroit Symphony Orchestra, a post he held until his death. Although Shael Sonenson greatly admired Mark Twain's work,

Ossip Gabrilowitsch (standing second from right), with his siblings and parents. Ossip, an accomplished musician, married Clara Clemens, the daughter of Mark Twain, in 1909. The Gabrilowitsch family were related to Shael Sonenson's family. The marriage of Ossip and Clara was kept a secret in the Sonenson family, though Shael Sonenson greatly admired Mark Twain. YESC, CH. SONENSON

the marriage of Ossip and Clara was never mentioned in his household, and came to light only because his brother Moshe spoke of it to his family.[51]

SHTETL PROSELYTES (GEREI ZEDDEK)

The traffic between religions went both ways: there were a number of proselytes — Christians who had converted to Judaism — in Eishyshok and the vicinity. Perhaps the most famous of these was a young Polish aristocrat, Count Valentine Potocki, known as the Ger Zeddek (Righteous Proselyte) of Vilna.

According to the most frequently told version of the legend, Count Valentine (d. 1749), a scion of the celebrated Potocki family, and another young Polish aristocrat named Zaremba, became friends with a Jewish tavern owner in Paris, where they had gone to pursue their studies. Intrigued by his total immersion in the Talmud, they asked him to teach them about Judaism. Eventually both Polish noblemen converted. Zaremba sensibly settled in Palestine. But Potocki returned to his native land — a risky act, since the conversion of a Catholic to Judaism was punishable by death at the time, and living in a place where he and his family were so well known meant he was always in danger of being exposed. After a lengthy period of wandering in search of a town that would serve as a refuge, he settled in the shtetl of Ilya, where he spent most of his time sitting and learning in the beth midrash. The people there knew who he was, but were honored to have him in their midst, so he felt safe from betrayal.

One day, however, a young boy disturbed him at his studies, and after repeated attempts to quiet the boy, Potocki pulled sharply on his ear; when the child reported this to his father, a crude tailor, the man was so enraged by what he considered to be the mistreatment of his son that he identified Potocki as a Jew to the local Polish government authorities. As Potocki was led away in chains, he cursed the tailor and his family. From then till the Holocaust, generation after generation of the tailor's family lived and died under that curse, many of them suffering from severe deformities, and only a few of them privileged to die a natural death.[52]

Potocki was tried and found guilty. Despite the pleas of his fellow aristocrats and of his mother, the aging countess, he was burned at the stake near the main cathedral of Vilna, dying a martyr's death, with a prayer on his lips. Moments after his death his mother received a letter from the Polish king, commuting the death sentence to life in prison.

A Jew disguised as a Christian bribed the executioner of the Ger Zeddek, so that he could collect some of the ashes for burial. He was also able to find a finger, which he buried along with the ashes in the Jewish cemetery (near the spot where the Gaon of Vilna would be laid to rest in 1797). Over this grave there grew a strangely shaped tree, in which many people saw the image of a mother weeping over her child, as Potocki's mother had indeed wept over him. Later a mausoleum was built at his grave site, and it became a place of pilgrimage. The day of his death was the second day of Shavuot, 1749, the anniversary of King David's death. For many years afterward that day was commemorated in the main synagogue of Vilna with a special prayer in memory of the Ger Zeddek, which was recited after the other prayers in memory of the dead.[53]

The Eishyshkian version of the legend of Count Potocki was quite different, adding a romantic dimension and moving the scene of the conversion to a neighboring village. According to this version, the events involved a branch of the aristocratic Potocki family who lived near Eishyshok. (This would have been an earlier generation of the same family whose cruelty to their Jewish land manager Avigdor Pachianko is recounted in chapter 9.) Their son was a student in Paris, but on one of his trips home for the Easter holidays he had an encounter that would change his life. Riding through the countryside with one of his friends that spring, he noticed a pretty girl drawing water from a well. The two young men stopped, dismounted, and went to the assistance of the young woman. During the course of their conversation with her, they became even more impressed, for her wisdom was as great as her beauty. The water she was drawing, she explained, was to be used in the baking of matzot for Passover. Water for the matzah dough is drawn the day before the baking and is left overnight; it is known as *mayyim shelanu*, "water that slept over the night." Intrigued by this information, since it made them wonder whether the stories they had always heard about Jews using the blood of Christian children for this purpose were perhaps not true, the two young aristocrats told her they would like to witness the baking of the matzot.

When the girl returned home, her father, the village innkeeper, was horrified by the story of her encounter at the well. Fearing that the aristocrats were in fact searching for a way to initiate a blood libel, he ran to the rabbi in Eishyshok for advice. But the rabbi advised him to comply with the request of the two young men, on the assumption that they had no evil intentions. So in the presence of Count Potocki and his friend, the innkeeper baked the matzot as he always did. The noblemen were so impressed with the cleanliness, the speed, and the joy with which all the Jews of the village baked their matzot that they began frequenting the inn. Soon they were spending their days studying Judaism with the innkeeper, their nights discussing their studies with his pretty, erudite daughter. Even after they returned to Paris they continued their studies, which ultimately led to their conversion. But when Potocki returned to his native land and his family found out what he had done, the innkeeper and his family had to flee the village in order to escape their wrath. And before his eventual capture and execution, Count Potocki himself hid out in Eishyshok's Old Beth Midrash.[54]

By way of commemorating this local legend, the memorial plaque in the Old Beth Midrash placed "Avraham ben Avraham Potocki, the Righteous Proselyte," at the very beginning of its list of illustrious names. There followed the names of all the other notables — prominent rabbis, pious citizens, and martyred saints — who had resided in Eishyshok. Also by way of commemoration, prayers for the soul of the Ger Zeddek were offered up on every holiday when the Yizkor (a prayer for the dead) was recited.[55]

The Eishyshok version of the Ger Zeddek story, with its romantic dimension that makes it quite different from the standard version, does have the advantage of explaining something that had always puzzled the historians and biographers: why Count Potocki ran the risk of returning to his native land. Perhaps he returned to marry the young woman he met at the well!

Less legendary converts to Judaism in the vicinity of Eishyshok included the Gotovicki family on Goyishker Street, who retained some Christian traditions and were not considered Jewish by their fellow Eishyshkians, even though they were said to have converted decades earlier. Other Eishyshok families, including the Kalekos and the Polaks (later known as the Polaczeks), were full-fledged, observant Jews who maintained that their ancestors were Christians who had converted to Judaism when they worked on Jewish farms.[56]

The last convert to Judaism prior to the Holocaust was Piczicz, a Catholic from Kalesnik who fell in love with a young yishuvnik woman from the same village. Eventually Piczicz married his Hayya, and converted to Judaism. But his lack of respect for his new religion was notorious. On Yom Kippur he would walk out of services when the prayers got too long, get drunk in a nearby

Christian-owned tavern, and return to the synagogue only when it was time to take his wife home. When the Germans occupied Eishyshok in June 1941, he abandoned his wife and once more embraced Catholicism. And when the Jews of Eishyshok were murdered by the Germans and the Lithuanians, there stood Piczicz among the murderers. Hayya, however, was able to escape the massacre, and went into hiding with Christian friends. Her biggest fear was that her husband would discover her whereabouts and betray her, or murder her himself.

THE HOLOCAUST AND ITS AFTERMATH

The Nazi definition of what constituted a Jew was purely racial. Baptism counted for nothing; all Jewish converts to Christianity were Jews according to the Nuremberg Laws, and were rounded up and shipped to their deaths, or massacred on the spot, along with the rest of their people. This is what happened, for example, to all two thousand apostates in Ghetto Warsaw. Though Monsignor Marceli Godlewski tried to save them, their baptismal certificates proved useless. In the end they were loaded onto trucks and deported to the death camp at Treblinka.[57]

In Eishyshok, however, perhaps due to lack of time, the Nazis did not search out the converts. Nonetheless, at least one former Jew chose to share the fate of his Jewish brethren. When the Nazis herded the Jews of Eishyshok into the synagogue and the Old and New batei midrash on the eve of Rosh Hashanah 1941, Meir Hilke's Catholic wife left him, and he ran to the shulhoyf. Screaming "I am a Jew, I want to die as a Jew," Hilke pleaded with the guards to lock him up with the rest of their prisoners. In the midst of his weeping and begging, he collapsed, fell to the ground, and died. After the massacre, his body was tossed into the huge trench in the Old Cemetery together with those of all the other Jews.

Some of the apostates in the area tried to help their fellow Jews. A blacksmith from the village of Kilkie, for example, went to warn the Jews of Olkenik that they were about to be killed. But he was too late. By the time he arrived, they had all been taken to Eishyshok and murdered there.

One of the most valiant of the Eishyshok-area apostates was Goldke, who offered shelter to a number of Eishyshkians, including Dr. Benski, the last Jewish doctor in the shtetl. Nonetheless, other Jews who were in hiding nearby did not trust her, fearing that she would betray them. Their fears proved groundless. Avraham Aviel Lipkunski, who would eventually get to Eretz Israel, where he would be the youngest witness at the Eichmann trial, remembers hiding with his father and brother in a barn near Goldke's house, and fearing her even more than they did the Christian neighbors. But when Jews were caught and led to their death, Avraham Aviel Lipkunski and his father watched through a crack in the wall of the barn and saw something that surprised them. As the local Poles crossed themselves and jeered, Goldke stood among them with tears streaming down her face. In the end Goldke herself was betrayed by Christian neighbors. Her reddish hair ablaze against the white snow, she was driven to the gallows and hanged.

Apostates in Ghetto Radun were betrayed by their Christian neighbors, some of them for hiding Jews, and duly executed. Dangling from the gallows, their bodies cast shadows over the home of the Haffetz Hayyim and the building that had once been his world-renowned yeshivah.

Peshke Ejszyszki and her two pretty, talented daughters survived the war, though her husband was not so fortunate. He was killed in 1939 by his Polish comrades, members of the Armia Krajowa, for the crime of having married a Jewess.

In the aftermath of liberation in Eishyshok there were two known conversions from Judaism. One was ideological, the other theological, and, so far as is known, they were the only voluntary conversions that weren't motivated by romance in the last two hundred years of the shtetl's history. Ziske Matikanski is said to have converted out of the belief that the best hope for peace in the region was a strong, independent, Catholic, Polish state. In an attempt to put his belief into practice, he dressed up in the uniform of the Polish army, in which he had served prior to the war, and walked into the forest in search of the headquarters of the Polish partisans, who were known as the Armia Krajowa (home army), or AK. There he expected to be welcomed by his countrymen and his new coreligionists, all of them wearing the same uniform, a symbol of their dedication to the Republic of Poland as it had existed before the Nazi invasion. But apparently he never had the chance to state his beliefs. He was murdered by neighboring AK farmers and his body was never found.[58]

The second convert to Catholicism was a young woman who survived the Holocaust thanks to the kindness of a mother and daughter who belonged to the Polish nobility. After witnessing the horrible fate of the shtetl Jews, and the contrast between that and the good fortune of the local Poles who were able to take over the land, houses, and money of their murdered neighbors, she came to a theological conclusion: The Christian God took better care of his followers than the Jewish God did. Therefore she chose to join the Christian God's flock. But her conversion did not last. A Jewish soldier in the Lithuanian Brigade heard about the incident, and went to the village where the young woman resided to see if he could reason with her.* Eventually he brought her back to Judaism, married her, and took her to Israel, where they raised a family.

A rural Christian family who converted to Judaism after the war, the Kuzmickis, seem to have been motivated by none of the factors usually mentioned to explain proselytes: theology, mystical experience, romance, and marriage. Nor, of course, could it be explained by the desire for career advancement, economic gain, or social prestige, since as Christians they stood only to lose such advantages by casting their lot with a persecuted minority. The Kuzmickis' decision to live as Jews arose solely from their deep affection for Szeina Blacharowicz, a Jewish woman from nearby Eishyshok whom they had helped to save from the Holocaust. By the time the war ended, they had become so attached to Szeina that they could not imagine parting from her. They chose to follow her through all the travails of a displaced person's postwar wanderings through Europe, and to embrace her faith as well. Though Szeina, concerned for their well-being, tried to dissuade them from doing so, they wanted to share her lot, and indeed the daughter, Marushka, identified very actively with her new faith: she spoke Yiddish and Hebrew, participated in Zionist activities, and dated Jewish men.

During the repatriation period the Kuzmicki family left their native land and traveled with Szeina to Poland, probably the only "Jews" on that long train ride to travel with a cow. From Poland they went with Szeina to Germany, making illegal border crossings with the help of *Briha*, an underground Zionist organization dedicated to making it possible for Jews to get to Israel. (The word *briha* is Hebrew for "escape" or "flight.") In Germany they all lived in a DP camp with other Jewish refugees. Eventually Szeina moved to the United States, while her adoptive family moved to Canada, after having (with difficulty) reestablished their Christian identity in order to be eligible for the land grants being offered to Polish farmers. Separated by physical

*The Lithuanian Brigade was made up of Lithuanian citizens living in the Soviet Union who fought alongside the Russians; it included a significant number of Jews among its troops.

distance, Szeina and Marushka nonetheless remained close, meeting occasionally over the years, talking in their shared language of Yiddish (especially when Marushka didn't want her Ukrainian-born husband or her Canadian children or grandchildren to understand what was being said).

Though a few Jews returned to Eishyshok after liberation, eventually all but one — Haikl Kanichowski and his family — left. Itzle (later known as Iris), his daughter by a former marriage, married a non-Jew, but conversion was no longer a prerequisite by then. When they eventually settled in Israel, she went as a Jew, he as a Christian.

There are no longer any Jews in Eishyshok. Nor is it likely that there will ever be any more converts to Judaism from Eishyshok, since the only thing a proselyte stands to gain is the spiritual wealth of the beth midrash, and the town no longer has a beth midrash.

PAUL TILLICH HAS WRITTEN, "JUDAISM IS MORE RELATED TO TIME AND HISTORY THAN to space and nature." This has always been true, but since the Diaspora, the Jews turned to time more than ever for their basic sense of orientation in the world.

Jewish time is divided into two fundamental dimensions: the sacred and the profane. According to the great twentieth-century scholar Rabbi Joseph B. Soloveitchik, the Jew, by creating this dichotomized view of experience, creates a stronghold of peace and abiding hope for himself, a barricade against mundanity, a shield against the indifference of nature and the fluctuations of life.

· 18 ·
HOLIDAYS

THE BASIC CRITERION WHICH DISTINGUISHES FREE MAN FROM SLAVE IS THE KIND OF RELATIONSHIP EACH HAS WITH TIME AND ITS EXPERIENCE. FREEDOM IS IDENTICAL WITH A RICH, COLORFUL, CREATIVE TIME-CONSCIOUSNESS. BONDAGE IS IDENTICAL WITH PASSIVE INTUITION AND RECEPTION OF AN EMPTY, FORMAL TIME-STREAM.

Joseph B. Soloveitchik
"KODESH VE-HOL"
(SACRED AND PROFANE)

The resulting duality dominates all of Jewish life and halakhah (law). Its most obvious manifestation is the Jewish lunisolar calendar, which divides the days of the year into sacred and secular, holidays and ordinary days, and dictates that life be led in accordance with that division. Many mitzvot (precepts), for example, can be carried out only on specific dates, at specific times of day and night. The Sabbath and holidays begin and end at a precise minute. The holidays are governed by the clock, by the revolutions of sun and moon, with each new moon beginning a new month, and the full moon arriving on the fifteenth of the month.[1] Rosh Hodesh (head of the month), the day of the new moon, is itself a holiday. Originally, in the time of the First Temple, all work was suspended in honor of Rosh Hodesh. It was also observed in the shtetl, but more modestly, with special prayers, a half-day off from school for heder boys, and the suspension of certain tasks (like laundry and other nonessential housework). The day had its own atmosphere, slightly more decorous and festive than that of the other days of the month.

And so it goes, year in, year out: The cycle of the week, the phase of the moon, the passing of the seasons, and the arrival of each of the prescribed holidays — these circumscribe and inform the life of every Jewish community, family, and individual, as they have done for thousands of years. The ability of Jews to transport this highly ritualized and regulated sense of time to wherever they live, to impose it on daily life, to use it to make a Jewish homeland outside the original homeland, has allowed the Jews to remain Jewish throughout the two thousand–plus years of the Diaspora.

At least some aspects of life in the Christian world have conformed to Jewish time. As noted in chapter 14, weekly market days as well as monthly or yearly local and regional fairs followed the Jewish calendar or at least attempted to avoid conflicting with it. And just as the Christians acknowledged Jewish time, Jews were very aware of the Julian calendar, especially with regard to important fairs that were associated with Christian holidays or saints. The famous Lublin fair was also known as the Gromnice fair, and was referred to as such in the pinkas of the Lithuanian Jewish communities, Gromnice being Polish for Candlemas, the Christian holiday that occurs on February 2. The Lithuanian Council's pinkas of 1627–44 also make note of the Christian holidays of Swiety Jan (honoring John the Baptist) and Swiatki (another saint's day), both of them summertime festivals associated with important commercial fairs.

The mutual awareness of each other's calendars was a crucial factor in the economy of both Christians and Jews, for it facilitated maximum attendance at their respective fairs, and fueled the manufacture and sale of holiday-related merchandise. For Jews, becoming familiar with the Christian calendar was also a safety precaution: On certain Christian holidays, especially Easter and Christmas, Christian animosity toward Jews was at its peak. Every shtetl Jew, from the youngest heder boy to the oldest man

The Matikanski family seated at the Passover Seder table in the 1930s. The father, Reb Dovid, is wearing a white kittel. To his left are his children Yitzhak, Haikl, and Malka, and his wife Nehama. On the table are photos of their children who had emigrated to America and France. Malka eventually made aliyah; Reb Dovid was murdered in the September 1941 massacre. Nehama, Haikl, Yitzhak, and their wives were killed at Majdanek. YESC, RUBIN

in the beth midrash, knew the dates of Christian holidays in order to avoid being in the wrong place at the wrong time. On Christmas Eve, for example, heder classes ended early so that the students could be sure of returning safely to their homes before nightfall.

Though Jews were well aware of the Julian calendar, it had a merely practical significance to them, which was completely external to their fundamental experience of life. All intimate, important, internal aspects of their lives, from birth to death, were dominated by the Jewish calendar. The dates in all correspondence and record keeping, public and private, referred to the Jewish calendar, and to important days on that calendar, as in "My father-in-law died on the fifth candle of Hanukkah"; or "During World War I, the Russians occupied Eishyshok on Yom Kippur"; or "Time is moving on: Not long ago it was Pessah [Passover], and here it is already seven weeks after Pessah and Shavuot is coming, and so our lives pass . . ."

Frad'l Moszczenik sitting on the "fish, chicken, and onion bench" near the family house on Mill Street, preparing the pike for the Sabbath gefilte fish. Frad'l emigrated to America. YESC, A. ZIMMERMAN

The commemoration of the sacred days, the Sabbath and the holidays, each governed by its own special laws and customs, each observed with its distinctive prayers, rituals, food, and dress, brought the shtetl together into one family unit. All within that extended family shared a basic cultural orientation and ethos, and lived with the same communal, collective memory informing their everyday sense of the present.

THE SABBATH

MORE THAN THE JEWS
KEPT THE SABBATH,
THE SABBATH KEPT THE JEWS.
Ahad Ha'am

Every week the Sabbath rescued the shtetl from secular, profane time and ushered it into the holy zone. The weekly day of rest transformed every Jewish household from a family burdened by the woes of its earthly existence into carefree members of royalty, exulting in another domain altogether. No matter what one's economic or social status, and regardless whether one resided in the humblest of hovels on the outskirts of the shtetl or the grandest of the brick buildings lining the market square, each house became a palace and every man a king, every woman a princess ready to welcome the Sabbath Queen.

As soon as the horse-drawn wagons began pulling away from the market square on Thursday afternoon, the shtetl plunged into its frantic preparations for the Sabbath. Chickens in hand, children were dispatched to the shohet, so that the Sabbath table would be graced with boiled or roasted chicken. Every female in the shtetl began doing her cooking and baking chores, peeling potatoes for the tscholnt (batches), cutting up carrots for the tzimmes, preparing the pike for the gefilte fish. Soon the shtetl cats could be seen running from house to house, their mouths stuffed with pike bladders, or

A hallah cover from the Blacharowicz household in Eishyshok. The family buried it near the house during the Holocaust. PHOTO: MELVIN LEVIN, 1997. YESC, BLACHAROWICZ

smeared with the yolks of egg fresh from the slaughtered chickens. From every house could be heard the sound of sharp knives hitting wooden noodle-boards as sheets of folded dough were cut into fine noodles for chicken soup, or broad ones for kugel. By Friday morning the air was thick with the aroma of freshly baked hallah, the braided white bread eaten on Sabbath and holidays, and the sweet fragrance of cakes and cookies.

Every item in the house had to be scrubbed and polished for the Sabbath: candlesticks, kiddush cups, hallah trays, silverware, samovars, even the family shoes. All brass objects shone like mirrors, including the brass hats of the volunteer firemen. Linens were washed and starched earlier in the week so that on Fridays the beds could be laid with immaculately clean, pure white pillowcases, sheets, and quilt covers, and freshly starched monogrammed linen towels could be hung in the kitchen. In the olden days the clay floors were sprinkled with a fresh layer of gleaming yellow sand; in the twentieth century, when wooden floors had replaced the dirt ones, they were polished to a shine with a reddish wax.

Water carriers shuttled from house to house bringing buckets of water, which would be boiled and kept warm for the Sabbath day in funnel-shaped metal bottles known as leikes.

Liebke Kabacznik (née Moszczenik) drawing water for the Sabbath from the family well on Mill Street. The well was a present from family members who emigrated to America. Liebke and her family were murdered by the AK in February 1944. YESC, A. ZIMMERMAN

This was the method employed until shortly before World War I, when Mordekhai Yankl der Blekher (the tinman) introduced a new "technology" into the shtetl, a combination of thermos and samovar that had an insulated compartment for keeping the coals burning and the tea water hot. This was such a revolutionary innovation that throughout one Friday afternoon, people flocked to his house to see the marvel. Having brought one back with him from the big city (Vilna, probably), Mordekhai Yankl eventually made (or procured) these samovars for many other households in the shtetl, so that in time they became a standard feature in most homes.

As the Sabbath drew closer, the traffic in the streets increased. The men of the household were seen leaving for the public bath, bundles of clean clothing under their arms, their sons trot-

Members of the Lubetski family are dressed for the Sabbath and ready to welcome the Sabbath Queen. Standing at right is Batia, with sister Bluma and nephew. At the window are the third sister, Sarah-Hashke Dugaczanski, with husband Aron-Leib and daughter Leah'le. Batia emigrated to Eretz Israel; Bluma survived the war in Russia. The Dugaczanski family were murdered in the September 1941 massacre. YESC, B. KALEKO

The tall candlesticks of Hanneh-Beile Kudlanski (née Moszczenik). She took them with her when she emigrated to Detroit. PHOTO: MELVIN LEVIN, 1997. YESC, A. ZIMMERMAN

ting along beside them. Late Friday afternoon, people bearing the family tscholnt pot headed toward the bakery that had been assigned to their household, for this traditional meal of meat, potatoes, and legumes couldn't be baked at home, due to the prohibition against lighting a fire on the Sabbath. Instead, each family took its tscholnt pot (and a piece of firewood) to one of the community-supervised ovens located in certain designated bakeries, left it to bake overnight, then picked it up the next day.

The final preparations took place at home, when mothers washed and braided their daughters' hair, and all the females in the household dressed up in their Sabbath finery. All this hustle and bustle came to an abrupt end when the shammash went to the market square and announced, "Yidden, in shul arain" (Jews, go to the synagogue).

Lipe Weingarten was the last shammash to perform this duty in Eishyshok. After the Kiuchefskis opened their steam-operated flour mill in the winter of 1930–31, the blowing of the mill's whistle three times at dusk on Friday announced the coming of the Sabbath. As in many other places, machinery was replacing men whenever possible.[2] In this case, however, there was precedent, the three blasts dating back (like so many shtetl customs) to the period of the Second Temple. According to Flavius Josephus, at dusk on Friday a priest atop a tower in Jerusalem would blow a trumpet to announce the coming of the Sabbath and the cessation of all work.[3] And the Mishnah gives a detailed description of the three blasts of the trumpets on the eve of Sabbath. During the Babylonian exile this custom fell out of favor, but in little Eishyshok and other East European shtetlekh, the ancient custom was revived.

As soon as the announcement was made, by man or steam whistle, all shops were closed and all last-minute preparations ceased. The shtetl was ready to receive the Sabbath Queen. (When a wedding took place Friday afternoon, cessation of Sabbath preparations occurred at an earlier hour.) Now, eighteen minutes before sunset, with the sun just settling into the treetops, all the men and boys in the shtetl went to shul; and every married woman, wearing her Sabbath dress, surrounded by her daughters and preheder-age sons, began lighting the Sabbath candles. The candles were displayed in two tall silver or brass candlesticks, a wedding present that was usually a family heirloom. In addition to the traditional blessing, the women recited a tehinah, a Yiddish prayer chiefly for women. Some women also improvised their own prayers, expressing gratitude for what they had, and the hope that God would provide what was still needed. Many tears were shed during these adlibbed prayers.

Then at last, grace descended on the shtetl. The marketplace was empty. Sabbath candles shone from every window. The chanting of prayers from the shulhoyf filled the air. On a warm night, women would sit on their stoops chatting with their daughters and granddaughters, their friends and neighbors, while everyone awaited the return of the menfolk from the synagogue. When Zivia Hutner was a halutza living alone in Palestine in the 1920s, she used to comfort herself on Friday nights with the memory of those enchanted moments. In her mind's eye she could see the Sabbath candles in every window; her mother, Rebbetzin Kreindl, in her Sabbath dress and starched white apron; herself and her sisters sitting with their mother and watching their father, Reb Hertz Mendl Hutner the dayyan, as he made his way down the street flanked by the two angels who are believed to accompany every man and woman on Friday night. Imbued with the spirit of the Sabbath, Zivia had felt the presence of the ministering angels within her.

Of these two angels it is written in the Mishnah that they escort a man from the synagogue to his home. If upon arriving he finds the candles lit, the table set, and the couch covered with a fine cloth, the good angel declares, "May it be thus on the next Sabbath too," and the evil angel is obliged to answer "Amen." But if the house is not ready for the Sabbath, the evil angel declares "May it be thus on another Sabbath too," and the good angel is obliged to answer "Amen."[4]

In Eishyshok, as elsewhere, it was the custom for the men to bring guests with them when they came home from services. Some were regulars, such as the maggid who ate at the home of Dovid and Nehama Matikanski, or the two rashei yeshivot, Tiktiner and Zarenberger, who went to the home of Shael and Hayya Sonenson. Other guests were transients, who were assigned to their hosts by the platten system described in chapter 4. Upon entering the house and introducing the guests if necessary, the father blessed his children by placing his hands on their heads, just as Patriarch Jacob did. First the sons were blessed, then the daughters, after which the family moved to the Sabbath table, which was set with their best linens and tableware, and lit by the Sabbath candles. In honor of the two angels the *Shalom Aleikhem* hymn was

A starched white apron, hand-embroidered by Szeina Blacharowicz, who wore it in Eishyshok every Sabbath evening.
PHOTO: MELVIN LEVIN, 1997. YESC, BLACHAROWICZ-WISZIK

chanted: "Welcome in Peace, Angels of Service, Angels of the Highest." This was followed by a chanting of the "Woman of Valor" verses from Proverbs, in praise of the role played by the Jewish woman. "A woman of valor, who can find? Far beyond pearls is her price."[5]

Both this and the second of the three Sabbath meals began with reciting the kiddush over wine, thus sanctifying the Sabbath time, the Sabbath freedom, and the Jewish people. During the meal, traditional Sabbath foods were served, hymns were sung, and Torah-related subjects were discussed. Now at last the family had a chance to catch up with each other's doings during the preceding week, for in many families the Sabbath meal was the only occasion when everybody sat down together, with enough time to talk. This was particularly true in the pre–World War I era, when most males of the balebatim class spent the greater part of their time in the shul, beth midrash, heder, or yeshivah.

After the meal, the men returned to the beth midrash to study, which they continued to do once they came home again, sitting at a special study table that was set aside for this purpose. Each house generally had two tables in the common area: one where the three Sabbath meals were served, the other, with its own lamp, where the men sat and learned.[6] Though this study table (shulhan lomdim) remained a constant feature in Jewish homes in Eishyshok, during the years between the world wars the younger generation no long used it for studying sacred books. Rather, they stacked their newspapers and magazines on it, and even used it as a card table during weekdays. In fact, in some homes interesting news from the papers was a common topic during the Sabbath meals, with occasional verbatim readings from articles of special interest.

The second Sabbath meal took place Saturday at midday, after morning services. As the entire shtetl population made its leisurely way home from the shulhoyf, one or two members of each family, usually young people in their teens, would dash ahead, having been dispatched to the bakery where the family tscholnt pot had been left the day before. Holding the steaming pot in both hands, they would make their way back to their families and lead the entourage home. Like everything else in the shtetl, the tscholnt pot had its own legends and lore, its own fund of humorous stories associated with it. Many of these involved tscholnt pot mixups, for the shtetl pranksters loved to exchange pots "accidentally," so that the rich family went home with a meatless stew of potatoes and beans, and the shtetl pauper enjoyed the delicious tscholnt meant for the rich.

People sat down to the Seudah Shelishot (third meal) after the minhah (afternoon prayer) on Saturday. In most Eishyshok families this meal was eaten in the home of the grandparents. In the Sonenson family, for example, during the summer months the entire clan gathered around the round table in the gazebo in Hayya Sonenson's beautiful apple grove. During the rest of

A kiddush cup from Eishyshok belonging to the Blacharowicz family. During the Holocaust it was buried near the family house.
PHOTO: MELVIN LEVIN, 1997. YESC, BLACHAROWICZ-WISZIK

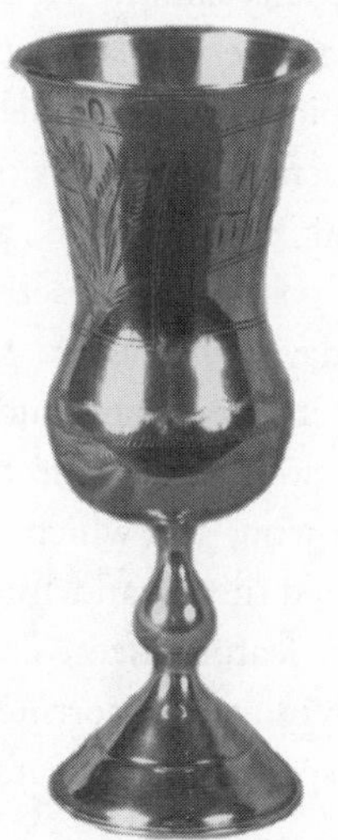

the year the family used the huge oblong table in the dining room.

SABBATH MEALS AND EVERYDAY MEALS

Eishyshok's standard Sabbath menus were typical for the region, with minor adjustments to conform to the local produce and culinary preferences. Each household also made its own further changes in the classic menu, changes that reflected the special skills and favorite recipes of the mother, grandmother, and other females in the family, some of whom brought knowledge of certain delicacies from other regions.

FRIDAY NIGHT The typical Friday dinner included: gefilte fish, which consisted of a whole pike, the flesh of which had been removed from the bones, then ground up with other ingredients and seasonings and stuffed into the fish from which it was taken; boiled or roasted chicken, or roasted goose or turkey, served with potato kugel (teigakhtz), pickles, sauerkraut, and, during the summer months, fresh radishes; chicken soup with fine noodles; and a dessert of baked apples and pears, or a compote, which was a cooked melange of fruit usually including apples, raisins, and prunes. There were also cakes, cookies, and varenie (a kind of marmalade), and, during the summer, various rhubarb dishes. Hot tea was served in a glass with chunks of sugar.

SATURDAY MORNING Only children ate breakfast, for one cannot eat before prayer and kiddush. For them breakfast consisted of babke (yeast coffeecake with raisins) and a cold rechisnik (a buckwheat pudding that was a local specialty), beer, lemonade, and kvass (a Russian fermented drink).

SECOND SABBATH MEAL The typical meal eaten after morning prayers on Saturday was gefilte fish with horseradish, chopped herring decorated with onion rings, chopped liver topped with shredded hard-boiled egg yolks, carrot tzimmes, sauerkraut with cranberries or gooseberries, and pickles; tscholnt made from potatoes, legumes, and often beef or veal, the whole thing topped with stuffed chicken neck or stuffed derma (intestinal casings); rechisnik and a broad-noodle kugel. Dessert was the same as on Friday night.

A silver box used for serving lumps of sugar decorated the Kudlanski family's Sabbath table. When they emigrated to America, they took it with them. PHOTO: MELVIN LEVIN, 1997. YESC, A. ZIMMERMAN

THIRD SABBATH MEAL In Eishyshok the custom was to wait six hours between meat and dairy, so during the short days of winter, when the full six hours wouldn't have elapsed between the midday and evening meals, the third meal was often pareve — that is, meatless and milkless. If desired, dairy could then be eaten at the final meal (or snack) of the day, the melaveh malkah. A typical meatless melaveh malkah meal in the evening consisted of gefilte fish, chopped herring, cold rechisnik, and an assortment of baked goods and desserts. During the long summer days, when there were six hours or more between the second and third meals, many families ate dairy at the third meal. A typical dairy menu, for which many grandmothers prepared their grandchildren's favorite delicacies, might feature cheese, cooked cold fish and potatoes in milk, an assortment of herring, and whatever special dairy treats the children requested.

MELAVEH MALKAH (ESCORTING THE QUEEN) The post-Sabbath meal was usually served quite late, and consumed either at home or at one of the community functions that frequently took place on Saturday nights. Its menu varied, sometimes consisting of dairy dishes, other times an array of desserts, and occasionally a more elaborate spread.

Regular weekday meals differed from the Sabbath meals most notably in that families rarely sat down to eat them together. But even without the sense of ceremony that prevailed on Sabbath, people in the shtetl ate well in times of plenty, on weekdays as on Sabbath, with the more affluent enjoying the more lavish meals, of course. Weekday menus were typically much less standardized, more diversified.

For breakfast there would be some combination of eggs, rolls, bagels, pumpernickel bread, butter, Dutch-style cheese from nearby Arodnoy, farmer-style cheese, herring, potatoes, buttermilk, milk, and tea. During the summer months, fresh sliced vegetables like cucumbers and radishes on buttered pumpernickel was popular.

During the winter months, there was often meat on the table at both afternoon and evening meals, with the meat dishes consisting mainly of beef, veal, and lamb, as well as liver, sweetbreads, and tongue. They were boiled, broiled, baked, or grilled, the grilling done on coals to which various kinds of wood were added to give a particular flavor. The fatter the meat the higher its quality was considered to be. There was also usually a soup course, typically consisting of borscht (beet soup) cooked with cabbage, fatty meat, and bones. Side dishes might include several of the following: whole boiled potatoes, sauerkraut, pickles, cranberries, barley, baked apples, potato kugel. Pumpernickel and scalding hot tea with lumps of sugar were served at each meal.

Many of the foods served during the winter — pickles, sauerkraut, and other preserved vegetables — were stored in wooden barrels in a cool cellar. Fats, marmalades, and honey were kept in clay jars covered with a white cloth. Apples were stored in the attic underneath piles of straw.

In summertime many chose to eat mainly dairy, forgoing the twice-a-day portions of meat consumed the rest of the year. Winter and summer alike, fish and herring were popular, as were a variety of starches, including potatoes, beans, barley, noodles, rolls, bagels, pumpernickel and other kinds of bread. The fish most frequently served were pike, carp, and a small local fish called platkes. They were broiled, grilled, baked, marinated, or fried. Fried herring served with "potatoes in pelts" (potatoes with their skins) and onion rings was a particular favorite. During the summer, fruits and vegetables were abundant, picked fresh from the garden or gathered from the forests, and often served with generous amounts of sour cream. Vegetables such as cucumbers, radishes, scallions, and tomatoes could be cooked or eaten raw, or made into cold soups like borscht and schav (made from greens), also served with sour cream.[7]

Although this diet seems extraordinarily rich in animal fats by today's standards, most people were not overweight, perhaps due to the fact that walking and physical labor were regular parts of their daily routine.

SABBATH PASTIMES

The Sabbath was a day of ease and refreshment, sustenance for body and soul, a day when people rested from their labors, as God rested from the work of creation. It was inspired by the biblical prohibition against labor on the seventh day, labor being defined as any of the thirty-nine categories of work that share in any aspect of the creation. These included sowing and such "offspring" as the watering of plants; plowing and such "offspring" as the weeding of a garden patch; kindling a fire and its "offspring," the adding of oil to a burning lamp or wood to a stove. For those categories of work that *had* to be performed — for example, the heating of the house during the bitter cold months of winter — there was a way around the prohibition: to hire a "Shabbes goy," a non-Jew on the payroll of the kahal who performed the forbidden work of maintaining a fire in the house-warming oven. At the appointed hours, he made his rounds from house to house, carrying out his responsibilities without having to be told what to do. In addition to his official pay from the community, some families gave him a tip, in the form of food and clothing as well as money. And every household paid the kahal a special tax for this service.[8]

The complete cessation of work resulted in what the twelfth-century philosopher and poet Judah Halevi viewed as a unique gift, whereby Jews consecrated a portion of their lives to spiritual and physical renewal. Even kings do not have such a privilege, such total relief from toil and distraction, he wrote.[9] And indeed, in welcoming the Sabbath Queen to his home every man in the shtetl felt himself a king, every male child a member of the royal family.

The shtetl woman, however, was not royalty; she was merely praised as a woman of valor, keeper of the Sabbath light, she who by her labor transforms an ordinary house into a Sabbath palace. During the week she was the dominant person in the house. Home was her domain, her husband and sons little more than guests there, however honored those guests may have been. On the Sabbath and on the holidays, however, her husband and the other males in the household became the central figures, conducting the rituals, leading the family and its guests in singing, Torah discourse, and learning. It was as if the male realm of the beth midrash had now extended into the home.

But women in the shtetl did create a special niche for themselves during the Sabbath, in which the social aspects of this day of rest rather than the ritual ones were central. There were a number of women's circles that gathered informally in each other's houses Saturday afternoon. The one that usually met in the home of Yakhe Dubitski, for example, was known for its elegance. The special dishes and pastries she prepared for her friends, the manner in which she served them, the quality of the gossip and the range of issues discussed, became an inspiration to other circles of women in the balebatim class.[10]

Fruml Cofnas's circle was known for its focus on acts of charity. Mere the seamstress, Elke Mere's (daughter of Mere), Frume the seamstress, Sheine-Reizl the melamed's wife, Perele Fischl the tailor's wife, Esther der Rubishker (from Rubishki), Soreh-Malke the wife of Benjamin di Lulke (the pipe), Ethel Simhe's (wife of Simha), Khiene Tzen Por Ploidern (the ten-layers-of-underwear lady) — they were all kind, God-fearing women whose main concern was the welfare of others. Fruml's youngest son, Pessah, thought of his mother's circle (all of them short of stature) as "The Little Women's Sabbath Afternoon Parliament." Their "secret" meetings took place behind closed doors, around a Sabbath table covered with a white tablecloth and adorned by two sparkling brass candlesticks.

Between mouthfuls of cooked chickpeas and sips of hot tea, they discussed their reading of the weekly portion from *Zeenah U-Reenah*, that seventeenth-century compilation of biblical stories and Aggadic and midrashic homilies which women of their generation were still using as a basic handbook of Judaism. Then they proceeded to the main business: a discussion of the needs of the shtetl's destitute. During one such Saturday-afternoon conversation, for example, they decided that Nohem the Pope should have more cooked food left for him in the women's gallery of the Old Beth Midrash; that Nohem's fellow meshuggener Arke could use a pair of woolen socks; that Sander der Rechisnik, another mentally ill man whose nickname derived from his craving for the local buckwheat pudding, needed some other warm nourishment; and that a poor young illiterate boy by the name of Motke needed reading lessons.

After identifying the various needs, the search for resources began. Fruml Cofnas donated her husband Gedalia's woolen socks, and her son Pessah's services as a tutor for young Motke. Feige Demitrowski the baker, Zisle Shlanski, Alte Katz, and Nehama Matikanski were all identified as potential resources for other needs, whom they would call upon for assistance as soon as the Sabbath was over.[11]

The Sabbath was also a time of family togetherness. The entire clan gathered around the Sabbath dinner table singing, talking, learning, discussing. Boys were tested on what they had learned the previous week in heder, the testing being done by a father, grandfather, or other erudite male member of his family, or by the melamed himself. Though boys did have to spend part of Saturday studying with the melamed, they also had time for games, and for a leisurely family stroll after the adults took their traditional Saturday afternoon nap.

Everyone in the shtetl turned out for the Saturday-afternoon walk, each family keeping to its own favorite itinerary. The Lewinson family took their stroll down Mill Street, while the Cofnas brothers and their friends preferred Radun Street. Some visited the ancestral lands once owned by their families; some went to the Seklutski forest, where many of the Zionist youth groups spent their time singing and discussing their dreams of Eretz Israel. Moshe and Zipporah Sonenson and their children, in company with family friends hazzan Moshe Tobolski, his wife Rivka, and their children, used to take Vilna Street, past the bridge, and on to the outskirts of the forest. The walks were a time for friends to meet and exchange the latest news and gossip. For little Yaffa Sonenson they were also exercise time: under her mother's watchful eye, she had to practice how not to walk pigeon-toed.

Following the Sabbath-day walk, the men returned to the synagogue for minhah (afternoon prayers), and then everyone went home in time to eat the third meal before the setting of the sun (though a few of the men, especially the elderly, remained in the synagogue for the third meal). Afterward, as the sun neared the horizon, Hayya Sonenson, like many another shtetl grandmother, would point to the fiery globe and tell all present that the Gehenna, whose flames died down during the Sabbath, just like those in the shtetl, was being reheated for the departed sinners. Their Sabbath rest, like everyone else's, was now ending, and they would shortly return to the flames. Scanning the sky for the appearance of the three stars that signaled the end of Sabbath, Hayya's grandchildren would rush to tell her the moment they spotted them. A few minutes later she would sadly recite the tehinah "God of Abraham."

And with that, the men who had stayed at the synagogue for the third meal returned home, and the whole family gathered for the havdalah (separation) ceremony. This was the ritual marking the end of the holy Sabbath, the beginning of the secular week, the separation between the sacred and the profane, between light and darkness, between the day of rest and all other days, between Israel and all other nations.

The four benedictions of the havdalah were recited over a goblet overflowing with wine, spices, and light that was reflected from the havdalah candle. Usually the youngest child held the candle, a colorful, braided one with many wicks. One of the many pieces of havdalah-related legend and lore was that if the child was a girl and she held the candle high, she would find a tall groom. As for the spices, they were mixed with the wine to cheer up the soul, which is saddened by the departure of the Sabbath.[12]

With the conclusion of the havdalah, the Sabbath magic evaporated. The house looked darker, the faces more somber and stern. Throughout the shtetl, the singing of the *Ha-Mavdil* hymn could be heard from each house, its chant the final step in the separation process:

The day has declined like the shade of a palm;
I call upon God who fills all my needs —
Open heaven's exalted Gate for me —
I call for thy help.
O grant redemption, in the twilight —
We are all potters' clay in thy hand —
Pardon our transgressions, both light and grand.

Saturday night was when most of the shtetl's community-wide events took place. Elections to the kahal and to the boards of the various charity organizations, the leasing of the korobka and the public bath, Zionist youth group parties, and the annual volunteer firemen's ball — all were usually held on Saturday night, and were often combined with the melaveh malkah meal, which honored the departing Sabbath Queen.

The melaveh malkah meal was accompanied by the singing of traditional songs, after which the shtetl artisans plunged into their frantic preparations for market day, still five days away, and the shtetl women returned to their workaday chores.

Just as the workdays gave way each week to the day of rest, so the secular days of every calendar year gave way to the sacred seasons and holidays — all determined by the waxing and waning of the moon. Holidays and special days occurred during eleven of the twelve months of the year (thirteen during leap year). During these holy days, every aspect of shtetl life was transformed.

THE MONTH OF ELUL

WAS MIR TUEN TUEN MIR
WAS MIR ZAINEN, ZAINEN MIR
OBER YIDDEN ZAINEN MIR
SHTEIT UF LE-AVODAT HA-BOREH.
(WHAT WE DO WE DO,
WHAT WE ARE WE ARE,
BUT WE ARE JEWS,
RISE FOR THE
DIVINE SERVICE!)

Sexton's wake-up call during Elul and the Ten Days of Repentance

Elul is the month preceding the High Holiday season, when the fate of each individual is decided. From the onset of the month of Elul (August–September, occasionally running into October) straight through the High Holidays, the entire population of the shtetl was gripped with fear and awe, their minds engaged in taking stock of their actions in the past year, their hearts set on making amends. This was the time for selihot, the prayers asking for forgiveness and mercy.[13]

Therefore, beginning on the morning of Rosh Hodesh Elul, and continuing through every morning from then until Yom Kippur, the predawn darkness would find the shammash making his way to the market square, and from there to every street and lane, to chant his special wake-up call. House by house, the melody of his call passed through the wooden shutters, and every man, woman, and child in the community rose early to go to shul. Soon the streets were filled with families, lanterns in hand, stumbling along in the early-morning chill. Footsteps echoing off the cobblestones, crisp autumn air with a touch of frost, darkness split by light from the lanterns — they were all part of the soul-stirring, awe-inspiring atmosphere of Elul.

During one selihot season, little Meir Wilkanski overslept. When he woke up, his father, mother, and older brother Yitzhak had already left. He awakened his older sister and asked her to go to the beth midrash with him. She peered through the curtain; it was pitch black outside, and the market square looked foreboding. Surely only the ghosts of the shtetl dead were roaming the streets. Meir cried. How would he get to services? He was concerned that the absence of one innocent heder boy from selihot would alter the balance of prayers in the shtetl.[14]

Each Elul service closed with the blowing of the shofar, from the many minyanim within each of the three houses of prayer. And on every one of the weekdays that followed during the month of Elul, there were interludes devoted to special ascetic and devotional practices, the purpose of which was to prepare the individual for the days of judgment and atonement soon to come and for the new year.

In a shtetl that had a yeshivah, like Eishyshok, the atmosphere was even more charged than in other shtetlekh. So intense did it become that many of the prushim at the yeshivah extended their study hours, and refused to carry on any conversation during the entire month of Elul, except on the Sabbath, out of the desire to avoid idle talk and gossip. The somber tunes of the prushim, studying well into the night, echoed through the dark, empty market square. Other prushim hoped to prove their merit by working with the shtetl's benevolent societies, helping the needy.

It was a common saying among the prushim that one must behave throughout the year as one does in the month of Elul. But Elul is Elul. Meir Wilkanski was convinced that even the early autumn skies of Elul looked different, their long, deep-red sunsets a warning of the heavy price to be paid in Gehenna for our earthly transgressions.[15]

Shammash Lipe Weingarten was still chanting his special Elul wake-up call on the eve of the great storm.

ROSH HASHANAH

THREE BOOKS ARE OPENED ON ROSH HASHANAH, ONE FOR THE COMPLETELY RIGHTEOUS, ONE FOR THE COMPLETELY WICKED, AND ONE FOR THE AVERAGE PERSONS. THE COMPLETELY RIGHTEOUS ARE IMMEDIATELY INSCRIBED IN THE BOOK OF LIFE. THE COMPLETELY WICKED ARE IMMEDIATELY INSCRIBED IN THE BOOK OF DEATH. THE AVERAGE PERSONS ARE KEPT IN SUSPENSE FROM ROSH HASHANAH TO THE DAY OF ATONEMENT. IF THEY DESERVE WELL, THEY ARE INSCRIBED IN THE BOOK OF LIFE, IF THEY DO NOT DESERVE WELL, THEY ARE INSCRIBED IN THE BOOK OF DEATH.

Rosh Hashanah, 16/b

The month of Elul was preparation for the even more awe-inspiring season to follow, that of the High Holidays. The first of the High Holidays was Rosh Hashanah, the Jewish New Year, the anniversary of creation itself, which fell on the first and second days of the month of Tishrei. The windows facing the market square were lit with glowing candles, the smells of holiday food, of fresh autumn apples and summer fruits, filled the air, the new moon rose. The Day of Judgment was at hand. This was a time of reflection and repentance, when all mankind stood before the divine throne to give a strict accounting of deeds committed during the previous year. One asked for mercy, not by virtue of one's own deeds, but on the merit of the Jewish people's matriarchs and patriarchs and other worthy ancestors, and the good deeds and faith of the Jewish people as a whole.

Though it is the custom to wear black when appearing before a court of law, when Jews appear before the ultimate court they wear white. On Rosh Hashanah and Yom Kippur "Jews should not appear depressed and in somber clothes, as supplicants before a human judge, but joyous, dressed in festive white, betokening a cheerful and confident spirit. They are to eat, drink and rejoice, in the conviction that God will perform a miracle for them."[16] Thus everyone in the shtetl flocked to the shulhoyf on the eve of Rosh Hashanah, and the two batei midrash and the summer shul became a sea of white: the women and girls in white dresses, their heads covered in flowing white scarves or fashionable white hats, their hair held back with white barrettes, the men wearing white kittels beneath their prayer shawls. The mood was festive and solemn, joyous and somber, all at the same time. At the conclusion of the evening prayers, people greeted each other with the words "Leshana tova tikatevu" (May you be inscribed [in the Book of Life] for a good year). The holiday meal that followed at home included an apple dipped in honey, that the year ahead should be a sweet one, and other fruits and vegetables to symbolize the hopes for a year of peace and plenty.

The next day, the weeping blast of the shofar pierced the morning air. From the shulhoyf to the empty market square, from street to alley, alley to lane, the one hundred notes of the shofar rang out in their specially prescribed patterns of tekiah, shevarim, and teruah. Each sounding of the shofar was a reminder of God's sovereignty, filling every heart with fear of his judgment, hope for his compassion.

In the afternoon of the first day of Rosh Hashanah (the second day if the first fell on a Sabbath), the entire population of the shtetl walked down to the banks of the Kantil to perform the ceremony of tashlikh, for the prophet Mikhah had said: "And thou will cast (ve-tashlikh) all their sins into the depth of the sea" (7:19). As Meir Wilkanski recounted:

Everyone in the shtetl — the worshippers from the Old Beth Midrash, the New Beth Midrash, and the synagogue — was streaming to tashlikh. The whole length of Vilna Street was filled with people and children. Some walked alone, others in groups, all the men bedecked in prayer shawls, with holiday mahzorim [Rosh Hashanah prayer books] in their hands . . .

We lined the banks of the river, whose waters gushed with ice chunks during the spring but were peaceful now. As we emptied our sins into the pure flowing waters, we prayed.

On the other side of the public bath, near the large meadow, stood a herd of white sheep . . . My brother Yitzhak laughed: "Those are not sheep, they are the women, wearing their white dresses. They, too, are casting their sins into the river, at the women's tashlikh. Somewhere in the stream the men's tashlikh and the women's tashlikh will unite, to be carried far away by the current.

After tashlikh we returned home. Rosh Hashanah is a holiday with plenty of good food and an abundance of fruits. But Father [Reb Layzer] is in a gloomy mood. One is not permitted to laugh, nor to engage in idle conversation. After the meal, it was back to the synagogue to recite Psalms until dusk.[17]

In the years between the two world wars, all Eishyshok still streamed down Vilna Street to tashlikh, still wearing white, but now it was a coed crowd. Families walked together, the children carrying the parents' mahzorim.

Another new custom was the sending of New Year's cards, mainly to and from America and Palestine. Though it had no origins in Jewish tradition, it caught on quickly, so that the post office was kept quite busy around this time of year. On a postcard depicting a little girl bearing a basket of goodies, Rachel Nunes wrote from Eishyshok to her cousin Sarah'le Moszczenik in America on August 30, 1931: "I hope that next year we will exchange Rosh Hashanah greeting cards in America." In 1937, Vela Dubczanski Portnoy sent her family a greeting card with a picture of herself, her husband, and their young son Itzhar at the seaport of Tel Aviv, its waters crowded with ships. Having barely made it to Palestine herself, after mishaps and adventures that included arrest, imprisonment, and deportation by the

British, Vela nonetheless wishes that everyone back home will have "a year of aliyah — emigration to Eretz Israel." Unlike Rachel Nunes, however, who did eventually get to America, Vela's parents, sister, and brothers never left Eishyshok, for they never received the certificates they needed to join their daughter in Palestine. They were among the thousands who made their last walk to the mass grave, two days after Rosh Hashanah in 1941.

Vela and Michael Portnoy with son Itzhar send New Year's blessings in Hebrew that express the hope that it will be a year of mass aliyah to the seaport in Tel Aviv. The greeting card was mailed to Vela's family in Eishyshok, 1937. YESC, V. PORTNOY

Meir Wilkanski mailed this New Year card in German and Hebrew from Eretz Israel, 1905. YESC, WILKANSKI

A New Year card from Jake Morris Goodman (Yaakov-Moshe Kudlanski) and his wife's sister Frad'l in America. (Jake's wife Hanneh-Beile had not yet emigrated.) The greetings in Yiddish include best wishes for a healthy, joyous year and much money in the bank. YESC, A. ZIMMERMAN

Atara Kudlanski (Goodman) with baby cousin Yudaleh Kabacznik on a New Year card. The good wishes are written in Hebrew and Polish. The card was sent from Eishyshok to their Aunt Sarah in Detroit. Yudaleh was murdered by the AK in 1944. PHOTO: REPHAEL LEJBOWICZ. YESC, A. ZIMMERMAN

Nahum Dwilanski sent his New Year's blessing in Portuguese from Buenos Aires to his cousin Moshe Dovid Katz in Eishyshok, 1937. YESC, Y. SONENSON

TEN DAYS OF REPENTANCE

During the Ten Days of Repentance between Rosh Hashanah and Yom Kippur, the shtetl was gripped with fear. There was a constant emphasis on the sincerity of repentance, as expressed in both prayer and good deeds.

On the afternoon of the Sabbath between Rosh Hashanah and Yom Kippur, the shtetl rabbi delivered one of the two sermons stipulated in his contract. During his sermon not a soul remained at home. The yishuvniks from the surrounding countryside came, too, for it was mandatory for them to spend the High Holiday period in the shtetl, so that they could perform their religious observances in the heart of the Jewish community, and feel themselves a part of it. There was standing room only in the summer shul. As a hushed silence fell upon the congregation, everyone paid heed to the rabbi's call for repentance. Typically he spoke about ethical conscience and moral responsibility, about self-examination and spiritual regeneration.

As Yom Kippur neared, the tension in the shtetl mounted. On the market day prior to Yom Kippur, shoppers went in frantic search of pure white roosters with red cockscombs for the men in their households, and snow-white chickens for the women. These would be used for the ceremony of kapparot (atonement), in which one symbolically transfers one's guilt to the fowl (a ceremony reminiscent of the use of the scapegoat during the days of the Temple).[18] After sunset on the eve of Yom Kippur, or before sunrise the following morning, the men grabbed their roosters, the women their hens (unless they were pregnant, in which case they took both), swung them around their heads three times, and recited the following: "This is my substitute, my vicarious offering, my atonement; this rooster [or hen] shall meet death, but I shall find a long and pleasant life of peace"— a ceremony that made an indelible, lifelong impression on some of their children. After the ceremony, the shohet slaughtered the fowl. The equivalent of each fowl's value was given to the poor, the intestines were thrown on the rooftops for the birds, and the slaughtered fowl were then eaten.[19]

Another ceremony that made a big impression, on old and young alike, was that of the thirty-nine lashes. Following afternoon prayer on the eve of Yom Kippur, thirty-nine lashes were inflicted on those who chose to atone in this manner — an echo of biblical times, when courts punished offenders with thirty-nine lashes. Prostrating himself on the floor of the polesh in the Old Beth Midrash, the penitent asked the shammash to administer the lashes. (Women were not eligible for this form of atonement, as it could compromise their modesty.) During the final days of the shtetl, this job was given to a poor person, who was chosen by the community and paid for his services by his "victims." But by the time of Shlomo Kik, the last man to hold the position, the lashes were little more than symbolic, for Reb Kik was a tiny man, who wielded a thin little rope that would barely hurt a fly. Nonetheless, there were those in the shtetl — and everyone knew who they were — who seemed to feel the pain, though perhaps that was symbolic too. Hayyim-Yoshke Bielicki, then a choirboy in the shtetl, remembered watching Reb Shmuel Malke's take the lash, his "Oy vay" ringing out before the rope even reached him. The memory of the sight and sound of that annual ritual never left him.

Both Reb Shmuel Malke's and Shlomo Kik were murdered by the Germans and their Lithuanian collaborators in September 1941, just a few days before they would have met up for another ritual lashing.

YOM KIPPUR: THE DAY OF ATONEMENT

ON ROSH HASHANAH IT IS INSCRIBED, AND ON YOM KIPPUR THE DECREE IS SEALED, HOW MANY SHALL PASS AWAY AND HOW MANY SHALL BE BORN; WHO SHALL LIVE AND WHO SHALL DIE. . . . BUT PENITENCE, PRAYER, AND CHARITY AVERT THE SEVERE DECREE.

Yom Kippur and Rosh Hashanah service

The Day of Atonement was the climax of the ten-day period of repentance, the emotional release for the tension that had permeated the shtetl ever since the beginning of Elul, the holiest of all the holy days of the Jewish year. Rosh Hashanah was the Day of Judgment, but Yom Kippur was the day when God's decision was actually made. On the eve of Yom Kippur, following the last meal prior to the fast that would be observed the next day, the father blessed his children. Many of the adults also went to be blessed, making their way to the most saintly of the rabbis and scholars in the community.

This was also the time to seek forgiveness. Since God will not grant forgiveness for matters that concern man's relationship with his fellow man until some reparation is made, the wrongdoer must first win pardon from the person he wronged. Only then can he ask God to expunge his guilt. So throughout the shtetl, people were busy making amends to one another for any wrongs committed, intentionally or otherwise. Parents and children, husbands and wives, other relatives and friends — all sought each other's forgiveness, so that they might begin Yom Kippur with a clean conscience. As the sun reached the treetops, people parted from one another, in some cases still not knowing whether forgiveness would be granted, or what the final verdict would be.

Soon the streets were filled with people hurrying toward the shulhoyf for the evening service, everyone carrying long wax candles that would be placed in the polesh in honor of the living and in memory of the dead. Everyone wore white, and since the wearing of leather was not permitted on Yom Kippur, everyone walked in their stocking feet. In the houses of prayer the floors had been covered in straw, to make it more comfortable for the unshod worshippers, and everything had been bedecked in white for the occasion, including the Holy Ark and the scrolls within.

Before the sun had set, while the last golden rays were still filtering through the tall windows, the rabbi and the shtetl notables approached the Ark, drew out the Holy Scrolls, and began to chant the Kol Nidre (Aramaic for "all vows"). In the stirring melody of this prayer, one hears fear of judgment, hope for ultimate deliverance; in the anguished sobbing that accompanied its three repetitions, the pain of centuries of Jewish suffering.

After the evening service, many of the men remained in the houses of prayer overnight. The following day, Yom Kippur, the Day of Atonement, the shtetl resembled a ghost town. All its inhabitants were praying in shul. Occasionally a young mother and her children could be seen rushing home; minutes later, the children's needs taken care of, the little family group would return to the shulhoyf. Men in their white kittels and prayer shawls would slip outdoors for a breath of fresh air, padding silently around the shulhoyf in their white socks or cloth slippers. Others checked on their loved ones in the prayerhouses, concerned about how they might be holding up under the stress of this day of fasting and prayer, soul-searching and repentance. Indeed, the shtetl's medicine men and women, and later its doctors, were often kept busy on this day. Each had his or her special methods for reviving those who succumbed, but sometimes all methods failed. One memorable Yom Kippur, in 1929, two people died during services: Layzer Remz and Szeina Blacharowicz's grandmother.

As the sun reached the treetops, signaling the end of Yom Kippur, the Neilah (closing prayer) was chanted. The entire congregation stood and faced the Holy Ark, all making their last effort of the day, one final appeal to be inscribed in the Book of Life. Finally the services were concluded, and the shofar was blown. Yom Kippur was now over, and the entire congregation enthusiastically sang "Next Year in Jerusalem." Mothers and grandmothers kissed their children and grandchildren, friends hugged, and all wished each other a happy holiday, a good verdict. Families picked up their burning candles from the sandboxes in the polesh and came together under the early-evening stars hovering above the shulhoyf. Stopping to bless the moon, they began the walk home. To anyone witnessing the scene, it would have appeared like a river of sparks flowing through all the channels of the shtetl. At home the havdalah was made over wine, the havdalah candle being lit with the candle brought home from the polesh. Now the fast was broken with a festive meal, and the joy of beginning the new year with a clean slate replaced the solemnity of repentance.

Later the calm of the night would be broken by the sound of hammers. It was time to start building the sukkah (booth).[20]

SUKKOT: FEAST OF TABERNACLES

YOU SHALL DWELL IN BOOTHS SEVEN DAYS — THAT YOUR GENERATION MAY KNOW THAT I MADE THE ISRAELITES DWELL IN BOOTHS.

Leviticus 23:42–43

The autumn festival of Sukkot (Hebrew for "booths") begins on the fifteenth day of Tishrei.

The Lubetski house with a number of its family members. The two squares on the roof are the hinged rooftops that were opened for the holiday of Sukkot. The open space was covered with fresh branches (skhakh), and the room beneath became the sukkah. PHOTO: YITZHAK URI KATZ. YESC, TOKATLI

It is a festival of joy and celebration, when one gives thanks for the fall harvest, and commemorates the temporary shelters the Jews found during their forty years of wandering in the desert before reaching the Promised Land. In Eishyshok it was celebrated with particular enthusiasm, because as an agricultural festival it had special meaning to a shtetl that had such an enduring and profound connection with the land.

Elsewhere the sukkah was usually a temporary dwelling that was put up in the backyard or alongside the house. But this was not the case in Eishyshok, where the sukkah generally consisted of a room in the attic with a hinged rooftop that could be opened to the skies. Most houses in Eishyshok were built with this special feature. To create the sukkah each year, the rooftop was opened and the space was overlaid with branches (*skhahk*, from which the name *sukkah* is derived) that were placed over beams in such a way as to conform to the prohibition against nails being used in the construction of the roof. On the market day preceding Sukkot, wagons came in from the countryside heaped with the cut pine branches Eishyshkians favored for this purpose. Once constructed, the canopy of the sukkah had to be thick enough so that there was more shade than sunshine, but not

Bill Goodman with his maternal grandparents, Reb Dovid and Leah Moszczenik, returning home from shul on Hoshana Rabbah, the seventh day of Sukkot, October 13, 1930. Bill emigrated to America, Reb Dovid died a natural death, and Leah was killed in the September 1941 massacre. YESC, A. ZIMMERMAN

so thick that rain or snow could not penetrate. For the eight days of Sukkot the family would take all its meals beneath this temporary roof (weather permitting).

Families brought fruits and vegetables from their garden into the sukkah, and they dressed the pine branches with paper lanterns, braids of onions and garlic, decorations made from apples and pears, and flying birds they constructed of eggshells with paper wings. The walls were hung with tapestries, paper cutouts, and other ornaments and decorations symbolizing the ushpizin (Aramaic for "guests") — the biblical heroes Abraham, Isaac, Jacob, Joseph, Moses, Aaron, and David — whom one invited into the sukkah each day. Pictures of great Lithuanian scholars such as the Gaon of Vilna and Rabbi Yitzhak Elhanan Spektor might also be included, as portraits of Theodor Herzl were after the rise of Zionism.

Mingling with the fresh aroma of the pine branches were the smells of the special holiday plants, hadassim (myrtle) and aravot (willow), tied together with the lulav (palm branch),*and the magnificent scent of the etrog (citron), which, being foreign to the region and hard to procure, was stored in its own special box wrapped in flax to protect it against damage, for it had to be perfect, without blemish. The Radunski family and others who had emigrated to Palestine used to send citron fruits to their friends and relatives in Eishyshok at this season. For special Sukkot services in the shul, the men walked in procession around the bimah, carrying the ceremonial branches and the etrog, singing as they went — much to the delight of the children.

At home the meals in the sukkah were accompanied by the singing of holiday songs, their melodies echoing throughout the shtetl, creating a mood of festivity. Young people walked from sukkah to sukkah, comparing decorations, sampling holiday delicacies. And the silhouette of the shtetl was transformed — with their hinged roof doors flung open, outspread like wings, the houses resembled birds.

HOSHANA RABBAH

The seventh day of Sukkot is known as Hoshana Rabbah (the great Hoshana; *Hoshana* means "Save now, we pray"). It is believed that on this day, God's decrees for the coming year are finalized. Thus the shtetl once again assumed a mood of solemnity. The walls of the Old Beth Midrash were covered with the shtetl's ancient parokhot, Ark coverings whose histories were recounted to the children on this once-a-year occasion when they were brought out of storage.[21] Men spent the night in the beth midrash, sitting and learning. In the early hours of the following morning, the women and children

*Since the palm is the biggest, the three plants bound together go by its name, *lulav.*

arrived with bundles of freshly cut willow branches, which the men then carried in procession around the bimah, while reciting the Hoshana prayers for a good harvest in the year to come. After seven encirclings of the bimah, the willow branches were beaten until their leaves fell off. The smashing of branches in the women's gallery echoed the sounds coming from the main sanctuary.

SIMHAT TORAH

The festive mood of Sukkot climaxed on the eighth and last day, Simhat Torah (Rejoicing in the Torah), when the annual reading of the weekly portions from the Torah is concluded, and a new cycle is begun. The townspeople celebrated with eating, dancing, and even drinking. The batei midrash and the synagogue were filled with circles of dancers, holy Torah scrolls in their hands, their children — waving Simhat Torah flags topped with apples and burning candles — on their shoulders. Linked together in long human chains, the men danced in front of the Holy Ark, around the bimah, out the door, from one house of prayer to another, and around the shulhoyf well. The women watched from the gallery upstairs, singing along.

The shtetl rabbi was always the Hatan Torah (the bridegroom of the Torah), who is given the honor of being called up to the Torah for the reading of the final portion of the Five Books of Moses. There were a number of Hatanei Bereshit (bridegrooms of Genesis), because each minyan selected its own person to read the first portion of the new cycle. The Hatan Torah was called up to the Torah with a special melody and hymn. From the synagogue he walked at the front of a long procession, with a huppah (wedding canopy) over his head, and the town notables behind him, carrying lit havdalah candles. Next came the Genesis bridegrooms, who were followed by the entire shtetl population. A kiddush (reception) given by the Torah bridegroom ended the day's festivities.

When Eishyshok was still an agricultural shtetl, before Eishyshkians had their lands taken away by tzarist decree, the kiddush took place in the shulhoyf, with everyone seated on bales of hay. The rabbi's wife was given the title *Kalat Torah* (bride of the Torah) and the women performed a special dance in her honor. In Olkenik, Shlomo Farber remembered how they held this picnic-style reception on the banks of the river, a custom that continued until World War I. Though Eishyshkians abandoned it long before then, many of them continued to see themselves as farmers and landowners, albeit displaced ones.

On the Sabbath following Simhat Torah, the Genesis bridegrooms gave a kiddush, and this last celebration brought the holiday period of the month of Tishrei to a conclusion. Everyone went back to their daily lives: Merchants and traders set out on long journeys, students returned to school, women to their housework and businesses, artisans to their workshops.

The last preparations for winter were made. The holy days now gave way to secular ones. In many households this was the season when weddings and other marriage-related matters took top priority.

HANUKKAH: FESTIVAL OF LIGHTS

THESE LIGHTS ARE SACRED
TO US THROUGHOUT THE
EIGHT DAYS OF HANUKKAH.

Hanukkah service

This eight-day holiday commemorates the heroic struggle that the Jewish Maccabees waged against the Syrians, from 168 to 165 B.C.E., culminating in a miraculous victory and the rededication of the Second Temple. Known as the Festival of Lights, Hanukkah is a celebration of religious freedom, symbolized by the lighting of a new candle on each of its eight nights.

When Hanukkah arrived on the twenty-fifth of Kislev (November–December), it did not dramatically alter shtetl life. A postbiblical holiday, it did not have the same impact that many of the other Jewish holidays did. But it was a time of family togetherness that brought a spirit of fun and games into the dark, cold season. Many a Hanukkah night found Eishyshok blanketed in snow, the light of burning candles glittering through frost-covered windows.

On the first night, the heder boys were dismissed early for the kindling of the first of the Hanukkah lights at home. On that same night, a ceremony was held in the Old Beth Midrash to light the huge Hanukkah menorah — an eight-branched candelabra topped by a ninth candle, which was used to light the other eight, one by one, night by night, until on the eighth night all the candles were lit.

As part of the holiday celebrations, children were given Hanukkah gelt (money) — the amount dependent on how generous their parents and grandparents were (and of course how much they had to spare). Some were extravagant, some played Scrooge. Shael Sonenson used to give his children and grandchildren a golden coin, while Yankl Kabacznik gave just a few kopecks. Deep-fried latkes (potato pancakes) served with sugar and applesauce were one of the foods traditionally associated with Hanukkah, as were jelly doughnuts. The traditional Hanukkah game was played with a dreidl, a four-sided wooden top inscribed with Hebrew letters standing for "A great miracle took place there."

The long winter evenings were a perfect time for storytelling. Grandparents recounted episodes from their youth — their days in the yeshivah, their near escapes from terrible blizzards, their childhood adventures with their sisters and brothers, and so forth. Sitting before the tile fireplace, basking in its warmth, giggling at these tales from the past, the youngsters would marvel to think that once their grandmother and grandfather had been young, just like them.

These peaceful evenings were sometimes violently disrupted in the occasional years when the end of Hanukkah overlapped with Epiphany, a Christian holiday celebrated January 6. Locally the holiday was known as Swieto Trzech Kroli, the Festival of the Three Kings. Dressed as the Magi, Christian villagers would burst into Jewish homes, demand money or other valuables, or simply run riot through the house. Children would take cover under the table while the adults — usually women, because they were the ones likely to be fluent in Polish — would handle the situation. In the 1920s and 1930s these visitations became more frequent and more violent.

With the rise of Zionism beginning in the 1900s, Hanukkah took on new significance and the holiday began to be celebrated with new rituals. Zionist youth organizations held coed parties for young men and women at the shtetl firehouse. Since this was a time when the Jews were actively planning on reestablishing a homeland, the themes of religious freedom, of the military courage of the Maccabees during the era of the Second Temple, became very popular, and the story of Hanukkah was told in plays and poems, dance and song, with present-day halutzim (pioneers in Palestine) being portrayed as the direct descendants of the Maccabees. Another new custom was a torchlight parade for the schoolchildren. Introduced by Peretz Kaleko, one of the shtetl's most ardent Zionists, it was modeled after the huge torchlight procession in Tel Aviv in which schoolchildren marched to the home of the national poet, Hayyim Nahman Bialik. Bialik would greet the children at the door with the blessing his mother had used when she lit the Sabbath candles: "May the eyes of our children shine forever with wisdom and knowledge, like the candles you have lit tonight." After Kaleko left Eishyshok, the school principal, Moshe Yaakov Botwinik, continued the tradition.

TU BE-SHEVAT: NEW YEAR FOR TREES

MAN IS A TREE OF THE FIELD.
Deuteronomy 20:19

New Year for Trees is celebrated six weeks after Hanukkah, on the fifteenth of Shevat, which is the first day of spring in Palestine. There the almond trees are beginning to blossom, but in Eishyshok it was the very heart of winter. Nonetheless, the shtetl managed to believe in the reality of the Jewish calendar, not the reality before their eyes. Meir Wilkanski described a Tu Be-Shevat sometime in the 1880s, when a snowstorm was raging outside, and he and his heder friends, their mouths stuffed with dried fruits from the Land of Israel, celebrated springtime. For the moment, they were living in a different climate zone from the one outside the heder windows, a land of figs, dates, and carob, not that wintry landscape where large, swaddled creatures struggled against snow and ice and blustering winds. And miracles could happen: The shtetl pinkas recorded that one Tu Be-Shevat the trees blossomed in the garden of the Christian pharmacist!

During the years between the two world wars, the holiday was celebrated with new vigor. Zionism was at its height, and in Palestine itself the day had been given a new significance as Arbor Day. In honor of the renamed Arbor Day, Eishyshok joined with Jewish communities all over the world to collect money for the planting of trees in Eretz Israel. To heighten the mood, the school building was decorated with cotton balls representing the blossoming of the almond trees, and songs about trees blooming in Eretz Israel echoed throughout the shtetl. Thus the sensation of dwelling in two lands became stronger than ever.

PURIM: FEAST OF LOTS

TODAY IS PURIM, TOMORROW IT'S OUT,
GIVE ME A GROSHN AND THROW ME OUT.
Epilogue to a Purim-shpiel

Purim was observed on the fourteenth day of Adar (February–March), or of Adar-Beth (the thirteenth month of a leap year). Adar was a month of joy, celebrating the victory of the Jews over Haman, minister to King Ahasuerus of Persia. Haman had convinced the king to kill all the Jews in the 127 countries in his kingdom by casting lots, but he was foiled by the heroism of Esther, the Jewish girl King Ahasuerus had chosen as his queen. Together she and her uncle Mordekhai successfully plotted Haman's downfall, as recorded in the Megillah (Scroll) of Esther.

Celebrated with readings from Esther that were repeatedly interrupted by children wielding noisemakers whenever the name of Haman was mentioned, this was the most raucous of the Jewish festivals. For Purim is a time when frivolous behavior is permitted and even encouraged: "Man is obliged to drink much wine on Purim so that he becomes incapable of distinguish-

One of the Purim customs is dressing up as a historical or modern character. A group of girlfriends in the early 1930s dressed as Gypsies: (top row, left) Malka Matikanski; (center) Esther Katz; (front row, right) Golde Kabacznik. Malka made aliyah to Eretz Israel. Esther emigrated to Colombia. Golde and her family were murdered during the Holocaust. PHOTO: ALTE KATZ. YESC, MATIKANSKI

ing whether he is cursing Haman or blessing Mordekhai."[22]

Among the other customs associated with Purim are the sending of gifts of money and food.[23] During the evening reading of the Scroll of Esther in the synagogue, money was collected for a special fund for the clergy. And families of means sometimes sent their own gifts of money to individuals like the melamed, members of the clergy like the zogerke, and to the poor. In Eishyshok the custom of "sending portions" (shalahmones) took the form of sending special foods — at least two different kinds — on plates covered with white linen napkins. They went to one's friends, to various members of the clergy, and to needy families who had been selected by the kahal. It was also the custom for brides-to-be to send gifts of sacred books to their fiancés.

In the late afternoon a festive meal took place, honoring the memory of the banquet at which Esther trumped Haman. Special foods associated with the holiday included a huge hallah; hamantaschen (Haman's ears); a three-cornered pastry stuffed with poppyseeds that is supposed to recall Haman's hat; and kreplach, meat-stuffed dumplings that are also triangular in shape. Kreplach were eaten three times a year: on Yom Kippur, when people were "beaten" with the thirty-nine lashes, on Hoshana Rabbah, when the willow branches were beaten, and on Purim, when Haman was beaten. Shtetl jokers used to say there was a fourth occasion: when one beat one's wife. Whatever the association between kreplach and beatings, it has long since faded from memory.

During the course of the festive meal, the homes of the balebatim were visited by the Purim shpielers, a group of performers who put on short comic plays. Ostensibly about characters from the Scroll of Esther, these playlets often portrayed thinly disguised local notables. In Eishyshok this tradition had its roots in an organization dating at least to the nineteenth century, and made up mainly of tailors, shoemakers, and other young artisan apprentices, who went by the name of Marah Levanah, meaning "white bile." The purpose of the group

Zipporah Lubetski (seated at left) emigrated to Eretz Israel in the 1920s with two of her sisters. One Purim there the three of them dressed as local Arabs. YESC, TOKATLI

Yehiel Blacharowicz dressed for a Purim party as a Cossack. Yehiel was murdered during the September 1941 massacre. YESC, RADUNSKI

After a Purim performance in 1936, the Hebrew kindergarten children pose for a photo: (top row, right to left) Yudaleh Kabacznik; name unknown; Elisha Koppelman; kindergarten teacher Dora Feller; (third row, right to left) (first name unknown) Slepak, Yitzhak Sonenson, Yehudah Schneider, Hannah Shawitski, Reizele Erlich; (second row, right to left) Pola Berkowicz, Gittele Sonenson, Mordekhai Bichwid, Arieh Krisilov; (sitting in front) Yaakov Kahanov (right) and Hayyim Gershowitz. Dora Feller emigrated to Eretz Israel, Yitzhak Sonenson survived the war, Yaakov Kahanov was killed in a car accident in the United States. Gittele Sonenson died from TB while in hiding in a pit during the war. PHOTO: BEN ZION SZREJDER. YESC, SONENSON

was to overcome the "black bile" of melancholy that pervaded the shtetl during hard times; they took it upon themselves to bring laughter into people's homes. They were at their best on Purim. Money paid them for their Purim performances was donated to needy artisans, or it went to purchase sacred objects for the artisans' minyan. The custom of charitable donations was continued in the twentieth century, when other groups took over the Purim shpiel tradition from the Marah Levanah.

Eishyshok monitored its Purim celebrations more vigilantly than other towns did. For example, yeshivah students in other shtetlekh (including Volozhin) put on special public performances in the yeshivah, but in Eishyshok this was strictly forbidden. Instead, the students were allowed to tell miraculous stories recounting the doings of local saints, scholars, and other personalities, such as Reb Avraham Shmuel Rabinowitch predicting the future, or the Haffetz Hayyim exorcising a dybbuk, or Rebbetzin Hendl Hutner delivering a hearty slap to one of the shtetl balebatim (not a miracle, but quite remarkable nonetheless). The ban on performances at the yeshivah was part of a general ban on public performances; Purim shpielers were restricted to presenting their playlets in private homes. But even in Eishyshok the time-honored tradition of drag — men and women wearing each other's clothes — was permitted.

During the interwar years, the restrictions of earlier years were eased, and both the shtetl drama club and theater revue put on special Purim performances — much acclaimed throughout the region — as did the schoolchildren.

PESSAH (PASSOVER): FESTIVAL OF FREEDOM

LET MY PEOPLE GO.

Exodus 7:26

Passover, a seven-day holiday, is the Festival of Freedom, celebrating the exodus of the Jews from Pharoah's Egypt, when God delivered the Jews from slavery.* It begins on the fifteenth of Nisan (March–April).

*Except for Yom Kippur, the sacred biblical festivals are celebrated one day more in the Diaspora than they are in Israel. This custom was introduced during the period of the Second Temple, when the lack of a printed calendar and the inability to communicate in a timely fashion over distances made it impossible to inform the Jews in the Diaspora of the precise date of the forthcoming festivals. By celebrating the additional day, Jews in the Diaspora could be assured that, for at least part of the time, they were celebrating the holiday simultaneously with Jews in Israel.

Passover may commemorate freedom, but for the women of the shtetl it brought anything but free time. Since the strict laws governing hametz (leavened food) dictated that the home had to be cleansed of everything that contained any leavening agent, or that had been in contact with any leavening agent, a round of frantic housecleaning took place in the days and weeks before Passover. From attic to cellar, every crumb had to be searched out and discarded. Every piece of furniture was scrubbed and polished. All dishes, crockery, and cutlery had to be replaced with a special set used only for Passover. Clothing was aired on the fences outside. And even books were cleaned with feathers, in case crumbs had been dropped between their pages.

The first place to be cleaned was a quiet corner, as far away as possible from the usual family traffic, which could be set aside for the making of mead. Though in medieval times mead was an alcoholic drink, in Eishyshok it seems to have been a nonalcoholic Passover drink that was made by water being dripped over raisins and filtered through a very fine cheesecloth. The slow, steady sound of the drops falling into a special wide-mouthed bottle was a sort of perpetual background music, heard day and night throughout the household during this season.

Another of the demanding Passover rituals was the making of matzah, a flat, unleavened bread, symbolic of "the bread of affliction that our fathers ate" when they fled Egypt in such haste that they could not wait for their bread to rise. This ritual was observed with varying degrees of strictness, but the most rigorous required that one eat only matzah shemurah — matzah made from wheat that was under rabbinical supervision at the time of reaping. This

A Purim Bear, *a play performed by the Hebrew day school on Purim, March 5, 1939, at the firehouse: (right to left) Elisha Epstein (the bear), Hayya Shlanski, Sheinke Dwilanski, a Hebrew teacher, and another student. Hayya emigrated to America. All the others were murdered in the September 1941 massacre.* YESC, SONENSON

supervision was the obligation of the shtetl dayyan. During one of his wheat inspection trips, Reb Layzer Wilkanski took his son Meir along with him to the estate of a Polish squire that was managed by Hayyim Dovid Shapira. There Meir observed the wheat being harvested under Reb Layzer's watchful eye, and saw how his father examined the barn where it would be stored, looking to make sure that the barn was watertight, with no possibility of raindrops or any other source of moisture coming into contact with the wheat. Thus he assured himself that the wheat would not become "leavened" (water being the source of fermentation, and fermentation the source of yeast). Months later, during the winter, this specially supervised and protected wheat would be brought to the shtetl by coachmen known for their reliability. The arrival of the shemurah wheat had its own ceremony, with the shtetl dayyan and other notables gathering at the center of the bridge to greet the coaches as they crossed over the river, and the coachmen being invited into Reb Layzer's home for a festive meal prepared by his wife, Batia.[24]

Until the last days of the shtetl, only handmade matzah was permitted in Eishyshok; no machine-made version was allowed. The baking of the matzah took place in several carefully supervised locations, which in the early post–World War I years included the homes of Zivia the kindergarten teacher on Mill Street, Aaron the Saltman on the market square, and the "cats' house," a house on the shulhoyf shared by a number of orphaned brothers and sisters. The water for the baking had to be drawn from a well owned by a Christian named Anton on Hazerim Gessl (Pigs Lane) — for reasons long since lost to memory, though presumably they had something to do with the fact that this well and the rest of Anton's property had once belonged to the Kabacznik family, which meant it had formerly been in the hands of Jews for many generations. By Reb Layzer's time, however, he had to go to Anton for special permission to draw water from this well.[25]

The making of the matzah was an elaborate process, every step of which was carefully monitored by the rabbi and the dayyan. First the dough was rolled out in sheets, then perforated into sections, then baked in a padrat (a special matzah oven) for a prescribed period of time. The matzah rollers were women who wore spotless dresses and white kerchiefs daily, and cleaned the rolling pins every few minutes. The matzah perforators were yeshivah students who were equally meticulous, washing their hands and the perforating wheel at frequent intervals. One could buy the matzah, or rent a padrat oven in one of these supervised locations and bake one's own.

All the rest of the special Passover foods were prepared at home, with the same highly ritualized attention to detail. The chicken fat used at Passover had been stored since Hanukkah; the utensils that were used had been set aside exclusively for Passover; and every time one worked on the cooking, or had any other contact with the Passover food, one had first to wash one's hands and change into clean clothes. In a letter to Sarah Rubin, her future sister-in-law, in 1905, Sarah Wilkanski described her mother Batia's Passover preparations: "Mother already wears her Passover clothes several times a day. She changes into them each time she goes over to check the wine and the matzah. And this is how she spends the day, changing her clothing."

In addition to doing all the cleaning, cooking, and baking, the women of the house were busy supervising the tailors, seamstresses, shoemakers, and stitchers who were at work making the customary new clothes and new shoes for Passover. So there were fabrics to be bought, patterns chosen, and measurements taken — not just for Passover clothes, but for summer clothes as well. (Summer clothes had to be ordered in early spring if they were to be ready when summer arrived, because after Passover a forty-nine-day mourning period known as the omer was observed, during which many restrictions were placed on everyday activities — including the buying of new clothes.) By the fourteenth of Nisan, on the eve of the first day of Passover, when the family finally sat down to the first of the two Seders (Passover ceremonial suppers), every corner of the house sparkled, the table was beautifully set, and the air was filled with that special aroma that was a combination of Passover cooking and Passover cleaning.

Now the Seder — the meal commemorating the flight from Egypt — could begin. Besides the matzah, the other symbolic foods on the table included a roasted lamb shank, signifying the sacrificial offerings brought to the Temple in honor of this day of freedom; a boiled egg, thought by some to commemorate the destruction of the Temple, as well as the cycles of life and death, renewal and destruction; haroset, a mixture of chopped nuts, apples, spices, and wine, representing the mortar the Jews used to lay bricks when they were slaves in Egypt; scallions and new potatoes (or whatever spring vegetables were native to the region) to represent springtime, for Passover is a spring festival; saltwater in which to dip the scallions and potatoes, signifying tears the Jews shed; and maror, the bitter herbs recalling the bitterness of slavery. In Eishyshok the local Passover specialties included khremslakh, a kind of pancake, and boiled dumplings made from grated raw potatoes stuffed with gribenes (fried chicken fat and onions).

At the head of the table, of course, sat the father, the king of the house, who wore a white kittel and reclined on beautiful pillows, some of them family heirlooms. He would lead the family through the readings from the Haggadah that recounted the Passover story.

Late at night, after each family had recited the last phrase of the Haggadah, "Next year in Jerusalem," the full moon shone down on a market square filled with young couples and their children returning home from their parents' and grandparents' Seder tables, their long shadows following them across the cobblestones. Some of the youngsters were hoping to meet up with the Prophet Elijah, who was believed to be a special visitor at Passover and was perhaps still making the last of his holiday calls.

It was the custom for the entire family to be together for this most festive of all holidays. Yeshivah students returned home from their studies in other shtetlekh and cities, all business traveling was suspended, and everyone who possibly could join their families did. But in the twentieth century, with emigration affecting almost every household in the shtetl, more and more family members were absent from these festive meals. To overcome his loneliness at the Seder table, Dovid Matikanski used to set a place for each child who had emigrated, and put photographs of the absent children on the table, facing their empty seats. Later Dovid, his wife Nehama, and their children Haikl and Yitzhak, who were never able to get their emigration certificates, were killed in the Holocaust. To mourn them, their daughter Malka in Tel Aviv set *her* Seder table with an empty chair for each loved one she had lost.

THE FORTY-NINE DAYS OF COUNTING THE OMER

Between the end of the second day of Passover, when the first of the new barley crop was brought to the Temple, and the beginning of Shavuot seven weeks later, when the Jews commemorated the giving of the Law at Sinai, were the forty-nine days of counting the omer, a time of semi-mourning. Maimonides pointed out that the counting out of these forty-nine days leading up to the Shavuot festival suggests the way one awaits one's most intimate friend at a rendezvous — counting the days and even the hours.[26]

It is because of the many tragedies that have befallen the Jewish people at this time of year that the counting of the omer is observed in such a somber manner, even though it happens to coincide with the most glorious weeks of springtime. The plague that decimated the students of Rabbi Akiva in the second century, the Crusades of 1096, 1146, and 1192, and the massacres of Bogdan Chmielnicki in 1648–49 — all occurred during this forty-nine-day period. As part of the mourning rituals observed during the omer, weddings are not permitted, nor are playing music, getting a haircut, wearing new clothes, or dedicating a new house.[27] Indeed, there was little the shtetl people were allowed to enjoy — not even a swim in the river on a hot day.[28] On the thirty-third day of the counting, however, came a break: Lag ba-Omer, considered a scholar's holiday because it honored the triumph of Rabbi Akiva and his students over the Roman legions. On this day heder students and their melamed went on an outing to the forest; during the interwar years, the outing turned into a picnic for all the schoolchildren.

SHAVUOT: FEAST OF WEEKS

YOU SHALL COUNT SEVEN WEEKS, FROM THE DAY WHEN THE SICKLE IS FIRST PUT TO THE STANDING GRAIN.

Deuteronomy 16:9

When Shavuot arrived on the forty-ninth day of the omer, the entire shtetl, especially the young people, breathed a sigh of relief. The anniversary of the covenant between God and Israel on Mount Sinai, it is also a late spring–early summer agricultural festival, and thus the shtetl was suddenly a very joyful place. In honor of Shavuot the windows of houses that faced the street were decorated with paper cutouts known as reyzele (roses),[29] and the interiors of the houses were decorated with fresh flowers, greenery, and herbs. The interiors of the synagogue and the batei midrash were garlanded so lavishly with freshly cut lilac and pine that the houses of prayer looked and smelled like greenhouses. Since this time of the Jewish year coincided with a Catholic blessing of the plants, great care was taken to cut all branches and flowers only from Jewish gardens, thus ensuring that nothing that entered a Jewish place of worship had been sprinkled with holy water.

Food and dress were also festive at this season. All the children were decked out in their new summer clothes for the first time, adding their own touches of brightness and color to the burgeoning spring. Since it is the custom to eat dairy food on Shavuot, Eishyshkians prepared cheese and honey cakes, cheese blintzes that were served

Sarah Wilkanski with her sister Esther's children Leora and Eli, who are bringing first fruits and newborn animals to a celebration of Shavuot in the Technion in Haifa, Eretz Israel, 1933(?). PHOTO: ORIENT PRESS PHOTO COMPANY, Z. KLUGER. YESC, WILKANSKI

with sour cream, and a long hallah filled with raisins, almonds, and cheese.

The men and boys spent the first of the two nights of Shavuot in the batei midrash, sitting and learning until dawn. According to tradition, the heavens split open for a fraction of a second at midnight on that night, as the covenant between God and the people of Israel is renewed. Eagerly awaited by the children, this is thought to be the moment when personal requests could be granted. Not surprisingly, the Eishyshok treasury of folklore contained many a tale of these requests and their manner of fulfillment. One oft-told tale concerned a pious but ignorant Jew named Shmuel Kolton, whose name signified his odd hairdo, which fell in a tangle of what were known as "elflocks." It was said that he acquired this hairdo one Shavuot midnight, when the skies opened and he asked God for *kol-tuv* (Hebrew for "all the best"), but mispronounced it as *kolton* (Yiddish for "elflocks"). Unfortunately, he got what he asked for, not the blessing he wanted. Parents and heder teachers used to tell the story of Shmuel Kolton as a cautionary tale about the trouble poor diction can cause.[30]

During the interwar years, the shtetl schools' celebration of Shavuot began to follow the new patterns established in Palestine, where the agricultural aspects of the holiday were stressed. Readings and discussions focused on Shavuot as the day when the first fruits of the spring harvest were brought to the Temple in Jerusalem.

The spirit of Shavuot set the tone for the weeks to follow, a time when the Jewish calendar merged with the season, the shtetl and nature were in accord, and people enjoyed the gifts of summer's abundance. Now was the time to take outings in the forest, go berrying and mushroom picking, swim in the river. This season of joy lasted until the seventeenth day of Tammuz (June–July), which ushered in another period of mourning, this one lasting three weeks.

TISHAH BE-AV AND THE THREE WEEKS BETWEEN THE STRAITS

IF I FORGET THEE, O JERUSALEM, LET MY RIGHT HAND FORGET HER CUNNING. LET MY TONGUE CLEAVE TO THE ROOF OF MY MOUTH.

Psalms 137:5–6

Once more, nature and the Jewish calendar diverged, as the glorious days of mid-summer were shadowed by mourning. Once more, the shtetl was engulfed in gloom.

The fast observed on the seventeenth day of Tammuz marks the breaking down of the wall of Jerusalem during the First Temple, 586 B.C.E., and the cessation of Temple worship during the siege of Titus in 70 C.E. Within the shtetl, sad tunes issued from the houses of prayer; visiting maggidim preached their most fiery, apocalyptic sermons; heder boys studied the accounts of the destruction of Jerusalem, and chafed against the ban on swimming.

During the last nine days of the three weeks, beginning with the first of Av, the spirit of mourning and grief deepened, with many formal mourning practices being observed (except on the Sabbath), including abstention from meat, and the forgoing of bathing, shaving, and haircutting. The mourning came to a climax on Tishah be-Av (the Ninth of Av), when people fasted, wore footcoverings of cloth rather than leather, and, in some cases, put ashes on their foreheads. The Holy Ark was stripped bare, its beautiful parokhet removed. In shul that evening the entire Book of Lamentations was recited, as were dirges from other sources, while the entire congregation sat on the floor, holding candles against the darkness. The following day, everyone adjourned to the cemetery after morning prayers, to visit the shtetl dead and watch the heder boys put on a special performance.

Though Tishah be-Av continued to be observed as a national day of mourning for the destruction of the Temples until the shtetl itself was destroyed, this three-week period of mourning did undergo changes in the 1920s and '30s. The prevailing mood remained sad, but not nearly so overwhelmingly so as it had once been, for there was more emphasis on positive activity. Zionist groups in the shtetl used the time to discuss their plans for rebuilding the Land of Israel and preventing future wars of destruction against the Jews. The major days of mourning they observed were the twentieth of Tammuz, which was the anniversary of the death of Theodor Herzl (on July 3, 1904), and the twenty-first of Tammuz, the anniversary of the death of National Awakening poet Hayyim Nahman Bialik (on July 4, 1934); much of the commemorative observance on these two days consisted of reading and discussing the two men's work. With the new emphasis on what could be done in the future, rather than what had happened in the past, the schoolboys' cemetery performances were also abandoned, probably sometime after World War I.

"COMFORT, O COMFORT MY PEOPLE"

Shabbat Nahamu, the first Sabbath after Tishah be-Av, ushered in seven Sabbaths devoted to prophecies of comfort, beginning with these words from Isaiah 40:1: "Comfort, o comfort my people."

Now nature and the Jewish calendar converged again, with the joy of summer days in harmony with the words pronounced in shul. All that had been forbidden in the season of mourning was now allowed. The shtetl barbers did big business, with the men eager to get their hair cut and their beards trimmed. The males of the shtetl, children and adults alike, rushed to the river to bathe and swim.

Women also rushed to the river — not to swim, but to do laundry, for they had a lot of catching up to do after the nine days when washing clothes was not permitted. A typical sight during this season was women and their maids carrying large wicker baskets filled with wet laundry, topped with large square cubes of homemade laundry soap and a blue whitener. The trip to the river was in fact only the conclusion of what was sometimes a three-day process, when items that had already been washed at home — boiled in a huge tin tub and scrubbed on a washboard — were checked for stains, and beaten with a piece of wood called a franik. Then the laundry was rinsed and spread out on the fresh meadows to dry.

And so another annual cycle drew to a close. These were joyous days, filled with walks in the forest, swimming and boating on the lakes and rivers, trips to dachas and, during the interwar years, to the summer resorts at Dumbla and Titiance.

Then a nip in the air and the turning of the leaves would put everyone on notice of the imminent departure of the glorious days of summer. Soon the harvest would begin, the digging of potatoes, the final gathering of summer vegetables from shtetl gardens. And soon the sounding of the shofar on Rosh Hodesh Elul would once again call the shtetl back to sacred time.

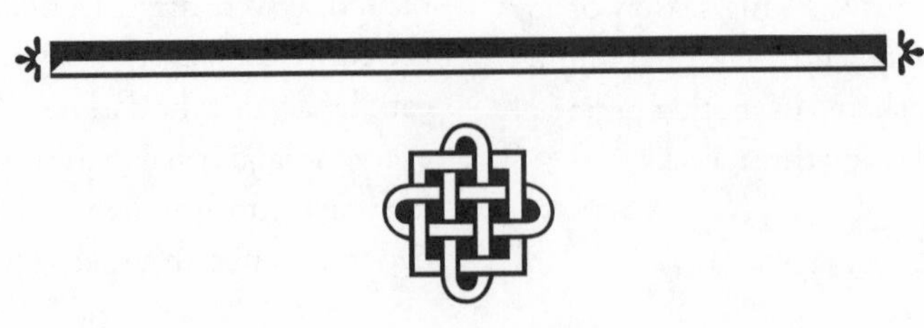

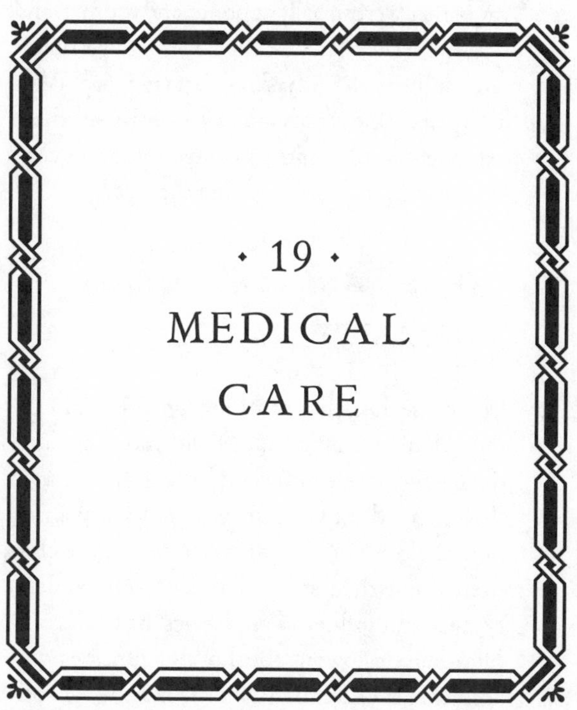

I HAVE HEARD THY PRAYER, I HAVE SEEN THY TEARS; BEHOLD, I WILL HEAL THEE.

Second Kings 20:5

HISTORIANS SPEAK OF THE "MIRACLE OF JEWISH DEMOGRAPHY" IN THE NINETEENTH century, the tremendous population explosion among the Jews of Europe. Population had been growing steadily since the mid-seventeenth century, but then began increasing exponentially in the early 1800s, and kept on doing so throughout the nineteenth century.

In the aftermath of the devastating Chmielnicki massacres of 1648–49, only about 1 million Jews were left in the entire world, about equally divided between Ashkenazim and Sephardim. By the end of the eighteenth century, they numbered 2.5 million, according to one estimate.[1] Their numbers jumped to 3.5 million by 1825, of whom about 2.75 million, more than 80 percent, lived in Europe, mainly Eastern Europe.[2] By 1850, there were about 4.35 million. And at the beginning of the 1880s there were nearly 7 million Jews in Europe, out of a total world Jewish population of 7.5 million. In 1914 there were 13.5 million Jews in the world, which represented an increase of 180 percent since 1850, or 16 per 1,000 annually. While the overall population of Europe was also growing rapidly at this time, the Jewish rate was much greater. From 1850 to 1900, for example, the population of Europe, North America, and Oceania is estimated to have grown by 11 per 1,000 annually (and the total population of the world by 6 or 7 per 1,000).

Fertility rates did not account for this Jewish population boom, for no significant difference between the number of births in Jewish and in non-Jewish families existed. In fact, toward the end of the nineteenth century, the relative fertility rate among Jews was lower. But infant as well as adult mortality decreased significantly among the Jews at this time. Thus the "miracle of Jewish demography" was attributable to falling death rates, not rising birthrates.

Part of the decrease in Jewish mortality can be accounted for by the same factors that were lengthening the lives of Europeans in general: better medical treatment for the sick, and improved sanitary conditions resulting from new ways of dealing with sewage, garbage, and the water supply. But part of it had to do with factors specific to Jewish culture. The greater stability of the Jewish family, the Jews' small number of illegitimate children, their low rate of alcoholism, their many community organizations that helped care for the sick, and their tradition of charity among both individuals and the community at large, even when it required major economic sacrifices — were important factors in Jewish longevity.[3]

In the matrilocal Jewish family, women held the central position in a multigenerational household. They made most of the important decisions about family life in Jewish households, and that included the care of the sick. Women and girls did most of the caretaking, too, if only because they were usually at home, and the men and boys were away (first at the heder and yeshivah, later at the beth midrash and synagogue). With a large battalion of females to summon, these extended-family units were able to devote considerable resources to nursing the sick.

Mordekhai Munesh Kaleko, father of the talented Kaleko children. He wrote about life in Eishyshok and the vicinity in the closing decades of the nineteenth century, including a detailed description of the death of his beloved first wife and infant firstborn son following childbirth. PHOTO: BOSTON (DURING HIS SHORT STAY IN AMERICA). YESC, KALEKO-ALUFI

INFANT AND MATERNAL MORTALITY

Of course, no amount of loving care could totally eliminate infant and child mortality, and during the nineteenth century and the first two decades of the twentieth virtually every shtetl household suffered the loss of one or more children. Some died at birth, others from cholera, typhus, and influenza epidemics, or from complications following the normal illnesses and accidents of childhood. But the number of children who survived greatly outnumbered those who died.

Maternal mortality was also a major problem. Until World War I, all the women in Eishyshok, as in most shtetlekh, gave birth at home. There they availed themselves of the services of midwives, Jewish, Christian, and Tatar, who were aided by the other women in the household and by women from the Ezrat Yoledet society. The expectant father and other males of the household did their share by reciting psalms.[4] Though many of the midwives earned stellar reputations, indeed some became legendary for their expertise, until the twentieth century childbirth remained the biggest killer among women of childbearing age. For this reason the New Cemetery contained row upon row of women who had died from complications of childbirth. Having given their lives while trying to bring the next generation into this world, they were honored as martyrs and buried in a section of their own.[5]

Mordekhai Munesh Kaleko left behind a detailed description of the perils of childbirth in the 1890s. When his first wife, Frieda, was nearing term with their first child, he took her to be examined by Dr. Bernitsky, the shtetl's Christian physician, and his wife, who was a midwife. Both were pleased with her condition, and a few days later Frieda gave birth to a son. Mordekhai Munesh was ecstatic. Soon he was planning not just the circumcision and the Pidyon ha-Ben, but the bar mitzvah, going so far as to calculate what the weekly portion would be when his son reached the age of thirteen. Mother and child did well until the fifth day, when Frieda developed a 102-degree fever and became very flushed. The doctor came to see her and gave her a prescription, but her fever kept climbing and her color grew ever more reddish. When the doctor suggested that a specialist be brought in from Vilna, a highly unusual step, Mordekhai Munesh took the coach to Bastun, and the train to Vilna, where the doctor demanded 150 rubles plus travel expenses and hotel accommodations. Though the price was steep, there was no cost the young husband would not pay to save the life of his beloved Frieda. Alas, when they finally reached her bedside, the specialist from Vilna said that it was already too late. After exchanging angry words with Dr. Bernitsky and the midwife, the specialist left the room and went home. His words to the anxious father left him with little hope. Mordekhai Munesh wrote later:

I understood that the situation was bad. I asked what would happen. He said that the next twenty-four hours would be critical. He gave me two prescriptions and said God should have mercy on her. Twenty-four hours passed and the situation worsened. In the interim, the baby also developed a high fever and died. He did not want to be an orphan. Prior to his departure the doctor told me that her suffering would last a few days. She swelled up terribly, and passed away a few days later. And I remained alone, a living corpse.[6]

It was only after seven years of mourning, during which the young widower spent many hours at the grave of his wife, that he decided to resume his life, at the age of twenty-three. When matchmakers suggested Mina Schneider, the eighteen-year-old daughter of Malke Roche's the shopkeeper, he agreed.

In the care of the sick all avenues were explored, including folk medicine, magic spells, the power of prayer, the merit of Torah study; the services of medicine men and women (both the babske feldshers, who practiced folk medicine, and the Haskalah-influenced feldshers, who were trained in more modern methods) and the shtetl doctor; visits to the local hospital, to the medical facilities and personnel in Vilna, and even — for those who had the financial resources — to those in Berlin, Vienna, and other world capitals of medicine.

The wealthy had access to the best medicine Europe could offer; the poor were provided for by the community. Everyone was covered, one way or another, and it was a given that the care of the sick would always be a top priority. If called to a sickbed, any medical practitioner, no matter what kind, was expected to be there within minutes, regardless of the time of day or night or of the weather conditions. Once when Rochel Kiuchefski was alone in her home she became very sick. When she finally managed to make it to her door to call for help, the only person on the street was one of the local meshuggoim, Hirshele Rohe Sheftle's from Olkenik. She asked him to go to the doctor's, which he dutifully did, but once there was unable to remember either her name or address. "New Street, New Mill, a stoop with three steps," he told the doctor — a riddle the doctor took seriously and, being intimately familiar with all the streets and homes of the shtetl, was able to decipher. Minutes later he was at Rochel Kiuchefski's bedside.

FOLK MEDICINE

As in other shtetlekh, folk medicine in all its many manifestations thrived for centuries in Eishyshok, and would continue to coexist with conventional medicine right up until the end. Some practitioners of the art cured with "words alone"— magic spells — while others supplemented them with concoctions of herbs and other elements. Each ailment had its corresponding magic spells. Reflecting Jewish mystical traditions as well as Christian and Muslim sources, they were recited in various languages, including Hebrew, Yiddish, Russian, and several local dialects, especially Tataric, since the Muslim Tatars were considered the best of all the folk practitioners. Here, for example, is a magic spell against toothaches, which was recited in Hebrew and was to be repeated three times:

Once as Job was walking on the road, he met the Angel of Death.

Said the Angel to Job: "Why are you so engrossed in pain?"

Job replied: "Because of my aching teeth."

And the Angel said to him: "As the desert has no seashore, so the teeth of the son/daughter of So-and-so will ache no more and will be mighty as the Hebrew letter Shin. In the name of the bone, Amen Sellah."

Another magic spell, also for toothaches, was in Russian mixed with other dialects, and it was addressed to the three tzars: the tzar of the high skies, the tzar of the fertile lands, and the tzar of the distant seas. It could only be recited at night, when the moon was shining. There were magic spells for snakebite, headache, and stomach cramps, one for the evil eye, and a blanket spell to cover all discomforts.

Worms were a common affliction in the region, and a number of spells were dedicated to the problem. The following one was in Yiddish, and it rhymed.

I stand on a rock alone
And make the worms swear, I alone.
I make them swear with ten Menorahs,
I make them swear with ten holy Torahs.

Two of the many magic spells used in the vicinity of Eishyshok. On the right is a general magic spell in Hebrew and Yiddish to mother superior and her one hundred and fifty angels. On the left is a magic spell in Yiddish against worms. YESC, SH. FARBER

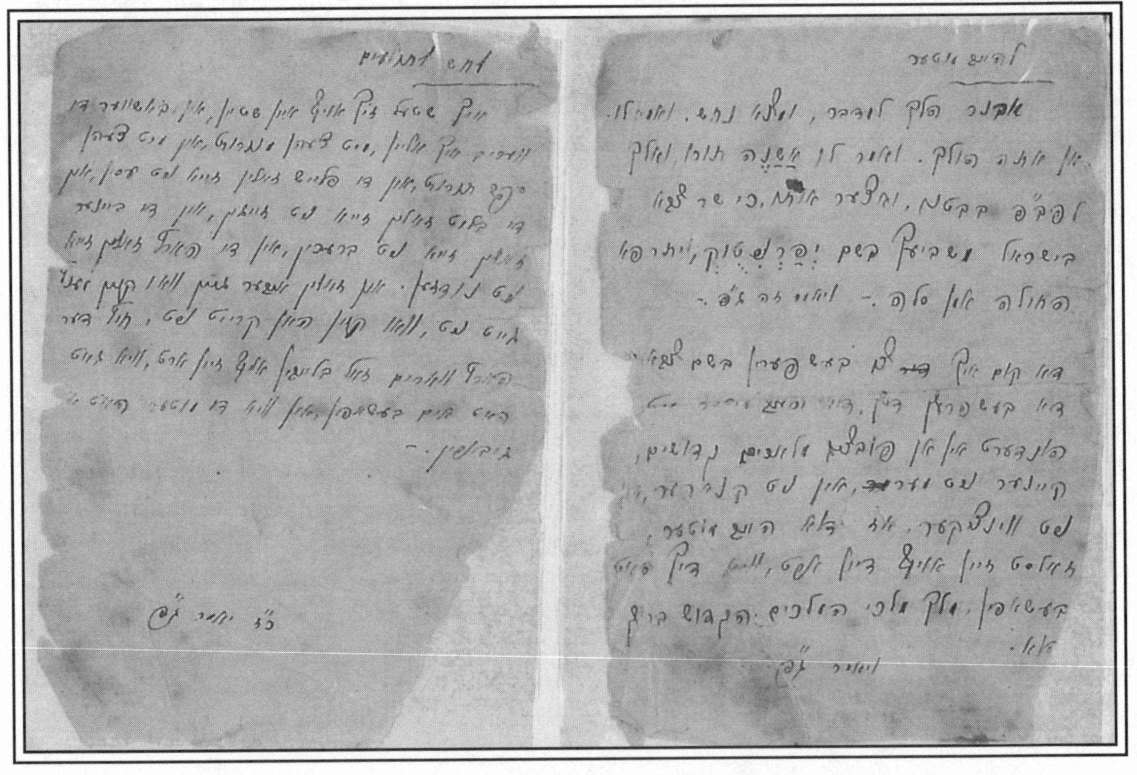

They should not eat my flesh to the bone,
And should not suck my blood till I'm prone.
My bones they should not break and abuse,
My heart they should not enter and use.
They should leave for a place where men
do not go,
Should depart for a land where roosters do
not crow.
The worm should stay where God in his
scheme created him
And where his mother in the earth gave birth
to him.[7]

One of the local magic-spell experts was Berl Vasilishki, who treated horses as well as people, and did an excellent business on market day, when the peasants came to town. There was also Hinde, who lived with her husband Yossel the shoemaker in a small wooden house on Mill Street, its windows decorated with an assortment of exotic feathers. She was known for talking to the animals, especially to her cow, with whom she engaged in dialogues that provided the shtetl youth with an abundance of material for mockery. Though she was expert in many kinds of spells, her specialties were toothaches and skin "roses." To assist her in her magic, she used cats whose tails were tied with red ribbons and roosters whose tailfeathers had been painted in bright colors. She was especially popular with Christian peasants, and was therefore very busy on market day. Though her spells were said to work magic, their powers failed in the face of a hail of bullets from the Einsatzgruppen; Hinde and Yossel met their deaths along with the rest of their fellow Eishyshkians in September 1941.

Berl Vasilishki, one of the local magic spell experts, October 17, 1926. He treated both people and horses. PHOTO: ALTE KATZ. YIVO INSTITUTE FOR JEWISH RESEARCH, 42904,21341

Another common practice in folk medicine was a ritual similar to a Rorschach test, which was used when a person was suddenly afflicted with fear, moodiness, restlessness, or depression. Lead would be melted in a frying pan and held over the head of the afflicted person until the lead solidified. Then the medicine man or woman asked the person to look at the shape of the lead and say what it looked like; the answer was a clue both to the source of the trouble and to the cure.

This ritual was almost put into action one summer day. Four-year-old Yaffa Sonenson had gone off to pick berries in the pine forest near her family's summer home in Titiance, and returned in a state of great excitement, telling a most peculiar story. It seemed she had met a man leading a camel along a forest path, and from the camel hung two huge shoe polish boxes, one on either side. The man allowed Yaffa to pet the camel, and even feed him berries. When Yaffa told her mother about this strange adventure, she feared that her little girl had eaten a poisonous mushroom or been stung by a dangerous insect, and was hallucinating as a result. Upon the advice of others, she called a medicine woman and the ritual of the molten lead was begun. However, just as Yaffa was about to be called upon to identify the images in the lead, the man and his camel, complete with shoe polish boxes swinging from the camel's sides, appeared in the vacation colony. Man and camel were from a traveling circus, and had been hired to advertise shoe polish.

The acknowledged experts in the use of spells as well as herbs were the Tatars, and when an illness was so serious that it could not be cured by the exorcism of a dybbuk or the use of conventional medicine, the Tatars were called upon for help. Though some Jews objected to the use of sorcery and magic in time of illness — either physical or mental — there seemed to be no firm halakhic grounds for their objection. When the issue was raised in the fifteenth century, Rabbi Israel Isserlin addressed it in his responsa, asserting: "We do not find any outright statement prohibiting the use of sorcery for the relief of sickness."[8]

Within the shtetl itself there were always a number of Jewish medicine men and women who did not use magic spells, but rather herbs and other folk remedies, good for man as well as beast. Shiyeh der Roiphe (the doctor) was a particular favorite, an expert with the cupping glasses, popular among both Jews and non-Jews. Assisted by his daughter Feige di Schneiderke (the seamstress), Shiyeh received patients in the small apartment he rented in a house on Mill Street. He also made house calls in the shtetl and in the surrounding villages.

Nehemia "der Feldsher" Virshubski, the shtetl's beloved medicine man, admired by adults and children alike, and daughter Sonia, who accompanied him on most of his house calls. Sonia Saposnikow later became a prominent pharmacist in Vilna. His favorite medical treatments were cupping (bankes) and enemas. At the end of World War I, he was shot by a Russian soldier. Sonia and her family disappeared during the Holocaust, most probably killed in Ponar, Vilna. PHOTO: YITZHAK URI KATZ. YESC, M. KAGANOWICZ

Around 1930 Shiyeh was succeeded by Bureh der Roiphe, who was especially popular with Jewish coachmen and Christian peasants since he was very effective at curing horses. Bureh der Roiphe's secret ingredient seems to have resided in the two stones, one black and one blue, he always carried with him, and from which he ground a powder that was his most frequently used concoction. He was also an expert in the use of leeches. Every Friday he could be found dispensing his services at the public bath, along with Alter Korelanski der Sherer (the barber) and the Tatar folk medicine specialists. At least one of Bureh's remedies was still in use some sixty years later: Former Eishyshkian Batia Lubetski Barkali averred that his technique of placing raw potato slices on a feverish brow, and replacing them with fresh slices as they warmed up, would lower a temperature almost immediately. She also swore by another of his fever remedies — a clay compress placed on the forehead — but said it was difficult to find the right kind of clay in Israel. When Bureh died in 1935, the mourners at his funeral included many Christians, who attended with their horses.

Shiyeh and Bureh belonged to a class of medicine men known in the shtetl as *babske feldshers* (practitioners of folk medicine). From the mid-1850s they were joined by a new kind of feldsher, followers of the Haskalah who believed that modernizing the medical practices within the shtetl was a crucial aspect of bringing Jewish life into conformity with the contemporary world. Though these modern feldshers did not attend medical school, they did study medical books and manuals, learn the basics of pharmacology, and visit hospitals where they could observe doctors at their work.

Nehemia der Feldsher was the epitome of this modern version of the medicine man. He was born in 1847 in the vicinity of Mir to a locally prominent family. His father, Reb Asher Amshel Suchowitski, had wanted all his sons to become rabbis and his daughters to marry rabbis. But Nehemia followed in the footsteps of his older brother Benyamin, born in 1838, who had so disappointed their father by becoming a feldsher that Reb Asher Amshel sat shivah for him; in other words, as far as he was concerned, his son was dead.[9] Another son, who went by the name Astramski, also became a feldsher.

Nehemia, who changed his last name to Virshubski so that he could avoid army service by claiming to be an only son, married Feige Dragootski of Eishyshok and settled there sometime during the 1870s.[10] Eventually their home on Vilna Street would become a cultural center for the shtetl intellectuals, and their children would form close friendships with the Wilkanski and the Kaleko children, for all the followers of the Haskalah tended to stick together.[11]

Nehemia's enlightened views extended to the way he charged for his services, which he modeled after the health insurance system his brother Benyamin used. Any household that wished to subscribe to it paid 1 ruble per year, which covered all its consultations with the feldsher, not including the cost of medications, cuppings, and enemas. Families that didn't subscribe paid for each visit, and poor families were paid for by the community.

Prescribing over-the-counter medications available in the local drugstores, Nehemia tended to favor quinine, castor oil, and enemas for any and all ailments. But perhaps it was his bedside manner — his good-natured smile and soothing voice — that made him the fine healer he was reputed to be. Always available to anyone who summoned him, at any hour of day or night and regardless of weather, he radiated kindness and optimism. Upon entering the room of a sick child, he used to say, "Little one, do not be afraid. I am here to bring you a cure and take away your sickness" — an approach that made him a special favorite with mothers. The presence of his daughter, Sonia, who frequently accompanied him on his house calls, clad in a white lace dress, was also reassuring. (She later became a pharmacist with her own pharmacy in Vilna.)

During the final days of World War I, Nehemia der Feldsher was shot by a Russian soldier while attending a patient. He died from his wounds a few months later, on Armistice Day, November 11, 1918. The Hebrew inscription on his tombstone in the New Cemetery, which read as an acrostic of his name, focused on his medical accomplishments:

Here is buried our honored father Nehemia
Son of Reb Asher Amshel.
He passed away on the 7th day of Kislev, 5679.
He saved many souls from death.
With his knowledge of pharmacology
He found a remedy for all of the suffering sick.
His honest ways and good deeds
All found favor with the Almighty in the heavens above.
May his soul be bound in the bonds of everlasting life.

PROFESSIONAL DOCTORS

When conventional medicine arrived in Eishyshok shortly after Nehemia in the 1880s, folk medicine continued to thrive right alongside it, and did so until the shtetl's final days. But the shtetl welcomed this new development, which began when the tzarist government built a hospital on the site of the Polish cemetery where the heroes of the 1863 rebellion were buried. In the years that followed, two doctors settled in Eishyshok, first a Jew, then a Polish Catholic.

It was the exception rather than the rule for a

small shtetl to have a doctor, much less two, during the nineteenth century. Even Volozhin, with its world-renowned yeshivah, made do without a doctor, until the death of a student and a subsequent school strike prompted the town to hire one.[12] Those doctors who did settle in shtetlekh rather than in one of the larger towns often came because they had experienced difficulties or disappointments of one kind or another.[13] Dr. Ezra, the Jewish doctor who came to Eishyshok in the early 1880s, was typical in this respect, having had his medical license revoked by the tzarist authorities because of an illegal abortion he had performed. Ironically, he was saved from exile to Siberia thanks to another abortion he had performed, this one on a beautiful Russian socialite. Out of gratitude she saw to it that her lover, who was a lawyer, defended Ezra at his trial, which he did with at least partial success.[14] After the trial, Dr. Ezra chose to settle in Eishyshok, since he had relatives there, among them the shtetl's beloved midwife, Shifra.

As one of the earliest proponents of the Haskalah in the shtetl, Dr. Ezra became a sort of living symbol of its modern ways. The clothes he wore, the fact that he sent his son to a Russian school in Vilna, his practice of bathing and swimming together with his wife, rather than at sex-segregated beaches — all these and many other departures from tradition acted as irritants to some of the balebatim. Yet he also had many admirers, particularly among the yeshivah students and the youth of the shtetl, and he became a frequent visitor to the Wilkanski household, where he made a vivid impression on the children of Reb Layzer and Batia. As for his medical practice, there was nothing radical about it; in fact, because he had had his medical license revoked and was therefore forbidden to perform surgery (his true calling) or prescribe anything but over-the-counter remedies, there was very little to differentiate him from Nehemia der Feldsher. Both prescribed quinine, gave enemas, and used cupping glasses. As Nehemia was assisted by his daughter, Dr. Ezra was assisted by his tall, silent wife.[15]

The second doctor to arrive in the shtetl was Dr. Bernitsky, a Catholic, who came sometime in the 1890s and resided in the home of the Polish pharmacist, along with his wife, who was a trained midwife. He introduced Eishyshok to the bicycle, and to an organized circle of Polish Catholic anti-Semites. With a government permit in hand, he used to raid the Jewish pharmacies in the hope of finding illegal prescriptions penned by Dr. Ezra. But since Dr. Bernitsky had no aversion to Jewish money, the occasional discreet bribe usually settled everything. Jews did not trust him, and whenever possible avoided his ministrations.

Dr. Adasse, an obstetrician (standing, left) and his nurse F. Sapocrynski (seated, right) were in Eishyshok for a short period. With them on March 3, 1924, were Hayyim-Leibl Glombocki (standing, right) and Uri Rozowski, the rabbi's son. Hayyim-Leibl emigrated to Argentina, Uri to Eretz Israel. PHOTO: YITZHAK URI KATZ. YESC, GLOMBOCKI

CHANGES IN MEDICAL CARE BETWEEN THE WARS

By the interwar years, Eishyshok had four doctors, including two gentiles, both of whom numbered many Jews in their practice. Dr. Religion had been a highly decorated and high-ranking officer in the tzarist army who after completing his military service came back to his native Eishyshok, where his mother, the widow of the Polish pharmacist, was still living. He left in 1935, much to the regret of the many shtetl women who had great trust in him.

Dr. Zytoner, an assimilated Jew from Warsaw, was the shtetl veterinarian in the 1920s and '30s. He lived with the Moszczenik family on Mill Street. Sitting in the Moszczenik dining room are (right to left) Atara Kudlanski, her brother Bill, Dr. Zytoner, Atara and Bill's mother Hanneh-Beile (née Moszczenik), her sister Liebke, and her daughter Connie. Hanneh-Beile and her three children emigrated to America. Liebke was killed by the AK. PHOTO: REPHAEL LEJBOWICZ. YESC, A. ZIMMERMAN

Dr. Lehr came to Eishyshok with the German army, and decided to stay after the war ended. He built his infirmary on a lot directly across the street from the hospital, which Lubetski the blacksmith sold to him. Perhaps the fact that the Polish government erected a huge cross in honor of the heroes of the 1863 uprising directly in front of the smithy had something to do with Lubetski's decision to sell the lot. Polish anti-Semites constantly taunted Lubetski, who had become blind in one eye, that his loss of eyesight was due to his refusal to look at the cross, rather than to a spark that had flown into his eye one day as he was hammering on a blazing horseshoe. Dr. Lehr himself was not above the occasional anti-Semitic gesture, as when he showed up for the hostile demonstration that local Christians staged as a sort of counterpoint to the celebrations in honor of the Schneider family's departure for Palestine in 1924. Nonetheless, he won the trust of many Jews in the shtetl, particularly mothers and young women, who had faith in both his diagnostic skills and his ability to keep a confidence.

Dr. Benski was one of the two Jewish doctors who came to the shtetl in the interwar years. (The other was a veterinarian.) He was very well liked, and along with a Jewish feldsher named Gurewitch he worked long, hard hours during the 1939–41 refugee influx to try to keep up with the medical needs of some 15,000 people fleeing the Nazis. During their years in the shtetl, Benski and Gurewitch used a health insurance policy similar to that of Nehemia der Feldsher. And as in Nehemia's time, poor families' medical bills were paid for by the kehilah.

Other medical personnel in the shtetl included Gurewitch's wife, who was a midwife; two female dentists, one married to Mr. Wien, the shtetl lawyer, the other, Fania, to the widowed Leib Tafshunski, who later became a dental technician and assisted his wife; and Dr. Zytoner, the veterinarian. Dr. Zytoner was an assimilated Jew from Warsaw, who was the first Jew in the shtetl to eat nonkosher meat in public and to violate the Sabbath. When Dr. Zytoner left the shtetl, the Polish Dr. Shemitkowski took his place

PHARMACIES

Prescriptions were filled in one of four drugstores in the shtetl. The Polish one was owned by Dr. Religion's mother, who hired an outspoken anti-Semite named Sharavei to work there after her husband died. (Sharavei and the local priest kept company with Dr. Lehr in the anti-Semitic demonstration that marred the Schneider family's departure celebrations.) The three Jewish drugstores were owned by Nahum Koppelman, Uri Katz, and Yitzhak Uri Katz, whose widow, Alte, managed the drugstore after his death.

In the interwar years, only the Polish drugstore was licensed to fill prescriptions, which caused much tension and even some fear in the shtetl. For example, when the teenage son of Yitzhak Uri and Alte Katz suffered an infection in his leg after a skiing accident in 1929, the Katzes had to go to the Polish drugstore to get the necessary medicine, which their own drugstore could not stock. When young Hayyim died a few days later, it was rumored that Sharavei had mixed poison into his prescription. Nonetheless, Jews continued to go to Sharavei, who was known as a tight-lipped man who could be trusted with secrets. He was the one they went to for birth control and other intimate products. Alternately, some patronized the Vilna pharmacy owned by Sonia Saposnikow, daughter of Nehemia der Feldsher, or the drugstore in Ivenitz owned by Nehemia's son Anshel. With all this competition, the Jewish drugstores within Eishyshok did what they could to hold on to their customers, outmaneuvering the law whenever possible by continuing to fill prescriptions.

Besides the over-the-counter and prescription medications sold in drugstores, many folk remedies continued to maintain their popularity. In addition to the cupping glasses and leeches, which had a multitude of applications, there were ice compresses for lowering temperature; urine compresses for use with animals; raw garlic to lower blood pressure; goosefat to prevent frostbite; blueberries to relieve diarrhea; stale bread or cobwebs (especially those found in barns) for boils; sugar cubes soaked in turpentine to cure worms, and many, many more. Some concoctions were family secrets, passed down from generation to generation, and sometimes sold in local stores, as Malke Roche's did with hers. Some of these are still being used to this day, in the various parts of the world where former Eishyshkians have settled: Seventy-odd years later, Hayya Sorele Lubetski's daughter Batia, for example, still swore by her mother's cure for hepatitis: a drink made of ground-up raspberry vines, dandelions, and carrots, followed by a drink of a fresh camomile infusion. Hayya Sorele also prescribed camomile baths for yeast infections, and infusions of camomile for colds.

BIG-CITY RESOURCES

The shtetl's elaborate health-care network could be supplemented, when necessary, by the medical facilities of the Jewish community in a nearby big city, which in Eishyshok's case usually meant Vilna. Acting as an umbrella organization to coordinate all public Jewish medical services, the Medical Council of Vilna could refer people to a sanatorium for tubercular children; a clinic for the care of children with joint diseases; a foundling home; the Zweriniecz Women's and Children's Hospital; the Mishmeires Holim Hospital and Clinic, which filled over four hundred prescriptions a day; the Jewish General City Hospital, and many other sources of help.[16]

With the inauguration of the bus line between Eishyshok and Vilna in 1929, more and more Eishyshkians chose to take advantage of the medical facilities in Vilna. They were motivated by a desire not just for the best in medical care but for privacy; it was impossible to keep a secret in the shtetl. Since illness in an unmarried girl, no matter how minor, could ruin her chances for a good marriage, and damage her siblings' prospects as well, privacy was a paramount goal for many people. Moshe Sonenson used to joke that he never met a sick single girl in the shtetl, or a healthy married woman!

When Batia Bastunski fell ill in 1936, her father Eliyahu wrote to her brother Zusl in California: "Imagine what kind of a time we are going through. All this being done in secret, for she is, after all, a young girl, and we do not want anyone to know about it — not even our daughters-in-law." Two months later Eliyahu Bastunski wrote to his son once more about Batia: "If only it would be possible for me, I would send her to Berlin or to Vienna." And what was this shameful illness that had befallen a young, single woman? The big secret turned out to be that Batia had had to have her tonsils removed.

To the regret of the Hertz Mendl Hutner family, the fact that their eleven-and-a-half-year-old daughter, Shoshana, had rheumatic fever was common knowledge. So their choice to go to Vilna for medical care was dictated not by the desire for privacy — it was too late for that — but the feeling that she needed more than what the shtetl facilities could provide. Kreindl Hutner left her five other children at home and traveled by coach to Vilna with her sick daughter. Once there, they found no bed was available in the Mishmeires Holim Hospital, but an elderly woman patient took pity on the feverish girl and shared her bed with her. A kindly German physician took an interest in Shoshana, and, after prescribing medicine, diet, and a daily routine free of physical labor, he reassured her mother: "With proper care, this young girl can live to be a mother and grandmother." She recovered, but had a relapse some five years later while on an outing with the Beitar Zionist group. Rushed back to Eishyshok by the Beitar commander, she was taken to Dr. Lehr, who ordered that she be sent to the hospital in Vilna immediately. The Vilna bus, driven by Yankele Krisilov, was about to depart for Radun, but instead detoured to the Hutner home, picked up Shoshana, and rushed her to the Mishmeires Holim Hospital. There she hovered for several days between life and death, after which she recovered slowly, and eventually proved the German doctor right. Shoshana lived long enough to become not just a mother and a grandmother, but a great-grandmother.

Jewish public health facilities in Vilna were

overcrowded with local patients, and therefore were reluctant to accept patients from the shtetlekh, especially those whose bills were paid by the community, for such payments were slow in coming, as the ongoing correspondence between the Zweriniecz Women's and Children's Hospital and the municipality of Eishyshok makes clear. On September 23, 1929, Eishyshok promised to pay all medical expenses incurred by Moshe-Reuven Michalowski on behalf of his daughter. But by January 29, 1930, the municipality of Eishyshok had still not paid the 96 zlotys for Hayya Michalowski's twelve-day stay in the hospital, which led to a threatening letter from a Dr. Kowarski, who said that if the bill were not paid within a few days he would take legal action and the municipality would end up having to pay much more.

Another dispute between the municipality of Eishyshok and the Zweriniecz Hospital focused on a 182-zloty bill for Eli, the child of Hersh Matikanski. Although the Matikanskis were not from Eishyshok, but from a village nearby, the municipality took responsibility for all the Jews in the vicinity, including the yishuvniks. This time Dr. Kowarski wrote in even more dire terms: "Due to the financial difficulties of the hospital, we can no longer extend any credit." All bills were eventually paid by the shtetl.[17]

People of means preferred private health clinics, and were willing to travel far to avail themselves of the best medical care. For example, Elisha Koppelman traveled to Carlsbad and Königsberg to be treated for tuberculosis; Szeina Blacharowicz's father went to Dr. Soloveichik's clinic in Warsaw; Yitzhak Dubitski went to Berlin to have a tumor removed.

The Bastunski letters were filled with medical reports about people in the shtetl, often accom-

Elisha Koppelman (standing second from left) at a private clinic in Carlsbad, where he was treated for tuberculosis. It did not save his life. YESC, N. FRISCHER

panied by a commentary on the cost of their treatment, or the lengths to which they had gone in search of help. There was "Yankele, who had three operations at a very high cost." "Altke Chashinkes is, alas, dying; she has already been to Italy." "Shael Sonenson passed away. He was ill for two years. He certainly was a very wealthy person, but he spent it all on his illness." And, referring to his own wife, Eliyahu writes, "Mother went to Vilna; her foot is, thank God, better, but she wants to go to a doctor."

After World War I, many women chose to give birth in hospitals rather than at home — either the local hospital in Eishyshok or, depending on their financial abilities, one of the public or private hospitals and clinics in Vilna. They felt that the hospital was a much safer place, for both themselves and their babies, and the drastically reduced maternal and infant mortality rates proved them right. During the interwar years only two women from Eishyshok died in childbirth, both of whom gave birth at home.

Many of those who went to Vilna to give birth were seeking status as well as safety: They preferred that on their child's birth certificate the place of birth should be "Vilna," the big city, rather than "Ejszyszki," the small shtetl that was the very archetype of obscurity. In general it was considered more prestigious to be from a city than from a shtetl. Expectant mothers of means would leave for Vilna a few weeks prior to their due date and stay with relatives or at a hotel, to be sure of giving birth in the clinic of their choice.

Despite the fact that medical care improved so greatly during this era, the size of the shtetl family was on the decline in the aftermath of World War I, both in Eishyshok in particular and in Poland in general. During the nineteenth century, the average shtetl family numbered between ten and twelve living children, and lost one or two children to death (a number that did not include mortality rates during epidemics). During the interwar years, as people began marrying at later and later ages and also began using birth control, families were smaller and smaller, as a look at the statistics for Eishyshok makes

Dr. Leon Gordon makes a house call. On the back of the photo is written in English "Sitting in my Packard, 1938 model." In the late 1930s Dr. Gordon moved to Vilna. He was a doctor in the ghetto. His fate in unknown. YESC, R. ROSENBLATT

The Jewish medical student fraternity at Vilna University, April 22, 1934. They were excluded from the Polish student fraternity. Seated second from left (marked by white arrow), is Jasza Saposnikow, son of Sonia and grandson of Nehemia der Feldsher. Seated fifth from left (marked by white arrow) is Leon Gordon, also a relative of Nehemia. Both disappeared during the Holocaust. YESC, R. ROSENBLATT

clear. In 1941, the number of children per family of childbearing age was as follows:

27 couples	*had*	*1 child*
53	*had*	*2 children*
45	*had*	3
15	*had*	4
4	*had*	7
2	*had*	8
2	*had*	9[18]

The increasing professionalization of medicine, the medicalization of childbirth, and the trend toward smaller families — all were representative of Eishyshok's march into modernity during the interwar years. In sickness as in health, there was no aspect of shtetl life left untouched by change, no twentieth-century innovation with which the shtetl was not at least familiar.[19]

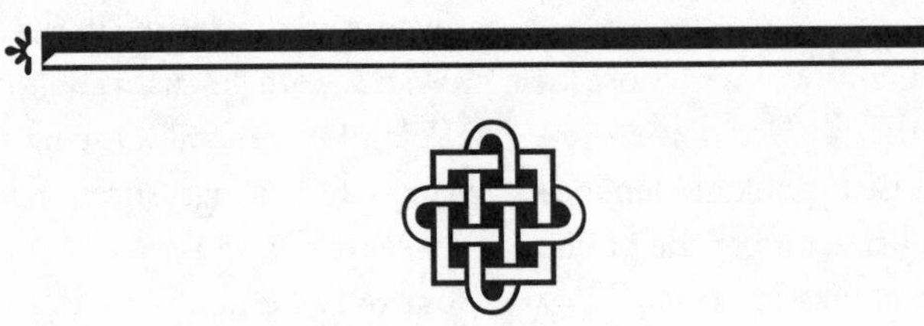

· FIVE ·
MODERN TIMES

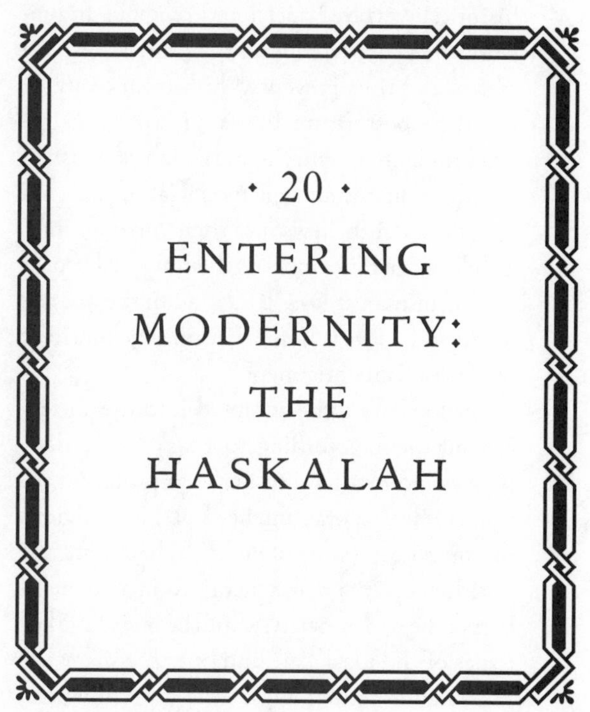

• 20 • ENTERING MODERNITY: THE HASKALAH

AWAKEN, MY PEOPLE!
HOW LONG WILL YOU SLEEP?
THE NIGHT HAS PASSED,
THE SUN SHINES THROUGH.

Judah Leib Gordon

AS INSULAR AND CUT OFF AS THEY WERE IN MANY RESPECTS, THE JEWS OF EASTERN Europe always eventually experienced and responded to the aftershock of major events in the rest of Europe. Both culturally and politically they felt the impact of turning points in European history. Thus the eighteenth-century European Enlightenment, with its emphasis on the universality of man and the rule of reason, had its Jewish equivalent in the Haskalah. Initially this movement met with fierce resistance from many if not most sectors of Jewish shtetl society, both because of its antitraditionalism and because many of its proponents, especially in Western Europe, believed in integrating the Jews into the surrounding society, even to the point of assimilation. But over the course of the nineteenth century, the Haskalah was eventually taken up — and transformed — by many of the best and brightest students, scholars, and teachers of Eastern Europe.

The Spring of Nations, the flowering of the spirit of nationalism in the 1840s that culminated in the consolidation of nation-states from Italy to Germany to the Balkans, found its Jewish equivalent in Zionism, resulting in waves of mass emigration to Eretz Israel (the Land of Israel), as the Jews called Palestine. And it too would eventually culminate in the consolidation of a nation-state, though not until 1948, when the Land of Israel became the State of Israel, and the dream of a spiritual, cultural, and national homeland for the Jews became a reality.

Some who did not believe that the problem of the Jews in Europe would be solved by the assimilationist tendencies of the Haskalah, and who did not wish to solve it by leaving their homes, for the Land of Israel or anywhere else (including the Americas), found an answer in socialism or Communism. Radical movements for the total overhaul of society, they would presumably result in freedom and justice for all. At the end of the nineteenth century, Jews founded their own socialist workers' movement, the Bund, and also joined — and in many places led — the revolutionary movements of their countrymen.

And so the Jews of Eastern Europe, who seemed to many people, including highly critical members of their own community, to be living in a benighted state of backwardness that had changed little over hundreds of years, gradually made their way into the twentieth century.

THE BERLIN HASKALAH

The Jewish Enlightenment, the Haskalah, was an offshoot of its European counterpart, with similar ideas about the brotherhood of man, similar ideals and aspirations for the ultimate triumph of reason. Like the European Enlightenment, it placed the individual at the center of the universe and aimed to liberate him from the historically evolved social and religious frameworks that interfered with the exercise of pure reason and thus prevented him from realizing his truest, best nature. In the spirit of the European Enlightenment, the Haskalah established as its most important goal the social and cultural integration of the Jews into their surroundings, as full-fledged members of the universal brotherhood of man at last. "Be a man in the outside world and a Jew at home" became the motto of the Jewish Enlightenment.

But for Jews to be accepted into the society around them, according to Haskalah leaders, they would first have to undergo profound social, cultural, moral, intellectual, and religious reform. The question of how to "rehabilitate" the Jewish people, to make them productive members of the wider society, would be one of the key issues of the Haskalah, and one that made the Haskalah a natural ally of the government in countries where the Jews had resolutely remained a people apart.

The German philosopher Moses Mendelssohn (1729–1786) was the father of the Haskalah movement. His acceptance of the separation of church and state as a basic principle of Enlightenment thought was a turning point for the Haskalah, for it meant the undermining of traditional Jewish authority within the community, since that authority was based on religious law. His book *Jerusalem* (1783) proclaimed that while the state had the right to exert coercion, religious issues should be resolved only by persuasion. By opposing the Jewish community's use of the weapon of herem (excommunication), an extreme and very powerful form of social coercion, Mendelssohn in effect wanted to render its legal jurisdiction over its members meaningless.

Mendelssohn's disciples Naphtali Herz Wessely (Weisel), David Friedländer, and Naphtali Herz Homberg were eager to implement the ideas of the Enlightenment, specifically through the reform of Jewish society, which would be accomplished via education. Thus Naphtali Herz Wessely responded enthusiastically to the 1782 Edict of Toleration issued by Austrian Emperor Joseph II, which extended many of the rights of the Jews but also endeavored to integrate them more fully into society by (among other measures) encouraging and even in some circumstances requiring their attendance at public schools, while discouraging the use of Hebrew and Yiddish in official documents.[1] Wessely's 1782 essay "Divrei Shalom ve-Emet" (Words of Peace and Truth) was a proposal to reform Jewish education by introducing secular subject matter into the curriculum. These new secular studies, he said, should be at least as important as the Bible, the Talmud, and the vast literature of ethical writings and religious legislation that were the traditional fundamentals of Jewish learning. "And thus, the children of Israel will also be men who accomplish worthy things, assisting the King's country by their actions, labor and wisdom."[2] The manifesto of the youthful Haskalah movement, this essay had both its strengths and its weaknesses: enthusiasm for the lofty universal ideals of the Enlightenment, but also denigration of Jewish culture as backward and primitive, a tendency toward self-deprecation before the representatives of secular power.

Several years before, at the initiative of Moses Mendelssohn, the first model Jewish school, Hinukh Nearim (Education of Boys), which anticipated and no doubt shaped Wessely's ideas, had been founded in Berlin in 1778. Mendelssohn and David Friedländer (1750–1834) coauthored a special textbook for the school. The focus was to be on secular studies, rather than the Bible and the Talmud. Reflecting the Berlin maskilim's intense dislike of Yiddish, which they regarded as a vulgar language that separated the Jews from the surrounding society and even stigmatized them, the language of instruction was German (and some French). "The Judeo-German way of speaking" (meaning Yiddish) had to be pushed out and eliminated in favor of German, so that the Jew would be integrated into the local population, as Friedländer wrote in an article that appeared as a special supplement to *Ha-Meassef* (The Collector), the leading organ of the Haskalah movement.[3] As for the Talmud, Friedländer regarded it as a "mystical book," the biggest stumbling block in the way of achieving a healthy, rational education. This hostility toward the Talmud came to be a major theme among those whose goal was to integrate the Jews into the surrounding society. Russian government officials and Jewish maskilim alike would try to undermine the traditional emphasis on Talmud studies.

Under the impact of the Haskalah, the Jewish schools in Western Europe changed rapidly. Even the Orthodox Jewish communities of Germany began to introduce secular studies into their schools. But as it traveled east, to the conservative, tradition-bound communities of Poland, Lithuania, and Russia, which had very little desire for closer contact with the non-Jewish world around them, the Haskalah would meet with considerably greater resistance.

THE GALICIAN HASKALAH

The Berlin Haskalah made its way eastward into Galicia, a region of the Hapsburg empire encompassing part of southeast Poland and the western Ukraine. There, because it fit in so well with the government's effort to integrate the Jews into the life of the nation, to persuade them to identify their own well-being with that of the state, the Haskalah would find considerable government support. Thus in the late 1780s the Hapsburgs appointed Mendelssohn disciple Naphtali Herz Homberg (1749–1841) to the post of chief superintendent of the newly established network of German-language Jewish schools. In 1788 Homberg directed a written proposal to the rabbinate that Jewish education be adapted to European culture, which was the overriding goal of his efforts as chief superintendent.

Homberg wrote special textbooks for the Jewish schools and advocated the teaching not just of German but of Hebrew. Learning to speak and write Hebrew as a living language was one of the innovations of the Haskalah, especially in Central and Eastern Europe, where it was seen as a greatly desired alternative to Yiddish as a common language for the Jews. Hebrew, after all, was not just the classical language of Judaism and the written language of its educated elite, it had enormous prestige in the non-Jewish world as well, since it was the language of the Bible.

In accordance with the new emphasis on practical subjects (for example, agriculture) that the maskilim felt would "redeem the moral character of the Jews" and contribute to their economic well-being, Homberg also commended the study of handicrafts, and he called for government censorship of Jewish books. In 1812 he published a German-language catechism, *Benei Zion* (Children of Zion), which established behavioral guidelines for young Jews. It was made a compulsory textbook in all Jewish schools within the Hapsburg dominion, and all young couples applying for secular marriage licenses were required to pass an examination in it. Most Jews of Galicia, however, resisted the law and were married in religious ceremonies without benefit of government license.

Both Homberg's schools and his publications were heartily disliked by most of his Jewish contemporaries, who saw them as vehicles for cultural assimilation at a time when that was not a popular goal. Homberg himself incurred the nearly universal hatred of the Jewish community, perhaps in part because of a personality so unpleasant that it would earn him a reputation as a "seducer and misleader."[4] Nonetheless, Galicia did become the cradle of innovative Jewish education in Eastern Europe, with schools under Jewish auspices adopting many of the features of those that were government-run.

In 1813 Joseph Perl (1773–1839), a leading figure in the Galician Haskalah, a Hasid turned maskil, opened the first of these modern Jewish schools. Beth Hinukh, located in Tarnopol, in eastern Galicia, was a coed school offering a mix of Jewish and secular studies that was perfectly in keeping with the spirit of the moderate wing of the Haskalah. A model for other schools throughout Galicia and Russia, Beth Hinukh was supported and directed by Perl until he died.[5]

THE RUSSIAN HASKALAH

Traveling further east, the Haskalah entered the Russian empire along Galicia's southern border and East Prussia's eastern border. In 1820 a school "according to the method of Mendelssohn" opened in Uman, the Ukraine. In 1826 maskilim in Odessa opened a school under the direction of a former teacher at the Perl school in Tarnopol; in 1835 the school started a section for girls. In 1838 another such school was founded in Kishinev, and more of these German-language, secular-influenced Haskalah schools would spring up throughout Russia during the 1820s and 1830s. (It would be several decades before the Russification efforts of the government would result in replacing German, the principal language of the Haskalah and the language of civilized discourse according to the bias of the time, with Russian.)

The Haskalah's principal Russian advocate was Isaac Baer Levinsohn (1788–1860), who had been influenced by Moses Mendelssohn; indeed, he became known as the "Russian Mendelssohn," the father of the Russian Haskalah. Levinsohn also came under the influence of prominent maskilim in Galicia, where he studied and taught school from 1813 to 1820, and the ideas he brought back with him would have a profound impact on Russian Jewish education.

In 1823 Levinsohn wrote *Teudah be-Israel* (Testimony in Israel), but because pious printers refused to print it, it was not published until 1828, when it came out in Vilna. Advocating major changes in Jewish education, the book quoted Talmudic and medieval sources to back up its arguments for studying Hebrew language and grammar, secular sciences, and handicrafts and agriculture. At the same time, *Teudah* severely criticized traditional heder education, with its Talmud-centered curriculum, its reliance on corporal punishment, its use of Yiddish, and the lack of any methodological training for its teachers. Despite its harsh criticisms of Jewish culture and the vehement opposition it aroused among the Hasidim, whose practices bore much of the brunt of his criticism, the book had an impact on many Russian Jews, among them yeshivah students who formed Russian and Hebrew study clubs to carry out its proposals.

Levinsohn's second major book, *Beth Yehudah* (The House of Judah), published in Vilna in 1839, outlined a five-point program for the reform of Russian Jewry. It not only became the official program of the Russian Haskalah during the reign of Tzar Nicholas I (1825–55), but because the maskilim in Russia developed such close ties with the government, and many of them were sympathetic to the government's goal of integrating the Jews into society, "Russifying" them, the book also influenced government policy toward the Jews. It called for the establishment of secular elementary schools for boys and girls of the lower classes, and recommended the teaching of a trade or craft. For gifted students, who alone should be encouraged to continue their academic education, central colleges should be established in the large urban centers of Jewish population — Warsaw, Vilna, Odessa, Berdichev — where Talmud and Codes as well as the sciences and various languages would be taught.[6]

Though the majority of Russian Jewry, Hasidic and non-Hasidic alike, opposed Levinsohn's recommendations for reforming heder and yeshivah education, the Russian government enthusiastically adopted them, seeing them as a vehicle not just for secularizing but indeed for Christianizing the Jews. And this was a result greatly to be desired, for anything that strengthened Christianity enhanced the authority of the state, since state and church were united in the person of the tzar, who was the figurative head of the Russian Orthodox church. The ultimate goal of the tzarist government with respect to the school system was succinctly expressed in a letter to Tzar Alexander from Count Speransky, a prominent member of the Russian nobility: "Christian teachings should be the basis not only of social order but even more so of education."

In line with this policy of emphasizing Christian piety, the Russian Ministry for Public Education merged with the Office of Public Worship, which resulted in an increase of general hostility directed against the Jews, and even stiffer resistance to public education among the Jews. Very few Jews opted to attend Russian schools.[7] Among other signs that the Russification of the Jewish people was not progressing well, this became a matter of concern to the authorities. In the words of an unsigned memorandum that may have been penned by P. D. Kisilev, Minister for State Domains under Tzar Nicholas I: "The Jews are still in a state of vagrancy and harmful to the well-being of the country."[8] The memo was aimed specifically at the religious teachings of the Jews (especially the Talmud), which the author believed were having a harmful impact on Russia and should be investigated. Special government-supervised schools for Jews were recommended as a corrective.

The government looked to the maskilim for help in organizing these schools. Count Sergius Uvarov, Minister of Public Education, had made a trip in the late 1830s to Germany, where he met with German maskilim for discussions about how to educate the Jews of Russia. In 1838, with the approval of Count Uvarov, the maskilim of Riga opened a school similar to the Hinukh Nearim of Berlin, under the directorship of Dr. Max Lilienthal, a young doctor of philosophy from Munich whose letters of recommendation included one from the king of Bavaria. The school soon received such glowing reports that Uvarov summoned Lilienthal from Riga and gave him the task of working out a systematic plan for the organization of Russian government-sponsored two- and four-year Jewish schools, and of inviting Jewish educators in Germany to come teach in the new schools.

In 1841, the year the government established a committee for the radical reorganization of Jewish life in Russia, principally through education reforms, Uvarov sent Lilienthal to many of the major cities to soften the Jewish community's opposition to the proposed schools. His reception, however, was mixed at best. In Vilna, the first city on Lilienthal's tour, the Jewish representatives clearly enunciated their fears: "We are sorry to state that we put no trust in the measures proposed by the ministerial council, and we look with gloomy foreboding to the future." In Minsk, too, he encountered strong opposition. In Berdichev and Odessa, however, he was warmly greeted, for the Society of Friends of the Enlightenment had made strong inroads in those cities.

To try to make the government schools more attractive to Jews, it was agreed that secular subjects — among them Russian language, history, and geography — could be taught by Jews as well as Christians. And the two theological seminaries the government was going to open, in Vilna and Zhitomir, would give their graduates privileges equal to those received by graduates of other government institutions. As hospitable to Jewish interests as these schools may have seemed, in true tzarist fashion their real agenda was made clear in a secret memorandum accompanying the legislation that established them: "The purpose of educating the Jews is to bring about their merger with Christian nationalities, and uproot those superstitions and harmful prejudices which are instilled in the teachings of the Talmud."

In 1843 the government called a meeting with the most prominent Russian rabbis, hoping to weaken their opposition, but to no avail. The rabbis, like the people they represented, understood that secular education would only encourage the Jews to abandon their own traditions, while offering them little improvement in their civil rights.

Religious and community opposition notwithstanding, the government imposed a special tax on Sabbath and holiday candles to finance the schools, and in 1844 the first of them were established, under the supervision of Max Lilienthal. While the maskilim acclaimed them, and praised Tzar Nicholas I in verse and prose, much as Naphtali Herz Wessely and his colleagues had praised Emperor Joseph II for his Edict of Tolerance, the majority of the Jews continued to view the schools as yet another of the "evil decrees" imposed by the Russian government, on a par with military service.

For the maskilim, the role they played in setting up these schools, thereby winning favor with the government of Nicholas I, was a turning point. Supported by the government, their voices were now heard. Henceforth the Haskalah would be a more visible and more powerful force in Russian Jewish life.

In 1845, however, one of its most important leaders, Max Lilienthal, departed quite abruptly for the United States, amid rumors that the Russian government had tried to get him to embrace the Russian Orthodox faith. In an article he wrote three years later, Lilienthal confirmed those rumors, saying: "Only when the Jews will bow to the Greek cross, will the Tzar be satisfied . . ."[9]

Lilienthal's replacement, A. L. Mandelshtan, with the assistance of a crew of maskilim composed Hebrew textbooks and translated the Bible, the Mishnah, and the works of Maimonides into German, the language of the Haskalah. Another of the maskilim who played an active role in the Russian pedagogical enterprise in the nineteenth century was Hayyim Zelig Slonimski, a native of Bialystok and, until he was expelled for his Haskalah opinions, a student at the Eishyshok yeshivah. Slonimski (1810–1904) was appointed Hebrew censor for South Russia, and government inspector of the rabbinical seminary in Zhitomir. In 1862 he would found *Ha-Zefirah* (The Dawn), a Hebrew-language newspaper devoted mainly to articles on popular science, which would become one of the most important of the Haskalah publications.

After the abortive but alarming Polish uprising of 1863, which seemed to validate the views of those who believed in taking a firm stand against minority groups within the empire, the Russian government intensified its Russification program in the government-supported Jewish schools of Poland and Lithuania, replacing German with Russian as the language of instruction, and reducing or altogether eliminating Jewish subject matter in the curriculum. Among a relatively small segment of the total Jewish population, these schools began to make headway, as the 2,045 Jewish students in Russian secondary schools in 1870 increased to 8,000 by 1880. Practical incentives for attendance were instituted, including a reduction in compulsory army service for graduates of Russian schools, and better employment opportunities.[10] By 1873, schools that would prepare Jewish students for entry into the general Russian schools had been opened, attracting parents who welcomed the economic advantages the Russian schools seemed to offer their children.

Another incentive for departing from tradition was the availability of education for girls. In response to the opening of exclusive schools for the daughters of the rich, known as "pensions," more affordably priced courses in the Russian language became available, some sponsored by the Russian government, some by Haskalah societies. Many of the teachers for these girls, both those at the pensions and those for the Russian government classes, were graduates of what would be, by 1886, the only Russian pedagogical seminary still in existence — the one in Vilna. As part of the more aggressively integrationist program of the Russian government from the mid-1860s on, the Vilna school had evolved from a rabbinical seminary, which graduated (though did not ordain) rabbis who never found much acceptance within the community, into an accomplished teachers' training institution, which produced teachers who were of such high quality that after some initial resistance they were ultimately welcomed.[11] Though the graduates were products of assimilation, with little knowledge of Jewish subject matter, some of them would nonetheless go on to become leaders of the new Jewish national education movement during the years between the two world wars in Russia, Poland, and Lithuania.

Despite the modest inroads the government seemed to be making with the "problem" of the Jews, and of Jewish education in particular, by the 1870s anti-Jewish sentiment was again on the rise in Russia, and incentives to attract Jewish students were being abandoned. Many maskilim now began reevaluating their optimistic ideas about assimilation. A variety of Jewish educational institutions and societies would reflect this change.

Hevrat Mefizei Haskalah (Society for the Promotion of Culture), for example, had been founded in St. Petersburg in 1863 by Baron Horace Guenzberg and a group of wealthy Jews dedicated to an assimilationist agenda. In line with their original ideals, they published Russian- and Hebrew-language textbooks for use in government-run Jewish schools. By 1874, however, their orientation had shifted to supporting Jewish education under Jewish auspices, private as well as public. They recognized the need to overcome the shortage of qualified, government-certified teachers for those schools, and therefore sponsored pedagogical training courses in Grodno that prepared Jewish teachers for the government-supervised exams in education. Graduates of those courses were among the best and brightest of their generation, excellent teachers whose impact on education would be significant. The society also published an education journal, *Vestnik* (The Announcer), which, like the courses, would eventually have an enormous impact on the Jewish national education movement not just in Lithuania and the other Baltic states, but in Palestine and the United States.

As part of this trend toward Jewish self-reliance, both institutional and economic, Jews who might once have cast their lot with the Russian government were actively pursuing other forms of education as well, such as vocational training. In 1880 the Society for the Development of Jewish Agriculture and Crafts was established in St. Petersburg, with Baron Guenzberg as one of its backers. ORT, as it was and still is known, after the initials of its Russian name (Obshchestvo Rasprostraneniya Truda Serdei Yevreyev), gave Jews their first opportunity to learn trades outside the system of family apprenticeships. By offering high-quality training to a much larger pool of workers, it played a significant role in improving Jewish employment opportunities, first in Russia, later worldwide.

Baron Guenzberg's organizations were practical responses to the new skepticism among some of the Jews who had formerly looked to integration, even assimilation, into Russia as an answer to poverty. A literary response can be found in the poetry of Judah Leib Gordon (also known as YALAG; 1831–1892), the foremost Russian Hebrew poet of the Haskalah. After Alexander II's emancipation of the Russian serfs in 1861, in the full flush of the enthusiasm he felt at witnessing what he thought was the dawn of a new era for all oppressed groups, Gordon wrote his poem "Hakiza Ami" (Awaken, My People). It would become the motto for a generation of maskilim anticipating their own emancipation:

Awaken, my people! How long will you sleep?
The night has passed, the sun shines through.
Be a man in the streets and a Jew in your home
A brother to your countryman and a slave
to your king.[12]

Less than a decade later, with young maskilim showing increasing indifference to Jewish values, unawareness of their heritage, and ignorance of Hebrew (the very language in which he wrote), at a time when there certainly was no evidence to suggest that these changes had resulted in any improvement in the lot of the Jews, Gordon published his most famous poem, "Lemi Ani Amel" (For Whom Do I Toil?):

My brothers, the Enlightenment brought us
knowledge,
But loosened our bonds to our people's tongue,
teaching
"Abandon the language whose hour has passed. . . .
Leave her for the language of the land."

For whom do I toil? To what avail?
Oh, who can foresee the future, who can say,
Am I the last of Zion's poets,
And you the last readers?[13]

As the earlier poem expressed the tenor of its time, so this one expressed changes that resonated with an increasingly large audience over the following decade. For a generation of Hebraists, who as children had to learn this poem by heart, it would become their manifesto.

EISHYSHOK MEETS THE ENLIGHTENMENT: THE WILKANSKI ERA

Like shtetlekh throughout Eastern Europe, Eishyshok was compelled to respond to or be swept away by the historical and intellectual currents of the late nineteenth century. Although it was more resistant to change than some others, it did change, and the changes were instigated by those at the very core of the community: its students and scholars, both native and visiting, and some of the younger, more forward-looking balebatim. Perhaps no group would play a larger role in this process than the children of the Wilkanski family, the sons and daughters of its esteemed dayyan Reb Layzer. Urged on by his much younger wife, Batia, who was determined that the generation gap pitting children against parents in so many other families would not divide theirs, Reb Layzer ultimately allowed his children a remarkable degree of intellectual freedom — though the decision to do so was a difficult one, at times very painful.

It wasn't until the late 1860s that the first Haskalah ideas seem to have begun to filter into Eishyshok, and then only very slowly. The literature and ideas of the Haskalah arrived via the Vilna and Lida coaches, in the books and journals yeshivah students hid between the pages of the Talmud. It took nearly a hundred years and many reincarnations for Moses Mendelssohn's ideas to travel the muddy, unpaved roads leading to this small Lithuanian shtetl — only to be met by fierce resistance. The resistance would prove relatively short-lived, however, perhaps because by the time the Haskalah came to Eishyshok there simply was no turning back. In any case, the result was that Eishyshok was able to benefit from the achievements of the Haskalah without experiencing many of its growing pains, thus escaping the lingering emotional scars that marked other shtetlekh where the struggle was more protracted.

The most courageous early attempt to bring the Haskalah to Eishyshok was in the field of education: a proposal for a two-year, Russian-language, secular school for Jewish boys and girls ages seven to twelve. In 1879 Moshe Faivl Kabacznik, then a resident of Lida but most likely a native Eishyshkian and member of the extended Kabacznik clan, petitioned the tzarist Ministry for Public Education in Vilna for permission to open the school. A certified teacher "who has passed the short examination at the Lida Teachers' Pedagogical School," Kabacznik included with his application a detailed ten-point description of the nature of the school, down to the fees it would charge and the number of students it would enroll, a letter attesting to the need for it and claiming the support of the shtetl deputies and householders, his certification from the school in Lida, a certificate from the police concerning his political reliability, and a certificate from the government-appointed Vilna rabbi, Dr. A. Gordon, concerning his good standing from the "religious point of view."

In typical Russian bureaucratic style, the response acknowledged the need for such a school: "I completely agree with the deputy's opinion, as expressed in his application, that since the densely populated town of Eishyshok does not have any [secular] teaching institution it is of vital importance that it should do so." But it stopped short of granting permission. Thus the school never became a reality. Some years later, however, after the Big Fire of 1895, a two-year, Russian-language school for girls was established. The subjects taught included reading, writing, arithmetic, and penmanship, and it attracted a handful of students, daughters of the Kiuchefski, Glombocki, Sonenson, and Senitski families. Perhaps permission had finally been granted, and this school was the long-delayed realization of Kabacznik's original plan.

One question that shall apparently never be answered is how Moshe Faivl Kabacznik was able, in 1879, to write a letter claiming the support of the shtetl deputies and householders, for 1879 was the year when Israel Isser Goldbloom was ousted from the Eishyshok yeshivah for his Haskalah views; it was during the tenure of Eliakim Shapira as shtetl rabbi and Naftali Shimshelewitch as head of the kahal, both of them staunch opponents of Haskalah innovations; it was a time when the sale of Haskalah books in the shtetl was still prohibited.[14] Perhaps Kabacznik cited their support knowing that they couldn't refute such a claim without appearing to the tzarist government to be active opponents of Russian culture. Or perhaps even then there was a dissident group among the balebatim who were willing to brave the shtetl authorities to help usher their children into the modern world.

THE MIXED HEDER (HEDER IRBUVIA) AND SECULAR EDUCATION

Not many years later, after all, it would be the Wilkanski children, under the leadership of Sarah, the oldest daughter, who fought for and won the right for the girls to attend heder. With the help of their father, whom they had at last won over to their side, Sarah and Esther (and, some years later, their younger sister Leah) were allowed to study at the school of a melamed known for his Haskalah sympathies. This was never an official heder irbuvia (mixed heder), for whenever a stranger walked into the melamed's house the Wilkanski girls had to hide under the table. Nonetheless, it was Eishyshok's first real advance in girls' education for centuries.

Until a decade or so into the twentieth century, tutors continued to be virtually the only route to an education for most girls whose parents wished them to have one. Polish tutors were particularly fashionable, since many parents of the merchant class thought that it would be economically advantageous for their daughters to learn language, literature, arithmetic, and social graces at the hands of these gifted teachers. Such knowledge could help the girls' families in their trade with the local Polish gentry and villagers. But there was also some anxiety about the possible consequences of so modern an education; and just as feared, one of the Eishyshok girls tutored by a Pole, Galke Weidenberg, became a physician (not considered a suitable occupation for a girl) and, worse still, was said to have married out of her faith. So some parents sought tutors who taught in Yiddish, and focused mainly on basic reading, writing, and arithmetic. Later, when the influence of the Haskalah had more thoroughly infused the shtetl, some of the most talented of the young women of Eishyshok were tutored by yeshivah students, who taught them the Bible and Hebrew language, grammar, and literature.

Yitzhak Wilkanski, the oldest of the children of Batia and Reb Layzer and one of the first Eishyshkians to pursue a secular course of study (in addition to his studies at the yeshivah, in Telz), was initially responsible for bringing the ideas of the Haskalah into their influential household. From there they made their way into the Eishyshok yeshivah, where Yitzhak's adoring younger brother Meir found an eager audience for them. A few years earlier, a contingent of students had come to Eishyshok from the Volozhin yeshivah, after it was closed down in 1891. Bringing with them a passion not just for the Talmud but for the Haskalah, Hibbat Zion, and even Russian socialist revolutionary movements, they had helped pave the way for new ideas. Thus, by the time Meir brought Yitzhak's letters from Telz to read them aloud to his fellow students, many of them were already secretly reading the Hebrew-language historical novels of Abraham Mapu (1808–1867), studying Russian, German, French, and even some Polish in preparation for the entrance exams they would need to take to get into the university, and subscribing to various Haskalah publications, among them *Ha-Zefirah* — a particular favorite since its editor, Hayyim Zelig Slonimski, was a former student at the Eishyshok yeshivah who had been expelled for his unorthodox views about education.

The intellectual traffic between the Wilkanski household and the yeshivah was two-way, for the books Meir found hidden within the walls of the Old Beth Midrash, disguised beneath the covers of the Gemara, concealed under trees in "Sin Grove" where students took their Sabbath and holiday strolls, would further inflame his imagination. *Hahavat Zion* (The Love of Zion, 1853) and *Ashmat Shomron* (The Guilt of Samaria, 1865), Abraham Mapu's novels depicting biblical characters as free people living on their own land, fascinated Meir, so much so that he persuaded his father to read them too. Like many of the new journals and newspapers coming into the shtetl, they were written in modern Hebrew, which the old guard considered to be a desecration of the language of the holy books. Indeed, there was hostility in Orthodox circles to language-learning of any kind. Nonetheless, the students had seen to it that the shelves of the Old Beth Midrash were discreetly but well stocked with books in many languages, and soon Meir was learning Polish from a primer given to him by a fellow parush. Always he was encouraged in his intellectual pursuits by Yitzhak, whom he would later describe in his memoir as having left the shtetl a zaddik (a righteous Jew), and returned on his first visit a taitchel (a German Jew who reads everything Jewish in translation).

Yitzhak promoted the study of Russian, German, and French, supporting his views with historical facts: Didn't Rashi know French, and Maimonides Arabic? And a knowledge of Polish, he presumed to tell his father, would greatly enhance his effectiveness as a judge, for then he could speak directly to the local Christians instead of relying on an interpreter.[15] But Hebrew was Yitzhak's true passion, and through the efforts first of himself and Meir, later of their talented sisters Sarah, Esther, and young Leah, Eishyshok was to become a virtual showplace of Hebrew learning.

Hebrew, of course, was one of the links between Haskalah and Zionism, so it was not surprising that the Wilkanskis would be pioneers in both. Thus, just as Reb Layzer Wilkanski lived to see his own home become one of the local breeding grounds for the Haskalah, though he had formerly been among those who opposed it, so he saw his children turn into avid Zionists, though he himself had believed that the return to Eretz Israel should await the coming of the Messiah. And he would prove a loving supporter to them during their years of struggle in Palestine, unlike the many parents who disapproved of the lives their children led there, some of whom went so far as to disown them — they had raised them to be scholars, not manual laborers, after all![16]

THE HEDER METUKAN

In 1903 the heder metukan (reconstructed or reformed heder) movement at last gained a foothold in Eishyshok, thanks mainly to the persistence of one man: Velvel Schneider, known as Velvel der Geller (the redhead). A descendant of one of the shtetl's oldest families and son of the shopkeeper Malka Roche's, he was a well-to-do shopkeeper himself and an ardent Zionist. Together with Meir Kiuchefski, he decided to see to it that the town had a modern school, lodged in its own spacious building rather than the home of a melamed, with a structured curriculum that would add secular subject matter as well as physical education and arts and crafts to the traditional religious subjects. Since Schneider was planning to emigrate to Eretz Israel, part of his motivation for founding such a school had to do with wanting his sons to be educated in the spirit of the National Awakening so that they would be well prepared for their new life. But his interest in the reconstructed heder was not just ideological; it was also rooted in personal dissatisfaction with the old heder, where his son Yaakov had earlier had an unhappy experience.

Any change in traditional education was at that time considered a dangerous move. When news of the plans for this new school reached the Haffetz Hayyim, he rushed to Eishyshok where, in the presence of Rabbi Zundl Hutner, he pleaded with Schneider and Kiuchefski to abandon their plans. Meir Kiuchefski could not stand up to the tearful Haffetz Hayyim and withdrew; Velvel Schneider, however, went forward.

The heder metukan opened under the leadership of a true maskil by the name of Archimowitz, whom Schneider brought to Eishyshok. Initially those who attended were mainly the sons of Velvel Schneider's relatives and friends, but eventually the school attracted an impressive number of boys. At the outbreak of World War I, Schneider brought in a second teacher, a devout Hebraist named Kupritz, who gave individual lessons on the side to eager students. Kupritz was a neatly dressed gentleman, unlike the typical melamed, and he expected his students to pay similarly close attention to their clothing and grooming. Eventually the school hired a third teacher, Shaul Litski, a returning POW who had been wounded during the war.[17]

The curriculum conformed closely to the spirit of the heder metukan movement. A physical fitness program of gymnastics, swimming, and nature walks was supervised by Shaul Litski. Each day's studies ended with the singing of *Hatikvah*, the Jewish national anthem, led by Mr. Kupritz.

Unfortunately, Shaul Litski's knowledge of Hebrew, unlike Mr. Kupritz's, was very limited, and when the fighting neared Eishyshok and

Mr. Kupritz had to leave the shtetl for a while to go help relatives who had been displaced by the war, the cause of Hebrew education suffered accordingly. Or so a story told by Peretz Kaleko suggests. As a student of Sarah Rubinstein, from whom he took extra classes on the side, Peretz Kaleko had gained a good enough command of Hebrew to sense Mr. Litski's weakness in the subject, and one day decided to put him to the test. When Mr. Litski came to class that day, he couldn't find his own copy of the Hebrew reader, which had the Yiddish translation of all the Hebrew words faintly penciled in, for Peretz Kaleko had hidden it. Just as the young prankster suspected would happen, poor Mr. Litski found himself at a loss for words as he faced the class.

Despite a few interruptions during the war, the heder metukan continued to function until sometime in the mid-1920s, when the Hebrew day schools run by Peretz Kaleko (now a teacher, and a very gifted one) and Moshe Yaakov Botwinik supplanted it. Whatever its limitations, during its brief life the heder metukan had presented such a challenge to the educational system of the shtetl that things would never be the same.

A SCHOOL FOR GIRLS

Another challenge to tradition arrived around 1911, when Mr. and Mrs. Yaffe and their family moved to Eishyshok from Russia. Both were graduates of a pedagogical institute in Grodno, where they had obviously imbibed the latest ideas, for the school they established in Eishyshok was for girls — the shtetl's second such venture, but a much more ambitious one than the two-year Russian-language school that had operated for a few years at the turn of the century. The Yaffskaya Shkola was located in a private house on Vilna Street. There Mr. Yaffe taught Yiddish and arts and crafts; his wife taught Russian, German, music, and social graces. All the traditional Jewish holidays were observed, as well as the New Year on the civil calendar, which was celebrated with a party where the girls read German and Russian poetry, sang, and danced.

The parents who sent their daughters to the Yaffskaya Shkola generally had a high level of commitment to the cause of girls' education, for they were paying dearly for it, both in terms of the tuition fee, which was large, and the price of their daughters' lost labor at home and in the family business. The brunt of this burden was usually borne by the mother of the family, who had to stretch the limited family resources to cover these additional expenses, and had to forgo the much-needed help.

Pessia Moszczenik was the daughter of one such mother. Before the Yaffskaya Shkola opened, Golde had sent Pessia to the heder teacher Meir der Lerer, to learn to read Hebrew and to read and write Yiddish. But that much of an education strained the family budget, for the Moszczeniks, although counted among the

The first school for girls in Eishyshok opened at the turn of the twentieth century. Among the girls in the photo are the four Glombocki sisters. Two are standing on the left, one is sitting on the ground, far right. Next to Ettl Glombocki (Gunzberg) standing second from right is a Kiuchefski. Third from right is Hinda Sonenson. A number of the Glombockis emigrated to Argentina. Ettl survived in Russia, Hinda was murdered with her four children in the September 1941 massacre. PHOTO: YITZHAK URI KATZ. YESC, GLOMBOCKI

balebatim, were of modest means. The father, Honeh, was a builder who could only count on working during the good weather of summertime; Golde was a trader on market days and, for extra money, a zogerke in the synagogue on Saturdays and holidays. Though some of their children had recently left for America and later sent substantial amounts of money back home, it was not yet flowing freely. Since on top of her two jobs Golde had several small children to take care of at this time, she surely could have used the help of her eldest daughter. Nonetheless, when the new school opened Golde enrolled Pessia in it. Parents now had aspirations not just for their boys but for their girls. As Pessia recounted years later: "I remember how my dear mother used to say that of me she would make a somebody. I would study and eventually become one of the notables in the shtetl."

Alas, Pessia's mother's aspirations for her were short-lived. When World War I broke out, the Yaffes left the shtetl, the school closed, and Pessia's education ended. Her talents found a new venue: the fields of neighboring villages, where she searched for potatoes in a desperate attempt to help her family ward off starvation. But the cause of education for girls was soon to be revived — if not in Pessia's family, in the shtetl at large. By the end of the war it would be an established fact, though the community had not yet made it compulsory.

The Yaffskaya Shkola, a school for girls founded circa 1911. The school's official languages were Russian and German, with courses in Yiddish. Sitting in the center is the founder, Mrs. Yaffe. To her left is Zipporah Lubetski (Tokatli). Zipporah and her sisters emigrated to Eretz Israel and America, as did a few other girls in the photo. The majority of the girls were murdered during the Holocaust in the September 1941 massacre and other locations. PHOTO: YITZHAK URI KATZ. YESC, TOKATLI

EDUCATION DURING WORLD WAR I

Soon after the Germans occupied Eishyshok in 1915, they launched a campaign against illiteracy, part of which involved opening a free coed elementary school, where four years of attendance was compulsory. (In other shtetlekh in the vicinity the requirement was for six years.) To lure the Jewish children to the new school, the German military orchestra played *Hatikvah* during the opening-day ceremonies. Though the school offered only the basics of reading and writing — in German — it was, of course, an advance for girls, since most of them had previously had to scramble on their own to pick up even the rudiments of literacy. As part of the literacy training, each child was given a special slate on which to practice writing and penmanship. Those who attended the school — and they were the majority, especially among the boys — recall it and the kindness of the teachers fondly.

At the same time that the new German school was attracting the lion's share of students, including many who might not otherwise have been able to get an education, the established Jewish educational institutions continued to function — even flourish: the hadarim, both traditional and reconstructed, and the yeshivah ketanah saw their student populations swell with the influx of refugee children. Decades later, World War I refugees like Hayyim Sonenson from Lubtch and Shlomo Farber from Olkenik still spoke of the excellent education they had received during those years in Eishyshok, attributing their fluency in Hebrew to their studies with Reb Tuviah der Yeremitcher.

Some of the shtetl's most gifted teachers, including Sarah Rubinstein, Esther Kiuchefski, Mr. Kupritz, and Moshe Yaakov Botwinik, founded a school for older girls, as well as for young girls whose parents were fearful of sending them to the German school or who wanted them to have a more ambitious course of study than was available there. The curriculum included Hebrew language and grammar, nature, geography, arithmetic, history, crafts, and music.

Though the community as a whole had not yet agreed to the principle of compulsory education for girls, most of the parents in the shtetl did make the effort to pay the necessary tuition. And it would not be long before the principle of education for girls was universally accepted. With all the opportunities that had become available, the presence of such gifted teachers, and the example of so many educated young women who were part of the refugee population, it was clearly an idea whose time had come.

The intensifying quest for education, for boys and girls alike, spread from Eishyshok to the Jewish villagers in the surrounding countryside. No longer was it only the most affluent of the yishuvniks who were committed to providing their children with an education. An ever-increasing number of yishuvniks' children attended classes and tutorials in Eishyshok, while others were educated by teachers who were employed by individual families, or by groups of families. As the sixteen-year-old Shaul Kaleko discovered when he was looking for a teaching position to ease his parents' economic burden, agencies existed that matched private tutors with prospective employers. On March 30, 1915, he wrote in his diary about his experience at one such establishment in Vilna:

With great difficulty I found the Katriel "palace." Located several steps below ground in a basement, the entire "palace" consists of one room with a kitchen along the eastern wall, and a long table down the center of the room. Around the table were many young men, of all kinds: some wore monocles, some did not; some wore caps, some brimmed hats; some had fine shoes, others torn ones. There were young men with full faces, gaunt faces, happy faces, somber faces. . . . Seated next to the young men, engaging them in conversation, were the villagers, a few with beards and earlocks, all smelling of pitch mixed with the fragrance of fields and forests.

Shaul Kaleko was hired on the very day of his arrival at the Katriel basement, for the villagers, as he later heard, had been impressed with his good looks as well as his learning. His employer was a Hasidic Jew who was leasing the village mill of Papernia from a Russian nobleman in St. Petersburg. Engaged for a five-month period, from April through August, Kaleko was paid 80 rubles per month, a bit less than the 100 he had asked for but superior to what he would have earned in tutoring fees in Eishyshok, minus a one-time service fee paid to Katriel.

Kaleko's charges, three boys ages twelve, nine, and seven, were not the typically wild yishuvnik youngsters, but children who were responsive and eager to learn. His employers were generous, the food was plentiful, his lodgings in a nearby Christian peasant's home were comfortable, and he enjoyed the additional pleasure of being able to spend time in the "lap of nature."

Study groups were established during the war, bringing together under the guidance of young tutors like Shaul and Simha Kaleko and the melamed Tuviah Rubinstein der Yeremitcher those with common intellectual interests in Hebrew language and literature, in Bible and in history. Reb Tuviah's daughter Sarah Rubinstein, who had assumed the leadership of Rak Ivrit, the Hebrew-language society, after founder Leah Wilkanski left for Eretz Israel in 1911 (see chapter 22), became one of the most gifted of the tutors in these groups. And it was she who would introduce into the shtetl the truly novel idea that women were capable of teaching men. Sarah Wilkanski had taught boys. But Sarah Rubinstein taught young men — a huge distinction by shtetl standards. Under her guidance, Rak Ivrit became a coed society, and the age of its participants was extended to the late teens. There and in her various other study groups she made a deep impression, as well as a long-lasting one: Seventy years later one of her students was still reciting literary and biblical passages she had learned with Sarah Rubinstein.

By war's end, the heder and yeshivah were clearly no longer the shtetl's most significant educational institutions. This in and of itself constituted a major innovation. In the years to come, most parents would opt for one or another of the new schools, so that the heder became mainly a late-afternoon school, offering Jewish students who in the first hours of the day attended other schools — Hebrew, German, and eventually Polish — an additional measure of Jewish education. Those parents who saw the heder as the last bastion of traditional Jewish education and life continued to send their children to it for several years prior to their entering Peretz Kaleko's or Moshe Yaakov Botwinik's Hebrew day schools, but they were only a handful, and generally from among the clergy. Elsewhere, particularly in the Hasidic communities of Eastern Europe, the people's allegiance to the heder remained unbroken. But Eishyshok had changed irrevocably.

HIGHER EDUCATION IN THE POSTWAR YEARS

With the ever greater acceptance of the idea of a Jewish homeland in the years following the Balfour Declaration of 1917, young Eishyshkians — young women as well as young men — looked to schools and universities to help prepare them for emigration. After World War I they flocked to Vilna, where a variety of institutions of higher learning offered courses to this end. I. N. Epstein, the Hebrew gymnasium at 4 Zavalna Street, attracted Peretz Kaleko and his cousins Yaakov and Shaul Schneider; Israel and Moshe Sonenson; Esther and Shoshana Katz; and Zipporah and Hayyim Wilenski. The Jewish Technikum, for training in engineering and other advanced vocational skills, drew another of the

Wilenskis, Dov, as well as the Glombocki brothers, Hillel and Faivl. There was also an ORT (Society for the Development of Jewish Agriculture and Trade) school for basic vocational training, and the Kahanshtam Tarbut teachers' seminary, where Peretz Kaleko went after he finished his studies at the gymnasium. The fact that none of these institutions was recognized by the Polish Ministry of Education did not bother the students from Eishyshok, for they expected to be living in Eretz Israel, not Poland, after graduation.

Like the Wilenski siblings, many brothers and sisters took divergent paths, in search of their own destinies. Esther and Shoshana Katz's older sister Zipporah studied photography in Lida, hoping one day to be able to open her own studio in Tel Aviv, while their brother David studied at the Radun yeshivah. Shaul Schneider continued his education in Paris, where he was certified as an agronomist, while brother Yaakov, very bright but never much of a student, married and emigrated to Palestine. Shtetl intellectual Shaul Kaleko, the older brother of Peretz, crossed over the border to Kovno, Lithuania, with their only sister, Rachel. Though it was illegal as well as dangerous to cross this now-closed border, they took the risk because during the new golden age of Jewish national autonomy in Lithuania, 1919–23, the educational opportunities for Jews were excellent. In fact, the Jewish school system in Lithuania was one of the best in all of Europe between the two world wars, and would remain so for the duration of the Lithuanian Republic, even when many other Jewish prerogatives fell by the wayside.

Rachel Kaleko studied at the Hebrew Reali gymnasium, while Shaul attended Kaunas (Kovno) University, which in 1922 had a nearly one-third Jewish enrollment, out of a student body of over 1,100.[18] Shaul supported himself by serving as a secretary to Max Soloveichik, the Minister for Jewish Affairs in the Lithuanian

Students at the Kahanshtam Tarbut teachers' seminary in Vilna on a winter outing, February 8, 1928. To the far left, on the sled, is Peretz Kaleko. YESC, KALEKO-ALUFI

government — a post that would soon be eliminated, when the short-lived golden age came to an end. Eventually Kaleko completed his studies at Berlin University, earning a Ph.D. with a dissertation on agrarian problems in Lithuania.

Like the Kalekos, Hayyim Zvi Hutner, son of the shtetl dayyan, went to Kovno to pursue his studies. But he was among the few Eishyshkians still attending a yeshivah — the Slobodka yeshivah, headed by his mother's brother, Rabbi Moshe Mordekhai Epstein (1866–1933) — and the reason he made the dangerous crossing was that his mother hoped that the closed borders between Poland and Lithuania would effectively isolate him from the secular Hebrew culture that was spreading so rapidly back at home. She specifically feared the secularizing spell of her son's best friend, Hayyim Wilenski, who was a student at the Epstein gymnasium. To a yeshivah boy, the gymnasium students seemed very glamorous. They affected big-city ways, sprinkled their conversation with new, unfamiliar terms, wore special student caps and insignia and dashing coats with shiny brass buttons.

Eishyshok's postwar years were marked by an avid quest for higher education, especially a Hebraist–Zionist education, which was seen as the avenue to a brighter future, in a new home. Wanting the best for their children, parents scrimped and saved in order to send them to good schools, an expensive proposition involving not just tuition but food, lodging, clothing, transportation, and other expenses. Many people could not afford it. Though a few students, like the Kalekos, were able to earn their own keep, most did not, which meant that education at this level remained largely the privilege of the children of the well-to-do balebatim.

A few students, of course, came from less affluent families, the children of artisans or small shopkeepers who had made a monumental

Albert Einstein speaking at a conference of Jewish university students in Germany, 1924. Among the organizers of the conference was Shaul Kaleko, a student at Berlin University. He is sitting to the left of Einstein against the wall. YESC, KALEKO-BARKALI

sacrifice in the hope it would pay off in the long run. And some young people of modest means were able to attend trade schools in the larger cities, returning to the shtetl as elite craftspersons catering to an affluent clientele. Rochel Szulkin and the Matikanski brothers studied fashion and design in Vilna, and earned good money afterward. But for many a bright young man and woman from the working class, education remained an impossible dream, and the shtetl's rigid economic and social barriers were thereby perpetuated, despite the mitigating influence of the Zionist cultural and political organizations.

Shaul Schneider (middle row, center) during his student years in Paris with fellow Jewish students, 1928. YESC, SCHNEIDER

ELEMENTARY SCHOOL EDUCATION AFTER THE WAR

In postwar Poland, education was mandatory for children between the ages of seven and fourteen. All elementary-school-age children, of every ethnicity, boys and girls alike, were supposed to receive a systematic education, at state expense.

Moreover, this education was to be ethnically appropriate. By the terms of the Minorities Treaty, which Poland signed on June 28, 1919, the same day that it signed the Versailles Treaty, the government of the new independent Poland guaranteed the rights of its minorities, who included nearly 5 million Ukrainians, 3.5 million Jews, and 1 million Germans and other national minorities (including Russians, Lithuanians, and Czechs) — about one-third of its population.[19] Articles 8, 9, 10, and 11 of the Minorities Treaty specifically addressed education, promising that all these peoples would be educated in their own languages, at their own schools, paid for by the Polish government. Indeed, the safeguarding of the rights of the minorities had been a condition of Poland's receiving its independence at the negotiating table in Versailles, and education was one of the most important of the rights guaranteed. Implementation of this policy would prove to be quite a different matter, however.

Other countries in the region did honor their minorities treaties, at least for a while — witness the liberal regime of Tomas Masaryk in Czechoslovakia, and the early years of the Lithuanian Republic, when the Jews enjoyed an autonomy in education, as in their other internal affairs, that was considered comparable to what they had had during the age of the Council of the Four Lands. Poland, however, was selective in its enforcement, establishing schools for other minorities but refusing to do so for the Jews. Only a small number of nominally Jewish elementary schools were ever opened under Polish auspices, and they offered very little Jewish content. Stepping into this vacuum, the main Jewish political parties established their own excellent educational networks, each of which served a different constituency.[20] The four major networks associated with the various Jewish political parties were CYSHO, Tarbut, Yavneh, and Horev.

CYSHO, the Yiddish-language network of the Central Yiddish School Organization, was founded by the Bund in 1921. Its students were the children of parents who were mainly secular in orientation, and mainly from the artisan class. Politically most of them were Bundists, Communists, or sympathizers with other socialist groups. In Poland the total number of pupils attending the CYSHO network of schools in 1934–35 was 15,486, which included students in kindergarten, elementary school, high school, and at two teachers' seminaries.[21]

The Tarbut (Hebrew for "culture") schools, established in March 1922, were Zionist in their ideology, with a curriculum that reflected that orientation, and they were mainly located in the Kresy, the towns of eastern Poland bordering on Lithuania and Byelorussia, in the Vilna/Bialystok region, where one of the largest concentrations of East European Zionists lived. Tarbut's main objectives were the revival of Hebrew language and culture, preparatory to a return to Eretz Israel and settlement of the land by a well-trained cadre of halutzim. Consequently, Hebrew was the language of instruction for all subjects, except for the government-mandated courses in Polish history, geography, and language; one-third of the Tarbut curriculum was devoted to the geography, flora, and fauna of the Jewish homeland. The inspiration for the Tarbut schools was the growing Hebrew school system in Palestine, which was also devoted to making Hebrew a living language.[22]

Tarbut experienced steady growth, despite the hostility of the Polish government, which, not surprisingly, viewed its strong commitment to Jewish nationalism with suspicion. In 1925–26 Tarbut operated 52 kindergartens and 113 elementary schools in Poland. By 1934–35 the numbers were 72 and 183. The Tarbut network also maintained 9 secondary schools (gymnasiums), 4 teachers' seminaries (Peretz Kaleko studied at the one in Vilna), 4 evening schools for adults and working teenagers, and 1 agricultural school, as well as sponsoring its own publishing program, which issued a steady stream of periodicals, textbooks, and curriculum-related materials. Tarbut attracted a mainly upper-middle-class group of students, for tuition fees were high. Overall enrollment increased from 24,000 students in 1927–28 to 44,780 in 1934–35.[23] With the British government's ever-stricter limits on emigration to Palestine, parents had begun to recognize that their children's future might for a while longer be in Poland, not in Eretz Israel, and Tarbut's enrollment began dropping accordingly.

The Yavneh school network was sponsored by Mizrahi, the religious Zionist party. Like Tarbut, it was committed to establishing Hebrew as a living, spoken language, and as the language of the Jewish homeland, but its focus was not just on Hebrew and the Land of Israel but on the Bible and other subjects from the traditional religious curriculum. Yavneh maintained elementary and secondary schools as well as a teachers' college in Poland, with an overall enrollment of 23,000 students in 235 schools by 1938.

Horev was the largest of the Jewish school networks, drawing its pupils from what was still the largest Jewish group within Poland: the ultra-Orthodox Jews, including the Hasidim. Operated by the anti-Zionist Agudat Israel party, which grew in strength during the 1930s as the Zionist party declined and the ultra-Orthodox became ever more conservative and more separate from the rest of the Jewish community, the Horev network had an enrollment of 110,000 students by 1934–35. There were Horev schools for boys and corresponding Beth Jacob schools for girls. Because Agudat Israel had no leftist political agenda and no nationalist agenda — indeed, it opposed Zionism and viewed Hebrew not as a living language but as the language of the sacred texts — its school system enjoyed a better relationship with the Polish government than the other educational networks did.[24]

In addition to the schools established by the various political parties, a substantial number of traditional yeshivot and hadarim continued to operate. The former, which were part of Rabbi Hayyim Ozer Grodzinski's Vaad ha-Yeshivot (Council of Yeshivot), totaled 136 schools in 1937, including both yeshivot and yeshivot ketanah (middle or preparatory yeshivot), with 12,000 students throughout Poland. During the 1930s some 50,000 students were still attending heder.

For those whose parents wanted them to be trained in a trade, there were also the ORT schools, which drew 5,000 students in 1934.

THE SCHOOLS IN POSTWAR EISHYSHOK

In postwar Eishyshok, the parents of the 800 children of kindergarten and elementary school age could choose from a variety of educational options to suit their particular political, religious, and ideological orientations. Eishyshok had no Yiddish network school, however, as the shtetl had too few people from the ranks of the working class — consisting of manual laborers and factory workers employed by the so-called ruling class — to warrant such an institution.

The few parents who still wanted their sons to have a traditional religious education could send them to heder, then to the yeshivah ketanah, an academy for boys of high school age, which had an excellent teaching staff. A small number — which would increase in later years as more people came to accept the idea of a future in Poland rather than Palestine — sent their children to the Polish public school (Powszechna) that was established in the early 1930s. There, under the extremely diluted provisions of the Minorities Treaty, they followed the standard Polish school curriculum with the rest of the class, in addition to which they received once-a-week instruction in Jewish subject matter, taught by Eli Politacki, a member of the Zionist Workers Party (Poalei Zion Left). If their parents wanted them to have a better grounding in Jewish studies, they could go to afternoon heder or Hebrew classes when the Polish school day ended.

For the majority of the community in Eishyshok, however, as in most of the rest of the Polish-Lithuanian border area, the Tarbut network, with its moderately secular orientation and strong commitment to Hebrew and Zionism, had the greatest appeal. For over a decade after the end of World War I, until the building of a community-controlled Hebrew day school which became the principal educational institution in the shtetl in the early 1930s, a number of small, private Hebrew schools offered a Tarbut-inspired curriculum. Some were housed in individuals' homes, others in the Old and the New Batei Midrash, and, weather permitting, in the summer shul and even in backyards. The two most popular of these were the courses offered by Peretz Kaleko, and the Hebrew day and afternoon schools run by Moshe Yaakov Botwinik.

Botwinik was a native of Minsk-Mazowieck who had married a woman from Eishyshok. A classic East European maskil, he had attended

Israel Szczuczynski (center) with Isaac Halperin and Isaac's sister doing their Hebrew homework. The Halperin children came from Bialystok to Eishyshok to stay with their maternal grandfather, Reb Dovid Remz, and attend the Hebrew school while there. Israel was murdered in the forest on June 16, 1943, during an attack by Germans and local collaborators.
PHOTO: J. RENDEL, BIALYSTOK. YESC, BLACHAROWICZ-WISZIK

both the famed Volozhin yeshivah and the university in Odessa, where he became close with the Odessa circle of maskilim, especially the National Awakening poet Hayyim Nahman Bialik and the historian Yossef Klausner. Bringing with him the innovative methodology he had acquired during his extensive studies, Botwinik would set new standards for Hebrew-language education in Eishyshok, and would preside over the education of several generations of students. During the 1920s he ran both a Hebrew elementary day school and a late-afternoon school for girls who worked during the early-morning and -afternoon hours when the day school was in session. In the 1930s the afternoon school was mainly for students who attended the Polish school for the first part of the day but whose parents wanted them to supplement their education with Hebrew studies.

The first class of Eishyshok's first coed Hebrew day school. The three Hebrew teachers are Moshe Yaakov Botwinik (right), Yaakov Schneider (left) and Rivka Rubinstein (sitting in the first row). The students: (first row, right to left) (first name unknown) Rosenblum, name unknown, Luba Ginunski, Shaike Segal, Shaul Schneider, (first name unknown) Slepak, and Esther Katz; (second row, right to left) Titinski, Paikowski (first names unknown); fourth girl is a Ginunski; (third row, right to left (first name unknown) Moszczenik, Taibke Kosowski, Luba Senitski, Dov Wilenski, and Miriam Lanski. PHOTO: YITZHAK URI KATZ. YESC, RESNIK

Botwinik was fluent in Russian, German, Yiddish, and Hebrew, but was particularly devoted to Hebrew — modern Hebrew literature as well as the traditional Jewish texts, all of which he was fiercely committed to teaching to his students. He was also passionate about his own studies, and, after the long day he put in at his two schools and his occasional stints helping his wife in their fabric store on the market square, he spent every night between 11 P.M. and 2 A.M. studying the Gemara, like the yeshivah student he had once been.

Until Peretz Kaleko left the shtetl to accept a teaching post in another town in 1930, he was Botwinik's chief competitor. The youngest of the six Kaleko children, Peretz had attended heder but not yeshivah, for he was a product of the shtetl's turbulent years of change and secularization. Like Botwinik, he was an innovative teacher, deeply devoted to Hebrew language learning, and, thanks to the education he had received at the Kahanshtam Tarbut teachers' seminary, well versed in the latest pedagogical trends.

After graduating with a teacher's diploma that was recognized by the Polish Ministry of Education, Peretz had returned to Eishyshok, only to discover that the Polish authorities would not let him accept a teaching post because his paternal grandfather had been born in a small village now considered part of Lithuania and they had decided he was a Lithuanian, not a Polish, citizen — part of the Polish government's extensive campaign to deprive "Litvaks" of citizenship. The fact that his mother, Mina, daughter of the legendary shopkeeper Malke Roche's, hailed from one of the original five founding families of the shtetl made no difference to the Polish authorities, who were similarly unimpressed by the claims of others from Eishyshok. Indeed, not a single Polish family residing in the shtetl or the surrounding area could prove their roots to the satisfaction of the government, though bribes to various Polish officials could be helpful, as they were in Peretz Kaleko's case. After a certain amount of tiresome correspondence with Polish officials in Lida, the district capital, Peretz was granted permission to teach in his hometown of Eishyshok.

The competition between Botwinik and Kaleko was fierce, with Botwinik attracting forty-five students to Kaleko's sixty-five. Presumably parents preferred Kaleko on the basis of personality and long-standing loyalty to a native son, since both men were highly qualified and both used a curriculum and textbooks that were Tarbut-based. Only when Kaleko left for Ivie in 1930, where he remained until his departure for Eretz Israel in 1933, did Botwinik's school become the dominant one in the shtetl, having outlasted the last challenge to centralized community Hebrew education.[25]

THE BUILDING OF EISHYSHOK'S HEBREW SCHOOL: DAWN OF A NEW ERA

One of the most important factors in the creation of a centralized system of education in Eishyshok was the construction of a school building. Previously classes had been held in a variety of constantly shifting locations throughout the shtetl. Now at last there would be one central, stable location, in a well-lighted, amply heated building. Though the need for a school building had been discussed for years, the shtetl did not have sufficient funds to undertake such a major project, and was able to do so only when it received a large donation from America in the late 1920s. The donor was philanthropist Harry Fischel (1865–1948), whose wife, Jane Brass, was a native Eishyshkian, related to the Lawzowski and the Zlotnik families, and one of the earliest of Eishyshok's emigrants to America.[26]

Though it had always refused to solicit donations from outsiders for its famed yeshivah, out of the desire to preserve its absolute independence in educational matters, the shtetl was now increasingly eager to receive such funds, from anyone who wanted to give them, which generally meant people in America — either former Eishyshkians themselves, or, as was the case with the school funds, people with family in Eishyshok. This eagerness for contributions did inevitably result in a certain loss of autonomy, which would be felt not only in education but in other aspects of shtetl life.

Events leading up to the construction of the school building were described in an unpublished memoir by Pessah Cofnas, the son of Gedalia the carpenter:

At the Coutsai store we can now purchase a newspaper — even the evening paper (Ovent Kurier) *— on* *the same day it comes out. But a building for the Hebrew school we still do not have.*

"Our children have had enough of wandering from building to building and from room to room," says Reb Itche der Shamesh in an agitated voice. The discussion takes place in the Old Beth Midrash between afternoon and evening prayers. The gentlemen present, who include Yankel der Baranovitcher, Shlomo Polaczek, Yekutiel Ginunski the shoemaker, Anschel the barber, and Shlomo the tailor, all nod their heads in agreement.

The kahal began to consider the topic at great length, but what was missing were the necessary funds from America. When at last the funds arrived, it was decided to begin construction immediately, whereupon a new topic began to dominate the discussions of the kahal: the question of where best to locate the building, for maximum educational benefit.

And so one beautiful warm spring day, from the windows of our carpentry shop we notice a number of people inspecting the grounds of the community-owned garden, which borders on my father Reb Gedalia's home and carpentry shop on one side, on the "orphans'" home on another. Yehuda Leib Smolianski is measuring out the plot with his feet. Mordekhai Replianski is jotting something down in his notebook. The teacher Botwinik is looking around. Our dayyan Hertz Mendl, to whose household the community garden is generally given over, is pacing back and forth near Reb Gedalia's stack of logs. Suddenly he stops abruptly, looks up in the sky, picks up the tail of his black summer coat, and sits down on the logs, whereupon he removes a small book from his pocket and begins to study it, while swaying back and forth. . . .

Mote, Reuven, and Leah, the three oldest orphans, are looking eagerly out their window, wondering what the balebatim are doing in the community-owned garden used by the dayyan. Suddenly Motl Replianski takes out a long wooden meter stick and begins to measure the garden, which quite naturally raises our curiosity level.

Nearby on Goyishker Street, Rabbi Szymen Rozowski was serenely engaged in taking his morning stroll, as was his daily routine. He passed us by without stopping, greeted various people along the way, then disappeared from view. On his return he made his way over to the balebatim clustered near Gedalia's workshop, and a young carpenter's apprentice came rushing over with a backless stool for the rabbi, which he positioned against the low picket fence between Hertz Mendl's and my father's gardens.

Yehuda Leib was the first to speak up. Pointing toward the garden, he explained: "We are ready to begin construction of the school building and trying to decide whether to build it here or on the plaza between the Old and the New batei midrash."

The rabbi thought for a while, then said, "Gentlemen, I see that you are facing a difficult dilemma. But, my dear fellow Jews, since we are discussing the building of a school, it is my opinion that the very choice of the location is an educational issue, and as such we must consult our educator, the distinguished Mr. Botwinik."

The teacher stood up, took a few steps toward the rabbi, and said, "This is the best spot for the elementary school building, in the middle of the garden. The building should be constructed in such a way that one side of the school faces the beth midrash and the other side faces the fields and the barns. A Jewish child should know where a loaf of bread comes from, should see barns stacked with fresh produce, should be familiar with plowing and planting. Let the Jewish child be close to nature and agriculture. Once we were a people who lived on the land in our own homeland. Now we must return to the land and work it. Therefore we must prepare our children for this holy task."

Our saintly dayyan, Rabbi Hertz Mendl, may his merit protect all of us, sat up straight on his log and said, "I too believe in 'And thou shall dwell on the land and conquer it.' If you were building a yeshivah, I would be ready to give up half of my garden for such a holy purpose."

Rabbi Rozowski stood up, leaned with both hands on his cane, and turned to the dayyan: "We will not cause any injustice. The garden will be fenced off and no harm shall come to your vegetables." To which the dayyan nodded his agreement, adding in his hoarse voice that we must "fence it off, fence it off."

Then the rabbi turned to Botwinik and expressed his full support, concluding the discussion by wishing the new endeavor much success.

It was several years until the new building was completed and students began to study there.

The resulting schoolhouse was a one-floor wooden structure with room for expansion, located on the shulhoyf to the right of the summer shul and the rear of the New Beth Midrash, in precisely the same place that was under discussion in the scene described by Pessah Cofnas. Its classrooms were spacious, and its special features included an assembly hall, an arts and crafts room, a large front yard, and a garden in the back — all on community property. Since it was a community endeavor, the school came under community jurisdiction for the first time. A coed school board was elected — this being only the second coed committee of the kehilah, the first being the soup kitchen relief committee founded during World War I. All the committee members, who included Miriam Kaganowicz, Avraham Kaplan, Ephraim Karnefski, Alte Katz, and Nahum Koppelman, were from the balebatim class.

With the election of the board, Botwinik's authority was curtailed, although he remained the

Faculty and students in front of the Hebrew school, Beit Sefer Klali Yivri, on the shulhoyf, May 31, 1936: principal Moshe Yaakov Botwinik (fifth row, center); four faculty members (in fourth row, right to left) Shaul Schneider, Malka Levittan Gayer, and A. Shainberg, and (first name unknown) Okun; of the students in the photo only seven survived the Holocaust: Hayya Shlanski (second row, eighth from left), who emigrated to America, and six boys who survived as teenage partisans: Reuven Paikowski (fourth row, second from right, with arms crossed); Layzer Ballon (to the right of teacher Okun); Leibke Kaganowicz (Leon Kahn) (second boy to the right of Botwinik); Avremele Botwinik, the principal's son (second-last row, far right); Leibke Pochter (same row, eleventh from right); and Israel Shmerkowitch (top row, far right). All other children and faculty members were murdered during the September 1941 massacre, in Ghetto Radun, Lida, Grodno, and by the AK. PHOTO: ALTE KATZ. YESC, SHLANSKI

A class of the Hebrew school in 1937: (first row) Avigdor Katz (left) and Yankele Kaganowicz; (second row, right to left) Sheinele Dwilanski, (first name unknown) Bichwid, Hayya Shlanski, Hebrew teacher Mr. Okun, (first name unknown) Narodowicz, name unknown, Leibke Portnoy; (top row, right to left) name unknown, Leah Michalowski, "The Rubishker," Altke Koutsai, Masha Dubczanski, Rachel Koppelman. Hayya emigrated to America, Rochke Koppelman was killed by the AK, the others were murdered in the September 1941 massacre. PHOTO: BEN ZION SZREJDER. YESC, Y. SONENSON

Yudaleh Kabacznik on his way to the Hebrew school while his proud father, Benyamin, watches him in front of their house on Mill Street. Both were killed by the AK. PHOTO: REPHAEL LEJBOWICZ. YESC, A. ZIMMERMAN

Hebrew school's principal and guiding mentor for the time being. Like all the other teachers and school personnel, he was now a community employee, his appointment subject to committee approval.

Accompanying the transfer of authority from Botwinik to the community was a change in the school's ideological orientation. Formerly a Tarbut school, it now came under the influence of Szymen Rozowski, the shtetl rabbi, who as a prominent member of Mizrahi opposed the secular orientation of the Tarbut curriculum. The Haffetz Hayyim of nearby Radun, an influential figure much revered in Eishyshok even by those who differed from his political and religious orientation, was also adamant in his opposition to secular tendencies.

Rabbi Rozowski's demand for more religious studies in the curriculum, in accordance with the Yavneh principles of the Mizrahi educational network, met with heated opposition. The struggle between the tradition-oriented Hebraists and the secular Hebraists was not unique to Eishyshok, of course, but was a continuation of battles that had been fought since the early days of Zionism, and were continuing to be fought in many places, including in Ivie, where Peretz Kaleko was now teaching. The Ivie school system broke into two camps over the issue, with Peretz playing one of the mediator roles in their eventual reunification.[27]

The struggle in Eishyshok proved to be an early indication of the power that outside financing would have in the shtetl, for Rabbi Rozowski won with the support of a Mr. Epstein, husband of Gita Lawzowski; the Lawzowskis, Mizrahi Zionists like Rabbi Rozowski, had secured most of the funds for the school building from their rich American relatives, Jane and Harry Fischel. Money from America was something the shtetl could not afford to reject, so the rabbi and his supporters had the upper hand.

Since the majority of the teachers at the school were graduates of the Kahanshtam Tarbut teachers' seminary in Vilna, or of similarly secular pedagogical institutions, and the Hebrew school had been part of the Tarbut network since the very beginning, introducing aspects of the Yavneh curriculum proved to be a difficult and delicate matter. But the changes were made, with the result that the curriculum was a mixture of subjects from three distinct educational entities: Tarbut, Yavneh, and, in grades seven and eight, to ensure that graduates would get a diploma that was valid in Poland, the Polish Ministry of Education.

By hiring a state-licensed teacher to teach courses in Polish history and geography, and by submitting to regular inspections from an official of the Ministry of Education, the Hebrew school made it possible for its matriculating students to be admitted to a Polish gymnasium. During the teaching of the Polish subjects, the boys removed the hats they wore the rest of the time, as the wearing of hats indoors was considered a Jewish custom, and forbidden by the Polish Ministry of Education.

The Yavneh component of the curriculum consisted mainly of religious and traditional subject matter, as well as certain religious observances. Thus the day began with morning prayers, the boys wore Yavneh school caps during all classes (except the Polish classes), and eventually the school even had its own Holy Ark, donated by the village of Nacha after it closed its synagogue. Under the personal supervision of Rabbi Rozowski, the students were taught the Torah, the Prophets, the weekly portion, and cantillations; and, beginning in fourth grade, for boys only, the Talmud. Following an old heder tradition, the rabbi visited the school every Thursday to test the students in these subjects — visits that were eagerly awaited by the children, as Rabbi Rozowski was a charismatic man who showed a lively interest in their accomplishments.

All other subjects in the school, including Hebrew language, literature, and history, the Land of Israel, nature, geography, mathematics, arts and crafts, and physical education, were taught according to the secular, nationalist-oriented Tarbut curriculum, following the Tarbut "Hebrew in Hebrew" methodology, and using textbooks and materials developed by the Tarbut network.[28]

A page from Atara Kudlanski's notebook on the subject of the giraffe and its unique characteristics.
PHOTO: MELVIN LEVINE, 1997. YESC, A. ZIMMERMAN

The Hebrew school offered many extracurricular activities, including school outings and agricultural projects. Three teachers — (right to left) a teacher from the shtetl of Belski, Mr. Okun, and Shaul Schneider — are supervising students working in the garden: (front row, right to left) Avigdor Katz, Moshe Kaplan, Elisha Koppelman, Sheinele Dwilanski; (back row, right to left) Hayya Shlanski, Rachel Koppelman, Leah Michalowski, (first name unknown) Zila, and a girl from the Narodowicz family. Hayya emigrated to America; Leah Michalowski was one of the girls raped by "White Jacket," the Gestapo commander of Eishyshok; Rachel was killed by the AK; the others were murdered during the September 1941 massacre.
PHOTO: BEN ZION SZREJDER. YESC, Y. SONENSON

Despite the presence of religious subject matter in the curriculum, the Hebrew school seemed light years away from the hadarim that had been the shtetl's only form of elementary education a mere three decades before. The building itself, the pedagogical methods employed, the preponderance of secular subjects — all were radically different from what children at the turn of the century had known. The new school also offered an unprecedented variety of nonacademic and extracurricular activities, ranging from the elaborate productions of the school's drama club, which were attended by everyone in the shtetl, to a school orchestra, and, during the annual summer vacation (itself a recent innovation), community-sponsored recreational camps that were set up in the pine forests of Dumbla and Titiance.

Even the holidays that were celebrated, which included days on both the Polish and Jewish calendars, were observed with a pomp and circumstance previously unknown, particularly when they could be related to Eretz Israel. On the anniversary of the death of the military hero Yossef Trumpeldor, his portrait was draped in black, and the battle with the Arabs in Palestine in which he lost his life in 1920 was recounted in song and drama, with many a repetition of his dying words: "Never mind; it is good to die for our country." On Tu Be-Shevat, the New Year for Trees, exhibits on the flora and fauna of Palestine were displayed, and native fruits that had been imported, compliments of the community, were distributed among all the children.

Teacher Leibke Botwinik, son of the school principal, with his class on winter vacation trip to the countryside to learn about nature. Only three boys survived the Holocaust as teenage partisans: Layzer Ballon (sitting in the snow, left, next to the teacher's feet); Moshe Edelstein (standing, third from left); and Reuven Paikowski (top row, third from left, biting his lips). Leibke Botwinik was severely wounded by the AK. Hirshke Mendelowitch (front row, fourth from right) was also an AK victim. The others were killed in the September 1941 massacre. YESC, Y. SONENSON

As the schoolyard echoed with songs and verses about the blossoming of the almond trees, the biting cold winds of Eishyshok seemed no more than the gentle spring breezes of Eretz Israel.

This sensation of dwelling in two lands was actively cultivated by the school's emphasis on all things relating to the future homeland. Every event in Palestine was closely followed in the classroom, and reported on by students and faculty alike in the school's "wall newspaper," a wall where handwritten articles as well as the Tarbut newspapers from Vilna and Warsaw were posted. Visitors from Palestine, particularly halutzim returning to see their families, were invited to the school to talk about their experiences in the old-new homeland. And considerable emphasis was placed on inculcating a respect for physical labor, in order to prepare the students to learn work that would be useful in their new lives. Thus there were many school outings to local Jewish farmers, fishermen, loggers, artisans, and tradesmen at their places of work. Returning home from these adventures by horse-drawn wagons or sleighs, the children would sing Hebrew songs and picture themselves as pioneers in the Land of Israel. At such times it seemed that Eishyshok was on the shores of the River Jordan, not the banks of the Kantil.

The shtetl took as much pride in its Hebrew school as it had once taken in its famed yeshivah, the glory of Eishyshok in former times. By bringing together into one oddly assorted coalition most of the community's various ideological factions, the school became the central unifying institution in the shtetl. Yet it was a basically middle-class institution, for it charged a tuition fee that few working-class parents could afford to pay. The kehilah did attempt to assure a Hebrew education to every child who wanted one. Funds from America were allocated to scholarships, and some of the well-to-do balebatim would occasionally provide tuition for those who couldn't afford it. But many children of modest means who might otherwise have gone to the Hebrew school were sent instead to the Polish school.

Rachel Kaleko with students of the Gani kindergarten, which she founded. They were dressed for a Purim performance. Rachel made aliyah to Eretz Israel.
PHOTO: YITZHAK URI KATZ. YESC, KALEKO-BARKALI

An entirely new educational venture in the shtetl during the interwar years was the Hebrew kindergarten, known as Gani. Founded by Rachel Kaleko upon her return from Kovno, where she had graduated from the Reali gymnasium and the teachers' seminary, it, too, was a private institution, and it too followed the "Hebrew in Hebrew" method of instruction. Soon Gani earned a reputation as a model kindergarten, whose little scholars were known for their fluency in Hebrew.

Many years later Rachel reminisced about the tots in her charge during those early years of the kindergarten's existence, recalling with special fondness one of their dramatic performances of Hebrew-language plays they gave on holidays, much to the delight of a loyal audience of family and friends:

In the deluge of blood that came down upon the world my little shtetl also drowned, my charming shtetl with its five streets that met at the market square. . . . I see you in front of my eyes as if you were alive . . . my darling Saraleh . . . my serious Miraleh . . . and Gitaleh Kumin, the famous little actress.

I remember Gani's first Purim performance, held at the stable of Yurdichenski di Praislikhe [the Prussian]. For the first time in your life, Gitaleh, you walked on the stage, a stage that Yoske Borshtein and Yankele the blacksmith's son had built with love and with all the technical know-how at their disposal. You marched onto that stage with so much poise and dash, without a hint of fear. You were only four! You sang, you recited, and you performed just like a real actress. Your parents and all those who heard you that night saw in you an actress par excellence, with a great future.

The place was so packed that Leibele, the son of Layzer Remz, could not get to the stage to perform his part. His father therefore hoisted him on his shoulders, from which "stage" he recited his part without any stage fright. He received a thundering ovation.[29]

When Rachel made aliyah in 1935, she opened a new kindergarten in Jerusalem, and left her school in Eishyshok in the capable hands of Dora Feller, a graduate of the Tarbut teachers' seminary in Vilna, who saw to it that her students maintained the same high level of fluency in Hebrew.

Thus, from the youngest to the oldest, the shtetl population had an impressive command of Hebrew that was much remarked upon. To a young halutz on his way to Palestine who spent five weeks teaching in Eishyshok, the town was a veritable marvel:

It served as a piece of homeland for a young Hebrew lad who was dreaming of aliyah, and the resurrection of the people and the language. Its Hebrew school has existed in a variety of shapes and sizes for close to three generations, before passing into the hands of its latest director. Three generations have received a systematic education in Hebrew, and Hebrew as a living, spoken language is known by almost everyone. Even heated debates with the teacher are conducted in pure Hebrew.[30]

The stormy debates in flawless Hebrew that so impressed this young man continued to rage for some time after his departure, many of them a continuation of an old conflict: the dispute over the religious content of the Yavneh curriculum, with one faction wishing to move the school back to an entirely Tarbut-based curriculum. Several attempts were made, but each ended in victory for the rabbi; as the chief administrator of the educational funds from America, he had the final say. The impact of American funding on shtetl affairs would only increase as time went on.

School principal Botwinik himself would become a victim of it. A complaint lodged by a student at the school eventually resulted in Botwinik's departure, for the student was closely connected not only to influential school board members but to one of the American families whose generous contributions kept the school afloat. Though some of the influential balebatim fought hard for Botwinik, their traditional power base had long since been eroded by all the changes that had occurred in the shtetl in the preceding decades, and they had no wealthy relatives in America to shore it up. Thus the man who was most responsible for creating the school now had to leave his beloved creation behind. After a brief period of working with his wife in their fabric store and tutoring students on the side, Botwinik left for Minsk-Mazowieck sometime in 1935–36. His son Leibke, a budding Hebrew scholar and graduate of a Tarbut teachers' seminary, remained behind and was appointed to a teaching position in the school — the only concession the pro-Botwinik faction was able to wrest from their opponents.

Quite apart from such conflicts and the distress over Botwinik's departure, the Hebrew school's enrollment declined after 1937, and the number of Jewish children attending the Polish Powszechna increased accordingly. This trend prevailed throughout the Vilna–Bialystok area, along the Lithuanian–Polish border, not because of Polonization, but as a response to the political and economic realities of the time. Thanks to new British immigration policies, the number of those able to make aliyah had declined from 13,256 in 1936 to 3,708 in 1937. The British White Paper of 1939 made things even worse.[31] To Jewish parents it seemed ever more likely that their children needed to be preparing themselves for a life in Poland, not in Eretz Israel — at least for the time being.

In Eishyshok, as elsewhere, children were sent to Polish schools to acquire a sound knowledge of Polish and a Polish diploma. Despite the vehement anti-Semitism of Eishyshok's Polish school principal, Jan Gurak, and the animosity of many of the faculty members, many a student was plucked out of the Hebrew school and forced to adapt to this new, hostile environment, all in the hope that they would thereby be able to advance themselves professionally. Though many parents did not explain why the change was being made, Leibke Kaganowicz's mother, Miriam — one of the original members of the Hebrew School board — made the practical reasons for her choice quite clear to him:

My mother . . . had aspirations for me to go beyond our little town. She was one of the most respected women of Eisiskes and wanted her sons to command the same respect. She decided that I should become an engineer and, knowing that I would not be accepted in an engineering university without fluency in Polish, she made up her mind that I would transfer to Polish school for my sixth and seventh years. I had no difficulty being accepted by the school, but I was certainly not accepted by the students. For the first time in my life, I was subjected to the full brunt of anti-Semitism. Centuries of hatred fed by the local Catholic clergy incited my Polish schoolmates to make daily attacks on me. I was beaten and kicked and teased unmercifully. I could not defend myself against these gang onslaughts and no one, not even my teachers, tried to defend me. Each day I would arrive home with bruises and cuts and torn clothes, and each day my mother would challenge me to return on the following day.

A class of the Polish Powszechna in Eishyshok. Principal Jan Gurak (center) worked with both the Germans and the AK in Eishyshok, Radun, and the vicinity during the war. A significant number of Jewish students were in this class. One of them was Leon Kahn (Leibke Kaganowicz) (third row, third from right), who survived the war as a partisan. PHOTO: BEN ZION SZREJDER. YESC, KAHN-KAGANOWICZ

"Of course, you can stay home, Leibke!" she would say. "We can apprentice you to the harnessmaker or maybe the baker!" knowing perfectly well that I would not give up my dream of becoming an engineer.

Her persistence won the day in the end. Gradually, the attacks decreased and in time I won a certain degree of respect from my fellow students and even from my teachers. This was not only the result of my stubborn refusal to quit, but also the result of my good progress in school. My tutor had provided me with a better grounding in Polish grammar than the rest of the class had. Eventually, even the anti-Semitic principal congratulated me on my achievement and assigned me a group of six Polish boys to tutor. They would walk home with me each day and over sweets and cakes we would review grammar. Although we never became good friends, at least they left me in peace after that.[32]

Other children also managed to adapt, and the school seems to have adapted to them. Jewish students were allowed to spend one hour once a week in religious studies. And the Polish and Jewish children participated in many joint activities, both inside and outside the classroom. There was even occasional contact between the Polish school and the Hebrew school, such as the orchestra, which drew students from both, and the soccer matches held on the athletic field at the new Horse Market — though these frequently ended in blows, regardless of who won.

The decline in attendance at the Hebrew school seems only to have encouraged its backers to strive for greater excellence, the better to lure students back. A revitalized education committee consisting of people who were fiercely devoted to the cause of Hebrew education lavished attention on the school, and secured additional funding, even at a time of political and economic hardship. The outbreak of World War II in 1939 found the Hebrew school at its educational zenith, about to begin a new school year with Moshe Yaakov Botwinik back at the helm — his opponents having emigrated to America.

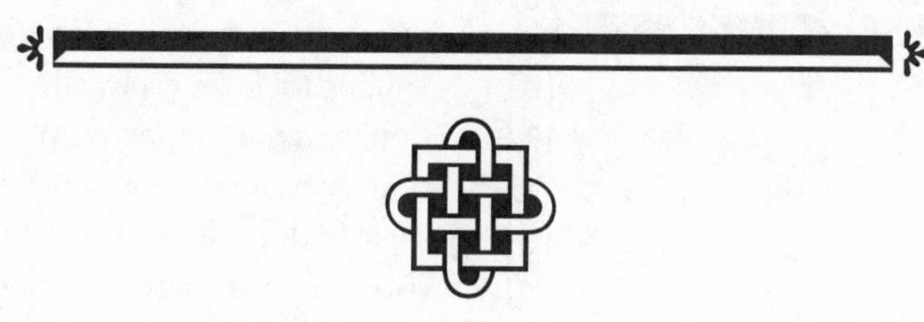

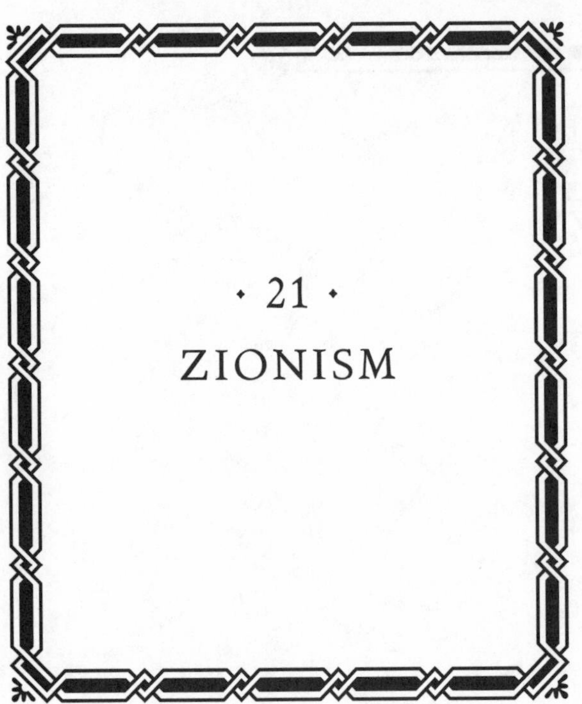

THE SAGE OF VOLOZHIN [RABBI NAFTALI ZVI YEHUDAH BERLIN] IS STILL DISCUSSING AT GREAT LENGTH HIS REPROOFS AND PROPOSALS [REGARDING THE SETTLEMENTS IN ERETZ ISRAEL], IT SEEMS THAT HE WOULD LIKE TO MAKE THE COLONIES INTO PLACES OF TORAH LIKE VOLOZHIN AND EISHYSHOK.

A letter from Moshe Leib Lilienbloom to Menahem Ussishkin, January 18, 1888, in Alter Droyanov ed. KETAVIM LE-TOLDOT HIBBAT ZION VE-YISHUV ERETZ-ISRAEL.

IN THE NINETEENTH CENTURY, MASKILIM WHO HAD GROWN CRITICAL OF THE MENdelssohnian Haskalah began promoting a new, nationalist ideology, one that called for the fostering of the Hebrew language and loyalty to the Jewish nation. Peretz Smolenskin's Hebrew-language newspaper *Ha-Shahar* (The Dawn) was their voice. Over the course of the sixteen years of the paper's existence, 1868–84, events would conspire to make the assimilationist goals of an earlier generation seem a pipe dream, new ideas a dire necessity.

The assassination of Tzar Alexander II in March 1881 led to anti-Jewish pogroms as well as anti-Jewish legislation, including the May Laws of 1882, which enacted various economic sanctions against the Jews, and the numerus clausus, a quota system barring them from Russian schools. Though staunch supporters of the Haskalah continued to believe in the possibility of progress even after 1881, other Jews, especially the younger generation, became supporters of the Russian revolutionary movement around this time. They put their faith in the radical reform of the basic institutions of society, believing that the fall of the tzars would lead to a new world, one in which freedom and justice for all would, of course, mean an end to the persecution of the Jews as well. A third group looked to the United States for their new world. And a fourth group, consisting of both older maskilim and young intellectuals, turned to Jewish nationalism with renewed vigor. They established the Hibbat Zion (Love of Zion) movement.

Unlike Peretz Smolenskin, whose sense of the Jews as a nation had a mainly spiritual, cultural dimension, this group had come to the conclusion that the situation of the Jews in Russia could not be remedied and that emigration to Eretz Israel was the answer. There the Jews would engage freely in productive occupations, revive their knowledge of Hebrew as a spoken language, and usher in the renaissance of a specifically Jewish culture. In order to realize their project, they called for an alliance with the Jewish masses, whose attachment to their culture, their traditions, and their languages (both Yiddish and Hebrew) was still intact. Hibbat Zion's platform was articulated first in the Russian-language paper *Rasvet* (the Dawn; 1879–83), later in the Hebrew-language papers *Ha-Melitz* (the Mediator; 1860–1904) and *Ha-Maggid* (the Declarer; 1856–1903).

Dr. Theodor Herzl (1860–1904), father of political Zionism and founder of the World Zionist Organization.

THE LONGING FOR ZION IN JEWISH HISTORY

Ever since the Jews were exiled from the Land of Israel into the Diaspora, the longing to return has been central to Jewish consciousness, and bound up inseparably with the longing for the Messiah, for when the Messiah comes, then shall all Jews be summoned by his trumpet to their homeland. Thus, long before modern nationalism made it a realistic possibility for the masses, the idea of the "return" to Israel constituted an integral part of the Diaspora experience, and the bond between the people and their homeland was thereby sustained.

Some people were able to make the idea a reality. Throughout the centuries a relatively small number of individuals, rich and poor, young and old, alone or as part of families or religious sects, did make aliyah to the Holy Land. Buoyed by love for Zion, fired with eschatological, messianic hopes, they made the perilous journey to Eretz Israel to settle near the holy places, or to have the merit of being buried in its hallowed ground. These people joined the Old Yishuv — the pre-Zionist community of Jews in Palestine.

For most Jews, however, the idea remained an idea, one destined to be realized only with the coming of the Messiah. But from the time of the destruction of the Second Temple in Jerusalem, it was an idea invoked at every important juncture of the individual's and the community's life cycle. Jewish redemption (geulah), when it finally occurred, would take the form of the complete ingathering of the exiles (Kibbutz Galuiot) from "the four corners of the world," and until it occurred it would remain the central aspiration of Jewish life: "If I forget thee, O Jerusalem, Let my right hand forget her cunning."[1]

At home and at synagogue, the Jews continually affirmed their commitment to the "return." Jews faced in the direction of Jerusalem to recite their daily prayers, concluded each Passover Seder celebration with the words "Next year in Jerusalem," consoled the bereaved with the traditional phrase "May God comfort you among the mourners of Zion and Jerusalem." The very calendar governing Jewish life is an expression both of universal ideas and the agricultural seasons in the Land of Israel. Thus the Jewish people lived for almost two thousand years in two time zones, one physical, the other spiritual. In the one they coped with exile; in the other they awaited redemption. Between these two poles swung the pendulum of Jewish history.

Then in the mid-nineteenth century, the two poles began to converge. The attitude toward redemption and the return to the Promised Land changed from the miraculous and the messianic to the realistic and the practical.

THE ROOTS OF MODERN ZIONISM

Religious messianism had always imagined the redemption of the Jews as an interaction between

Jews and God, with non-Jews playing various supporting roles in the drama: as a chastising rod in the divine hand, or as mere spectator, there to pay homage at the end of the play.[2] On the cutting edge of modern Zionism, in its most revolutionary expression, the essential dialectic was reimagined: it was now between Jews and non-Jews, the Jews and the nations of the earth.

Thus, in the mid-nineteenth century, the yearning for Zion began to assume nationalistic dimensions. The spiritual longing for Eretz Israel evolved into a practical wish to settle there, to resurrect Hebrew as a daily, spoken language. Partly this was in keeping with the spirit of the times, for the 1840s was the Spring of Nations, when concepts of nationhood and self-determination for individual peoples were spreading throughout Europe. But it was also a response to events afflicting the Jews specifically, causing them to doubt that they could ever find the universal acceptance that the Haskalah had promised them.

The notorious Damascus blood libel of 1840, when once again the Jews were accused of ritual murder during the festival of Passover, this time of a Capuchin monk who had suddenly disappeared, was one of these critical events. Prominent Jews from around the world, including James and Salomon Rothschild, of the banking family, the German socialist Ferdinand Lassalle, the French politician Adolphe Crémieux, the noted Orientalist Solomon Munk, and the British philanthropist Moses Montefiore, mounted a consolidated effort on behalf of the Jewish community—one of the first times they had acted together on such a large scale. Galvanizing international public opinion, they forced the release of those who had been arrested for the supposed murder. By their unified action they also awoke in their own people an understanding of the potential efficacy of Jewish solidarity.

These were stormy, interesting times. On the one hand, rumors were circulating in the Balkans and in Eastern Europe (as well as among Polish émigrés in Paris) that 1840 would see the coming of the Messiah, and there was great excitement over this impending event. On the other, Rabbi Yehudah Alkalai (1798–1878) was calling for the Jews to transform their messianic expectations into practical ones, to launch a realistic effort to settle in the Land of Israel. Alkalai was born in Sarajevo and, after studying in Jerusalem, had returned to Serbia where, since 1825, he had served as the rabbi of Semlin, Serbia's capital. Alkalai was greatly influenced not only by the Damascus case but by the successful national war of independence of the nearby Greeks, and the growing tide of nationalism in the Balkans, where the Serbs, among other nations, were mustering the strength to rise against the Turks.

Believing that the Jews needed to equip themselves with the attributes of a modern nation, Alkalai proposed that world Jewry unite into a single nation whose homeland was in Eretz Israel and whose common language was modern Hebrew. "I wish to attest," he wrote, "to the pain I have always felt at the error of our ancestors that they allowed our Holy Tongue to be forgotten. Because of this, our people was divided into seventy peoples, our one language was replaced by the seventy languages of the land of exile."[3]

Rabbi Hirsch Kalischer (1795–1874) was another early voice for Jewish nationalism. Born in Posen, he served as rabbi for forty years in the community of Thorn, and was more keenly aware than Alkalai of the growing misery of the Jews in Eastern Europe. He, too, was profoundly influenced by the swelling tide of nationalism, and preached Zionism as a solution to the persecution of the Jews.

Alkalai and Kalischer, in turn, were to have an influence on Reb Nathan Friedland, the maggid of Tabirg who became a pioneer of the modern Zionist idea in Lithuania. After meeting Kalischer in Thorn, Friedland became his devoted emissary with regard to the settlement of Eretz Israel. Seeking to raise funds and shape public opinion to Kalischer's ends, Friedland traveled to Paris, where he presented a memorandum stating the Zionist case to Napoleon III, and also met with Adolphe Crémieux and Dr. Albert Cohen; to London, where he met with Sir Moses Montefiore; and to shtetlekh throughout Lithuania. His book *A Cup of Deliverance (Kos Yeshuot)*, in which he called for a return to the Land of Israel without messianic intervention, was published in 1859. These efforts brought tangible results: the purchase of land on the outskirts of Yaffo, Palestine, in 1866, and the subsequent founding of the agricultural school Mikveh Israel in 1870. In 1882 Friedland himself settled in Palestine, where he died a year later.[4]

David Gordon (1831–1886) was another Lithuanian pioneer supporting Jewish settlement in the Land of Israel. Influenced by Kalischer, whose book *Seeking Zion (Drishat Zion)* he had read, and later by the Polish uprising of 1863 in which both Russians and Poles pressured the Jews to take sides — much to the eventual detriment of those who chose the losing (Polish) side — he made his journal, *Ha-Maggid*, one of the leading voices of the Hibbat Zion movement.[5]

Gordon had also been influenced by Moses Hess (1812–1875), a German Jewish socialist who was the first figure in Zionist history whose ideas were shaped less by Jewish tradition than by the European experience. Hess was at the Paris barricades in 1848, and, until he broke with him over the publication of *The Communist Manifesto* that same year, a close colleague of Karl Marx's. Hess's theory of Jewish nationalism, as expressed in his book *Rome and Jerusalem* (1862), was developed under the impact of the events that led to the unification of Italy in 1859. Hess saw the Jewish cause as "the last national problem" now that Italy had solved its own.

As these various voices of Jewish nationalism filled the air, efforts were begun to channel their ideas into organized group activities that could make them a reality. Meetings were held, societies were formed. In 1872 in Grodno sixty delegates organized themselves into Dorshei Zion ve-Yerushalaim (the Seekers of Zion and Jerusalem); in 1877 in Vilna a group calling itself Shaalu Shlom Yerushalaim (Seek the Peace of Jerusalem) was founded, a branch of which eventually made its way to Eishyshok. Both the Vilna- and the Grodno-based groups had as their agenda the settlement of Eretz Israel.[6]

HIBBAT ZION

Finally in 1881, in the aftermath of the pogroms that followed the assassination of Tzar Alexander II, the Hibbat Zion movement was founded in Russia. Since no strong defense of the Jews had been made by either the central government or the local authorities, much less by the Jews' Russian neighbors, the pogroms were a severe blow to the maskilim, the end of an era for many who had seen closer relations with the Russian people as an answer to the isolation of the Jews. Now many who had become estranged from the Jewish community in the process of seeking acceptance by the Russians came back. The idea of a Jewish homeland where the Jew would not be an alien, an outsider, took on new life. Hibbat Zion, and all the Zionist groups that were part of this umbrella organization, now supplanted the Haskalah as the leading voice for change among the Jews.

The first truly modern Zionist movement in history, Hibbat Zion was not just a response to the events of the moment, but the culmination of much activity by many different individuals and societies over the years, and its ideology was a sort of crystallization of what had long been said by the various Zionist forerunners who had been building the movement: Only in a country of their own could the Jews finally achieve freedom from centuries of anti-Semitism.

On November 6, 1884, in honor of the one

hundredth birthday of Sir Moses Montefiore, the British philanthropist who had long been a generous donor to settlements in the Land of Israel, the first conference of all active members of Hibbat Zion took place in Katowice. Most participants at the conference were from Russian associations; the rest were from Romania, Germany, and England. Much of the intellectual leadership was provided by two formerly ardent followers of the Russification goals of the Haskalah, Moshe Leib Lilienblum (1843–1910) and Dr. Leo Pinsker (1821–1891). In earlier days Lilienblum had written *Hatteot Neurim* (Sins of Youth), an autobiographical account of an East European shtetl prodigy who succumbed to the attractions of the Haskalah; now his energies were focused not on reforming the Jews so that they could be integrated into the surrounding society, but on resettling them. In *Auto-Emancipation* (1882), Pinsker called for a Jewish homeland bought with Jewish money and safeguarded by international guarantees.

The second Hibbat Zion conference took place in 1887 in Druskieniki, where it was resolved that the movement be called Hovevei Zion (Lovers of Zion). In an effort to wrest the leadership of the movement from the maskilim, Rabbi Samuel Mohilever of Bialystok attempted to make it into a religious movement headed by rabbis, but he was upstaged by younger, secular members, among them Menahem Ussishkin, who would later be instrumental in founding the heder metukan (reconstructed or reformed heder) movement. In a compromise, Pinsker was elected the head of Hovevei Zion, to serve with six advisers, including three rabbis, all of them from Lithuania: Rabbi Mohilever, Naftali Zvi Yehudah Berlin of Volozhin (the Neziv), and Mordekhai Eliasberg, originally of Eishyshok. The movement that resulted from this compromise was a blend of older religious groups and individuals longing for the coming of the Messiah and the restoration of Zion on the one hand, and younger, more secular groups committed to the modern spirit of nationalism and a revival of the Hebrew language on the other. Its agenda was moderate: the gradual settlement of Eretz Israel as a step in the direction leading to the ultimate goal — the total ingathering of the exiles.

Despite the fact that well-known religious figures were among its leadership, Hovevei Zion met with opposition from many in the Orthodox community, most prominently Rabbi Yaakov Lifshitz (1838–1921) of Kovno, a man who had once studied in Eishyshok and had also once been secretary to Rabbi Yitzhak Elhanan Spektor (who did not share his views). In an article that appeared in *Ha-Melitz* around this time, this opposition group was dubbed "the Black Office"; their activities marked the beginning of an organized anti-Zionist movement drawn from ultra-Orthodox circles.[7]

These activities notwithstanding, Hovevei Zion did make some progress toward its fund-raising and emigration goals. New settlements in Palestine included those at Rehovot, Haderah, Rishon Le-Zion, and Yissod Ha-Maalah; in addition, an earlier settlement in Petah-Tikvah was revived. Meanwhile, new Hovevei Zion associations were being established not just in Lithuania and Russia but in Galicia, Austria, and various places in Western Europe as well as the United States and Canada, and calls for an international meeting of all the groups began to be heard.

THEODOR HERZL

In 1897 they were heeded. The distinguished Viennese journalist Theodor Herzl (1860–1904) had joined the movement, publishing a book titled *Der Judenstaat* (The Jewish State) in 1896. Its arguments were similar to those of Leo Pinsker in *Auto-Emancipation*, but they met with a much wider, more enthusiastic response, not just in Eastern Europe, where people were moved by the return of this "Westerner" to his people, but in the West, too, because Herzl was well known there. His prestige as a journalist of international renown helped to overcome the indifference of many comfortably assimilated Western Jews, who had previously been uninterested in the concept of a Jewish national identity, much less a Jewish state. Herzl's physical appearance, which resembled that of an ancient prophet — or perhaps a great modern statesman — no doubt added to the power and resonance of his message. In the summer of 1897, at Herzl's urging, the First Zionist Congress was convened in Basel, Switzerland. The vast majority of Hovevei Zion societies now joined the new Zionist Organization, though the central leadership of Hovevei Zion, the Odessa Committee, continued to function separately until the Bolshevik takeover in 1919.

Herzl knew little about Hebrew language and culture. He saw the "Jewish question" as an international political issue requiring the attention of the world community — which the conference in Basel did much to galvanize. Like Pinsker, Herzl wanted the settlement in Palestine to be an autonomous Jewish state backed by international guarantees. Thus the First Zionist Congress had about it the aura of a Jewish world parliament, with Herzl acting as the head of state or prime minister. As Herzl noted in his diary: "In Basel I have created the Jewish State."

And the State now had its own official press, which was to appear in several languages, as well as its own bank, the Jewish Colonial Trust, which was established during the Congress as a means of supporting the nationalist movement through the buying of land in Palestine. Every member of the Zionist Organization paid a membership fee — called a shekel, after the biblical currency — which entitled him to voting rights; the number of shekels from a given region determined the number of votes that region had.

Herzl himself became the most prominent among the new national heroes of the Zionist movement, the men who were now eligible for a place in the Jewish pantheon formerly composed almost exclusively of rabbis. Stories told about his wisdom and concern for others rivaled those told about the Haffetz Hayyim. His birthday became an important day on the calendar. His picture was reproduced everywhere, in homes and synagogues, public places and private; it was to be found on watches, tapestries, Simhat Torah flags, and even in the sukkah.[8] When he died a premature death in 1904, thousands of male infants were named after him.

If Herzl was the political leader of the new state, Hayyim Nahman Bialik (1873–1934) was its poet laureate. Known as the poet of the National Awakening, as the Zionist movement was also known, Bialik spoke for both the nationalist and the cultural Zionists, for he believed that the Jews would achieve redemption as a people via the restoration of the Hebrew language and culture, *and* the establishment of their ancestral land as a nation among nations.

By the turn of the century, Zionism was well on its way to becoming a huge mass movement among Jews around the world, and nowhere more so than in Eastern Europe, where the Jews were suffering wave upon wave of violence as well as economic hardship, military conscription, prejudice, hatred, and discrimination. Perhaps a Jewish homeland would be the answer to all their problems.

EISHYSHOK CONTEMPLATES ZION

Like other small towns in the Pale of Settlement, especially in the Vilna–Grodno region, Eishyshok had for generations been saying farewells to the occasional pilgrim who made the treacherous journey to the Holy Land to join the Old Yishuv.[9] These rare departures were marked by a huge procession accompanying the oleh (emigrant) to the bridge that led from the shtetl, into the world beyond. Thus when Shifra the midwife decided to entrust her profession to younger hands and leave for the Holy Land, the old widow's carriage was followed by all the people of the shtetl, including many whom she herself had helped usher into the world. Clutching her famous lantern in her hands, the one she had carried to the bedsides of hundreds of women in labor, she sat looking out at the crowd surrounding her carriage. As she took her leave at the bridge, she promised to remember them all in her prayers in Jerusalem, where the same faithful lantern that had lighted her way through many a dark Eishyshok night would now guide her steps to the Western Wall.

Reb Layzer Wilkanski also wished to make aliyah, but was waiting for the summons of the Messiah's shofar. Still, it gave him pause when one day his long coat caught in the wheel of a carriage that was transporting another friend on the first stage of that same journey, and the friend turned to him and said: "It is an omen that you too will ascend to Eretz Israel."

Soon these occasional departures, many of which were undertaken in old age to satisfy the longing to die on holy ground, would give way to a flood of emigration, under the influence of the new Zionist movement. Reb Layzer himself would leave with his wife Batia in 1914, all six of their children having preceded them (as well as most of the grandchildren from Reb Layzer's first marriage).

Zionism, like the Haskalah, was imported into the shtetl by yeshivah students, both those who came from outside the shtetl and native Eishyshkians who studied elsewhere and returned aflame with all the new ideas. The shtetl also played host to a number of emissaries from the various groups promoting Jewish emigration, including, on at least one memorable occasion, Baron Maurice Hirsch's Jewish Colonization Association (ICA). The ICA aimed to facilitate the mass emigration of Jews from Russia not by sending them to Palestine, as the Zionists intended, but by establishing agricultural colonies in South America, particularly in Argentina and Brazil. Hirsch (1831–1896), a great philanthropist, and his wife Clara (1833–1899) had committed themselves financially to paying for the journey, purchasing vast tracts of land and funding the agricultural development of the fields, gardens, and orchards where, they believed, the downtrodden Jews of Russia could achieve the desired moral and economic rehabilitation.

When the ICA emissary-cum-bookseller arrived in Eishyshok in the early 1800s, he put the shtetl in an uproar. First there was the near scandal of the photograph. Among the standard photos of rabbinical personalities that booksellers routinely offered for sale was one that showed a husband and wife in a synagogue, he without a beard, she without a haircovering: Maurice and Clara Hirsch themselves. Then there was the question of what to do about the Hirsches' offer to pay for the journey to a new country — a particularly appealing offer to the many people who had lost their lands in recent times. The tzarist decree of 1869 that transferred land from Jews to non-Jews had fallen with particular force on many landowners from Eishyshok, and the May Laws of 1882 had displaced many of the farmers in the villages nearby. For all these people the Hirsches' offer was the chance to be real farmers again, and not merely cultivators of small garden plots.

From the beth midrash to the market square the debate raged, between those who wanted to add their names to the long list the emissary had compiled during his visits to other shtetlekh and those who were awaiting the coming of the Messiah. Abba Arikha the shoemaker, for example, had already heard the Messiah casting off his rusty broken chains, which meant that he was on his way, and that the entire shtetl would soon be lining up behind him and crossing to the Land of Israel on paper bridges. What would happen then to those who had gone to South America to become farmers? Would the Land of Israel extend all the way to Argentina and Brazil? Or would those who had left find themselves once more in the position of being owners of land in the Diaspora, subject to the edict of foreign governments who could deprive them of their property at will? It seemed the wrong time to sign up for land in Argentina. And so no one, at least no one who was willing to admit to it in public, signed up with the emissary of Baron Hirsch.[10] Nonetheless, documents show that a small contingent of Eishyshkians did indeed emigrate to Argentina around this time, though whether they went in response to this particular emissary's appeal or to that of a later representative of the ICA is not known.

By 1898, many people in Eishyshok, including Abba the shoemaker, had begun to see the possibility of imminent redemption in another form. Eishyshkians had begun to be intensely involved in the activities of Hovevei Zion, joining groups like Shaalu Shlom Yerushalaim (Seek the Peace of Jerusalem), Bnei Moshe (Sons of Moses), and others. So the speaker who addressed them one spring night in 1898 found a ready audience for his message:

A person has arisen, by the name of Dr. Herzl, who will bring redemption to his people. He will bring the people back to their homeland, with the sanction of the Sultan and of all the Kingdoms of the World. Thus the prophecy of Isaiah will be fulfilled: "And they shall bring thy sons in their bosom. And thy daughters shall be carried upon their shoulders." We are no longer discussing messianism, but the ingathering of exiles. The new Zionism is the continuation of Hibbat Zion but with a shortcut—first we establish a state, then the messiah comes.

For how long will we suffer in silence? Let us free ourselves. Let each Jew purchase a shekel and a share of the Jewish Colonial Bank. The Sultan himself will not be able to resist Herzl's charm, nor the power of the bank shares.[11]

This time the speaker invoking redemption was not a bearded maggid bedecked in a prayer shawl delivering a sermon in front of the Holy Ark in the Old Beth Midrash. It was a young man standing before a large crowd in the spacious new tavern built by Yaakov Seltskin, after his recent return from America. The walls were hung with pictures of Herzl; a table in the corner displayed books, newspapers, and pamphlets describing the new Zionist Organization; a glittering oil lamp cast a bright light on everything within its reach, including the speaker, eighteen-year-old Yitzhak Wilkanski, who was on spring recess from his studies in Telz. For the occasion he had had the family tailor alter his long, traditional kapote (coat) into a short, stylish one. And so there he stood, in the spotlight, fashionably dressed, proclaiming his faith in the Jewish State that Theodor Herzl was intending to establish in the old-new Jewish homeland.

That spring night of 1898, the first modern Zionist political organization was established in Eishyshok. Yaakov Pikarski was chosen as its president, and Naftali Ben Yehuda as secretary. Here, as elsewhere, one of the major activities of the Zionist movement was fund-raising, through sales of the shekel and of shares in the Jewish Colonial Bank. Presiding over these fundraisers, delivering their impassioned speeches, were emissaries sent by the regional Zionist Organization office, which was adept at matching the personality of the emissary to the dynamics of a particular shtetl. Thus the emissaries sent to Eishyshok were usually accomplished Talmudic scholars, eloquent maggidim known for their oratorical skills.

During a typical Zionist rally the Old Beth Midrash would be filled to capacity, mainly with yeshivah students and other young people, as well as members of the artisan class. A mere handful of the balebatim would attend, with most of them making their entrance only when it was time to recite the evening prayer. Nonetheless, the neeman of the kahal, Eliyahu Streltzer, was one of those who one night approached the table where the sales were transacted. His purchase of a shekel was viewed by many as official approval of Zionism. Soon after his dramatic gesture, Reb Eliyahu, his fourth wife, and their three-year-old daughter, along with a yeshivah student from Mezrich, set off for Jerusalem. As usual, a processional accompanied the small group to the bridge, but this one was even larger and more impressive than most, in deference to Reb Eliyahu's status. The Haffetz Hayyim himself gave the priestly benediction at the moment of leavetaking, and blessed the little girl, Hayya Leah, with "a long life." She lived to be ninety-seven.[12]

By the turn of the century, many Eishyshkians had demonstrated that they were committed body, soul, and pocketbook to the Zionist idea, for they had purchased 140 shares in the Zionist bank at a price of 10 rubles per share — a very substantial sum of money for the average Eishyshok Jew.[13] This generosity toward rebuilding and resettling the Land of Israel would henceforth be a hallmark of Eishyshok.

But it would be some time before most of the balebatim supported the movement. At the turn of the century the shtetl was divided, with the artisans and many of the young people on one side, and a significant number of the balebatim, especially those from the Old Beth Midrash crowd, on the other. For those in the tailors' and shoemakers' minyans, Herzl's Zionism promised to be the great equalizer, a people's movement that honored labor. They hoped it would free them from their class bondage and the social and economic stigma that had marked their lives for generations. For the young, Zionism was a noble cause that called to them. If they answered, it promised to put them on the magic road to the world beyond the bridge, the land of their forefathers. There they would build a Jewish homeland and be masters of their own fate, speakers of their own language, free at last of the fear of government decrees, of the harassment, prejudice, and violence that had been the lot of their people for as long as anyone could remember. For the balebatim, however, the class that had ruled the shtetl for hundreds of years, Zionism was a threat to their authority. With its political, secular ideology and its independent leadership, which operated at global as well as regional and local levels, Zionism presented a direct challenge to them, and to a way of life that had prevailed for centuries.

Indeed, just as feared, the Zionist Youth Organization in Eishyshok swiftly discarded one taboo after another. Coed and classless in a world that was in so many ways gender-segregated and class-bound, it held meetings at the home of its president, Yaakov Pikarski, that allowed young men and women from the shtetl to mix with each other and with students from the yeshivah, without regard for the usual social boundaries; Pikarski played on his violin new Zionist tunes that had been taught to him by Yitzhak Wilkanski; and together everyone sang Zionist songs, their haunting melodies and rousing lyrics overpowering the Talmud chant issuing from the Old Beth Midrash. "Bring to Zion your flags,/Flags of the Camp of Judah" could be heard echoing through the huge market square.

Young Meir Wilkanski would return home from these meetings at dawn and slip quietly under his covers. But Reb Layzer and Batia knew that their son was returning from a Zionist meeting, and not from a long night of study.[14] Their spirited daughter Sarah had also joined the Zionist camp. She even tried to turn their very house into a symbol of Zionist ideals: one day as she was painting its eastern wall, the mizrah, she decided to reduce the size of the square that was traditionally left unpainted as a reminder of the destruction of the Temple. When challenged, she defended her actions by claiming that the world no longer needed such a reminder since redemption was on the way. But Reb Layzer ordered her to repaint the wall and restore the unpainted square to its original size. She did.

The Wilkanski children became the undisputed leaders of the shtetl's Zionist movement. And once again Reb Layzer stood accused of harboring the evils of dissidence and innovation in his own household. First the mixed heder and the Haskalah, now Zionism (and with it the teaching of Hebrew as a living, spoken language, which many regarded as a violation of its sacredness).

Reb Layzer the dayyan, also known as Reb Layzer der Hokhem (the wise), was greatly perplexed over the issue of Zionism and went in search of advice. Alas, his two great mentors were divided. Rabbi Yitzhak Elhanan Spektor of Kovno was a great supporter of Hovevei Zion; in fact, the preparatory meeting for the appointment of local representatives to the Hibbat Zion meeting of 1884 in Katowice took place in Rabbi Spektor's home. But the Haffetz Hayyim, though a great lover of Israel, was awaiting messianic, not nationalist, Zionist redemption. Indeed, as a kohen, he purified himself daily by an immersion in the river so that he would at all times be prepared for the coming of the Messiah, and the subsequent resumption of his priestly duties in the rebuilt Temple in Jerusalem.

To resolve his dilemma Reb Layzer turned to his books, studying one rabbinic authority after another. Day by day his children watched as the cloud that sat on his wrinkled forehead slowly disappeared, until the moment when he rose from his book-laden table, stood next to his wife, and with a smile on his face announced: "If the Messiah has not yet come, his footsteps are already audible."[15] For the Wilkanski children and many other young people in the shtetl, Reb Layzer's statement was yet another sign that the establishment was giving official approval to the Zionist movement.

THE WILKANSKIS IN THE LAND OF ISRAEL

The Wilkanski children soon took action on their Zionist ideals. Voting with his feet in opposition to the Uganda Plan, which would have resettled the Jews in Africa rather than Palestine, Meir made aliyah in 1904, toward the beginning of the second wave of Zionist emigrations (which lasted until 1914, when World War I broke out).

As a participant in this Second Aliyah, Meir joined thousands of idealistic young Jews from all over the Pale of Settlement as well as other corners of the Russian empire, many of whom had been shocked into action by the 1903 Kishinev pogrom. Confronting the grim reality that the Russian authorities would not come to the defense of the Jewish community even in the face of wanton murder, rape, and torture, as well as massive destruction of homes and shops, and that many of the Russian people were indifferent to the resulting suffering, numerous Jews decided the time was right for a homeland of their own. They were also responding to events within the Zionist movement itself—the Uganda Plan, the death of Theodor Herzl in 1904, and the stagnation of the Palestinian colonies founded in the 1880s and 1890s by Baron Edmond de Rothschild—all of which aroused so much fear over the fate of the nationalist movement that Eastern European Jews felt compelled to flock to Palestine to offer their support.

For Meir the date of his arrival in Eretz Israel at the age of twenty-two became his second birthday, the beginning of a new life. He settled in Yaffo, the center of the Second Aliyah.

One of the rituals of the newly arrived halutzim was to walk through the country on foot, reestablishing the covenant with the land and following in the footsteps of biblical heroes like Abraham. As he did so, Meir was dismayed to discover his hallowed bonding with the land being violated by the sounds of fellow hikers who did not speak Hebrew. In the book he wrote to commemorate his journey, he complained bitterly of these so-called goyim: "To hike through the Galil, to walk among the Galil mountains, and the entire trip to hear only

Russian being spoken! One is in the Land of the Hebrews, and yet it sounds as if one walks in the streets of Moscow. It robs the entire trip of its unique charm."[16]

Meir was quick to learn that the Hebrew language had fared much better in his own shtetl than in the Land of Israel, where the Ashkenazim of the Old Yishuv spoke Yiddish, Baron de Rothschild's colonists promoted the study of French, and the majority of the halutzim spoke Russian.[17] Meir also learned early on that life in the new land was hard. Beneath the bright blue skies, Palestine was a bleak, malaria-ridden place demanding many sacrifices and presenting many dangers. The result was a life of often backbreaking manual labor, dedicated to reclaiming the barren land with one's own hands, and requiring a veritable "Religion of Labor," in the words of Aaron David Gordon (1856–1922), the Tolstoyan figure who was known as the secular saint and mystic of the Zionist movement. Not surprisingly, Meir Wilkanski embraced this new religion with as much fervor as he had observed the ancient traditions as a young child in the home of his parents. For him, as for so many others in the Second Aliyah, the dream of rebuilding a homeland and reviving the Hebrew language was brighter than the bleak reality. Publishing under the name Volkani-Elazari, he would prove one of the most optimistic chroniclers of that idealistic time, writing inspirational stories that depicted the lives of his fellow halutzim.

From 1904 to 1908 Meir worked as an agricultural laborer in Petah-Tikvah, Rishon Le-Zion, Mikveh-Israel, Rehovot, and wherever else he could find an honest day's work — which was not always easy, since the Jewish farmers of Baron de Rothschild's colonies preferred cheap Arab labor. He dug irrigation ditches in orchards, picked oranges, olives, and grapes, and dug wells. And always, despite the hard work and the scarcity of money, the idealistic young man was excited to find himself in a land where the chapters and verses of the Bible were constantly coming alive before his very eyes. "We are digging a well! We are doing what Abraham and Isaac did, and in the same land. We are enriching our beloved land with water."[18] What he had studied in books in heder he was now experiencing firsthand.

Sarah Rubin (center) at the train station about to start her journey to Eretz Israel in 1906. The Wilkanski siblings say goodbye to her, their future sister-in-law, bride of brother Meir. On the wall, on both sides of Sarah, is a Hebrew statement "From the land of the Diaspora to Zion." The Wilkanski siblings (right to left): Leah, Mordekhai, Sarah, Yitzhak, Esther, and a family friend. PHOTO: FROECK, KÖNIGSBERG. YESC, WILKANSKI

As might be expected, Meir was an avid correspondent, and his letters about the beauty of his new land, the joys of working to reclaim it through the labor of his own hands, were widely read throughout Eishyshok — not just in his sisters' Hebrew-speaking clubs and the various Zionist gatherings, but in the beth midrash as well. To many of his peers back home, Meir seemed the very embodiment of success: a young man who had had the courage to leave and thereby realized all his dreams. Some were inspired to follow in his footsteps; others who did not have the same courage (or the same support from their parents) took from his letters the hope that one day they too might reach Eretz Israel.

Meir was particularly fervent in encouraging his family to join him. In one of his letters he urged his father, Reb Layzer, to make the Passover promise of "Next year in Jerusalem" a reality.[19] And eventually the whole Wilkanski family would do so. First came Sarah Rubin, Meir's bride, and his siblings Mordekhai and Esther in 1906. They were followed by Meir's sister Sarah, their brother Yitzhak, and Yitzhak's wife Sarah (née Krieger) in 1908. Leah came in 1911.

In 1914 Sarah Wilkanski returned to Eishyshok to pressure her parents to join her and her siblings in their new homeland. Though Reb Layzer was hesitant to make aliyah, as he was still waiting for the Messiah to show him the way, he agreed to accompany Sarah to Radun, where they could seek the advice of the Haffetz Hayyim. The sage of Radun said to Sarah, "If you can promise that your father will receive the same loving care and respect in Eretz Israel as he did in Eishyshok, then he should go.'" "Definitely yes!" Sarah replied, in an emphatic voice. The Haffetz Hayyim gave his blessing: "Since Sarah says so, then it is all right for you to go." Later that year Reb Layzer and his wife Batia joined the rest of the family in Palestine.

The Wilkanski family poses for a photo in the newly established town of Tel Aviv: (right to left) Sarah (née Krieger) and husband Yitzhak; Sarah and Esther; Meir with wife Sarah (née Rubin) and baby daughter Temira. Lying on the ground is Mordekhai. YESC, WILKANSKI

THE GLOBAL POLITICS OF ZIONISM

By the turn of the century at least a few Eishyshkians were active in Zionist organizations not just on the home front, but at the national and international level as well, and many others were

avidly interested in what went on at the major gatherings. The Minsk Conference in August 1902, for example, which was to be the first as well as the last legal Zionist conference on Russian soil, was attended by Shmuel Senitski.[20] A native son of Eishyshok, member of one of its founding families, and former student at the Kibbutz ha-Prushim, Senitski was a lawyer who had been elected as the representative of his fellow Zionists in the shtetl. Though he was one of Eishyshok's earliest Zionists from among the balebatim, Senitski himself would never make it to Palestine. He, his wife, and his two daughters were among those murdered in 1941.

Also attending the conference was another former student at the Eishyshok yeshivah, Rabbi Yitzhak Yaakov Reines, who would later head his own yeshivah in nearby Lida. Rabbi Reines was one of the leaders of Mizrahi, the religious Zionist movement he had recently helped to organize. He and Shmuel Senitski shared a moving moment listening to Moshe Leib Lilienblum give the opening speech and a prayer of thanksgiving for the growth of the Zionist movement since the days of Hovevei Zion. How much had changed in the past several decades, years that had paved the way for this formerly forbidden, radical author — Lilienblum's memoir of a youth spent under the influence of the Haskalah had been banned from the yeshivah during their own student days — to assume a position of leadership, in a movement on the verge of becoming mainstream.

People in the shtetl, hungry for news of the latest events, eagerly awaited Senitski's return. The report he gave when he came back was comprehensive, encompassing both the many debates and discussions as well as what he called the "concrete" decisions. But since in Yiddish the word for "concrete" was very close to *kotlet*, the word for

A "who's who" of the political, ideological, and educational Zionist leaders of Eretz Israel in 1920: Chaim Weizmann (seated at table, center), later elected first president of Israel (1949–52); to his left is seated Sir Herbert L. Samuel, first high commissioner of Palestine (1920–25); standing behind Weizmann, underneath Herzl's portrait, is Yitzhak Wilkanski. PHOTO: AVRAHAM SUSKIN, YAFFO. YESC, WILKANSKI

"hamburger," there was great confusion in the shtetl about why hamburger had been a big issue at a Zionist conference. Once that confusion was sorted out, Senitski described the major issues that had dominated the conference, which were rooted in the divisions between the cultural Zionists, the political Zionists, and the religious Zionists.

The cultural Zionists, who tended to be secular in their orientation, focused on restoring Hebrew as the national language of the Jewish people, and as the basis for a revived national culture. One of their leaders was the Hebrew writer and educator Asher Zvi Ginzberg (1856–1927), known as Ahad Ha'am (One of the People). Ahad Ha'am opposed Herzl's political Zionism, for he felt it was too early to be thinking about founding a Jewish state, since a Jewish state that was not informed by and based on traditional Jewish culture and values would be meaningless. To prepare themselves for statehood, people needed to learn to see Eretz Israel as their cultural center, Hebrew as the language of everyday discourse. In his view, such cultural work was paramount, for it would serve as a catalyst in the moral and spiritual renaissance of the Jews, and a bulwark against assimilation in the years during which they were making themselves ready for emigration. Another of the leading cultural Zionists, the brilliant Menahem Ussishkin, delivered a three-hour speech in impeccable Hebrew, demonstrating beyond all doubt that it was indeed a viable, living language.

Rabbi Reines spoke for the religious Zionists when he expressed concern that so much emphasis on creating what was an essentially secular national culture would lead people away from religion. Mizrahi philosophy was summed up in the motto coined for it by Rabbi Meir Bar Ilan, son of the Neziv of Volozhin: "The Land of Israel for the people of Israel according to the Torah of Israel." Without the Torah, there could be no true homeland for the Jewish people, they believed. The eventual outcome of this divergence of concerns was that two committees for cultural affairs were established: the National Progressive faction, under the chairmanship of Ahad Ha'am, whose members included National Awakening poet Hayyim Nahman Bialik and Dr. Yossef Klausner, a native of Olkenik; and the National Traditional faction, under the leadership of Rabbi Reines. Some Mizrahi members who continued to be fearful of the secularizing tendencies of Zionism would eventually secede from the movement altogether, founding the ultra-Orthodox, anti-Zionist Agudat Israel in 1912.

Sarah Wilkanski was one of those who avidly followed the proceedings of the Minsk Conference, both as a member of the audience listening to Shmuel Senitski's report and a reader of the accounts provided in *Ha-Melitz* and *Ha-Zefirah*. Her already strong interest in cultural Zionism was reinforced by the speech given by Israel Belkind, one of the founders of Bilu, the early Zionist group that had sent a group of Russian Jews to Palestine in 1881, at the very beginning of the first wave of organized immigration — the First Aliyah.* Belkind (1861–1929) had come from Palestine to Minsk to make a plea for creating a national Jewish culture. This would be effected, he said, through the subject matter studied in the school system of the Yishuv (the Jewish settlement in Palestine, which at that time numbered 70,000 people), and through the restoration of Hebrew as the official language there.

Impressed by Belkind's speech, Sarah became all the more determined to make aliyah as soon as possible so that she could dedicate her life to national education and the Hebrew language.

But the keen interest Sarah and her fellow Eishyshkians showed in the various political

*Bilu was an acronym for *Beit Yaakov lekhu ve-nelka*, "House of Jacob, come ye and let us go" (Isaiah 2:5).

strains within Zionism never really descended into partisanship, because this was still a time when allegiances were constantly shifting. There were, of course, various Zionist political parties in Europe and in Palestine. Not until after World War I, however, would the internal life of the Jewish community crystallize into well-defined political parties with strong, fiercely guarded, and mutually exclusive ideological identities, and then only in Palestine. The all-engrossing dream of Zionists in Eishyshok, as in much of the rest of the Diaspora, was to make aliyah; their overriding loyalty was to the Land of Israel, not to any party.

Three Kaleko brothers and their Schneider cousin, rising young shtetl Zionist leaders during World War I, celebrating a successful day of grain distribution to the needy: (right to left) Shaul Kaleko, Shaul Schneider, Simha and Shmuel Kaleko. The entire Schneider and Kaleko family, with the exception of Shmuel, made aliyah to Eretz Israel before World War II. Shmuel and his family were murdered in Ghetto Grodno. PHOTO: YITZHAK URI KATZ. YESC, KALEKO-BARKALI

THE WAR YEARS

By the time World War I broke out, Zionism had become a mass movement of extraordinary potency, and a major political force throughout Eastern Europe. One of the biggest changes that occurred in the first couple of decades of the new century was the ascendance of a new generation of political leadership, under the aegis of Zionism. Over time, the Zionists became the majority in Eishyshok, and assumed all the leading positions in the kehilah.

For the first time, young people in their teens and early twenties were coming into positions of influence in the shtetl. They were participating in a wide range of Zionist and Zionist-influenced activities. During the war years the young people moved even more decisively into positions of power, becoming so indispensable that the leadership of the shtetl could only be exercised in unofficial alliance with the youth organizations and their representatives. Thus the distribution of grain to the needy, for example, became a joint effort: The key to the summer shul where the grain was kept was in the hands of kehilah member and staunch Mizrahi Zionist Reb Zvi Lawzowski; the actual work of distribution was done by young Simha Kaleko with the assistance of his cousin Shaul Schneider. The Billige Kikh, the soup kitchen that was established during the war, also operated as a coalition between the generations: Older members of the balebatim who were the traditional mainstay of the charitable organizations now joined with many of their young people to help feed the hungry. The soup kitchen became not just a multigenerational group, but the kehilah's first official coed institution. The sons and daughters of the artisan class also became partners in community leadership at this time, helping to care for the sick, the wounded, and the refugees, thereby crossing class boundaries in addition to generational and gender boundaries.

THE INTERWAR YEARS

For Eishyshok's young people, the prospect of making aliyah offered a legitimate opportunity to break away from the strict vigilance of family and community, to leave behind a class-conscious society for a place where yihus could be transcended, hard work could bring economic security, and degrading army service could be avoided.

The eventual flight of so many of those brilliant, vibrant, committed young people, many of whom were followed to Palestine not just by their spouses and children and siblings but sometimes by their parents as well, would change the character of Eishyshok dramatically by the mid-1930s. Together with the migrations to America (scant though they were, due to postwar quotas), these departures had a devastating impact on family life, and impoverished the shtetl both economically and culturally. As Batia Bastunski wrote her brother in California in 1935: "I have only one girlfriend now, but she too is thinking about going to Palestine. There are very few youth left in Eishyshok."

But for some years after World War I, a profusion of Zionist-inspired activities and organizations continued to spill over into every aspect of shtetl life, giving it enormous vitality, even as they were working toward their ultimate goal, which was to take people away from the shtetl to a new homeland. The spirit was so pervasive in Eishyshok that there were many self-proclaimed Zionists who had no intention of going to Eretz Israel themselves. As one wag has noted: "Who is a Zionist? A Jew who gives money to a second Jew to send a third Jew to Palestine."

During the war, emigration to Palestine had all but ceased; indeed, under the harsh rule of the Turks, and in the face of extensive Arab opposition to Zionism, many halutzim left Palestine during those years, quite a few of them returning to their hometowns. But the wartime experiences of the Jews of Eastern Europe convinced them anew that there could be no future for them in the shtetl. In Eishyshok the harsh treatment by each of the occupying forces of World War I — the Russians, Lithuanians, Poles, and Germans (with the Germans, ironically, being the kindest) — seemed an indicator of what life would be like when the war ended, under no matter whose jurisdiction. The postwar pogroms in the Ukraine and Poland were indeed quick to follow, as at least one Eishyshok family knew from personal experience: The Zlotniks, who owned a mill in a nearby village, were attacked by Polish Ulans, barely escaping with their lives. For Jewish war veterans such experiences were particularly dispiriting. Having shed their blood on all the battlefields of Europe, they were now shedding it again as victims of pogroms, often at the hands of their former comrades in arms. In the Ukraine, during the pogroms of the civil war of 1919–20, about 100,000 Jews were murdered.[21]

Hope was revived by the Balfour Declaration of 1917, which stated that the British government "views with favour the establishment in Palestine of a national home for the Jewish people," followed by the British occupation of 1918. The result was another wave of emigration after the war, the Third Aliyah, during 1919–23.

THE THIRD ALIYAH (1919–23) Eishyshok's own first postwar oleh was twenty-two-year-old Mordekhai (Motke) Rubinstein, son of Reb Tuviah der Yeremitcher. All the Zionists in the shtetl followed Motke's activities in Eretz Israel with enormous interest, for not only was he the first to leave in this latest wave of migrations, and the first to leave under the auspices of the new He-Haluz (Pioneer) movement, he immediately associated himself with two of the leaders who had the strongest claim on the imagination of the young: Vladimir Jabotinsky (1880–1940) and Yossef Trumpeldor (1880–1920).

Upon arriving in his new homeland, Rubinstein joined Jabotinsky in the defense he had mounted against Arab attacks on the Jews of Jerusalem during the Passover riots of 1920. For many young people, Jabotinsky was the very model of the new East European Jew: soldier, politician, poet. He was a brilliant orator who could keep audiences spellbound for hours in Hebrew, Russian, Yiddish, English, French, or German; an ardent supporter of Hebrew language and national culture, who also did excellent translations into Hebrew from other languages, some of which, such as "The Raven" by

Edgar Allan Poe, are still in use; a fierce and brave soldier who had fought alongside the British during World War I, as a volunteer with the Jewish fighting unit known as the Legion. Together with Yossef Trumpeldor and others, Jabotinsky had founded the Jewish Legion to help the British liberate Eretz Israel from the Turks. When the British demobilized their Legion after the war, then failed to give the Jews adequate protection from the Arabs during the Passover riots, Jabotinsky became one of the organizers of Haganah, the Jewish defense force for the Yishuv, which would eventually play the key military role in the 1948 War of Independence.

After the Passover riots had been suppressed, Mordekhai Rubinstein became one of the most active members of Gedud ha-Avodah, Palestine's first countrywide commune of Jewish laborers, which had been established by idealistic halutzim in August 1920 in memory of the recent death of storybook hero Yossef Trumpeldor. Its full name was Gehud ha-Avodah ve-Hahagana al Shem Yossef Trumpeldor (the Yossef Trumpeldor Legion for Labor and Defense). But for security reasons, having to do with fear of the British, the word *defense* was deleted from the official name. Founder and leader of the Russian branch of He-Haluz, Trumpeldor was a legendary and highly decorated soldier who was already a veteran of several battlefields by the time he died in March 1920, while defending Jewish settlements in upper Galilee from Arab attack.[22] After his death he became a symbol to an entire generation of young Zionists, who were brought up hearing poems, stories, and songs commemorating his bravery.

Mordekhai Rubinstein and his newly arrived sister Rivka were drawn by the Gedud's Tolstoyan vision of communal living, its idealism, its reliance on the mystical teachings of A. D. Gordon, its distinctly leftist sympathies.

The Gedud was organized into companies that were dispatched to various locations, wherever and whenever their services were needed. When members of the Gedud volunteered to serve in the British army, in order to replace the Egyptian laborers who had been doing all the army's menial tasks and whom they considered to be a threat to the security of the Yishuv, Mordekhai was among them.[23] He also joined with some other members of the Gedud to form the Sharona Shepherds, an organization dedicated to creating a new breed of sheep herders in the land: Jews. To enhance their authenticity, they advocated marrying Bedouin women. But here ideological commitment came up short: not a single such marriage materialized.

With the completion of the roadwork on which the majority of Gedud members had been employed, several companies were sent to the Valley of Jezreel to found Kibbutz Ein Harod in September 1921, and Kibbutz Tel Yossef (named in memory of Trumpeldor) in December. As settlers at Tel Yossef, Mordekhai and his sister

Mordekhai Rubinstein, looking through the tent opening, was one of the founders of Kibbutz Tel Yossef in Eretz Israel in 1921. YESC, S. RUBINSTEIN

Rivka were a magnet attracting other Eishyshkians, including their parents and two siblings.

As the conviction grew, even among the middle class and the affluent, that there was no future for the Jew in the shtetl, the promise of Zionism was constantly gaining momentum. Eishyshok between the two world wars saw the founding of local chapters of a seemingly endless succession of Zionist youth organizations, reflecting all the major trends within the Zionist movement — an astonishingly large and diverse range of groups for such a small shtetl. Indeed, there was almost no Zionist group that was not represented in Eishyshok at one time or another. Thus the shtetl fairly hummed with Zionist activities, which created a perpetually cheerful, dynamic mood.

During the week, the young Zionists labored hard, learning Hebrew and acquiring professional skills that they believed would prove useful for life in Eretz Israel. Some left the shtetl to attend vocational schools or institutes of higher learning. Others went to spend time on a hakhsharah, either the local one, which was a farm on the outskirts of town, or one of the regional farms. There they prepared themselves for communal living on a kibbutz, and did many kinds of physical labor: cutting wood, paving roads, quarrying stone, working in the fields. For the young men, most of them former yeshivah students who had never lifted anything heavier than a book, such tasks were a great strain. For the young women, however, their hakhsharah assignments seemed a normal part of life, since they were already accustomed to working in the family potato patch, milking the cow, tending chickens, weeding the vegetable garden, and doing all manner of domestic chores.

In 1921, twenty-one teenage girls, all Hebrew students and daughters of balebatim, established an apolitical friendship society and named it Club 21. Their younger sisters decided to establish a similar club, simply named Our Circle. Many of these young women emigrated or moved to larger towns during the 1930s. Among the Club 21 members: Matle Sonenson (front right) and her best friend Geneshe Kaganowicz; Zipporah Katz (third row, second from right); Leah Koppelman (top row, fourth from right). PHOTO: YITZHAK URI KATZ. YESC, Y. ELIACH

The Sabbath, too, was devoted to Zionist activities — mainly in the form of cultural events and ideological discussions. During the summer, after the midday Sabbath meal, members of the various Zionist organizations would walk to the edge of the shtetl, where town met country, to gather at an ancient abandoned castle, the Mayak. It was the favorite meeting place until Dr. Religion, a retired Polish general, renovated it and began living there, at which time its grounds were declared off-limits for Jewish youth.[24] The Seklutski forest then became the preferred rendezvous for the older groups, as the meadows along the banks of the Kantil River were for the younger ones. In wintertime they met indoors, in their respective clubs. There they would stay until late afternoon, singing, dancing, reading, discussing the latest political developments, and critiquing the latest books they had read, plays they had seen. One favorite pastime was the literary trial, in which a famous historical or contemporary literary figure was put on trial for his accomplishments, and cases for the defense and the prosecution were presented.

EARLY POSTWAR ZIONIST GROUPS The first of the new youth organizations to be established in postwar Eishyshok was a local chapter

In the late 1920s, only eight members of Club 21 remained in Eishyshok, among them Zipporah Katz (seated, right) and Geneshe Kaganowicz (left), hugging her best friend Matle Sonenson. The three young women later became sisters-in-law. Matle survived the war in Siberia, others were killed in the September 1941 massacre and Zipporah by the AK. PHOTO: YITZHAK URI KATZ. YESC, Y. SONENSON

Members of Our Circle: (seated, center) Malka Matikanski (right) and Goldke Kabacznik; Esther Katz (seated, far right); Miriam Koppelman (standing in center), next to Szeina Blacharowicz. Malka made aliyah to Eretz Israel, Esther emigrated to Colombia, Goldke and Miriam left for other shtetlekh after their marriages. Szeina survived the war in the forest; the others were killed in Eishyshok and other locations. PHOTO: YITZHAK URI KATZ. YESC, BLACHAROWICZ-WISZIK

of Poalei Zion (Workers of Zion), which was an amalgam of cultural Zionism, Jewish nationalism, and socialism. Led by Shaul Kaleko, Yossef Paikowski, and Moshe Dimitrowski, this group attracted former yeshivah students who had become secularized, as well as a number of the sons of shtetl artisans. During 1919–21, Herut ve-Tehyia (Freedom and Revival) dominated the shtetl. Organized by a group that included Shalom Sonenson, Shaul Schneider, Shaul and Simha Kaleko, Zeev Kaganowicz, Mordekhai Lawzowski, Shlomo Kiuchefski, Zipporah Lubetski, and Hayya Streletski, and dedicated to a rather elitist cultural agenda, it attracted a more homogeneous following, consisting for the most part of the sons and daughters of the balebatim. With its members dressed in white peasant-style garments, like the halutzim in Eretz Israel (or, closer to hand, the followers of Leo Tolstoy), they made quite a striking appearance, and their romantic, idealistic strain of Zionism was very attractive to the shtetl youth, and to many in nearby shtetlekh as well. Eventually an offshoot known as Pirhei Zion (a name that meant both Flowers of Zion and Young Cadets of Zion) was established for their younger brothers and sisters, ages ten to fourteen.

HE-HALUZ AND HALUZ HA-MIZRAHI In 1921 a much longer-lived and more powerful Zionist organization came to Eishyshok, via Reb Zvi Lawzowski. He had attended the twelfth Zionist Congress in Carlsbad, where he encountered the leadership of the He-Haluz movement. He-Haluz had been building in popularity ever since Yossef Trumpeldor organized a branch in Russia in 1918, and it was holding its first international conference at Carlsbad. Eventually it became the most popular and effective of all the organizations serving the needs of those who wished to make aliyah, particularly after 1925, when the British created a quota system to try to restrict immigration to Palestine. Members of He-Haluz had better access than most to the limited number of immigration certificates issued by the British, and they were also well served by the many illegal activities that He-Haluz mounted on behalf of would-be im-

Herut ve-Tehiya (Freedom and Revival), the most powerful Zionist organization in Eishyshok, was founded immediately after World War I. This photo was taken in 1921. Many of the members made aliyah to Eretz Israel. Those who remained in Eishyshok were murdered during the September 1941 massacre, in Ghetto Radun and by the AK. From the group who remained in Europe, only two survived. PHOTO: YITZHAK URI KATZ. YESC, Z. TOKATLI-LUBETSKI

A meeting of the leadership of Haluz ha-Mizrahi in Eishyshok, April 21, 1924: (seated, right to left) Zipporah Lubetski, Yankl Jankelewicz, Velvl Rochowski, "Itchke Hones" Moszczenik, Yossef Resnik, Nahum Radunski, and Peretz Kaleko. Zipporah, Itchke, and Peretz made aliyah to Eretz Israel. (Itchke returned to Eishyshok.) Yossef emigrated to Colombia. The others were murdered during the Holocaust in Eishyshok and other locations. PHOTO: YITZHAK URI KATZ. YESC, KALEKO-ALUFI

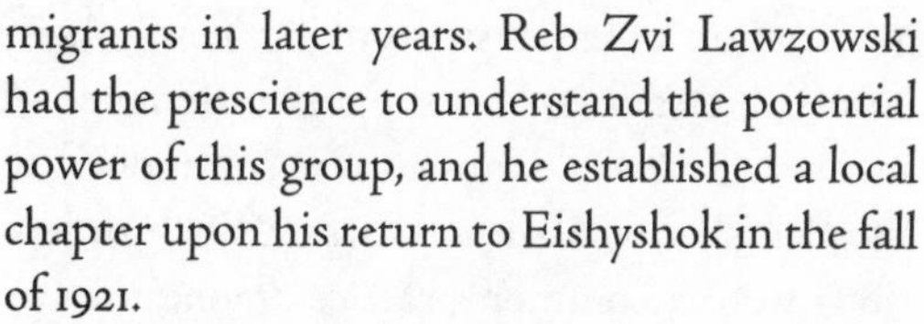

migrants in later years. Reb Zvi Lawzowski had the prescience to understand the potential power of this group, and he established a local chapter upon his return to Eishyshok in the fall of 1921.

It would take a while, however, for He-Haluz to come into its own in Eishyshok, for it was at first upstaged by Haluz ha-Mizrahi (The Religious Pioneer). The local chapter of this more religiously oriented Zionist group was founded in 1922 by a group that included Peretz Kaleko (chairman); Yossef Resnik (secretary), who had studied at the Reines yeshivah in Lida; Zipporah Lubetski; and Nahum Radunski, a graduate of the Ramailes yeshivah in Vilna. At its height in Eishyshok, it had about 120 members between the ages of eighteen and twenty.

Haluz ha-Mizrahi was very effective at helping its members to emigrate, and Eishyshok was particularly lucky in this respect, because of its close connection to one of the founders of Haluz ha-Mizrahi in Vilna, Yitzhak Munin. In the course of his work for the organization Munin became a frequent visitor to the shtetl, where he met, fell in love with, and eventually married one of the local members, Frume-Rochl Ratz. Until their aliyah in 1934, the Munins continued to be active in Haluz ha-Mizrahi, and Yitzhak proved very liberal in granting the group's allotment of the much coveted emigration certificates to his wife's fellow Eishyshkians. Among those who emigrated during this period were the three Radunski brothers, Zivia Hutner, Zipporah Lubetski, Pessia and Brakha Moszczenik, Hayya Streletski, Shalom and Leibke Sonenson, and many others.

It was Haluz ha-Mizrahi that created Eishyshok's hakhsharah. (Later, when that group went into decline, the farm was taken over by He-Haluz.) The group leased two large tracts of land on the outskirts of the shtetl, pitched a number of white tents just like those of the halutzim in Eretz Israel, cultivated the land, and built watchposts from which sentries guarded the precious produce at night. In addition to agricultural training, Haluz ha-Mizrahi also offered intensive courses in Hebrew, and even organized a soccer team. Given their deep feeling for the land, from which they had long felt exiled, Eishyshkians enjoyed the presence of the hakhsharah, while it lasted: The shtetl women were eager to purchase fresh vegetables from the farm, and everyone loved to see the halutzim in their pioneer-style garments and their worker-style caps, marching off to the farm at dawn with their sickles and spades on their shoulders, or passing through the shtetl atop wagons filled with freshly cut hay, singing songs of Zion in Hebrew.

Dora Zlotnik (center) posing with two friends for a farewell photo prior to her aliyah to Eretz Israel in 1931, Gitta Oshochowski (right) and Mira Iasinowski. Gitta, her husband, and their children were murdered in Ghetto Lida, May 8, 1942. YESC, BERKOWITCH

As always happened with Zionist organizations in the Diaspora, the success of Haluz ha-Mizrahi was its undoing: its most active members emigrated. In 1924 the revitalized He-Haluz picked up many of the remaining Haluz ha-Mizrahi members, among them the ubiquitous Peretz Kaleko, added new ones, and adopted a virtually identical program, minus the religious ideology, the daily services, and the distinctive hat.

With the advent of the certificate system in 1925, under which the various Zionist groups competed for a limited number of emigration permits granted by the British in Palestine, and tried to ensure that the candidates they sponsored were the most highly qualified, members spent more and more of their time preparing to pass the He-Haluz test. They were required to demonstrate fluency in Hebrew, a thorough knowledge of the history of Zionism, and familiarity with conditions in the Yishuv. A young man from Eishyshok named Hirshl failed his exam in Vilna, much to the surprise of the examiner, who knew that Eishyshkians were proficient Hebraists who generally performed very well. But Hirshl explained that the road to Vilna had been very bumpy, with the result that during the carriage ride all his highly organized knowledge had gotten scrambled up in his brain. Hirshl never did get his certificate, and was one of those murdered during the Holocaust.

Those who applied for certificates also had to prove to the British that they had financial stability. Passed from hand to hand, the same neatly packed valise filled with fine clothing and a collection of expensive-looking "family heirlooms" attested to the supposed affluence of many an Eishyshkian who was summoned to the British consulate in Warsaw. Such deceptions were a common practice among the halutzim hopefuls.

Uri Rozowski, Rachel Kaleko, Dora Zlotnik, Rivka, Rina, and Rachel Lewinson, Naftali Berkowitch and four of his five brothers, and the Lawzowski family were among the many He-Haluz members who successfully applied for certificates and made aliyah in these years.[25] But often, as with the Lewinson sisters and the Berkowitch brothers, each of whom received their certificates at a different time, the suspense about when and if the coveted piece of paper would ever arrive was enormous, and the effect on the family could be devastating.

Sometimes those who emigrated came back, especially in the wake of Palestine's economic depression of 1927–29. Many of those who returned at that time were from well-to-do families, including Shalom and Leibke Sonenson, Shoshana (Shoshke) Wine, Zeev Kaganowicz, Shlomo Kiuchefski, and Zeev Katz (later known

Aryeh (right) and Naftali Berkowitch prior to their departure for Eretz Israel in the 1920s. PHOTO: YITZHAK URI KATZ. YESC, ARYEH BERKOWITCH

Shaul Berkowitch on the Romanian ship Regele Carols, *sailing to Eretz Israel.* YESC, SHAUL BERKOWITCH

as Velvke, when he became a Communist), for to them their prospects seemed better back in Eishyshok. Others returned for other reasons, among them Pessia Moszczenik, who came back in 1926, sick and emaciated from a grueling seven-month stay.

Generally speaking, however, there were far more people who wanted to make aliyah than there were certificates, and many of the lucky ones who did eventually go left behind siblings, parents, and other relatives who each day went to greet the postman, in the hope that he would be bringing their own certificate.

HA-SHOMER HA-ZAIR AND BEITAR By the late twenties and early thirties the two dominant Zionist organizations in the shtetl were Ha-Shomer ha-Zair (The Young Guardians) and Beitar (an abbreviation of Berit Trumpeldor, the Covenant of Trumpeldor, honoring their soldier hero). The local chapter of Ha-Shomer ha-Zair was founded in Eishyshok in 1924 by Peretz Kaleko and Shaul Schneider. Though the national organization was socialist in its leanings, and would eventually move closer and closer to Marxist activism, the local chapter of Ha-Shomer ha-Zair focused only on the pioneering and scouting aspects of the program, which had once been its primary agenda. Its membership was drawn mainly from the sons and daughters of the balebatim, young teenagers who loved the emphasis on hiking and nature study, farming and manual labor. The local chapter's adherence to a scouting model was evident also in its structure, its division into peluga (company) and gedud (battalion), and into groups defined by age, with names like Kefirim (Cubs), Benei Midbar (Sons of the Desert), and Benei Massada (Sons of Massada). The members wore uniforms, and each group had its own flag.

Leaders of Ha-Shomer ha-Zair, October 25, 1925: among them are Peretz Kaleko (front, center); his future wife Leah Koppelman (second row, right) and Zipporah Katz (sitting next to Leah). Peretz and Leah made aliyah to Eretz Israel. PHOTO: YITZHAK URI KATZ. YESC, FRISCHER

At its height, the Eishyshok chapter of Ha-Shomer ha-Zair boasted about 150 members, many of whom grew up within its ranks and remained loyal to it, among them Dov Wilenski, Esther Katz, and Leah Koppelman. Beitar would command a similar loyalty from some of its members, but such firmly drawn ideological lines were relatively rare in the shtetl, where the various Zionist organizations often had overlapping memberships, and many people were involved in several at a time. Peretz Kaleko, for example, seems to have been active in some half dozen or so of these groups, often as a founding member. Moreover, it was common for people to switch from party to party in pursuit of those elusive emigration certificates, since sometimes one Zionist group had access to more, sometimes another.

Though Eishyshkians were keenly aware of partisan politics in the Yishuv — registering every tremor, every shade of ideology; analyzing and debating every political move by every prominent Zionist leader — for the most part they continued to live in a different emotional climate from that in Eretz Israel, love for the homeland being far more important to them than any party allegiance. With Ha-Shomer ha-Zair and Beitar, the shtetl did seem to be moving in the direction of a stricter partisanship, but the process was cut short by the Holocaust.

The aliyah of Ha-Shomer ha-Zair chapter founder Shaul Schneider and his family was a deeply inspiring event for his fellow party members, as it was for many others among the shtetl youth, for their departure was marked by a new kind of pageantry, symbolic of a new vision of what their destiny in that far-off land might be. In the time of Shifra the midwife, or even Meir Wilkanski, the processionals that escorted the emigrants to the bridge at the edge of town were mainly religious in nature, fitting send-offs for pilgrims to the Holy Land. By 1924, when the Schneiders left, the parades and ceremonies had a markedly nationalist, patriotic look to them, complete with uniforms, flags, marches, and a national anthem, for the emigrants were seen as pioneers going off to what they hoped would some day be a homeland of their own, a nation like all other nations. Upon their shoulders rested the destiny of their people.

An eyewitness account written in beautiful Hebrew by one of Sarah Rubinstein's former Rak Ivrit girls, Esther Katz, gives something of the flavor of the shtetl's elaborate farewell to the Schneiders, which exceeded in pageantry virtually all others, including the one celebrating the Balfour Declaration in 1917, when the entire shtetl danced in the streets to the music of a band of klezmers:

I am twelve years old, and a member of the Zionist group Ha-Shomer ha-Zair. The other day I took part in a parade that was organized by all our shtetl institutions and parties, for the purpose of saying farewell to a distinguished family by the name of Schneider, on the night of their departure for Eretz Israel.

It happened on a Saturday night, when the usual darkness of the shtetl was broken by the numerous candles and lamps burning in every window, in order to

In the mid-1930s other active members of Ha-Shomer-ha-Zair made aliyah. Munia Zahavi and Dov Wilenski posed with friends from various Zionist organizations for farewell photos on the steps of the house of Alte Katz, a popular spot among the shtetl Zionist organizations. Standing on the steps is Munia with his hand on the shoulder of Malka Matikanski, his girlfriend. Above him, Dov Wilenski holding the hand of his girlfriend Esther Katz. On the right, in front, is Motke Rubinstein with girlfriend Szeina Blacharowicz. At the top, center, is Shepske Sonenson. PHOTO: BEN ZION SZREJDER. YESC, MATIKANSKI

light the way for the olim and their escorts. An exceptionally orderly parade accompanied them, with each of the Zionist groups marching as a unit, displaying its own flag, and everybody joining together to sing songs expressing the love of Zion. Alongside the marchers rode young fellows on white horses, carrying burning torches, and behind them were the men, women, and children of the shtetl, people of all ages, singing and dancing.

We marched the length of Vilna Street until we reached the house of Rabbi Rozowski, our beloved Rabbi whose shining face, brilliant eyes, and gleaming white beard shone brighter than all the lights around us. He welcomed us from his porch, and, leaning against its railing, delivered a speech filled with blessings for the olim, and with hope for our persecuted people. Then we all sang Hatikvah, *the Jewish national anthem.*

Next we continued our march to the outskirts of the shtetl, where the parade came to a standstill before a platform, on which sat representatives of all the various organizations. Each one spoke a farewell on behalf of the members of their party. From there the parade continued to the bridge, where the Schneider family took leave of the shtetl and traveled on by carriage to the train station in Bastun. . . .

Our hearts were filled with hope that we too would one day make aliyah and join in building the land.

The Schneider family's emigration made a lasting impression on the entire shtetl. Inspired by their example, many people, including a number from the middle class, followed in their footsteps. For this was the time of the Fourth Aliyah (1924–28), also known as the Grabski Aliyah, after the Polish cabinet minister whose anti-Jewish economic policies had begun to take their toll on people who had once lived in comfort, even affluence. Now that they were no longer economically secure, they were more willing to uproot themselves.

Despite the departure of some of its most active members, Ha-Shomer ha-Zair continued to function, but Beitar began to surpass it in popularity.

Founded in Riga in 1923, Beitar was brought to Eishyshok in 1926, courtesy of Faivl Glombocki, Meir Shimon Politacki, and Dov Slepak, among others. But only in the late 1920s and early 1930s did it assume its role as the dominant youth organization in the shtetl. It was so popular that it sometimes even split families. For example,

Zipporah Katz, and her sister Esther belonged to Ha-Shomer ha-Zair, while their younger siblings, Shoshana and Avigdor, became devoted Beitar members, as did their mother, Alte (although her Beitar membership was just one of several Zionist affiliations she held).

Beitar's structure was similar to that of Ha-Shomer ha-Zair, as was its emphasis on pioneer life, and it used similar scouting terms. Like many other Zionist organizations, it was also dedicated to Hebrew language and culture, and to the goal of making aliyah by any means, legal or illegal. What set Beitar apart, however, was its militaristic stance, inspired by the martyred military man Yossef Trumpeldor and Vladimir Jabotinsky.

In 1925 Jabotinsky established the Revisionist Party, whose mandate was the establishment of a Jewish state — a return to Herzl's explicitly nationalist, political vision. Beitar then became the youth arm of the Revisionists. By the early 1930s, Jabotinsky had begun to call for the rapid evacuation of the Jews from Eastern Europe, for he believed they were in great danger. In urging mass emigration to Eretz Israel he broke with many of his fellow Zionists, who were unwilling to defy the British and believed that the settling of Palestine should take place legally, gradually, step by step, all in good time — time that Jabotinsky believed was running out.[26] Beginning in 1935, as a gesture toward Jabotinsky's vision of a "greater" Jewish state spanning both sides of the Jordan River, Beitar members had to take an oath upon joining the movement: "I de-

A farewell photo in honor of the aliyah of Malka Matikanski (front left). Shepske Sonenson (center) was among the last young Zionist men his age left in Eishyshok. With them are fellow Zionists Esther Katz (front right), Fania Botwinik (back right), Goldke Kabacznik, Szeina Blacharowicz, and Malka Nochomowicz. Malka Matikanski and Esther emigrated, Szeina survived the war, the others were murdered in Eishyshok and other shtetlekh. PHOTO: BEN ZION SZREJDER. YESC, BLACHAROWICZ-WISNIK

The founders and leaders of the Beitar movement in Eishyshok pose for a farewell photo on June 10, 1930, in honor of the departure of Shaul Berkowitch (seated, right) to Eretz Israel and Faivl Glombocki (seated, left) to Argentina. Standing (right to left) are Meir Shimon Politacki, Shepske Sonenson, and Zvi Hirshke Schwartz. Meir Shimon was captured and presumably killed by the Germans while in the Polish army. Shepske and Zvi Hirshke were killed in the September 1941 massacre. Shaul and Faivl were reunited in Israel fifty-five years after they left Eishyshok. PHOTO: ALTE KATZ. YESC, GLOMBOCKI

vote my life to the rebirth of the Jewish State with a Jewish majority on both sides of the Jordan."

Jabotinsky's distrust of British policies was borne out when the British further restricted immigration, issuing "White Papers" in October 1936 and again in May 1939 that severely limited the number of emigration certificates that could be distributed.[27] His fears about the fate of the Jews of Eastern Europe began to be realized very soon thereafter.

Eishyshkians loved Beitar's military-style uniforms, which its members wore with great pride. Many also enjoyed watching their martial drills, and were delighted to see them assisting the Polish police on market day. The appeal of the group was manifold: its respect for religion made many of the more devout young people feel welcome, among them Shoshana and Zipporah Hutner, granddaughters of Rabbi Zundl Hutner; the sharp appearance of its members, especially the boys, who looked so handsome in their uniforms, won others over; and some loved it for

A group of young Beitar girls with two of their commanders: (right to left) Shifra Berczanski, Hanna Szczuczynski, (first name unknown) Koppelman, Matke Slepak, (first name unknown) Portnoy, name unknown, Sarah'le Tatarski, Zvi's sister, and Zvi Hirshke Schwartz. Shifra made aliyah. Zvi survived the war as a partisan. Hanna was killed by Pietka Barteszewicz, the caretaker of the Polish school she attended, and a member of the AK. The others were murdered in the September 1941 massacre. PHOTO: BEN ZION SZREJDER. YESC, KABACZNIK

its ideology, a unique mix of pioneering and legionism, political and cultural Zionism. Beitar was also known locally for its Saturday-night parties, which took place in the homes of Sorl Kabacznik, Yossl Weidenberg, and Alte Katz (mother of members Avigdor and Shoshana, and, as noted above, an enthusiastic dedicated Beitar member herself).

These gatherings were very popular, and, as was typical in the shtetl, even at a time of rising partisanship they attracted members of many different groups. For example, Szeina Blacharowicz, who belonged to Ha-Oved ha-Zioni (The Zionist Worker), her brother Yehiel, a leader of Ha-Shomer ha-Zair, and "Mule the teacher" from Ha-Poel ha-Zioni (The Zionist Laborer) could all be found in attendance, as could youth from nearby Radun, and Beitar members who worked on the hakhsharah in Aran (Varena). There was nothing surprising about this, for close friendships existed between the members of various parties, and it was quite common to find in one household brothers, sisters, mothers, fathers, and even grandparents with different party affiliations. All worked and socialized together, in acknowledgment of their common goal: emigration to Palestine.

Some even took part in fictitious marriages in order to emigrate. For example, Hayya Gruznik of Beitar married Hayyim Streletski of Ha-Shomer ha-Zair because he had a certificate and she did not, and this was the only way she could make aliyah. Three months later, her purpose served, they divorced. A significant number of Eishyshok women chose this route to emigration, which caused their parents great anxiety; they feared the husband in one of these fictitious marriages might take advantage of a helpless young girl, or even refuse to divorce her later.

The various Zionist parties coexisted peacefully enough that their activities — known as Blue and White activities — were all coordinated by one all-inclusive Zionist Federation. The only occasion they all routinely observed together, however, was the anniversary of Theodor Herzl's death.

Beitar did sometimes clash with other groups. The approach of election day often saw tempers flaring, voices rising. As the rift widened during the 1930s between the followers of Jabotinsky on the one hand and the more leftist, even socialist Zionists on the other, some physical skirmishes took place, with the brown shirts of the Beitar members coming in for special abuse. But the most notorious confrontations were those between Beitar and the Communists.

OTHER POLITICAL MOVEMENTS

Zionism and its goal of emigration were the dominant political force in early-twentieth-century Eishyshok, but a small number of revolution-minded individuals hoped for radical change within their homeland, which they thought they could help bring about by aligning themselves with various socialist and Communist movements.

THE BUND

The Bund, short for Algemeyner Yiddisher Arbeiter Bund in Lite, Poylin, un Rusland (General Jewish Workers Union of Lithuania, Poland, and Russia), was founded in Vilna in October 1897 by representatives of Jewish socialist circles who had decided that the Jewish workers had special interests and needs that were not being addressed by other workers' parties. They felt themselves tied by an "indissoluble bond" to the non-Jewish proletariat, but wanted an equal partnership with, not a membership in, the general labor movement. This dualism was to be the cause of many years of ideological oscillations, giving rise to the famous remark that Bund members are seasick Zionists.[28]

Despite the fact that Eishyshok was only forty miles from Vilna, it never became a Bundist stronghold, for it had virtually no industry, and therefore no population resembling the classic proletariat from which the Bund typically drew most of its membership. Yet the Bund had a few sympathizers in Eishyshok, especially among the apprentices to the tailors, the bootmakers, and the shoemakers. For a short period, between 1897 and 1905, they had gained enough numerical strength that they even had their own circle with its own official stamp. Bund sympathizers in Eishyshok closely followed events in Vilna and elsewhere, held meetings, sang Bundist songs about the plight of the workers and the heroism of those who had lost their lives fighting for their rights. Bootmaker Hirsh Lekert (1880–1902) was a particular hero in Eishyshok. He had made an attempt on the life of the governor of Vilna after the governor ordered the whipping of a group of workers (including twenty Jews) during the May Day demonstrations of 1902. Lekert was executed on June 2, a date that was observed for many years thereafter by the leftist youth of the shtetl.

The closest Eishyshok ever came to experiencing serious labor actions was during the general train strike of 1905, when the Bastun coachmen returned to town from the train station without passengers or cargo, their carriages empty. The events were discussed at great length in Eishyshok's beth midrash, but young men and women who sought action rather than talk had to leave the shtetl for Vilna, as the occasional frustrated revolutionary who landed in Eishyshok, most notably A. Weiter (see chapter 6), discovered.

Local membership in the Bund peaked during the revolution year of 1905, but then fell off; shortly thereafter the group was disbanded. No further Bund activities seem to have taken place in Eishyshok until the 1930s, when three young men, Meishke and Hayyim-Itche the tailors and Rufke the bootmaker, tried to organize a local

Luba Ginunski (second from left), the leading Communist of Eishyshok and the vicinity. She survived the war in Russia. YESC, L. GINUNSKI

chapter, but failed. There were, however, about five card-carrying Bund members in the shtetl who belonged to a chapter elsewhere.

THE COMMUNIST PARTY

The Communist Party was illegal in Poland between the two world wars. But there were about fifty Communists operating clandestinely in Eishyshok during this period, about forty of whom were Jewish. Many of them were highly committed political activists, willing to fight, and suffer, for what they believed in. Some spent difficult years in Polish jails, others even gave their lives to the cause. In the 1930s Moshe Szulkin spent years in Vilna's infamous Lukishki prison, and in Kartuz-Breze, the Polish concentration camp for political prisoners, especially Communists.[29] His sister Rochel Szulkin, an elite seamstress for the rich, remained in a jail in Lomza for four years. Defiant upon her release, Rochel donned red stockings as a symbol of her Communist loyalties. Luba Ginunski was imprisoned in Lukishki and in Fordon, a maximum-security jail for women, where her clandestine lectures on Marx and Lenin were so popular that she became a jailhouse celebrity. In fact, she was such a dynamic leader that the official history of the Communist Party in Lithuania, which managed to exclude all the other Jews (some of whom had been among its most active members), did include Luba Ginunski. Luba bore the scars of her prison torture for life, and she was unable to bear children. Two other Eishyshkians, David Shuster and Nahum Hayyim Leib Cofnas, were murdered in Russia as Trotskyites.

The Communists considered the government of Poland their enemy, and made violent attacks on the Polish police. When members of Beitar assisted the Polish police on market day during the mid-1930s, the Communists sometimes fought with them, too. Occasionally hostilities spilled over into other venues, including, at least once, the synagogue. That much-talked-about event occurred at the height of the Simhat Torah celebration when a young Communist named Motke Shneur's grabbed hold of the Holy Scrolls and denied the existence of God. Reb Scholem Wilenski, the shtetl rosh yeshivah and mystic, himself a former revolutionary in his native Bobriusk, rushed toward Motke Shneur's, wielding a heavy Gemara in his hand. Members of Beitar, in full uniform, took over the fight from their beloved teacher. The Communists then blocked all the exits, but Beitar won the battle, as they did the next one, when the Communists struck again on a Friday night. Subsequently, one young Communist took the attack on religion to the New Cemetery, but that too ended in a kind of defeat, as is recounted in chapter 9. Aside from these episodes, the usual form of combat between Zionists and Communists was verbal: open debates were conducted, with Hayyim Paikowski as spokesman for the Communists and Simha Kaleko representing the Zionists (the latter could also claim credentials as a laborer and man of the people, since he was a cartwheel maker).

Though the Communists were a much embattled, tiny minority in the shtetl, they did enjoy at least one supreme moment of inspiration and triumph in the years before the 1941

Soviet occupation, when they would have their own brief reign. The news of the departure of Eishyshok's first post–World War I halutz, Mordekhai Rubinstein, from Palestine for the Soviet Union in 1927 came as a ringing affirmation of the Eishyshok Communists' own ideology, a sign that the Zionist emigration was a mistake, just as they had been saying all along.

In 1922–23 a rift had developed between various groups in the Tel Yossef kibbutz, and one group went to Ein Harod, while a more leftist group, led by Mendel Elkind, stayed at Tel Yossef. Mordekhai and Rivka were part of the latter group. Peace did not come to Tel Yossef after the split, however; disputes continued to rage for three more years, with Elkind and his followers experiencing a growing disenchantment with the kind of socialism that was emerging in the Eretz Israel labor movement. Moving ever further to the left, Elkind's group confronted their opponents, who included future prime minister of Israel David Ben-Gurion, across what came to seem an unbridgeable gap.[30]

Throughout the years of ideological struggle, Elkind maintained contact with Russia, even visiting the Soviet Union sometime in the early 1920s, where he met with high-ranking Soviet officials as well as with the editorial staff of the Yiddish Communist newspaper *Der Emmes* (The Truth). In October 1927 Elkind and his followers decided to take the drastic step of leaving Palestine for Russia. To the stunned shock of the Yishuv, 102 adults and their young children, 65 of whom were members of Tel Yossef, the others Communist sympathizers from Tel Aviv, Jerusalem, and other parts of Israel, departed for the land that had been oppressing Jews for centuries.

Members of the group included Mendel Elkind and his wife and two sons, Mordekhai Rubinstein and his wife Hayya (née Schneider), and sister Rivka.[31] Rivka's presence, however, was due only to an odd twist of fate, for her commitment was to the Land of Israel, and to the man she loved, Moshe Blaj, who shared her ideology. But Moshe, who was also a member of the Gedud, had run into trouble when he attended a secret Communist cell meeting in Tel Aviv, where the question of returning to Russia was being debated. While delivering a fiery speech in favor of remaining in the Land of Israel, the only place he felt that true socialism could be achieved, Moshe was interrupted by a British police raid and arrested. Despite the content of his speech, Moshe was ordered deported to the Soviet Union, a victim of British anti-Bolshevik phobia. So when Elkind's group finalized their plans, Rivka had to choose between two loves — her love for Eretz Israel, and her love for Moshe Blaj. She chose Moshe.

Another person who joined the Elkind group was Szyrke (Shira) Gorshman, a beautiful single mother with three little daughters who was originally from the Lithuanian shtetl of Krok. While in Krok, she had studied Hebrew with Mordekhai and Rivka's sister Sarah, and thus

Shira Gorshman on the left with her sister Brakhu. Shira worked for the novelist Shmuel Yosef Agnon in Jerusalem prior to her departure for Russia with the Elkind group in 1927. Agnon's book Shira *was inspired by her. Her Hebrew teacher was Sarah Rubinstein from Eishyshok.* YESC, SH. GORSHMAN

had a perfect command of the language when she arrived in Eretz Israel. Szyrke, who was a member of the Ratisbon chapter of the Gedud in Jerusalem, worked as a maid in the home of the future Nobel Prize–winning novelist Shmuel Yosef Agnon. Agnon first met Szyrke in the home of the philosopher Hugo Bergman, and, impressed by her gefilte fish, her sparkling blue eyes, her ideology, her witticisms, and her colorful stories, he asked her to come work for him. Twenty-two years old at the time, she was a vivacious free spirit who had left her husband out of her belief in free love. Agnon would later write a book titled *Shira*, named after its protagonist. Though much has been written about the symbolism of the name, which means "song," the critics overlooked the fact that there was a real flesh-and-blood Shira who was in all likelihood the inspiration for the character, since she was greatly admired by him.[32]

The Elkind group's journey to Russia was financed by the Soviet government. As part of the deal, Elkind signed a letter denouncing Zionism. But once the group arrived at their destination, a barren, salty stretch of land in Crimea where they were to establish their new commune, Elkind realized he had made a terrible mistake. The courtship between him and the Soviet authorities came to an abrupt end.

Because of official Soviet opposition to Hebrew, the group could not even give a Hebrew name to their commune. Via Nova, an Esperanto phrase meaning "new life," was their compromise. The Hebrew-speaking kindergarten teachers of the Via Nova children, including Elkind's wife, Mania, were replaced with Yiddish-speaking teachers and soon with Russian-speakers. Members of the commune were informed that the Communist Party would uproot and destroy anything to do with their Jewish and Zionist past: "The past is an obstacle in our forward march toward the future" was the slogan constantly thrown in their faces.[33] Failing crops, hunger, lack of clothing, and total dependence on an ineffectual central bureaucracy was their lot. Szyrke Gorshman's description of Elkind during this period deserves to be quoted:

Mendel Elkind, the chairman of the commune, enters the kitchen and remains standing. He smooths his thick, black curly hair and keeps shifting from one foot to the other, both feet clad in shoes for the right foot. He is offered some soup, but takes only a piece of bread before disappearing as unexpectedly as he appeared.

For a moment there is silence. Suddenly Nehomke remarks, very seriously, "Let's petition to the central committee to request the purchase of a normal pair of shoes for Elkind . . ."[34]

Eventually most of the Gedud members (or ex-Palestinians, as they became known) left the commune and settled in various cities in Russia. Elkind moved to Leningrad, his native city; Mordekhai Rubinstein, the rebel from Eishyshok, to Moscow, where he worked in its very bowels, helping build its famed subway system with the skills he had acquired in the Gedud; and Mordekhai's sister Rivka and her husband Moshe Blaj to Kiev, whence they made many futile attempts to return to Palestine. But none of this part of the story was known to the Communists back in Eishyshok. For a long time no one there knew what had happened to the Elkind group. Reb Tuviah Rubinstein and his wife Elka would die many years later without knowing, and it wouldn't be until the 1960s that the indomitable and resourceful Sarah, Mordekhai and Rivka's big sister, was able to track them down.

The majority of the shtetl Communists survived the Holocaust, having either fled to the Soviet Union or been exiled there by the time the Germans arrived. In a stunning reversal, they who had once denounced the Zionists, who had sought to reform what they saw as the parochial ethnicity of shtetl life so that the Jews could move beyond that stunted identity to the Communist ideal of a universal brotherhood, ended up as staunch Zionists and fierce defenders of their Jewish, shtetl roots. For them, as for many in the Elkind group, life in the Soviet Union proved the best antidote of all to their Communist fervor, better even than the years spent in harsh Polish jails. Taking advantage of a post–World War II repatriation act, most of them left the Soviet Union and returned to Poland, from whence they were eventually able to make their way to Canada, the United States, and Israel.

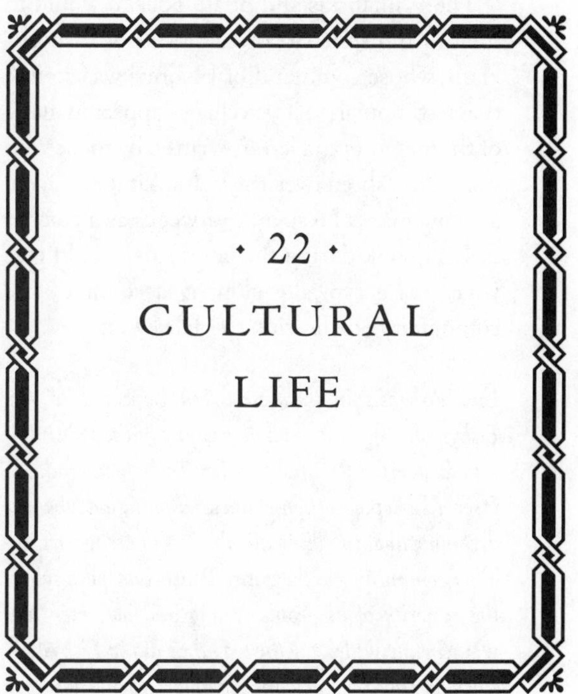

22 CULTURAL LIFE

THE JEWS WERE REDEEMED FROM EGYPT DUE TO FOUR PRAISEWORTHY MERITS. THEY DID NOT CHANGE THEIR NAMES, DID NOT CHANGE THEIR LANGUAGE, DID NOT REVEAL THEIR MYSTERY AND DID NOT ABOLISH CIRCUMCISION.

Midrash Shoher Shoher-tov 114

THE HEBREW LANGUAGE MOVEMENT

THE REVIVAL OF HEBREW AS AN EVERYDAY SPOKEN LANGUAGE WAS ONE OF THE hallmarks of the Haskalah in Russia, and a major goal of the Zionist movement — particularly that sector of the movement that was embraced by Eishyshok. Adopting Hebrew as the common language of the Jews meant building on a well-established tradition, for Hebrew had remained the written language of the educated male elite throughout the centuries. With few exceptions, all rabbinic writings, scholarly books, public and private letters, legal documents, and official records, including those of the Council of the Four Lands and the Lithuanian Council, as well as many community pinkasim (record books) were written in Hebrew.

Many family records, such as the family tree or scroll of origin (megilat yuhasin), were also kept in Hebrew, and many families prided themselves on their fluency. Indeed, some families told a special genre of stories describing their loyalty to the Hebrew language — stories so cherished that they became featured highlights of the family history, told and retold down through the generations. The Coutsai family in Eishyshok, for example, who were descendants of the thirteenth-century tosafist Rabbi Shimshon, the Noble of Coucy, took as much pride in their family's historical commitment to the Hebrew language in its purest, most elegant form (the Sephardic) as they did in their illustrious ancestry.[1] And a similar pride would come to be the trademark of many Hebrew-speakers in Eishyshok, perhaps inspired by the example of the Coutsais, who had been the main Torah readers in the shtetl ever since settling there centuries before, and would continue to be until the very end. That pride could only have been enhanced by the achievements of a number of Eishyshok's native sons and daughters in the world beyond the shtetl walls.

Meir Wilkanski, his older brother Yitzhak, and later Shaul Kaleko, three of the shtetl's most accomplished Hebraists, were among those who had been greatly impressed by hearing the Coutsais read in the synagogue and the beth midrash during the days of their youth, and all of them went on to distinguish themselves as Hebraists in the outside world. Meir, for example, was to become a writer of some renown, publishing several volumes of memoirs as well as a number of short stories in such Hebrew-language publications as *Ha-Omer* (The Sheaf), *Ha-Meorer* (The Awakener), and *Ha-Poel ha-Zair* (The Young Laborer). Yitzhak published under several different names, writing on subjects as various as agriculture, labor, politics, and literature.[2] And Shaul Kaleko became a renowned Hebrew grammarian.

The Wilkanskis and Shaul Kaleko would in their turn inspire later generations of Eishyshkians, whose command of Hebrew was so fine that testimonials to its excellence appear in many of the memoirs and letters written by those who visited the shtetl over the years. Yitzhak Ogen, a young man who spent five weeks as a teacher in Eishyshok during the late 1930s, would give what was a typically glowing account of the community's dedication to Hebrew:

Like an oasis in the desert you appeared to me, Eishyshok, a Jewish shtetl flourishing in the Polish Diaspora desert, a Jewish shtetl of an enchanted kind.... It served as a piece of homeland for a young lad who was dreaming about making aliyah.... There wasn't another community in the entire Polish Diaspora where the majority of its people, young and old, men and women, knew Hebrew the way they did in Eishyshok. Even the children knew the language, having absorbed it from their mothers, who sang them to sleep with Hebrew melodies and Hebrew folk songs.[3]

The Wilkanski household became the center for Hebrew-language learning in Eishyshok. First Yitzhak and Meir mastered it, then they began to teach others, including their two talented sisters, blond Sarah and dark-haired Esther. The two younger children, Mordekhai, born in 1890, and Leah, born in 1896, were practically brought up in the Hebrew language by their older siblings. Though Yiddish remained the language in which the children conversed with their parents, they spoke Hebrew among themselves.

The Wilkanski household became a center for Hebrew language study: (right to left) Sarah, Mordekhai, Leah, Meir, and his bride, Sarah Rubin, were all known for their perfect Hebrew. They were teachers, writers, and founders of Hebrew-speaking clubs. YESC, WILKANSKI

One by one, the older Wilkanski children left the shtetl in pursuit of university studies and training in professions that they thought would be essential for the rebuilding of the Land of Israel. During their years in Switzerland, Germany, Prussia, and Russia, they became apostles for the Hebrew language, and among its most graceful representatives. Their tall, slim figures, their beautiful Hebrew, and their active pens became well known. Among them, they would eventually contribute to virtually every major Hebrew newspaper of the first half of the twentieth century.[4] And always they were devoted letter writers; much of their correspondence described their activities on behalf of the Hebrew language: teaching it, reading it, proselytizing for it. Esther, for example, taught Hebrew four hours a day in a girls' elementary school in Mariampole during 1903; later that year she moved to Vilna, where she pursued her own studies while also teaching Hebrew to seventy young girls up to the age of thirteen, as she described in a letter to Meir:

I teach them to respect Hebrew and praise its beauty... I explain to them that every nation must

love its own language and its own country and we too must love our people, our land, and our language. Only by loving one another will we attain our goals and become a nation like all other nations who dwell in their own land, on their own soil.

She includes in her letter an account of her current reading, the popular serialized novel *Zikhronot Le-Veit David* (Memories from the House of David) running in *Ha-Zefirah*. Each new installment was awaited with bated breath by the Wilkanski siblings, who closely followed the adventures of its beloved heroes and heroines.[5] Reb Layzer himself was a secret fan, as Meir discovered the night he saw his father reading it when he thought everyone was asleep.

In the summer of 1904 Esther was joined in Vilna by Sarah, who had been studying at the university in Königsberg, and the two of them lived rent-free in a house that Esther was taking care of for its vacationing owners. But with Hebrew students being scarce that season — their only students were the children of a relative — they had very little to live on, so Meir, who was then living in the Lithuanian port city of Memel, sent them money.

Soon the peripatetic Esther would go on to Ponivezh, a shtetl near her hometown, where she studied for her university entrance exams. There she had better luck finding Hebrew students, including her landlord's sister and the shtetl rabbi's daughter, as well as several members of the socialist organization Poalei Zion (Workers of Zion), and "people from among the 'masses,'" as she put it, in what must have been a reference to other Jewish socialists. "Our language is dear to me and I try to spread it among many," she wrote Meir in June 1905.

Meanwhile, Meir had fallen in love with a first cousin on his mother's side, Sarah Rubin of Luknik. She was not fluent in Hebrew, so with typical Wilkanski zeal Meir set about teaching her Hebrew in Memel, then asked his sisters to continue the task in Eishyshok when Sarah went there to spend time with her future in-laws. Soon she too was fluent, so much so that she was able to engage in an exchange of beautiful, poetic love letters that may be among the first in modern Hebrew. As soon as she mastered Hebrew, Meir asked her to destroy the few letters he had written to her in "jargon"—Yiddish.

LEAH WILKANSKI'S RAK IVRIT

Wherever they went, the Wilkanski siblings eagerly followed the progress of their little sister Leah back home in Eishyshok. From Berlin University, Yitzhak wrote in 1904 asking what textbooks she was using, who her teacher was, whether she was studying Russian and mathematics, and whether she had learned to speak Hebrew yet. Leah would more than live up to her brothers' and sisters' expectations of her; with regard to Hebrew, she eclipsed them: By 1905 Esther was writing her nine-year-old sister to congratulate her on having founded Rak Ivrit (Hebrew only), a Hebrew-speaking society for six-to-twelve-year-old girls, which went on to became one of the most important, influential, and enduring educational institutions in the shtetl.[6]

My dearest, I envy you on the big step you have taken. I have not as yet proved worthy to take such a giant step. But you who are so diminutive in size and tender in years have achieved so much. . . . I am ashamed to look you in the eye, knowing all the difficulties you faced before you were able to establish your wonderfully named Rak Ivrit society, and wondering why I myself have been unable to translate my own plans for establishing a society for Hebrew-speaking individuals into reality. I do not know whether the blame lies within myself or the times, which perhaps are not ripe for such a step.

From that time on, Rak Ivrit became the central theme in the Wilkanskis' voluminous correspondence, with each letter from Leah to her siblings documenting in the minutest detail every event in the life of this extraordinary society. Leah's brothers and sisters vigorously supported her fledgling project and gave generously to it, in whatever way they could. Meir, who had left for Palestine in the summer of 1904, supplied her with materials published in the Holy Land, and corresponded with several members of the society. He also occasionally corrected her Hebrew and admonished her not to fall into sloppy habits. Yitzhak, in addition to mailing her all the newspapers to which he was by then a contributor, also sent money. "I am sending you 20 rubles, 7 for yourself, the rest for your society," he wrote in 1906. And Sarah and Esther involved themselves with Rak Ivrit on a daily basis whenever they were in Eishyshok, giving private lessons to the girls, guiding the group in its various activities, offering advice during meetings, researching the music for new Hebrew songs, purchasing books, and providing assistance with the Hebrew-language crossword puzzles that had begun to appear in the newspapers.

Sarah also founded an offshoot of Rak Ivrit called Ivriah (sometimes spelled Ibriah), a Hebrew-language society for teenagers in Eishyshok, which later became a chapter of the international organization of the same name.[7] Like Rak Ivrit, it required its members to conduct all their cultural activities in Hebrew: singing songs, reading books, performing plays. Thus Leah was responsible for establishing Hebrew as the mother tongue for the entire generation of Eishyshok girls born in the closing years of the nineteenth century, while Sarah taught their older sisters — and later, on a private basis, their brothers as well. Together they and their siblings revolutionized the shtetl's attitude toward Hebrew as a daily, spoken, secular language. And when some of the little girls of Rak Ivrit grew up and emigrated, they took with them their knowledge of the mother tongue. In this way Leah's work lived on for many years and in many places, even though she herself lived only to the age of twenty-one.

As its name indicates, Rak Ivrit required its members to speak Hebrew only, at all group functions and meetings, and in all other places where two or more members were present. Girls who broke the rules and slipped into "jargon" (Yiddish) were fined a kopeck per mistake, and even expelled. Though its members were all girls under the age of thirteen, like many organizations it was not above politics. Its three officers, after the second election was held, were Mina Berman, chair; Leah Wilkanski, secretary; and Kreine Chelikowski, treasurer, who replaced Szeina Katzenelenboigen after Szeina engaged in a power struggle with Mina and subsequently lost the post she had won in the first election. Mina may have won the struggle in Rak Ivrit, but she paid a high price for her activism at home, where members of her family who vehemently opposed the teaching of Hebrew as a secular, spoken language beat her and locked her up.

Despite its stiff rules and the internal and external battles its members fought, Rak Ivrit flourished, attracting local interest as well as international fame. At the local level, Leah was invited to establish a branch of her society in nearby Olkenik in 1906. Accompanied by her older sister, Esther, Leah traveled to Olkenik but had to return home before accomplishing her mission because of illness in the family. International attention first came via the well-known Hebrew writer A. Zarhi, who had spent time with Leah's group shortly after it was founded and in November 1905 published a long and eloquent letter addressed to "The Girls' Society of Rak Ivrit in Eishyshok" in *Ha-Hayyim ve-ha-Teva* (Life and Nature), a Hebrew journal for children:

My little sisters! . . . I am writing to you from our Holy Land. Though it is winter . . . the soil under my feet is bedecked in green and . . . the air is perfumed. . . . Like a dreamer I wander during the day and night, my heart full, my mind free. Then I forget the entire world and before my eyes there appears another place, filled with beauty and refinement, magic and song. During such hours I recall the sights I witnessed, day in and day out, during the months I dwelled among you . . .

I remember . . . your songs filled with joy and longing, power and confidence. "We shall take what is ours, Shall carry our banners to Zion!"

I recall all the games that you played, the parties that you made . . . And in my mind's eye I follow the clusters of women fighting to be near you, the mob of "jargon-girls" attempting to mimic your songs and repeat the few Hebrew words their ears have caught . . . I see boys and girls passing before me holding books from your library, wearing the embroidered Rak Ivrit society insignia over their hearts. I hear the public readings you gave, the joyful laughter that was always erupting like a storm in your midst . . .

Here in the land of the Hebrews there are many boys and girls and most of them know some Hebrew, but only a few speak it among themselves, and barely a handful attempts to enforce such speech among their friends as you do. They do not have your noble ideals, your bold goals; there are no public readings, no social gatherings of like-minded individuals, no games, no songs. They are missing the joy of life, the play of the imagination . . .

The magic of your society has captivated my soul . . . My heart fills with sadness when I reflect that not only is there no other society like yours in the Diaspora, but even in Eretz Israel there is none like it. You have taken an oath not to speak among yourselves any other language but Hebrew, and the walls of the houses, the cobblestones in the streets bear witness that you have not broken your oath. Here such things are still strange to them, and young and old they assault the ear with their "jargon." You little Hebraists in your forgotten corner of the Diaspora are to be for them a model. And what you have accomplished in one year must be written up as a paragon for all to follow!

Meir Wilkanski added to the renown of his sister's undertaking by publishing a letter about it in the children's journal *Olam Kattan* (Small World), to which Leah also contributed. A group of girls in Meir's town of Yaffo, Palestine, were so impressed by what they read about the Rak Ivrit of Eishyshok that they established a similar society by the same name. Modeled after Leah's group — though it soon became coed — it was both thrilling and anxiety-producing for Leah, who worried that it would not live up to its name or her own high standards. Meir tried in a letter of July 8, 1906, to calm his sister's fears: "To speak in Hebrew is not a big miracle here, as it is in our small town! I gave them a picture of you and they look at it frequently."

In Eishyshok the society continued to grow by leaps and bounds, despite having expelled a number of girls who persisted in speaking "jargon" against the rules. Nor was the harsh political climate a deterrent, though in 1906, when thousands of Russian Jews were being murdered in the riots that occurred in the aftermath of the revolution of 1905, Leah decided against putting on an anniversary banquet: "We did not celebrate by giving a party in this bloodthirsty, accursed Russia, for here we would be going to a party, while in another town our brothers' blood is being spilled!" she wrote to Meir.

By opening many of its functions to the public, Rak Ivrit won further support among the shtetl populace and made money, too. Its November 1905 staging of the Hebrew play *Ha-Hamsan Ha-Kattan* (The Little Thief), for example, was repeated twice and, at a price of 30 kopecks per ticket, brought in a healthy total of 15 rubles, 6 of which went to production expenses, 9 to purchase books for the new Hebrew library.

THE NORMALIZATION OF HEBREW

Hebrew language learning went through several phases in the relatively brief period of its revival in Eishyshok. The Wilkanski era was a time of founders, visionaries, and idealists, when the cause was so young that many everyday words could not be found in the sacred texts and had to be made up. Words for the musical notes, for straw hats, for librarian even, had not yet been coined. But the language was still supple enough that Meir Wilkanski and his future wife Sarah could write highly poetic love letters in it, as did Frume-Rochl Ratz and her future husband, Yitzhak Munin, some years later.[8] During this era many young people began to work toward the goal of Hebrew as the language not just of the sacred texts, and not just of those who studied those sacred texts, but of daily discourse.

When the Wilkanskis emigrated, their role in Hebrew language learning was assumed by the Rubinsteins, who also left, one by one, during the early 1920s, and by the Kalekos, who had inherited their grandmother Malke Roche's Schneider's flamboyance, and their father Mordekhai Munesh Kaleko's flair for writing. During the era of the Rubinsteins and the Kalekos, teaching Hebrew to the shtetl children, and integrating it in all the youth activities, became standard practice. Hebrew teachers were in great demand, among them Alte Paltiel, wife of the shtetl dayyan, and Moshe Yaakov Botwinik, later to become the Hebrew school principal.

By the mid-1920s, Hebrew in Eishyshok was no longer just the language of the young visionaries. It had spread throughout the shtetl, even to the older balebatim, who were making the effort to speak it. In many cases their children

Rak Ivrit (Hebrew only), the coed Hebrew-language society founded by Leah Wilkanski. The white bow on their chests indicates that Hebrew is the wearer's daily language, not Yiddish. In the third row, fifth from left, is Sarah Rubinstein, one of the shtetl's most gifted Hebrew teachers, who introduced the novel idea that women are capable of teaching men. Shlomo Kiuchefski is sitting on the ground, fifth from right. The little girl in the second row, far right, is Esther Katz. Fourth row, standing to the right of Sarah Rubinstein, is Shaul Kaleko and his brother Simha; the boy directly behind Sarah is Moshe Sonenson. Behind him in the last row is his brother Shalom, wearing a black outfit. A significant number of the people in the photo made aliyah and emigrated to various other countries. Those who remained in the shtetl were murdered during the Holocaust in various locations by the Germans, their local collaborators, and the AK. PHOTO: YITZHAK URI KATZ. YESC, Y. ELIACH

encouraged them, some more forcefully than others. Frume-Rochl Ratz, for example, would speak only Hebrew on the Sabbath, extending her usual practice to her mother's generation as well.

Still, even the most ardent Hebraist in the shtetl did not impose a Hebrew-only policy in traditional life-cycle ceremonies. At weddings, for example, old Yiddish songs and entertainments thrived side by side with Hebrew; at funerals, eulogies were delivered in Yiddish; newborn babies were given the Yiddish names of their deceased ancestors, as well as (in the case of male children) Hebrew names drawn mainly from the Bible. The first to break with this last tradition was Peretz Kaleko. When his first-born son arrived, he called him Amiram, a modern Hebrew name, instead of one of the accepted biblical Hebrew names that were the rule. Rabbi Rubinstein of Vilna, where the baby was born, refused to enter the name on a birth certificate, claiming it was not a Jewish name. Only when Peretz showed him that the name appeared in *Davar*, a Hebrew newspaper published in Eretz Israel, did the rabbi concede.

Ettl(?) Dubitski, one of the many Hebrew students and great admirers of Shaul Kaleko. The Hebrew inscription on this photo from 1919 reads: "To my darling, forever and ever, Shaul, my lover and dear one. From your lover, Dubitski." Ettl was murdered during the September 1941 massacre. PHOTO: YITZHAK URI KATZ. YESC, KALEKO-BARKALI

Like the Wilkanskis and the Rubinsteins, all the Kalekos (with the exception of one brother, Shmuel) eventually left the shtetl, to study and teach on behalf of Zion and Hebrew culture, and ultimately to make aliyah. But before they went to Palestine, they left their mark, and not just in the shtetl. While studying and working in Berlin, Shaul Kaleko, for example, became one of the key figures in the dissemination of the Hebrew language among Germany's Jews. His book *Hebraish fur Jeder Mann* (Hebrew for Everyman) became such a standard that it was the text from which Adolf Eichmann would later study Hebrew. Kaleko also wrote an extremely popular weekly column in the German Jewish newspaper *Yiddishe Rundschau*, where he created a mini-course in Hebrew, complete with grammar, vocabulary, a smattering of history, and homework exercises. It ran for years, until the paper was shut down in the wake of Kristallnacht in 1938.

By the time the last of the Kalekos had left Eishyshok — Rachel, in 1935 — Leah Wilkanski's Rak Ivrit had been officially dissolved for six years, and the evangelical excitement of the early days of Hebrew language learning had dissipated. Hebrew had become standard, and was now known and spoken throughout the shtetl. Indeed, less than three decades after Leah Wilkanski had started her "Hebrew only" girls' club, a multigeneration tradition of Hebrew speakers had been established. In the Katz family, for example, the grandmother, Alte, had studied with Sarah Wilkanski; her daughter Zipporah and son-in-law Moshe Sonenson had studied with Shaul Kaleko, while Moshe's brother, Shalom Sonenson, had studied with

Sarah Rubinstein; and Moshe and Zipporah's son Yitzhak was in Rachel Kaleko's kindergarten.

All Zionist youth organization functions were conducted in Hebrew; the majority of the children in the shtetl attended the Hebrew school; Rabbi Szymen Rozowski, the shtetl rabbi, issued all communications in Hebrew only; shtetl tots sang the latest Hebrew songs, while their baby brothers and sisters were rocked to sleep with Hebrew lullabies about Trumpeldor. In the census of 1932, 32 percent listed Hebrew as their native language.

Eishyshkians exulted in their reputation for speaking Hebrew with a purity and fluency that few people, even in Palestine, could match. Thus they loved to recount the story of Malka Matikanski's close call with the British immigration authorities, which came to a happy end largely because of her knowledge of Hebrew. As she was disembarking from the *Polonia*, the ship most Eishyshkians took to Palestine, an elderly gentleman remarked to her in Yiddish: "It is beyond me why such a pretty young girl has come to suffer in such a hard land." To which Malka responded in perfect Hebrew: "A beautiful motherland deserves beautiful daughters." Yitzhak Ben Zvi, (1884–1963), a high-ranking member of the leadership of the Yishuv, overheard her and was so impressed that he went to her aid when he noticed that she was having difficulty proving the legality of her immigration papers (which had been obtained through a fictitious marriage). "The fact that you speak such a fluent Hebrew and are from little Eishyshok, where I also have relatives, merits all the assistance I can give you."*

But at the same time that Hebrew had become an institutional reality within the shtetl, its chief promoters — men and women like Malka Matikanski — had departed. The intellectual vacuum they left behind was never filled.

And soon their legacy would be threatened not just by their absence, but by the restrictive immigration policies of Palestine and America, which required would-be olim to momentarily forgo their dreams of life in a new land and try instead to adapt to the grim economic realities of anti-Semitic Poland in the late 1930s. This meant that an increasing number of Jews sent their children to Polish schools, learned to speak Polish, and even read Polish newspapers, which began to be found in many shtetl homes alongside the Yiddish papers from Warsaw and Vilna.[9]

With the Soviet occupation of 1940–41, the Hebrew language legacy came under active attack — by local Jewish Communists. They closed the Hebrew day school and reopened it as a Yiddish school. Hebrew and all Zionist activities were banned. In the shtetl that had once regarded its commitment to reviving the ancient language as one of its very trademarks, Hebrew had to go underground. Those children who continued to study Hebrew — many with the help of relatives who had once been members of Rak Ivrit — did so in hiding, chanting their lessons in secret from behind warm ovens and in shadowy corners.

Leah Wilkanski wrote to her brother Meir in 1906 that life in tzarist Russia was worse than life during the Inquisition in Spain. Her remark applied to Soviet Russia in 1941 as well. Ironically, a number of Eishyshok's Communist "inquisitors" were fluent in Hebrew, having perfected it in Leah's Rak Ivrit.

*Yitzhak Ben Zvi was at that time chairman of the Vaad Leumi, the executive branch of the provisional government of the Yishuv. Later he would become the second president of the State of Israel. His eagerness to go to the aid of an Eishyshkian was partly due to the fact that it was another Eishyshkian, Akiva Rabinowitz, the grandson of Reb Layzer Wilkanski, who had helped him obtain a false passport in 1907.

THE PUBLIC LIBRARY

In 1905 the girls from the Rak Ivrit and Ivriah societies, led by nine-year-old Leah Wilkanski, founded a new library, the first public, coed library in the history of Eishyshok.

The new public library was, of course, not the only library in the shtetl. A number of traditional, religious libraries, large and small, were already in existence. The most important was the extensive collection of scholarly books that Eishyshok had been building for centuries in the beth midrash, but it was for men only, and its shelves were stocked exclusively with sacred books. These books, worn with age and use, had been shaping the minds of shtetl men for generations. In this book-oriented culture, every Jewish man was expected to have a bookshelf at home; thus most individual households had their own libraries, ranging from a handful of the most basic religious texts to thousands of books encompassing the wealth of Torah scholarship through the ages. Densely packed bookcases were a family's pride and joy, a status symbol attesting to their scholarship and, in some cases, to their membership in a dynasty of rabbis and scholars. When people left Eishyshok to make aliyah or emigrate to America, often the bundles they carried across the shtetl bridge on the way to their new homes held only their most precious family heirlooms: books, the portable homeland of the Jew.

In such a culture the new public library was both familiar and innovative — familiar because books were an integral part of everyone's life, innovative because it was a place where females as well as males, artisans as well as balebatim, were welcome, and because the collection ranged far beyond the traditional religious subject matter. The new library soon became an important center of learning for the shtetl youth — especially, of course, for girls and young women, who had no access to the library in the beth midrash, and for the sons and daughters of the artisans, since their parents generally could not afford the cost of tuition. Eventually the library collection contained all the classics in Hebrew, Yiddish, and Russian, some works of German literature, books on Zionism, socialism, zoology, and botany. The reference section had dictionaries, encyclopedias, and the Bible in various translations.

The growing demand for such an institution was paralleled by the shtetl's hunger for all the latest publications of the popular press. To pay the high price of these papers, which few could afford but many wished to read, families would pool their resources and subscribe to them jointly. Each issue was then passed from hand to hand, the order of distribution determined by the amount contributed. Thus the smallest investor received the paper last, by which time the print was not always even legible![10] In this and in other ways the people of the shtetl made sure that they kept up with current events, which they were passionately interested in. Newspapers reporting on contemporary issues of particular relevance to the shtetl populace were even pasted on outside walls, where all could read them. More than seventy years later, Moshe Szulkin could recall, almost verbatim, the text of two articles he had read on such a "wall newspaper": about the Beilis blood-libel trial of 1911 and the sinking of the *Titanic* in 1912.

Eishyshok had come a long way since Reb Layzer Wilkanski's time, when newspapers were so rare and extraordinary that they seemed to be God's writing on the wall (with the ever-present possibility of interference from Satan). In the spirit of that earlier time, three of Reb Layzer's contemporaries read a newspaper article about an impending shower of meteors and donned their shrouds to await what they felt sure was their imminent death. When the designated day came and went without incident, instead of rejoicing the women felt deeply disappointed at their discovery that a newspaper could be fallible. Reb Layzer himself rejoiced when he first saw a copy of the Jerusalem paper *Ha-Zevi* — at last he was privileged to hold in his hands a paper published in the Holy City. But his joy quickly turned to pain when he read an article attacking prominent rabbis for mismanaging charity funds in the Holy Land. Reb Layzer could not understand how one Jew could attack another in print.[11] The children of Reb Layzer and the generations that succeeded them never mistook the newspapers for God's word, but found them indispensable as hotlines to worldly knowledge, their link to the outside world.

A private house on Radun Street, rented for 15 rubles a month, was the library's first home. In 1908 Radun Street burned down, but the library devotees were able to save all the books, and eventually to transfer them to the library's new home, in a house on Vilna Street. In the summer of 1915 the library was again threatened with destruction, this time by rampaging Cossacks, but a number of the books were saved and hidden in people's homes until the library could be brought back to life. When the Russians retreated and the German occupation began later that year, introducing a period of relative peace and order, the library, like so many other cultural institutions, was enabled to flourish.

As a member of the comitet, the central community organization for emergency activities during World War I, young Shmuel Kaleko was assigned the task of helping to rebuild the library, while fellow comitet members Avraham Berl Paikowski and Benyomin Tshorny went door to door collecting the books that had been saved from the Cossacks. Soon the library had resumed its role as a vital cultural center in the shtetl, never more welcome than in wartime, when the German-imposed curfew left the shtetl youth with many idle hours in the evening. What better way to spend house arrest than in the company of a good book?

The library, staffed by volunteers, was open afternoons, Sunday through Wednesday. Most of the funding for the library, both for routine upkeep and for the acquisition of new books, came from membership dues, from private donations, and from the income produced by the many plays, concerts, banquets, and raffles that were put on for its benefit. The Germans could be counted on to purchase choice seats at high prices.

All library matters were coordinated through a central committee composed of representatives from the various youth organizations, who were among the shtetl's most ardent kultur treggers (culture carriers). And, as such, they also represented the two divergent cultural trends that were claiming different sectors of the shtetl youth: Hebrew versus Yiddish.

The Hebraists were generally Zionists, looking forward to life in a new land, with its own language and its own culture. The Yiddishists were mainly socialists, Bundists, and Communists, still hoping to improve life in the land of their birth. They viewed Yiddish as the language of the oppressed, toiling masses, with whom they identified; to speak Yiddish was part of their very ideology. A few people had a foot in each camp: as Zionists they had a strong allegiance to Hebrew as the classical language of the Jews; as proud carriers of shtetl culture they wanted to preserve Yiddish as an integral part of that culture, without regard to political ideology.[12] In the library, the common ground, the two camps were united in an uneasy alliance, but the unity sometimes gave way to fierce skirmishes.

Having been founded and supported by members of Hebrew-only cultural societies, during its early years the library tended to focus on the classics of the Hebrew Enlightenment — books by the likes of Abraham Mapu, Moshe Leib Lilienblum, Peretz Smolenskin, Judah Leib Gordon, Ahad Ha'am, and Micha Josef Berdyczewski, as well as Hebrew-language magazines and journals, many of them donated by Alte Katz and other subscribers in the shtetl.

Shaul Kaleko enjoying one of the Hebrew books from the library. PHOTO: YITZHAK URI KATZ. YESC, KALEKO-BARKALI

Authors like Y. L. Peretz and Mendele Mokher Sefarim, who wrote in both Yiddish and Hebrew, were also represented.

During World War I, Hebrew language learning continued to flourish, and the number of Hebrew readers greatly increased, because of the arrival of a critical mass of dedicated, activist Zionist war refugees in the shtetl. Because German rule created an oasis of relative stability in Eishyshok, during the several years of the occupation many outsiders sought shelter in the shtetl, including a number of highly educated young men and women who had studied at universities and teachers' seminaries in the larger cities. Thus the widening of cultural horizons was accelerated.

Some of the outsiders were relatives of local families, some former Eishyshkians, some strangers. Some came alone, some came with their entire families, especially from the province of Kovno, where the tzarist government expelled all the Jews in May 1915. But with their sophisticated foreign ways, which found expression not just in books they had read and languages they knew but in their fashionable grooming and clothes, in the new political causes they championed, and in the revolutions they anticipated, they all contributed to the unprecedented cosmopolitan atmosphere that prevailed at this time — much to the awe of many native residents of the shtetl.

The refugees were a diverse lot, many of whom might at other times have found their ideas and behavior under attack in the shtetl. But during wartime, all were welcomed with open arms. Shmuel Senitski's sister, for example, was a graduate of the University of Kharkov and a so-called naturalist (a believer in the redemptive powers of nature and the innate goodness of the body) for whom no topic was taboo. Her liberated speech made even Shaul Kaleko, a young intellectual who was a champion of change, "blush like a red lobster."[13] Less extreme but equally impressive in their way were the Hutner girls, Hava and Luba, who had come from their home in Warsaw to take shelter with their grandparents, Rabbi Zundl and Rebbetzin Hendl Hutner. The young women of the shtetl were dazzled by the Hutner sisters' knowledge and erudition, their commitment to Zionism and social change, and their beauty as well.

Astramski der Feldsher fled to Eishyshok from a small town near Poniviecz, bringing to the household of his brother Nehemia Suchowitski (also a medicine man) his six daughters and four sons. All the children were well educated and elegantly dressed. Soon Nehemia's home became a salon for the young intellectuals of Eishyshok, a place where they could spend the long curfew nights of World War I reading poetry, engaging in literary and political discussions, singing and playing musical instruments. To them the Astramskis seemed the very model of a shtetl family who had exchanged their small-town ways for big-city sophistication.[14]

Zipporah Katz (Sonenson), one of the shtetl's Hebrew librarians. Zipporah was murdered by the AK in 1944. PHOTO: YITZHAK URI KATZ. YESC, Y. SONENSON

Members of the library named in honor of Y. L. Peretz, including (first row, left) Batia Bastunski and Mordekhai (Motl) Replianski; Velvke Katz (fourth from left); (middle row, left) Velvke Kaganowicz; Eli Politacki (third from left); Malka Matikanski (top row, second from left). Batia emigrated to America, Malka to Eretz Israel. Most of the people were murdered in the September 1941 massacre. PHOTO: BEN ZION SZREJDER. YESC, MATIKANSKI

AFTER WORLD WAR I

The overwhelming proliferation of activities by and for the Hebraists resulted in a rift with the Yiddishists in 1918. Claiming that the major share of the financial support for the library came from their activities, while the majority of the books then being purchased were in Yiddish, the champions of Hebrew decided to split off and found their own library. The proceeds from performances of Peretz Hirschbein's play *Der Intelligent* were to provide seed money for this new Hebrew library.

Meir Kiuchefski, Eishyshok's very talented and civic-minded community leader during World War I, requested that money brought in by the play be used to aid the families of the hundred people who had died in the typhus epidemic of 1918. But the library committee, all of whom were young people, objected, claiming that such problems were the responsibility of the community leadership, not the library. The shtetl lined up on either side of this issue, prepared to do battle, but the discussion proved academic: library committee member Hayya Streletski, with 500 German marks in hand, had already gone to Vilna to purchase the Hebrew-language books. Faced with a fait accompli, the shtetl leadership had to accept the decision of the library committee. Once again the young had made their power felt.

The division between the two libraries did not last long. But even after they were reunited under one roof again, the conflict between Yiddish and Hebrew continued, and the tensions between them required an occasional outlet. Sometimes they were expressed ideologically: Candidates for posts in the various Zionist organizations had to declare themselves on one side or another of the rift during their election campaigns. Occasionally they were expressed more directly: The Hebraists would block the entrance to the library on the Yiddish evenings, when the Yiddish librarians were in charge, and the Yiddishists would block the entrance on the Hebrew evenings. In one such confrontation, Hebraist Peretz Kaleko ended up with a torn shirt, and his opponent, Moshe Sonenson, defender of the Yiddish language (although he was also a student at the Epstein Hebrew gymnasium in Vilna), suffered a bloody nose. But these battle lines were easily crossed: The librarian on duty that night, Zipporah Katz, was a Hebraist but was also Moshe Sonenson's girlfriend and future wife.

Eventually a more lasting peace prevailed, and the library was named after Y. L. Peretz, an author who wrote in both languages and was revered by members of both factions. Though the truce between the factions enhanced the cultural activities of the library for a while, in general there was a falling-off in all nonessential activities throughout the shtetl during the 1930s, and the library was one of the many cultural institutions that suffered. This was a time when the Polonization policies of the government in combination with the emigration of so many of the shtetl's most dynamic, creative people had begun to take a severe toll on the quality of daily life.

There were other reasons, too, for the library's loss of centrality in the shtetl. Each of the Zionist organizations eventually established its own mini–Hebrew library, and when the centralized Hebrew day school was finally built, in 1932, it too installed an excellent library. Eishyshkians also had access to libraries outside the shtetl. Once the modern system of roadways was completed in 1929, the bus lines that connected Eishyshok with the larger towns in the vicinity put such outstanding libraries as the Strashun in Vilna within reach.[15]

In addition, private family libraries were increasingly being stocked with secular as well as sacred texts. Certain individuals in the shtetl were particularly known for their collections of the latest books, as well as their subscriptions to a variety of journals and newspapers. Uri and Alte Katz ran a virtual salon (popularly known as the Vagsal, or train station) for those who wanted to keep up with the latest publications, listen to Yiddish records, drink tea, and eat pastries. They even produced a match between readers of the same paper: Alexander Zisl Hinski and Shoshana Hutner, both fans of the afternoon edition of the Warsaw *Haint*. Ida Goide-Sonenson, wife of Avraham Sonenson, subscribed to Yiddish and Polish as well as Hebrew publications, which were supplemented by frequent shipments of new reading material from her wealthy family in nearby Lida, all of which she generously shared. (Her mother-in-law, Hayya Sonenson, kept Ida's books on a different floor from the shelves that housed the collections of her Kabacznik ancestors and her late husband, so that the sacred and timeless works would not have to mix with the secular and the temporal.)

Ironically, despite its diminishing role in the shtetl, the library began to receive community funding in 1933, when the kahal gave it 500 zlotys — the same amount allocated to the Hebrew day school, which had become the shtetl's central educational institution, attended by a majority of the shtetl children.[16] Such a generous allocation was essentially an expression of the community's support of Yiddish culture, for the library was by then a mainly Yiddish institution (and the only one in the shtetl). Ever since 1925, when Bundists in Vilna founded YIVO (Yiddisher Visenshaftlikher Institut), an organization dedicated to promoting the study of Jewish history, language, and culture in Eastern Europe, the Yiddishists had been gaining strength in the shtetl. By 1933 most of the young Hebraists had emigrated, but the younger generation of Yiddishists, who were mainly the sons and daughters of artisans, had stayed on, still looking to socialism and Communism to deliver on the dream of a just and equitable world — while living in a shtetl that was clearly in decline.

Even in decline, the Y. L. Peretz library could on occasion put on a grand show, as it did in 1936 when it celebrated the centennial of the birth of another author who wrote in both Yiddish and Hebrew, the extremely popular and widely translated Mendele Mokher Sefarim (Mendele the Itinerant Bookseller, the pen name of Shalom Jacob Abramovich). The anniversary was commemorated with a special postcard, a decorative library stamp, and a variety of cultural events culminating in what was to have been a public lecture by the distinguished

Yiddish author Daniel Charney. As Charney later recounted in two charming articles he wrote about the occasion, when Mordekhai Replianski asked him to deliver the lecture he offered him the very inflated honorarium of 70 zlotys (20 being about the standard). When Charney asked why, Replianski replied that it was a matter of ambition and local pride, for little Eishyshok was determined to upstage Vilna by celebrating the centennial of Mendele's birth before Vilna had even begun to make plans.

Given a truly red-carpet reception when he got to Eishyshok — lavish food, a luxurious room in Szeina Katzenelenboigen's hotel, greetings from all the Zionist leaders and other community notables of the shtetl — Charney showed up the next evening to give his lecture to a packed audience at the firehouse. But before he could do so, Mordekhai Replianski explained, he would have to be officially welcomed by the representatives of the organizations sponsoring his lecture. So the eight shtetl dignitaries who were seated on the stage, bearlike presences in the heavy fur coats and tall fur hats they wore against the bitter chill of the unheated hall, would each be taking a turn at the lectern to offer a brief greeting, not to exceed five minutes apiece. Over three hours later, at 11:45, in the midst of what turned out to be the last round of speechifying, the room went black and a Polish policeman ordered everyone to leave. Public assemblies were outlawed after midnight in towns — like Eishyshok — that were close to the Russian border. Charney never delivered his Mendele Centennial lecture.

Nonetheless, he was paid in full, for, as Mordekhai Replianski later reassured him, the event had been a success: ticket sales had brought in 80 zlotys, each of the eight organizations whose representatives sat at the dais and spoke that night contributed an additional 5, so even after payment of the honorarium the library was left with a profit of 50 zlotys — and the honor of having been the first to celebrate the centennial!

The postcard issued by Eishyshok's Y. L. Peretz library in honor of the centennial celebration of the birth of Mendele Mokher Sefarim (1836–1936). Mendele's image is flanked by photos of the library jubilee committee. Below Mendele's image is the photo of the Yiddish author Daniel Charney, the keynote speaker of the event. PHOTO: ALTE KATZ AND BEN ZION SZREJDER. YESC, KALEKO-ALUFI

Most of the organizers of the Mendele Centennial were among those murdered in 1941. All that remains of the event are Charney's two articles about it and a photograph by Alte Katz and her assistant Ben Zion Szrejder.[17]

The Mendele celebration was a rare bright spot in the library's period of decline during the 1930s. In 1937 the American-funded Jewish aid agency known as the JDC (Joint Distribution Committee) offered this gloomy and all-too-accurate account of its sad state:

The community library, named after Y. L. Peretz, has a large section of Yiddish, Hebrew, Polish, and Russian books, which are never looked at. During the summer the library has about ten members, and during the

winter about thirty. But there is a heavy layer of dust on the books. Last year EKOPO *[the Jewish Loan Association of Eastern Europe] of Vilna sent the library a large number of Yiddish and Hebrew books. The community allocates the library an annual subsidy of 120 zlotys.*[18]

By cutting the library's 500-zloty allocation of 1933 down to 120 four years later, the community was simply acknowledging reality. In the face of the emigration of so many of the library's most dynamic leaders, and the loss of so many of its most enthusiastic members, the institution had failed to restructure itself to serve the changing needs of the community. Even the handful of activists who remained in the shtetl, or had returned to it, couldn't be counted on. People like Szeina Katzenelenboigen-Schwartz, one of the original founders of the library along with Leah Wilkanski, Zipporah Katz Sonenson, once one of its most active volunteer librarians, and Shalom Sonenson, who was one of those who had returned from Palestine, were now preoccupied with the demands of business, marriage, and child-rearing. Many other energetic young men and women were members of various Zionist organizations who spent most of their time away from the shtetl at a model farm where they were learning the manual skills they would need for their new life in Palestine. If they needed the latest information about conditions in their intended homeland, they went to the Strashun library to get it.

There was still to be one last glorious chapter in the history of the Eishyshok public library, however. From 1939 to 1941, when thousands of refugees passed through Eishyshok, the library was in great demand. Once again the books on its dusty shelves beckoned to readers, lifting the gloomy spirits of those who were running toward the unknown. As it happened, the only library books to survive World War II were those taken out of the shtetl by the refugees. The long journeys of some of them ended successfully, and the books they carried with them are treasured mementos of their escape.

During the Soviet occupation of 1940–41 the Jewish Communists closed the library. Some of its books were clandestinely taken into people's homes, as they were in World War I. But this time the ultimate fate of the books was different. During the subsequent German occupation, all the shtetl's sacred books, whether publicly or privately owned, were used as heating fuel by German troops and local Poles. Ironically, many of them were library books that had originally been purchased with the generous help of the occupying German soldiers of World War I.

Leah Wilkanski never learned the fate of the library she had founded at the age of nine. She died in Eretz Israel after a brief illness in 1917, only twelve years after her remarkable accomplishment.

SOCIAL CLUBS

During the 1920s and '30s an extraordinary variety of activities to suit a wide spectrum of tastes was available to Eishyshok's young people. Something was going on — a gathering to join, a performance to attend, a project to work on — virtually every night of the week.

In addition to the political and educational groups, there were social clubs, like Club 21, which consisted of twenty-one young women bound by no particular ideology other than the desire to be together, enjoying the simple pleasures of youth, among others of their class (the balebatim). Our Circle was another social club, for the younger sisters of the women in Club 21.

Cultural groups included the literary society named in honor of the Hebrew writer Yossef Hayyim Brenner, who had been murdered by Arabs in Yaffo, Palestine, during the riots of May 1921.[19] Brenner's psychologically acute portrayals of an uprooted generation struck a special chord with many of the young people, for even if they were not contemplating life in a new land, they were feeling the psychic strain of living in a time of transition, entering a new cultural era. Some of the young Eishyshkians were such ardent fans that they could recite whole sections of Brenner's writings by heart. The passion for his work apparently generated other kinds of passions as well: Peretz Kaleko and Leah Koppelman were the Brenner Club's first match, and there would be several more.

LEISURE AND VACATIONS

As the shtetl entered modernity, leisure and vacation activities assumed an unprecedented importance. Previously, leisure had been looked upon as a non-Jewish way of wasting precious time, time that could be better spent on Torah study, charity, and community work. Shtetl people had only to observe the local gentry to confirm this negative view. Hunting, drinking, and partying their time away on their country estates, when they weren't engaged in these or equally frivolous pastimes in the urban centers of Western Europe, the nobility seemed degenerate and dissolute. For the shtetl Jews, the only appropriate conception of leisure was as an integral part of the Sabbath and the Jewish holidays; as such, its main function was to restore the spirit so that one could serve God and study his law with new vigor the rest of the week. But during the twentieth century, Eishyshok arrived at a new understanding of leisure, and an appreciation of its positive impact on the well-being of the family in general, children in particular.

In the modern view, leisure was part of a preventive-medicine approach to life, its purpose being to forestall sickness among the healthy, and improve the health of the afflicted. For children it was deemed essential. Hence the new vogue for summer camps for children; country retreats for families; travel to mineral water spas; swimming, sports, and games. All became an integral part of shtetl life during the interwar years.

SWIMMING, SPORTS, AND GAMES

Swimming had been popular among the Jews of Eishyshok for centuries, perhaps because it was mentioned approvingly in the Talmud. Thus most of the men and boys of the shtetl knew how to swim (only a few of the out-of-town

Young friends on a summer vacation enjoy a boat ride, July 2, 1927: Rachel Kaleko (left), brother Simha (third from left), and three friends. The inscription on the back of the photo reads, "Rochale, when you will forget us, let the picture remind you." The Kaleko family made aliyah to Eretz Israel in the 1930s. YESC, KALEKO-ALUFI

A young men's swimming club. Leibke Sonenson (back row, left) was the club's leader. The majority of the young men in the photo were murdered during the Holocaust. YESC, BERKOWITCH

yeshivah students did). For those who were still learning, inflated cattle bladders and corks were used as floats. Eishyshok had two separate swimming spots, one for men, near the old water mill, and one for women, in a secluded area downriver. Until World War I, men swam nude. Women wore long white dresses, which became heavy in the water and thus made swimming very difficult.[20]

In the early 1890s the taboo against mixed swimming was broken by Dr. Ezra and his wife, and a young Polish lawyer and his wife, who swam together in the nude, in full view of passersby! The lawyer and his wife also made a practice of going to the old mill on Friday afternoons in the summer, so that they could watch the young boys and men who chose to perform their weekly ablutions in the river rather than in the public bathhouse.

By the interwar years, coed swimming, though not in the nude, became standard, and swimming as both a competitive sport and a social activity acquired great popularity in Eishyshok. Families and youth organizations went on outings that featured swimming, there was a young men's swimming club that competed successfully in many local contests, and children learned to swim at their summer camps. As swimming attracted more and more Jewish participants, it became a target for young Polish extremists, who liked to throw the swimmers' clothes into the river, and, more seriously, to attack them with stones and dogs. Since one of their leaders was the brother of the priest at the church in nearby Juryzdyki, the anti-Semites felt free to attack with impunity, until members of Beitar, the militaristic Zionist youth movement, pledged their protection: "United from

The Kudlanski (later Goodman) and Dubrowicz families enjoy a trip to a local lake, October 25, 1930. Among the seven family members are Hanneh-Beile Kudlanski (née Moszczenik) (second from right), daughter Atara, Leah Dubrowicz, and brother Shaul. The Kudlanski family emigrated to America, the Dubrowiczes were killed during the Holocaust. YESC, A. ZIMMERMAN

market square to the river," they proclaimed. Under the leadership of Leibke Sonenson (who had learned self-defense in Palestine) and Hillel and Faivl Glombocki, Beitar saw to it that the attacks on swimmers decreased in frequency, but they nonetheless continued until the outbreak of World War II.

Competitive sports such as bicycle racing also found a welcome in the shtetl. And there was a local soccer team that played against other Jewish teams from nearby shtetlekh, and a soccer team in Warinowa called the Vulcans that some

Two competitors in the Ha-Shomer ha-Tzair bicycle race, Hanan Polaczek (leaning on his bike, right), and Dov Wilenski (standing with his bike, left), on their return to the shtetl. To Dov's left, in a beret, is his girlfriend Esther Katz; to his right, in a hat, is Rina Lewinson. Standing barefoot on Rina's right is Meishke Michalowski. Front row, kneeling (right to left): Israel-Itchke Zlotnik (holding on to Dov's bike), Yehiel Blacharowicz, and Munia Zahavi. Standing on the right, dressed in a suit, is Shmuel Berkowicz. Shmuel, Hanan, Dov, Rina, and Munia made aliyah. Esther emigrated to Colombia. The others were murdered during the Holocaust. The photo was taken on the road behind the Old Beth Midrash. PHOTO: BEN ZION SZREJDER. YESC, D. WILENSKI

The Vulkan soccer team from Warinowa. The photo was dedicated to Eishyshok soccer player Velvke Saltz, May 26, 1924. YESC, SALTZ-SCHULTZ

Fraddie Shlanski and his favorite hand-carved wooden horse. Fraddie emigrated to America. YESC, SHLANSKI

Little Feigele (Fanichke) Saltz with her doll. Feigele emigrated to America. YESC, SALTZ-SCHULTZ

Israel and Matle Shereshefski with son Oscar (Asher) posing with one of his teddy bears. They survived the war in Russia.
YESC, M. SHEFSKI

of the better soccer players from Eishyshok joined. Occasionally Jewish boys even played on the local Polish team. Many parents and grandparents now followed their children's sports activities with as much interest as they followed their progress in school.

Families also changed their attitude toward children's toys and games. Previously, most of the games children played, like the toys they used, were associated with religious holidays. Chess, because it was considered a healthy challenge for the mind, was one of the few exceptions, and it could be found in virtually every household. A few handcrafted wooden toys were passed down from generation to generation, so that it was quite common for a child to ride the same rocking horse that his grandmother had ridden before him. But the interwar years saw a sudden profusion of mass-produced toys, which many of the old-timers objected to as having no relevance to Jewish values or customs. What could children learn from these machine-made dolls and clowns, cars and trains? they complained. Out of a belief that there were valuable skills to be acquired from making their own toys or mending existing ones, traditionalists like Hayya Sonenson taught their grandchildren how to construct buildings and bridges from small crabapples and sticks, how to carve walking sticks, how to make birchbark boats. Old Shaye Ginunski molded toys from wax for children of his acquaintance, and Avraham Shmuel der Shtepper (the stitcher) taught children the old-time games and dances every Saturday afternoon. But much to the regret of the older generation, the modern toys and games slowly conquered the shtetl, for the children insisted on having them, just as many of their parents were energetically embracing other manifestations of modernity.

RESORTS AND CAMPS

Following the lead of the sophisticates from Vilna, the more affluent Eishyshkians flocked to the countryside for vacations. Summer colonies in the pine forests and on the banks of nearby lakes and rivers were popular, with Dumbla and Titiance favored by the shtetl's fashionable set. By the mid-1930s the Vilna crowd had staked out its own preferred resort colonies, disdaining to mix with the shtetl vacationers.

A few days prior to summer vacation, the maids would depart for the families' summer dachas, traveling by coach, accompanied by suitcases and boxes filled with everything that would be needed in the months to come: blankets, pillows, linens, kitchen utensils. Once the schools closed, mothers and children would arrive to find immaculate cottages, well stocked with food, tables adorned by fresh summer flowers. Husbands, fathers, and other working relatives joined them on weekends, arriving by bicycle, coach, and horseback. The children were expected to improve their health by drinking milk fresh from the cow, and by eating butter straight from the churn, new-laid eggs, and just-picked berries and mushrooms. Outdoor activities in the salubrious air of the pine forest were

Yaffa Sonenson feeding her chickens in June 1941 in front of her family's summer home in Titiance. PHOTO: ALTE KATZ. YESC, Y. ELIACH

Gaining weight during summer vacation was considered a great accomplishment. Sonia Saposnikow was weighed at her family's dacha near Vilna. PHOTO: ROSALIND ROSENBLATT (NÉE FOSTER). YESC, R. ROSENBLATT

Moshe Sonenson holding his daughter Yaffa on the road leading to dachas in Titiance in June 1941. Moshe and Yaffa survived the war in hiding. PHOTO: ALTE KATZ. YESC, Y. ELIACH

Freshly laid eggs were a summer staple. Rosalind Foster, granddaughter of Nehemia der Feldsher, during her visit from America, brought fresh eggs to the family dacha, August 17, 1932. YESC, R. ROSENBLATT

considered essential for strong lungs, so the children went fishing, rowing, and swimming in the lakes and rivers, horseback riding and walking in the forest. There they could follow animal trails, pick mushrooms, berries, and wildflowers, or simply while away a summer day.

With so many of the shtetl intelligentsia gathered together in the countryside, it was natural that there should also be a variety of cultural activities: meetings with returning pioneers who could tell them about Eretz Israel, literary discussion groups at which poets and authors talked about their latest works, Saturday study

Rabbi Tuvia Rothberg (left) and Rabbi Shimon Schkopp vacationing in the pine forest near Luna, 1932. Rabbi Rothberg was murdered during the Holocaust. YESC, SH. FARBER

groups related to the weekly portion, and bonfires around which people sang the latest Hebrew songs. Alternately, one could stretch out on a hammock, the very symbol of the vacationer, and read, doze, or do nothing but gaze at a sky framed by pine branches.

Vacationing had become so respectable that even prominent rabbis did it. The Haffetz Hayyim, along with an entourage of family members and students, spent his summers in the pine forest of Dugalishok. Founded by Jewish farmers from Eishyshok's Paikowksi and Lipkunski families, Dugalishok was a summer resort village that became popular enough to be an important source of income for them. Rabbi Tuvia Rothberg, a former head of the yeshivah in Eishyshok, spent his summers in the pine forest around Olkenik, as did Rabbi Shimon Schkopp, Rabbi Avraham Yeshayahu Karelitz, who was an outstanding Talmudic scholar known as the Hazzon Ish, and a number of yeshivah students.[21]

By the 1930s, summer camps for children, located in Dumbla and Titiance, had become popular, particularly among Zionists. Organized by various community, school, and parents' associations, and by private investors as well, the camps conducted all their activities in Hebrew, and were visited frequently by Eishyshok's rabbi,

The Hebrew-speaking Zionist summer camp in Titiance. The adults in the third row (right to left) are hazzan Moshe Tobolski, Mordekhai (Motl) Replianski, an unidentified man, and Benyamin Kabacznik. Standing on the left is the camp owner, Aaron the Saltman. Among the campers are Leibke Kaganowicz, Avraham Hafetz, Leibke Bastunski, and Blumke Kremin. Most of the children and all of the adults were murdered in the September 1941 massacre and by the AK. YESC, D. & I. DIMITRO

Newlyweds Peretz Kaleko and wife Leah (née Koppelman) on summer vacation relaxing on a hammock in a pine forest. Both made aliyah to Eretz Israel in 1933. YESC, KALEKO-ALUFI

A group of friends enjoying sleigh rides in the shtetl, January 12, 1932: (right to left) Malka Matikanski, Szeina Blacharowicz, Motke Burstein, Esther Katz, an unidentified woman, Shepske Sonenson, Miriam Koppelman, Malka Nochomowicz, and another friend. Malka Matikanski emigrated to Eretz Israel, Esther Katz to Colombia. Szeina Blacharowicz survived the war in hiding. The others were murdered during the Holocaust. PHOTO: ALTE KATZ. YESC, Y. ELIACH

Benyamin Sonenson (left) and brother Shmuel skiing and sled riding, 1938. Both were murdered in the September 1941 massacre. PHOTO: BEN ZION SZREJDER. YESC, Y. SONENSON

Szymen Rozowski. The Dumbla camp was under the supervision of the Eishyshok hazzan Moshe Tobolski. Children whose parents could not afford to pay their camp fees were sponsored by the community, or by individual balebatim.

For children who were not strong enough to tolerate the strenuous physical activities at these summer camps, there was an alternative: a special camp run by Golda Levin and her sisters at their home in the pine forest of Dumbla. These children mainly ate and rested in hammocks, it being the fond hope of their parents that they would gain weight over the summer vacation. In general, a successful summer was measured by the number of pounds a child gained.

During the interwar years, vacations were no longer confined to summertime. Hotels and pensions at hot mineral springs like Druskieniki (Drozgenik) were year-round favorites. The Haffetz Hayyim, who suffered severe back pain, found relief at the springs, as did Alte Katz, who was cured of the pain in her legs that had made walking almost impossible. After her cure she visited the springs at Druskieniki several times a year, usually accompanied by members of her family. Those who could afford it traveled to ski resorts in Zakopane (a famous winter as well as summer vacation spot in Poland, south of Cracow); those of more modest means went cross-country skiing around Eishyshok, or skated on the frozen river under the first bridge on Vilna Street. Many took leisurely sleigh rides into the surrounding countryside. It wasn't unheard-of for Eishyshkians to travel to Vilna simply to eat a lavish meal at a favorite restaurant.

THE THEATER

The theater was one of those institutions that arrived in the shtetl only in the twentieth century. Or rather, it was only in the twentieth century that the shtetl version began to resemble our notions of conventional theater. During the centuries before, the people's innate sense of pageantry, which was rooted in religion, tradition, and local lore, had found expression in a different kind of theater, one in which every member of the community had his or her own role to play, and the stage was the shtetl itself: synagogue, marketplace, and home. Celebrations of the numerous holidays on the religious calendar, as well as of personal milestones like

The Frankel Hotel in Druskieniki near mineral springs. The hotel and the springs were favorite places of the Haffetz Hayyim and Alte Katz. YESC, ARIEL-FRANKEL

births and weddings, provided opportunities for a rich display of song, dance, rituals, processionals, and drama.

With the rapid secularization of the shtetl, such life-integrated pageantry diminished. The curtain call for Leah Wilkanski's production of *The Little Thief* in 1905 was the beginning of Act I in the life of the theater in Eishyshok — conventional theater, where the stage is not part of life but an imitation of life.

THE WAR YEARS

The German occupation of Eishyshok in 1915 proved a real boost to the theater, for the Germans in general were great lovers of culture, and the commander of Eishyshok in particular had a strong interest in the stage and in music. A kind, considerate, cultivated man, he was romantically involved with a young Jewish woman in the shtetl and it was rumored that he was a

Zipporah Katz Sonenson (right) with daughter Yaffa and sister Shoshana Katz, winter 1940. Yaffa lost her white hat skating on the frozen river and replaced it with a red one. Her mother was embarrassed that it did not match her white coat. PHOTO: BEN ZION SZREJDER. YESC, Y. ELIACH

One of the German commanders of Eishyshok during World War I with his local Jewish girlfriend, Gittl Rochowski, during one of their regular Sunday rides. They were always accompanied by the commander's beloved dog. Before the next war, Gittl made aliyah to Eretz Israel. PHOTO: GERMAN MILITARY PHOTOGRAPHER. YESC, M. KAGANOWICZ

Lemke, one of the most popular German soldiers in the shtetl during World War I, with a number of his Jewish girlfriends. Standing to his right is Rivka Remz, to his left Hayya Gershupski. Sitting on the extreme right is Menuha Salacki (Shlanski). Rivka survived World War II in France, the others were murdered by the Germans. PHOTO: GERMAN MILITARY PHOTOGRAPHER. YESC, M. KAGANOWICZ

Christian convert who had been born a Jew. While in Eishyshok he eagerly scanned the German press for news of the Yiddish theater in Vilna. Articles by author Arnold Zweig and artist Herman Struck, which compared the Vilna Troupe, the Yiddish theater group in Vilna, to the leading companies of Germany and the rest of Europe encouraged him and many of the other German military officers and enlisted men in the area to attend the local productions.[22] In fact, many of them, including Eishyshok's commander, became such fans that they ended up offering assistance to theater companies in the shtetlekh under their command, helping move props and heavy equipment when necessary, subsidizing the buying of costumes, and building an orchestra pit in the Eishyshok firehouse.[23] In some shtetlekh such assistance included participation: non-Jewish soldiers (as well as non-Jewish locals) sometimes acted in Jewish theater clubs.

During the first year of the German occupation, a teacher named Sarah Pinon established a drama club in Eishyshok. Charter members included Frume-Rochl Ratz (Eishyshok's answer to Esther Rachel Kaminska, the first lady of the Yiddish theater), Shmuel Gross, Shaul Kaleko, Szeina Katzenelenboigen, and Leibl Kaplan, who would later be joined by his son Avraham Meishke. This amateur theater group was generously supported by German officers, who attended regularly and purchased the most expensive tickets in the house — the "house" at the time consisting of the huge stable that belonged to Arie-Leib Dragutski "der Grober" (the fat one).[24] Its stage was constructed of barrels and lumber planks, the curtains were of homespun linen, the stage lighting consisted of lamps borrowed from the drugstores of Katz and Koppelman, the decorations were colorful paper lanterns, and the seating consisted mainly of benches donated by interested balebatim, usually the parents of drama club and library members. The best seats in the house were front-row chairs; the backless benches behind them were much less expensive. During the performances, the horses were either moved to another stable or kept in a far corner, where it was hoped they

A few charter members of the drama club with friends in the Seklutski forest: (front, center) Frume-Rochl Munin Ratz, the star of the Eishyshok theater; (middle row, from right): a Hebrew teacher; Miriam Shekowitski, Shaul Kaleko, leaning against Hannah Glombocki; Gita Lawzowski; two unidentified people; (back row) Ettl Dubitski, with hand on Shaul's shoulder, and (first name unknown) Ginzberg. Frume-Rochl, Miriam, and Shaul made aliyah. Ginzberg emigrated to Boston, changing his name to Goodwin. Gita and Ettl were murdered in the September 1941 massacre. PHOTO: YITZHAK URI KATZ. YESC, GLOMBOCKI

Szeina Katzenelenboigen was one of the leading personalities of the Eishyshok theater, greatly admired by the Germans during World War I. She was fluent in Hebrew, Yiddish, Russian, Polish, and German. She owned a hotel, and during the German occupation of Eishyshok during World War II the Gestapo used her hotel as one of their headquarters. They liked her perfect German, good food, and comfortable accommodations. But they murdered her in the September 1941 massacre. PHOTO: I. KENDEL, BIALYSTOK. YESC, BLACHAROWICZ-WISZIK

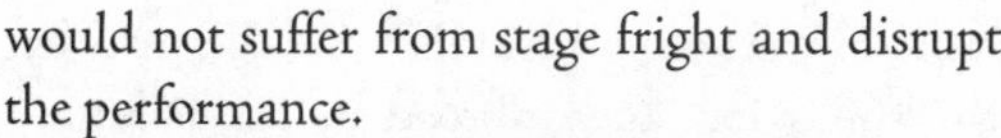

would not suffer from stage fright and disrupt the performance.

Hasia the Orphan by Jacob Gordin (1853–1909) was the first play to be performed under the direction of Sarah Pinon. And Gordin's plays, including *The Jewish King Lear, The Kreutzer Sonata, God, Man and Devil, The Slaughter,* and *Mirele Efros,* all of them written in Yiddish, would continue to be the major part of the repertoire during the early years of the theater, for Eishyshkians, like audiences in New York, Warsaw, and Vilna, responded to Gordin's understanding of the Jewish masses. That Y. L. Peretz referred to his work as "halfway between lit and shit" (kunst und shund) mattered little to them. What did matter was that though Gordin was (from 1891 on) a resident of New York, he had created a body of work that was in keeping with much that was traditional in Eastern European Jewish art, from the simplest Yiddish folktales to nineteenth-century drama. Writing with a realism that derived from Tolstoy, Gorky, and Ostrovsky, Gordin was a product of the Haskalah who nonetheless acknowledged and affirmed the ethnicity of the Jewish people.[25] Thus to Eishyshkians his work ranked even higher than that of Abraham Goldfaden (1840–1908), the father of the Jewish theater.

Memories of seeing Gordin's plays performed on the primitive stage in Arie-Leib's stable remained vivid decades later. Rina Lewinson remembered seeing *The Jewish King Lear* when she was ten, an initiation into the magic of show business that made her a lifelong theatergoer. For young Zipporah Lubetski, the impact was more immediate. Her first play, *The Slaughter,* told the story of the symbolic murder of a fragile young girl: her parents force her to marry a vile rich man whom she hates. This was a play that contained, in the words of the New York journalist Hutchins Hapgood, "indescribable violence and abuse." For Zipporah the stage and reality became one. When the heroine's life was threatened, Zipporah passed out. Shmuel Gross, who played the role of the rich man, recalled how the drama momentarily shifted from the stage to the audience until Zipporah could be revived. The show did go on then, but with Zipporah's seat having been upgraded from a backless bench to a chair in the front row. Another Gordin play, *The Wild Man*, starring Shaul Kaleko and Frume-Rochl Ratz, had a similar impact on the audience, resulting in not one but several fainting spells.[26]

The Eishyshok drama club kept current with what was happening on the Jewish stage in Warsaw and Vilna, and later in the new Hebrew theater, Habimah, which was founded in Moscow after the war and eventually moved to Tel Aviv. When Sarah Pinon left the shtetl, sometime during the war years, Shaul Kaleko took over as director of the drama club, and the repertoire expanded to include many biblical and historical plays. *Amnon and Tamar* by Sholem Asch (1880–1957), *King David and His Wives* by David Pinski (1872–1959), and *Shulamit, Bar Kohba*, and *Ben Ami* by Abraham Goldfaden were among the biblical dramas that were mounted in these years, often in a Hebrew translation from the Yiddish.

Casting under Shaul Kaleko tended to be quite consistent. Goldfaden's plays, in which music was prominent, generally featured Shmuel Gross and Ruben Boyarski, the shtetl cantor, in the main singing roles — though Boyarski had to sing his role from off stage, because Rabbi Zundl Hutner deemed it improper for the hazzan to appear in such a performance. Shaul Schneider, Kaleko's cousin, always played villains, while Peretz Kaleko, Shaul Kaleko's much younger brother, played kind-hearted protagonists.

THE 1920S AND '30S

The political ferment of the years between the two world wars was reflected in every aspect of shtetl life, including its cultural institutions. Thus the Zionist commitment to Hebrew language learning did not go unchallenged. Indeed, disagreements about what constituted the true cultural legacy of the Jews, about Hebrew versus Yiddish, secular versus sacred texts, modern versus traditional entertainments and celebrations, all of which had been set in motion during the years before the war, would continue and proliferate in the years to come, ending only when the shtetl itself ceased to exist.

For a brief period after World War I, the conflict between the Hebraists and the Yiddishists — an ideological struggle that was both local and representative of trends in the larger Jewish world — carried over into the drama club, which split in two, one group putting on performances in Yiddish, the other in Hebrew. The division did not last long, however, and the two were soon reunited, with Hebrew as the dominant language.

During the 1920s and early '30s, more and more of the young Hebraists and Zionists left the shtetl for study abroad or for Palestine, among them the Rubinsteins, the Kalekos, the Schneiders, the Wilenskis, the Glombockis, and the Lewinsons. Those Hebraists who remained behind, like the Sonensons and the Kiuchefskis, tended to be caught up in their family, community, and business responsibilities, with little energy to spare for other activities. With dedicated Yiddishists like the Ginunskis and the Szulkins now playing a bigger role in the cultural life of the shtetl, the drama club came under more Yiddish influences, including the renowned Vilna Troupe, the Yiddish theater company that the occupying Germans had so admired. The Eishyshok drama club's repertory became more diversified than ever. Yiddish plays by Peretz Hirschbein (1881–1948) became new favorites. *The Golem* by H. Levick (1881–1962), a writer who was helping to keep Yiddish culture alive in the United States, also found its way to Eishyshok, even though it is a very complicated play with elaborate and difficult staging.

One Yiddish play that left a lasting impression on many Eishyshkians was *Night at the Old Marketplace* by Y. L. Peretz, an author who wrote in both Hebrew and Yiddish. The German director Max Reinhardt described *Night at the Old Marketplace* as "a rare specimen of a universal symbolist play." For another man it came to be much more; indeed, it would assume almost mythical dimensions in memory. During the long subzero winter marches he was forced to take as a prisoner in the Siberian gulag from 1945 to 1953, Moshe Sonenson — one of those shtetl-lovers who was as avid to preserve Yiddish as to restore Hebrew — used to warm himself with what he remembered of the splendid Yiddish dialogue from the Peretz play. The imaginary conversations he had with Peretz's ghosts of the past — the water carrier, the jester, the other characters who came back from the cemetery to the market square to speak their piece — kept him going. When asked many years later why those memories had meant so much to him, he explained: "To cling to the present, to dare to hope for a future, I had to stay in close touch with the ghosts of the past." Perhaps the fact that they were Peretz's ghosts, rather than his own, was helpful; his own might have been too painful.

The Olkenik klezmer orchestra in 1921. They frequently performed in Eishyshok. YESC, SH. FARBER

Many factors beyond ideology had an impact, for better or worse, on the shtetl theater. Emigration was particularly influential, not just because it altered the balance between the Hebraists and the Yiddishists, but because many of the most talented people left. Leading lady Frume-Rochl Ratz left for Vilna when she married the Zionist leader Yitzhak Munin in the mid-1920s, returned for a while, then left for Palestine in 1934. Director Shaul Kaleko left for Kovno after the war, never to return, since it was too dangerous to cross the border between Lithuania and Poland; his brother Peretz left for the nearby shtetl of Ivie in 1930 (and from there Palestine). Fire, too, wrought its havoc: Arie-Leib's stable burned down. But a new theater with a new director, Yossef Michalowski, and many new members arose from the ashes of the old. This one was located in a huge stable on Vilna Street belonging to Yurdichenski di Praislikhe (the Prussian), a woman with a great love of the theater.

Modern technology had a role to play in the shtetl theater, too. With the opening of the bus line between Eishyshok and Vilna in 1929, the day-long journey was reduced to a two-hour ride, and the traffic increased accordingly. This included traffic back and forth between the theaters. Eishyshok theater lovers made it a cultural ritual, bordering on a religious experience, to go see the Vilna Troupe perform S. Anski's *Dybbuk.* And actors from the theater groups of Vilna played summer stock in Eishyshok, their professionalism rubbing off on the local actors. In fact, a starring member of the Vilna Troupe, a man from the Adler family, which was (and continued to be in the United States) one of the first families of the theater, spent several summers in Eishyshok.

Eventually the Eishyshok theater found a permanent home, in the firehouse in the center of the market square (which also served as the shtetl movie house). Now it was firefighting equipment, not horses, that had to be moved out before each performance. But the firehouse had two great advantages over the stables: an orchestra pit, which had been built by the music-loving German commander during World War I, and electricity. In these newly professional surroundings the theater had one of its greatest hits, *The Two Kuni Lemels* by Abraham Goldfaden. A hilarious play ridiculing forced matches, it found a ready audience among the young people of the shtetl, who by this time (the mid-1930s) were generally free to choose their own spouses. But soon after the great success of *The Two Kuni Lemels* many of the most talented members of the cast emigrated.

The theater group's final performances, under the Russian occupation in 1940–41 and approved by the local Jewish Communists, who forbade the use of Hebrew once they took power, were of *The Provocateur* by Shmuel Bergman and *The Big Win* by Sholem Aleichem. Both featured Berl Slepak and Mordekhai Replianski in the leading roles. Many in the audience found a local connection to the title of the Bergman play, since Velvke Katz — a Zionist turned Communist turned informer for the Polish authorities, and the man who was most responsible for bringing Communism to Eishyshok — had long been known as "the provocateur," an allusion to his duplicity.

REVUES Beginning in 1920, a new form of theater became popular with sophisticated Jews in Poland. The Kleinkunst (literally, "small art") was a sort of cabaret revue, switching rapidly back and forth among music and dance, monologue, and comic sketches. The two best-known revue companies were the Azazel of Warsaw

The members of the theater group at the end of a performance. The most talented performers moved to Eretz Israel, South America, or larger towns. Those who remained in Eishyshok were killed during the September 1941 massacre or murdered by the AK.
YESC, MATIKANSKI

(Azazel being the biblical name for hell) and the Ararat of Lodz (Ararat being the mountain on which Noah's ark came to rest). By the 1930s Eishyshok had its own revue, which, like those it imitated, became a forum for social and political commentary, humor, and scandal, concerning people and events at both the local and the global level. Stories of hard times, lost or thwarted love, and emigration to Eretz Israel — including many a chapter from the chronicle of Mordekhai Rubinstein's adventures — were particularly popular. So, too, were accounts of hometown conflicts.

Thus the story of Yude-Mendl Kremin and the Lida coachmen readily found its way into the revue's repertoire. It seems that the Lida coachmen broke Yude-Mendl's leg in a brawl that erupted over the right to transport goods between Eishyshok and Lida. Yude-Mendl had formed a cooperative to buy a truck that would essentially break the coachmen's monopoly, and the coachmen, seeing this as a threat to their livelihoods, resorted to violence. "About the coachmen he gave no hoot/So he suffered a broken foot" was the chorus to one of the Yude-Mendl revue songs that became a shtetl favorite.[27]

Another dispute chronicled with great relish by the revue was that between Yehuda Leib Solomianski, a jeweler, and Meir "Bonaparte," a poor tavern owner so known because he had a great interest in Napoleon, specifically in the time he had spent in the region during the Napoleonic wars. Using money sent him from America, Solomianski built a two-story brick house on Vilna Street which cast Meir Bonaparte's humble, one-story tavern into perpetual shadow. Christian customers stopped frequenting the tavern, choosing to go elsewhere to have a drink of samagonke (homemade spirits) and get a bite of herring on a fresh roll or bagel. Meir Shimon Politacki, a gifted comedy writer, captured the highlights of this battle for the revue theater, casting it as a dialogue between rich and poor. Only a few lines from this big hit live on,

The Eishyshok fire department orchestra of Poles and Jews. Among the Jews in the orchestra were (top row, right to left) Bere-Leibke Garmenishki, Shepske Sonenson, and Motl Narodowicz; (third row, second from left, with glasses) Menahem Politacki; Eishke Levin (second row, far left). The Polish conductor Gotowicky is in the center of the second row. Menahem made aliyah; Motl survived the war as a partisan. PHOTO: BEN ZION SZREJDER. YESC, Y. ELIACH

Mickey Mouse was very popular on stage and on the streets of Eishyshok and its vicinity. He poses with Esther Lapp here in the mid-1930s. She and her Olkenik family were murdered in the September 1941 massacre. YESC, M. BARAN

locked in the memory of a cousin of Politacki's, who was still able to recite them nearly five decades later.[28] Politacki himself was taken prisoner while serving in the Polish army during World War II; when the Germans learned he was Jewish, they beat him to death in his Polish uniform.

For weeks in 1937, Eishyshkians were singing a Hebrew halutzim song about a young man who met a girl and took her to a dance. But the Eishyshkians were singing it with a slight revue-inspired variation, in which the halutz, about to emigrate to Palestine with his sweetheart, loses her to a visitor to the shtetl, who is in fact his cousin. This was based on a real-life triangle involving Dov Wilenski, Esther Katz, and Dov's cousin Yossef Resnik, a former Eishyshkian. Resnik came to Eishyshok on a family visit and returned to his home in Colombia with a beautiful young bride.

Like so many other cultural activities in the shtetl during the 1930s, most of the revue performances were a joint production of the Zionist youth organizations, the Bundists, and the Communists, and they generally benefited the library. Sometimes the various groups split off from each other, the Zionist organizations sponsoring an event at one time, the non-Zionists at another — and sometimes both on the same evening. The only non-Jewish participation in the cultural life of the shtetl was in the fire department orchestra, a joint venture between Christians and Jews.

MOVIES

Eventually even the movies came to Eishyshok, arriving in 1931 soon after the introduction of electricity to the shtetl. The same firehouse building that was home to the theater also served as the movie house. It was known as Swjat (the World), and showed a mixed repertoire of Yiddish, American, and European hits, with occasional shorts from Palestine.[29] The Yiddish and Israeli movies were frequented mainly by Jews, the others by a mixed audience.

By the time movies arrived in town, Eishyshkians had been hearing about them, and then seeing them in nearby cities and shtetlekh, for years, and therefore took them in stride. But the early days of the cinema had found people quite unprepared for what they were seeing. The first reports of this strange phenomenon were carried by emigrants who returned from America to the shtetl. Indeed, one such man, Arie Leib Kudlanski, whose sons had brought him over to the United States for a visit in the hope that he would settle there, blamed the movies for his inability to adjust to the new world: "How can one trust a country where people walk on the walls?" was his commentary. His objections were shared by many religious leaders and other moralists, especially from nearby Radun. They read the fact that a movie had to be viewed in the dark as a metaphor for the spiritual darkness one entered in a movie theater, and could foresee nothing but bad coming from such an invention.

Nonetheless, the theaters conquered one shtetl after another. In Volozhin, local entrepreneur Michael Wand-Pollack converted an old stable into a movie house. When he took his mother-in-law, Sarah Rodanski, to the showing of the first movie, she became hysterical at the sight of a horse-drawn chariot charging across the screen, for she feared the horses might trample her. Later, at home, after she calmed down, she turned to her son-in-law and said with great admiration: "My dear Michael, I didn't know that you are such a wealthy man, who owns horses, carriages, maids, servants, and palaces." From that time on she greatly revered her son-in-law.[30]

Like so many other twentieth-century phenomena, the movies found a ready home in the small shtetl of Eishyshok, which by then had been exposed to influences from all over the world. But this aspect of shtetl life — its resilience, its flexibility, its adaptability, its surprising degree of cultural sophistication — has been forgotten. More than eight decades after Leah Wilkanski's first theater production in Eishyshok, and nearly five decades after the drama club's last one, which was soon to be followed by a conflagration that would destroy all evidence of the vibrant culture that had flourished for centuries, Yaffa Sonenson Eliach and her husband, David, visited the town, now under Lithuanian rule and known as Eisiskes. Pointing to the New Beth Midrash, which had been converted into a theater, a local Lithuanian resident proudly announced to them: "This is the first theater Eisiskes has ever had. At last the Lithuanians have brought culture to this place."

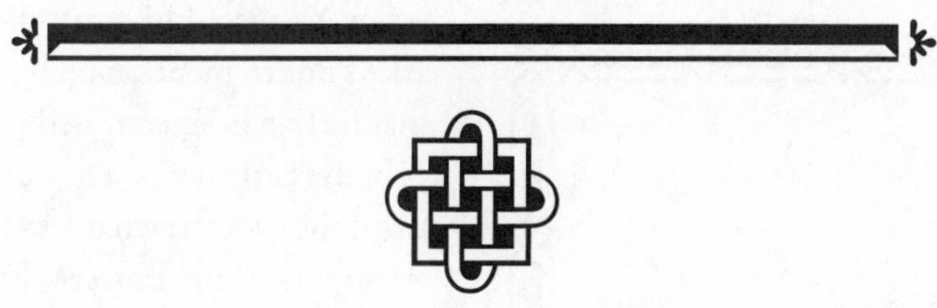

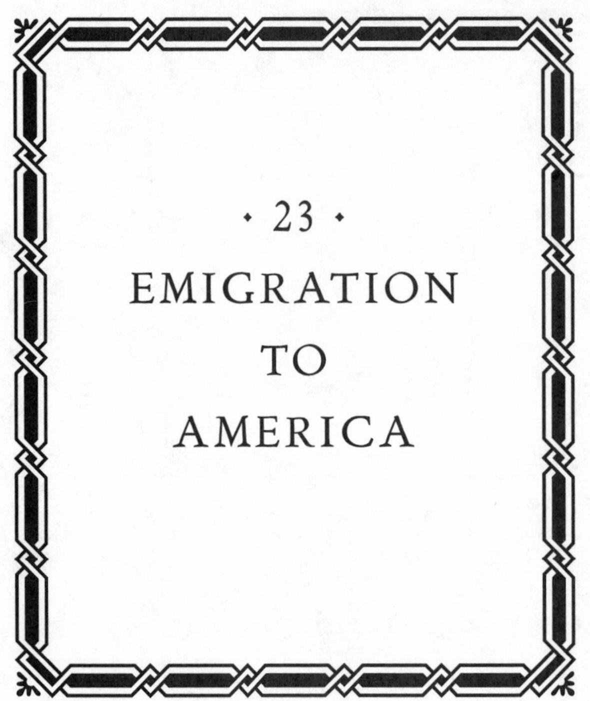

• 23 • EMIGRATION TO AMERICA

IN THE SHTETL PEOPLE HAVE BIG HEADS AND SMALL STOMACHS. AFTER THEY EMIGRATE TO AMERICA, THEY HAVE SMALL HEADS AND BIG STOMACHS.

Shtetl proverb

WHILE EMIGRATION TO PALESTINE CAME TO BE VIEWED AS THE FULFILLMENT OF BOTH a spiritual and an ideological commitment on behalf of the Jewish people as a whole, emigration to America was originally regarded within the shtetl as an act of severing, not affirming, one's communal, religious, and family ties. America was perceived as a barbaric country, materialistic in its values, devoid of any spirituality, hospitable to thieves and other lawbreakers. Although some may have looked to it as the place where the streets were lined with gold, respectable people in the shtetl saw it as a place where the very cobblestones with which the streets were paved were treif — nonkosher. Hence the term *Treife Medine* (nonkosher land) to describe the United States. Eventually, with changing times and changing values, the stigma faded. Yet in some families it seems never to have entirely disappeared. As late as 1930, when Yitzhak Uri Katz died, his widow was asked not to mention on his gravestone the fact that he had been educated in America!

In the early 1870s, a few unmarried men from Eishyshok joined what was then just a trickle of emigrants from Eastern Europe to America. When the occasional early emigrant to America did leave — usually someone who was in either dire economic straits or some kind of trouble with the law — his departure was marked by none of the ceremony and pageantry with which the shtetl bade farewell to the olim (emigrants to Eretz Israel). Quite the opposite, in fact: the departure was viewed as a tragedy, even a blemish on the family reputation, and families tried to keep the news a secret. In Eishyshok, as in other shtetlekh, such secrets soon became common knowledge, however, and then a mood of sadness and grief would descend upon the shtetl, as though on the eve of a funeral.

A man named Karna, who was a relative of the nineteenth-century local Robin Hood, Yehudah the Brigand (and of a similar lawbreaking disposition), was among the first Eishyshkians to leave for America during the 1870s. And though he was leaving after one of his run-ins with the law, the shtetl mourned his departure as though he were one of its most esteemed citizens. Meir Wilkanski described the scene: "When Karna left for America the entire town was in an uproar; everyone came to the house to weep and to lament about his departure. Even now [the 1880s] people still cry bitterly about those who leave for America. But now many people go there; at that time only Karna left."[1]

The Broida family was among the largest families from Eishyshok who emigrated to America. Morris Broida and wife Mildred, with their daughters Mathilda, Tereza, Isabel (baby), and Hannah (with basket). Mildred refused to allow Morris to leave for America without her and the children. The photo was taken in 1899(?) prior to their emigration. Today family reunions are attended by hundreds of Jewish Broidas, and Broidas who converted to various Christian denominations. All share an interest in family history. YESC, ANN GREENSTEIN

EMIGRATION IN THE WAKE OF THE MAY LAWS

After the assassination in 1881 of Tzar Alexander II, who had been relatively sympathetic to the Jews in his domain, a massive outbreak of anti-Semitism found expression in the so-called Southern Tempests, the pogroms that afflicted 215 Jewish communities all over southern Russia.[2] These were soon to be followed by the repressive May Laws of 1882, which deprived many Jews — including hundreds of people from the dozen or so villages under the jurisdiction of Eishyshok — of their lands. Called "Temporary Rules" when they were first announced, the May Laws stayed in effect until the fall of the tzars in 1917.

The Southern Tempests and the May Laws were devastating to Russian Jewry. Though many towns, among them Eishyshok, were geographically far removed from the pogroms and did not suffer any direct losses from them, the shadow the pogroms cast loomed over the entire Pale of Settlement. And the May Laws had an immediate and direct effect on virtually every community where Jews lived, inside and outside the Pale. As recounted in chapter 21, the combination of physical violence and legal economic sanctions contributed mightily to the rise of Zionism; soon it would also change the trickle of emigration to America into a torrent.

Many of the emigrants to America from 1882 to 1895 were the uprooted victims of the May Laws: farmers who had been thrown off the land, and villagers, mainly small shopkeepers and artisans, who had had to abandon their businesses. Since competition was already stiff in the typical shtetl, with most people there eking out only the most marginal of livings, the displaced villagers knew that moving there was not the answer; they would have to look elsewhere for a future. So large numbers of them, mainly young men in their teens and twenties, some single, some married, went off by themselves in search of new opportunities, promising to send for their wives, children, and other relatives as soon as they had made enough money.

Though the occasional reprobate disappeared without ever contacting his family again, and some men were never able to make enough money to bring the rest of their families over, the usual pattern was for that first emigrant to be followed by scores of other family members. The emigration saga of the Kirschner family was typical in this respect. Over a period of a couple of decades, dozens of Kirschners (and

Abramofsky'ses and Abramses) left Eishyshok for the shores of America, eventually fanning out to cities and towns all across their new land.

Jacob Kirschner was born in Eishyshok in 1861, one of the five surviving children of Simon-Chanoch and Basha Kirschner. Probably in order to avoid army conscription, Jacob changed his last name to Abramofsky, which would eventually be shortened to Abrams. In 1888 he emigrated to New York, leaving behind his pregnant wife Jeanette and their three young children, as well as parents, siblings, and other relatives. Once he passed the Castle Garden customs and immigration screening, Jacob made his way to the Lower East Side, where he spent his first five years working as a peddler, then a tailor. In 1893, when he had enough money to bring his family over, he returned to Eishyshok to fetch them.

In addition to his wife and their four children (Sarah, age twelve; Marie, ten; Israel, six; and Reuben, three), Jacob brought his brother Samuel, and they all went to Chicago. There Samuel moved in with Jacob and his family, and the two brothers worked as tailors. Later Samuel got married and had two children, and Jacob and Jennie eventually had three more. In 1906 Jacob and Samuel were joined by a third brother, George (Gedalia) and his wife and their two children. And in 1907, their uncle Ephraim (from their father's side) and some of the members of his large family came. Eventually all five of Ephraim's children by his first wife emigrated, as did the four by his second wife, among them the future presidential adviser, Walter Kirschner (1893–1974), as well as Ephraim's sister Rikla and her husband.

Two of Jacob Kirschner's sisters, however, never came. Thus Feiga and Ester-Malka, along with virtually all the members of their immediate families, were among the millions murdered in the Holocaust. And in this respect, too, the Kirschner family was typical, for few of those who stayed behind would survive the war.[3]

During this period of emigration most of the people who came to America were from the lower ranks of society. Having always been poor, they became desperate in the aftermath of the May Laws, and now looked to the Treife Medine for economic salvation. America continued to be viewed by the more affluent, more "respectable" members of shtetl society as a godless country, a destination for those who were poor at best, scoundrels at worst. The occasional husband who deserted his family by emigrating did nothing to enhance the image of America in the shtetl. However, there was one man who left Eishyshok around this time who didn't fit in to anyone's preconceptions about the kind of person who would choose America. In fact, no one in the shtetl understood why such a fine man had gone to such a terrible place.

Aharon Don Pachianko, a descendant of the

Aharon Don Becker (formerly Pachianko) (front right), during one of his visits from America to Eishyshok, his hometown. He always brought money from the New York Eishyshker society and unlimited praise for his adopted country. Seated with him are (right to left) Sarah Kaganowicz; Hayyim and Sarah Pachianko. Standing (right to left) are Libe-Gittel Rudzin, Shael and Miriam (née Rudzin) Kaganowicz, and Itta-Malka Pachianko. Sarah Kaganowicz died a natural death. Some of the others were murdered in the September 1941 massacre. Miriam Kaganowicz and her mother Libe-Gittel died at Majdanek. Shael was murdered by the AK. PHOTO: YITZHAK URI KATZ. YESC, L. KAHN-KAGANOWICZ

martyred farm manager Avigdor Pachianko (see chapter 10), was a well-to-do lumber merchant whose wife ran a grocery store.[4] When he went to America, he intended his stay to be a temporary one, lasting only until he had made enough money to expand his business in Eishyshok and build a more spacious house. He soon found himself enamored of his new home, however. Not just its material advantages, but other qualities, virtues that Eishyshkians had never heard mentioned in conjunction with America, impressed him. Instead of describing America as a sinful country and writing about how homesick he was for Eishyshok, birthplace of his ancestors, holy city of Torah and Talmud, he was singing the praises of the new land. To the distress of his family and the astonishment of his fellow Eishyshkians, Aharon Don had become a great advocate of American democracy:

It is a beautiful country, the land of freedom. Here a Jew does not feel the Diaspora. Wherever he wants to move he can go, whatever he wants to accomplish he can attain. There are those who speak against America, that it is the land of sweatshops. But sweat is a command from the Torah: "In the sweat of thy face shalt thou eat bread" (Genesis 3:19). The essence is bread with honor. And as to honor, the President of America is dependent on a Jew, the son of the son of Patriarch Abraham. If the Jew chooses to vote for him, he will be elected, and if he chooses not to vote for him, the President becomes just an ordinary person.[5]

While the letters of Aharon Don Becker (as he had become known in America)* signaled the beginnings of a new, more positive image of the Treife Medine, Eishyshok's Big Fire of 1895 was to prove a major turning point in the shtetl's perception of America.

EMIGRATION FROM THE 1890S TO 1914

In the Big Fire of May 1895, the entire shtetl of Eishyshok with the exception of a few houses on Radun Street went up in flames. Four hundred buildings were burned and three thousand people left homeless, with no source of livelihood. Though assistance came from the Rothschild family at the request of the Haffetz Hayyim, and from all across Russia in response to accounts of the disaster that appeared in the Haskalah newspaper *Ha-Melitz*, the largest amount of money came from America.[6] Some was sent to the community as a whole from the newly formed landsmanshaft in New York, the Hevrah Bnei Avraham Shmuel Anshei Eishyshker; and much more was donated by individual immigrants to members of their families. Elisha the postman staggered under the weight of all those heavy envelopes stuffed with green dollars. It was observed that people with relatives in America fared the best in this disaster: their houses were usually the first to be rebuilt. The shtetl began to reconsider its view of America, remembering those letters from Aharon Don, wondering if they might have contained a kernel of truth. Perhaps America could make a man not just rich but generous; perhaps the ties of family and community could remain intact even across those thousands of miles; perhaps America had a soul after all.

But Eishyshkers' new appreciation of America went beyond gratitude for help received.

*Pachianko, the name the family had taken to commemorate their ancestor Avigdor, "the burned one," got changed to Becker because when he tried to explain to the immigration officer the meaning of his name, he used the image of the baker who burns the bread, and all the officer could comprehend from the long explanation was the word *baker* — hence Becker.

With their homes and their businesses destroyed, many people, including not just the lower ranks of society but for the first time a number of the balebatim and eventually even the clergy, began to consider America as a possible home. Finding themselves at a crossroads, having to decide whether to rebuild in Eishyshok or make new lives abroad, they considered their options. In the years following the Big Fire and preceding the outbreak of World War I, many Eishyshkians emigrated to Palestine; a few moved to larger cities in the Pale of Settlement; about fifteen families went to England; a small group left for Argentina with the assistance of the Jewish Colonization Association, and some even headed for South Africa. The largest contingent, however, which probably totaled more than 1,500 people, left for America. Of these, a substantial proportion were not from Eishyshok proper, but from the villages and farmlands under its jurisdiction.[7]

Once again it was the men who went off first, later to be followed by their wives, children, and often many other family members.

For example, Jacob Broida (1857–1932) set off for America in the late 1880s, settled in Pittsburgh, and in 1891 sent for his wife Anna (1856–1914), who came over with their children Morris (1878–1947) and Joseph (1882–1934). She left behind Rose (1887–1955), Sam (1888–1973), and newborn Max (1891–1966), who stayed with grandparents; these three children were not to be reunited with their parents in America until adulthood. Their daughter Sarah remained behind because she was engaged, but she eventually came over sometime in the 1930s. The Broidas' oldest son, David (1875–1923), had actually preceded his father, having gone to stay with one of Jacob's uncles, who were part of the earlier wave of emigration. The uncles were the beginning of what would eventually be a three-generation migration to America, as one by one the Broidas came over and then sent steamship tickets back to the other Broidas still in Eishyshok.

Sheinke (left) and Taibke Broida. After a long struggle, they joined the rest of their family in America. PHOTO: BRUDNER, VILNA. YESC, ANN GREENSTEIN

Jacob's two brothers also emigrated around the same time: Peter (1835–1935) brought his wife and all nine of his children, and Joseph (1882–1934) brought his wife and their eight children. All this was accomplished in an incredibly short period of time. In fact, Morris Broida, Peter's son, who came over in 1900, was among the last to arrive (until Sarah came over in the 1930s), his wife Mildred having refused to allow him to go without her and their five little girls, for she was one of an increasing number of women who were beginning to object to the usual "men first" pattern of emigration. Mildred Broida was also something of a pattern-breaker in her post-emigration life, for unlike most of the women from shtetl backgrounds, few of whom were educated, she went to business school and learned bookkeeping, and, again unlike the typical shtetl-born woman in America, became a full participant in her family's various businesses. She wasn't just "helping out" or supplementing the family income, she was working full time — first as a bookkeeper at a department store in Pittsburgh, then as both bookkeeper and cigar-roller in the cigar business her husband ran when they moved to Youngstown, and later in the dry goods business they opened in St. Louis.

Although the Broidas fanned out over much of America, St. Louis was to become family

Annie Virshubski, daughter of Nehemia der Feldsher, emigrated in the 1890s. In America, she married David Foster (formerly Michalowski), also from Eishyshok. YESC, R. ROSENBLATT

headquarters. Jacob and Anna's sons Morris and Joseph moved there in 1901, later to be joined by their parents, and a number of their cousins lived in St. Louis as well, including the abovementioned Morris and his wife. There, as elsewhere, the family businesses — dry goods and cigars — were similar to those they had had in the shtetl. Various Broidas also worked as peddlers, clerks, salesmen, and eventually store owners, and one branch of the family went into real estate. In the years since, the American Broidas have come to number in the thousands, and, moving far beyond their original business interests, they have become Hollywood actors and moguls, research scientists and academicians.[8]

Like the Broidas, many of the people in the wave of emigration to America that began in the 1890s and climaxed before World War I had been shopkeepers and other small business owners in the old country. However, the social and economic backgrounds of the emigrants were constantly changing, so that eventually a veritable cross-section of shtetl society came to be represented in the new land.

Increasingly it was not just heads of young families but young single people who looked to America as a place where they could advance themselves socially and educationally as well as economically. They aspired to previously unheard of forms of self-fulfillment and self-betterment. And again, it was not just the impoverished or desperate young people who left, but young men and women from comfortable backgrounds. Five of the seven children of Dovid and Fradl-Leah Kiuchefski moved to America, for example, even though their parents were among the richest balebatim in the shtetl. Of the other two, one went to England, and Meir, later to become one of Eishyshok's most outstanding leaders, studied law in Moscow and then returned to his hometown, where he remained until his death. Eventually two of Meir's sons emigrated to America. The list of Dovid and Fradl-Leah Kiuchefki's descendants in America reads like a veritable "Who's Who" of professional accomplishment, including labor leaders, presidential advisers, judges, authors, academics, scientists, business people.[9]

All of the children of Nehemia der Feldsher also left Eishyshok. Daughter Annie went to America, followed by two sisters. There Annie married former Eishyshkian David Michalowski, who was now David Foster, courtesy of an Ellis Island clerk. David had gone into the meat business — the family occupation in Eishyshok — and founded the Foster Beef Company, which proved very successful.[10] Annie and David thereby joined the ranks of the many Eishyshkians who were known to be prospering in the new land.

For young women with limited opportunities for upward mobility, America could seem especially promising. Success stories like that of the three daughters of Shlomo the engraver, who had all married rich men in America, became part of the daily gossip in the shtetl. It was also said that girls who had been homely in the shtetl turned into beauties in America. Thus even an ardent Zionist like Ezra the shtetl doctor considered sending his four daughters to America. He reasoned that if homely young women from humble backgrounds did well in America, then his four beautiful, educated daughters would surely do brilliantly and end up marrying very wealthy men there.[11]

Many young people went without any plan to bring their families over. Morris Shlanski, for example, emigrated in 1905 at the age of seventeen, very much against his parents' wishes. His mother Zisle had wanted him to be a rabbi and had sent him to the Haffetz Hayyim's yeshivah in Radun. But Morris had other ideas. He was interested in science and geography, not religion, and continued to read his secular books even in Radun. In fact, it was one of those books that seems to have propelled him right out of the shtetl.

In that book was written up how to make ice. So one night I sat up, and I took all the ingredients — water, salt — and I kept on mixing them. And I succeeded in making ice. . . . Well, then I didn't want any more of the talmudic learning. I wanted to know.

. . . That's what was burning in me — to know. To know things. I knew about the world and I was longing to see it. And that's what made me know I had to get away from that place.

Then I made up my mind. I will not get anywhere here, because there is nothing at all.[12]

Dora and Yossef Michalowski, parents of David Foster, emigrated to America after the May Laws of 1882, which caused much damage to their business in Eishyshok. YESC, R. ROSENBLATT

Beautiful and strong-willed Ida Pochter emigrated to America at the age of sixteen. She married Julius Novakoff, who opened a tailor shop for naval uniforms in Boston, across from the Navy Yard. He became friendly with many prominent personalities, including Eleanor Roosevelt and Joseph Kennedy, who spent much time in his store. The Novakoffs' son Edward was a GI guard at the Nuremberg trials. YESC, R. ROSENBLATT

Unlike other towns in Lithuania, Eishyshok sent only a small number of émigrés to South Africa. Among them were the Radowsky family. This is one of their first family portraits taken in Cape Town: (right to left) Rose, baby Reuben (born in Cape Town), father Michel, Gershon, mother Bertha, and Joshua. YESC, S. RADOWSKY

When he emigrated, his parents wrote him that they would be sending him money for a return ticket so that he could come back home immediately. Morris replied: "Never in my life will I ever come back. I went away because I did not see my future — nothing at all. Here I will make do. I came for something." In America Morris studied medicine and became a doctor.

Eventually he would be joined there by his younger brother Louis. Just before the outbreak of World War I, a former Eishyshkian who was visiting the shtetl met Louis Shlanski and said to him, "Why does a young, smart boy like you stay in Eishyshok, a place without a future?" Louis took the remark seriously, went to his father, Avraham-Mordekhai Shlanski, a Vilner coachman, and told him that he would like to

Morris Gold (formerly Moshe Zlotnik), like a significant number of East European immigrants, left his wife and child behind, changed his name, remarried, and established a new family in America. His father, Shlomo Zlotnik, was able to trace him in America, force him to send divorce papers to his wife in Eishyshok, and establish contact with his beautiful, talented daughter, Dora. YESC, BERKOWITCH

The widow Mine Zlotnik (née Kabacznik), with three of her children: (right to left) Philip (Rephael), Leibke, and Goldke. After the death of her husband, she saw no future in Eishyshok for her and her younger children. She emigrated to Canada, remarried, and lived a comfortable life. PHOTO: YITZHAK URI KATZ. YESC, SCHNEIDER

leave for America. "Travel in good health," his father told him, handing him 200 rubles from the pocket of his coat. His mother, however, was furious. She kept saying, "In America, even the stones are not kosher." But to no avail. Louis made the necessary arrangements, packed his valise, and left. Years later he would be joined by another brother, Zelig. In America Louis married Ida Boyarski, sister of Ruben Boyarski, the shtetl hazzan.

Ruben himself had made his way first to England and then to America, where he settled in Detroit, home to many former Eishyshkians, who were delighted to be able to hear his magnificent voice again. He was part of a new phenomenon in the saga of Jewish emigration: the coming of the clergy to America. Having shunned the Treife Medine for over a quarter of a century, clergy from Eishyshok, as from other towns and cities throughout Eastern Europe, began to join the torrent of emigrants in ever-increasing numbers. Perceiving a critical mass of their countrymen in the new land, they felt that their services would be needed and their economic lot possibly improved.

Rabbis, shohatim, mohalim, melamdim, and hazzanim were all part of this new wave. But for many of them, life in the new land proved very difficult, for whatever else one might say about America at that time, it did not offer much in the way of material rewards for its spiritual leaders. Shael Sonenson's brother Rabbi Pinhas Sonenson had such a struggle in America that his brother Shael back home had to support him for some time — the reverse of the usual American success story. And Rabbi Ezekiel Aishishkin (who changed his name from Slepak so that he might always be reminded of his beloved birthplace) earned only the most pitiful of salaries until the day he died in 1935, nearly three decades after first stepping ashore in America. Like Ruben Boyarski, he had moved to Detroit, where he had a large following drawn from his

Though Eliyahu Bastunski disliked America, two of his sons loved it: Sol (Shlomo) on the left and Alexander (Zusl), shortly after Zisl's arrival in California from Eishyshok, 1922. YESC, BASTUNSKI

Alexander (Zusl) Bastunski and daughter Judy in their garden in Oakland, California. Judy developed a great love for her family's roots and the shtetl of Eishyshok. YESC, BASTUNSKI

fellow Eishyshkians, and a number of duties in addition to his rabbinical ones. He founded the Bnei Yehudah yeshivah, served as rabbi to a number of congregations, among them Bnei David, also known as the Rusisher Shul (the Russian synagogue), oversaw the slaughter and preparation of kosher meats, tended to the poor in Detroit and beyond, and lived a life of scholarship besides. Nonetheless, he and his wife and five children endured many hard times, which was typical of the lot of the clergy, and helps to explain why so few of them were followed to America by their extended families.[13]

For most emigrants to America, however, the new world was proving to be a land of opportunity and freedom, which beckoned ever more irresistibly to those left behind.

NEXT YEAR IN AMERICA: THE POST–WORLD WAR I ERA

In September 1923, a young man named Hatzkele in Eishyshok sent a greeting card in honor of Rosh Hashanah to his sweetheart in America, Sarah'le Moszczenik, daughter of Dovid der Kichier. It opened with the words "Next Year in America!" And indeed this had become the wish of many young people in Eishyshok after World War I. America had achieved a new respectability, thanks both to the

Rabbi Ezekiel Aishishkin (formerly Slepak) was among the first clergymen from Eishyshok to emigrate to America. In this picture taken at his son Joseph Askin's wedding to Ida, June 21, 1925, in Detroit, he is in the front row (center) with (left to right) Sarah Levine, Jennie Aishishkin, Akivah Drasnin, daughter Fanny Drasnin, daughter Katie Levine, daughter Anna Belensky with son Mayer on her lap, Akivah Belensky, bride Ida Askin and Sarah Drasnin. Standing (left to right) are son Peter Aishishkin, Sam Drasnin, Louis Levine, Jake Belensky, and Joseph Askin (son and groom). YESC, M. SARUYA

A New Year postcard with the blessing "Next Year in America," mailed by a young Eishyshkian to his sweetheart Sarah'le Moszczenik in America, September 4, 1923. YESC, A. ZIMMERMAN

caliber of people who had begun moving there since the turn of the century and to the news they sent back home about the lives they were leading. Unlike the shtetl, which to a restless young man like Morris Shlanski seemed a "small, forgotten place," a place where "you could be born, grow up, have children and die, and nobody ever knew about you," America offered unlimited hope, if not always unlimited opportunity.[14] Thus emigrants from Eishyshok were settling in almost every state in the union and much of Canada besides, with the largest concentrations in New York, Boston, St. Louis, Chicago, and Detroit.

During the difficult years after the war, the continuing financial generosity of those who had left Eishyshok toward those who remained behind only enhanced the reputation of the country the shtetl had once seen as godless. Money mattered more to people than it had before, and perhaps it was also true that religion mattered less. The shtetl zogerke Golde Moszczenik said in defense of her three children in America, whose generosity had enabled Golde and her husband to build themselves a beautiful new brick house on Radun Street: They had performed such acts of charity that God himself surely wouldn't require them to fast, even on Yom Kippur.

Again there was institutional as well as personal charity. After wartime hostilities had ended and communication between the shtetl

In the mid-1930s, Reb Dovid Moszczenik traveled from Eishyshok to America to visit his children and their families: (back row) granddaughter Lillian (right) and daughter Fradl; (middle row, right to left) son Saul, Reb Dovid, daughter Sarah; (bottom row, right to left) Saul's two sons and their mother, Isabelle. YESC, A. ZIMMERMAN

In 1933, when she was thirteen years old, Atara Kudlanski (Goodman) Zimmerman (shown here in her high school graduation photo), with mother Hanneh-Beile, brother Bill, and sister Connie, joined their father Jake in America. Atara was interested in the family history, the shtetl, and its people. She wrote, "You can take Atara away from Eishyshok, but you can't take Eishyshok away from Atara." YESC, A. ASNER

and America had been resumed, one of the first postwar visitors from abroad was Aharon Don Becker, who came as an emissary of the Hevrah Bnei Avraham Shmuel Anshei Eishyshker of New York. He brought with him a substantial sum of money, which was to be used to help the shtetl recover from the devastation of the war as well as the recent typhus epidemic, a sum much larger than the one sent after the Big Fire of 1895, when the group was still in its infancy.

Unfortunately, just as America was becoming more respectable, it was also becoming less accessible. In 1922 the U.S. Congress enacted a quota system, radically reducing the number of emigrants from Italy and from Eastern Europe. Now many people had to wait years for their quota numbers to come up, which was especially hard on families who had been separated by the war and had counted on being reunited once hostilities ended — families like Golde and Honeh Moszczenik's. Their children in America, Max, Sam, and Hannah-Leah, had been generous not just with money and clothing for their family back home, but with tickets to bring two of their remaining siblings over. But Yonah and Yitzhak Moszczenik never got to use their tickets, since their quota numbers never came up. Both brothers and their families were murdered during the Holocaust. Their sister Pessia, who had gone to Palestine with another sister, Brakha, but had had to return in 1926 because she became ill, decided that she could not wait for her quota number to be called. She and her husband traveled to Warsaw to get a visa for Brazil, and arrived in Rio de Janeiro December 1929. Another sister, Sarah, also emigrated to South America.

Thanks to a family unification policy, a few lucky people in the shtetl were able to go to America even during these days of extremely limited emigration. Four of the daughters of Dovid der Kichier, the above-mentioned Sarah'le Moszczenik and her sisters Esther, Fradl, and Ida (no relation to Golde Moszczenik's family) were among the recipients of the much coveted low quota numbers.

A fifth daughter, Hanneh-Beile Goodman, had to wait a long time, however, for her husband, Jake Morris Goodman (formerly Yaakov-Moshe Kudlanski in Eishyshok), was one of a number of Eishyshkians who emigrated to America illegally, having gone first to Cuba, then sailing aboard a fishing boat to a landing place somewhere near Miami in 1920. As an illegal alien he could not apply to bring his wife and children over, but in 1931 he applied for and was granted amnesty, under the terms of a 1929 act of Congress, and two years later was joined by Hanneh-Beile and their three children. Once in America Hanneh-Beile joined her sisters and their spouses in giving generously to the needy back home, sending the money to their father, Reb Dovid, for distribution. In fact, thanks to his children he had so much money at his disposal that the traditional balance of power within the shtetl was altered.[15]

In these postwar years, when a person's quota number was called the shtetl celebrated, though not as lavishly as for the halutzim, the pioneer emigrants to Eretz Israel. The American ceremony began with the photo session at the cemetery, where the soon-to-be-emigrant posed near the tombstones of his relatives, especially that of his namesake. Next there would be a photo with the living, including family and friends, and a formal photographic portrait of the emigrant, to be distributed among his loved ones before he left. Parties were held at school, in various youth organizations, and at home, all of them immortalized by the shtetl photographers. And at last came time for the final departure ritual, the farewell at the bridge, which was also commemorated in photographs, although it was a relatively simple affair, without the dancing and singing that accompanied the farewells to the halutzim. Now was the moment when the parents of those who were leaving would humbly approach, their own portraits in hand, with the request that their children hang them in their new homes, as a reminder that they would always be under the watchful eyes of their parents.*

When the natural reluctance of the old people to start new lives in a new land was compounded by their inability to do so, thanks to the quota system instituted in the United States, the result was that these portraits were often all that the members of these divided families had to remember one another by. These were stressful, sometimes heartbreaking times for families who had lost hope of seeing each other again.

America had reneged on her promise. The "huddled masses, yearning to breathe free" would have to look elsewhere.

*In 1987, when I interviewed Leah Cnaani, a woman then in her nineties, I saw hanging across from the bed in her modest kibbutz apartment in Israel a large portrait of her father, a bearded Jew with wise eyes beneath the typical pointed Lithuanian yarmulke. This handing over of the parental portraits was one of the rituals that all the emigrants had in common, regardless of their destination.

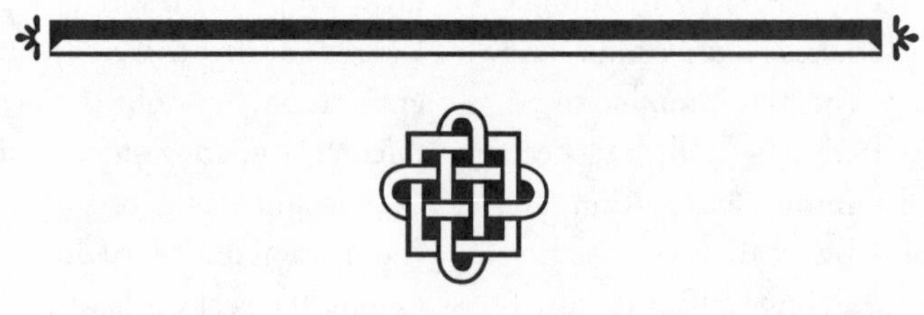

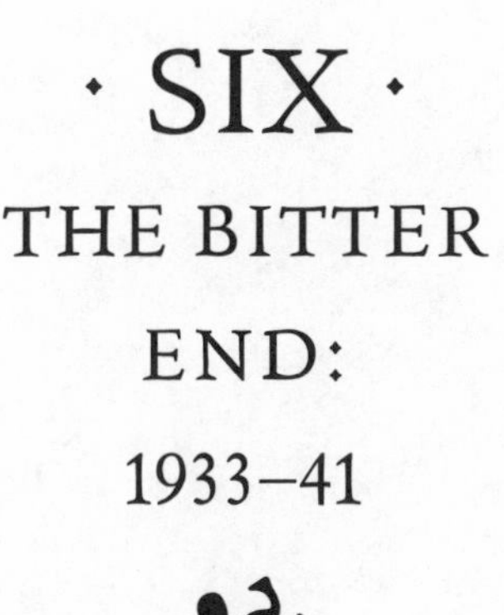

· SIX ·

THE BITTER END: 1933–41

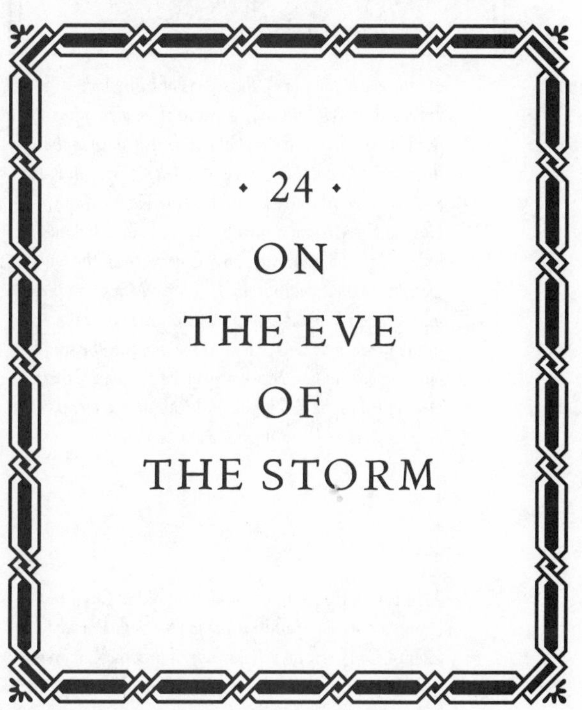

• 24 • ON THE EVE OF THE STORM

IT BURNS, BROTHERS DEAR, IT BURNS!
OUR POOR LITTLE SHTETL IS ON FIRE!
FURIOUSLY ANGRY WINDS STORM,
MADLY AROUND THE WHIPPED FLAMES
SWARM,
EVER WILDER GROWS THE FIERCE BLAZE —
EVERYTHING'S ON FIRE!

AND YOU STAND AROUND AND STARE
WHILE THE FLAMES GROW HIGHER,
AND YOU STAND AROUND AND STARE
WHILE OUR SHTETL BURNS.

Mordekhai Gebirtig,
OUR SHTETL IS BURNING
(written in 1938, after the pogrom in Przytyk)

ON THE OUTSIDE, THE SHTETL OF EISHYSHOK DURING THE YEARS 1933–41 APPEARED very much the same as it had in past decades. On Thursdays the market square hummed with the usual bustling vitality, the sounds of man, beast, and steel-rimmed carriage wheels coming together in the same special market day symphony that had been heard for centuries. The ceaseless activity of the work week gave way with predictable regularity to the serenity and beauty of the Sabbath and the religious holidays. At work, at rest, at prayer, and in celebration, the shtetl seemed stable yet flexible, well prepared both to protect its essential identity and to adapt as needed to the turbulence of the twentieth century. Survival mechanisms developed over hundreds of years, the culmination of experiences stored in collective as well as private memory, the expression of an ideology, an ethos, a faith that had oft been tested but always sustained, seemed to bode well for the continued life of the shtetl. But no one at that time knew what the twentieth century had in store.

Still, even in Eishyshok, the well-trained eyes of some of its native citizens detected ominous signs. Some of the signs were subtle, while others were writings on the wall spelling doom in huge, bold letters. On the market square, for example, the shrieking voice of Adolf Hitler joined the familiar cacophony of shtetl life. The few people who had radios shared with the many who didn't by turning up the volume and opening their windows whenever Hitler was giving one of his speeches. Some even set up rows of chairs on the cobblestones facing their homes to accommodate the crowd of eager listeners. At such times the shtetl's German mavins were in great demand. Eishyshkians looked to World War I veterans who had done time in German prison camps — such men as Yekutiel Ginunski and Eliyahu Plotnik — for help with both translation of the language and interpretation of the national character. The hotel owner Szeina Katzenelenboigen, who was fluent in German, was another of these mavins.

Over a glass of steaming tea or an ice-cold kvass or beer they would analyze the speeches for the benefit of their fellow Eishyshkians. Hitler was a foreigner to the Germans, a boor and a thug, and would surely not be tolerated for long by such a cultured, refined people, they concluded. Mordekhai Munesh Kaleko took issue with that optimistic view. Quoting from the letters of his son Shaul, who was at that time

On the eve of the storm, the streets of Eishyshok appeared peaceful. In 1940 a group of women, after a relaxing stroll, pose for a photo at the entrance to the shtetl from Radun Street: (right to left) Zipporah Katz Sonenson, Masha Michalowski, Alte Katz, Maite Gurewitch, Miriam Sonenson, and Shula, Miriam's little girl. Just a year later, on this very street, the Jews were led to their death from the Horse Market to their mass grave. When Zipporah was murdered by the AK in 1944, her body was placed in the morgue, the small building behind her. Masha survived the war. Others were killed in the Eishyshok and Radun massacres. PHOTO: BEN ZION SZREJDER. YESC, Y. ELIACH

Members of the election commission of Ha Oved Ha-Zioni, assisting in fund-raising for the 20th World Zionist Congress, 1937: They hoped that the Congress would be able to influence the British to open the gates to Palestine for mass emigration, as the writing on the wall states. (Right to left) Eli Politacki, Shuster, Shalom Kahn, Israel Szczuczynski, Szeina Blacharowicz, and Yankl Levin. None was able to obtain a certificate for aliyah. Only Szeina survived the war, in the forest; the others were murdered. YESC, BLACHAROWICZ-WISZIK

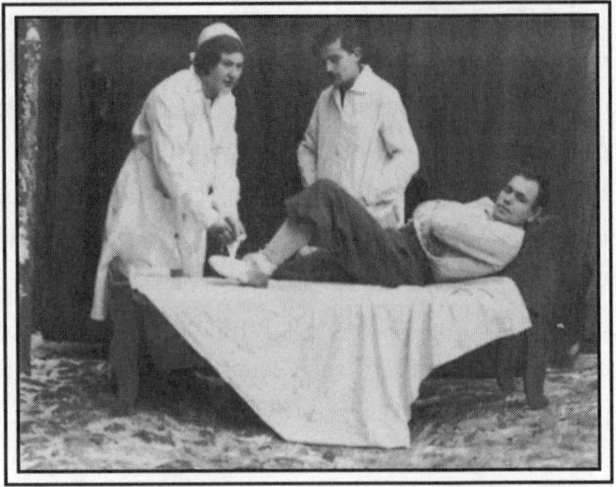

Many in Eishyshok hoped to overcome the British immigration restrictions and make aliyah. The young Zionists still in the shtetl attended a hakhsharah to prepare. Sarah Plotnik, in a hakhsharah in Oshmiani, being trained as a nurse, learning first aid in a hot climate. Sarah made aliyah. YESC, PLOTNIK-AVRAHAMI

attending Berlin University, Mordekhai offered a much darker interpretation of contemporary events. He shared Shaul's concern for the Jews of Germany, but went beyond that to worrying about all of European Jewry, whom he felt to be in great danger. The shtetl's young Zionists were in full agreement with Kaleko. Thus even as Eliyahu Plotnik, for example, was playing down the sense of danger in Europe, his Zionist daughters were looking to a safe future in Eretz Israel. Sarah, the oldest, was in a hakhsharah, preparing herself for aliyah by attending a nurses' training course that concentrated on first aid in hot climates. Her younger sisters, the twins Mikhle and Breine, were not old enough to be in the hakhsharah, but they, too, were active in the shtetl's Zionist activities.

On the whole, the shtetl simply didn't know what to make of Hitler, how seriously to take him. The menace he represented was still remote enough from their daily reality that with that typical shtetl mixture of humor and hostility, irony and derision, they could use his name to insult one of their own: a little German-speaking boy named Elisha. This child was the son of Nehama Koppelman Frischer, who had

Yehiel Blacharowicz (left) with friends at a hakhsharah at Oshmiani learning logging and forestry. Yehiel did not get an aliyah certificate and was murdered in the September 1941 massacre. YESC, PLOTNIK-AVRAHAMI

Elisha Frischer (later Professor Elisha Efrat) on his first day of school in Danzig. In 1935, Nehama Koppelman Frischer visited Eishyshok with her son Elisha, who spoke German. Eishyshkians, angered that the son of an ardent Hebraist and Zionist should converse in the language of the Führer, nicknamed him "Hitleruk." YESC, KOPPELMAN-FRISCHER

emigrated from Eishyshok to Palestine, where she met and married a fellow halutz from Poland. Later, because of her husband's poor health, they had moved back to Danzig, where they were raising their little boy. When Nehama visited Eishyshok in 1935, bringing Elisha with her, Eishyshkians nicknamed him "Hitleruk"— their way of expressing their hurt that the son of one of the shtetl's most ardent Zionists and Hebraists should converse in the language of der Führer. (Many traumatic events later, little Elisha would eventually learn Hebrew.)

ANTI-SEMITISM UNLEASHED

Following the death in May 1935 of Marshal Jozef Pilsudski, the president of the Polish Republic, the shtetl's interest in Hitler and the fate of Germany's Jews gave way to a sense of deep concern for themselves and the rest of the 3.5 million Jews in Poland. The feeling was that Marshal Pilsudski's quasi-dictatorial leadership had been the last and only curb on Poland's deeply ingrained anti-Semitism, which would now flourish unchecked.[1] Very shortly after the moving funeral in which Pilsudski's heart was buried in Vilna, that fear was vindicated by a number of events.

At the local level, Zalman Lubetski, who was serving in the Fifth Infantry Regiment of the Polish army for the mandatory eighteen months, was told by his anti-Semitic comrades: "Your grandfather is dead; there is no longer anyone in Poland to protect you."

At the national level, things looked very ominous indeed. With Pilsudski dead, his followers in the Sanacja Party, eager to maintain their edge over the increasingly powerful, anti-Semitic Endecja Party, gave official approval to anti-Jewish activity — all the while expressing some mild disapproval of its more violent manifestations. One of the first of their anti-Jewish measures was a bill introduced in February 1936 by Janina Prystor, a Sanacja member of the Polish parliament and, as it happened, a native of a village near Eishyshok, who proposed to ban shehita, the ritual kosher slaughter of animals. This was simultaneously an attempt to force the Jews out of the meat trade, to deprive them of religious freedom, and to take away a major source of income from the community. An amended and somewhat abbreviated version of this law was eventually passed in January 1937.[2] Around the same time, an increasing number of Polish organizations began to include in their bylaws restrictions against Jews. "Aryans" and "Christians by birth" were welcome; those "of Jewish descent" were not.

One of the leading voices in the ever-louder chorus of anti-Semitism belonged to Cardinal Augustyn Hlond, the primate of the Catholic church in Poland. Hlond made virulently anti-Semitic statements, even as he was warning that acts of outright violence against the Jews were of course "un-Christian." His pastoral letter of February 1936, which was read from the pulpits of all the churches in Poland, denounced the Jews as free-thinkers, Bolsheviks, usurers, and white slavers. Three and a half million Jews on Polish soil were 3 million too many, he said; half a million would suffice.[3]

Polish anti-Semitism was greatly reinforced by the momentum of the Nazis in Germany. Though the extreme nationalism of Poland's Endecja Party had predisposed it to enmity toward Germany in the past, a shared hatred of Jews helped the Nazis and the Endecjas bridge the ancient abyss of animosity between their countries.[4] The ideological connections between the anti-Semitism of the Nazis and that of the Poles during the latter half of the 1930s could most readily be seen in the racist writings and activities of two leading Polish personalities, both from Vilna: Stanislav Cat-Mackiewicz, editor of the newspaper *Slowo* (The Word), and Professor Wladyslaw Stadicki. Through their articles in the press, speeches on the radio, and lectures at the university, these influential members of the intelligentsia explained and justified the actions of the Nazis in Germany, while vilifying the Jews in Poland as outsiders who were destroying their country from within.

The years 1935–37 saw a number of anti-Jewish pogroms in Poland, such as the ones in Grodno in 1935, Przytyk and Minsk-Mazowieck in 1936, Czestochowa and Bszesc nad Bugiem in 1937. Zalman Lubetski happened to be in Przytyk in 1936, and heard eyewitness accounts of that pogrom. But when he tried to tell people at home what he had heard, or described his own experiences of anti-Semitism in the army, most of his townsmen turned a deaf ear. Surely nothing like what he was talking about would happen in Eishyshok: The business ties between the Eishyshkian Jews and their Polish neighbors were so strong that the Poles needed the Jews for their very livelihood.

Zalman's visit to Eishyshok coincided with an anti-Semitic attack on his relative Israel Yekutiel, who lived in the nearby village of Poshitva. Polish thugs beat him with an iron bar, crushing the bones of his skull. Though Dr. Lehr operated on him at the hospital in Eishyshok and was

Zalman Lubetski (Sol Lubek) with two of his sisters, Bluma (left) and Etele. On his lap is his niece Leah'le. After the death of Marshal Pilsudski, Zalman's anti-Semitic comrades in the Polish army told him "your grandfather is dead. There is no longer anyone in Poland to protect you." Zalman survived the war as a partisan, Bluma in Russia; Etele and Leah'le were murdered in the September 1941 massacre. YESC, LUBETSKI-LUBEK

able to save his life, after which he had further surgery in Vilna, he lived in constant pain for his few remaining years. Still, Eishyshkians reassured themselves that Eishyshok was not Poshitva.

Among the older people, there was considerable annoyance with what they regarded as the alarmism of their sons and daughters. They discounted the similarities the young people pointed out between the Nuremberg Laws in Germany and the various official acts of anti-Semitism in Poland (such as the Janina Prystor bill and the "ghetto benches" that had been introduced into academic institutes). They viewed the rising tide of anti-Semitism in their own country, as in Germany, as nothing more than a passing phase. And some of the young people agreed with them, or at least hoped they were right. Szeina Blacharowicz, writing to her best friend Malka Matikanski in Palestine in October 1936, told her: "At the present no changes have taken place in Eishyshok. It is the same Eishyshok. The only noticeable alteration is anti-Semitism. It has finally reached us, but I hope that we will outlive our enemies."[5]

There were plenty of troubles closer to home for people to be preoccupied with, after all. In 1935 the Polish lawyer Maracewicz burned down all of Vilna Street — an unintentional consequence of trying to burn his own home in order to collect the insurance money for it. Many people lost their homes in that fire, and in the fires set by a local Jewish underworld gang known as *padpalshchiki* — the firestarters — who lived up to their name by torching homes and then stealing the contents of those homes as they were being removed from the flames. The frequent fires kept the volunteer fire department very busy during these years. This mixed group of Jews and Poles — the only integrated group of adults in Eishyshok — was notable not only for its bravery and dedication, but for its camaraderie. The flames of anti-Semitism died down at the door to the fire department, where men like Moshe Sonenson — the head of the volunteers — were highly esteemed by their fellow firefighters.

As had happened after the Big Fire of 1895, people who had suffered losses in the various fires of the 1930s took stock of their lives and considered whether to rebuild or emigrate — but now, due to all the restrictions on emigration, their options were limited. Mordekhai Munesh Kaleko was one of the lucky ones. After his house on Vilna Street burned down, he decided to leave. Shortly after receiving the highly coveted certificates of emigration from their children in 1935, he and his wife Mina made aliyah. For years Mordekhai had been quoting the dire warnings of his children in Germany and Palestine, and the speeches of Zionist leaders Yitzhak Gruenbaum and Vladimir Jabotinsky, who were rivals in many areas but agreed on one thing: the necessity of large-scale Jewish emigration from Poland. Now at last Mordekhai was following his own advice.

The Dubczanski family, who also lost a house to the Vilna Street fire, were less fortunate. Their daughter Vela Portnoy was not able to get them a certificate to join her in Palestine, and their

The Kaleko family pose for a photo prior to their aliyah in 1935: (right to left) Mordekhai Munesh; son Peretz with wife Leah (née Koppelman) and their son Amiram; son Yehudah, and Mordekhai Munesh's wife Mina. Amiram and his brother Elisha were killed during the 1956 Arab-Israeli War. PHOTO: REPHAEL LEJBOWICZ. YESC, KALEKO-ALUFI

The Dubczanski family in their newly rebuilt house on the third night of Hanukkah, 1938: (right to left) Hannah, Rivka, father Hayyim-Moshe, mother Sarah, Masha, and Shlomo. All were murdered during the September 1941 massacre. YESC, PORTNOY-DUBCZANSKI

Moshe Ginunski, a bright, talented young man, son of Yekutiel the shoemaker, brother of Gedalia the hazzan and Luba, the shtetl's leading Communist. Moshe was murdered in the September 1941 massacre. PHOTO: BEN ZION SZREJDER. YESC, SHLANSKI

daughter Gale Laufer was unable to get them emigration papers to join her in America. They rebuilt their house on Vilna Street. Leibke Sonenson, whose house had burned in 1936 in a padpalshchiki fire on Radun Street, also rebuilt. Though his brothers Moshe and Shepske pleaded with him not to do so, quoting Mordekhai Gebirtig's prophetic lines, "It burns, brothers dear, it burns!/Our poor little shtetl is on fire!", Leibke responded, "You may be pleased to raise your children in a rented house, but not me and Geneshe." Soon a beautiful new house was going up on the site of the old one, where Radun Street met the market square. Moshe Sonenson and his family continued to reside in the house he rented from Eliezer Remz. Moshe also took the precaution of converting a substantial portion of his income into gold, always considered a reliable currency in times of trouble. Later he would begin burying part of his gold in the ground.

On the edge of the abyss, the shtetl continued to go on with its life as normally as possible. In 1934 a fund-raiser for Vaad ha-Yeshivot, the umbrella organization for the yeshivot of Eastern Europe, successfully solicited donations from a number of Eishyshkians, including, of course, the always dedicated Rabbi Szymen Rozowski, who was active as both the local campaign organizer in Eishyshok and as a contributor. By 1939, however, a similar fund-raiser was proving less successful. Thus a March 1939 letter to Vaad ha-Yeshivot from Rabbi Zusha Lichtig, the head of Eishyshok's yeshivah ketanah, regretfully announced: "We have not as yet collected all the pledges. Those who are usually active in community work did not want to be involved with this, and we have had to find new people to do the collecting."[6] Attached to the letter was a list of those who had contributed thus far, mainly balebatim in their forties or older. The younger people in the shtetl felt that in such hard times money collected in the shtetl should remain there, since its own yeshivah was underfunded.

The younger people were also continuing to monitor the events of the world with ever-increasing intensity, scanning the headlines for any relevant information they could glean. In a May 26, 1939, letter to his friend Fishke Shlanski (son of Zelig), in New York, Moshe "Deutch" Ginunski (so nicknamed because his father had been a POW in Germany) expressed their hunger for news, and for some understanding of how these global matters would affect them:

Dear Fishke,

The Eishyshkian news you know. All is as usual; here nothing ever changes. In the world things sound bad. Black clouds are gathering, with the latest instance being the quarrel over Danzig. Who knows what tomorrow will bring as a result? Surely we can anticipate some very unpleasant surprises. As for me, not so far in the future my turn as a soldier will come up.

Dear friend, write to me how in your part of the world they are assessing the situation. Here in the local press there is not a thing about the situation in Poland. We are unable to find out anything about it. This is why I am asking you to write me what the American press is saying about it.

Moshe would be murdered in Eishyshok, along with his father, on September 25, 1941.

THE EARLY DAYS OF WORLD WAR II

In August 1939, Rabbi Rozowski was still valiantly trying to fulfill his obligations as fund-raiser for the entire region, despite the resistance from within the shtetl and his own bad health. On September 1, 1939, the Germans invaded Poland, and two days later England and France declared war on Germany. Rabbi Rozowski would soon be attending to matters much more urgent than fund-raising, as he immediately understood. "A shepherd must remain with his flock. They need me more than ever," he told his son Uri and daughter-in-law Fania, who were visiting from Palestine when World War II broke out, and who pleaded with him to accompany them on their return.

The people of Eishyshok, like people everywhere in Poland, were stunned by the overwhelming success of the German blitzkrieg and the quick collapse of the Polish army. After all, the army was under the command of the much admired general Edward Smigly-Rydz, who had been appointed to the post by Pilsudski himself.

Despite years of increasingly anti-Semitic policies on the part of the Polish government, Eishyshkians had a sense of loyalty toward Poland and toward its army, in which so many of them had served, and indeed were still serving when war broke out. During the month of Elul, which began shortly after the war did, the sounding of the shofar each morning was followed by the reading of a chapter from Psalms, dedicated to the safety of the Polish soldiers. While other minorities in the vicinity were eagerly awaiting the downfall of Poland, Eishyshok's Jews were praying for her, and hoping that the western Allies would go to her aid.

On September 17, 1939, right before the surrender of the Polish army, Russian tanks and armored trucks entered the shtetl, part of the Russian invasion that had been agreed to in the secret nonaggression pact signed by Russia and Germany on August 23. Though at first there were rumors that the Red Army had come to fight alongside the Polish army against the Germans, Eishyshkians were quick to assess the new political reality and to understand that Russia was not on Poland's side. But confusion reigned about Russia's role. "[Russia] is a riddle wrapped in a mystery inside an enigma," Winston Churchill declared in one of his radio broadcasts, on October 1, 1939. With the partition of Poland between Russia and Germany, the meaning of the Russian invasion became clearer.[7]

Eishyshok and the area around it fell to the Soviets. The day the shtetl Communists had been waiting for had finally arrived. Under Soviet rule a regional revolutionary council known as the Revkum was established, which was responsible for Eishyshok and all the towns and villages in its vicinity. Headed by Hayyim Shuster, the

Revkum began its program by attacking all the "reactionary" Zionist organizations and activities within the shtetl. Thus the Hebrew school was abolished and a Yiddish school for the children of the proletariat was opened; the speaking of Hebrew was forbidden; and the young people were pressed to join Communist rather than Zionist organizations.

With the outbreak of war, Luba Ginunski, who had been released from a Polish prison in 1938 but forbidden to return to Eishyshok, was at last free to come home — home to the Communist shtetl she had been dreaming of for years. But first she had to make her way eastward from Warsaw, where she had been living in exile, and to cross territory that was under continuous strafing by German planes. Together with twelve other people, she set out on foot, and somehow managed to outmaneuver the low-flying German aircraft and their guns. In Brest she joined forces with two escaped Eishyshkian POWs, one Jewish, one Polish, still wearing their Polish army uniforms: Yitzhak Polaczek, and an outspoken anti-Semite who was the son of Dakinewiczowa, owner of the pork store on the market square. After three weeks of exhausting travel on roads clogged with refugees, Luba arrived in Eishyshok, to a heroine's welcome from her comrades.

On October 6, 1939, which was Simhat Torah, Zalman Lubetski also returned to Eishyshok. He, too, had been on the run from the Germans. Having been called back into the Polish army during the general mobilization of August 1939, he had fought at the front until the general surrender, then set out for home, in company with four other Polish soldiers, one of them a Jew from Lida. After two days on the road, however, the Christian soldiers decided to part company with the Jewish soldiers. "Why should we stay with you," they asked, "when Hitler is searching for Jews to kill, not Poles?" Many adventures and several weeks later, Zalman finally arrived in

Hayyim Shuster (left) with his friend Etchke Jurdyczanski (Isaac Juris). Hayyim, the shtetl's leading Communist and anti-Zionist, ordered the closing of the Hebrew school and banned all Zionist organizations and the speaking of Hebrew. Etchke survived the war in Russia, according to some testimonies. Hayyim was killed by fellow Russian partisans. YESC, JURIS-JURDYCZANSKI

Eishyshok, on a bicycle given to him by a Christian friend. When people came to welcome Zalman, he told his many well-wishers all about the horrors he had witnessed on the road. Though he urged them to run away, his contemporaries were still hoping to wait out the war at home. With young children as well as aging parents to take care of, and virtually no possibility of legal emigration, they thought that would be the best strategy.

EISHYSHOK'S FINEST HOUR

At the end of October 1939, Poland ceded Vilna and the surrounding region to Lithuania; the shtetl had changed hands once again. As the Russians retreated, most of the shtetl population breathed a sigh of relief. But the Russians didn't go far; they maintained army bases in strategic locations nearby, including one on the outskirts of Vilna, and Lithuania was clearly in the Russian sphere of influence, if not directly under Russian control. The exiled shtetl Communists did not have to go very far either, most of them settling in next-door Radun and other towns in Soviet Byelorussia. This group included Moshe Szulkin and his wife and children; Moshe's sister Elka Jankelewicz and her husband and children; Hirshke and Fruml Slepak; and Hayyim-Yoshke Szczuczynski. Luba Ginunski, however, who had been asked to remain in Lithuania to keep the Communist flame burning (and also to supply information), spent most of her time traveling, in semi-hiding.

Lithuanian rule in Eishyshok was ushered in by a ceremony on the market square, during which the entire shtetl swore allegiance to the Lithuanian flag and the Lithuanian president, Antanas Smetona. So began eight months of Lithuanian government — a time when all the shtetl's strengths were tested and proved, the finest hour of Eishyshok's last days.

With the fall of Warsaw to the Germans in 1939, the Lithuanian city of Vilna had become the center for all Eastern European Jewish activities, and the area's only remaining door to the free world — for Jews and non-Jews alike. According to the Joint Distribution Committee report of February 1940, there were then 30,000 refugees in Lithuania, an estimated 14,000 of whom were Jews.[8] (This of course was just the official count. The actual numbers were much higher.) Fleeing both German- and Soviet-occupied territories, the Jewish refugees went from door to door of the various consulates, immigration organizations, and relief agencies now headquartered in Vilna. Vilna was their last hope. Using whatever connections they had, they worked at getting papers for America, applied for visas to Shanghai and other Far Eastern destinations reachable via the Trans-Siberian Railway (sometimes with an eye to traveling from there to America), tried (though usually in vain) to secure emigration certificates to Palestine, bribed officials they thought might be able to help them, and asked for aid from the charitable groups.

Because of its proximity to Vilna and its location a mere two miles from the border of Byelorussia, Eishyshok tended to an estimated 15,000 refugees who passed through the town limits between October 1939 and June 1940. Most of them were on their way to Vilna, hoping to go on from there to Palestine; others, especially those with leftist sympathies, fled eastward into Byelorussia. The surrender of the Polish army resulted in hundreds of fleeing Polish soldiers, who were warmly welcomed by the Jewish community and given civilian clothing, hot tea and bread, and overnight lodging in the firehouse when necessary.

As noted in previous chapters, the shtetl took multiple measures to cope with the overwhelming number of refugees and to ensure that no aspect of their needs was overlooked: Rabbi Rozowski established and led a Refugee Committee; all of the mutual aid societies, including several that had been dormant for years, were activated; and virtually every house in the shtetl became a haven, as did the two batei midrash and the shul.

Refugees who were caught by Lithuanian border police as they tried to cross illegally were ransomed by the Eishyshkians. Unfortunates who were shot were buried in the New Cemetery. Others were fed and clothed, given proper papers (which Eishyshkians obtained from contacts in Vilna or forged themselves) and put on the bus to Vilna, or smuggled over the border into Byelorussia. People's medical problems, including many cases of frostbite, were tended to by Dr. Benski, the shtetl's various medicine men and women, and the three Jewish drugstores. One of the many accounts that describe the generosity of the Eishyshok community is this one from M. Hodorowski:

"Money, money, money" demanded the Lithuanian policemen. "We do not have any more valuables; we have given everything to the other policemen" [we replied]. "You don't have any more valuables?" They took us to the jail in Eishyshok, where we found other

candidates for aliyah. Through the jail windows we saw the faces of Eishyshkian Jews. Despite the cold weather, many left their houses and came to us. They brought us breakfast, they promised us help, they encouraged us.

"Do not be afraid, we will free you . . ."

During the day we were visited by the shtetl's community leaders. They brought us food, underwear, and more encouragement. Around the jail the shtetl children gathered, too, asking us what our needs were.

The shtetl elders gave instructions, sent delegations, attended one meeting after another, and paid ransoms until we were all free. . . . Eishyshok well deserved the name "Haven for Refugees." To the fifteen thousand refugees who passed through the shtetl she offered comfort, security, and encouragement. She took care of the refugees' physical needs and in addition provided them with spiritual sustenance to last them on their long, perilous journey to the motherland.

And if you had the good luck to arrive in Eishyshok without being captured by the border police, in the middle of the dark night you could knock on any Jewish door in Eishyshok. They were all open. Eishyshkians got up to make you a warm glass of tea, and to help you and your children. They offered you their bed, and their children's beds . . .[9]

Among the many who enjoyed the warm hospitality of Eishyshok was Menachem Begin, the future prime minister of Israel, who in later life often recounted his experiences there. Begin, who was at the time the leader of Beitar, having succeeded to the post after the death of Vladimir Jabotinsky in 1940, stayed at Eliyahu Bastunski's house, and in Alte Katz's spacious dining room gave a talk on the importance of the Zionist cause.

Eishyshok was so absorbed with helping the refugees that it overlooked its own dire situation and was lulled into a false sense of purpose and security. Even older people, like Honeh and Golde Moszczenik, for example, seemed to worry as much about the refugees as about their own strained resources. Having weathered the difficult years of World War I, the Moszczeniks were sure they could get through this new war, too; but with affluent children abroad, they were hoping for help. Honeh wrote to their daughter Pessia in Brazil in December 1939: "Already we can get a lot more food in the market. But everything is very expensive, especially clothing. We would very much like to hear from you, to receive letters, money, and packages. There is a great need to help the many refugees."

Meanwhile, Leibke and Geneshe Sonenson were moving into their beautiful new brick house, not far from Honeh and Golde Moszczenik's. In honor of the occasion the Sonensons threw a big party, which was attended by family and friends as well as a number of refugees, the latter marveling at the fact that Jews were building houses and giving parties during such troubled times.

Many people did have a sense of urgency about the situation, of course, but their options were extremely limited. Among the guests at the Sonenson party, for example, were Leibke's oldest sister Hinda Tawlitski and her four children. For five years she had been trying to emigrate to America to join her husband, Rabbi Ben Zion Tawlitski, but to no avail. Hinda failed the test given by the American consul in Warsaw and was found "non-competent." The questions to which she was unable to supply the correct answers were: "How many hairs did President Lincoln have in his beard?" and "How many feathers does a goose have in its tail?" Although her brother Shalom Sonenson accompanied her to the American consulate several times and tried to challenge this line of questioning, he was not successful. The consul was willing to give quota numbers and visas only to the four children, and both Hinda and her mother, Hayya, opposed their going alone. During the Lithuanian rule another Sonenson brother, Shepske, the youngest, tried to get the necessary papers for Hinda and her children. But after traveling to

Vilna and meeting with a number of officials, he too failed to overcome the obstacles. When he tried to comfort Hinda that things would somehow work out, she responded, "Speak to your brother Moshe; he knows the truth."

The Shlanski family were luckier. Zelig Shlanski, who had followed his brothers Morris and Louis to America, was able to get papers to bring his wife Rose and their five children over. As the family of an American citizen, they were given permission by the German government to travel through Nazi territory to board their ship in Italy. Zelig's sister, her husband, an American citizen, and their two daughters also received their papers at this time, and they made the necessary preparations for leaving. But at the last minute one of their daughters came down with the mumps. By the time she had recovered it was too late. The Soviets had occupied Lithuania, and the borders were closed.

As for emigration to Palestine, ever since 1925 the British restrictions had gotten tighter and tighter, and in 1939 the most restrictive of all the British White Papers effectively sealed the fate of the many families who were still hoping to leave. Even then, however, a few people managed to get through, sometimes against the longest and most dangerous odds.

Sarah Plotnik, the young Zionist who'd taken a nursing course on a hakhsharah, eventually made it to Palestine, thanks to a fictitious marriage, dated not long after her real marriage to a man she loved, Pessah Avrahami. Before she left

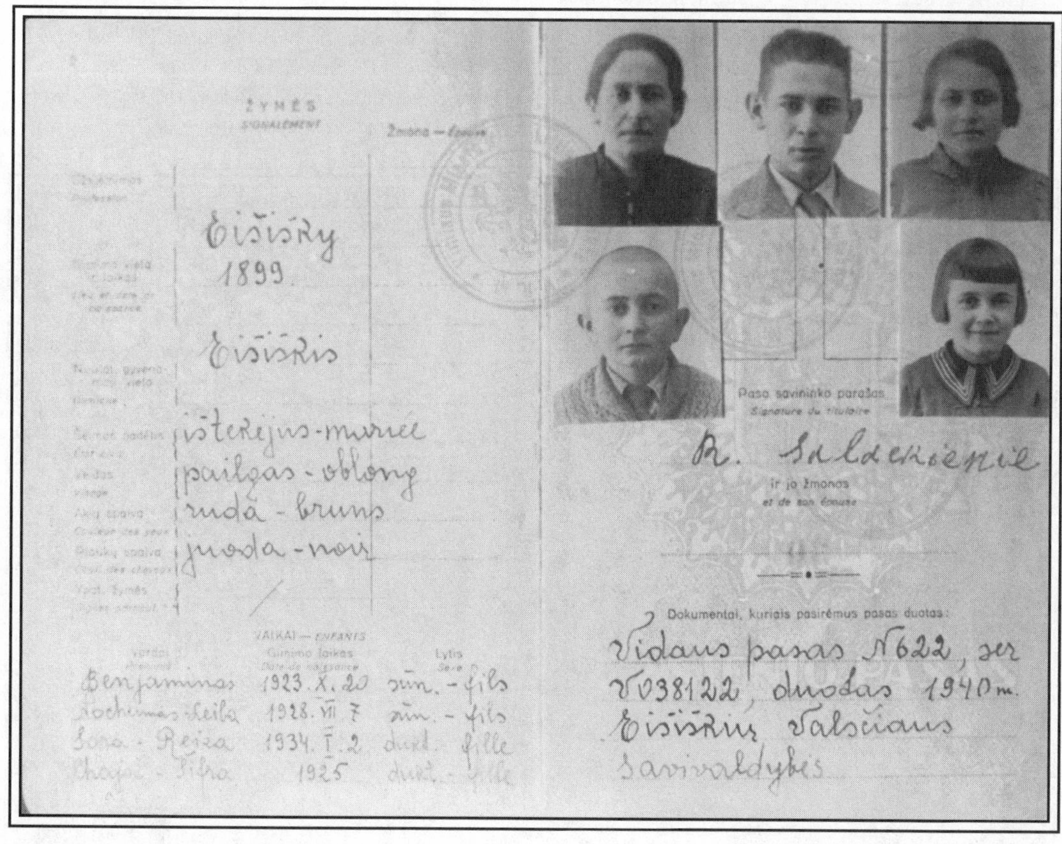

ŽYMĖS
SIGNALEMENT
Žmona — Épouse
Eišiškių
1899.
Eišiškis
ištekėjus - mariée
pailgas - oblong
rudā - bruns
juoda - noirs
VAIKAI — ENFANTS
Benjaminas 1923. X. 20 sūn. - fils
Jochimas-Leiba 1928. VII 7 sūn. - fils
Sora - Reiza 1934. I. 2 dukt. fille
Paso savininko parašas
Signature du titulaire
R. Salackienė
ir jo žmonos
et de son épouse
Dokumentai, kuriais pasirėmus pasas duotas:
Vidaus pasas N622, ser VO38122, duotas 1940 m. Eišiškių valsčiaus savivaldybės

The passport of Rose Shlanski (Salacki) and four of her children. An older son had left with their father Zelig for America at an earlier date. YESC, SHLANSKI

Eishyshok she tore her real wedding ketubbah in two and placed one half in her real husband's shoe, one in her own. Like many parents of young women in such circumstances, Sarah's father Eliyahu was extremely anxious about this arrangement, and spent many a sleepless night worrying about her. It would be several months before he received a letter from Palestine announcing that she and her real husband had remarried, and now had a new ketubbah, issued on the fourth day of Nissan, 5700 (April 12, 1940).

Together with his family, the little German-speaking boy the shtetl had earlier nicknamed Hitleruk had entered Palestine illegally. But the end of 1940 saw Elisha Frischer, his little sister Shulamit, and his parents, Nehama and Yitzhak, about to set sail out of Palestine, on the ill-fated ship known as the *Patria*. The British had chartered the *Patria* to deport illegal immigrants from several ships — the *Milos*, the *Pacific*, and the *Atlantic* — to the island of Mauritius. However, on November 25, 1940, after the passengers from the *Atlantic* had boarded the *Patria*, which was docked in the harbor of Haifa, the *Patria* exploded. It had been mined by members of Haganah (the Jewish Defense Organization), who meant to disable the engines and thus prevent the expulsion, but ended up killing 260 of those passengers they had hoped to keep in Palestine.[10] Although some 1,600 of the illegals were eventually deported as planned to Mauritius, the Frischers were among the *Patria* survivors

The wedding of Sarah Plotnik and Pessah Avrahami, one of the last in Eishyshok. Sitting at the table (right to left): Mr. Hamarski, his daughter Dvorah, Benyamin Kabacznik, wife Liebke, son Yudaleh, Reb Arieh-Leib Kudlanski, Reb Dovid Moszczenik, and Eliyahu Plotnik, father of the bride. Second row (right to left): Mrs. Hamarski; five family members; twin sisters of the bride, Mikhele and Breine; the bride and groom; Zipporah, mother of the bride; and two relatives. Back row: family youngsters. Only the bride and groom, who made aliyah to Eretz Israel, survived. Reb Dovid died a natural death; Benyamin, Liebke, and Yudaleh were murdered by the AK; the majority were killed in the September 1941 massacre; a few were killed in Ghetto Radun and Lida. YESC, ZIMMERMAN

Passport photo of Rivka Schwartz (Svarc), 1940. The Schwartz-Shlanski family received visas to emigrate to America to join their family. Prior to the departure, Rivka came down with the mumps. When she recovered, it was too late: the Russians had closed the borders. Her parents were murdered in the September 1941 massacre. She was killed a few months later. YESC, SHLANSKI

who were permitted, for so-called humanitarian reasons, to remain in Palestine (after a year-long internment at the detention camp at Atlit, near Haifa). But for every survivor who remained, the British made a deduction from the total number of emigration certificates that had been allocated under the 1939 White Paper.

Sarah Plotnik and Nehama Koppelman Frischer were the lucky ones. The families they left behind, like those of so many other Eishyshkian emigrants, were not so fortunate. Once the Soviets took over Lithuania, there would be no further emigrations to any part of the free world.

SOVIET RULE: THE FINAL YEAR

On June 15, 1940, the Soviet army crossed the Lithuanian border. On August 3, the Supreme Soviet announced that it was pleased to fulfill the "request" of the three Baltic Republics of Lithuania, Latvia, and Estonia to be incorporated into the Union of Soviet Socialist Republics. Now that Eishyshok was under Communist rule again, the local Communists who had fled to Radun and Lida, or across the border into Byelorussia, applied for repatriation. Told to register, most of them did so — only to find themselves deported, as punishment for their "disloyalty" to Mother Russia. With typical Soviet logic, they were told they should consider all Russia their homeland, not just the little Lithuanian shtetl of their birth. So instead of being sent back to Eishyshok, they were loaded on cattle cars and exiled to Siberia. Little did anyone realize in their unhappiness at this unexpected turn of events that their punishment would in the end become their passport to life, sparing them the fate that would soon claim their townspeople.

This time around, during the second Soviet occupation, the local Jewish Communists — those who remained — had more of an opportunity to implement their Marxist ideology. Luba Ginunski was the head of the local party, which included among its most active members Hayyim Shuster, his girlfriend Meitke Bielicki, Ruvke Boyarski di Bulbichke (the potato), Velvke Katz, and Pessah Cofnas. Among Luba's first priorities was the redistribution of land and property. The estates of the great Polish magnate Seklutski and those of other members of the Polish nobility were parceled out among five hundred Polish peasants. But anti-Semitism was so rampant that even the beneficiaries of Luba's act were not uniformly grateful: "A dirty

Jew Communist has no right to Polish land," she was told during the celebrations, after vodka had loosened some tongues.

The Soviet leadership in Lithuania was quick to realize that Luba's formidable talents — her administrative skills, her command of Marx's and Lenin's writings, her eloquence on the stump — were too valuable to be wasted on a small Jewish shtetl and a few hundred local Polish peasants. She was appointed to the Finadel (the Communist Party's finance department) in nearby Troki. There she lectured to factory workers throughout the region, talking mainly about German atrocities against the Polish people.

Luba Ginunski, one of the shtetl's leading Communists, distributed land to five hundred poor Polish peasants in the autumn of 1940. Here their leaders are celebrating the event with Luba (dressed in black and speaking to a woman with a white kerchief). YESC, L. GINUNSKI

According to Luba, most of the subsequent activities of the Communists in Eishyshok were implemented by the comitet — the local Communist governing committee — in her absence. As noted in chapters 3 and 17, Rabbi Szymen Rozowski was thrown out of his spacious house, and the property of many of the most affluent members of the community was nationalized, their houses confiscated, including those of the Abelovs, Kiuchefskis, Koppelmans, Katzes, and Weidenbergs, and Leibke and Geneshe Sonenson's brand-new one.

To cope with the dire economic situation, the "bourgeoisie" had to find new ways of earning a living. Markl Koppelman, Nehama Frischer's brother, previously successful in the textile business, found a job in a drugstore in Vilna; the well-to-do Motl Abelov became a blacksmith; and Alte Katz went to work as an employee in her own drugstore and photography studio. Permitted to reside in the back rooms of her spacious house in exchange for a monthly rent of 510 rubles, she could not make ends meet. In April 1941 she wrote to her daughter Esther in Colombia: "This month I am 110 rubles short. It is simply impossible to pay. Shepske Sonenson is trying to help me by negotiating with the authorities."

Deportation to Siberia was another threat issued to the well-to-do, and to whoever else was thought to "pose a danger to Communism." From Vilna and the vicinity, about 8,000 people were deported to Siberia, including 3,500 Jews.[11] Among the deportees were Matle Sonenson Shereshefski and her family, who had been residing in Baranowicz, and Benyamin Kabacznik and Etl Glombocki Ginzburg from Vilna, all of them former Eishyshkians. Within Eishyshok itself, the shtetl Communists had prepared a list of people to be deported, but as a personal favor to Moshe Sonenson, Luba Ginunski removed the names of the Sonenson family as well as those of their friends the Kiuchefskis, for Moshe had helped the Ginunski family through some hard times.

Life was difficult, but people managed as best they could. On the black market of Vilna and of Eishyshok itself, anything could be bought for a price. The Plotnik family, for example, managed to buy a short winter jacket, warm woolen boots, and galoshes for Eliyahu. They built a small oven to warm the house, purchased enough corn, potatoes, and pickles to last an entire winter, and even planned for a happier future, buying quilts, linens, and tablecloths for the trousseaux of the twins, Mikhle and Breine.

Twin sisters Mikhle (left) and Breine Plotnik. Mikhle's letters to her sister Sarah in Eretz Israel were among the last mailed from the shtetl. Both sisters were murdered in the September 1941 massacre. PHOTO: BEN ZION SZREJDER. YESC, AVRAHAMI-PLOTNIK

Alte Katz was also concerned with trousseau matters, for her daughter Shoshana was now engaged to Leibke Botwinik. She hid the magnificent trousseau she had put together for Shoshana in the home of poor, blind centenarian Reb Itche Berkowitch der Melamed. But local Communists (whom Reb Itche was able to identify by the sound of their voices) stole the trousseau and transported it over the border to Radun. Though Moshe Sonenson used all his connections to try to retrieve the stolen treasure for his sister-in-law, he had little success. Alte was devastated by the loss.

Despite the many restrictions imposed by the Communists, the shulhoyf and its three houses of worship were allowed to remain open and the shtetl was able to continue its public celebration of the religious holidays. Thus on Yom Kippur of 1940 Moshe Sonenson appeared in the synagogue to buy Maftir Yonah — the privilege of reading the Book of Jonah — as his family had been doing for hundreds of years. But instead of reading it himself, he called Reb Shaye Ginunski to the bimah. With his long white beard gleaming against the snow-white kittel he wore beneath his prayer shawl, Reb Shaye looked every inch the biblical sage. As he approached the bimah, however, most of the balebatim stood up and walked out in protest. The purchase of the right to read the Book of Jonah on Yom Kippur had traditionally resided with the Sonenson family, and most of the balebatim in the shtetl were not prepared to abandon that tradition. Nonetheless, Rabbi Szymen Rozowski, hazzan Moshe Tobolski, Reb Scholem Wilenski, Reb Zusha Lichtig, and several other clergy and balebatim as well as the entire population of the women's gallery remained seated, listening as Reb Shaye Ginunski chanted the Book of Jonah.

Those who stayed in their seats understood Moshe Sonenson's gesture as an act of good will, a political statement intended to make peace between the forces of religion and Communism. As a deeply religious man who was also the father of two daughters who were Communists and the uncle of the most renowned of the area's Communists, Luba Ginunski, Reb Shaye Ginunski seemed the perfect symbol for the possibilities of reconciliation. But those who walked out did not acknowledge such possibilities. They were abiding by a centuries-old Lithuanian tradition, observed throughout much of Eastern Europe, that Maftir Yonah can never be transferred.[12] It was a privilege purchased at a high price, believed to bring luck in the form of prosperity to its purchaser, and it belonged exclusively to that purchaser.

Moshe Sonenson went further in his attempts to bridge the differences between the two camps in the shtetl, attending Communist celebrations as well as religious ceremonies. Unlike most of his fellow balebatim, he showed up at the firehouse for parties given by the Communists in honor of special days on their political calendar. His dances with Luba Ginunski and the beautiful Bluma Lubetski were the talk of the region. But he was also as attentive as ever to family-centered celebrations. Alte Katz, writing in April 1941 to her daughter Esther in Colombia, described what was to be the shtetl's last Passover: "Moshe, Feigele [Zipporah], and the children were all with us for the First Days, as always. Thank God we managed to have matzah, wine, gefilte fish, and dumplings. We celebrated the Seder in your room, which serves as the dining room."

Despite the traditional celebration, which they had somehow managed in the face of severe scarcities in the food markets, the letter is permeated with a sense of distress. The family ate, as noted, in what had been Esther's bedroom — because Alte Katz now occupied only the back rooms of her own house. And though she expressed a wish to see her grandchildren in Colombia, she also made it clear that she doubted such a visit would ever happen.

The letters of beautiful young Mikhle Plotnik were filled with a similar sense of darkness and despair. When she wrote to her sister Sarah in Palestine in May 1941, just a couple of months after Sarah's arrival there, she thanked her for her letters about life on the kibbutz — the kind of letters that in earlier times had always been shared throughout the shtetl — but explained that the letters had not been discussed outside the family: "Because during these days it is better to stay home, for one does not know what to anticipate outside." Several weeks later Mikhle wrote: "I miss you very much. Here we are closed in. The world is trapped between two huge raging storms. Perhaps we will never again have the chance to see those who are so dear to us and for whom we long so deeply."

Mikhle Plotnik's words proved prophetic. On June 23, 1941, twenty-five days after her last letter to Sarah, the Russians scattered like leaves in a whirlwind, followed by the shtetl Communists, and the deadly Nazi storm crossed the bridge onto Vilna Street.

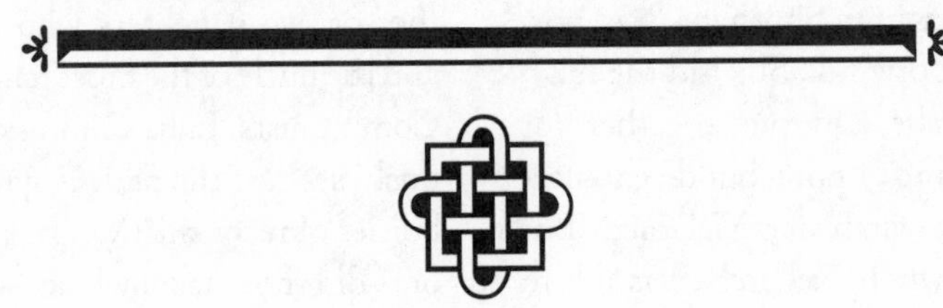

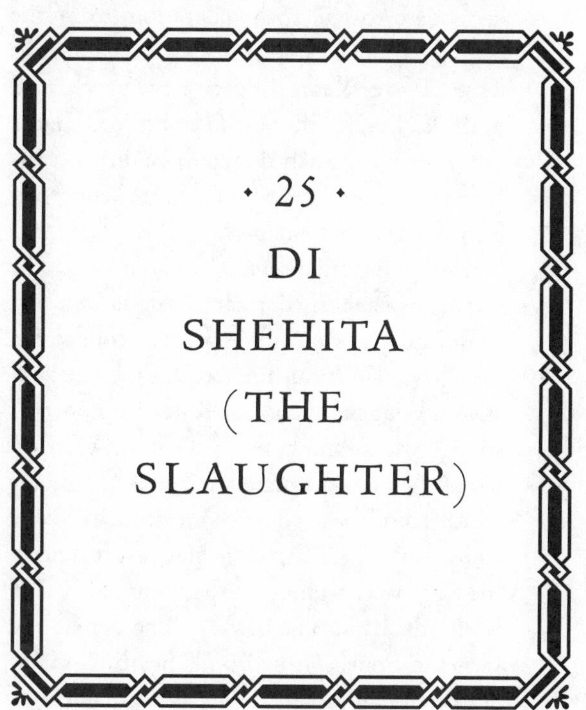

GET UP! GO TO THE CITY
OF SLAUGHTER —
THE SUN SHONE, THE
ACACIA BLOSSOMED
AND THE SLAUGHTERER
SLAUGHTERED.

Hayyim Nahman Bialik
IN THE CITY OF
SLAUGHTER, *1904*

THE NAZI INVASION

ON JUNE 22, 1941, WITH NO ADVANCE WARNING, THE GERMANS LAUNCHED OPERAtion Barbarossa (Red Beard), the massive invasion of the USSR. All night, the earth around Eishyshok rumbled as the Wehrmacht advanced and the Russians fled, with many of the shtetl Communists in tow. German aircraft flew so low over Eishyshok they seemed almost to touch the chimneys, to skim the stork nests.

According to the Wehrmacht report of June 29, 1941, on the first day of the invasion German Luftwaffe planes destroyed 1,811 Russian planes, many of them before they ever had a chance to leave the ground. German losses numbered a mere 35 planes.

On Monday, June 23, the German troops arrived in Eishyshok. First to cross the Vilna Street bridge were soldiers who roared into town on bucket-seat motorcycles. They were followed by the elite armored fighting division known as the Panzer Corps, and by row upon row of other armored divisions along with their tanks, their cannons, and an assortment of heavy artillery and other equipment. As the windows of their houses rattled and the ground beneath their feet shook, all the Jews remained inside behind locked doors. Peering out from behind closed shutters and drawn curtains, they watched the seemingly endless columns of the German army marching down the streets of Eishyshok. This was a far cry from the response described in a German song that had become a shtetl favorite in World War I:

> *The girls opened all the windows and doors,*
> *To greet the German soldiers during the wars.*

But for some the old song still rang true. Marching to whatever rhythm was being beaten out by whoever the latest conquerors were, just as they had always done, the Dakinewiczowa family were quick to change with the times. Their two beautiful blonde daughters sallied forth to welcome the German invaders with bouquets of flowers, and were joined by a steadily growing crowd of Poles.

The mob was quickly apprised of the invaders' intentions by leaflets proclaiming the end of the reign of the "Jews of Moses with his seven heavens, the friends of Roosevelt, Churchill and Stalin who brought Bolshevism, abuse and exploitation into the world." Soon the Jews would be gone and all would be well, the leaflets promised, for "we have come to liberate you from this unwanted element." Joyfully reading from the leaflets, the cheering Poles lined the highway and stood on opposite sides of the market square to hail their "liberation" from "the Jew-Communist exploiters." Even the illiterates were able to celebrate the good news proclaimed in the leaflets, for those who could read shared the contents with those who couldn't. As the Germans kept marching, the cheers kept growing in volume and intensity.

During the initial days of the occupation, the Germans established their headquarters and command posts in buildings they confiscated from Jews. The beautiful home of the Kiuchefskis on Vilna Street, Szeina Katzenelenboigen's spacious home and hotel on the northwest corner of the market square, the Kabacznik home which stood near the Dakinewiczowas' pork store on the Mill Street corner of the square, the Kaganowicz home on the corner of Radun Street, the handsome new dwelling Leibke and Geneshe Sonenson had built nearby, and the large building in which Alte Katz maintained her home as well as her photography studio, pharmacy, and bakery — all were taken over by the Germans, as were many other Jewish-owned buildings in the shtetl. The soldiers made themselves at home, drinking beer, playing cards, and eating food cooked for them by their Jewish "hosts."

Some of the Germans were friendly, reassuring their hosts that it would be a short war: "Here today, Moscow tomorrow" was the refrain. Older Eishyshkians breathed a sigh of relief, remembering the kind Germans of World War I and telling their sons and daughters that the refugees who had been pouring into the shtetl for the past two years had no doubt exaggerated when they described the atrocities committed against the Jews in Germany and Poland. Other Germans, however, sounded an ominous note: "Too bad that you are Jews," the Wehrmacht soldiers kept saying; "bad times are in store for the Jews."

One of the two yellow stars Shalom Sonenson wore in Ghetto Radun, October 1941–May 1942. YESC, SHALOM SONENSON-BEN-SHEMESH

Meanwhile, the shtetl continued to buzz with war-related activity, as soldiers and heavy military equipment kept streaming eastward over the highway that ran through the center of town. Accompanying the Wehrmacht were units manned by Spanish soldiers, who had difficulty communicating their needs to the local shtetl population because of the language barrier. They quickly acquired a reputation for stealing pigs from the Poles, and making sexual advances toward the Jewish girls.

As the front lines kept moving eastward, the Wehrmacht commanders were replaced by the Gestapo, and Lithuania was transferred from German military rule to German civil administration, becoming part of the Reikskommissariat (Reich protectorate) of Ostland, which consisted of all the occupied territories of the east. These changes took place between the end of July and early August. Any hopes for an amicable occupation were soon dispelled. Humiliation, torture, and other atrocities, eventually including murder, were to be the lot of the Jewish population of Eishyshok.

THE JUDENRAT

In fact, the grim signs of what was to come had started to emerge even before the new administration, just a few days after the occupation, with the arrival of two Polish Volksdeutschen — ethnic Germans who had lived in Poland for many years, some for generations. Dressed in civilian clothes, the two men went to see Rabbi Szymen Rozowski at the modest Vilna Street apartment he had been living in since the Communists had expelled him from his official residence. Ordered to establish a Judenrat (Jewish council), the rabbi summoned fifty of the shtetl's traditional leaders to the already desecrated Old Beth Midrash; all refused to serve. When the Volksdeutschen threatened to kill the rabbi if a Judenrat was not organized immediately, twelve men were selected by lottery, including Moshe and Leibke Sonenson, Shmuel Bastunski, and Shlomo Polaczek.

In places with ghettos the Judenrat had administrative responsibilities within the Jewish community, helping to provide food, lodging, education, medical attention, and other necessities pertaining to the physical and social welfare of their people. In places like Eishyshok, however, which had no ghetto, the Judenrat had no function whatever with regard to the internal life of the Jewish community.[1] Reporting to the Gestapo, the Judenrat existed to serve the Germans, supplying them with goods and services on demand. And they had another important function as well: As the Germans' primary and most public target of victimization and abuse, the men on the Judenrat served as a terrifying symbol to the Jews of what was in store for the rest of them. But just as the Germans used the spectacle of their mistreatment to spread fear among the entire Jewish community, they also recognized how effective it could be in gaining the support of the non-Jewish population.

One Sunday, June 29, which was the Polish Catholic holiday of Boze Cialo (Corpus Christi), a shot rang out near the church in Juryzdyki. No one was injured, but the police chief reported to the Germans that the Jews had attempted to kill a German patrol. The Judenrat was then ordered, on penalty of death, to find the person who had fired the shot. If the culprit was not named within one hour, all members of the Judenrat, beginning with Rabbi Rozowski, would be executed. After bribing some local Poles with money supplied him by members of the Jewish community, Moshe Sonenson learned that the shot had been fired by one of two German soldiers who had been showing off their guns to one of the villagers. Moshe gave his account to a German soldier who believed him and called a halt to the imminent execution.

Though the men on the Judenrat were thereby saved from immediate death, the Germans were not to be denied the pleasure of tormenting them. The entire population of the shtetl as well as all the Catholic worshippers from the Juryzdyki church were ordered to gather on the west side of the market square to witness the special form of humiliation the Germans had devised as a punishment. It began with a speech by the German commander stating that the Jews had tried to bribe the Germans with fifty eggs and two chickens — this being a reference to the food gathered by one of the Judenrat members that day, who, unaware of the crisis, had innocently kept going about his assigned task of providing the Sunday supply of food for the six Gestapo members living in Szeina Katzenelenboigen's house. "But what else could be expected of the sons of Moses, followers of Stalin, friends of Roosevelt and Churchill and destroyers of Poland?" the commander asked. Then all the members of the Judenrat were compelled to march through the market square with twig brooms on their shoulders screaming "Fifty eggs and two chickens" in German. Their fellow Jews wept for them, while some of the young Poles shouted with joy. When it was all over, Moshe Sonenson went home and shed bitter tears. The humiliation had been too much for him. His children had never before seen him cry.

On another occasion around this time, one of the Germans stationed in Eishyshok died. Dressed in full uniform and wearing a huge crucifix, the body in its casket was taken to a freshly plowed field on the outskirts of town, where it was placed atop a specially built platform. All the shtetl Jews as well as the local Poles were ordered to attend the funeral. After the usual speech by the German commander about the sons of Moses and his seven heavens, the Jewish Bolsheviks, destroyers of Poland, friends of Stalin, Roosevelt, and Churchill, the funeral featured yet another episode involving the persecution of the Judenrat: One by one, starting with the rabbi, each member was ordered to pass before the casket and bow down to the ground in front of it until his nose touched the black earth, then confess to being responsible for the death of every German during the current war.

Once again the Jews in the crowd wept as the Germans, Volksdeutschen, and many of the local Poles howled with laughter. After this "ceremony" the Judenrat members were commanded to run into the river, fully clothed, and clean up. With the German dogs nipping at their heels, the men hurled themselves into the river. A very pregnant Zipporah Sonenson tried to protect her children from the sight of their father's fresh humiliation, telling them to close their eyes, but her mother-in-law, Hayya, told her that the children should watch what was happening, so that they would always remember, never forget.

The persecutions were ceaseless. The very next day, a Sunday in July, members of the Judenrat were ordered to report to the spacious yard behind the Kiuchefski house at the hour when prayers were ending at the church in Juryzdyki and the worshippers from Eishyshok would be coming back to the shtetl. Three members of the Judenrat were missing, however, having been out on their Sunday food-gathering mission for the Gestapo when the orders were given. As punishment for their absence, the other men were lined up in two facing rows and instructed to beat each other up. When Moshe Sonenson administered a gentle slap to the man facing him, his brother Leibke, one of the Germans gave a demonstration of how a proper beating should be carried out. Moshe Sonenson's face was swollen for days afterward. When

In a bitterly cold climate all Eishyshkians owned fur coats or jackets of varying quality and cost. Zipporah Sonenson (right), daughter Yaffa, husband Moshe, and son Yitzhak dressed in theirs, winter 1940. All of the fur coats were taken by the Germans. PHOTO: BEN ZION SZREJDER. YESC, Y. ELIACH

Young women in fashionable fur and fur-trimmed coats, standing on the bridge on Vilna Street: (right to left) Bluma Lubetski, Sonia from Vilna, Geneshe Kaganowicz, Etele Yurkanski, and Masha Kaganowicz. Only Bluma survived the Holocaust. All the others were killed in the September 1941 massacre. YESC, JURIS-JURDYCZANSKI

the beating ceremony came to an end and there was still no sign of the three missing men, the members of the Judenrat, some with bloody, swollen faces, were ordered to run around the well in the Kiuchefskis' yard. Shlomo Polaczek, a man in his fifties who had eight children, collapsed and fell to the ground, but no one was allowed to go to his aid.

Life became more difficult and restrictive with each passing day. Jews were forbidden to walk on the sidewalks and were required to obey a strict nightly curfew. As the Gestapo issued one demand after another for supplies and valuables, the men of the Judenrat were kept busy requisitioning and gathering gold, silver, foreign currency, fur coats, fine linens, light bulbs, medical supplies, coffee, tea, cocoa, and other items from their friends and neighbors. From all corners of the shtetl, Jews could be seen carrying their belongings to designated depositories. Radios, one of their last links to the rest of the world, were also requisitioned. The Jewish women in the shtetl were put to work cooking, cleaning, and doing laundry and other domestic tasks for the Germans. Some were forced to perform particularly difficult and demeaning jobs like cleaning the weeds and moss from between the cobblestones in the market square, then scrubbing the stones down with soap and water.

The new administration that was put in place by early August had a number of different components. The Gebietskommisar (German for "head of a territory") for the immediate region was Commander Hans Christian Hingst, whose aide for Jewish affairs was Franz Murer. Gebietskommisar for the entire district of Vilna was a man named Dr. Wulf. Within Eishyshok itself the new command appointed by the Germans included a number of Polish Volksdeutschen, who were quite popular with the local Poles, in part because of their anti-Semitism;[2] a former army officer named Ostrauskas who had been aligned with the collaborationist wing of the Lithuanian army and was appointed chief of police in Eishyshok; and a unit from the TODT, the German army organization responsible for large-scale construction work in support of the military goals of the Third Reich. It was named after its founder, engineer Dr. Fritz Todt.

Every morning at dawn, most of the Jewish men between the ages of sixteen and sixty reported to the TODT for work on the various projects under way in the area: they repaired the highway, planted trees, and worked at the German garrison stationed at Titiance, about eleven miles from Eishyshok. The workday lasted from 7:00 A.M. to 9:00 P.M., after which everyone was ordered to perform military-style exercises and marches. There were severe beatings at the hands of the Polish Volksdeutschen, under the command of a German soldier named Webber. Jews with beards were especially popular targets for humiliation and abuse.

While most men worked outside the shtetl, a few who had young sons who could pass for sixteen and take their father's places remained at home. For example, Zvi Michalowski replaced his father, Maneh, at the Titiance garrison. Other men worked alongside the women in the shtetl, serving the Germans. The Matikanski family, for example — Dovid, his wife Nehama, and their sons Haikl and Yitzhak, who were considered the elite among the shtetl tailors — were all kept busy making elegant suits and jackets for the occupation forces. Since Dovid had spent time in Paris visiting another son, Albert, his tailoring had a special fashionable flair much favored by the Germans. Indeed, a certain Nazi commander in Eishyshok, a particularly cruel one, was nicknamed "der Weisser Rekele" after the white jackets he always wore, hand tailored for him by Dovid and Haikl Matikanski. The jacket matched his beloved white poodle, who went everywhere with him.

Besides being assigned the odious task of requisitioning their fellow Jews' valuables, the men of the Judenrat were also supposed to follow up on information about their community that the local Poles eagerly provided. The Germans wanted lists of the prettiest girls, the best tailors, the wealthiest balebatim; they wanted to know who the local Jewish Communists were, who had overseas relatives. Supplying food for the German officers was one of the Judenrat's most onerous responsibilities. Two hundred eggs, ten chickens, and large quantities of milk, cheese, butter, fresh vegetables, berries, mushrooms, and firewood had to be collected from an overworked, undernourished, impoverished shtetl population each day. And the German horses, which were now stabled in what had been the beautiful summer shul, had to be fed too.

Some of the Germans did display an occasional glimmer of humanity. When Moshe Sonenson's wife was about to have her baby, he approached the same officer who had believed his story about the gunshot incident and asked him to excuse him from his Judenrat duties when her time came. Permission was granted. The very next day, Zipporah Sonenson gave birth to a healthy baby boy with a little strawberry mark on his left arm. Pointing to his birthmark, the midwife whispered, "This means a black future for all of us." And indeed, days far darker than those they had just endured were to begin soon after the birth of that child.

The newly furloughed Moshe Sonenson was summoned back to duty almost immediately. He and the other members of the Judenrat reported to the Katzenelenboigen house, where the Gestapo ordered them to come up with ten thousand cigarettes within the next twenty minutes. Each of the members ran to his own private source, and the cigarettes — loose and in packages, machine made and hand-rolled — appeared before the deadline. The Germans took the cigarettes and then most of them headed eastward, leaving Eishyshok to a new German command, this one even more sadistic than its predecessor. Their job was to prepare the ground for the arrival of the Einsatzgruppen ("Action Groups"), the mobile killing squads the Germans used in the Soviet Union. Deployed principally against the Jews, they had other targets as well, including Gypsies, Communists, and other political groups.

After the departure of the "cigarette Gestapo" (as Moshe Sonenson called them), the Lithuanian commander Ostrauskas stayed on, and he was approached by the members of the Judenrat, asking to be released. For a hundred-dollar bribe he agreed, whereupon Rabbi Rozowski had to assemble a new Judenrat, once again via lottery. The new members included Eliyahu Bastunski's son-in-law Avraham Kaplan, who was made chairman; Shalom Sonenson, deputy chairman; Hanan Michalowski, Markl Koppelman, Mordekhai Kaganowicz, and eight other men.[3]

The new Gestapo command had a never-ending supply of diabolical ideas for tormenting the Judenrat and the rest of the shtetl population. On one occasion they summoned 250 Jews with beards to appear in the center of the market square, then ordered them to form two long lines facing each other and to pull each other's beards. On another occasion Shalom Sonenson and Mordekhai Kaganowicz were told to climb onto a roof, while Shalom's brother Moshe was ordered to try to knock them off with a stream of water from the fire department's hose. If they fell they would be shot to death; if they managed to remain on the roof they would be spared. Holding on with all their might, they managed to survive the ordeal, which was hugely enjoyed by a large crowd of cheering Germans and Poles.[4]

DENIAL

Even in the midst of all the torments, some remnants of the old way of life managed to be preserved. In a dark, shuttered room in the home of Zipporah and Moshe Sonenson, the new baby was secretly circumcised, in a ceremony attended by Reb Aaron Katz of Lida, who was Zipporah's uncle and the godfather of her first son. Having risked his life to come to Eishyshok, he now acted as sandak (godfather) to his niece's second son, who was named Shaul after his paternal grandfather.

Rumors were now reaching Eishyshok that Jews elsewhere in the vicinity were being murdered, indeed whole populations annihilated. But many townspeople found this impossible to believe. Shoshke Wine, for example, was warned by a Pole named Szczesnolewicz, who had been a hangman — and a former customer in her bar — during the "good old days" of the Polish Second Republic, that German killing squads (assisted by local collaborators) were massacring Jews in one shtetl after another, and they were getting closer and closer to Eishyshok. Since she lived near the outskirts of town, he urged her to escape across the border into Byelorussia, along with her son Ben-Zion and cousin Zlatke Garber. Thanking him for his concern, she gave him a drink of vodka, on the house, and sent him on his way; he was very disappointed that she would not listen to him. After he left, Shoshke turned to Zlatke and said, "All this terrible story for a free glass of vodka."

Hayya Sonenson was another naysayer. She did not believe that the Germans would kill old women and children. Moreover, she said, she belonged to Eishyshok and would rather be buried in the New House of Eternity with her ancestors and husband than in any strange town. Alte Katz also felt sure the Germans would revert to being civilized as soon as the front was far from Eishyshok. Thus Moshe Sonenson found himself unable to leave. Though he himself did believe the warnings, and set about burying more of his gold in the ground for possible future use in time of danger, he could convince neither his mother nor his mother-in-law to run away. And without her mother, his wife also refused to leave.

Rabbi Rozowski was convinced that the stories he was being told by Christian farmers were true. He knew that the destruction of his community was imminent. Thus when many of the shtetl Jews, fearful for their property as well as their lives, began transferring their valuables to the homes of Christian friends and neighbors, Rabbi Rozowski warned them not to, for he felt that by turning over their wealth they would be creating an incentive for those Christians to hasten their deaths. Few heeded his warnings, however.

Then on September 11, in the wake of rumors about a massacre in nearby Aran, a trustworthy Christian who had been sent there came back with firsthand confirmation: the entire community had been destroyed, and the streets were filled with the bodies of Jews. Rabbi Rozowski called a meeting to suggest buying ammunition in order to put up a fight and die with honor: "Let us not go as sheep to the slaughter!" he proclaimed. "Let us die with the Philistines." But still there were people who refused to believe the end was near, who were sure that the Germans were only after Jewish property and money, not Jewish lives, and the meeting ended in dissension.[5]

Police chief Ostrauskas told the Judenrat that he would save Eishyshok from its terrible fate if he were given one thousand rubles in gold. Opinion was divided, but the money was duly collected and turned over to him.

THE ROUNDUP

On Sunday, September 21, 1941, the eve of Rosh Hashanah, tension in the shtetl heightened. Dr. Wulf, the Gebietskommisar of the district of Vilna, came to Eishyshok and toured it that day — an ominous sign, since his name had come to be associated with the murder of Jews in other shtetlekh in the vicinity.[6]

Accompanying Dr. Wulf were a few members of Strike Commando 3, which reported to Dr. Franz Walter Stahlecker, the head of one of the four Einsatzgruppen companies. Stahlecker's Einsatzgruppe A, numbering about a thousand men, was attached to Army Group North, whose area of operations covered the Baltic states as well as all the territory between their eastern border and the district of Leningrad. The SS had begun training members of the Einsatzgruppen in early May, even before Operation Barbarossa, for the men chosen for the mobile killing squads had to be carefully prepared for their murderous job. Their targets, according to the instructions transmitted in a meeting on July 2, 1941 — the first time instructions regarding the Einsatzgruppen had been issued in writing — were Soviet political officials and "Jews in the [Communist] Party"; in reality, however, their chief objective was the death of all the Jews, not just the Communist ones.

That morning of September 21 a written decree was issued in the name of Gebietskommissar Wulf, and signed by police chief Ostrauskas and the mayor of Eishyshok (a Polish official the Germans had put in charge of the shtetl), stating that within two hours the Jews were to hand over all their remaining gold, silver, and other valuables; later that day they were to report to one of the three houses of prayer in honor of Rosh Hashanah. The Judenrat was responsible for implementing the decree.

Avraham Kaplan, the chairman of the Judenrat, came to Moshe Sonenson to discuss the situation. Moshe gave Kaplan his assessment: The shtetl is standing on the edge of the grave. Then he handed over to Kaplan a huge, black, brass-trimmed trunk and various family valuables, which were carried away by other members of the Judenrat.[7] Moshe's daughter Yaffa was very upset, for the trunk was what she sat on in order to reach the kitchen table, and she thought of it as belonging to her.

Lithuanian shaulisti (shooters) appeared in the shtetl around noon.[8] The shaulisti, local collaborators with the Germans, included both civilian volunteers and former members of the Lithuanian army, so while some of them were in uniform, others appeared in the simplest of peasant garb, barefoot, with their pants held up by ropes instead of belts. Armed with knives as well as guns, the shaulisti took up their positions throughout the shtetl, on every street and alley as well as the market square.

Dr. Franz Wulf (center), Gebietskommisar of the district of Vilna, with Theodore von Renteln (left), the German commissioner general of Lithuania, and Petras Kubiliunas, the Lithuanian commander.
YESC

Rumors started to circulate that a ghetto would be formed. Women, children, and the elderly would be housed in the ghetto, while able-bodied men would be sent away to labor camps. The rumors about the ghetto in combination with the permission to attend Rosh Hashanah services created false hope. But by then the sacred buildings were three empty, desecrated shells, and the presence of so many agents of death could not be ignored. Debates about what to do — comply with the orders or run away — were taking place in homes throughout the shtetl.

In the Kabacznik family the debate was fierce. The widow Sorl went to her old friend Yossl Weidenberg for advice. Yossl, one of those who had opposed Rabbi Rozowski's call to arms in the belief that the Germans were interested only in robbing the Jews, not killing them, suggested they stay in the shtetl and wait for the ghetto to be built. But Yossl was overruled by Sorl's children, Meir, Miriam, Shepske, and Goldke, who had decided that they had to flee. In the Lubetski home, Zalman and his brother Akiva also

The family of school principal Moshe Yaakov Botwinik: (top row, right to left) Layzer, a relative; daughter Fania-Aliza; and son Leibke; (middle row, right to left) two relatives named Rakow; Shoshana and Moshe Yaakov. Standing in front of his father is the youngest son, Avremele; next to him is daughter Zipporah. Sitting on the floor are sons Hilel (right) and Yitzhak. They all managed to escape the September 1941 massacre, but only Avremele survived the war, as a partisan; the rest of the family were killed in Ghetto Radun by the AK and Russian partisans. PHOTO: ALTE KATZ. YESC, EPSTEIN-BOTWINIK

decided to escape, confident that their many Christian and Tatar friends in the countryside would help them; the Lubetski brothers would then be able to smuggle food into the ghetto to sustain their aging parents and other family members. The Kaganowicz men — Shael and his sons Leibke and Benjamin — made a similar decision. Since it was believed that the men were more at risk than the women and children, they thought it best to leave while they still could, and they would meet up with the women — mother, daughter, and aging grandmother — later.[9] The Botwinik family escaped en masse: school principal Moshe Yaakov, his wife Alte, daughter Fania, and four sons, Leibke, Yitzhak, Hillel, and Avremele. Leibke took his leave of his fiancée, Shoshana Katz, promising to come back for her as soon as he had secured a safe hiding place.

When Moshe Sonenson found that he could not convince his wife Zipporah to escape, he decided to proceed with plans to save his two older children, nine-and-a-half-year-old Yitzhak and four-and-a-half-year-old Yaffa. He told Yaffa to go to the house of her nanny, Zoszka Aliszkewicz, on Pigs Lane. Yitzhak was to go to the nearby home of Zoszka's brother Jaszka. Dressed in their festive Rosh Hashanah clothing — Yitzhak in a gray suit, Yaffa in her black patent leather shoes and a powder blue dress with a white lace collar and a smocked bodice — the two children said goodbye to their parents and kissed their baby brother, who slept peacefully in their mother's arms. As they made ready to leave, the house looked calm and festive, the table set with beautiful silver candlesticks for the holiday meal, the air filled with the aroma of freshly baked hallah. Though they had no way of knowing they would never see that house again, they knew something was terribly amiss, and just as they were about to set out they heard their mother ask their father to take off his wedding band. She took it from him, removed her own as well, and, together with a pair of family-heirloom earrings, hid them in a cavity behind a picture on the wall, saying, "This I will never give to the Germans!"

With that, the children were sent on their way, taking separate paths to their two different destinations. After they left, Moshe did too, hoping to find a place to hide until he could collect his children, and make some kind of arrangements for Zipporah and baby Shaul.

Late that afternoon, as Rosh Hashanah was about to begin, the shaulisti went from house to house, brandishing their knives and their guns, looting whatever they could conceal beneath their clothes, and chasing the Jews to the synagogue. Soon the streets were filled with Jews, racing to comply with the orders. At the entrance to each of the three houses of prayer the Germans stood with baskets and pails, commanding the Jews to throw in all their jewelry and currency. Velvke Katz, the shtetl turncoat, tried to bargain with the Germans to spare his wedding band, but to no avail.[10]

The crowd at the New Beth Midrash included Maneh Michalowski and his family, who were huddled together on the floor, trying to find sitting space for themselves. Maneh was deeply concerned about what would happen to his daughter Judith, who was on the German wanted list as a Communist.[11] Already the Germans had killed one Jewish family for being Communists. When his son Zvi noticed that a window in the tailors' shtibl was open and unguarded, he took Judith by the hand and climbed out with her. Under cover of night, the two of them walked, undetected, the eight miles to Radun.

The same open window allowed Moshe Sonenson to enter the New Beth Midrash that night to speak to his wife. Pleading with her to leave with him, he told her that the Germans would kill the men first, and then the women and children; that there was no hope for any of them unless they escaped now. But she still refused to go without her mother, who remained convinced that all would be well in the end. Once again he left his wife, swearing that he would somehow save her. The next step in his plan was to pick up his children. As he was racing through the gardens behind Pigs Lane on his way to Zoszka's, the Lithuanian shaulisti opened fire on him. Through the window of Zoszka's house Yaffa saw a man fall to the ground amid a burst of gunfire, but she did not realize the man was her father. Unwounded, Moshe lay low until just before dawn, when he continued his flight, realizing that it was not yet safe for him to try to be reunited with Yaffa and Yitzhak. On the outskirts of Mill Street he saw the Gestapo evacuating Lipa the blacksmith, and he was once again fired upon by the shaulisti. But again he was able to evade the hail of bullets, and this time he made it to the border, crossing over the river near Rubishok into Byelorussia.

That same Monday morning found Zvi Michalowski back in Eishyshok. In the darkness just before sunrise, he planned to save his brother David, just as he had rescued his sister. But the window to the tailors' shtibl in the New Beth Midrash was now closed and guarded, and Zvi was spotted by several shaulisti, who hauled him away to the Old Beth Midrash. There conditions were so crowded that it was impossible to find a place to stand. Things got even worse when the men from Olkenik, Leipun, and Selo were brought to Eishyshok, and many of them were added to the crowd in the Old Beth Midrash. Later, some of the women and children were brought in, too. The stench and the noise of so many people kept in such a confined space, without food, drink, or any place to relieve themselves, were overwhelming.

Conditions became even more hellish in the Old Beth Midrash when the Germans appointed about two hundred of the mentally ill from Selo as "overseers."[12] The Germans stood on the bimah in the center of the room enjoying the spectacle of the Seloyer meshuggoim lording it over everybody else. Everywhere one looked, the "overseers" were jumping over people, beating them, screaming hysterically. What had been a sacred space for the expression of a people's highest aspirations — their love of learning, their charity, their compassion for all mankind — was now transformed into a hall echoing with wild, subhuman laughter. Zvi Michalowski nearly lost his life as a powerful meshuggener picked him up and tried to squeeze him into the small sink in the polesh.

Szeina Blacharowicz was part of the crowd in the main synagogue, where her brother Yehiel was sitting with Shepske Sonenson and Mordekhai Replianski, talking about the possibilities for escape. But Replianski, one of the last of the shtetl kultur treggers (culture carriers) was more of a realist: "Soon we will all be gone. Only the walls of the shul will stand as silent witnesses to what happened to us." As Szeina looked out the window the morning of September 22, she saw Rabbi Rozowski being led down the street to the Old Beth Midrash by two men in civilian clothes. Walking with his head held high, the rabbi was wearing his formal attire: black silk coat, striped pants, and top hat.

That afternoon Yaffa Sonenson stood looking out another window. Yaffa, who had not stopped crying for her mother since arriving at the home of Zoszka Aliszkewicz, was watching the slow, rumbling procession of carriages filled with goods that had been looted from Jewish homes. For while the Jews remained locked in the three prayerhouses, Poles from Eishyshok and the vicinity were busy plundering their neighbors' homes, taking everything they could pile into their wagons and carriages. On top of one of the carriages Yaffa spotted some of her own family's belongings: furniture, candlesticks, a clock, a beautiful porcelain dog, her favorite doll.

Later a shepherd boy came by Zoszka's house. Moshe Sonenson had paid him to take his children out of Eishyshok. Zoszka and her brother Jaszka put peasant outfits over the children's fancy Rosh Hashanah clothing, and then the shepherd led Yaffa and Yitzhak to the outskirts of town, where their father awaited them. As the family crossed the river on their way to the village of Paradin, Yaffa saw the bodies of Hayya Fradl Zlotnik Broide and her sister Bluma Zlotnik Michalowski lying in a puddle of blood on the riverbank. "Why are they sleeping by the river?" she asked. "They were killed last night," Moshe explained. "Now they are dead, and dead people never wake up from their sleep."

Sisters Bluma Zlotnik Michalowski (right) and Hayya Fradl Zlotnik Broide. They were murdered by Lithuanian shaulisti as they tried to escape the September 1941 massacre. Their dead bodies were the first Holocaust victims little Yaffa Sonenson witnessed. YESC, BERKOWITCH

In Paradin they briefly took refuge with the Mitnatz family, Polish friends in whose home they saw many of their own looted belongings, including a lamp with a hand-engraved brass base that was a favorite of Zipporah's. From Paradin they went to Radun, arriving there Wednesday night, but in Radun some of the local Poles were assisting the Gestapo in the hunt for escaped Eishyshkians, so they immediately left Radun for Vasilishok, where they had good friends. Wednesday night they slept in the home of a Jewish farmer outside Radun, Thursday night in the home of another Jewish farmer outside Vasilishok, and Friday they finally arrived in Vasilishok — in great uncertainty and suspense about what had happened to Zipporah and Shaul and the rest of their family.

TO THE HORSE MARKET

Wednesday, September 24, dawned cloudy and foggy. After three nights and two days of being locked up without food, water, or toilet facilities of any kind, on the third day the Jews of Eishyshok saw the doors of their prisons flung open. Driven outside and told to proceed to the Horse Market, they looked at one another in the dim light of that day, and saw they did not resemble the people who had entered the prayerhouses on Sunday. Years had been added to their faces.

The march to the Horse Market began. Nearly five thousand tired, thirsty, hungry, and frightened Jews filled the streets, their numbers drawn not just from Eishyshok itself, but from Olkenik, Leipun, Selo, and from many of the small villages under Eishyshok's jurisdiction, including Kalesnik, Dumbla, Arodnoy, Nacha, Rubishok, Dociszki, and Okla. Many of the children could barely walk. It was the Fast of Gedalia, but many of the Jews were already on their third day of fasting, having given whatever food they had with them to the children, the elderly, and the sick.[13]

Fruml Blacharowicz, her son Yehiel, her daughters Szeina and Gutke, her brother Leibke Kaganov and his wife Ida, along with their two small children Motele and Shifrale, were part of this exhausted group moving toward the Horse Market. As they passed through the market square, Szeina looked back at their house, its doors and windows wide open so that the lace curtains fluttered in the wind as if waving goodbye. Her aunt Ida said, "They are going to kill us," pointing to the Germans and Lithuanians who seemed to be everywhere, standing guard, and the Poles who were walking around carrying shovels. Szeina remembered a line from *Hatikvah*, the anthem of the Zionist movement. "Our hope is not yet lost," she hummed. "You must have lost your mind," her sister Gutke told her. "I will not let them shoot me in the back," Szeina responded, and at that moment she had a premonition that they would escape.

Poles stood around watching the commotion in the market square, laughing, looting, and keeping an eye out for valuables, for many people did not have the strength to continue carrying the few items they'd managed to take with them into the prayerhouses. Others, like Zlatke Garber, who was carrying her cousin Gutke Kanichowski's little daughter Itzle while Gutke struggled along with her two younger children, had to cast their bundles aside so that they could help their friends and families.

As the Blacharowicz family was about to enter the Horse Market, which was surrounded by Lithuanian shaulisti along with a handful of Germans, Yossl Kaplan, hatmaker and moving spirit of the shtetl theater, fell to the ground. When people rushed to help him, a German soldier from Strike Commando 3 chased them away and shot him in the head. His body was left where it lay, so that people had no choice but to trample over it as they were herded through the wooden fence. Once inside, families huddled together in the huge field, trying to protect and comfort one another. Zvi Michalowski's younger brother David, a boy in his early teens, whom Zvi had been unable to spirit out of the New Beth Midrash, was so frightened that he hid under his mother's skirt.

A Lithuanian came into the Horse Market, list in hand. Reading from the list, which had been supplied by local Poles, he called out the names of a number of the prettiest girls in the shtetl, who were then taken away. When they came back late that afternoon, their clothes were ripped, their faces scratched, their hair disheveled. Some cried nonstop; others stared blankly into space, oblivious of their surroundings. They had been gang raped by the Germans and the Lithuanian shaulisti.

Rabbi Szymen Rozowski was also taken away. Two Germans ordered him to show them where the Jews had buried their treasures, but when they returned later that day, they were empty-handed, and the rabbi was unharmed. The sight of their rabbi, so dignified and composed, and miraculously showing no signs of the four-day ordeal, gave strength to the people.

Rabbi Rozowski now addressed his congregation for the last time. In a loud, clear voice he said, "My dear Jews, we are lost and doomed!" The yeshivah students in the Horse Market then began to recite the Shema Israel, the Jewish proclamation of faith, the prayer that was forever on the lips of Jewish martyrs everywhere. All joined in the prayer, young and old alike, down to the littlest ones in their mothers' arms, and even the lunatics from Selo, the tearful voices of the entire crowd issuing from the depths of their hearts and souls: "Hear, O Israel, the Lord our God, the Lord is One!"

Ostrauskas kept circling the Horse Market on his motorcycle, gunning the motor and barking out orders: "All must remain seated, and anyone who has any valuables must turn them in immediately. Anyone who disobeys these orders will be shot." His Lithuanian henchmen, the police and the shaulisti, were clubbing people with their rubber truncheons, demanding, "Jews, give money!" Some Jews, like Hayyim Berkowski from Olkenik, tore their money into shreds rather than give it to the wild, screaming bandits; but most others tried to hide their money, which they saw as their last hope, something that could perhaps be used for bribes and barter if they ever managed to escape.[14]

A light rain began to fall. Exhausted by the events of the last four days and overcome by the fresh air of the outdoors after the stench of their prison, many people fell asleep; others continued to recite Psalms in the darkness. Around one or two o'clock that night, about ten SS men from Strike Commando 3 arrived on motorcycles. Their capes bore the skull-and-bones insignia, and they aimed their huge flashlights on the crowd, seeming to take special pleasure whenever they caught a bearded man in their beams. This would cause them to burst into laughter and screech insults about the "Ostjuden" (East European Jews). As they kicked their way through the crowd, stepping on people and spitting at them, their flashlights revealed a beautiful young girl. They ordered her to stand up and undress. She stood but did not undress. When they told her she would be shot if she did not obey, she continued to stand, motionless, until the Germans encircled her and began to rip off her clothing. She fell to the ground, striking out against her attackers while trying to hold on to her clothes. Suddenly they let her go, drew their machine guns from their shoulders, and emptied them into her body. Then they drove away on their motorcycles, leaving a deadly silence in their wake.[15]

THE SLAUGHTER OF THE MEN

On Thursday September 25 at six o'clock in the morning, as people were in the midst of their morning prayers, the Lithuanian police and the shaulisti ordered all the adult males in the Horse Market to stand. Selecting 250 young, healthy men, many of them leaders of the community, they ordered the group to line up five abreast and prepare to march into the Seklutski forest, where they would build the ghetto for the women and children. As the men were about to leave the Horse Market, Alte Katz ran after her two sons, David and Avigdor, and gave them a jar of honey, "to give you energy for your work."

Rabbi Szymen Rozowski, the hazzan Moshe Tobolski, and Rabbi Avraham Aaron Waldshan, the rabbi of Olkenik, were at the head of the procession. As they neared the Old Cemetery they began to chant the Vidduy, the confession recited on the verge of death. Back at the Horse Market, the sounds of machine-gun fire echoed in the air, from the direction of the Old Cemetery.

Three hours after the first group of men left, the shaulisti returned to the Horse Market and ordered the remaining men to stand up. As the Lithuanians began to make their selection, pandemonium broke out, for many people now clearly understood that the men were being taken off to be killed. Berl Lifshitz from Olkenik was discovered hiding under his wife's coat, with his little girl on top of him. When the shaulisti found him, they clobbered him about the head with their truncheons and ordered him to join the group that was lining up. As he was led away, his wife Sarah kept screaming, "Berl, escape, run away, avenge our deaths!" About this same time, the daughter of Shlomo the Amalekite began to give birth, as the midwife Gurewitch and several other women rushed to assist her.

Amid all the screaming and the hysteria, the Lithuanians began to shoot into the crowd. Fearing that the chaos would develop into a riot and that people would escape in droves, they soon switched tactics, however. Water was brought into the Horse Market and distributed, and reassuring words were spoken. "Why do you scream? Your men are working; no harm has come to them." Then a Yiddish-language letter was read, supposedly written by Leibe Milikowski to his wife. "All is well," he was quoted as saying. "Some men are at work on the highway, others are building a ghetto for the women and children." The shots they had heard were harmless ones fired into the air, according to the letter.

Berl Lifshitz did not believe a word of it. As his column began to move, he could think of one thing only: escape. At a bend in the road he ran away, Lithuanian bullets whistling after him as he jumped a wooden fence and raced toward a big barn. Hiding in the hay, he was so close to the Horse Market he felt sure he could hear the voice of his wife calling, "Berl, Berl," and his daughter Rive-Rochele softly crying, "Papa, Papinka . . ."[16]

By the early hours of Friday morning, Berl had made his way to Radun, where he described what was happening in Eishyshok, a mere eight miles away, and tried to warn the Jews of Radun that the same thing would soon happen to them. Some thought that he had lost his mind. Others felt that the events could be explained rationally by the fact that Eishyshok had a number of prominent Jewish Communists, or else by the fact that Eishyshok was a "wealthy" shtetl, nothing like Radun, a poor little rural shtetl where the grave of the Haffetz Hayyim was the only interesting feature. Since Berl's prime concern was to try to save the lives of his wife and child, he had no time to argue. Instead, he located a Christian who was willing to go to Eishyshok and attempt to sneak his loved ones out of the Horse Market.

Late Thursday afternoon, the Germans and Lithuanians had fallen behind schedule in their executions. To hasten the proceedings, some of the Jewish men were taken away on carriages driven by local Poles. When Yehiel Blacharowicz was pushed onto a carriage being driven by Yashka Sinkewicz, his sister Szeina ran after him and offered Sinkewicz ten dollars to take her, too, but he refused. Lithuanian policemen chased her away.

As the last group of men began to line up five abreast, Zvi Michalowski made a sixth as he went to join his father, Maneh Michalowski, who was standing with his son David and three other men. The Lithuanians were driving them like cattle, beating them with the butts of their guns and their rubber truncheons. This last group was joined by carriages transporting the sick, who had been taken from their hospital beds.

When they reached the Old Cemetery, Zvi saw that the deep trenches that had once served the purpose of keeping cattle away from the sacred ground were now a mass grave. The trenches were filled with the bodies of men, overflowing with a river of blood. Nearby was a huge pile of clothing. Zvi's group, too, were told to undress, and to add their own clothes to the pile. As Zvi undressed he stood next to his rosh yeshivah, Rabbi Zusha Lichtig, who was comforting his sons and reciting Psalms 91:2–3 with them: "I will say of the Lord, who is my refuge and my fortress, My God, in whom I trust, that He will deliver thee from the snare of the fowler . . ."

Grabbing his own father's hand as they neared the edge of the grave, Zvi envied Zusha's sons for having a father who was such a pillar of strength even in the face of death.

Just before the next volley of gunfire rang out, Zvi noticed a German gunman kneeling near the pile of clothing, a machine gun cradled in his lap. At precisely that moment Zvi felt Maneh pushing him into the grave, then falling on top of him, mortally wounded, his body Zvi's shield. Then came more shots, and more bodies.

Zvi lay still for a long time. It became darker and darker in the grave, and wet and hot and stifling. Some men kept moaning for a while, and occasional shots continued to sound. Then all fell silent. Immobilized at first by the weight of the bodies around him and the stiffness of his own, which was covered in dried blood, Zvi gradually managed to push the bodies aside and crawl out of the open grave. Except for a stinging sensation at the back of his neck where he had been slightly wounded, he seemed unharmed.

He walked shivering in the night, stopping at several houses to ask for shelter. Everywhere he was told, "Jew, go back to the grave where you belong." Finally he came to a farmhouse about two miles outside the shtetl. When the frightened woman who answered the door gave him the same response, he told her he was Jesus Christ who had come down from the cross on an earthly mission. Zvi was let into the house, given food and fresh clothing, and allowed to clean himself off, before going back out into the darkness.[17]

THE SLAUGHTER OF THE WOMEN

After the men had been killed, only a few shaulisti remained to guard the women in the Horse Market, for it was assumed they would be too frightened to try to escape. Most of the killers were out on the town, celebrating the murder of the men; other soldiers had been sent to Troki to get more bullets for the murder of the women and children, for supplies were running low. Thus on Thursday it was possible for a few brave souls to approach the women and discuss plans for getting them out. Moshe Sonenson's and Shoshke Wine's families both owed their lives to the eleventh-hour interventions of these local Poles, as did a number of other people, including Dobke Kremin, the Blacharowicz women, and the Kaganowicz women (Miriam, her daughter Freidke, and her mother Libe-Gittel Rudzin, whose rescuer extracted payment in the vodka he knew they had hidden in their house).

According to the plan Moshe Sonenson had worked out with them before leaving Eishyshok, Jaszka and Zoszka Aliszkewicz went to the Horse Market that afternoon to try once again to get his wife Zipporah to leave. She begged her mother and her sister, one last time, to come with her, but Alte Katz, still trusting that the Germans would turn out to be as civilized as their fathers had been in the last war, again refused to go. And Shoshana would not go unless her mother did. This time Zipporah decided she would have to part company with them if she were to have any chance of saving her infant son Shaul and being reunited with her husband Moshe and her other two children. Donning a kerchief that the Aliszkewiczes had brought so that she would look like a peasant, she tried to slip through the crowd at the entrance, but one of the shaulisti became suspicious. To buy his silence she gave him her beautiful embroidered sheepskin jacket, then climbed aboard the Aliszkewicz carriage. A local Pole recognized Zipporah, however, even beneath the kerchief, and tipped off the Lithuanian police.

A few minutes later Jaszka Aliszkewicz realized they were being followed. Stopping by a nearby field, he found a haystack where Zipporah and the baby could hide, then continued on his way. When their pursuers caught up with him, they searched the carriage but could find nothing. They were similarly unsuccessful as they thrust their pitchforks into the haystacks that lined the road, for Zipporah and Shaul had hidden in a haystack that was far back in the field. The Lithuanian and the Pole finally returned to Eishyshok without their quarry. Later that evening Jaszka retraced his path back to Zipporah, who was waiting for him with the baby sleeping in her arms. Their next stop was Radun, where Moshe had arranged for them to be sheltered by the Rogowski family. But by the time Zipporah and Shaul arrived Thursday night, Moshe and the children had already left and started on their way to Vasilishok.

Back at the Horse Market, Yashka Sinkewicz, who had transported many of the Jews to their death in his horse-drawn carriage, managed to speak with the beautiful Shoshke Wine early Thursday evening. "All the men have been killed," he said. Pointing to the coat he was wearing, which had belonged to a man she knew well, and which he hoped would demonstrate the veracity of his account, he told her, "Benyomin Tshorny is dead, too. He gave me this coat before he was shot. Now that all the men are dead, they will start killing the women and children. Tonight I will come back and help you escape." Standing near them was one of the few Lithuanian shaulisti who was native to the area, and was therefore acquainted with many of the people he had just helped to murder. He was newly returned from the killing fields, and clearly drunk. "How could you do it?" Shoshke demanded. "It was difficult to shoot the first Jew," he whispered. "But they gave us a lot to drink, and then it was easier to kill the rest of the ———."

That night Sinkewicz returned, along with another old friend of Shoshke's, Szczesnolewicz the hangman, who had tried to convince her to run away some days earlier. Through a hole in the wooden fence they helped Shoshke, her son Ben-Zion, and a number of her relatives to escape. They had a close call when a shaulist noticed them and fired a shot; but Sinkewicz told him that Shoshke's son was his nephew, and the man let them go. Shoshke's cousin Zlatke Garber, Shoshke's sister Gutke Yurkanski Kanichowski, Gutke's three children, and Gutke's sisters-in-law Kreinele Kanichowski and Ida Kanichowski Kaganov and Ida's two children all got out. Earlier that evening Shoshke had asked other relatives to join them in their escape attempt, including one of the girls who had been raped, and a married woman, but they declined. The girl felt that after what had happened to her, life was worthless; in the wake of the death of her husband and other family members, the woman also found life too meaningless to go through the struggle she knew lay in store for them.

Three of the women in the photo managed to escape from the Horse Market, with the help of Yashka Sinkewicz: (standing, right), Ida Kanichowski Kaganov; seated Sarah Moszczenik, her sister Liebke (standing), Shoshke Wine, and Marsha Kanichowski Yurkanski. Ida, Shoshke, and Marsha escaped with their children; Liebke had run away a few days earlier with her husband and son. Sarah emigrated to America, Marsha survived the war, Shoshke was killed by a Russian partisan, Ida by local Poles, Liebke by the AK.
PHOTO: YITZHAK URI KATZ. YESC, YORK-YURKANSKI

After leaving the Horse Market, Yashka Sinkewicz led them all to the stable in back of his house on Radun Street. His wife, however, came to warn them away. Festively attired in looted clothing and jewels — items that belonged to people they all knew, people who were at that very moment sitting in the Horse Market waiting to be executed — she told them they would have to leave, for there was a crowd in the house, including a number of shaulisti, who were having a drinking party in celebration of the death of the Jews. They quickly went out into the dark, moonless night, where they could see the dim

Zlatke Garber Paikowski ran away from the Horse Market with her cousin Shoske Wine. Zlatke survived the war as a partisan. YESC, PAIKOWSKI

shadows of other escapees, one of whom, Nehama Matikanski, joined them. Together they made their way to the home of a Christian friend in the village of Dociszki, who welcomed them with open arms and fed them bread, honey, and warm milk. After they had rested, Sinkewicz took them to Radun.

One of the other groups who escaped that night consisted of Fruml Blacharowicz and her two daughters, Szeina and Gutke. Their dream was that they would somehow survive long enough to reach Eretz Israel and be reunited with Fruml's brother, Szymen Kaganov. They too were noticed by one of the shaulisti as they were about to escape through a gap in the wooden planks of the fence. The young, barefoot man, clad in pants held up by a rope, was armed. Szeina offered him her ring as a bribe for his silence, but he refused it, and allowed them to go. From the Horse Market they made their way to the house of Yashuk Kapitan, who lived at the end of Mill Street on the way to Rubishok — a non-Jew who spoke a fluent Yiddish and was known to them as a good, loyal friend. When they knocked on his door, he let them in. His wife was already in bed, her head barely visible amid piles of pillows and goosedown quilts looted from Jewish homes. The escapees slept in the barn that night, then hid in the hayloft the next morning, when workers came to the barn to thresh the wheat. Whenever the threshing stopped they could hear shooting from the direction of the Christian cemetery in Juryzdyki.

That night, Friday, Yashuk Kapitan asked them to leave; the situation was too dangerous. Nearing the village of Korkuciany, Szeina knocked on the window of a farmhouse where one of her Singer sewing machine customers lived. The farmer let them in, fed them bread, honey, and hot milk, and agreed to take a note from Szeina to the Rogowski family in Radun. When he returned he had a note from the Rogowskis: "All is safe. Come to Radun." Rallying quickly to the emergency, the Jewish community of Radun had bribed local officials to obtain residency papers for the refugees from Eishyshok, in order to protect them from the Gestapo's efforts to ferret out those who had escaped the nearby massacres. For the moment Radun was a haven.

The shots the Blacharowicz family had heard from the direction of Juryzdyki Friday morning, September 26, were the sounds of the women and children being killed. Once again the killings took place at the hands of the Lithuanian shaulisti and the soldiers of German Strike Commando 3. Anxious to be more efficient about the process than they had been with the men, especially since the combined total of women and children was approximately twice the number of the men, they used horse-drawn carriages to transport many of them, particularly the elderly, as well as the mothers with very young children. Thus Friday's victims were quick to reach their final destination, a huge, freshly dug pit near the Catholic cemetery in Juryzdyki. By the time Berl Lifshitz's emissary reached the Horse Market that day, all the women and children, including

Hayya-Rochl Layzerowski was one of several women who gave birth in the Horse Market. On September 26, 1941, she and her baby were taken to the killing fields in a horse-drawn carriage with the other women and children. YESC, ELLIS

On September 26, 1941, horse-drawn carriages stopped in front of the hospital and took to the mass graves the sick, as well as mothers who had just given birth and their newborn infants. Nehama Paikowski (right) was among the patients who were taken from the hospital to the killing fields. Her friend, Freeda Yurkanski, was also murdered that day. YESC, PAIKOWSKI

Berl's wife and daughter, had been taken away. He returned to Radun that night, empty-handed.[18]

As it happened, two young men who had escaped the massacre the day before, Leibke Kaganowicz and his brother Benjamin, had found shelter behind the stone walls of that cemetery, and thus became accidental witnesses to all that followed. As they scanned the huge crowd of women and children, they were unable to locate their mother, sister, and grandmother. Hardly daring to hope that they had escaped, the two brothers saw horror after horror unfold before their eyes. They saw women with babies in their arms and older children clinging to their bodies marched to their deaths, the gun butts and the rubber truncheons of their murderers hurrying them on their way. They watched as all were made to undress.

Then many of those who were young were separated from the others and dragged into the bushes to be raped, and raped again by soldier after soldier and policeman after policeman. . . .

My mouth opened to scream, but I could not. I wanted to close my eyes, but they would not close.

"Don't look, Leibke! Don't, Leibke!" Benjamin sobbed, and pulled at me to leave the wall.

I didn't want to look, but I couldn't stop looking. I saw the Lithuanians shoot the breasts off some of the women, and shoot others in the genitals. . . . I saw my aunt die in a volley of gunfire. I saw my beautiful cousin raped and raped until death must have been the only thing she longed for.

My fingers slipped from the wall and I fell beside my brother, retching and sobbing. He clung to me.[19]

The horrors went on and on. Ostrauskas separated some of the youngest children from their mothers. As the women screamed for their children, whom they wanted to hold and comfort during these last moments of their lives, Ostrauskas carefully carried out his own plans for them. After requesting a coat he could wear to shield his uniform, he picked the children up, one by one, and smashed them against some nearby boulders, spattering his hands and the coat he had borrowed with the blood of his small victims.

Hayya Sonenson went to her death surrounded by members of her family: her daughter Hinda Tawlitski and Hinda's four children, who were never able to get the papers they needed to emigrate to America, where Hinda's husband awaited them; her daughter-in-law Geneshe and Geneshe's little son Meir; and her daughter-in-law Ida with her two sons. According to the account Jaszka Aliszkewicz gave Moshe Sonenson, Hayya was praying at the edge of the grave:

Was she saying the Viddui, the confession of the dying? Was she praying for the safety of her three sons who had managed to escape, and who would perhaps one day reach Eretz Israel?

Was she grateful for the fact that she would be buried in the soil of Eishyshok, as her ancestors had been for eight hundred years?

A volley of bullets mowed down the Sonenson family, one after another.

One of Hinda's children screamed, "Help me, I have a father in America!" And then she too fell into the grave.

Alte Katz met her death standing beside her daughter Shoshana and the wife of Mordekhai Replianski. Was it only when she arrived at the killing fields that she finally understood how different these new Germans were from the old Germans in whom she had had so much trust? As she fell into the common grave, one of the villagers who had gathered to watch the massacre shouted in Polish: "Pani Katzowa, I need some medicine; take my picture, I am posing for you!"

Friday at sundown, after having been kept alive in order to witness wave after wave of death at the killing fields, after having been forced to watch the murder of thousands of people from his beloved flock, the rabbi himself was finally killed. According to some eyewitness accounts he was shot; according to others, a machine gun was fired over his head and he was then buried alive.

At sunset the murderers returned to town, singing and laughing and drinking. After removing his bloodstained coat, Ostrauskas joined the other Lithuanians and the Germans in the caravan of motorcycles that descended upon the shtetl. Once back in town, der Weisser Rekele, the Nazi commander whose elegant white jackets had given him his nickname, put a bullet through the head of his beloved white poodle, which had accompanied him to the killing fields. Asked why he had destroyed his constant companion, he explained he had had to do so because the dog had become smeared with Jewish blood.

No Sabbath chants were heard issuing from the desecrated shulhoyf that night; no Sabbath candles shone from the bare windows of the looted Jewish homes. A drunken Polish peasant who had dressed himself in the rabbi's holiday attire — his long black coat and silk top hat — was the only reminder of nine centuries of tradition, now ended. Standing in the middle of the market square, vodka bottle in hand, he was calling out in slurred, mocking Yiddish: "Yidden, in Shul arain!"

The German document in which the actions of Strike Commando 3 are recorded shows that 137,346 Lithuanian Jews were killed between July 4 and November 25, 1941. In an inventory of the dates and places of the massacres and the numbers of people killed in each, there is a one-line entry for Eishyshok.[20] It reports that on September 27, 1941, 989 Jewish men, 1,636 Jewish women, and 821 Jewish children from Eishyshok were killed, totaling 3,446 in all. This entry gives the lie to the much-vaunted accuracy of German documentation, for not one item in it is correct. The date of the massacre was not

September 27; the killings took place over two days, September 25, when the men were murdered, and September 26, when the women and children were murdered. By September 27, when the murders supposedly took place, all was quiet in Eishyshok and the vicinity, but for the numerous drinking parties attended by the Germans and Lithuanians and many of the local Poles as well. The murdered Jews were not just from Eishyshok; close to 1,500 from other villages were also among the victims. The total number of murdered Jews was not 3,446, but something closer to 5,000.

Detailed community studies that are based on firsthand accounts, census lists, and other local documents raise serious questions about the credibility of all German documentation, suggesting that there may be many hundreds of thousands of Jews unaccounted for in the official records. Perhaps the mistakes in this case could be attributed to alcohol — to the sloppiness of the local Strike Commando 3 official who may well have sent in his report after returning from one of the drunken gatherings celebrating the deaths of the Jews. But that is only speculation — unlike the facts concerning the number of Jews killed, and their places of origin.

On Sunday, September 28, 1941, the tolling of the bells at the Juryzdyki church called the people to worship, just as it did every Sunday, and the sanctuary was filled to capacity, just as it always was. The pews were lined with people in their Sunday best, which in many cases had been the Sabbath best of their dead Jewish neighbors, whose homes they had looted. Ostrauskas was there, too, and was observed to make confession. While the freshly covered graves were still moving and spouting blood, the parishioners listened to their priest explain to them that the Jews had at last been called to account for the killing of Christ. The priest himself had not advocated killing them; nor did he approve of the looting of Jewish homes. In fact, at least one account says that he asked anyone in the congregation wearing stolen Jewish clothes to leave (though no one did). But he seemed to feel that the murder was understandable. Even if it was wrong, a kind of justice had been done.

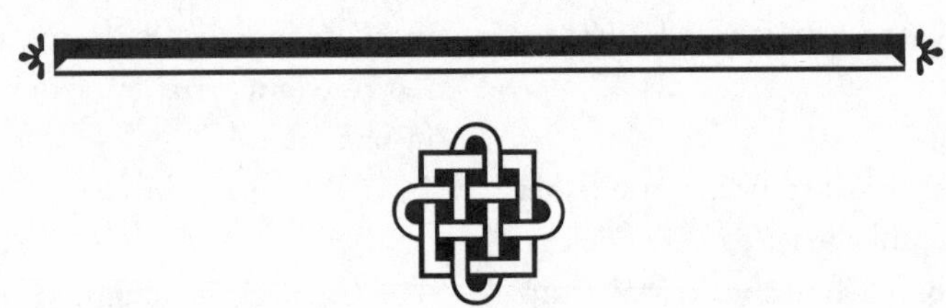

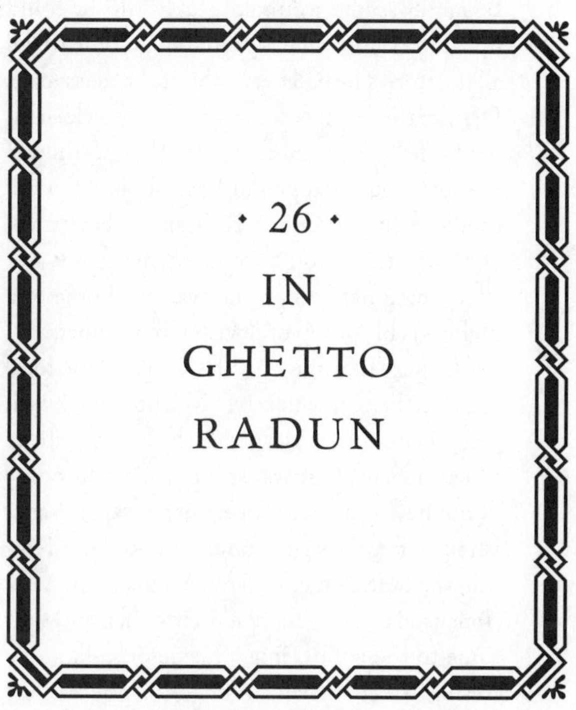

HERE IN RADUN WE WILL BE SAVED, SINCE THE GRAVE OF THE HAFFETZ HAYYIM WILL PROTECT US.

A common statement in Ghetto Radun

ABOUT 720 JEWS FROM EISHYSHOK AND THE VICINITY — OLKENIK, LEIPUN, SELO — managed to escape the massacre.[1] The majority of the males who were able to get away did so by ignoring the order to report to the three prayerhouses on September 21. At the time, many people believed that a ghetto was going to be built for the women and children, and that all the able-bodied men would be sent away to build it. Thus men were considered to be at the greatest risk, and many therefore decided that it was in their own as well as their families' best interest for them to go into hiding. From there they would perhaps be able to provide for their families, to remain in contact with them, and ultimately to spirit them away.

It was only when it became obvious that the men were not being sent away but were being massacred, and that the women and children were next, that women began considering escape. Most of the women and children who fled did so with the help of Christian friends.

Some of the escapees went into hiding with Christian and Tatar friends; most, however, went to the homes of Jewish friends and relatives in the vicinity. About 260 Eishyshkians found shelter in next-door Radun; about 70 fled to Warinowa; others went to Astrin, Vasilishok, Lida, and Grodno.

The escape of Moshe Sonenson and his family was typical. There were moments of great peril and interludes of safety; acts of hostility on the part of people they encountered as well as gestures of great kindness; deprivation and exhaustion followed by an occasional day of peace and plenty; and, wherever they went, glimpses into the ordinariness of life still being lived by people who thought they were exempt from danger.

After they left Radun to escape the Gestapo, Moshe and his two older children, Yitzhak and Yaffa, walked the nineteen miles to Vasilishok over the next two days, stopping to rest in the forest, eating berries and nuts. Farmers and shepherds who saw them asked, "Why do you try to escape? They will soon catch you and kill you." Some of the farmers had been in Eishyshok when the massacre took place, and they described everything they had seen. But no one tried to harm the Sonensons, or to detain them.

Arriving in Vasilishok on Friday, September 26, just as the massacre of the last group of women and children in Eishyshok was taking place, and Rabbi Rozowski was about to be killed, the Sonensons went directly to the home of Elchik Waletsinski, a former business associate and family friend. The table was set for the Sabbath, the air filled with the aroma of freshly baked hallah. It seemed to Moshe and his children that they had landed on another planet. Throughout the meal, with the entire Waletsinski family seated around the table, Moshe could not stop crying as he repeated in graphic detail all the stories he had heard about the massacres. Despite this grim account of events so close by, the Waletsinkis were convinced that nothing of the sort would happen in Vasilishok. After all, they concluded, unlike Eishyshok their town was not situated on a major highway, was not near a national border, and was not home to a highly visible group of Jewish Communists.

The next morning the Gestapo and the local Polish police came to arrest Moshe. Along with a number of other escaped Eishyshkians, about fifteen men in all, he was sent to jail for the crime of not having a resident permit to stay in Vasilishok. A few days later, on the fast of Yom Kippur, the police chief ordered Yitzhak and Yaffa Sonenson to bring food to their father, and they came to the jail bearing a bottle of milk and a freshly baked hallah. When the police chief brought out a gray-haired man with a swollen face all covered in blood, he asked the children if they knew this man, who was wearing their father's navy blue jacket and dark pants. Both shook their heads no. "Well, you don't want to feed strangers, do you?" And with that he threw the bottle of milk to the floor, shattering it into small pieces, and trampled the hallah beneath his feet. The man who was wearing their father's clothing stood there making strange, unintelligible noises, his mouth all swollen, his tongue hanging out like a piece of raw meat, until finally they managed to understand what he was saying: "I am your papa, I am your papa."[2]

After the men had languished in jail for nearly two weeks, members of the Vasilishok Judenrat were able to negotiate their freedom, by paying a handsome bribe to the police chief. The night of his release, Moshe Sonenson decided he and his two children had to leave Vasilishok, where he knew they were in danger, and begin their journey back to Radun, where they hoped to rejoin what was left of their family (for by this time, news of the safe arrival of Zipporah and baby Shaul had made its way from Radun). They spent the night hiding in a freshly dug, empty grave in a Christian cemetery in Vasilishok, then began their nineteen-mile walk to Radun at dawn. Little Yaffa was too tired to walk, but her father could not carry her for long distances because the wounds he had received in jail had left him weak. Finally, about five miles outside Radun, he stopped a Christian farmer going by in his carriage and asked him for a ride, paying him with the sweater he was wearing under his navy blue jacket.

In Radun, husband, wife, and three children were at last reunited in the home of Zalman Zakrowski, where Zipporah had gone to stay. Crying and hugging for a long time, Moshe and Zipporah, Yitzhak and Yaffa attempted to comfort one another on the murder of their entire extended family of 236 relatives. Meanwhile, baby Shaul slept peacefully on a pillow in the corner.

The day Moshe and his children arrived in Radun was Sunday, October 12, which was Hoshana Rabbah, the seventh day of the fall harvest festival of Sukkot. Soon after their arrival, the Sonensons went to see the Rogowskis, old family friends who were among the wealthiest families in Radun. At the Rogowski home they found the holiday preparations well under way, and the house filled with other refugees from Eishyshok. The sukkah was decorated, the house smelled of the willow sprigs that had been beaten against the ground in the annual ritual, and the spacious kitchen was the scene of elaborate preparations for Simhat Torah, the eighth day of Sukkot and the most festive day of the Jewish year. Szeina Blacharowicz and several other women from Eishyshok were part of the crowd cooking special holiday dishes.

Unlike many other people in Radun, the Rogowskis believed the accounts they had heard about the atrocities occurring nearby. Though they were attempting to celebrate the holidays in the traditional fashion, they knew that for thousands of people from the neighboring towns and villages, this was a season of deepest sorrow and loss, not joy and thanksgiving. One of their own sons had lost his wife in the previous month's massacres in Aran, and the young man himself had barely escaped to tell the terrible tale. Now the Rogowski home resounded with the stories of other escapees, those from Eishyshok, who were busy informing one another about the latest tragedies. Mrs. Rogowski told the Eishyshkian refugees, "The house is yours. You should make yourselves at home and take whatever you need, for if you don't it will soon be taken by our enemies."

Mr. Rogowski, however, felt sure that the Jewish community of Radun would be spared the worst horrors. Earlier that day Moshe Sonenson had picked up one of the beaten willow branches and said to his host, "This is how we look, bare and broken. Does God see our suffering? What does he want with the tears of Rabbi Rozowski, of my sainted mother . . ." — at which point Mr. Rogowski cut him off, reassuring him, "Here it will not happen. The grave of the sainted Haffetz Hayyim will protect us. Besides, we are in Byelorussia, where the Jews will be much safer than in Lithuania."

Shortly after Hoshana Rabbah, a ghetto was formed in Radun: the shtetl's Jews were forced to live within its boundaries. All Jews had to wear a yellow star and remain within the confines of the ghetto, unless they were sent out on a work detail. Except for a few Communists, most of the Eishyshkians were able to get residency rights in the ghetto by obtaining forged identification documents that stated they were natives of Radun.

Since the Rogowskis' and the Zakrowskis' spacious homes were outside the ghetto limits, they and all their guests had to find other housing. The Rogowskis were taken in by relatives; the Sonensons and a number of other refugees from Eishyshok and elsewhere moved in with Dobke di Gevirte (the rich woman), who had a large house as well as a big stable that could be used as living quarters. To maintain some illusion of privacy, each family marked off its own little corner of space with curtains made of sheets or jute sacks.

The ghetto was ruled by a German Gestapo group, which included one particularly friendly man who was nicknamed der Gutter Deutch (the good German), and another very cruel man by the name of Kopke, who was never seen without a cigar in his mouth. One of Kopke's favorite amusements was to watch people twisting slowly to their deaths on the gallows that he had ordered to be built in the center of the ghetto. He also enjoyed killing people himself, execution style, especially young girls.[3]

The other powerful group presiding over Ghetto Radun was the local police force, which was made up of Byelorussians, Lithuanians, and Poles. Some of the Poles were from Eishyshok, including Jan Gurak, former principal of the Polish school there, who now had a prominent desk job with the police force; Pietka Barteszewicz, a former caretaker at the Polish school; and a man named Zalusky, who had been a policeman in Eishyshok. There were also unarmed Jewish police in the ghetto: Yaakov Kowalski, who would survive the war; Lippa Skolski from Aran, formerly a high-ranking officer in the Polish army, who would also survive; Leibke Rogowski, later killed in Ghetto Grodno; and Leibke Haffetz from Eishyshok, who would eventually be murdered by the White Poles. All the police reported to Burgermeister (Mayor) Kulikowski, a former captain in the Polish army.

Though Kulikowski had been appointed to his job as administrative head of Radun by the Germans, he did not share their attitude toward the Jews. In fact, he employed a number of Jews in his home — especially pretty Jewish girls — and treated them well. Nonetheless, when required, he exhibited all the anti-Semitic ferocity his German masters expected of him.

Kulikowski was on particularly good terms with Noah Dolinski, the head of the Radun Judenrat, which made life in the ghetto easier than it would otherwise have been — though not for anyone suspected of being a Communist. The two men shared an intense dislike of Communists, each having had his own terrible experiences at their hands. Kulikowski's wife and children had been deported to Siberia, and he himself had narrowly escaped the 1940 deportation of Polish officers who were sent to Russia and later murdered in the Katyn forest.[4] Dolinski, one of the wealthiest men in Radun, had had both his home and his flour mill confiscated by the Russians. Thus when Radun police officer Pietka Barteszewicz denounced a woman from Eishyshok as a Communist, reporting her to Kulikowski, her fate was sealed.

The young woman was Judith Michalowski, who had been on a special wanted list in Eishyshok. Having escaped the massacre with the help of her brother Zvi, she had managed to reach Ghetto Lida and secure false papers in the name of Freilich, and from there to make her way to Radun, where unfortunately she was recognized by Barteszewicz, also from Eishyshok. Kulikowski turned the whole matter over to Dolinski, who asked some of the Eishyshkians who worked with the Judenrat, including Shalom Sonenson, whether the information regarding Judith's Communist past was true. Though Zvi emerged from his hiding place in the countryside to try to save his sister, it was to no avail. Dolinski had no sympathy for Communists, and sent Judith back to Lida. There her true identity was revealed, and she was executed.[5]

Berl Lipkunski was also accused of being a Communist, though in his case it was a false accusation made by a Christian farmer with whom he had once had a dispute over a bicycle. Berl's wife, fourteen-year-old son, and nine-year-old daughter were shot in the middle of the ghetto. Berl himself was taken to Lida and hanged.[6]

The Poles from Eishyshok who served on the Radun police force proved unpredictable to their former townsfolk, sometimes, as with Judith Michalowski, singling them out for death or for torture, sometimes assisting them in a variety of ways. Jan Gurak, for example, issued fake identity papers to a number of his fellow Eishyshkians, among them alumni of his school, such as the Kremin sisters Dobke and Blumke, Zlatke Garber and her cousin Shoshke Wine, and many others.

Life in the ghetto was hard. Healthy young people of both sexes were drafted to work in the Mieszczanca forest, cutting firewood for the German army. Used as virtual slave labor by the Germans, Poles, Lithuanians, and Byelorussians, they were given unrealistically high quotas, then punished severely when they couldn't meet them. Each week's contingent of slaves returned to the ghetto on Friday, to be replaced by the next shift, who would set off on the six-mile march in the bitter cold to perform their own grueling week of labor.

Men also worked in the nearby flour mill, on food details that supplied provisions for the German soldiers on the eastern front, and at various other tasks for the Germans as well as for the local Poles. Leibke Kaganowicz once went out with a group of shepherds charged with transporting two thousand sheep to the railway station at Bastun. Those who were employed as shepherds were in constant danger, for their Lithuanian escorts were cruelly ingenious in their punishments. There were beatings, of course, but also a "game" that was a particular favorite with the Lithuanians, in which they placed their victims in a pile, one atop another, to see how many they could kill with one bullet. To return alive to the ghetto after such an assignment was little short of a miracle.[7]

The Germans established a number of workshops in the ghetto itself, among them a tailor shop where men and women were put to work sewing uniforms as well as civilian clothing for the Germans and Poles. Most of these tailors were former Eishyshkians, including Moshe-Reuven Michalowski, Szeina Blacharowicz, and Nehama Matikanski and her sons Haikl and Yitzhak. Nehama was one of the women who had escaped the massacre by sneaking out of the Horse Market the night before; her sons had escaped by never reporting to the prayerhouses. Her husband Dovid, however, was lying in the mass grave at the Old Cemetery.

As the harsh winter descended on the ghetto, life became ever more difficult. Many hoped that the cold that was making things so hard for them would also help to hasten the defeat of Hitler's army on the eastern front. A minyan of ten men endangered their lives by going to pray at the grave of the Haffetz Hayyim, where they asked God to alleviate their suffering and to end the war. Instead, on January 5, 1942, one of the two assistants to the Gebietskommisar of Lida, a six-foot-tall German named Werner, arrived in Radun accompanied by his dog Donner (German for "thunder"). Everyone knew that Werner's visit meant death.

While little children in the ghetto were being hidden away and dosed with a liquid of boiled poppyseeds, in hopes that they would fall into a deep, silent sleep, Werner entertained himself with a hunting party in the woods near Radun. Returning empty-handed and angry, he and his men set out on another kind of hunting expedition, a house-to-house search for Jews from Lida who had no residence permits for Ghetto Radun. The Aktion (Oblawa in Polish) yielded about forty Jews — forty men, women, and children who had hoped to escape the severe hunger of the ghetto in Lida for a slightly more comfortable life in Radun. Now they were driven from the ghetto and told to run for their lives. As they did so, the Germans gunned them down, thus bringing Werner's hunting party to a successful conclusion. The Gebietskommisar's assistant was pleased. He had the bodies loaded onto sleds that were pulled back into the ghetto, leaving a trail of red blood on the white snow.

The police ordered the people of the ghetto to bury the dead, but the earth was frozen so hard that it was impossible to dig a grave. A native of Radun led them to a place he knew on the way to Bastun, a bomb crater from World War I, now filled with water from melting snow. Roaring with laughter, one of the Germans, Kopke the cigar-chewer, looked into the pit and announced: "Good to know they will have something to drink!" One little boy was discovered to be still alive, and the Jews managed to smuggle him back into the ghetto, but he died a few days later from his wounds.[8]

The suffering caused by beatings, sickness, cold, and grief was amplified by hunger. Trying to feed one's family was a never-ending task, worrying about it a ceaseless preoccupation, awake or asleep. Some were more fortunate than others, either in their own access to resources or in their connection to Christian friends who were able to get them much-needed supplies. Shalom Sonenson's maid Jasza smuggled enough food into the ghetto to feed him and his wife Miriam and their two little girls for the entire nine months they remained there. The Blacharowicz family were also blessed with help from a marvelous Christian friend, their former maid, Juszka.

Moshe Sonenson was at first fortunate enough to work for the local Catholic priest, who gave him bread. Later he was transferred to the flour mill, where he had another piece of luck, for his supervisor proved to be someone for whom he had once done a great favor. Some years before, the Polish agricultural minister, Stankewicz, had been visiting Eishyshok, when the car transporting him and his wife and several other notables overturned. Stankewicz and his wife were both slightly injured, and the driver of the car was put on trial. But Moshe Sonenson, who had been one of the passengers in the car, testified on behalf of the driver, thus saving him from a prolonged jail sentence. That driver was now his supervisor and was in a position to repay the favor, which he had never forgotten. He gave Moshe flour from the mill as well as food from his own home — gifts more valuable than gold. Moshe's young son Yitzhak, who was also on the work detail at the mill, used to smuggle those precious gifts back to the ghetto, hidden beneath a towel wrapped around his stomach, under his shirt. Back at home the Sonensons shared their good fortune with the other families in their overcrowded quarters, including Rebbetzin Fischer of Vilna and her two young children, Ita and Isser, who had no other source of food. The Fischers would survive the war and emigrate to the United States.

But some weeks the supervision at the mill was so strict that it was impossible to smuggle anything out. During those times the children were so hungry that they scratched the walls and ate paint. The baby was given melted snow sweetened with the taste of leaves.

Despite all the hardships, every effort was made to hold on to some of the old traditions and values. Clandestine services were conducted in private homes. People would get together to study a page of the Gemara. Certain families held occasional classes for small groups of children, and some people even managed to arrange private tutoring, using bread as payment, and hiring teachers like Moshe Yaakov Botwinik and his son Leibke, or Yitzhak Perski, a former teacher at Botwinik's Hebrew school who had married a woman from Radun. (He is part of the family that also produced Israeli politician Shimon Peres, who changed his name from Persky, and American actress Lauren Bacall, née Betty Joan Perske.)

Events on the religious calendar continued to be observed. On the eve of Hanukkah, in an attic facing the gallows, children were taught about the Festival of Lights. At Passover, matzot were baked from flour smuggled in from the mill. Occasionally even joyous personal events took place: Haikl and Yitzhak Matikanski both married girls they met in the ghetto. Szeina Blacharowicz gave birth to a beautiful little baby, Sarah'leh, who never met her soldier father, Motke Burstein, during her brief life.

Of course, many deviations from tradition had to be made. Acknowledging the reality of hunger, no less a figure than Rabbi Hillel, a member of the Haffetz Hayyim's family and the spiritual leader of the Radun ghetto, gave permission to the young and the sick to eat nonkosher meat (but forbade them to suck on the bones, so that they would not enjoy it too much). The children's games were also concessions to the drastically altered world they lived in, though the children themselves accepted that world as normal. Using dolls made of rags, they played games of make-believe around such themes as burying the dead who had been shot, telling the babies not to cry when the Germans and the police were nearby, and smuggling food past guards. And they quickly learned to divide the world into two types of children: those with grandparents, who were from Radun, and those without, who were from Eishyshok.

Winter slowly gave way, and spring came even to the gloomy ghetto. But many Eishyshkians became more depressed with each spring sunrise. They knew that the earth would soon be thawed, and it would once again be possible to dig mass graves.

One Friday night the Kabacznik family heard a knock on the window: it was Kazimierz Korkuc, a well-to-do Christian farmer from Korkuciany, come to take them away from Ghetto Radun. He had had a terrible dream about their impending fate, and wanted to save them. After a brief debate, Meir, Miriam, and Shepske once again overruled their mother, Sorl. Quickly packing their few belongings, they followed Korkuc into the darkness. Just outside the ghetto, his carriage was awaiting them. But the kindness of Korkuc was the exception, not the rule.

On Friday, May 8, 1942, the ghetto was surrounded, and the police received reinforcements. All working groups were returned to the ghetto, and no new details were sent in their place. Though the Germans had spread a rumor that they were about to depart, and many Radun natives dared to hope it might be true, the Eishyshkians knew that the Radun shehita was about to begin. There was more than enough evidence to validate their fear, and confirmation came from several key sources. Polish Burgermeister Kulikowski had tipped off the people working in his household — several pretty girls as well as Yossele Hamarski from Eishyshok — that the end was near. And Moshe-Reuven Michalowski, who was a tailor in one of the ghetto workshops, had asked Kopke what would happen to the Jews who had worked for the Germans. Kopke took his cigar out of his mouth and said, "We will murder you all." Other Germans, however, were completely closemouthed: one Gestapo man, a tailor by profession who had formed the habit of taking afternoon tea with Noah Dolinski, the head of the Judenrat, came to Dolinski's apartment as usual and said not a word about the impending danger.[9]

In each family, debates were raging about whether to run away, and who would stand a chance of surviving if they were to go into hiding. Clearly some individuals were stronger than others, and it would be necessary for families to split up. But that was a decision too painful for most to contemplate. Gutke Kanichowski, whose husband Haikl had already escaped the ghetto and gone into hiding in the countryside, was now alone with their three small children, whom she had rescued from the Horse Market in Eishyshok. With one baby in her arms and two little ones clinging to her sides, she said, "If three such beautiful angels have to go to the slaughter, I don't care to try to survive the war. Let Hitler win." Her sister, Shoshke Wine, couldn't accept that. She grabbed Gutke's older girl, Itzle, covered her up under her shawl, and together with her own son Ben-Zion, who was disguised as a shepherd boy, managed to escape from the ghetto.

Gutke's sisters-in-law Kreinele Kanichowski and Ida Kaganov, with Ida's two children Shifrale and Motele, left around this time also, as did Gutke and Shoshke's cousin Zlatke Garber, though it took two tries. After removing her yellow star, Zlatke tied a kerchief around her head, babushka-style, as the local peasants did, and started to walk over to the Aryan side of town. But somebody recognized her and shouted out that she was a Jew, and she had to run back. Her second attempt was successful. She walked through the backyard of the police station, expecting a bullet in the back every second, and passed unrecognized. Or so she thought. After liberation, Pietka Barteszewicz, one of the Polish policemen from Eishyshok, told her he saw her that day but decided to let her go.

On Saturday, May 9, when two truckloads of German soldiers arrived from Warinowa, it became clear to everyone that the ghetto was about to be liquidated. Some families went into hiding within the ghetto, other people took their chances at escaping, but most stayed put, not knowing what else to do. Mina Lipkunski, a native of Eishyshok, told her family that each of them must make an attempt to save themselves. Twelve-year-old Yekutiel, the youngest of her three sons, dressed himself up as a shepherd and tried to escape. But he was caught and told to pull his pants down, whereupon his circumcision betrayed him. After a severe beating, he was sent back to the ghetto to await the mass execution.

Meanwhile, Christian farmers began driving their carriages in from the countryside, ready to begin looting once the Jews were led to their deaths.

The next day, early in the morning, the Germans selected a hundred healthy men, including Moshe-Reuven Michalowski, Mina's husband Moshe-Dovid Lipkunski, Meir Stoler, and many other Eishyshkians, all of whom were given shovels and told they would be going to the cemetery to dig graves. Ordered to line up and start marching, they were closely guarded on both sides by a number of Polish, Lithuanian, and Byelorussian police, and led down the road toward the cemetery by two mounted Gestapo men, including the cigar-smoking Kopke, who was wearing a handsome uniform made for him by the Matikanski brothers and Moshe-Reuven Michalowski.

Suddenly, back in the ghetto, shots were heard from the direction of the cemetery — not the shots of an execution but of a rebellion, under the direction of Meir Stoler, a tall, husky Eishyshkian blacksmith known for his strength and heroism. Even the terrible humiliations of ghetto life had been unable to rob him of hope, or dampen his pride. At the head of the line of gravediggers, on the way to what he knew was his imminent death, he had hatched a plan for an uprising. The word was passed, reverberating down through the rows of marching men. "Since our fate is sealed, we must make an attempt to run away" was his reasoning. There was a place in the road where the bushes were high and the forest was near, and when they got to it he would tackle the two mounted Gestapo, Kopke and Berliner, while the others took care of the policemen. "It is shovels against automatic weapons, David against Goliath," he said, but they had nothing to lose and he was determined to try.

As they reached the designated place in the road, Stoler bent down, grabbed a handful of dirt, sand, and stones and threw it into the horses' eyes. Blinded, the horses went wild and started to gallop away, throwing their riders. In the resulting chaos the other men attacked the policemen, then scattered into the bushes. Kopke and Berliner gave chase on foot, their automatic weapons blazing. When Kopke spotted Moshe-Reuven Michalowski running down the road toward the bushes, he shot him in the face and leg, but his victim kept running and Kopke was unable to catch up to him. All in all, about twenty-five men were able to escape, including Stoler himself, as well as Moshe-Dovid Lipkunski and Moshe-Reuven Michalowski. The rest were killed.[10]

Back in the ghetto, many families had gone into hiding, including Moshe Sonenson's family. After outmaneuvering a German guard, the Sonensons made their way to an attic hayloft above a carriage house, but they were nearly ejected by the other Jews who were already hiding there. Nobody wanted a family with a baby, for fear that its crying would betray the hiding place. Stories about such incidents circulated from ghetto to ghetto, with the result that life for those with small children was even more precarious than for everybody else. At first Moshe tried to talk his way into the attic, assuring the others that the baby was well drugged with poppyseeds and would be kept so, but the ladder was pulled up and access denied, until, after an ugly struggle, Moshe managed to force his way in.

Moshe's brother Shalom also went into hiding, joining a number of other people who had found a place in the cellar of a house facing the gallows. But many, even those who could have found a hiding place, including Shalom's wife Miriam, refused to try. They saw no hope for Jewish survival under a Nazi occupation that had the overwhelming support of local collaborators, some of whom were the Jews' former friends, neighbors, and teachers. Miriam decided to go to the slaughter, and to take her two daughters, Gittele and Shulamit, with her. She dressed herself and the two girls in their best outfits and sprayed them all with perfume, for, as she said to the children, "We must look our best when we are at last reunited with our families in heaven." Miriam was joined by a number of other women from her building, whose husbands pleaded with them, but to no avail.

After the uprising near the cemetery, the Germans switched tactics. The next group of a hundred men they selected were issued geller schein (yellow cards) — the much-coveted passports to life. Each man in possession of the yellow permit, they were told, would be taken to the cemetery to help dig the mass grave, but he would be able to save himself, his wife, and two of his children from the general execution. As the hundred men stood waiting for their marching orders, they were forced to strip to the waist, then severely beaten with rubber truncheons. Moshe Yaakov Botwinik collapsed under the brutality of the beating, and was shot to death. The rest of the gravediggers, who included Pinhas, the seventeen-year-old son of Moshe-Dovid and Mina Lipkunski, Israel Szczuczynski, and a number of other Eishyshkians, marched off to the cemetery. This time they were guarded by no fewer than a hundred policemen as well as a German army unit; the Germans were taking no chances.

Kopke stayed behind in the ghetto to oversee the evacuation of the rest of the Jews. He stood in the center of the ghetto, wearing yet another elegant uniform, having freshened his appearance after being thrown from his horse that morning, and barked out orders via loudspeaker. All Jews were to leave their homes immediately and line up. The Germans and the local police went from house to house to make sure everybody complied. The old, the sick, and the very young — all those who could not walk as fast as the Germans wanted — were shot on the spot.

Through a crack in the wall in his attic hiding place, Moshe Sonenson was able to watch the death procession, which included many people who had been his friends and neighbors all his life. Rabbi Hillel was at the head of the line, wearing his phylacteries, his white kittel, and his prayer shawl. Shoshana Szczuczynski, his next-door neighbor from Eishyshok; fifteen-year-old Avraham Lipkunski, the second son of Moshe-Dovid and Mina, a former yeshivah student who had taken his meals in the Sonenson home during his studies at the yeshivah ketanah; people who had returned from Palestine, from America, from Cuba, preferring their little shtetl in civilized Europe to the new world; and even his brother Shalom's wife Miriam and her two daughters — he could see them all. Praying in unison, "Shema Israel, Hear, O Israel, the Lord our God, the Lord is One!" they marched toward the cemetery, as shots were fired all around them.

But then a momentary halt was called, for the murderers were behind schedule with the gravedigging because of the morning revolt. Everyone was told to kneel, while Burgermeister Kulikowski delivered one of the obligatory anti-Semitic speeches over the loudspeaker, telling them that they were being punished for the killing of Jesus Christ. After a long stay on their knees, they were told to get up. The march proceeded to the cemetery.

It was a beautiful spring day. Sunlight glanced off the tin roof of the Haffetz Hayyim's mausoleum, and the trees were in bud. Near the mausoleum was a huge, freshly dug grave, at the far side of which stood a field kitchen with food, vodka, and other refreshments for the killers. The gravediggers were standing behind the long, shallow trench they had dug, which served to separate them from the rest of the crowd.

Now it was time for the first wave of killings to begin. The people at the head of the procession were told to undress, and to sort out their clothing into piles — one for shoes, one for underwear, one for outerwear. Then they were ordered to stand at the edge of the grave, which they would conveniently topple into as they were shot. (Later, when the grave was filled to the top with bodies, the next victims were ordered to sit on top of the other bodies to await their execution.) The first group of executioners, consisting of about twenty Germans, Poles, Lithuanians, and Byelorussians, began to shoot. Other groups were standing ready to relieve them in due course, for there was a lot of killing to be done. Some parents instinctively tried to shield their children from the spray of machine-gun fire; others hoped for a direct hit, that they might be spared the agony of a slow death. And even in the midst of the gunfire, some could be heard praying, saying the Shema, or asking the Haffetz Hayyim to protect them.

Suddenly there was an order to stop the shooting. Kopke announced over the loudspeaker that all gravediggers with yellow permits could now call out the names of their wives and two of their children, but they had to wait on their side of the shallow trench for their loved ones to join them. Liba Ahuva Shlosberg's husband began screaming out for her, but no one answered, for unbeknownst to him, she and many of his relatives had gone into hiding after he was taken away.[11] In desperation he started to run toward the crowd to search for her, and was shot for disobeying orders. Israel Szczuczynski shouted, "Shoshana Szczuczynski!" Two naked women jumped out of the grave, his wife and his unmarried sister, both named Shoshana, and both of course bearing the same last name. Kopke told him he could save only one. He chose his wife. Kopke shot the other Shoshana at her brother's feet. Next a young girl ran out of the grave, saying she was Israel's daughter. He went along with the deception (and later adopted her). Gittele Sonenson, also in the grave and already wounded in one ear, tore herself from her mother Miriam's embrace, climbed out of the grave, and ran over to Israel saying that she too was his daughter. He acceded to this deception as well, and Gittele was saved.

In all the commotion of families being reunited, young Avraham Lipkunski spotted his older brother Pinhas among the gravediggers. Since he was still dressed, he thought he might be able to join Pinhas without being noticed. His mother, unaware that her husband had escaped and lacking any hope for the future, told him to say the Shema and die like a Jew. But

The two sisters-in-law named Shoshana Szczuczynski: Israel Szczuczynski's wife (right) and his unmarried sister. During the massacre in Ghetto Radun, on May 10, 1942, Israel was given a yellow card that permitted him to save his wife and children. When he shouted "Shoshana Szczuczynski," two women jumped out from the mass grave he had been forced to help dig, his wife and sister. Since he could select only one, he chose his wife. His sister was shot at his feet. In the inscription on the back of the photo is written in Hebrew, "Shoshana with Shoshana, can you tell us apart?" Israel and his wife were murdered in the forest on June 16, 1943, by local collaborators, Lithuanians, Byelorussians, Ukrainians, and Poles. YESC, N. SHUSTER

Avraham let go of her hand and left her and his younger brother Yekutiel behind. As he made his way toward Pinhas, alternately jumping over people's heads and crawling wherever there was a space, he was spotted by a German and stopped. When he told the German that he was a blacksmith — a useful occupation in wartime — and had a yellow permit, the man let him go. Avraham joined his brother in the group of permit-holders.

In hiding places throughout the Radun ghetto, people could hear echoes of the gunfire from the cemetery, and the roar of motorcycles racing

Mina Lipkunski with her three sons: Pinhas (right), Yekutiel, and Avraham. Mina and Yekutiel were murdered in the Radun massacre, May 10, 1942. Pinhas was killed by Poles, Germans, and neighbors near his home in the village of Dugalishok. Avraham witnessed his death. He survived as a partisan and was a witness at the Eichmann trial in Jerusalem, 1962. YESC, LIPKUNSKI-ARIEL

through the streets as the Germans looked for anyone who might have escaped the roundup. Baby Shaul slept peacefully in the attic hayloft where the Sonensons had taken shelter, until the sharp report of a motorcycle in the street below awoke him and he began to whimper. Zipporah attempted to nurse him, but he refused. Nor would he suck on the cloth in which she had wrapped the poppyseeds that were supposed to induce sleep. As he continued to whine, all but one of the sixteen adults who were hiding in the hayloft along with Zipporah surrounded the mother and child. Shmaye-Mendl, an older man with a yellowish beard, father of Liba Shlosberg, and one of the most highly respected men in Radun, stated their case: "He is just a baby. We are all adults. Because of him we are all going to be murdered."

Just then the doors below swung open. Through the cracks between the attic's floor planks, two young Germans could be seen, machine guns on their shoulders, their motorcycles decorated with streamers, as though they were headed for a parade. Shmaye-Mendl took off his coat and threw it over the baby, then put his hand on the coat and motioned to all the others to do the same. They did, as Yitzhak and Yaffa watched in horror. Zipporah remained motionless, big tears frozen on her face, holding her dead son in her arms.[12] From that moment on, Yaffa began to fear all adults.

Late that afternoon they heard Yiddish-speaking people marching through the streets. It was the gravediggers and their families, coming back to the ghetto. In the ensuing confusion, a number of the people who had been in hiding, including the Sonensons, returned to their ghetto dwellings.

Public announcements were made ordering all who had survived to register. Many of those still in hiding, however, were reluctant to do so, for fear that this was just another trap. A rumor circulated that only people with geller scheins as well as physical proof that they had been at the cemetery would be spared; the others would be shot instantly. "Proof" was a back covered with marks from the gun butts and rubber truncheons with which everyone had been beaten at the cemetery.

Moshe Sonenson took off his leather belt and, with tears streaming from his eyes, slashed the bare backs of his wife and children. Then he handed the belt to his wife for her to administer the same to him. Zipporah refused. "I am not taking part in this new, mad world," she declared, as she walked over to the crib and began rocking her dead baby. Moshe stepped outside and screamed, "Jews, have mercy on me and beat me up." A young Eishyshkian did, giving him a beating that was a far cry from the thirty-nine gentle Yom Kippur lashes of tiny Shlomo Kik. Whereupon Moshe registered himself and his family.

All whose names were registered were ordered to lie face down on the cobblestones near the gallows, bare backs up, as the Polish police and the Germans surrounded them. This ordeal lasted three days, during which time Burgermeister Kulikowski and assistant Gebietskommisar Werner walked back and forth across the bodies, as though over a thick red carpet. Moshe Sonenson kept his hands stretched out over the heads of his wife and children, pressing them to the ground so that they would not move. Occasionally Werner put his revolver to someone's head and fired, completely at random. People with lash marks on their backs were shot, as well as people without; people with yellow permits, and people without. The Polish police and the Germans were on a shooting spree, drunk on vodka and Jewish blood.

Werner had come back to Radun, once again bringing his dog Donner with him, as part of an inspection tour of all the mass killings the Germans were conducting in the vicinity. The Einsatzgruppen had massacred 5,670 Jews in Ghetto Lida on May 8, and they'd also been active in Zaludek, Vasilishok, and Warinowa. About 2,500 were murdered in the May 10 Radun massacre — although there is no record of it in any German source.[13]

Elia Margolies was one of those who escaped the Radun massacre by fleeing into the nearby forest, along with several Eishyshkians, among them Dr. Benski and Mirale Shiffel. The day after the killings, which was yet another beautiful spring day, Elia sat in the forest about two and a half miles away, listening to the call of a cuckoo bird. It rang out very clearly, eight times. "What is the message?" Elia wondered. "Does it mean the war will end in eight days, eight weeks, eight months, or eight years?" Neither he nor anybody else who was with him in the forest that day would survive to learn the answer.[14]

Werner's coming meant new orders in Radun: The size of the ghetto was reduced, to just a few houses in the vicinity of the gallows, in addition to the spacious home of the Haffetz Hayyim's dynasty, and the yeshivah. All Jews, regardless of age, yellow-card status, or registration, were "invited" to stay in the ghetto. Many who had run away or gone into hiding to escape the massacre returned and registered, so that the ghetto now numbered a few hundred Jews (though some accounts say as many as nine hundred).

Among those who returned to the ghetto at this time was Moshe-Reuven Michalowski, who had been living in the forest since the gravediggers' uprising. Wounded in his face and foot, bleeding heavily, and covered with mud, he had gone to a Christian home to ask for help. So alarming a sight did he present that the peasant woman thought he was a demon and begged him to spare her. Her husband, worried that his wife would die of fright, gave Moshe-Reuven a towel to bandage his wounds, and bread to eat, then pleaded with him to leave before anything terrible happened to his wife. When shepherds Moshe-Reuven met in the forest told him that living Jews were once again walking the streets of Radun, he went back to see whether his family were among them. The first person he encountered in Radun was his eight-year-old daughter Breinaleh, who had somehow managed to survive and was wandering about in a daze, completely on her own. His wife and his other children had been murdered.

Barteszewicz, the Polish policeman from Eishyshok, recognized Moshe-Reuven shortly after his return to Radun, but he did not report him for his role in the uprising. Barteszewicz was not always so lenient, however. Just moments before his encounter with Michalowski, he had come across another Eishyshkian, sixteen-year-old Yitzhak Asner, who had once been a student at the Polish school where Barteszewicz had served as caretaker, and had had some sort of disagreement with him in those days. Now was Barteszewicz's chance for revenge. Accusing Asner of being a Communist, he shot and killed him on the spot.

The first order of business in the newly organized ghetto was to bury the dead, sort their clothing and shoes and other belongings, and take everything to the train station for shipment to Germany. Liba Shlosberg found her own husband's new sweater as she was sorting through the piles of garments, but she refused to believe he was among the dead. Hugging the sweater to her chest, she kept saying, "He must have given his sweater to someone else and escaped." Later she was told by the people who buried the dead that they had found his body near the grave that he himself had helped to dig.[15]

Barteszewicz and a fellow policeman named Zalusky, who was also from Eishyshok, assigned most of the Eishyshkian men to burial detail, a most demanding task as the attics, cellars, and streets were filled with the dead, as was the area within the vicinity of the cemetery. Barteszewicz put Moshe Sonenson in charge of the collecting and burying of the dead. As he said, "Your family was always in the Hevrah Kaddishah. Now you can bury more dead bodies in one day than your whole family did in a lifetime."

Those who had been assigned this horrible task were afraid to leave their families in the ghetto — if they still had families, that is — so they took them along. They saw many of their friends and relatives among the dead: old people who'd been shot sitting in their chairs, their prayer books in their hands; babies dead in their cribs, the contorted, desperate bodies of their mothers nearby, frozen in the position they'd been caught in as they tried to shield their children from the bullets.

The corpses were carried away in four wagons. Zipporah Sonenson, however, would not surrender her baby son to one of the wagons. Taking his small, yellowed body from the crib, she cradled him in her arms and walked to the cemetery with her husband and two children. As they followed the corpse-filled wagons to the burial ground, the trees were budding with fresh green leaves, the birds were singing, and the Germans and their collaborators were drinking and laughing. They saw Leibke Kaganowicz and his group trying to lift the bloated, bullet-riddled body of their beloved teacher and principal, Moshe Yaakov Botwinik. During the days he had been lying there, pigs had further mutilated his corpse. They saw Avraham Asner chasing away a cat who had been eating the body of a baby in its dead mother's arms. And they saw the Germans and the local police, still feasting on the supplies laid in at the field kitchen.

When it was time to start the burials, the very earth around them seemed to be moving. The men placed the bodies in the huge grave, and Zipporah put baby Shaul at the very corner of the grave facing the mausoleum of the Haffetz Hayyim. Next to her own child she placed the bodies of other little babies, cradling them in her arms before she relinquished them to the earth. Yaffa bent down and kissed her baby brother goodbye.

And then they covered the grave with soil and lime, and drowned it in tears. Kaddish was recited, in a kind of counterpoint to the sound of German and Polish laughter in the background.

The dead were now buried, their belongings shipped off in neat packages to Germany. The ghetto was clean.

New rumors began to circulate that the young and the healthy and people with special skills would be sent to Ghetto Lida, where their services were needed, while older people and families with young children would be sent to Szczuczin. Nehama Matikanski and her sons Haikl and Yitzhak, together with the wives they had married in Ghetto Radun, were among those shipped to Lida in June 1942. They hoped that the demand for their tailoring skills would keep them alive, since a number of the German officers in Lida, including Werner, the assistant to the Gebietskommisar, were among their admiring "clientele." After a while in Ghetto Lida, however, they realized that that ghetto, too, was about to be liquidated, its last inhabitants "resettled." Haikl urged his family to escape. But Nehama said that she was too old and tired to run again, and they should escape without her, in the hope that they could one day be reunited with their brother and sisters in Palestine and America. Unwilling to leave their mother alone, they were last seen boarding the death train to Majdanek with her, on September 19, 1943.[16]

For those faced with going to Szczuczin, the choices were grim. These survivors of the Eishyshok and Radun massacres were, needless to say, no longer naive, but even in the wake of the most recent round of horrors, the decision to try to flee was still not an easy one, for it had become clear to the Jews that their former friends in the countryside were turning their backs on them, and in some cases becoming full-fledged collaborators with the Germans. Who, then, would help them? Who could be trusted? Moreover, for many people, especially the very young and the very old, the hardships of life on the run would be too great.

The issues debated by the Kaganowiczes, who had escaped the Radun massacre by hiding in a cellar, were typical of the dilemmas faced by many multigenerational families. When Leibke Kaganowicz decided he would run away to the forest, decisions had also to be made about a course of action for the rest of the family: brother Benjamin, sister Freidke, father Shael, mother Miriam, and aging grandmother Libe-Gittel Rudzin.

That night I sat down with my father to tell him that I had decided to go into the forest to find the partisans. Benjamin and Freidke came to listen.

"I've got to go, papa! I can't wait around to be killed." I knew he'd been thinking about this, too, so I pressed my advantage. "It's the only place we can be safe! Lots of our people are there now, whole families of them, and they're safe. They sleep nights and they get enough food so their stomachs aren't growling all the time! We won't escape from Szczuczin, father!"

My brother and sister nodded, agreeing with me, and then they urged father to take the whole family there. Father was more cautious.

"We'll leave Radun," he said at last, "and we'll see if some of our old friends will hide us . . . at least for a time. After that, if there is no other way . . . we'll have to go to the forest."

I had to accept his decision.

We went to tell my mother. I believe she had always known that it would come to this because our family was so determined to live. But we were not prepared for her answer.

"No," she said. "You'll have to go without me. Grandmother could never make the journey, and she could never adjust to that kind of life at her age. I must stay here to look after her."

We begged her to change her mind, but she remained adamant. Grandmother had no one left now but my mother, and mother felt it was her duty to look after her. We all knew that grandmother was too old to go to the forest, but somehow we had expected that she would accept the fact she had lived her life, and generously she would tell mother to go with her husband and family. But grandmother never opened her mouth. "You go and save yourselves!" mother told us. "This is my own decision and none of you is responsible. You must go and I must stay here to care for mother. You have to understand . . . I can't come with you."

For four days and nights the arguments raged. We all knew that Szczuczin was just another trap.

My grandmother remained silent throughout the whole argument. My father was brokenhearted. In the end, he realized he had to leave mother behind and lead his children to safety.

Our parting will remain forever on my mind and my conscience. We hugged and kissed goodbye again and again; then at the door I turned to look back, to take one last mental picture of my dear mother. I can still see her, her dark wavy hair now prematurely grey, but her beautiful strong features unchanged. I was torn between my fear of dying and my conviction that I was betraying her, letting her down when she needed me. A hundred times I told myself to stay, a hundred times my terror forced me to leave my adored mother. . . .

To this day, I still wonder if we had insisted more, or begged just a little longer, she might have relented. Somehow I feel certain that with mother with us, my parents would have made different decisions and all of us would have survived.

My only comfort is the prayer that in those last moments before she and my grandmother were led into the gas chamber, she found consolation in the thought that her husband and children were still alive.[17]

To Moshe Sonenson it had become clear that with Ghetto Radun about to be liquidated, death was waiting just around the corner. Once again he began to plot an escape, this time to include his wife, children, brother, and niece. A man from Eishyshok who had lost his entire family got wind of Moshe's plan and came to suggest an alternative. There was no way, he said, that such a scheme would work, since small children could only be a hindrance, as Moshe already knew from his experience in the attic on May 10. The two of them should join forces and run away alone. "I will stay with my family," Moshe replied, "and I will save my family. And we will outlive Hitler and his local henchmen!"

On Sunday May 24, 1942, the day after Shavuot, when the Germans, the local police, and many of the peasants were at church, Moshe set his plan in motion. He had everyone dress like peasants. Zipporah, Yaffa, and Gittele tied kerchiefs on their heads. Moshe, Shalom, and Yitzhak rolled their pants legs up (as the peasants did to avoid fraying or soiling the cuffs), and tied their shoes together so they could sling them over their shoulders (as the peasants did to save the soles). Since Shalom had plenty of food, they took as much as they could, including a red enamel container shaped like a milk can that was filled with honey.

Prior to their escape, Moshe told the group what would be expected of them, without revealing any details of his plan. First he apologized to his wife and his brother, for requiring that henceforth they strictly obey all his orders. With his characteristic mixture of seriousness and humor he then announced: "I am your captain from this moment until Hitler and his armies are dead — naked, frozen, and defeated by Russian General Winter. You do not listen to anyone but me. You do whatever I tell you to do. When I tell you to run, you run. When I tell you to keep quiet, you keep quiet. In return I promise you that I will do my best to save us all."

When they walked out of the ghetto, no one chased them. Only a distant shot was fired when they reached the river. Deep, swift, and still filled with chunks of ice in May, the river was a perilous barrier between them and freedom. Moshe carried the members of his family, one by one, to the other side, leaping from one block of ice to another. Once in the forest on the other side, they sheltered under a tall fir tree whose branches reached down to the ground, offering them both a roof and camouflage. Moshe gave detailed instructions to his family about how to behave in the forest. He knew forests well, both from the two years he had spent on the road when he was in the fur trade, and from the teachings of his mother, Hayya, whose family had owned forests, and who had therefore known everything about the flora and fauna of the vicinity.

Moshe waited for a full moon to light the way. They were headed toward Korkuciany. There, on the estate of Kazimierz Korkuc, he hoped to find a hiding place.

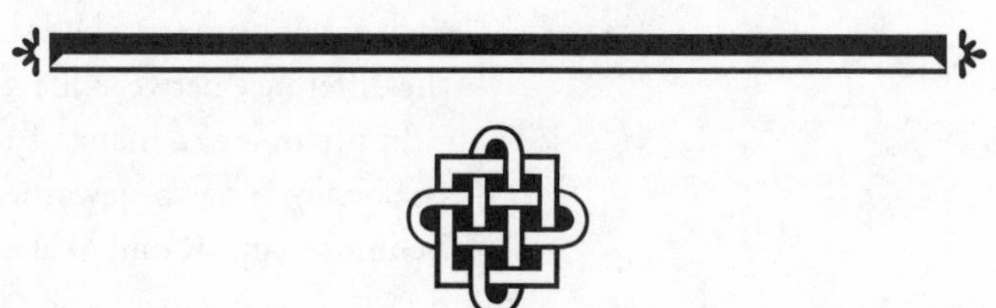

THOSE WHO HAD MANAGED TO ESCAPE THE 1941 MASSACRE IN EISHYSHOK — MANY OF whom then had to flee similar mass executions that later took place in Ghetto Radun, in Lida, Warinowa, Marcinkonys, and elsewhere — found that the hardest thing for them to accept was that their worst, most dangerous enemies were not the German invaders, but the local Poles, Lithuanians, and Byelorussians. Now that the Jews were on the run, these gentile neighbors, families their own families had associated with for generations, people they had known for years and counted among their most trusted friends, colleagues, customers, teachers, and doctors, were becoming active collaborators with the Germans.

In fact, the Germans could not have done their job of extermination without these collaborators. For despite the Nazi ideology that Jews are a distinct race with distinct physical characteristics, the Germans in the occupied countries could not tell the Jews from the rest of the local population unless the Jews were dressed in ultra-Orthodox garb, with beards and earlocks. In the vicinity of Eishyshok, as elsewhere throughout Eastern Europe, lived many blue-eyed, blond Jews, and many dark-haired, brown-eyed non-Jews. Photos of Adolf Hitler and many of his top Nazi officials show that they themselves did not have the pure Aryan look.

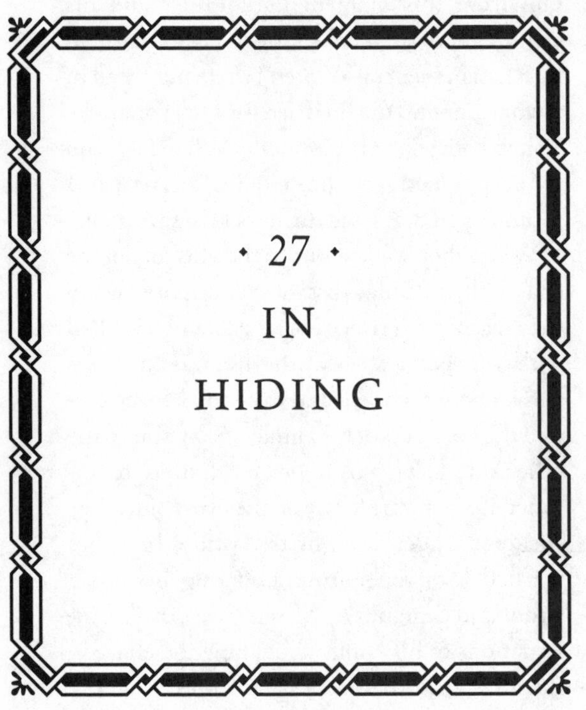

• 27 • IN HIDING

FOR EACH OF US WHO SURVIVED, THERE WAS A GOOD CHRISTIAN. FOR EACH OF US WHO WAS MURDERED, THERE WAS A CHRISTIAN COLLABORATOR.

Moshe Sonenson
June 29, 1977

For the Germans to be able to pick out the Jews in hiding, they needed the help of the local residents. It was the locals who guided their ostensible enemy down narrow, unknown country roads to the dense forests, marshes, and small hamlets where Jews had found shelter, the locals who told the Germans who was who.

On the other hand, it was also in many cases the locals who gave the Jews food, shelter, and other kinds of help. And those Christians and Tatars who aided the Jews did so at risk of their own lives and those of their families. The duration of the help, and consequently of the risk, varied widely. For some rescuers it was a spontaneous, one-time act that happened in the space of seconds, minutes, or hours; for others it may have involved days, weeks, months, and even years of continuous aid. But regardless of the duration, each act of humanity had the potential to make the difference between life and death.

In urban areas, many of the rescuers did not personally know the Jews they were saving. Oskar Schindler and Raoul Wallenberg, for example, were total strangers to virtually all of the hundreds and thousands to whom they offered protection.[1] But the rescuers who helped shtetl Jews had generally known them well since childhood, in some cases through friendships that spanned several generations within their respective families. But so, too, had the murderers and betrayers.

Generalizations about who became a rescuer, who a collaborator, were and are impossible to make. Those who were rescuers defy any effort at classification. Religion, social and economic class, level of education, political views, age and gender — all fail to serve as predictors of this kind of altruistic behavior.[2]

Thus it was extremely difficult for the Jews to determine who might have turned foe, who remained a friend. On the run, these decisions had to be made instantly. Which lighted window on a dark night might mean a loaf of bread and warm shelter, which a hail of bullets? Which doorway must one avoid even in a raging storm? There were surprises of both kinds lurking behind those rural windows.

Many Jews, for example, had left their family valuables with Christian friends during both the Russian and the German occupations. Everything from fur coats to fine linens, jewelry to furniture, had been deposited with these people, in whom they had total faith. For the Kaganowicz family the trusted friend was Mrs. Carolowa. Her home in the village of Lebiedniki was not just their storehouse, but the place they had all run to, separately and without advance planning, after escaping the massacre in Eishyshok.

From there they had all gone to Ghetto Radun, and after Shael Kaganowicz, his sons Leibke and Benjamin, and his daughter Freidke escaped that massacre, they found shelter in the countryside with a farmer named Bobkin and his brother-in-law. Bobkin was known as a Jew-hater; he used to get drunk on market day and beat up Jews. Yet now he was willing to hide them in his barn — for a price. In order to pay him for their stay they went to Mrs. Carolowa to ask for some of their possessions. When Shael and Leibke appeared at her window under cover of night, she could not hide her distress at seeing them alive. She told them they must go away immediately, since the police were in the vicinity. When they later learned that she had been lying they returned, and demanded several bolts of the cloth they had left with her. A few minutes later she thrust a small bolt of cotton cloth through the window, but would not give them any more, even though Shael explained that this would be insufficient as a payment to Bobkin. Realizing that she would probably turn them in to the police before surrendering their possessions, they had to give up the effort.[3] Rabbi Rozowski had proved to have been correct when he warned his congregation not to deposit their goods with their friends and neighbors, for fear the valuables would prove too strong an incentive to hasten their deaths.

Since the Bobkins refused to hide them without pay, the Kaganowiczes were soon on the run again, going from farmer to farmer, begging a loaf of bread here, a night's shelter in a hayloft or pigsty there. Most farmers were kind and let them stay for a day or two, but they were too frightened to keep them longer than that. Finally they found shelter with Zoludzewicz, a farmer who had been in partnership with Shael Kaganowicz: he raised sheep from whose skins Shael had made leather. Zoludzewicz was glad to see his old friend, and for two weeks Shael and his family had a home. But Zoludzewicz's son feared that the farmers in the vicinity would betray them, burn the house down, and kill everyone in it. The young man was so frightened that he stopped eating and drinking, and out of concern for his son, Zoludzewicz had to ask the Kaganowiczes to leave.

After several more weeks on the run they found the cold, the hunger, and the lice too much to bear. Having heard that life in Ghetto Marcinkonys was relatively easy, they hired a guide to take them there (paying him with leather that had been stored on the Zoludzewicz farm), and indeed found it to be a small paradise in the heart of hell. The ghetto was so livable that when the Jews went out to the forest to gather mushrooms for the Germans on the eastern front — that being their main job — they didn't even need to be guarded; everyone returned voluntarily. Unfortunately, although there were other Eishyshkians who had found a home in Marcinkonys, the Judenrat was not willing to give a residence permit to the Kaganowicz family. Thus by October 1942 they had to leave. From there they made their way to Ghetto Grodno, which they escaped in late December, a few days prior to the January 1943 Aktion, when 10,500 Jews (among them a number of Eishyshkians) were deported to Auschwitz.[4] After the escape from Grodno, Leibke finally won his father over: they would join the partisans in the forest, rather than trying to rely on local farmers for shelter.

By then many Eishyshkians knew the story of the Rogowskis' sons, and were coming to realize how perilous it could be to depend on old friends. The three Rogowski brothers, Leibke, Moshe, and Niomke, and their sister Hayya, had escaped Ghetto Radun on May 9, 1942, and had gone to live in the forest. One night the three young men and a friend of theirs went to the Shiemaszka family, Christian friends who had been entrusted with a large portion of the Rogowskis' quite considerable stock of valuables. Between the wealthy Rogowskis and the very well respected Shiemaszkas there existed a bond that had endured for generations. Thus it was only to be expected that Mr. Shiemaszka would welcome them with a big smile and a warm handshake. However, he was also carrying a machine gun. Why was he armed? Niomke asked. Because dangerous Russian criminals were roaming the forests at night, looking for places to rob, was the answer.

Moments later another of the Shiemaszkas joined them, also armed with an automatic weapon. He told his father to invite everybody in so that they could eat and refresh themselves. In the midst of a dinner-table conversation, at very close range, one of the young Shiemaszkas opened fire on the Rogowskis. Niomke started to run. "No, no," the Shiemaszka boy screamed as he gave chase. "It was a mistake; please come back."

Wounded in the hand and foot, Niomke made it to the house of another farmer, where he was later joined by his older brother Leibke and their friend, both of them unharmed. In the morning the farmer went to the Shiemaszka home to inquire about the shooting he had heard the previous night. When he returned, he quoted Shiemaszka as saying, "Russian bandits came and we shot one of them, who we think is dead. But they carried his body away with them." The two brothers understood that to mean that their younger brother Moshe, who had managed to escape the German massacre in Radun, had been murdered by the family's most trusted friends, who had then disposed of his body.

Upon their return to the forest, Leibke Rogowski told his wife, "After what happened at the Shiemaszkas', I cannot stay in the forest any more. If the Germans don't kill us, our Christian friends will." He took his wife and two young children to Ghetto Grodno, where they all perished. Niomke, however, continued to take his chances in the forest.

Another family who split up over the question of safety was the Lipkunskis. Moshe-Dovid Lipkunski was one of the men who escaped during the gravediggers' uprising in Radun; so did his teenage sons, Pinhas and Avraham, who ran away to the forest. From there they made their way to Dugalishok, the village their family had founded in the previous century, after the Russian general Stalewitch gave them a large tract of land as an expression of gratitude for their help during the Polish uprising of 1831. In Dugalishok they were reunited with their father. Like the rest of the Dugalishok Jews, Moshe-Dovid was tall — over six feet — strong, and husky. A veteran of the tzarist army and a blacksmith by profession, he was a man people looked up to, a hero who was known for always going to the aid of those in trouble. Confident that his Christian friends in the vicinity would take care of him as he had taken care of so many others, he would not listen to his sons' pleas to join them in the forest. Thus they decided to part. While his sons went to the forest to search for the partisans, Moshe-Dovid hid in a pit beneath the clay floor of a barn belonging to a man named Anczelewicz.

Anczelewicz was an educated peasant whose family had become part of the Polish petty nobility (szlachta). Like most of the local Poles, he was friendly with the AK in the area, but in his case this did not mean he was anti-Semitic. Generally speaking, however, the AK and those who were sympathetic to its goals did tend to be hostile to the Jews.

The AK was the Polish underground army in occupied Poland, a conglomerate of many different factions from what had been, before the German occupation, the army of the Polish Republic. It was established in 1939, after the fall of Poland, and remained active until January 1945. Known officially as the Armia Krajowa (Home Army) or AK, and known locally as Akowtsy or Biale Polaky (White Poles), the AK operated under the auspices of the Polish government-in-exile in London. Though its overriding goal was to defeat the Germans (as well as the Communists), and see to it that the government-in-exile was brought back to Poland at the end of the war, the major target of the AK in the vicinity of Eishyshok, as in many other areas of Poland, was not the Germans but the Jews. "Polska bez Zydow" (Poland without Jews) was adopted as the slogan of the White Poles. Anti-Semitism took precedence over all other goals. This is not, however, the way the official records of the AK read, nor was it necessarily the intent of the government-in-exile.[5]

In February 1942, the operational command of the AK information and propaganda office created a section for Jewish affairs, directed by Henryk Wolinski, the purpose of which was to gather information about the underground resistance activities of Jews in Poland and to send that information on to London, in order that support for those activities could be more adequately directed. Such efforts notwithstanding, it must be noted that during the Warsaw ghetto uprising of April–June 1943 no AK members fought alongside the Jews; whereas during the Polish uprising of August 2–October 2, 1944, over a thousand Jews converged on Warsaw, individually and in small groups, to help their compatriots.[6] Some had been inmates in the Gesia Street concentration camp established in Warsaw after the ghetto uprising, many others came from what was left of the Jewish resistance movement (the Jewish Fighting Organization) from within and around Warsaw.

Despite the loyalty of many Jews to Poland, they — not the Germans and not the Russians — bore the brunt of AK attacks as the enemies of Poland. In fact, a shaky cooperation existed at times between the AK and the Russian partisans against their common enemy, the Germans, even though the Poles were competing with the Russians for control of a number of regions, including western Byelorussia and Vilna and vicinity. But no such cooperation ever prevailed between the AK and the Jews. Quite the opposite: Jews in hiding as well as in partisan units were sought out and killed by the AK in a number of regions, including that of Eishyshok.[7]

By the end of 1942, the AK had become increasingly active, and as it grew in size and strength, the number of Polish nationalists willing to offer help to the Jews dwindled significantly. Anczelewicz was thus in the distinct minority.

Because of his friendships with the White Poles, Anczelewicz received their underground literature; he also listened to Polish-language broadcasts from London over his radio, thereby keeping up with the latest word from the government-in-exile. His familiarity with AK activities in the area ended up being of little use to the Lipkunski brothers, however, for it was not the AK but the Radun police who ambushed them as they were on their way to meet their father at Anczelewicz's one night early in October 1942. Pinhas was killed in front of his father's blacksmith shop, where he had spent many happy days in his childhood. Avraham escaped. Afterward the man who had organized the ambush, a Lithuanian from a branch of the same Shiemaszka family who had murdered Moshe Rogowski, took over the Lipkunski house, land, and blacksmith shop. Pinhas's bullet-riddled body was tied to a horse's tail and dragged through the streets of his native village, the town that his own ancestors had helped to found.

A few days later, Avraham came back to the Anczelewicz home to commiserate with his father over Pinhas's murder. When the Anczelewicz family saw him they fell to their knees, certain that they were witnessing a resurrection, for they had thought both brothers had been murdered in the ambush. Once again Avraham begged Moshe-Dovid to come with him to the forest. Anczelewicz concurred. "Our people, the White Poles, do not like you. They are liquidating all the Jews." His warning was well founded. The commander of the AK in the Eishyshok area, Jan Borysewicz, known as Krisha, hated Jews even more than he hated the Germans and Russians, and so did the men under his command. Since many of these were locals, working their farms by day, serving as vigilantes by night[8] — especially by the end of 1942, when AK members were to be found in virtually every village with a Polish population — they knew who in the vicinity had longstanding friendships with Jews and might be suspected of harboring them. Those families were singled out for frequent raids in search of Jewish fugitives as well as Jewish goods. This meant that hiding on a farm had become a highly risky venture for both the Jewish guests and their protector.

But Moshe-Dovid Lipkunski simply couldn't believe that any harm could befall him at the hands of his friends and neighbors in Dugalishok. The murder of his own son, and of Moshe Rogowski, did not change his mind. Nor did the murder of Faivl Lipkunski and his son, two members of Moshe-Dovid's extended family who lived in Dugalishok. The man who had given them shelter, to whom they had entrusted their possessions as well as their lives, was their executioner.

Making one last effort to get his father to join him, Avraham Lipkunski visited Moshe-Dovid again on Passover, April 20, 1943. His pleas were refused. "I know all the farmers and all the farmers know me," Moshe-Dovid said, still as confident as ever of his own safety. With that, Avraham left for the Nacha forest, to join the group of partisans headed up by his boyhood friend, Elke "Todras" Ariowitch of Radun. A few weeks later, on the eve of Shavuot, May 5, 1943, Moshe-Dovid Lipkunski, age forty, and four other Jews from the Dugalishok vicinity were murdered by the AK. The handful of remaining Jewish survivors in Dugalishok were killed by the AK a few weeks later.[9]

Moshe-Dovid Lipkunski (seated on the ground, second from right), posing with the captain and other Polish immigrants prior to their emigration to South America. Moshe-Dovid returned to Europe, since his wife Mina refused to join him in a godless country where she could not observe Judaism. Moshe-Dovid Lipkunski escaped the Radun massacre but was killed with a group of other Jews by the AK on May 5, 1943. YESC, ARIEL-LIPKUNSKI

THE KORKUC FARM

Hiding on Polish farms was becoming more difficult with each passing day. The farmers themselves, as Rabbi Rozowski had warned, had an interest in eliminating the rightful owners of the goods that had been deposited with them. If that weren't enough of an inducement, the Germans and the local occupation government officials and police offered tax exemptions, or a few kilograms of salt, for the capture of Jews in hiding. Moreover, the individual collaborators were greatly strengthened by the organized, military-style raids on the Jews that were staged by the AK. But the occasional courageous Christian or Tatar farmer continued to risk his life and his property to offer shelter to Jews. Such a man was Kazimierz Korkuc.

Even for those who had the good fortune to find one of these righteous rescuers, and the financial resources to pay him, survival required both skill and luck. Life in the compound of Kazimierz Korkuc, where Moshe Sonenson took his family after they escaped from Ghetto Radun, was typical of the many hazards faced by Jews in hiding, although Korkuc himself was a completely honorable and generous man, who helped dozens, even hundreds, of Jews in the vicinity.

In the midst of wheatfields, lakes, pastures, and woods, all belonging to the Korkuc family, was the Korkuc homestead, on a huge plot of land enclosed by a wooden fence with two large gates on opposite sides. Within the fence were a large barn, a stable, a blacksmith workshop, and a storage house where grain, grinding equipment, and flour were kept. At the center of the yard was a well, and facing the well was the main house, which had two wings flanking a central entrance.

Korkuc, then a dashing bachelor of the petty nobility, lived to the right of the entrance in the modern wing, which had wooden floors, a tile fireplace, contemporary furniture, and a gramophone. Even the religious icons on his walls looked more modern than those in the old wing, where his mother, Pani (Mrs.) Korkucowa, the family matriarch, maintained her own living quarters. The large public area of Pani Korkucowa's wing had clay floors, wooden benches lining the walls, a few spinning wheels, and a large wooden table at the end of the room. On the wall above the windows near the table hung the icons of the holy family. Off this main room was a large storage pantry, and between the pantry and Pani Korkucowa's bedroom was an immense oven. The flat top of the oven was so large that six people could sleep on it in cold weather. The bedroom itself had only one bed, but the room served as home not just for Pani Korkucowa but for sheep and their kids, sows and their piglets, chickens, geese, and a variety of sick animals that needed special attention, especially in wintertime.

The bedroom also concealed an intricate passageway to one of the numerous underground shelters where the family hid their Jewish friends and neighbors. A trapdoor near the bed, covered with straw and manure, led to a narrow shaft, which in turn led to a tunnel that was connected to a pit, a cavelike space beneath and beyond the house, with an air shaft consisting of a hole beneath a cherry tree. This was the pit in which Moshe, Zipporah, and their two children hid, along with Shalom Sonenson and his daughter Gittele. Moshe paid the Korkucs 60 rubles in gold, monthly, for his pit dwellers — 10 rubles a head being the going rate for hiding a Jew.

In contrast to the world-famous attic in Amsterdam where Anne Frank's family hid, most of the hiding places around Eishyshok, as elsewhere in the Eastern European countryside, consisted of pits like this one, dug deep in the ground and located beneath farmhouses, pigsties, barns, stables, potato shacks. With only straw to line the walls and soak up moisture, the pits were always damp, and with only a pail for people to relieve themselves, the air was always

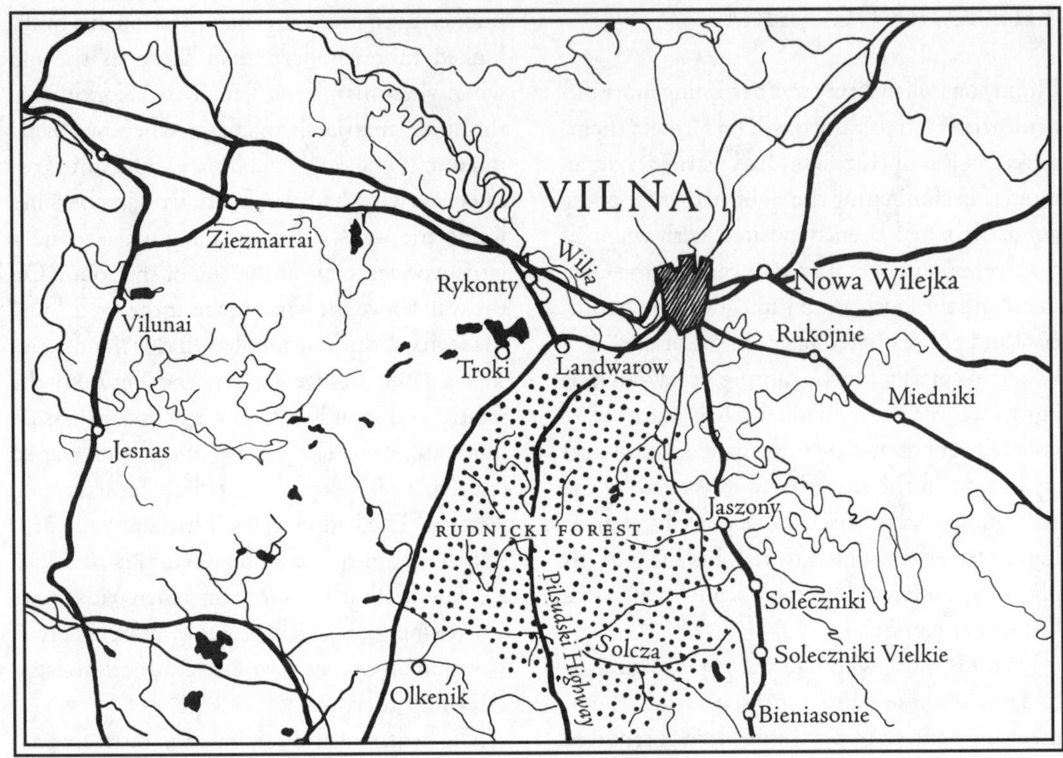

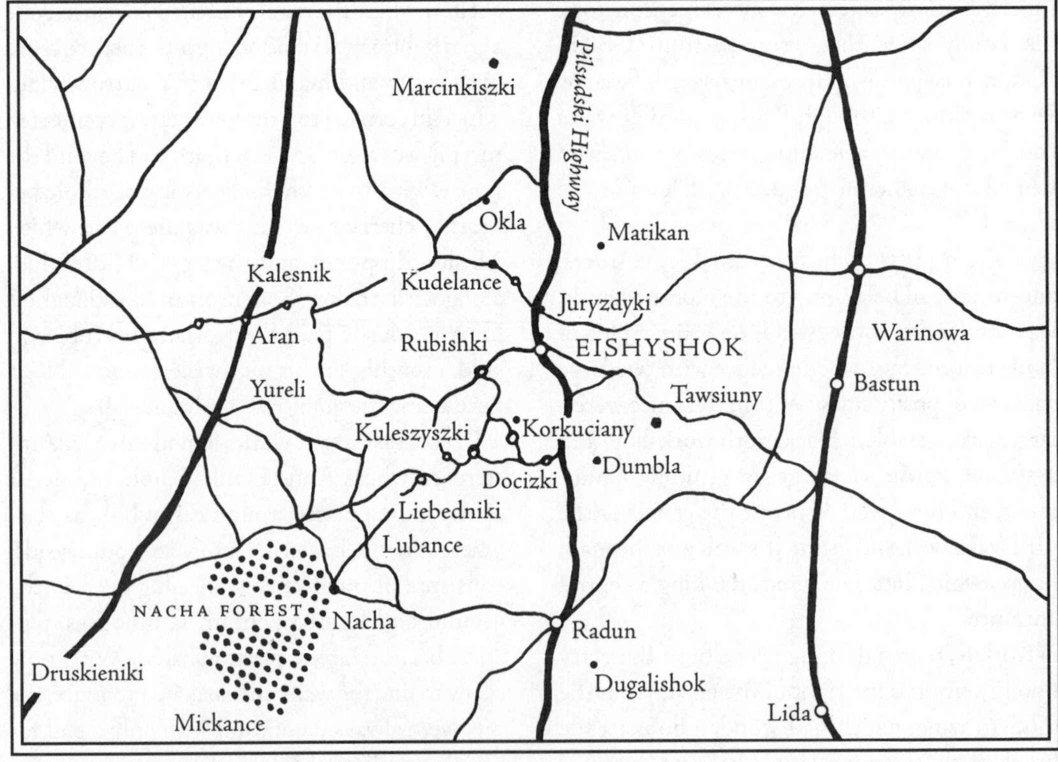

Two maps of the Holocaust period. Top: Vilna and its vicinity. Bottom: Eishyshok and its vicinity.

M. MAGARIL

foul. But uncomfortable as they were, the pits were safer than many other kinds of hiding place: Their concealed trapdoors, made of the same clay or mud as the ground above, and their small, hidden air shafts were so well disguised that even a Sherlock Holmes would have had difficulty finding them.

To live in such circumstances required extraordinary fortitude, as well as the most meticulous vigilance among both the rescued and their rescuers. A highly refined art of survival developed under duress, with caution governing every word uttered, every facial expression, every response to every sign in the environment. The sharp-eyed peasants in the countryside missed nothing. The ways Jews could reveal their presence seemed never-ending. On one occasion when Zipporah Sonenson was slicing cooked beets for the harvest feast, Pani Korkucowa told her not to slice them so evenly, "Jewish style," for that would be a dead giveaway. Similarly, Zipporah learned to weave linen at the Korkucs' and when her freshly spun linen was placed on the grass for bleaching, a farmer passing by remarked, "That's Jew linen, very fine." Pani Korkucowa told him he was blinded by the sun. "It's the same type of linen I always spin," she insisted.

In one of her several hiding places, Miriam Kabacznik nearly lost her life on account of her dumplings. A neighbor who belonged to the AK ate soup with dumplings that had been cooked by Miriam. "These dumplings could only have been cooked by a Jewess," he remarked to the farmer on whose land Miriam was hiding. That very night Miriam was on the run again, in search of a new shelter. The purchase of a newspaper by an illiterate Pole was another clue, a signal that the man might have Jews on his farm, people who were eager for news from the front.

There were also seasonal hazards. During the winter every footprint in the snow was a signal to the enemy (while conversely, every snowstorm was also a blessing because the killers were likely to remain indoors). On a winter's morning, fresh footprints in the snow leading to a house but not from it could mean that Jews had come in from the night for shelter. Moshe and Zipporah's daughter Yaffa used to envy the foxes in the snow, noting that they covered their own tracks with their bushy tails. Too little snow on the roof of a barn might mean that Jews were hiding in the hayloft, their body heat melting the snow. But winter did have one advantage: it made it easy to spot potential enemies at a great distance. In the summer, when the leaves were full and the grain in the fields grew high, an unwanted visitor could materialize quite suddenly.

During safe hours the Sonenson family would surface from their pit and help out with the Korkucs' household chores: cooking, cleaning pigs' intestines for the making of sausages, smoking ham, making cheese, churning butter, braiding onions and garlic, weaving, spinning, making ropes, whips, baskets, and brushes, mending shoes, boots, and saddles. In times of danger, the Sonensons would disappear from sight like mice, crowding into the narrow shaft, then crawling through the tunnel until they reached the pitch-black, lice-infested pit where they always slept. At times they had to stay in the pit for days. But even in the midst of such squalor they tried to maintain something of their way of life. Zipporah taught her daughter to read and write by inscribing the Hebrew letters on the damp clay wall of the pit, and she and Moshe recited to the children all that they could remember from their own school days with Shaul Kaleko, Sarah Rubinstein, and Moshe-Yaakov Botwinik in Eishyshok, and from the Epstein gymnasium in Vilna. Moshe lit up the gloom of the pit, making everybody forget the cold and the hunger with his humorous stories about Eishyshok and its characters. Shalom's contribution was to tell about his experiences as a halutz in Eretz Israel. The holidays were observed with the help of a Jewish pocket calendar.

The Korkuc estate — the house as well as the land around it — was a maze of shelters. As

Kazimierz Korkuc recalled, "The entire farm was intersected with tunnels, and all over were hiding places." Besides the Sonensons' pit beneath Pani Korkucowa's bedroom, there were spaces beneath the main house, beneath Korkuc's quarters, and beneath the stable, as well as additional hiding places in the barn and the grain storage house. Each one was a little world unto itself, some of them entirely unaware of the existence of the others. The Sonensons, for example, did not at first know that their cousins the Kabaczniks were also in residence on the Korkuc property.

In the pit beneath the stable lived nine members of the Kabacznik family, several of whom Kazimierz had secretly transported from Ghetto Radun one night, on the strength of an ominous dream he had had, as noted in chapter 26. Sorl Kabacznik, the matriarch of the family, viewed that pit beneath the stable as Noah's ark, from which the members of her family would one day emerge to perpetuate the Jewish people. So she felt responsible for saving as many members of her family as she possibly could, the better to ensure the continuity of the Jews after the war. Sorl was committed not just to the physical survival of the Jews, but to their spiritual continuity. Thus she had managed to obtain, at a high price, a small Sefer Torah (scroll) and a prayer book for use in her family's religious observances.

When it came to her family, Sorl was unstinting with money. She paid handsomely, in gold, for each resident of her pit, and installed as many relatives as she could in that underground dwelling. She gave Jaszuk, Kazimierz Korkuc's brother, 100 gold rubles to go to Ghetto Vilna and fetch her mother's youngest sister, the sister's husband, and their two sons. When the Solomianski family refused to leave the ghetto, Sorl did not give up, but at the cost of another 100 rubles sent Jaszuk once more to Ghetto Vilna. And then she sent him yet a third time, until finally he returned with the parents, Hayya and Muleh Solomianski, and their younger son Yankl, a medical student. The son who stayed behind was eventually murdered in the Ponar section of Vilna. Sorl also rescued a teenage nephew, Yitzhak Levin, from Ghetto Ivie, and Sonia Kowarski, who later became Sorl's son Meir's wife. But Sorl's indomitable will failed with her own older, married daughter Goldke, who had a hideaway that Korkuc had found for her on a nearby farm but was simply unable to endure the difficulties of life in hiding, opting instead to go to Ghetto Ivie, taking her two young children with her. There they all perished.

Another of the Korkuc farm fugitives was a young Lithuanian Jewish woman named Itta, who usually hid in the house. Since she was not a local who could be recognized by any of the neighbors, the Korkucs were able to pass her off as a relative of theirs, whose poor knowledge of Polish was easily explained by the fact that she was from Lithuania. Itta eventually took over the running of the Korkuc household, and endeared herself to a number of their secret guests as well. The Sonensons considered her virtually a relative, and took her into the pit with them whenever some unusual danger arose. Sorl Kabacznik, however, was not so friendly toward her, for she resented Itta's central position in the household, and was even more unhappy about the fact that her cousin Yankl and Itta fell in love with each other, thus foiling Sorl's plans to marry her older son Shepske off to Itta.

In addition to providing the honeycomb of hiding places on his own land, Kazimierz Korkuc helped about two hundred Jews from Eishyshok and other nearby shtetlekh build shelters in the vicinity. Such a project required not just money, which Korkuc obtained from his paying guests, but careful planning, stealth, caution, and all manner of clever deceptions, for any slip could spell death. First was the problem of obtaining the nails and wood and other materials without arousing suspicion. Korkuc purchased his nails from as far away as Lida and Vilna so that no one in the immediate vicinity would know. Wood

Itta Solomianski with her brother. Itta survived on the Korkuc farm, where she met her future husband, Dr. Yankl Solomianski. YESC, SOLOME

was cut in a faraway forest for the same reason. Once construction began, the nails would have to be hammered at the same time that some other repair or construction project was taking place aboveground, so that the noise could be easily explained. The freshly dug soil had to be deposited many miles away, dumped into lakes and rivers, or, if the soil were of a similar type, onto freshly plowed fields.

Whatever the Jews in his area needed — food, a night or two's shelter on his own land, or materials for building a shelter elsewhere — Korkuc seemed willing to supply it. His farm had become one of the few places where a Jew on the run could seek help. When asked many years later how he accounted for his willingness to risk his life on a daily basis, as well as the lives of his mother and other members of his household, he explained it in terms of his Christian duty: "All nations are brothers to one another. The whole planet belongs to God Almighty, to our Lord Jesus . . ." As to why he was one of only a few who tried to help the Jews: "It could not be helped if there were saboteurs among us."

Korkuc also used his faith to try to explain the genocide committed by the Germans and their collaborators. Korkuc saw the mass killings of the Jews as a punishment for the killing of Christ. One day several of the Jews on Korkuc's estate saw him driving off in his Sunday carriage, dressed in his Sunday best. Where had he been? he was asked on his return. "To see the Jews being led to their slaughter" in a nearby shtetl, he replied. And why would a man like him wish to see such a sight? "When Christ was led to the crucifixion you lined the streets to Jerusalem. Now, when you are led to your death we line the streets."[10] But however "understandable" the killing of the Jews was to Korkuc, he never wavered in his own treatment of them. Indeed, he seemed more willing to risk his life for a fugitive than the Jews themselves were at times.

One of the unfortunates to whom the Korkuc family gave occasional help was Mr. Wien, who had been the shtetl lawyer. Wien had escaped the Eishyshok massacre, dressed in his Rosh Hashanah best, but his two daughters and his wife, who was one of the shtetl's two dentists, were murdered. Wien also escaped the Radun massacre, and since then had been living in the Dumbla swamps. Still dressed in his top hat and tails, now all in tatters, with his pants held up by a rope and his swollen feet wrapped in rags, he cut quite a strange figure. But whenever he showed up at the Korkucs', Itta would serve him a hot meal, wash his lice-infested rags, and give him some food to take back to the swamp.

Unbeknownst to Wien, his old friends the Sonensons were at that time living at the Korkucs'. Wien had been Moshe's lawyer, his wife their family dentist, and his two little girls the best friends of Gittele and Shulamit, Shalom Sonenson's daughters. Zipporah Sonenson insisted that it was only human for them to make themselves known to Wien; her brother-in-law Shalom agreed. But Moshe was against it, and reminded them, as he did on many such occasions, that he was the boss, the one who would make their decisions. "It is not a matter of humanity; it is a matter of survival. The Wien you knew in Eishyshok is not the Wien from the Dumbla swamp. He is on the verge of insanity."

A few weeks later, after what turned out to be Wien's last visit to the Korkuc farm, Wien was betrayed by a shepherd for a kilo of salt. Wien was then taken to Eishyshok, where he was severely tortured by the police, all of whom knew him personally. They pulled his fingernails out, one by one, offering to spare him if he would reveal the names of other Jews in hiding. Eventually he did give them several names, after which he was taken to the mass grave that contained all the women of Eishyshok, including his wife and daughters. There he was shot, as were the Jews whose names his torturers had forced him to reveal.

Because he had to, Korkuc offered hospitality to many of the Jews' enemies as well. Among the visitors were heavily armed Russian criminal prisoners who had been released from jail to do heavy labor for the Russian army, but chose not to return when the army withdrew. These deserters lived in the forest and preyed upon the countryside, confiscating food and supplies and threatening to shoot anyone who did not accede to their demands. Jewish partisans also came to Korkuc's farm, though they did not loot, since they knew him well and everything he stood for.

A daughter of the shtetl lawyer Mr. Wien. She was murdered with her sister and mother, one of the two shtetl dentists, in the September 1941 massacre. Wien managed to escape and hid in the Dumbla swamps. Though his clothing was in tatters, he managed to keep photos of his wife and daughters in his pockets. Betrayed by a Polish shepherd for a kilo of salt, he was murdered in Eishyshok on the women's grave by the local police. YESC, GILLIOT

The most frequent visitors were the AK, who used to come to the Korkuc farm to rest up prior to a major sortie. Dressed in either civilian clothing or their old Polish army uniforms, they would march into Korkuciany in the full light of day, confident that no one in that Polish village would betray them to the Germans. At night they would camp out at the Korkuc farm, eating, drinking, and partying with girls from the village for hours on end. When they finally left, they carried bundles of food the Korkucs prepared for them.

Sometimes the AK arrived with virtually no advance warning. On one occasion Antoni Gawrylkewicz, the teenage shepherd on the Korkuc farm, saw a long column of AK heading their way; he ran so fast to deliver a warning that he collapsed on the floor when he arrived. Thanks to Antoni, the Korkucs and their young maid Marushka Iwanowska were able to supply their pit dwellers with food to tide them over during the AK visitation, and to conceal the entrances properly. Down in their pit the Sonensons could hear much of what was being said — the boasting about the killing of the Jews, the fanatical zeal for a Poland free of Jews, Communists, and Germans — and could also recognize many of the voices, since they belonged to people who had been their longtime friends, neighbors, and associates.

Korkuc of course would join in these drinking parties, adding his voice to the chorus toasting the freedom of Poland. But his vision of a free Poland, which he could not share with his visitors, was different from theirs, for he viewed the Jews of Eishyshok as loyal Polish citizens, with hundreds of years of local history behind them, who ought by right to be part of the nation that would emerge from the ruins of war. He recalled the rejoicing of the Jews when World War I ended and the Polish Republic was founded, he remembered how devoted the Jews had been to Marshal Pilsudski, he knew that many Jews had served in the Polish army, and he remained committed to them as his fellow Poles.

Unfortunately, rumors began to circulate that Korkuc, as hospitable as he was to the AK, was also the "father of the Jews." He was arrested by the Eishyshok police, and tortured both by them and the Gestapo. Though they knocked out several of his teeth and slashed his face, he continued to maintain his innocence, insisting that he knew nothing about the location of either the Jewish partisans or the Jews in hiding. Eventually he managed to escape and go into hiding himself, where he was slowly nursed back to health. When it seemed safe to do so, he quietly returned to his farm, but the rumors about him persisted. Finally his mother became so nervous that she was unable to sleep, and trembled constantly from fear.

On Christmas night, 1942, Korkuc asked all the Jews on his farm to leave. There was much weeping on all sides, with the Jews pleading to stay, and Pani Korkucowa telling them that she loved them all very much, especially little Sonia (as she called Yaffa). But her love for her son and her fear for the lives of the other members of her household forced her to take this step, she explained. Korkuc managed to find new shelters for the Kabaczniks, the Sonensons, and Itta, sending them to various farms in the vicinity. So in January 1943, during a severe storm that would cover up their tracks, the Sonensons set off for their new home.

As they reached the edge of the forest, the thick falling snow was pierced by what appeared to be scores of lights: the gleaming eyeballs of a pack of hungry wolves. Moshe managed to hold them at bay, and for the rest of the night carried his niece Gittele on his back, since she was too exhausted to walk.

Their new hiding place was under the farmhouse belonging to the brother of the Korkucs' maid, Marushka Iwanowska. Little more than a shack, the Iwanowskis' house had been built without a chimney so the family could avoid the chimney tax, and it was therefore filled with smoke. The overcrowding was severe, since the shack was home not only to five or so Iwanowski children, but all the farm animals as well; the resulting filth was so bad that even the table was covered with manure. In fact, the underground pit that Korkuc had constructed at the Iwanowskis' was actually a more pleasant place than the dwelling above, but it too was very crowded, for the Sonensons had been preceded there by a number of other Jews, including Shepske Kabacznik and a woman named Hayya from Kalesnik. Food was scarce, for the Iwanowskis as well as for the Jews in hiding, and space was so limited that people had to sit on top of one another.

Moshe Sonenson soon realized that even if his family were to survive the raids of the AK, they wouldn't survive the dire conditions of their new underground shelter. Moreover, he feared being discovered by Piczicz, Hayya's Lithuanian husband, who had converted to Judaism when they married but had now joined the Lithuanian collaborators and had made it his mission to find and murder his wife. So off Moshe went one stormy night in search of a new shelter. One by one his old friends rejected him; some would not even allow him to set foot in their homes. After a few nights he went to Lebiedniki to see a Pole named Binkewicz, a man who had been a close friend and owed him a few favors for help rendered in the past. He would love to be able to help out, Binkewicz told Moshe, despite what the priest in Juryzdyki had said in his sermon about the Jews, but out of concern for the safety of his family he could not. And what had the priest in Juryzdyki said? Moshe wanted to know. That the punishment of the Jews was well deserved, and that for hundreds of generations to come they would still be paying for the crucifixion of Jesus, was the reply.[11]

Despite his concerns for his old mother and

three young children, Binkewicz did offer Moshe and his companions — his son Yitzhak and Yoshke Mordekhai's Bleicharowicz, their former coachman whom they had encountered wandering about in the blizzard — three days of shelter in his pigsty.

Moshe finally found a place for his family in the home of a man named Fredik Kodish, who also lived in the village of Lebiedniki, where he was not much liked on account of his Tataric origins. Because Fredik had a beautiful blonde wife whose hunger for money he had trouble appeasing, he was willing to court danger by renting the Sonensons the space under a potato shack attached to his house. There the Sonensons built another pit shelter, this one with a ceiling of wooden logs. But the backbreaking labor was very hard on Moshe, who became deathly ill and developed a huge boil on his neck. When the boil became so large that it threatened to strangle him, his little daughter Yaffa finally lanced it with a razor blade and then used an old healing method she had learned about from Pani Korkucowa: Yitzhak and Yaffa gathered spider webs and mildew in the barn, and applied them to the open wound. Their father did indeed recover, albeit slowly.

During this period a close relationship developed between Zipporah Sonenson and Fredik's wife, who both became pregnant around the same time. Mrs. Kodish, whose first child had died in infancy, was eager to learn everything she could from Zipporah, which was part of the bond between them. But unlike her new friend, who looked forward to the birth of her child with joy, Zipporah knew that for her family a new baby would be a burden, not a blessing, and that the baby itself would have little chance of surviving. Hoping to miscarry, she volunteered for all kinds of heavy work on the farm, but her pregnancy continued.

The seasons changed and the time passed in relative peace, as the Sonensons watched the comings and goings in the outside world through a small window in the potato shack. Unaware that some of their most intimate moments were being closely monitored by six pairs of eyes, people in the vicinity went about their lives, burying their dead, celebrating their weddings and agricultural festivals, harvesting their crops, relieving themselves and even copulating in those same fields.

Then came Sunday February 20, 1944. Shots pierced the open air from the direction of the nearby farm of Mrs. Aneza Bikewiczowa, followed by the screams of a familiar voice: "Don't shoot! I am a captain in the Polish army! I wore the same uniform you are wearing. I have protected the same land!" It was the voice of Benyamin Kabacznik, a cousin of Sorl's and of Moshe and Shalom Sonenson's. The Sonensons ran to the window of Fredik's house in time to see a crowd of AK in Polish army uniforms aiming their weapons at a number of Eishyshkians tied to a wooden fence: Benyamin Kabacznik,

Benyamin Kabacznik, an officer in the Polish army and a great Polish loyalist, in a 1928 portrait. He was murdered by the AK on February 20, 1944, with his wife, son, ten other Jews, and Aneza Bikewiczowa, the righteous Polish woman who hid them in a pit on her farm. PHOTO: YITZHAK URI KATZ. YESC, ZIMMERMAN

his wife Liebke (the only one of Dovid der Kichier Moszczenik's six daughters who had not emigrated to America), and their thirteen-year-old son Yudaleh, a classmate of Gittele Sonenson's; Avraham Sonenson, oldest brother of Moshe and Shalom; Hirshke Melzer; Yankl Koppelman; Shlomo Matikanski, his wife, and their little girl. Now a volley of gunfire rang out. In the middle of the yard, one woman remained standing: Mrs. Bikewiczowa. "Now you will join your Jews!" the White Poles shouted at her. "It is people like you who are preventing a Poland without Jews." As another volley of gunfire echoed throughout Lebiedniki, Mrs. Bikewiczowa fell to the ground, the red of her blood seeping into the white snow. Minutes later, the entire farm and everyone on it was put to the torch by the AK.

Fredik's wife became hysterical and told the Sonensons they had to leave the house immediately. Moshe calmed her down, promising to leave as soon as night fell and they could sneak out undetected, without endangering her or her unborn child. Later that afternoon Fredik, pale and trembling, told them of the events that had led to the massacre. Aneza Bikewiczowa had received a visit from the AK, under the leadership of Krisha, the local commander. Despite the fact that her two older sons were members of the AK, they had come to search her farm for Jews. When one of them slammed his gun against the table, it went off accidentally and hit Mrs. Bikewiczowa in the arm. The blood so frightened her little girl that the child ran over and said, "Please do not kill my mother. I will show you where the Jews are hiding." Whereupon she led them to the pit beneath the stables. The subsequent shooting left all nine Jews wounded, some of them severely; but they were still alive when they were set on fire. One Eishyshkian, Benyamin Kanichowski, survived by hiding in a pile of wood near the stable. And the AK spared Mrs. Bikewiczowa's daughter.

After darkness fell, the Sonensons departed, with no place to go on a cold, snowy night. Zipporah was now four months pregnant. For several nights they slept in a nearby forest, under a fern tree, while Moshe made forays to the homes of various farmers to seek shelter. But everyone knew the fate of the Bikewiczowa family, and no one was willing to take such a risk. Gittele started to cough blood. Food was running out. It was bitter cold. With a pregnant wife and three young children, one of them apparently quite sick, Moshe knew that going off and joining the partisans was not an option. He could think of no other alternative than to return to the farm of the Korkuc family, and throw himself on their mercy.

When the Sonensons entered the Korkuc house, Pani Korkucowa fell to her knees and began to cry. Moshe fell to his knees also, and begged her to let them stay. He reminded her that his wife's parents, Yitzhak Uri and Alte Katz, had saved her son from death during World War I. They had pulled him out from under the corpses of Polish soldiers and, with the help of the Koppelman family, who also had a pharmacy, nursed him back to health. Had they been discovered, they would all have been shot by the Russians. Moshe also promised that he would once again pay them generously for their help, and would in addition give them property in Eishyshok, starting with the slaughterhouse. After a long negotiation with many tears shed on both sides, they were permitted to stay. Their gratitude on returning to their pit knew no bounds.

Soon after their return, the Sonensons learned that in the wake of the murder of Aneza Bikewiczowa and her Jews, all the other Korkuc pit dwellers had also returned. Like the Sonensons, they had all been turned out of their hiding places, and had all found themselves with nowhere to go. The Kabaczniks were back in their pit beneath the stable; Itta had returned too. Everyone had horrible stories to tell. And their stories were but individual entries in a long ledger of horrors, for as bad as things had been in the past, the heightened activities of the local AK were resulting in new levels of death and devastation for Jews who had thus far managed to survive in hiding.

The accelerating aggression of the AK was a response to a growing sense of hopefulness that the war might soon be over. As the news from the eastern front became more encouraging, the AK began to plan for the future of Poland, a crucial component of which was the extermination of all the Jews still within its borders. A "Poland without Jews" was the only way to ensure a free Poland, unthreatened by the dangers of Communist ideology and uncontaminated by an alien presence.

On January 25, 1944, a meeting had been convened by local AK commander Krisha and the Polish Catholic pharmacist Sharavei, at which all the Polish elite of Eishyshok were present, including Dr. Shemitkowski, the veterinarian, in whose home the meeting was held; Jan Gurak, former principal of the Polish school in Eishyshok and an official with the Radun police force during the German occupation; Stanislav Katowietski, the former chief of police in Eishyshok; Dr. Lehr, a longtime resident of Eishyshok who had numbered many Jews among his patients; a miller named Krolowitz, once a close friend of Avraham Dubitski, as well as his tenant; and two young priests, assistants to Father Maczulski at the Juryzdyki church. Their agenda: how to resolve "the Jewish question" in time for the return of the London-based government-in-exile at the end of the war, which was now felt to be imminent. [12]

Their decision was that all Poles now needed to make a renewed effort to ferret out and kill every Jew in hiding or in the forest. To make sure the message got out to as wide an audience as possible, they forced Father Maczulski to present it in a sermon from the pulpit in Juryzdyki.

At the beginning of 1944, besides the Jews living in nearby forests either as partisans or fugitives there were close to two hundred still in hiding with Christian and Muslim families in the vicinity. Most were from Eishyshok, though some were friends and relatives from other towns. The sermon that was duly delivered on a Sunday in February proved a death sentence for most of those two hundred. The killing at Aneza Bikewiczowa's in late February was just one of scores of such incidents. Many of them took place at the hands of Christians whom the Jews had considered their friends.

A number of the Koppelman cousins. The first three children from the right, Beila, Rachel, and Elisha, were murdered with their parents Markl and Mina Koppelman by a member of the AK with an ax. Four other children were killed in the September 1941 massacre. The child on the left, Elisha Peretz, was killed in the Arab-Israeli War in the Sinai Campaign, 1956.
PHOTO: ALTE KATZ. YESC, N. FRISCHER-KOPPELMAN

Markl Koppelman, his wife Mina, and their children Beila, Rachel, and Elisha managed to survive the massacres in both Eishyshok and Radun, but not the hospitality of their good friend Kadishon of Dociszki. Having deposited some of their most precious possessions with him, they took refuge in an underground pit on his farm. One night while the Koppelmans were asleep, Kadishon murdered them all with an axe, then scattered the pieces of their bodies on the ground for the pigs and other animals to eat. After learning of the tragedy from Kazimierz Korkuc, Moshe Sonenson left his hiding place on the Korkuc farm to gather what was left of their remains. With the help of Meir Kabacz-

Standing on Vilna Street bridge are Yaakov Kaganov (right) with his two cousins Shifrale and Motele Kaganov. Shifrale and Motele, with their mother Ida Kaganov, her mother, and Ida's sister Kreinele Kanichowski hid in the forest. They were betrayed by a Christian friend and murdered by the local police on the women's mass grave in Eishyshok. Shifrale was Yaffa Sonenson's best friend. Yaakov emigrated to Israel and later to America. YESC, BLACHAROWICZ-WISZIK

A group of friends on an outing to the Seklutski forest: (right to left) Miriam Kabacznik; a Hebrew teacher; Kreinele Kanichowski; Shepske Sonenson; Shoshana Katz; two Hebrew teachers; Frumele Abelov; Yehiel Blacharowicz; and Dina Weidenberg. Only Miriam survived the war; all the others were murdered in the 1941 Eishyshok massacre and by the Poles in other locations. PHOTO: BEN ZION SZREJDER. YESC, KABACZNIK

nik, he carried them into the forest, where he buried them in an unmarked grave and said Kaddish over them, returning to his hiding place before dawn.

Hirshl Yurkanski and his wife Mariyasl were murdered by the Poles who had been sheltering them. In happier times Mariyasl had been one of the shtetl scribes, a woman much loved by the local Polish peasants for whom she wrote letters. Honeh Michalowski the hatmaker was killed by his Christian friends. A number of the Paikowskis were killed by their former friends. Alter Kabacznik was caught in Paradin, begging for food. A local Pole who knew him very well put him and his daughter Golde in a carriage — Alter accepting his fate quietly, eleven-year-old Golde sobbing bitterly and asking for mercy — and drove them to the police station in Eishyshok to collect his reward. Kreinele Kanichowski, her sister Ida Kanichowski Kaganov, and Ida's two young children Shifrale and Motele, who had been in hiding in the forest, were betrayed by a Christian friend and brought back to Eishyshok, where they were murdered near the women's mass grave. Esther Kiuchefski, the daughter of former Eishyshok mayor Meir, along with her husband Yeffim Shiffel and daughter Mirale were murdered by the AK.

Shlomo Kiuchefski, brother of Esther, scion of one of the leading families of Eishyshok, and at one time the man considered Eishyshok's most eligible bachelor, was also murdered by the AK. Trying to talk his way out of death, he told his killers of his illustrious background as the descendant of well-known Polish patriots. It was his grandmother, Fradle-Leah Kiuchefski, who had hidden Ludwik Narbutt, the local commander of the Polish uprising of 1863, in her bedcovers, thereby saving him from certain death at the hands of the Russians. Wild laughter, a chorus of voices chanting "Poland without Jews!", and a hail of bullets was the response he got.

The wife and two daughters of theater director Yossef Michalowski were killed in Korkuciany by the AK. Michalowski and his son were murdered in another nearby village, where Korkuc had built them a shelter. Tanhum Ballon, his wife, two sons, and a daughter were murdered. So, too, were Asher the shohet and one of his grandsons. (Eishyshok's other shohet, Reb Itche Burstein, had been killed in Eishyshok on September 22, 1941, his throat slit with his own ritual slaughter knife.) Shlomo the baker, his wife, and their two children were murdered by Christian friends. These victims constitute but a fragment of a long list of Eishyshkians murdered by their Christian neighbors, a list compiled by two of their townsfolk.[13]

The AK became increasingly popular in the vicinity, presenting themselves as protectors of Polish lives and property, who would save the local farmers from the depredations of the Russian and Jewish partisans in the countryside. They were the voice of the true Polish government, the government-in-exile in London, and it was they who would retrieve this area of Poland from Lithuania, ensuring its return to its rightful owner. This platform appealed to many, even to moderate Poles, and the AK took almost complete control of the numerous Polish-populated villages in the region of Eishyshok.

The AK penetrated even the Korkuc stronghold, when Kazimierz Korkuc's seventeen-year-old nephew announced that he was joining. Czeslaw was the son of Kazimierz's older brother, who had been exiled to Siberia by the Russians. An honest, intelligent young man, Czeslaw had no personal animosity toward the Jews, but a strong belief in the AK as the agent of a free Poland. He was well aware of the Jews hiding on his uncle's land, and indeed had spent many hours being tutored in math by Miriam Kabacznik, who was helping him toward his goal of becoming an engineer. Though they felt Czeslaw would not intentionally do anything to harm them, he had an almost compulsive honesty that made them fear he would accidentally reveal their hiding place.

His big test came in March 1944. Krisha and an elite unit of the AK were once again in residence at the Korkuc farm, using it as their home base, and this time staying around nine days, which was longer than usual. Down in the pit, the Sonensons thought they had reached the end. Every move they made needed to be planned; even relieving oneself in the pail had to be coordinated with the movements of the livestock above. In the dark, airless pit, where everyone sat motionless for hours on end, only the lice roamed freely.

The family had had time to put in but a meager supply of food, which Moshe rationed out in tiny pieces of cheese and bread, and small drops of honey. Yaffa's hands and legs felt as if they had become detached from her body, to float like white feathers in the darkness. But remembering the fate of her baby brother in the attic in Radun, she did not complain. Gittele's cough was the biggest hazard, which she tried to contain by stuffing her mouth with rags. When

Shlomo Kiuchefski (right) with future brother-in-law Zeev Kaganowicz. Shlomo was murdered by the AK, though his family had been very loyal to Poland. They supported the Polish uprising of 1863, his grandmother endangering her own life to save Narbutt, the regional commander of the uprising. Zeev was murdered in one of the ghettos. PHOTO: YITZHAK URI KATZ. YESC, BERKOWITCH

she removed them they were always stained with blood.

From above, they could hear every noise, every voice. They could hear Krisha, they could hear the guards circulating about the house with their dogs, and most heart-stoppingly of all, they could hear Czeslaw. Every time he opened his mouth they wondered what would come out of it.

After a few days Krisha started to complain about the stench from the animals in Pani Korkucowa's room, which he found unbearable. He ordered that the animals be taken out and the room cleaned. This would have meant death for Korkuc as well as his Jews, for the trapdoor to their underground pit would be seen once all the clutter and the livestock were removed. But just as the evacuation of the animals was about to begin, a messenger arrived to inform Krisha that a fierce battle being waged with the Russian partisans required the aid of his troops. They left in great haste. Czeslaw had passed his test with honor, for the AK were none the wiser about the Sonensons' presence after their lengthy stay on the Korkuc farm.

When the Sonensons emerged from their cave, they had been so motionless for so long that they had to learn to walk again. Gittele had suffered the most from the cold and the damp, but everyone was miserable, and at night they all sat covered in sheepskins, warming themselves on the huge oven outside Pani Korkucowa's room. Meanwhile, their clothes had been tossed into a huge pot of boiling water to kill the lice.

Toward the end of May 1944 the holiday of Shavuot came around. Like all other holidays they celebrated in the pit, it was observed by the telling of stories about the history of the holiday, the saying of whatever prayers Moshe and Shalom were able to remember, and reminiscences about how they had celebrated the holiday in happier times. But the biggest event was the "eating" of the special food associated with that holiday. Zipporah would ask everyone their favorite holiday dish, and then "prepare" it by naming each of its ingredients. "Dishing it out," she would allow everyone plenty of time to savor it, before asking them their opinion. This make-believe game was much enjoyed by everyone. On this Shavuot, Gittele most enjoyed the imaginary blintzes, and even asked for seconds. When they played their other favorite game, "What will I do after liberation," Gittele was once more an avid participant. She said that after liberation she intended to redesign the obituary pages of the newspaper, to make them look more cheerful. One morning a few days later, Yaffa, who shared a blanket with Gittele, tried to wake her up. But she was cold as ice. Gittele had died of tuberculosis at the age of thirteen.

Gittele's father's first reaction was to blame Yaffa, claiming that she had grabbed too large a share of the blanket, causing Gittele to take sick. This was followed by a fierce and bitter exchange between the two brothers, with Moshe reminding Shalom of all that he had done for him and his daughter. He had carried Gittele on his back on that terrible night in January 1943, when he ought to have been carrying his own children; he had been paying out gold every month to support Shalom and Gittele in their underground pit since May 1942, though Shalom had never spared so much as a morsel of the generous supplies of food he and his family had received from their former maid in Ghetto Radun. Finally they ran out of recriminations, and the two brothers fell into each other's arms, crying.

When night fell they buried Gittele on the road leading to Lebiedniki. Her face shone up at them out of the grave they had dug, round and pale as the moon. They trod repeatedly over her grave, back and forth, so that there would be no trace of fresh soil visible in the morning. Shalom and Moshe Sonenson, her father and uncle, and Meir and Shepske Kabacznik, her cousins, recited the Kaddish, not just for Gittele but for all those who had died during the last few months.

Now that Zipporah was nearing her time, she slept near the "heart," as the air shaft venting into the hole beneath the cherry tree was called. On Monday June 8, she went into labor, and Moshe walked her out of the pit into the stable, where she lay on a bed of fresh straw amid the sheep and cows. Pani Korkucowa came in with boiled water and towels, and Sorl Kabacznik and Hayya Solomianski emerged from the pit beneath the stable to attend the birth. Suddenly Marushka the maid began to scream, "Jesus, it's a baby boy!" Pani Korkucowa crossed herself, saying, "It is just like the birth of our Lord Jesus." And Moshe, ever ready to see the humor in even the grimmest of circumstances, responded, "This is our eternal problem: nobody ever allows our women to have their babies peacefully in their own home."

The next night, Antoni the shepherd came to them with a basket padded in flax, and they placed the baby inside it, with a nugget of sugar wrapped in cloth for the baby to suck on. Attached to the basket was an envelope with some money, and a note explaining that the child had been born out of wedlock to a girl from the Polish nobility. As Moshe and Korkuc took the baby away, Zipporah pressed her daughter close, telling her, "Your babies will be born in hospitals, free, proud Jews!" Moshe and Korkuc tied the basket under the eaves of a home that belonged to a Polish peasant and his sister, a nun, who were known for their willingness to raise abandoned children.

That same night, Russian bombers flew over the area, dropping packages of food supplies for the partisans, and leaflets that announced their imminent arrival. Some of the farmers in the area therefore suggested that the mystery baby be named "parachutist"; others suggested he be named Jan — which was also the request in the note on his basket — since he was born close to the holiday of St. John the Baptist. His parents privately named him Hayyim, in memory of Moshe's mother, Hayya, and because the word means "life." He was baptized Jan in the church at Juryzdyki, before a crowd that included Fredik Kodish's wife, holding her own infant son in her arms. She guessed the baby's true identity but told no one.

The Sonensons and the Kabaczniks were now among the last handful of Jews still in hiding with Christian friends in the vicinity. Almost all the other surviving Jews were in the forests.

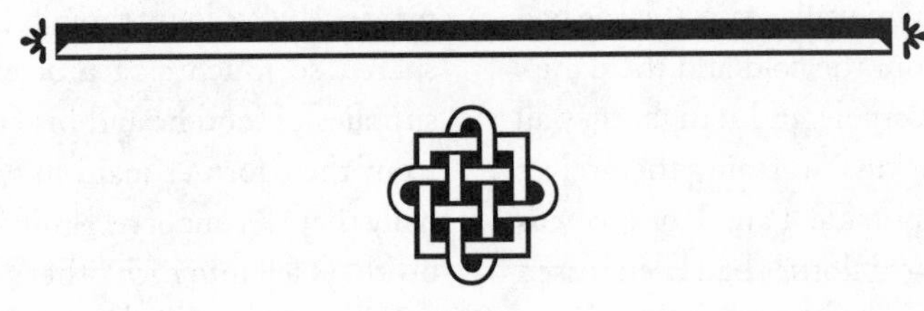

AT THE END OF 1943, AK ACTIVITY INTENSIFIED AND BECAME MORE OPEN, ESPECIALLY in the southwest Vilna region and southeast of Lida. The vicinity of Eishyshok was in the center of the attacks launched by the White Poles, the result of a local official agreement they reached with the Germans in Lida. Details of the agreement are included in a secret, urgent report mailed January 18, 1944, by Dr. Wulf, the Gebietskommisar of the Vilna region, to Dr. A. V. Rentein, the generalkommisar of Lithuania.[1]

It stated that the White Poles did not want to fight against the Germans, and could kill about 800 Bolsheviks in a specified area. As part of the agreement, the White Poles received a supply of 120,000 bullets of infantry ammunition, twelve to fifteen machine guns, and several grenades. The Germans also granted the Poles medical supplies and care for the wounded. There was no need for the Germans to provide food, since the White Poles were being taken care of by the peasants in the area. In Eishyshok and Varena (Aran), the AK force numbered about 200.

The information in the supposedly secret document was common knowledge. It was openly discussed by the AK with the local population, since the villages and estates of the well-to-do farmers, such as that of Kazimierz Korkuc, served as their meeting places and food supply centers.

Though the official document refers to the Bolshevik gangs, the Jews became the main target of the White Poles. The Jews quickly realized that since the AK had German support, they would have to leave their hiding places with the Polish peasants and seek shelter in the forests, despite the harsh winter weather of 1944.

In addition to the increased danger, the Jews were finding it more and more difficult to pay their righteous rescuers. Although Yad Vashem, Israel's Martyrs and Heroes Remembrance Authority, in its definition of a "Righteous Among the Nations," includes the requirement that "remunerations [were] neither requested nor received by the rescuer for the action or aid," most rescuers in the vicinity of Eishyshok were too poor to have provided food and shelter for the Jews they hid had they not received some money. Even some of the more affluent rescuers, like Kazimierz Korkuc, collected money from those who could afford it, because it enabled them to help many others.

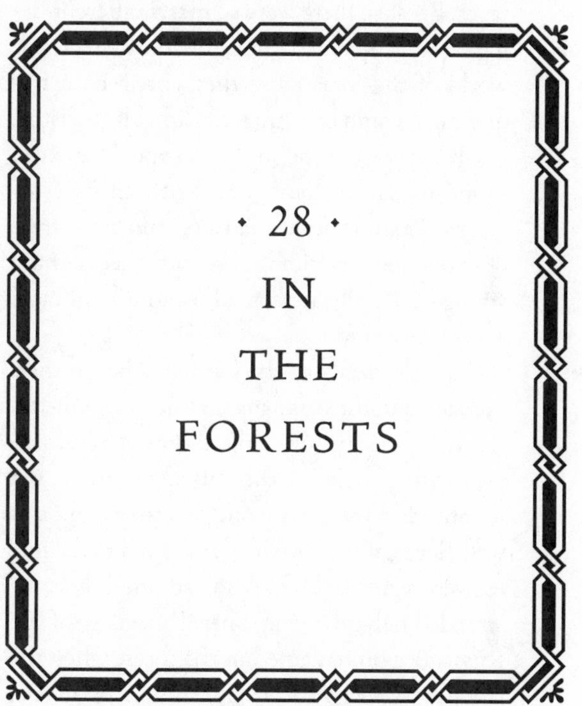

FROM THE GHETTO'S PRISON WALLS,
TO THE FOREST'S WONDERS,
ON MY HAND THERE ARE NO CHAINS,
BUT A GUN THAT THUNDERS.
WHEN ON DUTY, MY DEAR GUN
KISSES NECK AND SHOULDER.
WITH MY FRIEND TO GIVE ME HEART,
I GROW BOLDER AND BOLDER.

Shmerl Kaczerginski
THE PARTISAN
JEW

Those who took to the forest lived in a variety of situations, some on their own, some within the partisan community, some in family units or in groups bound by ties of friendship and geography, some in larger communal groups. And many people changed their living situations depending on the season, circumstances, and shifting alliances. Each way of life had its own difficulties and hazards, its own advantages. Because there were so many different living arrangements within the dark, secretive world of the forest, and they changed so frequently, it could be extremely difficult to distinguish between friend and foe, sometimes even more so than in hiding. Yet with all its challenges, life in the forest had a certain air of freedom that those in hiding never breathed. For the young, especially, it seemed a more honorable way of surviving.

From the very day the Germans began their invasion and the Russians their retreat, June 22, 1941, the forest became a place of refuge and survival, particularly for the Russians, and as the months and years wore on, for other groups as well. Some of the Russians who lived in the forest were regular soldiers who had simply become stranded behind enemy lines. But many of the Russians who remained in the forest when the troops moved on had been criminal prisoners, including rapists and murderers, who had been released from jail to work for the Russian army as laborers on large-scale construction projects like military airports, fortifications, and roads. Several contingents of these criminals had been brought in to do work in the area around Eishyshok.

When the Russian army retreated it left in great haste, abandoning large quantities of ammunition, which the former prisoners seized. Making themselves at home in the forests, they became roving bandits who threatened the nearby farmers with death whenever their demands for food and other supplies were not met. Occasionally they worked as farmhands during the sowing and harvest seasons, but mainly they sustained themselves by theft and thuggery. When other groups began looking to the forest for refuge as well, these heavily armed criminals constituted a serious menace—especially to young women. Eventually many of these Russian ex-cons joined various Russian partisan groups. Though they could be tough, aggressive fighters against the mutual enemy, the number of drinkers, anti-Semites, and rapists within their ranks made them a continuing source of danger to fellow partisans and especially women.

As early as May 1942, after the slaughter in Ghetto Radun, some of the Jewish escapees decided to take their chances in the forest, rather than hiding with Christian friends. In the forest they lived in groups of three basic kinds.

Some individuals hid together in the forest, linked by ties of friendship and/or family, without any central leadership and generally without any significant means of self-defense. A second category consisted of family camps who allied themselves with a group of armed men and women, under the leadership of a single charismatic personality. In some cases these groups went beyond agendas of food, shelter, and self-protection, to rescue and revenge operations, and even to aggressive action against the enemy. The third group were full-fledged partisan fighting battalions (atriads) organized on military lines, some of them all Jewish in makeup, some of them Russian partisan brigades who reported to Moscow and received substantial support in the form of training, troops, ammunition, and medical supplies. Wounded Russian partisans could even be flown out of the forest and into military hospitals in Russia for emergency medical treatment. There were also Lithuanian and Lithuanian–Communist partisan units. This pattern of diversity pertained throughout the forests of Eastern Europe.

INDIVIDUALS IN THE FORESTS AROUND EISHYSHOK

From mid-1942 until liberation, groups of friends and relatives as well as occasional isolated individuals were constantly roaming the large, dense forests (puszcza) of Nacha, Rudnicki, and Mieszczanca in the vicinity of Eishyshok and Radun, as well as smaller wooded areas. They lived either in underground shelters, usually close to fir trees because of the protection and camouflage provided by the low-hanging branches, or in temporary, aboveground shelters called *buda* (Polish for "booth"), constructed of fir tree branches. Some of the groups consisted of just three or four people, who preferred the smaller size because they felt the risk of detection by hostile farmers and shepherds was less; others wanted more of a sense of community, a feeling that they "lived among Jews," and they opted for life in larger groups.

The Blacharowicz women, Fruml and her daughters Szeina and Gutke, lived in one of these more extended communities, along with a number of other Eishyshkians and people from nearby shtetlekh, including Liba Shlosberg and her aging parents, Shmaye-Mendl and Freidl, and the Davidowicz family, Moshe the Lubaver and Dvora, with their three surviving daughters, all of them adults. (A fourth had been killed when they were fleeing Ghetto Radun.) By the summer of 1942 the group numbered about forty people, who moved from one temporary shelter to another in the Nacha and Mieszczanca forests. The group would maintain two budas at a time, each one measuring about six feet by six, a space so cramped that people had to sleep sardine-style. Inside was a small oven built of bricks and stones. The building of the shelter and the oven was a community task, but each individual was responsible for providing his or her own food and clothing. Though some of the partisans in the area, men like Zvi Michalowski and even the legendary Elke Ariowitch (popularly known as "Todras"), would occasionally bring food and other items to the family groups, for the most part people had to find local supply sources.

Since everybody in the group was from the area, be it Olkenik, Radun, or Eishyshok, they all had Christian and Tatar friends and associates nearby to whom they could turn for help. Of course, just as those Jews who were in hiding on farms did, they had to learn to distinguish between those who had remained friends and those who had turned against them. But once they had located their own trustworthy farmer or peasant, they were likely to keep the source a secret from the others, out of concern both for themselves and for the farmer (because the fewer who knew, the less danger for the farmer).

Having traveled the countryside for years selling her Singer sewing machines, Szeina Blacharowicz was very well known in the area, which was both a blessing and a curse. She maintained two primary points of contact with the outside world, one a poor Polish farmer and his wife, the Abrashuks, and the other a much more affluent couple, Marushka and Stashek Kuzmicki. Szeina knew Marushka well, from the days when Marushka was growing up in Eishyshok, in an apartment on Bathhouse Lane.

Marushka's father was a skilled laborer who worked on the paving of the Pilsudski highway, and had been involved in a tragic accident that resulted in the death of his son during the course of that project. Marushka herself was a beautiful girl who attracted a great deal of attention from the opposite sex, and was eventually courted by Stashek Kuzmicki, a member of the Polish szlachta (petty nobility), despite her humble origins.

Stashek was the only one of the Kuzmicki sons who did not pursue an education in Vilna or one of the other European capitals where the family sent their children, for his sole ambition was to farm the land. Since the Kuzmickis considered themselves far above Marushka in station, with their large estate and their beautiful manor house, they were not happy about the impending marriage, but eventually they acceded to it, after Marushka and Stashek were able to put together a substantial dowry with the help of some of their Jewish friends. Now they lived on the Kuzmicki estate with their three young daughters, in a relatively humble building that was located at a considerable distance from the main manor house — which turned out to be very fortunate for Szeina, since all the other Kuzmicki sons were members of the AK and the manor house served as one of the bases the local AK used prior to their raids.

Stashek and Marushka provided Szeina with food, occasional amenities like soap and a place to wash up, and even newspapers, which they could buy without attracting any suspicion, since they were part of the educated, literate Polish elite. They also tried their best to keep her spirits up. Unlike most of the other farmers who helped the Jews, but whose usual practice was to begin each encounter with a disheartening recitation of all the latest casualties and mishaps that had befallen other Jews in the vicinity, Stashek and Marushka doled out the news in reverse order, highlighting the positive and saving the grim facts for last.

Each time the Kuzmickis assisted Szeina, they were putting themselves and their three daughters in danger, especially since members of their own family were dedicated Akowtsy. But their commitment to Szeina was unwavering, and it meant the difference between life and death, not just to Szeina herself but to the others in her group as well, for some of the supplies they gave her — for example, two shovels, which were worth their weight in gold because the group was establishing new camps so frequently — were absolutely crucial for survival.

Despite the difficult conditions in the forest, several members of Szeina's group observed not just the Jewish holidays but many of the traditions and even the dietary laws, somehow managing not to eat nonkosher food, and to bake matzot at Passover. Avraham Lipkunski, who was with the partisans at that time, used to come to them in the forest to warm himself with a bit of Jewish tradition, sometimes making his own contribution to the holiday observance, as when he brought white chickens for the Yom Kippur ceremony of kapparot. Years later he remembered the theological reservations he had that Yom Kippur as he took part in the group's prayer of atonement. "We are guilty," he recited, while thinking to himself that the prayer should read, "*They* are guilty."[2]

The cold of the winter that followed that Yom Kippur proved too much for old Shmaye-Mendl. His body turned as white as his beard, and his legs became seriously frostbitten. Though his daughter Liba managed to get goosefat from Marushka Kuzmicki which she rubbed into her father's feet, nothing seemed to help him. "When

Szeina Blacharowicz (second from left) visits Marushka Kuzmicki (second from right) in Canada. Marushka helped Szeina survive the Holocaust. The two young men are Marushka's grandsons. At right is Elka Zubizki, who was also helped by Marushka and her husband Stashek.

YESC, BLACHAROWICZ-WISZIK

is Gromnice?" he kept asking Liba, referring to the Christian lighting of candles in honor of Jesus that is traditionally the occasion for a major trade fair in the region; and indeed it was on Gromnice, February 2, 1944, that he finally succumbed. He seemed to have predicted both his own death and his child's life, for he told Liba that she would survive the war, and she did. Shmaye-Mendl was given a proper Jewish burial, in a wooden coffin Liba made for him, and with the Kaddish she recited over his grave.[3]

Despite the familylike atmosphere and the observance of Jewish tradition, some of the young people in the group were clamoring to join the partisans, seeing that way of life as far superior. Twenty-year-old Gutke Blacharowicz was one of them, and she pleaded with her mother and sister Szeina to allow her to leave. They strongly objected, for they felt the partisan groups, many of them including ex-convicts in their ranks, were far too rough for a young woman. Against their wishes, Gutke took off one day, but she never made it to the partisans. Ambushed by the AK, she was tortured to death, cut up piece by piece as they tried to force her to reveal the hiding place of her family and other Jews in the forest. She died without betraying them.

The AK were increasing their activities in the forest around this time, just as they were doing in the villages. Another of their attacks took the lives of a number of members of the group with whom an Eishyshkian named Benyamin Frankl was hiding. Returning to search for survivors, Frankl found a little boy, covered in blood, lying next to his dead mother. When he took the boy to Szeina Blacharowicz's group, they accepted him, but no one really wanted the burden of caring for a child in the forest. As things turned out, Liba Shlosberg ended up as his principal caretaker, because of a bargain she had made with God one day: Out on a food-gathering mission, she was ambushed by the AK, and with bullets flying all around her she had vowed that if she survived, little Barukh'l would have a mother. Fulfilling her part of the bargain, she became an extraordinarily loving and devoted protector.

Szeina Blacharowicz (right) with younger sister Gutke. Gutke was caught by the AK in the forest, raped, tortured, and murdered. YESC, BLACHAROWICZ-WISZIK

March 19, 1944, was a beautiful day, the birthday of Pilsudski's namesake, St. Joseph. Marushka Kuzmicki warned Szeina that the AK contingent who were staying at her mother-in-law's manor house were planning a "rabbit hunt"— an obvious euphemism for killing Jews. Before Szeina's group had time to escape, they heard the frozen earth crackle beneath the boots of the AK. Everyone began running away wildly. Liba, wearing only one boot, grabbed her mother Freidl, her beloved Barukh'l, and her prayer book, and made a dash for it. Of the three, only Liba made it. Barefoot Szeina took off, holding her mother's hand and pulling her along from bush to bush, as bullets whizzed by and ricocheted off the trees of the forest. Suddenly her mother panicked, for the Akowtsy was directly in front of them, and she ran for cover. As Szeina hid behind a thick tree trunk, she could see a pleasant-looking, clean-shaven Polish youth just a few feet away, aiming his short French gun straight at her mother. He fired; Szeina ran, and she kept on running, trying to outmaneuver the bullets, until the forest fell silent.

Sitting under a tree, trying to rub some life back into her numb, frozen legs, she suddenly heard the sound of footsteps close by. Then through the branches she glimpsed a familiar face, that of Avraham Teikan from Olkenik, another of the forest dwellers. He had come to search for survivors. Teikan warmed her feet until she regained feeling in them, and wrapped them in rags so she could walk. Eventually she was able to reach the house of Stashek and Marushka Kuzmicki. It was no longer possible for them to present things in the most positive light in order to give their friend hope, as they usually did. Stashek told Szeina that he had buried her mother. Szeina was now the sole survivor of her family. Of the seven family members who had escaped the Horse Market with the help of their Christian friends, all but Szeina had been killed by Poles between 1942 and 1944: her mother Fruml, her sister Gutke, her aunt Ida, Ida's children Shifrale and Motele, and Ida's sister Kreinele Kanichowski. Only eighteen of their forest group had survived the AK hunt, which took place a mere four months before liberation.[4]

The survivors regrouped in a new location, building new budas and maintaining their way of life. Not once during the twenty-six months they spent in the forest did any member of their group, either before or after the AK massacre, take food from anyone by force. They either received it as a gift from the local farmers and villagers or from the occasional partisan — Todras in particular being a generous supplier of food and soap — or they paid for it from the meager possessions they had deposited with their Christian friends.

THE PARTISAN FAMILY CAMPS (SEMEINIE LAGRIE)

Large groups of noncombatants made up mainly of women and children and the elderly joined together in Jewish family camps that were linked to Jewish partisan fighting units. Unlike the Russian partisans, who viewed their main task as fighting the Germans and who therefore refused to accept anyone who could conceivably be a hindrance during a military action, the Jewish partisans had a dual agenda: fighting the enemy, as the Russian partisans did, but also saving Jewish lives (and avenging Jewish deaths). This put them at odds with the Russians, resulting in a great deal of tension and hostility between the two groups.

One of the largest of the partisan family camps was established by Tuvia Bielski and his brothers Asael, Zusya, and Aharon of Navaredok, who were based in the Naliboki forest. Like many of their fellow Jewish partisans, the Bielskis were dedicated to saving Jews and to retaliating against local murderers of Jews. Thanks to a camp that was large and well enough organized to support workshops, a maintenance crew, a medical staff, and even a small hospital, they were able to provide food and shelter for those who had escaped into the forest from the ghettos, as well as for their own people. Any pregnant woman had expert assistance when her time came, and those who chose to terminate their pregnancies were also helped. In fact, abortions were of such high priority that on one occasion, when there were three abortions to perform, the doctor knew that the situation gave him considerable bargaining power and he refused to attend to the women until he was given three pairs of boots (for his wife, his assistant, and himself). "No boots, no abortions," he said to the three women in Tuvia Bielski's headquarters. In a matter of hours Tuvia saw to it that three pairs of boots were provided.[5]

Eishyshkians living in partisan family camps included Basha Shuster Landsman and her mother Hodl and daughter Hava, who arrived in the forest of Nipiczansky toward the end of 1942. They had left Eishyshok with Basha's husband Moshe in 1939, shortly after the war broke out, because they feared becoming the targets of reprisals against Basha's brother Hayyim Shuster, one of the shtetl Communists. Hoping that Byelorussia would be safer, they had moved to Lida, and when the Communists were expelled from Eishyshok during the Lithuanian occupation, Hayyim moved there too.

Lida was occupied by the Germans on June 30, 1941. On July 8, 1941, eighty Jewish intellectuals and professionals were murdered by the Nazis, who picked their victims by examining people's hands, and allowing those with calluses — the mark of manual labor — to live. Moshe Landsman was among the dead. Shortly afterward Basha led her mother and daughter to Ghetto Zhetl (Dyatlovo), where she somehow secured the lifesaving yellow permits for all three of them, despite the fact that her daughter was too young to qualify for one, and her mother too old. In Zhetl they survived a major Aktion in April 1942 by hiding in an underground bunker (schron) for seven days. While in hiding, Basha's sixty-two-year-old mother had a heart attack, and Basha herself suffered an attack of retinitis pigmentosa, a blinding disease, but still they kept going.

When they realized that Ghetto Zhetl was probably going to be liquidated, the ghetto leaders made contact with the partisans, who included Hayyim Shuster, to form a resistance group that would smuggle people out of the ghetto and into the forest. Unfortunately, when Hayyim sent one of his contacts to get his own family out, they were unable to leave because nine-year-old Hava had scarlet fever at the time. The doctor Basha consulted told her, "If you take her to the forest she will die, because there are no medicines or doctors there. Here she has half a chance."

Accepting the doctor's advice, Basha remained in the ghetto until August 1942, by which time Hava had recovered and the three of them were able to escape and to find their way to the home of Vashka, the farmer Hayyim had earlier sent to rescue them. He took them to the Nipiczansky forest, where they were expecting to rejoin Hayyim, Basha and Hayyim's sister Rivka, and Rivka's husband. But when they arrived at the partisans' family camp, they learned that Hayyim was dead. One of the roving Russian criminals who had attached himself to the partisan movement had killed him.[6]

Basha, Hava, and Hodl were nonetheless taken in by the camp, where their home consisted of a carefully camouflaged underground space of the kind many partisans in the forests had constructed, known in Russian as a *ziemlanka.* With the onset of winter, however, the camp was ceaselessly on the move, hunted down wherever they went by the Germans and the AK, who were constantly launching raids on the partisan camps.

On January 31, 1943, Rivka went into labor. She was twenty-three and this was her first child. Unlike the Bielski camp, the camp in the Nipiczansky forest had no doctor, nurse, or midwife. Determined to see to it that her sister delivered her child safely, Basha set off in the 40-below-zero cold wearing only the flimsiest of shoes, in search of another partisan camp where she could get help. The same determination that had enabled her to quit school and go to work in her widowed mother's store at the age of nine, and that had seen her and her mother and her daughter through every crisis of the war years, was now brought to bear on the problem of finding a midwife for her sister. After walking miles and miles, she found one and brought her back to Rivka in time for the delivery. Though the Germans chose this moment to stage one of their infamous raids (oblawas), and the ziemlanka where Rivka was giving birth was so deep underground that it was flooded with water which had to be bailed out by the pailful, both baby and mother survived. And Hava recovered from the typhus she had contracted around this time as well.

The baby was named Joseph. Hodl, the boy's grandmother, took upon herself the responsibility for his welfare. Whenever there was an attack on the camp, Hodl would grab her grandson and run with him. As people all around them were being shot, Hodl and her small charge always somehow managed to evade the fusillade of bullets. Joseph also escaped the lot of many other infants in hiding: suffocation. Whenever the AK or the White (anti-Communist) Russians were spotted in the vicinity of their ziemlanka, the adults would clap their hands over the mouths of any babies or children who might give away their hiding place. Sometimes, as had happened with the Sonenson baby in Ghetto Radun, the result was death. But Joseph survived every danger, including that one. And indeed all the Shuster women, as well as little Joseph, would survive the war.

Not all elderly women were as lucky as Hodl Shuster. When the Yurkanski brothers ran to the forest in the early days of 1944, their mother, Zirl, could not keep up with them, and they left her behind in the snow. Zirl, a descendant of one of the five founding families of Eishyshok, was picked up by Poles, former customers who had bought leather from her tannery for years. They took her back to Eishyshok, where she was tortured, and later murdered, then buried near the mass grave.

Elke Ariowitch, known as Todras, in Radun, July 7, 1938. In 1942 he became one of the most beloved partisans in the vicinity. He was the only camp commander who protected unmarried young Jewish women from rape by fellow partisans. He was murdered by Communist partisans, among them two Jews. YESC, BEN-ARI

The Nacha forest group headed by Elke Ariowitch "the Cossack," also known as Todras, was another of the partisan camps that drew a number of Eishyshkians. Todras had been fascinated with the military since childhood, sometimes at the expense of his studies at Radun's Yavne Hebrew school (where he often got help from Avraham Lipkunski, even though Avraham was several years his junior). As a teenager Todras was a member of the quasi-militaristic Zionist organization Beitar. From Beitar member to partisan leader was a natural transition for Todras, who seemed born to wear a uniform. Dressed like a Russian Cossack, and always on horseback, Todras the partisan cut quite a figure. The Jews, the Russians, and the local peasants were all impressed by him.

Todras established his camp in the Nacha forest during the summer of 1942, after the slaughter in Ghetto Radun, to give shelter to his friends from the area. A number of other Jewish partisan camps were established in the dense forest of Nacha, including ones led by Niomke Rogowski, the Asner brothers, and Yoske Lubetski, and two Russian ones, made up of soldiers and ex-convicts, which were known as the Sashka and the Kolka.

Well organized and well supplied, the Todras group had its own herd of cows and its own shepherd, so that meat and milk were never lacking. Additional supplies were obtained from local farmers. Todras also saw to it that his men were well armed, with the best weaponry available in the vicinity.

Because Todras was very protective of his followers, and willing to take people other groups had rejected, his camp became a haven for young Jewish women on their own, who were extremely vulnerable to attack in the dark, dangerous world of the forest. Drunken ex-convicts from the Sashka and Kolka groups were notorious for raping Jewish women, and some of the other partisan groups, Lithuanian and even Jewish, were also a danger to unprotected young women. Miriam Ribak, for example, had been brutally attacked by Lithuanian partisans after her escape from Ghetto Radun. They shot at her, and when their guns ran out of bullets they pierced her hands with their bayonets, then left her for dead. When Avraham Teikan and Isaac Levo found her, she was in such deplorable condition that no group they approached would take her, until they went to Todras. He accepted her into his camp, nursed her back to life, and assigned a young man to guard her against any further assaults.

Todras was loved by some of the local farmers, hated and feared by others. Relations with the locals were often volatile and unpredictable. But generally speaking, the farmers who lived in villages that were hospitable to the Jewish partisans found a good friend in Todras, for he and his men assisted them during the harvest season, helped them make their illegal vodka, known as Samagonka, and protected them against German raids on their food supplies. Farmers in villages that were hostile to the Jews suffered at the hands of Todras and his men. Their food was confiscated by force, and the murders they committed against innocent Jewish victims were avenged. On one occasion Todras's visit to a village coincided with a Polish wedding. Among the guests, he spotted a Polish policeman who had actively participated in the Ghetto Radun massacre. Todras accosted the man and marched him into the forest, where he shot him to death.

As Todras's name was becoming increasingly well known, to both his friends and his enemies, a new Russian partisan group known as the Leninski Komsomol Atriad was being established in the area, as part of an effort being coordinated from Moscow to organize the Russian partisan groups along military lines. In February–March 1943, seven Russians came to the Nacha forest from the east to carry out this mandate, among them a lieutenant named Anton B. Stankewitch, who took charge of the Leninski battalion. Many able-bodied men and some young women as well left the family camps, including Todras's, to enlist with Stankewitch's atriad, and with other military camps. Avraham Lipkunski and several of his Paikowski relatives from Dugalishok, Avraham Asner and his girlfriend Liebke, Avremele and Yankl Botwinik, Leibke Kaganowicz, Niomke Rogowski, and Yossele Hamarski were among those who signed on with Stankewitch. (Leibke Kaganowicz also joined Stankewitch, but his father Shael and sister Freidke remained behind with the Todras group, as did his brother Benjamin, who was planning to join Stankewitch as soon as he obtained a rifle.) Taking their weapons with them, these young men and women left the family camps virtually defenseless. Todras, however, was able to rearm his group, as usual with the best of weapons.

Though they might have been expected to be at odds with each other, in fact Lieutenant Stankewitch admired Todras so much that a warm relationship characterized by camaraderie and mutual respect developed between the two commanders. Nonetheless, a number of Stankewitch's men did not share his feelings; Todras had many enemies in the Leninski battalion, including some of the ex-convicts, a Polish Communist who had been a friend of the Radun policeman whom Todras executed, and several hard-core Jewish Communist partisans who disapproved of Todras's devoting so much energy to the welfare of his followers — like other partisans, they wanted to focus on attacking the Germans and their collaborators rather than rescuing Jews.

Soon Todras's enemies would have their day,

for Lieutenant Stankewitch was called back to the east for a military meeting, and they swiftly took advantage of his absence. Convening a military court, they found Todras guilty of taking food by force from some of the nearby villages — an offense of which they themselves were far more guilty. While under arrest, Todras was approached by his guard, Yossele Hamarski from Eishyshok, with the suggestion that the two of them run away together. But Niomke Rogowski advised against escape, and since Todras saw no imminent danger to his life, he accepted the verdict and the punishment: demotion from his position as commander of his family camp. The next stage of his punishment was that he was removed from his camp altogether, and his people were disarmed. Though some of the ammunition was later returned to the Todras group because Todras's judges feared the injustice of the verdict might prompt a general uprising among the partisans, it was only a token amount.

Under orders to join the Leninski battalion, Todras went out on a mission a few days later, with the very people who had judged and sentenced him. He never came back. The peasants of the village of Lipkunce, many of whom loved and revered Todras, later reported how he was killed: First he was shot in the feet, then in the back of his head. As his killers were torturing him, one old woman in her seventies approached them, weeping profusely, to ask, "What are you doing to him? He is like a God to us."[7]

After his death, two of Todras's seconds-in-command assumed the leadership of his camp, but it was soon to be all but obliterated by a new threat: a sixteen-day land and air assault on the forest of Nacha, which started on June 16, 1943. German planes flew low and bombed the forest relentlessly, especially the family camps, and when the bombers weren't flying, the German ground troops went on the attack, led by Lithuanian, Byelorussian, and Ukrainian collaborators familiar with the local topography. This was the first time the Germans had penetrated the forest.

Perhaps heeding an early warning, Lieutenant Stankewitch and most of his battalion had already left the area, never to return; but some of his men, mainly refugees from Eishyshok, Radun, Nacha, and Dugalishok who knew both the local farmers and the local terrain, had been out on intelligence- and food-gathering missions when their battalion decamped, and they were left behind, stranded.

The losses in the family camps were staggering. In the Todras camp alone some seventy people were killed, about three-quarters of the members. With little ammunition, no leader to plan their escape, and no warning of the attack, they didn't stand a chance. Shael Kaganowicz and his son Benjamin and daughter Freidke were among the few survivors.

Two days after the attack ended, some of the men Stankewitch had left behind — Avraham Lipkunski, Benyamin Frankl, Avraham Asner, and several of the Paikowskis — returned to the site of their former camp. Nothing remained. As for the Todras camp, the devastation they found there and elsewhere in the vicinity was beyond their worst imaginings. What had once been human beings were now unrecognizable as such. The bodies of yeshivah students whose heads had been filled with Torah learning, and of mothers whose hearts contained nothing but love and hope, were now filled to overflowing with masses of crawling worms. The stench was unbearable.

Although these partisans prided themselves on their toughness and thought of themselves as people who had seen everything in the way of human suffering, they were so overwhelmed by the scene that only four of them could bring themselves to bury the dead. "Ezekiel's vision of the dry bones was nothing in comparison to what we saw," Avraham Lipkunski later recalled.[8] They did what they could to identify the bodies, though they had only a few clues — a shoe, a hat, a scrap of cloth — to help them in their grisly task. Then they said Kaddish over the bodies, and carved the date, June 16, 1943, on a tree trunk. Among the dead were Israel Szczuczynski and his wife Shoshana, whom he had saved from the grave in Radun at the cost of his sister's life, as well as the little girl whom he had also been able to save there and then adopted, and his last surviving sister, Rochke. Now another grave had claimed them, too. Other Eishyshkians who died in other family camps during the June 1943 attack included Shoshke Wine's teenage son Ben-Zion; Israel the Fisherman and his son Berele, Shalom-Gershke Mackewicz, Meir the Rubishker, and many others.

Those who survived the massive forest blockade now had to reassess their strategies for survival. So, too, did people who had been hiding on farms, for the AK were claiming more and more victims as 1943 wore on.

Moshe Edelstein, a scion of one of the founding families of Eishyshok, the Azrielis, joined the Bielski brothers' camp in early spring 1944, at the age of seventeen. By then he had survived two and a half years of daily encounters with death, beginning with his escape from Eishyshok on September 21, 1941. Having failed to persuade his father and his older brother to run away with him, he left Eishyshok with two other boys, then made his way from Ghetto Radun to Warinowa and back again, until May 10, 1942, when he escaped the Radun massacre. For a while he had wandered from one Christian friend to another, paying for his hiding places with goods that had been left for safekeeping with family friends (among whom was Staniwicz, the former minister of education in the Polish government). But as the AK steadily increased its activities in 1943, life in the farmhouses became too dangerous, and Moshe and his friend Zvi Michalowski escaped to the forests of Nacha and Rudnicki. After the forest attack of June 1943, Zvi and Moshe parted company,

Rochke Szczuczynski with a friend, Hayyim-Yoshke Bielicki in Rochke's garden in Eishyshok. Rochke was murdered in the forest during a massive assault by German planes and local collaborators: Lithuanians, Byelorussians, Ukrainians, and Poles. YESC, SZCZUCZYNSKI

Moshe Edelstein, the teenage partisan who joined the Bielski camp, groomed the fifteen horses belonging to the Bielski brothers and the other commanders. YESC, EDELSTEIN

Zvi to form alliances with different partisan groups for varying periods of time, Moshe to join the Bielski camp, where he was given the job of grooming the fifteen horses belonging to the Bielski brothers and the other commanders.

Other Eishyshkians who had been hiding in the forest had a much harder time finding a new living situation. The Kremin sisters Dobke and Blumke, Dobke's boyfriend Israel Dimitrowski, Blumke's husband Eliyahu Eliashewicz, and their friend Nahum Dimitrowski (no relation to Israel) found themselves on their own as winter 1943–44 approached, unable to join the partisans if they wished to stay together. Nahum, an excellent carpenter, built them a ziemlanka. Under cover of night they would go to Christian friends and barter for food and clothing, exchanging for them family belongings that had been hidden with farmers in the villages nearby.

One evening a Polish friend, whom they all knew well, treated them to an elaborate meal. They did not suspect this was meant to be their last supper. But suddenly, as they were eating, the door opened and a group of armed AK men burst into the house and began to shoot at the guests sitting at the table. The cool-headed Nahum immediately smashed the lamp, throwing the room into darkness, and shot the AK commander, a man he knew very well from market day in Eishyshok. Nahum, Israel, and Eliyahu jumped out the windows; the sisters took shelter under the oven, in the katukh, and later they too escaped through the windows. Regrouping in the frozen fields outside the village, they saw that Israel had been wounded in the head, with blood from the wound forming a frozen patch on his face. They found shelter in the barn of a friendly farmer, who they hoped would not betray them. In the bitter cold they warmed themselves against the feverish body of the wounded man.

From June 1943 until liberation, Israel, Eliyahu, Dobke, and Blumke stayed together in

The Kremin family. Second from right is Dobke Kremin, first and second from left are Eliyahu Eliashewicz (Ellis) and wife Blumke Kremin. Dobke, Blumke, Eliyahu, and Israel Dimitrowski, Dobke's boyfriend, survived an AK attack in the house of Christian friends. All the others in the photo were murdered in the Eishyshok, Radun, and Grodno massacres. YESC, ELIASHEWICZ-ELLIS

Israel Dimitrowski (left) and Dobke Kremin hid together in the forest. They were married in the Sonenson house after liberation. His two friends are Yoshke Jurdyczanski (right) and Shneur Glombocki. Shneur survived as a partisan. YESC, JURIS-JURDYCZANSKI

Three Jewish partisans under the command of Jurgis: (right to left) Zvi Tarbutshin, who escaped from Ponar, Itchke Moshetowitch, and Zalman Lubetski (Sol Lubek) from Eishyshok. YESC, LUBEK-LUBETSKI

their own small group, alternating between shelters in the forest and hiding places made available to them by farmers in the vicinity. Cold, starving, emaciated, and covered in boils and lice, they struggled on. Dobke nearly died. It was only through the dedication of her boyfriend (and later husband) Israel that she survived. He would sneak into the kitchens of the local peasants while they were asleep and steal food from their pots, which he would bring to Dobke.

As a single man, their friend Nahum Dimitrowski was able to join a partisan group, a Lithuanian one that was under the direct command of the powerful leader known as Jurgis. Scores of Nahum's fellow Eishyshkians — those who were young and strong and male and unattached — were drawn to Jurgis's camp, or to one of the many other camps in the vicinity that were now being organized along military lines.

THE MILITARY PARTISAN CAMPS

The camp that Nahum Dimitrowski joined was in the Rudnicki forest, about twenty-five miles south of Vilna, in the place where Marshal Pilsudski used to hunt. Jurgis, one of the most important leaders in the Lithuanian partisan movement, had been put in charge of all the partisan groups in southern Lithuania. The Lithuanians would never have given him such a high-level command had he not hidden his true identity — as Henrik Ziman, a Jewish teacher who had escaped from Ghetto Kovno.

Nahum became one of Jurgis's favorite scouts, for he was very knowledgeable about the area, which made him an excellent forest guide and resourceful supplier of food. This familiarity was a double-edged sword, however, since it meant he could be recognized by farmers who were part of the AK, or were collaborating with the Lithuanians and Germans. Nahum survived many a hostile encounter with the nearby villagers, including those from Pircupi, the village that would later become a shrine to Lithuanian heroism during the Nazi occupation. Yet it was true that many of the villagers from Pircupi did assist the partisans, for which some of them paid a terrible price — being rounded up and buried alive by the Germans. Other villagers, in Pircupi and elsewhere, were traitors to their own people and to the partisans, and some of them also paid a terrible price, in loss of life and the destruction of their homes: they were victims not of the Germans but of the partisans.

Other Eishyshkians who joined Jurgis's camp included Reuven Paikowski, then a teenager, and his father, Shmuel-Leib. They had been living in hiding with a farmer named Ivashka, but with the danger from the AK increasing, and the resources with which to pay their host diminishing, they thought their chances of survival would be better in the forest. Their fellow Eishyshkian Haikl Kanichowski, who had worked with a number of the partisan camps at various times and knew the forest well, led them to the Jurgis camp. Despite Jurgis's attempt to hide his Jewish origins, he inadvertently revealed himself to the Paikowskis one day. Hearing Shmuel-Leib ask Reuven in Yiddish for a pocketknife, Jurgis offered his own.

The Russian partisan units in the forests had begun to emerge as a major military force in 1943, and many Jews were eager to join these battalions, too. For them it was an opportunity to fight the Germans and the AK, and to settle scores with local collaborators. However, the Russians would accept only armed, able-bodied, young men, and a few select Jewish women.

Leibke Kaganowicz was one of the Jews who joined up with the Russian partisans. Leaving the Todras camp, which he and his father Shael, brother Benjamin, and sister Freidke had been with off and on since early 1943, he went to the Leninski atriad under the command of Lieutenant Stankewitch, while Shael and Freidke remained in the Todras camp. Benjamin was also intending to join the Leninski battalion, as soon as he obtained a gun, but the farmer who had agreed to sell him one killed him with it instead. At the Leninski camp Leibke was trained in guerrilla warfare, with a specialty in railroad sabotage. Posted in the Marcinkonys–Aran (Varena) area, where they were advised by Russian military experts and supplied with weapons, explosives, and medical provisions, all of which were parachuted in to them, Leibke and his unit were responsible for blowing up German trains on their way to the eastern front. They were also charged with the task of securing a certain amount of food for the atriad.

After their raids on local food supplies, Leibke would try to pay a visit to the Todras group to see his sister and his father, so that he could give them whatever food he could spare, make plans for the coming few weeks, and exchange news. On October 26, 1943, after the completion of one of these food raids, Leibke went to see his family. He was accompanied by the men from his demolition unit, Dr. Babisch the commander, a Ukrainian partisan named Cymbal, and Isaac Levo, an old family friend from Aran. There was also another unit from the Leninski atriad with them, which included a few Russians (among them a pilot who had been parachuted into the forest), as well as Niomke Rogowski and Aaron Berkowicz from Radun, who had known the Kaganowicz family in Eishyshok, and had maintained contact with them in the ghetto and forest during the war years.

For Leibke this was a special reunion, for winter was approaching and, since his family would be leaving the forest to go into hiding on a farm during that harsh season, it would be harder to stay in touch in the months to come. After the usual embraces and news updates, Leibke talked

Teenage Reuven Paikowski and his father Shmuel-Leib joined the Lithuanian partisan battalion under the command of Jurgis. Shmuel-Leib was killed by an AK mine. Reuven survived. YESC, PAIKOWSKI

to his sister and father about their plans for the near future, trying to identify which local farmers might be willing to hide them.

While they were absorbed in this discussion, Leibke's fellow partisans began to drink—a frequent pastime of the Russian partisans, and of a number of Jewish fighters as well, for alcohol helped numb them to the terrible realities of their lives. It also caused many problems, military misjudgments as well as brawls among themselves and sexual attacks on women.

After a night-long drinking party, which ended only when the alcohol ran out in the early morning, the sentries posted at the edge of the forest came across a farmer named Nowicki. He explained that he was there simply to search for a lost cow, which had perhaps wandered into the forest that bordered his grazing fields. Isaac Levo recognized Nowicki as someone he had encountered on market day, and on occasional business trips into the countryside. Nowicki clapped Levo on the back and told him he would never do anything to hurt his people. But Shael Kaganowicz, who also knew Nowicki, was worried.

Shael Kaganowicz. He was severely wounded by the AK and died a few days later. His daughter Freidke and son Benjamin were also murdered by the AK. PHOTO: YITZHAK URI KATZ. YESC, KAGANOWICZ-KAHN

As Nowicki was leaving, Isaac Levo called after him, "Bring me back two bottles of vodka." When Nowicki returned, he brought the AK rather than vodka. The partisans waged a fierce battle, but they were outnumbered by scores of heavily armed AK, and the only machine gun in their possession jammed. In the chaos that followed, as Leibke tried desperately to protect his sister and his father, Shael Kaganowicz was badly wounded:

"Leibke! Leibke! I've been hit!" he said.

"Where, papa, where?"

He undid his shirt and I almost fainted at the sight. The wound was enormous. I could put my fist into it and his lifeblood poured out of him in a river before my horrified eyes!

"It's nothing, papa," I said. "You'll be alright. Sit by the tree for a moment and rest. Where is Freidke? Where is Freidke?" I looked out and saw her. Three of her pursuers were almost upon her, bayonets poised as she fled in front of them.

I raised my rifle, aimed and fired! "One down, Freidke!" I shouted. Then I fired again and as the next one fell, I screamed, "One more, Freidke! Run, Freidke, run!" Again I fired, but this time I missed. Her attacker was closer. I tried to fire again and my gun jammed!

As in a slow motion movie, I saw her fall as her pursuer poised his blade over her. I cursed my gun and its impotence as the bayonet entered my poor sister's defenseless body.

As in a dream, I heard my father shouting over and over, "Hold them back, Leibke! Hold them back!" But it was too late for Freidke. Too late for my little sister. She fell to earth like a wounded bird, and as her life ebbed away, I wept with sorrow. "Goodbye, my Freidke . . . Goodbye, my little sister . . ."

But there was no time for mourning in the forest. No time for prayers or tears as our pursuers closed in on us. Just the terrible need to run, to escape. And so we ran, my father, his flesh torn open by the bullet which had ripped his body apart, and me holding on to him.[9]

A few days later Shael Kaganowicz died from his wounds, despite Leibke's devoted care. Somehow, even in the darkness, Avraham Widlanski, an old family friend who was one of the freelance partisans, now with one group, now with another, found his way through the forest to Leibke. "I heard the Angel of Death come for your father," he told Leibke, "and I heard your father struggle with him. He cried out many times but finally he could resist no more. He is at peace now, Leibke, be comforted." With the assistance of some of the local farmers, Leibke and Avraham took Shael's body back to the forest and buried him, as he had requested, next to his murdered son Benjamin. Near the graves stood a tree, its top blasted by lightning. Leibke chanted the ancient Kaddish, but found no solace in it.

Though Leibke Kaganowicz's entire family had escaped the slaughter in Eishyshok and lived through the massacre in Ghetto Radun as well, Leibke was now the sole survivor. His mother and grandmother had gone up in smoke in Treblinka, and his brother, father, and sister had all been murdered by Poles.

Lieutenant Stankewitch's Leninski atriad attracted a considerable number of local Jewish partisans like Leibke, for Stankewitch valued them highly. He considered them to be loyal, brave, and sober (unlike the many heavy-drinking Russians), and he also appreciated them for their familiarity with the terrain and its local inhabitants. In fact, he was one of the relatively few Russian partisan commanders who approved of — indeed actively assisted in — retaliatory raids against farmers who were responsible for the deaths of members of his Jewish fighters' families. Niomke Rogowski, for example, together with a number of other partisans from Stankewitch's group, avenged the death of his brother Moshe by killing the farmer Shiemaszka, and burning his entire farm to the ground.

Leibke Botwinik, son of school principal Moshe Yaakov, served in the Polish army and was a Hebrew teacher in Eishyshok. Gravely wounded by the AK, Leibke begged his brother Yitzhak to put an end to his misery. He complied. Yitzhak was later killed by the Russian partisans in the Leninski battalion, because he was caught sleeping while on guard duty. YESC, EPSTEIN-BOTWINIK

Avremele Botwinik, teenage partisan in the Leninski battalion. He is the sole survivor of the Botwinik family. YESC, EPSTEIN-BOTWINIK

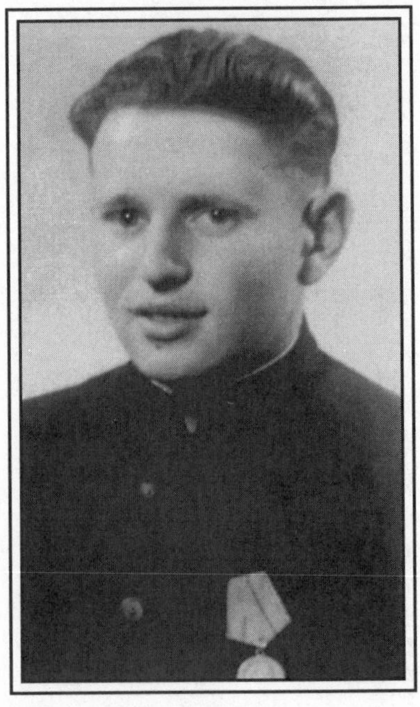

Despite his young age, teenager Israel Shmerkowitch was an inspiring partisan, an excellent marksman, and familiar with every forest path. He served as guide when partisans were sent to Ghetto Vilna to rescue Jews. YESC, PAIKOWSKI

Yitzhak Botwinik and his teenage brother Avremele were also part of the Leninski atriad. Like the Kaganowiczes, the Botwinik family had escaped the mass killing in Eishyshok, and three of them — Leibke, Yitzhak, and Avremele — had escaped the Ghetto Radun slaughter as well. (Their father Moshe Yaakov, their mother Shoshana Alte, sister Fania, and probably brother Hillel all died there.) The three surviving sons had made their way to the forest, where Leibke was gravely wounded in an AK attack (led by a man from Eishyshok). Knowing that he stood no chance of recovery, Leibke begged Yitzhak to put an end to his misery. With a single bullet, Yitzhak killed his own brother, once a bright, promising young Hebrew schoolteacher, veteran of the Polish army, and fiancé of Shoshana Katz, now also dead.

Like Leibke, Yitzhak, too, had served with the Polish army, where he had learned to be an excellent fighter, and he was therefore a great asset to the Leninski battalion, and highly valued. However, Lieutenant Stankewitch's affection and respect for his Jewish fighters was not shared by many of the Russian partisans, particularly the hard-core criminals, who viewed themselves as the real masters of the forest. Whenever Stankewitch was away on one of his trips to the east, they terrorized the Jewish partisans in the group — sometimes with the help of the Jewish Communists. Like Elke "Todras" Ariowitch, Yitzhak Botwinik would become a casualty of one of Stankewitch's absences. Caught sleeping while on guard duty, Yitzhak was court-martialed, found guilty, and sentenced to death. He was then ordered to march into the interior of the forest. When he refused, he was shot on the spot, in full view of his comrades, including his brother. Avremele, the last surviving Botwinik brother, fainted and fell into the arms of Zlatke Garber.

Zlatke, too, had faced tragedy in the Leninski battalion. When she and her cousin Shoshke Wine left Ghetto Radun, they were guided to the forest by other Eishyshkians. Some time later Niomke Rogowski brought them to Stankewitch's group, where they became two of the few women to be accepted. Just days later, catastrophe struck. With Stankewitch and a number of the other partisans away on a raid, the women were easy prey for some of the men who remained behind, including the notorious Russian rapist Vanka, now a member of the Leninski battalion. After a drinking spree they went on the attack. When Shoshke tried to shield her young cousin, she was murdered by Vanka, and Zlatke was wounded in the head.

Beautiful, brave Shoshke, who had once been a pioneer in Palestine but had returned to Eishyshok, was dead. Shoshke the tavernkeeper, beloved by Christian and Jew alike, protector of her Christian friends whose husbands would otherwise have drunk their market-day earnings away and abused their wives, rescuer of numerous members of her family, had been murdered by a drunken rapist. Vanka was tried, found guilty, and executed by a partisan court.[10]

Eventually most of the Jewish women in the Leninski battalion were asked to return to the family groups, for Stankewitch felt it was too difficult to protect them from attacks like the one that took Shoshke's life. Zlatke, however, was one of the few allowed to remain until liberation.

Among the best-known partisans from Eishyshok and the vicinity were Israel Shmerkowitch and the four Asner brothers, Yankl, Hayyim, Avraham, and Aaron. Israel Shmerkowitch was only a teenager when he escaped the slaughter in Eishyshok with his father Yekutiel. Despite his youth, Israel had a sense of responsibility and devotion to his fellow Jews that would have befitted a much older person. And he had the skills to put his commitment into action. An excellent marksman, he never missed a target. His sense of direction in the forests of Nacha and Rudnicki was similarly impeccable; every forest path was as familiar to him as the streets and lanes of his native town. When Israel led partisans through the woods, they knew they would reach their destination.[11] Thus it was Israel whom Lieutenant Stankewitch appointed to guide the partisans he sent to rescue Jews from Ghetto Vilna in April 1943. But this mission proved ill-fated.

Once they'd reached the ghetto, Niomke Rogowski, who was in command of the rescue group, encountered resistance from the leaders of the ghetto's underground, including the legendary Abba Kovner (1918–1988). After discussing the matter at great length, Kovner, other leaders, and members of the FPO (Polish initials for Ghetto Vilna's United Partisan Organization) argued that the time was not ripe; it would be better for people in the ghetto to be organized into a well-trained partisan force, which could go into the forest as a unified group. Abba Kovner was planning to stage an uprising within the ghetto once this partisan unit was organized. The decision not to allow Rogowski and his comrades to take Jews out of Ghetto Vilna was confirmed by Jacob Gens (1905–1943), the head of the Vilna Judenrat, who believed that the key to the ghetto's survival lay in cooperation with the Germans, and by Salek Dessler, the liaison between the ghetto leadership and the Gestapo. Ordered to leave the ghetto or else be turned over to the Gestapo, Rogowski, Shmerkowitch, Yankl Asner, and the other would-be rescuers returned to the forest, taking with them about forty people who left despite their leaders' opposition to their departure. On the way, however, the group was attacked by Germans and Lithuanian collaborators, and only about fifteen of the forty survived the attack.

In September 1943, after the failure of the uprising that Abba Kovner had planned, the policy in Ghetto Vilna changed, and Israel Shmerkowitch was again sent there, this time to guide Kovner and his followers to the forest. He led about 150 people to safety.[12] Leibke Katz and his sister Luba, from Olkenik, were two of the

Leibke Katz was the assistant to Anton Stankewitch, the commander of the Leninski battalion. On February 15, 1944, after Stankewitch was shot by the AK, Leibke carried him on his back. Both were brought down by AK bullets. YESC, LUBA KATZ

Ghetto Vilna Jews who followed Israel back to the Leninski camp; Lieutenant Stankewitch was so impressed with Leibke that he chose him as his personal assistant. Leibke's presence made life easier for a lot of the Jews in Stankewitch's company, but he did not succeed in convincing Stankewitch to accept many women.

The Asner brothers, known as "the Yitzkutsi" after Yitzhak, the founding patriarch of the family, were among the bravest and most feared partisans in the Nacha and Rudnicki forests. Being natives of the village of Nacha (which was under the jurisdiction of Eishyshok) and descendants of its founders, they, too, were familiar with every path, road, swamp, village, and farmer in the vicinity. Their military skills had been honed during years of service in the Polish army, which meant they were excellent sharpshooters and horsemen, and also that they had many acquaintances in the AK, for a number of those men had been their comrades in the army. But they, unlike their Polish former comrades, had never been promoted to any position of rank in the army; their superb leadership abilities had not been sufficient to outweigh the fact that they were Jewish.

Of the four brothers, only Avraham, along with the young woman who later became his wife, Liebke, joined the Leninski atriad. She was eventually expelled, when Stankewitch made it his policy to exclude women. After that Avraham, who always alternated between fighting alongside his brothers and within the Leninski atriad, spent more time with his brothers, who had formed their own partisan group, which sometimes acted independently, and sometimes joined with other partisan groups on specific actions, such as the rescues from Ghetto Vilna. They established their camp in a swampy area, which was very safe because it could be penetrated by only a few local people who knew their way around the mysterious terrain. In addition,

Luba Katz, sister of Leibke Katz, survived as a partisan. Her husband, Ilya (Eliyahu) Margalit, kept a diary in Polish about the partisans' activities. He was murdered by the AK near Vasilishok after liberation, but his diary survived. YESC, LUBA KATZ

Avraham Asner in Russian uniform during World War II. He was a member of the Leninski battalion and one of the four fighting Asner brothers, who were among the bravest and most feared partisans in the Nacha and Rudnicki forests. YESC, ASNER

Aaron Asner (right) with four Jewish friends in 1939, during his service in the Polish army. He was severely wounded by the AK and later died from his wounds. YESC, ASNER

Avraham Asner in the Polish army during the 1930s. Despite his outstanding achievements, he was never promoted to a higher rank because he was Jewish. He survived several AK attacks, including one that left a bullet lodged in his leg. YESC, ASNER

mists rising from the swamp helped to obscure the fires the partisans built for cooking and for warmth.

The four kept in close touch, meeting regularly in the home of a friendly farmer named Shepkowski, who lived a mile and a half from Nacha. One of their planned rendezvous coincided — by chance or by betrayal — with a visit by the AK, who surrounded the farm. Avraham and Liebke were not there at the time, but Yankl, Hayyim, and Aaron were just about to enter the house when the AK opened fire. Yankl and Hayyim escaped unharmed. Aaron was severely wounded, his leg bones shattered. Despite his injury, he managed to crawl to some bushes on the outskirts of the farm, where he collapsed. There he lay for three days as the first snow of the season fell, concealing him and covering the bloodstained earth. When his brothers were finally able to go to him they found he had a huge hole in his foot. "May Hitler have such a hole in his heart!" Avraham raged when he saw his brother's deep wound.

With the help of some nearby farmers, they carried Aaron to their ziemlanka, where a round-the-clock watch was mounted at his bedside. Avraham Lipkunski, Yankl, and Yankl's girlfriend Etke (from Eishyshok) watched over him day and night, trying to ease his pain and keep his wound clean. And then came the day when the color returned to his face and he began talking again. Just as it seemed that his condition was improving, however, he succumbed to blood poisoning. Aaron, beloved youngest brother of Hayyim, Yankl, and Avraham, was buried a few feet away from the ziemlanka.

The three remaining Asner brothers continued to fight, battling the Germans, the AK, and the local collaborators with even greater determination. Though Stankewitch wanted to send Avraham to officer training school in Russia, he declined the offer, because it would have meant being away from Liebke and he felt his time would be better spent fighting the enemy. Avra-

Four Asner cousins. Rachel and sister Itzle (second and third from right), having survived the Eishyshok and Radun massacres, stayed in the Asner partisan camp. In May 1944, the Asner camp was attacked by the AK. Seven people were murdered, including Itzle. YESC, ASNER-WELTMAN

ham later took part in an attack on a German dairy depot that was a major food center for the eastern front. That operation, though ultimately successful, cost Stankewitch twenty-four of his men, most of whom were killed by the AK, not the Germans. Many were wounded as well, including Avraham Asner. Shot in the leg, he bandaged himself and managed to return to his battalion in the forest, but the bullet remained lodged in his body. It was still there when he emigrated to the United States.

During another mission, in Bierozowce, Poland, on February 15, 1944, Stankewitch himself was severely wounded. His assistant, Leibke Katz from Olkenik, carried his wounded commander on his back, until both were brought down by AK bullets. After the death of Lieutenant Stankewitch, a number of Leninski atriad members joined the Asner group, including Niomke Rogowski and Avraham Lipkunski.

Victory now seemed within reach. During May 1944 the earth rumbled with the sound of shells being fired. At night the Asner camp partisans could see the huge red lights of the Russian rockets hanging in the distant skies. But as the eastern front approached, with the Germans in retreat, hostile activities intensified from all sides and made it ever more difficult for the Asner camp to operate independently. The Germans were making their last stand, even as they were retreating, and the AK were doing everything they could to ensure a "Poland without Jews" at war's end. One day during these dangerous but hopeful times, the Asner camp dispatched five of its members, including Yankl and Avraham Asner and Niomke Rogowski, to the partisan battalion under the command of Major General Kapusta. Their dual mission was to obtain both information and assignments, for they were trying to coordinate their activities with the Kapusta battalion's.

While they were gone, their own camp came under surprise attack. In the small tent shared by Avraham Lipkunski and Yossele Hamarski it sounded as though the world were coming to an end. As they tore out of their tent and raced away, bullets flew in every direction and they could see that the AK had surrounded the camp, stationing themselves within fifteen to thirty feet of every tent. Seven people were murdered, including Hayyim Asner, his cousin Itzle Asner, plus three others from Eishyshok, and two from Radun. The traitor who had led the AK through the difficult terrain of the swamp to the Asner camp was a local Pole, who had been made a confidant of the partisans. In retaliation for the deaths of the seven, the partisans murdered the informer and torched his farm.

What was left of the Asner camp felt they had little chance of surviving as a small, independent fighting unit, and they joined the Kapusta battalion. One of their assignments was to keep on the lookout for German soldiers who were fleeing to the forests. Revenge was sweet: Now it was the Germans, sons of the "master race," who were the underdogs, tired, unshaven, their uniforms hanging from them in rags. Hundreds of them were being rounded up and disarmed, then herded through the forest by individual young Jewish partisans.

But that didn't mean Jewish lives weren't still being lost in the forests. On June 3, 1944, the twelfth of Sivan, just a few weeks before liberation, Shmuel-Leib Paikowski, who was with the partisan battalion under the direct command of Jurgis in the Nacha forest (puszcza) was sent on a sabotage mission with four other Jews, three from Vilna, and one from Smargon. Before they could accomplish their goal, which was the cutting of telephone lines, they were blown up by mines. Local farmers buried them in the village of Salkes. According to Shmuel-Leib's son, Reuven, no prior scouting had been done of the area, which was heavily mined. Now there were only two members of "the Zalkutzki" (as they were called after their founding patriarch, Bezalel), only two Paikowskis, left, Reuven and an uncle. A family as well known for its strength and bravery as the legendary Asners, a family whose lives had for generations enriched the fabric of their native Eishyshok, and of Nacha, the village that Bezalel had co-founded with the Asners, was now almost entirely wiped out.

In July 1944 the Russians surrounded Vilna. Nahum Dimitrowski was one of the partisans Jurgis sent in to the city to wipe out the remaining German resistance, which consisted in part of snipers who were taking aim at the Russian troops from church steeples. The liberation of Vilna cost Jurgis 150 of the 350 fighters in Nahum's battalion.

Zalman and Akiva Lubetski's battalion, also under Jurgis, was not permitted by the Russian army to participate in the liberation of Vilna. "We can do it without your help," they were told, and were then sent to the front, where Zalman virtually retraced (in reverse) the escape route he had taken when the Polish army was defeated in 1939. Now he was marching with the victorious Russian army, under the command of Sasha Kazakov; the following year, as part of a Russian partisan unit, he would become one of the liberators of Berlin.

Since Jews did not fight as a unified force in the partisan movement, but instead joined with Russian and Lithuanian partisan groups to repel the German invaders, it is difficult to separate out their contribution to the war effort, and to value it accordingly. But one measure has been provided in *The Encyclopedia of the Holocaust*, where the partisan movement in Lithuania, a significant minority of which was made up of Jews (numbering about 1,650), is credited with 461 train derailments, the destruction of 288 locomotives, and the injuring and killing of 3,663 Germans. Besides blowing up railroad tracks, they destroyed bridges, cut telephone and telegraph lines, and performed other acts of sabotage.[13] Partisans from Eishyshok contributed their fair share to all these actions.

What the *Encyclopedia* does not include are the Jewish partisans' many actions that were directed not against the Germans, but against local collaborators and the AK. And the tallying up of casualties does not include the partisans lost in those battles, nor the many other Jews who died in the forests or in hiding at the hands of those local collaborators and the AK. That total exceeded the number of Jews killed by the Germans during military missions or other kinds of clashes.

OTHER EISHYSHKIANS DURING WORLD WAR II

Jews from Eishyshok, both those who had emigrated and those who were still living there when war broke out, played many different roles in many different places during World War II. Besides fighting with the partisans, some were soldiers in the Russian and other Allied armies, some were taken captive as POWs, some tried to pressure their governments on behalf of relatives who they knew were being engulfed by the flames of the Holocaust. And others, it must be said, showed little or no interest in the fate of relatives left behind in Europe.

Mote Yosl Kremin (in the bed), brother of Dobke and Blumke, served in the Polish army. He survived the war in a POW camp, in Germany. YESC, DIMITRO-DIMITROWSKI

Shneur Glombocki was serving in the Polish army when he became one of the 160,000 POWs taken in September 1939. Shneur managed — on his fifth attempt — to escape, and later joined the partisans in the forest. During an attack on a German train station that he and his fellow partisans mounted, he found a pile of clothing belonging to people who had been deported to Treblinka and murdered. His wife's sweater was in the pile. Glombocki's fellow Eishyshkians Mote Yosl Kremin, the brother of Dobke and Blumke; Berke Kaganowicz; Eli Slonimski; and the shtetl photographer Rephael Lejbowicz

Moshe Baram (kneeling, fourth from right), with fellow members of the Jewish Brigade in Paris, near the Arc de Triomphe. The Jewish Brigade fought alongside the British in Europe against the Germans. YESC, BARAM-BLACHER

Hayyim-Yoshke Bielicki (left) fought in the Russian army, participated in the battle of Stalingrad, was wounded, and was highly decorated for his achievements. YESC, WEISSMANN-BIELICKI

Benjamin Shlanski (second from right) emigrated to America with his family on the eve of the Holocaust. He was drafted into the American army and killed fighting in Italy. YESC, SHLANSKI

were also Polish POWs. About the subsequent fate of Kaganowicz and Lejbowicz nothing further is known. But Kremin survived the entire war in a POW camp in Stalag VIII A 49 in Gepruft, Germany; and Slonimski, like Glombocki, was able to escape and subsequently joined the partisan movement.

Hayyim-Yoshke Bielicki fought in the Russian army, as did a number of other Eishyshkians, and participated in the battle of Stalingrad. He was present on February 2, 1943, for the surrender of General Friedrich von Paulus, the commander of the German Sixth Army, and Paulus's 91,000 German troops.

David Ejszyszki served in General Anders's army for a short while.[14]

Moshe Baram, a relative of Yitzhak Uri Katz who had made aliyah, was among the five thousand members of the Yishuv who served in the Jewish Brigade and fought alongside the British against Nazi Germany. Vela Portnoy's cousin Dave Durbin, whose family had emigrated from Eishyshok to England, served in the British army, fighting against Rommel at El Alamein, under the command of Lieutenant General Bernard Montgomery.

Benjamin Shlanski, son of Zelig and Rose, who were fortunate enough to have been able to emigrate to America just prior to the outbreak of World War II, served in the American army, as did many other Eishyshkian emigrants. He trained at Fort McClellan, Alabama, and left for Italy in May 1943. Shortly after he arrived in Italy he was killed in action against the Germans.

Walter Kirschner, who had emigrated from Eishyshok to America at the beginning of the twentieth century, was too old to serve in the armed forces. But he brought the plight of the European Jews to the attention of President Franklin Roosevelt. A heavy contributor to Roosevelt's campaigns and a family intimate, called "Popsy" by the president's children, Walter built a ranch in Indio, California, to serve as a retreat for Roosevelt, dined frequently with him in the White House, and slept in the historic Lincoln bedroom when he was there. Roosevelt used to love to hear Kirschner's stories and jokes, all recited in his heavy Yiddish accent.

One night, after a round of story- and joke-telling, Kirschner raised the topic that had been burning within him like a fire: to save the Jews in Europe. The president's response: "I don't want you to talk about the Jews to me, now or ever. I haven't time to hear any Jewish wailing." Thereafter the president would wisecrack to his family in Kirschner's presence: "Watch out for Popsy. He may turn out to be another Gold-

Shaul Berkowitch, who had emigrated to Eretz Israel, served in the British army. YESC, BERKOWITCH

Walter Kirschner, who emigrated from Eishyshok, was a close friend and financial supporter of President Roosevelt. He asked the president to save the Jews during the Holocaust. Roosevelt saw Kirschner's request as a political criticism, and feared that Kirschner was turning Republican. PAINTING BY PRES. DWIGHT D. EISENHOWER

man"— a reference to a wealthy Jewish supporter of FDR's during his race for governor of New York, who had switched sides one month before the election.

Roosevelt's policy with regard to the rescue of European Jews did not change. And Walter Kirschner never spoke against the president, not even after FDR's death, always praising him as a great man. However, the story about the presidential bust he had commissioned for the then quite princely sum of five thousand dollars suggests more complicated feelings. The marble bust was always displayed in a flood of light, like a relic in a shrine, until the day Kirschner picked it up and threw it out his ninth-floor window, smashing it to pieces.[15]

New York's Eishyshker landsmanshaft, Hevrah Bnei Avraham Shmuel Anshei Eishyshker, made up of emigrants from Eishyshok and their descendants, showed considerably less concern than Walter Kirschner about the fate of their fellow Jews under Nazi occupation. During the entire war, not a word of anxiety about the Jews in general, or the Jews of Eishyshok in particular, is to be found in the minutes of the society's wartime meetings. The minutes of the meeting of September 27, 1941, one day after the massacre, when the earth around Eishyshok was still pooled with blood, and the graves were still moving, read as follows:

A regular meeting took place in our synagogue at 180 Clinton Street. It was chaired by president-brother Sam Rudsin and vice-president-brother Reuven Jankelewitch.

The president reported that brother Jonah Poretz was sick for six weeks and received $42 sick benefits. Jonah Poretz returned the money to the society and asked the president to use it according to his discretion and give it to the needy. The president asked for advice. Brother Rabinow proposed that the $42 be given to Salberg, a society brother who was currently in need. Fourteen society members voted for the proposal, one opposed.

Benny Astrow, who also received sick benefits for two weeks, donated $4 to the synagogue for a lamp. Brother Sam Schaffer gave a donation of $25 for the synagogue to be painted. For seats in the synagogue, $148 was already collected in cash. The seat sales will bring in a total of $200. Brother Harry Gordon presented the candidacy of son Max for membership in the society. Max, who is twenty-eight years old, is an engineer.

Barnet Salkow wants to return to our society. It was suggested that prior to taking a vote the books should be checked to see how much money he owes the society. Brother Rudsin read a letter from Harry Salberg. He writes that his health is improving and he is wishing all the brothers a healthy year.

Nominations for society officers took place [and there follows the list of all the nominees for all the electoral offices].

Brother Yehiel Levin reported at the meeting that brother Reuven Levin would like to purchase two burial plots in the Washington cemetery. It was suggested by brother Rabinow that Reuven Levin pay $800 for the plots. The proposal was voted on and all agreed. The brothers Levin were pleased with the price.

It was proposed that the society use the money only for the purchasing of plots in other cemeteries. The president put the proposal to a vote; ten brothers voted in favor of the proposal. It was not opposed by anyone.

The meeting was closed.

Reported by Secretary A. Sklar.

It is certain that Walter Kirschner was not present at that meeting, because he had been expelled from the Eishyshker society in 1936. He had violated the society's bylaws and was found to be a Jew who was not in good standing.*

*Kirschner was expelled from the society on August 9, 1936. His daughter Adaire Harris thinks the reason might have been his marriage to a Japanese woman.

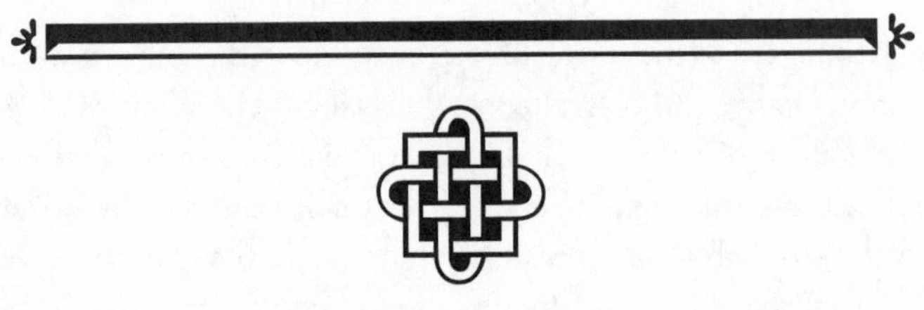

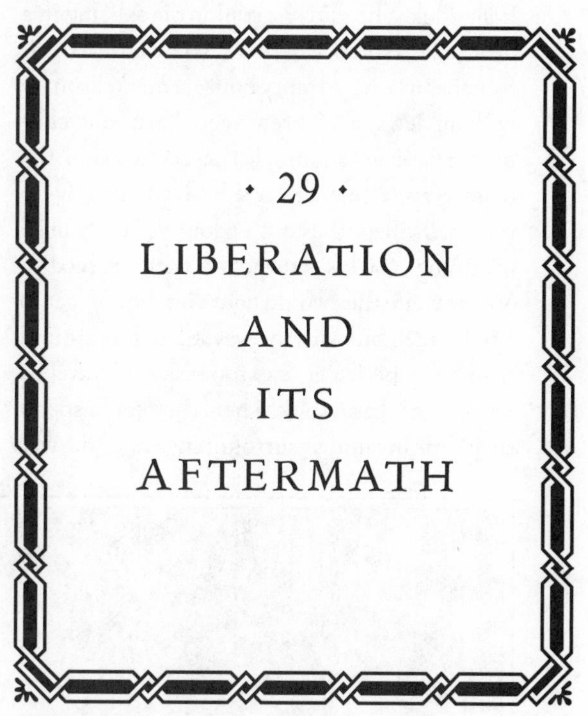

AFTER THE WAR ALL OF THE NATIONS COUNTED THEIR LOSSES. WE COUNTED OUR SURVIVORS.

Gideon Hausner, chief prosecutor at the Eichmann trial

BY JULY 1944, THE BATTLEFRONT WAS NEARING EISHYSHOK. A NUMBER OF THE SURviving Jewish partisans went off to join the advancing Red Army, eager to fight the Germans openly and hasten the day of liberation. But the promise of liberation brought danger as well as hope to the few surviving Jews who remained in hiding in the countryside. Even as the earth beneath their feet rumbled to the rhythms of the Russian army's approach, and the night skies lit up with the long red arcs of the shells fired by the Russian cannons, the Jews who had lived through the horrors of the Holocaust wondered whether they would live to see freedom. They feared they would either be murdered by the AK, who were searching out the last Jews with renewed intensity, or incinerated by one of the German or Russian shells that were landing all around them.

Heavy fighting broke out near the farm of Kazimierz Korkuc, but the farm itself was spared, as were all its inhabitants, including the Jews to whom Korkuc was giving shelter. As the battlefield came ever closer, the Jews consulted their host and decided to leave their underground pits for hiding places in the wheatfields that were then in full growth. Shielded by the tall, dense stalks of the wheat, they reveled in the glories of nature. There beneath the open skies they could see the sun, feel the wind on their face, fill their air-starved lungs — and put their ear to the ground to hear the rumbling of the earth growing stronger and stronger. They felt that despite all the dangers, freedom was at last marching in their direction. Zipporah Sonenson helped her daughter weave a crown of blue cornflowers to wear in honor of liberation. Moshe Sonenson, however, remained as vigilant as ever, and reminded his family that he was still their "captain." The eve of liberation, he cautioned, was a very dangerous time; there would be many hazards still to come.

On July 13, 1944, after a long discussion with Korkuc, Moshe and his cousin Meir Kabacznik paid a secret visit to Eishyshok to see whether it would be safe to return. Making their way carefully through the dark streets of the shtetl, they looked up a number of old family friends who had remained loyal to them, and asked their opinion of the situation. Jaszka Aliszkewicz, who worked in the Sonenson tannery and whose wife had worked in the Sonenson home, was one of the people they consulted. Since Jaszka had joined forces with his sister Zoszka to help

Moshe save his family from the 1941 massacre, at considerable risk to their own lives, they knew he was trustworthy, and decided to accept his opinion that they could return in safety.

Back at Korkuc's, however, Moshe had to talk his wife into this plan of action, which was part of an overall strategy he had worked out to retrieve the baby boy they'd had to give up at birth. Zipporah Sonenson did not want to return to Eishyshok. She said she couldn't face being in a dead Jewish shtetl, where she would have to confront her mother's empty house, a market square without Jews, a Hebrew school without children, a deserted shulhoyf, a desecrated shul, the mass graves. She preferred to go directly to the small village the baby's adoptive family lived in, arrange for his return, and then proceed to Vilna, where they would figure out how to get to Eretz Israel. But with the war still raging around them, Moshe felt it was too risky to travel as far as Vilna. Eishyshok, where they could spend their time in familiar surroundings until the war came to an end, and he could try to recover some of their money and family belongings, was the logical first station on their long journey to a new homeland, he insisted. Zipporah very reluctantly accepted her husband's decision.

Before they left, Korkuc gathered all "his" Jews together for some farewell remarks. Since the AK were still out in force, hoping to ferret out and kill all the remaining Jews and their res-

The majority of the Eishyshkians who survived the war, more than sixty-two, did so in Russia. Some were ardent Communists, others admirers of Communism. Members of the Russian contingent in a DP camp in Germany held a memorial service commemorating the victims of the September 1941 massacre. Standing at far right are Luba Ginunski and husband. Standing, second from left, is Aaron Velvke Rosenblum; fourth from left, Hayyim Motke Narodowitch. Sitting in the center row (right to left) are a Jankelewicz daughter; Feigl Szulkin, her son Robert and daughter Betty; Fruml Slepak and daughter Zipporah; Elka Jankelewicz with two children. Sitting on the ground (right to left): Hayyim-Yoshke Bielicki, Meir Rosenblum, Moshe Szulkin. YESC, SZULKIN

cuers, they had to leave under cover of night, he warned them. Moreover, they had to be careful not to reveal to anybody where they had hidden during the war. Addressing the children Yitzhak and Yaffa directly, he explained that if they were ever to mention his name to anyone, it would mean the death of him and his mother.[1]

THE RETURN

In the predawn darkness the Jews silently departed the Korkuc estate. Hiding in the woods until daylight, they appeared as from nowhere on the streets of Eishyshok — much to the shock of the remaining residents. They could not believe their eyes. "Where did you come from?" they wanted to know — and their astonishment was not always marked by joy. Though some were indeed happy to see their old friends still among the living, and crossed themselves in gratitude for the miracle they had just witnessed, many others had hoped and believed that Poland was at last free of Jews. And now it appeared that the Jews had risen from the dead, perhaps to reclaim their homes, furniture, clothing, and money, to resume their control over the shtetl.

Indeed, included among these few returning Jewish survivors were members of the town's oldest, wealthiest, and most powerful families: the Sonensons, the Kabaczniks, and the Yurkanskis. Owners of big houses, large tracts of land, all three of the town's tanneries, the slaughterhouse, and the wax factory, they all had deep roots in the shtetl and many connections. The greedy among the Poles must have taken some comfort in the fact that none of the Kiuchefskis had returned, since that family had owned the electric sawmill, part of the electric power station, several beautiful buildings on Vilna Street, and a number of other properties. But despite the slaughter of the Kiuchefskis and nearly five thousand other Jews from Eishyshok and the vicinity, there were still too many Jews left, in the opinion of a number of their former neighbors.

Some voiced their resentment in words, saying that Hitler had not done a good enough job. Others drew their hands across their throats in a silent miming of the fate they wished upon those who had returned. The shtetl lunatics also joined the chorus of dismay, making their contribution in their own highly animated, dramatic fashion.

The shock and distress were entirely mutual, for the Jews saw many of their old neighbors, including people who had once been their friends, wearing clothes that had formerly belonged to Jews, living in homes that had been owned by Jews, and going about their normal business as though nothing had changed in the years between September 1941 and July 1944.[2] Apart from the absence of the people who had been the majority of the population, the town appeared much as it had before. It was true that some houses were empty, too damaged to be lived in, with gaping holes where the doors and windows had been, so that they looked like wounded shells of their former selves, forever mourning their dead owners. But all in all, the town and its Christian inhabitants had come through the war remarkably intact.[3]

What was to become of the Jews who were now beginning to return? In fact, the issue of how to deal with Jewish property and Jewish jobs that had been taken over by Poles during the war had been addressed as early as August 1943 (though not in a form the Christian citizens of Eishyshok would have had access to). Anticipating that some Jews might survive the Holocaust, the Polish government-in-exile had had Roman Knoll, a member of its foreign affairs office, draft a memo on the subject:

In the Homeland as a whole — regardless of the general psychological situation at any given moment — the position is such that the return of the Jews to their jobs and workshops is quite out of the question, even if the number of Jews were greatly reduced. The non-Jewish population has filled their places in the towns and cities; in much of Poland this is a fundamental change, and final in character. The return of masses of Jews would be perceived by the population not as an act of restitution but as an invasion against which they would have to defend themselves, even by physical means . . . The Government is correct in assuring world opinion that anti-Semitism will no longer exist in Poland; but it will no longer exist only if the surviving Jews do not endeavor to return to Poland's cities and towns en masse. Considering the difficult situation, the Homeland sees only one way out: the Polish Government must take the initiative — immediately if possible — with the aim of creating a national centre for the Jews of Eastern Europe. This project should be drawn up in co-operation with Jewish Zionist circles; [it] should focus on an East European territory for the future Jewish state, in preference to Palestine — which is too small for the purpose, too exotic, and has aroused conflict with the Arab world — and in preference to some tropical colony to which the Jews will refuse to emigrate. It may be too early to decide precisely what territory should be considered. Our attitude in this matter should be philo-Jewish rather than anti-Jewish. . . .[4]

In Eishyshok, as in shtetlekh throughout Eastern Europe, the Red Army's liberation of Nazi-occupied territories was followed by the return of the Jews — that is, if there were any native Jews who had survived long enough to make such a return; and if they chose to take a chance, once again, at living with neighbors who had at best tolerated the slaughter and deportation of the local Jews, at worst actively collaborated in them. The hope was that the Russian occupying forces would act as a guarantor of their safety (though in many places the Russians were too few in number to be effective, and the local police forces they appointed were too small).

Slowly, one by one or in small groups, Eishyshok's few remaining Jews began trickling back into town, accompanied by friends and relatives with whom they had survived the war. They reclaimed a few houses from the Poles who had moved in, among them Hayya Sonenson's "Long House," so called because it ran the length of an entire block, Leibe Glombocki's house across the backyard from the Sonenson house, the Kabacznik house two houses away from the Sonensons' at the corner of the market square and Mill Street, and Haikl Kanichowski's house on Vilna Street.

The Kabacznik and Sonenson houses became the central gathering places for the survivors. Sorl Kabacznik and her three surviving children took in Israel Shmerkowitch and his father Yekutiel as well as most of the single people, who were usually the sole survivors of their families, among them Reuven Paikowski, Szeina Blacharowicz, and Yitzhak Levin. All told, their household, which they called the Kabacznik kibbutz, numbered about twenty people. The Sonensons housed a number of married couples, among them Moshe's good friend Alter Michalowski and his wife Masha, and an occasional single as well. Since people could not bring themselves to enter the empty, desecrated prayerhouses, which had once served as community forums, Moshe Sonenson also turned his mother's Long House into a meeting place, where the now pitifully reduced community could discuss its joint concerns.

As one of only two survivors who had served on the kahal (the other being his brother Shalom), it was somehow natural that Moshe should have become the unofficial leader of the community. Without ever being asked, he simply took it upon himself to do what needed to be done, assuming responsibility for both the living and the dead. He tended to the gravestones in the Old and New Cemeteries, and hired people to build a fence around the women's mass grave. He responded to the letters that began to arrive from relatives in distant places inquiring about their families. With the exception of one note to a relative of the Kabaczniks', all the letters he sent bore sad tidings. Typical is the postcard he wrote on August 24, 1944, to Eishyshkian Hayyim-Yoshke Bielicki, who had served as a soldier in the Red Army:[5]

My Dear Friend Bielicki,

Your letter was received. From your family no one survived. All perished at the hands of the Hitlerite murderers. The shehita took place in September 1941. From our shtetl only 35 people survived.

The shehita was a hundred times more horrible than what is described in the newspapers. Children were buried alive. I do not have the strength to write. . . .

Your friend,
Moshe Sonenson

Of course Moshe's most immediate concern upon his return to the shtetl was to reclaim the baby son he had left at the home of the Polish brother and sister in the countryside. Because he had feared that the infant might be harmed or killed if it were known that he was Jewish, the note tucked into the little basket that carried him had identified him as the illegitimate child of Polish nobility, and now Moshe had to establish himself as the real father. First he went, incognito, to the home of the peasants who had taken the baby in, so that he could identify the child. The brother recognized Moshe from prewar times but did not make any connection between Moshe and one of "his" children, and Moshe in turn recognized the baby but did not reveal his relationship to him. After Moshe engaged in an energetic negotiation with officials from the church in Juryzdyki, and made handsome payments to the church and to the kindly foster parents, baby Hayyim was returned to his own parents. He was about ten weeks old. From the moment Zipporah first held her son in her arms again, the tear that had seemed permanently frozen on her cheek since the death of her infant baby son in the Radun attic disappeared.

Life for the survivors who returned to Eishyshok ricocheted constantly between the mundane to the tragic. People were trying to get back to normal, using their prewar connections to begin buying, selling, and trading again, in a weekly market that was only the dimmest reflection of what had existed before. But nothing could really distract them from the utter abnormality of it all. No matter where they turned, memories and death lurked in every corner. And always the shadow of fear loomed over them, making them wonder when the AK and their sympathizers would resort to violence. As the danger was quite real, the Russians enforced a curfew from late evening to sunrise to try to protect the Eishyshkians.

The overriding preoccupation of everyone was the dead: how to honor them, commemorate them, pray over them. Twice the survivors came together to say Kaddish at the huge common graves, once at the grave for the men, once at the grave for the women and children. The men's grave, in the ditch around the Old Cemetery, was still visible, for even with the thousands of bodies piled within, the level of the ditch was still lower than the high ground of the cemetery. The women's and children's grave, which adjoined the Christian cemetery, was now covered over with grass, yellow buttercups, purple clover, and white daisies. Butterflies flew gracefully from flower to flower there, and birds sang in the trees of the carefully manicured cemetery beyond. Zipporah Sonenson attended both of these Kaddish gatherings with baby Hayyim cradled in her arms and a new crystal tear shining on her face.

The survivors were also concerned with recovering the bodies of their loved ones who had died in the countryside so that they could recite the memorial prayers over them, invoking the "perfect rest" that is the goal of those prayers: "Merciful God in heaven, grant perfect rest to the soul of . . . who has passed to his eternal habitation; may he be under thy divine wings among the holy and pure who shine bright as the sky; may his place of rest be in paradise." They felt that they could never be at peace with themselves until they had given a proper Jewish burial to those who had died in hiding, or while fighting with the partisans. Though going back into the countryside was a dangerous undertaking because of the roving gangs of White Poles, they nonetheless made serious attempts to find those lonely, unmarked graves and bring the remains back for burial in a Jewish cemetery.

Accompanied by a few Russian soldiers who came along to protect them, Shalom Sonenson, his brother Moshe, and Alter Michalowski exhumed the body of Shalom's daughter Gittele, which was buried in the middle of a dirt road leading to Lebiedniki on the Korkuc estate. Her body was intact. With black hair framing her pale face, and a peaceful cast to her features, she seemed simply to be sleeping. Gittele was buried in the New Cemetery near her grandfather Shael Sonenson.

Reuven Paikowski was very anxious to retrieve the body of his father, Shmuel-Leib, killed at age forty-four during a partisan mission only a month before. But with the area teeming with AK, Reuven's quest turned out to be impossible.

Leibke Kaganowicz was more fortunate than Reuven Paikowski. Like many local partisans (as well as men who were members of the Communist Party), he had been appointed to one of the new police forces organized by the Russians to help them maintain control of the territories they were occupying. As a member of the Aran police force, Leibke was able to get a truckload of Russian soldiers to accompany him and Avraham Widlanski to the outskirts of the Yureli forest, where Leibke's father and brother, and several members of the Levo family who were Widlanski's relatives, were buried. Describing the disinterment, Leibke later wrote:

We unearthed the bodies of Benjamin and father and all the Levos, who were Abraham's kin, and took them to Varena [Aran]. There we interred them in the Jewish cemetery. It was one of the most heartbreaking tasks I have ever performed, but I knew that I must do it.[6]

Ever since liberation, Avraham Lipkunski had dreamed practically every night about his brother Pinhas, who was murdered in Dugalishok on October 21, 1942, near their father's blacksmith shop. Now he was determined to give Pinhas the proper Jewish burial he had been denied. Since Avraham worked for the Russian secret police, the NKVD, which had extended its authority to all the Soviet-occupied territories, he was hoping that the Radun unit, where he was employed, would give him a police escort into the countryside; but his request was denied. Despite the danger from the local White Poles — the very people who had killed his father — Avraham set off for Dugalishok alone. It was the end of August, 1944.

Armed with a gun and a pistol, Avraham accosted a peasant from Radun and ordered him to harness his horse to a wagon and take him to Dugalishok on what he described as a special mission he'd been given — to unearth the body of a partisan and bring it back to Radun for burial. After the successful completion of this mission, he told the man, he would be free to return home. The peasant drove Avraham into Dugalishok, where he entered his old family home, which was now inhabited by Shiemaszka, the man who had organized the ambush of his brother and subsequently buried him. When Shiemaszka saw Avraham Lipkunski, gun in hand, he turned pale as a ghost. Avraham reassured him that he had not returned on a mission of vengeance, nor to reclaim family property. The only thing that mattered to him was to reclaim Pinhas's body.

Shiemaszka joined the Radun peasant at the front of the carriage, while Avraham sat behind them with his gun drawn. They passed near the place where Pinhas was killed, and continued on until they reached a small hill covered with grass and cattle dung, which Shiemaszka identified as Pinhas's grave. Avraham ordered them to dig. When they reached the skeleton, Avraham recognized his brother's clothing. He also recog-

In September 1944 four weddings took place on one day at the Sonenson house in Eishyshok. After the wedding, Shalom Sonenson (right) posed with his new wife, Miriam Ribak, a friend, and Berl (Dov) Lifshitz of Olkenik. Both Shalom and Miriam had lost their spouses during the Holocaust. Berl escaped the September 1941 massacre as he was being led to the killing fields. YESC, SH. FARBER

nized the leather strap of Pinhas's phylacteries. Now he knew that these were his brother's remains, for Pinhas had never parted from his phylacteries during even the worst moments of the Holocaust. Avraham had them put the remains in a blanket, and checked to make sure that not a single fragment of bone had been left behind. He would later write about that moment:

I saw that he was not alone on his grave. He took with him his faith in God — the leather strap of his phylacteries hung from his skeleton . . . For that split second, a ray of joy penetrated my heart. I had found my big brother Pinhas. He was resurrected. His spirit was hovering above me. I was not alone anymore. My dear Pinhas, I did not forget you. I will never forget you. I will reunite you with our loved ones, so that you will never be alone anymore.[7]

And so he did. Accompanied by a minyan of Jews, Avraham took Pinhas's remains to the Jewish cemetery in Radun, site of the huge mass grave that contained the bodies of those killed in the May 10, 1942, massacre, including their mother Mina and brother Yekutiel. After he'd given Pinhas the proper Jewish burial that would bring him to the long-awaited "perfect rest," Avraham felt such relief that it was as though he had been liberated a second time.[8]

Liba Shlosberg wanted to bring her father back to the Radun cemetery, too. Since she herself had buried him earlier that year, she had no difficulty locating his grave. With the help of a Christian friend who drove a horse and wagon into the forest to the burial site, she brought old Shmaye-Mendl back to Radun and buried him next to the mass grave, in a coffin she made of broken furniture she'd found in their house. Now Shmaye-Mendl and the infant he had helped suffocate, Shaul Sonenson, were together again, this time below ground instead of two stories above it, in an attic.

Liba returned once more to the forest to search for the bodies of her mother and the other five people she'd buried after they were all murdered by the AK in the "rabbit hunt" of March 19, 1944. Unlike her father's body, which was intact, these six bodies were decomposed beyond recognition. However, the size of the skeletons and the scraps of clothing that still hung from them allowed her to make the necessary identifications. They, too, were transported to the Radun cemetery and buried next to the mass grave.[9]

Even as people were burying their dead, they were trying to rejoin the living. So there were weddings as well as funerals. One day in September 1944 four Jewish weddings took place at the Sonenson home in Eishyshok: Shalom Sonenson, whose first wife had refused to flee and thus had been murdered in the Radun massacre, married Miriam Ribak from Olkenik, whose first husband had barely emerged from the wedding canopy when he was shot by a Lithuanian shaulist; Shalom and Miriam had first met in

Ghetto Radun. Moshe Yurkanski, whose wife and two sons had been murdered in the Eishyshok massacre, married Feigl from Zelva, whom he had met in the forest. The other marriages were of forest couples, too: Dobke Kremin and Israel Dimitrowski, both native Eishyshkians, and Esther Wilenchik and a man named Kaufman from Grodno. Reb Moshe Davidowicz der Lubaver (from Luba) performed the group wedding.

Reb Moshe was an accomplished Talmudic scholar, as well as a relative of the Haffetz Hayyim. But despite his training and his family background, he had never held an official position as a rabbi. In prewar times the Haffetz Hayyim's court refused to accept him because of his great admiration for secular studies. Excluded from the court but wanting to stay in Radun, where he had attended yeshivah and met and married his wife, he had opened a restaurant/tavern that became popular with Jews and Christians alike. His manner of doing business made him so well loved and respected by all that when he and his wife and three daughters lived in the forest during the Holocaust (in the same group with Liba Shlosberg and Szeina Blacharowicz), it was Christian former customers of his who helped them survive for the twenty-six months they were there. Now, in one of those strange twists of fate, this man who had once been criticized for being too secular and modern had become the keeper of the flame of tradition, the spiritual leader for what remained of the Jewish communities of the two illustrious yeshivah towns of Radun and Eishyshok. He also served as the ritual slaughterer of meat, and at least once as mohel (when he circumcised Hayyim Sonenson).[10]

At the group wedding at which he officiated, attempts were made to bring something of a festive atmosphere to the occasion. The ceremony was the traditional one, and during the reception that was held afterward, Zipporah Sonenson and her brother-in-law's new bride, Miriam Ribak, served some of the usual wedding foods. But none of the other customs could be observed. The market square and shulhoyf through which the wedding procession would once have marched were empty; the klezmers were silent; only a handful of Jews were still alive to witness the ceremony. The survivors, however, then as always, felt that the spirits of the several thousand Jewish martyrs buried nearby were in attendance.

Soon after the wedding it was time to prepare for the High Holidays, but where to hold the Rosh Hashanah and Yom Kippur services was in doubt. Emotions ran high among the survivors as this holy season approached, bringing with it memories of the terrible Rosh Hashanah of three years before, which had immediately preceded the massacre. The idea of restoring a portion of the main synagogue was brought up, as it had been when people first returned to Eishyshok. Only a small area would be needed, since what was left of the Jewish community would not even fill two of the benches in the sanctuary, plus a few seats in the women's gallery above. But those among the survivors who had spent three terrifying days locked in the main synagogue or one of the two batei midrash during the 1941 High Holidays vehemently opposed the idea. Szeina Blacharowicz and several others declared that they would never be able to enter any of those buildings again, or indeed any synagogue at all. The only incentive they could imagine for ever again setting foot in a house of prayer was to remember the dead and to register a complaint against the Almighty for abandoning his people during the war.

Moshe Sonenson suggested that the High Holiday prayers be held in the Sonenson house. Sorl Kabacznik objected, saying that the prayers should be held in *her* house, because she owned the only Sefer Torah in Eishyshok — the one she'd had in the pit beneath the Korkuc stable — and because the majority of the survivors were living in her home. So the services were held in the Kabacznik home. They were attended not just by the local Jews, but by a number of Russian soldiers as well. Though they, too, were Jewish, for some of them it was the first Jewish service they had ever witnessed. Overflowing with tears of grief and remembrance, this was a Rosh Hashanah that would remain forever engraved in the memories of all who were present. Equally memorable was the Kaddish that was said at the mass graves on the third anniversary of the massacre, when the very earth beneath the survivors' feet seemed to tremble.

NEW DANGERS, NEW LOSSES

A few nights later, on Yom Kippur, the dangers the survivors still faced were brought vividly home to them. Several people in the Kabacznik "kibbutz" nearly lost their lives, thanks to what Miriam Kabacznik believed was a plot to murder the members of her household. When Miriam had gone shopping for food in Vilna and asked for baking soda to use in the traditional hallah, she was sold another white powder — either by accident or on purpose — which was later revealed to be detergent. The screams of pain that issued from the Kabacznik home that night were so loud that they could be heard two doors away at the Sonenson's house. Despite the curfew, the doctor and Sharavei, the pharmacist of the Polish drugstore, were called, and they managed to save those who had nearly succumbed to the poisoning. Ironically, Sharavei had been present at the meeting a mere nine months before where it was decided that the answer to what remained of "the Jewish question" was to ferret out and kill every last Jew who still survived. Though Sharavei's ties of friendship with the Kabaczniks apparently prevailed over ideology this time, the poisoning episode left the survivors feeling newly vulnerable.

Adding to this feeling of vulnerability was the fact that during this same period, the Russian army left Eishyshok to follow the front, which was now to the west.[11] All that remained to represent the occupying force were three members of the militia, the local police force appointed by the Red Army, which meant that the Jews were now virtually defenseless. With the departure of the Russians, rumors began to circulate about a new AK attack on the Jews in Eishyshok. Jaszka Aliszkewicz and other friends among the local Poles confirmed the rumors, and added that a significant number of young Eishyshkians were joining the AK, including two young sons of a man named Merzuk, who in pre-Holocaust days was the watchman at the Sonenson slaughterhouse. Previously the Sonensons had had great confidence in Merzuk, and indeed had entrusted him with many family valuables when they had to flee. Now Merzuk's sons Ivan and Waclaw had gone over to the AK, and Merzuk himself was refusing to return the Sonensons' property, claiming that Lithuanians and Germans had seized most of the fur coats and the silver and gold family heirlooms that had been left with him.

Moshe Sonenson became very concerned about this latest turn of events, so much so that he and his cousin Shepske Kabacznik took the risk of traveling the dangerous road to Vilna to appeal to the Russian military headquarters for protection. The Russian in charge there assured them they had nothing to fear. The White Poles would not dare to attack anybody in a town under Communist rule, he told them; the roads were perhaps still not safe, but the towns were secure, the days of AK atrocities were reaching an end. Besides which, he explained, no Russian soldiers could be spared, because they were all needed at the front.

Nonetheless, at about five o'clock in the afternoon on Thursday, October 19, 1944, two soldiers from the Red Army arrived in Eishyshok to investigate the reports of trouble with the AK. The two men, a captain who was a member of the Russian Counterintelligence, Smersh, and his sergeant driver, stayed at the Sonensons'. At the same time that they were in Eishyshok another Red Army man was also in town, his mission being to requisition potatoes for the nearby troops.[12] He stayed in the home of a Christian woman known for her friendship with soldiers during the war and post-liberation.

With rumors flying about a possible attack, the Jewish community was very tense. Miriam Kabacznik pleaded with her family and the other members of the Kabacznik kibbutz to leave at once. Despite her pleas, they chose to remain at home. But they did make several concessions to the impending danger, such as going to bed in their clothes in case they had to flee in the middle of the night, and posting a guard outside.

The Sonenson household was perceived as being more secure, since it was a very sturdy brick building with two armed Russian soldiers staying there, as well as Alter Michalowski, who was also armed because he was one of the three members of the local Russian-appointed militia. For reasons of safety several of the other Jews in Eishyshok — Zvi Michalowski, Moshe Edelstein, Dobke Kremin Dimitrowski, and Esther Wilenchik Kaufman — also decided to take refuge in the Sonenson house that night.

At the same huge dining table where the entire Sonenson family had once shared its festive Sabbath and holiday meals, Moshe and what was left of his family, along with their assorted guests, now sat down to eat. This meal, too, was festive in its odd way, with frequent interludes of storytelling and singing to punctuate the evening. After the meal, everybody departed to the sleeping quarters they had been assigned. The Russian captain ordered his driver to sleep in the truck, which was parked in the stable, while the captain himself took the front room near the main entrance to the house. Yitzhak and Yaffa slept in the room at the end of the dining room, the bedroom that had once belonged to Grandmother Hayya. Moshe, Zipporah, and baby Hayyim, Shalom and Miriam Sonenson, Alter Michalowski, and all the other guests retired to bedrooms on the second floor, once the apartment of Avraham Sonenson, the oldest of Hayya Sonenson's children, and his wife and two sons, who were all murdered in the Holocaust. Soon everyone was asleep.

Sometime after eleven that night, Miriam Kabacznik heard noises outside. A voice was giving orders in Polish for an imminent attack, which would be launched first against the Sonensons, "since the people there are armed," and then against the Kabaczniks. "Polska bez Zydow" — Poland without Jews — was the rallying cry he trumpeted to his followers. Reuven Paikowski, Szeina Blacharowicz, and several others who had heard the footsteps of the AK echoing off the cobblestones below ran through the house with Miriam, trying to awaken all the members of the Kabacznik kibbutz before it was too late. People jumped from the windows and ran through the back door into the dark moonless night, going wherever their feet and their instinct for survival would take them. Miriam and Reuven ran to the backyard of what had once been the Botwinik home, where they hid in a ditch. Szeina hid in a pigsty outside the Dakinewiczowa house. Zvi Michalowski and others found shelter in the Kabacznik garden, while still others hid in nearby barns and pigsties. Those who hid in the garden heard the AK march on the Sonenson house.

The next sound was the loud noise of something crashing through the window of the room where Yitzhak and Yaffa Sonenson were sleeping. Immediately awake, Yitzhak grabbed his sister's hand and pulled her out of bed, making for the staircase leading to their parents' room. One second later the grenade that had been lobbed through the window exploded in Yaffa's bed, sending a cloud of feathers up to the ceiling. As the sound of shooting filled the air, people began fleeing for their lives. Dobke Kremin

Zipporah Sonenson (right), holding little Yaffa in her arms in the late 1930s, in front of the Sonenson house, where she would be murdered by the AK with another baby in her arms, on October 20, 1944. At left are Ida Sonenson with son Mulke (Shmuel). Behind Zipporah are Geneshe Sonenson with her son Meir. In the center is Hayya Sonenson, the owner of the house. To her right is her niece Yetta Wolotzki, a visitor (with flower from Eretz Israel); and Miriam Kabacznik. Top row (right to left): Dov (Berele) Wolotzki, Yetta's brother; a relative; and Golde Kabazcnik with son Yossef. Miriam and Yaffa survived in hiding, Dov at Dachau; the others were murdered in the September 1941 massacre and in other locations. YESC, WOLOTZKI

Dimitrowski and Esther Wilenchik Kaufman jumped from the second-floor windows and began to run toward Hayya Sonenson's apple grove. Shalom and Miriam Sonenson ran to the outdoor toilet and stood in excrement practically up to their necks. Meanwhile, Alter Michalowski and Moshe Sonenson fired machine guns through the second-floor windows, trying to keep the mob at bay. When their bullets ran out, Alter jumped out the window, and was joined by Moshe Edelstein. The two men ran to the apple grove, where they met up with Moshe Yurkanski, and together they all ran to the river.

Moshe ran back to his wife to plead with her to follow the others through the window. Baby Hayyim would have to be left behind in the crib for now, but Moshe, Zipporah, Yitzhak, and Yaffa would be able to jump and make a dash to safety. Zipporah refused. "I am not going to sacrifice another child. You can jump with Yitzhak and Sheinele" (Yaffa's Yiddish name, which her mother used only in times of great emotion). Since Zipporah refused to leave the baby, Moshe took the whole family to a hiding place in an atticlike closet above the steps and off a second-floor room. Hoping to camouflage the doorway to the attic closet, he pulled a piece of furniture against it. Once inside the cramped space, Moshe crawled to the back of the closet where the sloping roof met the floor, and lay flat, trying to take up as little room as possible, so that his family would not be too uncomfortable. Yitzhak sat in front of him, while Zipporah sat facing the door, in the most spacious area of the hiding place, with Yaffa in back of her and the baby in her arms. Miraculously, none of the commotion — guns firing, grenades exploding, people screaming — disturbed Hayyim. He slept peacefully throughout.

Below, all was chaos, as the AK tore the house apart looking for them. From their hiding place in the atticlike closet they could hear men's voices screaming at the Russian captain to tell them where the family was, and cursing every time they mentioned Moshe Sonenson's name. Finally, sometime past midnight, the Sonensons heard footsteps on the stairs leading to the second floor, and more voices — many of them voices they recognized as belonging to people they knew. Then they heard another round of chaos as the men ran through the upstairs rooms, smashing furniture and exploding in a frenzy of frustration at being unable to find their prey. Then one of the men noticed the telltale scratch that had been etched into the floor when

Moshe dragged the piece of furniture across the room.

Silence. Then, breath held, they listened to the sound of the chest being moved. As the men opened the door, Zipporah Sonenson walked out from the hiding place, still holding her sleeping infant. She knew her murderers, among them Anton Sharavei the pharmacist's son; Stanislaw Bulgak; and seventeen year-old Waclaw Merzuk and his brother Ivan, age twenty-two, the sons of the former Sonenson employee. Well acquainted with the way the AK worked, she did not plead for her life. But, addressing Anton and Stanislaw by name, she did ask that she be killed first so she would not have to witness the death of her son. Nine shots answered her plea; baby Hayyim was killed in his mother's arms. Yaffa, who had learned to count in the pit beneath the Korkuc pigsty, counted the nine. And then she counted fifteen more. Zipporah, who had taught her daughter her numbers, fell backward on top of her. As the hail of bullets rained down and the killers screamed with joy, Yitzhak pleaded for mercy in Polish, but apparently no one recognized that it was his voice they were hearing, not Zipporah's, for they did not realize there was anyone else in the closet. With a final fusillade of bullets, which flew around the closet gleaming like little red fireflies, the men left. Had they aimed their guns lower, Moshe and his two older children would have been killed.

At first Yaffa thought she *had* been killed. Her body felt heavy and numb. She was sure that ants and worms were already eating her flesh. As daylight began to enter the windows, they could hear people down below, speaking in Yiddish. The broken voice of Shalom Sonenson was telling people that Moshe, Zipporah, and the three children had been murdered. He and Miriam, hiding in the outhouse, had heard Zipporah and Yitzhak's voices talking to the murderers, and then gunfire, and then silence. People spontaneously began saying Kaddish when Shalom stopped talking.

Yaffa Eliach in 1997 on the spot in her grandmother's house in Eishyshok where her mother Zipporah Sonenson and brother Hayyim were murdered by the AK, pointing to the door of the attic-closet where the family hid.
PHOTO: KEVIN CLOUTIER. YESC, Y. ELIACH

Yaffa, Yitzhak, and Moshe crawled out of their hiding place. Yaffa was covered in the blood of her mother and baby brother, blood that had also formed two puddles on the floor, one large, one small. Moshe led the children downstairs, through the ruin of their grandmother's house. Feathers were still drifting through the air, blown about by the breezes that came through the smashed windows; splintered furniture littered their path. So this was what the aftermath of a pogrom looked like. Later they would hear that a search of the house by survivors had turned up several unexploded grenades and a number of empty ammunition shells.

As they walked out to the street through the main door, people looked at them in disbelief. "Zipporah and the baby are dead," Moshe told them, and burst into uncontrollable sobbing. Miriam, still covered in excrement, tried to comfort him, telling him he must be grateful for the survival of his two older children. But it was to no avail. Moshe could not stop crying.

Now they heard that there had been another victim that night. The Russian soldier who had come to requisition potatoes for the army was murdered in his sleep. As for the Russian captain who had slept in the Sonenson house, he had disappeared without a trace, along with all the official documents he was carrying. Later it was learned that the AK had taken him prisoner and subsequently murdered him. Neither his body nor his papers were ever found.

Members of the Kabacznik household had all escaped injury, but the house itself had been sacked, every item in it, valuable or otherwise, gone or destroyed. Most of the inhabitants' meager possessions had consisted of the few things they had been able to retrieve from Christian neighbors upon their return, and now they were gone again. Even the small Sefer Torah that Sorl Kabacznik had purchased at such expense and had kept in the pit beneath the stable at Korkuc's, the only Torah left in Eishyshok, was among the looted items.

The same night of the murders the municipal building, about half a mile away, had been attacked by a crowd of about 150 Poles, 80 of whom were sworn members of the AK, the rest Eishyshkians who were sympathizers. The attackers were the same men who had staged the pogrom against the Sonenson and Kabacznik households. Among the targets of the municipal-building attack were the official seals of the new Russian government of Eishyshok, which the marauders stole in order to be able to forge official documents.[13]

The Russian captain's driver, who had slept in the truck that night, was lucky. While the AK were still busy looting the Kabacznik home and the municipal building, he had been able to drive away unnoticed. He drove twelve and a half miles to Aran, where he called on the militia for

Yaffa Eliach in 1997 at the attic-closet, with (right to left) husband David, daughter Smadar-Zipporah, granddaughter Moriah, and grandson Moshe-Ariel.
PHOTO: KEVIN CLOUTIER. YESC, Y. ELIACH

help. Aran policeman Leibke Kaganowicz and a truckload of his fellow militia men (known locally as "Green Hats") immediately drove to Eishyshok, but they were too late. The attacks were over and the murderers had fled.[14]

Alter Michalowski had also gone for help that night, running and walking all the way to Radun. He, too, returned with a truckload of men, soldiers from the Russian army.[15] The Green Hats from Aran and the Russian soldiers from Radun joined forces and, together with Reuven Paikowski, Israel Shmerkowitch, Zvi Michalowski, and several other young local Jewish partisans, they went searching for the murderers and looters of the previous night. With the help of some local Poles, they were able to find and arrest about fifty people, most of them members of the AK. However, the killers of Zipporah Sonenson and her baby were not among them.

As the search for the killers proceeded, it was necessary to attend to the burying of the dead. The bodies of Zipporah and Hayyim were brought down to the main dining room, which was cleared of feathers, bullets, grenades, and broken furniture. Only hours before, Zipporah had served dinner to a houseful of people in that dining room. Now she and her child lay on the floor, feet facing the door, in accordance with custom. They did not, however, undergo the usual cleansing rituals. In keeping with the Jewish law pertaining to those who die violent deaths, Zipporah remained dressed in her bloody clothes, the baby in his bloody swaddling and blanket, and together they were wrapped in shrouds made from white sheets. Moshe returned his baby son to the crook of his wife's arm, which had remained bent, in death, as if she were still holding him. "They must never part," he said. "This was her wish."

Though Jewish law required immediate burial, the Russian commander from Radun would not allow it. While he awaited orders from headquarters in Vilna, the bodies of Zipporah and Hayyim and that of the slain Russian soldier were transferred to the morgue near the hospital.

Fearing that the AK might still present a threat to the remaining Jews, the commander suggested that they all go to Radun for the night. Most did, including Yitzhak and Yaffa, but Moshe refused to go, because he was afraid that the White Poles and their collaborators might mutilate his loved ones' bodies, or spirit them away from the morgue. He, Reuven Paikowski, Alter Michalowski, and several other former partisans remained in Eishyshok.

On Sunday morning, October 22, the Jews of Eishyshok returned from Radun for the funeral. Reuven Paikowski and Moshe Davidowicz der Lubaver had taken it upon themselves to make all the arrangements, and had managed to obtain a horse-drawn carriage to transport the coffin to the graveyard. Following in the wake of Moshe and his children and a few of their friends, who were holding on to the carriage, a small procession of Jews accompanied them on the walk to the graveyard. Local Poles lined the street, some of them friends of the Sonensons' who were weeping, others making no attempt to hide their satisfaction that Poland was two deaths closer to the goal of being rid of its Jews. The procession went directly to the New House of Eternity, without making the traditional stop at the now desecrated summer shul.

As Yaffa walked with girlfriend Bashke Yurkanski, the cobblestones on the way to the cemetery all seemed to look up at her, each one bearing the face of her mother or baby brother or one of the other thousands of murdered souls she'd seen in the mass grave in Radun. Looking up, she saw smiles on the faces of many of the local Poles, smiles that seemed like replicas of the smile Assistant Gebietskommisar Werner had worn as he marched across their bare backs in Radun over two years before, and the smiles of her mother's murderers just over two days before.

Zipporah and Hayyim were buried next to

Shortly after the murder of Zipporah Sonenson and her baby, the Russian soldier Abrascha-Arluk-Lawit (center) was sent to Eishyshok to investigate the crime, as a member of a committee in Lida, under the command of General Petrov, that looked into the atrocities of the AK during the Holocaust and its aftermath. He is shown here during his partisan days in the Naliboki forest, 1943, with partisan Meyer Isckowicz (right) and Dvora Retzkin. PHOTO: YEHEZKIEL OKUN. YESC, ABRASCHA-ARLUK-LAWIT

the tombstone of Shael Sonenson and the fresh grave of Gittele. As newly dug earth was shoveled onto the coffin containing the bodies of her mother and baby brother, Yaffa felt as if it were thudding against her own body.

The murders of Zipporah Sonenson and her infant son marked the beginning of the end of the last tragic chapter of Jewish life in Eishyshok. People understood at last that there could be no future for Jews in Poland, that it was not just the Nazi invaders but the Poles themselves who wanted to see all the Jews dead. "Hitler gut, Jude kaput" was a popular saying of the time. And the White Poles (and their collaborators) seemed to be doing what they could to ensure the truth of it.

Ziske Matikanski, for example, was murdered by White Poles — ironically enough, since he was among the few who still believed in the possibilities of peaceful coexistence. A grandson of Eishyshkian Nehama Gershonowitz was also murdered by White Poles. Having come to Eishyshok to see if any of his relatives had survived the massacre, he was informed that all of his family in both Lida and Eishyshok had been killed, and then he himself was killed on his way back to Lida. Rachel Pochter's oldest son Yoske was ambushed and severely wounded by the White Poles on the highway between Vilna and Eishyshok. After a year of suffering, he finally succumbed to his wounds in Lodz.[16] Luba Katz, a partisan from Olkenik, lost her husband Elia Margolies, a fellow partisan, when he was murdered by White Poles as he was giving a lecture.[17] Luba was once more alone, having lost her last living blood relative when her brother Leibke was shot while trying to save Lieutenant Stankewitch.

Jews began leaving Eishyshok and all the other small towns and villages to which they had so tentatively ventured to return a short while before. In Eishyshok, the Kabaczniks were among the first to leave, moving to Vilna, along with most of the rest of the members of their "kibbutz."

REVENGE

Other Jews, however, were more concerned with settling scores than with their personal safety, and stayed on to help bring to trial the local murderers and collaborators responsible for the death of their loved ones. Those who had fought in Russian partisan units were able to help by working with the NKVD (the Russian secret police) and the militia. Considered a great asset by the military, since they were so familiar with the local language, populace, and countryside, many of the Jewish partisans were drafted into prominent positions where their knowledge of local politics and personalities could be put to use. Near Eishyshok, for example, the Russians had ordered local partisans Leibke Kaganowicz,

Niomke Rogowski, Avraham Asner, and Lippa Skolski to establish a police station in Aran, under the command of a man named Ratner, a pre–World War II member of the local Communist party.

It was men like these whom the Russians trusted to identify and track down their mutual enemies: members of the anti-Communist White Poles (in areas that were largely Polish) and Green Partisans (in areas that were largely Lithuanian); civil officials and others who had collaborated with the Germans and specifically with the Einsatzgruppen (the mobile killing squads); Nazi sympathizers who had been responsible for the murder of Jews. Charged with finding collaborators as well as Germans who were still hiding in the forest, they put their lives on the line daily. Ironically, the same local farmers who had once been so helpful in capturing Jews now helped in the capture of Germans. They would invite the fugitive Germans to their homes for a lavish meal and alert the police to their presence — a performance that had been polished to perfection by earlier run-throughs in which it was the Jews who were invited and the Germans, White Poles, and other murderers who arrived unannounced.

Among the many collaborators captured by the Aran police force was a man named Baderas, who had been one of the busiest executioners at the Eishyshok massacre in September 1941. Leibke Kaganowicz, an inadvertent witness to the massacre of the women and children from his hiding place behind the Christian cemetery wall, recognized Baderas and orchestrated his capture. The most wanted man on their list was the Lithuanian commander Ostrauskas, who, in his capacity as police chief of Eishyshok under the Germans, had presided over the massacre with great gusto. Though they failed to capture him, they did find his wife. Since they did not hold her responsible for her husband's horrendous crimes, however, they did not arrest her.[18]

Eishyshok at first had no strong NKVD presence after liberation, unlike Aran and Radun. But after the October 19–20 attacks, there was a drastic change, apparently in response to the fact that the situation had gotten so out of control that in one night a large mob had killed a civilian Jewish woman and her infant son, murdered a Russian soldier, attacked the municipal building, and abducted a Russian captain, who subsequently disappeared, along with a number of important documents, before being killed. Now, trying to reassert their authority over the area, the Soviets established an NKVD post in Eishyshok, which seemed to promise a new era of security for the few Jews who remained in Eishyshok and total Russian control of the area.

The NKVD station was staffed by a contingent of Russian officers: Major Bazarov, Captain Shabaiov, Captain Krushenko, Lieutenant Soloviev and Lieutenant Aliushka. Immediately after their arrival, Moshe Sonenson met with them and told them that he intended to dedicate his life to finding, arresting, and bringing to trial the AK murderers of his wife and infant son, and that he would never rest until he had accomplished his mission. In addition to Moshe Sonenson, who played an important albeit unofficial role in the search, other local Jews who became involved in tracking down the killers were Alter Michalowski, in his capacity as chief of police, the post to which the Russians had appointed him, Israel Dimitrowski, Zvi Michalowski, Israel Shmerkowitch, and Reuven Paikowski. Though they were allowed (indeed encouraged) to go along on various NKVD missions, unlike the Jews of Aran and Radun, the Jews of Eishyshok did not have the legal right to search for and arrest their prey independently.

Moshe Sonenson and the commander of the NKVD station, Major Bazarov, were very impressed with each other and became instant friends. Bazarov's friendship didn't in any way diminish the danger to Moshe's family, however. Life for Moshe's children became more difficult with each passing day. They lived in constant fear that their father would be killed in an ambush or a clash with the AK during one of his numerous missions into the countryside with the NKVD. They were also aware that they themselves were not welcome members of the community to which they had returned. One day Major Bazarov had ordered the teacher of Yaffa's first-grade class to take all the children to the Sonenson house to see the place where Yaffa's mother and brother had been murdered. As the group looked at the bloodstains on the floor, Yaffa noticed that the only one who was visibly moved by the sight was her friend Bashke Yurkanski. Many of the children as well as the teacher herself were related to one of the 150 people who had participated in the October attacks.

Concerned for the safety of his children,

Yitzhak Sonenson (front) with three of the partisans with whom he lived in Aran in fall 1944: (right to left) Leibke Kaganowicz, Niomke Rogowski, and Hayyim Berkowitch (known as Pietka). YESC, Y. SONENSON

Moshe pondered what to do. He felt Yaffa was too young to live apart from her family, but he decided to send Yitzhak to Aran to stay with friends: Partisans Leibke Kaganowicz, Niomke Rogowski, Hayyim "Pietka" Berkowitch, and Lippa Skolski were all living in a household run by Zlatke Garber and Niomke's sister Hayya Rogowski, also former partisans. All were well known to the Sonensons, and the household had become the center for Jewish life in the vicinity. When Shalom and Miriam Sonenson decided to go to Aran as well, Yaffa asked them to take her along, but her uncle refused. Newly married, he didn't want the burden of taking care of his brother's child.

Hostilities between the AK and their pursuers kept intensifying as the Russian-led search missions turned up more and more incriminating documents. During an NKVD raid on AK headquarters, for example, Moshe discovered minutes from the January 1944 meeting where it was decided that all the still-surviving Jews who were hiding in the vicinity should be tracked down and murdered. Other searches turned up a variety of other kinds of damaging evidence, such as the agreement of December 1943 between the White Poles and the Germans. There were letters written by survivors of the massacre in which they agreed to give up their property in Eishyshok in exchange for food and shelter — a very bad exchange at times, since the very people to whom they wrote those letters often betrayed them. In many village homes there were Jewish family memorabilia, religious items, heirlooms, fur coats, and other valuables, some of which could be readily identified by the family names or initials that appeared on them. Some had been deposited with people believed to be family friends, who nonetheless refused to redeem them when the original owners came back to claim them; some had been stolen during the sacking of Jewish homes that followed the massacre; some had been taken from Jews who were murdered while in hiding or while serving with the partisans. When the search missions uncovered such caches of goods, the items were returned if the owner or anyone from his family was still alive. If not, the NKVD men would sometimes divide the property among themselves.

During these searches, ambushes and face-to-face battles took place constantly between the Russians and the AK, with casualties on both sides. The dead bodies of the AK, most of them dressed in at least one or two remnants of their old Polish army uniforms, were put on public display on the market square. The rows of frozen corpses remained there for weeks, growing longer and longer as new truckloads of bodies were added. Soon the rows extended to Radun and Vilna Streets. One winter day the body of Krisha, the AK commander of the northern group was brought in. As the murderer of numerous Russians, Jews, and Poles who had given shelter to Jews, including the saintly Aneza Bikewiczowa, who had taken in nearly a dozen Jews at her farm, Krisha was given a central place in the grisly market square display.

Still defiant, the AK staged another attack on Eishyshok on the night of December 6–7, 1944. This time their target was the jail on Vilna Street, where many of their members had been imprisoned. Although they did free their friends, a number of AK members were killed during the fierce resistance they encountered.[19] This latest violence was a turning point for Moshe. After that, he took his daughter Yaffa to Aran.

On the way there the Russian army truck they were traveling in was attacked by the AK, but after an exchange of gunfire in which no one in the truck was injured, they proceeded to Aran, where Yaffa joined her brother Yitzhak in the partisans' household run by Zlatke Garber. Though Zlatke was very young herself, she took care of Yaffa as though she were her own child.

Partly because it had a railway station, Aran was teeming with life. Trains filled with soldiers were constantly coming and going, carrying their human cargo to and from the front. There was also a medical supply train based in Aran, which serviced the Third Armored Division of the Russian army. The medical train was under the command of a high-ranking Russian Jewish officer named Tevl Zinberg, who, after a brief courtship, married one of the young Jewish partisans, beautiful blond Hayya Rogowski, and took her to live with him on the train. The train soon became Yaffa's second home, too, for Zinberg arranged to have several of his men tutor her, and she often spent days at a time on board, even when it went off on one of its missions into the countryside. The presence of Zinberg and other high-ranking Jewish officers and soldiers made Aran a hospitable place for all the Jews, especially after Tevl and Hayya's marriage.

Tevl Zinberg, the high-ranking Russian Jewish officer who married the beautiful blond Jewish partisan Hayya Rogowski. YESC, PAIKOWSKI

After Moshe Sonenson took Yaffa to Aran, his commitment to apprehend the AK murderers of his wife, son, and other Jews and to secure the return of looted Jewish property intensified. Day and night he went to various locations to find them, despite the danger. But unlike other Jews who killed the White Poles when they caught them, Moshe Sonenson influenced local members of the NKVD to bring the murderers to trial instead. He wanted the murders of his wife, son, and numerous Jews during the Holocaust to be recorded and become common knowledge.

With the arrest and interrogation of members of the AK, details of their attack on Eishyshok on October 19–20, 1944, began to emerge. The 150 AK members were under the general command of Krisha (Jan Borysewicz). The attack was led by former schoolteacher Michal Babul ("Gaj"), Jozef Chiniewic ("Grom"), Nikolas Tapper ("Zhaba"), and Golmont Henrik ("Gront").

While staging the attack on Eishyshok, each of three units had its special mission, such as plundering the Kabacznik and Yurkanski tanneries, invading the administration building to burn the official documents and take the official seals, and kill the Jews and loot their homes.[20]

According to the testimony in January 1945 of Michal Iwaszko, who was in the "placowka" unit, their commander, Jozef Chiniewic, ordered them to plunder and kill the Jews. According to his testimony, it was Stanislaw Bulgak (Buak) who murdered one Jewish woman and her baby: Zipporah Sonenson and her son Hayyim.[21] This confirms the testimony of Moshe Sonenson that Bulgak was one of the murderers, and that the AK came to kill the Jews, not the Russians, as claimed by many Poles.

Perhaps it was the command of Chiniewic that the people in the Kabacznik house heard on October 19, 1944, at eleven P.M., to kill the Jews because Poland should be without Jews. The evidence also includes material on the Russian captain who slept in the Sonenson house and the other Russian soldier, as well as details on the AK attack of December 6–7, 1944, on the Eishyshok jail to free arrested White Poles, among them Stanislaw Bulgak.

A significant number of AK members who were under Michal Babul's command during the October attack stood trial in Vilnius on April 2–5, 1945. Some were sentenced to death, others were exiled to Siberia. Among those convicted and executed were Babul (b. 1914), Jozef Chiniewic (b. 1919), and Nikolas Tapper (b. 1913), who was a local Catholic priest. A number of the AK members involved in the October attack and the murder of Zipporah Sonenson, the baby, and the Russian captain and soldier were never caught, having escaped to Poland.

A STALINIST REALIGNMENT

Unfortunately, the winds of change would soon begin to blow again, fanning the flames of anti-Semitism. This was a time when the Lithuanian Green Partisans and the AK were both dwindling in numbers and power in the Eishyshok–Vilna region, their membership decimated by casualties, their morale sapped by defeat. Once it became clear that their dreams of an independent Lithuania and Poland would not be realized, they were no longer able to muster the energy to fight, and so ceased to pose much of a threat to the Russians. At that point, in the spring of 1945, the Jews became irrelevant to the overall strategy of the Russians, and the tactics the Russians used to control the occupied territories entered a new phase.

Overnight they began to remove former partisans, particularly the Jewish ones, from the positions of power they had only recently appointed them to in the police stations that worked with the NKVD. Jews were replaced with non-Jews, also locals; the Russians overlooked their shady behavior during the period of the Nazi occupation when it suited them to do so. This was all part of official Stalinist policy, which dictated the severing of all connections with the Jews. A mutual dislike for the Jews would serve as a strong bond between the local population and the occupying force.

It was not just the local Jews who were eliminated from their central positions in the NKVD stations, but also a significant number of those

Russians who were Jewish themselves or had worked closely with the Jews. They were replaced with new NKVD members who had no sympathy for the Jews, and no interest in seeing to it that those few who had survived would be able to redeem their lost property, or memorialize their loved ones. The new Russian administration allowed the local population increasing access to Jewish property, and gave legal permission to their local employees to eliminate all traces of Jewish life from their towns. Jewish cemeteries were destroyed, and the Jews were robbed even of their martyrdom by signs identifying the mass graves as belonging to "Victims of Fascism, 1941–1944." The fact that all those victims were Jews went unacknowledged.

In Aran the change was so swift that the Jewish policemen were caught entirely unawares. One afternoon, with no advance warning, a Russian sergeant appeared in the police station and informed Leibke Kaganowicz and Niomke Rogowski that they were being replaced — by him. To support his claim that he was the new chief of police, he produced the relevant documents. They simply refused to believe him, and went to nearby Alytus to complain to their superior. There they found a new and completely unsympathetic colonel who stared coldly at them and asked them what they had to say in their "defense." "We were partisans, sir! We fought side by side with the Russian people!" "The day of the partisans is over" was the cold response. "Take off your belts! Hand over your pistols! You will face trial for your crimes against the Lithuanian people!" Yesterday's heroes had become today's criminals.

The two were speechless. All they could see before their eyes was a vision of years in Siberia. They had to control their impulse to shoot their way out. The ringing of a telephone saved them: they managed to slip away while the colonel took the call. Once outside, they met a high-ranking Russian officer who was recruiting men for the new NKVD training program in Vilnius, as Vilna was now called. All recruits had to be members of the Communist Party or former partisans. After a few drinks, the two former partisans managed to get themselves recruited. But since the training center itself was still under construction, they volunteered to work on it, one as a carpenter, the other as a mechanic. When the colonel found out, he swore that he would see to it they would face trial after graduation. In April 1945, Kaganowicz and Rogowski eluded arrest once again by volunteering to serve in the Russian army, which allowed them to make a safe exit from the training center (where they and another man had been the only three Jews among hundreds of Lithuanians). Eventually both men managed to obtain Polish repatriation papers and leave for Poland.[22]

An even more dire scenario was acted out in Meretch, where Yankl Asner, the head of the local police, was arrested and tortured when he showed up for work one day. Knowing what his fate would be, he apparently shot himself immediately. After the death of Yankl, whose heroic exploits in the forest had been legendary, Avraham Asner became the sole survivor of the remarkable Asner brothers' partisan group.

In Eishyshok, too, the new Stalinist policy guidelines resulted in a shift in power, but the mechanics of the transfer were complicated still further by longstanding local rivalries. Moshe Sonenson, who had been accepted as an insider at the NKVD station in Eishyshok, thanks to his friendship with Major Bazarov and his own stake in tracking down the AK, was soon to become victim to those old rivalries. Moshe had always been one step ahead of the executioners during the Holocaust, but he failed to see the writing on the wall that winter of 1944. Intent on seizing and bringing to trial the murderers of his wife and son, he became blind to all warning signals.

As part of the change in administration, a new Russian NKVD commander named Kovalov arrived in Eishyshok with a group of his own people.

Kovalov immediately made friends among the local Poles, and also among a handful of Jews who disliked the whole Bazarov–Sonenson crowd. Alter Michalowski sensed the impending danger and left Eishyshok with his wife Masha. Moshe Sonenson stayed on, absorbed not just in the pursuit of the murderers of his own family members, but in the case he was helping to prepare against the murderer of the Koppelman family as well. The Koppelmans' good friend and supposed rescuer, Kadishon of Dociszki, had hacked them to death in their sleep, and Moshe had gone out in the middle of the night to gather what was left of their remains and bury them. Now he was acting as chief witness and activist in the case. A search he had conducted of Kadishon's farm had turned up Koppelman family pictures and memorabilia as well as the fur coats, silver, and other household goods and valuables they had left with him for safekeeping.

The three Yurkanski siblings: (right to left) Yitche-Mendke, Rochke, and Layzerke. Yitche-Mendke was responsible for the arrest of Moshe Sonenson and much of the false evidence used against him. In 1969, Yitche-Mendke York (Yurkanski) invited Moshe Sonenson to forgive him publicly in front of a large group of Eishyshkians in Detroit, Michigan. Sonenson accepted, but the event never took place. Moshe's sister Matle Shereshefski died just before it was to take place. In 1973, Yitche-Mendke came to Israel and planned a public forgiveness party at a hotel in Tel Aviv, but the Yom Kippur War broke out and Yitche-Mendke rushed back to America. He was never able to fulfill his wish to be forgiven in public. YESC, YORK-YURKANSKI

Knowing that Moshe had enough evidence to prove he was the murderer, Kadishon set about exploiting the ancient rivalries and animosities between the Sonenson–Kabacznik clan and the Yurkanskis. Perhaps Kadishon could engineer a preemptive strike against his accuser. He offered the Yurkanski men a large sum of money — money he had stolen from the Koppelmans — to go to Captain Kovalov and testify against the Sonenson–Bazarov group, on the grounds that they were bandits who had used their forays into the countryside in search of the AK as a pretext for robbing many innocent Poles in the vicinity, himself included. The Yurkanskis, under the leadership of Yitche-Mendke, struck the deal — this despite the fact that they were related to the Koppelmans. The enmity with the Sonensons outweighed all other considerations, including ties of friendship and obligation that had been forged between individual members of the two families in times of trouble. (During the Holocaust, for example, Moshe had lent gold to Shoshke Yurkanski Wine, so that she could buy a gun for her teenage son. And Moshe's daughter Yaffa was even now close friends with Yitche-Mendke's daughter Bashke, as Moshe himself was with Yitche-Mendke's cousin Moshe Yurkanski, who was not part of the plot.)

Kovalov and his superior in Troki were happy to go along with the scheme to frame Sonenson because it complemented their own plans to depose Bazarov and his associates. A generous gift of gold made them even more eager, and events unfolded rapidly from that point. Moshe Sonenson, Israel Dimitrowski, Zvi Michalowski, Captain Shabaiov, Lieutenant Soloviev, and Lieutenant Aliushka were all arrested for stealing, while Major Bazarov was demoted and removed from his post. The arrest was so sudden that Moshe Sonenson was hurled into jail without so much as a chance to put on a coat.

In fact, the accusations against him would eventually focus on another coat — a man's coat trimmed with a beautiful silver fox collar, which he was charged with stealing from a Pole. He had indeed taken the coat from a Pole, for he had found it in the man's house, along with many other Sonenson family possessions that had been stolen during the war. It had belonged to Moshe's younger brother Shepske, who had been killed in the September 1941 massacre. Family memorabilia that Moshe had managed to retrieve after liberation included a number of pictures of Shepske wearing his coat, but the pictures were never accepted as evidence. Although it was suggested that Moshe's children, Yitzhak and Yaffa, travel to Moscow with the photographs to make an appeal to higher authorities, perhaps even to Stalin himself, Major Bazarov opposed the idea. The danger was too great, he explained, for if they were apprehended on the road they would be classified as orphans, made wards of the state, and placed in an orphanage. It would be only too easy for them to vanish without a trace, forever lost in the tangled web of the Soviet bureaucracy. His advice was accepted, and the children never traveled to Moscow. In general it was thought best to keep them away from all Russian offices.

They did, however, visit their father in jail. Brought to Eishyshok from Aran under armed guard, they were shown to a bare, freezing cell, where they found him sitting on a pile of hay. He explained to them that all the charges against him and the others were groundless. Their real "crime" was trying to track down the murderers of their loved ones, but the crime they had been arrested for was their attempt to retrieve some small fraction of the Jewish possessions that were still in Polish homes. Meanwhile, he said, "people with Jewish blood on their hands are free. They will probably die of old age while sleeping in Jewish beds covered with Jewish quilts in formerly Jewish-owned homes."

He also directed them to where some of the family gold was hidden. When Yaffa told her father that she wanted to be able to attend a regular school, he suggested she go stay with Rachel

Shepske Sonenson (right), wearing his gray coat with the silver fox collar, the coat his brother Moshe was accused of stealing from a Pole, one of the causes for his arrest. With Shepske are his sister Matle Shereshefski, three relatives, and Matle's husband Israel. YESC, Y. SONENSON

Pochter in Vilna, since a new Jewish school had recently been established there. He assured her that the gold she would find hidden among the stacks of firewood near his mother's home would make her a welcome guest, since Rachel needed the money to buy medicine for her son, wounded earlier that year in an AK ambush. As father and children parted, he assured them he would soon be free and they would start on their journey to Eretz Israel. In fact, close to seventeen years would pass before they were all together again.

Many attempts were made to intervene with the Russians on Moshe's behalf. Though his brother Shalom Sonenson was too fearful for his own safety to be active in these efforts, Reuven Paikowski and Miriam Kabacznik took it upon themselves to knock on every possible official door in both Vilna and Troki. Nothing helped. Eventually Moshe and the other Jewish prisoners were transferred to the infamous Lukishki jail in Vilna. It was then that everybody understood the Russians had decided to treat the Eishyshkians as serious political offenders, and make their trial a major event, perhaps even a show trial, as yet another step in their public relations campaign to win over the local populace. Anti-Semitism would once again be invoked to bind people together, uniting diverse religions, ethnic groups, and political aims.

In March 1945 there was one last serious attempt to free Moshe Sonenson — this one a plot to enable him to escape. With the cooperation of high-ranking Russian officials who were in on the plot, Moshe was to be granted permission to attend the Vilna wedding of his cousin Meir Kabacznik and Sonia Kowarski (both survivors from the pit under the Korkuc stable). While at the wedding his guards would be plied with liquor, and on the way back to jail Moshe would make his escape. However, once more he was betrayed. Friends of the Yurkanskis' found out about the scheme, and Moshe was never granted permission to attend the wedding.

JEWISH LIFE IN VILNA: PRELUDE TO REPATRIATION

While her father was awaiting trial, Yaffa moved to Rachel Pochter's in Vilna, as he had suggested. Her dream had come true: she was attending a regular school, the new Yiddish academy that had been founded that fall at 12 Zigmond Street, where it would remain until it was closed by Soviet authorities in 1950. It was an excellent school, despite the fact that its student population was in constant flux because of the extreme instability of their lives. To accommodate the many students who were orphans, the school had a dormitory that housed about eighty children. Many of the students as well as their teachers had hair-raising stories to tell about their wartime experiences, particularly the children who had been with the partisans; they loved regaling their classmates with tales of their exploits in the forests.

The teachers were a loving, dedicated group, most of them fully committed to the official Communist ideology of the school. Each morning began with the singing of the *Internationale* in Yiddish. Among the teachers, however, were a few secret Zionists, who discovered that Yaffa knew Hebrew. Her proficiency in the language was a source of great interest and pride to them, but they were careful to warn her not to let on to the other students or teachers.[23]

While school was a paradise for Yaffa, life with Rachel Pochter was hell. Every penny Yaffa gave her was used to purchase medicine for her badly wounded son, so that they often went without food. The building where the Pochters lived had been so severely damaged by bombing that what had been an interior staircase was now an outside one, and with each snowfall it seemed about to collapse. The unheated building was so cold that one day while doing her homework Yaffa found that her frozen fingers could not grip the pencil. With that, she decided to leave, and to throw herself on the mercy of her uncle Shalom, who was also living in Vilna by then. Appearing on his doorstep, her knapsack on her back, she asked him to take her in. Though he was reluctant, both his pregnant wife Miriam and Miriam's father, David Ribak, intervened on her behalf. Miriam went down on her knees and begged; her father put a few golden coins on the table as payment for the child's upkeep. Yaffa remained with her uncle and aunt from then on.

Shalom and Miriam had come to Vilna, along with many other Jewish survivors from Eishyshok and the vicinity, because by the winter of 1944–45 Vilna had become a Jewish center. All the Eishyshok-area survivors lived near one another, the majority, including Shalom and Miriam, in one building that had come through the war only slightly damaged. The building was home to the Kabacznik group, and thus became known, like their former residence, as the Kabacznik kibbutz. Like most surviving buildings in post-liberation Vilna, it had no running water, for either toilets or drinking and bathing. To get fresh drinking water, one had to stand in line near one of the few outdoor faucets that had miraculously escaped the devastation.

About 6,000 Jews were living in Vilna at this

time, only about 2,500 of whom were from Vilna originally. Most of the Jewish inhabitants were young (few old people having survived the rigors of the Holocaust), and they included former partisans and people who had survived in hiding, inmates from the Baltic concentration camps, and people who had served in the Russian army. Striving to renew something of Vilna's glorious Jewish past, glimpses of which were still visible in the standing walls of the Gaon's kloiz, the Strashun library, and the YIVO archive, these survivors built on that legacy. They founded the Yiddish school and orphanage at 12 Zigmond, built a Jewish museum, and established a memorial to the 100,000 Jewish victims at Ponar. Their meeting place was the beautiful choral synagogue, which had also survived the bombing. Once the perils of war had subsided and the Soviet occupation was more securely established, the Soviet government would eventually suppress all signs of the cultural life of Vilna's Jewish community, secular or religious, just as they were doing in the small towns and villages surrounding Vilna. But for this brief period something resembling a Jewish revival was taking place.[24]

REPATRIATION: FIRST STEP TO EMIGRATION

Vilna was both a refuge and a point of embarkation for the Jews. Most had come to Vilna to apply to the Soviet offices that were issuing Polish repatriation papers, either because they wanted to return to Poland or because they viewed Poland as the first step on their journey to Eretz Israel (where it was still illegal for them to go) or to other destinations, particularly America. The repatriation program permitted the return to Poland of all former Polish citizens currently residing in Soviet territories — Jews included — who had lived in Poland until September 17, 1939 (the day the Soviet army crossed the Eastern frontier and occupied parts of Poland).

There are still many unanswered questions about why Russia made such a generous offer, since its borders had been kept sealed from the beginning of the Soviet regime. There are at least as many questions about why the Polish government agreed to it, since the redrawing of Poland's boundaries and the destruction of its Jewish population had created a Poland practically free of minorities, just as the Poles had long hoped for. However, the brief period during which the repatriation policy remained in effect constituted a miracle for hundreds of thousands of people, among them many Jews.

By mid-1946, about 200,000 of the 400,000 Polish Jews who were still alive had repatriated. The majority were Jews who had lived out the war in Russia or had served in the Polish army. Those who had survived the war under Nazi occupation made up a much smaller minority. Advised by the Polish government not to return to their pre-Holocaust residences, which had generally been taken over by local Poles, the Jews who chose to stay in Poland tended to settle mainly in the western territories, which before the war had belonged to Germany.[25]

Most of the Jews who returned, however, were hoping to go elsewhere eventually, principally to the United States or the Land of Israel — neither of which was opening its doors to them even now. The British Mandate in Palestine continued to refuse to issue certificates of immigration to Jews, and the United States had a quota system. For the many Polish Jews knocking futilely on these nations' doors, Poland thus became a kind of limbo, a corridor, an escape route to who knew where. Thousands of the maapilim — "illegal" immigrants to Palestine — got started on their journeys in Poland.

None of the Eishyshok Jews who were applying for Polish repatriation papers, in either Vilna or Aran, had any intention of staying in Poland. They saw little advantage in leaving what was now Soviet-occupied Lithuania, where Jews were being pushed out of all the positions of responsibility they had briefly enjoyed in the early days of liberation, to go to a country whose slogan had been "Poland without Jews." The virulence of the anti-Semitism they had experienced during the Holocaust, and now during liberation, had convinced them that the Jews had no future in either Poland or Lithuania. Though each of the survivors owed his or her life to friendly Poles, each of them had close relatives, friends, and neighbors who had been betrayed and murdered by Poles. Most painful of all was the fact that many of the Poles who had turned against them — even to the point of the most savage kind of murder, as in the case of Kadishon and the Koppelmans — had been trusted family friends.

Had they entertained any hopes whatsoever for peaceful coexistence with their Polish neighbors, those hopes ended with the murder of Zipporah Sonenson and her baby in October 1944. That murder had the same impact on the Eishyshok Jews that the July 4, 1946, pogrom in Kielce, Poland, would have on much of the rest of Polish Jewry nearly two years later. In Kielce, in broad daylight, forty-two Jews were killed by Poles and dozens more were injured. As a result, 100,000 Jews fled Poland in panic, headed for the DP (displaced persons) camps in Germany, Austria, Italy, and other locations.

Even the Yurkanski family, who had collaborated with the new round of Soviet officialdom under Captain Kovalov, understood early on that there was no future for Jews in Eishyshok. Having used the Yurkanskis to engineer the downfall of Major Bazarov and the Jews who had worked closely with him, Kovalov now warned the family that they, too, were on a wanted list and should leave town immediately. The Yurkanski men left in great haste for Lodz, Poland, followed shortly thereafter by the women and children.

Reuven Paikowski and Israel and Yekutiel Shmerkowitch were among the Eishyshkians who sought repatriation papers in the winter of 1944–45. They headed to the office in Aran, but they almost never made it, because the three heavily armed former partisans in their horse-drawn sleigh were ambushed by the AK. The alertness and skills they had acquired during their years in the forest served them well once again, however, and they managed to escape.

The Eishyshkians who went to Vilna to get their repatriation papers had a great advantage, because one of the people who worked in the Vilna office was Kazimierz Korkuc. He and his aging mother had had to leave their large estate in the countryside because Korkuc, labeled "the father of the Jews," was on the AK's most-wanted list. Traveling with an NKVD escort to Vilna, he had joined the Soviet-backed Polish People's Army, founded by the Polish Communist poet Wanda Wasilewska in 1943.[26] After liberation, it had deployed a number of its soldiers in the offices where repatriation papers were granted. Kazimierz Korkuc had the good fortune to secure one of these office jobs. For Korkuc, the army meant safety for himself and his mother, because as an enlisted man he was heavily armed and constantly protected. It also meant an opportunity to help not just dozens or hundreds of people as he had done during the Holocaust, but thousands, thanks to the power he now had to speed the process of repatriation, so that those who were in danger could leave the Soviet Union.

Some people, however, weren't ready to leave yet. The Sonensons — Yitzhak, Yaffa, their uncle Shalom, and his wife Miriam — were staying in Vilna, hoping that the prison gates would open and Moshe would walk through them. Dobke Kremin Dimitrowski, the wife of one of the other Eishyshkian Jews awaiting trial, was also hoping for her husband Israel's freedom. The trial was scheduled for that summer.

Before Moshe appeared at his own trial, he went before a military court in another trial, as a witness for the prosecution. On May 28 and

29, 1945, in one of the several anti-AK trials, he testified against a number of AK members he had helped bring to justice, including the murderers of his wife and son. Based on his testimony and that of many other witnesses (not including his children, whom Moshe wanted to protect against possible retaliation), the court found the AK members guilty and sentenced them to hard labor in Siberia. The length of their terms varied with the seriousness of their crimes, ranging from five years for robbery to twenty years for murder. In 1954 an attempt was made to appeal the longer sentences, but it was denied. According to the military court decision of June 31, 1954:

As is clear from the archival files of the guilty, the organization Armia Krajowa carried out two attacks on the town of Eisiskes [Eishyshok]. In these attacks the local municipal building was destroyed, citizens were robbed, the civilian Sonenson and her son were killed as well as a Russian Army soldier.

The judgment was followed by a listing of all the AK members who had been found guilty.[27]

In the last week of June 1945, Moshe Sonenson, Israel Dimitrowski, Zvi Michalowski, and the Russian NKVD officers they had worked with were put on trial. As had been predicted, the Russian authorities turned it into a show trial, holding it in Vilna, in one of the imposing government buildings that the Russians had taken over. There, on July 1, 1945, before a huge audience that filled the auditorium to capacity, the verdicts were issued: all guilty. Bazarov and the other Russian officers were sentenced to three years. In light of their service during the war, however, they were pardoned and given their freedom (though Bazarov's rank was not restored). But apparently there were no mitigating circumstances applicable to the Jews. Their agony during the war, the tragedy suffered by Moshe Sonenson after liberation, the cooperation they had extended to the Soviet regime — none of these factors counted for anything. Moshe Sonenson was sentenced to ten years of hard labor in Siberia, Israel Dimitrowski to eight, and Zvi Michalowski to six.

After the sentencing, Moshe Sonenson asked permission to share one of Krylov's animal fables with the court. "Once there was a singing contest," he recounted, "between a nightingale with a magnificent voice and a hoarse crow. The loser was to have one of his eyes gouged out by the winner. The judge of the contest between the two birds was a pig. The nightingale lost the contest, and an eye. With blood still flowing from his fresh wound, the nightingale said: What hurts me most is not losing the contest, for I know that I have a more beautiful voice than the crow, or even being blind in one eye, for I can live with that. What hurts me most is the disposition of the judge who presided over the contest."

Shalom Sonenson felt that after the publicity around the trial, and his brother's Krylov-inspired riposte to the court, it would be advisable for the family to leave Vilna as soon as possible. With help from Korkuc, who rushed their papers through and saw to it that Yaffa was issued papers in the name of Shalom's dead daughter Shula, Shalom, Miriam, and Yaffa left for Poland on August 12, 1945. In her shoe, Yaffa had stashed photos of her father, mother, brother, and grandmother Alte Katz.

It was her brother Yitzhak who had given her the picture, for he had decided to stay behind in Vilna, still hoping for a change in the court's disposition that might lead to their father's release. Dobke Kremin Dimitrowski also chose to stay behind. Yitzhak and Dobke spent long hours waiting for the opportunity to deliver packages to Moshe and Israel in the Lukishki jail, and devoted many futile days to the attempt to get their loved ones set free.

During the winter of 1945–46, Moshe was deported to Siberia in a transport of "political" prisoners, which included many prominent Lithuanian clergymen. He would not be released until 1953, following the death of Stalin. Before his deportation he advised his son to leave Vilna, which Yitzhak did in March 1946. Together with former partisan Lippa Skolski, Yitzhak boarded a repatriation train in Bastun and left for Poland, a point of departure for what would prove a long, dangerous, and difficult journey to the Land of Israel.

Israel Dimitrowski was spared the worst of the punishment intended for him thanks to his wife Dobke. Having obtained false identification papers, she got a job as a waitress in a restaurant frequented by high-ranking Soviet army officers and government officials. The close ties she was able to establish with a number of influential people (attributable in part to the many bottles of vodka she plied them with) enabled her to prevent her husband's deportation to Siberia. She continued to work in the restaurant, eventually being promoted to head waitress, until her husband's release on July 1, 1949. In 1957, the Dimitrowskis and their daughter left Vilna for Israel, where they stayed for two years before emigrating to the United States, so that Dobke could be near her sister Blumke and Blumke's husband Eliyahu. The four who had lived together in the forest were now together again, in Brooklyn, New York.

Zvi Michalowski fared better than either Dimitrowski or Moshe. In November 1945, he was in a camp named Rosa from which he was going to be deported to Siberia. On November 11, 1945, he escaped, and made his way to the home of Avraham and Liebke Asner in Druskieniki (Drozgenik). They assisted him in obtaining false repatriation papers in the name of one of his murdered relatives, and eventually all of them left for Poland, whence they made their separate ways to their ultimate destinations.

PASSAGES: TO NEW COUNTRIES, MARRIAGES, AND FAMILIES

Most Eishyshkian survivors chose to take advantage of the repatriation program as a step in their journeys, with a few exceptions. Hayya Rogowski stayed in Vilna to be with her friend Dobke Kremin Dimitrowski, for Hayya's husband Tevl Zinberg had left her for the sister-in-law of his dead wife. In 1957, shortly after Dobke left for Israel, Hayya and her little girl followed. Meir Stoler, the Eishyshok blacksmith who organized the gravediggers' uprising that disrupted and delayed the Radun massacre of May 10, 1942, stayed in Radun, where he married a Byelorussian Christian woman.

The Eishyshkians who survived the Nazi occupation were not the only ones who saw the repatriation program as their passport to a new life. About sixty-two Eishyshkians who had fled to or had been deported to the Soviet Union did so as well. Former Communists and deportees alike shared a profound revulsion toward Communism, and were quick to take advantage of this unprecedented opportunity to leave. Unlike the survivors' contingent, most of whom hoped ultimately to make their way to Eretz Israel, most of the Russian contingent, former Communists, intended to settle in the United States and Canada. That was not true for all, however. One of the most ardent of the prewar Eishyshok Communists, Luba Ginunski, had become an equally ardent Zionist, her destination Eretz Israel. Fruml and Hirshke Slepak and their two children — in company with the Singer sewing machine which had kept them alive during the hard years of exile in Siberia — went to Eretz Israel, where once again Fruml's dressmaking skills saved the day. Elka Jankelewicz (daughter of Nahum Szulkin, the last undertaker of Eishyshok) emigrated to Eretz Israel along with her husband Yankl and their five children, where they eventually lived a comfortable life as farmers. David Ejszyszki and his family also became farmers in Israel. Rivka Rubinstein, who had left Palestine in 1927 to follow her deported husband Moshe Blaj and the rest of the Elkind group to the Soviet Union, would at last return in 1967. Old, sick, and blind, she spent the last years of her life in a nursing home.

A certain few never left the Soviet Union. Rivka Rubinstein's brother Mordekhai Rubinstein, who left Palestine for Russia in 1927 as a member of the Elkind group, continued to live in Kiev with his Russian wife and their daughters. Motke Kiuchefski and his wife and children also remained in Moscow. Yankele Krisilov (the man who rescued Fruml Slepak's sewing machine for her when she and her family had had to flee Eishyshok), had survived the war as a driver for the Red Army. After the war he settled in Vilna with his new wife and their two sons, and stayed there until his death.

The first postwar family portrait of the Sorl Kabacznik family, in honor of daughter Miriam's wedding: (seated, right to left) Luba, wife of Shepske; Sorl; Miriam, the bride; and Sonia, Meir's wife; (standing, right to left) Shepske Kabacznik; Yitzhak Levin (a relative who was saved by the Kabaczniks); Nahum Shulman, the groom; and Meir Kabacznik. Nahum was a relative of Sorl, a partisan from Lubtch who lost his first wife and two children in the Holocaust. The wedding took place at a DP camp in Cremona, Italy. Shepske and Luba were also married at the same camp. YESC, KABACZNIK

THE DP CAMPS

Before they could emigrate, hundreds of thousands of Jews spent months and sometimes years being shunted from one displaced-persons camp to another. But they didn't let that stop them from making up for their lost years. Eager to pick up the frayed threads of their lives, they married in the camps, they had children, they established educational and cultural programs, they became active in political groups to pressure the British into allowing Jewish immigration to Palestine, they even organized sports teams.

Among the Eishyshkians who joined the rush to create new lives and new families were the following men and women who got married in DP camps: Zvi Michalowski, who married Paula Lefkowicz of Sosnowiec, Poland, at the DP camp of Bad Reichenhall, near Munich; Avraham Meishke Kaplan, who married a woman from Berlin in a DP camp in Germany; Zlatke Garber and Reuven Paikowski, both former partisans who had known each other since childhood in Eishyshok, and who were married by Reb Moshe Davidowicz der Lubaver in October 1945 at a DP camp in Leibnitz; Miriam Kabacznik, who married Nahum Shulman, a former partisan from Lubtch, in a DP camp in Cremona; and Miriam's brother Shepske, who married a woman named Luba in the same DP camp in Cremona. A number of these marriages were second marriages for one or both partners, because the first spouse had died during the Holocaust.

Some people married even before reaching the DP camps. Itta and Yankl Solomianski, whose romance had begun in the pit under the stable on the Korkuc farm in 1942 — the same pit where Miriam and Shepske Kabacznik lived — got married in Vilna, immediately after liberation, where Yankl had begun attending medical school. He continued his studies while living in a DP camp near Munich, where Itta gave birth to a daughter.

Reuven Paikowski and Zlatke Garber, former partisans who had known each other since childhood, were married at the DP camp in Leibnitz in October 1945. The photo was taken in Nastra, Italy, on their way to Eretz Israel. YESC, PAIKOWSKI

Zvi Michalowski and Paula Lefkowicz married at the DP camp of Bad Reichenhall near Munich. Standing in the back are (right to left) Moshe Yurkanski and wife Feigl (Fanny), who were married post-liberation in the Sonenson house, and Hayyim-Yoshke Bielicki. PHOTO: FOTO SCHNEIDER BAD REICHENHALL. YESC, FANNY YORK

DESTINATIONS: THE SEARCH FOR A HOMELAND AND A HOME

After the war there were millions of refugees roaming throughout Europe, in search of a place to settle, to rebuild their lives. But out of all these millions, only the Jews of Eastern Europe were virtually cut off from any possibility of return to their former homes. The dangers were just too great. For them, new lives would mean not just new places of residence, but new countries, languages, and customs. Of course many non-Jewish Eastern Europeans would also, for political reasons, have to find new homes, but for them it was often possible to settle nearby, in places where the language and culture were familiar to them.

For example, Kazimierz Korkuc and his mother, unable to return home in safety because of the help they had given the Jews, settled in Wroclaw, Poland (which until the war had been the German city of Breslau). In 1971 Yaffa Eliach and Miriam Kabacznik Shulman brought Korkuc to the United States for a visit. In New York, he received the key to the city from Mayor John Lindsay.

Antoni Gawrylkewicz, the faithful shepherd on the Korkuc estate, who had also helped to save the Jews, settled in Plock, Poland.

Just one Jewish native of Eishyshok remained in the town itself: Haikl Kanichowski. He and his family were the last living Jews in the dead Jewish shtetl. When his daughter Itzle finally emigrated to Israel in 1967 with her Christian Polish husband and their daughter, Haikl and his second wife and their three daughters followed soon after. With their departure, all that remained of the Jews of Eishyshok were the two mass graves.

Between 1945 and 1952, most Eishyshkians,

survivors of the Nazi occupation as well as those who had lived out the war in Russia, managed to leave the continent. From the DP camps all over Europe, the detention camps in Cyprus to which thousands of "illegal" emigrants to Palestine were deported, and a variety of other temporary residences, they fanned out all over the world.

The destinations of the Eishyshkians were as follows:

USA	50
Israel	33
Canada	21
Brazil	3
Germany	2
England	1

Counting the 4 who remained in the Soviet Union, the total was 114. The number includes those native to Eishyshok itself and to the villages under the shtetl's jurisdiction.[28] Sixty-one of the 114 were people who had been through the Holocaust: 38 men (12 of whom were partisans), 15 women (3 partisans), and 8 children. Generally speaking, the survivors were young people in their teens, twenties, and thirties; two notable exceptions were the matriarchs Sorl Kabacznik and Hodl Shuster, both widows who had been heads of their households since the end of World War I.

Many of those trying to emigrate were helped by the Berihah movement, the underground operation whose name means "flight" in Hebrew. Between 1944 and 1948, the Berihah moved tens

Kazimierz Korkuc receiving the key to New York City at City Hall from Mayor John V. Lindsay in 1972, in honor of saving the Sonenson, Kabacznik, and Solomianski families and many other Jews. Right to left: Yaffa Sonenson Eliach, Itta Solome (Solomianski), Mayor Lindsay, Korkuc, Dr. Yankl Solome, his parents Shmuel and Hayya Solomianski. YESC, Y. ELIACH

of thousands of Jews across the European borders on their journeys to Eretz Israel and elsewhere. Members of the Berihah obtained false papers for people, acted as trail guides through forests and over mountains, and put individual maapilim in touch with other would-be participants in the Aliyah Beth (as this wave of "illegal" immigration was known).

ERETZ ISRAEL

Avraham Lipkunski, wanted by the NKVD, spent two years on the run, crossing one illegal border after another in the attempt to get to Palestine. With the help of the Berihah movement, he finally made it in 1946. Not long after arriving, this former partisan found himself fighting in another war — the Israeli War of Independence — and at a later date he would testify as one of the chief witnesses at the trial of Adolf Eichmann.

*

Antoni Gawrylkewicz, a faithful shepherd on the Korkuc estate, who helped to save Jews during the war. YESC, Y. ELIACH

On July 11, 1947, Zvi Michalowski and his wife Paula boarded the *Exodus* at the French port of Sete, along with about 4,500 other maapilim who were bound for Eretz Israel. Zvi's friend Moshe Edelstein, with whom he had roamed the forests of Nacha and Rudnicki in the days of the partisans, was with them as well. The British Royal Navy intercepted the *Exodus* mid-sea, and, after a brief battle in which three Jews were killed and thirty wounded, the maapilim were returned to their point of departure, and thence to Hamburg, Germany. But the plight of those aboard the *Exodus* — captured most vividly in a famous newspaper photo of a small child being carried on the shoulders of a tall, handsome teenager, who was none other than Moshe Edelstein — was to touch hearts around the world.[29] Their suffering seemed so symbolic of both the perennial plight of European Jewry and the struggle for the establishment of a Jewish state, that it resulted in an international outcry, which helped hasten the UN agreement for the

Avraham Aviel Lipkunski (right) in Italy in 1945, on his way to Eretz Israel. YESC, AVIEL-LIPKUNSKI

Avraham Aviel Lipkunski testifies at the Eichmann trial in Jerusalem, 1962. YESC, AVIEL-LIPKUNSKI

Moshe Edelstein, who had survived the war as a partisan, shown here with a child on his shoulders aboard the Exodus *in 1947. The British Royal Navy intercepted the* Exodus*, returning it to Hamburg, Germany. Zvi and Paula Michalowski were also on the ship. All three eventually made it to Eretz Israel.* YESC, EDELSTEIN

partitioning of Palestine, in November 1947. As for Zvi and Paula and Moshe, they and their fellow passengers on the *Exodus* eventually made it to Eretz Israel. And soon Zvi and Moshe, like Avraham Lipkunski, would be fighting on another battleground, in the War of Independence, where both were wounded.

On August 23, 1946, Reuven Paikowski and his wife Zlatke Garber, together with 1,024 other "illegal" immigrants, boarded a ship that sailed from Italy to Eretz Israel, only to be intercepted by the British, who attacked them with tear gas and water hoses. From Haifa they were deported to Cyprus, where they remained until February 1947, after which they finally made it to their destination.

Shneur Glombocki and his new wife Esther (his first wife and baby having been murdered at Treblinka) traveled the Lublin–Romania route of the Berihah. But once in Romania only his wife was granted a certificate for Eretz Israel, so he sent her on and joined up with the Berihah himself, spending the next year smuggling other Jews (among them Eishyshkians Alter and Masha Michalowski) across the Alps from Austria to Italy — work for which his years with the partisans in the forest was good preparation. Shneur finally rejoined his wife and baby son in Eretz Israel in June 1945, after a perilous journey on a nameless fishing boat with thirty-five other illegal immigrants.

Shalom and Miriam Sonenson, with Shalom's niece Yaffa, went from Poland to Prague to Carlsbad — where Miriam gave birth to a baby girl — and on to a number of other waystations in Germany until finally they reached the DP

Zlatke Garber Paikowski (left) with a friend, Leah Slodovnik from Radun, in a Cyprus camp, where they were exiled upon arriving in Eretz Israel in 1946, along with 1,024 other "illegal" immigrants. YESC, PAIKOWSKI

Yaffa Sonenson with her aunt Miriam and cousin Bilinka, arriving in Jerusalem on the eve of Passover, 1946. YESC, SAHAROFF

camp at Neue Freimann near Munich. Their border crossings had been facilitated by private smugglers as well as by the Berihah, which helped them with false papers. While in Neue Freimann Shalom learned that, thanks to the fact that he had established residency in Palestine during the 1920s, he was entitled to a British passport and certificates of immigration for himself and his family, which meant that they were among the fortunate few who had a legal right to emigrate there. Even so, Shalom had difficulty securing the papers he needed in Neue Freimann and was forced to make a dangerous journey back to Prague, leaving his wife, his newborn daughter, and his niece behind for a month. When at last he returned to the DP camp he had the necessary papers for everybody, including Yaffa, who was listed as his daughter so that she too would be eligible to immigrate legally. After further journeys and mishaps, during one of which Yaffa was parted from her uncle's family and nearly lost contact with them, they all left together for Paris, and from Paris to Marseilles to board a ship that would take them to Eretz Israel by way of the Suez Canal. From Port Said, Egypt, they took a train to their final destination. On April 5, 1946, with tears in their eyes, they kissed the Eretz Israel ground.

*

Trying to cross from the British Zone of Germany to the American Zone, from which he believed he would have a better chance of getting to Palestine, Yaffa's brother Yitzhak was arrested by American MPs who accused him of being a Soviet spy. He was sent to a DP camp at Fahrenwald, where he spent part of the spring of 1946, and from there to Monaco, where he and a number of other youngsters had been told they would receive their certificates of immigration. In Monaco they were warmly welcomed, as guests of the prince of Monaco and the Jewish community of Nice. Even Winston Churchill paid them a visit. But after a number of months on the French Riviera they were told there were no more certificates, and that their best hope was to join the Aliyah Beth, the "illegal" immigration movement. Yitzhak organized a group of eleven teenagers who set out for Port-de-Bouc, France, where they were to set sail to the Land of Israel on the *Lanegev*. After twenty-one perilous days at sea, the *Lanegev* and its 750 maapilim were intercepted outside Haifa by three British gunboats, which opened fire on them. Yitzhak was among the many who were captured while trying to swim ashore. From

Moshe Sonenson after his release from his imprisonment in Siberia in 1953, following the death of Stalin. YESC, RESNIK

Yitzhak at last made it back to Haifa, in August 1947 — nearly a year and a half after his parting from his father in Vilna. Soon afterward, he volunteered to fight in the War of Independence — which he was able to do only by lying about his age — and became one of a number of Eishyshkians to be wounded in that war. In March 1954, on the anniversary of the death of Israel's heroic warrior Yossef Trumpeldor, former Beitar mem-

there they were deported to a refugee camp in Cyprus that bore a terrible resemblance to a concentration camp, complete with barbed wire and watchtower. After nearly dying of typhus,

In 1954, Moshe Sonenson obtained a special permit to travel to Vilna from Siberia. With the assistance of Dobke and Israel Dimitrowski, he was able to gather ten Jews to make a minyan. They traveled together to Radun and Eishyshok and recited Kaddish on the mass graves. On the men's mass grave in Eishyshok, in the Old Cemetery, the ditches and the pits where the men were shot and buried were still very visible. On the mass grave in the front row at the far right is Moshe Sonenson. Second row (left to right) are Dobke and Israel Dimitrowski; Hayya Rogowski is fourth from left. Behind Dobke is Meir Stoler, who organized the uprising in Ghetto Radun. To the left of Meir, top row center, is Hayyim Paikowski. YESC, PAIKOWSKI

ber Yitzhak married a woman from Wyszkow, Poland, named Shoshana Bergazin.

Moshe Sonenson was released from his imprisonment in Siberia in 1953, following the death of Stalin. However, he was required to remain in Karaganda in central Kazakhstan for two additional years, during which he had to report to the local authorities on a regular basis. There he met and married Mania Braverman, a Romanian widow with a young son named Alex, and together they had another son whom they named Hayyim, after the baby who had been shot and killed in the Sonenson house in Eishyshok. In 1954 Moshe obtained a special permit to travel to Vilna. There he was able to make contact with Israel Dimitrowski, who had remained in Vilna after his release from jail in 1949. Moshe, Israel, Israel's wife Dobke, and a number of other Jews living in the region — enough to make a minyan — traveled together to Radun and Eishyshok to recite Kaddish over the mass graves in both towns. In Eishyshok, to his surprise, Moshe was warmly received by his Polish friends, who included former colleagues in the fire department and various town officials. In 1956 Moshe and his second family arrived in

In September 1997 Yaffa Eliach brought fifty-seven people to Eishyshok in order to document the shtetl's past. Standing on the men's mass grave, following a memorial service, at the right near the tombstone is Zvi Michalowski with daughter Edna. He survived the September 1941 massacre. In the baseball cap is Reuven Paikowski, who was responsible for building the tombstones on the mass graves. On the extreme right is Bill Goodman. On the left is Yitzhak Sonenson embracing Antoni Gawrylkewicz, the friendly Polish shepherd who helped to save Jews. Next to Yitzhak are Dobke (Dora) and Israel Dimitrowski (Dimitro), who were on the mass grave with Moshe Sonenson in 1954, David and Yaffa Eliach with two of their grandchildren, Moshe Ariel and Moriah Rosensweig. Among the others standing on the grave were members of the Bastunski, Berkowitch, Zlotnik, Shlanski, Shereshefski, Saltz, Wilkanski-Rabinowitch, Siegal, and Shuster families.
YESC, Y. ELIACH

Rosh Hashanah greetings from the Landsman-Shuster family in Berlin, 1947. Evelyn (Hava) (left), cousin Joseph, born while the family was in hiding in the forest, and his mother Rivka. BLACHAROWICZ-WISZIK, YESC

Yossele Hamarski, the sole survivor of his family, in 1948 on board the ill-fated Altalena, *sitting in front of the life ring. Yossele survived the clash between the Irgun and the Israeli army and the sinking of* Altalena. *But the sight of Jew fighting Jew was too overwhelming. Yossele left Israel to join his family, the Goodmans, in Detroit.* YESC, CAMARONE-HAMARSKI

Israel, with the help of his children Yitzhak and Yaffa, who took advantage of a Russian law that permitted the reunification of families who had been divided by the Iron Curtain.

NORTH AMERICA

Leibke Kaganowicz was one of a number of Eishyshkians who never made the attempt to emigrate to Palestine. Though he worked for a while as a Berihah guide helping others to get there, he had set his own sights on the United States, where the prospect of a peaceful future seemed very inviting. When members of the Irgun, an Israeli military defense organization that had been active in recruiting in the DP camps, approached him to join the fight against the British, he declined, explaining that his fighting days were over. Leibke had vivid memories of the stories told about his uncle Aharon Don Becker, whose letters from America had been so full of praise for his new home that they had persuaded many people in the shtetl to regard the United States as a land of freedom, not the godless, materialistic place they had previously supposed it to be. Now Leibke's greatest desire was to see that land for himself. Like many others in the DP camps, he asked a member of the Joint Distribution Committee to help him compose a notice to be placed in a Jewish newspaper in New York: "Leibke Kaganowicz, of Eishyshok, Lithuania, son of Shael and Miriam Kaganowicz, and grandson of Benjamin Kaganowicz, is looking for relatives in New York. He is looking particularly for his uncle, Aharon Don Becker." Becker's daughter saw the ad, and a few days later Leibke received a telegram from his uncle, followed by many warm, loving letters and an offer to sponsor him in America.

But when 1948 rolled around and Leibke was still a long way down on the quota list for emigrants from Poland, he began to despair. Canada had opened its doors, and his relatives advised him it would be an easy matter to transfer from Canada to the United States. This proved not to be the case, but Leibke so quickly made a home for himself in Canada that the U.S. quota list ceased to matter. He loved Vancouver for its beauty, and for the hospitality of its people.[30] In the years to come, Leibke Kaganowicz — now Leon Kahn — would marry a woman from Eishyshok whom he met in New York, have children, and become a very successful businessman as well as a leader in his community.

*

Liebke and Avraham Asner, fellow partisans who married and emigrated to Canada after liberation. YESC, A. ASNER

Szeina Blacharowicz and her second husband, Isaac Wiszik (front), whom she married at the DP camp in Bergen Belsen, on their way to board a ship that would take them to America, March 7, 1950. YESC, BLACHAROWICZ-WISZIK

Evelyn Landsman, the woman Leon Kahn married, was part of the three-generation family of women headed by Hodl Shuster who had spent the war years under the protection of a partisan group in the forest of Nipiczansky. Evelyn (formerly Hava) was the daughter of Basha, and granddaughter of Hodl. The three of them plus Basha's sister Rivka and Joseph, the little boy Rivka gave birth to while in the forest, emigrated to New York in 1947.

Like Leibke Kaganowicz, Yossele Hamarski was the sole survivor of his family. His mother was murdered in Eishyshok, father in Radun, and sister in Lida. And like Leibke, he had been a partisan, in the Asner camp. But unlike Leibke, Yossele did not feel his fighting days were over, and was determined to participate in Israel's War of Independence. He joined the Irgun, and in June 1948 traveled to Port-de-Bouc, France, to board the *Altalena*, an Irgun ship that was carrying hundreds of volunteers and a large quantity of arms to the newly declared State of Israel.[31] But the new government of Israel had outlawed the Irgun and sent its troops to intercept the ship when it arrived in Kfar Vitkin. A total of seventeen Irgun members were killed during the bloody clashes that ensued. Yossele was one of many who were taken from the ship and transported to shore, where they were held prisoner, until eventually they were released after a hunger strike. But the sight of Jews fighting against their fellow Jews caused Yossele to reconsider his commitment to Israel. This was not what he had had in mind when he enlisted in the struggle to create a safe homeland for the Jews. Yossele joined his relatives the Goodmans in Detroit, where he found a warm welcome, and a new name — Joe Camarone.

Yossele's fellow partisans Avraham Asner and Avraham's cousin Rachel both emigrated to North America. Avraham, the only one of four brothers to survive, married his partisan girlfriend Liebke immediately after liberation, and the two eventually made it to Canada. Rachel Asner, who married a Holocaust survivor from Poland, moved to Los Angeles.

*

Szeina Blacharowicz journeyed through the DP camps of Europe with her dear friends Marushka and Stashek Kuzmicki and their three daughters, who had helped her during her days in hiding in the forest and couldn't bear to say goodbye to her when the war ended. Out of solidarity with their friend, they had converted to Judaism. At the DP camp in Bergen Belsen, Szeina met and married Isaac Wiszik, a hero of the battle of Stalingrad. After several unsuccessful attempts to get to the French port city of Sete to board the *Exodus*, and another abortive effort to reach Rome in time to board another ship headed toward Palestine, they lost heart when Israel's War of Independence broke out. Unable to face the prospect of another war, they decided to take advantage of the new immigration policy that President Truman had initiated in 1948. The Displaced Persons Act, which authorized the admission of 205,000 people considered to be DPs after World War II, enabled some 90,000 Holocaust survivors to enter the United States, regardless of whether the quota for their nationalities had been filled.[32] Szeina and Isaac moved to Chicago, where she had cousins from Eishyshok. Over the years Szeina was able to pay the occasional visit to the Kuzmicki family, who had settled in Canada.

Hayyim-Yoshke Bielicki, who had served in the Russian army during the war, and Avremele Botwinik, a former partisan, both of whom were the last surviving members of their families, were among a number of Eishyshkians who, like Szeina Blacharowicz Wiszik and her husband, were able to emigrate to the United States thanks to the Truman immigration policy. So, too, were Israel Shmerkowitch and his father Yekutiel, Itta and Yankl Solomianski, who came to New York in 1950 with their daughter, who had been born in a DP camp, and Pessah and Rivka Cofnas, who came with an older daughter and their twins, a boy and a girl, all of whom were born while they were living in the Beth Bialik DP camp near Salzburg.

Zalman Lubetski was also part of the Truman immigration. He had served in the Polish army, and fought with both the Lithuanian and the Russian partisans. After various postwar adventures, including a brief stay in Vilna's notorious Lukishki prison, he repatriated and, in 1952, made his way to the United States.

Miriam Kabacznik Shulman and her husband Nahum, who had both been active Zionists since childhood, gave up on getting to Palestine after several foiled attempts. Nahum's brother in Los Angeles helped them get visas, and on March 3, 1948, their first wedding anniversary, Nahum and Miriam (who was pregnant with their daughter Gloria) left their DP camp in Italy for America. Miriam's mother, Sorl, would eventually join them there, after she decided she did not care for life in Brazil, where her sons Shepske and Meir had bought large ranches.

Avraham Meishke Kaplan, one of Eishyshok's great theater talents, married Annaliese Edith Ephraimson, who was from Berlin and served in the British Army, in Boston. Though he never acted again, he enjoyed telling his wife wondrous stories of his beloved Eishyshok, which was, to hear him tell it, "much bigger than Berlin!"

Matle Sonenson Shereshefski, whose family had been exiled to Siberia during the Soviet occupation of 1940 and who had thus lived out the war in relative safety, moved with her husband Israel and two sons to Memphis, Tennessee, where Israel had family. There Matle became Mollie, their sons Asher and Yossef became Oscar and Joe, and Shereshefski became Shefski — a transformation of a kind that was very common in the United States and Canada. The Yurkanskis (now the Yorks) settled in Detroit, next to relatives from Eishyshok. Moshe Szulkin and his family moved to Boston, also next to relatives from Eishyshok.

BUILDING NEW LIVES

Some emigrants were warmly welcomed and given generous help, others faced disappointments. But eventually most of them achieved economic security, in part thanks to the well-inculcated shtetl work ethic, which prompted both husband and wife to work, and work hard.

Those people who moved to Israel after the war were particularly likely to be greeted with open arms, for in many cases family members had preceded them in the 1920s and '30s, whereas most Americans with roots in Eishyshok were apt to have emigrated before World War I (because restrictive quotas had put a halt to most immigration after the war), and many were therefore meeting their newly arrived Eishyshkian relatives for the first time.

Immediately upon arriving in Israel, all the young Eishyshkian men went directly from the boat to the army. Yitzhak Sonenson, sitting (right) on the front of an armored vehicle, during the War of Independence in Jerusalem, 1948. He was slightly wounded but after recovering, he continued to fight and was among the liberators of Eilat in 1949. YESC, Y. SONENSON

The generosity of the Eretz Israel people to the Holocaust survivors from Eishyshok was remarkable. When Shalom Sonenson arrived, for example, they had arranged a job for him, and provided a furnished apartment, complete with flowers on the table and food in the icebox. All of this was courtesy of an ancient institution that the former Eishyshkians had brought with them, the Gemilut Hessed. Among the founders of the Eretz Israel branch of this financial aid society were Uri Razowski, son of Miriam and Szymen Razowski, Eishyshok's last rabbi; Alexander Zisl Hinski, son of Taibe-Eidl and Reb Israel Yossef Hinski, Eishyshok's last upper shammash; Naftali Berkowitch, Moshe Kaganowicz, and Israel Goldstein — men who would have remembered the Gemilut Hessed as an invaluable component in the shtetl's network of benevolent societies, providing a safety net to many a needy family, most recently during the hard times in the 1930s.

Desperate for word of their families from those newly arrived, the first-generation Haluzim were devastated when they received it. The

Zvi Michalowski became a father during the War of Independence. He holds his firstborn daughter, Nehama. YESC, MICHALOWSKI

Reuven Paikowski (left) served in the reserve in Abu-Gush, 1952. YESC, PAIKOWSKI

Yaffa Sonenson at the dedication ceremony of the Kfar Batia School in 1952 represented her fellow students, all Holocaust survivors and Sephardic immigrants. She made a speech in the fluent Hebrew she had learned in Eishyshok. Listening are (right to left) Rabbi Kerenshenblum from America; Monnet B. Davis, the American ambassador to Israel (1951–54); Rabbi Zeev Gold, chairman of the Mizrahi movement; Rabbi Unterman, chief rabbi of Tel Aviv–Yaffo; Dvorah Rabinowitz, director of Amit in Israel; Bessie Gotesfeld, national president and founder of Amit; and Rose Halpern, national president of Hadassah. YESC, Y. ELIACH

horrors the survivors described exceeded their worst fears. Everyone had lost people dear to them. In at least one case, the news prompted a suicide. Hannah Kiuchefski learned that she had lost her mother, five of her seven siblings (two brothers had lived out the war in Russia, where they had gone to study), and numerous nieces, nephews, aunts, uncles, and cousins. Unable to bear the graphic description of their deaths, one bright sunny day in Jerusalem Hannah Kiuchefski threw herself under the wheels of a passing bus.

The Israeli War of Independence of 1948–49 slowed down attempts at normalcy, as many able-bodied Eishyshkians, having survived the killing fields of Europe, found themselves in a combat zone once again — as they, and their sons, would do in the Sinai Campaign of 1956, the Six-Day War of 1967, and the Yom Kippur War of 1973. Nonetheless, most of the emigrants to Israel, like their counterparts in the United States and Canada, did eventually go on to achieve lives of material comfort and security. Certainly their adjustment was made easier by the fact that, coming from a fervently Zionist, Hebraist shtetl, they were familiar not just with the religion, politics, and history of their new home, but with the language. Long known for the excellence of their Hebrew, the Eishyshkians were so fluent that sometimes they had trouble convincing people that they were new immigrants, fresh off the boat.

MEMORY AND MOURNING

But young or old, in Israel or North America or wherever they had settled, none of the survivors have ever ceased to be tormented by the loss of their loved ones. Leibke Kaganowicz, who was a teenager during the war, and firsthand witness to the death of his sister Freidke and father Shael in the forest, described the feelings well:

. . . I am still haunted by the question, "Why me?" Why did I survive when so many others died? I wish with all my heart I knew the answer, but perhaps I am not meant to know. I try to live from day to day and forget the trauma of the past, but just as I think I am succeeding, events that seem ordinary to anyone else have the power to revive all the old horrors . . .

Yaffa's brother Yitzhak Sonenson and bride Shoshana, in Haifa, Israel, March 1954.
YESC, Y. ELIACH

Wedding portrait of Yaffa Sonenson Eliach. She married David Eliach, a seventh-generation Jerusalemite, in Jerusalem, August 1953.
PHOTO: RUBIN, JERUSALEM. YESC, Y. ELIACH

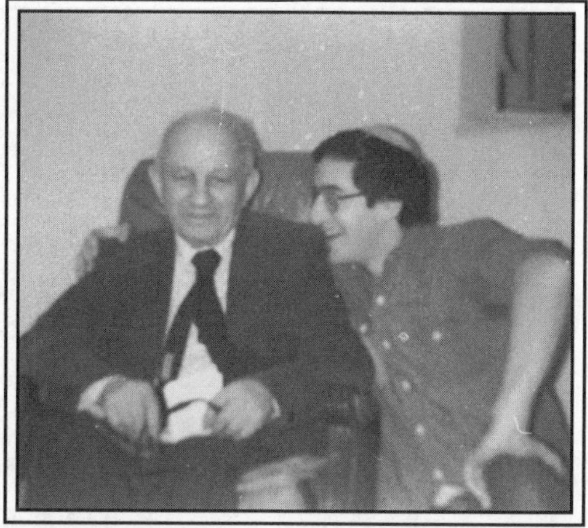

Moshe Sonenson with his oldest grandson, Yotav Eliach, in 1979. Yotav inherited his grandfather's sense of humor.
YESC, Y. ELIACH

At a football game when the crowd shouts, "Hold that line! Hold that line!", I am back in the forest . . . with my father shouting, "Hold them back! Hold them back!" I fire my gun, but the murdering Poles come closer and closer and my bullets go right through them and they don't stop, and Freidke runs in slow motion toward me with the glint of the murderer's bayonet at her back. "RUN, Freidke, RUN!"

But Freidke is dead. And father is dead.

I stop at a rail crossing to wait for a freight train to pass. Suddenly it is my mother and grandmother who press against the slats of the cattle cars on their way to extermination in Treblinka. Every click of the wheels marks off the seconds until they die all over again.[33]

Older survivors, men and women born prior to World War I, who had already come into their own as active members of the community, only to see that community irreparably shattered by the Holocaust, mourn more than just their families. For them the loss encompasses a heritage they feel they can never communicate to anyone else, a way of life that can never be restored. Yossef Kaplan of Radun, the only member of his large family to survive the Holocaust, settled in London after the war, and remembers his aunt,

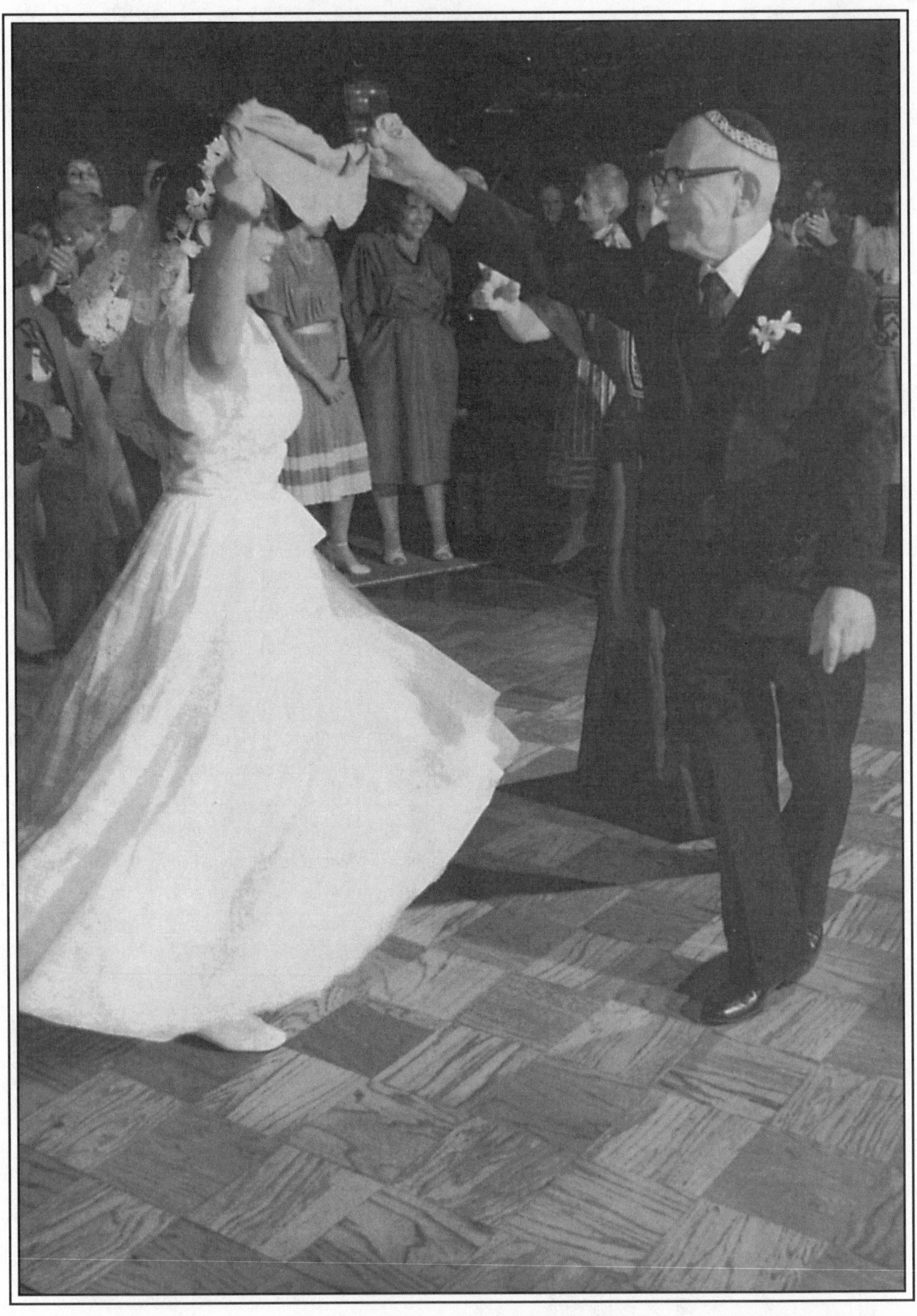

Moshe Sonenson dancing with the bride, his beloved granddaughter Smadar-Zipporah Eliach, August 23, 1983. Moshe died three days later, during the celebration of the Shevah-Brakhot (Seven Benedictions). YESC, Y. ELIACH

who had emigrated early, asking him: "Yossele, how do the Jews of London treat you?" His answer speaks for many:

Dear Auntie, they treat me like a bastard. How else can they treat me? Do they know the gentle, dear Jews who were my parents? Do they know my father? Do they know my mother's lofty origins? The war turned all of us survivors into bastards, for it destroyed our illustrious past. Do you know what Hitler has done to us? He turned us into broken vessels that can never be mended . . .

For many the loss goes deeper still, straight to the heart of their faith. After his return from the gulag, Moshe Sonenson, formerly a prosperous businessman in Eishyshok, became a farmer in Israel. In a world devoid of humanity, he decided, it was better to work with animals and the soil, "since they are more faithful than God or man." If there was a God at all, Moshe wished to voice his quarrel with him. For surely he was a God of transgressors, of a "world turned upside down . . . in which the rich are become poor, and the lawless have prospered beyond their own wildest dreams. To the sweet sound of their cash registers, preferably with a blond shikse at their side; occasionally they open their purse but never their heart. This, my child, is the new Jew that Hitler has fashioned into being."

The words of these survivors describe a condition of unspeakable loss. They can only hope that something of their vanished shtetl will live on in memory. It was with that hope that so many of them allowed their voices to be heard in these pages, knowing that if they weren't preserved here, they would go to the grave unheard. By speaking up, they believed, in the words of Moshe Sonenson, that "at least the people, and perhaps even God, will remember that there once was a world filled with faith, Judaism, and humanity."

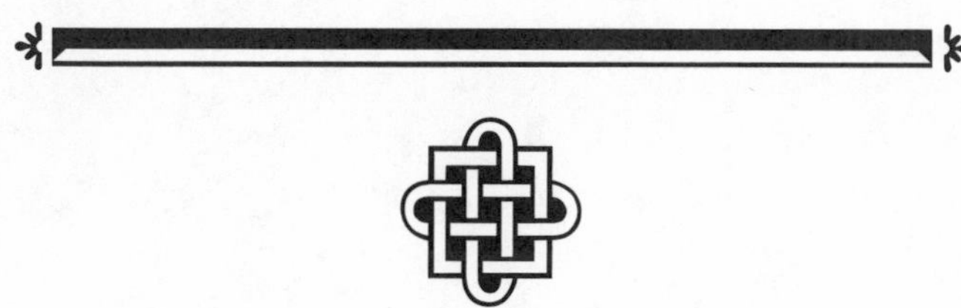

NOTES

INTRODUCTION : : THE QUEST FOR EISHYSHOK: RESTORING A VANISHED PAST

Information for this chapter also came from interviews with Shira Gorshman, Elke Szulkin Jankelewicz, Nahum Shulman, and Hayyim Sonenson.

1 Shaul Kaleko, "Fun Yiddishen Folklore in Lite," *Die Velt*, Kovno, June 1924.

2 *Lietuvos* TSR *Urbanistikos Paminklai*, no. 6, p. 61, note 333. In the Lithuanian encyclopedia published in English in the United States, the Jews of Eishyshok are not mentioned, neither during the centuries prior to World War II nor during the Holocaust, when they came to their tragic end. See *Encyclopedia Lituanica*, vol. 2, p. 145.

3 See Shira Gorshman, *Izranie Stranitski, 1939–1979*, vol. 1, pp. 180–82.

CHAPTER I : : ORIGINS AND HISTORY OF EISHYSHOK: 1065–1941

Information for this chapter also came from interviews with Avraham Asner, Shalom Sonenson Ben-Shemesh, Alexander Zisl Hinski, Hayya Streletski Kosowski, Hanoch Kosowski, Zippi Melamud, Asia Friedman Paamoni, Reuven Paikowski, Dr. Morris Shlanski, Moshe Sonenson, and Malka Matikanski Zahavi; from the unpublished diary of Moshe Kaplan; and from the unpublished notebook of Szeina Blacharowicz Wiszik.

1 Singer, *Meshugah*, p. 31. I am grateful to Judy Baston for bringing the source to my attention.

2 *Lietuviskoji Enciklopedija*, vol. 7, pp. 606–7; Koreva, *Materiali*, p. 737; *Wielka Encykopedia*, vol. 17–18, p. 1011; Polujanski, *Opisanie Lasow Krolewstwa Polskiego i Gubernij Zachodnich Cesarstwa Rossyjskiego Pod Wzgledem Historycznym, Statystyznym i Gospodarczym*, vol. 2, p. 83; *Lietuvos Metrastis, Bychovco Kronika*, pp. 46, 47; *Polnoe Sobranie Russkeich Letopicei Chroniki: Litovskaia i Shomoitkaia i Bychovtsa Letopici Barkylabovskaia, Averki i Pantsyrskovo*, vol. 32, p. 130.

3 Saduikis, *Eisiskes Praeityje*, p. 2.

4 D. Wieski, *Ejszyszki, Ziemia Lidska*, p. 20. Wieski explains that some historians believe that the historian T. Narbutas invented the story that Eishyshok was founded in the thirteenth century rather than in the eleventh century.

5 On tombstones in the Old Cemetery, the Jewish burial ground, see Koreva, *Materiali*, p. 573; Bershadskii, *Litovskie Yevrei*, p. 153; Biblioteka Jegiellonska, Dzial Rekopisow, Sygn. 6320, IV, p. 44 (Jagiellonian Library Department of Manuscripts); Saduikis, *Eisiskes Praeityje*, p. 2; Tarasenka, *Lietuvos Archelogijos Medziaga*, p. 127; Minor, *Kratki Istoricheski Ocherk o Yevreiach v. Polshi Litvi i Russi*, p. 4.

6 *Lietuviu Enciklopedija*, vol. 5, p. 405; Vanagas, "Eisiskes Ikure Eiksys," p. 7.

7 Jurginis, Baudziavos Jsigalejimas Lietuvoje, p. 168; *Lietuviskoji Enciklopedija*, vol. 7, pp. 606–7; Rouba, *Przewodnik*, p. 60. According to Rouba, the Crusaders were in Eishyshok in 1392 and 1402. Saduikis, *Eisiskes Praeityje*, pp. 2–3; D. Wieski, *Ejszyszki*, p. 20.

8 Saduikis, *Eisiskes Praeityje*, pp. 2–3; Maskovcevas, *Ka Jus Zinote*, p. 3.

9 For information regarding the multiple spellings of Eishyshok, see Mokotoff and Sack, *Where Once We Walked*, p. 83; C. Cohen, *Shtetl Finder*, p. 23; Eliach, *Hasidic Tales of the Holocaust*, pp. 50–55.

10 *Lietuvos* TSR *Urbanistikos Paminklai*, no. 6, p. 56.

11 *Slownik Geograficzny Krolestwa Polskiego*, vol. 2, p. 319. On the general history of the Karaites, see Ankori, *The Karaites in Byzantium*; Baron, *Social and Religious History of the Jews*, vol. 5, 209–85; J. Mann, "Karaism in Lithuania and Poland"; Nemoy, trans. and ed., *Karaite Anthology*.

12 Re Karaite practices in Eishyshok: Every morning when he came home from synagogue services Eliyahu Plotnik would remove the four-fringed garment known as a zizit and hang it on the wall, whereupon his wife Zipl (Zipporah) would invariably remark, "What do you think, you are a Karaite that you hang your zizit on the wall for the rest of the day?" Since the Karaites follow only Scripture, they do not observe the laws in the

Mishnah and Talmud calling for the zizit to be worn all day. Another possible clothing-related carryover occurred in the Streletski family during Passover. For many generations it was the practice of the man who conducted the first Seder on Passover to wear a special embroidered kippah, a headcovering similar to that worn by Karaites from Crimea. The kippah is still in the possession of the Streletski family in Israel, and is still worn during the family Seders. I saw very similar headcoverings at the Karaite Museum in Troki, August 10, 1987. See chapter 9 re commemoration of Hevrah Kaddishah anniversary; see chapter 6 re use of the word *kibbutz* in the Eishyshok yeshivah's name.

13 Abramauskas, *K Voprosy Geneza Krepostney Sooryshenii Tipa Kastle v Litve,* p. 73.

14 *Regesty i Nadpysy,* vol. 1, no. 178.

15 D. M. Lippman, *Le-Toldot ha-Yehudim be-Lita-Zamut,* p. 21.

16 The charter was based on one given to the Jews of Poland by King Boleslav the Pious in 1264. For the text of the charter, see Bershadsky, *Litovskie Yevrei.*

17 *Lithuania Past and Present,* pp. 18–19.

18 Davies, *God's Playground: A History of Poland,* vol. 1, pp. 122–23; *Lietuvos TSR Urbanistikos Paminklai,* no. 6, p. 7.

19 *Lietuvos SR Urbanistikos Paminklai,* no. 6, p. 9, note 37.

20 *Encyclopedia Lituanica,* vol. 2, p. 145.

21 Koreva, *Materiali,* p. 573; Ziminskas, "Eisiski Isgyvrentos Nelaimes."

22 *Lietuvos TSR Urbanistikos Paminklai,* no. 6, pp. 30–31.

23 *Encyclopedia Lituanica,* vol. 2, p. 145; *Lietuvos TSR Urbanistikos Paminklai,* pp. 30–31.

24 Lukowski, *Liberty's Folly: The Polish Lithuanian Commonwealth in the Eighteenth Century, 1647–1795,* pp. 76–77.

25 *Lietuvos TSR Urbanistikos Paminklai,* no. 6, p. 43; Buchaveckas, *Salcios Zeme,* p. 203.

26 *Yahadut Lita* (Lithuanian Jewry), vol. 1, pp. 26–27.

27 VUB (Vilnius University Library), RS file 5, A85 N 12631; *Lietuvos TSR Urbanistikos Paminklai,* no. 6, pp. 32–33.

28 Halpern, comp., and Bartal, ed., *The Records of the Council of the Four Lands,* (English title) vol. 1, Introduction by Shmuel Ettinger, p. 15.

29 See Ben-Sasson, ed., *A History of the Jewish People,* p. 679; *The Records of the Council of the Four Lands,* Introduction, p. 20.

30 For details of the elections and tax collection, see Dubnow, ed., *Pinkas ha-Medina,* pp. 239–42, for the minutes of the Lithuanian Council. All subsequent references to the pinkas — the official record book of the Council — will state only the short title followed by date of the meeting and the number of the paragraph in the minutes. For this citation, then, the reference would be: *Pinkas ha-Medina,* 1700/906–909.

31 *Pinkas ha-Medina,* 1691/862. The decision to hold the next meeting in Olkenik, 1695/904, the year the meeting took place.

32 The pinkas of the Council of the Four Lands was edited, annotated, and published by the historian Israel Halpern in 1945. The second edition was published in 1990 (see note 28). The pinkas of the Lithuanian Council survived in Grodno, under the auspices of the leaders of the kahal. In 1806 they authorized the copying of the pinkas, to be performed with "special care and accuracy, letter by letter, to assure that nothing will be changed from beginning to end, so that it will be kept as evidence for generations." Eliakim Shlomo Shapira, the rabbi of Grodno and previously rabbi of Eishyshok, whose love of books and scholarship extended far beyond sacred texts, gave a copy of the pinkas to historian Simon Dubnow, who published it in 1925 (see note 29). Since then it has been the major historical source concerning Lithuanian Jewry of the seventeenth and eighteenth centuries. See Rabin, ed., *Grodno,* pp. 42, 139–42.

33 Lukowski, *Liberty's Folly,* pp. 77–82.

34 Nathan of Hanover, *Yeven Mezulah,* pp. 31–32.

35 *Pinkas ha-Medina,* 1649/452; 1650/460.

36 Ibid., 1650/461.

37 This happened despite the efforts of the communities, immediately following the 1648–49 massacres, to tell little orphans about their families. Amulets were put around their necks inscribed with the names of their murdered parents. See *Gzerot Tah ve-Tat Shevet Yehudah,* p. 292.

38 Among the many chroniclers who documented the tragedy were: Nathan of Hanover, *Yeven Mezulah;* Shulberg, *Petah Teshuvah;* Feitel, *Tit ha-Yeven;* Shabbtai b. Meir Cohen, *Megilat Eifa.* For detailed figures about the death toll, see Weinryb, *The Jews of Poland,* pp. 192–95 and notes 23–35, pp. 362–63.

39 *Pinkas ha-Medina,* 1650/463–68; 469.

40 See *Regesty,* no. 971, re Tzar Alexis's banishment of the Jews.

41 Rivkes, preface, *Beer Ha-Golah.*

42 *The Memoirs of Gluckel of Hameln,* pp. 19–22.

43 Maskovcevas, *Ka Jus Zinote* IV, 2, p. 3.

44 Saduikis, *Eisiskes Praeityje*, November 11, 1959, p. 4; D. Wieski, *Koscioly w gm. Ejszyskiej–Ziemia Lidzka*, p. 29.

45 John III Sobieski was also the king who punished the participants in anti-Jewish riots in Brest-Litovsk, and who ordered the Sejm to actively oppose the blood libels that were more and more frequently being leveled against the Jews. His greatest claim to fame, however, was heading up the Christian armies that joined together to defeat the Turks in 1683, delivering Vienna from Muslim Turkish occupation.

46 On Swedish cruelty toward the Jewish population of Poland and Lithuania, see Halpern, ed., *Bet Yisrael* vol. 1, pp. 87–90.

47 On the Great Northern War and its consequences, see Davies, *God's Playground*, vol. 1, pp. 496–504; Riasanovsky, *A History of Russia*, pp. 244–50; Klyuchevsky, *Peter the Great*, pp. 62–74; Sumner, *Peter the Great and the Emergence of Russia*, pp. 101–9.

48 Nikolaev and Parry, *The Loves of Catherine the Great*, pp. 82–128.

49 There are some slight differences of opinion about the number of people taken by each of the three countries. See Riasanovsky, *A History of Russia*, pp. 298–99; Davies, *God's Playground*, vol. 1, pp. 521–22.

50 Wiernik, *History of Jews in America*, pp. 95–98.

51 For details concerning the military career of Berek Joselewicz, a career that was brilliant despite the anti-Semitism of the Polish army, see Mstislavskya, "The Jews in the Polish Revolt of 1831"; Luninski, *Berek Joselewicz i Jego Syn*; Ringelbaum, *Zydzi w Powstaniu Kosciuszkowskiem*; *Yahadut Lita*, vol. 3, p. 173.

52 Baron, *The Russian Jews under Tzars and Soviets*, index; Greenberg, *The Jews in Russia*, vol. 1, pp. 8–9.

53 On the titles of kahal officers in various communities, see Levitats, *The Jewish Community in Russia, 1772–1844*, pp. 88–139.

54 Wilkanski, *Ba-Heder*, pp. 80–81. Passages quoted here translated by Yaffa Eliach.

55 Wilkanski, *Mi-Gal El-Gal*, pp. 16, 103.

56 *Ethics of Our Fathers*, A:3.

57 Re the 1827 statute, see A. Lewin, *Kantonistn, 1827–1856*, pp. 39–47.

58 Nahum Sokolow (1859–1936), ed., *Sefer Hashanah*, quoted in Greenberg, *The Jews in Russia*, vol. 1, p. 48, note 94.

59 Nahum Sokolow, *Sefer Ha-Yovel Le-Khvod*, quoted in Greenberg, *The Jews in Russia*, vol. 1, p. 49, note 95.

60 Quoted in Ginsburg, *Historishe Werk Yiddishe Kantonistn*, vol. 3, p. 16.

61 Herzen, *My Past and Thoughts*, pp. 219–20.

62 For folk songs and memoirs from the cantonist period, see Lewin, *Kantonistn*, p. 214–313.

63 Ginsburg, *Historishe Werk Yiddishe Kantonistn*, vol. 3, p. 99.

64 Ibid., pp. 131–35.

65 Slutski and Kaplan, eds., *Hayalim Yehudim be-Zivot Eiropa*, pp. 112–13; pp. 110–12.

66 In 1782 there were said to be 76 Jewish houses in Eishyshok with 446 people, as well as 4 Tatar households numbering 28 people. In 1790, there were about 60–63 houses with chimneys (meaning payers of the chimney tax); in 1796 their number increased to 64. See Buchaveckas, *Salcios Zeme*, pp. 199–200. In 1820 there were 69 houses with chimneys, 52 of them belonging to Jews. See *Lietuvos TSR Urbanistikos Paminklai*, no. 6, p. 47.

67 JDC/AR 33-44/891. The JDC document erroneously states that Eishyshok was founded by the Gypsy king in the nineteenth century and named after him.

68 *Lietuvos TSR Urbanistikos Paminklai*, no. 6, pp. 44, note 200.

69 Ibid., p. 47.

70 *Yahadut Lita*, vol. 1, pp. 84–85.

71 Ariel Lipkunsky, *Dogalishok*, p. 15.

72 Buchaveckas, *Salcios Zeme*, p. 201.

73 Gelber, *Die Juden und der Polnische Aufstand*, no. 159.

74 *Lietuvos TSR Urbanistikos Paminklai*, no. 6, p. 54.

75 Ibid.

76 Ibid., p. 57, note 289.

77 Ibid., p. 56; Ziminskas, "Eisiskes XVIII–XIX Amziuje," p. 3.

78 Wilkanski, *Mi-Gal El-Gal*, p. 64.

79 *Ha-Melitz*, June 4, 1895; June 30, 1895; September 14, 1896.

80 *Lietuvos TSR Urbanistikos Paminklai*, no. 6, p. 58; *Yahadut Lita*, vol. 1, p. 104.

81 *Lietuvos TSR Urbanistikos Paminklai*, no. 6, p. 58.

82 Wilkanski, *Ba-Heder*, pp. 39–40.

83 *Lietuvos TSR Urbanistikos Paminklai*, no. 6, p. 59.

CHAPTER 2 : : THE SYNAGOGUE AND BETH MIDRASH

Information for this chapter also came from interviews with Shalom Sonenson Ben-Shemesh, Rabbi Kalman Farber, Shmuel Gross, Rebbetzin Zipporah Hutner Kravitz, Mordekhai Lawzowski, Iris (Itzle) Kanichowski

Makowski, Asia Friedman Paamoni, and Reuven Paikowski.

1 Ezekiel 11:16; Megillah 29/a.
2 Philo, *Legatione ad Gaium*, 132f, 156; Tosefta Megillah, 83:6; Maccabees III 7:20.
3 Flavius Josephus, *Life*, p. 200; Eiruvin 101/b; Josephus, *Antiquity*, 19:305; Josephus, *Wars*/2:285–9; Mark 1:21; Shkalim, Talmud Yerushalmi, chapter 2. The synagogue of the Tarsians (carpenters) existed in Lod and Tiberias.
4 Ketubot 105/a; Megillah, Talmud Yerushalmi, chapter 3.
5 Krauss, *Synagogale Altertamer*, p. 247; Weiss, *The Synagogue in the Roman Diaspora in the Time of the Mishna and the Talmud*, pp. 123–44.
6 Sifri Deuteronomy 41; Sukkah 53/a; Taanit 9/a.
7 Megillah, Talmud Yerushalmi, chapter 3.
8 Maimonides, *Mishneh Torah*, Hilkhot Tefila 11:1.
9 Josephus, *Antiquity* 14:258; Acts 16:13.
10 Tosefta Megillah, 4:23; *Shulhan Arukh Orakh Hayyim*, 150:1–3; Maimonides, *Mishneh Torah*, Hilkhot Tefila 11:2.
11 Eizenshdat and Gelbert, eds., *Kamenetz-Litovsk, Zastavije and Colonies*, pp. 35–36.
12 Jeshurin, ed., *Wilno*, p. 10.
13 *Lietuvos* TSR, *Urbanistikos Paminklai*, no. 6, pp. 42–43.
14 Wilkanski, *Ba-Heder*, pp. 30–31. Builders falling to their death during construction seems to have been a common occurrence; see Davidowicz, *Synagogues in Poland and Their Destruction* (English title), p. 147.
15 Etlinger, *Binyan Zion*, p. 9. He approves of planting trees in the shulhoyf, but this opinion was not accepted in most locations in Lithuania. I am grateful to Rabbi Dr. Michael Rosensweig for bringing this source to my attention. Nahmanides on Deuteronomy 16:21.
16 Wilkanski, *Ba-Heder*, p. 98.
17 Piechotka, *Wooden Synagogues*, pp. 21–22. Krinsky, *The Synagogues of Europe*, pp. 225–26. For classic three-tiered synagogues, see also Holzsynagoge/Litauen/The Central Archives for the History of the Jewish People, Jerusalem, file PL/449; Wisniewski, *Synagogues and Jewish Communities in the Bialystok Region*, p. 107.
18 Farber, ed., *Olkeniki in Flames*, pp. 69, 81.
19 Wigoder, *Story of the Synagogue*, pp. 96–105; Krinsky, *Synagogues of Europe*, pp. 223–25. Dawidowicz, *Synagogues in Poland*, pp. 33–34.
20 Dawidowicz, *Synagogues in Poland*, pp. 33–34; Ran, *Jerusalem of Lithuania*, vol. 1, p. 108 (see also p. 105); Wigdor, *The Story of the Synagogue*, pp. 97–99; Zinowitz, "Batei Midrashot Historyim Be-Vilna." The Vilna synagogue inspired many artists and was painted by Francizsek Smuglewicz (1745–1807), Ben Zion Zakerman (1890–died in Samarkand, 1944), Wolf Vittel Kaplanski (perished at Treblinka), and Marc Chagall; and was also photographed by Roman Vishniac. See Dawidowicz, plates no. 6, 7, and 8. The Old Kloiz survived the Second World War as a gutted ruin, only to be burned down entirely during the infamous Doctors' Trial of 1952. The Gaon's Kloiz, though damaged, also survived the war. But the entire courtyard complex was later demolished and subsequently replaced with drab modern buildings. I visited the ruins of the shulhoyf in 1945, and the buildings on the site in 1987 and 1997. Also see Ran, *Jerusalem of Lithuania*, vol. 2, pp. 519–22, 530–31.
21 Ha-Rema, *Darkei Moshe*, Hilkhot Beit Knesset, 150/3.
22 Dawidowicz, *Synagogues in Poland*, p. 96.
23 Feinstein, *Iggrot Moshe Hoshen Mishpat*, p. 230, paragraph 42.
24 Wilkanski, *Ba-Heder*, pp. 30–31.
25 Wilkanski, *Mi-Gal El-Gal*, p. 64.
26 Ibid., p. 90.
27 Ibid.
28 Ibid., p. 94.
29 Piechotka, *Wooden Synagogues*, p. 26.
30 Ibid. The women's gallery has its origins in the Temple in Jerusalem; see Zahariah 12:12; Sukkah 51/b-52/a; Safrai, ed., *The Ancient Synagogue*, pp. 57–58.
31 Wigoder, *Story of the Synagogue*, p. 108.
32 About women reciting Kaddish, see Bachrach, *Havat Yair*, p. 222; Margaliot, *Mateh Ephraim*, 4:8 (he was against women reciting Kaddish); Henkin, *Kitvei ha-Gria Henkin*, vol. 2, pp. 3–6; Wolowelsky, "A Review of Avraham Weiss, *Women at Prayer: A Halakhic Analysis of Women's Prayer Groups*."
33 The unheated synagogues were referred to by different names in the various communities, e.g., "the cold synagogue" in Minsk (as in Eishyshok). Shoshan, ed., *Minsk, Jewish Mother City* (English title), vol. 1, pp. 89–90.
34 Elijah the prophet is associated with circumcision. He complained during the reign of Ahab and Jezebel that the Jews "have foresaken your covenant" (Kings I 19:10). According to the commentators, "your covenant" refers to circumcision. See also Zohar Breishit 93:1.
35 Psalms 130:1; *Pinkas Navaredok Memorial Book*, p. 69.

36 Wilkanski, *Mi-Gal El-Gal*, p. 95.
37 Farber, ed., *Olkeniki in Flames*, p. 71. Re similar wooden Holy Arks, see Wisniewski, *Synagogues and Jewish Communities in the Bialystok Region*, p. 107; and Yargina, *Wooden Synagogues*, pp. 189, 194–96, 211–12.
38 Wilkanski, *Mi-Gal El-Gal*, p. 94.
39 Farber, ed., *Olkeniki in Flames*, pp. 80–81.
40 On the elevated status of those who were granted the title *morenu*, see *Pinkas Vaad ha-Kehilot be-Lita*, 1667/592; 1687/805; Fine, *Kirya Neemana*, p. 37.
41 *Pinkas Vaad ha-Kehilot be-Lita*, 1695/881; 1761/974.
42 Kaleko, "Fun mein zeiduns zikorn," pp. 531–32.
43 *Shulhan Arukh, Orakh Hayyim*, 63.
44 In the only existing photograph, only a section of the Old Beth Midrash is visible, and nothing at all of the New Beth Midrash. According to Reuven Paikowski, the two masonry structures were identical, and similar to many batei midrash throughout the region.
45 Replianski, *Unzer Hilf*, p. 4.
46 In the event of a husband's death, the shtot remained in his wife's possession. *Pinkas Beth ha-Midrash he-Hadash be-Rehov Palangian ba-Yir Telz*, pp. 2–4.
47 Bloom, *A Shtetele in Poilen*, pp. 24–27.
48 Wilkanski, *Ba-Heder*, pp. 82–83.
49 Re a dybbuk leaving the body through a finger, see ben Israel, *Nishmat Hayyim*, 3/10; Nigal, *Dybbuk Tales*, pp. 54–60.
50 Told to me by Rabbi Moshe Blau, who heard it from Rabbi Cahaneman on Purim, while a student in the Lithuanian yeshivah of Telz.
51 Rabbenu Gershon, known as "the Light of the Diaspora," made legal provisions and guidelines pertaining to the delay of the Torah reading. The practice was especially widespread among small Ashkenazic communities where everyone knew each other. In the sixteenth century, the Council of the Four Lands offered additional guidelines. The practice remained widespread, especially in the shtetlekh of Eastern Europe. See Leoni, ed., *Volozhin*, pp. 240–41; Finkelstein, *Jewish Self-Government in the Middle Ages*, pp. 15–19, 48–49, 128–29, 242–43.
52 Ben-Sasson, ed., *A History of the Jewish People*, pp. 506–7.
53 Jacob Katz, *Tradition and Crisis*, pp. 99–101.

CHAPTER 3 : : RABBIS AND REBBETZINS

Information for this chapter also came from interviews with Shalom Sonenson Ben-Shemesh, David Ejszyszki, Rabbi Kalman Farber, Shlomo Farber, Rebbetzin Zivia Hutner Hadash, Alexander Zisl Hinski, Shoshana Hutner Hinski, Rabbi Yehoshuah Hutner, Peretz Kaleko-Alufi, Arieh Kopelowitch, Hayya Streletski Kosowski, Mordekhai Lawzowski, Reuven Paikowski, Sonia Hutner-Kagan-Rockler, Abrashke (Adam) Rogowski, Fania (Mrs. Uri) Rozowski, Moshe Sonenson, Moshe Szulkin, and Rabbi Moshe Zinowitz.

1 Numbers 27:18–23. In our time, when ordination in the ancient sense (the placing of the hands on one's successor) no longer exists, the certificate of admission to the rabbinate is still called *semikhah*, as it was in early times, but it is based on a thorough examination in the field of halakhah by an outstanding authority in Talmud and Psakim.
2 Israel Isserlin, one of the foremost rabbis of fifteenth-century Germany, complained that ordination was given too freely: "The ordained are many but the knowledgeable are few" (*Psakim U Ketavim*, paragraph 255). His responsa provides an excellent resource re contemporary Jewish life. Similarly, Don Yitzhak Abrabanel of Spain, who was exiled to Italy with his Jewish compatriots in 1492, despite years of devoted service to King Ferdinand and Queen Isabella, wrote about ordination in his new country: "All are ordained and ordaining. I do not know from where they have taken this liberty, probably they have learned it from the gentiles who were handing out the title 'doctor,' so they do the same" (*Nahlat Avot*).
3 Israel Meir Ha-Konen (1838–1933) was known as the Haffetz Hayyim ("he who wants life"), after the title of his first book, published in 1873, which was devoted entirely to an exposition of the primary importance of the laws of slander, gossip, and tale-bearing.
4 In 1529, Sigismund II Augustus was formally elected to the Polish throne at the wish of his father, Sigismund I, and began to rule, under his father's guidance, as grand duke of Lithuania. Sigismund the Elder had his seat in Cracow; the Younger in Vilna. See Davies, *God's Playground: A History of Poland* vol. 2, pp. 144–45.

5 Re privileges granted by Sigismund II, see Bershadsky, ed., *Russko-Yevreiskii Arkhiv*, I. 1882, #139, 147; and A. L. Feinstein, *Ir Tehilla*, pp. 21–22, 164–65.
6 Maimonides, *Hilkhot Talmud Torah*, 1:7.
7 Ketubot, 106/a.
8 Jacob Katz, *Tradition and Crisis*, pp. 122–34.
9 Klausner, *Vilna be-Tekufat ha-Gaon*, pp. 9–10.
10 Y. H. Soloveichik, *Hadoar*, April 21, 1961, p. 40; Seidman and Federbush, eds., *Hokhmat Israel be-Maarav Eiropah*, p. 96ff.
11 *Pinkas Medinat Lita*, 1628/169. See also *Bava Batra*, 8/a-b, re the RaHaSh, a tax distributed among the rabbi, hazzan, and shammash, for attending and officiating at various ceremonies. All three members of the clergy also had the privilege of being exempt from taxes.
12 Zinowitz, "Mir," pp. 38–40.
13 Grade, *Rabbis and Wives*, p. 5.
14 Dov Katz, *Tenuat ha-Mussar*, vol. 2, pp. 28–29.
15 Grade, *Rabbis and Wives*, p. 6.
16 *Pinkas Medinat Lita*, 1623/48; 1626/103; 1628/171; 1628/141; 1628/143.
17 Alufi and Barkali, eds., *Eishyshok Koroteah ve-Hurbanah*, p. 16.
18 Ibid., p. 12.
19 Klausner, *Vilna be-Tekufat ha-Gaon*, p. 92; Shteinshneider, *Yir Vilna*, p. 87. Rabbi Moshe was the author of *Sefer Ekronot*, and of a responsa volume titled *Halaka-le-Moshe*. He was also an expert in the intricate calculations of the Jewish calendar, which involve synchronizing the solar and lunar cycles.
20 Zinowitz, "Mir," p. 20. When he studied at the Navaredok Kibbutz ha-Prushim, Reb Avraham Shmuel was a friend and student of Rabbi Alexander Ziskind and Rabbi Eliyaho Kalish. Zinowitz, *Etz Hayyim, Toldot Yeshivat Volozhin*, pp. 106, 120.
21 Wilkanski, *Ba-Heder*, p. 135.
22 Zinowitz, "Mir," p. 20.
23 Wilkanski, *Ba-Heder*, p. 135. The same story is told about several other East European rabbis, including the Baal Shem Tov, founder of Hasidism.
24 Zinowitz, "Mir," p. 39; pp. 20–22.
25 Wilkanski, *Ba-Heder*, pp. 134–35.
26 Meirowitch, *Ahavat David*, sermon 7.
27 Ibid.
28 Yossef Zundl Hutner, *Ulam ha-Mishpat*, foreword.
29 Ibid., foreword by grandson Rabbi Yehoshua Hutner.
30 Yossef Zundl Hutner, *Bikkurei Yossef*, foreword.
31 Hershberg, *Pinkas Bialystok*, vol. 1, p. 202.
32 Yudson, "Deretchin Fun Meine Kinder Yorn," pp. 47–51.
33 Ibid., pp. 47–51.
34 *Ethics of Our Fathers*, A:3.
35 Hutner, *Ulam ha-Mishpat*, p. 5.
36 Rabbi Yossef Zundl Hutner's works included: *Bikkurei Yossef* (Vilna, 1871); *Ulam Ha-Mishpat* (Warsaw, 1880; Jerusalem, 1971); *Hevlei Yossef; Hadrei Deah* (Warsaw, 1908; Jerusalem, 1971); *Hok Ha-Ezrah* (Warsaw, 1922), a work concerning divorce laws, published posthumously by Rebbetzin Hendl and their son Rabbi Yehudah Leib Hutner; *Ginzei Hayyim* (Warsaw, 1928), published posthumously by his son Rabbi Hertz Mendl Hutner.
37 Israel Meir Ha-Kohen, known as the Haffetz Hayyim, asked Hutner to write an endorsement for his book *Likkutei Halakhot*, on the tractate of *Zevahim*. Other endorsements were penned by men who were among the greatest scholars of Lithuania.
38 Zivia Hutner Hadash, July 10, 1980.
39 These dates, which not everyone agrees upon, were provided in an interview with Reb Zundl's granddaughter, Zivia Hutner Hadash, July 10, 1980.
40 Bernard Malamud based his 1966 novel *The Fixer* on the Beilis case, which was fought in the courts of Kiev from 1911 to 1913. The actual trial took place September 25–October 28, 1913.
41 *Eishyshok Koroteah ve-Hurbanah*, p. 29.
42 Ibid.
43 Rabbi Moshe Mordekhai Epstein (1866–1933), a brother of Zivia's mother, Rebbetzin Kreindl Hutner, headed up the Slobodka yeshivah after it moved to Hebron. See Avissar, ed., *Sefer Hebron*, pp. 409–38.
44 A. Lewin, *Mi-Pinkaso Shel Moreh Mi-Yehudia* (published in English as *A Cup of Tears*), pp. 9, 10.
45 Ibid., p. 154.
46 Nineteenth-century Kapolia is well documented in the autobiographical works of Mendele Mokher Sefarim (1835–1917).
47 Warhaftig, *Palit ve-Sarid, be-Yemei ha-Shoah*, pp. 136–40. Shalom Holavski's classification of Rabbi Szymen Rozowski as a member of Poalei Zion is an erroneous one. See Holavski, *Al Neharot ha-Neiman ve-ha-Dnieper*, p. 336.
48 See Alperowitch, ed., *Sefer Telz*, pp. 67–125, 206–16.
49 Rabbi Szymen Rozowski, *Unzer Fund*, 1936, quoted in *Eishyshok Koroteah ve-Hurbanah*, p. 126. Rabbi Rozowski was a frequent contributor to Torah and Halakhah scholarly publications, like the monthly

Shaarei Zion, published in Jerusalem. See *Shaarei Zion*, Adar Nissan, 1927, no. 6–8; Kislev-Shvat, 1928, no. 3–5; Adar Nissan, 1928, no. 6–7; Nissan-Iyar, 1929, no. 8–9. I am grateful to Rabbi Tzvi Rothberg, grandson of Rabbi Tuvia Rothberg from Eishyshok, for sharing this material with me.

50 R'Avraham Aaron Waldshan's daughter was being married to Yaakov Zeldin, a student at the Beit Yossef yeshivah in Bialystok. Farber, ed., *Olkeniki in Flames* pp. 62, 88–89; Hershberg, *Pinkos Bialystok*, vol. pp. 335–38.

51 Chaim Grade, "Talmidei Hakhomin in Lite," quoted in *Olkeniki in Flames*, p. 224, English trans. by Yaffa Eliach.

52 *Eishyshok Koroteah ve-Hurbanah*, p. 126.

53 Shalom Sonenson Ben-Shemesh, in *Eishyshok Koroteah ve-Hurbanah*, pp. 57–66.

54 On rumors circulating among the Jews about the fate that awaited them from the Einsatzgruppen, see German report of September 12, 1941, in Hilberg, *The Destruction of the European Jews*, vol. 1, p. 295, note 14.

55 *Eishyshok Koroteah ve-Hurbanah*, pp. 63–64. The quote is from the Book of Judges 16:30.

56 Holavski, *Al Neharot ha-Neiman ve-ha Dnieper*, p. 165.

57 Shalom Sonenson Ben-Shemesh, interviewed by a member of Dr. Philip Friedman's committee, Munich, 1946. On Dr. Friedman's work in the DP camps, see Friedman, "Bibliography of Bibliographies, on the Period of Disaster."

CHAPTER 4 : : OTHER MEMBERS OF THE CLERGY

Information for this chapter also came from interviews with Shalom Sonenson Ben-Shemesh, Luba Ginunski Deutch, Shmuel Gross, Rachel Shekowitski Hadash, Alexander Zisl Hinski, Elke Szulkin Jankelewicz, Evelyn (Hava) Landsman Kahn, Leon Kahn, Mordekhai Lawzowski, Moshe-Reuven Michalowski, Zvi Michalowski, Rivka Remz, Shaul Schneider, Miriam Kabacznik Shulman, Hayyim Sonenson, and Moshe Sonenson; from the unpublished notebook of Szeina Blacharowicz Wiszik; and from a letter from Hyman Boyer.

1 Isaiah 45:19.

2 Dinur, *Be-Mifneh ha-Dorot*, pp. 97–100, 133–36; Ben-Sasson, *Hagut ve-Hanhagah*, pp. 34–54, 254–56; Ben-Sasson, "The Personality of Elijah the Gaon of Vilna and His Historical Influence" (English title).

3 For example, Reb Benyamin Shekowitski, the Minsker maggid, a native of Eishyshok, continued to preach in Tel Aviv. See Rebbetzin Rachel Hadash (née Shekowitski), "Beit Avi, ha-Maggid mi-Minsk," in Shoshan, ed., *Minsk, Jewish Mother-City*, vol. 1, pp. 504–15. Ben Zion Yadler, the famous maggid in Jerusalem, was a native of Lithuania. The Nobel-winning novelist Shmuel Yosef Agnon's colorful character Yakum Purkan was based on him.

4 Luntschitz, *Ammudei Shesh*, n. p.

5 H. R. Rabinowitz, *Dioknaot Shel Darshanim*, pp. 297–303; M. Tempkin in *Jewish Review*, February 3/March 3, 1971.

6 Hadash, "Beit Avi ha-Maggid mi-Minsk," p. 509; Genechowski, *Stories of Jerusalem* (English title), pp. 159–62.

7 See, for example, Yaakov Kranz, the Maggid of Dubno, *Mishlei Yaakov* (The Parables of Jacob), 1885. These are parables culled from his works. Taken out of their homiletic context, however, the parables, while retaining a historical significance, lose most of their artistic impact. There is also an unpublished collection of parables by a nineteenth-century maggid from Eishyshok, Rabbi Hersh Margaliot.

8 Wilkanski, *Ba-Heder*, pp. 219–20.

9 Hadash, "Beit Avi, ha-Maggid mi-Minsk," p. 511.

10 Shazar, *Morning Stars*, pp. 32–38.

11 Hadash, "Beit Avi," p. 513.

12 Ibid., p. 508.

13 Ibid., p. 506.

14 Quoted in Gitelman, *Jewish Nationality and Soviet Politics*, p. 310.

15 Hadash, "Beit Avi," p. 515.

16 Shazar, *Morning Stars*, pp. 32–38.

17 Deuteronomy 16:18–20.

18 Mahler, *Yahadut Polin*, pp. 204–7.

19 Tory-Golub, ed., *Mariampole*, pp. 95–96; *Yahadut Lita*, vol. 3, p. 76.

20 Deuteronomy 25:1–3.

21 Horodezky, *Shlosh Meot Shanah Shel Yahadut Polin*, pp. 15ff; Tchernowitz, *Toledot ha-Posekim* (*Biographies of Decisors*), vol. 3, pp. 38ff.

22 See L. I. Rabinowitz, *Herem-ha-Yishuv*; and Levitats, *Jewish Community in Russia, 1772–1884*, for information re specific laws and regulations governing the various categories of excommunication in Eastern European communities.

23 Maimonides, *Yad Sanhedrin* 2:7.
24 Gittin 10/b.
25 Wilkanski, *Ba-Heder*, p. 88.
26 Wilkanski, *Mi-Gal El-Gal*, pp. 18, 27.
27 Yevamot, Talmud Yerushalmi, chapter 12, Halakha 6.
28 Wilkanski, *Ba-Heder*, pp. 31–32.
29 For the various duties of the shammash, see *Pinkas Medinat Lita*, 1623/17 and 54–56, 1627/113, 1628/129 and 157, 1670/545.
30 Tiferet Bahurim was founded by Reb Eliakim Gezl Levitan during the nineteenth century, and spread throughout Poland and Lithuania. Its charge was to teach working-class youth Torah and the Rashi commentary. In Vilna it also became a mutual aid society with its own synagogue, and medical and financial funds.
31 Caro, *Shulhan Arukh Orah Hayyim*, 53:4ff.
32 *Pinkas Vaad ha-Kehilot be-Lita*, 1623/62.
33 Jeshurin, ed., *Wilno*, pp. 848–55.
34 Rema on *Yoreh Deah, Hilkot Shehita*, 1:1. See *Yad Shaul* on the Rema. Maimonides, *Hilkhot Shehita*, 4:4. On the issue of a shohetet, see Azulai, *Birkei Yossef Yoreh Deah*, 1:1, and *Mahazik Brakha Yoreh Deah*, 1:1. I am grateful to Rabbi Dr. Michael Rosensweig, my son-in-law, for bringing these sources to my attention.
35 *Pinkas Vaad ha-Kehilot be-Lita*, 1632/258.
36 Wilkanski, *Ba-Heder*, p. 88.
37 On the importance of the shehita in the early days of the Hasidic movement, see Shmeruk, "The Social Significance of Hasidic Shehita."

CHAPTER 5 : : HEDER EDUCATION

Information for this chapter also came from interviews with Shalom Sonenson Ben-Shemesh, Naftali Berkowitch, Moshe Edelstein, Shlomo Farber, Alexander Zisl Hinski, Moshe Kaganowicz, Peretz Kaleko-Alufi, Avraham Aviel Lipkunski, Temira Wilkanski Orshan, Rivka Remz Rewzin, Shaul Schneider, Miriam Kabacznik Shulman, Hayyim Sonenson, Moshe Sonenson, Mordekhai Zanin, and Philip Zlotnik.

1 Balaban, "Hayyei Israel ve-Tarbutum ba-Meah Ha-16 & 17."
2 Wilkanski, *Ba-Heder*, pp. 10–11, 12; idem, *Mi-Gal El-Gal*, p. 174; Mordekhai Munesh Kaleko, unpublished diary, notebooks.
3 In Nikalsburg, an attempt was made to require melamdim to have a formal education, but it did not succeed, and no further attempts are known to have been made by any communities, large or small. *Educational Encyclopedia*, vol. 4, p. 393.
4 Avot 5:24.
5 Ketubot 50/a.
6 Well-to-do farmers always hired melamdim for their sons, but this was not the case with poor farmers. Since the number and gender of their children was not always known to the shtetl kahal, they were sometimes able to get away with this. A. M. Lifschitz, "Ha-Heder," in *Hatekufa*, vol. 7, pp. 297–99.
7 *Educational Encyclopedia*, vol. 4, pp. 579–80.
8 Biographical facts concerning Kallir are shrouded in mystery, including even the question of when he lived. The first known mention of his name is in 857.
9 Lifschitz, "Ha-Heder," p. 327.
10 Rabbi Moshe ben Henich Brantshpigl, in a musar book of the seventeenth century.
11 Wilkanski, *Ba-Heder*, pp. 5–7.
12 Lifschitz, "Ha-Heder," pp. 301–2.
13 Avraham Hayyim Schorr, quoted in *Educational Encyclopedia*, vol. 4, p. 388.
14 Bialik, *Aftergrowth and Other Stories*, pp. 60–63.
15 Lifschitz, "Ha-Heder," pp. 328–29.
16 Hagiga 9/b.
17 Lifschitz, "Ha-Heder," pp. 318–19.
18 Wilkanski, *Ba-Heder*, p. 130. The name of the children's society dedicated to the funding of sacred book purchases was Pirhei Shoshanim. The society was common in Lithuania and Byelorussia.
19 Caro, *Shulhan Arukh Yoreh Deah* 285; Maimonides, *Mishneh Torah, Hilkhot Talmud Torah* 2:2.
20 Wilkanski, *Ba-Heder*, p. 36.
21 Ibid., pp. 105, 114–15; Wilkanski, *Mi-Gal El-Gal*, p. 138.
22 Maimonides, *Mishne Torah*, Hilkhot Talmud Torah 2:2.
23 Wilkanski, *Ba-Heder*, pp. 91–92; 8–10.
24 Ibid., p. 100.
25 Ibid., p. 8.
26 Bava Batra 2/a.
27 Maimonides, *Mishneh Torah, Hilkhot Talmud Torah* 2:2.
28 Wilkanski, *Ba-Heder*, pp. 148–50.
29 Ibid., pp. 25–26.
30 Peah, Talmud Yerushalmi, chapter 1.
31 Y. Meltzer, *Be-Derekh Etz ha-Hayyim*, vol. 1, p. 62.
32 Yoma 66b; Sota Talmud Yerushalmi, chapter 3, Halakha 4; Sota 20/b; see also Maimonides, *Mishneh Torah, Hilkhot Talmud Torah* 1:1, 13.

33 See Henry and Taitz, *Written Out of History*, pp. 48–53.
34 Zborowski and Herzog, *Life Is with People*, pp. 124–28.
35 Founding charter of Agudat Bnei Moshe, Central Zionist Archives of Jerusalem, 35A/13; Klausner, *Sefer ha-Zionut ha-Datit, be-Reshit Yesud ha-Mizrahi*, vol. 1, p. 369; Ziporah Rice, "Jewish Religious Education of the Mizrahi Movement in Poland Between 1920–1930," M.A. thesis, Brooklyn College, May 1990, pp. 134–43.
36 Lifschitz, "Ha-Heder," 340–42.
37 *Educational Encyclopedia*, vol. 4, p. 687; vol. 2, chapter 5.
38 Interview with Rebbetzin Amital, granddaughter of Rebbetzin Beile Hinde Meltzer, January 17, 1987; I. Z. Meltzer, *Even ha-Azel*, vol. 3, Introduction (Rosh Davar).
39 Wilkanski, *Mi-Gal El-Gal*, p. 178.
40 Ibid.
41 Quoted in Lifschitz, "Ha-Heder," p. 343.
42 Quoted in *Educational Encyclopedia*, vol. 4, p. 678.
43 Karon, "Ha-Kursim ha-Petagogim be-Grodna"; Broides, *Vilna ha-Zionit ve-Askaneha*, pp. 154–58.
44 *Educational Encyclopedia*, vol. 4, p. 682.
45 Ibid., p. 685.
46 Alufi and Barkali, eds., *Eishyshok Koroteah ve-Hurbanah*, p. 30.
47 Wilkanski, *Ba-Heder*, p. 49–50.

CHAPTER 6 : : THE YESHIVAH: TOWN AND GOWN

Information for this chapter also came from interviews with Naftali Berkowitch, Rina Lewinson Fenigstein, Yossef Resnik, Moshe Sonenson, and Moshe Szulkin.

1 Rabbi Simhah Zisl Broida (1824–1898) was the disciple of Rabbi Israel Lipkin Salanter, the founder of the Musar movement. In the frequent variations of the quote that is attributed to him, the location of the parliament is changed, from London to Paris to Washington, D.C. For a recent example, see Rabbi Aharon Ben Zion Shurin, "Der Yeshiveh-Boher fun Eishyshok un der Pariser Parliament," *Forward*, June 17, 1994, pp. 11–23.
2 Generally the heads of the yeshivot were prominent rabbis (or sons-in-law or relatives of prominent rabbis). Notable scholars and rectors of yeshivot in Poland and the vicinity until the closing decades of the sixteenth century are listed in Gans, *Tzemah David*, pp. 140–47.
3 Among the outstanding rabbis who objected to pilpul in the Ashkenazic yeshivah were Yehuda Lowe ben Bezalel (the Maharal), and Yeshayahu ben Avraham Ha-Levi Horwitz (the Holy Shelah, 1565?–1630). For more information on the opposition to pilpul and hilluk, see Assaf, ed., *Mekorot le-Toledot ha-Hinukh be-Israel* (Sources for the History of Jewish Education), vol. 1, pp. 46–51; Etkes, *Mossad ha-Yeshivah*, pp. 13–29; Zinberg, *A History of Jewish Literature*, vol. 6, pp. 21–44.
4 Nathan of Hanover, *Yeven Mezulah*, pp. 83–87.
5 *Pinkas Vaad ha-Kehilot be-Lita*, 1623/46; 1623/49; 1628/141; 1655/513; 1662/528; 1667/586; 1676/608–9; 1679/638–9; and many more.
6 See Lewin, *Aliyyat Eliahu*, p. 16.
7 Reb Hayyim's other great master was Reb Aryeh Gunzberg, author of *Shaagat Aryeh*. See "Letters of Reb Hayyim of Volozhin" in *Ha-Peles*, Berlin, 1902, pp. 141–43, re the factors that prompted him to establish the yeshivah.
8 The educational philosophy of Reb Hayyim of Volozhin is contained in his posthumously published book, *Nefesh ha-Hayyim*, sections 3, 4; N. Lamm, *Torah Lishma: Torah for the Sake of Torah in the World of Rabbi Hayyim Volozhin and His Contemporaries*.
9 In 1825 the Volozhin yeshivah's budget was 16,675 silver rubles, of which 6,000 was spent on the support of the students (with juniors receiving 2 to 4 rubles a month, seniors 4 to 10), 3,618 on teachers' salaries, and the rest on other expenses. On the budget of the yeshivah in its last years, see Stampfer, *Ha-Yeshivah ha-Litait be-Hithavutah*, pp. 183–92.
10 Rabbi Hayyim Zalman Bressler was born in Stolaptzi and served as rabbi of Setz, the birthplace of the Gaon of Vilna. According to his contemporaries, he was an accomplished scholar. Moshe Zinowitz, *Mir*, pp. 38–39.
11 The other rabbis on the Mir beth din were Rabbi Dov Berush Meisels of Warsaw, Rabbi Issac Harif of Slonim, and Rabbi Yehoshuah of Nizvic.
12 Rabbi Meisels in a letter to Rabbi Spektor, quoted in Zinowitz, "Mir," pp. 39–40.
13 Rabbi Spektor, letter to Rabbi Yitzhak Blazer, reprinted in *Talpiot*, no. A-b, 1951.
14 Bar-Ilan, *Mi-Volozhin ad Yerushalaim*, pp. 17–18.
15 Reb Hayyim of Volozhin was succeeded at his death (1849) by his son, Reb Yitzhak, known as Itzele of Volozhin. Reb Yitzhak's two sons-in-law

were Reb Eliezer Yitzhak Fried and Naftali Zvi Yehudah Berlin, the Neziv. The Neziv (1817–1893) was appointed head of the yeshivah, and some years later, in 1849, was joined by Reb Hayyim's grandson, Reb Yossef Baer Soloveitchik (1820–1892). The Neziv remained to guide the yeshivah for over forty years, but Rabbi Soloveitchik would leave in 1865, after a bitter dispute over the method of instruction, which involved pilpul. In 1878 he became the rabbi of Brest-Litovsk (Brisk). Reb Raphael Shapira (1837–1921), son-in-law of the Neziv, replaced Rabbi Soloveitchik as co-head of the academy. One of the great scholars at Volozhin was Reb Hayyim Soloveitchik (1853–1918), son of Yossef Baer, and husband of Reb Raphael Shapira's daughter. The last heads of the Volozhin yeshiva were Reb Yaakov Shapira (d. 1936) and his son-in-law Hayyim Wulkin, both of whom perished in the Holocaust. For a detailed summary of the Soloveichik dynasty, see Leoni, ed., *Wolozin*, pp. 152–59; and Meiselman-Soloveitchik, *The Soloveitchik Heritage*.

The Soloveitchik family still plays a significant role in Jewish intellectual life. Rabbi Professor Joseph Baer Soloveichik (1903–1993) was a world-renowned Talmudic scholar, religious philosopher, and political leader. His son, Professor Hayyim Soloveichik, is a prominent medieval scholar, teaching at Yeshivah University in New York. The late son-in-law of J. B. Soloveitchik, Professor Rabbi Isidore Twerski, was chairman of Yale's Department of Near Eastern Languages and Civilization. The younger son-in-law is Rabbi Dr. Aharon Lichtenstein, codirector of the Har Ezion yeshivah in Israel.

16 Bar-Ilan, *Mi-Volozhin ad Yerushalaim*, pp. 31–35. Rabbi Meir Bar-Ilan was the son of the Neziv from his second marriage.

17 Ethical literature incorporated into the Musar curriculum included works by such authors as Jonah ben Abraham Gerondi, Moses ben Jacob Cordovero, and Moses Hayyim Luzzato.

18 See Chaim Grade, "My Quarrel with Hersh Rasseyner," in Howe and Greenberg, eds., *Treasury of Yiddish Stories*, pp. 579–606; Grade, *The Yeshiva*; and D. Fishman, "Musar and Modernity: The Case of Novaredok." On the musar movement see Etkes, *Yisrael Salanter ve-Reshita Shel Tenuat ha-Mussar*; Goldberg, *Israel Salanter, Text, Structure, Idea*.

19 Ben-Sasson, ed., *A History of the Jewish People*, p. 843.

20 Menes, "Patterns of Jewish Scholarship in Eastern Europe," p. 207.

21 Wilkanski, *Ba-Heder*, pp. 137–38.

22 Zinowitz, "Eishyshok Ayeret ha-Prushim."

23 Cited in Menes, "Patterns of Jewish Scholarship in Eastern Europe," pp. 206–7.

24 Hafetz, *Melekhet Harash*, introduction.

25 Uri David, *Apirion David*, introduction.

26 The title *Haffetz Hayyim* is taken from Psalms 34:13–14: "Who is the man that *desireth life* and loveth the days that he may see good therein? Keep thy tongue from evil and thy lips from speaking guile."

27 See obituary, *New York Times*, September 16, 1933.

28 Kaganowicz, ed., *Sefer Zikaron le-Kehilat Ivie*, pp. 206–213.

29 M. Greenbaum, *The Jews of Lithuania*, pp. 101–2.

30 To name just a few of the many students who studied in Eishyshok and had an impact on Torah Judaism: Hayyim Leib of Stavisk Mishkovski (1835–1896), one of the great Lithuanian rabbis, who was known for his scholarship and ethics, was a friend of the Haffetz Hayyim, and wrote *Peni ha-Arieh ha-Hai*; Rabbi Malkiel Zvi Tenenbaum, author of responsa *Divrei Malkiel*; Rabbi Moshe Danishevski (d. 1909), rosh yeshivah in Slobodka, rabbi in Eishyshok in 1855–57 (during the two-year absence of Rabbi Avraham Shmuel), author of *Beer Moshe*; Reb Simha-Meir ha-Cohen of Dvinsk (1843–1926), who studied in Eishyshok during his bar mitzvah year with Rabbi Moshe Danishevski, was a close colleague of Reb Zundl Hutner, became a dedicated public servant and a participant in most of the major rabbinic conferences of his time, and wrote *Or-Sameah*, which made him one of the best-known Talmudic scholars of his time; Rabbi Yehonatan Abelman (1854–1903), author of responsa *Torat Yehonatan* and *Zikhron Yehonatan*; Ben Zion Alfas (1851–1940), author of ethical (musar) books and many popular books for women; Avraham Mordekhai Raziel-Rosenson (1880–1961), educator in Tel-Aviv, father of David Raziel, who was commander of EZL, and of Esther Raziel, a member of the Knesset; Reb Hayyim-Shalom Tuvia Rabinowitz (1860–1931), a rosh yeshivah in Slobodka and Telz, whose special teaching methodology was known as "Reb Hayyim's Way"; Shlomo Zvi Goldman "Shalmon" (1862–1933), author, public activist, journalist, Zionist, and Hebrew educator, father of Dr. Nahum Goldman and brother of author Shmuel ben Avigdor; Reb Mordekhai from Palangian, teacher, author, chief proofreader in the Romm publishing house in Vilna; Benyamin Eliyahu Ramigulski (1871–1930), a rabbi and political leader of Mizrahi, author of

halakhic works including *Hadrat Benyamin;* Hayyim Natanson (1838–1904), rabbi and accomplished artist, author of responsa *Divrei Hen;* Yehoshua-Yossef Preil (1858–1896), author of excellent articles in *Ha-Melitz* and a number of books, including *Eglei Tal;* Yossef Avigdor Kessler (1885–1956), rabbi in Lithuania and New York, author of books including *Tiferet Ziv* and *Tiferet Yossef;* Hayyim Uri Cohen (1857?–?), dayyan in Vilna, author of many books, including *Menahem Zion,* a eulogy of Rabbi Yitzhak Elhanan Spektor; Zalman Aharon Dat (1859–1916), who published in *Ha-Melitz* and other papers and was the author of *Toldot Aharon,* a charitable man and a rabbi who refused to accept payment for his clerical duties and instead supported his family by managing a drugstore; Yaakov Lewinson (1875–1955), rabbi in Chicago, head of Mizrahi Teachers Seminary, honorary chairman of Yeshivah University and the Mizrahi movement; Shmuel Idelzek (1862–1947), rosh yeshivah in Eishyshok in 1899, founder of two yeshivot in Israel, author of *Divrei Shmuel,* and a man well known for his public activism; Yaakov David Gordon (1873–?), rabbi in Norfolk, Virginia, author of *Hed ha-Zman;* Israel-Nissan Krek (1867–1938), a dayyan in Kovno, ardent supporter of Zionism and delegate to the twelfth Zionist Congress, who made aliyah in 1927 and became chairman of Mizrahi after World War I; Iliyahu Klachkin (1852–1932), a rabbi who was fluent in Greek, German, French, Russian, Polish, and English, knowledgeable in mathematics, medicine, and geography, deeply interested in world literature, art, and music, a genius in halakha who responded to questions from around the globe, author of many halakhic books, including *Dvar Halakha,* he made aliyah in 1928 and became a leading dayyan in Rabbi Hayyim Zonenfeld's Jerusalem court. Many prominent individuals who studied at the Eishyshok yeshivah are mentioned in Ben Zion Eisenstadt, *Dor Dor ve-Sofrav* (Vilna, 1901).

31 Wilkanski, *Mi-Gal El-Gal,* pp. 29–30.

32 E. Friedman, *Sefer ha-Zikhronot* pp. 124–25. Eliezer Eliyahu Friedman, who later went on to become a founder of the newspaper *Ha-Zofeh,* (The Observer) published in Kovno, was a student in Eishyshok at the time, a frequent visitor in the home of his relatives, the Wilkanskis, and an eyewitness to these events.

33 Israel Isser Goldbloom, *Ha-Shahar* (The Dawn), Adar 1878, no. 4.

34 Stampfer, *Ha-Yeshivah ha-Litait be-Hithavutah,* pp. 158–59.

35 G. Kressel, *Leksikon,* vol. 1, pp. 409–10. Goldbloom is known by the acronym Yafaz, standing for Israel Isser Goldbloom of Neistadt Shirvint, Lithuania.

36 Wilkanski, *Mi-Gal El-Gal,* p. 30; p. 209.

37 Ibid., pp. 39–41.

38 Ibid., pp. 206–7.

39 Ibid., pp. 41–42.

40 Ibid., p. 39.

41 The Volozhin yeshivah was closed when its leadership resisted the attempts of the tzarist government to impose a secular curriculum in addition to the regular yeshivah curriculum. See Bar-Ilan, *Mi-Volozhin ad Yerushalaim,* pp. 109–14; Zinowitz, *Etz Hayyim;* Jacob J. Schacter, "Haskalah, Secular Studies and the Closing of the Yeshiva in Volozhin in 1892"; Stampfer, *Ha-Yeshivah,* pp. 215–17.

42 Wilkanski, *Mi-Gal El-Gal,* p. 7.

43 On the Telz yeshivah, see Alperowitch, ed., *Sefer Telz,* pp. 57–155. For more on the student experience in Telz, see Ben-Zion Dinur, "Shnataim Be-Yeshivat Telz," in Etkes, ed., *Mossad ha-Yeshivah,* pp. 155–74.

44 Wilkanski, *Mi-Gal El-Gal,* pp. 156–57.

45 A. L. Ha-Kohen, *Mikhtavei Haffetz Hayyim,* p. 85. I am grateful to Professor Sid Z. Leiman for bringing the source to my attention.

46 A. Weiter, *Ketavim* p. vi.

47 Ibid., p. xxxii.

48 Ibid., pp. xxxi–xxxii.

49 Moshe Zinowitz, "Yeshivat Radun," in *Yahadut Lita,* vol. 1, pp. 222–25.

50 *Ha-Zefirah,* 1913, no. 218.

51 Wilkanski, *Mi-Gal El-Gal,* pp. 218–19. These are the concluding paragraphs of the book.

52 Kaleko, *Yomon* (unpublished diary; the correct Hebrew word is *Yoman,* but it did not exist in 1914). Dr. Kaleko kept his diary from June 1914 until Kristallnacht, November 9, 1938. After his arrival in Eretz Israel that same month, until his death in 1975, he made sporadic entries. He specified in his will that his diary be destroyed if his death preceded the completing of the writing of his memoirs, as it did. A few months prior to my meeting in 1987 with his widow, Raya Kaleko-Barkali, she carried out his wishes and burned it. However, their daughter Leora Barkali Yoav informed me that one section from the diary, concerning the Eishyshok period, had been saved. This she graciously shared with me. Sections on Kovno, Berlin, Tel Aviv, and Jerusalem had been destroyed. I am grateful to Leora Yoav for

sharing with me the diary, as well as many other important documents.

53 Ibid., pp. 2–9.

54 *Educational Encyclopedia*, vol. 4, p. 582.

55 In the 1930s, there were about a hundred students in the yeshivah ketanah of Eishyshok, but it faced many financial difficulties. YIVO, Vaad Ha-Yeshivot, file #7, 117–18.

56 Zinowitz, "Yeshivat Radun," p. 225; Warhaftig, *Palit ve-Sarid, bi-Yeme ha-Shoah*, p. 141.

CHAPTER 7 : : THE BATHHOUSE: THE PERFECT REST

Information for this chapter also came from interviews with Dora Kremin Dimitro (Dobke Dimitrowski), Reuven Paikowski, Miriam Kabacznik Shulman, and Szeina Blacharowicz Wiszik.

1 Vaikra Rabba 34:3.

2 Yalkut Kohelet 972.

3 Sanhedrin 17/b.

4 Shabbat 33/b.

5 Ibid.; Avoda Zarah 44/b.

6 Baron, *Social and Religious History of the Jews*, vol. 4, p. 37.

7 Dinur, *Israel ba-Golah*, vol. 2, pp. 628–29.

8 Brakhot, Talmud Yerushalmi, chapter 9, Halakha 6; Brakhot 60/a.

9 Sandhedrin, Talmud Yerushalmi, chapter 7.

10 Wilkanski, *Mi-Gal El-Gal*, pp. 52–53.

11 Wilkanski, *Ba-Heder*, pp. 140–41.

12 Leviticus 11:36, 12:1–7, 15:17; Caro, *Shulhan Arukh Yoreh Deah*, "Hilkhot Niddah," 195:9, 197.

13 Shabbat 2:6.

14 Bava Metzia 84/a.

15 Wilkanski, *Ba-Heder*, p. 102.

16 Ibid., p. 85.

17 Ibid., p. 89.

18 On the similarity between the public bath in Eishyshok and those in other shtetlekh, see *Pinkas Navaredok Memorial Book*, pp. 137–38.

19 Rashi in Shabbat 10/a; Bava Batra 67/b.

20 Wilkanski, *Ba-Heder*, p. 85.

21 Genesis 9:21–23; Wilkanski, *Ba-Heder*, p. 75. On the issue of adult males bathing with youngsters and other male relatives in the public bath, see Wolf, *Sefer Toldot Adam*, pp. 106–7.

22 Isaac Bloom, *A Shtetele in Poilen*, p. 72.

23 Wilkanski, *Ba-Heder*, p. 90.

CHAPTER 8 : : MUTUAL AID SOCIETIES

Information for this chapter also came from interviews with Sarah Plotnik Avrahami, Shalom Sonenson Ben-Shemesh, Rina Lewinson Fenigstein, Gita Giliot, Alexander Zisl Hinski, Shoshana Hutner Hinski, Hayya Streletski Kosovski, Mordekhai Lawzowski, Reuven Paikowski, Yossef Shanzer, Louis Shlanski, and Malka Matikanski Zahavi.

1 Addison, *The Present State of the Jews*, chapter 25.

2 Ben Sira 7:35.

3 Gittin 61/a; Shabbat 127/a.

4 In *Orhot Hayyim* (Paths of Life), an ethical work dating from eleventh-century Germany and attributed to Rabbi Eliezer ben Isaac the Great, it is written: "Visit the sick and lighten their suffering. Pray for them and leave. Do not stay long, for you might inflict upon them additional discomfort. And when you visit a sick person, enter the room cheerfully." Rabbi Yehuda he-Hasid of Regensbourg (d. 1217), a poet, scholar, and mystic, advises that when visiting the sick, the poor person should be given preference, since the rich are visited by many. Margaliot, ed., *Sefer Hasidim*, pp. 361ff.

5 Genesis 18:1; Sota 14/a.

6 Alufi and Barkali, eds., *Eishyshok Koroteah ve-Hurbanah*, p. 39.

7 Maimonides, *Hilkhot Avel*, 14:a; Gittin, Talmud Yerushalmi, chapter 5, Halakha 9.

8 In Poland there were special street carnivals on Purim, with entertainers who solicited donations for poor brides. Y. L. Peretz, "Hakhnasat Kalla."

9 Bava Batra, Talmud Yerushalmi, chapter 1, Halakha 6.

10 Genesis 18:18; Bava Metzia 86/2.

11 Shabbat 127/a; Avot 1:5.

12 Quoted in Farber, ed., *Olkeniki in Flames*, p. 81.

13 See Mendele Mokher Sefarim (Shalom Jacob Abramovich, 1835–1917), *The Travels of Benjamin the Third*, for a description of the unique subculture of the beggars.

14 Dating back to the days of the Lithuanian Council — at least — beggars were described as a burden on the community, deceptive, immoral,

patrons of houses of ill repute. *Pinkas Vaad ha-Kehilot be-Lita* 1623/84.

15 Wilkanski, *Ba-Heder*, pp. 150–51.
16 Ibid., p. 138.
17 Ibid., p. 107.
18 Horayot 13/a.
19 For listings of most of the landsmanshaften, see Rosaline Schwartz and Susan Milamed, *A Guide to YIVO's Landsmanshaften* (New York: YIVO Institute for Jewish Research, 1986). This guide does not include Eishyshok. See also Weisser, *A Brotherhood of Memory: Jewish Landsmanshaften in the New World*; for Eishyshok, see index.
20 *Constitution der Hevrah Bnei Avraham Shmuel Anshei Eishyshker*, established 1891. Printed in New York by Avraham Yitzhak Teigman, 1926.
21 Peah 1/a.

CHAPTER 9 : : THE OLD AND NEW HOUSES OF ETERNITY

Information for this chapter also came from interviews with Shalom Sonenson Ben-Shemesh, Simcha Dembrow, Shlomo Farber, Shneur Glombocki, Elka Szulkin Jankelewicz, Moshe Hayyim Kaplan, Gershon Katz, Zvi Michalowski, Reuven Paikowski, Hayyim Sonenson, Israel Sonenson, Moshe Sonenson, Malka Matikanski Zahavi, and Philip Zlotnik.

1 Heschel, *The Earth Is the Lord's*, p. 20.
2 Tukachinski, *Gesher ha-Hayyim*, vol. 1, p. 17.
3 Hagiga 3/b, Rashi; Nida 17/a; Brakhot 18/b.
4 For the Hebrew *bet olam* (house of eternity), see Ecclesiastes 12:5. For the Aramaic form, *bet almin*, see Sanhedrin 19/2. In Hebrew the cemetery is also known as *beit Kevarot* (place of the Sepulchers), Nehemiah 2:31, and *beit moed le-khol hai* (the house appointed for all living), Job 30:23, or euphemistically *beit hayyim* (house of the living).
5 Bava Batra 25/a.
6 Alufi and Barkali, eds., *Eishyshok Koroteah ve-Hurbanah*, pp. 7–9.
7 Dr. Shaul Kaleko Barkali, "The Holy Martyr's Grave," in idem, *Eishyshok*, a booklet issued by the Lemel School, Jerusalem, 1969, as part of the Yad Vashem project in which schools across Israel "adopted" the destroyed Jewish communities of Europe. Peretz Kaleko-Alufi, Shaul's younger brother, was then the principal of the Lemel School, which "adopted" his native Eishyshok.
8 Re the custom of marrying off two orphans in the cemetery, see Mendele Mokher Sefarim (Shalom Jacob Abramovich), "Sefer ha-Kabzanim," pp. 97–98.
9 Wilkanski, *Ba-Heder*, pp. 112–13.
10 Tenenbaum, *Divrei Malkiel*, vol 2, p. 154, paragraph 94; Shapiro, "Rabbi Malkiel Tenenbaum, Rav of Lomza."
11 See M. Lamm, *The Jewish Way in Death and Mourning*, pp. 211–15.
12 Krajewska, *A Tribe of Stones*, pp. 11–41; for Jewish tombstones in other regions of Eastern Europe, see Goberman, *Jewish Tombstones in Ukraine and Moldava*.
13 Genesis 49:9; *Ethics of Our Fathers* 5:23.
14 Proverbs 31:18; Genesis 60:167.
15 Numbers 20:1–2.
16 On the custom of visiting the cemetery during Elul, see Tukachinski, *Gesher ha-Hayyim*, vol. 1, pp. 303–12.
17 Wilkanski, *Ba-Heder*, pp. 112–13.
18 Taanit 16/a.
19 There is another version of this story that is not based on family sources: see Krohn, *Around the Maggid's Table*, pp. 218–20.
20 Pessia Moszczenik Skir, *Zikhronot, 1910–1980*, pp. 7–9. The unpublished manuscript was given to me by her son Zeev Skir, June 24, 1986, Israel.
21 For use of the term *hevrah kaddishah* and information re the evolution of the brotherhood and its functions, see Ezekiel 39:14; Targum Jonathan and Rashi; Ketubot 8/b; Niddah 24/b; Moed Kattan 24/b; Tobit A, 17–19, B, 4–9. Rabbenu Nissim Girondi, Responsa 75; *Magen Avraham, Orah Hayyim*, 84/7; *Pinkas Lita*, 1761/572.
22 Wilkanski, *Ba-Heder*, p. 143.
23 Ibid., p. 141.
24 Shneur Zalman of Lyady, the founder of the Habad Hasidic dynasty, was accepted as an assistant (shammash) in the Hevrah Kaddishah at the age of five, and as a member at thirteen. In gratitude for the honor, his grandfather undertook to supply wood to the synagogue and made a donation of 18 gulden. Steinman, *Beer ha-Hassidut, Sefer Mishnat Habad*, vol. 1, p. 31.
25 The death charts that follow are based on the official death records of Eishyshok in the years 1891–1905 and 1906–1940.

DEATHS 1891–1914 — TZARIST RUSSIA

AGE / DATE		MALES 0–3	4–10	11–18	19–59	60		FEMALES 0–3	4–10	11–18	19–59	60	TOTAL M & F
1891	33	11	3	5	8	6	16	0	1	1	7	7	49
1892	46	20	9	5	4	7	13	0	0	0	8	5	59
1893	34	12	4	3	9	6	20	4	1	1	6	8	54
1894	25	10	0	0	7	8	18	1	0	1	9	7	43
1895	BIG FIRE — NO OFFICIAL RECORDS												
1896	27	9	1	4	5	8	12	0	0	0	7	5	39
1897	30	7	5	6	2	10	19	0	1	0	6	12	49
1898	33	16	2	3	5	7	23	5	2	0	8	8	56
1899	24	6	2	3	8	5	15	3	1	1	7	3	39
1900	30	10	2	6	4	8	18	6	0	1	5	6	48
1901	23	9	5	1	3	5	16	4	3	1	1	7	39
1902	23	9	0	3	6	5	24	7	3	0	7	7	47
1903	34	12	2	6	7	7	19	3	1	0	7	8	53
1904	22	7	1	2	4	8	10	0	0	2	4	4	32
1905	20	5	0	2	7	6	13	1	1	2	2	7	33
1906	16	2	1	1	5	7	8		1		1	6	24
1907	19	3	2	2	3	9	6				3	3	25
1908	24	3	2		5	14	9	1	1			7	31
1909	18	2	2		3	11	8				1	6	*
1910	15	6		1	5	3	12	1			7	4	27
1911	21	6	1		1	13	16	3	2	1	3	7	37
1912	20	5	3		3	9	10	1			1	8	30†
1913	21	7	2	1	3	8	7		1		2	4	28‡
1914	15	7	2		1	5	18	2			2	14	33**
TOTAL	513	184	51	54	105	175	330	42	19	11	104	153	875

Chart based on F.728 A.4 B.430 VCIA (Vilnius Central Historical Archive)
*One age not recorded.
†Note: Two males died at age 102.
‡Note: Pinkas recorded incorrect figures for male deaths.
**Pinkas missing a page thus missing records of 1 male and 1 female death.

DEATHS 1915–1939 — WORLD WAR I AND SECOND POLISH REPUBLIC

AGE / DATE	MALES						FEMALES						TOTAL M & F
		0–3	4–10	11–18	19–59	60		0–3	4–10	11–18	19–59	60	
1915	NO RECORDS												
1916	24				6	17	23				4	19	43*
1917	41	2		3	12	24	31		1	2	8	20	72
1918	32		1	5	11	15	29		1	2	10	14	61†
1919	31		2	3	8	18	31			3	9	15	62‡
1920	19		1	1	2	15	17		2		3	10	36**
1921	NO RECORDS												
1922	9		1		2	6	3				1	2	12
1923	9	1	1	1	1	5	9	1			2	4	18††
1924	13	1			2	8	13			1	4	5	26‡‡
1925	8				2	6	9				2	7	17
1926	8				2	6	17	1			3	12	25***
1927	5				1	4	6				4	2	11†††
1928	9					9	10				2	8	19
1929	12				5	7	9			1		8	21
1930	4				2	2	12				2	10	16
1931	10	1	1	1	1	5	18		1		7	10	28‡‡‡
1932	11		1		3	7	4				1	3	15
1933	11	1	1		1	8	13				4	9	24****
1934	17	2	1	2	3	9	5		1			4	22
1935	12				2	10	6					6	18
1936	16	4			2	10	12	1	1	1	1	8	28
1937	11	2			3	6	16			1	7	8	27
1938	9	3		2	3	1	9			1	5	3	18
1939	12			1	1	10	6				1	5	18
TOTAL	333	17	10	19	75	208	308	3	7	12	80	192	637

Chart based on F.728 A.4 B.430 VCIA (Vilnius Central Historical Archive)
*One male age not recorded.
†Two female ages not recorded.
‡Four female ages not recorded.
**Two female ages not recorded.
††Two female ages not recorded.
‡‡Two male ages not recorded, 3 female ages not recorded.
***One female age not recorded.
†††One male died at age 100.
‡‡‡One male age not recorded.
****One male died at age 102.

CAUSES OF DEATH — CHILDREN

	MALES			FEMALES		
AGE	0–3	4–10	11–18	0–3	4–10	11–18
Sickness	1					
Meningitis	1	1			1	1
Bolezni odrow	1					
Pneumonia	6		1		1	
Leukemia			1			
Typhus		2				
Inflammation of intestine	1					
Inflammation of kidneys		1				1
Inflammation	1		1		1	
Scarlet fever	1					
TB			1			
Intestinal complication	1					
Blood infection				1		
Hit by lightning						1
Congestion	1					
Cold	1					
Chickenpox	1					
Bronchitis	1					
Poisoned (self)			1			
Blood poisoning			1			

TZARIST RUSSIA 1891–1914

CAUSES OF DEATH — ADULTS

	MALES			FEMALES		
AGE	19–35	36–59	60–	19–35	36–59	60–
Cancer					1	
Typhus	9	4		7	4	3
Childbirth				9	2	
Drowning			1			
Hemorrhage	2	2		2	2	1
Weakness		2	9		2	13
Old age			37			30
Asthma	2	4				
Fever	3	2		2		
TB	6	2	3	2	5	2
Inflammation	1					1
Pneumonia	1					
Encephalitis					1	
Poison	1					
Proploxy		1				

Chart based on State Historical Archives, Vilnius, Lithuania, F.728 H.4 B.430.
Notes:

A. In 1892, one male killed, no age given — thus was not recorded on chart.

B. In 1897, 1898, 1899, 1900 very few recorded causes for death. Therefore number of deaths does not correspond to number of causes.

C. In 1901, 1904–1914 — no causes of death recorded.

D. In 1903, only 1 recorded cause for death — drowning.

E. According to files from private archives scores of infants died at birth and mothers during childbirth.

CAUSES OF DEATH — ADULTS

	MALES			FEMALES		
AGE	19–35	36–59	60–	19–35	36–59	60–
Old age			19			23
Various heart disease	1	3	22	5	5	16
Inflamed bladder		1	2			
Inflammation		1	3			2
Various cancer		6	6	1	3	10
Suffocated			1			
Inflammation of kidneys		1				2
Asthma		1				2
Pneumonia		1	10		1	9
TB		3	2	3		
Intestinal inflammation		1			1	
Cold		1	1			1
Meningitis						1
Blood poisoning				1		
Flu						1
Colitis			1			
Sclerosis			2			
Diabetes			1			
Drowned (self)		1		1	1	
Killed	1	2				
Apoplexy					1	
Sudden death		1				
Brain attack		1	1			
Killed by horse		1				
Prolonged paralysis	1					1
Sore uterus						1
Sepsis					1	
Stroke		1				
Typhus			1			

Notes:

A. 1916, 1920, 1926 — No cause of death recorded — records are retroactive.

B. 1919, 1924, 1925 — only one cause of death recorded for each year.

C. No records for 1921.

D. 1916, 1925, 1927, 1928, 1930, 1935, no children's deaths recorded.

E. 1931 — death of one male from cancer — age not recorded.

F. 1922, 1923, 1927, 1928, 1929, 1930, 1931, 1932, 1933 — Many have no causes for death.

G. Death caused by various complications were listed by major cause; for example, "dangerous influenza complicated by pneumonia" was listed under *pneumonia*.

H. During WWI a few hundred Eishyshkians and refugees who stayed in Eishyshok died from a typhus epidemic. It is excluded from the public record.

26 Other popular dates for the Hevrah Kaddishah feast were those for the weekly portions Vayehi (death of the patriarch Jacob) and Hukat (death of Aaron), as well as the 19th of Kislev (March). See Shneur, *Pandrei ha-Gibor*, vol. 2, pp. 105–6.
27 Genesis 23.
28 Farber, ed., *Olkeniki in Flames*, pp. 52–53.
29 Brakhot 64/a.
30 *Hatam Sofer, Yoreh Deah* 327.
31 Szeina Blacharowicz Wiszik, *Notebook;* Tukachinski, *Gesher ha-Hayyim*, vol. 1, p. 117.
32 Caro, *Shulhan Arukh Yoreh Deah*, 361:1; Brakhot 18/a.
33 Tukachinski, *Gesher ha-Hayyim*, vol. 1, pp. 114–16.
34 Avoda Zarah 35/b.
35 *Pinkas Vaad ha-Kehilot be-Lita*, 1761/972.
36 Jeremiah 22:18–22; Sanhedrin 82/b.
37 Gitelman, *A Century of Ambivalence*, p. 85.
38 Caro, *Shulhan Arukh Yoreh Deah* 364:1; 368:1.
39 Deutscher, *The Non-Jewish Jews*, pp. 20–21.
40 Zvi Michalowski, quoted in Livingston, *Tradition and Modernism in the Shtetl Aisheshuk, 1919–1939*, pp. 67–68.

CHAPTER 10 : : AGRICULTURE

Information for this chapter also came from interviews with David Ejszyszki, Rina Lewinson Fenigstein, Temira Wilkanski Orshan, Reuven Paikowski, Moshe Sonenson, Moshe Szulkin, and Szeina Blacharowicz Wiszik.

1 Telushkin, *Ha-Torah ve-ha-Olam*, vol. 3, pp. 209–10.
2 *Slownik Geograficzny Krolestwa Polskiego*, vol. 2, p. 319.
3 Eishyshok was in the center of a predominantly agricultural region. According to a JDC survey in 1937 (JDC 4/21/37), the total number of people in the Eishyshok Township, consisting of Eishyshok and the surrounding villages and countryside, was 18,976, 83 percent of whom (15,758) were peasants. There were 38,947 hectares of land, only 16.7 percent of which (5,516 hectares) was infertile. In hectares, the fertile land consisted of:

Land fit for plowing	19,913
Prairie land	6,533
Pastures	5,502
Forests	483

How much of the land once belonged to Jews, or belonged to them at the time of the survey, is difficult to determine.
4 On the grain trade, see Davies, *God's Playground: A History of Poland*, vol. 1, pp. 256–92.
5 On Jews living in Lithuanian villages, see Kagan, *Jewish Cities, Towns and Villages in Lithuania*, pp. 642–701.
6 Farber, ed., *Olkeniki in Flames*, p. 20; *Recueil de materiaux sur la situation economique des Israelites de Russie*, vol. 2, p. 330; *Ha-Melitz*, no. 33.
7 One surviving member of the family traces the date of their receipt of the land that later became Dugalishok to the early decades of the eighteenth century (Ariel Lipkunsky, *Dogalishok*, p. 15). All that we can find in the official documents is that, according to the tax records of April 1858, the Lipkunski family were by then well-established farmers in the vicinity of Eishyshok (Vilnius Central Historical Archives, F515 a25, b81).
8 For the text of the 1804 Statute, see Levanda, ed., *Polnyi khronologicheskii sbornik zakonov i polozhenii kasaiushchiksia Yevreev*, pp. 54–60; on the anti-Jewish legislation concerning village Jews, see pp. 119–20, 216–17; see also Gessen, *Yevrei v Rossii*, pp. 31, 37, 109, and 315ff.
9 Greenberg, *The Jews in Russia*, vol. 2, pp. 30–32.
10 Frederic, *The New Exodus*, p. 130.
11 Wilkanski, *Ba-Heder*, pp. 33–34.
12 JDC file 891, April 30, 1937.
13 Greenbaum, *The Jews of Lithuania*, pp. 10–11.
14 This kind of torture of Jews was common in the Vilna region. See Klausner, *Vilna Yerushalaim de-Lita*, pp. 38–40; 78–79.
15 Interview with Elka Szulkin Jankelewicz, July 4, 1983. Elka was the daughter of Dina Malka, whose first husband was Avigdor Pachianko's son. In 1939 two researchers from a Vilna archive interviewed Dina Malka Szulkin in Eishyshok to verify documents concerning the tragic story of Count Potocki and his estate manager. Elka was present for the conversation. Dina Malka was murdered in Eishyshok on September 26, 1941, at the age of seventy-five.
16 Quoted in Mendelsohn, *Class Struggle in the Pale*, p. 2.
17 Maimon, *An Autobiography*. The autobiography of the Jewish philosopher Salomon Maimon (1754–1800) is an excellent source on the tensions between his Jewish arendator grandfather and the Polish magnate who owned the land, Prince Radziwill.
18 *Pinkas Vaad ha-Kehilot be-Lita*, 1644/404; 1623/87; 1627/121.
19 Ibid., 1623/46; 1628/202; 1623/73; 1627/120; 1623/83.
20 Ibid., 1628/145; 1623/95.

21 Wilkanski, *Mi-Gal El-Gal*, pp. 117–18.
22 Ibid., pp. 65–66.
23 Wilkanski, *Ba-Heder*, pp. 51, 56, 67. Wilkanski refers to him as "Reb Zvi the Chatterbox"; in Yiddish he was called "Reb Hersh, der Gorten Maggid."
24 Wilkanski, *Mi-Gal El-Gal*, pp. 180, 185, 200–202.
25 Wilkanski, *Ba-Heder*, pp. 15–16.
26 Shaul Schneider published a number of articles in the agricultural paper *Sadeh ve-Hadar*, and in *Davar*, winter 1932, the latter articles having been written at the request of Berl Katznelson.
27 On emigration to Argentina, see *Ha-Zefirah* and *Ha-Melitz*, August 2, 1889; see also Sanders, *Shores of Refuge*, pp. 170–71.

CHAPTER 11 :: COMMERCE

Information for this chapter also came from interviews with Naftali Berkowitch, Hayya Gruznik Dworkin, Gitta Politacki Ginsberg, Yossef Goldstein, Gitta and Shmuel Gross, Peretz Kaleko-Alufi, Basha Shuster Landsman, Rina Fenigstein Lewinson, Reuven Paikowski, Moshe Sonenson, Szeina Blacharowicz Wiszik, and Kunie Zlotnik.

1 Lithuanian Council, 1623/80.
2 Mordekhai Munesh Kaleko, *Zikhronot* (unpublished notebook III), pp. 1–3.
3 JDC/AR 33-44/891, p. 5, re borrowing from Gemilut Hessed Kassa.
4 Chaim Finkelstein, *Hajnt, A Zeitung bei Yidn*, p. 80.
5 *Unzer Hilf*, Eishyshok, December 11, 1936, p. 7.
6 *Haint*, May 17, 1928.
7 Wilkanski, *Mi-Gal El-Gal*, p. 117.
8 *Pinkas Vaad ma-Kehilot be-Lita*, 1639/358; 1676/713; Netzer, *Ma-avak Yehudei Polin*, pp. 190–92.
9 Szeina Blacharowicz Wiszik, notebook.
10 Wilkanski, *Ba-Heder*, p. 234. According to *Lietuvos TSR Urbanistikos Paminklai*, p. 53, the first match factory was built by J. Stalewitch from Vilna; the second was built in 1893 by Z. Brudman from Smargon.
11 Alufi and Barkali, eds., *Eishyshok Koroteah ve-Hurbanah*, p. 39; Wilkanski, *Mi-Gal El-Gal*, pp. 132–34, 140. Alufi and Barkali attribute the closing of the factory to high taxes.
12 Wilkanski, *Mi-Gal El-Gal*, pp. 31–32.
13 See Replianski, "Eishyshok in Likht fun Handl un Melokhe," pp. 2–3, for an exact breakdown. The same report, with slight variations, appears in English as JDC/AR 33-44/891, April 19, 1937. The 1937 total count given here, and the information about specific factories that follows, reflects additional information provided by Moshe Sonenson and Reuven Paikowski.
14 JDC/AR 33-44/891, p. 8.
15 On Rabbenu Gershon ben Judah, and the prohibition against reading another person's mail, see *Talmudic Encyclopedia*, vol. 17, pp. 452–54.
16 Wilkanski, *Mi-Gal El-Gal*, p. 90.
17 Ibid., pp. 102–3.
18 JDC Reconstruction Report re Volksbanks in shtetlekh in the Vilna district. JDC/AR 21-32/401; JDC/AR 33-44/891.
19 Levin, "10 Yor Gemilut Hessed Kassa."
20 Mordekhai Replianski, JDC/AR 33-44/891.
21 Ibid.
22 The Vilna *Unzer Hilf* was edited by Moshe Shalit, and had been published twice a month since June 1921 by EKOPO. See A. Y. Goldshmidt, "Di Yiddishe Presse in Vilne in di Yoren 1914–1922," in Jeshurin, ed., *Wilno*, p. 356.

CHAPTER 12 :: HANDICRAFTS

Information for this chapter also came from interviews with Moshe-Reuven Michalowski, Joe Weissmann (Hayyim-Yoshke Bielicki), and Rachel Asner Weitman, and from Szeina Blacharowicz Wiszik's notebooks.

1 JDC/AR 33-44/891.
2 *Unzer Hilf*, December 11, 1936, p. 10.
3 Ibid., p. 9.
4 See chart, p. 719.
5 Mordekhai Replianski, JDC/AR 33-44/891, pp. 4, 12.

CHAPTER 13 :: TRANSPORTATION

Information for this chapter also came from interviews with Elka Szulkin Jankelewicz, Moshe Kaganowicz, Yossef Kaplan, Reuven Paikowski, Rivka Lewinson Shanzer, Louis Shlanski, Fruml Slepak, Moshe Sonenson, Szeina Blacharowicz Wiszik, Joe Weissmann, and Dov Wilenski.

1 Wilkanski, *Ba-Heder*, p. 27.
2 For a similar incident involving the murder of a coachman, see Wilkanski, *Ba-Heder*, pp. 127–28.

CRAFTS IN EISHYSHOK, 1936

OCCUPATION	JEWISH	NON-JEWISH	JEWISH APPRENTICES	NON-JEWISH APPRENTICES	
Shoemaker	32	37	19	20	
Tailor	22	1	12	5	
Blacksmith	7	2	4	5	
Stitcher	7	1	4	—	
Baker	6	—	5	—	
Seamstress	12	—	10	10	
Seamstress (underwear)	5	—	2	3	
Carpenter (construction, furniture)	5	6	7	1	
Hatter	5	—	2	—	
Leathergoods maker	4	—	2	—	
Housepainter	4	1	2	1	
Tinsmith	3	—	1	—	
Glazier	3	—	—	—	
Box maker	2	—	2	—	
Photographer	2	—	—	—	
Barber	3	—	2	—	
Locksmith	—	4	2	4	
Bookbinder	1	—	—	—	
Mason	9	1	6	—	
Potter	2	—	—	—	
Watchmaker	2	—	1	—	
Felt boot maker	1	1	1	1	
TOTAL	139	55	88	50	332

Unzer Hilf, p. 9.

3 *Pinkas Vaad ha-Kehilot be-Lita*, 1752/947 [957].
4 Wilkanski, *Mi-Gal El-Gal*, p. 30.
5 Ashkenazi, *Terumat ha-Deshen*, paragraph 196; He-Hassid, *Sefer Hasidim*, pp. 191–92, paragraph 200.
6 *Yahadut Lita*, vol. 1, p. 371.
7 Slutski, ed., *Bobruisk Memorial Book*, vol. 3, p. 671.
8 Baer, "Mickiewicz un di Yiden fun Navaredok." S. Melzer, "Maaseh ha-Rav u-Baal ha-Agalah."
9 Wilkanski, *Mi-Gal El-Gal*, pp. 116, 123.
10 *Zaveti Lenina*, Vilnius, January 23, 1969.

CHAPTER 14 : : MARKET DAY

Information for this chapter also came from interviews with David Ejszyszki, Hillel Glombocki, Moshe-Reuven Michalowski, Shaul Schneider, and Moshe Szulkin.

1 Baron, *A Social and Religious History of the Jews*, vol. 4, p. 175.
2 Mahler, *Yahadut Polin*, pp. 100–1; Rabin, ed., *Grodno*, pp. 29–30.
3 Nathan of Hanover, *Yeven Mezulah*, pp. 86–87.
4 *Lietuvos TSR Urbanistikos Paminklai*, no. 6, pp. 12–15, has several references to Eishyshok as a major market town in the sixteenth and seventeenth centuries, including mention of John III Sobieski, king of Poland (1629–1696), granting Eishyshok the Magdeburg Charter, which gave Eishyshok and its residents commercial privileges usually granted only to much larger towns.
5 Wilkanski, *Ba-Heder*, pp. 60–61.
6 Ibid., p. 54.
7 Bloom, *A Shtetele in Poilen*, pp. 30–32.
8 Ibid., pp. 31–32.
9 Wilkanski, *Mi-Gal El-Gal*, pp. 161–62.
10 Wilkanski, *Ba-Heder*, p. 62.
11 Kahn, *No Time to Mourn*, pp. 12–13.
12 Ibid.
13 Wilkanski, *Ba-Heder*, p. 61.
14 Ibid., p. 160.
15 Ibid., pp. 62–63; Wilkanski, Ha-Rabbi, pp. 7–8.
16 Rabin, ed., *Grodno*, pp. 247–55.

CHAPTER 15 : : THE SHTETL HOUSEHOLD

Information for this chapter also came from interviews with Shalom Sonenson Ben-Shemesh, Arieh Berkowitch, Dora Zlotnik Berkowitch, Moshe Kaganowicz, Dr. Yehudit Berlin-Bar-Ilann Liberman, Rivka Remz Rewzin, Jean Rothstein, Miriam Kaplan Shapira, Moshe Sonenson, and Shoshana Sonenson.

1 According to S. D. Goitein's work on Jewish life in the Mediterranean basin between the tenth and thirteenth centuries, however, the Jewish family there was both patriarchal and patrilocal. Young couples established their households in the husband's father's home, which was usually in an extended-family compound. And the patriarchal, patrilocal family that Goitein describes as prevalent in medieval Egypt had much in common with the traditional Moroccan Jewish family of the eighteenth and nineteenth centuries. In Morocco, as in Aleppo, Syria, and in other Jewish societies in Muslim countries, Jewish women were largely confined to the home, with the men being responsible even for food shopping in the local market. See Goitein, *A Mediterranean Society: The Jewish Communities of the Arab World as Portrayed in the Documents of the Cairo Geniza*, vol. 3, *The Family*; and Deshen, "The Jewish Family in Traditional Morocco."
2 Etkes, "Marriage and Torah Study Among the Lomdim in Lithuania in the Nineteenth Century," pp. 158–59.
3 Leviticus 19:29; Sanhedrin 76/2.
4 R. Ha-Kohen, *Torat Yekutiel*; Lithuanian Council of 1761; for a comprehensive essay on the subject, see Halpern, *Eastern European Jewry*, pp. 289–309.
5 Maimon, *An Autobiography*, pp. 31–33.
6 Landau, *Noda be-Yehudah*, Sect. 2, Q 52, pp. 45–46.
7 N. Berlin, *Ha-Amek Davar*, commentary on Exodus 1:7.
8 Leoni, ed., *Wolozin*, p. 106.
9 *Yahadut Lita*, vol. 3, p. 592.
10 De Vaux, *Ancient Israel*, pp. 19–55.
11 Genesis 21:12.
12 Etkes, "Marriage and Torah Study," pp. 166–70.
13 A. Mapu, *Mikhtavim*, p. 185.
14 Grade, *My Mother's Sabbath Days*; Nedava, ed., *The Image of the Woman as Seen by V. Jabotinsky* (English title), pp. 51–54.

15 *Yahadut Lita*, vol. 3, pp. 593–94.
16 *Pinkas Vaad ha-Kehilot be-Lita*, 1623/44.
17 Epstein, *Mekor Barukh*, vol. 4, chapter 46.
18 On the lives of women in the immigrant generation, see Glenn, *Daughters of the Shtetl*, and S. Weinberg, *The World of Our Mothers*.
19 Some of the letters written to the *Jewish Daily Forward* over a period of sixty years, including a number by Lena Kaganowicz, were collected and published in book form: Isaac Metzker, ed., *A Bintel Brief*, Ballantine Books, 1972.
20 Moshe Kaplan, *Korot Hayyai* (unpublished manuscript), pp. 10–11, 19, translated from the Hebrew, Israel, 1973. I am grateful to Dr. Motti Melamud and Zippi Avrahami Melamud for entrusting me with their uncle's manuscript.
21 *Pinkas Vaad ha-Kehilot be-Lita*, 1628/128; 1632/258.
22 Ibid., 1629/145-46, 1634/281.
23 Mordekhai Aaron Guenzburg (1795–1846), one of the leading spokesmen for the Haskalah in Vilna, was active in the attempt to remove girls and women from commerce, out of concern for their moral well-being. See Guenzburg, *Kiryat Sefer*, p. 59.
24 From the beth din pinkas of Williampole (Vilijampole), Lithuania. The Central Archives of the Jewish People, Jerusalem, RU/82.
25 Wilkanski, *Ba-Heder*, p. 122. Interview with Rifka Remz.
26 Y. Meltzer, *Be-Derekh Etz ha-Hayyim*, vol 1, p. 16.
27 The edition of the Haffetz Hayyim's *Sefer Ahavat Hessed* published in New York by Pardes in 1946, for example, contains a "strict warning" that nobody can publish this or any other of his books, in this or any other country, without the permission in writing of Rebbetzin Freide Kagan (his second wife) and Rabbi Aaron Kagan (his son by his second marriage).
28 The model of Olkenik was made for the Museum of Kibbutz Lohamei ha-Gettaot (Ghetto Fighters House), Israel.

CHAPTER 16 : : RITES OF PASSAGE

Information for this chapter also came from interviews with Shalom Sonenson Ben-Shemesh, Rina Lewinson Fenigstein, Shneur Glombocki, Alexander Zisl Hinski, Shimon Hutner, Moshe Kaganowicz, Peretz Kaleko-Alufi, Gershon Katz, Mordekhai Lawzowski, Moshe-Reuven Michalowski, Temira Wilkanski Orshan, Vela Dubczanski Portnoy, Rivka Remz Rewzin, Shaul Schneider, Hayyim Sonenson, Moshe Sonenson, Zipporah Lubetski Tokatli, Szeina Blacharowicz Wiszik, Malka Matikanski Zahavi, and Philip Zlotnik (Avraham Fishl), and from Mordekhai Munesh Kaleko's notebooks.

1 Bava Batra 16/b.
2 Niddah 31/b; Bava Batra 6/b.
3 Genesis 22:17.
4 The Lithuanian Council objected to wachnacht. See *Pinkas Vaad ha-Kehilot be-Lita*, 1667/604.
5 Shternbuch, *Hilkhot Hagra u-Minhagav*, pp. 189–90.
6 Wilkanski, *Ba-Heder*, pp. 99–100.
7 After the incident with the Golden Calf, the Levites were consecrated into lifelong service to the Lord, taking the place of the firstborn males from the other Tribes of Israel. Numbers 8:14–19.
8 *Divrei Malkiel*, p. 83.
9 See Magen Avraham on *Shulhan Arukh Orah Hayyim*, 225:2.
10 Yevamot 63/a; 62/b.
11 Megila 27/a; Yevamot 113/a; Kiddushin 7/a.
12 Sota 2/a.
13 Kiddushin 70/a; Sota 3/b; Taanit 4:8; BB 109/b; Kiddushin 49/2; Pesahim 49/b; Yev 44/b; Sanhedrin 76/a–b.
14 Avot 5:21; Kiddushin 29/b; 30/a; Yevamot 63/b; Ketubot 63/a; Sota 4/b; Kiddushin 29/b.
15 Shabbat, 150/a; Psikta De-Rav Kahana, B.
16 *Pinkas ha-Medina*, 1623/34; 1623/36.
17 Information is based on marriage certificates, genealogies, personal interviews, and public archival records from 1891 to 1940. See, for example, the charts on pp. 722–729 based on material from the pinkas, 1891–1939.
18 Zborowski and Herzog, *Life Is with People*, p. 276.
19 Wilkanski, *Ba-Heder*, pp. 141–42.
20 Ketubot 102/a. The phrase "betrothal terms" is inaccurately translated as "prenuptial agreement" in the English version of Etkes, "Marriage and Torah Study Among the Lomdim in Lithuania in the Nineteenth Century," p. 160.
21 Y. L. Cohen, *Yiddishe Folkslider mit Melodies*, pp. 260, 257–73.
22 Wilkanski, *Mi-Gal El-Gal*, p. 110.
23 On the impact of the Haskalah on the East European Jewish family, see Biale, "Childhood, Marriage and the Family in Eastern European Jewish Enlightenment."
24 Wilkanski, *Mi-Gal El-Gal*, pp. 150–51.
25 Stampfer, "Marital Patterns in Interwar Poland."
26 Wilkanski, *Mi-Gal El-Gal*, p. 99.

MARRIAGES 1891–1903 TZARIST RUSSIA*

YEAR	TOTAL SUM OF MARRIAGES RECORDED IN PINKAS	INDIVIDUAL MARRIAGES RECORDED IN PINKAS	LOCAL GROOMS	OUT OF TOWN GROOMS	WIDOWED GROOMS	DIVORCED GROOMS
1891	22	19	14	5	3	
1892	30	15	10	5	4	
1893	23	8	4	4	2	
1894	52	22	8	14	3	
1895**	25	6	4	2		
1896	24	14	7	7	1	
1897	45	22	5	17	2	
1898	23	19	8	11	3	
1899	39	21	8	13	3	
1900	35	19	10	9	5	
1901	35	10	2	8	2	
1902	47	24	14	10	1	1
1903	63	20	8	12	3	
TOTAL	463	219	102	117	32	1

Chart based on 171 + 306 Hop ZAGST (Vilnius Vital Records Archive)
*F.728.A4, Marriage Records 1891–1903 Ejszyszki, Valstybinis Istorigos Archyvas
**Due to the Big Fire of 1895, the record is not complete.

AVERAGE AGE	LOCAL BRIDES	OUT OF TOWN BRIDES	WIDOWED BRIDES	DIVORCED BRIDES	AVERAGE AGE	SUM OF RUBLES LISTED IN KETUBAH HIGH AND LOW	
Mid 20's	18	1			Early 20's	300	100
Early 20's	14	1	2		Early 20's 2–18 yrs	700	100
Mid 20's	8		1		Early 20's	250	150
Mid 20's	22		2		Early 20's 1–19 yrs	600	100
Mid 20's to 31 yrs	6				Early 20's 1–18 yrs	300	100
Late 20's	10	4	1		Mid 20's	400	50
Late 20's	21	1	1	1	Early 20's 1–19 yrs	1000	50
Mid 20's	18	1			Early 20's 1–18 yrs	600	200
Upper 20's	13	8	1		Early 20's	500	50
Late 20's	19		5	1	Early 20's	1000	35
Mid 20's	7	3			Early 20's	500	50
Mid 20's	20	4	1	1	Early 20's	1000	50
Mid 20's 1–18 yrs	20		1			800	50
	196	23	15	3			

MARRIAGES 1904–1914 TZARIST RUSSIA

YEAR	TOTAL SUM OF MARRIAGES RECORDED IN PINKAS	INDIVIDUAL MARRIAGES RECORDED IN PINKAS	LOCAL GROOMS	OUT OF TOWN GROOMS	WIDOWED GROOMS	DIVORCED GROOMS
1904	14	14	2	2	1	
1905	10	10	2	8	1	2
1906	11	11	2	9	3	
1907	12	12	7	5	2	1
1908	11**	10	2	8	1	1
1909	9	9	1	8	1	
1910	7	7	3	4		
1911	4	4	1	3	1	
1912	16	16	2	14	3	
1913	7	7	3	4	1	
1914	9	9	1	8	1	
TOTAL	110	109	26	83	15	4

Chart based on 171 + 306 Hop ZAGST (Vilnius Vital Records Archive)
*Some grooms younger than brides
**One marriage missing from the records

AVERAGE AGE*	LOCAL BRIDES	OUT OF TOWN BRIDES	WIDOWED BRIDES	DIVORCED BRIDES	AVERAGE AGE	SUM OF RUBLES LISTED IN KETUBAH HIGH AND LOW	
Mid 20's	13	1		1	Low 20's 2-19's	1000	50
Mid 20's 1-30	10			1	Low 20's 2-19's 1-25	500	50
20's 1-50 2-30's	4	7	2		Low 20's 1-35 1-42	1000	50
20's 1-48 1-30 3 NA	6	6	2		Low 20's 1-45 3 NA	300	50
20's 1-35	7	3			20's	400	50
Late 20's 1-18	7	2			20's 1-19 1-32	300	50
Mid 20's 1-17	4	3			20's 1-32	200	50
2-19 1-25 1-46	1	3		1	20's 1-33	200	50
20's 1-18 1-36 1-40 1-69	12	4			20's 2-19 2 Mid 60's	200	50
20's 1-61	3	4	3		Low 20's 1-19 1-52	200	50
20's 1-17 1-62	6	3	1		20's 1-18 1-37	200	50
	73	36	8	3			

YEAR	TOTAL SUM OF MARRIAGES RECORDED IN PINKAS	INDIVIDUAL MARRIAGES RECORDED IN PINKAS	LOCAL GROOMS	OUT OF TOWN GROOMS	WIDOWED GROOMS	DIVORCED GROOMS
1916	3	3	1	2		
1917	4	4	3	1		
1918	5	5	2	3		
1919	2	2	2			
1920	5	5	3	2		
1921	NO RECORDS					
1922	12	12	7	5	1	
1923	16	16	6	10	1	
1924	14	14	10	4	1	
1925	15	8	7			
1926	8	8	4	4		
1927	5	5	4	1		
1928	10	10	8	2		
1929	17	17	9	8	1	1
1930	14	14	6	8	1	1
1931	7	7	5	2		

AVERAGE AGE	LOCAL BRIDES	OUT OF TOWN BRIDES	WIDOWED BRIDES	DIVORCED BRIDES	AVERAGE AGE
Mid 20's	3				Mid 20's
Low 20's	4				Low 20's
2-20's 2-30's 1-58	4	1			20's 1-48
1 NA 1-25	2				1 NA 1-26
1-18 3-20's 1-30	4	1			2 late teens 3-20's
20's 30's 1-40	9	3	1		1-17 20's 1-30
1-17, 20's, 1-31, 1-46	13	3	1		20's 1-36
20's 1-31, 1-71	12	2			1-19 20's 1-33
20's 3 Early 30's 1-NA	12	3			20's 1-32 1-NA
20's 1-40	7	1			20's 1-18
20's	5				20's
5-20's 5-30's	8	2			20's
20's 2-40's 2-50s 1 NA	15	2			1-18, 1-19 20's, 1-31 1-40
20's 2-30's 1-40	12	2			1-18, 20's
20's 1-39 1 NA	6	1			20's, 1 NA

(continued on next page)

YEAR	TOTAL SUM OF MARRIAGES RECORDED IN PINKAS	INDIVIDUAL MARRIAGES RECORDED IN PINKAS	LOCAL GROOMS	OUT OF TOWN GROOMS	WIDOWED GROOMS	DIVORCED GROOMS
1932	14	14	5	9		
1933	17	17	8	9	1	
1934	7	7	1	6*		
1935	8	8	7	1		
1936	6	6	3	3		
1937	7	7	3	4*		
1938	11	11	4	7		
1939	5	5	5		1	
TOTAL	210	210	113	91	7	2

Vilnius State Archives (VVA) Vilniaus Valstybimis Archyvas.
1916–1923, all records were recorded retroactively in 1924.
*One groom from Palestine
**A marriage took place in 1921 recorded in 1938 for purpose of visa for children to emigrate to the U.S.A.
Notes:
A. All marriages recorded in Polish. No record of money in Ktuba.
B. Marriage in years 1916–1923 retroactively recorded in the year 1924 during the Second Polish Republic.
C. In 1931 different Polish form from previous used to record marriage.
D. In 1932 and 1933 different Polish form from previous two used to record marriage. Also used a Hebrew form. Some marriages therefore recorded both in Hebrew and Polish.
E. In 1934–39 Polish form same as used in year 1931. One groom from Palestine.
F. In 1936 some couples have year of birth given instead of age.
G. In 1937–38 year of birth of couples recorded, not age. One groom from Palestine.
H. In 1939 some couples have year of birth, not age.
I. All records are in Polish. Government did not permit to record in Hebrew as it was done during Tzarist Russia.

AVERAGE AGE	LOCAL BRIDES	OUT OF TOWN BRIDES	WIDOWED BRIDES	DIVORCED BRIDES	AVERAGE AGE
20's 1-34	14				20's, 1-30
20's 2-30's 1-65	10	7	1		1-19, 20's, 3-30, 1-49
20's 2-30	7				20's
20's 1-30	8				20's 2-30's
20's 1-41	6			1	20's, 1-39
1-18 20's 3-30's	4	3			20's
20's 1-48	9	2			20's, 3-30's**
1-19, 20's 1-30's	4	1			20's 1-31 1-40
	178	34	3	1	

27 Ibid., pp. 157–58.
28 Ibid., p. 44.
29 Genesis 24:60.
30 In the original Yiddish: "Wos is libe?/Di libe is a likht/brent ois-mitn block/du kukst zikh arum es iz finster zurick." This appeared in a mazel tov letter written in rhymes sent from Eishyshok to America, in honor of Zipporah Levin's marriage to David Levin (born Portnoy; changed name to immigrate), on August 10, 1923.
31 In the original Yiddish: "Di gebbers zeinen vi a samovar/Mi brent in shtub un mi shaint afn tretovar."
32 Wilkanski, *Mi-Gal El-Gal*, pp. 59–61.
33 Wilkanski, *Ba-Heder*, p. 28.

CHAPTER 17 : : LIFE ON THE FRINGE

Information for this chapter also came from interviews with Shalom Sonenson Ben-Shemesh, Dora Zlotnik Berkowitch, Naftali Berkowitch, Hayya Gruznik Dworkin, David Ejszyszki, Shlomo Farber, Rina Lewinson Fenigstein, Elka Szulkin Jankelewicz, Moshe Kaganowicz, Leon Kahn, Peretz Kaleko-Alufi, Hayyim Moshe Kaplan, Yossef Kaplan, Moshe-Reuven Michalowski, Reuven Paikowski, Vela Portnoy, Rivka Remz Rewzin, Miriam Kabacznik Shulman, Moshe Sonenson, Yitzhak Sonenson, Moshe Szulkin, Zipporah Lubetski Tokatli, and Szeina Blacharowicz Wiszik (and her notebooks).

1 Avot 1:12.
2 Deuteronomy 24:1; Isaiah 50:1; Jeremiah 3:8; Ketubot 72/a; Sota 25/a; Yevamot 56/b.
3 Ketubot 77/a; PDR 3:126; Ishuth 13:4–14:8.
4 Ketubot 65/b.
5 See charts, pp. 732–735.
6 Wilkanski, *Mi-Gal El-Gal*, pp. 96–97.
7 Ibid., pp. 16–17, 27, 52.
8 Ibid., p. 42.
9 *Yahadut Lita*, vol. 1, p. 378. In Spektor's two-volume responsa, *Ein Yitzhak*, there are over seventy questions regarding agunot in vol. 1.
10 Wilkanski, *Mi-Gal El-Gal*, pp. 8–9.
11 Ibid., p. 130.
12 Leviticus 21:9. See Commentary by Rashi.
13 Wilkanski, *Mi-Gal El-Gal*, pp. 19–24, 43.
14 Ibid., p. 29.
15 Re comparative divorce rates: In 1897, for example, Russian Jewish males in the larger cities of the Pale of Settlement had a divorce rate of 5.4 per 1,000 marriages, versus an overall 2.2 among the males in other ethnic and religious groups. For Jewish and non-Jewish women, the divorce rates were 19.1 and 5.4, respectively. (The reason the divorce rate for Jewish women was so much higher than for Jewish men was that once a person remarried, he or she no longer appeared as a divorce statistic, and many more men than women remarried, in large part because of the stigma against divorced women.) While the non-Jewish divorce rates appear particularly low due to the inclusion of so many Roman Catholics, for whom divorce is forbidden, the Jewish rate was still substantially higher than that of any other group in the region at that time.

During the interwar years in Poland, the divorce rate of Jewish urban males was 2.8 per 1,000 in 1921 (a particularly low rate, which was probably a reflection of the fact that it took a while for things to get back to normal after the war, or else that the records were inaccurate), and 6.8 in 1931, versus 3.5 and 7.9, respectively, for non-Jewish males in the same cities. For Jewish females the rates were 9.6 and 17.3, respectively; and for non-Jewish females 6.9 and 14.8, respectively.
16 Wilkanski, *Ba-Heder*, p. 109.
17 Trumot 81, Talmud Yerushalmi; Hagiga 3/a.
18 Bava Kama 8:4 (Mishnah).
19 Caro, *Shulhan Arukh Hoshen Mishpat* 235/2; Hatam Sofer, *Responsa Orah Hayyim*, no. ff.3/2.
20 See Falk, *The Law of Marriage*, p. 143; *Shulhan Arukh Even ha-Ezer* 44/2.
21 Farber, ed., *Olkeniki in Flames*, pp. 19–20.
22 Ibid., p. 47.
23 Luba Ginunski Deutch denies that she had any part in the eviction of the rabbi, claiming that she learned about it only after her return to Eishyshok from Troki, at which time she was very surprised to hear that her colleagues had made such a drastic move (interview, June 13, 1988).
24 Wilkanski, *Mi-Gal El-Gal*, p. 100.
25 Taanit 23/A.
26 For a slightly different version of Arke's last days under German occupation, see Kahn, *No Time to Mourn*, pp. 29–30.
27 Wilkanski, *Ba-Heder*, p. 114.
28 See *Talmudic Encyclopedia*, vol. 17, pp. 435–569; to safeguard mute and deaf women from sexual abuse, marriage was recommended.

29 The character of Nohem the Pope served as an inspiration for the protagonist Nahummadman in a 1977 play by Yaffa Eliach and Uri Assaf, *The Last Jew.* For a number of descriptions of Nohem the Pope, see Livingston, *Tradition and Modernism in the Shtetl Aisheshuk: 1919–1939*, pp. 87–90.

30 Kahn, *No Time to Mourn*, p. 22.

31 Interview with Reuven Paikowski; for a different account of his death, see Kahn, *No Time to Mourn*, p. 23.

32 Farber, ed., *Olkeniki in Flames*, p. 54; Eliach, *Hasidic Tales of the Holocaust*, pp. 50–55.

33 Prinz, *Popes from the Ghetto.*

34 In the integration of converts into the nobility, see Ciechanowiecks, "A Footnote to the History of the Integration of Converts into the Ranks of the Szlachta in the Polish-Lithuanian Commonwealth."

35 See Endelman, ed., *Jewish Apostasy in the Modern World.*

36 "Report of the Procurator of the Holy Synod for 1825–55"; "Otchet Ober-Prokurator Sviateishago Synoda, 1825–1855"; *Sbornik Imp. russkago istoricheskago obshchestva* 98 (1890): 457–60.

37 Ginsburg, "Yiddishe Kantonistn" (Jewish Cantonists); A. Lewin, *Kantonistn.* Lewin was married to Luba Hutner, Rabbi Zundl Hutner's granddaughter.

38 Ginsburg, *Meshumodim in Zarish Russland* (Converts in Tzarist Russia), pp. 194–206.

39 Ibid., pp. 119–56; Tzitron, *Meshumodim: Tipn un Siluetn fun Noentn Over* vol. 2, pp. 3–38; and anonymous entry in *Yevreiskaia, Entsiklopediia*, vol. 15, pp. 584–87.

40 Jacob Brafman's book was *Kniga Kahala* (The Book of the Kahal). See Ginsburg, *Meshumodim*, vol. 2, pp. 145, 147, 223.

41 Klausner, *Vilna, Yerushalaim de-Lita*, p. 79.

42 Stanislawski, "Jewish Apostasy in Russia: A Tentative Typology," pp. 189–206.

43 On Antoni Slonimski's attitude toward Jews and Judaism in the pre- and post-Holocaust era, see Low, "Antoni Slonimski in Hebrew."

44 Farber, ed., *Olkeniki in Flames*, p. 18.

45 David Osishkin (Ejszyszki), *Zikhronot: Me-Ejszyszok ve-ad Kfar Hess*, pp. 1–2. (The memoir is a 74-page typed Hebrew manuscript, translated from the original Yiddish, which he wrote for his children and grandchildren. I have both the Hebrew and the Yiddish manuscripts.) In the folklore surrounding conversion, there is a frequent association between Yom Kippur and apostasy.

46 Since the days of the Lithuanian Council, the amount of money to be spent retrieving Jews who sought conversion was subject to local community discretion (*Pinkas Lita*, 1670/646). Apparently, the bulk of the financial burden in such cases fell upon the family.

47 Osishkin (Ejszyszki), *Zikhronot*, p. 67.

48 Arendt, *The Origins of Totalitarianism*, pp. 68–79.

49 Livingston, *Tradition and Modernism in the Shtetl Aisheshuk, 1919–1939*, p. 68.

50 On kugel and meshumodim, see Schwarzbaum, *Studies in Jewish and World Folklore*, pp. 334–42.

51 Clemens, *My Husband Gabrilowitsch*, pp. 6–7, 31–32, 52–53, 156–57, 306–9; Hill, *Mark Twain, God's Fool*, pp. 44–45, 215.

52 Aviva, "Parashat Ger ha-Zeddek" (The Case of the Ger Zeddek), in Kopelowicz, ed., *Sefer Ilya, Yizkor Bukh*, pp. 23–34. (This is the memorial book to Ilya, the shtetl where the Ger Zeddek was betrayed. In order to preserve the shtetl's good name, the article dedicated to this illustrious proselyte is silent about his betrayal by an Ilya resident, an event that for two hundred years was an enigma to the shtetl.) Litwin, "Graf Potocki der Ger Zeddek."

53 Among the earliest sources for the story of the Ger Zeddek was the non-Jewish author I. Krashevski. Other sources include *Yevreyskaya Biblioteka*, vol. 3, pp. 229–37; Litwin, *Yiddishe Neshomes*, vol. 1, pp. 1–8. See also Klausner, *Vilna, Yerushalaim de-Lita*, p. 79.

54 Interview with Elka Szulkin Jankelewicz. Elka said this account of Potocki's conversion was told by her mother, Dina Malka Szulkin, to the two researchers from a Vilna archive to whom she also told the story of Avigdor Pachianko and his death at the hands of the Potocki family in the nineteenth century. In the Szulkin version of the eighteenth-century Ger Zeddek story, the name of the young Count Potocki is Adam rather than Valentine, and the Potocki family estate was managed at that time by an Eishyshkian Jew named Avigdor — details that suggest the two different Potocki family stories from two different eras got conflated in the Ger Zeddek story recounted to the archivists. See also note 15, chapter 10.

55 Wilkanski, *Ba-Heder*, p. 20.

56 In an interview, Shlomo Farber said that in the course of his research on Olkenik he came across

YEAR	NAME OF HUSBAND	AGE	NAME OF WIFE	AGE
1891–1902	NO DIVORCES			
1903	Feivel ben Shlomo Yurkanski	25	Yitzle bat Eliezer	20
1904–1908	NO DIVORCES			
1909	Zalman ben Yitzhak Weinstein	26	Beila bat Yerachmiel Popko	27
1910	Mordechai ben Yitzhak Becker	29	Esther Rivka bat Nachum-Ber Ganzterowitch	24
1911	Reuven ben Yitzhak Michalowski	27	Nechama bat Aron Vishyski	31
	Yitzhak ben Wolf Becker	72	Zipa bat Avraham Lubetcki	54
1912–1913	NO DIVORCES			
1914	Eliyahu ben Lazar Kantor	39	Dabrushe bat Moshe Galub	23
TOTAL:	6 Divorces			

F.728.A.4. B. 340 VCIA (Vilnius Central Historical Archive)
Recorded in Hebrew and Russian.

DATE OF DIVORCE	REASON FOR DIVORCE	TOWN OF HUSBAND	TOWN OF WIFE	GRANTERS OF DIVORCE
July 4	No Reason	Eishyshok	Eishyshok	Rabbi & Bet Din
March 2	No Reason	Michalishok	Warinowa	Rabbi Zundl Hutner. Witnesses: Moshe Yehuda ben Avraham Stalewitch, Asher ben Yossef Marcus
February 21	No Reason	Olkeniki	Malawa	Rabbi Zundl Hutner. Witnesses: Moshe Yehuda ben Avraham Stalewitch, Yitzhak ben Moshe Ilitowitch
October 25	No Reason	Eishyshok	Eishyshok	Rabbi Zundl Hutner. Witnesses: Shlomo Heller, Moshe Paikowski
December 18	Amicable	Eishyshok	Eishyshok	Rabbi Zundl Hutner. Witnesses: Shlomo Heller, Moshe Paikowski
July 16	Amicable	Novy Dvor	Vasilishok	Rabbi & Beth Din

DIVORCES 1922–1939 POLISH SECOND REPUBLIC*

YEAR	NAME OF HUSBAND	AGE	NAME OF WIFE	AGE
1922	Nutel, son of Owseja Arjowicz	24	Rosa, dghtr of Josel Oranski	24
1928	Chaim Leib, son of Lejzer Pruczanski	NG	Cype, dghtr of Boruch Kabacznik	NG
1928	Lejb, son Szlomo Tawszunski	47	Sora, dghtr of Uri Katz Festensztejn	32
1930	Israel, son of Chaim Berkowicz	73	Rochela, dghtr of Mejacha Pupko	60
1931	Judel, son of Lejzer Wolak	23	Sima, dghtr of Lejby Jankielewicz	24
1931	Berko, son of Abram Rajch	23	Judisa, dghtr of Chaim Hirsza Plotnik	19
1935	Wolf, son of Abram Szmuel Wajn	31	Szosia, dghtr of Pinchos Jurkansk	31
1938	Yankiel, son of Szmuel Rogowski	62	Mira, dghtr Josiel Bass	33
TOTAL:	8 Divorces			

Recorded only in Polish, since the usage of all other languages was prohibited in the recording of official documents. See Shlomo Netzer, *The Struggle of Polish Jewry for Civil and National Minority Rights 1918–1922*, p. 177.

*No divorces recorded retroactively from 1915 through 1921.

DATE OF DIVORCE	REASON FOR DIVORCE	TOWN OF HUSBAND	TOWN OF WIFE	GRANTERS OF DIVORCE
July 24	Not Given	Radun	Eishyshok	Rabbi Rozowski. Witnesses: Jeko Jlutomicz, Je Sonenson
June 3	Not Given	Eishyshok	Eishyshok	Rabbi Rozowski. Witnesses: Juda Stolewicz, Jeko Jlutowicz
Oct. 17	Not Given	Eishyshok		Rabbi Rozowski. Witnesses: Juda Stolewicz, Jeko Jlutowicz
July 3	Not Given	Eishyshok		Rabbi Rozowski. Witnesses: Jeko Jlutowicz, Jankiel Hamarski
March 18	Not Given	Swieckong		Rabbi Rozowski. Witnesses: Jeko Jlutowicz, Jankiel Hamarski
Dec. 8	Not Given	Vilna		Rabbi Rozowski. Witnesses: Jeko Jlutowicz, Meyer Jeko Mackiewicz
April 7	Not Given	Buenos Aires, Argentina	Eishyshok	Rabbi Rozowski. Witnesses: Jeko Jlutowicz, Israel Chinski
Nov. 2		Wydynianczy		Rabbi Rozowski. Witnesses: Yzrael? Ilowsira, Mowsa Tabolski

entries in the *Seimeni Pisok*, the book where all births were registered, that supported this belief.

57 Pat, *Ash un Fajer*, pp. 24–28; Bartoszewski and Lewindwna, *Ten Jest Z Ojczyzny Mojej*, pp. 816–19.

58 After the Holocaust a number of ideologically motivated conversions took place throughout Europe, among them those of the chief rabbi of Rome and Brother Daniel, who was from a shtetl near Eishyshok. See Tec, *When Light Pierced the Darkness: Christian Rescue of Jews in Nazi-Occupied Poland*.

CHAPTER 18 : : HOLIDAYS

Information for this chapter also came from interviews with Sarah Plotnik Avrahami, Shalom Sonenson Ben-Shemesh, Hayya Gruznik Dworkin, David Ejszyszki, Shlomo Farber, Rina Lewinson Fenigstein, Nehama Koppelman Frischer, Gitta Gross, Rebbetzin Zivia Hutner Hadash, Szymen Hutner, Elka Szulkin Jankelewicz, Peretz Kaleko-Alufi, Hayya Streletski Kosowski, Reuven Paikowski, Rachel Lewinson Peres, Rivka Remz Rewzin, Moshe Sonenson, Joe Weissmann, Dov Wilenski, and Malka Matikanski Zahavi, and from Pessia Skir's unpublished memoir and Szeina Blacharowicz Wiszik's notebook.

1 The Jewish calendar must meet two requirements, both solar and lunar. The balancing of the solar and lunar results in the following sequences: years are grouped in cycles of nineteen, twelve of these years consisting of twelve lunar months, and seven of them, the leap years, consisting of thirteen months. See Spier, *The Comprehensive Hebrew Calendar*, pp. 217–28.

2 See Slutski, ed., *Bobruisk Memorial Book*, 1967, vol. 2, p. 675.

3 Flavius Josephus, *Wars*, vol. 2 19/12.

4 Shabbat 19/b.

5 Proverbs 31:10–31.

6 Wilkanski, *Mi-Gal El-Gal*, pp. 166–67.

7 Wilkanski, *Ba-Heder*, pp. 108, 116–17.

8 On the many aspects of this issue, see Katz, *The Sabbath Gentile*.

9 Judah Halevi, *Kuzari*, 3, 10.

10 Szeina Blacharowicz Wiszik, notebook.

11 Pessah Cofnas, "Di Kleine Vaibalakn," in *Mein Shpetiker Shnit*, unpublished memoir, 1977, pp. 122–25. The shtetl also provided the poor with food for the three mandatory Sabbath meals, and also for Saturday night's melaveh malkah meal.

12 Zohar, Vaikra 35:2.

13 In some communities, selihot did not last the entire month but began during the last week of Elul. Caro, *Shulhan Arukh Orah Hayyim*, 581/a.

14 Wilkanski, *Ba-Heder*, p. 37.

15 Ibid., p. 76.

16 Rosh Hashanah, Talmud Yerushalmi, chapter 1, Halakha 3.

17 Wilkanski, *Ba-Heder*, pp. 37–38.

18 *Mahzor Vitry*, p. 373.

19 Wilkanski, *Ba-Heder*, pp. 38–39.

20 Ibid., pp. 123–26.

21 Wilkanski, *Mi-Gal El-Gal*, pp. 143–44.

22 Megillah 7/b.

23 Esther 9:22.

24 Wilkanski, *Ba-Heder*, pp. 58–61, 92.

25 Ibid., p. 23.

26 Maimonides, *The Guide for the Perplexed*, 3:43.

27 Goren, *Moadei Israel*, pp. 292–309.

28 Wilkanski, *Ba-Heder*, p. 105.

29 On this form of folk art, see *Tracing An-Sky Jewish Collections from the State Ethnographic Museum in St. Petersburg*, p. 47.

30 Wilkanski, *Ba-Heder*, p. 115.

CHAPTER 19 : : MEDICAL CARE

Information for this chapter also came from interviews with Batia Lubetski Barkali, Hayya Gruznik Dworkin, Moshe Edelstein, David Eszyszki, Shlomo Farber, Hillel Glombocki, Shoshana Hutner Hinski, Moshe Kaganowicz, Leah Koppelman Kaleko, Peretz Kaleko-Alufi, Reuven Paikowski, Rivka Remz Rewzin, Moshe Sonenson, Zipporah Lubetski Tokatli, Reuven Vasilinski, Szeina Blacharowicz Wiszik, and Atara Kudlanski (Goodman) Zimmerman.

1 Ruppin, *The Jews in the Modern World*, p. 423.

2 Lestchinsky, "The Economic and Social Development of the Jewish People."

3 A survey carried out in Frankfurt in 1855, for example, showed that the average life span of Jews was about 49 years, versus about 37 years for non-Jews. In Pest, Hungary, in 1872, the number of Jewish children under the age of 14 was 33 percent

of the total Jewish population, while in the non-Jewish population children under the age of 14 were only 10 percent of the total. Ben-Sasson, ed., *A History of the Jewish People*, pp. 790–93.

4 Wilkanski, *Mi-Gal El-Gal*, p. 92.

5 Rabbi Malkiel Tenenbaum, former student at the Eishyshok Kibbutz ha-Prushim, described this burial practice in his *Divrei Malkiel*, vol. 2, p. 154, paragraph 94.

6 Mordekhai Munesh Kaleko, unpublished notebook.

7 These two spells are from Shlomo Farber's collection of regional magic spells. I purchased the original parchments from him and translated them. See also J. Shaked, *Magic Spells and Formulae*.

8 Isserlin, *Psakim u-Ketavim*, p. 13.

9 Based on the research of Benyamin's granddaughter by marriage Dr. Barbara Flood (who is a descendant of a *Mayflower* Pilgrim). Benyamin had ten children, four by first wife Malkele, and six by second wife Dinah. The six by Dinah emigrated to the United States and changed their name to Suhoff.

10 Information based on August 28, 1944, Standard Certificate of Death, the State of New Hampshire, for Annie Foster, who was the eldest daughter of Nehemia der Feldsher. I am grateful to Rosalind Foster Rosenblatt, Annie's daughter and Nehemiah's granddaughter, for her extensive research on the family, and for sharing the family archive with me.

11 Kaleko, *Yomon*, pp. 51–52.

12 Stampfer, *Ha-Yeshivah ha-Litait be-Hithavutah*, pp. 142–44; Bar-Ilan, *Mi-Volozhin ad Yerushalaim*, pp. 108–11.

13 *Pinkas Navaredok, Memorial Book*, pp. 76–78.

14 Wilkanski, *Mi-Gal El-Gal*, pp. 13, 116.

15 Ibid., p. 13.

16 For a detailed report concerning the organizations under the umbrella of the Medical Council, known as the OSE, see JDC/AR 2132, files 324–412.

17 JDC/AR 2132 #G-37.

18 The numbers are based on Szeina Blacharowicz Wiszik's notebooks; interviews, birth certificates, passports, and photographs. See also Dobroszycki, "The Fertility of Modern Polish Jewry."

19 See charts, pages 738–39.

CHAPTER 20 : : ENTERING MODERNITY: THE HASKALAH

Information for this chapter also came from interviews with Avraham Botwinik Epstein, Shlomo Farber, Hannah Glombocki Gunzberg, Shoshana Hutner Hinski, Peretz Kaleko-Alufi, Gershon Katz, Zvi Michalowski, Reuven Paikowski, Fania Rozowski, Shaul Schneider, Miriam Kabacznik Shulman, Hayyim Sonenson, Moshe Sonenson, Yitzhak Sonenson, Zipporah Lubetski Tokatli, and Szeina Blacharowicz Wiszik; from Pessah Cofnas's unpublished *Mein Shpetiker Shnit*; and from Pessia Skir's unpublished memoir.

1 For an English translation of Joseph II's *Toleranzpatent*, see Mendes-Flohr and Reinharz, eds., *The Jew in the Modern World*, pp. 34–36.

2 Ibid., pp. 62–67, for additional excerpts in English translation of "Words of Peace and Truth."

3 *Ha-Meassef* was a Hebrew-language journal published by the proponents of the Haskalah in Germany during the last decade of the eighteenth century and the first of the nineteenth. See Zinberg, *A History of Jewish Literature*, vol. 8, pp. 117–18.

4 Ibid., pp. 109–12.

5 Mahler, *Ha-Hasidut ve-ha-Haskalah*, pp. 155–208; A. Rubinstein, "Ha-Haskalah ve-ha-Hasidut: Peiluto Shel Yossef Perl," vol. 12, pp. 166–78; *Educational Encyclopedia*, vol. 4, pp. 585–87.

6 For his Five-Point Program, see Levinsohn, *Beth Yehudah*, pp. 348–54.

7 In 1835, out of 1,906 university students in Russia, 11 were Jews; in 1840, out of 2,866 students in higher institutions of learning in Russia, 15 were Jews, and out of the total of 80,017 students in primary and secondary schools, 48 were Jews.

8 The historian Simon Dubnow believes this anonymous memorandum was penned by Kisilev. See *Voskhod*, 1901, books 4 and 5, pp. 29–40 and 3–9.

9 Max Lilienthal first settled in New York City, where he directed a private boarding school, and later, until his death, was rabbi of a prominent congregation in Cincinnati. He taught at Hebrew Union College there and was a trustee of the University of Cincinnati. On his activities in Russia, see Dubnow, *History of the Jews in Russia and Poland*, vol. 2, pp. 50–59; Ginsburg, "Max Lilienthal's Activities in Russia: New Documents"; Hessen, "I. B. Levinsohn

YEAR	MALES	FEMALES	TWIN MALES	TWIN FEMALES	TWINS 1 BOY 1 GIRL	
1891	42	55				
1892	35	28				
1893	34	25				
1894	51	23	1 set			
1895	BIG FIRE — NO OFFICIAL RECORDS					
1896	60	19				
1897	55	22				
1898	43	27				
1899	44	23				
1900	40	28				
1901	48	22				
1902	32	23		1 set		
1903	47	20				
1904	31	19	1 set			
1905	28	15				
1906	21	5	1 set			
1907	14	19				
1908	16	17			1 set	
1909	27	18				One male born in 1909, birth recorded in 1936
1910	33	7	1 set			One male born in 1910, birth recorded in 1936 One female born in 1910, birth recorded in 1937
1911	17	5				
1912	28	6				One female born in 1912, birth recorded in 1935 One set of female twins born in 1912, births recorded in 1935. One male born in 1912, birth recorded in 1936. One female born in 1912, birth recorded in 1937.
1913	27	1				One male born in 1913, birth recorded in 1937.
1914	11	5			1 set	One male born in 1914, birth recorded in 1936. One female born in 1914, birth recorded in 1936.
TOTAL	784	433	4	1	2	

Chart based on F.728. A.4. B.337. VCIA (Vilnius Central Historical Archive) and Iapy, ZAGS (Vilnius Records Archive) 340.
Records inscribed in Russian and Hebrew.
Dates of circumcision inscribed in most cases.

YEAR	MALES	FEMALES	TWIN MALES	TWIN FEMALES	TWINS 1 BOY 1 GIRL	
1915	NO RECORD					One female born in 1915, recorded in 1936.
1916	17*	11	*Records record 19 males, only 17 males listed.			Two females born in 1916, recorded in 1936. One female born in 1916, recorded in 1937.
1917	13*	14	*Records record 12 males, 13 males listed.			
1918	10	3				Two males born in 1918, births recorded in 1937.
1919	6	8	Note: 2 couples had 2 children in same yr.			
1920	11	4				One male born in 1920, birth recorded in 1937.
1921	NO RECORD					
1922	16	13				
1923	19	15				
1924	29	5			1	One male born in 1924, birth recorded in 1937.
1925	20	8				
1926	30	8				
1927	28	5				
1928	31	11				
1929	22	5				
1930	7	5				One male born in 1930, birth recorded in 1937.
1931	23	11			1	
1932	26	5				
1933	23	13	1			
1934	19	16				
1935	20	13				
1936	23	21				
1937	35	18				
1938	17	12			1	
1939	9	9				

*1916–1923 — retroactively recorded in 1924.
Note: Records inscribed only in Polish.
1916–1923 — all records were recorded retroactively in 1924 during the Second Polish Republic.
1929–1930 Different Polish format used from previous years to record births.
1931–1939 Change in Polish format used to record births. Age of parents given.
1937–1939 Year of birth of parents given (not age).
1935, 1936, 1937 — Figures include births of previous years but recorded in 1935, 1936, 1937 (see above).

and Dr. M. Lilienthal"; Philipson, "Max Lilienthal in Russia"; Stanislawski, *Tsar Nicholas I and the Jews*, pp. 49–96.

10 Greenberg, *The Jews in Russia*, vol. 1, p. 75.

11 The rabbinical seminary from which the Vilna pedagogical seminary evolved had operated between 1847 and 1873. See Slutski, "Beit ha-Midrash le-Rabbanim be-Vilna."

12 Excerpts from Judah Leib Gordon's "Awaken, My People," *Ha-Karmel*, April 6, 1866.

13 *Ha-Shahar* 2 (1870–71), no. 8, pp. 353–43. According to Gordon's biographer, "For Whom Do I Toil?" was not an expression of failure or despair, but one of Gordon's periodic ponderings on the meaning of his life, venting the frustration he felt as a lonely campaigner for moderate reform of the life and culture of the Jews of Russia. See Stanislawski, *For Whom Do I Toil?*, p. 105.

14 *Ha-Shahar*, Adar 1878, no. 4.

15 Wilkanski, *Mi-Gal El-Gal*, pp. 114–15.

16 Poet Nathan Alterman (1910–1970) in his play *Kinneret Kinneret* referred to the halutzim of the Second Aliyah as "one big orphanage," an allusion to the many children (albeit adults now themselves) who had cut their ties with their parents back home, or had been disowned by them.

17 Alufi and Barkali, eds., *Eishyshok Koroteah ve-Hurbanah*, p. 30.

18 The exact figure was 31.5 percent Jews out of a total of 1,168 students. Dov Lipec, "Ha-Hinukh ha-Ivri ve-ha-Tenuah ha-Ivrit be-Lita Ha-Atzmait 1920–1940."

19 Davies, *God's Playground: A History of Poland*, vol. 2, pp. 401–10. Davies uses a figure of 3 million Jews, but that doesn't include the Jews in the territories annexed by the Second Polish Republic.

20 M. Eisenstein, *Jewish Schools in Poland, 1919–1939*, p. 4.

21 Kazdan, *Die Geschichte fun Yiddishen Shulvezen in Umuphengiken Poilen*, p. 549. For a somewhat lower figure — 15,166 (versus 15,486) — see Mauersberg, *Szkolnictwo Powszechne Dla Mniejszo Sci Narodowych W Polsce W Latach 1918–1939*, p. 167.

22 M. Eisenstein, *Jewish Schools in Poland*, p. 24.

23 Plantovski, *Le-Toldot Mosdot ha-Hinukh Shel Tarbut be-Polin*; Scharfstein, *Ha-Hinukh ve-ha-Tarbut Ha-Yivrit be-Eiropa Bein Shtei Milhamot ha-Olam*, 1957. Figures differ, however. According to the Tarbut Schools' own census, taken in 1921, total enrollment was 25,829; by mid-1923 there were 30,672 (and as many as 12 high schools); by 1934–35 the number had risen to 35,000. Mendelsohn, *The Jews of East Central Europe Between the World Wars*, p. 66.

24 M. Eisenstein, *Jewish Schools in Poland*, p. 80.

25 Kaleko-Alufi, "Beit ha-Sefer ha-Yivri be-Ivie," pp. 368–70.

26 Goldstein, ed., *Forty Years of Struggle for a Principle: The Biography of Harry Fischel*, pp. 23, 50, 308, 318.

27 Kaganowicz, ed., *Sefer Zikaron le-Kehilat Ivie*, pp. 365–70.

28 During the years between the two world wars, Tarbut faced a great demand for textbooks and other printed educational materials. Most of the textbooks they published were in Hebrew and Yiddish, and most — 75 percent — were published in Poland. Scharfstein, "Sifrei Limud ve-Zramin Hinukhyim."

29 Rachel Kaleko Abiri (Strikowski), "'Yizkor' Ziyun Nefesh le-Peutei Gani," pp. 130–31.

30 Ogen, "Ka-Halom Yauf," p. 128.

31 On the nature and impact of the "White Papers," see Lissak, ed., *The History of the Jewish Community in Eretz-Israel Since 1882* (English title), vol. 1, pp. 310–17, 426–32.

32 Kahn, *No Time to Mourn*, pp. 13–15.

CHAPTER 21 : : ZIONISM

Information for this chapter also came from interviews with Sarah Plotnik Avrahami, Shalom Sonenson Ben-Shemesh, Naftali Berkowitch, Luba Ginunski Deutch, Yitzhak (Munin) Drori, Rabbi Zfania (Munin) Drori, Hayya Gruznik Dworkin, David Ejszyszki, Faivl Glombocki, Hillel Glombocki, Shira Gorshman, Zvi Harris, Shoshana Hutner Hinski, Elka Szulkin Jankelewicz, Peretz Kaleko-Alufi, Mordekhai Lawzowski, Temira Wilkanski Orshan, Rachel Lewinson Peres, Moshe Szulkin, Dov Wilenski, Dov Wolotzky, and Malka Matikanski Zahavi; from a letter from Yossef Resnik; and from Esther Katz Resnik's and Pessia Skir's unpublished memoirs.

1 Psalms 137:5.

2 On the three-way covenant between God, Jew, and gentile with regard to redemption and catastrophe, see Ravitzky, *Messianism, Zionism, and Jewish Religious Radicalism* (English title), pp. 277–305.

3 Alkalai, "The Third Redemption, 1843," p. 106.

4 *Yahadut Lita*, vol. 1, p. 490.

5 Ibid.

6 Ibid., pp. 101–2, 491–93.

7 Ibid., pp. 512–14.

8 On the image of Herzl in art, see *Herzl in Profile: Herzl's Image in the Applied Arts.*
9 For the travels and settlement of Lithuanian Jews in the Holy Land, see Morgenstern, *Messianism and the Settlement of Eretz-Israel* (English title), pp. 94–132; Etkes, *Lita be-Yerushalaim.*
10 Wilkanski, *Mi-Gal El-Gal,* pp. 7–8.
11 Ibid., p. 169.
12 Ibid., pp. 195–97.
13 Alufi and Barkali, eds., *Eishyshok Koroteah ve-Hurbanah,* p. 29.
14 Wilkanski, *Mi-Gal El-Gal,* pp. 170–71, 197–99.
15 Ibid., p. 172.
16 Wilkanski, *Ha-Galila/Beer Hafarnu,* p. 9.
17 On the Hebrew language during the Second Aliyah, see Greenzweig, "Maamada Shel ha-Yivrit be-Yemei ha-Aliyah ha-Shnia," p. 198.
18 Wilkanski, *Ha-Galila/Beer Hafarnu,* pp. 115–16.
19 Wilkanski, *Senuniyyot,* pp. 133–35.
20 On the Minsk Conference, see Norok, *Veidat Zionei Russia be-Minsk, 1902;* Maor, *Ha-Tenuah ha-Zionit be-Russia,* pp. 198–208; Even-Shoshan, ed., *Minsk Ir Va-Em,* vol. 1, pp. 373–82.
21 Sanders, *Shores of Refuge,* pp. 328–58.
22 On the life of Trumpeldor, see Lipovetsky, *Joseph Trumpeldor;* Freulich and Abramson, *The Hill of Life.*
23 The popular name for the Gedud group that served the British army was the "gyps," short for "Egyptians" (whom they were replacing). On the "gyps," see Pishi, *Memorial Volume, 1901–1991,* pp. 11–12.
24 *Eishyshok Koroteah ve-Hurbanah,* pp. 9–10.
25 On certificates granted to students, see Leichter and Milkov, eds., *Sefer Olei ha-Sartifikatim* (Students' Rescue by Aliyah).
26 Vladimir Jabotinsky's writings have been collected in volumes published in Hebrew in Tel Aviv, 1947–59, by his son Avi. The essence of his philosophy of Jewish history and life is best expressed in his biblical novel *Samson the Nazarite* (1930). The Zionist leader Chaim Weizmann's memoir *Trial and Error* (1950) is an excellent account of this most stormy era of Zionist history.
27 On the impact of the "White Papers," see Lissak, ed., *The History of the Jewish Community in Eretz-Israel Since 1882* (English title), vol. 1, pp. 310–17, 426–32.
28 Made by the Russian Marxist Georgy Plekhanov to Zeev Vladimir Jabotinsky.
29 *Kartuz-Breze: Our Town Memorial Book* (English title), pp. 22–24.
30 For details on the ideological dispute between left and right in the Gedud, see *Mitokh Maavak ha-Raayoni, Teudot u-Mikhtavim,* file no. 16, Beth Trumpeldor Archives, Tel Yossef, especially *Mi-Hayyenu,* no. 56, 28 Av, 5684 (August 28, 1924); A. Cnaani, "'Hasemol Ba-Gedud," *Yediot mi-Vaad ha-Poel shel ha-Histadrut,* January 13, 1927, document no. 61, the last document in the minutes from a stormy meeting. David Ben-Gurion was among the many participants; see Shapira, *Berl Katznelson: A Biography,* vol. 1, pp. 227–31; 283; Shapira, *Visions in Conflict* (English title), pp. 157–207.
31 Mintz, "Zikhronot al Menahem Elkind," p. 129. "Reshimat Havrei Gedud ha-Avoda she-Yardu le-Russia," file no. 17, Beth Trumpeldor Archives, Tel Yossef (the list was updated in 1984 by Zahava Erlich). Isserson, "Meshak Tel Yossef Nesiat Elkind."
32 Agnon spent many evenings in the company of Szyrke Groszman and her fellow halutzim in Jerusalem; see Erez, ed., *Sefer ha-Aliyah ha-Shlishit,* vol. 1, p. 441. See also Barzel, ed., *Love Stories of S. Y. Agnon* (English title), pp. 132–34. Mordekhai Dayagi, a contemporary of Szyrke Groszman who shared many of the same experiences in Tel Yossef and in the Gedud, and who later visited her in the Soviet Union during the 1960s, said in an interview that her being the inspiration for *Shira* was a matter of fact rather than speculation.
33 Mintz, "Me-Eretz-Israel le-Sibir u-Vehazara."
34 Szyrke Grosztman, *33 Nowele,* p. 82.

CHAPTER 22 : : CULTURAL LIFE

Information for this chapter also came from interviews with Sashka Frankl Ariel, Shalom Sonenson Ben-Shemesh, Yitzhak (Munin) Drori, Rabbi Zfania (Munin) Drori, David Ejszyszki, Rina Lewinson Fenigstein, Faivl Glombocki, Hillel Glombocki, Avraham Shmuel Gross, Alexander Zisl Hinski, Peretz Kaleko-Alufi, Hayya Streletski Kosowski, Avraham Aviel Lipkunski, Moshe-Reuven Michalowski, Reuven Paikowski, Hadassah Berlinski Rabinowitz, Esther Katz Resnik, Shaul Schneider, Miriam Kaplan Shapira, Miriam Kabacznik Shulman, Hayyim Sonenson, Moshe Sonenson, Moshe Szulkin, Zipporah Lubetski Tokatli, Szeina Blacharowicz Wiszik, and Malka Matikanski Zahavi, and from a letter from Antoni Gurak.

1 Rabbi Shimshon dealt with many of the major public issues that affected the Jews of his time, including the wearing of the "badge of shame" imposed by the Lateran Council in 1215. See Urbach, *The Tosaphists: Their History, Writings and Methods* (English title), pp. 281–83.

2 Wilkanski, *Mi-Gal El-Gal*, p. 205. On Meir Wilkanski's place in and contribution to Hebrew literature and the Second Aliyah, see G. Shaked, *Ha-Siporet ha-Yivrit, 1880–1980*, pp. 55–59; Smilanski, *Mishpahat ha-Adamah, vol. 4, pp. 282–87; Thon, "M. Wilkanski, Mi-Zayarei ha-Aliyah ha-Shnia"*; Govrin, *Maftehot*, pp. 14–15; Govrin, *Ha-Omer*, pp. 86–89, 142–45, 243–45; Keshet, *Maskiyot*, pp. 109–21; Ehud ben Ezer, "Be-Yemei ha-Aliyah le-Meir Wilkanski," *Ha-Aretz*, August 27, 1971. Meir also translated selections from Goethe into Hebrew. Yitzhak Wilkanski was a contributor to most of the major publications of his time, writing under the names E. Zioni, I. Avuyah, and Yitzhak Elazari-Volcani Wilkanski. His writings were gathered in ten volumes. He was also considered the architect of modern agricultural techniques in Eretz Israel. See *Davar*, February 3, 1950, and Sdomi, *Siah Rishonim*.

3 Ogen, "Ka-Halom Yauf," p. 128.

4 Yitzhak and Meir Wilkanski were invited by many editors in the Diaspora and in Eretz Israel to contribute to a wide range of newspapers and journals. Under his various pen names, Yitzhak Wilkanski published articles in David Frishman's *Hashiloah* (named after a spring near Jerusalem), Bener's *Ha-Meorer* (The Awakener), *Ha-Zefirah* (The Dawn), *Ha-Olam* (The World), *Hedim* (Echoes), *Maabarot* (Passages), *Ahdut Haavodah* (Unity of Labor), *Revivim* (Raindrops), *Rassviet* (The Dawn), *Hazofeh-Warsaw* (The Spectator). Meir published in *Ha-Poel ha-Zair* (The Young Laborer), and *Ha-Omer* (The Sheaf), among others. Even Leah, during her very short life, published in *Haolam ve-Hateva* and *Olam Kattan* (Small World).

5 Wilkanski, *Mi-Gal El-Gal*, pp. 29–30; Friedberg, *Zikhronot le-Veit David*, based on an original text by Herman Rekendorf. The ongoing adventures of its characters were popular among the generation who grew up in the Haskalah era, when the Hebrew language was being revived, and remained popular with young people well into the twentieth century.

6 Barkali and Alufi, eds., *Eishyshok Koroteah ve-Hurbanah*, p. 31, erroneously attributes the founding of Rak Ivrit to Sarah Wilkanski.

7 During a convention for Hebrew culture in Berlin in 1910, Dr. Yossef Klausner reported that there were 127 chapters of Ivriah in various countries. *Ha-Olam*, January 1910, p. 18.

8 I am grateful to Rabbi Zfania (Munin) Drori, son of Frume-Rochl and Yitzhak Munin, for giving me access to the letters.

9 The Warsaw *Haint* (Today), and the Vilna papers, *Zeit* (Time), *Der Vilner Tog* (The Vilna Daily), *Der Ovent Kurier* (Evening Courier), and various Polish dailies were among the most popular newspapers in the shtetl during the '30s, after the highway was paved, which allowed papers to be delivered to the shtetl on the day of publication. Bar, ed., *The Jewish Press That Was*, pp. 17–43, 223–36.

10 *Yahadut Lita*, pp. 212–13.

11 Wilkanski, *Mi-Gal El-Gal*, p. 165.

12 Tory-Golub, ed., *Mariampole*, p. 14.

13 Kaleko, *Yomon* (unpublished diary), p. 44.

14 Ibid., pp. 51–52.

15 On the Strashun library, see Jeshurin, ed., *Wilno*, pp. 273–87, 739–40.

16 JDC, 4/21/37.

17 Charney, "Ikh For Kain Eishyshok" and "Ikh Were a Kunanmakher." I am grateful to Dina Abramowitz from YIVO for bringing the source to my attention.

18 JDC/AR 33-44/891, p. 3.

19 For more on the life and work of Brenner, see Waxman, *A History of Jewish Literature*, vol. 4, pp. 92–105.

20 Wilkanski, *Ba-Heder*, pp. 105, 114–15.

21 Farber, ed., *Olkeniki in Flames*, pp. 94, 87; Chaim Grade's Yiddish poem "The Scholars of Lithuania" has a section about the Hazzon Ish vacationing in Olkenik.

22 Zilberzweig, "Di Vilner Trupe," pp. 575–76.

23 Another such fan was Commander Hoffman in Ivie; see Kaganowicz, ed., *Sefer Zikaron le-Kehilat Ivie*, p. 388. On theater audiences of the time, see Tory-Golub, ed., *Mariampole*, p. 117.

24 Alufi and Barkali, eds., *Eishyshok Koroteah ve-Hurbanah*, pp. 34–36.

25 See Sandrow, *Vagabond Stars*, pp. 132–63.

26 The same plays were performed in other shtetlekh in the vicinity. See Avinadav, ed., *Kehilat Ostila*, pp. 205–6.

27 In the original Yiddish: "Yude-Mendl der Katchap/Hot gekhapt a guten Klap/Farn Otobus/A make em in fuss." Interview with Joe Weissmann (Hayyim-Yoshke Bielicki).

28 In the original Yiddish: "Zogn di Kabzonin zu di reikeh leit/Mir zainen mahatonim gleikh mit aikh/Yeder oreman mit zain bisl mintz/Endingt zain gewins glaikh mit aikh." Interview with Joe Weissmann.
29 N. and Y. Gross, *Haseret ha-Ivri*, pp. 116–22.
30 Leoni, ed., *Wolozin*, pp. 336–37.

CHAPTER 23 : : EMIGRATION TO AMERICA

Information for this chapter also came from an interview with Ellen Broida Hawley and from Pessia Skir's unpublished memoir.

1 Wilkanski, *Ba-Heder*, pp. 16–17.
2 For an account of the pogroms accompanied by fine original source material, see Greenberg, *The Jews in Russia*, vol. 2, pp. 19–26.
3 Most of the information on the Kirshner-Abrams families is based on Maynard Abrams with the assistance of his wife Gertrude, *The Ancestors of Our Children*.
4 In the records of the Hevrah Bnei Avraham Shmuel Anshei Eishyshker he appears as "Aharon Don"; in Wilkanski, *Mi-Gal El-Gal*, he is simply "Don."
5 Quoted in Wilkanski, *Mi-Gal El-Gal*, p. 97.
6 *Ha-Melitz*, June 4, 1895; June 30, 1895.
7 The number of immigrants is based on public and private records; burial plots of the Eishyshker society in New York, New Jersey, Boston, Chicago, and Detroit; interviews with immigrants and their descendants.
8 I am grateful to Ann Greenspan, daughter of Nathan Greenspan and granddaughter of Sarah Broida-Greenspan, for gathering this information about the Broida family from cemetery headstones, city directories, old letters, and family history files. A letter regarding the family history from Hilda Fish Broida, granddaughter of Jacob and Anna Broida, to Ann Greenspan, dated July 21, 1990, Jerusalem, was particularly helpful.
9 I am grateful to Rosalind Rosenblatt, granddaughter of Nehemia der Feldsher, for assembling all the birth and death records, family photos, and headstone photos of the Kiuchefksi family, as well as their up-to-date records.
10 On David Foster and the family business, see *Adath Yeshurun Synagogue, Silver Anniversary, 1912–1937* (Manchester, N.H., 1937), p. 36; James Lenane, "Twenty Million Pounds of Meat," in *New Hampshire Profiles*, November 1965, pp. 24–29.
11 Wilkanski, *Mi-Gal El-Gal*, pp. 91–92.
12 Quoted in Livingston, *Tradition and Modernism in the Shtetl*, pp. 12–13.
13 Aishishkin, *Sefer Dvar, Ezekiel.*
14 Quoted in Livingston, *Tradition and Modernism in the Shtetl*, p. 12.
15 I am grateful to Atara Goodman Zimmerman for giving me the original family records.

CHAPTER 24 : : ON THE EVE OF THE STORM

Information for this chapter also came from interviews with Sarah Plotnik Avrahami, Shalom Sonenson Ben-Shemesh, Luba Ginunski Deutch, Hayya Gruznik Dworkin, Professor Elisha Efrat, Nehama Koppelman Frischer, Sol Lubek (Zalman Lubetski), Vela Dubczanski Portnoy, Fania Rozowski, Gilad Shoshani, Moshe Sonenson, and Moshe Szulkin; and from letters and documents given to me by Zippi Avrahami and Dr. Motti Melamud.

1 Balaban, "U trumny budowniczego."
2 On ritual slaughter in Poland, see E. Melzer, *Maavak Medini be-Malkodet: Yehudei Polin, 1935–1939*, pp. 97–110, 243–50.
3 Heller, *On the Edge of Destruction*, pp. 112–14.
4 E. Melzer, "Anti-Semitism in the Last Years of the Second Republic."
5 I am grateful to Malka Matikanski's daughter Nehama Gil-Ad and granddaughter Malka Matikanski, namesake of her murdered grandmother, for sharing this correspondence with me.
6 Rabbi Szymen Rozowski, Tevet 5, 5695 (December 11, 1934); Rabbi Zusha Lichtig, *Shusham Purim*, Adar 15, 5699 (March 6, 1939), YIVO, Vaad ha-Yeshivot files no. 117–118.
7 For a detailed description of the outbreak of World War II, see Davies, *God's Playground: A History of Poland*, vol. 2, pp. 435–41.
8 From a memo on the refugee problem in Lithuania, submitted by a Mr. Beckelman, February 1940, JDC/AR 33-44, 1933–1944, file no. 875. According to Beckelman, on January 31, 1940, there were 9,824 refugees registered with the Jewish refugee committee under the auspices of the JDC (and of course

many thousands who were not registered — hence the disparity between the 9,824 figure and the 14,000 figure), 7,415 of whom were men, 1,926 women, and 483 children. Broken down by occupation, these 9,824 included 2,500 halutzim, 500 doctors, lawyers, and journalists, 2,000 yeshivah students, as well as labor leaders, educators, teachers, and community workers. For eyewitness accounts, see Rindzionski, *Hurban Vilna*, pp. 13–20; Fishoff, "Iber Vilne, Telz un Japan," 1990, pp. 22–24.

9 M. Hodorowski, "Do Not Be Afraid, We Will Free You." For more descriptions of Eishyshkian hospitality, see Alufi and Barkali, eds., *Eishyshok Koroteah ve-Hurbanah*, pp. 50–55.

10 For an eyewitness account, see Versano, "The Last Days of the Patria" (English title). See also Steiner, *The Story of the Patria.*

11 Rindzionski, *Hurban Vilna*, p. 23.

12 The tradition of not transferring Maftir Yonah is recorded in the Yom Kippur guidelines from the shtetl of Slonim. See file RU/82, Central Archives for the History of the Jewish People, Jerusalem.

CHAPTER 25 : : DI SHEHITA (THE SLAUGHTER)

Information for this chapter also came from interviews with Gershon Katz, Sol Lubek, Zvi Michalowski, Reuven Paikowski, Zahava Garber Paikowski, Miriam Kabacznik Shulman, Moshe Sonenson, Szeina Blacharowicz Wiszik, and Malka Matikanski Zahavi.

1 For more on the Judenrat, see Gutman and Haft, eds., *Patterns of Jewish Leadership in Nazi Europe, 1933–1945*, and Trunk, *Judenrat: The Jewish Councils of Eastern Europe Under Nazi Occupation*. Unfortunately, these fine studies of the Judenrat totally exclude the Judenrat in non-ghetto communities during 1941, during the height of the Einsatzgruppen activities, as well as in many small communities like Radun, which did have ghettos.

2 Brown, "The Third Reich's Mobilization of the German Fifth Column in Eastern Europe."

3 Shalom Sonenson Ben-Shemesh, "Hurban Eishyshok." In this article he did not mention the first Judenrat. When asked about the omission, he stated that the editors of the book had condensed the sufferings of the two different Judenrate into one. My own article (written when I was ten years old) in the same volume was also significantly edited and altered.

4 Ibid.

5 Ibid., pp. 63–64.

6 Ran, ed., *Jerusalem of Lithuania: Illustrated and Documented*, vol. 2, p. 430.

7 The gold he gave to the Germans on this day is listed on his reparation request, Moshe Sonenson Case, #10773, a file spanning the years 1956–1972.

8 For a history of the shaulisti, which omits any mention of their collaboration with the Nazis, see *Encyclopedia Lituanica*, vol. 5, pp. 74–77.

9 Kahn, *No Time to Mourn*, pp. 36–38.

10 Lehmann, *Du wirst Leben und dich rachen: Die Geschichte des Juden Zwi Michaeli*, pp. 26–27.

11 Lehmann, *Du wirst Leben*, pp. 30–34.

12 Shalom Sonenson Ben-Shemesh, testimony given to a Jewish historian, Munich, 1946. Other testimony estimated the number of lunatics "overseeing" the crowd in the Old Beth Midrash at sixty to seventy.

13 B. Lifshitz, "In Shturm," pp. 245–46.

14 Ibid.

15 Ibid., p. 247.

16 Ibid., pp. 249–50.

17 Eliach, "Jew, Go Back to the Grave," in idem, *Hasidic Tales of the Holocaust*, pp. 53–55.

18 Lifshitz, "In Shturm," p. 251.

19 Kahn, *No Time to Mourn*, pp. 40–41.

20 Hilberg, ed., *Documents of Destruction*, pp. 47–55.

CHAPTER 26 : : IN GHETTO RADUN

Information for this chapter also came from interviews with Avraham (Avremke) Asner, Shalom Sonenson Ben-Shemesh, Yossele Hamarski (Joe Camarone), Kazimierz Korkuc, Moshe-Reuven Michalowski, Zvi Michalowski, Zahava Garber Paikowski, Miriam Kabacznik Shulman, Moshe Sonenson, and Szeina Blacharowicz Wiszik.

1 Moshe Sonenson, during the ten years of his Siberian exile, 1945–55, compiled a list of 720 escapees, about 520 of them from Eishyshok itself. According to his brother Shalom Sonenson Ben-Shemesh, 490 escaped; see "Yameah ha-Ahronim Shel Eishyshok," p. 65.

2 Yaffa bat Moshe Sonenson, age ten, "Be-Mahboim," pp. 67–68. The editors took some liberties with my article.
3 Kahn, *No Time to Mourn*, p. 57.
4 On the Katyn massacre, see Lukas, *The Forgotten Holocaust*, index; Karski, *The Great Powers in Poland, 1919–1945*, index.
5 In Lehmann, *Du wirst Leben und dich rachen*, pp. 48–51, the entire blame is placed on Dolinski and the Judenrat. The fact that it was Pietka Barteszewicz who disclosed her true identity is never mentioned.
6 Avraham Lipkunski Aviel, Yad Vashem, 03/508. See also A. Aviel Lipkunsky, *Dogalishok*, p. 82.
7 Kahn, *No Time to Mourn*, pp. 53–54. Similar descriptions of this time come from an unpublished diary kept by Elia Margolies, who was born in Warsaw, spent time in Ghetto Radun, and later became a partisan. The daily entries in his diary, written in Polish, with segments in French and Russian, give an eyewitness account of his experiences in the ghetto and with the partisans. I am grateful to Luba Katz for making me aware of this diary. See Margolies diary, Section I, p. 28, April 3, 1942, Yad Vashem, Kaf-5.
8 Avraham Lipkunski Aviel, Yad Vashem 03/508; Kahn, *No Time to Mourn*, p. 57. On the postwar trial of Werner, see Manor, Ganusowitch, and Lando, eds., *Sefer Lida*, pp. 383–85.
9 Kahn, *No time to Mourn*, p. 57–58. Noah Dolinski was a relative of Kahn's. They lived in the same apartment in the ghetto.
10 Margolies diary, Section A, p. 34, May 10, 1942.
11 Liba Ahuva Shlosberg, *Mi-Labat Esh*, pp. 40–44.
12 Lossin, *Pillar of Fire*, p. 315; Yaffa bat Moshe Sonenson, "Be-Mahboim," pp. 68–69. In *Mi-Labat Esh*, p. 46, Liba Shlosberg tells the story — which concerns her father, Shmaye-Mendl — in a different version; see also Kahn, *No Time to Mourn*, pp. 65–66.
13 Re the Lida massacre, see Manor et al., eds., *Sefer Lida*, p. 281; re the Radun massacre, a list of the Jews in Ghetto Radun is in the archives of the former Soviet Union, but the list is inaccurate, missing a few hundred people.
14 Margolies diary, Section A, pp. 34–36, May 11, 1942.
15 Shlosberg, *Mi-Labat Esh*, pp. 52–53.
16 Manor et al., eds., *Sefer Lida*, pp. 305, 327.
17 Kahn, *No Time to Mourn*, pp. 70–73.

CHAPTER 27 : : IN HIDING

Information for this chapter also came from interviews with Kazimierz Korkuc, Niomke (Benyamin) Rogowski, Miriam Kabacznik Shulman, Ida Solome, Moshe Sonenson, and Yitzhak Sonenson.

1 Keneally, *Schindler's List*; Yaffa Eliach and Bonnie Gurewitsch, eds., *Center for Holocaust Studies Newsletter*, 1988, vol. 3, no. 4, pp. 18–21; Yahil, "Raoul Wallenberg: His Mission and His Activities in Hungary"; Anger, *With Raoul Wallenberg in Budapest: Memories of the War Years in Hungary*.
2 On rescuers in Nazi-occupied Europe in general and on Poland in particular, see Oliner and Oliner, *The Altruistic Personality: Rescuers of Jews in Nazi Europe*; Tec, *When Light Pierced the Darkness: Christian Rescue of Jews in Nazi-Occupied Poland*.
3 Kahn, *No Time to Mourn*, pp. 44–45, 76–77.
4 Rabin, ed., *Grodno*, pp. 521–614. In Hebrew.
5 See Gutman, ed., *Encyclopedia of the Holocaust*, vol. 1, "Aid to Jews by Poles," pp. 9–11, and "Armia Krajowa," pp. 88–89. Unfortunately, these entries omit all mention of the hostility of the AK toward the Jews, as well as the murder of many Jews by Poles who did not belong to the AK.
6 Krakowski, *The War of the Doomed*, pp. 276–77.
7 On the killing of Jewish partisans by the AK, see Gutman and Krakowski, *Unequal Victims*, p. 131; Krakowski, *The War of the Doomed*, pp. 41, 133; Lipkunsky, *Dogalishok*, pp. 250–55; Cholawski, *Soldiers from the Ghetto*, p. 162.
8 Yaffe, *Be-Ghetto Novogrudek u-ba-Tenuah ha-Partizanit*, p. 251.
9 Lipkunsky, *Dogalishok*, pp. 189–90; Avraham Lipkunski Aviel, Yad Vashem 03/508, pp. 51–73, 80–81.
10 Bryk, "The Struggles for Poland."
11 Kazimierz Korkuc, in a 1986 interview, presented a significantly different view of the character of the priest in Juryzdyki, and of the nature of his anti-Semitic sermons. He portrayed him as a compassionate individual, sensitive to Jewish suffering.
12 The decisions made at this meeting were put in writing. Moshe Sonenson saw the signed document in the files of the NKVD in Eishyshok in the fall of 1944.
13 The list was compiled by Moshe Sonenson, with additions and corrections by Reuven Paikowski. Moshe Sonenson carried this list with him to the day of his death, when it was found in his suit pocket.

CHAPTER 28 : : IN THE FORESTS

Information for this chapter also came from interviews with Miriam Ribak Sonenson Ben-Shemesh, Dora (Dobke) Kremin Dimitro, Moshe Edelstein, Shneur Glombocki, Yossele Hamarski (Joe Camarone), Adair Kirschner Harris, Evelyn (Hava) Landsman Kahn, Avraham Aviel Lipkunski, Sol Lubek, Reuven Paikowski, Zahava Garber Paikowski, Niomke (Benyamin) Rogowski, Avraham Teikan, Joe Weissmann, Avraham Widlanski, and Szeina Blacharowicz Wiszik.

1 I am grateful to Svenja Kadegge for assisting me in finding these records. German federal archives, Koblenz, file no. R6/369.
2 Avraham Lipkunski Aviel, Yad Vashem 03/508, pp. 97–108; Shlosberg, *Mi-Labat Esh*, pp. 58–59.
3 Lipkunski Aviel, ibid.; Shlosberg, ibid., pp. 65–69.
4 Shlosberg, ibid., pp. 84–87.
5 Bielski and Bielski, *Jews of the Forest* (English title); Yaffe, *Be-Ghetto Novogrudek u-ba-Tenuah ha-Partizanit*; Eliach and Gurewitsch, eds., *Center for Holocaust Studies Newsletter*, vol. 3, no. 7, 1991 (final issue), pp. 50–55; Tec, *Defiance: The Bielski Partisans*.
6 Interview with Evelyn (Hava) Landsman Kahn. According to other accounts, Hayyim Shuster was killed by Jewish partisans.
7 Lipkunsky, *Dogalishok*, pp. 191–95; Lipkunski Aviel, Yad Vashem 03/508. Eckman and Lazar, *The Jewish Resistance*, pp. 86–87; Elia Margolies, unpublished diary, section II, p. 45, June 10, 1943.
8 Lipkunsky, *Dogalishok*, pp. 207–11; Lipkunski Aviel, Yad Vashem 03/508, p. 94. See also Margolies diary, section II, pp. 47–49, June 17 and 19, 1943.
9 Kahn, *No Time to Mourn*, p. 145.
10 Lipkunsky, *Dogalishok*, p. 179.
11 Lazar, *Destruction and Resistance*, pp. 150–54.
12 For more on the departures from Ghetto Vilna in 1943, and the disputes that were waged between the partisans, the leaders of the ghetto underground, and the ghetto administration, see Arad, *Ghetto in Flames: The Struggle and Destruction of the Jews of Vilna in the Holocaust*; N. Dworzecki, *Jerusalem of Lithuania in Revolt and Holocaust* (English title); Einat, *Libel Without Disgrace* (English title); Lipkunsky, *Dogalishok*, pp. 187–88.
13 Cholawski and Levin, "Partisans," p. 1117.
14 On the Jews in General Anders's army, see Nussbaum, *Story of an Illusion: The Jews in the Polish People's Army in the USSR* (English title).
15 Hecht, *A Child of the Century*, pp. 567–70.

CHAPTER 29 : : LIBERATION AND ITS AFTERMATH

Information for this chapter also came from interviews with Avraham Asner, Miriam Ribak Sonenson Ben-Shemesh, Shalom Sonenson Ben-Shemesh, Dora (Dobke) Kremin Dimitro, Israel Dimitro, Moshe Edelstein, Yossele Hamarski, Moshe Kaganowicz, Avraham-Meishke Kaplan, Betty Yurkanski Kaplan, Yossef Kaplan, Zvi Michalowski, Reuven Paikowski, Miriam Kabacznik Shulman, Fruml Slepak, Moshe Sonenson, Yitzhak Sonenson, Szeina Blacharowicz Wiszik, and Feigl Garber Yurkanski.

1 It was a common phenomenon in post-liberation Poland for Poles who had saved Jews to keep their heroic behavior a secret, out of fear of revenge from their friends and neighbors. See Borwicz, "Polish-Jewish Relations, 1944–1947," p. 193.
2 Moshe Sonenson, quoted in Lossin, *A Pillar of Fire*, p. 409. The book is based on a TV documentary in which Moshe Sonenson appears.
3 The statement in Lithuanian sources that Eishyshok was destroyed during July 1944 is not accurate. See Buchaveckas, *Salcios Zeme*, p. 206.
4 Quoted by Yisrael Gutman in his excellent essay, "Polish and Jewish Historiography on the Question of Polish-Jewish Relations During World War II," p. 182; for additional information, see Engel, *Facing a Holocaust: The Polish Government in Exile and the Jews, 1943–1945*.
5 I am grateful to Joe Weissmann (Hayyim-Yoshke Bielicki) for giving me the postcard.
6 Kahn, *No Time to Mourn*, p. 150.
7 Lipkunsky, *Dogalishok*, p. 266.
8 Ibid., p. 267.
9 Shlosberg, *Mi-Labat Esh*, pp. 108–9.
10 Lipkunsky, *Dogalishok*, pp. 212–15.
11 Michalowski, "Hitnaplut ha-Partizanim ha-Levanim al Eishyshok," p. 85.
12 KGB file reprinted in Polish translation, "From the Ejszyszki Municipality About the AK Activities in the Vilna Vicinity After July 1944," in *Kurier Wilen*, August 5, 1992.
13 Moshe Sonenson's testimony about the AK attack on October 20, 1944, before the NKVD War Tribunal in Lithuania, SSR, on May 28–29, 1945, as well as other testimonies. See Criminal Case No. 3710, accused Ptak P.L. and others. Archive file no. 28621/3, Archives of the KGB, Lithuania's Council of Ministers.

14 For names of the participants in the attack by the Armia Krajowa and in the murder of Zipporah Sonenson and her son, for detailed testimonies from members of the AK as well as the head of the municipality of Ejszyszki, and for the Bill of Indictment by the State Security Committee, see NKVD/KGB file no. 28621/3, especially pp. 48, 136, 146–87, 267–77, 301–10, 322–25, 332–34. See also Kahn, *No Time to Mourn*, pp. 184–85, but note that Kahn's version of the sequence of events is inaccurate. The attacks on the Kabacznik and Sonenson homes and the municipal building occurred on the night of October 19–20, 1944; a second attack, on the jail, was made during the night of December 7, 1944. Also the account that Moshe Sonenson and his two older children fled, leaving Zipporah and the baby behind, is inaccurate.

15 Michalowski, "Hitnaplut ha-Partizanim," p. 86. Michalowski's testimony is inaccurate with regard to the baby's age and gender. See also Gilbert, *The Holocaust*, p. 759, and my letter to the *New York Times Book Review* regarding Gilbert's inaccuracy, and Gilbert's apology, March 30, 1986, p. 29.

16 Rachel Pochter, "Im Ha-Partizanim," p. 75.

17 Various Polish groups and individuals in the United States, Canada, and Poland challenge the historical fact that members of the AK murdered Jews during the war and after liberation. These groups and individuals, including the AK historian Jaroslav Wolkonowski, have chosen the murder of my mother and baby brother as the focus of their attacks. The material published by the Poles regarding the October 19–20, 1944, pogrom and other tragic events in Eishyshok is inaccurate, and manages to avoid citing any of the historical data concerning atrocities committed by the AK. For articles on the controversy between myself and the Poles, see Richard Z. Chesnoff, "Poles Can't Hide from History of Anti-Semitism," op-ed page, *New York Daily News*, July 5, 1996; Yaffa Eliach, "The Pogrom at Eishyshok," op-ed page, *New York Times*, August 6, 1996; "Poles Have Yet to Face Their Postwar Past," letters, *New York Times*, August 13, 1996; Danuta Swiatek, "Mur w glowach rosnie coraz wiekszy," *Zucie Warszawy*, August 22, 1996, pp. 1–2; Adam Michnik, "On the Murders at Ejszyszki" (English translation), *Gazeta Wyborcza*, August 8, 1996.

18 Kahn, *No Time to Mourn*, pp. 175–84.

19 Witness Moishes [Moshe] Sonenson's interrogation, NKVD/KGB file no. 28621/3, pp. 322–32; *Kurier Wilen*, August 5, 1992.

20 NKVD file P-18850-LI, vol. 4.

21 Michal Iwaszko to NKVD Senior Lieutenant Chalif, January 15, 1945, NKVD file P-18850 LI, vol. 2.

22 Kahn, *No Time to Mourn*, pp. 189–95.

23 About the school in Vilna, see Dov Levin, "The Final Chapter of Public Jewish Schools in the Soviet Union."

24 For photos and documents of Vilna in 1944–45, see Ran ed., *Jerusalem of Lithuania*, vol. 2, pp. 519–29.

25 Gutman, "The Jews of Poland, From Liberation to Immigration, 1944–1948," pp. 113–15; Dobroszycki, "Restoring Jewish Life in Post-War Poland."

26 Stalin himself supported the People's Army, because he knew the Russians would need the backing of the Polish political left when they entered Poland to take it from the Germans. Wasilewska's army had 1,500 Jewish officers, including 159 women. See Nussbaum, *Story of an Illusion: The Jews in the Polish People's Army in the USSR* (English title), pp. 80–84, 233–357.

27 Letter of the assistant to the military prosecutor of the Baltic Military District, Vilnius, June 31, 1954, NKVD/KGB file no. 28621/3, pp. 210–18.

28 The numbers changed slightly during the years, as Eishyshkians moved from one country to another. See Eliach, "Survivors of a Single Shtetl: A Case Study of Eishyshok." There is a slight difference between the number of immigrants I cite in this 1990 article and the statistics I cite here.

29 Kimche and Kimche, *The Secret Roads*, p. 129. For a new interpretation of the illegal immigration, see Zertal, *From Catastrophe to Power: Jewish Illegal Immigration to Palestine, 1945–1948* (English title).

30 Kahn, *No Time to Mourn*, pp. 203–7.

31 Department of State, Division of Communication and Records, Control 5302, file no. 9/20 Kaf. 4, the Jabotinsky Archive, Tel Aviv.

32 Dinnerstein, *America and the Survivors of the Holocaust*; idem, *Anti-Semitism in America*, p. 161.

33 Kahn, *No Time to Mourn*, pp. 209–10.

SOURCES

UNPUBLISHED MANUSCRIPTS

Cofnas, Pessah. *Mein Shpetiker Shnit* (My Later Harvest). 1977.
Ejszyszki (Osishkin), David. *Zikhronot: Me-Ejszyszok ve-ad Kfar Hess* (Memoirs from Eishyshok to the Kfar Hess). 1913–90.
Kaleko, Shaul, *Yomon* (Diary). 1914–15.
Kaleko, Mordekhai Munesh, *Mahbarot* (Notebooks). 1890–1945.
Kaplan, Moshe, *Korot Hayyai* (Events of My Life). 1915–79.
Margolies, Elia. Diary. 1941–44.
Skir, Pessia Moszczenik. *Zikhronot* (Memoirs). 1902–80.
Resnik, Esther-Etele Katz. *Zikhronot* (Memoirs). 1924.
Wiszik, Szeina Blacharowicz. *Notebooks*. 1912–90.

INTERVIEWS

Rebbetzin Amital
January 17, 1987
Sashka Frankl Ariel
August 20, 1980
Avraham (Avremke) and Liebke Asner
September 23, 1986
September 23, 1987
September 4, 1996
Avraham Lipkunski Aviel
August 7, 1980
February 8, 1987
Sarah Plotnik Avrahami
June 23, 1982
August 28, 1990
Batia Lubetski Barkali
January 29, 1994
January 16, 1996
Miriam Ribak Sonenson Ben-Shemesh
June 19, 1984
August 29, 1990
Arieh Berkowitch
January 6, 1993
Dora Zlotnik Berkowitch
January 7, 1987
January 6, 1988
Naftali Berkowitch
July 6, 16, 1980
Hadassah Rabinowitz Berlinski
January 16, 1995
Joe Camarone (Yossele Hamarski)
September 4, 19, 1986
Leah Cnaani
January 19, 1989
Mordekhai Dayagi
January 23, 1985
Simcha Dembrow
November 17, 1988
Luba Ginunski Deutch
August 27, 1980
June 26, 1985
January 14, 1988
June 13, 1988
Dora Dimitro (Dobke Kremin Dimitrowski)
March 16, 1988
June 18, 19, 1995
Israel Dimitro (Dimitrowski)
March 16, 1988
Nathan Dimitry (Nahum Dimitrowski)
May 1991
Yitzhak (Munin) Drori
January 1, 1985
Rabbi Zfania (Munin) Drori
June 22, 23, 1983
Hayya Gruznik Dworkin
June 21, 1984
June 21, 24, 1989
Moshe Edelstein
June 23, 26, 1983
June 26, 1986
April 17, 1997
Professor Elisha Efrat (Frischer)
January 17, 1996
David Ejszyszki (Osishkin)
June 26, 1984
June 26, 1989
Avraham Epstein (Botwinik)
September 15, 1991

Rabbi Kalman Farber
February 8, 1987
Shlomo Farber
June 6, 1980
August 10, 11, 1980
June 13, 1984
Rina Lewinson Fenigstein
August 24, 25, 28, 1980
January 13, 1988
Ethel Friedman
February 28, 1991
Nehama Koppelman Frischer
January 13, 1988
Gita Giliot
August 24, 1990
Gitta Politacki Ginsberg
June 25, 1985
Faivl Glombocki
December 24, 26, 1986
Hillel Glombocki
December 24, 26, 1986
Shneur Glombocki
February 19, 26, 1987
Yossef Goldstein
July 10, 1980
Shira Gorshman (Szyrke Gorszman)
January 20, 1992
April 6, 1998
Gitta and Shmuel Gross
August 28, 1980
Hannah Glombocki Gunzberg
June 23, 1986
Rebbetzin Rachel Shekowitski Hadash
January 15, 1987
Rebbetzin Zivia Hutner Hadash
July 10, 1980
Meir Stoler Haimowitch
August 9, 1987
Adaire Kirschner Harris
November 15, 1992
Zvi Harris
June 28, 1983
Ellen B. Broida Hawley
October 18, 1992
Alexander Zisl Hinski
July 9, August 9, 1980
Shoshana Hutner Hinski
July 8, 10, 1980
Szymen Hutner
January 11, 1987
Rabbi Yehoshuah Hutner
January 19, 1987
Elka Szulkin Jankelewicz
June 23, July 4, 1983
July 4, 1988
Moshe Kaganowicz
July 14, 15, August 14, 1980
June 12, 1985
Evelyn (Hava) Landsman Kahn
January 4, 14, 1982
September 19, 1994
Leon Kahn (Leibke Kaganowicz)
November 10, 1984
July 11, 1995
Leah Koppelman Kaleko
July 9, 1980
Peretz Kaleko-Alufi
July 6, 9, 23, August 14, 1980
June 17, 18, 1984
January 21, 1987
Betty Yurkanski Kaplan
June 27, 1995
Hayyim Moshe Kaplan
November 3, 1982
September 1984
Yossef Kaplan
September 7, 1981
Gershon Katz
June 19, 1984
Arieh Kopelowitch
June 26, 1984
Kazimierz Korkuc
May 30, 1986
Yashuk Korkuc
Winter 1942
Hanoch Kosowski
March 28, 1994
Hayya Streletski Kosowski
August 29, 1980
Rebbetzin Zipporah Hutner Kravitz
January 19, 1987
Aharon Lahav
January 19, 1989
Batia (Basha) Shuster Landsman
August 16, 1981
November 8, 1984
Mordekhai Lawzowski
August 17, 18, 1980

Sol Lubek (Zalman Lubetski)
June 15, 1994
September 16, 1994
June 19, 1996
Iris (Itzle) Kanichowski Mazowski
June 29, 1980
Zippi Avrahami Melamud
July 31, 1994
Moshe-Reuven Michalowski
June 26, 1983
June 27, 1987
Zvi Michalowski
November 11, 1979
September 14, 1980
September 14, 1988
October 4, 1992
June 17, 19, 1995
Temira Wilkanski Orshan
July 21, 1980
January 23, 24, 29, 1989
Asia Friedman Paamoni
June 29, 1985
Reuven Paikowski
January 23, 1983
June 23, 24, 1986
October 20, 22, 1986
November 8, 11, 14, 23, 1986
February 24, 1987
January 14, 18, 1988
January 16, 1989
January 16, 1990
September 16, 1990
June 1, 11, 1995
April 16, 1998
Zahava (Zlatke) Garber Paikowski
October 22, 1986
Yair Pishi
March 3, 1994
Vela Dubczanski Portnoy
December 23, 1990
January 4, March 4, 1991
Rachel Lewinson Peres
January 21, 1988
Esther Katz Resnik
March 1, 1993
Rivka Remz Rewzin
May 30, 1984
Abrashke (Adam) Rogowski
June 9, 1986
Niomke (Benjamin) Rogowski
February 14, 1954
March 16, 1954
December 16, 1964 (interviewed by Dov Levin)
Rosalind Foster Rosenblatt
January 3, 1990
Jean Rothstein
February 1, 1989
Fania Rozowski
August 31, 1980
Shaul Schneider
July 15, August 9, 1980
August 30, 1982
Rivka Lewinson Shanzer
January 13, 1988
Yossef Shanzer
January 30, 1994
Miriam (Merele) Kaplan Shapira
January 20, 1987
Louis and Ida Shlanski
June 25, 1987
Dr. Morris Shlanski
June 13, 1978
Gilad Shoshani
February 8, 1995
Miriam Kabacznik Shulman
November 3, 1982
November 3, 1983
January 13, 1984
April 13, 1984
May 24, 1984
June 16, 19, 1991
July 17, 1994
June 19, 1995
Nahum Shulman
April 13, 1984
Sara L. Siegel
March 28, 1995
Fruml Slepak
June 19, 1983
Ida Solome
September 4, 1979
Hayyim Sonenson
January 4, 1987
Israel Sonenson
December 27, 1989
Moshe Sonenson
June 18, 29, 1977
June 27, 1978
May 30, 1980
July 19, 1980
August 1, 14, 17, 20, 27, 1980
June 22, 1982

June 19, 22, 23, 1983
August 13, 18, 26, 1983

Shalom Sonenson Ben-Shemesh
Fall/Winter 1946
March 2, 4, 1980
June 24, 1980
August 1, 18, 20, 1980
June 19, 20, 24, 29, 1983
July 3, 1983
June 18, 19, 1984
July 1, 1984
August 18, 19, 1984

Shoshana Sonenson
March 7, 1994

Yitzhak Sonenson
December 1978
August 10, 1980
June 24, 1986
August 23, 1990

Moshe Szulkin
May 18, 22, 1984

Avraham Teikan
August 30, 1983

Zipporah Lubetski Tokatli
January 19, 1987
January 10, 11, 1988

Mordecai Tsanin
December 28, 29, 1986

Reuven Vasilishki
June 21, 1986

Joe Weissmann (Hayyim-Yoshke Bielicki)
August 17, 22, 1990
January 13, 1991

Rachel Asner Weltman
November 3, 1982
January 10, 1985

Avraham Widlanski
September 8, 1982

Dov Wilenski
June 27, 1983

Szeina Blacharowicz Wiszik
May 30, 1984
June 19, 1985
June 10, 1988
December 20, 1989
June 13, 16, 17, 19, 24, 1991
October 29, 1993
November 2, 1993
July 25, 1994

Dov Wolotzky
January 18, 1993

Feigl Garber Yurkanski
June 27, 1995

Malka Matikanski Zahavi
August 20, 1980
January 21, 1988

Atara Kudlanski (Goodman) Zimmerman
September 17, 1986

Rabbi Moshe Zinowitz
February 10, 1987

Kunie Zlotnik
January 15, 1990

Philip Zlotnik
November 11, 1984
November 11, 1989

PRIVATE FAMILY ARCHIVES

The following are family archives with more than fifty documents, obtained by the author. The names of those who assisted in gathering the family archives are in parentheses.

Avrahami (Sarah Plotnik Avrahami and Zippi Avrahami Melamud)
Bastunski (Judy Baston)
Berkowitch (Dora and Naftali Berkowitch; Penina Ivzan)
Berkowitch, Arieh (Reuven Barkai-Berkowitch)
Boyarski (Hyman Boyer)
Broida (Ann Greenspan Greenstein)
Cofnas (Rivka and Pessah Cofnas)
Dragutski, Kiuchefski, Sachowitski (Rosalind Rosenblatt née Foster Michalowski)
Dubczanski (Vela Dubczanski Portnoy)
Farber (Shlomo Farber)
Glombocki (Hillel and Faivl Glombocki and sister, Ethel)
Hutner-Hinski (Zisl and Shoshana Hinski and Hutner family members)
Juris (Bluma and Isaac Juris Jurdiczanski)
Kabacznik (Miriam Kabacznik Shulman)
Kaleko (Peretz Kaleko-Alufi, Raya Barkali, Neora Barkali Yahav, and Binyamin Strikowski Abiri)
Katz (Esther Katz Resnik)
Koppelman (Nehama Koppelman Frischer and Professor Elisha Efrat)

Lewinson (the Lewinson sisters: Rivka Shanzer and her husband Yossef, Rina Fenigstein, Rachel Peres)
Lubetski (Sol Lubek [Zalman Lubetski], Zipporah Lubetski Tokatli, Batia Lubetski Kaleko-Barkali)
Matikanski (Malka Matikanski Zahavi, Pauline Braunstein and Nehama Giladi)
Paikowski (Reuven and Zahava Paikowski)
Portnoy-Levin (Al Levin and Alfred Feld)
Rubinstein (Edna Cohen)
Saltz-Schultz (Phyllis Schultz-Saltz)
Schneider (Shaul Schneider, Yossef Shalgi-Schneider)
Shereshefski (Oscar and Darlene Shefski)
Shlanski (Shirley Shlanski Grynbal)
Smith-Shmidt (Dr. Harold Smith)
Sonenson (Yitzhak Sonenson)
Szulkin (Moshe Szulkin, Professor Robert Szulkin, Elka Szulkin Jankelewicz)
Wilkanski (Temira Wilkanski Orshan, Hadassah Rabinowitch Berlinski, Shmuel and Rachel Rabinowitch)
Wiszik (Szeina Blacharowicz Wiszik)
Zimmerman (Atara Kudlanski [Goodman] Zimmerman)
Zlotnik (Kunie Zlotnik, Philip Zlotnik, Dora Zlotnik Berkowitch)

PUBLIC ARCHIVES

The Bernardin Convent, Vilnius District of the AK, 1941–44 (contains 110 files)
Beth Trumpeldor Archives, Tel Yossef, Israel
Biblioteka Jegiellonska Dzial Rekopisow (Jagiellonian Library, Department of Manuscripts), Cracow
Central Archives for the History of the Jewish People, Jerusalem
Central Zionist Archives, Jerusalem
Eisiskes City Archives
German Federal Archives, Koblenz
Ghetto Fighters House Archives, Kibbutz Lohamei ha-Gettaot, Israel
Hagana Archives, Tel Aviv
Hevrah Bnei Avraham Shmuel Anshei Eishyshker Archive, Brooklyn, NY
Jabotinsky Archive, Tel Aviv
Joint Distribution Committee (JDC) Archives, New York
LCVIA (State Historical Archives), Vilnius
National Archives, Washington
NKVD War Tribunal Archives, Vilnius
Roosevelt Library Archives, Hyde Park, N.Y.
Stadtarchiv, Frankfurt on the Oder
United States Holocaust Memorial Museum, Research Institute, Washington
VCMA (State Civil Vital Records Archive), Vilnius
Vilnius University Library
VVA (Vilnius State Archives)
Yad Vashem Archives, Jerusalem
YIVO Institute for Jewish Research, New York
ZAGS (Vilnius Vital Records Archive)

BIBLIOGRAPHY

Abiri (Strikowski), Rachel Kaleko. "'Yizkor' Ziyun Nefesh le-Peutei Gani." In *Eishyshok Koroteah ve-Hurbanah*, edited by Peretz Alufi and Shaul Barkali.
Abrabanel, Yitzhak, *Nahlat Avot*. Venice, 1545.
Abrahams, Israel. *Jewish Life in the Middle Ages*. New York: Athenaeum, 1969.
———. "Jews and Letters." *Jewish Chronicle*, January 1890.
Abramauskas, S. *K Voprosy Geneza Krepostney Sooryshenii Tipa Kastle V Litve* (On the Questions of the Genesis of Castle-Type Defense Constructions in Lithuania). Lithuanian Scientific Work of Higher Education.
Abramovitch, Raphael R. "The Jewish Socialist Movement in Russia and Poland (1897–1919)." In *The Jewish People, Past and Present*, vol. 2, 369–98. New York: CYCO, 1948.
Abramovitch, Zeev. "The Poale Zion Movement in Russia, Its History and Development." In *Essays in Jewish Socialism, Labour, and Cooperation, in Memory of Dr. Noah Barou, 1899–1955*, edited by Henrik F. Infield, 63–72. London: Thomas Yoseloff, 1961.
Abrams, Maynard, and Abrams, Gertrude. *The Ancestors of Our Children*. Jacksonville, Fl.: Mendelson Printing Co., 1984.
Abramsky, Chimen. "The Crisis of Authority Within European Jewry in the Eighteenth Century." In *Studies in Jewish Religious and Intellectual History, Presented to Alexander Altmann on the Occasion of His Seventieth Birthday*, edited by Siegfried Stein and Raphael Loewe, 13–28. University of Alabama Press, 1979.
———. "Emdat Lenin Kelapei ha-Yehudim" (The Stand of Lenin on Jews). In *Hartzaot be-Knasei ha-Iyyun be-Historia*, 363–74. Jerusalem: Israel Historical Society, 1973.
Abramsky, Chimen, Jachimczyk, Maciej, and Polonsky, Antony, eds. *The Jews in Poland*. Oxford: Basil Blackwell, 1986.

Adam, Monya M. *Vital Link, Signals in the Hagana — A Personal Account* (English title). Tel Aviv: Ministry of Defense, 1986.

Adams, Arthur et al. *An Atlas of Russian and East European History*. New York: Praeger, 1967 and 1970.

Addison, Lancelot. *The Present State of the Jews*. London, 1675.

Adler, Ruth. *Women of the Shtetl Through the Eyes of Y. L. Peretz*, Rutherford, N.J.: Associated University Press, 1980.

Agnon, S. Y. *Shira*. Translated by Zeva Shapiro. Syracuse, N.Y.: Syracuse University Press, 1989.

Agranowski, G., and Guzenberg, I. *Litowski Yerushalaim* (Lithuanian Jerusalem). Vilnius: Lituanus, 1992.

Ainsztein, Reuben. *Jewish Resistance in Nazi-Occupied Eastern Europe*. London: P. Elek, 1974.

———. "Poland's Anti-Semitic Mania." *Midstream* 14, no. 7 (1968): 3–27.

Aishishkin, Ezekiel. *Sefer Dvar Ezekiel* (The Sayings of Ezekiel). 1921. Reprint. Jerusalem/Brooklyn: Moriah Offset Co., 1990.

Algemeine Encyclopedia. Paris: Dubnow-Fund, 1935.

Alkalai, Yehudah. "The Third Redemption, 1843." In *The Zionist Idea: A Historical Analysis and Reader*, edited by Arthur Hertzberg. 1959. Reprint. New York: Athenaeum, 1982.

Almog, Shmuel, ed., *Transition and Change in Modern Jewish History*. 2 vols. Jerusalem: Historical Society of Israel and the Zalman Shazar Center for Jewish History, 1987.

Alon, Gedaliahu. "Yeshivot Lita" (The Yeshivot of Lithuania). In *Mehkarim be-Toledot Yisrael*, vol. 1, 1–11. Israel: Ha-Kibbutz ha-Meuhad, 1957.

Alperowitch, Yitzhak, ed. *Sefer Telz* (Telz Book). Tel Aviv: Irgun Yotzei Telz be-Israel, 1984.

Alpert, Nachum. *The Destruction of Slonim Jewry*. New York: Holocaust Library, 1989.

Altbauer, Moshe. "I. Schipper's Study of the Khazar-Jewish Element in Eastern Europe" (English title). In *Sefer Yizhak Shipper*, edited by Shlomo Eidelberg, 47–58. New York, 1966.

Altshuler, Mordecai. "The Attitude of the Communist Party of Russia to Jewish National Survival, 1918–1930." YIVO *Annual* 14 (1969): 68–86.

Alufi, Peretz, and Barkali, Shaul, eds. *Eishyshok Koroteah ve-Hurbanah*. Jerusalem: Ha-Vaad le-Nizole, Eishyshok be-Medinat Israel, 1950.

Anger, P. *With Raoul Wallenberg in Budapest: Memories of the War Years in Hungary*. New York: Holocaust Library, 1981.

Ankori, Zvi. *Karaites in Byzantium: The Formative Years, 970–1100*. 1959. Reprint. New York: AMS Press, 1968.

Anolik, Benjamin. *Memory Called* (English title). Tel Aviv: Beit Lochamei Haghetaot, 1990.

Apenszlak, Jacob, ed. *The Black Book of Polish Jewry*. New York: American Federation for Polish Jews, 1943.

Arad, Yitzhak. *Ghetto in Flames: The Struggle and Destruction of the Jews of Vilna in the Holocaust*. New York: Holocaust Library, 1982.

Arendt, Hannah. *The Origins of Totalitarianism*. New York: Meridian, 1958.

Aronson, Chil. "Wooden Synagogues in Poland." *Menorah Journal* 25 (1937): 326–32.

Aronson, Gregor et al., eds. *Di Geschichte fun Bund* (The History of the Bund). 3 vols. New York: Unser Tsait, 1960–66.

Ashkenazi, Rabbi Israel ben Petahia. *Terumat ha-Deshen*. Venice, 1519.

Assaf, Simha, ed. *Mekorot le-Toledot ha-Hinukh be-Israel* (Sources for the History of Jewish Education). 4 vols in 2. Tel Aviv: Dvir, 1954.

Atamuk, Shlomo. *Yidn in Lite*. Vilnius: Lituanus, 1990.

Avinadav, Arieh, ed. *Kehilat Ostila* (Uscilug). Tel Aviv: Association of Former Residents of Uscilug, 1961.

Avissar, Oded, ed. *Sefer Hevbon*. Jerusalem: Keter, 1970.

Aviva, A. Avi. "Parashat Ger ha-Zeddek" (The Case of the Ger Zeddek). In *Sefer Ilya, Yizkor Bukh*, edited by Arie Kopelowicz. Yhud Yotsei Ilya be-Israel, 1962.

Azulai, Hayyim Yossef David. *Birkei Yossef Yoreh Deah*. Livorno, 1774.

Bachrach, Yair. *Havat Yair*. Reprint. Jerusalem, 1973.

Baer, Mark. "Mickiewicz un di Yiden fun Navaredok" (Mickiewicz and the Jews of Navaredok). In *Pinkas Navaredok*, 188–91. Israel: Alexander Harkavy Navaredker Relief Committee in U.S.A. and Navaredker Committee in Israel, 1963.

Baker, Zachary. "Bibliography of Eastern European Memorial Books: Updated and Revised." *Toledot* 3, nos. 2–3 (1979–80): 7–42.

Balaban, Majer (Meir). *Bibliografia historii Zydow w Polsce i w krajach osciennych za lata 1900–30* (Bibliography of the History of the Jews in Poland and Neighboring Lands for the Years 1900–30). Warsaw, 1939. Reprint. Jerusalem: World Federation of Polish Jews, 1978.

———. "The Great War, 1648–1666" (English title). In *Beth Israel be-Polin*, edited by Israel Halpern, vol. 1, 81–90. Jerusalem: Youth Department of the Zionist Organizations, 1948.

———. "Hayyei Israel ve-Tarbutum ba-Meah ha-16 & 17." In *Beit Israel be-Polin*, edited by Israel Halpern,

vol. 1, 65–80. Jerusalem: Youth Department of the Zionist Organizations, 1948.
———. "The Kahal's Organization in Poland" (English title). *Kwartalnik posweicony badaniu przeszlosci Zydow w Polsce* 1, no. 2 (1912): 17–54.
———. "U trumny budowniczego." *Nasz Przeglad*, September 15, 1935.
———. *Di Yidn in Poyln: Shtudies un shilderungn*. Vilna: B. Klatzkin, 1930.
———. "Zydzi w powstaniu 1863 r. (Proba bibliografii rozumowanej)" (Jews in the 1863 Uprising [An Attempt at a Bibliography]). *Przeglan Historyczny* 34 (1937–38): 564–99.
Bar, Arie, ed. *The Jewish Press That Was* (English edition). Jerusalem: Jerusalem Post Press, 1980.
Bar-Ilan, Meir. *Mi-Volozhin ad Yerushalaim*. Tel Aviv: Yalkut, 1939.
Barkali, Shaul (Kaleko). *Eishyshok*. Jerusalem: Lemel School, 1969.
Bar-On, A. Zwi. "The Jews in the Soviet Partisan Movement." *Yad Vashem Studies* 4 (1960): 167–89.
Baron, Salo W. *The Russian Jew under Tsars and Soviets*. New York: Macmillan, 1964. 2nd ed., rev. and enl., Macmillan, 1976.
———. *A Social and Religious History of the Jews*. 19 vols. New York: Columbia University Press, 1952–93.
Baron, S. W., Dinur, B., Ettinger, S., and Halpern, I., eds., *Yitzhak F. Baer Jubilee Volume* (English title). Jerusalem, 1960.
Bartal, Yisrael, comp. *Ha-Sufot ba-Negev* (The "Storms in the South"). Course reader. Jerusalem: Akademon, 1976.
Bartoszewski, Wladyslaw. *The Blood Shed Unites Us*. Warsaw: Interpress, 1970.
———*Righteous Among Nations: How Poles Helped the Jews, 1939–1945*. London: Earlscourt, 1969.
Bartoszewski, Wladyslaw, and Lewin, Zofia. *The Samaritans: Heroes of the Holocaust*. New York: Twayne, 1970.
———*Ten Jest Z Ojczyzny Mojej* (This One Is from My Country). Cracow: Wydawnictwo Znak, 1969.
Barzel, Hillel, ed. *Love Stories of S. Y. Agnon* (English title). Israel: Bar-Ilan University, 1980.
Bass, David. "Bibliographical List of Memorial Books Published in the Years 1943–1972." *Yad Vashem Studies* 9 (1973): 273–321.
Bauer, Yehuda. *Flight and Rescue: Brichah*. New York: Random House, 1970.
Benayahu, Meir. "The Revival of Ordination in Sefed" (English title). Jerusalem: Historical Society of Israel, 1960: 248–69.
Ben Ezer, Ehud. "Be-Yemei ha-Aliyah, le Meir Wilkanski" *Ha-Aretz*, August 27, 1971.
Ben-Menachem, Naftali. *Hakhmei Lita*. Jerusalem: Mossad Harav Kook, 1959.
Ben-Sasson, Hayyim Hillel. *Hagut ve-Hanhagah* (Theory and Practice: The Social Views of Polish Jews at the End of the Middle Ages). Jerusalem: Mossad Bialik, 1959.
———. *Continuity and Variety* (English title), selected by Joseph R. Hacker. Tel Aviv: Am Oved, 1984.
———. "The Personality of Elijah the Gaon of Vilna and His Historical Influence" (English title). *Zion* 31 (1966): 29–86, 197–216.
———. "Wealth and Poverty in the Teaching of the Preacher Reb Ephraim of Leczyca" (English title). *Zion* 19 (1954): 143–66.
———, ed. *Ha-Kehilah ha-Yehudit bi-Mei ha-Beinayim* (The Medieval Jewish Community). Issues in Jewish History, no. 4. Jerusalem: Zalman Shazar Center/Historical Society of Israel, 1976.
———, ed. *A History of the Jewish People*. Cambridge, Mass.: Harvard University Press, 1976.
Ben-Shemesh, Shalom Sonenson. "Hurban Eishyshok." In *Eishyshok Koroteah ve-Hurbanah*, edited by Peretz Alufi and Shaul Barkali, 61–62. Jerusalem: Ha-Vaad le-Nizolei Eishyshok be-Medinat Israel, 1950.
———. "Yameah ha-Ahronim Shel Eishyshok." In *Eishyshok Koroteah ve-Hurbanah*, edited by Peretz Alufi and Shaul Barkali, 57–66. Jerusalem: Ha-Vaad le-Nizolei Eishyshok be-Medinat Israel, 1950.
Berdyaev, Nicholas. *The Russian Idea*. Boston: Beacon Press, 1962.
Berenbaum, Michael. *The World Must Know*. Boston: Little, Brown, 1993.
Berlin, Isaiah. *The Crooked Timber of Humanity*. New York: Vintage, 1992.
Berlin, Naftali Zvi. *Ha-Amek Davar*. Vilna, 1879–80.
Bershadskii, Sergei A. *Litovskie Yevrei* (Lithuanian Jews: A History of Their Legal and Social Status in Lithuania from Vitovt to the Union of Lublin, 1388–1569). St. Petersburg, 1883.
———, ed. *Russko-Yevreiskii Arkhiv*. (Russian Jewish Archive: Documents and Materials for the History of the Jews in Russia, 1388–1569). 3 vols. St. Petersburg, 1882.
Bettan, Israel. "The Sermons of Ephraim Luntshits." *Hebrew Union College [of Cincinnati] Annual* 8–9 (1931–32): 443–86. Also in idem, *Studies in Jewish Preaching*, 273–316. Cincinnati: Hebrew Union College Press, 1939.

Biale, David. "Childhood, Marriage and the Family in Eastern European Jewish Enlightenment." In *The Jewish Family*, edited by Steven M. Cohen and Paula E. Hyman. New York: Holmes & Meier, 1986.

———. *Power and Powerlessness in Jewish History*. New York: Schocken, 1986.

Bialik, Hayyim Nahman. *Aftergrowth and Other Stories*. Translated by I. M. Lask. Philadelphia: Jewish Publication Society, 1939.

Bielski, Tuvia, and Bielski, Zusya. *Jews of the Forest*. Tel Aviv: Am Oved, 1946.

Bikerman, I. *Cherta Yevreiskoi Osedlosti* (The Pale of Jewish Settlement). St. Petersburg, 1911.

Bloom, Isaac. *A Shtetele in Poilen*. New York: Farlag Bloom, 1939.

Blumenthal, N., ed. *Memorial Books Mir*. Jerusalem: Encyclopedia of the Diaspora, 1962.

Bornstein, Chayim Jehiel. *Mishpat ha-Semikha ve-Koroiea*, 1919.

Borwicz, Michal. "Polish-Jewish Relations, 1944–1947." In *The Jews in Poland*, edited by Chimen Abramsky, Maciej Jachimczyk, and Antony Polonsky. Oxford: Basil Blackwell, 1986.

Boyarin, Jonathan. *Polish Jews in Paris: The Ethnography of Memory*. Bloomington: Indiana University Press, 1991.

Boyarsky, Joseph. *The Life and Suffering of the Jew in Russia: A Historical Review of Russia's Advancement Beginning with the Year 987 A.D. to the Close of the Nineteenth Century: A Description of the Special Laws Enacted Against the Jews and Reasons Thereof*. Los Angeles, 1912.

Breier, Alois; Eisler, M.; and Grunwald, M. *Holzsynagogen in Polen* (Wooden Synagogues in Poland). Vienna, 1934.

Broides, Yitzhak. *Agadot Yerusalem de-Lita*. Tel Aviv: Sefer, 1947.

———. *Vilna ha-Zionit ve-Askaneha*. Tel Aviv: Hozaat Histadrut Olei Vilna ve-Hagalil be-Tel Aviv, 1939.

Bronsztejn, Szyja. "The Jewish Population of Poland in 1931." *Jewish Journal of Sociology* 6, no. 1 (July 1964): 3–29.

Brown, X. M. "The Third Reich's Mobilization of the German Fifth Column in Eastern Europe." *Journal of Central European Affairs* 19/2 (July 1959): 128–48.

Browning, Christopher. *Ordinary Men: Reserve Police Battalion 101 and the Final Solution in Poland*. New York: Harper Perennial, 1992.

Bryk, Andrzej. "The Struggles for Poland." In *Polin*, edited by Antony Polonsky, vol. 4, 377–79. Oxford: Basil Blackwell, 1989.

Buchaveckas, Stanislovas. *Salcios Zeme* (Land of Salcia). Vilnius: Mintis, 1992.

Buloff, Joseph. *From the Old Marketplace*. Cambridge, Mass.: Harvard University Press, 1991.

Cantor, Aviva. *Jewish Women, Jewish Men*. San Francisco: HarperCollins, 1995.

Charney, Daniel. "Ikh For Kain Eishyshok" and "Ikh Were a Kunanmakher." In *Vilne*, 265–81. Buenos Aires: Central Farband fun Poilishe Yiden in Argentine, 1951.

Chesnoff, Richard Z. "Polish Can't Hide from History of Anti-Semitism," *Daily News*, Op Ed page, July 5, 1996.

Chew, Allen F. *An Atlas of Russian History: Eleven Centuries of Changing Borders*. Rev. ed. New Haven, Conn.: Yale University Press, 1970.

Cholawski, Shalom. *Beleaguered in Town and Forest* (English title). Tel Aviv: Moreshet & Sifriyat Poalim, 1973.

———. *Soldiers from the Ghetto*. New York: Herzl Press, 1980.

Cholawski, Shalom, and Levin, Dov. "Partisans." In *Encyclopedia of the Holocaust*, edited by Israel Gutman, vol. 3, 1108–18. New York: Macmillan, 1990.

Choron, Rose. *Family Stories: Travels Beyond the Shtetl*. Malibu, Calif.: Joseph Simon/Pangloss Press, 1988.

Ciechanowiecks, Andrzej. "A Footnote to the History of the Integration of Converts into the Ranks of the *Szlachta* in the Polish-Lithuanian Commonwealth." In *The Jews in Poland*, edited by Chimen Abramsky, Maciej Jachimczyk, and Antony Polonsky. Oxford: Basil Blackwell, 1986.

Clemens, Clara. *My Husband Gabrilowitsch*. New York: Harper and Brothers, 1938.

Cohen, Benjamin. "The Jurisdiction of the Wojewoda over the Jews in Old Poland" (English title). In *Studies in Jewish History Presented to Professor Raphael Mahler on His Seventy-fifth Birthday*, 47–66. Merhavia, Israel, 1974.

Cohen, Chester. *Shtetl Finder*. Bowie, Md.: Heritage Books, 1989.

Cohen, Shabbtai ben Meir. *Megilat Eifa*. Reprint. Hanover, Germany, 1924.

Cohen, Steven M., and Hyman, Paula E., eds. *The Jewish Family Myths and Reality*. New York: Holmes & Meier, 1986.

Cohen, Y. L. *Yiddishe Folkslider mit Melodies*. New York: YIVO, 1957.

Cronbach, Abraham. "Social Action in Jewish Lithuania." *Hebrew Union College [of Cincinnati] Annual*, 23, part 2 (1950–51): 593–616.

Cygielman, Shmuel Artur. *The Jews of Poland and Lithuania Until 1648 (5408)* (English title). Jerusalem: Zalman Shazar Center for Jewish History, 1991.

———. "Leasing and Contracting Interests (Public Incomes) of Polish Jewry and the Founding of the Council of Four Lands" (English title). *Zion* 47 (1982): 112–44.

———. *Mekorot le-Toledot Yehudei Polin ve-Lita* (Sources for the History of the Jews in Poland and Lithuania). Ben Gurion University, Department of Jewish History, 1978.

Czacki, Tadeusz. *Rozpravva O Zydach I Karaitach*. Cracow: Biblioteka Polska, 1860.

David, Uri. *Apirion David*. Eidetkugen, 1873.

Davies, Norman. *God's Playground: A History of Poland*. 2 vols. New York: Columbia University Press, 1982.

Davitt, Michael. *Within the Pale: The True Story of Anti-Semitic Persecutions in Russia*. New York: A. S. Barnes, 1903.

Dawidowicz, David. *Omanut ve-Omanim be-Vattei Kenesset Shel Polin* (Art and Artists in Polish Synagogues). Israel: Ha-Kibbutz ha-Meuhad, 1982.

———. "Polish Synagogues with Four Pillars" (English title). In *Sukenik Memoril Volume*. Jerusalem, 1967. Also in idem, *Omanut*, 95–103.

———. "Toward the Origins of the Use of Wood for Religious Building by the Jews of Poland" (English title). In *Sefer Ze-evi*, edited by Y. Siegelman, 94–103. Haifa: Ha-Mo-adon le-Sifrut, 1966. Also in idem, *Omanut*, 129–37.

———. *Synagogues in Poland and Their Destruction* (English title). Jerusalem: Mossad Harav Kook and Yad Vashem, 1960.

Dawidowicz, Lucy S. *From That Place and Time: A Memoir, 1938–1947*. New York: Norton, 1989.

———, ed. *The Golden Tradition: Jewish Life and Thought in Eastern Europe*. New York: Holt, Rinehart and Winston, 1967.

De-Nur, Daniella. *Jewish Liberators and Survivors* (English title). Tel Aviv: Hagana Archive, 1993.

de Vaux, Roland. *Ancient Israel*. New York: McGraw-Hill, 1961.

Deshen, Shlomo. "The Jewish Family in Traditional Morocco." In *The Jewish Family*, edited by Steven M. Cohen and Paula E. Hyman. New York: Holmes & Meier, 1986.

Deutscher, Isaac. *The Non-Jewish Jews*. New York: Oxford University Press, 1968.

Dienstag, Israel. "Rabbi Elijah of Vilna: A Bibliography" (English title). *Talpiot* 4 (1949): 269–356, 861–62.

Dinari, Yedidya Alter. *The Rabbis of Germany and Austria at the Close of the Middle Ages: Their Conceptions and Halakha-Writings* (English title). Jerusalem: Mossad Bialik, 1984.

Dinnerstein, Leonard. *America and the Survivors of the Holocaust*. New York: Columbia University Press, 1982.

———. *Anti-Semitism In America*. New York: Oxford University Press, 1994.

Dinur, Ben-Zion. *Be-Mifneh ha-Dorot* (Historical Writings). Jerusalem: Mossad Bialik, 1955.

———. *Israel ba-Golah* (Israel in the Diaspora). 2 vols. Tel Aviv/Jerusalem: Dvir and Mossad Bialik, 1961–72.

——— (Dinaburg). "Tochniyotav shel Ignatiev le'Pitron Seelat ha-Yehudim uveidot netsigei hakehillot be-eterburg beShenot 5641–42" (The "Plans" of Ignative for Solving the "Jewish Question" and the Meetings of Representatives of Communities in St. Petersburg, 1881–82). *He'avar* 19 (1963): 5–60.

Dobroszycki, Lucjan. "The Fertility of Modern Polish Jewry." In *Modern Jewish Fertility*, edited by Paul Ritterband. Leiden: Brill, 1981.

———. "Restoring Jewish Life in Post-War Poland." *Soviet Jewish Affairs*, 1973, no. 2, 58–72.

Droyanov, Alter, first ed.; Laskov, Shulamith, new ed. *Ktavim Le-Toldot Hibbat Zion Ve-Yishuv Eretz Israel*. Tel Aviv: University of Tel Aviv, 1888; 1982.

Dubnow, Simon M. *Divrei Yemei am Israel* (History of the Jewish People). 10 vols. 2d ed. Tel Aviv: Dvir, 1958.

———. *A History of the Jews in Russia and Poland*. 3 vols. Philadelphia: Jewish Publication Society of America, 1916–20. Reprint. New York: Ktav, 1975.

———. "How Military Service for Jews Was Introduced in 1827." *ES* 2 (1909): 156–65.

———, ed. *Pinkas ha-Medina*. Berlin: Ayanot, 1925.

Dubnow-Erlich, S., and Hertz, J. S. *Di Geschichte fun Bund* (History of the Bund). New York: Unser Tsait, 1972.

Dworzecki, N. *Jerusalem of Lithuania in Revolt and Holocaust*. (English title). Tel Aviv, 1951.

Eckman, Lester, and Lazar, Chaim. *The Jewish Resistance*. New York: Shengold, 1977.

Educational Encyclopedia. 5 vols. Jerusalem: Ministry of Education and Culture, and the Bialik Institute, 1961–69.

Ehrenburg, Ilya, and Grossman, Vasily, eds. *The Black Book*. Translated by John Glad and James S. Levine. New York: Holocaust Library–Schocken Books, 1982.

Eidelboim, Meir. *Di Yidn-Shtot Mezeritch*. Buenos Aires: Mezeritcher Landsleit in Argentina, 1957.

Einat, Amela. *Libel Without Disgrace* (English title). Israel: Yediot Ahronot, 1994.

The Einsatzgruppen Reports. Edited by Y. Arad, S. Krakowski, and S. Spector. New York: Holocaust Library, 1989.

Eisenstein, Judah David, ed. *Ozar Yisrael: An Encyclopedia*. 10 vols. 1907. Reprint. 10 vols, in 5. Jerusalem: Shiloh, 1980, 1984.

Eisenstein, Miriam. *Jewish Schools in Poland, 1919–1939*. New York: Columbia University, King's Crown Press, 1950.

Eizenshdat, Shmuel, and Gelbert, Mordekhai, eds. *Kamenetz-Litovsk, Zastavye and Colonies*. Tel Aviv: Townsmen Organizations in Israel and the United States, 1967/1970.

Eliach, Yaffa. *Hasidic Tales of the Holocaust*. New York: Oxford University Press, 1982.

———. "The Pogrom of Eishyshok," *New York Times*, Op Ed page, August 6, 1996.

———. "The Russian Dissenting Sects and Their Influence on Israel Baal Shem Tov, Founder of Hassidism." *American Academy for Jewish Research, Proceedings* 36 (1968): 57–83.

———. "Survivors of a Single Shtetl: A Case Study of Eishyshok." In *Sheerit Hapleta, 1944–1948*, edited by Israel Gutman and Avital Saf, 489–508. Jerusalem: Yad Vashem, 1990.

Eliach, Yaffa, and Assaf, Uri. *The Last Jew*. Israel: Alef-Alef Theater Publications, 1977.

Eliezer, Rabbi ben Isaac the Great. *Orhot Hayyim* (Paths of Life). Lublin, 1572.

Encyclopaedia Judaica. 16 vols. Jerusalem: Keter, 1973.

Encyclopedia Lituanica. Edited by S. Suziedelis. Boston: J. Kapocius, 1970.

Endelman, Todd H., ed. *Jewish Apostasy in the Modern World*. New York: Holmes & Meier, 1987.

Engel, David. *Facing a Holocaust: The Polish Government in Exile and the Jews, 1943–1945*. Chapel Hill: University of North Carolina Press, 1993.

———. *Semantics and Politics in the Description of Polish–Jewish Relations* (English title). Tel Aviv: Tel Aviv University, 1990.

Epstein, Rabbi Barukh Ha Levi. *Mekor Barukh* (1928).

Erez, Yehuda, ed. *Sefer ha-Aliyah ha-Shlishit*. 2 vols. Tel Aviv: Am Oved, 1964.

Ertel, Rachel. *Le Shtetl, la bourgade juive de Pologne*. Paris: Payot, 1982.

Etkes, Immanuel. "Ha-GeRa ve-ha-Haskalah-Tadmit u-Meziut" (The Gaon of Vilna and the Haskalah: Image and Reality). In *Studies in the History of the Jewish Society . . . Presented to Professor Jacob Katz*, edited by I. Etkes and Y. Salmon, 192–217. Jerusalem: Magnes, 1980.

———. *Lita be-Yerushalaim*. Jerusalem: Yad Ben Zvi, 1991.

———. "Marriage and Torah Study Among the Lomdim in Lithuania in the Nineteenth Century." In *The Jewish Family: Metaphor and Memory*, edited by David Kraemer. New York: Oxford University Press, 1989.

———. *Mossad ha-Yeshivah*. Jerusalem: Hebrew University, 1989.

———. *Yisrael Salanter ve-Reshita Shel Tenuat ha-Mussar* (Israel Salanter and the Beginning of the Musar Movement). Jerusalem: Magnes Press, 1982.

———, ed. *The East European Jewish Enlightenment* (English title). Jerusalem: Zalman Shazar Center for Jewish History, 1993.

Etkes, Immanuel, and Salmon, Y. "Ha-Yesodot ve-ha-Megamot be-Itzuv Mediniuto Shel ha-Shilton ha-Rusi Kelapei ha-Yehudim im Halukot Polin" (The Bases and Goals in the Formation of Russian Government Policy Toward Jews with the Partitions of Poland). *He'avar* 19 (1972): 20–34.

Ettinger, Shmuel. *History and Historians* (English title). Jerusalem: Zalman Shazar Center for Jewish History, 1992.

Ettinger, S.; Fox, A.; and Stern, M. *The Great Man and His Age* (English title). Lectures delivered at the eighth convention of the Historical Society of Israel, December 1962. Jerusalem: Historical Society of Israel, 1963.

Ettingler, Jacob. *Binyan Zion*. Jerusalem: Dvar, 1989.

Even-Shoshan, Shlomo, ed. *Minsk Ir Va-Em* (Minsk, Jewish Mother-City). 2 vols. Israel: Ha-Kibbutz ha-Meuhad, 1975.

Ezekiel Feiwel ben Zeev Wolf. *Sefer Toldot Adam*. Reprint. Jerusalem: Meorot ha-Galil, 1987.

Ezrahi, Shulamit. *Ze-Ha-Yish Toldot Hayyav Shel ha-Hafetz Hayyim*. Jerusalem: 1986.

Fajnhauz, David. "Dwor I karczma zydowska na Litwie w polowie 19 w" (Jewish Tavernkeepers in Lithuania in the Mid-Nineteenth Century). In *Sefer Raphael Mahler*, edited by S. Yeivin, 62–76. Merhavia, Israel: Sifriat Poalim, 1974.

———. "Ludnosc zydowska na Litwie I Bialoruse, a powstanie styczniowe" (Jewish Population in Lithuania and White Russia and the January Insurrection). BZIH 37 (1961): 3–34; 38; 39–68.

Falk, Zeev. *The Law of Marriage*. Jerusalem: Meisharim, 1983.

Farber, Shlomo, ed. *Olkeniki in Flames*. Tel Aviv: Association of Former Residents of Olkeniki and Surroundings, 1962.

———. *Vilna — My Origin Land* (English title). Israel: 1984.

Federbush, Simon, ed. *Hokhmat Israel be-Maarav Eiropa*. 3 vols. Jerusalem/New York: Reuven Mass, "Ogen" of Histadruth Haivrith of America, 1958–65.

Feinstein, Aryeh Leob. *Ir Tehilah*. Warsaw: M. Y. Alter, 1886.

Feinstein, Rabbi Moshe. *Iggrot Moshe Orah Hayyim*. New York: Chorav and Gross Brothers, 1959–73.

Feitel, Samuel Feivish ben Nathan. *Tit ha-Yeven*. Venice, 1650.

Feuchtwanger, Oscar. *Righteous Lives*. New York: Bloch, 1965.

Fine, Rabbi Shmuel Yossef. *Kirya Neemanah*. Vilna, 1915.

Finkelstein, Chaim. *Hajnt, A Zeitung bei Yidn, 5668–5699* (*Hajnt*, a Jewish Newspaper, 1908–1939). Tel Aviv: Y. L. Perets, 1978.

Finkelstein, Louis. *Jewish Self-Government in the Middle Ages*. New York: Phillip Feldheim, 1964.

Fishman, David E. *Embers Plucked from the Fire: The Rescue of Jewish Cultural Treasures in Vilna*. New York: YIVO Institute for Jewish Research, 1996.

———. "Musar and Modernity: The Case of Novaredok." *Modern Judaism* 8, no. 1 (1958): 41–64.

Fishman, Joshua (Shikl) A. *Never Say Die: A Thousand Years of Yiddish in Jewish Life and Letters*. The Hague: Mouton, 1981.

———, ed. *Studies on Polish Jewry, 1919–1939*. New York: YIVO Institute for Jewish Research, 1974.

Fishoff, Yehiel Ben Zion, "Iber Vilne, Telz un Japan." *Dos Yiddishe Vort*, Kislev 5750 (1990).

Flinker, David; Rosenfeld, Shalom; and Tsanin, Mordechai. *The Jewish Press That Was*. Jerusalem: Jerusalem Post Press, 1980.

Florinsky, Michael T. *Prophecy and Politics: Socialism, Nationalism, and the Russian Jews, 1862–1917*. Cambridge: Cambridge University Press, 1981.

———. *Russia: A History and an Interpretation*. 2 vols. New York: Macmillan, 1959.

———. *Their Brothers' Keepers*. New York: Crown, 1957.

Fogelman, Eva. *Conscience and Courage*. New York: Doubleday, 1995.

Frederic, Harold. *The New Exodus: A Study of Israel in Russia*. New York: Putnam, 1892.

Freulich, R., and Abramson, J. *The Hill of Life*. New York: Thomas Yoseloff, 1968.

Friedberg, Abraham Shalom. *Zikhronot le-Veit David*. Warsaw: Ahiassaf, 1893–99.

Friedman, Eliezer Eliyahu. *Sefer ha-Zikhronot, 5618–5686 (Book of Memoirs, 1858–1926)*. Tel Aviv, 1926.

Friedman, Philip. "Bibliography of Bibliographies, on the Period of Disaster." *Kiryat Sefer*. Vol. 28, 1952–53, 410–415. Vol. 29, 1953–54, 162–71.

Friedman, Tuvia. "From the Reminiscences of the First Jewish Student in Russia." In *Perezhitoe*, 1–50, St. Petersburg, 1908.

Frischman, David, ed. *Hatekufa* (a quarterly), vol. 7. Warsaw: Stiebel Publishing House, 1920.

Gachelet. Tel Aviv: Association of the Lithuanian Jews in Israel, January 1992.

Gans, David. *Tzemah David*. Prague, 1592. Reprint. Jerusalem: Magnes Press, 1983.

Gelber, Nathan Michael. "A Jewess' Memoirs of the Polish Uprising of 1863." YIVO *Annual* 13 (1965): 243–63.

———. *Die Juden und der Polnische Aufstand* (The Jews and the Polish Revolt: The Memoirs of Yaakov Halevi Levin from the Days of the Polish Revolt in the Years 1830–31). Wien, 1923, no. 159, 1863.

Genechowski, Dov. *Stories of Jerusalem* (English title). Jerusalem: Karta, 1989.

Gessen, Iulii. *Yevrei v Rossii*. St. Petersburg, 1906.

Gilbert, Martin. *The Holocaust*. New York: Holt, Rinehart and Winston, 1985.

Gilboa, Menucha. *Hebrew Periodicals in the Nineteenth Century: The Precursors, 1691–1856* (English title). Israel: Tel Aviv University, the Chaim Rosenberg School of Jewish Studies, 1986.

Gilboa, Yehoshua. *The Black Years of Soviet Jewry, 1939–1953*. Boston: Little, Brown, 1971.

Ginsburg, Saul. "Die Antstehung fun der Yiddisher Rekrutchina" (The Introduction of the Jewish Army Service). *Zeitshrift* (Minsk) 2–3 (1928): 89–106.

———. "Max Lilienthal's Activities in Russia: New Documents." *Publications of the American Jewish Historical Society*, 1939.

———. *Meshumodim in Zarish Russland* (Converts in Tzarist Russia). Historishe Werk, vol. 2. New York: CYCO Bichar-Farlag, 1946.

———. "Yiddishe Kantonistn." In idem, *Yiddishe Leiden in Zarish Russland*. Historishe Werk, vol. 3. New York, 1937.

Ginzberg, Louis. "Israel Salanter." In idem, *Students, Scholars, and Saints*, 145–94. Philadelphia: Jewish Publication Society of America, 1928.

Gitelman, Zvi. *A Century of Ambivalence.* New York: Schocken, 1988.

———. *Jewish Nationality and Soviet Politics.* Princeton, N.J.: Princeton University Press, 1972.

Glenn, Susan A. *Daughters of the Shtetl.* Ithaca, N.Y.: Cornell University Press, 1990.

Gluckel of Hameln. *The Memoirs of Gluckel of Hameln.* 1896 Reprint. Translated by Marvin Lowenthal. New York: Schocken, 1977.

Goberman, D. *Jewish Tombstones in Ukraine and Moldava.* Moscow: Image Publishing House, 1993.

Goitein, S. D. *A Mediterranean Society: The Jewish Communities of the Arab World as Portrayed in the Documents of the Cairo Geniza.* 5 vols. Berkeley: University of California Press, 1967–88.

Goldberg, Hillel. *Israel Salanter: Text, Structure, Idea.* New York: Ktav, 1982.

Goldbloom, Israel Isser. *Ha-Shahar,* Adar 1878, no 4.

Goldhagen, Daniel Jonah. *Hitler's Willing Executioners.* New York: Knopf, 1996.

Goldhagen, Eric."The Ethnic Consciousness of Early Russian Jewish Socialists." *Judaism* 23 (1974): 479–96.

Goldin, Judah, ed. *The Jewish Experience.* New York: Bantam, 1970.

Goldstein, Herbert S., ed. *Forty Years of Struggle for a Principle: The Biography of Harry Fischel.* New York: Bloch, 1928.

Goodwin, Richard N. *Remembering America.* Boston: Little, Brown, 1988.

Gordon, Harry. *The Shadow of Death: The Holocaust In Lithuania.* Lexington: University of Kentucky Press, 1992.

Goren, Shlomo. *Moadei Israel.* Tel Aviv: Yediot Ahronot, 1983.

Gorshman, Shira (Szyrke Gorszman). *Chana's Sheep and Cattle* (English title). Israel: Israel Book Publishing House, 1986.

———. *Izranie Stranitsi 1939–1979.* Moscow: Isvestsia, 1978.

———. *Survival* (English title). Israel: Israel Book Publishing House, 1992.

Gorszman, Szyrke (Shira Gorshman). *33 Nowele.* Warsaw: Idisz Buch, 1961.

Govrin, Nurit. *Ha-Omer.* Jerusalem: Yad Ben Zvi, 1980.

———. *Maftehot.* Tel Aviv: Ha-Kibbutz ha-Meuhad, 1978.

Gra, Gershon. *Ha-Shomer.* Israel: Ministry of Defense, 1985.

Grade, Chaim. *My Mother's Sabbath Days.* New York: Schocken, 1987.

———. *Rabbis and Wives.* Translated by Harold Rabinowitz and Inna Hecker Grade. New York: Vintage Books, 1983.

———. *The Yeshiva.* 2 vols. Translated from the Yiddish by Curt Leviant. Indianapolis: Bobbs-Merrill, 1976–77.

Graetz, Heinrich. *Geschichte der Juden von den altesten Zeiten bis auf die Gegenwart.* 11 vols. Leipzig: O. Leiner, 1853–76.

Greenbaum, Alfred A. *Jewish Scholarship and Scholarly Institutions in Soviet Russia, 1918–53.* Jerusalem: Hebrew University Center for Research and Documentation of East European Jewry, 1978.

Greenbaum, Masha. *The Jews of Lithuania: A History of a Remarkable Community, 1316–1945.* Jerusalem: Gefen Books, 1995.

Greenberg, Louis. *The Jews in Russia.* 1944–51. Reprint. 2 vols. New York: Schocken, 1976.

Greenstein, Yehiel, and Kaganovich, Moshe, eds. *Leksikon ha-Gevura* (Lexicon of Heroism). 2 vols. Jerusalem: Yad Vashem, 1965–68.

Greenzweig, Michael."Maamada Shel ha-Yivrit be-Yemei ha-Aliya ha-Shnia." In *Ha-Aliya ha-Shnia 1903–1914,* edited by Mordechai Naor. Jerusalem: Yad Ben Zvi, 1985.

Gross, Nathan, and Gross, Yaakov. *Haseret ha-Ivri.* Jerusalem, 1991.

Gruber, Ruth. *Raquela: A Woman of Israel.* New York: New American Library, 1978.

Guenzburg, Mordekhai Aaron. *Kiryat Sefer.* Vilna, 1847.

Gursan-Salzmann, Ayse. *The Last Jews of Radauti.* New York: Dial Press, 1983.

Gusev, A. *Zakony o Yevreiakh* (Collection of active laws concerning Jews extracted from code of laws of Russian Empire). Kharkov, 1889.

Gutman, Israel (Yisrael)."Ha-Am ha-Polani Nochah Hashmadat ha-Yehudim" (The Polish Nation Facing the Destruction of the Jews). *Molad* 7 (1975): 77–90.

———."The Jews of Poland, From Liberation to Immigration, 1944–1948." In *Eastern European Jewry: From Holocaust to Redemption, 1944–1948* (English title), edited by Benjamin Pinkus. Sde Boker: Ben Gurion University of the Negev, 1987.

———. *"Polish and Jewish Historiography on the Question of Polish-Jewish Relations During World War II.* In *The Jews in Poland,* edited by Chimen Abramsky, Maciej Jachimczyk, and Antony Polonsky. Oxford: Basil Blackwell, 1986.

———, ed. *Encyclopedia of the Holocaust.* 4 vols. New York: Macmillan, 1990.

Gutman, Israel, and Krakowski, Shmuel. *Unequal Victims: Poles and Jews During World War II*. New York: Holocaust Library, 1986.

Gutman, Israel, and Haft, C. J., eds. *Patterns of Jewish Leadership in Nazi Europe, 1933–1945: Proceedings of the Third Yad Vashem International Historical Conference*. Jerusalem, 1979.

Gutman, Yisrael.; Mendelsohn, Ezra; Reinharz, Jehuda; and Shmeruk, Chone, eds. *The Jews of Poland Between Two World Wars*. Hanover, N.H.: University Press of New England, 1989.

Gzerot Tah ve-Tat Shevet Yehudah. Vilna, 1862. Reprinted in Yiddish by Rabbi Krausz, Brooklyn, 1960.

Hadash, Rebbetzin Rachel. "Beti Avi, Ha-Magid Mi-Minski" In *Minsk Ir Ve-Em Mother-City*, edited by Shlomo Even-Shoshan, vol 1. Tel Aviv: Ha-Kibbutz ha-Meuhad, 1975.

Hafetz, Yehezkiel. *Melekhet Harash*. Vilna, 1875.

Ha-Kohen, Arieh Leib, ed. *Mikhtavei Haffetz Hayyim* (The Letters of the Haffetz Hayyim). Reprint. Bnei Brak, 1986.

Ha-Kohen, Israel Meir (Haffetz Hayim). *Sefer Ahavat Hessed*. New York: Pardes, 1946.

Ha-Kohen, Rephael. *Torat Yekutiel*. Berlin, 1772.

Halevi, Judah. *Sefer ha-Kuzari*. Vilna, 1905.

Halevy, Zvi. *Jewish Schools Under Czarism and Communism: A Struggle for Cultural Identity*. New York: Springer, 1976.

Halperin, Meir. *Ha-Gadol Mi-Minsk*. Jerusalem: Feldheim, 1991.

Halpern, Israel. "Additions and Supplements to Pinkas ha-Medinah." *Horev* 2 (1934–35): 67–86; 123–200.

———. "The Beginnings of the Lithuanian Council and Its Relations with the Council of Four Lands" (English title). *Zion* 3 (1937): 51–57. Also in idem, *Yehudim*, 48–54.

———. "On the Threatened Expulsion of Polish and Lithuanian Jewry in the Latter Half of the Seventeenth Century" (English title). *Zion* 17 (1952): 65–74. Also in idem, *Yehudim*, 266–76.

———. "Some Words about the Extent of Karaite Settlement in the Mid-Seventeenth Century" (English title). In *Sefer ha-Yovel Dr. Nathan Michael Gelber*, 35–38. Tel Aviv: 1962. Also in idem, *Yehudim*, 401–4.

———. *Yehudim ve-Yahadut be-Mizrah Eiropah* (Eastern European Jewry: Historical Studies). Jerusalem: Magnes Press, 1968.

———, ed. *Beit Yisrael be-Polin* (The House of Israel in Poland). 2 vols. Jerusalem: Youth Department of the Zionist Organizations, 1948, 1953.

Halpern (Halperin), Israel, comp., and Bartel, Israel, ed. *The Records of the Council of the Four Lands* (English title). 2 vols. Jerusalem: Bialik Institute, 1990.

Halpern, Leopold. *Polityka Zydowska w Sejmie I Senacie Rzeczypospolitej Polskiej 1919–33* (Jewish Politics in the Sejm [Parliament] and Senate of the Republic, 1919–33). Warsaw: Instytut Badan Spraw Narodowosciowych, 1933.

Harkavy, Alexander. *Navaredok*. New York: Grayzel Press, 1921.

Hayyim of Volozhin. *Ha-Peles* (Letters). Berlin, 1902.

Hecht, Ben. *A Child of the Century*. New York: Simon & Schuster, 1954.

Heinemann, Benno, ed. *The Maggid of Dubno and His Parables* by Jacob ben Wolf Kranz. New York: Feldheim, 1967. 4th rev. ed., 1978.

Helfand, Jonathan I. "Assessing Apostasy: Facts and Theories." *Jewish History* 5, no. 2 (Fall 1991).

———. "Passports and Piety: Apostasy in Nineteenth Century France." *Jewish History* 3, no. 2 (Fall 1988).

Heller, Celia S. *On the Edge of Destruction: Jews of Poland Between the Two World Wars*. New York: Columbia University Press, 1977.

Helzel, Florence B. *Shtetl Life*. Berkeley, Calif.: Judah L. Magnes Museum, 1933.

Henkin, Rabbi Yehuda Herzl. "Amirat Kadish al Yedei Isha Vetseruf Laminyan Me-Esrat Nashim." *Hadarom*, no. 54 (1985): 34–48.

Henkin, Rabbi Yossef Eliyahu. *Kitvei ha-Gria Henkin*, vol. 2. New York: Ezrat Torah, 5789 (1989).

Henry, Sondra, and Taitz, Emily. *Written Out of History*. New York: Biblio Press, 1983.

Herford, Travers R. *The Pharisees*. New York: Macmillan, 1924.

Hershberg, Avraham Shmuel. *Pinkos Bialystok* (The Chronicle of Bialystok). 2 vols. New York: Bialystok Jewish Historical Association, 1949–50.

Hertzberg, Arthur, ed. *The Zionist Idea*. New York: Athenaeum, 1982.

Herzen, Alexander. *My Past and Thoughts*. 1855. Reprint. Translated by Humphrey Higgins. New York: Knopf, 1968.

Herzl in Profile: Herzl's Image in the Applied Arts. Tel Aviv: Museum Publications, 1978.

Heschel, Abraham Joshua. *The Earth Is the Lord's*. New York: Farrar, Straus & Giroux, 1986.

Hessen, Iulii. "From the History of the Korobka Tax in Russia." ES 4 (1911): 305–347, 484–512.

———. "K istorii vyzeleniia evreev iz sel I dereven" (Toward a History of the Expulsion of Jews from Villages). *Voskhod* 4 (1903): 3–34; 5 (1903): 3–28.

Hessen, J. I. "I. B. Levinsohn and Dr. M. Lilienthal." *Perezhitoye* 111, 1911, 1–37.

Hilberg, Raul. *The Destruction of the European Jews.* 2 vols. New York: Holmes & Meier, 1985.

———, ed. *Documents of Destruction.* Chicago: Quadrangle Books, 1971.

Hill, Hamlin. *Mark Twain: God's Fool.* New York: Harper & Row, 1973.

Hodorowski, M. "Do Not Be Afraid, We Will Free You." *Haboker,* 22 Adar 5706 (January 24, 1946).

Hoffman, Eva. *Shtetl: The Life and Death of a Small Town and the World of Polish Jews.* Boston: Houghton Mifflin, 1997.

Holavski, Shalom. *Al Neharot ha-Neiman ve-ha-Dnieper.* Tel Aviv: Moreshet and Sifriat Poalim, 1962.

Holtz, Avraham. *Marot u-Mekomot.* Tel Aviv: Schocken, 1995.

Horodezky, Samuel A. *Le-Korot ha-Rabanut* (On the History of the Rabbinate). Warsaw: Tushiyah, 1914.

———. *Shlosh Meot Shanah Shel Yahadut Polin* (Three Hundred Years of Polish Jewry). Tel Aviv: Dvir 1946.

Howe, Irving, and Greenberg, Eliezer, eds. *A Treasury of Yiddish Stories.* New York: Schocken, 1973.

Huberband, Shimon. *Kiddush Hashem: Jewish Religious and Cultural Life in Poland During the Holocaust.* Hoboken, N.J.: Ktav, 1987.

Hutner, Yehudah Leib. *Ginzei Hayim.* Warsaw, 1928.

Hutner, Yossef Zundl. *Ulam ha-Mishpat.* Warsaw, 1880. Reprint. Jerusalem, 1971.

Isaac of Troki. *Hizzuk Emunah.* In *Tela Ignea Satanae,* edited by Johann Christoph Wagenseil, 61–480. Altdorf, 1681.

Isserles, Moses ben Israel. *Darkei Moshe.* Fiorda, 1760.

———. *She-elot u'Teshuvot* (Responsa). Edited by Asher Siev. Jerusalem, 1970.

Isserlin, Israel ben Petahia Ashkenazi. *Psakim u-Ketavim/Terumat ha-Deshen.* Venice, 1519.

Isserson, Zeev. "Meshak Tel Yossef Nesiat Elkind." *Davar,* October 20, 1927.

Jabotinsky, Vladimir. *Samson the Nazarite.* Translated by C. Harry Brooks. London: Martin Secker, 1930.

Jacobs, Noah J. "Solomon Maimon: An Annotated Bibliography" (English title). *Kiryat Sefer* 41 (1965–66): 245–62.

Janowsky, Oscar. *The Jews and Minority Rights (1898–1919).* New York: Columbia University Press, 1933.

Jeshurin, Ephim H., ed. *Wilno.* New York: Wilner Branch 367, Workmen's Circle, 1935.

Josephus, Flavius. *Jewish Antiquities,* books 17–19. Translated by Louis H. Feldman. Cambridge, Mass.: Harvard University Press, 1931.

———. *The Life of Flavius Josephus, Antiquities of the Jews.* 4 vols. Grand Rapids, Mich.: Baker, 1984.

Jurginis, Juozas. *Baudziavos Isigalejimas Lietuvoje* (Establishment of Serfdom in Lithuania). Vilnius: Valstybine Politines ir Mokslines Literaturos Leidkyla, 1962.

———. *Lietuvos Valstieciu Istorija V* (History of Lithuanian Peasants). Vilnius: Mokslas, 1978.

Kaczerginski, Shmerl. "The Partisan Jews." Translated by Esther Zweig. In *Anthology of Armed Jewish Resistance, 1939–1945,* edited by Isaac Kowalski, 385. Brooklyn, N.Y.: Jewish Combatants Publishing House, 1991.

Kagan (Kahn), Berl. *Jewish Cities, Towns and Villages in Lithuania* (English title). New York: B. Kohen, 1991.

———. *Sefer Haprenumerantin.* New York: Jewish Theological Seminary and Ktav, 1975.

Kaganowicz, Moshe, ed. *Sefer Zikaron le-Kehilat Ivie* (Ivie Memorial Book). Tel Aviv: Irgun Yotzei Ivie in Israel and in America, 1968.

Kahn, Leon, as told to Marjorie Morris. *No Time to Mourn: A True Story of a Jewish Partisan Fighter.* Vancouver, B.C.: Laurelton Press, 1978.

Kaleko, Mascha. *Kleines Lesebuch fur Grobe.* Berlin: Rowohlt, 1935.

Kaleko, Shaul. "Fun mein zeiduns zikorn." Kovno: *Die Welt,* no. 35, September 5, 1924.

———. "Fun Yiddishen Folklore in Lite." Kovno: *Die Welt,* June 1924.

Kaleko-Alufi, Peretz. "Beit ha-Sefer ha-Yivri be-Ivie." In *Sefer Zikaron le-Kehilat Ivie,* edited by Moshe Kaganowicz. Tel Aviv: Irgun Yotzei Ivie in Israel and in America, 1968.

Kalmanovitch, Zelig. "A Diary of the Nazi Ghetto in Vilna." YIVO *Annual* 8 (1953): 9–81.

Kaminski, Andrzej. *Lithuania and the Polish-Lithuanian Commonwealth, 1000–1795.* A History of East Central Europe, vol. 4. Seattle: University of Washington Press, forthcoming.

Kamzon, Y. D. *Lithuanian Jewry: Its History in Pictures.* Jerusalem: Mossad ha-Rav Kook, 1959.

Kantautas, Adam, and Kantautas, Filomena. *A Lithuanian Bibliography: A Check-List of Books and Articles Held by the Major Libraries of Canada and the United States.* Edmonton: University of Alberta Press, 1975.

Karon, Aharon. "Ha-Kursim ha-Petagogim be-Grodna." In *Yahadut Lita* (Lithuanian Jewry), vol. 1, 566–71. Tel Aviv: Am ha-Sefer and Igud Yotzei Lita, 1959.

Karski, Jan. *The Great Powers in Poland, 1919–1945.* New York: University Press of America, 1985.

Kartuz-Breze: Our Town Memorial Book (English title). Tel Aviv: Organization of the Survivors of Kartuz-Breze, 1993.

Katz, Benzion. *Le-Korot ha-Yehudim be-Rusia, Polin ve-Lita* (On the History of the Jews in Russia, Poland, and Lithuania in the Sixteenth and Seventeenth Centuries). Berlin, 1899. Reprint. Tel Aviv: Zion, 1970.

Katz, Dov. *Tenuat ha-Mussar* (The Musar Movement). 5 vols. Tel Aviv: Bitan Ha'sefer-A. Zioni, 1952–63.

Katz, J. "The Semikha Controversy Between R. Jacob Berab and Ralbach." *Zion* 16 (1951): 28–45.

Katz, Jacob. "Between 1096 and 1648" (Hebrew, English summary). In *The Yitzhak Baer Jubilee Volume*, edited by S. W. Baron et al., 318–37. Jerusalem: Historical Society of Israel, 1960.

———. *The Sabbath Gentile* (English title). Jerusalem: Zalman Shazar Center, 1983.

———. *Tradition and Crisis*. New York: Schocken, 1971.

Kazdan, Chaim Shlomo. *Die Geschichte fun Yiddishen Shulvezen in Umuphengiken Poilen* (The History of Jewish Education in Independent Poland). Mexico City: Kultur un Hilf, 1947.

Keneally, Thomas. *Schindler's List*. New York: Simon & Schuster, 1982.

Keshet, Yeshurun. *Maskiyot*. Tel Aviv: Hozaat Agudat ha-Sofrim, 1953.

Kimche, John, and Kimche, David. *The Secret Roads*. London: Secker and Warburg, 1954.

Klausner, Israel. "Bereshit Yisud ha-Mizrahi." In *Sefer ha-Zionut ha-Datit*, vol. I. Jerusalem: Mossad ha-Rav Kook, 1977.

———. "History of the Jews in Lithuania" (English title). In *Yahadut Lita*, 23–73.

———. "Tazkir al Baayat ha-Yehudim be-Russia Me-et Sar ha-Pelech ha-Vilnai Pahlen" (A Memorandum on the Jewish Problem in Russia by Vilna Province governor Pahlen). *He'avar* 7 (1960): 91–122.

———. *Toldot ha-Kehilah ha-Ivrit be-Vilna* (History of the Jewish Community in Vilna). Vilna, 1938. Reprint. Jerusalem, 1969.

———. *Vilna be-Tekufat ha-Gaon* (Vilna in the Days of the Gaon). Jerusalem: Reuven Mass, 1942.

———. *Vilna, Yerushalaim de-Lita: Dorot Rishonim*, vol. 1. Jerusalem: Mossad ha-Rav Kook, 1977.

Klier, John D. "The Ambiguous Legal Status of Russian Jewry in the Reign of Catherine II." *Slavic Review* 35 (1976): 504–517.

Klyuchevsky, Vasili. *Peter the Great*. New York: Vintage, 1958.

Kochan, Lionel, ed. *The Jews in Soviet Russia Since 1917*. 3d ed. Oxford: Institute of Jewish Affairs, Oxford University Press, 1978.

Koestler, Arthur. *The Thirteenth Tribe: The Khazar Empire and Its Heritage*. New York: Random House, 1976.

Koreva, A. *Materiali*.

Kosover, Mordechai. "The Domestic Trade of Polish Jews in the Sixteenth and Seventeenth Centuries" (English title). *Yb* (1937): 533–43; 15 (1940): 182–201.

Krajewska, Monika. *A Tribe of Stones*. Warsaw: Polish Scientific Publishers, 1993.

Krakowski, Shmuel. *Lehima Yehudit be-Polin Neged ha-Nazim, 1942–1944* (Jewish Resistance in Poland Against the Nazis, 1942–1944). Jerusalem: Yad Vashem, Hebrew University Institute for Contemporary Jewry, 1977.

———. *The War of the Doomed*. New York: Holmes & Meier, 1984.

Kramer, David, ed. *The Jewish Family: Metaphor and Memory*. New York: Oxford University Press, 1989.

Kranz, Yaakov, *The Parables of Jacob*. Cracow, 1985.

Kremer, Moses. "Jewish Artisans and Guilds in Ancient Poland." YIVO *Annual* 11 (1956–57): 210–42.

Kressel, Getzel. *Leksikon ha-Sifrut ha-Ivrit ba-Dorot ha-Aharonim* (Lexicon of Hebrew Literature in Recent Generations). 2 vols. Merhavia, Israel: Sifriat Poalim, 1965–67.

Krinsky, Carol Herselle. *Synagogues of Europe*. Cambridge, Mass.: MIT Press, 1985.

Krohn, Paysach J. *Around the Maggid's Table*. Brooklyn: Mesorah Publications, 1992.

Kruk, Herman. "Diary of the Vilna Ghetto." YIVO *Annual* 13 (1965): 9–78.

Kuznets, Simon. "Economic Structure and Life of the Jews." In *The Jews: Their History, Culture, and Religion*, 3d ed., edited by Louis Finkelstein, vol. 2, 1597–1666. New York: Harper and Brothers, 1960.

Lamm, Maurice. *The Jewish Way in Death and Mourning*. New York: Jonathan David, 1969.

Lamm, Norman. *Torah Lishma: Torah for the Sake of Torah in the World of Rabbi Hayyim Volozhin and His Contemporaries*. New York: Ktav, 1989.

Landau, Yehezkael Segal. *Noda be-Yehudah*. Jerusalem: Pardes, 1960.

Lazar, Chaim. *Destruction and Resistance*. New York: Shengold, 1985.

Lehmann, Reinhold. *Du wirst leben und dich rachen: Die Geschichte des Juden Zwi Michaeli*. Munich: List, 1992.

Leichter, Sinai, and Milkov, Chaim, eds. *Sefer Olei ha-Sartifikatim*. (Students' Rescue by Aliyah). Jerusalem: Magnes Press, Hebrew University, 1993.

Lenane, James. "Twenty Million Pounds of Meat." *New Hampshire Profiles*, November 1965.

Leoni, Eliezer, ed. *Wolozin*. Tel Aviv: Wolozin Landsleit Associations of Israel and the United States, 1970.

Lestchinsky, Jacob. "Aspects of the Sociology of Polish Jewry." JSS 28 (1966): 195–211.

———. "The Economic and Social Development of the Jewish People." In *The Jewish People, Past and Present*, vol. 1. New York: CYCO, 1946.

Levanda, V. O., ed. *Polnyi khronologicheskii sbornik zakonov i polozhenii, kasaiushchikhsia Yevreev* (Completed Chronological Collection of Laws and Ordinances Relating to the Jews, 1649–1873). St. Petersburg: Tip. K. V. Trubnikova, 1874.

Levin, Dov. "The Final Chapter of Public Jewish Schools in the Soviet Union." In *Eastern European Jewry: From Holocaust to Redemption, 1944–1948* (English title), edited by Benjamin Pinkus, 88–112. Sde Boker: Ben Gurion University of the Negev, 1987.

———, ed. *Pinkas ha-Kehillot* (Encyclopedia of Jewish Communities from Their Foundation Till After the Holocaust — Lithuania). Jerusalem: Yad Vashem, 1996.

Levin, Nora. *While Messiah Tarried: Jewish Socialist Movements, 1871–1917*. New York: Schocken, 1977.

Levin, Yaakov. "10 Yor Gemilot Hessed Kassa." *Unzer Hilf*. Ejszyszki, December 11, 1936.

Levinsohn, Isaac Baer. *Bet Yehudah*. Vilna, 1839.

Levinsohn, Yitzhak Baer. *Teuda be-Israel*. Vilna, 1828. Reprint edited with an introduction by E. Etkes. Jerusalem: Zalman Shazar Center, 1977.

Levinson, Yosif. *Skausmo Knyga: The Book of Sorrow*. Vilnius: Vaga Publishers, 1997.

Levitats, Isaac. *The Jewish Community in Russia, 1772–1844*. New York: Columbia University Press, 1943.

———. *The Jewish Community in Russia, 1844–1917*. Jerusalem: Posner and Sons, 1981.

———. "Le-Bikoret Sefer ha-Kahal Shel Brafman" (Toward a Critique of Brafman's Book of the Kahal). *Zion* 3 (1937–38): 170–78.

Lewin, Abraham. *Kantonistn, 1827–1856* (Cantonists). Warsaw: Hutner, 1934.

———. *Mi-Pinkaso Shel Moreh mi-Yehudia*. Israel: Ha-Kibbutz ha-Meuhad, 1969. Translated and edited by Antony Polonsky, *A Cup of Tears: A Diary of the Warsaw Ghetto*. Oxford: Basil Blackwell, 1988.

Lewin, Isaac. "The Herem as an Executive Instrument of the Council of Four Lands." *Yearbook of the World Federation of Polish Jews* 1 (1964): 79–109.

Lewin, J. *Aliyyat Eliahu* (The Ascension of Elijah). 4th ed.

Lewinsky, A. *Le-Toledot ha-Yehudim be-Polin ve-Rusia* (History of the Jews in Poland and Russia in the Eighteenth Century). St. Petersburg, 1912.

Lewinsky, Yom-Tov. *Encyclopedia of Folklore, Customs and Traditions in Judaism*. 2 vols. Tel Aviv: Dvir, 1975.

Lietuviskoji Enciklopedija. 7 vols. Edited by Vaclovas Birziska. Kaunas: Spaudos Fondas, 1939.

Lietuviu Enciklopedija. 36 vols. Boston: Lietuviu Enciklopedijos Leidykla, 1953.

Lietuvos Metrastis, Bychovco Kronika (Lithuanian Chronicles, Chronicle of Bychovo). Vilnius: Vaga, 1971.

Lietuvos TSR Urbanistikos Paminklai, no. 6. Vilnius: Mokslas, 1983.

Lifschitz, A. M. "Ha-Heder." In *Hatekufa*, vol. 7. Warsaw, 1920.

Lifshits, Ezekiel. *Badkhanim un Leitsim by Yidn*. Vilna, 1930.

———. "Ha-Pogromim be-Polin ba-Shanim 1918–19, Vaadat Morgenthau u-Misrad ha-Hutz' ha-Amerikai" (The Pogroms in Poland, 1918–19, the Morgenthau Commission and the American State Department). *Zion* 23–24 (1958–59): 66–97.

Lifshitz, Berl. "In Shturm." In *Olkeniki in Flames*, edited by Shlomo Farber. Tel Aviv: Association of Former Residents of Olkeniki and Surroundings, 1962.

Linenthal, Edward T. *Preserving Memory: The Struggle to Create America's Holocaust Museum*. New York: Viking, 1995.

Lipec, Dov. "Ha-Hinukh ha-Ivri ve-ha-Tenuah ha-Ivrit be-Lita ha-Atzmait 1920–1940." In *Yahadut Lita*, vol. 2, 113–31.

———. "Ishim be-Yahadut Lita." In *Yahadut Lita*, vol. 3, 97–98.

———. "The Karaites in Lithuania" (English title). In *Yahadut Lita*.

Lipkunsky, A. Aviel. *Dogalishok*. Tel Aviv: Ministry of Defense, 1995.

Lipovetsky, P. *Joseph Trumpeldor*. Jerusalem: Youth and he-Halutz Department, World Zionist Organization, 1953.

Lippman, D. M. *Le-Toldot ha-Yehudim be-Lita-Zamut*. Keidani: Mofshowicz and Cohen, 1934.

Lippman, Eliezer. *Nefesh ha-Hayyim*. (Soul of Life). Vilna, 1824.

Lippman, Rabbi Yom Tov. *Kvod Yom Tov*. Vilna, 1817.

Lipstadt, Deborah E. *Denying the Holocaust*. New York: Free Press, 1993.

Lissak, Moshe, ed. *The History of the Jewish Community in Eretz-Israel Since 1882* (English title). Jerusalem: Israel

Academy for Sciences and Humanities, Bialik Institute, 1993.
Lithuania, Past and Present. New York: American Lithuanian Literary Association, 1965.
Litwin, A. (Sh. Horowitz). "Graf Potocki der Ger Zeddek." In *Wilno*, edited by Ephim H. Jeshurin. New York: Wilner Branch 367, Workmen's Circle, 1935.
———. *Yiddishe Neshomes.* New York: Farlag Folksbildung, 1916.
Livingston, Ellen. *Tradition and Modernism in the Shtetl Aisheshuk, 1919–1939.* Princeton, N.J.: Princeton University Press, 1986.
Lossin, Yigal. *Pillar of Fire: The Rebirth of Israel—A Visual History.* Jerusalem: Shikmona, 1982.
Loukomski, George K. *Jewish Art in European Synagogues: From the Middle Ages to the Eighteenth Century.* London: Hutchinson, 1947.
Low, Richard. "Antoni Slonimski in Hebrew." In *Studies on Polish Jewry* (English title), edited by Ezra Mendelsohn and Chone Shmeruk, 173–77. Jerusalem: Hebrew University of Jerusalem, 1987. In Hebrew with English titles and summaries.
Lukas, Richard C. *The Forgotten Holocaust: The Poles Under German Occupation, 1939–44.* Lexington: University of Kentucky Press, 1986.
Lukowski, Jerzy. *Liberty's Folly: The Polish Lithuanian Commonwealth in the Eighteenth Century, 1647–1795.* New York: Routledge, 1991.
Luninski, Ernest. *Berek Joselewicz I jego syn: zarys historyczny* (Berek Joselewicz and His Son: A Historical Sketch). Warsaw: Orgelbrand, 1909.
Luntschitz, Ephraim Shlomo ben Aaron. *Ammudei Shesh.* Prague, 1617.
Luria, Y. "The Communities of Lithuania and the Karaites: Tax Assessment and Collection from Karaites in the Sixteenth and Seventeenth Centuries" (English title). *He-Avar* 1 (1918): 159–71.
Maciejowski, Waclaw. *Zydzi w Polsce, na Rusi I Litwie* (The Jews in Poland, Russia, and Lithuania). Warsaw, 1878.
Mahler, Raphael. "Anti-Semitism in Poland." In *Essays on Anti-Semitism*, edited by Koppel Pinson. New York: Conference on Jewish Relations, 1942.
———. "A Budget of the Council of Four Lands in the Eighteenth Century" (English title). *Yb* 15 (1940): 64–86.
———. "A Fragment About Jewish Commerce between Lithuania and Poland in the Sixteenth Century: A Hebrew-Yiddish Toll Register from Bielsk and Lukow, 1580" (English title). *HS* 2: 180–205.
———. *Ha-Hasidut ve-ha-Haskalah* (Hasidism and Haskalah in Galicia and Congress Poland in the First Half of the Nineteenth Century: Social and Political Bases). Merhavia, Israel: Sifriat Poalim, 1961.
———. *Yahadut Polin* (History of Jews in Poland). Tel Aviv: Sifriat Poalim, 1946.
Maimon, Salomon. *An Autobiography.* 1792. Reprint translated by Moses Hadas. New York: Schocken, 1947.
Mairantz, Baruch. *My Jewish Shtetl Recreated in Raffia and Wood* (English title). Tel Aviv: Amir, 1972.
Malamud, Bernard. *The Fixer.* New York: Viking Penguin, 1994.
Mann, Jacob. "Karaism in Lithuania and Poland." In idem, *Texts and Studies in Jewish History and Literature.* 1934. Reprint. New York: Ktav, 1972. Vol. 2, 553–1407.
———. *Texts and Studies.* Reprint. New York: Ktav, 1972.
Mann, Yitzhak, ed. *Herman Shtruk.* Tel Aviv: Dvir, 1954.
Manor, Alexander. "Ha-Miflagot be-Yahadut Polin Bein Shtei Milhamot ha-Olam" (The Parties in Polish Jewry between the Two World Wars). *Sefer ha-Shana/Yorbuch* 3 (1970): 233–78.
Manor, Alexander; Ganusowitch, Itzchak; and Lando, Abba, eds. *Sefer Lida.* Tel Aviv: Irggun Yozei Lida be-Israel u-Vaad ha-Hazalah be-Arzot ha-Berit, 1970.
Maor, Yitzhak. *Ha-Tenuah ha-Zionit be-Russia* (The Zionist Movement in Russia). Jerusalem: Magnes Press, Hebrew University, 1986.
———. "Tehum ha-Moshav ha-Yehudi be-Russia" (The Pale of Jewish Settlement in Russia: Its Origin, Development, and Abolition). *He'avar* 19 (1972): 35–53.
Mapu, Avraham. *Mikhtavim*, August 5, 1862. Reprint. B. Dinur, 1971.
Marcus, Jacob R. *Communal Sick-Care in the German Ghetto.* Cincinnati: Hebrew Union College Press, 1947.
Margaliot, Ephraim Zalman. *Mateh Ephraim.* Jerusalem, 1954.
Margaliot, Reuven, ed. *Sefer Hasidim* by Rabbenu Yehudah he-Hassid. Jerusalem: Mossad ha-Rav Kook, 1957.
Marrus, Michael R. *The Unwanted European Refugees in the Twentieth Century.* New York: Oxford University Press, 1985.
Maskovcevas, D. *Ka Jus Zinote* (What Do You Know). March 30, 1963.
Mauersberg, Stanlislaw. *Szkolnictwo powszechne dla mniejszosci narodowych w Polsce w latach 1918–1939.* Wroclaw: Zaklad Narodowyim. Ossolinskich, 1968.

Meir of Szczebrzeszyn and Nathan N. of Hanover. *Sippurei ha-Gezerot bi-Shnot Tah ve-Tat* (Texts on the Massacres of the Years 1648–1649). Introduction by M. Rosman. Texts and Studies, Ben Zion Dinur Center for Research in Jewish History, no. 19. Jerusalem: Merkaz Dinur, 1981.

Meirowitch, Shalom David. *Ahavat David.* Vilna, 1872.

Meirtchak, Benjamin. *Jewish Military Casualties in the Polish Armies in World War II.* 4 vols. Tel Aviv: Association of Jewish War Veterans of the Polish Armies in Israel, 1994.

Meiselman, Shulamit Soloveitchik. *The Soloveitchik Heritage: A Daughter's Memoir.* Hoboken, N.J.: Ktav, 1995.

Meizelish, Shaul. *Brit Milah.* Tel Aviv: Modan, 1988.

Meltzer, Isser Zalman. *Even ha-Azel.* 3 vols. Jerusalem: Defus ha-Ivri, Shel Yehiel Verker, 1928–38.

Meltzer, Yadael. *Be-Derekh Etz ha-Hayyim.* 2 vols. Eretz Israel: Arzei ha-Hen, 1986.

Melzer, Emanuel. *Maavak Medini be-Malkodet: Yehudei Polin, 1935–1939.* Tel Aviv: Tel Aviv University Press, 1982.

———."Anti-Semitism in the Last Years of the Second Republic." In *The Jews of Poland Between Two World Wars,* edited by Israel Gutman et al., 126–37. Hanover, N.H.: University Press of New England, 1989.

Melzer, Emanuel, and Engel, David, eds., *On the History of the Jews in Poland.* Tel Aviv: Tel Aviv University, 1973.

Melzer, Shimshon."Maaseh ha-Rav u-Baal ha-Agalah." In *Sefer ha-Shirot, ve-ha-Balladot,* 137–41. Tel Aviv: Dvar, 1950.

Menashe ben Israel. *Nishmat Hayyim.* Warsaw, 1796.

Mendele Mokher Sefarim (Shalom Jacob Abramovich)."Sefer ha-Kabzanim." In *Kol Kitvei Mendele Mokher Sefarim.* Tel Aviv: Dvir, 1951.

———. *The Travels of Benjamin the Third.* Translated by Moshe Spiegel. New York: Schocken, 1949.

Mendelsohn, Ezra. *Class Struggle in the Pale: The Formative Years of the Jewish Workers' Movement in Tsarist Russia.* Cambridge: Cambridge University Press, 1970.

———. *The Jews of East Central Europe between the World Wars.* Bloomington: Indiana University Press, 1983.

———. *The Jews of East Central Europe between the Two World Wars: A Selected Bibliography.* Jerusalem: Zalman Shazar Center, Historical Society of Israel, 1978.

———. *Zionism in Poland: The Formative Years, 1915–1926.* New Haven, Conn.: Yale University Press, 1982.

Mendelsohn, Ezra, and Shmeruk, Chone, eds. *Studies on Polish Jewry: Paul Glikson Memorial Volume* (English title). Jerusalem: Hebrew University of Jerusalem, 1987.

Mendes-Flohr, Paul R., and Reinharz, Jehuda, eds. *The Jew in the Modern World: A Documentary History.* New York: Oxford University Press, 1980.

Menes, Abraham."Patterns of Jewish Scholarship in Eastern Europe." In *The Jews: Their Religion and Culture,* edited by L. Finkelstein, vol. 2, 177–227. New York: Schocken, 1971.

Menes, Abraham."The Jewish Socialist Movement in Russia and Poland (from the 1870s to the Founding of the Bund in 1897)." in *The Jewish People, Past and Present,* vol. 2, 355–68. New York: CYCO, 1946.

———."Legal Documents of the Troki Karaite Community" (English title). *Kiryat Sefer* 33 (1957–58): 260–68.

———."The Yeshivot in Eastern Europe." In *The Jewish People, Past and Present,* vol. 2, 108–18. New York: CYCO, 1946.

Michalowski, Alter."Hitnaplut ha-Partizanim ha-Levanim al Eishyshok." In *Eishyshok Koroteah ve-Hurbanah,* edited by Peretz Alufi and Shaul Barkali.

Michnik, Adam."On the Murders at Ejszyszki" (English title). *Gazeta Wyborcza,* August 8, 1996.

Minor, Z. *Kratki istoricheski ocherk o yevreiach v Polshi Litvi i Russi* (Brief Historical Essays about the Jews in Poland, Lithuania, and Russia). Moscow: Kaplan, n.d.

Mintz, Israel."Me-Eretz-Israel le-Sibir u-Vehazara." *Migvan,* January 1981, 55–57.

———."Zikhronot al Menahem Elkind." *Hedim* no. 106 (July 1977).

Miron, Dan. *The Shtetl Image.* Tel Aviv: I. L. Peretz, 1981.

Mirsky, Samuel Kalman, ed. *Jewish Institutions of Higher Learning in Europe: Their Development and Destruction* (English title). New York: Ogen, 1956.

Mishinsky, Moshe."Kol-Kordi Shel Irgun Mahapchani Russi Neged ha-Pogromim be-Shenat 1881" (Proclamation of the Russian Revolutionary Organization against Pogroms in the Year 1881). In *Mekharim be-Toledot Am Yisrael ve-Eretz Israel,* vol. 4, 253–67. Haifa University, 1978.

———."Regional Factors in the Formation of the Jewish Labor Movement in Czarist Russia." YIVO *Annual* 14 (1969): 27–52.

Mokotoff, Gary, and Sack, Sallyann Amdur. *Where Once We Walked.* Teaneck, N.J.: Avoteynu, 1991.

Morgenstern, A. *Messianism and the Settlement of Eretz Israel* (English title). Jerusalem: Yad Ben Zvi, 1985.

Mstislavskya, S."The Jews in the Polish Revolt of 1831" (English title). *Yevreyskaya Starina* 3 (1910): 61–80, 235–52.

Mysh, Mikhail. *Rukovodstvo k russkim zakonam o Yevreiakh* (Guide to Russian Laws on Jews). 3d ed. St. Petersburg, 1904.

Nadel, B. *Di eldste yiddishe Yeshuvim in Mizrah Eiyrope* (The Oldest Jewish Settlements in Eastern Europe). Warsaw, 1961.

Naor, Mordechay. *A Living Bridge* (English title). Tel Aviv: Ministry of Defense, 1993.

———, ed. *Ha-Aliyah ha-Shneia 1903–1914* Jerusalem: Yad Yitzhak Ben Zvi, 1985.

Nathan of Hanover. *Yeven Mezulah*. Venice, 1653. Hebrew edition with notes by Israel Halpern, Tel Aviv: Ha-Kibbutz ha-Meuhad, 1945, 1966.

Nedava, Yossef, ed. *The Image of the Woman As Seen by V. Jabotinsky* (English title). Tel Aviv: Hamerkaz, 1963.

Nemoy, Leon, trans. and ed. *Karaite Anthology*. New Haven, Conn.: Yale University Press, 1980.

Netzer, Shlomo. *Ma-avak Yehudei Polin al Zechuyotehem ha-Ezrahiyot ve-ha leumiyot* (The Struggle of Polish Jewry for Civil and National Minority Rights, 1918–1922). Tel Aviv: Tel Aviv University Press, 1980.

Neugroschel, Joachim, ed., *The Shtetl*. New York: Richard Marek, 1979.

Nigal, Gedalyah. *Sippurei Dibbuk be-Sifrut Israel* ("Dybbuk" Tales in Jewish Literature). Jerusalem: Rubin Mas, 1994.

Nikolaev, Vsevolod A., and Parry, Albert. *The Loves of Catherine the Great*. New York: Coward, McCann and Geoghegan, 1982.

Nissem, Girondi ben Reuben. *Responsa*. Reprint. Jerusalem: Makhon Shalem, Tsefunot Kadmonim, 1984.

Nizoz. Biweekly Hebrew Paper, published by the Central Zionist Organization of the D.P. Munich, Germany, January 21, 1946.

Norok, Mordechai. *Veidat Zionei Russia be-Minsk, 1902* (The Conference of Russian Zionists in Minsk, 1902). Jerusalem: Ha-Sifria ha-Zionit, 1963.

Noy, Dov, and Ben-Ami, Issachar. *Folklore Research Center Studies*. Jerusalem: Magnes Press, 1970.

Nussbaum, Klemens. *Story of an Illusion: The Jews in the Polish People's Army in the USSR* (English title). Tel Aviv: Diaspora Research Institute, Society for Jewish Historical Research, 1984.

Obitzinski, Levi. *Nahlat Avot*. Vilna, 1894.

Ofer, Dalia. *Escaping the Holocaust: Illegal Immigration to the Land of Israel, 1939–1944*. New York: Oxford University Press, 1991.

Ogen, Yitzhak. "Ka-Halom Yauf." In *Eishyshok Koroteah ve-Hurbanah*, edited by Peretz Alufi and Shaul Barkali.

Oliner, Samuel P., and Oliner, Pearl M. *The Altruistic Personality: Rescuers of Jews in Nazi Europe*. New York: Free Press, 1992.

Opalski, Magdalena, and Bartal, Israel. *Poles and Jews: A Failed Brotherhood*. Hanover, N.H.: University Press of New England, 1992.

Oppenheim, Israel. "He-Haluz be-Russia ba-Shanim 1918–1922" (He-Haluz in Russia, 1918–1922). *Meassef* 1 (1971): 3–55.

Orgad, Dorit. *Abducted Jewish Children in the Czar's Army*. Israel: Zalman Shazar Center, 1986.

Orshanskii, Ilia. *Yevrei v Rossii* (Jews in Russia — essays on the economic and social life of Russian Jews). St. Petersburg, 1877.

———. *Russkoe zakonodatelstvo o Yevreiakh* (Russian Legislation on Jews). St. Petersburg, 1877.

Osherowitch, Mendel. *Shtet un shtetlekh in Ukraine* (Cities and Towns in the Ukraine). 2 vols. New York: M. Osherowitsh Yubiley-Komitet, 1948.

Pat, Jacob. *Ash un Fayer* (*Ashes and Fire: Through the Ruins of Poland*). New York: CYCO Bicher-Farlag, 1946.

Peretz, Y. L. "Haknasat Kalla." 1924.

Philipson, D. "Max Lilienthal in Russia." *Hebrew Union College Annual* 12–13 (1937–38).

Philo of Alexandria. *Legatio ad Gaium*. Edited, translated, and with commentary by E. Mary Smallwood. Leiden: Brill, 1961.

Piechotka, Maria, and Piechotka, Kazimierz. *Wooden Synagogues*. Warsaw: Arkady, 1959.

Pinkas Beth ha-Midrash he-Hadosh be-Rechov Palangian be Yir Telz, 1870.

Pinkas Navaredok. Israel: Alexander Harkavy Navaredker Relief Committee in USA and Navaredker Committee in Israel, 1963.

Pinsker, Leo (Judah Leib). *Auto-Emancipation*. Berlin, 1882.

Pinson, Koppel S. "Arkady Kremer, Vladimir Medem, and the Ideology of the Jewish Bund." *JSS* 7 (1945): 233–64.

Pipes, Richard. "Catherine II and the Jews: The Origins of the Pale of Settlement." *Soviet Jewish Affairs* 5, no. 2 (1975): 3–20.

Pishi, Raphael. *Memorial Volume, 1901–1991*. Israel: Kibbutz Yifat, 1992.

Plantovski, N. *Le-Toldot Mosdot ha-Hinukh Shel Tarbut be-Polin*. Jerusalem: Kiryat Sefer, 1947–48.

Pochter, Rachel. "Im ha-Partizanim." In *Eishyshok Koroteah ve-Hurbanah*, edited by Peretz Alufi and Shaul Barkali.

Polnoe sobranie Russkeich letonisei chroniki: Litovskaia i Shomoitkaia i Bychovtsa Letonici Barkylabovskaia, Averki i Pantsyrskovo (Complete Collection of Russian Manuscripts: Lithuanian, Samogitian, Bychovo, Barkulabovskaian, Averki and Panturski Chronicles). M. Nauka, 1975.

Polonsky, Antony. *Politics in Independent Poland, 1927–1939*. Oxford: Oxford University Press, 1972.

Polujanski, A. *Opisanie lasow krolewstwa Polskiego i gubernij zachodnich cesarstwa Rossyjskiego pod wzgledem historycznym, statystycznym i gospodarczym* (Description of the Forests of the Polish Kingdom and Western Territories of the Russian Kingdom, Historical, Statistical, and Economic). Warsaw, 1854.

Porath, Jonathan. *Jews in Russia, The Last Four Centuries: A Documentary History*. New York: United Synagogue of America, 1974.

Prinz, Joachim. *Popes from the Ghetto*. New York: Schocken, 1968.

Rabin, Dov, ed. *Grodno*. Encyclopedia of the Jewish Diaspora: Memorial Book of Countries and Communities, vol. 9. Jerusalem: Grodno Society, 1973.

Rabinowicz, Harry M. *The Legacy of Polish Jewry: A History of Polish Jews in the Inter-war Years, 1919–1939*. New York: Thomas Yoseloff, 1965.

Rabinowitch, Avraham Shmuel. *Amud Esh*. Vilna, 1875.

Rabinowitsch, Wolf Zeev. *Lithuanian Hasidism*. New York: Schocken, 1971.

Rabinowitz, Hayyim Reuven. *Dioknaot Shel Darshanim* (Portraits of Jewish Preachers). Jerusalem: Rubin Mas, 1967.

Rabinowitz, Louis Isaac. *Herem-ha-Yishuv*. London: E. Goldstein, 1945.

Rabinowitz, S. P. "Traces of Freedom of Opinion in the Polish Rabbinate in the Sixteenth Century" (English title). Translated from the Russian by Y. D. Abramski. Jerusalem: Akademon, 1959.

Raeff, Marc. *Understanding Imperial Russia*. New York: Columbia University Press, 1984.

Ran, Leyzer, ed. *Jerusalem of Lithuania: Illustrated and Documented*. 2 vols. New York: Vilno Album Committee, 1974.

Ravitsky, Aviezer. *Messianism, Zionism and Jewish Religious Radicalism* (English title). Tel Aviv: Am Oved, 1993.

Rechtman, Abraham. *Yiddishe Ethografie un Folklor*. Buenos Aires: YIVO, 1958.

Recueil de matériaux sur la situation economique des Israelites de Russie. Jewish Colonization Association. 2 vols. Paris: Alcan, 1906.

Regestry i Nadpysy: Svod Materialov dlia Istori Yevreev v Russii (Documents and Requests: Materials for the History of the Jews in Russia, 80–180). 3 vols. St. Petersburg, 1899–1913.

Rekendorf, Herman. *Zikhronot le-Veit David*. Warsaw: Ahiassaf, 1893–99.

Replianski, Mordekhai. "Eishyshok in Likht fun Handl un Melokhe." *Unzer Hilf*. Eishyshok, December 11, 1936.

Riasanovsky, Nicholas V. *A History of Russia*. New York: Oxford University Press, 1977.

Rice, Zipporah. "Jewish Religious Education of Mizrahi in Poland Between 1920 and 1930." Master's thesis, Brooklyn College, May 1990.

Rindzioniski, Alexander (Senia). *Hurban Vilna*. Israel: Ghetto Fighters House, 1987.

Ringelbaum, Emanuel. *Zydzi w Powstaniu Kosciuszkowskiem* (Jews in the Kosciuszko Uprising). Warsaw, 1938. Yiddish version with additions by R. Mahler, Warsaw, 1937.

Rivkes, Moshe. *Beer ha-Golah*. Amsterdam, 1661–66.

Robbins, Richard G., Jr. *Famine in Russia, 1891–1892*. New York: Columbia University Press, 1975.

Rogger, Hans. "The Beilis Case: Anti-Semitism and Politics in the Reign of Nicholas II." *Slavic Review* 25 (1966): 615–29.

Rosenthal, Shraga Fish, ed. *Sefer ha-Yasher* (Responsa). 1898.

Roskies, Diane. *Heder: Primary Education Among East European Jews — A Selected and Annotated Bibliography of Published Sources*. Working Papers in Yiddish and East European Jewish Studies, no. 25. New York: YIVO, 1977.

Roskies, K. Diane, and Roskies, G. David. *The Shtetl Book*. New York: Ktav, 1975.

Rubinstein, Avraham. "Ha-Haskalah ve-ha-Hasidut: Peiluto Shel Yossef Perl" (Haskalah and Hasidism: Activities of Joseph Perl). *Bar-Ilan* 12 (1974): 166–78.

Rubstein, Benzion. "Di Yiddishe Innerliche Iber vanderung in Russland" (Jewish Internal Migrations in Russia, Including the Congress Kingdom). In *Naye Lebn*, 97–106 (39–48). New York, 1910.

Ruppin, Arthur. *The Jews in the Modern World*. London: Macmillan, 1934.

———. "Die russischen Juden nach der Volkszahlung von 1897" (Russian Jews According to the Census of 1897). *Zeitschrift für Demographie und Statistik der Juden*, yr. 2, vol. 1 (January 1906): 106; vol. 2 (February 1906): 17–22; vol. 3 (March 1906): 39–45.

Saduikis, C. *Eisiskes Praeityje* (Eisiskes in the Past). October 28, November 11, 1959.

Safrai, Zeev, ed. *The Ancient Synagogue*. Jerusalem: Zalman Shazar Center, 1986.

St. John, Robert. *Tongue of the Prophets*. New York: Doubleday, 1952.

Salmon, Yosef. *Sbornik materialov ob ekonomicheskom polozhenii Yevreev v Rossi* (Collection of Materials on the Economic Situation of Jews in Russia). 2 vols. St. Petersburg, 1904.

———. "The Yeshiva of Lida: A Unique Institution of Higher Learning." YIVO *Annual* 15 (1974): 106–25.

Sanders, Ronald. *Shores of Refuge*. New York: Schocken, 1988.

Sandrow, Nahma. *Vagabond Stars: A World History of Yiddish Theater*. New York: Harper & Row, 1977.

Schachter, Jacob J. "Haskalah, Secular Studies and the Closing of the Yeshiva in Volozhin in 1892." *Torah u-Mada Journal*, 1990, 76–133.

Schall, Jakob. *Historja zydow w Polsce, na Litwie i Rusi* (History of the Jews in Poland, Lithuania, and Ruthenia). Lwow: Polska Niepodlegia, 1934.

Scharfstein, Zevi. *Ha-Heder be-Hayyei Amenu* (The Heder in the Life of Our People). New York: Shilo, 1943. Rev. enl. ed., Tel Aviv: M. Neumann, 1951.

———. *Ha-Hinukh ve-ha-Tarbut ha-Yvrit be-Eiropa Bein Shtei Milhamot ha-Olam* (Jewish Education and Culture in Europe Between the Two World Wars). New York: Ogen, 1957.

———. "Sifrei Limud ve-Zramin Khinukyim." In *Kovetz Ribelow*, edited by M. Ribelow, 260–75. New York, 1937.

Schipper, Ignacy (Yizhak). "The Beginnings of Jewish Life in Poland and Russia" (English title). BFG 12 (1960): 25–59. First published in *Almanach Zydowski*, 1918.

———. *Geshikhte fun Yiddisher Teatrkunst un Drame* (History of Jewish Theater and Drama from Earliest Times to 1750). 4 vols. Warsaw, 1923–28.

Schochat, Azriel. "Ha-Hanhaga be-Kehillot Russia im Bitul ha-Kahal" (Leadership in Russian Kehilot After the Abolition of the Kahal). *Zion* 42 (1977): 143–233.

Schoenburg, Nancy, and Schoenburg, Stuart. *Lithuanian Jewish Communities*. New York: Garland, 1991.

Schulman, Faye. *A Partisan's Memoir: Woman of the Holocaust*. Toronto: Second Story Press, 1995.

Schwartz, Rosaline, and Milamed, Susan. *A Guide to YIVO's Landsman Shaftn*. New York: YIVO Institute for Jewish Research, 1986.

Schwarzbaum, Haim. *Studies in Jewish and World Folklore*. Berlin: de Gruyter, 1968.

Sdomi, Isaac. *Siah Rishonim*. Beth Dagan, Israel: Merkaz Volcani, 1988.

Sefarim. *See* Mendele Mokher Sefarim.

Segal, B. "A Jew in the Russian Army During the First World War." *Rhode Island Jewish Historical Notes* 7 (1975): 104–39.

Segal Halevi Horowitz, Rabbi Moseh ben Aaron. *Sefer Ekronot*.

Shabbtai ben Meir Cohen, *Megilat Eifa*. Reprint. Hanover, 1924.

Shaked, Gershon. *Ha-Siporet ha-Yivrit, 1880–1980* (Hebrew Narrative Fiction in the Land of Israel and the Diaspora). Israel: Ha-Kibbutz ha-Meuhad and Keter, 1983.

Shaked, Joseph Naveh Shaul. *Magic Spells and Formulae*. Jerusalem: Hebrew University, Magnes Press, 1983.

Shalit, Moshe, ed. *Di Ekonomishe Lage fun di Yidn in Poilen un di Yiddishe Kooperatsie* (The Economic Situation of the Jews in Poland and Jewish Cooperatives). Vilna, 1926.

Shapira, Anita. *Berl Katznelson: A Biography*. 2 vols. Tel Aviv: Am Oved, 1980.

———. *Visions in Conflict* (English title). Tel Aviv: Am Oved, 1989.

Shapiro, Chaim. "Rabbi Malkiel Tenenbaum, Rav of Lomza." *Jewish Observer*, March 1987.

Shatskin, I. "From the History of the Participation of the Jews in the Polish Revolt of 1863." ES 8 (1915): 29–37.

Shatzky, Jacob. "The First History of Yiddish Theater" (English title). YIVO *filologishe shriftn* 2 (1928): 217–63.

Shazar, Zalman. *Morning Stars* (*Kokhvei Boker*). Translated by Sulamith Schwartz Nardi. Philadelphia: Jewish Publication Society, 1967.

Shimoff, Ephraim. *R. Yitzhak Elhanan Spektor: Toledot Hayyav ve-Igrotav* (Rabbi Y. E. Spektor: His Life and Letters). Jerusalem: Yeshiva University, 1961.

Shlosberg, Liba Ahuva. *Mi-Labat Esh*. Jerusalem: L. A. Hershkovits, 1987.

Shmeruk, Choneh. "The Social Significance of the Hasidic Shehita" (English title). *Zion* 20 (1955): 47–72.

———. "Young Men from Germany in the Yeshivot of Poland" in *Yitzhak F. Baer Jubilee Volume*, edited by S. W. Baron, B. Dinur, S. Ettinger, and I. Halpern, 304–17. Jerusalem: Historical Society, 1960.

Shneur, Zalman. *Pandrei ha-Gibor*. Tel Aviv: Dvir, 1958.

Shoskes, Henry. *Poilen — 1946: Eindruken fun a Raize* (*Poland — 1946: Impressions from a Trip*). Buenos Aires: 1946.

Shteinshneider, Hillel Noah Maggid. *Yir Vilna*. Vilna: Ha-Almana Ve-he-Ahim Romm, 1900.

Shternbuch, Moshe, *Hilkhot Hagra u-Minhagav*. Jerusalem: Shternbuch, 1993.

Shulberg, Gavriel ben Yehoshua. *Petah Teshuvah.* Amsterdam, 1651.

Shurin, Aaron Ben Zion. "Der Yeshiveh-Boher fun Eishyshok." *Forward,* June 17, 1994.

Siamahka, Yurgen. *Armia Krajowa na Belarusi.* Minsk: Belaruskaia, Vidavetskae Tavaritsva "Hata," 1994.

Siev, Asher. *Rabeinu Moshe Isserles.* 2d ed., rev. New York: Yeshiva University, 1972.

———. "The Rema." *Tradition* (1959): 132–44.

Silverman, Peter; Smuschkowitz, David; and Smuszkowicz, Peter. *From Victims to Victors.* Montmagny, Quebec: Marquis/Canadian Society for Yad Vashem, 1992.

Singer, Isaac Bashevis. *Meshugah.* New York: Farrar, Straus & Giroux, 1994.

Slepak, Edna. *Zikhronst mi-Sham.* Tel Aviv: Saar, 1990.

Slownik geograficzny Krolestwa Polskiego (Geography of the Polish Kingdom). 15 vols. Warsaw: Filip Sulimierski and Wladyslaw Walewski, 1880.

Slutski, Yehudah. "Beit ha-Midrash le-Rabbanim be-Vilna." In *The East European Jewish Enlightenment* (English title), edited by Immanuel Etkes. Jerusalem: Zalman Shazar Center for Jewish History, 1993.

———, ed. *Bobruisk Memorial Book* (English title). 2 vols. Tel Aviv: Tarbut ve-Hinukh, 1967.

Slutski, Yehudah, and Kaplan, Mordekhai, eds. *Hayalim Yehudim be-Zivot Eiropa.* Israel: Maarakhot, 1967.

Smilanski, Moshe. *Mishpat ha-Adamah.* Tel Aviv: Am Oved, 1944.

Soloveitchik, Yossef Halevi. "Reb. Hayyim Heller Z"L - Shmuel ha-Kattan Shel Dorenu." *Hadoar,* April 21, 1961.

Soloveitchik, Hayim. "Rupture and Reconstruction: The Transformation of Contemporary Orthodoxy." *Tradition* 28:4. New York: Rabbinical Council of America, 1994.

Soloveitchik, Joseph B. "Kodesh & Hol" (Sacred & Profane). In *Shiurei Harav* (Lessons of the Rabbi). Edited by Joseph Epstein. Hoboken, N.J.: Ktav, 1994.

Sonenson, Yaffa bat Moshe. "Be-Mahboim." In *Eishyshok Koroteah ve-Hurbanah,* edited by Peretz Alufi and Shaul Barkali. Jerusalem: Ha-Vaad le-Nizolei Eishyshok be-Medinat Israel, 1950.

Spektor, Yitzhak Elhanan. *Ein Yitzhak.* Vilna, 1889–95.

———. Letter to Rabbi Yitzhak Blazer. In *Talpiot,* no. A-B, 1951.

Spier, Arthur. *The Comprehensive Hebrew Calendar.* New York: Behrman House, 1952.

Stampfer, Shaul. *Ha-Yeshivah ha-Litait be-Hithavutah* (The Lithuanian Yeshivah). Jerusalem: Zalman Shazar Center for Jewish History, 1995.

———. "Marital Patterns in Interwar Poland." In *The Jews of Poland Between Two World Wars,* edited by I. Gutman, et al., Hanover, N.H.: University Press of New England, 1989.

———. "Shalosh Yeshivot Litaiot Ba-Meah-Ha '19" (Three Lithuanian Yeshivot in the Nineteenth Century). Ph.D. diss. Hebrew University, Jerusalem 1981.

Stanislawski, Michael. *For Whom Do I Toil?* New York: Oxford University Press, 1988.

———. "Jewish Apostasy in Russia: A Tentative Typology." In *Jewish Apostasy in the Modern World,* edited by Todd Endelman, 189–206. New York: Holmes & Meier, 1987.

———. *Tsar Nicholas I and the Jews: The Transformation of Jewish Society in Russia, 1825–1855.* Philadelphia: Jewish Publication Society of America, 1983.

Steiner, Gershon Erich. *The Story of the Patria.* New York: Holocaust Library, 1982.

Steinman, Eliezer. *Beer ha-Hasidut: Sefer Mishnat Habad.* 2 vols. Tel Aviv, 1900.

Stern, Kenneth S. *Holocaust Denial.* New York: American Jewish Committee, 1993.

Sternberg, Ghitta. *Stefanesti: Portrait of a Romanian Shtetl.* Oxford: Pergamon Press, 1984.

Stessel, Zahava Szasz. *Wine and Thorns in Tokay Valley.* Madison and Teaneck, N.J.: Fairleigh Dickinson University Press, 1995.

Sumner, B. H. *Peter the Great and the Emergence of Russia.* New York: Collier, 1969.

Swiatek, Danuta. "Mur w glowach rosnie coraz wiekszy." *Zucie Warszawy,* August 22, 1996: 1–2.

Szajkowski, Zosa. "The German Appeal to the Jews of Poland, August 1914." *Jewish Quarterly Review* 59 (1969): 311–20.

Talmudic Encyclopedia. 22 vols. Jerusalem: Yad Harav Herzog, 1995.

Tarasenka, Petras. *Lietuvos Archelogijos Medziaga.* Kaunas: Svietimo Ministerijos Knygy (Lithuanian Archaeological Materials, An Issue of the Ministry of Education Committee for Book Printing). no. 147, 1928.

Tchernowitz, Hayyim. *Toledot ha-Posekim* (Biographies of Decisors). 3 vols. New York: Jubilee Committee, 1947.

Tec, Nechama. *Defiance: The Bielski Partisans.* New York: Oxford University Press, 1993.

———. *When Light Pierced the Darkness: Christian Rescue of Jews in Nazi-Occupied Poland.* New York: Oxford University Press, 1986.

Telushkin, Nissan. *Ha-Torah ve-ha-Olam.* New York: Shulsinger Brothers, 1995.

Tenenbaum, Malkiel Zvi. *Divrei Malkiel*. Vilna-Pietrekov, 1891. Reprint. 2 vols. Jerusalem, 1987.

Thon, Yaakov. "M. Wilkanski, Mi-Zayarei ha-Aliyah ha-Shnia." *Davar*, December 9, 1949.

Tobias, Henry J. *The Jewish Bund in Russia from Its Origins to 1905*. Stanford, Calif.: Stanford University Press, 1972.

Tory-Golub, Avraham, ed. *Mariampole (Maryiampol)*. Tel Aviv, 1983.

Trachtenberg, Joshua. "Jewish Education in Eastern Europe at the Beginning of the Seventeenth Century." *Jewish Education* 11, no. 2 (1939): 121–37.

Tracing An-Sky Jewish Collections from the State Ethnographic Museum in St. Petersburg. Zwolle; Amsterdam; and St. Petersburg: Waanders; State Ethnografic Museum; Joods Historisch Museum, 1992–94.

Trunk, Isaiah. *Judenrat: The Jewish Councils of Eastern Europe Under Nazi Occupation*. New York: Macmillan, 1972.

Tsanin, Mordecai. "Solving the Khazar Problem." *Judaism* 13 (1964): 431–43.

———. *Tel Olam — Masa Al Penei 100 Kehillot Neheravot* (Eternal Ruin — A Trip Through 100 Destroyed Communities). Tel Aviv: Menora, n.d.

Tukachinski, Yehiel Mikhal. *Gesher ha-Hayyim*. 3 vols. Jerusalem: Solomon Printing Press, 1960.

Urbach, Ephraim E. *The Tosaphists: Their History, Writings and Methods* (English title). Jerusalem: Bialik Institute, 1955.

Vago, Bela, and Mosse, George, eds. *Jews and Non-Jews in Eastern Europe, 1918–1945*. New York: Wiley, 1974.

Vanagas, Aleksandras. "Eisiskes Ikure Eiksys" (Eishyshok Was Founded by Eiksys). *Gimtasis Krastas* (Native Land), August 29–September 4, 1991.

Vereta, Meir. "Polish Suggestions for a Territorial Solution to the Jewish Problem" (English title). *Zion* 6 (1940–41): 148–55, 203–13.

Versano, Samy. "The Last Days of the Patria" (English title). *Yalkut Moreshet*, August 1987, 13–38.

Vital, David. *The Origins of Zionism*. Oxford: Clarendon Press, 1975.

Voskhod (1881–1906). 1901 Books 4–5.

Wahrman, Nahum. *Mekorot le-Toldot Gezerot Tah ve-Tat* (Sources for the History of the Decrees of 1648–49). Jerusalem, 1949.

Wandycz, Piotr. "Die Karaer" (The Karaites). *Zeitschrift für Demographie und Statistik der Juden*. 10 vols. September–October 1914: 132–37.

———. *The Lands of Partitioned Poland, 1795–1918*. Seattle: University of Washington Press, 1974.

Warhaftig, Zorach. *Palit ve-Sarid, bi-Yeme ha-Shoah* (Refugee and Remnant). Jerusalem: Yad Vashem, 1984.

Waxman, Meyer. *A History of Jewish Literature from 1880 to 1935*. 6 vols. 2d ed. New York: Thomas Yoseloff, 1960.

Waysblum, M. "Isaac of Troki and the Christian Controversy in the Sixteenth Century." *Journal of Jewish Studies* 3 (1952): 62–77.

Weinberg, Jeshajahu, and Elieli, Rina. *The Holocaust Museum in Washington*. New York: Rizzoli, 1995.

Weinberg, Sydney Stahl. *The World of Our Mothers: The Lives of Jewish Immigrant Women*. Chapel Hill: University of North Carolina Press, 1988.

Weinryb, Bernard D. *The Jews of Poland*. Philadelphia: Jewish Publication Society of America, 1973.

Weintraub, Wiktor. "Tolerance and Intolerance in Old Poland." *Canadian Slavonic Papers* 13, no. 1 (1971): 21–43.

Weiss, Avraham. *Women at Prayer: A Halakhic Analysis of Women's Prayer Groups*. Hoboken, N.J.: Ktav, 1990.

Weisser, Michael R. *A Brotherhood of Memory: Jewish Landsmanshaftn in the New World*. Ithaca, N.Y.: Cornell University Press, 1989.

Weiter, A. *Ketavim* (Writings). Vilna: B. A. Kletskin, 1923.

Weizmann, Chaim. *Trial and Error*. New York: Harper, 1950.

Wengeroff, Pauline. *Hasidim u-Mitnagdim*. 2 vols. Jerusalem: Mossad Bialik, 1970.

———. *Memoiren einer grossmutter* (Memoirs of a Grandmother). Berlin: M. Poppelauer, 1913–19.

Werner, Eric. *A Voice Still Heard: The Sacred Songs of the Ashkenazic Jews*. University Park: Pennsylvania State University Press, 1976.

Wertheimer, Jack. *Unwelcome Strangers: East European Jews in Imperial Germany*. New York: Oxford University Press, 1987.

Wielka Encyklopedia. Warsaw, 1896.

Wiernik, Peter. *History of the Jews in America*. New York: Jewish Press, 1912.

Wieski, D. *Ejszyszki, Ziemia Lidska* (The Lida Territories). January 1937, no. 2.

———. *Koscioly w gm. Eszyskiej–Ziemia Lidzka* (Churches in the Eishyshok Vicinity–Lida Territory). March 1937, no. 3, Lida.

Wigdor, Geoffrey. *The Story of the Synagogue*. Jerusalem: Domino Press, 1986.

Wilkanski, Meir (Elazari). *Ba-Heder*. Tel Aviv: A. I. Shtibel, 1933.

———. *Be-Yemay ha-Aliyah*. Tel Aviv: Sifriat Tarmil, 1982.

———. *Ha-Galila/Beer Hafarnu.* Tel Aviv: Sifriat Tarmil, 1978.

———. *Ha-Rabbi.* Jerusalem: Ashkolot, booklet II, n.d.

———. *Mi-Gal El-Gal.* Tel Aviv: Am Oved, 1943.

———. *Senuniyyot.* Tel Aviv/Jerusalem: Hozaat Sfarim M. Newman, 1963.

Wischnitzer, Mark. "Bibliography for the History of the Jews in Poland and Lithuania" (English title). *Istoria Yevreiskogo naroda* II: 505–16.

Wischnitzer-Bernstein, Rachel. *The Architecture of European Synagogues.* Philadelphia: Jewish Publication Society of America, 1964.

Wisse, Ruth R. *A Shtetl and Other Yiddish Novellas.* Detroit: Wayne State University Press, 1986.

Wolakanowski, Jaroslaw. *Okreg Wilenski Zwiazku Walki Zybrojnej Armii Krajowej.* Warsaw, 1996.

Wolf. *See* Ezekiel Feiwel ben Zeev Wolf.

Wolowelsky, Joel B. "A Review of Avraham Weiss, *Women at Prayer: A Halakhic Analysis of Women's Prayer Groups.*" *Judaism* 2, no. 4 (Fall 1993).

———. "Women and Kaddish." *Judaism* 44, no. 3 (Summer 1995).

Wyszkowski, Charles. *A Community in Conflict: American Jewry During the Great European Immigration.* Lanham, Md.: University Press of America, 1991.

Yaffe, Yehoshua. *Be-Ghetto Novogrudek u-ba-Tenuah ha-Partizanit.* Tel Aviv: Irggun Yozei Novogrudek be-Israel, 1988.

Yahadut Lita (Lithuanian Jewry). Edited by Natan Goren. 4 vols. Tel Aviv: Igud Yotzei Lita be-Israel, 1959–84.

Yahil, Leni. *The Holocaust.* New York: Oxford University Press, 1990.

———. "Raoul Wallenberg: His Mission and His Activities in Hungary." *Yad Vashem Studies* 15 (1983): 7–54.

Yarden, Shmuel. *Sipura Shel Motele.* Jerusalem, 1979.

Yarmolinsky, Avrahm. "The Khazars: A Bibliography." *Bulletin of the New York Public Library* 42 (1938): 695–710.

Yerushalmi, Yosef Hayim. *Zakhor: Jewish History and Jewish Memory.* New York: Schocken, 1989.

Yevreiskoe Statisticheskoe Obshchestvo. *Yevreiskow naselenie Rossii* (The Jewish Population of Russia). Petrograd, 1917. Reprint. Tel Aviv: Aticot, 1970.

Yshdavinis, V. *Tragedia Sela Pirchupis* (Tragedy of the Pirchupis Village). Vilnius: Gospolitnychizdat, 1963.

Yudson, Shlomo. "Deretchin Fun Meine Kinder Yorn." In *Sefer Dereczyn.* Tel Aviv: Deretchiners Societies in Israel and USA, 1971 or 1972.

Zborowski, Mark, and Herzog, Elizabeth. *Life Is with People.* New York: Schocken, 1952.

Zenkovsky, Serge A., ed. *Medieval Russia's Epic Chronicles and Tales.* New York: Dutton, 1963.

Zertal, Idith. *From Catastrophe to Power: Jewish Illegal Immigration to Palestine, 1945–1948* (English title). Tel Aviv: Am Oved, 1996.

Zilberzweig, Zalman. "Di Vilner Trupe." In *Wilno,* edited by Ephim H. Jeshurin. New York: Wilner Branch 367, Workmen's Circle, 1935.

Ziminskas, J. "Eisiskes XVIII–XIX Amziuje" (Eishyshok in the Eighteenth and Nineteenth Centuries). *Ateitis* (Future), no. 44 (347), February 22, 1944, 3.

———. "Eisiski Isgyvrentos Nelaimes" (What the Town of Eisiskes Suffered). *Ateitis* (Future), no. 38, February 15, 1994.

Zinberg, Israel. *A History of Jewish Literature.* 12 vols. Cincinnati, Ohio: Hebrew Union College Press; New York: Ktav, 1977.

Zinowitz, Moshe. "Betei Midrashot Historyim be-Vilna." *Beth ha-Kneset* no. 5, 1948.

———. "Eishyshok Ayeret ha-Prushim." *Yahadut Lita,* vol. 1, p. 220.

———. *Etz Hayyim, Toldot Yeshivat Volozhin.* Tel Aviv: Mor, 1972.

———. "Mir." In idem, *Toldot Yeshivat Mir.* Tel Aviv: Mor, 1980.

Zipperstein, Steve J. *The Jews of Odessa: A Cultural History, 1794 to 1881.* Stanford, Calif.: Stanford University Press, 1986.

Zitron, Samuel Leib. *Meshumodim: Tipn un Sulvetn fun Nontn Ovar* (Apostates: Types and Silhouettes from a Near Past). 4 vols. Warsaw: Ahisefer, 1923–28.

GLOSSARY

ADAR Twelfth month of the biblical calendar, sixth of the civil (February–March). During a leap year, Adar Beth is added. Within a cycle of nineteen years, seven years have thirteen months with Adar Beth as the addition.

AGGADAH Name given to those sections of the Talmud and Midrash containing homiletic expositions of the Bible, stories, legends, folklore, anecdotes, or maxims. In contradistinction to HALAKHAH.

AGUDAT ISRAEL (Union of Association of Israel) Anti-Zionist movement founded in 1912 by German and East German Jews.

AGUNAH, *pl.* AGUNOT Woman unable to remarry according to Jewish law, because her husband has deserted her or is missing but cannot be presumed dead.

AK *see* ARMIA KRAJOWA.

ALEPH BETH The Hebrew alphabet.

ALIYAH (*Hebrew,* "ascent") (1) The coming of Jews to the Land of Israel. Emigrants to Israel are *olim.* (2) Being called to read the Torah at a synagogue.

ALTER BESOYLEM (*Yiddish*) The old house of eternity — the Old Cemetery.

AMIDAH (*Hebrew,* "standing") Main prayer recited at all services; also known as Shemone Esreh (Eighteen Benedictions) and Tefillah.

AMORAIM Jewish scholars in Eretz Israel and Babylonia in the third to sixth centuries who were responsible for expounding the Mishnah and compiling the Talmud.

ARENDA The system by which a Jew leased a magnate's land.

ARENDATOR Leaseholder. A Jew who leased an estate for a fixed rate.

ARMIA KRAJOWA (*Polish,* "home army") Polish underground army run by the Polish government-in-exile in London during World War II. They were also known as AK, Akowtsy, and White Poles. In the vicinity of Eishyshok, they murdered hundreds of Jews and the Poles who rescued Jews. They continued their anti-Jewish policy after liberation.

ARON KODESH Holy Ark.

ASHKENAZIM (*Hebrew,* "German") Since the ninth century, a term applied to the German Jews and their descendants, in contrast to the SEPHARDIM. After the Crusades, many Ashkenazic Jews settled in Eastern Europe and from there migrated to Western Europe and America. In recent centuries they have constituted the overwhelming majority of the world Jewish population.

ATRIAD Partisan battalion in World War II.

AV or MENAHEM-AV Fifth month of the biblical calendar, eleventh of the civil (July–August).

AV BETH DIN Head of the rabbinic court.

AVODAH (*Hebrew,* "work") The sacrificial system in the Temple was applied to prayer, referred to as "avodah of the heart."

BAALAGOLEH Coachman.

BABSKE FELDSHERS Practitioners of folk medicine.

BADKHAN (*Hebrew*) Jester, joker, entertainer, and master of ceremonies who entertained wedding guests in semi-improvised rhymes.

BAHELFER An assistant (helper) to the melamed.

BAHUR (*Hebrew*) Young man; a young man who has studied Torah.

BALEBATIM Householders, petty bourgeois.

BALE-MELOKHE The artisan and plebeian class.

BALFOUR DECLARATION The British government's statement of sympathy for Zionist aspirations in the Land of Israel, November 2, 1917.

BANKE, *pl.* BANKES (*Yiddish*) Cupping glasses used by physicians and medicine men and women to draw blood to the skin, as a remedy for various maladies, especially colds. It is also part of the shtetl proverb treasury. "It will help as bankes for a dead person" meant to be useless and ineffective.

BAR "Son of. . . ," frequently appearing in personal names.

BAR MITZVAH Ceremony marking the initiation of a boy at the age of thirteen into the Jewish religious community. He is thereafter personally responsible for his religious acts for the rest of his life.

BATEI MIDRASH *pl.* of BETH MIDRASH.

BEDDER Bathhouse manager.

BEITAR Abbreviated name for Berit Trumpeldor (the Covenant of Trumpeldor), an activist Zionist youth movement founded in Riga in 1923.

BEKIUT (*Hebrew*) Proficiency, especially in Talmud and its literature.

BEN "Son of. . . ," frequently appearing in personal names.

BERIHAH (*Hebrew,* "flight") Underground movement that assisted Holocaust survivors to escape from Europe and reach Palestine. Approximately 250,000 Jews used the Berihah routes, though not all of them reached Israel.

BETH DIN (*Hebrew; pl.* batei din) Rabbinic court of law.

BETH MIDRASH (from *Hebrew,* "house of learning"; in *Yiddish, besmedresh; pl.* in *Hebrew,* BATEI MIDRASH, in *Yiddish, bote-medroshim*) In the Talmudic age, a school for higher rabbinic learning where students assembled for study and discussion, as well as prayer. In the post-Talmudic age most synagogues had a beth midrash or were themselves called by the term, insofar as they were places of study. The beth midrash served the double function as a house of prayer and house of study, primarily for Talmudic literature, for individuals, various societies (havurot), and as a yeshivah. All major community events took place in the beth midrash, since in many Eastern European towns the principal synagogue was not heated during the winter, while the beth midrash was.

THE BIG FIRE The fire that burned down Eishyshok on Thursday market day in the first week of May 1895.

BIKKUR HOLIM (*Hebrew*) A charitable organization dedicated to the welfare of the sick.

BILLIGE KIKH Soup kitchen to aid the needy.

BILU Hebrew initials of Beit Yaakov Lekhu ve-Nelkha, "House of Jacob, come ye and let's go" (Isaiah 2:5), an organized group of young Russian Jews who returned to Eretz Israel in 1882 in reaction to the pogroms of 1881. It was the first modern movement of pioneering and agricultural settlement in Palestine, founded in 1882 in Kharkov, Russia.

BIMAH Synagogue platform on which stands the table from which the Scriptures are read.

BNEI HAIL (*Hebrew,* "sons of valor") Charitable organization of Jewish war veterans formed in Eishyshok during World War I to assist Jewish soldiers.

BORERIM (*Hebrew*) Laymen chosen as arbitrators instead of the shtetl dayyan (judge).

BRITISH MANDATE Responsibility for the administration of Palestine conferred on Britain by the League of Nations in 1922; mandatory government; the British administration of Palestine.

BUDA (*Polish*) Booth.

BUND (*Yiddish,* "union") In full, Algemeyner Yiddisher Arbeiter Bund in Lite, Poylin, un Rusland. General Jewish workers' union in Lithuania, Poland, and Russia. A Jewish socialist party founded in Vilna in October 1897, supporting Jewish national rights; it was Yiddishist, and anti-Zionist.

CANTONISTS Young Jewish boys who were forcefully taken into the Russian army during the reign of Tzar Nicholas I, 1825–55. Many boys were kidnapped and most were baptized. This dark period of history is known in Hebrew as *Hatufim* — the kidnapped.

CERTIFICATES Immigration papers issued by the British in Palestine, from 1925 to independence.

COUNCIL OF THE FOUR LANDS (Vaad Arba Aratzot) The autonomous national organization of Polish–Lithuanian Jewry, originating in the sixteenth century and taking its name from the four "provinces": Great Poland, Little Poland, Ruthenia, and Volhynia. It was dissolved in 1764.

DAYYAN, *pl.* **DAYYANIM** A judge in a rabbinical court who is competent to decide on cases involving monetary matters and civil law, as well as questions of religious or ritual character. Member of the BETH DIN.

DIASPORA Originally, the Greek term used by Hellenistic Jews for all Jewish settlements that were dispersed outside Eretz Israel; all lands of dispersion outside the Land of Israel.

DIN A law (secular or religious), legal decision, or lawsuit.

DIN TORAH (*Hebrew,* "judgment," "law") Lawsuit presented before an individual or individuals well versed in Jewish law.

DP Displaced persons: individuals who did not return to live in their homes following World War II. For Jews, especially those from Eastern Europe, it was due to strong anti-Semitism. DPs lived in temporary camps in the Allied zones and Italy. At the end of 1946, the number of Jewish DPs was estimated at 250,000: 185,000 in Germany, 45,000 in Austria, and 20,000 in Italy.

DYBBUK (from *Hebrew,* "to cleave") In Jewish folklore and popular belief, a spirit of a dead person or an animal that enters into the body of a living person. The dybbuk cleaves to the soul, causes mental illness, talks with a strange voice through the mouth of the possessed, and represents a separate and alien personality.

EIN YAAKOV A popular Aggadic work, a compilation of the legendary (*Aggadetah*) sections of the Talmud first published in Salonica in 1516. It became a textbook of special adult study groups also called Ein Yaakov. The author was Rabbi Yaakov Ibn Haviv (1460–1516).

EINSATZGRUPPEN (*German*, "Action Groups") The Nazis' mobile killing units, deployed in the USSR, eastern Poland, the Baltics, and Serbia. Probably over 2 million Jews were murdered by the Einsatzgruppen with assistance of local collaborators.

ELUL Sixth month of Biblical calendar, twelfth of the civil (August–September). Precedes the High Holiday season in the fall.

ENDECJA Poland's National Democratic Party, known for its anti-Semitic policies.

ENDEKES Members of Endecja.

ERETZ ISRAEL Land of Israel; Palestine.

ESSEN TEG (*Yiddish*, literally "eating days") Yeshivah students who ate on designated days in homes of balebatim.

EVEN HA-EZER Section of SHULHAN ARUKH.

EZRAT YOLEDET A charitable society that provided midwife and postnatal care for mother and child.

FELDSHER (*Yiddish*, from the German for "field surgeon") Old-time barber-surgeon; medicine man (or woman).

FIRST ZIONIST CONGRESS Organized by Theodor Herzl, it took place August 29–31, 1897, in Basel, Switzerland.

FROYEN FARAIN (*Yiddish*, "union of women") Official union of the women's charitable societies.

GABBAI (*m.*); GABBAIT (*f.*); GABBAIM (*pl.*) (*Hebrew*) Official of the synagogue. Originally a tax collector.

GALUT (*Hebrew*, "exile") The condition of the Jewish people in dispersion.

GAON (*Hebrew*, "genius") The spiritual and intellectual leader of Babylonian Jewry in the post-Talmudic period, from the sixth through the eleventh centuries. The title gaon is occasionally applied in a general honorific sense to a very eminent scholar, such as the gaon of Vilna.

GEBIETSKOMMISAR (*German*, "head of a territory") Regional Nazi commander.

GEDUD HA-AVODAH (Labor Battalion) An idealistic Jewish road-building and defense group established in Palestine in 1920 in honor of Yossef Trumpeldor.

GELLER SCHEIN (*German*, "yellow certificate") Document issued to Jews by the German occupying forces during the Holocaust granting temporary permission to survive.

GEMARA, *pl.* GEMAROT (*Aramaic*, "completion") A book containing traditions, discussions, and rulings of the Amoraim, commenting on and supplementing the Mishnah, and forming part of the Bavli and Yerushalmi Talmuds.

GEMATRIA A system of exegesis based on the interpretation of a word or words according to the numerical value of the constituent letters in the Hebrew alphabet.

GENIZAH (*Hebrew*, "hiding place") A storeroom for worn-out sacred writings called SHEMOT (divine names) because they contained God's name or reference to God. The sanctity attached to them forbade disrespectful disposal. Each synagogue had a genizah. The most famous is the Cairo genizah.

GET (*Hebrew*) Bill of divorce.

GEULAH Redemption.

GILGUL, *pl.* GILGULIM (*Hebrew*, "turning over of the soul") Metempsychosis; transmigrated soul that enters but does not take over a living being.

GOY Gentile (non-Jew).

GRAF A Polish count.

GRAFINA A Polish countess.

GROSZ, *pl.* GROSZY One-hundredth of a zloty: a Polish penny.

GUBERNIA Province. During the reign of Catherine the Great, tzarist Russia was divided into fifty administrative units; each unit was a gubernia.

HAFTARAH, *pl.* HAFTAROT (*Hebrew*, "conclusion") The portion from the Books of the Prophets recited after the synagogue reading from the Pentateuch on Sabbaths and holidays.

HAGANAH (Jewish Defense Organization) Clandestine group working for armed self-defense in Palestine under the British Mandate, which eventually evolved into a people's militia and became the basis for the State of Israel's army.

HAGGADAH (*Hebrew*, "telling") Set form of benedictions, prayers, biblical quotations, Psalms, midrashic commentary, and songs recited at the Seder during Passover. It is based on the service prescribed in the Mishnah (Pesahim 10).

HAKHNASAT KALLA (*Hebrew*, "the ushering of the bride under the bridal canopy") A charitable society that provided the dowry for poor brides, often helping poor non-Jewish brides as well.

HAKHNASAT ORHIM (*Hebrew*, "hospitality") Charitable organization.

HAKHSHARAH (*Hebrew*, "preparation") Organized training farm in the Diaspora of future HALUTZIM.

HAKAFOT (*Hebrew*, "circuit") A ceremonial circular procession.

HALAKHAH, *pl.* HALAKHOT; *adj.* HALAKHIC (*Hebrew*, "way"; derived from the verb *halakh*, "to go" or "to follow") An accepted decision in rabbinic law. Also refers to those parts of the Talmud concerned with legal matters. The legal part of Talmudic and later Jewish literature, in contrast to AGGADAH, the nonlegal elements. In the singular, *halakhah* means "law" in an abstract sense or alternatively, a specific rule or regulation; in the plural, *halakhot* refers to collections of laws.

HALIZAH (*Hebrew*) Biblically prescribed ceremony (Deuteronomy 25:9–10) performed when a man refuses to marry his brother's childless widow; the ceremony enables her to remarry.

HALLAH, *pl.* HALLOT (*Hebrew*) Special soft white bread, often in a braided shape, eaten on the Sabbath and holidays.

HALUTZ, *pl.* HALUTZIM Pioneer, especially in agriculture, in Eretz Israel.

HALUTZA, *pl.* HALUTZOT A female halutz.

HA-MEASSEF The major publication in Hebrew of the proponents of the Haskalah in Germany in the last decades of the eighteenth century and the first of the nineteenth.

HA-MELITZ (The Mediator) First Hebrew publication in tzarist Russia, founded by Alexander Zederbaum. It expressed the philosophy of the Russian Haskalah, later of Hibbat Zion.

HAMETZ Leavened foods that may not be eaten nor owned during the Passover holiday. Hametz is disposed of in three ways: by burning, annulling, and selling. Since disposing of hametz may result in financial hardships, especially when large quantities are involved in business, the hametz can be sold to a non-Jew for the duration of the holiday. The sale must be of a legal nature, carried out by means of a bill of sale. Any hametz a Jew has kept over Passover may never be used by him.

HANUKKAH (*Hebrew*, "dedication") Eight-day festival commemorating the victory of the Maccabees over Antiochus Epiphanes in 165 B.C.E. and the subsequent rededication of the Temple in Jerusalem and the miracle of the cruse of oil.

HA-OVED HA-ZIONI (The Zionist Worker) A labor movement founded in 1935.

HA-POEL HA-MIZRAHI Pioneering religious labor movement founded in 1922. Its ideology is expressed in the statement of Torah Ve-Avodah (Torah and Labor) after the saying: "The world stands on three things: Torah, divine service and deeds of loving kindness" (Avot 1:2).

HA-SHOMER HA-ZAIR (The Young Guardians) Zionist socialist organization established in Poland in 1913–14.

HASID, *pl.* HASIDIM Member of the pietistic sect of Hasidism.

HASIDISM (1) Religious revivalist movement of popular mysticism among Jews of Germany in the Middle Ages. (2) Religious movement founded by Israel ben Eliezer, the Baal Shem Tov (Master of the Good Name) in the first half of the eighteenth century in Eastern Europe.

HASKALAH Enlightenment. The movement for disseminating modern European culture among Jews from the 1750s to the 1880s. It advocated the modernization of Judaism, the Westernization of traditional Jewish education, and the revival of the Hebrew language.

HATIKVAH (*Hebrew*, "the hope") Anthem of the Zionist movement, later national anthem of the State of Israel. The poem was written by Naphtali Herz Imber, probably in 1878.

HATUFIM. *See* CANTONISTS

HAVDALAH (*Hebrew*, "differentiation, distinction") Ceremony marking the end of the Sabbath and holidays.

HAVER, *pl.* HAVERIM Friend. Title given to bar mitvah boys who failed to earn the more prestigious MORENU designation.

HAZAKA (*Hebrew*), HAZOKE (*Yiddish*) Claim to, right of possession, right to title, tenure.

HAZZAN, *pl.* HAZZANIM Cantor who intones the liturgy and leads the prayers in synagogue; in earlier times a synagogue official.

HEDER, *pl.* HADARIM (*Hebrew*, "room") School for teaching boys the fundamentals of Judaism. It figured prominently in traditional Jewish education in Eastern Europe.

HEDER IRBUVIA A mixed heder that boys and girls attended together, started during the Haskalah.

HEDER METUKAN Reconstructed or reformed heder.

HEDER YINGL Heder boy.

HEKDESH Consecrated property; property dedicated to the needs of the Temple. In the post-Talmudic times, *hekdesh* without qualifications came to mean property set aside for charitable purposes or for the fulfillment of any other MITZVAH. In the Middle Ages the hekdesh became a communal shelter and hospital for the poor, transient, and sick. In Yiddish *hekdesh* became synonymous with disorder and disarray of the home, in a room, or concerning a person.

HEREM, *pl.* HARAMOT Excommunication, imposed by rabbinical authorities for purposes of religious and/or communal discipline; originally, in biblical times, that which is separated from common use either because it was an abomination or because it was consecrated to God.

HESHVAN *or* MAR-HESHVAN Eighth month of the biblical calendar and second of the civil calendar (October–November).

HEVRAH BNEI AVRAHAM SHMUEL ANSHEI EISHYSHKER The Eishyshok society of America, founded in 1889.

HEVRAH KADDISHAH (Sacred Brotherhood) The burial society. Its duty was to assure a dignified burial for the dead.

HEVRAT MISHNAYOT Mishnah learners society.

HEVRAT SHAS Talmud learners society.

HEVRUTA A study partner in the yeshivah.

HIBBAT ZION. *See* HOVEVEI ZION

HIGH HOLIDAYS Also known as the Days of Awe. ROSH HASHANAH and YOM KIPPUR, autumn holidays dedicated to spiritual regeneration and religious rehabilitation.

HILLUKIM (*Hebrew*) Subtle distinctions or refined analyses in interpretation of the TALMUD or other rabbinic texts. Hebrew, divisions, or analysis method in the study of Talmud.

HOSHANA RABBAH The seventh day of SUKKOT, the harvest festival. Climax of the festival in the time of the Temple, when seven processions were made around the altar and verses of *Hoshana* (O Save) were sung.

HOVEVEI ZION (Lovers of Zion) Federation of Hibbat Zion, early (pre-Herzl) Zionist movement in Russia.

HUPPAH (*Hebrew*) Canopy under which the bride and groom stand during the wedding ceremony.

IKUV KRIAH The stopping of the reading of the Torah in the synagogue as a social protest.

ILLUI Outstanding scholar or genius, especially a young prodigy in Talmudic learning.

IRGUN ZEVI LEUMI (IZL-EZEL) Underground Jewish military organization in Eretz Israel founded in 1931, which engaged from 1937 in retaliatory acts against Arab attacks and later against the British mandatory authorities.

IYAR Second month of the biblical calendar, eighth of the civil (April–May).

JARGON A derogatory term of the Yiddish language sometimes used by detractors of Yiddish.

JEWISH LEGION Jewish units in British army during World War I.

JUDENRAT (*German*, "Jewish council") Committee set up by the Nazis in Jewish communities and ghettos in occupied Europe to execute the Nazis' instructions. The order to establish Judenrate (*pl.*) was issued by Reinhard Heydrich on September 21, 1939. Small communities had twelve-member Judenrate; in communities with more than 10,000 people twenty-four members were appointed to the Judenrat.

JUDENREIN (*German*, "clean of Jews") In Nazi terminology, the condition of a locality from which all Jews had been eliminated.

KABBALA The Jewish mystical traditions; the mystical religious movement in Judaism and/or its literature. The term *Kabbala* came to be used by the mystics beginning in the twelfth century to signify the alleged continuity of their doctrine from ancient times.

KADDISH (*Aramaic*, "holy") Ancient prayer, originally used after the study period, now recited publicly at the death of parents and other close relatives for the first eleven months and on the anniversary of the death.

KAHAL The semi-autonomous Jewish community organization and government officially sanctioned by the Russian authorities until the middle of the nineteenth century. Also, Jewish congregation; among Ashkenazim, KEHILAH.

KANCHIK (*Yiddish*) A disciplinary whip used by the melamed to discipline the heder boys.

KAPOTE Long black coat once worn by Eastern European Jews and now worn by most Hasidic men.

KAPPAROT The custom, practiced on the eve of Yom Kippur, the Day of Atonement, of swinging a fowl over one's head while praying that the fowl, when slaughtered, will expiate the sins of the individual as his substitute. The practice was sanctioned by some rabbinic authorities and ridiculed or banned by others.

KARABELNIK Peddler.

KARAITES A Jewish sect, originating in the eighth century in and around Persia, which rejected the oral Torah law and wished to interpret the Bible literally and to deduce from it a code of law without reliance on Talmudic tradition. Major factors in the evolution of the Karaites were their ardent messianic hopes and their ascetic tendencies.

KASHER Ritually permissible food.

KASHRUT Jewish dietary laws.

KATUKH An opening under the oven used as a hen roost.

KEDUSHAH Main addition to the third blessing in the reader's repetition of the Amidah in which the public responds to the cantor's introduction.

KEHILAH, *pl.* KEHILOT Congregation; governing body. *See* KAHAL

KEST (*Yiddish*) Room and board, especially offered by a family to its new son-in-law to enable him to continue his studies without financial worries.

KETUBBAH (*Hebrew*) Marriage contract, stipulating husband's obligations to wife.

KIBBUTZ, *pl.* KIBBUTZIM (1) In modern times, a collective settlement in Israel based mainly on agriculture but engaging also in industry. (2) In earlier times, a community of scholars studying Talmud and its commentaries; a yeshivah, where community support (money, food) was equally shared and divided by all the students.

KIBBUTZ GALUIOT Ingathering of the exiles.

KIBBUTZ HA-PRUSHIM OF EISHYSHOK The yeshivah, an academy for Torah learning where the PRUSHIM learned to become rabbis, judges, teachers, and preachers. The academy was known as a *kibbutz*, meaning "together," because the students shared everything given to them by the community.

KIDDUSH (*Hebrew*) Prayer of sanctification of time, recited over wine or bread before the evening and morning meals on Sabbath and festivals.

KIPPAH, *pl.* KIPPOT A head covering for Jewish males.

KISLEV Ninth month of the biblical calendar, third of the civil (November–December).

KITTEL White robe worn by Jewish men on the High Holidays, under the wedding canopy, and other occasions, symbolizing remembrance of death, and purity.

KLEI KODESH Holy vessels: the clergy.

KLEZMERS (*Yiddish*) Musicians.

KLOGERINS (*Yiddish*, from "lament") Professional female mourners who were hired to fall on the graves, weeping and wailing.

KLOIZ A Central and Eastern European institution, usually with synagogue attached, where Talmud was studied perpetually by adults.

KLOIZNIK (*Yiddish*) A yeshivah student who sat and learned in a kloiz, usually by himself.

KOHEN, *pl.* KOHANIM Priest. Kohanim are descendants of Aaron, the brother of Moses.

KOL NIDRE ("all vows") Ancient prayer in Aramaic recited at sundown on the eve of Yom Kippur.

KOROBKA A basket tax levied on certain consumer items, particularly kosher meat.

KRISTALLNACHT (*German*, "crystal night," meaning "night of broken glass") Organized destruction of synagogues, Jewish houses, and shops, accompanied by mass arrests of Jews, which took place in Germany and Austria under the Nazis on the night of November 9–10, 1938.

KUGL, *pl.* KUGLEKH (*Yiddish*, "ball") A kind of a pudding made from potatoes or noodles, a traditional Sabbath and holiday dish.

KULTUR TREGGERS (*Yiddish*) Culture carriers.

KUPPAT HOLIM In the shtetl, a fund to assist the sick. In Israel, the major institution of socialized medicine.

KVASS Nonalcoholic fermented Russian drink.

KVORESMAN (*Yiddish*, "graveman") The shtetl undertaker.

LAG BA-OMER Thirty-third day of the omer period, falling on the eighteenth of Iyar; a semi-holiday. Very popular in the shtetl among heder boys and their melamdim.

LANDSMANSHAFT, *pl.* LANDSMANSHAFTEN Social and philanthropic organization formed by Eastern European immigrants in the United States.

LEVIRATE MARRIAGE Compulsory marriage of a childless widow to the brother of her deceased husband (in accordance with Deuteronomy 25:5); release from such an obligation is effected through Halizah.

LINAT ZEDDEK (*Hebrew*, "righteous bedside") A charitable organization dedicated to offering personal care to the sick.

LITVAK A Lithuanian Jew. A cultural and character description regardless of the changing political and geographic borders of Lithuanians. A person who is rationalistic, intelligent, learned, diligent, stubborn, and an opponent of Hasidism.

LUBLIN UNION Agreement signed in Lublin July 1, 1569, between Poland and Lithuania. It brought Lithuania under firm Polish influence.

LUFTWAFFE German air force.

LULAV Palm branch. One of the four species used on Sukkot together with hadus aravah and etrog.

MAAPILIM "Illegal" Jewish immigrants to Eretz Israel during the Holocaust and its aftermath.

MAARIV Evening prayer; also called *arvit*.

MAGGID, *pl.* MAGGIDIM (*Hebrew*, "preacher") A preacher, scholar, and rabbi. The folksy, storytelling maggid was very often the voice of the people.

MAGGID MEISHARIM, *pl.* MAGGIDEI MEISHANIM (*Hebrew*) Preacher of the Righteous.

MAHZOR, *pl.* MAHZORIM Festival prayer book.

MALBISH ARUMIM A charitable society that clothed the poor.

MAOT HITTIM (*Hebrew,* "wheat money") A tax paid by the community that provided the poor with matzot and wine for Passover.

MAR-HESHVAN Popularly called Heshvan; eighth month of the biblical calendar, second of the civil (October–November).

MARAH LEVANAH ("white bile") A society whose function was to cheer up people who were melancholic.

MASKIL, *pl.* MASKILIM An adherent of the Haskalah.

MAY LAWS OF 1882 Restrictions against Jews in tzarist Russia.

MEAD A drink used for Passover made from honey and a spice called *hoppn.*

MEASSEFIM Contributors to *Ha-Meassef,* which, in the late eighteenth century, served as the major organ of the Haskalah movement in Germany.

MEGILLAH A scroll; tractate in the Mishnah.

MELAMED, *pl.* MELAMDIM (*Hebrew*) Teacher; generally applied to a teacher in an old-time heder.

MELAVEH MALKAH Saturday-evening meal and ceremony to bid farewell to the Sabbath Queen.

MENORAH Candelabrum; seven-branched oil lamp used in the Tabernacle and Temple; also eight-branched candelabrum used on Hanukkah.

MESHUGGOIM (*Yiddish, pl.*) Mentally ill people.

MESHUMAD, *pl.* MESHUMADIM (*Hebrew,* "one who is destroyed") Apostates; Jewish converts to Christianity.

MESHUMEIDESTE (*Yiddish*) Female apostate.

MESSIAH (*Hebrew,* "anointed") Originally a king or priest anointed with holy oil and consecrated to carry out the purpose of God. Later the focus of a prophetic vision of the restoration of Israel and establishment of the just kingdom on earth. The yearning for the Messiah's coming is part of the Jewish tradition.

MEZUZAH (*Hebrew,* "doorpost") Parchment scroll with selected Torah verses, Shema, and two other biblical passages concerning the love of God, placed in a container and affixed to gates and doorposts of houses occupied by Jews in fulfillment of an injunction of Deuteronomy 6:4–9; 11:13–21.

MIDRASH (*Hebrew,* "exposition") Homiletic commentary on the Scriptures elucidating legal points (Midrash Halakhah) or teaching lessons with stories and anecdotes (Midrash Aggadah). Also a collection of such rabbinic interpretations.

MIKVAH, *pl.* MIKVAOT (*Hebrew,* "a collection of water") Ritual bath for purification. The ritual immersion of women in the mikvah seven days after the end of the menstrual flow is a fundamental halakhic principle governing Jewish family purity.

MINHAH Afternoon prayers.

MINSK CONFERENCE First and last legal conference of Russian Jews in tzarist Russia attended by delegates, August 1902. Among its main issues was the discussion between secular and religious Zionists about the cultural image of the Zionist movement. Two committees for culture and education were set up expressing ideologies of the two groups.

MINYAN Group of ten adult male Jews, the minimum required for communal prayer.

MISHNAH The legal codification containing the core of the post-biblical oral Torah, compiled and edited by Rabbi Judah Ha-Nasi at the beginning of the third century.

MITNAGGED, *pl.* MITNAGGEDIM (*Hebrew,* "opponents") Originally Eastern European Jews, chiefly in Lithuania, opposed to Hasidism. Used as a synonym for Lithuanian Jews.

MITZVAH, *pl.* MITZVOT (*Hebrew,* "command") (1) The 613 divine commands (precepts) in the Torah. They are classified as being either positive or negative. There are 365 negative precepts corresponding to the 365 days of the solar year, and 248 positive, corresponding in number to the parts of the human body (Makoth 23/b). There are many additional categories of the mitzvot, like the time-bound positive mitzvot from which women are exempt if they belong to the affirmative category. (2) A good deed.

MIZRAH Hebrew for Eastern. The wall in the synagogue facing east, toward Jerusalem, along which sat the most highly respected males, mainly scholars, notables, and well-to-do individuals.

MIZRAHI (term coined from some of the letters of the Hebrew words *merkaz ruhani,* "spiritual center") Religious Zionist movement founded in 1902. Its aim was expressed in its motto "The Land of Israel for the People of Israel according to the Torah of Israel" (coined by Rabbi Meir Berlin-Bar Ilan).

MOHEL, *pl.* MOHALIM The person qualified to perform ritual circumcision, who was pious, thoroughly conversant with the laws of circumcision, and trained in the most advanced techniques of surgical hygiene.

MONOPOLKA The exclusive concession to sell liquor and alcoholic drinks.

MORENU "Our teacher." A coveted title that signified a high level of scholarship.

MUSAR (*Hebrew*) (1) Traditional Jewish moral literature. (2) Ethical movement for the education of the individual toward strict ethical behavior in the spirit of halakhah developed in the latter part of the nineteenth century among the Orthodox yeshivah community in Lithuania, founded by Rabbi Israel Lipkin Salanter.

NAYER BESOLEM (*Yiddish*) The new house of eternity — the New Cemetery.

NEEMAN HA-KAHAL Trustee, head of the Jewish community. *See* ROSH HA-KAHAL

NEILAH (*Hebrew*) The closing service of the Day of Atonement, Yom Kippur, at sunset, when, according to tradition, the gates of the Temple were closed and the heavenly "gates of judgment" are sealed.

NIKOLAIEVTZY Soldiers who served in the tzarist army.

NINTH OF AV. *See* TISHA BE-AV

NISAN First month of the biblical calendar, seventh of the civil (March–April).

NUREMBERG LAWS Nazi laws excluding Jews from German life, and setting other anti-Jewish policy, issued September 15, 1935.

OHEL, *pl.* OHALIM (*Hebrew,* "tent") Mausoleum built over a grave.

OLEH, *pl.* OLIM Emigrant to Eretz Israel.

OMER First sheaf cut during the barley harvest, offered in the Temple on the second day of Passover.

OMER Forty-nine days counted from the day on which the omer was first offered in the Temple (according to the rabbis, the 16th of Nisan, i.e., the second day of Passover) until the festival of Shavuot; now a period of semi-mourning.

OPERATION BARBAROSSA The invasion by the Wehrmacht of the USSR on June 22, 1941.

ORAH HAYYIM Section of SHULHAN ARUKH.

ORLA TISH Table in the synagogue vestibule on which the circumcised foreskins of baby boys were placed.

ORT (Obshchestvo Rasprostraneniya Truda Serdei Yevreyev) Society for the Development of Jewish Agriculture and Trade, established in 1880, in St. Petersburg.

PALE OF SETTLEMENT Twenty-five provinces of tzarist Russia where Jews were permitted permanent residence, between 1791 and 1917; the borders of the Pale of Settlement were always in flux.

PARASHAH, *pl.* PARASHOT (*Hebrew,* "section") In the synagogal reading of the Pentateuch, either the weekly portion (sidrah) or, more particularly, the smaller passages read to or by each person who is called to the reading of the Torah.

PARNAS, *pl.* PARNASIM (from the Hebrew *parnes,* "to foster" or "to support") Chief synagogue functionary, originally vested with both religious and administrative duties, but since the sixteenth century an elected lay representative.

PAROKHET, *pl.* PAROKHOT Curtain (curtains) for the Holy Ark.

PASSOVER Spring festival beginning on the 15th day of Nisan, continuing for seven days in the Land of Israel and eight days in the Diaspora, that commemorates the Exodus from Egypt. No leaven may be eaten; matzot replace bread. The ceremonial commemorative meal, the Seder, is conducted on the first night and in the Diaspora also on the second night.

PESSAH Passover.

PIDYON SHVUYIM (*Hebrew*) The ransoming of captives.

PILPUL (*Hebrew,* "to search, to argue") In Talmudic and rabbinic literature, a clarification of a difficult point. Later the term came to denote a sharp dialectical distinction or, more generally, a certain type of Talmudic study emphasizing dialectical distinctions and introduced into the yeshivot of Poland by Jacob Pollak in the sixteenth century. Pejoratively, the term means "hairsplitting."

PINKAS, *pl.* PINKASIM The official record book of the Council of the Four Lands, communities, and various societies. Each unit kept its own pinkas. In the official pinkasim, the entries were in Hebrew. For the tzarist government, the records were entered in Hebrew and Russian, in Poland during the interwar years only in Polish.

PIYYUT, *pl.* PIYYUTIM A Hebrew liturgical poem. The practice of writing such poems began in Palestine, probably around the fifth century, and continued throughout the ages, enriching the Jewish prayer book.

PLATTEN Pieces of wood on which were engraved the names of the people who had agreed to serve as Sabbath hosts for those who were visiting the shtetl.

POALEI ZION (Workers of Zion) Socialist youth Zionist organization.

POLESH The vestibule of the synagogue.

PRUSHIM (*Hebrew,* "abstainers") Yeshivah students who left their families for months or years to go study Torah.

PUD Unit of measure: 1 pud is 40 Russian pounds.

PURIM (*Hebrew*, "the lots") Festival held on the 14th of Adar in commemoration of the delivery of the Jews of Persia in the time of Queen Esther.

RABBANITE Adherent of rabbinic Judaism. In contradistinction to Karaite.

RAD KROMEN Row shops.

RAHASH Acronym for *rabbi, hazzan,* and *shammash.* The name of the tax paid at a wedding to those three officials.

REB Honorary title like Mr.

REBBETZIN (*Yiddish*) Wife of a rabbi.

RECHISNIK Buckwheat pudding.

RESPONSUM, *pl.* RESPONSA Written opinion given in reply to a question on aspects of Jewish law by qualified authorities; (*pl.*) collection of such queries and opinions in book form.

ROSH HA-KAHAL Head of the community. In some communities he was known as *neeman ha-kahal.*

ROSH HASHANAH The Jewish New Year, beginning on the first day of the month of Tishrei, start of the High Holidays. Since early times, a day of reflection and repentance, concerned with the individual and his relation to God and to his fellow men. A prominent feature is the sounding of the shofar.

ROSH HODESH New moon, marking the beginning of the Hebrew month.

ROSH YESHIVA, *pl.* RASHEI YESHIVOT The principal or director of a Talmudic academy or yeshivah.

RUBLE Russian currency.

SAMAGONKA Illegal vodka made by the local population.

SANDAK (*Hebrew*) Godfather.

SEDER (*Hebrew*, "order, sequence") Ceremony celebrated at the dining table in the home on Passover night, according to the order prescribed in the Haggadah. During the ceremony, four cups of wine are drunk, a meal is eaten, and adult male members sit in a reclining position to symbolize that they are free men.

SEFER TORAH Manuscript scroll of the Pentateuch for public reading in the synagogue.

SEJM Polish parliament.

SELIHOT (*Hebrew*, "pardon") Penitential prayers. In most communities, it is customary to begin the recital of selihot on Saturday midnight prior to Rosh Hashanah.

SEMIKHAH (*Hebrew*, "placing [of the hands]") The practice of ordination whereby Jewish teachers, beginning in the Talmudic age, conferred on their best pupils the title *rabbi* and authorized them to act as judges and render authoritative decisions in matters of Jewish law and ritual practice.

SEPHARDIM (*Hebrew*, "Spanish") The Jews of Spain and Portugal and their descendants, wherever resident, as contrasted with Ashkenazim. The term *Sephardim* is applied particularly to the Jews exiled from Spain in 1492 who settled all along the North African coast and throughout the Ottoman empire, at the present most non-Ashkenazic Jews.

SHABBAT HA-GADOL The Sabbath before Passover.

SHABBAT TESHUVAH The Sabbath between Rosh Hashanah and Yom Kippur.

SHADKHAN (*Hebrew*) A marriage broker, or a matchmaker.

SHAHARIT Morning service.

SHAMMASH The servant of the people in the synagogue or beth midrash or the rabbi's personal assistant, the beadle.

SHAULISTI (*Lithuanian*, "shooters") Local Lithuanians who collaborated with the Germans in murdering the Jews of Eishyshok on September 25 and 26, 1941.

SHAVUOT (*Hebrew*, "weeks") The second of the three biblical pilgrim festivals, originally marking the wheat harvest, but after the destruction of the Temple commemorating especially the covenant between God and Israel and the giving of the Torah on Mount Sinai.

SHEGETZ, *pl.* SHKOTZIM A non-Jewish boy or youth.

SHEHITA Slaughter of animals according to Jewish law. The term is also used by Jews to refer to the murder of the Jews by the Einsatzgruppen and their local collaborators during World War II.

SHEKEL, *pl.* SHEKALIM A coin minted in Eretz Israel since biblical days and a present-day unit of Israeli currency. During the First Zionist Congress (1897), the name *shekel* was given to the fee and card of Zionist membership. Its price was fixed but varied according to currency in each country: in the United States 50 cents; in Russia 40 kopecks, and so on. The shekel also served as a voting certificate for elections to the Zionist Congress (1960); the number of delegates allocated to a certain country was calculated on the basis of the total number of shekalim sold there.

SHEKHINAH A term used to imply the presence of God in the world, in the midst of Israel, or with individuals. In contrast to the principle of divine transcendence, Shekhinah represents the principle of divine immanence.

SHEMA ISRAEL "Hear, O Israel . . ." (Deuteronomy 6:4), Judaism's confession of faith, proclaiming the absolute unity of God. Recited at daily prayers and before death.

SHEMINI ATZERET The final day at the end of the Festival of Tabernacles, or Sukkot. *See* SIMHAT TORAH

SHEMOT (*Hebrew*, "names") Timeworn sacred writings that may contain God's name and were buried in the cemetery. *See* GENIZAH

SHEVAT Eleventh month of the biblical calendar, fifth of the civil (January–February).

SHIKSE (*Yiddish*) A non-Jewish girl or young woman.

SHIURIM Classes in school.

SHIVAH (*Hebrew*, "seven") The seven days of mourning following burial of a close relative.

SHLIAH ZIBBUR "The messenger of the congregation"; the person who leads the congregation in prayer.

SHLOSHIM (*Hebrew*, "thirty") The thirty days of mourning following burial of a close relative.

SHOFAR The horn of a ram, sounded on Rosh Hashanah, at the conclusion of Yom Kippur, and on other occasions.

SHOHET, *pl.* SHOHATIM Ritual slaughterer of animals and poultry in accordance with Jewish laws.

SHOK A currency used by taxpayers in Lithuania during the Middle Ages. The Yiddish translation of *shok* was the number 60.

SHTADLAN (*Hebrew*, from the *Aramaic*, "persuader") A Jewish representative or lobbyist, skilled in diplomatic negotiations and having access to high officials. The shtadlan carried on his activities to promote the welfare and interests of the Jewish community.

SHTANDER (*Yiddish*) Lectern, pulpit.

SHTARKE "The strong ones"; rugged individuals in the shtetl who sometimes imposed their own "law and order."

SHTETL, *pl.* SHTETLEKH (*Yiddish*, from *German stadt*, "town") Small market towns in Eastern Europe ranging in size from 1,000 to 20,000 people. Most shtetlekh had between 1,000 and 5,000 people, with the majority of the population being Jewish.

SHTIBL, *pl.* SHTIBLEKH (*Yiddish*, "little house") Prayerhouses, especially Hasidic. In Eishyshok, prayerhouses of the various artisan groups; tailors' shtibl, shoemakers' shtibl.

SHTOT (*Yiddish*) Family-owned seat in the synagogue or beth midrash.

SHULHAN ARUKH Joseph Caro's code of Jewish law in four parts: *Orah Hayyim*, laws relating to prayers, Sabbath, festivals, and fasts; *Yoreh Deah*, dietary laws; *Even ha-Ezer*, laws dealing with women and marriage; *Hoshen Mishpat*, civil, criminal law, court procedure.

SHULHOYF The synagogue courtyard, the spiritual and social center of shtetl life.

SIDDUR The volume containing the daily and sabbath prayers (as distinct from the mahzor, containing those for the festivals).

SIMHAT TORAH Eighth day of Sukkot; holiday marking the completion of the annual cycle of reading the Pentateuch; in Eretz Israel observed on Shemini Atzeret (outside Eretz Israel on the following day).

SINAI CAMPAIGN Brief campaign in October–November 1956 when the Israeli army reacted to Egyptian terrorist attacks and blockade by occupying the Sinai peninsula.

SIVAN Third month of the biblical calendar, ninth of the civil (May–June).

SIX-DAY WAR War in June 1967 when Israel reacted to Arab threats and blockade by defeating the Egyptian, Jordanian, and Syrian armies.

SOFER Scribe.

SS (abbreviation of *German Schutzstaffel*, "protection detachment") Nazi unit established in 1925, which later became the "elite" organization of the Nazi party and carried out central tasks in the Holocaust.

STAROSTA ("elder") Official in the tzarist government.

SUGIA A problem, especially in the Talmud and its literature; a subject for study.

SUKKAH Booth or tabernacle erected for Sukkot. For seven days (eight in the Diaspora), religious Jews "dwell" or at least eat in it (Leviticus 23:42).

SUKKOT Festival of Tabernacles; last of the three pilgrim festivals, beginning on the 15th of Tishrei.

SWIETO TRZECH KROLI (*Polish*) The festival of the three kings, a post-Christmas holiday.

SZELENZE (*Polish*) A tax paid by innkeepers.

SZLACHTA Polish nobility.

TAANIT ESTHER (Fast of Esther) Fast on the 13th of Adar, the day preceding Purim.

TAHARAH SHTIBL Small house at a cemetery in which dead bodies are cleansed before burial.

TAHARAH BRET The board on which dead bodies are laid for cleansing before burial.

TAKHRIKHIM (*Hebrew*) Burial shrouds.

TAKHSHITIM (*Hebrew*, "jewelry") Rascals, troublemakers.

TAKKANOT Regulations supplementing the law of the Torah; regulations governing the internal life of communities and congregations.

TALLIT Four-cornered prayer shawl with fringes (tziziot) at each corner.

TALMID HAKHAM Talmudic scholar.

TALMUD (*Hebrew*, "study, learning") The major body of Jewish teachings, consisting of the Mishnah, in Hebrew, and the Gemara, in Aramaic. Written by generations of scholars and jurists in two centers, Babylon and Palestine, in the third to fifth centuries, the Talmud concerns itself with every area of human activity and experience. The Babylonian (Bavli) Talmud and the Jerusalem (Yerushalmi) Talmud.

TALMUD TORAH Schools organized by volunteer Jewish community associations to provide tuition-free instruction in the law and lore of Judaism for children of poor parents. Ultimately the term came to be applied to Jewish public religious schools in general.

TAMMUZ Fourth month of the biblical calendar, tenth of the civil (June–July).

TANNA (*pl.* TANNAIM) Any of the teachers mentioned in the Mishnah, or in literature contemporaneous with the Mishnah, and living during the first two centuries C.E.

TARBUT (*Hebrew*, "culture") A network of Zionist Hebrew schools, from kindergarten through teachers' college during the interwar years.

TARGUM (*pl.* TARGUMIM) The Aramaic translation of the Bible. There are three Targumim to the pentateuch: Targum Onkelos, Targum Jonathan, and Targum Yerushalmi.

TASHLIKH (*Hebrew*, "thou wilt cast") The custom, observed on the first day of Rosh Hashanah, of praying near a stream or body of water and (at one time) throwing breadcrumbs to the fish.

TEFILLIN Two black leather boxes fastened to straps worn on the arm and head by an adult male Jew, starting with the bar mitzvah, especially during the weekday morning prayer. The boxes contain four portions of the Pentateuch written on parchment.

TEHINAH, *pl.* TEHINOT A prayer said by women. Devotional books in Yiddish, intended for women, also came to be known as tehinot.

TEVET Tenth month of the biblical calendar, fourth of the civil (December–January).

THIRD SABBATH MEAL Most spiritual and mystical of the three meals eaten on the Sabbath. It is stated in the Talmud that the obligation to eat three meals on the Sabbath is reflected in the threefold repetition of the word *today* in Exodus 16:25.

TISHAH BE-AV Ninth day of the month of Av (July–August). Fast day commemorating the destruction of the First and Second Temples in Jerusalem.

TISHREI Seventh month of the biblical calendar, first of the civil (September–October). Rosh Hashanah falls on the first two days of Tishrei.

TODT Organization in Nazi Germany for large-scale construction work, particularly in the military and armaments field. It was named after its founder, the engineer Dr. Fritz Todt (1891–1942).

TOKERIN, TOKERKE (from the Yiddish "to immerse") Female attendant in the mikvah (ritual bath).

TORAH (*Hebrew*, "teaching, instruction") The first five books of the Bible, also known as the Five Books of Moses, or the Pentateuch. Also used to refer to the Pentateuchal scroll for reading in the synagogue, and for the entire body of traditional Jewish teaching and literature.

TOSAFISTS The French and German scholars of the twelfth to the fourteenth centuries who produced critical and explanatory notes on the Talmud. Among the most famous of the tosafists are Rabbenu Tam, Rabbi Samuel ben Meir, and Rabbi Isaac of Dampiere.

TOSAFOT (*Hebrew*, "addenda") Critical and explanatory notes on the Talmud by the tosafists.

TREIFAH Nonkosher food forbidden by Jewish tradition.

TREIFE MEDINE Nonkosher land (America).

TSCHOLNT (*Yiddish*) A kind of stew kept in a community oven in the shtetl, and served at noon on Saturday, since cooking on the Sabbath is forbidden.

TU BE-SHEVAT The 15th day of Shevat (January–February), the New Year for Trees; date marking a dividing line for fruit tithing; in modern Israel celebrated as Arbor Day.

TZARSKI DVOR The Tzar's Court. This is how the powerful household of the Haffetz Hayyim in Radun was known.

UGANDA PLAN At the Sixth Zionist Congress in Basel, 1903, Herzl introduced Britain's plan: Uganda as a homeland for the Jews instead of Palestine. Herzl wanted to accept it as a "temporary shelter for a difficult time." The Russian Zionist delegates vehemently opposed it. The Uganda Plan was totally rejected at the Seventh Zionist Congress in 1905.

ULANS (*Polish*, "lancers") Anti-Semitic political group of the Polish army.

VARENIE Jam, preserves.

VATIKIN Pious, diligent individuals who rise early in the morning so that their morning prayers coincide with sunrise (Brakhot 9/b). This quorum was known as *minyan vatikin*.

VIDDUY (*Hebrew*, "confession") Prayer recited on several occasions, as when a Jew realizes he is about to die. It must be recited while the person is fully conscious.

VIGAN The community-owned pasture.

VOLKSDEUTSCHEN (*German*) Ethnic Germans living outside of Germany.

WANNSEE CONFERENCE Nazi conference held on January 20, 1942, at which the planned annihilation of European Jewry was endorsed.

WAR OF INDEPENDENCE War of November 1947–July 1948 when the Jews of Israel fought off Arab invading armies and ensured the establishment of the new State.

WEHRMACHT The armed forces of Germany from 1935 to 1945.

WHITE PAPERS Reports issued by the British government, frequently statements of policy, especially restricting Jewish immigration to Palestine.

WHITE POLES. *See* ARMIA KRAJOWA

WOJEWODA (*Polish*) The governor of a province.

YAD VASHEM Israel's Martyrs and Heroes Remembrance Authority, a national institute in Jerusalem dedicated to perpetuating the memory of the victims of the Holocaust through exhibits, research, documentation, and publications. The name is taken from Isaiah 56:6.

YARMULKE A skullcap worn by Jewish men during prayer, and by religious Jews at all times.

YAVNEH A school network from kindergarten through teachers' college sponsored by Mizrahi, dedicated to Hebrew Zionism and Jewish tradition.

YEKOPO Acronym for Yevreyski Komitet Pomoschi Zhertran Voyny, Jewish Relief Committee for War Victims, formed after the outbreak of World War I.

YERID A fair.

YESHIVAH, *pl.* YESHIVOT A traditional Jewish academy devoted primarily to the study of the Talmud and rabbinic literature.

YEVSEKTSIA Jewish section of the propaganda department of the Russian Communist Party from 1918 to 1930. Their goal was systematic destruction of Zionist and religious life.

YIHUS Pedigree, prominent roots.

YISHUV (*Hebrew*, "settlement") The Jewish community of Eretz Israel in the pre-State period. The pre-Zionist community is generally designated the "Old Yishuv" and the community evolving from 1880, the "New Yishuv."

YISHUVNIK A rural Jew; an uneducated person from a village under the shtetl jurisdiction.

YIVRIT BE-YIVRIT "Hebrew in Hebrew." Method for the teaching of Hebrew as the mother tongue.

YOM KIPPUR (*Hebrew*, "Day of Atonement") A solemn fast day observed on the tenth day of the Hebrew month Tishrei and serving as the culmination of the Ten Days of Penitence. It is the day when Jews are to cleanse themselves from sin and to beg for the forgiveness of God through confession, prayer, and atonement.

YOREH DEAH A section of SHULHAN ARUKH.

ZADDIK, *pl.* ZADDIKIM (Hebrew, "a righteous man") Person outstanding for his faith and piety.

ZEMAN, *pl.* ZEMANIM (Hebrew, "time") Semester in the heder and the yeshivah. From Sukkot to Passover was first semester, zeman rishon, approximately October–April; from Passover to Rosh Hashanah, the second semester, zeman sheni; in between semesters, bein hazemanim.

ZIEMLANKA (*Russian*) An underground dwelling used by partisans during World War II.

ZIZIT Rectangular garment of linen, cotton, or wool with woolen tziziot (*Hebrew*, "fringes") on its corners, worn during the day by observant male Jews. The number of threads and knots in each fringe is prescribed (Numbers 15:37–41; Deuteronomy 22:12).

ZOGERKE Woman who reads prayers in the women's section of the synagogue, for the other women to repeat.

INDEX

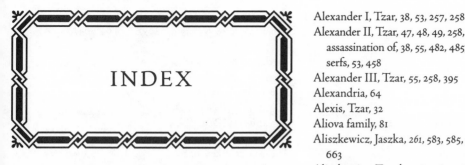

PAGE NUMBERS IN *italic* INDICATE ILLUSTRATIONS.

Aaron the Saltman, 324, 430, *533*
Abba Arikha (Abba ben Aivo). *See* Rav
Abba Arikha (shoemaker), 168, 488, 489
Abbahu, 168
Abelov, Frumele, *272*, *625*
Abelov, Motl, 572
Abelowitch, Leizerke, 220
Abelowitch, Meishke, 233
Abelowitch, Reb Isser Velvl, 42
Abelowitch brothers, 220–221
Abramauskas, S., 22
Abramofsky, Jacob. *See* Kirschner, Jacob
Abramovich, Shalom Jacob. *See* Sefarim, Mendele Mokher
Abrams, Jacob. *See* Kirschner, Jacob
Abrashuk family, 631
Acosta, Uriel, 87
Adam, Reb. *See* Krapovnitzki, Eliezer David Mordekhai
Adamowicz, 304
Adasse, Dr., *442*
Addison, Lancelot, 211
Adler family, 539
Agnon, Shmuel Yosef, 8, *510*, 511
Agobard, Archbishop, 313
agriculture, 255–269; and anti-Semitic legislation, 257–261; education and, 473, *476*, 502; Jewish merchants and, 274; in South America, 488
Agudat Israel movement, 107, 112, 113, 189, 190, *374*, 375, 469, 495
agunah (abandoned woman), 379, 380
Ahiezer (Grodzinski), 191
Aishishkin, Jennie, *553*
Aishishkin, Peter, *553*
Aishishkin, Rabbi Ezekiel (Slepak), 552, *553*
AK. *See* Armia Krajowa
Akiva, Rabbi, 162, 431
Aleichem, Sholem, 319, 398, 540
Alexander I, Tzar, 38, 53, 257, 258
Alexander II, Tzar, 47, 48, 49, 258, 455, 488; assassination of, 38, 55, 482, 485, 545; emancipation of serfs, 53, 458
Alexander III, Tzar, 55, 258, 395
Alexandria, 64
Alexis, Tzar, 32
Aliova family, 81
Aliszkewicz, Jaszka, *261*, 583, 585, 589, 590, 593, 655, 663
Aliszkewicz, Zoszka, 583, 584, 585, 589, 655
Aliushka, Lieutenant, 670, 675
Aliyah ("ascent") to Eretz Israel, 56; First (1881–1904), 495; Second (1904–1914), *16*, *194*, 491, 492, 740n16; Third (1919–1923), 497–499; Fourth (Grabski Aliyah; 1924–1928), 505. *See also* Wilkanski, Meir
Aliyah Beth immigration movement, 685, 687
Alkalai, Yehudah, 484
Altalena (ship), 11, *690*, 691
Alter, Reb (the Long), 206
Alter der Dumbler, 259
Alter der Sherer (the barber), 207
Altshul brothers, 355
Alvokove family, 205
Alytus, 674
Amalekites, 293n
Amsterdam, 33, 178, 615
Anczelewicz, 613, 614
Anders, General, 652
Anozewicz, 275
Anschel the barber, 473
Anski, S., 539
anti-Semitism: and agriculture, 255–256; of Armia Krajowa, 613, 629; and attacks on travelers, 302; in Austria, 68; and Christian holidays, 406–407, 425; and Christian servants, 338–339; economic effects of, 261–262, 285–287; of Jewish converts, 396; and Jewish millers, 279–280; legislation supporting, 257–261, 262; in Lithuania, 26; on market days, 324–326; in military, 45–48, 53–54, 86, 221, 332; in Poland, 55, 208, 220, 284, 443, 444, 480, 505, 529, 561–563, 571, 658, 673, 676–677, 679; in Prussia, 68; in Russia, 36, 38, 45, 119, 284, 332, 482, 485, 545; in Sweden, 33; and Zionism, 485. *See also* Armia Krajowa; May Laws; pogroms
anti-Zionism, 173, 189, 486. *See also* Agudat Israel movement
Apirion, Uri David (Rabbi of Old Zager), 187
apostates (meshumodim), 394–400
Aran (Varena), 242, 300, 507, 629, 676, 678, 679; massacre in, 116, 581, 597; and military service, 38,

49; and partisan camps, 642, 672; police force in, 660, 667–668, 670, 674; and post-liberation, 671–672
Archimowitz (teacher), 461
arendators (leaseholders), 263–265, 397
Arendt, Hannah, 398
Arie-Yankel, 324
Ariowitch, Elke (Todras), 614, 631, 634, 636, 638, 642, 645
Arke der Shtarker, 304
Armia Krajowa (Home Army; AK), 19, 43, 257, 583, 613–629, 649; arrest of members, 673; attack on Sonenson house, 664–667, 747n14; and converts, 402–403; and liberation, 655, 656, 659, 660, 663, 664, 669, 671, 673, 679; and official agreement with Germans, 629; and partisan camps, 629–650; and Russian army, 670–673
Arodnoy, 40, 264, 586
Aronowicz, Jozef, 36
Aronowitch, Yoshke, 389
artisan class, 43, 64, 120, 288, 289–299, 303; and Bund, 289, 292–293, 294, 295; burial of, 233; and Communism, 41, 289, 291, 292, 293, 294, 295, 327; and education, 160, 468, 521; marriages of, 358; tailors in, 294–295; women of, 338; in World War I, 496; and Yiddish, 224, 525; and Zionism, 490, 500. *See also* handicrafts
Asch, Sholem, 538
Asher, Avraham, *221*
Asherowitch (Ben Asher) family, *258*
Asher the shohet, 625
Ashkenazi, Jacob, 169
Ashkenazic Jews, *40*, 65, 69, 144, 177, 244, 435, 492; and education, 147, 148, 175, 176, 188, 189
Ashmat Shomron (The Guilt of Samaria; Mapu), 460
Askin, Ida, *553*
Askin, Joseph, *553*
Asner, Aaron, 646, 648
Asner, Aryeh-Leib, *236*, 248, 249
Asner, Avraham, 201, 257, 607, 646, 648, 649, 670, 674, 681; emigration to Canada, 691; in Leninski battalion, 637, 638, 647
Asner, Beile, *236*
Asner, Bezalel, 248
Asner, Ed, *236*, 249, *257*
Asner, Hayyim, 646, 648, 649
Asner, Itzle, 649
Asner, Liebke, 647, 648, 681, 691
Asner, Morris, *257*
Asner, Rachel, *649*, 691
Asner, Yankl, 646, 648, 649, 674
Asner, Yitzhak, *257*, 606, 647
Asner family, 58, 86, *249*, 256–257, 636, 646, 647, 648, 650, 691
Astramski der Feldsher, 441, 523
Astrin, 595
Astrow, Ben, 654
Augustus II (Poland), 34, 76
Augustus III (Poland), 34
Auschwitz, 124, *141*, 143, 612
Auschwitz-Birkenau, 3
Austria, 34, 35, 36, 68, 256
Auto-Emancipation (Pinsker), 486
Av Beth Din, 94, 96
Aviel Lipkunski Avraham. *See* Lipkunski, Avraham
Avigdor, Rabbi Shmuel ben (of Vilna), 129
Avigdor (the martyr), 262–263
Avraham-Hayyim (coachman), 199
Avraham-Heshl (divorce scribe), 356–357, 380, 381
Avrahami, Pessah, 569, *570*
Azrieli family, 18, 19, 639
Azzai, ben (Talmudic sage), 354

Baal Shem Tov (Master of the Good Name; Rabbi Israel ben Eliezer), 145, 179, 704n23
baal-tefillah (everyday cantor), 142, 143
Babisch, Dr., 642
Babul, Michal (Gaj), 673
Babylonia, 6, 19, 28, 64, 147, 151, 160, 166
Bacall, Lauren (Betty Joan Perske), 600
Baderas (Polish collaborator), 670
balebatim (householders), 40–44, 49, 53, 79, 82, 228, 270, 279; and artisan class, 289, 290, 291, 292, 293; burial of, 233; and charity, 211; and education of children, 298; and election of rabbis, 93, 96; and holidays, 427, 428; and leasing, 204; marriages of, 358; on Sabbath, 411; shoemakers in, 295; view of Zionism, 490
bale-melokhe (artisans), 289, 292, 298
Balfour Declaration (1917), 107, 111, 465, 497, 504
Ballon, Layzer, *474*, *477*
Ballon, Tanhum, 625
Baram, Moshe, *651*, 652
Baranowicz, 353, 572
Barkali, Batia Lubetski, *409*, 440, 445
Barkali, Shaul. *See* Kaleko, Shaul
Bar Kokhba, 162
bar mitzvah, 350–353
Barteszewicz, Pietka, *273*, *507*, 597, 598, 601, 606, 607
Barukh'l, 633
Baston (Bastunski), Judy, 13, 552

Bastun, 87, 188, 193, 265, 274, 308, 365, 437, 508, 598, 599, 681
Bastuner, der, 193, 194, 197
Bastunski, Alexander (Zusl), 279, *342*, 362, 363, 445, *552*
Bastunski, Altke. *See* Kaplan, Altke Bastunski
Bastunski, Batia, *276*, 283, 285, *311*, 316, 375, 385, 445, 497, *524*; emigration of, 279, 363
Bastunski, Eliyahu, *43*, 142, 276, 279, 325, 445, 447, *552*, 568, 580; on marriage, 362–363, 375
Bastunski, Ettl, *276*
Bastunski, Judy. *See* Baston, Judy
Bastunski, Leibke, *533*
Bastunski, Mordekhai, 277
Bastunski, Moshe, *351*
Bastunski, Shlomo (Sol), 142, 276, 552
Bastunski, Shmuel, *277*, 362, 577
Bastunski, Yankl, *277*, *310*, 447
Bastunski, Zusl (Alexander), 279, *342*, 362, 363, 445, *552*
Bastunski family, 13, 265, *689*
batei midrashi (prayerhouses), 63–64, 66–68, 70–71, 78–84, 85, 88, 89; women's gallery in, 123, 142–143, 169, 185, 217. *See also* New Beth Midrash; Old Beth Midrash
bat mitzvah, 353–354
Battle of Grunwald, 23
Battle of Poltava, 34
Battle of Stalingrad, 652, 692
Bazarov, Major, 670, 671, 674, 675, 676, 679, 680
Becker, Aharon Don. *See* Pachianko, Aharon Don
Begin, Menachem, 568
Beilis, Mendel, 383
Beilis blood-libel case, 107, 125, 521, 704n40
Beitar (Zionist youth group), 10, 325, 445, 503–508, 509, 529, 530, 568, 636, 688
Beit Sefer Klali Yivri (Hebrew school), *474*
Belensky, Akivah, *553*
Belensky, Anna, *553*
Belensky, Jake, *553*
Belensky, Mayer, *553*
Belkind, Israel, 495
Ben-Asher family, 18, 19
Benchke der Meshuggener, 388
Benei Zion (Children of Zion), 453
Ben-Gurion, David, 510
Ben-Sasson, H. H., 85
Ben-Shemen (Israel), *268*
Ben-Shemesh, Shalom. *See* Sonenson, Shalom
Ben-Yossef family, 18, 19
Ben Zvi, Yitzhak, 520
Benski, Dr., 402, 444, 567, 606
Berczanski, Shifra, *507*
Berdichev, 455
Berdyczewski, Micha Josef, 522
Berele (son of Israel the Fisherman), 639
Berenbaum, Michael, 5
Berger, Reb Hayyim, 117
Bergman, Hugo, 511
Bergman, Shmuel, 540
Berihah movement, 684–685, 686, 687, 690
Berkowicz, Aaron, 642
Berkowicz, Israel, 301, 302
Berkowicz, Leib (der Pochter), *43*
Berkowicz, Pola, *428*
Berkowicz, Shmuel, *530*
Berkowitch, Aryeh, *503*
Berkowitch, Dora Zlotnik, *283*, 345, 374, 502, 551
Berkowitch, Golde Kabacznik, 333–334
Berkowitch, Hanche, *287*
Berkowitch, Hayyim, 54
Berkowitch, Hayyim (Pietka), 671
Berkowitch, Naftali, *302*, *372*, 374, 502, *503*, 693
Berkowitch, Rachel Kabacznik, 334
Berkowitch, Reb Itche (the melamed; Itche der Shammes), 77, 137, 159, 202, 333, 573
Berkowitch, Reuven-Beinush, *43*, 283, 333–334, 374, 375
Berkowitch, Shaul, *503*, *506*
Berkowitch family, *689*
Berkowski, Hayyim, 587
Berlin, 650, *690*
Berlin, Naftali Zvi Yehudah (the Neziv), 182, 183, 196, 333, 336, 486, 495, 708n15
Berliner (Gestapo), 602
Berl the Cantonist (Nikolaievitz), 47, 185–186, 218–219
Berman, Mina, 516
Bernitsky, Dr., 436, 437, 443
Bershadsky, Sergei, 23
Beruria, 171
Berz, Shlomo, 385
Besoylem Gessl (Eternity Lane), 209, 230, 233
Beth Hinukh (modern school), 454
Beth Jacob schools, 469
Beth Yehudah (The House of Judah; Levinsohn), 454–455
Bezalel, 71
Bialik, Hayyim Nahman, 155, 180, 183, 232, *260*, 425, 434, 471, 575; as Zionist, 172, 487, 495
Bialystok, 50, 100, 101, 103, 114, 300, 456, 469, 486. *See also* Grodno-Bialystok region
Bible, 482; Enlightenment view of, 452, 453; in Israel, 492; teaching of, 460, 469; translation of, 456
Bichwid, Mordekhai, *428*

Bichwid family, 475
bicycles, 305–306, 530
Bielicki, Hayyim-Yoshke, 292, 420, 639, 652, 656, 659, 683, 692
Bielicki, Meitke, 571
Bielski, Aharon, 634
Bielski, Asael, 634
Bielski, Tuvia, 634
Bielski, Zusya, 634
Bielski brothers, 634, 635, 639, 640
Big Fire. *See* Fire of 1895
The Big Win (play; Aleichem), 540
Bikewiczowa, Aneza, 622, 623, 624, 672
Bikkur Holim, 212, 213
Bilu (early Zionist group), 495
Binkewicz (Polish Christian), 621–622
"A Bintel Brief" (A Bundle of Letters; newspaper column), 337
Blacharowicz, Fruml, 277, 586, 591, 631, 633, 634
Blacharowicz, Gutke, 586, 591, 631, 633, 634
Blacharowicz, Sarah'leh, 600
Blacharowicz, Szeina, 307, 309, 310, 410, 446, 500, 534, 658; on anti-Semitism, 563; in Ghetto Radun, 597, 599, 600; grandmother of, 421; in hiding, 631, 632, 633, 634, 662; and Kuzmicki family, 403; and liberation, 664, 692; and massacre of 1941, 584, 586, 588, 591; repatriation of, 692; as sewing machine saleswoman, 291, 292, 303, 340; and Zionism, 505, 506, 507, 560
Blacharowicz, Yehiel, 148, 261, 272, 427, 530, 561, 625; and massacre of 1941, 584, 586, 588; and Zionism, 507
Blacharowicz, Zlate, 277
Blacharowicz family, 408, 411, 589, 599
Black Death, 23, 26, 204
black suitcase blood libel case, 382–383
Blaj, Moshe, 510, 511, 682
Bleicharowicz, Yoshke Shneur Mordekhai's, 304, 622
Bleicharowicz, Honke, 304
blood libels, 22, 30, 39, 54, 57, 401, 701n45; Beilis case, 107, 125, 521, 704n40; black suitcase case, 382–383; Damascus (1840), 484; Saratov, 395
Bnei Hail Society, 58
Bnei Moshe (Sons of Moses), 170, 489
Bobkin (Polish farmer), 611
Bobruisk, 304, 509
Borshtein, Yoske, 479
Borysewicz, Jan. *See* Krisha
Botwinik, Avremele (Epstein), 351, 352, 474, 583, 637, 644, 645, 692
Botwinik, Fania, 310, 506, 583, 645
Botwinik, Hillel, 583, 645
Botwinik, Leibke, 477, 479, 573, 583, 600, 645
Botwinik, Moshe Yaakov, 583; death of, 603, 645; in Ghetto Radun, 600, 607; as principal, 425, 474–475, 479, 481, 518; and schools, 114, 462, 464, 465, 470–473, 617
Botwinik, Shoshana Alte, 583, 645
Botwinik, Yankl, 637
Botwinik, Yitzhak, 583, 645
Botwinik, Zipporah, 583
Botwinik family, 583, 645, 664
Boyarski, Alte, 140
Boyarski, Ida, 140, 551
Boyarski, Ruben, 84, 140–141, 538, 551–552
Boyarski, Ruvke, 115, 251, 270, 387, 571
Brafman, Jacob, 395–396
Brantshpigl, Moshe ben Henich, 152
Braverman, Alex. *See* Sonenson, Alex Braverman
Brenner, Yossef Hayyim, 527–528
Breskin, Yehudah, 189
Breslau fair, 313
Bressler, Rabbi Hayyim Zalman, 181, 182
Briha ("flight;" Jewish rescue organization), 403
Brisk (Brest-Litovsk), 23, 26, 29, 91, 92, 129
British Mandate, 125, 678
British White Papers (1936, 1939), 480, 507, 569, 571
Broida, Anna, 548
Broida, Hannah, 545
Broida, Isabel, 545
Broida, Jacob, 548
Broida, Joseph, 549
Broida, Mathilda, 545
Broida, Mildred, 545, 548, 549
Broida, Morris, 545, 549
Broida, Rabbi Simhah Zisl (Grand Old Man of Kelme), 175
Broida, Sheinke, 548
Broida, Taibke, 548
Broida, Tereza, 545
Broida family, 548–549
Broide, Hayya Fradl Zlotnik, 345, 585
Broide, Yitzhak, 142, 143, 345
Bukeika (Polish official), 390, 393
Bulgak, Stanislaw (Buak), 666, 673
Bund (General Jewish Workers Union of Lithuania, Poland, and Russia), 184, 198, 250, 468, 508–509, 525, 542; and artisan class, 289, 292–293, 294, 295; founding of (1897), 107, 173, 451, 508
Bureh der Roiphe, 440
Burstein, Altke, 371

Burstein, Motke, *287, 310, 534*
Burstein, Yitzhak (Reb Itche der Shohet), *145, 371*, 626
Butchan, Reb Yitche der (the stork), 137, 163, 165, 166
Byelorussia, 27, 87, 110, 115, 201, 226, 326, 566, 571, 581, 584, 597, 613, 635

Camarone, Joe. *See* Hamarski, Yossele
Camus, Albert, 3
cantonists, 40, 45–48, 185, 186, 332, 384, 395, 396, 397. *See also* Nikolaievtzky
Carlsbad, 446, 500, 686
Caro, Rabbi Yossef, 102, 189
Carolowa, Mrs., 611
Carter, Jimmy, 3, 5
Caruso, Enrico, 84, 140
Casimir IV (King of Poland and Lithuania), 261–262
Catherine the Great, 34, 36, 38, 45
Catholicism, 25, 57, 382, 432, 480, 562, 577; and Communism, 116; conversion to, 20, 395, 396, 399. *See also* Christianity
Cat-Mackiewicz, Stanislav, 562
cemeteries, 228–252. *See also* New Cemetery; Old Cemetery
Center for Holocaust Studies (Brooklyn College), 8
Central Yiddish School Organization: Yiddish-language network (CYSHO) of, 468–469
Chafetz, Berl, *189*
Chafetz, Reb, *189*
charity (zedakah), 210, 223, 227, 233. *See also* mutual aid societies
Charles XII, King (Sweden), 33, 34
Charney, Daniel, 526
Chashinkes, Altke, 447
Chelikowski, Kreine, 516
children, 343, 344–347, 348–354, 377, 388
Chiniewic, Jozef (Grom), 673
Chmielnicki, Bogdan, 31, 32, 38, 39, 178, 210–211, 431
Chmielnicki massacres, 431, 435
Christianity: conversion to, 24, 47, 48, 149, 185, 394, 395, 399, 402, 455, 456, 729nn45, 46, 54, 736n58; in Lithuania, 22, 23, 24, 25–26, 27, 52, 231; and military, 54; and plagues, 204. *See also* Catholicism
Christians, 256, 381, 606, 657; as collaborators, 57, 581, 594, 598, 601, 610–628, 670; conversion to Judaism of, 394, 400–402; as friends, 303, 583, 588, 595, 596, 599, 631, 662; holidays of, 406–407, 425; and Jewish businesses, 272, 273, 278, 290, 293, 294, 303; mentally ill, 393–394; as neighbors, 6, 10, 18, 116, 207; as servants, 338–339. *See also* Korkuc, Kazimierz
Churchill, Winston, 565, 575, 577, 578, 687
circumcision, 137, 167, 212, 348–349, 437, 513, 601, 662
class structure: artisans in, 289–290, 294–295; coachmen in, 300–305; and emigration, 279; and marriage, 360–364; and mentally ill, 384. *See also* balebatim
Clemens, Clar, 399
clergy, 44–45, 119–146; in America, 552–553; wives of, 93, 94–95, 97, 126. *See also* rabbinate
Cnaani, Leah, 556n
coachmen (baaleagoleh), 300–305
Cofnas, Fishke, 141
Cofnas, Fruml, 414–415
Cofnas, Gedalia, *296*, 415
Cofnas, Nahum Hayyim Leib, 509
Cofnas, Pessah, *296, 297, 305*, 325, 389, 414, 415, 472, 474, 571, 692
Cofnas, Rivka, 692
Cofnas family, *308*
Cohen, Albert, 485
Cohen, Margolia der Feldsher, *341*
Communism, 107, 111, 191, 325, 355, 624, 681; and artisan class, 41, 289, 291, 292, 293, 294, 295, 327; and maggid, 120, 123; sympathizers with, 311, 389, 451; and Yiddish, 469, 520, 522, 525, 677; and Zionism, 508–512, 566, 681
The Communist Manifesto (Marx), 485
Communist Party, 129, 293, 509–512, 660, 670, 674; in Eishyshok, 226, 327, 509; Finadel (finance department) of, 572; Revolutionary Committee of, 115–116; Yevsektsia (section of), 111, 125, 127
Communists, 250, 338, 571–576, 598, 645; attack on Hebrew, 520, 540; and Beitar, 508, 509; of Eishyshok, 124, 174, 201, 251–252, 270, 382, 503, 527, 540, 542, 571, 588, 596, 606, 635, *656*, 670; and Nazis, 580, 582, 584
Confederation of Warsaw (1704), 33
Council of the Four Lands, 28–31, 69, 87, 92, 139, 210, 358, 468, 513, 700n32; dissolution of (1764), 129, 130, 180, 256; and education, 151, 177, 178; judicial system and, 128–129. *See also* Lithuanian Council
Council of Lithuanian Lords, 24
Coutsai family, 513
Cracow, 25, 33, 36, 69, 74, 177
Cracow Ordinance, 147–148, 158
Crémieux, Adolphe, 484, 485
Cremona, Italy, 682
Crimea, 19, 26, 48
Crusades, 6, 16, 20, 22, 23, 24
Cumpulsory Sunday Rest Law, 272, 273

A Cup of Deliverance (*Kos Yeshuot*; Friedland), 485
Cymbal (Ukrainian partisan), 642
CYSHO. *See* Central Yiddish School Organization

Dakinewiczowa family, 325, 327, 566, 575, 576, 664
Danzig, 35
Davar (Hebrew newspaper), 519
Davidowicz, Dvora, 631
Davidowicz, Reb Moshe (der Lubaver), 631, 662, 668, 682
Davidowicz family, 631
Davis, Monnet B., *694*
dayyan (judge), 128–134
Deguchinski, Rashi, *301*
Dekeshene. *See* Selo
the Deluge (war of 1650s-1690s), 32, 38, 178
Demitrowski, Feige, 337, 415
Demitrowski, Gittke, *291*
Derechin, 100, 101, 102
Dessler, Salek, 646
Deutch, Dobke (Dvorah), *261*
Deutscher, Isaac, 251, 252
Devenishki, Issic Meir (A. Weiter), 197, 198, 508
Devenishki, Reb Yehoshua Heshl, 197
Diaspora, 6, 7, 28, 32, 64, 65, 128, 203, 246, 517; and yeshivah, 175, 181; and Zionism, 483, 489
Diet of Piotrkow, 26, 27
Dimitrowski, Dobke Kremin (Dora Dimitro), 206, 651, 681; and attack on Sonenson house, 664–665; in Ghetto Radun, 598; in hiding, 640, 641; and Israel Dimitrowski, 662, 679, 680; and massacre of 1941, 589; and minyan to mass graves, *688*, 689
Dimitrowski, Dodke, 386
Dimitrowski, Israel, 640, 641, 662, 670, 675, 679, 680, 681, *688*, 689
Dimitrowski, Moshe, 500
Dimitrowski, Nahum, 640, 641, 650
Dimitrowski, Shoshke, 386
Displaced Persons Act, 692
displaced persons (DP) camps, 679, 682–684, 687, 690–692
Disraeli, Benjamin, 394, 398
D'Israeli, Isaac, 394
divorce, 356–357, 376–384, 730n15, 732–735
"Divrei Shalom ve-Emet" (Words of Peace and Truth; Wessely), 452
Dobke di Gevirte (the rich woman), 597
Dociszki, 40, 586, 591, 624, 675
doctors, 263, 441–443. *See also individual doctors*
documents: photographic, 4–5, 10, 11, 13–14; private *vs.* official, 7–8, 12–13; in United States, 11–12
Doig (Daugai), 257, 318
Dolgoruky, Prince, 51
Dolinski, Noah, 598, 601
Dolinski family, 125
Dorshei Zion ve-Yerushalaim (Seekers of Zion and Jerusalem), 485
Dov Bear, the Great Maggid of Mezrich, 120
DP camps. *See* displaced persons (DP) camps
Dragutski, Arie-Leib der Grober, 285, 536
Dragutski, Margolia. *See* Kaplan-Gottlieb, Mary
Drasnin, Akivah, *553*
Drasnin, Fanny, *553*
Drasnin, Sam, *553*
Drasnin, Sarah, *553*
Dreyfus family, 245
Druskieniki (Drozgenik), 486, 535, 681
Dubczanski, Hannah, *564*
Dubczanski, Hayyim-Moshe, *564*
Dubczanski, Masha, *475*, *564*
Dubczanski, Rivka, *564*
Dubczanski, Sarah, *564*
Dubczanski, Shlomo, *176*, 279, *564*
Dubczanski, Vela. *See* Portnoy, Vela Dubczanski
Dubczanski family, 563
Dubitski, Avraham, 43, 624
Dubitski, Ettl, *519*, *537*
Dubitski, Meir Shalom, 107
Dubitski, Reuven, 130
Dubitski, Yakhe, 414
Dubitski, Yitzhak, 321, 447
Dubno, 120
Dubnow, Simon, 700n32
Dubrowicz, Leah, 529
Dubrowicz, Shaul, *20*, *309*, *529*
Dubrowicz family, *529*
Dugaczanski, Aron-Leib, *409*
Dugaczanski, Leah'le, *409*
Dugaczanski, Sarah-Hashke Lubetski, *409*
Dugaczanski, Shlomo, *148*
Dugalishok, 201, 256–257, 398, 533, 612, 614, 637, 638, 660, 717n7
Dumbla, 40, 51, 256, 265, 434, 586, 619; summer camps in, *141*, 142, 477, 531, 533, 535
Dumbla blotes (marshes), 259
Dumbla River, 22, 33
Dumblianski family, 265
Durbin, Dave, 652
Dvinsk (Dunaburg; Latvia), 100, 101
Dvorcen, Reb Yossef, 77
Dwilanski, Alte Rochel, 234
Dwilanski, Avigdor, 234, 235, 344

Dwilanski, Benyamin (Niomke), *260*
Dwilanski, Hayyim, 344
Dwilanski, Nahum, *419*
Dwilanski, Rachel, *372*
Dwilanski, Rivka, 337, 344, 347
Dwilanski, Sheinele, *475, 476*
Dwilanski, Sheinke, *429*
Dwilanski, Yudl, *43*
dybbuk, 83, 428
Dybbuk (Anski), 539
Der Dzhik (the wild one), 378

Edelstein, Moshe, 174, *477*, 639–640, 664, 665; on *Exodus*, 685, 686
Edelstein family, 19, 255
Edict of Toleration (1782), 452, 456
education: and agriculture, 473, *476*; of boys, 147–174, 350; and class, 298; and Diaspora, 175–176; elementary-school, 468–470; and emigration, 465; higher, 465–468; of Jews in Russia, 454–455; in Middle Ages, 152, 176; vocational, 457, 466, 468; of women, 94–95, 168–171, 191, 340, 342, 457, 459–460, 462–463, 464, 471; during World War I, 464–465; of yishuvniks, 464. *See also* heder; yeshivah
Eichmann, Adolf, 519
Eichmann trial, 201, 402, 655, 685, *686*
Einsatzgruppen (Action Groups), 580, 582
Einstein, Albert, *467*
Eishyshok: aerial photo of, *51*; after liberation, 655, 657, 683; Armia Krajowa in, 629; arts in, 55; beggars in, 218; castle of, *22*; Church of the Ascension in, *25*; class structure in, 14, 233–235; courtship in, 194; crime in, 324–325; death and burial in, 233–235, 245–249; early settlers in, 18–20; electric power in, 283, 297, 387, 657; founding of, 16–17, 228; under German rule in World War I, 55, 211, 223, 522, 527, 535; girls' clubs in, *499, 500*; history of, 15–59; Jewish, 17–20; land appropriation in, 52; leaseholding near, 264–265; leisure in, 528–535; liberation from Germans (July 1944), 8, 9, 10, 229; under Lithuania, 20, 22, 115, 174, 201, 326, 543; maggidim in, 122–124; maps of, *58, 616*; as market town, 28, 316–324; Mendele Nokher Sefarim Centennial in, 526; names for, 16, 17; and Napoleon's retreat from Russia, 50; Nazi occupation of (1941), 9, 55, 57, 78, 116, 138, 174, 208, 226, 389–390, 393, 401–402, 527, 574, 575–581, 584; New Plan in, 51; nineteenth-century, 49–54; number of Jews murdered in, 7–8, 594; origins of, 15–24; 1850 plan of, *50*; post–World War I schools in, 470–481; public bath (bod) in, 66, 81, 161, 163, 164, 203–209, 243; public library in, 521–527; quest for, 3–14; rabbis of, 97–117; Refugee Committee of, 115, 226, 567; refugees through, 115, 226, 252, 527, 567–568; relief societies in, 211–227, 474; under Russian rule, 36, 38, 105–106, 257; St. Petersburg–Warsaw telegraph tower in, 50, *51*; social clubs in, 527–528; under Soviet rule, 115–116, 123, 174, 226, 251, 270, 274, 326–327, 387, 520, 527, 540, 565, 571–574; streets in, 55, 130, 209, 230, 233, 258, 430; students in, 188–192, 708nn30&32; Swedish army in, 33; swimming in, 528–530; synagogue of, *64*, 65–78, 227, 232, 252; theater in, 309, 398, 427–428, *429*, 535–543; in twentieth century, 54–59, 115; villages of, 256; Vilna Street bridges in, 310; yeshivah in, 186–187, 261, 284. *See also* Fire of 1895; Kibbutz ha-Prushim yeshivah; Massacre of September 1941
Eishyshok Society of America (Hevrah Bnei Avraham Shmuel Anshei Eishyshker), 12, *42*, 99, 223–226, *546*, 554; and Fire of 1895, 53, 70, 224, 547, 555; constitution of, 223–*224*; fifty-second anniversary of, *225*; original record books of, *224*; and World War II, 653–654
Eisiskes. *See* Eishyshok
Eisys, 16, 18
Ejszyszki, Benyamin, *397*
Ejszyszki, David, 325, *397*, 398, 652, 682
Ejszyszki, Gedaliah, *397*
Ejszyszki, Hannah, 397
Ejszyszki, Israel, *397*
Ejszyszki, Peshke, 397–398, 402
Ejszyszki, Zipporah, *397*, 398
EKOPO (Jewish Loan Association of Eastern Europe), 286, 527
Elazari-Volcani, Mordekhai. *See* Wilkanski, Mordekhai
Elazari-Volcani, Yitzhak. *See* Wilkanski, Yitzhak
Ele, Reb, 206
Eli (son of Esther Wilkanski), *432*
Eliach, David, 5, 543, *667, 689, 695*
Eliach, Yaffa Sonenson, 4, 5, 22, 191, 202, *213, 260*, 324, *346*; and Armia Krajowa, 666, 668, 672; bat mitzvah of, 354; escape from Eishyshok, 582, 583, 584, 585, 595, 596; and folk medicine, 439–440; in Ghetto Radun, 605, 607, 609; great-grandmother of, *332*; in hiding, 615, 617, 621, 622, *625*, 626, 627; and Kazimierz Korkuc, 683, *684*; and liberation, 657, 664, 665, 669, 671, 675, 676, 677, 679, 680, 683, *684*; maternal grandparents of, *361*; parents of, *261, 275, 307, 309, 347, 370, 532, 535, 578*; and repatriation, 686, 687, 690; return to Eishyshok, 543, *666, 667, 689*; on Sabbath, 415; wedding of, *695*

Eliach, Yotav, *695*
Eliasberg, Mordekhai, 486
Eliashewicz, Blumke Kremin, *533*, 598, 640, 651, 681
Eliashewicz, Eliyahu (Ellis), 640, 681
Eliezer ben Hyrcanus, Rabbi, 168, 170
Elisha the postman, 284–285, 547
Elke Mere's, 414
Elkind, Mania, 511
Elkind, Mendel, 510, 511, 512
Elkind group, 682
Emancipation of the Serfs (1861), 258, 294
emigration, 53, 54, 240, 274, 465, 539; and agriculture, 268–269, 277; to Argentina, 269, *419*, *462*, 488, 489, *506*, 548; to Brazil, 269, 488, 555, 568, 684, 692; to Canada, 269, 681, 684, 690, 691, 692, 694; to Colombia, *275*, *307*, *371*, *426*; to Cuba, 298; and Eishyshok economy, 276, 279, 284–285; to Great Britain, 56, 548, 684; and holidays, 431; and marriage, 355, 361; to Palestine, 53, 54, 56, 108, 109, 112, 114, 115, 120, 125, 128, 213, 274, 298, 303, 389, 444, 451, 488, 497, 502–505, 544, 548, 569, 658, 682, 694; restrictions on, 286, 298; and role of women, 336–337; of scholars, 178; to South Africa, 548, *551*; to South America, 269, 298, 488, *500*, *501*, *530*, 555; to Soviet Union, 8, 9–10; and weddings, 375. *See also* Eretz Israel; United States; Zionism
Der Emmes (The Truth; Yiddish Communist newspaper), 510
Encyclopedia of the Holocaust, 650
Endecja Party, 325
Endekes (anti-Semitic gang), 302, 325
Enlightenment, European, 6, 55, 69, 122, 394, 452. *See also* Haskalah
Ephraimson, Annaliese Edith. *See* Kaplan, Annaliese Edith Ephraimson
epidemics, 33, 51, 72, 211, 233, 243, 343, 524, 555
Epstein, Avremele. *See* Botwinik, Avremele
Epstein, Elisha, *429*
Epstein, Faivl, *43*
Epstein, I. N., 465
Epstein, Mr. (husband of Gita Lawzowski), 475
Epstein, Rabbi Moshe Mordekhai, 467
Erdvilas, duke of Samogitian tribe, 16
Eretz Israel (Land of Israel; Palestine), 7, 39, 59; Aliyah to, *16*, 56, *194*, 491, 492, 495, 497–499, 505, 740n16; Amit in, *694*; and Bible, 114–115; as cultural center, 495; depression of 1927–1929 in, 502; emigration to, 10–11, 78, 99, 108, 241–242, 451, 497, 502–506, 556, 678, 681, 683, 693; kibbutzim in, *498*, 499, 510; and liberation, 685–692; May 1921 riots in, 527; River Jordan in, 163; scholars in, 160; Sharona Shepherds in, 498; socialism in, 510; synagogues in, 64; Yaffo in, 491, 517, 527, *694*; Yishuv in, 483, 487, 492, 495, 498, 502, 504, 510, 520, 652; Zionist leaders (1920) of, *494*. *See also* emigration; Palestine; Zionism
Erlich, Israel, *309*
Erlich, Reizele, *428*
Erter, Dr. Isaac, 198
Esther der Rubishker, 414, *475*
Ethel Simhes, 414
Etke (girlfriend of Yankl Asner), 648
Exodus (ship), 685, 686, 692
Ez Hayyim (yeshivah in Amsterdam), 178
Ez Hayyim, Volozhin Yeshiva, 180, 187
Ezra, Dr., 204, 380, 442, 443, 529, 550
Ezrat Yoledet society, 436

fairs, 313–315; Eishyshok Horse Fair, 27, 49, 185, 274, 315; Lublin, 29, 178, 314, 355, 406
family life, 331–347
Farber, Hanneh-Feige, 258
Farber, Shlomo, 8, *64*, 74, 77, 78, 258, 345, 424
Farbshtein, Heshl, 273
Feibush, Shraga, 207, 322
Feige di Schneiderke, 440
Feller, Dora, *428*, 479
Fenigstein, Rina Lewinson, 213
Ferdinand I, 313
Fiddler on the Roof, 95
Finkel, Eliezer Yehudah, 104
Finkl, Neta Zvi Hirsh, 195
Finland, 395, 396
Fire of 1895 (Eishyshok), 9, 52–55, 131, 196, 264, 268, 340, 459; and America, 547–548; and Eishyshok Society, 224, 547, 555; losses in, 44, 112, 244; rebuilding after, 70–78, 133, 134, 193, 197, 199, 284, 563
Fischel, Harry, 472, 475
Fischel, Jane Brass, 472, 475
Fischel family, 177
Fischer, Isser, 600
Fischer, Ita, 600
Fischer, Rebbetzin (of Vilna), 600
Fischl, Perele, 414
Fishl, Avraham, 351
Flavius Josephus, 65, 162, 409
folk medicine, 437–441, 444; magic spells in, *438–439*; practitioners (babske feldshers) of, 440
food, 407–408, 412–413; holiday, 417–418, 423, 427, 428–431, 432; matzah, 429–431
Fordon prison, 509

forests: hiding in, 265, 303, 629–654; near Eishyshok, 300, 301; products from, 274–276. *See also individual forests*
Foster, Annie Virshubski, 250, *341*, 549, 737n10
Foster, David. *See* Michalowski, David
Foster, Rosalind, 250, *532*
Frank, Anne, 615
Frank, Menachem Mendl, 91, 92, 129
Frankl, Benyamin, 633, 638
Freidl (mother of Liba Shlosberg), 631, 633
Friedland, Nathan, 484–485
Friedländer, David, 452, 453
Frischer, Elisha (Elisha Efrat), 560–561, 570
Frischer, Nehama Koppelman, *372*, 560–561, 570, 571, 572
Frischer, Shulamit, 570
Frischer, Yitzhak, *372*, 570
Froyen Farain (Union of Women), 42, *211*
Frume the seamstress, 414
Frumkin, Esther, 124, 127
funerals, 233–235, 245–249; of yishuvnik (rural Jews), 248–249

Gabrilowitsch, Ossip, 399
Gani (Hebrew kindergarten), 478–479
Garadie, 275
Garber, Zlatke. *See* Paikowski, Zlatke Garber
Garmenishki, Bere-Leibke, *541*
Gawrylkewicz, Antoni (shepherd), 620, 628, 683, *685*, *689*
Gayer, Malka Levitan, *474*
Gebirtig, Mordekhai, 559, 564
Gedalia the carpenter, 472, 473
Gediminas, Prince (Grand Duke of Lithuania), 20, 22, 23
Gemilut Hessed Kassa, 285–287, 298
Gemilut Hessed societies, 219, 693
Gens, Jacob, 646
gerei zeddek (proselytes), 400–402
German language, 158, 454, 456, 464
Germany, 10, 176, 193, 649; invasion of Poland by (1939), 20, 327, 565, 678; Jews from, 6; occupation of Eishyshok by (1941), 9, 55, 57, 78, 116, 138, 174, 208, 223, 226, 389–390, 393, 401–402, 527, 574, 575–581, 584; prisoners of war in, 222–223; in World War I, 55, 57, 211, 222, 223, 464, 522, 523, 527, 535, *536*, 540, 575, 576
Gershom ben Judah, Rabbenu, Light of the Diaspora, 284, 376, 384
Gershonowitz, Nehama, 669
Gershowitz, Hayyim, *428*
Gershupski, Hayya, *536*
Ger Zeddek. *See* Potocki, Count Valentine
Gestapo: in Eishyshok, 576–580, 584, 585, 591, 595, 596, 601, 602, 621; in Ghetto Radun, 597; and Ghetto Vilna, 646
Gimpel (German yeshivah student), 359
Gimpel der Maskil, 193, 195, 196
Ginsberg, Gitta Politacki, *291*, *292*
Ginunski, Gedalia, 124, 141, 143, *564*
Ginunski, Luba, 115, 141, 270, *471*, *564*, 571, 573, *656*; and Eretz Israel, 124, 681; and eviction of Rabbi, 387, 730n23; imprisonment of, 509; return to Eishyshok, 566, 567; and Soviets, 572
Ginunski, Moshe, 124, 565
Ginunski, Reb Shaye, 120, 124, 531, 573
Ginunski, Yekutiel, *223*, 303, 473, 559, *564*, 565
Ginunski family, *471*, 538
Ginzberg (emigrated to Boston; changed name to Goodwin), *537*
Ginzberg, Asher Zvi (Ahad Ha'am), 172, 407, 495, 522
Ginzberg, Tamar, *346*
Ginzberg, Yossef, *346*
Ginzburg, Etl Glombocki, 572
Glauberman (photographer), *275*
Glombocki, Esther, 686
Glombocki, Ettl. *See* Gunzberg, Ettl Glombocki
Glombocki, Faivl, 9, 466, 505, *506*, 530
Glombocki, Hannah, *537*
Glombocki, Hayyim-Leibl, 442
Glombocki, Hillel, 466, 530
Glombocki, Leibe, 658
Glombocki, Shneur, 343, 352, 640, 651, 652, 686
Glombocki family, 459, *462*, 466, 538, 686
Gluckel of Hameln, 32
Godlewski, Monsignor Marceli, 402
Goide-Sorenson, Ida, 525
Gold, Morris (Moshe Zlotnik), *551*
Gold, Rabbi Zeev, *694*
Goldbloom, Israel Isser, 192, 193, 271, 381, 459
Golde, Hashe, 268
Golden Pinkas. *See* pinkas
Goldfaden, Abraham, 537, 538, 540
Goldke di Hilzerne ("wooden Goldke"), 320
Goldstein, Israel, 693
Goldstein, Yossef, 182
The Golem (play; Levick), 538
Golmecziszki, 397
Goodman, Atar Kudlanski, *419*
Goodman, Bill, *423*, *689*
Goodman, Hannah Beile. *See* Kudlanski, Hanneh-Beile Moszczenik

Goodman, Jake Morris (Yaakov-Moshe Kudlanski), 419, 556
Goodman (Kudlanski) family, 412, 529, 555, 690, 691
Gordin, Jacob, 335; Yiddish plays of, 537–538
Gordon, Aaron David, 492, 498
Gordon, David, 485
Gordon, Dr. A., 459
Gordon, Harry, 654
Gordon, Judah Leib (Yalag), 15, 188, 451, 458, 522
Gordon, Leon, 447
Gordon, Max, 654
Gordon, Rabbi Eliezer, 195
Gordon, Y. L., 70
Gorky, Maxim, 128, 537
Gorshman, Szyrke (Shira Gorshman), 8, 510–511, 741n32
Gotesfeld, Bessie, 694
Gotovicki family, 401
Gotowicky (Polish conductor), 541
Gottlieb (Jewish apostate), 396
Grade, Chaim, 113, 335
Granowsky, Count, 68, 76
Great Northern War (1700–1721), 33, 38
Greece, 484; Jewish communities in, 65
Grodno, 53, 282, 300, 325, 326, 335, 356, 595; castle of, 23; Ghetto, 48, 154, 496, 612; history of, 23, 24, 26, 29, 34, 46, 258, 314, 700n32; 1935 pogrom in, 562; and Polish Rebellion, 50; teacher training in, 457, 462; Zionism in, 485
Grodno-Bialystok region, 67, 68, 71
Grodzinski, Reb Hayyim Ozer, 190–191, 351, 469
Gromnice (Lublin) fair, 406
Gross, Gitta, 277, 278
Gross, Shmuel, 84, 277, 278, 536, 538
Gross, Yehoshuah, 278
Gruenbaum, Yitzhak, 273, 563
Gruznik, Hayya, 507
Gruznik, Mickhe, 305
Gruznik, Zvi Hayyim, 280
Gruznik family, 264
Guenzberg, Horace, 457
Guenzburg, Mordekhai Aaron, 721n23
Gulf War, 11
Gunzberg, Ettl Glombocki, 462
Gurak, Jan, 480, 597, 598, 624
Gurewitch (feldsher), 444
Gurewitch (midwife), 588
Gurewitch, Maite, 560
Guterman, Belinka Ben-Shemesh, 687
Gypsies, 49, 218, 315, 322, 323, 426, 580
Ha'am, Ahad. *See* Ginzberg, Asher
Habimah (Hebrew theater), 538
Ha-Boker (The Morning; student newspaper), 183
Hadash, Aaron, 108
Hadash, Meir, 362
Hadash, Rachel Shekowitski, 119, 125
Hadash, Shulamit, 108
Hadash, Zivia Hutner, 108
Hadassah, 694
Hafetz, Avraham, 533
Hafetz, Rabbi Yehezkiel, 187
Haffetz, Leibke, 597
Haffetz Hayyim (Rabbi Israel Meir Ha-Kohen), 72, 89, 91, 188, 201, 344, 487, 600, 662, 703n3, 704n37, 708n26, 721n27; anti-Zionism of, 107, 112–113, 189, 190, 191; and coming of Messiah, 104, 491; and emigrants, 490, 493; and exorcism, 83, 428; funeral of, 238, 239; grave of, 238, 239, 588, 597, 599, 603, 607; and heder metukan, 173, 461; and Kibbutz ha-Prushim, 98, 188–190, 198; in Radun, 604, 606; and Radun yeshivah, 93, 189, 198, 402, 550; and rebuilding of Eishyshok, 197, 547; secularism of, 475; on vacation, 256, 533, 534; wife of, 189
Haganah (Jewish Defense Organization), 498, 570
Ha-Hamsan Ha-Kattan (Hebrew play), 517
Hahavat Zion (The Love of Zion; Mapu), 460
Ha-Hayyim (The Life; student newspaper), 183
Ha-Hayyim ve-ha-Teva (Hebrew journal for children), 516
Haifa, 686, 687, 688
Haint (Today; Warsaw newspaper), 291, 525
"Hakiza Ami" (Awaken, My People; Gordon), 458
Ha-Kohen, Israel Meir, *See* Haffetz Hayyim
halakhic laws, 349, 371, 376, 379, 383, 405. *See also* Judaism: halakhic
Halevi, Judah, 414
Halperin, Isaac, 470
Halperin family, 470
Halpern, Israel, 700
Halpern, Rose, 694
Haluz ha-Mizrahi, 500, 501–502
Ha-Maggid (the Declarer; Hebrew-language newspaper), 482, 485
Haman, 426–427
Hamarski, Dvorah, 570
Hamarski, Mr., 570
Hamarski, Mrs., 570
Hamarski, Yossele (Joe Camarone), 11, 601, 637, 638, 649, 690, 691
Hamburg, 32, 685, 686

Ha-Meassef (Haskalah newspaper), 171, 453
Ha-Melitz (Hebrew-language newspaper), 99, 192, 193, 381, 482, 486, 495, 547
Ha-Meorer (Hebrew-language publication), 514
handicrafts, 289–299, 453, 457, 461
Hannah (wife of Zvi the Tailor), 340
Ha-Omer (Hebrew-language publication), 514
Hapgood, Hutchins, 537
Ha-Poel ha-Zair (Hebrew-language publication), 514
Harkavy, Abraham Elijah, 19
Ha-Shahar (Hebrew newspaper), 245, 271, 482
Ha-Shomer ha-Zair, 362, 375
Hasia the Orphan (play; Gordin), 536–537
Hasidism, 18, 111, 124; in Eishyshok, 40, 41, 98, 145; establishment of, 83, 93, 145, 179, 704n23; and Haskalah, 198; and maggidim, 120; opponents (mitnaggedim) of, 39, 179, 198, 454; and schools, 465, 469
Haskalah (Jewish Enlightenment), 47, 98, 103, 134, 280, 394, 451–481; attitude to Talmud, 172, 453, 454; in Berlin, 452–453; classics of, 522; critics of, 482; in Eishyshok, 41, 458–463; Galician, 453–454; and handicrafts, 453, 457, 461; and Hasidism, 198; and heder education, 147, 171; influence on authors, 537; and Jewish stereotypes, 298; on marriage, 359, 360; and medicine, 437, 440–441; publications of, 284; punishments for, 271, 381; reaction to, 192–194, 196, 197; Russian, 454–458; and teaching of Hebrew, 95, 453, 456, 457, 458, 460, 461, 513; women and, 170, 171, 335, 340, 460; and yeshivah students, 183, 198, 494; and Zionism, 461, 484, 485. *See also* Gordon, Judah Leib
Hassia (daughter of Menuha), 380–381, 382
Hatikvah (Jewish national anthem), 461, 464, 505, 586
Hatteot Neurim (Sins of Youth; Lilienblum), 198, 486
Hausner, Gideon, 655
havdalah (separation) ceremony, 415–416, 422, 424
Hayya (from Kalesnik), 621
Hayyim-Barukh, 133–134, 377–378
Hayyim der Tregger (porter), 186
Hayyim-Itche the Tailor, 508
Hayyim of Volozhin, Reb, 180, 181, 182, 187, 707n15
Ha-Zefirah (newspaper), 193, 456, 460, 495, 515
Hazerim Gessl (Pigs Lane), 258, 430
Ha-Zevi (newspaper), 522
Ha-Zofeh Le-Veit Israel (The Watchman of the House of Israel; Erter), 198
hazzan (cantor), 139–142, 139–143
Hazzan, Sarah Shekowitski, *125*
Hazzon Ish. *See* Karelitz, Avraham Yeshayahu
Hebraish fur Jeder Mann (Shaul Kaleko), 519
Hebrew language: cemetery inscriptions in, 231, 232; and Communism, 540, 677; of Eishyshkians, 44, 115, 134, 143, 694; in Israel, 492; and Jewish Enlightenment, 95, 453, 456, 457, 458, 460, 461–462, 513; modern, 460, 484, 515; movement for, 513–520; normalization of, 517–520; in official documents, 29, 452; record books (pinkasim) in, 244, 513; revival of, 469, 482, 484, 486, 487, 492, 495, 498, 499, 513; societies for, 465, 504, 515–521, 742n7; teaching of, 150, 156, 158, 170–173, 194, 200, 453, 454, 462, 464, 471, 472, 479, 491, 502, 511, 617; *vs.* Yiddish, 172, 236, 462, 514, 522, 524, 525, 538, 539, 566; and Zionism, 114
Hebrew University (Rehovot): Volcani Institute of, 269
heder (religious elementary school), 8–9, 147–174, 176; amusements in, 163–166; criticism of, 454; early-childhood, 151–156; Gemara, 160–161, 165; Humash (middle), 156–160, 169; mixed (heder irbuvia), 168–171, 459–461, 465; punishment in, 166–167; reconstructed (heder metukan), 171–173, 461–462, 486; rhythms of life in, 161–168; and swimming, 163; twentieth-century, 173–174
He-Haluz (Pioneer) movement, 109, 478, 497, 498, 500–501, 502
Heine, Heinrich, 359, 394
hekdesh (homeless), 218, 248, 338, 351, 382, 392; at weddings, 369, 372
Heller, Professor Rabbi Hayyim, 93
Henrik, Golmont (Gront), 673
herem (excommunication), 40, 41, 87–88, 92, 131, 452
Herford, Robert Travers, 63
Hersh, Reb, 201
Herzen, Alexander, 46–47
Herzl, Theodor, 191, *260*, 423, *483*, 486–487, 489, *494*; death of, 173, 361, 434, 491, 508; eulogy for, 121; opponents of, 495; Zionism of, 107, 120, 490, 506
Hess, Moses, 485
Hevrah Kaddishah (burial society), 240, 242–245, 246–247, 248, 249, 286, 290, 351, 607
Hevrat Mefizei Haskalah (Society for the Promotion of Culture), 457
H.I.A.S. (Hebrew Immigrant Aid and Sheltering Society), 301
Hibbat Zion (Love of Zion) movement, 460, 482, 485–487, 489, 491. *See also* Zionism
Hiene di Frume (the pious one), 186, 393
Hiene di Krume (the lopsided one), 225
highways: Pilsudski, 300, 307, *307*, *309*, 325, 388; and wedding travel, 365

Hilke, Meir, 399, 402
Hilke, Mendl the builder, 399
Hillel, Rabbi, 600, 603
Hillel the Elder, 92, 203
Hinde, 439
Hingst, Hans Christian, 579
Hinski, Alexander Zisl, 136, *148*, 173, *176*, *199*, *239*, 352; emigration to Eretz Israel, 138; and Gemilut Hessed, 693; and Yiddish, 525
Hinski, Avraham-Yaakov, *138*, *199*
Hinski, Golda-Brahah, *138*
Hinski, Hayya-Sheine, *138*
Hinski, Israel Yossef (Reb Israel der Shamesh), 136, 138, 693
Hinski, Masha, *138*
Hinski, Shoshana Hutner, 108, 445–446, 507, 525
Hinski, Taibe-Edl Kabacznik, 138, 693
Hinski, Yekutiel, *138*
Hinukh (Education) society, 172
Hinukh Nearim (Education of Boys; school), 452, 455
Hirsch, Baron Maurice, 384, 488, 489
Hirsch, Clara, 488
Hirschbein, Peretz, 524, 538
Hirsh, David, *239*
Hirshele Rohe Sheftle's, 386–387, 393, 437
Hishveh (from Golmecziski), *148*
Hitler, Adolph, 115, 389, 560, 561, 566, 601, 610, 648, 657, 669, 697; defeat on Eastern front, 599, 609; speeches on radio, 559
Hlond, Cardinal Augustyn, 562
Hodorowski, M., 567–568
holidays, 162–163, 405–434; Arbor Day, 426; Catholic, 432; Fast of Gedalia, 586; forty-nine days of counting the omer, 431; gifts on, 342, 350; Hanukkah, 80, 81, 162, 234, 235, 287, 424–425, 430, 600; High, 417; Hoshana Rabbah, 423, 427; Lag ba-Omer, 162, 431; month of Elul, 416–417, 421; Ninth of Av, 18, 78, 163, 222, 239, 240; Passover (Pessah), 154, 162, 198, 215, 216, 218, 268, 428–431, 483, 484, 493, 574, 600, 614, 632, 700n12; Purim, 83, 162, 216, 426–428, *429*, *478*, 479, 710n8b; Rosh Hashanah, 80, 96, 117, 138, 162, 266, 417–419, 420, 421, 581, 582, 583, 585, 662–663; Rosh Hodesh, 115, 405, 416; Rosh Hodesh Elul, 434; Sabbath, 96, 407–416, 433; Shabbat Nahamu, 433; Shavuot, 135, 431, 432–433, 609, 614, 627; Simhat Torah, 34, 89, 162, 201, 202, 423–424, 487, 509, 566, 596–597; Sium (completion) celebration, 163; Sukkot, 154, 162, 422–423, 596; Ten Days of Repentance, 420; Tishah Be-Av, 162, 163, 433; Tu Be-Shevat, 162, 425–426, 477; Yom Kippur, 9, 79, 80, 96, 105, 106, 127, 138, 142, 162, 206, 208, 242, 251, 416, 417, 420–422, 427, 573, 596, 632, 662, 663
Holocaust Commission, 3, 4, 5, 7
Holocaust Memorial Museum, United States: Tower of Life at, 5, 12
Holy Ark, 69, 71, 73–76, *74*, *75*, 114, 186, 476, 489; coverings of, 77, 78, 80, 202, 217; and excommunication, 87; and maggid, 123
Homberg, Naphtali Herz, 452, 453–454
Honeh the builder. *See* Moszczenik, Dovid Elhanan
Honi-ha-Me'aggel (Jewish Rip Van Winkle), 389
Horcanus, Rabbi Eleizer ben. *See* Hyrcanus Rabbi Eleizer ben
Horse Fair, 27, 49, 185, 274, 315
Horse Market, 117, 146, 209, 481, 585–587, 634
Hovevei Zion (Lovers of Zion), 112, 486, 487, 489, 491, 494. *See also* Hibbat Zion
Huna, Rabbi, 92
Hus, Jan, 24
Hutner, Hava. *See* Kook, Hutner Hava
Hutner, Hayyia Dvorah, 100
Hutner, Hertz Mendl (Naftali Menahem Hutner), 42, 101, 105, *108*, 109, 111, 250, 352, 410; as acting rabbi, 107–108; daughters of, 72, 445; at funeral of Haffetz Hayyim, *238*; and school building, 473
Hutner, Rebbetzin Kreindl Epstein, 105, *108*, 109, 410, 445
Hutner, Luba. *See* Lewin, Luba Hutner
Hutner, Naftali Menahem. *See* Hutner, Hertz Mendl
Hutner, Rebbetzin Hendl, 100–*101*, 102–109, 110, 111, 303, 428; children of, *108*, 523
Hutner, Shimon, *108*, 238, *352*
Hutner, Shoshana. *See* Hinski, Shoshana Hutner
Hutner, Yehoshuah, 110
Hutner, Yehudah Leib, 101, 108, 109
Hutner, Yossef Zundl (Reb Zundl), 83, 91, 99–110, 130, 140, 164, 197, 317, 343; children of, *108*, 523; death of, 45; grandchildren of, 340, 507; and heder metukan, 173, 461; and theater, 538; and Wilkanski family, 134; works of, 100, 704n36
Hutner, Zipporah. *See* Kravitz, Zipporah Hutner
Hutner, Zivia, 108, 109, *220*, 303, 340, 352, *362*, 410, 501
Hutner, Zvi Hayyim, 109, 467
Hutner family, 108, 109, 198

Iasinowski, Mira, *502*
ICA. *See* Jewish Colonization Association
Ignatiev, Count Nikolai Pavlovich, 55, 258
Ilan, Meir Bar, 495

Ilya, 100, 400
Der Intelligent (play; Hirschbein), 524
Irgun, 11, 690, 691
Isckowicz, Meyer, *669*
Israel, State of, 125; agriculture in, 268–269; establishment of (1948), 451; kibbutz movement in, 184, 298; War of Independence for (1948), 11, 498, 685, 686, 688, 691, 692, 694. *See also* Eretz Israel
Israel the Fisherman, 639
Isserles, Rabbi Moses ben Israel (the Rema), 69, 144, 177, 189
Isserlin, Rabbi Israel, 440
Isserson, Reb (meshuggoim), 385–386
Itche der Shammes. *See* Berkowitch, Reb Itche
Itzele, Reb, 333
Ivashka (farmer), 641
Ivenitz, 444
Ivie, 190, 472, 475, 539; Ghetto, 618
Ivriah (Ibriah; Hebrew-language society), 516, 521, 742n7
Iwanowska, Marushka, 620, 621
Iwaszko, Michal, 673

Jabotinsky, Vladimir, 15, 335, 497, 498, 506, 507, 508, 563, 568, 741n26
Jadwiga (Polish princess), 20, 24
Jagiello, Grand Duke Alexander, 26, 177
Jagiello (King of Poland), 24, 25, 176
Jankelewicz, Elka Szulkin, 133, 229, 240–241, 567, *656*, 681, 717n15, 731n54
Jankelewicz, Sarah, *291*
Jankelewicz, Yankl, *287*, *501*, 681
Jankelewicz family, *656*
Jankelewitch, Reuven, 653
Janow, 169
Jaroslav, 29, 314
Jasza (Sonenson's Catholic maid), 339, 599
Jerusalem, 488; destruction of First Temple (586 B.C.E.) in, 64, 162, 239; destruction of Second Temple (70 C.E.) in, 64–65, 90, 162, 239, 483; Hadassah Hospital in, 14; Labor Battalion in, 8; Passover riots of 1920 in, 497, 498; reenactment of capture of, 162–163, 239; schools in, 479; Second Commonwealth in, 147; synagogues in, 65; Temple in, 7, 22, 39, 64, 74, 78, 92, 104, 189, 490, 491
Jerusalem (Mendelssohn), 452
Jeszance, 301
Jewish Colonial Bank, 487, 489, 490
Jewish Colonization Association (ICA), 151, 269, 488, 489, 548
Jewish Cooperative People's Bank (Volksbank), 285–286
Jewish Court, 129, 130; and din-Torah, 129–130
Jewish Daily Forward (newspaper), 337
Jewish Distribution Committee, 283, 292
Jewish Loan Association of Eastern Europe (EKOPO), 527
Jewish National Fund, 112
John III Sobieski, 33, 701n45, 720n4b
John of Capistrano, 262
Joint Distribution Committee (JDC), 526, 567, 690
Jordan river, 7, 163, 478, 506
Josefowicz-Hlebickis family, 394
Joselewicz, Berek, 36
Joseph II, Emperor of Austria, 452, 456
Josephowitch (ben Yossef) family, *260*
Judah the Prince, 135
Judaism, 697; conversion to, 394, 400–402; and death, 247; halakhic, 64, 65, 103, 104, 111, 112, 156, 169, 183, 191; Liberal, 69, 70; Orthodox, 41, 189, 190, 203, 460, 469; and public bath, 203; and rabbinate, 94, 117–118; and scholarship, 169; and women, 169, 170
Judenrat (Jewish Council), 28–31, 38–39, 581, 582; in Eishyshok (Juden Kommittet), 116–117, 577–580; position of rabbis in, 29; in Radun, 598, 601. *See also* kahal; *individual councils*
Der Judenstaat (The Jewish State; Herzl), 486
Jud family, 394
Jurdyczanski, Etchke, *305*, *566*
Jurdyczanski, Shimon, *310*
Jurdyczanski, Yoshke, 640
Jurgis (Henrik Ziman), 641, 642, 650
Juris, Isaac. *See* Jurdyczanski, Etchke
Juryzdyki, 18, *50*, 105, 231, 577, 591; Catholic Church in, 25, 34, 66, *88*, 89, 132, 232, 381, 398, 399, 529, 578, 591, 594, 621, 624, 628, 659, 745n11b
Juszka (Blacharowicz family maid), 599

Kabacznik, Alter, 625
Kabacznik, Avraham, *148*
Kabacznik, Benyamin, *279*, *302*, *475*, *533*, *570*, 572, 622–623
Kabacznik, David, 246, 333–334, 351
Kabacznik, Golde (daughter of Alter), 625
Kabacznik, Golde (daughter of David). *See* Berkowitch, Golda Kabacznik
Kabacznik, Golde (daughter of Sorl), 310, 426, 500, 506, 582
Kabacznik, Liebke Moszczenik, *259*, *408*, *443*, *570*, *590*, 623
Kabacznik, Luba, 682

Kabacznik, Meir, 269, 582, 600–601, 624–625, 627, 655, 677, *682*, 692
Kabacznik, Mendl, 274
Kabacznik, Miriam. *See* Shulman, Miriam Kabacznik
Kabacznik, Moshe Faivl, 459
Kabacznik, Rachel. *See* Berkowitch, Rachel Kabacznik
Kabacznik, Shepske, 269, 272, 582, 600–601, 621, 627, 663, 682, 692
Kabacznik, Sonia, *682*
Kabacznik, Sorl, 284, 390, 582, 601, 667, *682*, 684; and Beitar, 507; in hiding, 618, 622, 628; and Kabacznik kibbutz, 658, 662, 664; repatriation to United States, 692
Kabacznik, Taibe-Eidl. *See* Hinski, Taibe-Eidl Kabacznik
Kabacznik, Yankl, 425
Kabacznik, Yossef, *665*
Kabacznik, Yudaleh, *266*, *419*, *428*, *475*, *570*, 623
Kabacznik, Zalman, 138
Kabacznik family, 53, *64*, 130, *239*, 459; and Armia Krajowa, 667; as founding family, 243, 255; and gentiles, 321; in Ghetto Radun, 582, 600; in hiding, 618, 621, 623, 628; home of, 576; and liberation, 669, 675, 677, *684*; property of, 430; return to Eishyshok, 657, 658; tannery of, 280, 283–284, 673
Kaczerginski, Shmerl, 629
Kadishon of Dociszki, 624, 675, 679
Kaganov, Ida Kanichowski, *259*, 586, 590, 601, 625, 634
Kaganov, Judith, 279
Kaganov, Leibke, *259*, 586
Kaganov, Motele, 586, 601, 625, 634
Kaganov, Shifrale, 586, 601, 625, 634
Kaganov, Szymen, 279, 591
Kaganov, Yaakov, *625*
Kaganov, Yankele, 279
Kaganowicz, Basha, 277
Kaganowicz, Benjamin, 583, 592, 608, 611, 637, 638, 642, *643*, 644, 660, 690
Kaganowicz, Berke, 651–652
Kaganowicz, Freidke, 589, 608, 611, 637, 638, 642, 643, 694–695
Kaganowicz, Geneshe. *See* Sonenson, Geneshe Kagnowicz
Kaganowicz, Hannah Kiuchefski, *283*, 371, 693, 694
Kaganowicz, Leibke (Leon Kahn), *309*, 321, 392, 474, 480, *533*, 583; in Canada, 690, 694; in Ghetto Radun, 598, 607, 608; in hiding, 592, 611–612, 637; and liberation, 660, 668, 669, 670, 671, 674, 691; and Russian partisans, 642, 643, 644
Kaganowicz, Lena, 336–337
Kaganowicz, Masha Kiuchefski, *52*, *283*, 348, *578*
Kaganowicz, Miriam Rudzin, *42*, 474, 480, *546*, 589, 608–609, 690
Kaganowicz, Mordekhai, 580
Kaganowicz, Moshe, 153, 264, 283, *287*, 346, 371, 693
Kaganowicz, Sarah, *42*, *546*
Kaganowicz, Shael, *42*, *546*, 583, 608, 660, 690; death of, 644, 694, 695; in hiding, 611, 637, 638, 642, 643
Kaganowicz, Velvke, *52*, 524
Kaganowicz, Yankele, *475*
Kaganowicz, Zeev, *283*, *287*, 500, 502, *626*
Kaganowicz der Kapeliushnik, Reb Benyomin, 213
Kaganowicz family, 576, 608, 611, 612, 642, 645
kahal (local Jewish government), 29, 38–44, *42*, 55, 69, 79, 700n32; and commerce, 270; election of, 81, 82, 416; and holidays, 426; and land managers, 262; and leaseholders, 263, 264; and livestock, 267, 268; and markets, 326; members of, *41*, *276*, 658; and meshuggoim, 387; on orphans, 343; and Shabbes goy, 414; and Yishuvniks (country people), 265
Kahaneman, Yosef, 104
Kahanov, Yaakov, *428*
Kahanshtam Tarbut teachers' seminary, 466, 472, 475, 479
Kahn, Leon. *See* Kaganowicz, Leibke
Kahn, Shalom, *560*
Kaleckis, J., 33
Kaleko, Amiram, 519, *563*
Kaleko, Elisha, *563*
Kaleko, Frieda Yankelewitch, 358–359, 362, 436
Kaleko, Leah Koppelman, *339*, 362, *499*, 504, 528, *533*, *563*
Kaleko, Mina Schneider, *154*, 200, 272, 362, 472, 563
Kaleko, Mordekhai Munesh, *154*, 200, 272, 355, 358–359, 362, 436–437, 518, 559, 560, 563
Kaleko, Peretz, 153, 154, 362; and Brenner Club, 528; emigration to Palestine, 539, *563*; and Hebrew, 462, 519, 524; at summer home, *533*; as teacher, 470, 472, 475; and theater, 538; in Vilna, 465, 466, 469; and Zionism, 425, 501, 502, 503, 504
Kaleko, Rachel, *154*, *287*, 342, 466, 478–479, 502, 519, 520
Kaleko, Shaul (Shaul Barkali), *154*, 345–346, 617; at Berlin University, 268, 467, 519, 559–560; diary of, 200, 232–233, 464–465, 709n52; as Hebraist, 513, 514, 518, 523; in Kovno, 342, 466, 539; and theater, 536, *537*, 538; and Zionism, 107, *496*, 500
Kaleko, Shmuel, *154*, *496*, 519, 522
Kaleko, Simha, *154*, 200, *272*; debates with Communists, 509; and Hebrew, 465, *518*; and Zionism, 496, 500

Kaleko, Yehudah, 297, 563
Kaleko-Alufi, Peretz, 10, 14, 58, 112
Kaleko family, 391, 401, 441, 467, 496, 518, 519, 538
Kalesnik, 40, 249, 256, 293, 586, 621
Kalinin, Mikhail Ivanovich, 128
Kalischer, Rabbi Hirsch, 484, 485
Kallir, Rabbi Eleazar, 152
Kalman, Reb, 170–171
Kameneta-Litovsk, 65
Kaminetski, Itchke, 387
Kaminetski, Leibke, 387
Kaminska, Esther Rachel, 536
Kanichowski, Benyamin, 623
Kanichowski, Gutke Yurkanski, 259, 586, 590, 601
Kanichowski, Haikl, 259, 302, 404, 601, 642, 658, 683
Kanichowski, Itzle (Iris), 77, 404, 586, 601, 683
Kanichowski, Kreinele, 272, 590, 601, 625, 634
Kantil river, 7, 22, 143, 163, 205, 209, 231, 478, 499
Kapitan, Yashuk, 591
Kaplan, Altke Bastunski, 342, 363
Kaplan, Annaliese Edith Ephraimson, 692
Kaplan, Asher, 338
Kaplan, Avraham, 363, 474, 580, 582
Kaplan, Avraham Meishke, 293, 692
Kaplan, Leibl, 536
Kaplan, Miriam, 343
Kaplan, Moshe, 57, 337–338, 351, 476
Kaplan, Rochke Yurkanski, 381
Kaplan, Yoshke, 381
Kaplan, Yossef, 695, 697
Kaplan, Yossl, 586
Kaplan-Gottlieb, Mary (Margolia Dragutski), 280
Kapolia (Kopyl), 107, 110, 111
Kapusta, Major General, 649
karabelniks (peddler-coachmen), 301, 302
Karaite Jews, 18, 19, 184, 244, 699n12, 700n12
Karelitz, 364
Karelitz, Avraham Yeshayahu (Hazzon Ish), 533
Karna (emigrant to America), 544
Karnefski, Ephraim, 474
Karnowski, Ephraim, 117
Kartuz-Breze (Polish concentration camp), 509
Kashka (Polish Catholic maid), 339
Kasimierz, King Jan (John Casimir), 65
Katowice, 486, 491
Katowietski, Stanislav, 624
Katriel school, 464–465
Katyn forest, 598
Katz, Alte (Rahel-Yehudit) Dwilanski, 4, 307, 340, 344, 346, 353, 354, 361, 560, 680; businesses of, 115, 309, 323–324, 338, 362, 444, 526, 576; children of, 235; and Communists, 572–573; at daughter's wedding, 373; and German invasion, 327; and Hebrew, 474, 522; on last Passover, 574; and massacre of 1941, 587, 589, 593; and Nazi occupation, 581; and Nohem the Pope, 393; on Sabbath, 415; salon (Vagsal) of, 525; as student, 519; on vacation, 534; in World War I, 321, 623; and Zionism, 505, 506, 507, 568
Katz, Avigdor, 306, 309, 346, 351, 352, 475, 476, 506, 507, 587
Katz, Esther. *See* Resnik, Esther (Etele) Katz
Katz, Hannah-Batia, 235
Katz, Hayyim, 444
Katz, Leibke, 646, 649, 669
Katz, Luba, 646, 647, 669
Katz, Moshe Dovid (David), 148, 307, 419, 466, 587
Katz, Rabbi Avraham Yaakov, 235
Katz, Reb Aaron, 353, 580
Katz, Shaul, 353
Katz, Shoshana, 307, 323, 346, 466, 535, 573, 583, 625, 645; and Hebrew, 465; and massacre of 1941, 589, 593; and Zionism, 506, 507
Katz, Uri, 444
Katz, Velvke, 502–503, 524, 540, 571, 583
Katz, Yitzhak Uri, 33, 234, 340, 346, 353, 361–362, 373, 525, 652; drugstore of, 444; education in America, 235, 544; in World War I, 321, 623
Katz, Yossele, 234
Katz, Zeev. *See* Katz, Velvke
Katz, Zipporah. *See* Sonenson, Zipporah Katz
Katzenelenboigen-Schwartz, Szeina, 516, 526, 527, 536, 537, 559, 576, 577, 580
Katz family, 519, 536, 572
Kaufman, Esther Wilenchik, 662, 664, 665
Kazakov, Sasha, 650
kehilah (community), 28, 86, 284, 290, 363
Keidan, 193
Kelme, 175, 183, 332
Kerenshenblum, Rabbi, 694
kest (room and board offered to a newly married son-in-law in a matrilocal marriage), 331–332, 334, 338, 345, 357, 358, 359, 361, 366, 378
Kfar Batia School, 694
Kfar Vitkin, 269, 691
Khazar Kingdom, 19
Khwolson, Daniel, 149, 394, 395, 398
Kibbutz Galuiot (ingathering of exiles), 483, 486, 489
Kibbutz ha-Prushim yeshivah, 89, 261; changes in, 192–196, 202; decline of, 196–198; food distribution of, 201; founding of, 97, 131, 184; golden age of, 80,

98, 119; students at, 52, 70, 81, 104, 129, 138, 175, 255, 302, 355, 494
kibbutzim, 184, 298, *498*, 499, 510; Kabacznik, 658, 662, 664
Kichier, Reb Dovid der. *See* Moszczenik, Reb Dovid
Kiczie, 302
Kielce, 679
Kiev, 258, 511, 682
Kik, Shlomo, 420, 605
Kilkie, 402
Kirschner, Basha, 546
Kirschner, Ephraim, 281, *282*
Kirschner, Ester-Malka, 546
Kirschner, Feiga, 546
Kirschner, Jacob (Jacob Abramofsky; Jacob Abrams), 546
Kirschner, Jeanette, 546
Kirschner, Simon-Chanoch, 546
Kirschner, Walter, *281*, 546, 652–653, 654
Kirschner family, 545, 546
Kishinev, 454; 1903 pogrom in, 107, 125, 491
Kisilev, P. D., 455
Kitchie, 265
Kiuchefski, Berl, *52*, 283
Kiuchefski, Dovid, 277, 549
Kiuchefski, Esther. *See* Shiffel, Esther Kiuchefski
Kiuchefski, Frade-Leah, *52*, 277, 549, 625
Kiuchefski, Hannah. *See* Kaganowicz, Hannah Kiuchefski
Kiuchefski, Masha, *52*, 348
Kiuchefski, Meir (Mayor of Eishyshok), *41*, 107, 130, *220*, 301, 461, 524, 549, 625
Kiuchefski, Mordekhai (Motke), *52*, *214*, *310*, 682
Kiuchefski, Rochel, *52*, 277, *278*, 437
Kiuchefski, Shlomo, *52*, *283*, *287*, *310*, 362–363, *518*; and meshuggoim, 385, 387; murder of, 625, *626*; return from Palestine, 502; and Zionism, 500
Kiuchefski, Sonia, *52*
Kiuchefski, Yossef, *52*
Kiuchefski family, *52*, *53*, 265, 285, 459, *462*, 538; electric power plant of, *283*, 297, 387, 657; home of, 572, 576, 578, 579; in liquor trade, 277; mill of, 280, 389, 409, 657
Kkuzmicki, Marushka, 403–404
Kkuzmicki family, 403
Klausner, Amos (Amos Oz), 385
Klausner, Yossef, 385, 471, 495
Kleck, 275
Klei Kodesh (Holy Vessels), 94, 135, 138, 139, 144, 145
Kletskin, B. A., 386
klezmers (musicians), 382, *539*; at weddings, 365, 366, 367, 368, 372
Knoll, Roman, 657
Kock, 35
Kodish, Fredik, 622, 623, 628
Kodish, Mrs. Fredik, 622, 623
Kolka partisan camp, 636
Kolton, Shmuel, 432
Königsberg, 171, 192, 446, 515
Kook, Hutner Hava, 110, 523
Kook, Rabbi Avraham Yitzhak ha-Cohen, 110, 210, 212
Kopke (Gestapo officer), 597, 599, 601, 602, 603, 604
Koppelman, Avraham Asher, 390
Koppelman, Beila, 624
Koppelman, Elisha, *260*, *339*, *351*, *428*, 446, *476*, 624
Koppelman, Elisha Peretz, *624*
Koppelman, Golda, *138*
Koppelman, Leah. *See* Kaleko, Leah Koppelman
Koppelman, Malka, 390–391
Koppelman, Markl, *43*, 190, 572, 580, 624
Koppelman, Mina, 624
Koppelman, Miriam. *See* Rushkin, Miriam Koppelman
Koppelman, Nahum, 190, 444, 474
Koppelman, Nehama, *339*
Koppelman, Rachel, *475*, *476*, 624
Koppelman, Yankl, 623
Koppelman, Zlate, *339*
Koppelman family, 321, *507*, 536, 572, 623, 675, 679
Korelanski, Alter (the barber), 218, 440
Korkuc, Czeslaw, 626, 627
Korkuc, Jaszuk, 618
Korkuc, Kazimierz, 321, 600, 601, 609, 615, 618, 619, 624, 625, 626, 627, 628, 629; and liberation, 655, 656, 679, 680; in New York, 683, *684*, 745n11b
Korkuc farm, 615–628, 655, 656, 657, 660, 662, 666, 667, 677, 682
Korkuciany, 591, 600, 609, 620, 625
Korkucowa, Pani, 615, 617, 618, 621, 622, 623, 627, 628
Korna, Rabbi, 92
korobka (kosher meat) tax, 39, 82, 86, 93, 119, 126, 133, 145, 204, 213, 219; and yeshivah students, 183
Kosciuszko, Tadeusz, 36
Kosolewicz, Rabbi, 234
Kosowski, Daniel, *362*
Kosowski, Hayya Streletski, 90, 112
Kosowski, Taibke, *471*
Koszczuk (informer), 277
Koutsai, Altke, *475*

Kovalov, Captain, 674–675, 679
Kovner, Abba, 646
Kovno, 109, 127, 167, 342, 539; expulsion of Jews from, 523; Ghetto, 641; Kaunas University in, 466; rabbi of, 99, 181, 245, 303, 486, 491; teachers' seminary in, 478
Kowalski, Yaakov, 597
Kowarski, Dr., 446
Kranz, Yaakov ben Wolf, 120
Krapovnitski, Eliezer David Mordechai (Reb Adam), *148*, 173
Krashunski, Hayya, *237*
Krashunski, Notl, *237*
Kravitz, Zipporah Hutner, 72, *108*, 507
Krechmer, Reb Yehudah Leib, 100
Kremin, Blumke. *See* Eliashewicz, Blumke Kremin
Kremin, Dobke, Dobke Kremin, *See* Dimitrowski
Kremin, Hayyim-Itchke, *237*
Kremin, Hirsh-Faivl, *48*, *237*, 293
Kremin, Mote Yosl, *43*, 651
Kremin, Yude-Mendl, *237*, 309, 541
Krisha (Jan Borysewicz), 614, 623, 624, 626, 627, 672, 673
Krisilov, Arieh, *428*
Krisilov, Avraham, 308, *309*
Krisilov, Israel, *287*
Krisilov, Moshe-Leib, *234*
Krisilov, Yankele, 292, *307*, 311, 445, 682
Krisilov family, *22*
Kristallnacht, 519
Krizova, 301
Krok, 8, 511
Krolowitz (miller), 624
Krudlanski, Kreine, *250*
Krushenko, Captain, 670
Kruzh, 97
Krylov, 680
Kubiliunas, Petras, *582*
Kudlanski, Arie Leib, 542
Kudlanski, Atara. *See* Zimmerman, Atara Goodman (Kudlanski)
Kudlanski, Bill, *443*
Kudlanski, Connie, *443*
Kudlanski, Hanneh-Beile Moszczenik, 229, *250*, *370*, *409*, *419*, *443*, *529*, 556
Kudlanski, Reb Arieh-Leib, *570*
Kudlanski, Yaakov-Moshe. *See* Goodman, Jake Morris
Kudlanski (Goodman) family, *412*, *529*, 555, *690*, 691
Kulikowski, Burgermeister (Mayor), 597–598, 601, 603, 606
Kumin, Gitaleh, 478, 479
Kuppat Holim (sick fund), 213
Kupritz (heder metukan teacher), 461, 464
Kuzmicki, Marushka, 631, 632, 633, 634, 692
Kuzmicki, Stashek, 631–632, 634, 692
Kuzmicki family, 692

Lachowice, 275
Lakish, Rabbi Reish, 163
land: anti-Semitic legislation on, 257–261; Jewish managers of, 261–263, *279*; Jews' attachment to, 259–261; New Plan, 280
Land of Israel. *See* Eretz Israel
Landsman, Basha Shuster, 634, 635, 691
Landsman, Evelyn (Hava), 634, 635, 690–691
Landsman, Hodl, 634, 635, 636, 691
Landsman, Moshe, 634, 635
Landsman-Shuster family, *690*, 691
Lanegev (ship), 11, 687
Lanski, Miriam, *471*
Lapp, Esther, *541*
Lassalle, Ferdinand, 484
Laufer, Gale, 564
Lawit, Abrascha-Arluk, *669*
laws: anti-Semitic, 257–261, 262; on apostates, 394; on commerce, 270, 272–274; on leaseholding, 263. *See also* May Laws
Lawzowski, Gita, 475, *537*
Lawzowski, Mordekhai, 80, 374, 500
Lawzowski, Yehuda, 84
Lawzowski, Zvi, 496, 500, 501
Lawzowski family, 198, 472, 502
Layzerowski, Hayya-Rochl, *592*
leaseholders (arendators): Jewish, 263–265
Lebiedniki, 611, 621, 622, 623, 627, 660
Lebowicz family, 319
Lehr, Dr., 443, 444, 445, 562, 624
Leib, Reb, 243, 379
Leib der Grober (the Fat One), *221*
Leibnitz, 682, *683*
Leibowitz, Rina Shekowitski, *125*
Leipun, 256, 584, 586, 595
Lejbowicz, Rephael, *56*, *273*, 651–652
Lejbowicz, Sarah, *272*
Lekert, Hirsh, 508
Lemel the tailor, 322
"Lemi Ani Amel" (For Whom Do I Toil?; Gordon), 458
Lemke (World War I German soldier), *536*
Lenin, Vladimir, 326, 509, 572

Leningrad, 511, 582
Leora (daughter of Esther Wilkanski), *432*
Leszczynski, Stanislaw, 33
Die Letzte Naeis (Yiddish newspaper), 149
Levick, H., 538
Levin, A., *301*
Levin, David, *363*, 730n30
Levin, David Leib, *272*
Levin, Eishke, *541*
Levin, Ella Kirschner, *282*
Levin, Golda, 534
Levin, Solomon, *282*
Levin, Yankl, *287*, *560*
Levin, Yitzhak, 618, 658, *682*
Levin, Zipporah (née Levin), *363*, 730n30
Levine, Katie, *553*
Levine, Louis, *553*
Levine, Sarah, *553*
Levinski, Elhanan Leib, 192, 193
Levinsohn, Isaac Baer, 454, 455
Levitan, Breine, *241*
Levitan, Hayyam, *241*
Levitan, Henia-Hayya, *241*
Levitan, Mina, *241*
Levitan, Reb Eliakim Gezl, 706n30
Levittan, Motke, *372*
Levo, Isaac, 637, 642, 643
Levo family, 660
Lewin, Abraham, *109*, 110
Lewin, Luba Hutner, 109–110, 523
Lewin, Ora, 110
Lewinson, Ephraim, *281*
Lewinson, Itte, 281
Lewinson, Pesie, *281*
Lewinson, Rabbi, *189*
Lewinson, Rachel, 502
Lewinson, Rina, 266, 361, 502, *530*, 537
Lewinson, Rivka, 220, 502
Lewinson, Yehiel, 201, 281, 303, 308
Lewinson family, 198, 415, 538
Lewinson sisters, *220*
Lichtig, Rabbi Zusha, 201, 564, 573, 588
Lida, 16, 20, 24, 51, *237*, 264, 300, 353, 459, 466, 525, 541, 566, 580, 618, 691; as administrative district, 38, 472; and Armia Krajowa, 629, 669; Communists in, 571; escapees in, 595, 599, 610; Ghetto, *502*, 598, 606, 607; and Haskalah, 458; manufacturing in, 282, 283; in 1941 occupation, 635; rabbis in, 107, 130; thieves from, 325; travel to, 301, 308; yeshivah in, 84, 191, 198, 494, 501
Lieberman, Aaron, 198
Liebke (girlfriend of Avraham Asner), 637
Lifshitz, A. M., 147
Lifshitz, Berl, 587, 588, 591–592
Lifshitz, Rive-Rochele, 588
Lifshitz, Sarah, 587
Lifshitz, Yaakov, 98, 486
Lilienblum, Moshe Leib, 198, 486, 494, 522
Lilienthal, Max, 455, 456
Lilith (Queen of the Demons), 167
Lindsay, Mayor John, 683, *684*
Lipa the blacksmith, 584
Lipkunce, 638
Lipkunski, Avraham, 402; and Eichmann trial, 201, *686*; in Ghetto Radun, 603, 604; in hiding, 612; and liberation, 660–661, 685; as partisan, 614, 632, 636, 637, 638, 648, 649; and War of Independence, 686
Lipkunski, Berl, 598
Lipkunski, Faivl, 614
Lipkunski, Mina, 601, 602, 603, *614*, 661
Lipkunski, Moshe-Dovid, 602, 603, 612–613, 614
Lipkunski, Pinhas, 603, 604, 612, 614, 660, 661
Lipkunski, Yekutiel, 601, 604, 661
Lipkunski family, 256–257, 533, 614, 717n7
Lippman, Rabbi Yom Tov, 182
Lithuania, 3, 6, 15, 16, 17, 55; acquired by Russia, 257; agriculture in, 268; as center for scholarship, 179; Christianization of, 25–26, 66; during Cold War, 7; early history of, 20–34; Eishyshok ruled by, 20, 22, 115, 174, 201, 292, 326, 389, 543; fairs in, 313; farmers of, *26*; independence of, 12, 107, 115; Jewish autonomy in, 23; Jewish farmland in, 260; Jewish schools of, 456, 466; Jews of, 7, 18, *39*, *40*, 110, 231; landowning in, 25, 30, 52; leaseholders in, 264; nobility of, 25–26, 27, 261; paganism in, 22, 23, 24, 25, 66; Polonization of, 25, 27–28; postwar, 678–679; refugees in, 567; and Second Partition of Poland, 35; settlement of Jews in, 19; social mobility in, 25; tolerance toward Jews, 22, 23; union with Poland, 24
Lithuanian Brigade, 403
Lithuanian Chronicles, 16, 65, 230
Lithuanian Council, 28, 29, 30, 31–32, 248, 256, 349, 700n32; on bar mitzvahs, 351, 352; on Christian holidays, 406; on Christian servants, 338–339; and circumcision, 349; and commerce, 270; and Hebrew, 513; and leaseholders, 263, 264; and liquor trade, 276; on marriage, 355; on mentally ill, 383; and morenu issue, 78; and rabbis, 92; and shohet, 144; on weddings, 215, 366, 368–369; on women, 302, 336
Lithuanian Duchy, 16

Lithuanian Socialist Republic, 229, 466, 468
Litski, Shaul, 461
The Little Thief (play), 535
Livonian Knights, 23, 24
Lodz, 669, 679
Loewenstein, Zvi Hirsch, 139
Loewenstein-Strashunski, Joel David, 139
Lomza, 93, 98, 509
Lubek, Sol. *See* Lubetski, Zalman
Lubetski, Akiva, 582, 650
Lubetski, Batia. *See* Barkali, Batia Lubetski
Lubetski, Bluma, *305*, *409*, *562*, 574, *578*
Lubetski, Etele, *305*, *562*
Lubetski, Hayya-Sorele, 364, 445
Lubetski, Israel Yekutiel, 562
Lubetski, Leah'le, *562*
Lubetski, Yoske, 636
Lubetski, Zalman (Sol Lubek), 561, 562, 566, 582, *641*, 650, 692
Lubetski, Zipporah. *See* Tokatli, Zipporah Lubetski
Lubetski the blacksmith, 443
Lubetski family, 583; house of, *422*
Lublin, 120, 131, 177; Church of St. Stanislaw in, 27; fairs in, 29, 178, 314, 355, 406
Lublin Union, 16, 25, 26–27, 28
Lubtch, 464, 682
Luknik, 515
Lulke, Benjamin di, 414
Lunski, Haikl, 217
Luntschitz, Ephraim Shlomo ben Aaron, 120
Luski, Yankele Hazkl, 308
Luther, Martin, 158
Lutsk, 20

Maccoby, Hayyim Zundel, 120
Mackewicz, Shalom-Gershke, 639
Maculski, Zisl, 390
Maczulski, Father, 624
Magdeburg Rights, 33, 720n4b
maggid (preacher), 119–128; and Eishyshok, 122–124; eulogies of, 121, 123; and revolutionary movements, 120, 122; and women, 121, 122
Maggid Meisharim (Preacher of Righteousness), 97, 119, 126
Maggid of Dubno, 120
Maharal of Prague, 244
Maimon, Salomon, 332
Maimonides, 92, 132, 191, 215, 377, 431, 456, 460
Majdanek, 294, 608
Malke's, Shmuel, 420
Mandelshtan, A. L., 456
manufacturing, 279–284
Mapu, Abraham, 335, 460, 522
Maracewicz (Polish lawyer), 563
Marah Levanah (organization), 427
Marcinkonys, 610, 611, 642
Margalit, Ilya (Eliyahu), *647*
Margolies, Elia, 606, 669, 745n7
Mariampole, 129, 514
Maricewicz (Pole), 308
markets, 255, 313–327, 406
Markus, Asher, 141
Markus, Lolke, 141
marriage, 331–334, 354–375; bigamous, 384; and divorce, 376; and holidays, 424; levirate, 379, 380; and mentally ill, 383–384
Marushka (maid), 628
Marx, Heinrich, 394
Marx, Karl, 326, 394, 485, 509, 572
Marxism, 503
Masaryk, Tomas, 468
Massacre of September 1941 (Eishyshok), 3, 4, 6, 7–8, 9, 57, 58, 97, 209, 226–227, 252, 575–594, 610; aftermath of, 671; revenge for, 670
Massalski, Bishop, 36
Matikan, 265
Matikanski, Albert, *292*, 579
Matikanski, Baruch, *43*
Matikanski, Dovid, 290, *292*, *406*, 410, 431, 579, 599
Matikanski, Eli, 446
Matikanski, Haikl, *290*, 294, *371*, *406*, 431, 579, 599, 600, 607, 608
Matikanski, Hersh, 446
Matikanski, Malka Zahavi, *310*, *371*, *406*, *426*, 431, *500*, *505*, *506*, 520, 524, *534*, 563
Matikanski, Nehama Pecker, *290*, *406*, 410, 415, 431, 579, 591, 599, 607, 608
Matikanski, Shlomo, 623
Matikanski, Yitzhak, *199*, *290*, *406*, 431, 579, 599, 600, 607
Matikanski, Ziske, 403, 669
Matikanski family, 265, 468, 602
Ma-Yafit, Rabbi Zvi Hirsh, 133, 196, 197
May Day demonstrations (1902), 508
May Laws (1882), 38, 119, 257, 482, *550*; and emigration, 269, 546; and land, 258, 488, 545; and yishuvniks (country people), 211, 265
Mazovia, 36
Megillah, 65
Meir "Bonaparte," 541
Meir der Lerer (Meir the teacher). *See* Shewitski, Meir (der Lerer)
Meir the Rubishker, 639

Meir "the wicked butcher," 365–366
Meirowitch, Reb Shalom David, 99
Meishke the tailor, 508
Meltzer, Fruma-Rivka, 342
Meltzer, Rabbi Isser Zalman, 170, 342
Meltzer, Rebbetzin Beile Hinde, 170
Melzer, Hirshke, 623
Melzer, Shimshon, 305
Memel, 515
Mendelowitch, Hirshke, 477
Mendelssohn, Moses, 452, 453, 454, 458, 482
Mendl the peddlar, 365
mentally ill (meshuggoim), 383–394
Menuha (divorced shopkeeper), 380–381
Merchants and Artisans Alliance, 219
Mere the seamstress, 414
Meretch (Merkine), 259, 385, 674
Merzuk (watchman at slaughterhouse), 663
Merzuk, Ivan, 663, 666
Merzuk, Waclaw, 663, 666
Meshuggeneh, Henia Di, 391
Messiah, coming of, 189, 483, 484, 486, 488, 491, 493
Meyshe-Yude, Reb, 164
Mezrich, 120, 490
Michalowski, Alter, 658, 660, 664, 665, 668, 670, 675, 686
Michalowski, Bluma Zlotnik, *345*, 585
Michalowski, Breinaleh, 606
Michalowski, David (David Foster), 549, *550*, *584*, *586*, *588*
Michalowski, Dora, *550*
Michalowski, Eli Dovid, 305
Michalowski, Hanan, 580
Michalowski, Honeh, *345*, 625
Michalowski, Judith, 584, 598
Michalowski, Leah, *475*, *476*
Michalowski, Maneh, 173, *220*, 579, 584, 588, 589
Michalowski, Masha, *560*, 658, 675, 686
Michalowski, Meishke, *530*
Michalowski, Moshe-Reuven, 293, 446, 599, 601, 602, 606
Michalowski, Moshe Sheshko, *345*
Michalowski, Nehama, *693*
Michalowski, Paula Lefkowicz, 682, *683*, 685, 686
Michalowski, Sarah (Sorke), *345*
Michalowski, Sheshko, *345*
Michalowski, Yossef, 539, *550*, 625
Michalowski, Zelda-Bluma, *345*
Michalowski, Zvi, 251, 664, 670, 675; on *Exodus*, 685, 686; marriage of, 682, *683*; and massacre of 1941, 579, 584, 586, 588–589, 598; as partisan, 631, 639, 640, 668; return to Eishyshok, *689*; on trial in Vilna, 680, 681; and War of Independence, *693*
Mickiewicz, Adam, 304
Mieszczanca forest, 598, 631
Mihalowski, Hayya, 446
mikvah (ritual purification bath), 65, 66, 68, 205–206, 208, 247
Milikowski, Leibe, 588
Minke (unwed mother), 382
Minorities Treaty (1919), 468, 470
Minsk, 46, 91, 97, 103, 124–128, 181, 241, 289, 455
Minsk Conference (1902), 172, 494–495
Mir, 93, 97, 98, 188, 241, 364, 441; yeshivah at, 181, 182, 183, 184, 192
Mirele Efros (Gordin), 335
Miriam (daughter of Zvi the Tailor), 340
Mishnah Berurah (Ha-Kohen), 189
Mishnah society (Hevrat Mishnayot), 72, 247
Mishneh Torah, 377
Mitnatz family, 585
Mizrahi movement, 73, 170, 173, 469, 495, *694*; founders of, 84, 107, 191; members of, *91*, 109, 111, 112, 113, 115, *374*, 375, 475, 494, 496
Mogilev province, 258
Mohilever, Rabbi Samuel, 486
Moishe der Guss (the last), 322
Montefiore, Moses, 484, 485, 486
Montgomery, Lieutenant General Bernard, 652
Mordekhai, Moishe (woodcutter), 232
Mordekhai-Leib (the tailor), 249
Moreh Zedek (Teacher of Justice), 96
Moscow, 184, 511, 676, 682
Moshe, Rabbi Avraham, 181
Moshe, Reb. *See* Segal, Rabbi Moshe ben Aaron Halevi Horowitz
Moshetowitch, Itchke, *641*
Moszczenik, Brakha, 501, 555
Moszczenik, Dovid Elhanan (Honeh the builder), *143*, *296*, 463, 555, 568
Moszczenik, Esther, 555
Moszczenik, Frad'l, *407*, *419*, 555
Moszczenik, Gelle, *229*
Moszczenik, Golde, 143, *296*, 462, 463, 554, 555, 568
Moszczenik, Hannah-Leah, 555
Moszczenik, Ida, 555
Moszczenik, "Itchke Hones," *501*
Moszczenik, Leah, *266*, *267*, *423*
Moszczenik, Liebke. *See* Kabacznik, Liebke Moszczenik

Moszczenik, Max, 555
Moszczenik, Pessia, 242, 462, 463, 501, 568; return from Palestine, 503, 555
Moszczenik, Reb Dovid (der Kichier), *43*, 225, *226*, 265, *266*, *370*, *423*, 556, *570*; daughters of, 553, 555, 623; death of, 247
Moszczenik, Reb Zvi Hersh (Garden Preacher), *229*, 266
Moszczenik, Sam, 555
Moszczenik, Sarah, 418, 553, *554*, *555*, *590*
Moszczenik, Yitzhak, 555
Moszczenik, Yonah, 555
Moszczenik family, *471*, 555
Motke (illiterate boy), 415
Mule the teacher, 507
Munin, Frume-Rochl Ratz, 143, 501, 518, 519, 536, *537*, 538
Munin, Yitzhak, 501, 518, 539
Munk, Solomon, 484
Murer, Franz, 579
Musar movement, 183, 187–188
Muslims, 6, 10, 20, 66, 207, 256, 624, 720n1c
mutual aid societies, 210–227, 567; Bnei Hail (sons of valor), 221–223; and caring for the sick, 213, 224; and childbirth, 213–214; and clothing the poor, 215; and dowries, 214–215; and homeless shelters (hekdesh), 217–218; and hospitality, 216–219; and landsmanshaften, 223; and moneylending, 219; and ransoming of captives, 219–220; and soup kitchens, 212, 220, *221*; and Zionism, 226

Nacha, 86, 201, 248, *249*, 256–257, *268*, 476, 586, 638, 639, 647, 648, 650
Nacha forest, 300, 614, 631, 636, 637, 638, 646, 647, 650, 685
Naftali Ben Yehuda, 489
Naftolke (shepherd), 268
Nahman, Rabbi (of Braslav), 228
Nahum der Kvoresman, 250
Naliboki forest, 634, *669*
Naphtali (divorced from Menuha), 380–381, 382
Napoleon, 8, 36, 38, 50, 192, 259, 541; and Eishyshok horse fair, 315; and Olkenik synagogue, 68, 77, 217; on Vilna, 6–7
Napoleon III, 485
Narbutt, Ludwik, *52*, *53*, 277, 625, *626*
Nardowicz, Motl, *541*
Narodowicz family, *475*, *476*
Narodowitch, Hayyim Motke, *656*
Nathan of Hanover, 31, 39, 177–178, 314
National Awakening movement, 47, 155, 170, 171, 172, 180, 183, 461, 471, 495
nationalism, 469, 482; and Zionism, 451, 483, 484, 485, 486, 487, 491, 504
Natzir, Velvke, *189*
Navaredok, 20, 97, 183, 184, 275, 304, 634; castle of, *20*
Nehemia der Feldsher. *See* Virshubski, Nehemia
Nekraszunca, 66, 132
Neshwis, 275
Nes Ziona (Banner of Israel), 183
Neue Freimann camp, 687
New Beth Midrash, 78–81, 82, 88, 107, 227, 474; cantors in, 140, 141, 142; gathering at, 584; and Haskalah, 193; maggid and, 122–123; rebuilding of, 133, 197; supporters of, 130, 167; as theater, 89, 543
New Cemetery, 33–34, 233–242, 243, 250, 436, 509; burials in, 229, 660, 668; care of, 658; and refugees, 252, 567
Nezah Israel (The Eternity of Israel), 183
Nicholas I, Tzar, 53, 219, 258, 454, 455, 456; and cantonist period, 45, 47, 185, 186, 384, 395
Nicholas II, Tzar, 139, 140, 274
Nieszawa, Statute of (1454), 262
Night at the Old Marketplace (play; Peretz), 539
Nikolaievitz, Berl, 396
Nikolaievtzky (Jewish soldiers in Russian army), 40, 47, 185–186, 218–219, 248. *See also* cantonists; Nicholas I, Tzar
Nipiczansky forest, 634, 635, 690
NKVD (Russian secret police), 660, 669–674, 679, 680, 685
Noah (Eishyshkian builder), 71
nobility: Lithuanian, 25–26, 27, 261; Polish, 255, 261, 263, 264, 284, 294; Russian, 261, 263
Nochomowicz, Malka, *261*, *506*, *534*
Nochomowicz, Sander, *148*, *176*
Nochomowicz family, *308*
Nohem the Pope, 391–393, 414–415, 731n29
Nohum, Rivke, 186
No Time to Mourn (Kahn), 321
Novakoff, Edward, *550*
Novakoff, Ida Pochter, *550*
Novakoff, Julius, *550*
Nowicki (farmer), 643
Nunes, Rachel, 418, 419
Nuremberg Laws, 402

Odessa, 172, 454, 455, 471, 487
Ogen, Yitzhak, 514

Oholiab, 71
Okla, 40, 256, 586
Okun, Mr. (Hebrew teacher), 475, 476
Okun family, 474
Olam Kattan (children's journal), 517
Olbracht, King Jan, 26
Old Beth Midrash, 70, 76, 78–81, 89, 96, 106, 114, 166, 186, 190, 222, 227, 263; business transactions in, 81–82, 204, 219; cantors in, 140, 141, 142; and charity, 215; exorcisms in, 83, 164; and Gaon of Vilna, 179; and Haskalah, 192, 193, 460; and inauguration of rabbis, 96, 107; maggid in, 121, 122–123, 124; in Nazi occupation, 577, 584; rebuilding of, 133, 197, 202; and refugees, 88; supporters of, 130, 173, 198; in World War I, 242; and Zionism, 489; Zionist rally at, 489
Old Cemetery, 25, 143, 230–233, 252, 658, 688; ancient tombstones in, 16, 18, 19, 65, 228–229, 231; and massacre of 1941, 209, 587, 588, 599, 659
Olesh (Christian lunatic), 392
Olkenik, 30, 113, 159, 256, 345, 384, 385, 396; Ark of, 73, 74, 75, 76, 77, 217; fugitives from, 631, 634, 646; Hebrew teaching in, 516; Hevrah Kaddishah feast in, 245; klezmer orchestra of, 539; market day in, 315; and massacre of 1941, 4, 57, 117, 402, 584, 586, 587, 595; meshuggoim from, 386; Napoleon's visit to, 8, 49, 68, 259; Simhat Torah in, 424; students from, 188; synagogue in, 67, 68, 68, 69, 71, 74, 75, 77
O'Neill, Thomas P. (Tip), 4
Operation Barbarossa, 575, 582
ORT. *See* Society for the Development of Jewish Agriculture and Trade
Oshochowski, Gitta, 502
Ostland, Reich protectorate of, 576
Ostrauskas (Lithuanian chief of police), 117, 579, 580, 581, 582, 587, 592, 593, 670
Ostrovsky, 537
Otian, 201
Oz, Amos. *See* Klausner, Amos

Pachianko, Aharon Don (Aharon Don Becker), 42, 546–547, 555, 690
Pachianko, Avigdor (the martyr), 262–263, 400, 547, 717n15, 731n54
Pachianko, Hayyim, 546
Pachianko, Itta-Malka, 546
Pachianko, Sarah, 546
Pachianko family, 42
Paikowski, Avraham Berl, 522
Paikowski, Bezalel, 650
Paikowski, Hayyim Leibke, 221, 509, 688
Paikowski, Nehama, 592
Paikowski, Reuven, 389–390, 474, 477, 670, 676, 745n13b; in Kabacznik kibbutz, 658, 664; marriage of, 682, 683; as partisan, 641, 642, 650, 660, 668; repatriation of, 679, 686, 694; return to Eishyshok, 689
Paikowski, Shmuel-Leib, 641, 642, 650, 660
Paikowski, Yossef, 500
Paikowski, Zlatke Garber, 581, 591; in Ghetto Radun, 598, 601; in Leninski battalion, 645, 646; and liberation, 671, 672; marriage of, 682, 683; and massacre of 1941, 586, 590; repatriation of, 686, 687
Paikowski family, 51, 52, 53, 256–257, 471, 533, 625, 637, 638
Palangian, 99
Pale of Settlement, 18, 27, 36–38, 37, 68, 548; abolition of, 107; coachmen in, 300; and Eishyshok, 244, 487; emigration from, 122, 491, 545–547; and Jewish businessmen, 182n; and military conscription, 45, 46, 47, 185; schools in, 151; Zionism in, 120
Palestine, 9, 10, 30, 48, 56, 58, 159, 478; agriculture in, 268–269; Gedud ha-Avodah in, 498, 510, 511; and holidays, 425, 426, 432; Jews of Simonia in, 135; Mikveh Israel in, 485; 1947 partitioning of, 686; settlements in, 486, 487, 495; Yaffo, 485. *See also* emigration; Eretz Israel
Paley, Aaron, 48
Paltiel, Alte, 333, 343, 518
Paltiel, Hayyim, 247, 333, 343
Panashishok, 256
Papernia, 465
Paradin, 256, 264, 279, 585, 625
Paretski, Dovid, 282, 283
partisans, 56, 630–650, 745n7; family camps of (semeinie lagrie), 630, 634–641, 671, 672; Green, 670, 673; and liberation, 673, 678, 684; military camps of, 630, 636–640, 641–654; revenge of, 669–673. *See also* Armia Krajowa
partisans, Russian, 628, 630, 634, 635, 669, 692; and Armia Krajowa, 613, 626, 627; Leninski battalion of, 637, 638, 642, 643, 644, 645, 646, 647, 649
Patria (ship), 570
Pavlovna, Yekatrina, 128
Paulus, General Friedrich von, 652
Peer, Pastor Arthur, 395
Peres, Shimon, 600
Peretz, Avraham, 195
Peretz, Y. L., 193, 197, 198, 523, 539; on Jacob Gordin, 537; library named for, 524, 525, 526
Perkunas (pagan god), 23, 25, 66

Perl, Joseph, 454
Perlman, Reb Yeruham Yehudah Leib, 103
Perski, Yitzhak, 600
Pesachowitz, Hayyim (Red Maggid of Minsk), 120
Peter the Great, 34, 45
Petrov, General, *669*
Piczicz (convert to Judaism), 401–402
Piczicz (husband of Hayya from Kalesnik), 621
Piczicz, Hayya, 401–402
Pidyon ha-Ben (Redemption of the First Born), 350
Pierleone family, 394
Pikarski, Yaakov, 489, 490
Pilsudski, Marshal Jozef, 58, 274, 307, 561, *562*, 565, 621, 633, 641
Pilushki, Shlomo, *148*
pinkas (shtetl record book), 44, 70, 94, 101, 106, 228, 700n32; Golden, 286–287; Hebrew, 244, 513
Pinon, Sarah, 536, 537, 538
Pinsk, 29, 275
Pinsker, Leo, 48, 486, 487
Pinski, David, 538
Pircupi, 641
Plaszow, 3
Plock, 683
Plock, Reb Alter, 248
Plotnik, Breine, *570*, 572, *573*
Plotnik, Eliyahu, 222–223, 559, 560, 570, 572, 699n12
Plotnik, Mikhele, *570*, 572, *573*, 574
Plotnik, Sarah, 222, 223, 560, 569–570, 571, *573*, 574
Plotnik, Zipporah, *570*, 699n12
Pobedonostsev, Konstantin, 395
Pochter, Leibke, *474*
Pochter, Rachel, 669, 676, 677
Pochter, Yoske, 669
Poe, Edgar Allan, 498
pogroms, 482, 485; in Czestochowa (1937), 562; in Grodno (1935), 562; in Kielce (1946), 679; in Kishinev (1903), 107, 125, 491; in 1930s, 56, 562; Polish (1944), 252, 664–669; post–World War I, 497; under Russian rule, 45; Southern Tempest, 38, 54, 545; in Ukraine, 497
Polack (Polaczek) family, 401
Polaczek, Hanan, *530*
Polaczek, Mariyasl, *239*
Polaczek, Meir Yaakov, *239*
Polaczek, Mrs. Meir Yaakov, *239*
Polaczek, Shlomo, 473, 577, 579
Polaczek, Yitzhak, 566
Polak, Golde Roche, 264
Polak, Meir Yankel, 264
Polak, Moshe, 264
Poland, 3, 6, 10; anti-Semitic policies of, 284; during Cold War, 7; constitution of May 3, 1791, 36; conversion to Christianity, 24; fairs in, 313, 314; fall of, in World War II, 57; German invasion of (1939), 20, 327, 565, 678; Great, 35; independence of, 107, 468; Jewish schools in, 176, 456; Jews of, 18; Little, 177; nobility (szlachta) of, 255, 261, 263, 264, 284, 294; partitioning of, 34–36; Republic of, 244, 613, 620; Sejm (parliament) of, 33, 34, 35, 39; union with Lithuania, 24
Poland-Lithuania, 26–27, 33, 36, 38, 177, 263. *See also* Lublin Union
Polish army: Jewish soldiers in, 57, 86, 222, 277, 565, 621, 622, 647, *648*, 650, 651, 678, 692, 747n26; People's, 679, 747n26
Polish Kingdom, 16
Polish Republic, 270, 272–274; Second, 259, 274, 277, 282, 284
Polish uprisings: of 1794, 35; of 1831, 38, 50, 612; of 1863, 38, 51, 52, 277, 443, 456, 625, *626*; of 1944, 613. *See also* Kosciuszko, Tadeusz
Politacki, Avraham Ele, 287
Politacki, Eli, 470, *524*, *560*
Politacki, Meir Shimon, 505, *506*, 541–542
Politacki, Menahem, *541*
Politacki, Shlomo, 294
Politacki, Temke, 390
Pollak, Rabbi Jacob, 177
Polonia (ship), 520
Polukne, 301
Ponar, *641*, 678
Poniatowski, Stanislaw, 34
Ponivezh, 515
Popiski, 301
Popl, Avraham Dov, 129
Portnoy, David. *See* Levin, David
Portnoy, Itzhar, 418, *419*
Portnoy, Leibke, *475*
Portnoy, Michael, *419*
Portnoy, Vela Dubczanski, 418–419, 563, 652
Portnoy family, *507*
Portnoy's Complaint (Roth), 336
Posen, 484
Poshitva, 562, 563
Potocki, Count Valentine (Ger Zeddek), 237, 262–263, 400–401, 717n15, 731nn52, 53, 54
Powszechna (Polish public school), 470, 479, 480
Prague, 686, 687
prayerhouses. *See* batei midrashi
proselytes (gerei zeddek), 400–402
The Provocateur (play; Bergman), 540

Provoslavic Church, 126
Prussia, 34, 35, 36, 68, 95, 256, 315
Prystor, Janina, 87, 561–562, 563
Puzeritsky, Arkey, 280

rabbinate, 90–118; American Orthodox, 118; commercialization of, 92–93; of Eishyshok, 97–118; Russian, 456
Rabinowitch, Arke, 388–390, 393, 394, 414–415
Rabinowitch, Rabbi Avraham Shmuel (Amud Esh), 79, 80, 97–99, 102, 181, 187, 192, 223, 428
Rabinowitz, Akiva, 520n
Rabinowitz, Dvorah, *694*
Rabinowitz, Yehuda Leib (Leon), 193
Rachowsky, Yankl (der Cymbler), 167
Radowsky, Bertha, *551*
Radowsky, Gershon, *551*
Radowsky, Joshua, *551*
Radowsky, Michel, *551*
Radowsky, Reuben, *551*
Radowsky, Rose, *551*
Radun, 83, 125, 256, 315, 507, 542, 638, 668; Communists in, 566, 571, 573; and Eishyshok, 51, 115; escapees in, 584, 585, 588, 590, 591, 592–609, 659; police of, 614, 624, 660, 670; synagogue of, 72; Yavne Hebrew school, 636; yeshivah of, 89, 93, 115, 127, 138, 183, 188, *189*, 198, *199*, 201, 225, *238*, 466, 662. *See also* Haffetz Hayyim
Radun Ghetto, 339, 402, *576*, 595–609, 626, 627; escape from, 610, 611, 612, 615, 618, 619, 630, 634, 637, 639, 644, 645; 1942 massacre in, 602–607, 624, 631, 636, 661, 668, 681, 691; rebellion in, 602, *688*
Radunski, Beileh-Rivkeh, *291*
Radunski, Nahum, *501*
Radunski family, *261*, 423, 501
Ragachefski, Meir, 308
RaHaSh (rabbi, hazzan, and shammash) tax, 93, 135, 139, 704n11
railroads, 300, 315, 365
Rak Ivrit (Hebrew-language society), 465, 504, 515–517, *518*, 519, 520, 521
Rashi, 95, 156, 158, 159, 168, 207, 245, 460
Rasvet (Russian-language newspaper), 482
Ratner, Luba, 385, 393
Ratner (Communist), 670
Ratz, Frume-Rochl. *See* Munin, Frume-Rochl Ratz
Ratz, Mere, 143
Rav (Abba ben Aivu; Abba Arikha), 151, 166
"The Raven" (Poe): Hebrew translation of, 498
Reali Hebrew gymnasium (Kovno), 342
Reb Layzer the Wise, 53
refugees, 87–88, 115, 219, 464, 527, 567–568
Reina Batia (first wife of the Neziv), 336
Reines, Rabbi Yitzhak Yaakov, 84, 107, 191, 198, 494, 495
Reinhardt, Max, 539
Religion, Dr., 443, 444, 499
Remz, Eliezer, 391, 564
Remz, Katke, 391
Remz, Layzer, 421, 479
Remz, Leibele, 479
Remz, Reb Dova, *470*
Remz, Reb Yehuda Leib, 392
Remz, Rivka, 9, 121, 392, *536*
Rentein, Dr. A. V., 629
Renteln, Theodore von, *582*
Rephael (der Meller), *43*
Replianski, Mordekhai, 287
Replianski, Mordekhai (Motl), 473, *524*, 526, *533*, 540, 584, 593
Replianski, Shaul, *260*
Resnik, Esther (Etele) Katz, *275*, *307*, *371*, *426*, 466, *471*, *500*, *505*, *534*, 572, 574; and Hebrew, 465, *518*; marriage of, 542; and Zionism, 504, 506, *530*
Resnik, Yaakov, 198
Resnik, Yossef, *307*, 501, 542
Resnik family, *64*
Retzkin, Dvora, *669*
Reuven the Postman, 285
Revisionist Party, 506
Revkum (revolutionary council), 565–566
Ribak, David, 677
Riga, 455, 505
Rivkes, Rabbi Moshe, 32
Rochel-Leye (tokerin; bath attendant), 205
Rochowski, Gittl, *536*
Rochowski, Velvl, *501*
Rochowski, Yossl, *43*
Rodanski, Sarah, 542
Rogachewski, Shaul, *176*
Rogowski, Hayya, 612, 671, 672, 681, *688*
Rogowski, Leibke, 597, 612
Rogowski, Moshe, 612, 614, 644
Rogowski, Niomke, 612, 636, 637, 638, 642, 644–646, 649, 670, 671, 674
Rogowski family, 590, 591, 596–597
Rome and Jerusalem (Hess), 485
Rommel, General, 652
Roosevelt, Franklin D., *281*, 575, 577, 578, 652, 653
Roseini, 98
Rosenblatt, Rosalind Foster, 13
Rosenblatt, Yossele, 140

Rosenblum family, *471*
Rosenblum, Aaron Velvke, *656*
Rosenblum, Meir, *656*
Rosenheim, Rachel, 194
Rosenheim family, 197
Rosensweig, Moriah, *213*, *667*, *689*
Rosensweig, Moshe-Ariel, *667*, *689*
Rosensweig, Smadar-Zipporah Eliach, *667*, *696*
Roth, Philip, 336
Rothberg, Rabbi Tuvia, 201, *370*, 533
Rothschild, Baron Edmond, 491, 492
Rothschild, James, 484
Rothschild, Salomon, 484
Rothschild family, 197, 547
Rozowski, Avraham, 111, 113, 114, 117
Rozowski, Bat-Sheva, 111, 113, 114
Rozowski, Fania, 114, 565
Rozowski, Miriam, 111, 113, 114, 115, 116, 117, *373*, 693
Rozowski, Rabbi Szymen, 43, 107–108, 110–118, 137, 142, *189*, 353, 373, *374*, 375, 381, 573; on armed resistance, 117, 581, 582; on charity, 287; and Communists, 572, 577; and daughter's wedding, 375; and emigrants, 505; eviction of, 387; and funds from America, 247; and Gemilut Hessed, 693; and German invasion, 565, 581; and Hebrew, 520; and herem, 87; and illegitimate births, 382, 383; and Judenrat, 577, 580; and massacre of September 1941, *91*, *141*, 584, 586, 587, 593, 596, 597; and meshuggoim, 385; on Polish friends, 581, 611, 615; and prayerhouses, 80; and refugees, 226–227, 567; and schools, 201, 473, 475, 476, 564; and summer camps, 533–534
Rozowski, Uri, 111, 113, 114, 115, *442*, 502, 565, 693
Rubin, Ruth Matikanski, *271*
Rubinstein, Elka, 511
Rubinstein, Hayya Schneider, 510
Rubinstein, Mordekhai (Motke), 8, 497, 498, 499, *505*, 510, 511, 541
Rubinstein, Rabbi (of Vilna), 519
Rubinstein, Reb Tuviah, *195*; children of, 497, 511; as teacher, 8–9, 150, 174, 201, 464, 465
Rubinstein, Rivka, 8, 471, 498, 499, 510, 511, 682
Rubinstein, Sarah, 8, 462, 464, 465, 504, *510*, 511, *518*, 519, 617
Rubinstein family, 518, 519, 538
Rubishok, 40, 266, 584, 586
Rudna, 280
Rudnicki forest, 300, 631, 639, 641, 646, 647, 685
Rudsin, Sam, 653
Rudzin, Libe-Gittel, *42*, *546*, 589, 608–609
Rufke the bootmaker, 508
Rupin, Arthur, 269
Rushkin, Avraham, *311*, *371*
Rushkin, Elisha, *261*, *311*
Rushkin, Miriam Koppelman, *261*, *310*, *311*, *371*, *500*, *534*
Rushkin, Sarale, *311*
Russia, 6, 16, 22, 23, 55; annexation of land by, 256, 257, 259; anti-Semitic policies of, 36, 284, 482, 485; attitude to Jews, 45–49, 395; civil war in, 54, 107, 111, 125; Eishyshok under, 36, 38, 105–106, 257; invasions of Poland, 35, 565; Jewish education in, 172, 454–458; and logging trade, 276; and Poland-Lithuania, 32–34; revolution of 1905 in, 107, 198, 517; revolution of 1917 in, 36, 54, 107, 111, 125, 127, 250, 487; taxes imposed by, 280–281; White, 125, 184. *See also* Byelorussia
Russian army: and Armia Krajowa, 672, 673; deserters from, 620; drafting by, 332; Jewish soldiers in, 652, 655, 659, 692; and liberation, 658, 663, 667, 670, 674, 680. *See also* Nikolaievtzky
Russian language, 172, 454, 455, 459, 492, 511
Russo-Japanese War, 48, *223*

Sabbath Queen, 84, 136, 407, 410, 413, 414, 416
St. Petersburg, 34, 35, 182, 184, 457, 465
Salanter, Rabbi Israel Lipkin, 183, 187, 195
Salkes, 650
Saltz, Feigele (Fanichke), *341*, *530*
Saltz, Velvke, 214, *341*, *530*
Saltz family, *689*
Samogitian tribe, 16, 23
Samuel, Sir Herbert L., *494*
Sander der Rechisnik, 386, 415
San Remo Conference, 107
Sapocrynski, F., *442*
Saposnikow, Jasza, *447*
Saposnikow, Margolia, *273*
Saposnikow, Sonia, *440*, *441*, 444, *447*, *532*
Schaffer, Sam, 654
Schanzer, Rivka Lewinson, 212–213
Schindler, Oscar, 610–611
Schkopp, Shimon, 533
Schmidt, Hayya-Roche, *237*
Schneider, Malke Roche's, 159, 200, 271–272, 316, 437, 461, 472, 518; drugstore of, 272, 274, 320, 337, 380, 444–445
Schneider, Shaul, 159, 269, 465, 471, 504, 538; in Paris, 466, *468*; as teacher, *474*, *476*; and Zionism, 496, 500, 503
Schneider, Velvel, 159, 274, 374, 461
Schneider, Yaakov, 159, 374, 461, 465, 466, 471, *496*
Schneider, Yehudah, *428*

Schneider, Zipporah, 374
Schneider family, *64*, *220*, *496*; emigration of, 9, 444, 504, 505, 538
school networks: Horev, 469; Tarbut, 466, 469, 470, 472, 475, 476, 478, 479, 740nn23,28; Yavneh, 469, 475, 476, 479; Yiddish-language, 468–469, 470
schools, 151, 176, 456, 466; elementary, 468–470; Hebrew, 472–481; Polish, 470, 479, 480; secular, 459; Talmud-Torah, 96, 162. *See also* education; heder; yeshivah; *individual schools*
Schorr, Avraham Hayyim, 155
Schwartz, Dodke, *43*
Schwartz, Rivka, *571*
Schwartz, Zvi Hirshke, *506*, *507*
Sczervak, Shlomo, 258
seamstresses, 290–294
Second Polish Republic, 17, 34, 36, 53, 57
secularism, 111–114, 190, 198, 199, 249–252, 287, 310, 320, 354–355, 411
Seeking Zion (*Drishat Zion*; Kalischer), 485
Sefarim, Mendele Mokher (Shalom Jacob Abramovich), 203, 523, 525, *526*
Segal, Rabbi Moshe ben Aaron Halevi Horowitz, 97, 184–185, 704n19
Segal, Shaike, *471*
Sejm (Polish parliament), 33, 34, 35, 39; Four-Year (1788–92), 35
Seklutski (Polish magnate), 571
Seklutski forest, 84, 112, 142, 162, 231, 499, 537, 587, *625*
Selo (Dekeshene), 256, 384–385, 389, 393, 584, 586, 595
Seltskin, Yaakov, 489
Senitski, Luba, *471*
Senitski, Shmuel, 173, 391, 494–495, 523
Senitski family, 18, 53, 255, 459, 523
Sephardic Jews, 65, 102, 144, 157, 178, 189, 435, 513, *694*
Serfia, Duke, 102
Sforza, Bona (Queen of Poland), 92
Shaalu Shlom Yerushalaim (Seek the Peace of Jerusalem), 485, 489
Shabaiov, Captain, 670, 675
Shainberg, A., *474*
Shakhna, Shalom ben Yossef, 131, 177
Shalit, Moshe, 286
Shalom, Ima, 168
shammash (beadle, or sexton), 129, 134–138, 164, 216, 219, 246
Shanski, Menuha Salacki, *536*
Shanzer, David, *372*
Shanzer, Rivka Lewinson, 212–213, *372*
Shapira, Eliakim Shlomo, 459, 700n32
Shapira, Hayyim Dovid, 264, 429
Sharavei (pharmacist), 444, 624, 663
Sharavei, Anton, 666
Shavelis (shepherd), 268
Shawitski, Hannah, *428*
Shazar, Zalman, 125, 128
shehita (kosher animal slaughter), 86–87, 562, 662
Sheine-Reizl (melamed's wife), 414
Shekowitski, Aaron, *125*
Shekowitski, Miriam, *537*
Shekowitski, Mordekhai Yossef, 125
Shekowitski, Rabbi Benyamin Ha-Cohen, 124–*125*, 126–128
Shekowitski, Rachel, 127, 128
Shemitkowsky, Dr., 146, 624
Shemitkowsky, Mrs., 146
Shepkowski (farmer), 648
Shereshefski (Shefski), Asher (Oscar), *353*, *531*, 692
Shereshefski (Shefski), Israel, *260*, *531*, *676*, 692
Shereshefski (Shefski), Matle (Molly) Sonenson, *88*, *260*, *309*, *353*, *499*, *500*, *531*, *572*, *675*, *676*, 692
Shereshefski, Yossef (Joe), 692
Shereshefski family, *689*, 692
Sheshko, Yankele, *345*
Shewitski, Meir (der Lerer), *172*, *174*, *381*, *462*
Shiemaszka family, 612, 614, 644, 660
Shiffel, Esther Kiuchefski, 52, 464, 625
Shiffel, Mirale, 606, 625
Shiffel, Yefim, 52, 625
Shifra the midwife, 442, 487–488, 504
Shilat, Samuel ben, 166
Shimonowitch, Shalom, *199*
Shimonwitch, Layzer (Leo Simons), *268*
Shimonwitch, Tuviah (Ted Simons), *268*
Shimshelewitch, Naftali, 459
Shimshelewitch family, 18, 255
Shimshon, Rabbi (Noble of Coucy), 513
Shira (Agnon), 8, *510*, *511*
Shiyeh der Roiphe, 440
Shlanski, Avraham-Mordekhai, *43*, 551–552
Shlanski, Benjamin, 652
Shlanski, Fishke, 564–565
Shlanski, Fraddie, *530*
Shlanski, Hayya, *429*, *474*, *475*, *476*
Shlanski, Isaac, *43*
Shlanski, Louis, *43*, 551–552, 569
Shlanski, Morris, 9, *43*, 225, 550–551, 554, 569
Shlanski, Rose Salacki, 569, 652
Shlanski, Shmuel, *148*
Shlanski, Zelig, *43*, 551, 564, 569, 652
Shlanski, Zisle, 415, 550
Shlanski family, 77, 569, *689*

Shlomo the Amalekite, 293, 382–383, 587
Shlomo the baker, 626
Shlomo the engraver, 379, 549
Shlomo of Rasein, 76
Shlomo the tailor, 473
Shlomo the Vegetable Man, 186
Shlosberg, Liba Ahuva, 604, 605, 607, 631, 632, 633, 661, 662
Shmaye-Mendl, 605, 631, 632–633, 661
Shmerkowitch, Israel, *474*, *645*, 646, 658, 668, 679, 692
Shmerkowitch, Yekutiel, 646, 658, 679, 692
Shmidt, Nehamah Kremin, *237*
Shmuel Malke's, Reb, 420
Shneur's, Motke, 509
shoemakers, 294–296
shohet (ritual butcher), 66, 140, 141, 143–146, *145*, 407, 420
shopkeepers, 270–274
Shtepper, Avraham Shmuel der, 531
shtetl (small town), 44, 229–230, 266–268, 298–299, 331–347; definition of term, 6, 27
shtibl (small prayerhouse), 64, 72, 88
Shulhan Arukh (Caro), 102, 189
Shulman, Gloria, 692
Shulman, Kalman, 193
Shulman, Miriam Kabacznik, *272*, *311*, 582, 600–601, *625*, 663, 664, *665*, 676, 683; in hiding, 617, 626; marriage to Nahum Shulman, 682; repatriation to America, 692
Shulman, Nahum, 682, 692
Shuster, Basha, 270, 271
Shuster, David, 270, 509
Shuster, Hayyim, 115, 270, 387, 565, *566*, 571, 634–635, 746n6a
Shuster, Hodl, 270, 271, 273, 635–636, 684, 691
Shuster, Joseph (Rivka Shuster's baby), 635–636, *690*, 691
Shuster, Rivka, 635, *690*, 691
Shuster, Yossef, 270, 271
Shuster family, *560*, 635, *689*
Siberia, 53, 198, 571, 572, 598, 626, 673, 674, 692; escapees from, 681, 744n1b; Moshe Sonenson's deportation to, 10, 539, 680–681, *688*, 689, 744n1b
Siegal family, *689*
Sigismund I (King of Poland), 92
Sigismund II Augustus (King of Lithuania), 26, 27, 34, 92, 703n4
Simonis (Shimantzi), 111
Simons, Leo. *See* Shimonowitch, Layzer
Simons, Ted. *See* Shimonowitch, Tuviah
Singer, Isaac Bashevis, 15, 95
Sinkewicz, Yashka, 588, 590, 591
Sira, Ben, 212
Sirk, Lilly der Feldsher, *341*
Sirota, Gershon, 139, 140
Skolski, Lippa, 597, 670, 671, 681
Slepak, Benyamin, 307
Slepak, Berl, 84, 540
Slepak, Dov, 505
Slepak, Fruml, 292, 311, 567, *656*, 681, 682
Slepak, Hirshke, 292, 681
Slepak, Matke, *507*
Slepak, Mirshke, 567
Slepak, Zipporah, *656*
Slepak family, *428*, *471*
Slobodka yeshivah, 109, 110, 127, 167, 183, 194, 467
Slodovnik, Leah, *687*
Slonim, 101, 275
Slonimski, Antoni, 396
Slonimski, Eli, 651, 652
Slonimski, Goldke di Meshumeideste, 398, 399, 402
Slonimski, Hayyim Zelig, 396, 456, 460
Slonimski, Moshe, 308, *309*
Slonimski, Rochel, *291*
Slonimski, Yekutil, 398
Slowo (newspaper), 562
Slutsk, 29
Smargon, 197, 198, 650
Smersh (Russian captain), 664
Smetona, Antanas, 567
Smigly-Rydz, Edward, 565
Smolenskin, Peretz, 482, 522
Smolianski, Yehuda Leib, 473
socialism, 111, 122, 193–194, 197, 198, 389, 451, 460; in Eretz Israel, 510; and marriage, 355; and Yiddish, 522, 525. *See also* Bund
Society for the Development of Jewish Agriculture and Trade (ORT), 457, 466, 470
Society of Friends of the Enlightenment, 455
Sokolov, 149
Solcianski, Hayyim Zvi, *199*
Solome, Itta Solomianski, 618, 619, 621, 623, 682, *684*, 692
Solome, Yankl, *684*
Solomianski, Goldke, 618
Solomianski, Hayya, 618, 628, *684*
Solomianski, Itta. *See* Solome, Itta Solomianski
Solomianski, Meir, 618
Solomianski, Shepske, 618
Solomianski, Shmuel, 618, *684*
Solomianski, Sonia Kowarski, 618, 677

Solomianski, Yankl, 618, *619*, 682, 692
Solomianski, Yehuda Leib, 541
Solomianski family, 618, *684*
Soloveitchik, Dr., 446–447
Soloveitchik, Max, 466
Soloveitchik, Rabbi Joseph B., 405
Soloveitchik family, 708n15
Soloviev, Lieutenant, 670, 675
Sonenson, Alex Braverman, 689
Sonenson, Alter, 241
Sonenson, Avraham, 167, *239*, *260*, *275*, 353, 525, 623, 664
Sonenson, baby Hayyim (Jan), 656, 659, 662, 664, 665; birth of, 628; grave of, 229, 668–669; murder of, 666, 673, 679, 680, 689, 747n14
Sonenson, baby Shaul, 580–581, 583, 585, 589, 590, 596; burial of, 607; death of, 605, 659, 661
Sonenson, Benyamin (Niomke), *260*, *309*, 353, 354, *534*
Sonenson, Bilinka. *See* Ben-Shemesh Bilinka Guterman
Sonenson, Geneshe Kaganowicz, 88, *260*, 348, 499, 500, 564, 568, 572, 576, 578, 593, 665
Sonenson, Gittele, 339, *428*; burial of, 660; death of, 627, 669; in Ghetto Radun, 602, 604, 609; in hiding, 615, 619, 621, 623, 626
Sonenson, Hannah, 241, 242
Sonenson, Hayya Kabacznik, 4, *42*, 201, *211*, *240*, *332*, 353, 628, 664; and agriculture, 266–267, 281, 609; and ancestors' land, 259, *260*, 346; children of, 339, 344; on children's toys, 531; and Ezrat Yoledet society, 213–214; and German invasion, 327; and Hebrew books, 525; Long House of, 658, 665; and massacre of 1941, 214, 578, 581, 593; on Sabbath, 410, 411, 415; and sons' marriages, 361, 372–373
Sonenson, Hayya (wife of Naftali Eliezer), 332, 364
Sonenson, Hayyim (from Lubtch), 368, 464
Sonenson, Hayyim (named for murdered baby), 689
Sonenson, Hinda. *See* Tawlitski, Hinda Sonenson
Sonenson, Ida, *260*, 353, 593, 665
Sonenson, Israel, 167, *239*, *260*, 275, 465
Sonenson, Leibke (Aryeh), *88*, 214, *239*, *260*, *309*, 501, 564, 568, 576; and Communists, 572; and Judenrat, 577, 578; return from Palestine, 502, 530
Sonenson, Mania Braverman, 689
Sonenson, Matle. *See* Shereshefski, Matle Sonenson
Sonenson, Meir (son of Leibke), *353*, 593, 665
Sonenson, Miriam Ribak Ben-Shemesh, *260*, 339, *560*; in Ghetto Radun, 599, 602, 603, 604, 661–662, 679, 680; in hiding, 637; and liberation, 664, 665, 666, 671, 677; and repatriation, 686, *687*
Sonenson, Moshe, 4, 142, 167, 191, 201, 202, *307*, *370*, 445, 563, 564, 569, 745nn12b,13b; and Armia Krajowa, 663–666, 668, 670–674, 680; arrest of, 596; in business, 275, 281, 283, 284; and "case of the black suitcase," 383; and Communists, 572, 573; deportation to Siberia, 10, 539, 680–681, *688*, 689, 744n1b; and family, *239*, *260*, *261*, *346*; and gentiles, 321; and German invasion, 327; in Ghetto Radun, 597, 599, 600, 602–609; and grandchildren, *695*, *696*; and Hebrew, *518*, 519, 524; in hiding, 610, 615, 617, 619, 621–624, 626–628; in Israel, 269, 689–690; and Judenrat, 577, 578, 580; and last Passover, 574; and liberation, 655, 658–660, 662, 674–677, 679; marriage of, 361–362; and massacre of 1941, 581–585, 589, 590, 593, 595, 656; and meshuggoim, 389, 394; release from Siberia, 689; repatriation of, 689, 697; return to Vilna, *688*, 689; on Sabbath, 415; at summer home, *532*; on trial in Vilna, 680; in Vilna, 465; wedding of, 372–373; and Yiddish, 539
Sonenson, Moshe (brother of Shael), 400
Sonenson, Naftali Eliezer, 364–365
Sonenson, Rabbi Pinhas, 552
Sonenson, Reb Shael, 14, *41*, 42, 107, 167, 198, *211*, *239*, 241, 242, *260*, 281, *346*, 347, 399, 447, 552, 660; and "case of the black suitcase," 383; children of, 339, 344; on holidays, 410, 425; mother of, *332*; and slaughterhouse, 130; at son's wedding, 372, 373; tombstone of, 669
Sonenson, Ruhama, 241
Sonenson, Shalom Ben-Shemesh, *239*, 243, *260*, 324, 344, 351, *372*, 501, 568, 658; and Armia Krajowa, 664, 665, 666; in Ghetto Radun, 339, 598, 599, 602, 603, 609; and Hebrew, *518*, 519; and heder, 8, 165, 167; in hiding, 615, 617, 619, 622, 623, 627; and Judenrat, 580; and liberation, 660, 661, 671, 676, 677, 679, 680; marriage of, 361; and repatriation, 686, 687, 693; return from Palestine, 502, 527; yellow star of, *576*; and Zionism, 500
Sonenson, Shepske (Shabtai), *239*, 260, 261, 310, 385, *505*, *506*, *534*, *541*, 564, 568, 572, 584, *625*, 676
Sonenson, Shmuel, 353
Sonenson, Shmuel (Mulke), *260*, *534*, *665*
Sonenson, Shoshana Bergazin, 689
Sonenson, Shulamit (Shula), *260*, 339, *560*, 602, 619, 680
Sonenson, Yaffa-Sheinele. *See* Eliach, Yaffa Sonenson
Sonenson, Yitzhak (Yitzhak-Uri), 191, *307*, *309*, 324, 347, *353*, *428*, 520, *578*, 583, 584, 595, 596; and Armia Krajowa, 666, 668, 672; and family, *260*, *261*, *346*; in Ghetto Radun, 600, 605, 609; in hiding, 615, 622;

and liberation, 657, 664, 665, 671, 676, 679, 680, 681; and repatriation, 10–11, 687–689, 690; return to Eishyshok, *689*; and War of Independence, *693*
Sonenson, Yitzhak (der Minsker Illui), 241–242, 364–365
Sonenson, Zipporah Katz, 142, 201, *275*, *307*, 347, 354, *370*, *535*, *560*, 574; burial of, 668–669; in childbirth, 580–581, 627–628; and Club 21, *499*, *500*; and family, *260*, *261*, *309*, *346*; and gentiles, 321; in Ghetto Radun, 596, 605, 607, 609; grave of, 229, 252; and Hebrew, 519; in hiding, 615, 617, 619, 622, 623, 627, 628; and liberation, 655, 656, 659, 662, 664, 665; and library, 527; in Lida, 466; marriage of, 361–362, 372–373; and massacre of 1941, 583, 584, 585, 589, 590; and mother, *340*; murder of, *665*, 666, 668, 669, 673, 679, 680, 747n14; on Sabbath, 415; and Zionism, 191, *504*, 506
Sonenson family, *64*, *220*, *260*, 459, 538, 573, 589, 657; and Armia Krajowa, 663–667; in hiding, 617, 621, 626, 628; and liberation, 675, *684*
Sonia from Vilna, *578*
Soreh-Gittl, 318
Soreh-Malke, 414
Soreh-Reizl, 133–134, 377–378
Sorke Leah's, 390
Sosnowiec, 682
Soviet Union, 7, 12, 107, 284, 387, 510, 511, 575, 630, 681; Eishyshok under, 115–116, 123, 174, 226, 251, 270, 274, 326–327, 387, 520, 527, 540, 565, 571–574. *See also* Russia
Spektor, Rabbi Yitzhak Elhanan, 99, 181, 182, 245, 304, 379, 423, 486, 491
Speransky, Count, 455
Spinoza, Baruch, 87
Stadicki, Wladyslaw, 562
Stahlecker, Franz Walter, 581–582
Stalevich, Rabbi Meir, 15
Stalewitch, General, 257, 612
Stalewitch, Jossef, 280
Stalin, Josef, 327, 576, 577, 578; death of, 681, *688*, 689; policies under, 673–677, 747n26; purges of 1920s, 127n
Stanislawski, Michael, 396
Staniwicz (former minister of education), 639
Stankewicz (Polish agricultural minister), 599–600
Stankewitch, Lieutenant Anton B., 637, 638, 642, 644–649, 669
Statute of 1804, 257–258
Stoler, Meir, 602, 681, *688*
Strauss family, 197
Streisand, Barbra, 95
Streletski, Hayya, *362*, 500, 501, 524
Streletski, Hayyim, 507
Streletski, Reb Itche (Yitzhak), 42
Streletski family, 700n12
Streltzer, Eliyahu, 489–490
Streltzer, Hayya Leah, 490
Struck, Herman, 536
Suchowitski, Anshel, 444
Suchowitski, Astramski, 441, 523
Suchowitski, Benyamin, 441
Suchowitski, Reb Asher Amshel, 441
Sventsyan (Swieciany), 191
Swenczian, 282
synagogue (shul): Conservative, 69; of Eishyshok, *64*, 65–78, 227, 232, 252; Elijah chair in, 72; four-pillared style, 67–68; interior of, 71–73; in Jerusalem, 65; and Jewish community, 63–64; maggid in, 123; Old Kloiz, 68; origins of, 64–65; Orthodox, 69, 70; rebuilt, 197; Reform, 69; restrictions on style of, 65–66; in 1940s, 88; significance of bimah in, 69–70, 85; social protest in, 84; social significance of, 63; student, 114; women's gallery in, 71, 73, 81, 82, 85, 88, 105, 121, 142–143, 169, 217
Syria: synagogues in, 64
Szczesnolewicz the hangman, 581, 590
Szczuczin, 607, 608
Szczuczynski, Hanna, *507*
Szczuczynski, Hayyim-Yoshke, *305*, 567
Szczuczynski, Israel, *19*, *214*, *470*, *560*, 603, 604, 639
Szczuczynski, Layzer, *19*
Szczuczynski, Rochke, 639
Szczuczynski, Shoshana (sister of Israel Szczuczynski), 604, 639
Szczuczynski, Shoshana (wife of Israel Szczuczynski), 603, 604, 639
Szrejder, Ben Zion, 115, 323, 526
Szulkin, Avraham (Robert), *295*, 656
Szulkin, Betty, *656*
Szulkin, Dina Malka, 717n15, 731n54
Szulkin, Elka. *See* Jankelewicz, Elka Szulkin
Szulkin, Feigl, *295*, *656*
Szulkin, Matle, *295*
Szulkin, Moshe, 14, 112, *295*, 509, 521, 567, *656*, 693
Szulkin, Nahum, 229, 235, *236*, 241, 248, 681
Szulkin, Rochel, 291, *292*, 468, 509
Szulkin family, 538

Tabirg, 484
Tafshunski, Fania, 444
Tafshunski, Leib, 444

tailors, 290–294
Talmud, 45, 59, 83, 94, 95, 103, 104, 110, 176; on bathhouses, 203, 204, 207; on cemeteries, 230; and charity, 212; Enlightenment view of, 452, 453; and heder, 147, 156, 158, 160, 161, 163, 164; on hospitality, 216; logic *(higgayon)* in study of, 191; on marriage, 354–355, 357; opposition to, 456; on swimming, 528; on weddings, 366; and yeshivah, 177, 178, 179, 184, 187, 198
Talmud Torah, 148, 176, 218
tanneries, 283–284
Tapper, Nikolas (Zhaba), 673
Tarbutshin, Zvi, *641*
Tarnopol, 454
Tatars, 16, 20, 31, 32, 49, 66, 259, 701n66; as friends, 583, 595, 610, 615, 622, 631; at markets, 315, 319; medical skills of, 207, 263, 323, 438, 440
Tatarski, Hirshl, *237*
Tatarski, Rivka Kremin, *237*
Tatarski, Sarah'le, *507*
Tawlitski, Altke, *353*
Tawlitski, Hannkeh, *260*
Tawlitski, Hayyim, *260*, *353*
Tawlitski, Hinda Sonenson, *260*, *462*, 568–569, 593
Tawlitski, Leah, *260*
Tawlitski, Rabbi Ben Zion, 568
taxes: collection of, 28, 30, 31, 33, 39; on manufacturing, 280–281, 284; on small shopkeepers, 273; wheat money (maot hittim), 215–216
teachers, Hebrew (melamdim), 77, 137, 147–151, *153*, 160, 163–165, 173
Tebeli, Rabbi David, 97
Tehilim (Psalms) society, 246
Teikan, Avraham, 634, 637
Tel Aviv, 11, 125, 128, 418, 466, *493*, 510, 538, *694*
Telz, 112, 183, 184, 195, 196, 460, 489
tenaim (betrothal terms), 357–358
tendlerin (women peddlers), 302–303
Teudah be-Israel (Testimony in Israel; Levinsohn), 454
Teutonic Knights, 23
Third Lithuanian Statute of 1588, 394
Thirty Years' War, 38
Thorn, 35, 484
Three Kings, Festival of, 425
Tiferet Bahurim, 138, 706n30
Tiktiner (one of two rashei yeshivot), 410
Tiktinski, Avraham, 181
Tiktinski, Reb Hayyim Yehudah Leib, 181, 182
Tiktinski, Shmuel, 181
Tillich, Paul, 405
Titiance, 434, 439, 477, 531, *532*, 533, 579
Titinski family, *471*
Tobolski, Moshe, 117, 141–142, 143, 206, 415, 534, 573, 587
Tobolski, Rivka, 141, 143, 415
Tobolski, Sheindele, 141, 143
Tobolski, Zina, 141, 143
Tobolski family, 142
Todras (Elke Ariowitch), 614, 631, 634, 636, 638, 642, 645
Todt, Fritz, 579
TODT (organization for large-scale construction work), 579
Tokatli, Zipporah Lubetski, 361, 364, *372*, 385, *427*, *463*, 500, 501, 537–538
Tolstoy, Leo, 500, 537
Torah, 123, 156, 157, 246; and the poor, 210, 212; rabbis and, 94, 98, 99, 102, 103, 106, 107, 115, 117, 476; reading of, 69, 70, 71, 72, 73, 84–87, 423–424, 703n51; reverence for, 161, 185, 186, 187, 192, 199, 202; teaching of, 92, 150, 152, 178, 547. *See also* holidays: Simhat Torah
Torah studies, 78, 182, 186, 191; centers of, 176, 179, 198; decline of, 175; in Eishyshok, 7, 47, 185, 188, 192, 201, 521; and heder, 147, 153, 154, 156, 163, 167, 168; in Poland, 177–178; and yeshivah, 91, 97, 110, 184
Torczinowicz (Catholic priest), 396
transportation, 300–312, 315, 325, 355, 364–365
Treaty of Riga, 42
Treblinka, 3, 375, 402, 644, 651, 686, 695
Tribunal of the Starosta, 92
Trivash, Abba Yossef ben Ozer ha-Kohen, 245
Troki (Trakai), 572, 589, 675, 676, 700n12; castles of, *21*; early history of, 20, 23, 24, 26; entrance to, *22*; Karaite Jews in, *18*
Trotsky, Leon, 270, 509
Truman, Harry S., 692
Trumpeldor, Yossef, 48, 477, 497–500, 503, 506, 520, 688
Tshorny, Benyomin, *43*, 522, 590
Turetz (Lithuania), 97
Turkey, 10, 26, 31, 32, 497, 498, 701n45
Twain, Mark, 399
The Two Kuni Lemels (play; Goldfaden), 540
Tzarski Dvor (Tzar's Court; yeshivah in Radun), 93
Tzimbalist family, 266

Uganda Plan, 491
Ukraine, 7, 31, 35, 179, 274, 275, 453, 454, 497
Ulans (Polish army gangs), 280, 302
Uman (Ukraine), 454

United States: emigration to, 77, *225*, *229*, 269, 472, 482, 497, 544–556, 681, 684, 690–692, 694; Holocaust Memorial Museum in, 5, 12; immigration policy of, 56, 520, 678; Jewish soldiers in military of, 652; money from emigrants to, 53, 225, 276, 279. *See also* Eishyshok Society of America
Unterman, Rabbi, *694*
Unzer Hilf (Our Help), 286–287, *296*
Ussishkin, Menahem, 172, 486, 495
Uvarov, Count Sergius, 455

Vaad ha-Pletim (Refugee Committee), 88
Vaad ha-Yeshivot (Council of Yeshivot), 190, 469–470, 564
Vancouver, 690
Vanka (Russian partisan), 645
Varena. *See* Aran
Vashka (farmer), 635
Vasilishki, Berl, 322–323, 439
Vasilishok, 200, 585, 590, 595, 596, 606, *647*
Velvel, Reb Itche, 216
Vestnik (journal), 457
Vilkovisk, 100, 196
Vilna, 3, 6, 183, 290–291, 311, 385, 629, 656; and Bund, 107, 292–293, 508, 525; and Eishyshok, 16, 526, 527, 531; Epstein gymnasium in, 275, 617; Gaon of, 68, 69, 91, 97, 99, 110, 120, 132, 152n, 179, 180, 184, 185, 234, *235*, 237, 400, 422, 678; Ghetto, 618, *645*, 646, 647; Great Synagogue in, 68, 76, 77; and Haskalah, 458, 459; hazzanim of, 139, 140; history of, 20, 24, 25, 29, 32, 33, 35, 38, 50, 53, 106, 257, 272, 561, 566; as Jewish center, 7, 171, 173, 287, 514, 567; Jewish education in, 455, 456, 457, 464, 465, 468; Jewish Technikum in, 465–466; and liberation, 669, 673, 674, 677–679; Lukishki prison in, 509, 676, 680, 692; maggidim of, 119; manufacturing in, 282, 283; markets in, 262, 274, 572; medical services in, 445–447; in Nazi occupation, 579, 581; Ponar section of, 277, 281; rabbis in, 96, 112, 113, 129, 187, 245; Ramailes yeshivah in, 125, 199, 200, 501; refugees to, 87, 88, 105; Russian liberation of, 650, 663, 668; Strashun Library in, 68, 525, 527, 678; teachers from, 172, 457, 475, 479; temple to Perkunas in, 25, 66; thieves from, 325; tombstones from, 235; and trade, 262, 271, 572; travel to, 301, 308, 310, 539; in twentieth century, 107, 115; United Partisan Organization (FPO), 646; yeshivah in, 184, 188; Yiddish theater in, 535–536, 538; Zalkind department store in, 386; Zaretche cemetery in, 237; Zionism in, 226, 469, 485. *See also* Zalman, Rabbi Eliyahu ben Shlomo
Vilna-Grodno region, 297, 487
Vilna Hazzanim Quartet, 141
Vilna University, 447
Vilner Tog (newspaper), 384
Vilnius. *See* Vilna
Virshubski, Annie. *See* Foster, Annie Virshubski
Virshubski, Anshel, 59, *250*
Virshubski, Feige Dragootski, 441
Virshubski, Nehemia (der Feldsher), 250, *341*, *440*, 441, 442, 444, 447, 523, *532*, 549, 737n10; granddaughter of, *273*
Virshuki River, 22, 33, 65, 231
Vishniver, Shlomo, *189*
Vistula River, 22, 163
Vitebsk province, 258
Vladimir, Prince, 22
Volga River, 47
Volkani-Elazari. *See* Wilkanski, Meir
Volksbank (Jewish Cooperative People's Bank), 219
Volozhin, 111, 196, 442, 542; and students, 188, 194, 195; yeshivah in, 98, 110, 180–184, 190, 192, 193, *234*, 333, 385, 460, 471, 707n9, 709n41
Vronki prison, 338
Vytautas the Great (Grand Duke Witold), 16, 19, 23, 24, 25

Waldshan, Rabbi Avraham Aaron, 117, 587
Waletsinski, Elchik, 596
Walkin, Shmuel, *189*
Wallenberg, Raoul, 610–611
Wand-Pollack, Michael, 542
Warinowa, 57, 231, *267*, 530, 595, 601, 606, 610, 639
Warsaw, 3, 15, 35, 108, 139, 300, 402; fall of, 567; Gesia Street concentration camp in, 613; ghetto uprising of 1943, 613; Jewish Fighting Organization in, 613; occupations of, 33, 36; Yehudia School for girls in, 109
Washington, George, 36
Wasilewska, Wanda, 679, 747n26
Webber (Nazi official), 116, 579
weddings, 364–375
Weidenberg, Dina, *272*, *625*
Weidenberg, Galke, 460
Weidenberg, Yossl, 117, 273, 507, 582
Weidenberg family, 572
Weingarten, Lipe, 409, 417
Weiter, A. *See* Devenishki, Issic Meir
Weitz, Herman, 277
Weizmann, Chaim, *494*, 741n26
Di Welt (newspaper), 345
Werner (assistant to Gebietskommisar of Lida), 599, 606, 607, 668

Wessely (Weisel), Naphtali Herz, 452, 456
White Jacket (der Wiesser Rekele; Gestapo commander of Eishyshok), 208, *476*, 579, 593
White Poles. *See* Armia Krajowa
Widlanski, Avraham, 644, 660
Wien, Mr., 444, 619–620, *620*
Wiesel, Elie, 4, 5
Wilenski, Dov, *297*, 466, *471*, 504, *505*, *530*, 542
Wilenski, Hayyim, 465, 467
Wilenski, Mekhil, 198
Wilenski, Rabbi Scholem, *189*, 201, 209, 509, 573
Wilenski, Zipporah, 465
Wilenski family, *64*, 538
Wilja river, 17
Wilkanski, Batia Altshul, 102, 111, 196, 303, 321, 359, 361, 429; and Big Fire of 1895, 70; children of, 12, *132*, 134, 194, 195, 442, 458, 460, 490, 491; and divorce, 377–381; emigration to Palestine, 10, 110, 488, 493; on holidays, 430; marriage of, 95, 355–356; and mixed heder, 170; at wedding, 369, 370
Wilkanski, Esther, 342, 360, *432*, *492*, 493; and Hebrew, 461, 514, 515, 516; and mixed heder, 170, 171, 459; in Vilna, 514, 515
Wilkanski, Leah, 342, *492*; emigration to Palestine, 465, 493; and founding of library, 521, 527; and Hebrew, 461, 514, 515–517, *518*, 519; and mixed heder, 170, 171, 459; in Russia, 520; and theater, 535, 543
Wilkanski, Meir, 47, 59, *194*, 267, 285, 305, 342, 349, 377, 396; on autopsies, 243; on bathhouses, 207, 208; on Berl the Cantonist, 186; and Big Fire of 1895, 70, 71; and brother Yitzhak, 196, 199, 742n4; on elections to kahal, 43–44; on Elhanan Leib Levinski, 193; on emigration to America, 544; emigration to Palestine, *16*, 59, 269, 491, 492, 493, 504; and Haskalah, 359, 460, 461; as Hebraist, 513–518; and holidays, 416–417, 418, *419*, 425, 429; on Holy Ark of Eishyshok, 73, 74, 76; and homeless shelter (hekdesh), 217; and Hutner family, 134; as journalist, 742n4; and Leah Wilkanski, 520; on leasing of meat tax, 82; on maggid, 123; on market days, 315, 318, 322; marriage of, 360–361; on melamed's household, 148–149; and mixed heder, 170, 171; publications of, 10; on Reb Layzer, 133, 207; on ritual slaughter, 144; on school days, 152–153, 154, 161, 163, 165, 166, 169; style of dress of, 194–195; in Telz, 199; on visits to family graves, 239–240; on Volozhin students, 195; on Zechariah the shammash, 135–136; and Zionism, 490
Wilkanski, Mordekhai (Mordekhai Elazari-Volcani), 269, *492*, 493, 514
Wilkanski, Reb Layzer, 52, 98, 131–134, *132*, 190, 196, 267, 358, 520n; at bathhouse, 207; and Big Fire of 1895, 70, 340; children of, 10, 12, *132*, 134, 194, 195, 199, 359, 361, 442, 458, 460, 490, 491, 515; and divorce, 377–381; and Eretz Israel, 107, 132, 488, 493; grandchildren of, 54, 388; and Haskalah, 192, 461, 491; on holidays, 418, 429, 430; and illegitimacy, 382; and mixed heder, 170, 491; and newspapers, 521–522; and wife, 95, 102, 303, 321, 356; and Zionism, 491
Wilkanski, Sarah, 134, 170, 194, *377*, *432*, *492*; emigration to Palestine, 493; and Hebrew, 461, 465, 514, 516, 519; and mixed heder, 170, *171*, *459*; in Vilna, 515; and Zionism, 490, 495, 496
Wilkanski, Sarah Krieger, *268*, *360*, 493
Wilkanski, Sarah Rubin, 360, 430, *492*, 493, *514*, 515, 518
Wilkanski, Sarah (sister of Yitzhak), 342, 430
Wilkanski, Temira, *493*
Wilkanski, Yitzhak (Yitzhak Elazari-Volcani), 12, 44, 170, 195–196, 199, *268*, 342, *360*, 416–417, 489, *492*, 515; and Haskalah, 460–461; as Hebraist, 513, 514, 516; in Israel, 268–269, 493; as journalist, 742n4; and Zionism, 59, 489, 490, *494*
Wilkanski, Zafrira, *268*
Wilkanski family, 33, 56, 280, 388, 441, 442, 458, 459, 514, 518; in Israel, *16*, 107, 132, 134, 389, 461, 488, 491–493, 519
Wilkanski-Rabinowitch family, *689*
Wine, Ben-Zion, 581, 590, 601, 639
Wine, Shoshana (Shoshke) Yurkanski, 277, *278*, 324, 675; in Ghetto Radun, 598, 601; in hiding, 639; and massacre of 1941, 581, 589, 590, *591*; murder of, 645, 646; return from Palestine, 502
Wine, Zeev, *278*
Wishnowitz, 275
Wiszik, Isaac, *691*, 692
Witold, Grand Duke (Vytautas the Great), 16, 19, 23, 24, 25
Wolinski, Henry, 613
Wolkonowski, Jaroslav, 747n17
Wolotzki, Dov (Berele), *272*, *665*
Wolotzki, Yetta, *665*
Wolpa, 68
women: in agriculture, 266; of artisan class, 338; and bar mitzvahs, 352; in bathhouses, 204, 205, 206; burial of, 233; and burial society, 243–244, 245; and childbirth, 436; conversions of, 396; and daughters, 339–341; and divorce, 376–377; education of, 94–95, 168–171, 191, 340, 342, 457–464, 471, 521; and

education of sons, 159, 161, 168, 169; and emigration, 336–338; eulogies of, 247; gallery for, 71, 81, 82, 85, 88, 105, 121, 142–143, 217; and Haskalah, 170, 171, 335, 340; and holidays, 414–415, 418, 428–430, 434; and Judaism, 169, 170; and kahal, 43; Lithuanian Jewish, *39, 40*; and maggidim, 121, 122; in market, 271–272, 320–322; and marriage, 331–334; as matriarchs, 334–338; and menstruation, 205, 206; and modernization, 336, 342; and mutual aid societies, 212, 213; non-Jewish, as domestics, 264; and partisans, 630, 637, 643, 645; and prayer minyan, 83; as rabbis' wives, 93, 94–95, 97, 110; and rites of passage, 348–350, 353–354; as ritual slaughterers, 144; on the road, 302–303; as seamstresses, 290–294; as shopkeepers, 271–272; and socialism, 122; and soup kitchens, 220; in synagogues, 71–72; in Talmud, 168; tombstones of, 236–237; and Torah, 85, 186; Yiddish and, 169; and Zionism, 122, 170

World War I: economic effects of, 282; and Eishyshok, 55, 73, 104–105, 125, 134, 221, 242, 522, 523, 524, 623; end of, 127, 620; Germans of, 55, 57, 222, 223, 464, 523, 527, *536*, 540, 575, 576; heroes of, 48, 498; hunger in, 211; Minsk in, 126–127; outbreak of, 107, 200, 223, 461, 463, 491, 496, 548, 550; refugees in, 201, 464, 523; Russians in, 77; soup kitchens (billige kikh) in, 212, 474, 496; typhus epidemic of, 72

World War II, 28, 33, 34; early days of, 565–571; and Eishyshok, 55, 59, 115, 542, 650–654; Jewish Brigade in, *651*, 652; "new" Germans of, 223; outbreak of, 481, 530; partisans in, 11; soldiers in, *647*

Wroclaw (Breslau), 683

Wulf, Franz (Gebietskommisar of Vilna region), 579, 581, 582, 629

Yaakov, Reb, 73, 76

Yaari, Meir, 375

Yache (the zogerke), 143

Yad Vashem (Israel's Martyrs and Heroes Remembrance Authority), 629

Yaffe, Mr., 462, 463

Yaffe, Mrs., 462, 463

Yaffskaya Shkola, 462, *463*

Yankel der Baranovitcher, 473

Yankele (blacksmith's son), 479

Yankelewitch, Beile, 359

Yankelewitch, Frieda. *See* Kaleko, Frieda Yankelewitch

Yankel-Layzer (shoemaker), 294

Yankl der Bleckher (the tinman), Mordekhai, 408

Yaroslav the Wise, 16

Yashinowa, rabbi of, 378–379

Yehudah (the Bandit), 82, 219, 324–325, 544

Yeketrinislav, 172

Yemenite Jews, 157

Yeremitch, 8

yeshivah, 161, 175–202, 427–428; and Bund, 184, 198; during Elul, 417; expulsions from, 271; German-style, 176–177; and Haskalah, 459, 460; ketanah (middle or small), 200–201, 470; Lithuanian models of, 176, 179, 183, 191; outstanding alumni of, 188–191; pilpul style of logic in, 176, 177, 179, 180; Reines, in Lida, 191, 198, 501; Volozhin-style, 180–184; and Zionism, 184, 196, 468, 488. *See also* Kibbutz ha-Prushim; *individual towns*

Yiddishe Rundschau (newspaper), 519

Yiddish language, 134, 158, 198, 249, 588, 652, 666; in ceremonies, 519; and Communism, 469, 520, 522, 525, 677; *vs.* Hebrew, 172, 236, 462, 514, 522, 524, 525, 538, 539, 566; in Israel, 492; as jargon, 515, 516, 517; in official documents, 44, 224, 452; and partisans, 642; plays in, 535–538; and socialism, 522, 525; in Soviet Union, 511; teaching in, 460, 462, 468–469, 470; under Tzars, 47; as vulgar language, 453, 454; and women, 169

Yidl, Yitzhak, *370*

yishuvniks (country people), 265, 358, 420

Yitzhak the Chicken (thief), 324

Yitzhok, Burnik Avraham, 294

Yitzkutsi (Asner brothers' partisan group), 647–650

YIVO (Yidisher Visenshaftlikher Institut), 525, 678

Yohanan, Rabbi, 92, 206

Yoshke Shneur Mordekhai's (coachman). *See* Bleicharowicz, Yoshke Shneur Mordekhai's

Yossef der Bedder (the bath attendant), 204, 207, 208

Yossel the shoemaker, 439

Yude-Yankl (shoemaker), 142, 206, 216, 295

Yudson, Shlomo, 101–102

Yurdichenski di Praislikhe (the Prussian), 479, 539

Yureli forest, 660

Yurkanski, Arie-Leib, 258

Yurkanski, Asher Leib, 79

Yurkanski, Bashke, 388, 668, 671, 675

Yurkanski, Etele, 578

Yurkanski, Feigl (Fanny), 662, *683*

Yurkanski, Freeda, *592*

Yurkanski, Hirshl, 625

Yurkanski, Layzer, 216, *675*

Yurkanski, Mariyasl, 324, 625

Yurkanski, Marsha Kanichowski, *590*

Yurkanski, Miriam Kanichowski, *259*
Yurkanski, Moshe, 662, 665, 675, *683*
Yurkanski, Rochke, *675*
Yurkanski, Yitche-Mendke, *259*, 675
Yurkanski, Zirl di Garberke (tannery owner), 216, *259*, 284, 381, 636
Yurkanski family, 53, 80, 255, 260, 657, 673, 677, 679, 693; tannery of, 283–284

Zabrowski, Zalman, 596
Zahavi, Malka. *See* Matikanski, Malka Zahavi
Zahavi, Munia, *297*, *505*, *530*
Zaidres, 398
Zakheim, Miriam, 378–379
Zakheim, Reb Benyomin, 378
Zakheim, Uri, 378–379
Zakopane (ski resort), 535
Zakrowski family, 597
Zalkutzki (Paikowski family partisan group), 650
Zalman, Rabbi Eliyahu ben Shlomo (Gaon [Sage] of Vilna), 39, *40*, 179, 180
Zalman Leib, 196
Zalman, Reb, 380
Zalmanovitz, Bat-Sheva Rozowski, *373*, 375
Zalmanovitz, Dvorah, *373*
Zalmanovitz, Rabbi David, 113, 114, *189*, 225, *373*, *374*, 375
Zaludek, 606
Zalusky (policeman), 597, 607
Zamut, 184
Zanin, Mordekhai, 149
Zaremba (Polish aristocrat), 400
Zarenberger (one of two rashei yeshivot), 410
Zargodian, der, 193–194
Zarhi, A., 516
Zarum, Zvi Hertz, 48
Zeenah U-Reenah (Go Forth and Gaze), 169, 414
Zelikowski, Lucjan, 274
Zelva, 662
Zemah, Rabbi Shimon ben, 92
Zhetl (Dyatlovo), Ghetto, *311*, 635
Zhitomir, 172, 456
Zikhronot Le-Veit David (Memories from the House of David), 515
Zikhron-Yaakov, 10
Zila family, *476*
Ziman, Henrik. *See* Jurgis
Zimmerman, Atara Goodman (Kudlanski), 13, *229*, *250*, *307*, *370*, *443*, *476*, *529*, *555*
Zinberg, Tevl, 672, 681
Zionism, 9, 10, 41, 54, 59, 128, *132*, 134, 298, 403, 482–512, 560; and apostates, 396; and artisan class, 289, 293, 294, 295; balebatim view of, 490; and cantors, 140, 142; and Communism, 508–512, 566, 677; cultural, 495, 507, 513, 527, 538; Diaspora and, 483; and education, 469; and Haskalah, 461, 484; and heder, 173; heroes of, 15, 48; and holidays, 422–423, 425, 426, 433; and liberation, 658; and maggid, 120, 121, 122; and marriage, 355, 360, 361; movements within, 84, 475; and mutual aid societies, 220, 225, 226; and nationalism, 451, 483, 484, 485; organizations of, *310*, 362; and politics, 493–496, 507; of rabbis, *91*, 107, 108, 111–114, 189; religious, 495; roots of modern, 483–485; and summer camps, 533; and weddings, 375; and women, 122, 170, 335; and yeshivah students, 184, 196, 468, 488. *See also* emigration; Eretz Israel
Zionist Workers Party (Poalei Zion Left), 470, 515
Zionist World Congresses: First (Basel; 1897), 107, 191, 487; Twelfth (Carlsbad), 500
Zionist youth organizations, 325, 415, 416, 487, 489, 490, 499, 542; Beitar, 10, 325, 445, 503–509, 529, 530, 568, 636, 688; Ha-Oved ha-zioni, 507; Ha-Poel ha-Zioni, 507; Ha-Shomer ha-Zair, 503–504, 505, 506, 507, *530*; and Hebrew, 520; Herut ve-Tehyia, 500, *501*; Pirhei Zion, 500; Poalei Zion, 500
Zivia (kindergarten teacher), 430
Zlotnik, Dora. *See* Berkowitch, Dora Zlotnik
Zlotnik, Goldke, *551*
Zlotnik, Hayya Fradl. *See* Broide, Hayya Fradl Zlotnik
Zlotnik, Israel-Itchke, *530*
Zlotnik, Kunie, *371*
Zlotnik, Leibke, *551*
Zlotnik, Mina Kabacznik, *551*
Zlotnik, Moshe. *See* Gold, Morris
Zlotnik, Philip, 246
Zlotnik, Philip (Rephael), *551*
Zlotnik, Shlomo, *345*, *551*
Zlotnik, Yehuda-Leib, *371*
Zlotnik family, 198, 280, 472, 497, *689*
Znamierovskis, J. (King of the Gypsies), 49
zogerke, 142–143, 463
Zoludzewicz (Polish farmer), 611, 612
Zubizki, Elka, *632*
Zubizki, Yaakov, *199*
Zundl, Reb. *See* Hutner, Yossef Zundl
Zvi the Tailor, 340
Zweig, Arnold, 536
Zytoner, Dr., *318*, 443, 444

A NOTE ABOUT THE TYPE

This book is set in Adobe Jenson, designed by Robert Slimbach. It is based on the roman by Nicolas Jenson, first used in *De Præparatio Evangelica* by Eusebius in 1470, and italic by Ludovico degli Arrighi. These classic Renaissance types served as models for several type revivals in the twentieth century, each with its own character, from pedestrian to refined. Slimbach's typeface is a fresh variation on the traditional theme, produced in a digital realm. It combines strength and economy with elegance. While consciously making the drawing of the letterforms more consistent, the designer deliberately retained some of the irregularities and idiosyncrasies of the original letterpress type.

A NOTE ABOUT THE AUTHOR

Yaffa Eliach is a pioneering scholar in Holocaust studies and the creator of the Tower of Life, which millions of visitors have described as the most moving exhibit at the United States Holocaust Memorial Museum in Washington, D.C. The founder of the first Center for Holocaust Documentation and Research in the United States, she has introduced new concepts in Holocaust documentation, both written and visual. She is a Professor of History and Literature in the Department of Judaic Studies at Brooklyn College, with areas of specialty in Eastern European history, Holocaust studies, and Hasidism. A member of President Carter's Holocaust Commission, she lectures frequently to academic and lay audiences and appears often on television at home and abroad. Her earlier book, *Hasidic Tales of the Holocaust,* is an international classic.